THE NATURE AND TYPES OF
SOCIOLOGICAL THEORY

THE NATURE AND TYPES OF SOCIOLOGICAL THEORY

Second Edition

DON MARTINDALE

University of Minnesota

HOUGHTON MIFFLIN COMPANY · BOSTON

DALLAS · GENEVA, ILLINOIS · HOPEWELL, NEW JERSEY · PALO ALTO · LONDON

To Edith

Library of Congress Catalog Card Number: 80-68142

ISBN: 0-395-29732-X

CONTENTS

PART II: SCIENTIFIC HOLISM

PART IV: HUMANISTIC HOLISM

PART V: HUMANISTIC ELEMENTARISM

PREFACE

When the first edition of *Nature and Types* appeared in 1960, sociological theory was dominated by structure functionalism, conflict theory was not generally viewed as a possible alternative, Marxism was primarily characterized as a dangerous anti-American philosophy, and symbolic interactionism was thought of as an interesting social psychology but hardly a general theory. Although Max Weber was widely consulted, his theories were not seen as constituting a research tradition. Neo-Kantian formalism was viewed as an historical curiosity and phenomenology as a microsociological curiosity. The field of theory as a whole was envisioned as divided between grand or global philosophizing and visionless empiricism, whereas falling somewhere between these a middle-range strategy was needed and deemed desirable. The first edition of *Nature and Types* attempted to change all that; the book presented the field as distributed into five major active theoretical divisions with their associated research traditions.

The first edition of *Nature and Types* was the culmination of work begun in 1947, when I was first charged with teaching sociological theory. To prepare for the assignment, I undertook a systematic review of all traditions called sociological theories. This endeavor was soon abandoned: the multiple classifications — I had counted more than eighty — were fragmentary and conflicting; the bases of classification schemes were ambiguous and inconsistent from case to case; the relations among theories and other Western intellectual trends were rarely traced in other than a sketchy, inconclusive manner; the field was cluttered with dead wood and historical curiosities. Sociological theory was in dire need of being mapped; the employment of a defensible set of criteria for classifying theories, as well as the tracing of their intellectual and social roots, was overdue.

If a sociological theory is taken to comprise a set of explanations of social life together with an associated research tradition, the most obvious criteria for the mapping of theories are (1) the basic concept of the nature of social life employed, and (2) the assumptions made as to the appropriate methods by which it is studied. From this point of view things quickly fall into place. Sociology was a nineteenth-century discipline arising in response to the needs of postrevolutionary men and women to explain the social world of the nation-states. Sociology defined itself primarily in opposition to the rationalism of the Enlightenment and proposed to treat society as an organism best studied by the positive methods that had proven themselves in the study of physical nature. Hence the most appropriate designation for the first general system of sociological theory was positivistic organicism.

Once developed as a growing body of explanations with an associated research tradition (the comparative method operating with historical materials), positivistic organicism became a semi-autonomous cultural tradition with its own history, a tradition reflecting both internal and external influences, against which alternative traditions could define themselves and to which it could respond. Alongside positivistic organicism, conflict theory soon materialized. In time, neo-Kantian formalism, social behaviorism (in three sub-forms), and structure-functionalism (in two sub-forms) also arose, each with a distinctive history of sources and antecedents. Moreover, as the map of theories was drawn, it became possible to trace with new precision the trajectory of individual careers of theorists who sometimes worked in more than one theory and research tradition.

Although a large part of the picture traced in the first edition of *Nature and Types* remains intact fully twenty years later, Western society and its cultural traditions have experienced major earth movements, volcanic outpourings, and typhoons in the 1960s and 1970s. A theorist can now explore possibilities of a Marxian sociology without being accused of anti-Americanism; conflict theory has revived; both the scientific and positivistic traditions have been questioned and the humanistic traditions of the West explored with new thoroughness for leads; elementaristic traditions have been developed with new vigor; a case has been made for a value-relevant sociology, which would place ideology at the core of sociology rather than at the periphery as a problem to be overcome; and paradigms have been offered as the ideal synthesizing principles of intellectual culture. Moreover, as could be expected, many new and yet fragmentary characterizations accompanying such developments have once again appeared, tending to blur or obliterate the general picture.

The second edition of *Nature and Types* proposes to remap the field of sociological theory in the light of developments that have occurred in the past twenty years.

All that remains sound from the first edition has of course been retained and updated. Instead of being presented against a backdrop of enlightenment rationalism, sociological theory has now been presented against the background of the humanistic and scientific traditions of the West. A review of the comparative value of ideologies and paradigms provides alternative strategies to theories and research traditions for organizing sociological culture. The basic criteria for isolating theory types have been both generalized and sharpened. In terms of their substantive differences, theories fall into either elementaristic or holistic types. In terms of the underlying assumptions of their research strategies, theories can be divided into humanistic and scientific types. In terms of a combination of its substantive view of social life and its primary research strategy (it requires both to constitute a theory), there are, thus, four major possible types of sociological theory: (1) humanistic elementarism; (2) humanistic holism; (3)

scientific elementarism; and (4) scientific holism. Subdivisions are, of course, possible in any of these categories. Moreover, it is important to remember that whereas the elementarism/holism distinction is a dichotomy (something can be one or the other but not both at the same time), the humanism/science distinction is a contrast between multivariate traditions that partly blur into one another, and hence differences are, at best, matters of degree. For example, it has been possible for recent adherents of symbolic interactionism, which took shape as a form of scientific elementarism, to tilt the theory, at least in part, toward humanistic elementarism.

Among the major differences between the conceptual bases of the second and the first editions of *Nature and Types*, thus, has been the generalization, sharpening, and simplification of the major typology of theories. Although the general types have been reduced from five to four, it has been possible to accommodate in the new scheme, not only the theories isolated in the first edition, but the rich developments of the last twenty years, including some shifts of direction and emphasis in the older theories.

Finally, whereas the first edition of *Nature and Types* concluded with a chapter on the integration of sociological theory (an objective that the structure-functionalists thought they had achieved, but which at best lay in the future) it was felt desirable in the second edition to direct attention to the residual problems of sociological theory. Only to the extent to which the basic problems are solved — even if this be, as John Dewey liked to say, discovering that they are pseudoproblems and can be dismissed as irrelevant — will the true integration of sociological theory be achieved.

DON MARTINDALE

PART I

THE CONTEXT

EVERY HUMAN DEVELOPMENT takes place in the midst of ongoing events. A new discipline does not appear suddenly, fully panoplied with ideas, distinctive procedures, methods, a tradition, institutional anchorage, facilities for training novices, and jobs in which they can be placed when they graduate. A discipline is first manifest as a new stress or emphasis within older disciplines from which it borrows until it acquires the momentum to continue on its own. The three chapters in the present section examine the complex reorganization that had to occur before a science of society became possible; the elements of Western tradition that supply the basic assumptions to which sociology responds; and the comparative value of paradigms, ideologies, and theories as organization principles of the subject matter of sociology.

In the first edition of *Nature and Types*, a chapter on "The Birth of the Social Sciences" reviewing the transformation from the rationalistic philosophy of the eighteenth century to the empirical social sciences of the nineteenth century was felt to be sufficient for describing how, once general condi-

tions were ripe, sociology acquired its distinctive characteristics among the social sciences. It was not necessary at that time even to raise the question of the role of theory in the formation of schools. Few assumptions were more widely accepted by all the social sciences than that ideas (worked up into systems of explanation — theories) were the defining components of sociological schools.

However, in the twenty years since the first edition of *Nature and Types*, the tendency of theorists to ransack the entire Western tradition for new approaches to sociological problems has made it essential that Western tradition as a whole be examined as the context in which the birth and development of the social sciences occurs. Moreover, a major attack has been launched on the scientific-positivistic tradition in sociology and suggestions have been made for organizing the discipline in terms of paradigms or ideologies rather than theories, necessitating that we take account of the implications of such alternative approaches to the schools and subcultures of sociology.

I

The Road to Sociology

With all historical time to develop in, sociology is only about a hundred years old. As far as we can tell, our intelligence is no greater than that of individuals of previous societies. There is no greater potential incidence of genius. We have a broader culture at our disposal than any earlier society, but culture has accumulated in other epochs and times without the appearance of sociology. We can, of course, simply dismiss the problem of why sociology did not appear much earlier as a historical accident somehow related to the peculiar conditions of our era. But it is not an isolated event. Sociology is a continuing activity distinctive of our time. It is not the creation of one or a few people of genius but an ongoing enterprise of research, study, and teaching, It provides careers for research workers and teachers. It offers knowledge and service to members of our society sufficient to justify their continuing support. If it did not, the entire enterprise would wither.

If we are to talk sensibly about sociology, we must first find out what it is that we are talking about. We might start out by defining sociology

very generally as "a body of thought about the individual's interhuman life," but this does not carry us very far because, in many respects, the same definition might apply to folk wisdom and magic and religion. We come closer to the subject when we call sociology the "science" of the individual's interhuman life. But even if we beg the question of what science is, we have still not really isolated sociology from competing disciplines, for historically sociology has had to fight for its own place in a noisy circle of social sciences — a battle that even today leaves it preoccupied with its identity. Perhaps, then, the best approach to a definition of sociology lies along the path of history. Sociology is a part of that great evolution of thought in Western civilization that passes from religion through philosophy to science. There are properties of modern sociology that can be accounted for only in terms of its birthright. The formula for the construction of science out of philosophy was in considerable measure fixed by the physical sciences, which pioneered the movement, and this fact has left a deep imprint on all the social sciences, in-

3

cluding sociology. By tracing the primary relations of sociology to the other social sciences, and by exploring its ties with the intellectual and ideological movements from which it historically emerged, we can come closest to establishing the boundaries of the area that sociology claims for its own.

SOCIOLOGY, FOLK WISDOM, AND THEOLOGY

As other sciences, sociology originated in the common experience and shared thinking or common sense of a particular society at a particular time and place. In all complex societies, the common thinking of its members contains, at the very least, distinctions between fact and fancy and generalizations of varying scope. Shared knowledge must have sufficient workability to permit the members of the social group to survive.

Most sciences soon reached the point where common-sense generalizations had to be modified or replaced. In physics, for example, the idea Aristotle adopted from common sense that motion is a product of the exercise of effort, eventually became an obstacle to an understanding of motion. The idea that combustion was due to a subtle substance named phlogiston also impaired the understanding of chemical change. Modern chemistry was created by the reconceptualization of combustion as a process.

It was perhaps inevitable that some persons interested in the development of sociology as a science should find common sense as the major obstacle to this desirable goal. No one in the postwar world has taken up the cudgels more vigorously for a scientific (conceived as naturalistic) rather than a common sense (which was taken as a euphemism for that which was hopelessly distorted by animism) point of view than William R. Catton, Jr.

> What I mean by animistic sociology is this: (1) the assumption that our common-sense notions about the nature of human nature are valid; (2) the conviction that these common-sense notions can and should

serve as the premises from which more elaborate sociological formulations are to be derived.[1]

In Catton's opinion there is no better example of common-sense animism in sociology than the widely held notion that people have values that are responsible for many of the things they do. Naturalistically, Catton maintains, all we know is that people act; we require no subjective or metaphysical entities to account for this. All values, even sublime values, are capable of naturalistic explanations. And Catton argues that no value is more sublime than love of wilderness. To illustrate his naturalistic approach, Catton reasoned that national park attendance rates constitute a measurement of the sublime value of wilderness, and went in search of a formula that would describe it. After rejecting other models, Catton finally advanced Kepler's laws of planetary motions,[2] to account for the behavior of people attracted by out-of-door experience on the one hand, but hindered by a variety of difficulties such as the distances they had to travel, the time it took, and the cost of gas on the other. Catton was convinced that he had the ideal paradigm for behavior that is usually animistically described as a response to sublime values.

Common sense, of course, would view Catton as having imposed an inappropriate model on his data, concealing more problems than he solved. People visit national parks for many reasons, of which love of wilderness is only one. Park attendance rates are responsive to many things other than a love of wilderness. Moreover, persons engaging in value behavior typically respond to value axiologies (sets of values ordered from higher to lower, as in a restaurant menu, for example, steak is higher in value than scrambled eggs) and may

[1] William R. Catton, Jr., *From Animistic to Naturalistic Sociology* (New York: McGraw-Hill, 1966), p. 47.
[2] (1) The planets travel in paths that are ellipses with the sun in one focus; (2) the areas swept out in any orbit by the straight line joining the centers of the sun and a planet are proportional to the times; (3) the squares of the periodic times that different planets take to describe their orbits are proportional to the cubes of their mean distances from the sun.

balance a number of conflicting values off against one another. And, in fact, if Catton is correct that Kepler's laws of motion do in fact describe ordinary value behavior such as dining in a restaurant, one wonders whether average individuals do not spoil the whole game by actually eating the steak they order rather than circulating indefinitely in its force field. Whatever its fate in sociology at large, common sense, in Catton's pages, suffered a resounding defeat.

As long as sociology remains close to common sense (a fact some sociologists find embarrassing — and the warm reception given Catton's book is among the evidences that many sociologists do), it has the unfortunate consequence of dividing the field into contesting factions. When Elbridge Sibley made a study of *The Education of Sociologists in the United States* in 1963 he took note of this conflict.

> There are sociologists who frankly deny the need, utility, or even the possibility of formal methodological rigor in sociology; who make no apology for comparing their work to that of novelists and journalists. There are others who reject as unscientific anything that is not stated in the language of mathematics or formal logic.[3]

The division between these factions has led to the ironic result that some sociologists construct elaborate mathematical models of social life based on questionable foundations (for they oversimplify some life to meet their mathematical assumptions), while others have been encouraged to make conceptual formulations so vague as to be virtually incapable of comprehension (concealing ideas so simple that they seem ludicrous). In felicitous phrases, Sibley was inclined to accept each faction's criticism of the other:

> If some of the pioneers in mathematical social science are rightly charged with building logically elegant

superstructures on naively simplistic assumptions, they can with equal justice berate their colleagues for failing to formulate their theories in terms susceptible to any rigorous analysis and testing.[4]

This state of affairs has not changed, though it has taken on a new character. In the 1960s and 1970s there has been a rapid development of points of view whose exponents have variously called themselves existentialists, phenomenologists, and ethnomethodologists. They have forthrightly insisted on conceiving the primary subject matter of sociology to consist of ongoing social life (with all of its common sense features). They have also argued in favor of a development of so-called qualitative methods. Their aim is to preserve the richness that they feel is lost in the attempt to apply the quantitative methods of their scientific-minded colleagues.

In any case, common sense was the original starting point of sociology. If the discipline does not preserve whatever is sound in common sense, in the long run, common sense will eliminate sociology. At the same time, the common sense of any given society tends to be time bound and normatively local and, in both respects, falls short of science. Folk wisdom is only one of the sources of sociological knowledge.

There are other things people do, or perhaps things that happen to them, which fall outside the framework of everyday events. They have accidents, they become ill and die. They lose loved ones. Tragedies sometimes strike in the midst of what began as great happiness. Such things tend to defy the explanatory formulas of folk wisdom. How, furthermore, is one to explain the fact that, even if two members of a society are equally diligent in the conducting of the affairs of everyday life, the good fortune of one may be matched by the misfortune of another? Even without the unexpected and tragic or extraordinary event, feelings arise out of ordinary life that are not always easy to accept or explain. Every social order prescribes goals for its members and the means for

---

[3]Elbridge Sibley, *The Education of Sociologists in the United States* (New York: Russell Sage Foundation, 1963), p. 134.

[4]*Ibid.*, p. 135.

attaining these goals. The stuff of life must be crammed into socially prescribed forms. The murderous or lustful impulse must be repressed. A man may be expected to go into battle knowing all too well that it may mean his life. The individual may in fact covet a neighbor's spouse. Modern psychologists have familiarized us with the suppressed antisocial impulse that takes its secondary revenge in the form of guilt arising in the face of repression. Finally, no social order privileges all its members equally, a fact that does not make the frustrations generated within the order easier to endure.

The psychological roots of religion seem universal to humankind. They appear to lie in the demand for emotional and intellectual "closure." Human beings must explain and accommodate themselves emotionally to the tragic, the unexpected, and frustrating events that take place within and around their lives. They feel the need even to explain and adjust to the fact of their own deaths. At bottom, religions seem to be collective institutional solutions to these problems.

Thus, beside the common-sense thinking of a society, another type arises with various subtypes of magical, theological, and mixed forms. In various ways this thought, too, may be concerned with the incidents of everyday life. But its point of gravity is elsewhere, in the hidden, the extraordinary, the transcendent. And when such thought is concerned with everyday events, it is often because of the unpredictable or uncontrollable factors. The magical spell is added as a warrant for the success of a hunting expedition, its intent being to control the unforeseeable accident. Black magic is worked to injure an enemy who would be dangerous to face directly. Such thinking addressed to the extraordinary — the explanation of health and illness, life and death, chance and fate — may undergo various degrees of organization, development, and sublimation. In its "purer" form, it becomes a speculative, ethical probing into the ultimate meaning of life.

A number of older theories found such theological reasoning to be the first form of abstract thought and its bearers — the "magician-priests" — the world's first professional intellectuals. But even at this time there was a subdivision of intellectual roles, with the old man or woman — the "sage" — being thought of as the respected advocate of common-sense knowledge in contrast to the "magician-priest-philosopher," who was defined as the specialist in the esoteric. However this may be, theology is no more the counterpart of sociology than is folk wisdom. In fact, if one searches previous societies or contemporary preliterates for the equivalent of sociological knowledge, it is not to be found. Nor will the "sage" or "magician-priest" substitute for the sociologist. Sociology lies somewhere in between.

Like common sense, sociology is concerned with the everyday, the average, the ordinary, the recurrent social event. In this respect, it differs most widely from magic and theology. However, unlike common sense, sociology is not a discipline bound to uphold the ethos of some particular social order. It seeks maximum freedom from value suppositions. On the other hand, sociology shares with the various disciplines concerned with the extraordinary a speculative and intellectual intent, but, unlike magic and religion, its speculative motives are dominated by the concept of the "natural" rather than the supernatural. One may thus conceive of sociology as either extending the intellectual and speculative concerns proper to religion into the area of the ordinary; or, in reverse, as the rise from notions about the ordinary toward general, abstract explanation.

A peculiar combination of "naturalism" and "speculation" is almost the badge of a world in which the primary form of institutionalized thought is science itself.

SOCIOLOGY AND PHILOSOPHY

The relation between sociology and philosophy is at once more direct and more subtle than its relation to folk wisdom or theology. Sociology was one of the late offspring of philosophy. Comte even called the new field "positive philosophy" before he accepted the name "sociology" for it. It was some time before sociology was sufficiently established as an independent discipline beside its parent for the two fields to find special subject matter in each other. It has finally become possible for the "philosophy of the social sciences" to appear as a special project within philosophy and for sociology to contemplate the study of social factors important for philosophic systems as aspects of the "sociology of knowledge."

Because philosophy was the matrix which gave birth to sociology in the nineteenth century, and because of the continuing interaction between the two disciplines, it is important to differentiate them. But first we must consider the still earlier emergence of Western philosophy itself out of magic and theology — one of the foundation developments in Western civilization, preparing the way for all subsequent intellectual movements. Philosophy had first to become distinct from magic, theology, and folk wisdom before, much later, science and, still later, sociology could become distinct from it.

The effects of magic upon intellectual life were primarily in the direction of a stereotyping of form and content. The incantation does not invite analysis. Magical tabooing of words, such as the occasional absolute prohibition on uttering the name of God, hardly promotes analysis. Or compare the taboo on many words relating to sex in our own society and the effect this taboo has on the child's understanding of sexual matters. The requirement of letter-perfect rendition of an efficacious magical formula may even restrict expressive fluidity — to say nothing of fixing an upper limit on rational analysis. Intellectual life dominated by magic is fixed by requirements external to intelligence itself.

The step in thought from theology to philosophy was an important achievement of the human mind, one which has had its effect on human thought ever since. When speculation about the nature of the individual and the world occurs outside the protective confines of sacred institutions, the competition of alternative explanations becomes especially sharp. A religious institution has powerful sanctions at its disposal in securing intellectual conformity. Apostates may be punished or excommunicated. On the other hand, believers who are challenged in their beliefs may retire to the protection of official doctrine. The very presence of official doctrine, "dogma," or a "party line" often involves many compromises and adjustments. If one observes a difference emerging between one's personal beliefs and the official dogma, life is always easier if the dangerous thought is put aside. But all this is incidental to the most important point of all: so long as thought is controlled by sacred sanctions the criterion of acceptability tends to be external — outside thought itself.

All this is changed when the reasoning process takes place outside religious institutions. Viewpoints multiply, for there is no established dogma against which to measure acceptability of ideas. Most important of all, ideas are forced to stand "upon their own merit." It may become necessary to find criteria for the acceptability of ideas within the thought process itself. *The Socratic method formalized the procedure central to the transition of thought from theology to philosophy — the search for a procedure establishing the criteria of truth within the thought process itself.*[5]

Logic as an Example of the Rational Proof. It is the amusing estimate of Bertrand Russell in his somewhat whimsical *History of Western Philosophy*[6] that if Socrates actually practiced the dialectic in the manner described in the *Apology*, the hostility centering on him is easily explained, for all the "humbugs of Athens" would have combined against

---

[5] According to Plato in the *Parmenides*, Socrates did not stop with the dialectical method but went on to develop the fundamental "hypothesis" that behind every term with an unequivocal denotation there is an ideal object accessible only to thought. Such conceptual objects are "ideas" or "ideal forms." The objects of the ordinary world are then viewed as of secondary reality, becoming what they are by virtue of their temporary participation in a corresponding form.

[6] Bertrand Russell, *History of Western Philosophy* (New York: Simon and Schuster, 1945), p. 92.

him. The dialectical method is an excellent way of establishing the truth whenever logical propositions are at issue. It leads to the formation of propositions into consistent logical systems and to the discovery of logical errors and inconsistencies.

Looking back from the standpoint of a scientific world, the Socratic method appears remarkably limited precisely at the point where things become crucial — the winning of new knowledge. Even logically it was limited. When it was pressed to the interpretation that contraries have some sort of capacity to generate higher truths, or that the truth-establishing process consists in the evocation of memories from previous lives, it was on the way toward mysticism. However, if one looks at the Socratic method from the standpoint of the magico-theological conceptions of a world still dominated by religion, the Socratic method is like an open window letting in light and fresh air. It marks the decisive point of transition from theology to philosophy, from an intelligence determined by external institutional criteria to an intelligence established on the basis of the principles of thought itself. There is a sort of poetic justice in the tradition that would transform Socrates from what he most probably was, the scion of an eminent family, into a "common man." Once one establishes truth as a property of the proper conduct of the thought process, anyone can establish truths. This important conceptual function is emancipated from social class, and a commoner is as able to find truths as an aristocrat.

The development of the Socratic method testifies to the central place occupied in Greek philosophy by the search for a way of conducting the thought process that would provide dependable results. The magnificent discovery that resulted, to be transmitted on as an imperishable ideal of the West, was the *rational proof*. The two outstanding achievements of Greek thought were the foundations of logic and the demonstration of the nature of mathematical truth.

Aristotle is ordinarily given credit for having laid the foundations of logic. The most important of his logical works is the *Prior Analytics*, which pre-

sents the theory of the syllogism — a three-termed argument resting on the logic of classes. The syllogism consists of a *major premise,* a *minor premise,* and a *conclusion.* The conclusion necessarily follows from the premises, and if the premises are true, then the conclusion must be true. Thus, with the major premise "all men are mortal," and the minor premise "Socrates is a man," the conclusion necessarily follows that "Socrates is mortal."

The theory of the syllogism is not as simple as this, and Aristotle went on to analyze its properties in great detail, but these ramifications, significant as they are in the history of Western thought, are not immediately relevant to the present discussion. What is most important for our purposes is the impetus that Aristotelian logic gave to the notion that the criteria for establishing the truth of anything lie within the thought process itself.

Modern students have raised three main criticisms of the syllogism. (1) There are formal defects in the system. Statements such as "all Greeks are men" do not, as Aristotle assumed, necessarily assert that Greeks exist. When the ambiguity of such a statement is resolved, it is seen to contain two statements: (*a*) "there are Greeks," and (*b*) "if anything is a Greek, it is a man." The latter statement is purely hypothetical, involving no necessary assertion of existence. (2) The logic of Aristotle overestimated the importance of the syllogism — leaving, for example, the whole area of mathematical truth outside its framework and obscuring its character. Finally, (3) it overestimated the importance of deduction. In Aristotle's writings, where questions are raised that transcend the problems of the syllogism, the discussion tends to become metaphysically obscure. This may be seen in his doctrine of "essences" (qualities of a thing which cannot be changed without a loss of its identity) and his doctrine of "substance" (presumed ultimate subjects of properties). These studies transferred the task of obtaining the first premises of the syllogism to metaphysics.

Deductive inference was thought by Aristotle to be syllogistic. It was necessary only to state all knowledge in syllogistic form to avoid all fallacies.

The historical fate of these brilliant logical beginnings was the transformation of Aristotelian logic into a medieval dogma and the continuance of this logical dogmatism into modern times, where it functioned as a stronghold of resistance against further development of logical analysis. The logical thought of the Greeks did not embrace the problem of deduction broadly enough to include mathematics.

Because of all these objections, many modern students are unwilling to accept Greek logic as one of the great achievements of the human mind and think of it rather as an obstacle to the general growth of logic. But such a judgment fails to take account of the sort of magico-theological thinking which Greek logic replaced. More impressive than the intrinsic logical limitations of the syllogism is the concrete demonstration that Aristotelian logic provided of the possibilities of rational proof and the dream to which it gave birth of a rationally ordered sphere that could encompass all knowledge. Syllogistic logic was a superb product of the drive in Greek philosophy toward rationality.

Mathematics as an Example of the Rational Proof. A much more universally acclaimed product of the same drive was the discovery of the nature of mathematical truth. The Greeks had inherited numerous mathematical propositions from Babylonia and Egypt. They transformed them into something quite new. The practical utilization of mathematics is reported of Thales, who is said to have measured the height of a pyramid by waiting until the time of day when the shadow of the king was the same height as the king and measuring the shadow of the pyramid. He is said also to have solved the problem of finding the distance of ships at sea. The Pythagoreans made numerous contributions to the development of mathematics and, incidentally, elevated mathematical reasoning to the status of a soul-purifying rite. They speculated on the meaning of "the square root of 2," the first irrational number to be discovered, and they devised methods to approximate its value. Pythagoras possibly discovered the theorem bearing his name.[7] As a product of the study of the square root of 2 and of other irrationals, Eudoxus (408–355 B.C.) developed a geometrical theory of proportion. He also developed the method of exhaustion later used with great skill by Archimedes.

The great work, however, was that of Euclid, slightly after Aristotle. He did for mathematics what Aristotle did for logic — to be sure with somewhat greater logical beauty. Euclid's elements begin with the definition of such basic concepts as point, line, plane, angle.[8] Next were presented certain principles or postulates or axioms which related the primitive terms. Finally a number of theorems (lemmas or corollaries) were proved by applying the postulates and definitions.

There were logical imperfections in the *Elements*.[9] Eventually the attempts to prove the postulate of parallels from other of Euclid's postulates led to important logical discoveries[10] and to the further evolution of mathematics. A variety of postulational systems have been explored, and it has been demonstrated that Euclid's system for plane geometry is satisfied by only one model. But all this should not obscure the tremendous importance of Euclid's system to the history of thought — the creation of a purely deductive system resting on undefined terms. It is another brilliant monument to the Greek drive toward rationality.

The great discovery of Greek philosophy so significant for the progress of Occidental thought was thus the rational proof. But this is not science, for science is more than logic. In fact, the very impressiveness of the logical discoveries of the Greeks strengthened the antiempirical movements in the Greek world by reducing empirical knowl-

[7]Sir Thomas L. Heath, *A History of Greek Mathematics* (Oxford: The Clarendon Press, 1921), I, 145.
[8]Strictly speaking, other terms used to define these basic concepts were left undefined. The clarification of them is somewhat comparable to the discovery of formal ambiguities in the syllogism.
[9]Corrected by David Hilbert and others.
[10]Such as those of John Bolyai and Nikolai Lobachevski.

edge to an inferior position. Euclid, for example, had a typical Greek contempt for the practical utility of his geometry. On the other hand, the discovery of rational proof was one of the essential steps toward science itself. Without the conception of an autonomous, rationally closed world of thought, the basis of which rests in the inner principles of thought itself, science could hardly have arisen. Furthermore, a major beginning was made toward the forging of mathematics into a powerful tool for the investigation of nature.

Greek Sophism as Protosociology. If science was not achieved, except whimsically and incidentally, in the Greek world, neither was social science. But philosophy in the West remained, thereafter, the guardian of bodies of thought which later separated into the special sciences. The first model for concept formation in the special sciences was often drawn from Aristotelian logic, and to this day the criticism is frequently directed against sociology that its conceptualizations rest on the foundations of an outmoded traditional logic.

The nearest approach to a social science in Greek philosophy was made by the Sophists, intellectuals originating as displaced persons who made their living by teaching. They included such men as Hecataeus of Miletus, Xanthus of Sardes, Hellanicus of Mytilene, Protagoras of Abdera. Xenophanes and Heraclitus had turned philosophic attention to religion and language; the Pythagoreans opened a tradition of the discussion of ethics and politics. Now these foreigners brought to philosophy an extensive comparative knowledge of customs and social forms. Sophism partly became a philosophy of civilization, studying the individual as a social being in terms of language, religion, art, literature, and politics. Moreover, the Sophists had strong empirical inclinations and they sought to amass as much knowledge as possible from all areas of human life. Such comparative knowledge was made the basis for inferences about the progress of human civilization, the origin and structure of language, the most efficient arrangement of social institutions for the development of the individual. The concept of

natural law was developed into a social critical formulation for the test of institutions, establishing the view in Sophistic circles that society rests on natural laws. They even called the institution of slavery to critical account.

But in the end, the knowledge of the Sophists was more practical than theoretical, and Sophism increasingly aimed at teaching the art of the control of life. Sophism was oriented to the education of the young and to the control of opinion through popular education. It developed courses for promoting practical efficiency in the conduct of private and public life. Sophists became expert in teaching the techniques of debate and the conduct of argument. They were denounced by Plato as "shopkeepers with spiritual wares."[11]

As a genuine movement toward social science, Sophism had serious limitations, and, as time went by, it aspired more toward systematic moral education than the extension of objective empirical-social knowledge. Thus, in the end, the contribution of Greek philosophy to social science was not direct — through Sophism — but indirect, by way of its discovery of the rational proof, which as a basic element of science ultimately was important for sociology as well.

SOCIOLOGY AND HISTORY

Philosophy became the discipline in the West that in more or less logical form summarized the knowledge available to the intellectual. In this it was a most bountiful queen of the sciences, bequeathing intellectual grants to serve as starting points for particular disciplines, including the kind of knowledge potentially important for sociology. On the other hand, the assemblage of sociological knowledge by philosophy was subject to intrinsic restrictions as long as its primary aim was moral instruction. For the establishment of a science, the simple assemblage and preservation of traditional wisdom is not enough, even though

[11]*Protagoras*, 313c.

this lore is partly transformed into logically consistent wholes.

Science lives by the extension of empirical knowledge, not in a discipline that may view such empirical knowledge as downright dangerous. The task of establishing and explaining new facts about society and developing criteria for ascertaining their authenticity fell to the lot of the historians of the Greek world rather than its philosophers. Indeed, if we desire a relatively full and accurate picture of the "facts" of the Greek world, we turn naturally to such persons as Herodotus, Thucydides, Xenophon, and Arrian. The Greek word ἱστορία meant "research" or "investigation." A progressive increase in the precision of investigation of social facts is the lesson of fundamental importance for social science contained in the development of historiography.

Some points of view in modern sociology have been determined by their opposition to history in all its forms. Some of the sociological formalists — for example, Leopold von Wiese — have felt that sociology could emerge only to the degree that it freed itself from history. Moreover, the recent school of small-group sociologists of the "group dynamics" persuasion have been overwhelmingly of the opinion that any use by sociology of historical materials is evidence of medievalism. The formalists and small-group theorists undoubtedly have good reasons for their contempt for history, but it should not obscure the slow, difficult steps by which objectivity in the establishment of social facts was won. It is difficult to conceive the possibility of sociology without the prior developments of historiography, beginning in classical Greece.

Historiography and the Evolution of Empirical Methodology. There are shadowy figures such as that of Hecataeus behind the work of Herodotus. From Herodotus' comments it is clear that Hecataeus was interested in geography and ethnology. Herodotus began his own work as a report of his travels. Born in Halicarnassus about 484 B.C., he spent time on the island of Samos and traveled in parts of the Persian Empire, Scythia, and Egypt, and he visited Athens and Thurii in

Magna Graecia as an Athenian colonist. Herodotus seems to have had the idea of systematizing geography and chronology and recording the myths encountered in his travels. He did not believe everything he reported. Once he began his account, the significance of the Persian wars for the appearance of Greek political freedom and the autonomy of the city-state became increasingly clear to him. Because Herodotus never abandoned a general religious interpretation of historical events, he was led ever and again to trace out the tragic sequence of well-being, insolence, folly, and disaster. But despite the ultimately religious character of his explanation and the errors of fact and even naïveté of reporting, his account ranges from climate to social custom, from geography to myth, meriting the characterization of Herodotus as the world's first ethnologist.

By contrast, Thucydides wrote about events occurring during his lifetime and in which he participated. He was one of the ten generals elected to direct political and military affairs and banished by the Athenians in 424 B.C. after his failure to relieve Amphipolis. Thucydides almost completely rejected Herodotus' type of theological explanation of social events. He opened his account with a quick synoptic history of Greece before the Peloponnesian War — an account marked by its thorough rationalism and skepticism. Hellas, he thought, was not regularly settled in ancient times. The original Greeks must have been migratory or semimigratory. They had no walls around their settlements. The richest districts were most subject to attack. Before the Trojan War, he believed, there was no common action in Hellas; in fact, the country did not even have a name as a whole. In ancient times both Hellenes and barbarians, as well as inhabitants of the coast and islands, began to find their way to one another by sea and had recourse to piracy. They were commanded by powerful cities grown rich from war booty. As wealth accumulated, cities were built on the seashore and fortified; peninsulas were occupied and walled off. As Hellas grew more powerful and the acquisition of wealth became more rapid, the revenues of the cities increased, and in many of them tyrannies were established where formerly there had been only hereditary kings with fixed prerogatives. Thus a political evolution parallels economic evolution.[12]

Thucydides rejects Herodotus' "external" cause of social events. The causes of economic and political events lie in the human sphere. Moreover, he distinguishes between biased opinion and observation, and he constantly specifies the need for firsthand information:

> Of the events of the war I have not ventured to speak from any chance information, nor according to any notion of my own; I have described nothing but what I either saw myself, or learned from others of whom I made the most careful and particular inquiry. The task was a laborious one, because eye witnesses of the same occurrences give differing accounts of them, as they remembered or were interested in the actions of one side or the other.[13]

A responsible social-scientific attitude is illustrated in the speeches that Thucydides put into the mouths of crucial actors in his account at critical times. He quite consciously separates his method of reporting such speeches from the methodology of the rest of his account:

> As to the speeches which were made either before or during the war, it was hard for me, and for others who reported them to me, to recollect the exact words. I have therefore put into the mouth of each speaker the sentiments proper to the occasion, expressed as I thought he would be likely to express them, while at the same time I endeavored, as nearly as I could, to give the general purpose of what was actually said.[14]

The conception of history contained in the works of Herodotus and Thucydides was dissipated in the work of the rhetoricians, such as Ephorus and Theopompus. But in the studies of Timaeus the Sicilian (fourth century) and even more in the work of Polybius (particularly his critique of Timaeus's use of controversial documents), a more adequate conception appears.

The Romans added practically nothing to historiography. Dionysius of Halicarnassus and Livy, while making a study of sources, reduced history to sketches from antiquity subordinated to literary aims. In the work of Cicero, the claims of Roman patriotism are everywhere predominant. And by the time of Suetonius (*Lives of the Caesars*), history had degenerated to the mere gossip of a court journalist.

In the medieval world, the conception of historiography degenerates still further. Eusebius of Caesarea introduced a world chronology that became basic for the Christian historians. In St. Augustine's *City of God*, philosophy of history on the grand scale was projected; but generally throughout the period the chronicle is typical, and it is dominated by fascination with the miraculous. The low level of historical responsibility is evidenced in outright historical forgeries such as the False Decretals and the Donation of Constantine.

The Renaissance carried with it a renewed sense of historical responsibility, as shown by Valla's attack on the Donation of Constantine. But it is only with the conflict between Protestantism and Roman Catholicism that the forces were fully set in motion for an increased responsibility in the writing of history. After the challenge presented by Luther and by the authors of the great Protestant ecclesiastical history known as the *Magdeburg Centuries* (1560–1574), the collection of sources by Protestant writers began in earnest. Cardinal Baronius in *Annales Ecclesiastici* (1588–1607) began even more thorough source collections, and thereafter collections proceed from both groups. Leibnitz even proposed the formation of an organization specifically charged with collecting historical source materials. Such activities led on to the modern archives. The basis was being laid as well for more secular philosophies of history, such as began to appear in the eighteenth century. The importance of the so-called philosophy of history is

---

[12]Thucydides, *History of the Peloponnesian War*, trans. Benjamin Jowett, in Francis R. B Godolphin, ed., *The Greek Historians* (New York: Random House, 1942), I, 575 f.

[13]*Ibid.*, p. 576.

[14]*Ibid.*

found in the fact that it lifts out the conceptual element in historical thought, separating it permanently from the field of myth. However, formulations such as St. Augustine's — conceiving the history of humankind as the successive revelation of a divine plan — could only lead to the subordination of history to dogma. Augustine's philosophy received its last full statement by Bossuet (*Discours sur l'histoire universelle*, 1681).

The historians of the eighteenth century (Voltaire, Montesquieu, Hume, Robertson, and Gibbon) changed all this. The exclusive connection of history with theology was severed; traditional authorities were questioned; the concept of a universal history was projected; other objects took their place in the historical account alongside politics and religion; the concept of "progress" was projected as a historical theme, and the idea of the triumph of reason presented as its goal. However, there was a certain inevitable shallowness implicit in the Enlightenment approach to history. To a point, the critique of tradition is valuable; but carried to extremes it becomes a scorn of the past per se. The anchorage of interest in supposed "principles of human nature" can lead to the dismissal of the individual event as accidental.

When Vico phrased the idea of a fundamental value of every age (*Scienza Nuova*, 1725–1744) and its function in preparing for the next, he emphasized the development of the historical series as a whole, posing the problem of its continuities and thus modifying the predominant interest merely in the "goal" of history. Winckelmann's study of Greek art left no doubt that there were periods of development that were unsurpassed in their own way, hence, not to be dismissed as mere stages in the progress of reason. Similarly, studies such as those of Justus Möser (1720–1794) lifted the examination of the locale to an importance equaling the study of universal human nature. Johann Gottfried von Herder (1744–1803) is particularly important in that he signalized a general shift from the historical interpretations of the Enlightenment to those of Romanticism. The principle of development became more important than "progress," and it was applied to cultural history (*Auch eine*

Philosophie der Geschichte zur Bildung der Menschheit (1774); *Ideen zur Philosophie der Geschichte der Menschheit* (1784–1791). Emphasis was on the whole historical series and not simply on the presumed "goal" of history.

As the new historical spirit fully emerged under the influence of the *Sturm und Drang* movement, new interests came to the fore. In contrast to the old emphasis on reason was the new appreciation of the role of the irrational in human affairs. Tradition was no longer dismissed out of hand as the irrational residue of the dead past, but treated with respect. Nationalism and the concept of the folk soul emerged as unifying concepts in place of universal human nature and the ideal of humanity. As already noted, development rather than progress became the watchword of the new history. In his concept of history as the realization of the absolute spirit in its dialectical struggle for freedom, Hegel summed up one aspect of the romantic theory of history.

Throughout the eighteenth and nineteenth centuries continuous gains in methodological exactness were registered. Editions of source materials were increasingly published during the eighteenth century. New historical tools were being forged. Philosophical criticism was applied to historical sources (Friedrich August Wolf, *Prolegomena ad Homerum*, 1795; Barthold Georg Niebuhr, *Römische Geschichte*, 1811–1812). The history of law was established as a special discipline (Savigny and Eichhorn). The synthesis of Enlightenment and romantic methods was secured and the establishment of the facts elevated to the status of the foremost historical duty (Leopold von Ranke, *Zur Kritik neuerer Geschichtschreiber*, 1824). The nation was proposed as a unit of historical analysis, particularly by Heinrich von Treitschke, *Deutsche Geschichte im neunzehnten Jahrhundert* (1879–1894). The history of science was contemplated as a special discipline (Ranke) and social and intellectual history brilliantly projected (Jakob Burckhardt, *Die Kultur der Renaissance in Italien*, 1860). Meanwhile the interrelation between special social institutions was brought under investigation (as in the studies of Henry Thomas Buckle, *History of Civilization in England*, 1857–1861, and in the work of Karl Marx).

Historiography and Sociology. This thumbnail sketch of the development of historical thought calls attention to two things. (1) Historical thought itself becomes fully possible only to the degree that objective secular knowledge of the actual world is possible and desirable. Historical thought appeared in the Greek world under the same general conditions that favored the discovery of the rational proof. Also, in parallel fashion, it went into comparative decline in the Roman world, where rhetorical and patriotic motives were dominant. Its deepest eclipse occurred in the medieval world, where the historical forgery testified to the domination of didacticism and propaganda over objectivity. It revived under the same circumstances as the rise of science, and indeed reached full development only as scientific history. (2) More important in the present context is the fact that to the degree that history makes its appearance and is extended to various areas of human life, an assemblage of dependable information about society occurs. Herodotus is sometimes called "the father of anthropology," and with justice: he recorded much of the varied data that an ethnological science finds indispensable. Or when Voltaire, in his *Essai sur les mœurs* (1754), attacked Bossuet's conception of history for its limitations and its reliance on miraculous procedure, he was performing two tasks essential to social science: (a) requiring dependable data, and (b) demanding a broader reporting of facts of social life than those narrowly relevant to a special theology.

Along the same lines, the movement from Enlightenment to romantic conceptions of history was also relevant for social science. A defective reporting of those social facts that some special philosophy would describe as "irrational" can hardly serve the full understanding of institutional phenomena. So, too, a social science will require information on the areas of social life isolated by romanticism: the developmental, the traditional, the local, and all the special cultural and institutional phenomena.

Philosophy, in its preoccupation with the good life, had traditionally been more concerned with the systematic cultivation of attitudes toward the world and the individual than with the patient assemblage of facts and the task of verifying them. In this last respect, the historian had more to teach the incipient sociologist than did the philosopher. (This is not to say, of course, that the system-building of the philosophers — a pioneering effort of thought — was not also essential for the growth of science.)

Philosophy and history together presided over the birth of sociology, as may be seen from the work of Auguste Comte (1798–1857), who has often been described as "the father of sociology."[15] Comte presented sociology as a polemic against traditional philosophy, which he denounced as "metaphysical." The very term *positivism* identifying the new field was intended to express this opposition. At the same time, the new "positive philosophy," or as Comte characterized it later, "sociology," relied directly upon history for its subject matter. The task of the new science was to establish laws of the regularities of social events. There was no doubt in Comte's mind that these events were supplied by history. "The historical comparison of the consecutive states of humanity is not only the chief scientific device of the new political philosophy. Its . . . rational development constitutes the substratum of the science, in whatever is essential to it."[16] The historians' work was thus fundamental for sociology. For this reason Comte tried to promote the establishment of professorships of history in the French universities. His polemic against traditional philosophy, however, should not obscure an important fact: his basic point of view was derived from philosophy, and the new field was thought of as a philosophic movement.

Not only did the disciplines of philosophy and history preside over the birth of sociology, but in the early days of the development of sociology,

[15]Comte's work is discussed in detail in Chapter IV.
[16]*The Positive Philosophy of Auguste Comte,* freely translated and condensed by Harriet Martineau (London: J. Chapman, 1853), II, 105.

when problems of a theoretical or methodological type arose for the new field, sociologists frequently turned to these disciplines for help. An extensive literature has developed on the interrelation of the fields; Dilthey and Rickert may be taken to illustrate the reaction of philosophy and history upon sociology at a later stage.

Dilthey, Windelband, and Rickert. To Wilhelm Dilthey (1833–1911), Comte's conceptions of society and human history seemed rather crassly materialistic. At the same time, he accepted the idea that empirical knowledge of historical materials is possible, and that these materials are precisely cultural in nature. He set about to examine the nature of knowledge in cultural history. (*Geistesgeschichte*).

The materials of history are acts of spiritual agents, but these, contrary to Comte's assertion, are not understandable on the basis of the methods of natural science. Knowledge in history occurs through the isolation of spiritual forms (*geistige Gebilde*) present in cultural phenomena. The common ideas, feelings, and aims of a period of humankind constitute the spirit of an age (*Zeitgeist*), which determines the attitudes of individuals. The study of a historical period consists in the analysis of the structural system present in its various tendencies, discovering what these tendencies have in common and how they combine. The common element is the peculiar essence (*Eigenwesen*) of the period. The concepts which it expresses will apply generally throughout the period. These are historical categories.

In life the relation of whole to part is not mathematical but "meaningful." Meaning provides the relation between whole and part whenever this relation is grasped. The meaning of life episodes is determined by memories and future possibilities. The task of historical understanding is the grasp of meaningful relations between whole and part, between the elements of experience and the desires that inform them. In history, where we pass from the meaning of elements of our own experience to the experience of others as embodied not only in written texts but in all forms of expression,

we utilize the various outer or external signs of activities as devices for inferring the inner meanings behind them.

Thus the comprehension of immediate experience of life is supplemented by "understanding," which grasps the nature of life through its external manifestations. The method of understanding consists in the act of thought moving from external forms (objectifications of life) to inner reality. This is done by "reliving"; such reliving consists in the imaginative reconstruction of another's experience in terms of one's own and passing to it by analogical inference. The method of history thus becomes a kind of empathic technique.

When sociologists began to experience difficulties with their theories and methods, one group turned to the discussions of Dilthey and his associates for guidance. However, the effect of accepting Dilthey's formulations would apparently have involved the abandonment of sociology as a natural science and the fusion of it with history and the humanities. One would thus, it seemed, be forced to abandon not only positivism but the science itself. This was hardly a view to go unchallenged. The leaders of the opposition to this view were Wilhelm Windelband (1848–1915) and particularly Heinrich Rickert (1863–1936). Both of these men, while admitting that the sociology of Comte was inadequate, raised serious criticisms of Dilthey's analysis, and the relation between sociology and history had to be reexamined.

Windelband, a major German philosopher of the nineteenth century, assumed, with Dilthey, that the task of philosophy is to find the meaning of life. This task, he maintained, is accomplished in the discovery of universally valid norms of pure reason, embodied in human activities and actualized in history. Their actualization in history is studied by the historical sciences (*Geschichtswissenschaften*). The two fundamental ways of dealing with subject matter are by laying down laws (in which case knowledge is *nomothetic*) or by describing individual facts (in which case knowledge is *idiographic*). Natural science is a nomothetic type of inquiry; history is idiographic.

Dilthey had found the materials of history to be

psychological, and in a psychological method he located the procedure of history. However, Windelband argues, psychology is a nomothetic rather than an idiographic discipline. The methods of all nomothetic disciplines are similar, and psychology must be returned to natural science. And if this is done, it is quite inappropriate for history.

The problem for historical understanding is found by Rickert in the determination of individuality. Historical knowledge attempts to grasp the meaning of a particular incident in its concreteness and individuality. The criterion of indivisibility is needed as the source of its uniqueness. The historical task is to trace the relation of individuals to values.

If one were to follow Dilthey, the problem of "meaningful" interpretations comes into prominence and the method of "empathic understanding" is required. Moreover, a sharp division is accepted between the cultural and natural sciences. If one follows Rickert, the results are different. Psychology and sociology are conceived as sciences. But now the lines are sharply drawn between science and history as alternative and antithetical forms of thought. To the extent that sociology insists on being a science but accepts the conceptual formulations of Rickert, it may well be set on the road toward abstract formalism.

The time was to come, as we have said, when sociology would experience theoretical difficulties, and Dilthey and Rickert serve as starting points for distinct schools of sociological theory.

ART, NATURAL SCIENCE, AND SOCIOLOGY

Like folk wisdom, sociology aspires to generalization about social events; unlike folk wisdom, it seeks abstract knowledge not bound by the normative patterns of a local time and place. Like religious thought, sociology aspires to abstract knowledge; unlike religious thought, it is neither metaphysically inclined nor subordinate to sacred institutions. Like philosophy, sociology aspires to a body of knowledge resting on intrinsic rather than extrinsic standards of validity — a knowledge formed into logically consistent wholes; unlike philosophy, it is empirical rather than social-ethical (as in the case of traditional philosophy). Like history, sociology aspires to empirical knowledge of social events; unlike history, it aspires to a knowledge of the general rather than the unique, for, when all is said and done, sociology is a scientific organization of knowledge.

But sociology did not immediately depart from traditional philosophy as one of the special sciences. In time, it was to emerge and find a body of data ready made in history, but this occurred only in an atmosphere in which science was already a going concern. The separation of sociology from philosophy was long anticipated by the departure of natural science therefrom. In fact, it was the great success attendant upon the separation of physical science from philosophy that provided a major motive for the establishment of independent social science. For this reason, special interest attaches to the factors promoting the independence of physical science.

As has already been indicated, the first step toward science was taken when Greek philosophy discovered the rational proof. The logic of Aristotle, however fragmentary from the standpoint of contemporary logic, represented an important beginning, for, together with Euclidean geometry, it was bearer of the ideal of a rationally organized world of thought. But Greek philosophy was primarily carried on by a stratum of thinkers remote from the workaday world. Moreover, the spirit of empirical investigation declined precisely with the rise of moral concerns. Nevertheless, the acquisition of the rational proof permitted philosophy to acquire an autonomy, a self-determination, which facilitated its separation from theology. When the truth-establishing function was located in the thought process itself, no institutional hierarchy was required to fix the truth. Mythological, theological, and magical types of thought were thoroughly undermined by the self-correcting power of the new philosophy. Furthermore, this same autonomy of thought was simultaneously being developed in the area of

mathematics, which was to become a fundamental tool of science. All this was transmitted directly on to science, which retains as a basic ideal of its own the formation of its concepts as nearly as possible into logically closed systems. Nevertheless, the point of gravity of science lies elsewhere.

The fundamental object of science is the advancement of empirical knowledge, the extension of knowledge of the facts of the actual world. The rational proof of philosophy is subordinated to this primary task of extending empirical information. With the advent of science, the mathematical achievements of philosophy cease to be an "end" of knowledge and become instead a means of empirical investigation. Only after this development is the ideal again restored of forming empirical concepts into logically closed systems.

Thus, from its earliest beginnings, science differed from philosophy in that it endeavored to find a systematic procedure for extending *empirical* knowledge, a general method of verifying statements about the empirical world. Only by generalizing the procedures of empirical proof could science hope to achieve the sort of autonomy which had been granted to philosophy by the discovery of the rational proof. Eventually such a procedure was found in the *experiment,* which performed the service for science which the rational proof had performed for philosophy. Science was thus emancipated from philosophy by a discovery equivalent to the one which had earlier freed philosophy from theology.

The interplay between thought, observation, activity, and thought once again, in such a way as to verify one's generalizations about the empirical world, was not new in human history. It has occurred in all societies, however primitive. The success of this movement is a measure of the progress of civilization. However, the transformation of the process into a conscious procedure is quite another matter. Isolated experiments are reported from the earliest days of Greek philosophy. But even the nearest approach to the modern scientist in the Greek world shows that science was still far in the future.

The closest foreshadowing of the modern synthesis of experiment and mathematics is provided by Archimedes of Syracuse (287–212 B.C.). The interplay between conceptualization and observation is illustrated by the principle that bears his name — that a body floating in a liquid displaces an amount equal to its weight. The principle is said to have occurred to Archimedes in his bath — showing the leap from observation to conceptualization. The trip back from conceptualization to manipulation is shown by his extension of this principle to the notion that equal weights of metals of different alloy will displace varying volumes of a liquid. Archimedes had, in fact, much of a scientist's delight in controlling things: he is said to have invented a screw for raising water for mining operations and irrigation; he moved great weights by systems of pulleys; he devised military equipment for the defense of Syracuse; he made great use of cut-out models in the service of his mathematical deductions. Furthermore, he employed experimental procedure, as shown in his use of the method of exhaustion in the measurement of a circle, leading to the discovery of the relation between the surface and volume of a sphere and its circumscribing cylinder within narrow tolerance limits. He proved that the ratio of the circumference to the diameter of a circle was between $3^{1}/_{7}$ and $3^{10}/_{71}$. From burning mirrors to weight-throwing machines for warfare, to attempts to determine the angle suspended by the sun's disk at the eye, an experimental mentality is evident.

But Archimedes was under the spell of the rational proof, and he never assigned to experiment anything like the importance that he attributed to rational demonstration. From a fascination with the lever, his interest quickly passed to the attempt to deduce its properties from a minimum-number of axioms.[17] He attempted to deduce his observations on the relative density of bodies from the concept of a fluid as a substance yielding to the smallest shearing stress. Orderly logical deduction from a limited number of postulates was the aim of

[17]He suggested two: (1) that equal weights placed at equal distances from the point of support balance, and (2) equal weights at unequal distances do not.

thought. Above all else, Archimedes minimized the importance of experiment. For Greek thought, science was remarkably close in possibility; and yet, psychologically, it was remote. Thus, for the person most completely approaching the modern synthesis, the elevation of experiment into a general method of thought was most completely out of the question. To achieve science, the enormous generalization of experimental procedure and its elevation to a position of prestige were required.

Science and Art. This increase of experimentation in prestige and the generalization of it into a rule of empirical procedure occurred in the workshops of the Renaissance artists. Both the social role of the artist and the nature of his activity were factors in the process. Art mediated the transition from philosophy to science.

The philosophers of ancient Greece were either eminent men or tutors in the households of eminent families. Their connection with the workaday world was indirect. The artist, on the other hand, is basically a craftsperson — however high a value society may place on a particular craft. Artists find themselves in the center of an activity, operating with a material medium: metals, stone, wood, leather, glass, paint, sound.

Moreover, not only does artistic activity require a high level of skill; it also demands a novelty of product. Here, in contrast to many other areas of life, *originality tends to be rewarded rather than punished.*[18] To the degree to which art becomes a "play" activity or an "aesthetic" activity, it becomes peculiarly uncommitted or "free" from any limitations other than those it establishes itself. A combination of dedication and activity without external commitment tends to emerge. When the capacity to surprise and delight are rewarded, innovation may become one of the artist's fundamental goals. The Renaissance artist was thus inspired to experiment systematically.

There is no better illustration than Leonardo da

Vinci (1452–1519). The son of a lawyer and a peasant girl, Leonardo was educated by his father and served in a number of courts, including Florence, Milan, and Rome. He was a painter, sculptor, engineer, architect, physicist, and biologist among other things. Of all persons of the ancient world, it was Archimedes (not Aristotle) who fired Leonardo's imagination, and he noted the names of friends and patrons who could procure copies of Archimedes' work for him.[19] However, while sharing Archimedes' great respect for mathematics, Leonardo arrived at a very different estimate of its place and importance. Mathematics, he thought, concerned mental materials and provided certainty in its realm. Experience is another matter. For Leonardo, experience also potentially provided certainty. Experience, he argued, is never at fault. Only judgment is in error. Experience offers a realm of universal causation. Experiment is the procedure for determining causes. Once we understand the causes, we no longer have need for experiment.[20] Experiment is lifted by Leonardo to a level of importance parallel to that of mathematics. It is the only way of attaining certain knowledge of the actual world. One is not, under such circumstances, to be surprised by the fact that Leonardo's notebooks read like one continuous lifelong collection of laboratory notes. Experiment after experiment is described. We learn that if we place the second finger under the tip of the third in a manner such that the whole of the nail is visible on the far side, any round object that is touched by the two fingers will seem double. To discover the north side of a magnet, fill a large tub with water and set the magnet floating in a wooden cup; it will turn toward the north star. A drop of dew with its perfect round affords an opportunity to observe the various functions of the watery sphere. A concave mirror, although cold when it receives rays of the fire, reflects them with undiminished heat. Experiments are recorded on

[18]At least this seems to be the case whenever artistic activity escapes from magical and religious contexts.

[19]This interest in Archimedes was not peculiar to Leonardo. Some of Archimedes' works were published in Latin by Tartaglia at the time.
[20]Edward McCurdy, *The Notebooks of Leonardo da Vinci* (New York: George Braziller, 1956), pp. 64 ff.

how to measure the thinness of water, on making fire with mercury and a siphon, on flowing liquids, fire, waves in water and air. Innumerable experiments are described and inventions proposed. There are inventions for drying up the marsh at Piombino; for a clock showing hours, minutes, and seconds; for measuring how great a distance one goes in an hour with the current of the wind; for learning from the quality and density of air when it will rain; for reckoning mileage at sea; for an apparatus designed to lift weights with ropes and pulleys; for descending below the surface of the water; for an alarm clock and a drilling machine; for making concrete; for constructing a bellows without leather; for producing a wind, and so on.

A thoroughgoing spirit of scientific naturalism pervades all Leonardo's work: he knew the experimental impossibility of perpetual motion; he developed Archimedes' concept of the pressure of fluids; he traced analogies in wave theory in water, sound, and light; he treated the realm of astronomy, naturalistically conceiving the celestial world as a sort of machine; he thought the earth could be interpreted naturally, and the presence of fossils was taken as indicating that areas now dry were once covered by ocean; he dissected a number of human bodies, and made numerous anatomical drawings; he anticipated the theory of circulation of the blood; he knew how an image is formed on the retina of the eye. Though Leonardo was clearly one of the outstanding men of all time, his activities were not a departure from his day.

Science Outside the Artists' Workshop.

The new faith in the possibility that experience could yield dependable knowledge if only method were sound diffused from the workshops of the artists to one area after another. Copernicus (1473–1543) revived the theories of Euphantus and Aristarchus from antiquity, maintaining that the earth revolves on its axis daily and around the sun yearly. He established the heliocentric theory, and Giordano Bruno was martyred for this and other opinions (1600). The study of animals was reopened in the sixteenth century, and the science of ichthyology

was founded. Theophrastus von Hohenheim, or Paracelsus (1493?–1541), broke away from the orthodox (Galenic) school of medicine, and opened the way to the application of chemistry to medicine. New studies in mineralogy and geology were opened by Agricola (1494–1555) and Jan Baptista van Helmont (1577–1644). Modern anatomy and physiology got under way with the work of Jean Fernel (1497–1558) and Andreas Vesalius (1514–1564). Vesalius particularly had seen many dissections, and extended knowledge of bones, veins, and abdominal organs. These developments led to the discovery of the circulation of the blood by William Harvey (1578–1657). Using the compound microscope (invented about 1590), Marcello Malpighi of Bologna (1628–1694) made numerous discoveries about tissues. Tycho Brahe (1546–1601) and Johannes Kepler (1571–1630) made systematic new observations in astronomy, providing — especially in Kepler's three laws of planetary motion — the theories and evidence that laid the foundation for Newton's great synthesis.

Galileo Models the Scientific Role.

The full transition from art to natural science is evident in the work of Galileo Galilei (1564–1642). He invented a thermometer. From stories of a glass that magnified distant objects, he drew on his knowledge of refraction and constructed a telescope, observing the surface of the moon, and hitherto invisible stars. He experimented extensively with inclined planes and established the science of dynamics on an experimental and mathematical foundation. He studied the composition of forces, the pressure of liquids. In all his careful studies, Galileo constantly aimed at the establishment of exact laws. It is not difficult to see why he is often treated as the first modern scientist.[21]

Strictly speaking, of course, Galileo was not the first scientist. The extension of the scientific attitude to almost every conceivable area was better illustrated by Leonardo. And many of Galileo's predecessors and contemporaries not only ob-

[21]See, for example, Bertrand Russell, *The Scientific Outlook* (New York: W. W. Norton, 1931), Chapter 1.

served and invented instruments for observation, but experimented as well. Galileo's importance lies not in his temporal priority but in the completeness or distinctness with which he represents the new scientific role. He is the very paradigm of the scientist. He demonstrates the value of systematic, continuous experimentation with limited aims, simultaneously motivated by the ideal of demonstrating mathematical relations between events and forming his ideas into a logically closed system. Copernicus and Kepler had shown that the motion of the heavenly bodies could be expressed mathematically. Galileo set out to discover the mathematical relations holding for falling bodies. Noting that bodies fall with increasing speed, he hypothesized that the increase is proportionate to the distance. Since measurement of bodies in free fall was beyond the scope of the available instruments, he designed special situations for studying slower rates of fall in inclined planes. He experimentally demonstrated that speed is proportionate to the time of fall. He also proved that a body running down an inclined plane will rise to an equivalent height on another except insofar as checked by friction, and that a body running down a plane will continue indefinitely in motion on a horizontal unless checked by friction. He proved that the swing of a pendulum is independent of the displacement, and that gravity increases the speed of the bob by equal amounts in equal times. Throughout this work, Galileo's aim was to arrive at the statement of the exact mathematical relations involved.

Newtonian Physics Models the Scientific Theory. If Galileo is the paradigm of the new man of science, the great achievement of Newtonian physics is the paradigm of the new scientific knowledge. Kepler had established his three laws of motion. Galileo had advanced a theory of the tides, and had developed some of the mathematical relations discoverable in motion. Sir Isaac Newton's *Principia* (1687) fused the two major elements of science—rational proof and experimental-observational evidence. From the three laws of motion and the law of gravitation, the movement of the solar system was explained by a system of mathematical deduction. So impressive was this logical schema that no fundamental criticism was carried through until Ernst Mach (1883) examined its logical structure and pointed out that Newton's definitions of mass and force were logically circular. But Newton had established the validity of terrestrial mechanics for celestial spaces. He annihilated, once and for all, the ancient and medieval view that the heavenly bodies are divine. In the course of his labors, like Leibniz, he invented infinitesimal calculus. He established the binomial theorem in mathematics. In astronomy he founded lunar theory. He also established hydrodynamics and the theory of the propagation of waves. Even his work in optics, had he done nothing else, was sufficient to place him in the forefront of science. But more than anything else, Newton's work emerged as a paradigm of organized scientific theory, much as Galileo supplied the paradigm of the scientific role.

Experimentation was therefore first established in the activities of the artists — activities which were peculiarly free and designed specifically for the creation of the aesthetically new. This area had invited systematization of the procedure by which the human mind moved into the unknown. The relevance of this for science was direct, for science itself can be conveniently described as a kind of *strategy of adventure*. It takes little insight to determine why the extension of experimentalism could be made from the workshop of the Renaissance artist to the physical world. For one thing, there was a coincidence of activity. Leonardo, like many of his contemporaries, was more than an artist. He was also an architect, engineer, and military expert. On occasion he sought work primarily as a civil and fortification engineer rather than as an artist. Techniques of procedure so useful in art were inevitably tried on other things.

But the reasons for the extension of experimentalism from art to physical nature are more than external and accidental. One could expect the extension of experimentalism only into areas relatively unencumbered by magical, religious, or traditional restrictions. Leonardo himself saw that unquestioned authority puts an end to thought. He suggested that whenever, in a discussion, authority is adduced, reliance is being placed on the memory rather than the intellect. He scorned the activities of the priests so far as they encouraged superstition and trade in miracles. At the same time, he recognized that religion claimed an unquestioned interpretation of the spiritual. But Leonardo did not fail to perceive that his researches could come into conflict with scripture. At the conclusion of his attempt to develop a natural theory of the origin of life, he observed that he spoke not against the sacred books that contain the supreme truth.

The extension of experimentalism to the physical world could only occur because at the time art was relatively outside magical and religious control. However, once science had been established as a procedure for dealing with physical events, its further extension was to be expected. Psychologists have proved than even a rat running a maze so complicated that it could not possibly comprehend will retain the favorable trials and gradually dismiss the unfavorable, until its behavior reduces to something approaching maximum economy. A creature's habits represent generalizations of its responses imposing a common behavioral form on a variety of particular situations. Habits form advance organizations of potential response. Only when these do not work does the rather painful process of readjustment occur.

Hence, there is no mystery about the fact that, when experimentation is once established as a method of exploring the physical world, it may expand beyond this sphere. Rather, at this stage the problem becomes one of explaining why it does *not* continue to spread, for the growth of science becomes largely self-perpetuating, and only repeated failure or the appearance of counter forces strong enough to overcome its momentum can halt its advance.

The very persons most directly involved with science have been the first to perceive the forces that oppose it. This is to be expected. Leonardo saw the potential conflict between his theories of the natural origin of life and the scriptures, and

made an appeasing gesture in the direction of religion. The scientific role was not only fully established with Galileo, but the fact that it was not a role without limits was made clear as well. Galileo became unpopular and his lectures were booed; Einstein was to have a similar experience in his lectures in Berlin. When Galileo invited the professors to look at Jupiter's moons through his telescope, they refused: Aristotle had said nothing of such. And toward the end of his life, Galileo was called before the Inquisition, and forced to recant. However, by the time the forces basically inimical to science were thoroughly awakened to the threat it represented, it was too late. Science had become linked to new social forces that it helped to implement.

The Dream of a Social Science Takes Shape. The importance of Francis Bacon (1561–1626), Lord Chancellor of England, was not in the extension of scientific results, but in the generalization of the scientific program to make it coextensive with thought itself. Also, he helped to popularize the scientific point of view. For Bacon, medieval theology ceased to be the center of thought. He attributed the backwardness of thinking to three things: (1) resistance from antiquity, (2) resistance from the prestige of thinkers important in the history of philosophy, and (3) resistance of public opinion.

With respect to antiquity, Bacon maintained that the opinion individuals have of it is of negligible importance. The old people of the world, he argued, are its true antiquity. We expect greater wisdom from older people than from younger people, because they have experienced more. This and only this is an antiquity of value. In modern times, Bacon indicated, distant journeys have become frequent and have revealed the nature of things in a manner casting new light upon philosophy. And surely it would be a disgrace to open the material world of sea, earth, and stars while the intellectual globe remains closed. The obstacles to thought represented by antiquity, authority, and popular opinion must be eliminated. Bacon urged that the full extension of the new method of experimentation would infinitely expand the power of humanity. He proposed a general program of recording all available facts and the performing of all feasible experiments. The tabulation of results, he thought, would permit the discovery of general laws holding between facts. The full mastery of nature and the betterment of humankind was visualized and the possibility of a social science was conceived.

SUMMARY

The entire structure of human culture is learned, and maintained, by habit. Its infinite plasticity is matched only by its amazing tenacity, for in the unceasing cycle of birth, learning, and death of individuals, the continuous introduction of individuals into the countless little acts that constitute culture make it incredibly adaptable in minor things but glacial in its responses to major things.

With all historical time to develop in, sociology is only about a hundred years old. For hundreds of thousands of years before this, people learned and transmitted to their children all the knowledge necessary for stability and successful life. The things essential for a science of social life were partly assembled in the folk wisdom of human societies. Other materials were refined and organized by theology. But neither the time-bound ethos of folk society nor the ethico-religious ethos provides the conditions for the secular pursuit of social generalizations. A significant step toward a general social science was taken by philosophy, which made general knowledge of a secular type possible.

The Greeks, however, who took this step, never quite achieved a clear social science. Where naturalistic attitudes were present, as in the Greek atomists, they were not applied to social phenomena. Where social phenomena were studied, as with the Sophists, they were subordinated to ethical and didactic requirements. For this reason, the great contribution of the Greeks to social science remained indirect by way of the discovery and elaboration of the rational proof. The real beginnings of Western mathematics and logic were laid by them. These beginnings formed basic elements in the imperishable heritage of rationalism that ever after remained fundamental components in Western philosophy and one of the primary factors in the rise of Western science.

For further insight into the sources of sociology and social science, one must therefore turn to history, where the accumulation of objective historical data about society was carried through. The development of historiography was also, in part, a development of objective empirical methods for assembling and evaluating social materials. The playback of historiography into social science continued into the nineteenth century, when Dilthey and Rickert pioneered special schools of sociology.

But the impulse for a genuine social science was to come from science itself. The scientific point of view needed, it seems, to have first proved its value by gains in nonsocial areas. Thus, sociology took its early points of view from philosophy, its first materials were supplied by history, but the model for its emergence was provided by natural science. Sociology comes into being with the extension of the scientific method (pioneered in art and confirmed in its applications to the physical world) to the social world of humanity itself.

II

The Humanistic and Scientific Poles
of Western Intellectuality

In the medieval world the classical spirit of Western thought went into eclipse: oriental mysticism walked the world, metaphysics and science were fused, and philosophy became the handmaiden of theology. In his reflections the typical church father combined demoniac and miraculous elements along with fragments of ancient thought. The second-century compilation of Christian allegories, the *Physiologue,* or *Bestiary*, illustrate medieval knowledge of natural history. Typical of its doctrinal intent was the idea that the lioness brought her cubs dead into the world, breathing between their eyes on the third day so that they woke to life, thus symbolizing the Resurrection of the Lord, the Lion of Judah.[1] In the hands of the church propagandists, history was transformed into apologetics. The medieval historian did not hesitate to resort to outright forgery in the name of the faith, as illustrated by the false Decretals and the Donation of Constantine:[2]

THE MEDIEVAL SCHOLASTIC

The dominant intellectuals of the ancient world in the Classical period were the philosophers. Though they might theorize profoundly about spiritual matters, they were secular intellectuals. Their thought was dominated by the striving for a rational synthesis of ideas. They rested their case

[1]Sir William Cecil Dampier, *A History of Science* (New York: The Macmillan Co., 1944), p. 72.
[2]Until the time of Gregory the Great, the supremacy of

Rome over the local churches outside its immediate area was more theoretical than factual. Gregory's statesmanship greatly enhanced the papal prestige. His successors employed this prestige in their bestowal of the temporal crown on Charles the Great in reward for his defense of spiritual power. Charles, in turn, asserted that absolute obedience was due in spiritual matters to the see of Peter. The authority ascribed to Rome by Charlemagne was bolstered by the False Decretals whose object was to limit the absolutism of local metropolitans by exalting the prerogatives of the papal see. Earlier in origin than the False Decretals was the document known as the Donation of Constantine by which that Emperor was represented as bestowing upon the Popes his imperial dignity in the West, with a spiritual principate over other patriarchs and local churches. The principal aim of these fabrications was to transform the Roman see into the final court of appeal for Christians.

for acceptance on adherence to standards of rational proof: the proper conduct of the thought process itself in terms of its own rules.

In the Hellenistic period all this began to change. Spokespersons, rivals of the philosophers, appeared among the leaders of popular sects, cults, and mystery religions. The heirs of the older philosophic positions, in turn, began to bend in the direction of these irrational popular faiths. Various forms of revelations and mystical intuitions began to take their place alongside the older rational arguments. The priest-theologians, the scholastics of the medieval world, who represented the end product of these developments and a starting point for modern developments, completed the amalgamation of faith and reason that was under way in the Hellenistic period by the subordination of reason to the requirements of faith.

The subordination of reason to faith is taken as the central clue to the scholastic and his thought by Sir Henry Slesser.

> The Catholic, perhaps, is the only modern man who can hope fully to appreciate the medieval scholastic philosophers, for he alone, like the School-men whom we have here to consider, without qualification accepts the Beatific Vision of God as the final end of man. Moreover, it is not possible to understand, much less to accept, the medieval mode of thought unless we grasp firmly the fact that, in any event, wherever speculation might wander, it took place within the ambit of revealed faith as disclosed in the Scriptures, the Fathers, and the tradition and teaching of the Church.
>
> Whether we study St. Augustine and wonder at his remark: "Whence shall we begin? With authority or with Reason? Authority should precede Reason when we wish to learn anything" . . . or begin with St. Anselm and his "I believe that I may understand" . . . or St. Thomas who, when distinguishing between faith and philosophy, said, "it is necessary that there should be a doctrine according with divine revelation, besides the philosophical disciplines which are pursued by human Reason, because man was ordained towards God as towards an end passing his comprehension"[3]

[3]Sir Henry Slesser, *The Middle Ages in the West* (London: Hutchinson & Co., 1950), p. 197.

Even philosophers who ran afoul the church, for example, Scotus Erigena and Abelard, subscribed to the primacy of faith over reason. Erigena is quoted as stating: "The Scripture is the chief source of our knowledge of God. Reason establishes its data." And against the severe persecution of Abelard by St. Bernard for overstressing reason at the expense of faith stands Abelard's own formulation: "We set the faith of the blessed Trinity as the foundation of all good."[4] In this characterization of the scholastic, Slesser automatically locates the modern intellectual on the other side of his equation.

St. Augustine may be taken as marking the end of the evolution of the intellectual in the Hellenistic period from the philosopher to the scholastic. He was also the greatest of the scholastics until the late Middle Ages. In his own life he epitomized much of the drama of the exploration of thought systems in the search for spiritual certainty that had come to dominate the learned of the Greco-Roman world.

St. Augustine (Aurelius Augustinus, 354–430 A.D.) was born at Tagaste, Numidia, of Roman parents. His mother had been a Christian from childhood; his father was baptized late in life. At the age of twelve St. Augustine attended the grammar school at Madaura, where he became thoroughly acquainted with Latin literature and superficially acquainted with Greek. He formed a liaison with a concubine, and was a father before he had reached twenty years of age. Shortly thereafter he came under the influence of Manicheanism, which he studied for nine years. Because of conceptual problems with Manicheanism, he turned to the popular teacher, Faustus, but after a time cast off his influence as well, and fell back on the skepticism of the Academy (Neo-Platonism). In 384 A.D. he departed for Milan to teach, where he fell under the influence of its bishop, Ambrose. In 387 A.D. he was baptized a Christian. He was ordained a priest by the Bishop of Hippo in 391 A.D., and in 396 A.D. he himself became Bishop of Hippo.

Having worked his way through Manicheanism

[4]*Ibid.*, pp. 197 ff.

and Neo-Platonism to Christianity, St. Augustine was familiar with many of the currents of pagan philosophy. He was able to turn many of its formulations to account in his defense of the faith. No one has summarized his synthesis of Christian philosophy more compactly than Rudolf Sohm.

> On Easter Eve 387, at the age of thirty-three, he was baptized by the great Bishop Ambrose at Milan. The duty of his life was henceforth two-fold: to proclaim, first, the gospel of sin and grace, and then the glory of the Church. Against the British monk Pelagius he developed the doctrine of Original Sin and of the salvation of man by Grace alone, making the doctrine of Grace, as Luther at first also made it, equivalent to the doctrine of Predestination. Against the African Donatists, who would have made the effectual working of the sacraments dependent on the worthiness of the minister, he set up the idea of the Church as an institution for dispensing salvation, as an institution possessing *objective* sanctity. The supreme value of the church — even of the outwardly visible Church constituted as she is — he expressed in the statement that she represents the "City of God" (*Civitas Dei*) upon earth. From this commonwealth salvation flows forth upon the individual. To serve this commonwealth, and in particular to lead back the erring (the Donatists) by force into the Church is the highest duty of the State. Only by doing such service to the Church will the State attain a value which does not otherwise belong to it. The middle ages are dawning. Catholicism, at least Western Catholicism, in claiming supremacy for the Church over the world, is embodied for the first time in Augustine's mighty personality. Even in his monkish convictions he is a Catholic. Flight from the world into the cloister is to him the perfection of the Christian life.
>
> Yet this man has the Reformation — Luther's Reformation — in him too. Side by side with his conception of the Church as a hierarchy, he holds the opposite idea of the true Church as the invisible Church of the predestined — the redeemed. In direct contradiction to his doctrine of the saving power of the Church, he lives by faith in grace freely given by God as the only source of salvation. He prepared a way for Catholicism by his doctrine of the Church, for Luther by his doctrine of Sin and Grace.[5]

St. Augustine worked elements of Hellenistic thought and Christian faith into a system of theology that was to remain the primary, uncontested framework of official church dogma for nearly a thousand years.

THE SCHOLASTIC DUEL WITH THE NEW URBAN INTELLECTUALS

St. Augustine brought many of the currents of ancient thought into a definitive synthesis within a framework of Christian faith at the very time the final collapse of the ancient city was imminent. The medieval heirs to the Greco-Roman intellectual were to be learned monks. In the Benedictine pattern of Western monasticism, from three to five hours a day were assigned to reading according to the season. As Butler observes:

> There can be little doubt that this reading was wholly devotional, confined to the Bible and the writings of the fathers, St. Basil and Cassian being recommended by name. Out of this germ grew in the course of ages those works of erudition and of historical science with which the Benedictine name in later ages became associated. . . . But the chief work of the monk was, in St. Benedict's eyes, neither field work nor literary work: all the services of Benedictines to civilization and education and letters have been but by-products.[6]

In the West there were long periods when the monastery was the only source of literacy. This was of inestimable value for the church, for again and again its literate popes and administrators were monastically trained. When new urban communities began to erupt through the floor of the medieval world and to displace its intellectuals, monasticism responded to the challenge with the development of powerful new orders:

> The "Four Orders" were (1) the Dominicans or Friars Preachers, often called Black Friars in England

---

[5]Rudolf Sohm, *Outlines of Church History*, trans. May Sinclair (Boston: Beacon Press, 1958), pp. 71–72.

[6]Dom E. C. Butler, "Monasticism," *The Cambridge Medieval History* (New York: The Macmillan Co., 1929), I, 538.

and Jacobins in France; (2) The Franciscans or Friars Minor, called in England Grey Friars, in France Cordeliers, and in Germany Barefoot Friars; (3) the Carmelites or Order of the Blessed Virgin of Mount Carmel, or White Friars; (4) the Austin Friars or Order of the Friar Hermits of St. Augustine. Many smaller Mendicant Orders also sprang up in the thirteenth century, but were suppressed, *i.e.*, forbidden to receive any more novices, by the Second Council of Lyons in 1274.[7]

The monastic orders rejected permanent endowments. Their members embraced a life of poverty, and undertook the reconciliation of secular and religious life. Many independent movements of this sort — organized groups of people devoting themselves to self-sacrifice, social work, and the imitation of Christ — appeared toward the end of the twelfth century. Among them were the Beguines and Beghars of the Low Countries, the Humiliati of Italy, and the Poor Men of Lyon. Between the Franciscans and the Poor Men of Lyon there was little difference other than the fact that the latter repudiated the Church. The Poor Men of Lyon were excommunicated as heretics, while the Franciscans were authorized as a religious order.

The Intellectual Ferment in the New Urban Communities. The conflict between the new urban communities and the church was inevitable. It was equally certain that the urban communities would give rise to a type of intellectual activity that would find its organization, in part, in opposition to the priest-theologian.

Pirenne has noted that as a general rule the lay princes favored the new urban communities. While they had nothing militarily or politically to fear from the bourgeoisie, it was to their economic advantage to protect them. The urbanites produced a new, taxable, moneyed wealth that helped the princes free themselves from dependency on the Church and the landed aristocrats. On the

other hand, the bishops who remained on the sites of the once thriving Roman cities regarded with suspicion the struggles by the bourgeoisie to achieve autonomy.

They were all the more suspicious because this autonomy was demanded by merchants. For the Church had an invincible objection to trade. It considered that trade endangered the salvation of souls, it accounted desire for gain as avarice, and in most commercial transactions it detected various forms of usury.[8]

The first struggle that cities arising in episcopal sees had to face was with the bishops. Pirenne has noted that the occurrences of insurrectional movements in episcopal cities were far too numerous not to be due to some common factor.

The earliest mentioned occurred at Cologne in 1074; two years later in 1076 one broke out at Cambrai. Then about 1080 there followed a revolt at St. Quentin, one at Beauvais in 1099, one at Noyon in 1108–1109, one at Amiens in 1113, one at Laon in 1115. There is no doubt that this tendency to revolt was fomented by the merchants. The important part they played is definitely proved at Cambrai and Cologne; at Beauvais the insurrection movement was led by the cloth merchants. The subsequent insurrections at Noyon and Laon present a slightly different character. Here it seems that we are concerned with an agitation less obviously provoked by the merchant class. Serfs and even priests were involved.[9]

However, where such insurrections are not directly traceable to the merchants, they were a precipitating factor. It is natural for class excitements to pull malcontents from other groups into their course.

These insurrections were no mere riots or occasions to let off steam, but directed movements. The merchants were determined to revise the laws and monetary arrangements sustained by the

[7]A. G. Little, "The Mendicant Orders," *The Cambridge Medieval History* (New York: The Macmillan Co., 1929), VI, 727.

[8]Henri Pirenne, "Northern Towns and Their Commerce," *The Cambridge Medieval History* (New York: The Macmillan Co., 1929), VI, 517.
[9]*Ibid.*, p. 518.

Church, which blocked the free exercise of their trade. They organized their movements into mutually sworn associations and proclaimed their communes in a revolutionary manner.

> The commune was, strictly speaking, the association of burghers, constituted by oath, who seized municipal power and undertook to defend both corporate and individual liberty against all attacks. It was the result of a conjuration and it sometimes even bore the name of Conjuration. Its members were conjurors (*coniurati*) and the same name *iuratus* or *jure* was adopted by the magistrates appointed at their head. It was thus essentially revolutionary, and it never appeared except in towns where self-government was gained as a result of a keen struggle. For this reason it is characteristic of episcopal cities, and especially of episcopal cities in Northern France.[10]

The aim of these revolutionary associations was to replace seigneurial law by an autonomous civic law and jurisdiction. When they succeeded, all inhabitants acquired similar status subject to the same courts and governed by the same council recruited from their members. The city became a distinct judicial territory. Their revolutionary origin did not prevent the communes from attaining a legal existence. Some revolutions were crushed, but many communes obtained charters from their overlord or king confirming their organization. Charters of communes such as were conceded only after insurrections in the eleventh century were frequently freely granted during the following century.

When the city so often arose as a revolutionary insurrection against the bishop, there is no question that it was providing an intellectual milieu for social roles other than that of priest. From the beginning the cities supported anticlerical types. Moreover, the city not only demanded different intellectual skills than a monastic or manorial community, but demanded them in far greater volume. In the monastic community the primary employment of literary skills was in devotional reading and study, and the keeping of monastic

annals and records. In the manorial communities the amount of administrative work and record-keeping was so slight that all correspondence and records could be kept by the manorial priest who was, at times, the only literate person in the castle. The city, on the other hand, presented a great range of activities for which the routine application of literary skills was an absolute essential: business correspondence, record-keeping, administration of its many guilds, legal problems, and all the complete judicial, legislative, and administrative activities of the city itself.

The cities were seedbeds for voluntary associations of all sorts: for religious, welfare, health, economic, and political purposes. The cities were creating unprecedented needs in both quantity and kind for trained persons, which the existing monastic and cathedral schools were not equipped to supply. Besides, when active tensions with the bishops so often accompanied the establishment of the cities, the local clergy could hardly be expected to supply the trained persons who would make such revolts possible. At the same time, it was not altogether to the disadvantage of the bishops to have the cities grow up around them once again. Urban populations supplied a source of wealth undreamed of in the rural subsistence economy for the bishops as well as for lay lords. The cathedrals developed in size and wealth, undertook new building programs, developed administrative staffs, and incidentally developed new training schools, primarily to train their own personnel but also, at times, to serve the urban community and reinstitute control over the urban population once again. However, whether these new educational institutions grew as voluntary guilds of students and teachers or by expansion of cathedral schools (the first was typical of southern Europe, the second typical of the north), an enormous expansion of secular education was under way to supply new requirements of the cities. Rashdall summarizes the basic patterns as follows:

> During the Dark Ages, whatever learning and education survived the barbarian cataclysm had their home almost exclusively in the monasteries and the

[10]*Ibid.*, pp. 518–519.

cathedrals; and during this period the monastic schools were perhaps slightly in advance of the secular. The period has been called the Benedictine Age. In the cathedrals themselves some of the best-known teachers had been pupils of the monks. A marked feature of the intellectual new birth which took place in the twelfth century was the transference of the intellectual primacy from the monastic schools to those of the secular clergy. In the north of Europe the universities were an outgrowth of the cathedral schools, not of the monasteries. Anselm of Bec was one of the last great monastic teachers; the great Abelard — the introducer of a new era in the scholastic philosophy, the true father of the scholastic theology, out of whose teaching, though not in his lifetime, the University of Paris may be said to have grown — was a secular who lectured in the schools of the cathedral, though accidentally, as it were, he ended his days as a monk. At a later date, regulars played a great role in connection with the universities, but the universities themselves were essentially secular, *i.e.,* non-monastic, institutions. In Italy culture was never so completely the monopoly of the clergy as it came to be in the dark ages of northern Europe. The lay professions of law and medicine were never wholly extinguished; and, when the intellectual revival came, the movement was not so closely connected with the Church. And the universities to which it gave birth, though like all medieval institutions, they had close relations with the Church, may be looked upon, on the whole, not only as secular but as lay institutions. This was one of the great differences which from first to last distinguished the universities of northern Europe from those of the south, or at least of Italy. In the northern universities . . . the scholar was *ipso facto* regarded for many purposes as a clerk; he wore, or was supposed to wear, the tonsure and the clerical habit, while the Master was still more definitely invested with the privileges and subject to the restrictions of the ecclesiastical life, including the obligation to celibacy. In Italy the teacher was more often a layman than an ecclesiastic; the scholar was not necessarily a clerk, and the control which ecclesiastical authorities exercised over the universities was only the kind which they exercised in all spheres of medieval life.[11]

The universities were the eventual institutionalization of a ferment of new ideas and the demand for new types of training at first supplied in the cities by voluntary associations of teachers and students. In the nature of the case, churchmen tried to take over or, at least, to guide the course of such movements, for if they did not, the control of society would slip out of their hands.

The Rise of the Universities. In the cities that had begun to take shape in Italy during the twelfth century, the typical institution of higher learning of the West was created — the university. Through Italy and Sicily in the twelfth century there was an influx of new knowledge into Europe from Arabic scholars, including the works of Aristotle, Euclid, Ptolemy, and the Greek physicians. The core of the new higher learning was made up of medicine and law.

In Salerno, south of Naples, in Lombard, and in Norman territory, the contact with the traditions of Greece was never completely lost. By the middle of the eleventh century, Salerno took shape as the foremost medical center of Europe around the teachings of Hippocrates amplified by developments in anatomy and surgery. In 1231 Frederick II regulated its degrees.[12] Meanwhile, in response to the revival of trade and the rise of town life, new demands were made for a law adequate to more complex social and economic conditions. Bologna became the center for the revival of Roman law as Salerno was for the revival of Greek medicine. By 1158 a student class of sufficient importance had appeared to receive a formal grant of rights and privileges from Frederick Barbarossa. The student corporation (university) was organized as a means of protection against the townspeople over the cost of rooms and supplies. The student organization was also employed to control the professors, who were put under bond and required to live up to detailed regulations guaranteeing the students their money's worth.[13]

[11]Hastings Rashdall, "The Medieval Universities," *The Cambridge Medieval History* (New York: The Macmillan Co., 1926), VI, 559–560.

[12]Charles Homer Haskins, *The Rise of Universities* (Ithaca: Cornell University Press, 1957), pp. 4 ff.
[13]*Ibid.,* pp. 7 ff.

Excluded from the universities of the students, the professors formed guilds or "colleges" requiring special qualifications ascertained by examination for admission.[14] The professor's certification of attainment that gave him license to teach became the earliest type of academic degree. At an early period Bologna had already developed standard academic degrees, a university organization, and special officials such as the rector.

Bologna was the model of university organization for Italy, Spain, and southern France. Frederick II founded the University of Naples (1224) on its pattern. Padua was founded two years earlier as a secession from Bologna. In northern Europe the university originated around the cathedral school of Notre Dame in Paris. By the beginning of the twelfth century schools attached to cathedrals included Liège, Rheims, Laon, Paris, Orleans, and Chartres. Paris received its first royal charter in 1200; by this time there were four faculties each under a dean: arts, canon law, medicine, and theology. Paris was the model for the northern universities as Bologna was for the southern group. Oxford developed in the twelfth century; Cambridge somewhat later. By the end of the Middle Ages eighty universities had been founded in different parts of Europe.

This growth of universities was a direct or indirect response to the new demand for experts on the part of the new communities. The rise of medicine was a product of the requirements of more wealthy and sophisticated persons who broke out of the framework of medieval conceptions and limitations. The establishment of the faculties of civil and canon law was in response not only to the growth of legal problems in conjunction with the rise of the cities and the rapid development of trade, but to the increasing legal requirements of church and state. (It is noteworthy that as long as the University of Paris was under religious domination it had a college of canon law but not one of civil law.) The appearance of a theological faculty also testifies to the increased need of the church for trained persons in the face of accelerating social developments.

The Reopening of the Controversy Between Classical Philosophy and Christian Theology. The transformation of urban-based voluntary associations for the acquisition of the knowledges and skills required by the changing times into the universities proper was accompanied by a reopening of the controversy between classical philosophy and Christian theology with which the ancient development had closed. Langlois phrased this succinctly:

> At the very moment when the new Aristotle and his Moslem commentators were introduced at Paris, the philosophical-theological system which was reigning in the schools was Platonic idealism or pseudo-Platonic, on the model of St. Augustine. Although St. Augustine had been almost dazzled by Greek metaphysics, yet he was one of the most violent contemners of reason: he subordinated the True to the Good, the Intelligence to the Will, and prostrated human thought in the dust. The disciples of this somber genius continued to maintain his fundamental theses, which were satisfactory to spirits inclined to obedience, to religious and mystical souls, to born defenders of orthodoxy, and to rhetoricians. For these reasons, Augustinianism has never ceased to have numerous partisans.[15]

Augustinianism represented a subordination of the classical philosophy to the requirements of faith; it was brilliantly adapted to a religious evolution on the threshold of withdrawal into agricultural subsistence communities. When the voluntary guilds of scholars and teachers emerged in the cities, it was because of a need for training in skills and knowledges not available in the monastic and cathedral schools. One must not be misled by the fact that some individuals associated with the church participated in the brilliant recovery of ancient thought that got under way in the twelfth century, the so-called twelfth century Renaissance.

[14]*Ibid.,* p. 11.

[15]Adapted from C. V. Langlois, in Lavisse, *Histoire de France,* Vol. III, Part II, 1901, p. 387; Dana Carleton Munro and George Clarke Sellery, *Medieval Civilization* (New York: The Century Co., 1910), p. 460.

It arose in response to the requirements of the emerging urban milieux — not those of the monasteries. However, it was equally evident that if the church was to remain in control of intellectual life, it must either destroy these trends or take them over.

> The rationalistic philosophy of Aristotle was received with distrust by theologians who followed the Augustinian tradition, because they judged it dangerous; but most scholars fell upon this new food with an avidity which is comparable only to the intoxication of the first humanists in the presence of the resuscitated Antiquity. Such a vigorous fermentation immediately set in that the ecclesiastical authorities attempted to stop it, in 1210 and 1215: "The Books of Aristotle on metaphysics and natural philosophy are not to be read." Nevertheless, the prohibition pure and simple could not be maintained. April 13, 1231, Pope Gregory IV gave absolution to the masters and students who had been excommunicated for having disobeyed orders by reading and interpreting Aristotle; in principle, he confirmed the prohibited decrees of 1210 and 1215, but "provisionally, until the books of the Philosopher had been examined and expurgated."[16]

The three major courses of study — philosophy, law, and medicine — of the primary university centers of the thirteenth century (Paris, Bologna, and Salerno) all had major nonreligious components in their origins. However, it was also true that at an early stage the religious authorities took cognizance of them. Speaking of this revival of intellectual activity in which the intersection of secular and sacred interests led to the institutionalization of the universities, Rashdall states:

> If the revived study of the Classics was prominent in the earliest phase of the movement — the phase represented by such teachers as Bernard of Chartres and such writers as John of Salisbury — these studies were never prominent at Paris, and were everywhere thrown into the background by the re-discovery of the lost works of Aristotle at the beginning of the thirteenth century. In Italy the movement, though it

began with a revival of literary study, and of Roman Law as a branch of ancient literature, soon concentrated itself on the study of Law which became increasingly scientific and professional. Broadly speaking, Paris was the home of scholastic Philosophy and Theology; Bologna was the great School of Law, and, in a subordinate degree, of Medicine. The contrast must not be overstated: there was a large body of canonists at Paris; Philosophy was studied at Bologna — though chiefly as a preparation for Medicine rather than Theology. And Medicine was studied in both; as a place of medical study, Bologna was inferior to Salerno, which was exclusively a Studium of Medicine. From a period considerably before the actual birth of the university organization, these three places — Paris, Bologna, Salerno — stood forth as the three great homes of highest culture. By the twelfth century they had come to be known as *Studia Generalia,* a term which at first meant simply, places of study resorted to by students from all parts.[17]

The rise of the orders of Mendicant Friars coincided with this great intellectual activity, one phase of which was the rediscovery of ancient learning, particularly Aristotle. After an outbreak of heretical teaching at Paris based on Aristotle, lecturing on Aristotle's natural philosophy was prohibited in the university by papal decree. However, the ancient learning was too brilliantly adapted to the new milieu to be put down, and the second phase of the interaction between ancient learning and Christian faith got under way. The reconciliation of Aristotle with Christian theology was taken over by the friars and carried through, particularly by the Dominicans. The two greatest thinkers of the Dominican Order were Albert the Great (c. 1200–1280) and Thomas Aquinas (1225–1274). The Dominicans reached their greatest power in Paris. The Franciscans, on the other hand, reached prominence at Oxford, where Robert Grosseteste became lecturer and produced the first of the *Summa* which were intended to synthesize the newly discovered Aristotle with Christian theology (1245). The greatest of the Franciscans were Roger Bacon, Duns Scotus (1270–1302), and William of Occam (c. 1320–1340).

[16]*Ibid.,* pp. 460–461.

[17]Rashdall, "The Medieval Universities," pp. 560–561.

Thus the Renaissance of the twelfth century was a major component in the stimulation of scholastic philosophy to the period of its most rapid evolution since the days of St. Augustine. The response of the church to it had roughly assumed three forms: the official recognition of the new intellectual movements by sanctioning the universities and, as far as possible, bringing them under church control; attempting by papal decree to prohibit that part of the new instruction deemed heretical; and encouragement of the great scholastic syntheses of the Franciscans and particularly the Dominicans.

From the beginning, in the rising universities there appeared essentially nonpriestly intellectuals. Such intellectuals were in the forefront of the reception of materials from classical antiquity that they immediately perceived to be more directly adapted to their requirements than much of the traditional church theology. From the beginning, the universities were battlegrounds of the priest-theologian and the humanist. The thirteenth century victory of the Scholastics was only temporary, however, as the humanist — the first fully distinctive modern intellectual type — was emerging.

THE WESTERN HUMANIST

It has frequently been observed that the nearest point of contact between the ancient and modern intellectual is found in the Western humanist. Like their oriental counterparts, the Western humanists were equipped with secular literary learning and were the bearers of an ideal of cultivated deportment. There are sociological reasons for the similarity.

To Burckhardt goes the credit for the brilliant discernment of the changing character of self-consciousness that accompanied the movement from the feudal world into the city. Under feudal conditions, he urged, individuals were conscious of themselves as members of some general category — a race, people, party, family, or corporation. However, in the cities, corresponding to the change in their objective community, people became conscious of themselves as spiritual individuals.[18] Dante's great poem would not have been possible in any other European country of the time, for most of Europe lay under the spell of traditional rural communities. Only Italy evoked the treasures of individuality that the poet set forth.

Burckhardt believed that despotism was a major source of individuality, for being persons operating outside the sphere of tradition, the tyrant and the *condottiere* had to rely upon their personal resources. Their secretaries, ministers, poets, and companions were also forced to call upon their personal abilities to meet their problems. Individuality was also promoted by the new wealth, the new culture, and the conflict between church and state. Such conditions precipitated the emergence of the political individual. The private person indifferent to politics and busy with individual interests also appeared, for members of defeated parties were involuntarily cast on their own resources. A heightened individuality inspired Agnolo Pandolfini (d. 1446) in his treatise on domestic economy that delineated the ideal of a private life more satisfactory than politics.

The cosmopolitanism emerging in cultivated circles of the city was itself a developed form of the individualism it expressed:

> Dante . . . finds a new home in the language and culture of Italy, but goes beyond even this in the words, "my country is the whole world," and when his recall to Florence was offered him on unworthy conditions, he wrote back: "Can I not everywhere behold the light of the sun and stars; everywhere meditate on the noblest truths, without appearing ingloriously and shamefully before the city and the people? Even my bread will not fail me." The artists exult no less defiantly in their freedom from the constraints of fixed residence. "Only he who has learned everything," says Ghiberti, "is nowhere a stranger; robbed of his fortune and without friends, he is yet the citizen of every country, and can fearlessly despise the changes of fortune." In the same strain an exiled hu-

[18]Jacob Burckhardt, *The Civilization of the Renaissance* (New York: Oxford University Press, 1945), pp. 81 ff.

manist writes: "Wherever a learned man fixes his seat, there is home."[19]

The new individualism was manifest in the frequent appearance of many-sided personalities. Merchants also served as statesmen. Both merchants and statesmen often acquired both classical languages. Private education was vigorously promoted by middle-class strata for daughters as well as for sons. Educated individuals valued wide learning that could range from ethics to politics, from Aristotle to Pliny.

Learned people eagerly assembled collections of natural history, sought to apply the geography of the ancients to modern conditions, and established libraries and museums. It was quite possible for the same individuals to translate the comedies of Plautus, serve as their own stage managers, and act in the parts. One and the same person was often magistrate, secretary, and diplomat by turns. Typifying the many-faceted individuals of the time, in Burckhardt's view, was Leon Battista Alberti (1404–1472).[20] When young he achieved unusual gymnastic prowess, and was unsurpassed in walking and riding. He learned music without a master well enough to compose creditably. He studied both civil and canon law; he painted and modeled with facility. In Burckhardt's words, "Leonardo da Vinci was to Alberti as the finisher to the beginner, as the master to the dilettante."[21]

Under such circumstances people ceased to identify the highest ideal of life as the status honor of the feudal individual. Many turned their highest energies to the pursuit of fame. Social recognition of this type of aspiration appears in the coronation of poets. Poets and individuals of letters were given honors formerly offered only to saints and heroes. The cult of the birthplaces of the famous was amplified by the cult of their graves. Cities engaged in rivalry with one another for possession of the bones of their own and foreign celebrities.

By the side of these local temples of fame, which myth, legend, popular imagination, and literary tradition combined to create, the poet-scholars built up a great Pantheon of worldwide celebrity.[22]

As a counterweight to an often overdeveloped individuality, Burckhardt notes, was the appearance of ridicule and wit. Petrarch pioneered the collection of witty sayings. Among the cities Florence was particularly famous for the cynicism and sharpness of its wits. Eminent wits were themselves celebrities. No person or institution escaped their mockery, which ranged from the caricatures of the lovelorn wails of Petrarch to the parodies of the church processions. Italy became, in Burckhardt's words, a school for scandal in a manner not to be approached again until the France of Voltaire.

The flowering of modern individuality in the cities of Renaissance Europe has many parallels in the princely courts of feudal China, in the royal cities of the Indian kingdoms and of the Jewish monarchical period, in the autonomous city-states of ancient Greece. In all times and areas an intensified individuality has accompanied the formative period of the community. The medieval priest-theologian is the Western counterpart to the religious hierarchs of the Shang and early Chou periods of China, to the Vedic priest of India, to the ro'eh and seer of premonarchical Judaism, and to the Homeric bard and soothsayer of the Greek Heroic period. The Western humanist was the counterpart of the mandarin, guru, of the Upanishadic period, and genteel, heterodox priest, prophet, Yahweh priest, and philosopher of the creative phase of the Axial period.

The Western humanists were the creative bearers of an awakened intellectual life in the formative phase of the Western city. They formed a stratum of literarily trained, many-sided individuals. They shared a common set of values, problems, and status situations — positions and points of view rather than a special philosophy.

The humanists were often statesmen, merchants, diplomats, secretaries, administrators, po-

[19]*Ibid.*, pp. 83–84.
[20]*Ibid.*, pp. 85–86.
[21]*Ibid.*, p. 87.

[22]*Ibid.*, p. 91.

ets, companions. They were almost as flexible as the citizen-intellectuals of the Classical Greek period. They were often self-taught, but above all in their circles the value of education was perceived. Many of them served as private tutors, and were often engaged in private teaching apart from the growing universities. They were all, though to varying degrees, learned in Latin and Greek antiquities. If they had a method of thought and life, it was the exploitation of ancient texts for guidance in their contemporary problems. They developed the methods of historical and philological criticism in the course of their researches and the promotion of an educational program based on the study of the classics. By the thirteenth century the humanists had established a distinctive point of view outside of, and partly in opposition to, the church and the scholastics who were fighting for control of the universities.

Humanism first became popular in the cities of Italy, spreading rapidly in cities and courts outside Italy and reaching its high point in the sixteenth century. The self-image of the humanist was clearly expressed by Petrarch (1304–1374). In a letter to Francesco Bruni, papal secretary in Avignon, he stated:

> "You make an orator of me, a historian, a philosopher, and poet, and finally even a theologian. . . . But let me tell you, my friend, how far I fall short of your estimation. . . . I am nothing of what you attribute to me. What am I then? I am a fellow who never quits school."[23]

Lorenzo Valla (1405–1457), who shared with many other humanists of his day an antipathy to Aristotle, to dialectic, and to the scholastics, illustrates the freedom of the humanistic mind in this early period in his cheerful attempt to reconcile reason and faith, philosophy and theology, paganism and Christianity. This, however, was quite distinct from the scholastic enterprise: faith was being subordinated to reason by Valla. More than any of his contemporaries he opened up the question of the philosophical basis of individual autonomy. This seems to have been his motive in freeing the problem of free will from Aristotelian and scholastic interpretations,[24] which led Ernst Cassirer to state:

> . . . for the first time since the days of the ancients the problem of Freedom was cited before a pure worldly forum, before the judgment chair of "natural reason. . . ." And still one traces above all in his work the power of the new critical-modern spirit which becomes conscious of its might and its intellectual tools.[25]

Marsilio Ficino (1433–1499) reveals the early Western humanist as reviver of a purified Platonism and as founder of the private school. With the patronage of Cosimo de Medici he established the Platonic Academy of Florence, which became the center for the revival of Platonism throughout Europe.[26] Ficino actively promoted the idea of the unity and universality of human aspiration. Religion and philosophy were conceived by him as dual manifestations of the individual's spiritual life, each necessary for achievement of the highest good. In his five questions concerning the mind,[27] he reasoned that all human desire can have only boundless truth and goodness as its objective. The human soul is a middle essence with affinities with all things above and below.

Giovanni Pico della Mirandola (1463–1494) expressed the humanistic outlook in still another way in his ideal of the dignity of the individual and his desire to see a universal harmony among philosophers. He published in Rome in 1486 nine hundred theses inviting all scholars to a great pub-

[23]Ernst Cassirer, Paul Oskar Kristeller, and John Herman Randall, Jr., eds., *The Renaissance Philosophy of Man* (Chicago: The University of Chicago Press, 1948), p. 34.

[24]Lorenzo Valla, "Dialogue on Free Will," in *The Renaissance Philosophy of Man*, pp. 155 ff.
[25]Ernst Cassirer, *Individuum und Kosmos in der Philosophie der Renaissance* ("Studien der Bibliothek Warburg"), (Leipzig and Berlin, 1927), X, 82. Quoted by Charles Edward Trinkaus, Jr., in *The Renaissance Philosophy of Man*, p. 152.
[26]Josephine L. Burroughs in *The Renaissance Philosophy of Man*, p. 185 ff.
[27]*Ibid.*, pp. 193 ff.

lic disputation. The latent tension ever present between priest-theologian and humanist here again became manifest after the earlier encounter in the university. Pope Innocent VIII suspended the debate, and appointed a commission to examine the theses. The commission condemned some of them as heretical. In the theses Pico advanced the proposition that the uniqueness of human beings consists of their lack of fixed properties, their power to share in the properties of other beings according to their own choice. The uniqueness of human beings lay not simply in their role as inventors of the arts and crafts, or even in their powers of speech and reason, but in their ability to form their own nature by their own free choice.[28]

Humanism rises like a rainbow over the Western city in its formative period. Yet anyone who would seize it in its essence often finds that it dances tantalizingly out of reach. For the humanists did not fix a position; they pioneered an outlook. They were often anticlerical; originally they were rarely antireligious. They were often anti-Aristotle in considerable measure because he had been taken over by the Scholastics, but some humanists freed Aristotle and even Scholasticism for fresh application to everyday life. They were often preoccupied with the classics, but in the early period the classics were rarely turned into fetishes; they were freed for application to contemporary life and reinterpreted in terms of contemporary forms. The humanists reopened the question of the nature of human beings and freedom of the soul, but differed widely in their answers to the questions they propounded.

Humanism was a manifestation of the awakened intellectuality of the Western city. It was produced in these new communities by intellectuals cast upon their own resources for the solution of unprecedented problems. It was the self-confident view of people relying on their own talents and scholarship to solve the problems they faced.

Early humanism assumed recognizable shape in the twelfth century. By the thirteenth it fought and

lost its first battle with scholasticism. It mounted rapidly to popularity in the Italian cities outside the universities, after having been partly blocked off within them, and soon spread to the cities and courts of northern Europe. It was not a point of view that could be permanently confined to private circles. It soon penetrated the upper ranks of the clergy and rallied its forces within the universities. By the sixteenth century early humanism had reached its height. Also, by the sixteenth century, powerful forces were at work that were to bring the early form of Western humanism to an end. The forces associated with the Protestant revolts (both in Protestant and Roman Catholic countries) created an atmosphere quite alien to the humanistic outlook, Besides, the institutions of the city were hardening in the face of extra-city forces.

It was of great significance to the West that at the very time the city had begun to lose its elasticity, the new community represented by the nation had begun to assume distinct enough form to take up where the city left off. One of the fundamental contrasts between the social roots of ancient and modern creativity is that while ancient creativity rested on one wave of community formation, modern creativity rests on two. The nation-state was not like the empire of ancient China, or like the Indian caste system, or the pariah community of Jewry, or the Macedonian or Roman Empires which represented in considerable measure a reduction and hardening of prior community elements. Rather, the nation-state was a genuine new community of greater complexity than the city. However, the nation-state was not merely a higher stage of the city, for though the city was a component in its growth, it sprang from independent roots, eventually coming into conflict with and partly supplanting the city.

Like the city before it in its formative period, the nation-state faced unprecedented problems. At the very time when the freedom of the individual was narrowing, within the city, it was expanding within the nation-state. In this new, more comprehensive framework, creative individuals were encouraged in a self-reliant manner to call upon their own natures as they did earlier in the

[28]Kristeller, in *The Renaissance Philosophy of Man*, p. 219.

city. To be sure, in this second phase, Western humanism was somewhat changed. Remnants of the older humanism had been taken up in theological circles and the universities, where classical learning had been transformed from a fresh approach to the contemporary social order into a basis for reaction. Hence the true heirs of the humanistic position in the new period were often disinclined to accept the classics (though much of the old humanistic nostalgia remains). When the issues were drawn, the humanists of the new period remained true to the critical spirit of early humanism. Moreover, the second phase of humanism enjoyed the strategic possession of a far richer cultural heritage than their predecessors, a heritage which included that of the early humanists.

By the seventeenth century the new intellectual ferment associated with the rise of the nation-state had as definitely gotten under way as was true for early humanism of the twelfth century city. By the eighteenth century it had achieved its classic fullness and a name of its own — *The Enlightenment.* The early humanists had raised the problem of the autonomy of the individual under the form of the problem of freedom of the will. The thinkers of the Enlightenment take as unquestioned that the human understanding is capable, by its own power and without recourse to the supernatural, of understanding and controlling the world.[29] The base values of the eighteenth-century humanists were the same as those of their Renaissance predecessors: hatred of ignorance and superstition, love of intelligence and learning, conviction of the innate dignity of the individual. Moreover, like their Renaissance predecessors, they shared an outlook rather than a fixed position. This was formulated clearly by Lecky:

> By the spirit of Rationalism . . . I understand not any class of definite doctrines or criticisms, but rather a certain caste of thought, or bias of reasoning. . . . It

leads men on all occasions to subordinate dogmatic theology to the dictates of reason and of conscience. . . . It predisposes men, in history, to attribute all kinds of phenomena to natural rather than miraculous causes; in theology to esteem succeeding systems the expressions of the wants and aspirations of that religious sentiment which is planted in all men; and, in ethics, to regard as duties only those which conscience reveals to be such.[30]

The Enlightenment thinkers often wore an impudent air of skepticism that was only the flimsiest of disguises for bubbling optimism and, at times, moral smugness. They were never more secure than in the conviction that they needed only to consult their own minds to arrive at the truth.

Corresponding to the cosmopolitan universalism of the earlier humanists was the international character of Enlightenment culture; there was also a corresponding flexibility of roles. French and Latin were used everywhere. Hume and Adam Smith were familiar in Paris salons; Montesquieu, Voltaire, and Rousseau spent time in England. Even scholars who did not travel (for example, Kant and the young Goethe) were usually in correspondence with leading scholars of the day, and familiar with all main intellectual developments in other circles.[31]

Their intellectual products have little national identification. Rousseau's *Social Contract,* for example, and More's *Utopia* avoid frontiers and national identifications. Voltaire's *Candide* presents a philosopher's progress in the world, and ends with the advice to mind one's own business, but between individual self-sufficiency and philosophic universalism there is no stopping point.

The highest ideal of cultivation is that of the universalistic scholar, not the specialist. This ideal inspired the French scholars to undertake with assistance of the Académie and royal government to compile an encyclopedia, the prospectus of which was published in 1750. Goethe and Voltaire each in his particular way came close to approximating

[29]Carl Becker, *The Heavenly City* (New Haven: Yale University Press, 1932); W. E. H. Lecky, *Rationalism in Europe* (New York: D. Appleton & Co., 1891).

[30]Lecky, *Rationalism in Europe,* I, 17–18.
[31]R. B. Mowat, *The Age of Reason* (Boston: Houghton Mifflin, 1934), pp. 36 ff.

the condition of the universal scholar. Goethe practiced law for a period before the imperial law courts; for ten years he was an official of the Duchy of Weimar. He hated war, and thought revolution was not worth the price in blood. His private loyalties were to learning and culture rather than to the state. His study and work ranged the entire field of letters and science. Voltaire was twice sent to the Bastille, where he spent his time writing plays. During his three years in England he earned his way by his pen. He spent some time in many of the courts of Europe. He was careful with his earnings, and planned to secure his own freedom by purchasing land in three European states. Condorcet observed that it would have required a league of the major European powers to silence him. Voltaire wrote plays, histories, and popular science, and in his way covered most of the world of letters.

Whatever the spirit of rationalism touched, it naturalized and tried to reduce to rational principles. In *De jure belli ac pacis* (1625) (*The Laws of War and Peace*), Hugo Grotius contemplated a system of universal jurisprudence resting on principles as self-evident as mathematical axions. So unconditionally valid, he thought, was his scheme of natural law to be as to hold for all reasoning beings including God. In *De Veritate* (1624) Lord Herbert of Cherbury visualized a rational theology resting not on authority and revelation but on universal principles immediately evident to the understanding of all people. Lord Herbert's study was a major influence in the development of a rational psychology and empiricist epistemology. Just as Grotius' influence was transmitted to Leibnitz and Christian Wolff, that of Lord Herbert was transmitted to theological rationalists (such as John Hales and Chillingworth), the Cambridge Platonists (Whichcote, John Smith, Cudworth, and Henry More) and the deists and freethinkers generally (John Toland, Anthony Collins, Herman Samuel Reimarus, Voltaire, Diderot, d'Alembert). In *Leviathan* (1651) Thomas Hobbes visualized the rational organization of the state by way of a formal contract to end the state of "war of each against all," which he assumed would characterize human beings in their natural condition. Hobbes'

views had general influence on most later political thinkers, including Locke, Rousseau, and Kant. In the *Spirit of the Laws,* which has at times been described as the greatest book of the eighteenth century, Montesquieu (1689–1755) accepted the rationalistic theory of human nature of his contemporaries and went beyond it to develop a natural and social environmentalism to explain why an identical human nature should in fact display such varied forms. In numerous special treaties the physiocrats laid the foundation for the first general form of the classical economic doctrines of Adam Smith's *Wealth of Nations* (1776). The physiocrats and classical economists conceived economic behavior as a natural product of rational human activity. In *Outlines of an Historical View of the Progress of the Human Mind* (1795), Condorcet synthesized the historical theories of the Enlightenment in his conception of the progress of the human mind as the central law of society.[32]

Like their humanistic predecessors, the individuals of the Enlightenment were a product of an open period of community formation. Like them, they found the point for the synthesis of their lives and philosophies in their own hearts and minds, in their intellectual and scholarly skills. Like them, they carried out the liquidation of traditional social forms standing in the way of new community formation. Like their predecessors, they partly originated outside the universities and other formal institutional hierarchies, but helped create the social forms of new communities and the dogmas of new academic disciplines. The early humanists were spokespeople for the cities, the later humanists for the nation. All helped to create the community that made their own situation impossible.

The humanists pioneered one form of the intellectual life of the free Western individual. By and large they were optimists, confident in the abilities of the human reason to solve the problems of humanity's destiny. Society, to them, was not the

[32]In addition to the various particular works cited, for other references see Ernst Cassirer, *The Philosophy of the Enlightenment,* trans. Fritz C. A. Koelln and James P. Pettigrove (Boston: Beacon Press, 1951).

end of individuals, but their instrument. Institutions were made for people, not people for institutions. The highest objective of society was the fullest possible development of human personality. In this form humanism represents the general foundation of Western liberalism.

THE WESTERN SCIENTIST

The debt of the West to the humanists is very great, for they presided over the birth of its two major community forms: the city and the nation-state. They helped free these communities from the dead hand of the past, provided the justifications for their expansion, indicated their aspirations, and helped to implement their new institutions. But in the end the humanists were not destined to give their signature to the epoch. We live not in an age of humanism, but in an age of science.

There is fairly widespread recognition of the fact, despite denials, that the humanist and the scientist are to some extent contrasting intellectual types. It hardly need be added that the contrast is not absolute, nor does it extend to every point. The very examples of a happy fusion are instructive — as when a humanist is also a scientist, or when a scientist wins recognition as a humanist. The point of gravity of the humanist is in the world of letters, in scholarship, in learning; the point of gravity of the scientist is in the world of experimental research. When scientists are said to be humanists, it is usually because over and beyond their successful conduct of research (laboratory or other), they are also persons of erudition; when humanists are said to be scientists, it is because over and beyond their scholarly achievements they are at home in research (usually experimental). At the other extreme from the scholarly person of letters who abhors the laboratory is the experimental-minded individual who is inclined to dismiss the world of letters as mere untested balderdash until such time as it has been processed through the laboratory.

The contrast between the humanist and the scientist, however, is more extensive than the mere location of the center of their activity between the world of letters and the laboratory. The fundamental difference between humanism and science is that between a normative and an empirical discipline. Humanism is a system of values and modes of conduct designed to secure them; science is evaluatively neutral pursuit of knowledge, renouncing all claims to prescribe what ought to be. At times, this difference has been confused by the evident fact that same types of social milieu negative to humanism are also negative to the pursuit of scientific objectivity. Hence, it is sometimes stated that science has at least that minimum value program that would make science itself possible. However, the only scientific proposition is: "If you wish to promote science, then certain specifiable social conditions are necessary." The further proposition, "science ought to be promoted," is not scientific.

Humanism locates ultimate value in the fullest self-realization of the human personality. This aspect of its theory was never more brilliantly formulated than by Kant in his various explications of the categorical imperative: so act that one's action can become a universal law. This meant, for Kant, that a type of individuality was the ultimate good. Nothing, he maintained, is more ultimately good than the good will. Hence the categorical imperative was capable of being reformulated: so act that one never uses other persons as means, only as ends. This formulation of the humanistic and enlightenment theory of individuality in its relation to society was not, as Kant knew, a scientific statement. It belonged not to the sphere of science but to the sphere of ethics. Kant was convinced that the nonscientific category of freedom was as crucial to the sphere of ethics as the category of causality was to the sphere of scientific explanation. This, however, was no grounds for confusing them.

Western humanists immediately strike us as the counterpart of the ancient intellectual because their knowledge, too, was always ultimately normative. Western humanists are the transitional intellectual type from the ancient to the modern intellectual. The reason why Western scientists immediately strike one as different from the ancient intellectual (and from the humanist) is that their knowledge always rests on empirical rather than normative considerations.

It is not unfair to describe scientific knowledge as instrumental, if one does not construe this too narrowly. It is certainly wrong to describe scientific knowledge as practically instrumental, though much of it is. The pure or theoretical scientist is concerned with the solution of problems arising out of the growing body of scientific knowledge in its relation to empirical events. Often pure scientists will give for their studies a practical justification, as it were, at second remove. So, for example, one often hears that, when one develops applied science at the expense of pure science, in the long run the sources from which applied scientists draw their ideas disappear. Thus, pure science is being justified by its value for practice after all; it is merely a prudent long-term annuity. This is not very satisfactory, since it also rests on the promise of results, though not very immediate results. Most persons prefer the bird in hand. In the face of this rather lame justification for science, many theoretical scientists maintain that they want to know for the sake of knowing, and that science is the pursuit of knowledge for its own sake. However, since science is never a knowledge which prescribes human ends, this seems to put scientists in a position comparable to that of misers toward their money; they too have converted a purely instrumental form of power into an end in itself. In any case, the ultimately instrumental character of scientific knowledge remains. In the argument that science increases humanity's ability to predict, to control, to master nature either immediately or in the long run remains the more convincing justification of scientific knowledge. That the possessors of instrumental knowledge should give their signature to an entire epoch is a most extraordinary fact. How and why this came about contains the ultimate mystery and paradox of the West.

Without pretending to solve the mystery of the rise of the Western scientist to a position of domi-

nance over other intellectual types, we will note some of the characteristics of the process of establishing empirical knowledge and the change in the intellectual's role that made it possible.

The roots of empirical knowledge are as deep as life itself. Every living creature contains sufficiently effective response-potential to the world around it to survive, or it does not exist long. Very often the instinctive adaptation of a creature to its environment is so subtle as, almost spontaneously, to evoke the characterization of it as a kind of biological wisdom. In the more complex creatures the location of the response potential of the creature tends to move to the higher brain centers, to be intellectualized. What is lost in instinctive fixity in this process is more than gained in adaptability.

In an address delivered on the occasion of the centennial celebration of the organization of the United States Patent Office, Otis T. Mason called up the image of what human beings must have been like before the rise of civilization:

> But, I ask you now, ... go with me to that early day when the first being, worthy to be called man, stood upon this earth. How economical has been his endowment. There is no hair on his body to keep him warm, his jaws are the feeblest in the world, his arm is not equal to that of a gorilla, he cannot fly like the eagle, he cannot see into the night like an owl, even the hare is fleeter than he. He has no clothing, no shelter. He had no tools or industries or experience, no society or language or arts of pleasure, he had yet no theory of life and poor conceptions of the life beyond.[33]

The all-important property of human beings, as Mason sees it, that could change all this is their faculty for invention:

> Through this faculty of invention, the whole earth is man's. There is no lone island fit for his abode whereon some Alexander Selkirk has not made a home. For every mineral, plant, and animal so far

[33]Otis T. Mason, *Proceedings and Addresses*, 1891, pp. 403–412.

known a place has been found . . . in his *Systema Naturae*. Every creature is subject to man; the winds, the seas, the sunshine, the lightning do his bidding. Projecting his vision beyond his tiny plane; this inventing animal has cataloged and traced the motion of every star.[34]

Their faculty for inventing, together with their capacity to retain what they have learned in their habits, potentially turns every invention, in Mason's phrases, into the very nursery of future inventions, into the cradle of a future Hercules. The original ancestors of the major nineteenth-century inventions were often quite humble: the ancestor of the steam plow was the digging stick sharpened and hardened by fire; the ancestor of the steam harvester was the stone sickle; of the thresher the roasting tray; of the cotton gin and power loom crude frames to aid the human fingers; of the sewing machine the needle or bodkin of bone with a leather cap over the ends of the fingers for a thimble.

The aspiration for more exact empirical knowledge is as old as human culture. Mason is quite correct: the basic process in the mastery of nature is invention or discovery. Moreover, for every invention or discovery there are perhaps a hundred tentative probings or accidents of thought which fail to work. An invention or discovery is an idea that practice has confirmed and society has accepted.

One should not think of inventions and discoveries as only, or primarily, material in nature. The greatest of all complexes of inventions is language, which lifted all others to a higher plane of generality and became the mechanism of all higher forms of civilization. A new form of social organization is as much an invention as a new kind of arrowhead, and may be more significant. However, an invention, material or nonmaterial, acquires significance only when accepted. If there are at least a hundred trial ideas for every one confirmed as an invention, there are at least a hundred inventions delayed in reception or by-passed for

every one accepted into the conserving complex of community formation.

Thus we are brought back to a point noted before: every community has a body of empirical knowledge about nature and humanity appropriate to it; new discoveries or inventions proceed from this base, being impeded or spurred on by the basic forces sustaining the particular community. Invention is possible in any community, but only a highly specialized community elevates the scientist to a key position among its social types.

The comparatively open periods of community formation are usually marked by extensive gains in the stock of empirical knowledge of humankind, though different types of communities vary in this. In the neolithic peasant village, the gains in empirical knowledge included domestication of plants and animals, many new features of weaving and spinning, pottery-making, the invention of the wheel and its adaptation to both vehicles and pottery-making. While there was a considerable extension of the empirical knowledge of the peasant village in the world's first cities, their more impressive inventions were of a nonmaterial nature — writing, the beginnings of science, the first foundations of mathematics, new forms of social organization (religion, government, etc.). There were also significant gains in empirical knowledge in the Axial period, particularly in Greece.

The occurrence of fresh empirical observation in the formative period of the Greek city-state has been traced by Farrington. In the pre-Socratic period, he observed, the ancient thinkers never lost sight of the fact that they were trying to understand nature. The Pythagoreans experimented with the relation between the pitch of tones and the length of string. Empedocles demonstrated the corporeal nature of air by thrusting a funnel into water with the upper end closed, proving that water could not enter until the hole was uncovered and the air released. Anaxagoras demonstrated the limits of accuracy of sense perception by taking two vessels, one filled with white liquid and one with black, and mixing them drop by drop until the eye could no longer discern a difference. "These and similar experiments show that they had taken the first step to a real technique of sys-

[34]*Ibid.*, p. 403.

tematic experimental investigation, although they did not get very far with it."[35]

However, the time rapidly approached in ancient Greece when the fresh observation of nature was seen as endangering the state cult. Farrington takes the most striking indication of change to be the expulsion of Anaxagoras from Athens. Anaxagoras was "an ideal embodiment of the spirit of Ionian science."[36] However, his naturalistic account of the heavenly bodies made him suspect. Plato by contrast defended the divinity of the heavenly bodies. However, to some extent "Aristotle saved his scientific soul by a break with Platonism."[37] The devaluation of empirical knowledge continued until "the very understanding that there was such a thing as science, except for a few languishing techniques such as medicine or architecture, almost died out under the Empire."[38]

As Sarton was to phrase the problem:

> However much one may admire Greek science, one must recognize that it was sadly deficient with regard to the (experimental) point of view which turned out to be the fundamental point of view of modern science.[39]

The experimental philosophy has been compactly and clearly summarized as follows:

> Establish the facts by direct, frequent, and careful observations, and check them repeatedly one against the other; these facts will be your premises. When many variables are related find out what happens when only one is allowed to vary, the others remaining constant. Multiply such experiments as much as you can, and make them with the utmost precision in your power. Draw your conclusions and express them in mathematical language if possible. Apply all your mathematical resources to the transformation of the equations; confront the new equations thus obtained with reality.[40]

The splendid triumphs of modern science are due to the application of the experimental method.

The real contribution of the Greeks to the development of modern science was not to be found in the many original experiments carried out by them or even in the brilliant syntheses of the scientific knowledge of the Hellenistic world by the Alexandrians. It lay rather in their discovery and preservation of the rational proof. Euclid (330–260 B.C.), who was trained at Athens probably by a pupil of Plato, carried out his synthesis of Greek mathematics in the *Elements of Geometry* at Alexandria. It was one of the primary monuments to, and future sources of, the influence of the rational proof. The Greeks were well aware of the fact that the rational proof was an important and unique development. Beside it, empirical knowledge seemed second-rate. This dominance of the rational proof over empirical considerations appears even in Archimedes (312–287 B.C.) of Syracuse, perhaps the nearest approach of a modern scientist in antiquity — with his mathematical conception of knowledge and extraordinary talent in handling mechanical problems. However, though Archimedes often made brilliant use of mechanical devices in arriving at his logical and mathematical demonstrations, he did not consider such knowledge on a plane with logical proofs. He usually presents his proof, but does not explain how he reached it. Hence, despite brilliant syntheses of earlier science like Aristarchus of Samos' (310–230 B.C.) heliocentric theory of the planetary system and attempts to measure the distances of the sun, moon, and earth, despite Archimedes' invention of the screw, and his studies of specific weights of metals and experiments with the lever, despite Eratosthenes' (276–194 B.C.) measurement of the earth, or Hipparchus's (190–120 B.C.) original astronomical investigations, and Ptolemy's (–170 A.D.) final astronomical summary of ancient knowledge and his experiments in optics, Singer

[35]Benjamin Farrington, *Science and Politics in the Ancient World* (New York: Oxford University Press, 1940), p. 58.
[36]*Ibid.*, p. 74.
[37]*Ibid.*, p. 230.
[38]*Ibid.*, p. 232.
[39]George Sarton, *The History of Science and the New Humanism* (New York: George Braziller, Inc., 1956), p. 100.

[40]*Ibid.*, pp. 101–102.

still speaks of the entire Alexandrian period in science as "a failure of nerve."[41]

The first ingredient of science is this same rational proof. Though it was partly thrust aside by medieval thought, and in the form of scholastic logic for a time made subordinate to theology, it was never completely lost in the West after the Greeks. Whenever the conception of rational proof was freed from extraneous influences (such as theology), it tended to evolve rapidly toward a mathematical conception of knowledge. As applied to science, it pointed toward the ideal of the concepts formulated with exactness and of proofs as certain as mathematical demonstrations — in fact, if possible, cast into the form of mathematical demonstrations.

Science only emerges, however, when the rational proof is subordinated to the achievement of empirical knowledge, a subordination requiring a special kind of social atmosphere. The domination of the pursuit of new empirical knowledge over the intellectual ethos was not possible in any of the world areas during the Axial period. Though the mandarin intellectuality of ancient China was plastic and free in its sphere, that sphere of application was socially and politically expedient. Nature was not an object of study on a par with the study of humanity; the naturalization of human beings was the violation of their essence. The thought of the Indian *guru* was confined within a narrow range of religious and moral concerns; it was concerned with *atman,* not *maya,* with timeless spiritual essences, not the snares and betrayals of spirituality by time-bound experience. The priests and prophets of Israel were dominated by political, religious, and ethical problems of another type that were also remote from systematic experimentalism.

Only in the secularized speculation of the citizens of the autonomous Greek city-states was there a near approach to the scientific ethos. One major effect of the elevation of the rational proof into central focus in Greek thought was democratiza-

tion, the process of truth establishment, for the basis of truth became the conduct of the thought process in terms of the criteria of thought itself. While this was not yet science, from this standpoint one can phrase the general conditions for the domination of science over the intellectual ethos: *it is possible for science to dominate the intellectual ethos only if a generalization of the procedure of empirical proof is carried through in a manner equivalent to the generalization of the rational proof of logical and mathematical thought.*

The two major institutional complexes of ancient Greece that prohibited the rise of science in the modern sense were militarism and slavery. In the time of its dominance, the autonomous city-state of the eastern Mediterranean was the bearer of the highest military technology of the world. The hoplite on land and the sailor on the seas were each unsurpassed in their spheres. The city-state was a warrior's community. In the long run military and political considerations had the decisive voice in events. When political and military considerations supply the authenticating badge of significance, thought is turned away from systematic experimentalism in nonmilitary spheres. Insofar as it may appear at all, experimentalism on everyday problems was primarily confined to lower social strata: metics, peasants, and slaves. Meanwhile, not all but significant blocks of the technology of the autonomous city-state were in the hands of slaves. Slavery inclines toward technological backwardness. The two systems — militarism at the top and slavery at the bottom — of ancient society were mutually self-supporting. The wars were always in considerable measure slave raids. The only technology of the classical city that was progressive was that of warfare. The presence of slavery required war and at the same time impeded nonmilitary technical advance.

Only among practitioners of the practical and fine arts could a progressive attitude toward the advance of empirical knowledge be anticipated, and these strata in the ancient city were trapped between the slaves from below and the soldiers from above. There was, however, in the ancient

[41]Charles Singer, *A Short History of Science* (Oxford: The Clarendon Press, 1941), pp. 56 ff.

city a stratum revealing this progressive pattern. The ancient city had a stratum of enfranchised persons. A large number had been former household slaves. The suggestion has been advanced that the number of persons enfranchised increased in economically troubled times, and declined in times of prosperity. Enfranchisement was one way in times of economic hardship by which a lord could reduce expenses of the household and shift the risk of bad times onto the former slave.[42]

The economic activity of enfranchised persons of antiquity was quite similar to that of the modern bourgeoisie. Enfranchised persons did not have full access to civic office, the priesthood, nor did they enjoy full connubium with the highest civic strata, though they were at times called to arms. However, the slaves who were permitted through their own free economic activity to buy their freedom were driven by unusually powerful incentives. While their masters now had only limited liability for them, the former slaves were inclined rationally to exploit every economic opportunity as fully and effectively as possible:

> Thus the enfranchised were the most important bearers of those economic forms which best display a character corresponding to modern petty capitalism. Under the circumstances, however, it signified the accumulation of wealth in a middle class in contrast to the typical *demos* of full citizens in the Hellenic city which monopolized political conditioned rents: state rents, daily allowances, mortgages, and land rents. The industrial schools of slavery operating under the possibility of the achievement of freedom were as powerful an incentive for rational economic conduct on the part of the unfree in antiquity as it has been in modern Russia.[43]

As a special stratum, the enfranchised appeared only for a short time in the precity period of the European Middle Ages. Serfdom and grades of semifree persons vanished in the city in accordance with the principle that city air makes people free. In contrast to antiquity, the medieval guild

reached its full development by ignoring nonurban status differences. The progressive attitude toward empirical knowledge and of a rational economic technology became a property of the entire urban community.

In the Western city, strata associated with the practical and fine arts were in a position to set the style for all the rest; in fact, to sound the keynote of its civilization. Moreover, the stratum in central position during the formative period of a community is not only able to impose its outlook on all others, but is freest of all the strata for self-development. In the Western city, industrial and merchant strata had their unparalleled opportunity for development.

The patricians who rose to power in the cities attained their positions by their successes in trade, commerce, and industry rather than by religious excellence, military prowess, or aristocratic family ties. They might occasionally adopt a feudal conception of rank in the course of their inner civic competition, and even aspire to own rural villas or castles and stables for horse-racing, but the fundamental content of their status striving was that of merchant adventurers. They imported art objects from distant places, turned their merchant talents to good effect in the creation of libraries and museums. They knew good craftsmanship when they saw it, and formed the perfect patrons for a brilliant flowering of art. When the fine arts emerged, that is, the production of objects to be enjoyed for their own sake or to be pressed into the decoration, enhancement, and celebration of life, it was in terms of clear standards of craft quality. The work of the better artists was known, valued, and sought after.

Two properties of the arts in the formative period of the Western city had considerable bearing on the rise of science: (1) the line between the practical and fine arts was not sharply drawn, for fine art was of a continuity with practical art, being, in considerable measure, merely a qualitatively superior example of it; (2) the lines between the different arts were not sharply drawn, making it quite possible for a given artist-craftsperson to display excellence in a variety of fields. When a given person is skilled in a number of areas, inspiration

[42]Max Weber, *The City* (Glencoe: The Free Press, 1958), p. 216.
[43]*Ibid.,* p. 218.

for the solution of problems is drawn in one area from another.

The artist is a bearer of a peculiar kind of knowledge — knowledge of characteristics of materials, of the nature of skills, of tools, and of mechanical processes. In the Western city, the many-sided artist was the counterpart in a different sphere to the many-sided citizen intellectual of the ancient city. The ancient Greek intellectual was often a soldier, administrator, diplomat, teacher, lawyer, and school founder. The artists of the early Western city were often craftspeople, painters, sculptors, metal workers, engineers, fortification experts, stage designers, architects, and even musicians.

The work of the fine artist is particularly noteworthy, for it presents the artisan as creator. It requires the highest level of information of the properties of materials, skills, tools, and mechanical processes — naturalistic, empirical knowledge. At the same time, the fine artist is expected to innovate. The situation is thus one involving a synthesis of empirical knowledge, demanding a high level of devotion, and yet with creativity at a premium. When the fine artist achieves something new, it will rarely be sheer accident — at least not by this alone. New results will usually only be obtained by projecting a new idea into an empirical situation and trying it out.

The essence of the Greek in contrast to the modern achievement is the pursuit of certainty in the world of thought in contrast to the pursuit of certainty in the world of experience. The Greeks solved their problem by the rational proof; the modern world solved its problem by systematic experiment. The distinction lies between the certainties of mathematics and those of experience. Leonardo da Vinci had already arrived at the view that in its sphere mathematics provides certainty:

> He who blames the supreme certainty of mathematics feeds on confusion, and will never impose silence upon the contradictions of the sophistical sciences, which occasion perpetual clamor.[44]

However, experience also gives certainty its sphere:

> Experience is never at fault; it is only your judgment that is in error in promising itself such results from experience as are not caused by our experiments.[45]

In the workshops of the Renaissance artists, firsthand observation and experiment were generalized as a method of knowledge and applied to almost every conceivable problem. Leonardo was not alone among the artists of the time, though without question he was the most able. His notebooks read like a continuous never-ending system of laboratory notes and he records observational and experimental knowledge turned up by his own reflections and work and that of others. To Sarton, Dürer and Leonardo epitomize the artist-scientist of the Renaissance:

> Dürer was a businessman, a man of substance, living in his own comfortable house; he was capable of taking some interest in scientific questions, but he was not a man of science. Leonardo, on the contrary, was a pure artist, a disinterested inventor, a man of science, a cogitator, a Bohemian; he was decidedly not a businessman or an administrator. He was anxious to obtain not money, or power, or comfort, but beauty and truth. He wanted to understand God, nature, art, himself, and other men. I admire them both, but I love Leonardo.[46]

In the sixteenth and seventeenth centuries the spread of the scientific point of view to ever wider spheres is evident. Nicolaus Copernicus (1473–1543) renovated the heliocentric theory from antiquity. Belon (1517–1564), Rondelet (1507–1564), Salvini (1514–1573), Gesner (1516–1565), and Androvandi (1525–1608) opened the modern study of animals. Andreas Vesalius (1514–1564) made the first significant advances in anatomy since Galen. William Gilbert (1546–1604) in his

---

[44]Edward MacCurdy, *The Notebooks of Leonardo da Vinci* (New York: George Braziller, 1956), p. 83.

[45]*Ibid.,* p. 64.
[46]George Sarton, *Six Wings: Men of Science in the Renaissance* (Bloomington: Indiana University Press, 1957), p. 232–233.

work, *On the Magnet and on Magnetic Bodies and Concerning the Great Magnet, the Earth, a New Physiology*, made the first great original contribution to science in England. Giordano Bruno (1547–1600) raised the demand for a new level of precision of observation.

For the full emergence of science, however, it was necessary not only to develop systematic observation and experiment, but to subordinate the establishment or rational proof to them. This was accomplished in the course of the transformation of mathematics into an instrument of physical investigation. François Viete (1540–1603) employed letters to represent numbers, and applied algebra to geometry in a manner anticipating analytical trigonometry. Simon Stevin (1548–1630) introduced the decimal scheme for representing fractions. He also experimented on the relative rates of the fall of bodies, and computed the pressure of liquids on any given point of a vessel, laying the foundation for hydrostatics. John Napier (1550–1617) discovered a general rule for roots of all degrees in the course of his attempt to systematize algebraic knowledge. He conceived the principles of logarithms, and computed the table of logarithms. Kepler developed the mathematics of conic sections. In his analytic geometry, Descartes introduced the conception of motion into the geometric field, displaying the basic correspondence of number and form. Blaise Pascal (1623–1662) advanced the theory of probability, and invented one of the first mathematical machines. John Wallis (1616–1703) anticipated differential calculus. Newton read Wallis' *Arithmetica infinitorum* (1655) and derived the binomial theorem from it. Wallis wrote the first mathematical work on the tides. Mathematical development and the advance in scientific knowledge were beginning to move hand in hand.[47]

In the work of Galileo Galilei (1564–1642) systematic experimentalism and the mathematical ideal of scientific knowledge were fused. Though trained in scholasticism and Aristotelianism, he soon began to modify this heritage in the course of his experimental researches. He worked from the conception of a world of calculable forces and measurable bodies. The whole modern science of dynamics was laid by Galileo. In the words of Bertrand Russell:

> Scientific method, as we understand it, comes into the world full-fledged with Galileo . . . and, in somewhat lesser degree, his contemporary, Kepler (1571–1630).[48]

As the first modern scientist, Galileo was destined to clarify another aspect of science over and beyond the synthesis of a mathematical conception of nature and experimentalism. For championing the Copernican theory of planetary motions in 1632, he came under censure of the Inquisition. In its censure the Inquisition called attention to its earlier criticism of Galileo in 1615. In its document the Inquisition indicated its own conception of the proper way to establish truth:

> The two propositions of the stability of the sun, and the motion of the earth, were qualified by the Theological Qualifiers as follows:
> 1. The proposition that the sun is the center of the world and immovable from its place is absurd, philosophically false, and formally heretical; because it is expressly contrary to the Holy Scriptures.
> 2. The proposition that the earth is not the center of the world, nor immovable, but that it moves and also with a diurnal action, is also absurd, philosophically false, and theologically considered, at least erroneous in faith.[49]

For offenses against the faith, the Inquisition declared:

> That the book Dialogues of Galileo Galilei be prohibited by a public edict, and We condemn you to the formal prison of This Holy Office for a period determinable at Our pleasure; and by way of salutary

[47]Charles Singer, *A Short History of Science* (Oxford: The Clarendon Press, 1941), pp. 189–195.

[48]Bertrand Russell, *The Scientific Outlook* (Glencoe: The Free Press, 1931), p. 20.
[49]Quoted by Russell, *Ibid.*, p. 25.

penance, We order you during the next three years to recite, once a week, the seven penitential psalms, reserving to Ourselves the power of moderating, commuting, or taking off, the whole or part of the said punishment or penance.[50]

The mode of establishing truth by the new science was at the opposite pole from the truth-establishment of the medieval church. Scientifically established truth could come into conflict with religion. The Inquisition stamped out the beginnings of science in southern Europe.

Of considerable importance for the further development of science was the Reformation, which broke the monopoly of the medieval ecclesiastical hierarchy and opened a new era in European culture as well as in church history. The Reformation reached its climax in the sixteenth century, but it had roots deep in the Middle Ages in sacred and clerical groups opposed to religious centralization. The Reformation reached particular intensity in the towns where the new urban freedom encouraged the emergence not only of free thinkers and nonconformists but a new, more individualized religious intensity. In place of the traditional primacy of the sacraments and ministrations of the priesthood, the Reformation offered a nonsacramental theory of the church which placed great emphasis on the religious conscience of the individual. In its area the Reformation eliminated the monastic ideal of religious life for a religious elite, while it imposed a new, more rigorous religious interpretation on the everyday life of lay religious persons. This new ideal of lay religiosity has often been described as inner-worldly asceticism. The role that the Reformation played in enhancing those trends in the cities and in the national economies that led on to modern capitalism, has been brilliantly traced by Weber.[51]

The Reformation not only broke up the spiritual monopoly of the church, thus establishing areas where the Inquisition was unable to carry out its opposition to science and other forms of modernism, but intensified those religious sentiments of Western civilization that were most nearly akin to the emerging scientific spirit. To a considerable degree the Reformation, modern capitalism, and modern science were simply different, though closely interrelated, aspects of the same process. Robert Merton has traced the relation between Protestantism and science in seventeenth-century England in a manner directly parallel to Weber's study of the interrelation between Protestantism and capitalism.[52]

Western science was to reach its highest development in the Protestant countries of northern Europe. If Merton is correct, science was borne primarily by the new Protestants. Moreover, the attitudes and norms of inner-worldly asceticism, which Weber was to find central to the formation of the capitalistic ethos were also capable of being transmuted into the scientific attitude and philosophy of experimentalism.

Humanism made its appearance as a form of intellectuality in the early period of the Western city. However, as the city developed and increasingly realized its potential, the point of gravity of its intellectuality tended increasingly to shift toward science. Moreover, leadership in the new science taking shape within the city was transferred to the newer community of the nation-state. This was observed by Butterfield:

> The whole story of the Renaissance shows within the limits of the city-state how the exhilarating rise of an urban civilization is liable to issue in a process of secularization — the priest as well as the noble loses the power that he was able to possess in a more conservative agrarian world. Something parallel has happened over and over again in the case of nation-states when not only have towns become really urban

[50]Ibid., p. 30.
[51]Max Weber, The Protestant Ethic and the Spirit of Capitalism, trans. Talcott Parsons (New York: Charles Scribner's Sons, 1948).

[52]Robert K. Merton, Science, Technology, and Society in 17th Century England (Bruges, Belgium: St. Catherine Press, Ltd. Osiris: Studies on the History and Philosophy of Science, 1938). Merton also carried out a number of shorter studies of this interrelation. See the bibliography of Robert K. Merton's Social Theory and Social Structure (Glencoe: The Free Press, 1949), pp. 409 ff.

in character — which is late the case of England, for example — but when a sort of leadership in society has passed to the towns, and literature itself comes to have a different character.[53]

At the height of the early phase of the Renaissance, it has been noted, philosophy was considered the queen of the sciences,[54] but this was rapidly undergoing change toward the end of the Renaissance. Francis Bacon complained about the divorce between observation and explanation. In the seventeenth century, when the autonomous Western city had passed its height and the nation-state was beginning to take shape, the new science got thoroughly under way.

> Not only did the science of mathematics make a remarkable development in the seventeenth century, then, but in dynamics and in physics the sciences give the impression that they were pressing upon the frontiers of mathematics all the time. Without the achievements of the mathematicians, the scientific revolution, as we know it, would have been impossible.[55]

> It is not until the seventeenth century that the resort to experiments comes to be tamed and harnessed, so to speak, and is brought under direction, like a great machine getting into gear.[56]

Science was rapidly becoming the distinctive thought of the West. Yet in the nature of the case, this was a growth outside the institutional thought of the day. Martha Ornstein has advanced the thesis that the science of the seventeenth century received little help from the university. Rather, the new science was its own sponsor in the scientific societies which supplied indispensable aid.[57]

The seventeenth century produced the microscope, telescope, machinery for grinding lenses, time-measuring instruments, thermometer, barometer, air pump, the apparatus of the modern physical laboratory, places and conditions where experimentation could be carried on, the modern observatory, and many other things necessary to exact observation and experimentation. Ornstein maintains that the leadership in promoting these technical developments, creating the conditions for scientific work, and publicizing their findings were unions of scientific workers which became the dominating feature of scientific activity after 1650.

These societies concentrated groups of scientists in single places, performed experiments and investigations impossible to individuals, became centers of scientific information, published and translated scientific works, promulgated scientific efforts, coordinated the scientific effort of different countries, concerned themselves about the application of science to trade and commerce, tools and machinery, and sought to dispel popular errors about science by means of lectures.

> But first and foremost they developed the scientific laboratory, devised, perfected, and standardized instruments, originated and insisted on exact methods of experimentation, and thus established permanently the laboratory method as the only true means of scientific study.

> The conclusion is thus inevitable that the organized support which science needed in order to penetrate into the thought and lives of people was not obtained from universities, but was derived from those forms of corporate activity which it had created for itself, the scientific societies.[58]

The major trends from the seventeenth century to the present have consisted in the institutionalization of science first in modern industry, second in the universities within which it has become a dominating influence, and finally the increased support of scientific research by the modern state. Step by step the contemporary world has been transformed into an age of science.

[53]H. Butterfield, *The Origins of Modern Science* (London: G. Bell & Sons Ltd., 1949), p. 183.
[54]*Ibid.*, p. 66.
[55]*Ibid.*, p. 77.
[56]*Ibid.*, p. 79.
[57]Martha Ornstein, *The Role of Scientific Societies in the Seventeenth Century* (Chicago: University of Chicago Press, 1928).

[58]*Ibid.*, pp. 260–261.

SUMMARY

Three major communities organized the medieval world out of which the contemporary world developed: peasant villages, manorial communities, and monasteries. Two of these, the manorial and monastic communties, sustained intellectual traditions of sorts: the epic and romantic literatures of chivalry and the theological literatures of the priest-theologians. The dominant intellectuals of the period were the priest-theologians who had replaced the philosophers of the ancient world and whose intellectual products reversed the order of elements of ancient thought, transforming reason into the handmaiden of faith.

When the cities arose in the eleventh century they provided milieux to which the priest-theologians on the one hand and the bearers of the feudal chivalric traditions on the other were ill adapted. The basic tension between the requirements of the church-dominated communities of the Middle Ages and the new urban communities is revealed by the frequency of the conflicts that occurred whenever a new city began to rise on the site of the old episcopal sees. The bishops perceived the rising bourgeoisie as a threat, and evaluated major phases of their commercial activities in religiously negative terms. For their part, the merchants perceived the ecclesiastics as an obstacle, and often formed sworn confederations that carried out revolutionary seizures of power from the ecclesiastical authorities. No communities that found it necessary to acquire power against the priests were going to find the priestly intellectual fully adequate to their needs.

The range of new intellectual requirements of the urban centers were first satisfied by voluntary organizations of students and teachers or by an expansion of the curriculum of the cathedral schools. The three great centers of learning that emerged in the early period were: Salerno, Bologna, and Paris, specializing in medicine, law, and philosophy respectively. For at least two centuries before the universities were formally organized, these centers continued to grow, drawing students from all parts of Europe and evolving into the highest centers of culture of the time. In connection with the growth of these intellectual centers a great recovery of ancient science, at first primarily from Moslem and Jewish sources, got under way.

So many medieval institutions, such as the urban administrations, the state, and eventually the church itself, began to look at these voluntary associations of teachers and students for a supply of trained persons that a competition for their control emerged. In the course of this competition the formal organization of the universities was carried through. Moreover, within the universities at an early stage a struggle broke out between the secular intellectuals and the monastically trained men. This pressed the scholastics to the highest level of intellectual activity to be seen in the West since the days of St. Augustine. The twelfth-century Renaissance was thus the foundation for the thirteenth-century scholastic synthesis of classical learning and Christian theology. Of the various *Summae* that were undertaken, the most famous was that of the Dominican, Thomas Aquinas, which was to become the official point of view of the Roman Catholic Church.

However, despite the fact that the final form of scholasticism was in part a product of the very forces that were lifting the city into the central experience of early modern humanity, the scholastics were destined to be the last of the medieval intellectuals though, to be sure, they still have heirs in the contemporary world. The intellectual patterns of the contemporary individual were destined to achieve their distinctive properties in the Western humanist and the scientist. Though a variety of priests and scholastics play a part in the contemporary world, humanist and scientist demark the two major poles of its distinctive intellectual life.

III

Ideologies, Paradigms, and Theories

The 1950s was a period of rare consensus in American society and American sociology. American society had emerged from World War II as the foremost power on earth militarily, politically, and economically. A generation whose aspirations had successively been frustrated and deferred by depression and war was anxious to transfer to the suburbs, settle down, raise families, and enjoy the hard-earned new affluence. The international Cold War and domestic McCarthyism tended to shut off and suppress radical dissent. At the same time, structure-functionalism, America's first endemic form of sociological holism, seemed about to swallow up the last traces of opposition.

However, the consensus both in the society and in sociology was to be short-lived. The minority movements, the rise and fall of the poverty program, the ugly course of the Vietnam War, the Watergate scandals, and, finally, simultaneous inflation and unemployment would dampen the nationalistic euphoria and transform the sense of domestic well-being into alienation and dismay. In sociology, theories that had long been out of favor were reexamined; the hard-won tradition of objectivity was challenged; arguments were advanced for an ideologically committed social science; humanism and science were conceptualized as antithetical, and a rift appeared between an antipositivistic sociology and a hardened positivism that paraded under the names of "theory construction" and "mathematical sociology."

In the course of conflicts between representatives of these positions even the definition of the primary business of sociology as the development of theories of society has been challenged. Suggestions have been made that ideologies or paradigms are better suited to the proper task of sociology than concern with the development of theories. It is impossible to understand recent developments in sociology without clarifying the difference between ideologies, paradigms, and theories.[1]

[1]For a school of sociology that sees the task of the discipline to be primarily ideological, see Chapter XXIII. Also there is a review of the positivism controversy in Chapter XXV.

THE CLASSICAL NOTION

No idea was more widely shared by the creators of sociology than that its task was to develop empirically adequate theories to explain society. Opinion divided over the further question whether sociologists should also assume responsibility for the applications of their theories. Eventually Max Weber developed the classical answer to this question.

In a lecture delivered in 1918 on "Science as a Vocation," Weber took up the issue of the place of values in science. "Today," he observed, "one usually speaks of science as 'free from presuppositions.' Is there such a thing? It depends upon what one understands thereby."[2]

Weber answered his rhetorical question: there is no such thing as complete freedom from presuppositions of any human activity, including science. Science assumes that the rules of logic and method are valid and it takes it for granted that the results of scientific work are worth knowing. This last supposition, it should be noted, cannot be proven by science, but can only be determined by an individual's attitudes toward life whether he or she is a scientist or not. What is true of science in general is true of the historical and cultural sciences that help us understand social phenomena in terms of their origin and development, but cannot answer the question whether these same social and cultural phenomena are worthwhile. This is a nonscientific or extrascientific question. This kind of question raises issues that belong to ethics and politics which are out of place in the scientific laboratory or lecture room, whether they are raised by the students or the professors. In fact, "Whenever the man of science introduces his personal value judgment, a full understanding of the facts ceases."[3] Among the basic tasks of the professor is to "teach his students to recognize 'inconvenient' facts."[4] This, of course, is not to say that the establishment of fact, the basic task of science, is without value. Science "contributes to the technology of controlling life by calculating external objects as well as man's activities"; it provides "methods of thinking and training for thought" and aids in the achieving of "clarity."[5]

A scientific sociology draws as clear a distinction as possible between explaining and evaluating. (Science thus is one kind of specialization of everyday thinking in which explaining and evaluating are usually intermixed.) In fact, one of the major ways in which science departs from common sense is by instituting the distinction between explanation and advocacy. On occasion, however, even common sense recognizes the danger of advocacy to objectivity. Advocates tend to gloss inconvenient facts, presenting only such evidence as is favorable to their preferred outcome. In a court of law this can be disastrous to an individual's cause as recognized in the folk saying: one who acts as one's own lawyer has a fool for a client. However, the superiority of science does not, for Weber, mean that it is a privileged form of thought. The facts cannot speak for themselves. It is the task of human beings as ethical and political agents to decide how science, with its superior equipment for obtaining the facts, is to be used. The last thing, however, Weber was interested in was the replacement of scientific explanation by ideology.

IDEOLOGIES

No one has played a more important role in the postwar attempts to dethrone scientific theory as the core of sociology and replace it with ideology than Alvin W. Gouldner, Max Weber Research Professor of Social Theory at Washington University of St. Louis. It is an anomaly that a man occupying a chair in the name of Max Weber felt called upon to denounce Weber as a monster and to describe anyone who consults his views on the

[2]Max Weber, "Science as a Vocation," *From Max Weber,* trans. Hans Gerth and C. Wright Mills (New York: Oxford, 1946), p. 143.
[3]*Ibid.*, p. 146.
[4]*Ibid.*, p. 147.

[5]*Ibid.*, pp. 150–151.

relations of values and social science as displaying "the first sign of professional senility."[6]

Gouldner argued that Weber's views on scientific sociology were "part of the ideology of a working group," which developed and thrived because of "its usefulness in maintaining both the cohesion and autonomy of the modern university, in general, and the newer social science disciplines in particular."[7] It was, he continues, a complaint against the unfair competition by professors responsible to student interests and intended to serve as a "Fair Trades Act." So concerned was Weber to safeguard the university from politics he was willing to pay any price for it, even if it detached the university from a basic intellectual tradition of the West, the exploration of the meaning of human life.[8] Weber's view provided a freedom from moral compulsiveness, leading sociologists "to ignore current human problems and to huddle together like old men seeking mutual warmth."[9]

In all of this, Gouldner claimed, Weber and the sociology that flows from his point of view represent a modern version of the medieval conflict between faith and reason for they create a gulf between science and values in a manner that in the end *"warps reason by tinging it with sadism and leaves it feeling smugly sure only of itself and bereft of a sense of common humanity."*[10]

Alvin Gouldner's denunciation of Max Weber's conception of the need for scientific objectivity inspired an assorted group of liberals and radicals to place (as did Gouldner himself) ideology at the core of the sociological enterprise.

This radical position has varied from the view (1) that all sociology, whatever its pretenses, is value committed; through the view (2) that what current sociology most needs is a sociology of relevance; to the view (3) that sociology can only be advanced by forthright partisanship. In response to the many-sided assault on the tradition of objectivity, sociologists of the positivistic tradition have, in turn, hardened their position with demands for rigorous theory construction. In the course of the ongoing debate the place of ideology in sociology has grown increasingly moot.

Superficially, it is not difficult to distinguish scientific theory from ideology. A scientific theory is a set of generalizations for explaining a body of phenomena; an ideology is a set of arguments advanced with persuasive intent. Scientific theory is oriented to description and explanation, to what "is"; ideology is oriented to action, to some person's view of what "ought to be." In composition a scientific theory is made up of hypotheses or laws that it forms into an explanation; an ideology is composed of values that it forms into an axiology. The criteria of scientific theory are truth and falsity, validity and invalidity; the criteria of an ideology are some person's notions of goodness and badness. These contrasts may be summarized as in Table 1.

Offhand it would appear that the differences between ideologies and social science theories are sufficiently evident to preclude confusing them. However, ideologies and social science theories are both anchored in the requirements of human social life. All human life involves both the necessity to take factual account of situations (to describe and explain) and the necessity to make choices and to act (to allocate priorities). Elements of evaluative preference are involved when one chooses a scientific career over others. Once launched upon a career, a scientist must choose some problems for study and omit others. There is no good reason to restrict the concept of ideology, as is sometimes done, to the more elaborate and bizarre forms of organizing preferences into an axiology such as those represented by the ideologies of classes, special interest groups, parties, and institutional elites. In the strictest sense, there is no possible human situation that could see an end of ideology. At best, one could expect the disappearance of some kinds of axiological systems

---

[6]Alvin Gouldner, "Anti-Minotaur: The Myth of a Value-Free Sociology," in *For Sociology: Renewal and Critique in Sociology Today* (New York: Basic Books, 1973), p. 3.
[7]*Ibid.*, pp. 4, 6–7.
[8]*Ibid.*, p. 10.
[9]*Ibid.*, p. 13.
[10]*Ibid.*, p. 24. Italics in original.

TABLE 1 *Ideology versus Scientific Theory*

Characteristic	Ideology	Scientific Theory
Objective	Prescriptive	Explanatory-Descriptive
Location of operation	The World of Action	The World of Thought
Component elements	Values formed into an axiology	Laws formed into an explanation
Criteria	Good and bad	True and false

in favor of others. At the same time the attempt to appraise facts objectively and to account for them without distortion, whether apart from or within the scientific process, should be seen as the difficult task it is. However, when it is accomplished, action becomes more efficient.

To compound the problems for the social sciences, a significant segment of their subject matter is made up of the ideas, notions, evaluations, and strategies of their human subjects. In other words, the ideological dimensions of interpersonal actions form much of the content of sociological study. Moreover, since much of the time the social scientist has personal values that differ from those of the subjects, an ever-present danger is the introduction, consciously or unconsciously, of private biases into the research. Furthermore, the subjects of research may recognize differences between their own values and those of the investigator and distort the findings either by giving what they think the researcher wants or needs, or by concealing from the investigator what they think might be disapproved of. For example, when research by black and white investigators of black subjects is compared, considerable discrepancies in findings appear.

In view of the multiple sources of bias, from the side of both the researcher and the subjects, it might seem that the safest route to scientific objectivity is to limit scientific research to neutral individuals (that is, those individuals without intense commitments). However, human affairs are never simple. When one seeks the best and fullest evidence in an area of human endeavor, one usually finds it necessary to consult the very persons who were drawn to the area by deep personal involvement. Much of the best evidence on Old Testament materials has been produced by Protestants who had been drawn to the study by their religious commitments. In a similar manner much of the best evidence on Jewish social history and Catholic social history has been produced by pious Jews and Catholics, respectively. Some of the most penetrating studies of blacks, Chicanos, and women are being currently produced by black, Chicano, and female sociologists.

Passionate interest in a particular outcome can create selective perception and distorted interpretation such that one sees only evidence and argument for one's cause. But only a scoundrel will manufacture evidence. Moreover, the exposure of carelessness and bias may do serious damage not only to a researcher but to the area of interest. A case in point is the recent exposure of methodological carelessness, and perhaps even the outright fraudulent fabrication, of data by Cyril Burt, the late authority on identical-twin-based studies of the genetic foundations of intelligence. At the same time, it is often people with no particular interest in an area who stop short of the full evidence or who permit themselves to be persuaded by superficial interpretations. The principle stands: In human affairs there is no major achievement without passion.

The confusion over the place of ideology in sociology is compounded further by the argument advanced by nineteenth-century collectivists and occasionally repeated by their twentieth-century followers: All social science *is* ideology. Much of the appeal of collectivism in the nineteenth century was based on the failure of their rationalistic predecessors to construct a rational picture of the world in which logical, empirical, and evaluative types of knowledge had a consistent and unambiguous place. The system of knowledge appeared to be in crisis. Empirical knowledge appeared to lack the certainty of logical knowledge; moral knowledge seemed to require presuppositions about action, such as freedom, that were in apparent direct contradiction with presuppositions about action in a context of scientific explanation. The answer by the collectivists was twofold: (1) that these were apparent contradictions due to analyzing thought from a static frame of reference; and (2) that they arose from analyzing thought from the standpoint of the experience of the isolated individual rather than the spiritual (mental) development of the entire community over time. Thus the holists argued that in the collective experience of the community over time, logical, empirical, and moral knowledge were interdeveloped. No truth is eternal, but rather relative to some particular set of historical circumstances. Contradictions are not only temporary but are necessary for development and are resolved in action, or as some of the collectivists were and are fond of saying, praxis.

This argument unavoidably committed its proponents to the conviction of an inseparable relation between thought and the rest of collective humanity's social condition, a relationship expressed in a terminology of super-, sub-, and infrastructures. It also carried with it the assumption that value commitments (ideology) are inseparable in principle from theory.

One of the few persons to confront the problem of objectivity directly from a collectivistic point of view was Karl Mannheim. He found himself faced with this question: If all social knowledge can only reflect a particular situation at a particular time, how is objective social science knowledge possible? He tried to solve the problem in two stages: (1) by drawing a distinction between relativism and relationism and (2) by counting on the intellectual to supply a transperspective perspective.

> Relationism . . . states that every assertion can only be relationally formulated. It becomes relativism only when it is linked with the older static ideal of eternal, unperspectivistic truths independent of the subjective experience of the observer, and when it is judged by this alien ideal of absolute truth.[11]

However, it should be noted that this formulation does not help much. Although it makes truth relational, it makes objectivity relative. Mannheim seriously toyed with the idea of resolving the problem of a relative objectivity by appealing to the unique perspective of a socially unattached intelligentsia, a characterization he borrowed from Alfred Weber. This characterization posited that intellectuals tend to be recruited from all classes and hence tend to reflect all social positions within their own.

> There are two courses of action which the unattached intellectuals have actually taken as ways out of this middle-of-the-road position: first, what amounts to a largely voluntary affiliation with one or other of the various antagonistic classes; second, scrutiny of their own social moorings and the quest for the fulfillment of their mission as the predestined advocate of the intellectual interests of the whole.[12]

This, however, is still not very satisfactory, for it is not made clear how intellectuals recruited from the laboring class will transcend their perspective by, say, also adding the perspective of the intellectual to it. Nor is it clear why they should agree

[11]Karl Mannheim, *Ideology and Utopia,* trans. Louis Wirth and Edward Shils (New York: Harcourt Brace, 1949), p. 270.
[12]*Ibid.,* p. 140.

with other intellectuals who combine an upper-class perspective with that of the intellectual. If he considered at all the possibility of a calculus of perspectives, Mannheim rejected it as absurd. He suggested rather:

> . . . when observers have different perspectives, "objectivity" is attainable only in a . . . round-about fashion. In such a case, what has been correctly but differently perceived by the two perspectives must be understood in the light of the differences in structure of these varied modes of perception. An effort must be made to find a formula for translating the results of one into those of the other and to discover a common denominator for these varying perspectivistic insights.[13]

Although the model for Mannheim's reasoning was provided by physical perception, it is clear that this was an analogy for dealing with differences in orientation between people when they possess varying value commitments. More important than his success in reconciling conflicts in a holistic position on the individual, society, culture, and social thought was the fact that in his effort to establish the possibility of the achievement of scientific objectivity, he was being forced, step by step, to reinstitute analytical distinctions between thought and action, value and fact.

Karl Mannheim was one of the first sociologists to assimilate the sociology of Max Weber. In the 1920s at Heidelberg he had tried to synthesize the sociology of Weber with the theories of Karl Marx. He continued these efforts at the London School of Economics after being forced into exile by the Nazis in 1933. Practically as well as theoretically, he was concerned with the relations between value and fact, politics and science. He tried to reconcile Weber's concept of the need for scientific objectivity with collectivistic suppositions of Marx that imply all thought systems to be ideologies.

When, thirty years later, Alvin Gouldner took up the problem again, this time not with the intention of restoring to sociology the task of achieving

objective knowledge, but of supplanting it with a forthrightly partisan sociology, Gouldner was not long in reacting to the manner in which other sociologists followed his suggestions. Arguing that "the value-free doctrine is about to be superseded by a new but no less glib rejection of it,"[14] he launched a major assault on Howard S. Becker and various other persons belonging to the same group, including Howard Brotz, Donald Cressey, John Kitsuse, Raymond Mack, David Matza, Sheldon Messinger, Ned Polsky, and Albert J. Reiss.

Howard Becker had written a paper on the topic "Whose Side Are We On?" in which he had taken as given Gouldner's proposition that sociology was unavoidably partisan: being either in the interest of subordinates or superiors. Becker's position, in Gouldner's opinion, was that "of a blasé referee announcing the outcome of a finished fight."[15] He and other members of his group represent "a school of thought that finds itself at home in the world of hip, drug addicts, jazz musicians, cab drivers, prostitutes, night people, drifters, grifters and skidders: the 'cool world'. Their identifications are with deviant rather than respectable society."[16] Now, if he were honest, Gouldner maintains, Becker would admit that he is on the side of whomever he is studying at a given time, "he would advocate the devotional promiscuity of sacred prostitution." However, for all his underdog sympathies he is really on the side of one of the "currently conflicting elites in the welfare establishment."[17] This, according to Gouldner, leads him to maintain a posture of emotional blandness as an antidote to partisanship. "Becker thereby creates a new myth, the myth of the *sentiment*-free social scientist."[18] All of this, in Gouldner's view, is in the interest of obtaining funding for the study of the underdog in response

[13]*Ibid.*, p. 270.

[14]Alvin Gouldner, "The Sociologist as Partisan: Sociology and the Welfare State," in *For Sociology*, p. 27.
[15]*Ibid.*, p. 28.
[16]*Ibid.*, p. 29.
[17]*Ibid.*, p. 32.
[18]*Ibid.*, p. 33.

to the paternalism of establishment bureaucrats. Gouldner concluded:

> The new underdog sociology propounded by Becker is, then, a standpoint that possesses a remarkably convenient combination of properties: it enables the sociologist to befriend the very small underdogs in local settings, to reject the standpoint of the 'middle dog' respectables and notables who manage local caretaking establishments, while, at the same time, to make and remain friends with the really top dogs in Washington agencies or New York foundations.[19]

While all of this might sound as if Gouldner intended to return to the position of Max Weber, this was not the case. Gouldner's objection to Howard S. Becker was not based on Becker's failure to substitute ideology for social theory, but his advocacy of the wrong ideology. Becker's was the ideology of liberalism, which was the target of Gouldner's scorn as "sacred prostitution." Only a radical ideology is acceptable to Gouldner.

The conflicts between Gouldner and Howard Becker illustrate the consequences of assigning to sociology an ideological mission: in the end the finding of fact is set aside and only violent partisan dispute remains. Thus, in view of all the forces against it, scientific objectivity, when it is in fact realized, has many of the characteristics of the moment of calm at the eye of a hurricane.

PARADIGMS

In a situation in which practitioners launch a vigorous attack upon traditional conceptions of sociological theory and the partisans of ideology can not agree, there is a temptation by persons who still wish to discuss the kinds of materials traditionally included in theory to look for neutral ground. The notion of paradigm was such a popular expedient in the 1960s and 1970s.

The use of models and examples for the training of the young in moral and ethical conduct has

long been practiced. Aesop's fables, for example, were moral or ethical paradigms. When linguistics and folklore were being transformed in the nineteenth century into intellectual disciplines, the concept of paradigm was borrowed from moral and ethical contexts and employed in the analysis of language and cultural formations.

In grammar, a paradigm is a set of all forms containing a particular element such as the set of all inflected forms of a single root, stem, or theme. It is also a display in fixed arrangement of such a set. Paradigm also has the secondary meaning of a pattern or example. By extension from the secondary meaning, paradigm has occasionally been employed as a euphemism for ideal type. An ideal type is a thought-model which combines ideas and evidence into an analytical construct. In Weber's words:

> An ideal type is formed by the one-sided *accentuation* of one or more points of view and by the synthesis of a great many diffuse, discrete, more or less present and occasionally absent *concrete individual* phenomena, which are arranged according to those one-sidedly emphasized viewpoints into a unified *analytical construct*.[20]

Still other meanings of the term appear in the 1950s with Robert Merton's usages. In his introduction to the second edition of his essays, Merton argued:

> As here construed, codification is the orderly and compact arrangement of systematized fruitful experience with procedures of inquiry and with the substantive findings which result from the use of these procedures. . . . At periodic points in the book, I use the device of the *analytical paradigm* for presenting codified materials.[21]

The first of his paradigms was an outline of concepts and problems thought to be important

[20]Max Weber, *On the Methodology of the Social Sciences*, trans. Edward A. Shils and Henry A. Finch (Glencoe: The Free Press, 1949), p. 90.
[21]Robert K. Merton, *Social Theory and Social Structure* (Glencoe: The Free Press, 1957), p. 13.

[19]*Ibid.*, p. 49.

for functional analysis; the second was a typology of possible behaviors resulting from cross-tabulating the orientation of individuals to cultural goals as positive or negative, and dichotomizing their willingness to use the legitimate means for attaining them as positive or negative. The third of Merton's paradigms consisted of a set of questions and an outline of possible answers, each designed to make uniform the systematic evaluation of a number of different positions on the sociology of knowledge. In the context of Merton's work paradigm had acquired the meaning of "summary outlines" and "heuristic check lists."

Merton discovered no fewer than five sterling virtues in paradigms of this sort for increasing the precision of qualitative analysis in sociology: (1) they provide an economical arrangement of central concepts; (2) they tend to make presuppositions explicit; (3) they advance the cumulation of theoretical interpretation; (4) they suggest systematic cross-tabulation of central concepts; and (5) they codify qualitative analysis in a manner approximating the empirical rigor of quantitative analysis.[22]

In 1962 the historian of science Thomas S. Kuhn gave the concept of paradigm new meaning and significance. In a manner that could not be without fascination to social scientists, Kuhn addressed himself to the endless disagreements that prevail in the "soft" sciences in contrast to the symphony of consensus that usually seems to prevail in the "hard" sciences. In view of the long-standing inferiority feeling of so many practitioners of the social sciences, it is small wonder that hearts leaped when Kuhn announced his discovery that the difference was not one of principle, but a condition of historical stage. The soft sciences are in the preparadigm, and the hard sciences are in the postparadigm, stage. In the first meaning he assigned paradigms as "universally recognized scientific achievements that for a time provide model problems and solutions to a community of practitioners."[23] A paradigm begins its life as an achievement sufficiently arresting to attract a company of devotees, but it is sufficiently ambiguous to leave all sorts of problems to be solved. Moreover, it would appear a paradigm contains a whole potential system of science within its scope.

> Achievements that share these two characteristics I shall henceforth refer to as "paradigms," a term that relates closely to "normal science." By choosing it, I mean to suggest that some accepted examples of actual scientific practice — examples which include law, theory, application, and instrumentation together — provide models from which spring particular coherent traditions of scientific research.[24]

The endless bickering of the soft sciences arises from the fact that they are still in the preparadigm stage. Having entered the paradigm stage, the hard sciences are privileged to engage in "normal" science, that is, the routine tasks laid down in the paradigm. "These three classes of problems — determination of significant fact, matching of facts with theory, and articulation of theory — exhaust, I think, the literature of normal science, both empirical and theoretical."[25]

Paradigm creation gives its creators an aura of charismatic genius; acceptance of a paradigm by a lay member of the scientific community is not so much a rational decision as a conversion, an act of faith; the paradigm provides the scientific community with a unified gestalt-like perspective. The ordinary conception of theory making is false: it is actually a form of puzzle solving. The ordinary conception of scientific method is false; it is actually a form of illustration. Science does not progress — at least not in a linear sense — but undergoes periodic convulsive revolutions as one noncomparable faith replaces another.

Few theses have enjoyed more instant popularity in the social sciences than Kuhn's 1962 study. The discovery was quickly made that in structure-functionalism, sociology had entered its long-awaited paradigm stage. In fact, only the last mopping-up operations remained. However, at the very time Kuhn's theses were being diffused,

---

[22]Merton, *Essays*, pp. 13–17.
[23]Thomas S. Kuhn, *The Structure of Scientific Revolutions* (Chicago: The University of Chicago Press, 1962), p. x.

[24]*Ibid.*, p. 10.
[25]*Ibid.*, p. 33.

the consensus developed in the name of structure-functionalism was breaking up. Hence there was some uncertainty as to whether sociology was still in the preparadigm stage or was just passing through its first phase as a mature, paradigm-dominated science, and was about to undergo convulsive reorganization under a new paradigm. However, the structure-functionalists largely refused to stampede, and after nearly ten years of erosion of the structure-functionalist point of view, Alvin W. Gouldner could announce as a personal discovery, in 1970, that there was a *coming* crisis of Western sociology represented by the fact that structure-functionalism was acquiring sociological rivals: "Functional theory and Academic Sociology more generally, are now in the early stages of a continuing crisis."[26] Hence some sociologists decided that either sociology was still in the preparadigm stage after all, or perhaps it was uniquely a multiple-paradigm science.

Robert Friedrichs (1970) made one of the most imaginative and ambitious attempts to reconstruct sociology from this point of view. He argued that sociology was not only characterized by multiple paradigms, but that its paradigms were multilayered, rising in two stages (first and second order).

> Kuhn finds that natural scientific revolutions hinge upon shifts in the fundamental image a discipline has of its *subject matter*. A social science may have to confront a more fundamental paradigmatic dimension if it is to comprehend or extrapolate radical changes in the former, a level that addresses itself to the grounding image the social scientist has of *himself as scientific agent*. The reason this may be necessary is quite simple. Social scientists interact with their subject matter in a much more intimate manner than do scientists dealing with biological and physical phenomena. . . . The paradigms that order a sociologist's conception of his subject matter . . . may themselves be a reflection or function, of a more fundamental image; the paradigm *in terms of which he sees himself.*[27]

It should be noted that Kuhn did not rest scientific revolutions on shifts in the fundamental image of a discipline's subject matter.[28] There were other novelties in Friedrichs's procedure. In contrast to Kuhn's assumption that mature science is measured by the unification of the entire scientific community behind a single paradigm, Friedrichs is more than half persuaded that sociology is fundamentally pluralistic. He does, however, toy with the idea that two antithetically constructed paradigms contest for dominance in sociology: the systems paradigm and the conflict paradigm, but that they may undergo dialectical synthesis in the future. Furthermore, Friedrichs departed from the Kuhnian formula by introducing the argument from the neo-idealists, and some of their humanistic followers, that sociology is unique in having humans as subjects; the self-image of scientists combines with the definition of the subject matter to provide a sociological paradigm with its peculiar relevance. In the case of sociology, the self-image of the scientist as priest combines with the systems conception of subject matter uniquely to qualify structure-functionalism for a pro-Establishment role; the self-image of the scientist as prophet combines with the conflict conception of subject matter uniquely to qualify Marxist sociology for an anti-Establishment mission, at least in non-Communist countries.

Another interesting feature of Friedrichs's paradigm analysis of contemporary sociology is the extent to which he has translated the major sociological paradigms into conservative and radical ideologies, respectively.

While sociologists were seeking to come to terms with Kuhn's yeasty, new concepts, those same concepts were arousing interest in philosophical circles as well. They were made subject of a discussion by a colloquium in the philosophy of science in 1965 at which various differences between Kuhn's formulations and those of Sir Karl Popper were brought into central focus. Papers worked up in connection with the colloquium were

---

[26]Alvin W. Gouldner, *The Coming Crisis of Western Sociology* (New York: Basic Books, 1970), p. 341.
[27]Robert W. Friedrichs, *A Sociology of Sociology* (New York: The Free Press, 1970), pp. 55–56.

[28]Differences in basic conception of the discipline's subject matter was one of the bases for the typology in the first edition of *Nature and Types* (1960).

brought to completion sometime after the conference and the proceedings were finally published in 1970, after the appearance of the Friedrichs study. Among them a paper by Margaret Masterman brought the various meanings assigned by Kuhn to paradigms under critical review.

She observed that Kuhn's quasi-poetic style made the ascertainment of his meanings difficult. She counted no fewer than twenty-one different meanings assigned to the term *paradigm* in Kuhn's 1962 study. Among them were: a universally recognized scientific achievement; a myth; a philosophy or constellation of questions; a textbook or classic work; a standard illustration; an anomalous pack of cards; a set of political institutions; an organizing principle that can govern perception; a general epistemological viewpoint; a new way of seeing; and something that defines the broad sweep of reality.[29]

For herself, Masterman argued, the one meaning of Kuhn's paradigm that represents an original contribution to the philosophy of science is recognition of an element that complements hypothetico-deductive theory. At times in scientific practice an artifact, which is also a concrete "way of seeing," is isolated and utilized analogically. "The trick which . . . starts off every new science, is that a known construct, an artifact, becomes a 'research vehicle,' and at the same moment, if successful, it becomes a paradigm, by being used to apply to new material, and in a non-obvious way."[30]

In applying the term *paradigm* to any and all of different situations that Masterman carefully documented in her 1962 work, the term was permitted by Kuhn to range freely from a total system of scientific practice imposed bindingly on a scientific community to any part thereof. The argument automatically became ambiguous and circular. In his reply to his critics, Kuhn acknowledged Masterman's criticism:

All of the objects of commitment described in my book as paradigms, parts of paradigms or paradigmatic would find a place in the disciplinary matrix, but they would not be lumped together as paradigms, individually or collectively. Among them would be: shared symbolic generalizations . . . ; shared models whether metaphysical . . . or heuristic . . . ; shared values . . . ; and other elements of the sort. Among the latter I would particularly emphasize concrete problem solutions, the sorts of standard examples of solved problems which scientists encounter first in student laboratories, in the problems at the ends of chapters in science texts, and on examinations. If I could, I would call these problem-solutions paradigms, for they are what led me to the choice of the term in the first place. Having lost control of the word, however, I shall henceforth describe them as exemplars.[31]

By the time George Ritzer[32] undertook the integration of sociology in a paradigm framework, he had at his disposal the published proceedings of the colloquium. Moreover, in 1970 Kuhn brought out a second edition of his book, in which he also proposed restricting the meaning of paradigm to exemplar. However, Ritzer chose not to follow Kuhn in his restriction of the meaning of paradigm to exemplar, but opted to continue the usage of the 1962 edition of *The Structure of Scientific Revolutions.*

Paradigms were interpreted to be matrices of normal science, or more specifically, to consist of metaphysical world views (an idea Ritzer mistakenly attributed to Masterman) taken together with an associated system of scientific practice and including: definitions of reality, exemplars, theories, and methodological preferences.

Ritzer maintains that three paradigms divide and organize sociology: social factism, social definitionism, and behaviorism. Social factism is best exemplified in the work of Durkheim. It defines social reality as social fact. It is theoretically elaborated in both systems (structure-functionalism and conflict theory). Methodolog-

[29]Margaret Masterman "The Nature of a Paradigm," in *Criticism and the Growth of Knowledge,* ed. Imre Lakatos and Alan Musgrave (London: Cambridge University Press, 1970), pp. 61–65.
[30]*Ibid.,* pp. 71–78.

[31]Thomas Kuhn, "Reflections on My Critics," in *Criticism and the Growth of Knowledge*, pp. 271–272.
[32]George Ritzer, *Sociology: A Multiple Paradigm Science* (Boston: Allyn and Bacon, 1975).

ically, it is purportedly characterized by a love of surveys and statistics. Social definitionism, which is said to be best exemplified in the work of Max Weber, is said to conceive social reality as primarily consisting of people's interpretations of definitions of situations. This paradigm is theoretically illustrated by social action theory, symbolic interactionism, existentialism, ethnomethodology and phenomenology. Social definitionism has a methodological preference for introspective procedures, participant observation, and for qualitative methodology generally. Behaviorism is exemplified in the work of B. F. Skinner. It defines social reality as social behavior. It is theoretically developed in behavioristic sociology and in the exchange theory of Peter Blau and George Homans. It is characterized by methodological preferences for laboratory experimentation.

Some selectivity was required to impose this formalism on the thought and practice of current sociology. It appears to overlook the fact that Weber and Durkheim are exemplars to persons of a variety of schools of sociology. Weber does not, as Ritzer himself notes, fit easily into the paradigm of social definitionism of which he is taken as an exemplar. There were other cases of poor fit. Also, no note was taken of the fact that while some problems lend themselves more easily to one kind of methodological procedure than others, there are no sound reasons why theorists of any persuasion should not exploit any or all of the discipline's methodological resources whenever they are suitable to the problem at hand. In any case, the tight gestalt-like unity that Kuhn postulated to hold through all phases of a paradigm-dominated discipline is lacking.

In general, there has been a failure by sociologists to consider the very different implications for a scientific community divided into a set of competing paradigms rather than domination by a single one. One could anticipate some of the differences that one finds between a church or ecclesia, on the one hand, and a set of denominations and sects on the other. A scientific matrix dominated by a single orthodoxy is one thing; a closely related set of competitive scientific matrices, each with its unique definition of reality, exemplars, theories, and methods, is quite another. One could expect either fierce politicization or the mutual unmasking of ideological bias and a competition of truth. In any case, a novice initiated into the second type of scientific milieu would never be without alternatives.

The one meaning Masterman was willing to leave to Kuhn when she sheared away the others — that is, paradigm conceived as a concrete example or procedure that entails a *way of seeing* — bears considerable similarity to Weber's conception of ideal types as one-sided accentuations of one or more points of view taken together with a synthesis of discrete, concrete, individual phenomena. Both the limits and functions that Masterman assigned to paradigm in this special sense are similar to those Weber assigned to the ideal type. Weber observed:

> This procedure can be indispensable for heuristic as well as expository purposes. The ideal typical concept will help to develop our skill in imputation in *research:* it is no "hypothesis" but it offers guidance to the construction of hypotheses. It is not a *description* of reality but it aims to give unambiguous means of expression to such a description.[33]

Weber assigned a critical role to ideal-type procedures in the rise of research traditions that superficially, at least, sound similar to those assigned by Masterman; he recognized heuristic roles played by ideal types in the transmission of scientific culture that sound similar to those assigned by Kuhn. However, Weber thought the essence of science was to be found in its theories, not in its ideal types.

THEORIES

In view of the difficulties that develop for sociology whenever scholars attempt to fit its materials

[33]Max Weber, *Methodology*, p. 90. Italics in original.

into a framework of ideologies (which are conflicting, noncomparable mixtures of evaluation and explanation) or paradigms (which are, by at least one definition, ideal types of scientific practice, but which are rarely parallel or comparable to one another), it is hardly surprising that after nearly twenty years of dalliance with these alternatives, sociologists are once again turning to theories to provide the organizing principle of sociological materials. Despite the antipositivism that inspired the experiments, the positivists still provide the most generally accepted account of scientific explanation. The remarks of Herbert Feigl, a member of the original Vienna circle of logical positivists and a prominent philosopher of science, sum up the major areas of agreement on the nature of scientific explanation, whether in the hard or social sciences.

> Scientific explanation differs sharply from the pseudo-explanations of the animistic, theological or metaphysical types in that the explanatory premises of legitimate science must be capable of test, and must not be superfluous (i.e., not redundant in the light of the principle of parsimony). The significance of the premises and verbalisms of pseudo-explanations is usually purely emotive, i.e., pictorial and emotional. It is also agreed that all legitimate explanation is never absolute but *relative,* in the following two regards: (a) any given explanation proceeds from premises which, although possibly capable of further explanation, are *assumed* or *taken for granted* in the given case. It is only at the price, and in the light, of such assumptions that we can account for the explicanda; (b) the explanatory premises, as regards their validity, are relative to the confirming evidence, and therefore subject to revision.[34]

From this point of view, the task of science, including sociology so far as it aspires to be a science, is explanation — the inductive-deductive derivation and descriptive propositions (facts) from general assumptions (laws, hypotheses, theoretical

postulates). Explanation is a procedure of inference in which facts are examined and defined. Logical necessity is bestowed on the facts by virtue of their "derivation" from laws and theories. There is, thus, a twofold movement: induction from facts; deduction from theories.

Feigl found it convenient to visualize scientific explanation in terms of various levels arising from a basic platform of descriptions — singular statements representing specific facts, events, or situations. Laws and theoretical constructions are or contain generalized statements (unlimited universal propositions), and hence are not classified as descriptions. They constitute a second level in the hierarchy of explanation. Laws, in turn, may be concluded in superordinate or higher theoretical assumptions, first-order theories. First-order theories may, in turn, be subsumed under higher or second-order theories, and so on. Reading from bottom to top:

Theories, second order	Still more comprehensive interpretations or higher constructs.
Theories, first order	Sets of assumptions employing high order constructs; the results of abstraction and inference.
Empirical laws	Functional relationships between relatively directly observable or measurable magnitudes.
Descriptions	Data; simple accounts of individual facts or events that are more or less directly observable.[35]

While in principle the process could repeat indefinitely, in practice scientific explanation usually stops at the second or third level. The top level at any given state of research covers all available descriptive data.

---

[34]Herbert Feigl, "Some Remarks on the Meaning of Scientific Explanation," in *Readings in Philosophical Analysis,* ed. Herbert Feigl and Wilfred Sellars (New York: Appleton-Century-Crofts, 1949), p. 510.

[35]Paraphrased from Feigl, "Meaning of Scientific Explanation," p. 512.

When scientific theory departs from the context of everyday activity and common-sense thinking, it defines and clarifies a sphere of its own. In time, previous scientific practice becomes the context from which further elaborations proceed. The movement of thought that leads to science more than any other process consists in establishing the distinction between what "is" and what "ought to be," between fact and value. Science is the specialized attempt to account for what "is" in the most general and abstract manner possible. Thus, every attempt to replace scientific theory with ideology is intentionally or inadvertently an attempt to destroy science. This, of course, does not mean that there may be no value in the periodic return to the matrix from which science emerged. And, in any case, in the background of every developed theory of science are accidents, chance findings, or, as Merton would express it, serendipitous findings. New theories often seem to originate as leaps of the mind to a new plane. At this stage they are mytho-poetic, frequently taking the form of metaphors or intuitive fusions of ideas and evidence that suggest relationships not previously suspected. Some studies have described these creative illuminations as "transcendent hypotheses."

> When first introduced, a transcendent hypothesis may be extremely vague, provided only that it entails the laws that it is intended to explain. When Huyghens tried to explain the diffraction and the interference of light by means of his undulatory theory, he had no clear idea of the nature of the waves he supposed to occur, but the wave-motion seemed to render some laws of optics intelligible and there was no rival suggestion that could do as much.[36]

It is quite evident that Masterman reinterpreted Kuhn's paradigms in such a way as to liken them to the notion of transcendent hypotheses. Paradigms were, she argued, a special class of analogies that involved both concrete examples of procedure and a new way of seeing. If one reserves the term *theory* for a worked-up, logically interrelated set of explanatory principles, a transcendent hypothesis (paradigm) is pretheoretical and, as both Kuhn and Masterman seem inclined to urge, can operate to institute the scientific process prior to the appearance of theory. If, however, one treats a transcendent hypothesis (paradigm) as the first crude form of theory and as a new way of organizing evidence, it should not be located outside theory, but rather is a most integral part of that theory. With considerable frequency, as a theory and its associated research tradition develop, an idealized version of the original way of looking at and handling evidence is utilized as a model (heuristic paradigm) for teaching purposes. Kuhn seems to have been most enamored of exemplars (heuristic paradigms) and models employed for socialization and the teaching purposes of a scientific tradition. Masterman is most interested in transcendent hypotheses, paradigms functioning in a context of discovery. Reichenbach's observations are pertinent to the kinds of paradigms that excited Masterman:

> The act of discovery escapes logical analysis; there are no logical rules in terms of which a "discovery machine" could be constructed that would take over the creative function of the genius. But it is not the logician's task to account for scientific discoveries; all he can do is to analyze the relation between given facts and a theory presented to him with the claim that it explains these facts. In other words, logic is concerned only with the context of justification.[37]

A curious thing has happened in the course of the recent discussion of the role of paradigms in science. A tendency has been present to separate the creative aspects of science from its routine hard work. This transforms the scientific process into flashes of genius (which are conceived as prescientific or extrascientific) and the formation of

---

[36]William Kneale, "Induction, Explanation and Transcendent Hypotheses," in *Readings in the Philosophy of Science*, ed. Herbert Feigl and May Brodbeck (New York: Appleton-Century-Crofts, 1953), p. 356.

[37]Hans Reichenbach, *The Rise of Scientific Philosophy* (Berkeley: University of California Press, 1953), p. 231.

cults and rituals of compulsively neurotic puzzle solving. The result is a caricature of the scientific process. Still the most satisfactory way of appraising the status of sociology, or of any science, is in terms of an inventory of its theories. Moreover, the fuller one's picture of the development of theory and its associated research traditions, from its foundation often in a powerful metaphor to the establishment of its principles of explanation through the translation of its laws into mathematical formulas, the better one's understanding of the nature and limits of the discipline's explanatory power. This may be illustrated by a few brief notes on the rise of sociological theory and a sketch of the current theoretical landscape of sociology.

The naturalization of social life in the seventeenth and eighteenth centuries that laid the foundation for the rise of the social sciences in the nineteenth century was immeasurably speeded by a favorite metaphor of the rationalistic social philosophers: the social contract. This suggested radical reappraisal of the relations between individuals and their associates in social groupings of most diverse sorts. It thrust the rational quid pro quo into central position regarding the estimation of social situations. Social relationships that had previously been left unexplored because of traditionalistic or religious reasons were examined, and sometimes surprising discoveries were made about them. In the process social life tended to lose dimensions of mystery and awe and were thus made open and down to earth. The conclusions became inescapable: much could be learned by applying to human social life the methods that had proved their worth in the study of the physical world.

In the nineteenth century, if one takes the conventional position which traces the rise of sociology to the influence of Saint-Simon and Comte, the metaphor of society as an organism presided over the birth of sociology proper. Organismic analogies of society were by no means new. However, the proposal to study simultaneously the social organism while employing the positivistic methodology of science was an interesting realignment of previously discrete and to some extent opposed traditions. The new science is accurately described in terms of its basic conception of social reality and its presuppositions as to how this is best studied as positivistic organicism. The conceptual resources of the new theory received their first elaboration in the works of pioneering figures such as Comte, Spencer, J. S. Mill, and Lester Ward. They constituted sociology's first school. Positivistic organicism was further elaborated and partially biologized under the influence of Darwinian biology. The theory was brought to its classic formulation in the work of persons such as Ferdinand Tönnies and Emile Durkheim.

There will always be a question as to when innovations in an emerging body of theory are so basic as to warrant the establishment of a new theory. Accident and personality variables, such as intransigence, ambition, and the like, often play a role. Sometimes traditions split off from the main body only to rejoin it at a later stage of their mutual development. Somewhat parallel to the manner in which the Marxians split off from the Hegelians, the conflict theorists in sociology split off from the positivistic organicists. The conflict theorists appealed to a wide spectrum of historical authorities, for example, Hobbes, Machiavelli, Polybius in Antiquity, and Ibn Kahldun in the Islamic Middle Ages, who were almost completely ignored by the positivistic organicists. They were the first sociologists to take Marx seriously, and when Marxism was eventually seen as a type of sociological theory, it was classified as a form of conflict theory. The conflict theorists virtually founded a series of new subdisciplines such as the sociology of power, the sociology of law, the sociology of stratification. The conflict theorists came to see themselves as a separate school of sociology. However, some of their heirs in the twentieth century seem prepared to join ranks with the twentieth-century heirs of positivistic organicism.

Toward the end of the nineteenth century and in the opening decades of the twentieth century, sparked in some measure by problems in Western society, a series of revolts was staged in the ranks of sociologists against both positivistic organicism and conflict theory. The revolt was directed against the holistic concept of social reality held by the first two schools of theory. Previously, society was considered analogous to an organism by the positivistic organicists and analogous to battlefield warfare by the conflict theorists. Social reality was now reconceptualized as interindividual activity or as the interactive process.

Again and again a richly suggestive metaphor appears at the beginning of what becomes, in time, a new movement in theory. However, only those metaphors that suggest new relationships and ideas that prove to possess explanatory power are useful; metaphors without such properties may do more harm than good (as the metaphor of an ethereal substance, phlogiston, which was thought to account for fire). Scientific explanation is a process, a development of ideas, often starting with a brilliantly evocative notion that is explored and tested and, sometimes, ending with a set of mathematical equations in which an idea is applied with precision. While some persons — possibly with the unconscious inclination to dazzle the peasants — are inclined to reserve the term scientific theory exclusively for the set of mathematical equations that occasionally crowns a development in science, the essential character of science is revealed in the whole process and not in the possible outcome alone.

SUMMARY

From the time of its origin in the nineteenth century through the 1950s, sociology was primarily viewed by its practitioners as a science whose main concern was the theoretical explanation of society. In the 1960s and 1970s, the discipline entered a period of conflict when vigorous minorities among sociologists undertook to downplay the role of theory and locate the organizing principle of sociology's subject matter in ideology or in paradigm. Ideologies are combinations of ideas and values formed into a strategy for realizing some individual or group's notion of the good life. Ideologies are an indispensable part of social life.

No study of social life that ignores them is complete. However, whenever ideologies are substituted for scientific theories the results are fatal to science. Ironically, the ultimate value of science to the adherents of any given ideology is increased to the extent that scientific explanation is kept free of ideology.

At the time the conflict was joined between persons defending scientific theory as the core of sociology and others proposing to replace it with ideology, Thomas Kuhn's *Structure of Scientific Revolutions* made its appearance. Kuhn's argument had obvious appeal to social scientists, for he was convinced that the struggles over point of view in the social sciences were perhaps more typical of science as a whole than the harmony of the hard sciences. The unity of opinion in the hard sciences, Kuhn maintained, was supplied by a paradigm, an ideal system of scientific practice to which everyone, or almost everyone, subscribed. In such paradigms, theory was reduced in importance to merely one of the puzzles of a paradigm left to be solved. Among the myths of science is the idea that it progresses. Kuhn brought the welcome news to sociologists that there was no more progress in the hard sciences than in the social sciences — there was merely a game of musical chairs. After a signal (the music of the paradigm stopped), everyone raced to a new seat. The only difference between the soft and the hard sciences, Kuhn indicated, was that the former were still in a preparadigm stage. To persons dismayed by the emerging dispute between positivists (protheory) and antipositivists (pro-ideology), the idea of paradigm seemed to present a middle way; they climbed aboard.

However, upon analysis, Kuhn's definition of paradigm was perceived to exist in so many variations (according to Masterman at least twenty-one), as to lack the solidity on which to build a new church. Nevertheless, analyses stimulated by the idea of paradigm sharpened realization of the role of social factors in the development of science and called to attention the problems associated with the appearance of new ideas. Meanwhile there has been a quiet return to the notion that the central concern of science is with theory.

PART II

SCIENTIFIC HOLISM

SOCIOLOGY IS A PRODUCT of Western attempts to understand the self and society. In the course of this endeavor, Western thinkers developed two basic perspectives: humanism and science. Humanism was an individual-centered social philosophy implemented by a variety of linguistic, stylistic, and philological skills, placing highest value upon direct firsthand participation in the social life it would understand and supplementing experience with archival collections of source materials. Science was originally centered on analysis of the physical world, developing methods eventually extended to the sociocultural world. The primary tool of scientists was laboratory experimentation, but when they were forced by the nature of their problems to conduct studies of situations over which they lacked physical control, they approximated laboratory conditions as far as possible with instruments for precise observation and measurement. These perspectives, humanism and science, took shape in the Western city, the community that dominated Western interpersonal life from the tenth through the sixteenth centuries; they were reshaped in the nation-state, which has dominated Western collective life since that time. Humanism and science are tool kits from which Western man and woman draw the procedures and techniques by which they seek to understand and control others and nature. Their importance is primarily methodological.

When one considers humanism and science as methodological orientations, it is useful to keep in mind the common-sense notions that a tool is designed to do a job and it is most beneficial when it is adapted to properties of the objects on which it is intended to be used. Humanism was originally adapted to the properties of people, society, and culture; science originally to the properties of things (see table: *Western Perspectives*).

When humanism and science took shape they displaced or reorganized pre-existing approaches to people and things. Much animistic and primitive religious thought was based implicitly, if not explicitly, on the notion that things (nature, natural events, physical objects) can be influenced by the same devices that influence people (entreaty,

Western Perspectives	
Orientation	Traditional Objects
Humanistic	Individuals and their behavior
	Society
	Culture
Scientific	Physical Nature

prayer — as in prayers for rain — and threats). One theory of social thought that enjoyed popularity with ethnologists and sociologists for a time held that magic was the first stage in the development of thought. Its attempts to control people, spirits, and deities were characterized as a science-like technology. Witches still do a thriving business and the belief is fairly widespread that, at least under some circumstances, psychic control over physical events is possible. When Skylab, which was intended to be the United States' first staffed space satellite, began to break down and threatened to fall to earth, one Indian mystic was reported in the world press to have announced that he intended to use his extraordinary psychic powers to hurl it into a higher orbit. Prescientific and prehumanistic thought persists in some cultures. However, wherever the lines between humanism and science are clearly drawn, devices effective in influencing people are not assumed to be effective in dealing with the nonorganic nor even the nonhuman world.

The general drift in Western thought has been toward the growth of humanism (as a secular philosophy of sociocultural life) at the expense of magic and religion, and of science at the expense of both. As magico-religious thought collapsed, some of its components fell into the sphere of humanism. Meanwhile, from the time of the Renaissance, the suggestion was made repeatedly to apply the methods that proved their worth in the hard sciences to the traditional subject matter of the humanistic disciplines. In the nineteenth century this suggestion turned into a virtual social movement.

When sociology made its appearance in the nineteenth century, its very name, in a sense, signaled its lack of concern for the traditional niceties of humanism: the name combined a Latin with a Greek term. However, more importantly, the new discipline proposed erasure of the lines between the traditional subject matters of humanism and science. Sociology proposed to deal with people, society, and culture as if they were things. The positivism conflict, which has haunted sociology ever since, was built into the discipline by the circumstances of its origin. Almost from the beginning, sensitive students of Western thought were aware of the potential conflict between sociology's subject matter and its methodological pretensions. Only the conditions in Western society that made this combination attractive and problems in Western thought that it appeared to solve, permitted sociology to develop into a permanent feature of nineteenth- and twentieth-century thought.

The holism of the first schools of sociology was an asset to the new discipline in the teeth of potential antipositivistic reactions to the application of scientific method to humanistic subject matter. The objects of study of sociology were society, humanity, and the whole of human history and culture. Individuals were not the subject matter of sociological study, though they were acknowledged to be bearers of society and culture. Moreover, society and culture were viewed holistically as entities. The implications of treating society and culture as things subject to the methods of physical science are, at least on the surface, less drastic than treating individuals in this manner.

The first school of sociological theory was a form of scientific holism. It treated society as a super-individual organism, proposing to study it with the positive methods of the sciences. The best name for this school of theory, thus, is positivistic organicism. However, even as the school of thought took shape, the antagonism between its positivism and its organicism began to have effect. In response to a series of pressures from both within and outside sociology, the theory underwent a series of changes from a pioneer to a classic phase and then collapse. Since the first edition of *Nature and Types* some developments have occurred among the last representatives of this school of theory.

The second major school of sociological theory, conflict sociology, was treated in the first edition under a section of its own. Conflict theory, however, also subscribed to both a positivistic methodology — in fact it sought to tighten up the positive program — and to a holistic theory of society, though in this case society was conceived as the product of dialectical tension between organized subgroups of society. Conflict theory also developed in response to the same general tensions between method and subject matter that motored the evolution of positivistic organicism. However, its adherents drew from different sources in the history of social thought and, though holistic, they held a more realistic picture of society than did followers of positivistic organicism. The present typology of theories has been lifted to a higher plane of generality than employed in the first edition of *Nature and Types*. Hence, both positivistic organicism and conflict theory are classified as subtypes of scientific holism. This, however, is not intended to erase the distinction between these two schools of theory, nor imply that they necessarily rise and fall together. In fact, conflict theory has experienced a brisk revival in the 1960s and 1970s while positivistic organicism has continued to decline.

IV

The Social and Philosophical Origins of Positivistic Organicism

Two things tend to be true of a scientific discipline in the early stages of its development: (1) it depends extensively on the surrounding intellectual context, and (2) its ideas become organized into "schools." It is inevitable that a new discipline will be more dependent on the intellectual context from which it emerges than an older, better established discipline. At the time of its origin, the new discipline has rarely invented many of the ideas that will eventually become central to it, and it will certainly have acquired few of the facts that it seeks to explain through its own research resources. Indeed, the first form of a new discipline is often only a new point of view in one of the older disciplines. Psychology had its origins in the epistemological branch of philosophy and in some theoretical aspects of political explanation; economics took shape out of ideas from ancient philosophy, applied medieval theology, and out of materials developed in large measure in the course of practical statecraft. Sociology represented a new departure among the ideas traditionally forming a part of philosophy. Many of the materials

for sociology had been assembled by history. In part, sociology took over programs from reformist politics. Both Comte and Spencer originally approached sociology from the standpoint of philosophy. Comte even called his study, "positive philosophy" before he adopted the term "sociology," and Spencer approached it by way of his "synthetic philosophy."

Once a discipline is organized it begins to institute standards, to accumulate materials, and to verify ideas on its own. It becomes increasingly autonomous. Recourse to outside disciplines diminishes and new points of view occur as departures within the context of the new science itself.

A second characteristic of the early stages of a science is the organization of its thought into "schools." The fertility of the human mind seems constantly to exceed the particular requirements of its time. The appearance of a new discipline depends not on this fertility alone but on a situation requiring the new thought. When social needs confirm the new discipline, the accumulation of knowledge and systematic research in one general direction can go forward. Social recognition and honors accrue to the persons satisfying the new demand. Competition for this recognition begins. And since the new area is, at first, unsettled in its theories, problems, materials, or methods, a variety of claimants appear. Thus in the early stages of a discipline alternative constructions of the basic ideas into "schools" is to be expected. The only person inclined to deny this fact is the partisan of some particular school: it seems to be normal to deny the very existence of every other than the one true faith.

Just as with the gradual maturity of the science the discipline becomes intellectually "self-sufficient" or "autonomous," although never completely so, there also tends to be a decline in the number of schools. We do not hear of "schools" of physical theory; we do hear of schools of psychology and sociology. This is to be expected in sciences of such different degrees of maturity. It is possible, of course, to grieve over the fact that sociology is still divided into schools; it is also possible to ignore this fact. Neither of these alternatives, however, is of any particular value to social theory, which must discover what the schools are and how they differ. Furthermore, it is unthinkable that any theorist should ever ignore the stimulation afforded by contrasting ideas.

The first theoretical construction of the new discipline of sociology may be designated as "positivistic organicism." It represented, in part, a fusion of opposed tendencies in philosophy. One could hardly find a more dramatic way to announce the appearance of a new discipline than in a formula combining previously opposed philosophic principles. The nature of these principles and the points at which they are in potential conflict is one of the most dramatically interesting problems in early sociological theory.

ORGANICISM AND PHILOSOPHICAL IDEALISM

The potential tension between "organicism" and "positivism" may be seen even in the most simple formulations of them. *Organicism* refers to that tendency in thought that constructs its picture of the world on an organic model. By an organismic metaphysics is meant the attempt to explain reality, or the world, or the universe, or the totality of everything as if it were a kind of organism or had properties like an organism such as being "alive," having a "vital principle," or displaying relations between parts like those between the organs of a living body. *Positivism,* on the other hand, refers to that tendency in thought which rigorously restricts all explanation of phenomena purely to phenomena themselves, preferring explanation strictly on the model of exact scientific procedure, and rejecting all tendencies, assumptions, and ideas that exceed the limits of scientific technique. Nothing is more immediately obvious than the fact that organicism commits one to assumptions about the nature of phenomena that exceed the limits of what is immediately presented in experience as well as the limits imposed by scientific technique. Organicism and positivism should have been in tension from the start. The fact that they were put together and accepted by the learned world of the time is demonstration of the need for a new discipline, for the learned world will not overlook contradiction unless it has good reasons for doing so.

Origins of Sociological Organicism in Philosophical Idealism. Popularly, *idealism* tends to refer to visionary and prophetic attitudes toward human affairs. It also tends to refer to the optimistic frame of mind. The person who dreams of a better future or better world, who looks at the bright side of every issue and who stoutly maintains cheerfulness in the face of difficulty tends to be described as an "idealist." Philosophically, idealism does not require this hopeful and forward-looking attitude toward human affairs, though many philosophical idealists have retained it. Philosophical idealism refers to the view that reality itself is somehow in the nature of ideas or, in more moderate forms, to the view that, among all the kinds of realities, ideas are the most significant.

Idealism has played an important role in the

history of Western thought.[1] It was deeply imbedded in that tradition in ancient Greece which was summarized in the philosophies of Plato and Aristotle. Plato's doctrine of ideas is typical. Ideas are the only things that really exist. Each thing is what it is only through the presence of the idea in it or through its participation in the idea. An idea as the "one" stands in opposition to the "many" — the plurality of actual things. For example, one idea "horse" refers to many actual horses. The world of actual things is constantly changing or becoming something else. The "many" are changeable: the "idea" remains always the same. All becoming, including human conduct, has its end and aim in a being. These ends can only be in the realization of that in which thought recognizes the unchanging primary patterns of things — ideas. Despite his many objections to Plato's theory of ideas, Aristotle accepted all its essentials. With Plato, he thought that only necessary and unchangeable forms can be objects of knowledge.

[1]See Guido de Ruggiero, "Idealism," in the *Encyclopedia of the Social Sciences* (New York: Macmillan, 1931), VII, 468–472. Among general works, see R. F. Alfred Hoernlé, *Idealism as a Philosophy* (New York: Doran, 1927); John Theodore Merz, *A History of European Thought in the Nineteenth Century* (Edinburgh: 1896–1914), Vol. 3, Ch. 5; and Josiah Royce, *Lectures on Modern Idealism* (New Haven, Conn.: Yale University Press, 1919).

The term *idealism* has not been popular through much of the twentieth century and an entry on the concept was not included in the *International Encyclopedia of the Social Sciences*. In H. B. Acton's entry on "Idealism" in the *Encyclopedia of Philosophy* (New York: Crowell Collier and Macmillan, 1968), IV, 110–118 the most recent bibliographical entry is Alfred Cyril Ewing, *The Idealist Tradition from Berkeley to Blanchard* (Glencoe: The Free Press, 1957). However, phenomenologists, existentialists, and the critical theorists of the Frankfurt school were developing the central ideas of both the subjective and objective idealists and with the decline in popularity of the logical positivists in the 1970s there has been some inclination to rehabilitate the term. Among new and reprinted works are: Nicholas Rescher, *Conceptual Idealism* (Oxford: Blackwell, 1973); Alfred Cyril Ewing, *Idealism: A Critical Survey* (London: Methuen, 1974); John Howie and Thomas O. Buford, eds., *Contemporary Studies in Philosophical Idealism* (Cape Cod, Mass.: C. Stark, 1975).

The idealistic traditions expressed in Plato and Aristotle became the dominant ones from the Greek world. They formed the basis for the theologies of the Middle Ages, which were established first on the basis of Platonism and Neo-Platonism, later on the basis of Aristotelian metaphysics. The theological idealism of the medieval world sharpened the distinction between heaven and earth. The activity of human kind became a pilgrimage toward eternal goals. The ultimate source of reality was the idea in the mind of God.

Modern forms of idealism appear most clearly in the more theologically inclined philosophers. Leibnitz, for example, conceived the world as a complex of individual monads. The soul of a person is a single monad which does not stand alone in nature. According to the law of continuity, by which there are no leaps in nature, we must assume infinite degrees of the kind of existence found in ourselves. *C'est partout et toujours la même chose, aux degrés de perfection près.* The law of continuity for Leibnitz originates in the principle of sufficient reason. The appearance of consciousness in nature can only be explained in terms of more obscure forms and degrees of psychic life, of impulse and efforts that awake to full consciousness in the higher forms of life.

Transcendent Idealism and Subjective Idealism. Ancient idealism may be described as "transcendent idealism," since it located the *idea* in some world beyond the world of the senses. Modern idealism as typified by George Berkeley may be called "subjective," for it tends to relocate the idea at the core of experience. Berkeley arrived at it by way of a critique of the empiricist tradition he shared. Philosophers since Locke had tended to make experience the starting point for the analysis of the world and the mind. Experience was believed to show properties that belonged to each: there were some qualities like weight, extension, existence in time, that belonged to real things; there were others like smell, color, etc., that were subjective. Berkeley, however, argued that this distinction of qualities cannot be maintained. The experience of weight is just as subjective as the experience of color. We have no more basis for assuming the existence of a real thing corresponding to a weight than we do the existence of a real thing in nature corresponding to a color. In fact, if we stick purely to what experience gives, the world consists of ideas. To account for the fact that when we awake day after day it is to the same sights, sounds, smells, and weights, Berkeley urged that there must be a Divine Mind where things exist when they are not present in the individual mind.

Objective Idealism. While a kind of personalized and subjective idealism was developed in the work of Leibnitz and Berkeley, a modern form of "objective idealism" appeared in the work of Hegel. Like the subjective idealists, Hegel was strongly theological in orientation. His philosophy represents a new departure in idealistic philosophy attempting to overcome some of the individualistic and atomistic characteristics of subjective idealism. Hegel maintained that ordinary consciousness develops into speculative thought by stages. The truth is a process in which substance and subjectivity are phases. The individual consciousness is an incident in the development of the world spirit. History itself is the development of the consciousness of humankind. History is rational, and the task of philosophy is to grasp the reason contained in it. The ethical world is the state of social affairs representing reason as actualized self-consciousness. Thought is the last product of a world process. Reflection itself is a sign that an epoch is drawing to a close. The Owl of Minerva takes its flight only when the shades of night are gathering. The mind of humanity develops in much the same manner as that of a single individual from infancy to intellectual maturity.

Irrational Idealism, Idealism of the Will. Another important form of idealism that developed in the nineteenth century along somewhat different lines was a kind of negative or irrational idealism. It remains idealistic in the most basic of all senses — the world is ultimately conceived as a living process. However, instead of discovering the world to

be modeled after the more rational actions of the human mind, this model of the world is conceived after feelings and will. Schopenhauer argues that the world as immediately given corresponds to changes in our bodies. Space, time, and causality are various ways in which the immediately given sensation is comprehended. Science deals with this world. Science can do nothing other than present a materialistic explanation of phenomena. However, Schopenhauer believes the world as idea is only a surface manifestation, a relatively superficial level of existence. There must be a thing-in-itself that is a substratum of all this. The will is the essence of a human being as a thing-in-himself or -herself. The will must also represent the essence of the world. This makes striving, wishing, experiencing pleasure, pain, hope, fear, love, and hate as the most important aspects of humanity and the world. These are only the infinitely varied, different forms of the will to live, which in nature is manifest as the crude force. Here is a type of idealism taking not rationalism but blind irrational will to explain what the world is really like.

Modern types of idealism thus have a threefold source. From subjective and personal idealism like that of Berkeley, from objective idealism like that of Hegel, from irrational idealism like that of Schopenhauer, the modern world has also witnessed new versions of irrational idealism, illustrated by Henri Bergson.

All types of philosophic idealism have been represented as an extension of the organic analogy.[2] Once the analogy is applied, it leads to such characteristic results as: (1) the teleological concept of nature; (2) the view that nature, society, history, and what not are integral wholes which lose their peculiar property (their "life") when dissected (analyzed); and (3) the idea that the relation between the subparts of nature, society, history, or civilization are like the relation between the organs of a living body. From idealism, early sociology

[2]Harald Høffding, A *History of Modern Philosophy,* trans. B. E. Meyer (New York: Macmillan, 1935), I, 348.

took the organismic concept of society, history, and civilization.

THE PHILOSOPHICAL AND SOCIAL BACKGROUND OF "POSITIVISM"

Positivism is that movement in thought that rests all interpretation of the world exclusively on experience.[3] Since science has been the mode of thought most successful in the modern world in dealing with the data of experience, positivism takes its point of departure from natural science, seeking a unified view of the world of phenomena, both physical and human, through the application of the methods and extension of the results of the natural sciences. Positivism arose as a reaction to traditional philosophy, being an attempt to cut through its complexities and variations and to establish thought on a definite foundation.

Ancient Positivism. In the ancient Greek world the closest approaches to a positivistic orientation are found in the atomists and the Sophists. Democritus, for example, conceived all changes in nature as due to the ceaseless joining and separation of uncreated atoms. Qualities were thought to depend on the size, shape, and arrangement of the atoms. Love, hate, and the other emotions were conceptualized as motions of the primary substance. Thinking was viewed as changes in the soul-body. Knowledge was thought to be derived from observation, and the imperfections of

---

[3]The two major forms of positivism, nineteenth and twentieth century, are both heirs of eighteenth-century rationalism. Nineteenth-century positivism, which was reviewed by Guido de Ruggiero in "Positivism," *Encyclopedia of the Social Sciences* XII, 260, has actually been the major influence on sociology throughout the nineteenth and twentieth centuries: encouraging the application of scientific methods to society with a preference for measurement, scaling, and quantitative data, and an interest in social problems. See Walter M. Simon, *European Positivism in the Nineteenth Century: An Essay in Intellectual History* (Ithaca, N.Y.: Cornell University Press, 1963). Among typical works which reveal the spirit of nineteenth-century positivism (which, incidentally, also had an influence on such American pragmatists as John Dewey) are the works of Comte (cited further on in this chapter); T. H. Huxley, "The Scientific Aspects of Positivism," in *Lay Sermons, Addresses, and Reviews,* 3d ed. (London and New York: 1870); Marcel Boll, *La Science et l'esprit positif chez les penseurs contemporains* (Paris: Larousse, 1921); Ernst Mach, *The Science of Mechanics,* trans. Thomas J. McCormack (La Salle, Ill.: Open Court Publishing Co., 1942) and *The Analysis of Sensations and the Relation of the Physical to the Psychical,* trans. C. M. Williams and Sydney Waterlow (Chicago: Open Court Publishing Co., 1914); and John Dewey, *Experience and Nature* (Chicago: Open Court Publishing Co., 1925; New York: Dover Publications, 1958).

Twentieth-century positivism, which is presented by Abraham Kaplan in "Positivism," *International Encyclopedia of the Social Sciences* (New York; Crowell Collier and Macmillan, 1968), XI, 389–395, is sometimes described as logical positivism or logical empiricism. It was inspired by developments in logic and mathematics, particularly Alfred North Whitehead and Bertrand Russell, *Principia Mathematica,* (1910–1913) 2nd ed. (London: Cambridge University Press, 1957). In the 1920s a circle of scholars formed in Vienna to promote an updated positivism, taking as one of its major texts the work of Russell's student Ludwig Wittgenstein, *Tractus Logico-*

philosophicus, first American edition (New York: Harcourt Brace, 1922).

No attempt will be made to list all the works of the logical positivists, though some persons and works important for various subbranches of the movement may be noted: the English Branch is illustrated by Alfred J. Ayer, *Language Truth and Logic* (London: Gollancz, 1936); the Austrian Branch, Rudolf Carnap, *The Logical Structure of the World and Pseudo Problems in Philosophy* (Berkeley, University of California Press, 1964); the German branch, Hans Reichenbach, *The Rise of Scientific Philosophy* (Berkeley: University of California Press, 1951); the American branch, Charles W. Morris, *Signs, Language and Behavior* (Englewood Cliffs, N.J.: Prentice-Hall, 1946). Excellent collections of positivistic texts appear in the symposia: Herbert Feigl and May Brodbeck, eds., *Readings in the Philosophy of Science* (New York: Appleton, 1953) and Herbert Feigl and Wilfred Sellars, eds., *Readings in Philosophical Analysis* (New York: Appleton, 1949). Good recent summaries of positivism and its influence on sociology are Anthony Giddens, ed., *Positivism and Sociology* (London: Heinemann, 1975) and Anthony Giddens "Positivism and its Critics," *A History of Sociological Analysis,* Tom Bottomore and Robert Nisbet, eds. (New York: Basic Books, 1978), pp. 237–286.

sense-perception were one of the primary sources of error.[4]

These ideas of Democritus could appear remarkably promising to a modern positivist. However, Democritus' ideas were not established on the basis of observation, nor were his notions of such things as atoms and primary motions confirmed by scientific procedures. He seems rather to have deduced them from his central principles. Democritus' sensualism did not lead him to oppose the existence of the gods but to a naturalistic explanation of them. He thought that beings of human form inhabit space. They are superior to people in size and length of life. The images that they send out appear to people in waking and sleep, and are believed to be gods.

Actually much closer to modern positivism was the sophistical movement in Greek thought. In the long run, the major philosophic traditions in Greece, although not eliminating observation, relegated it to second place. This was not the case with the Sophists. The Sophists abandoned metaphysical inquiries, and taking their stand on experience, they sought to amass the greatest amount of knowledge in all departments of life. They developed ideas on the possibility of knowledge, on the beginning and progress of human civilization, on the origin and structure of language, on the appropriate and efficient arrangement of the life of the individual and society. Their method was empirico-inductive. Sophism tried to maintain its analysis strictly on the foundation of experience itself; furthermore, like modern positivism, it showed an inclination to extend its method to the solution of everyday problems and to social life. Another impulse typical of positivism appears in sophistic enterprise: the practical twist given to knowledge. For the Sophists, "knowledge was only valuable in so far as it formed a means to the control of life. The sophist cannot be thought of without pupils. His aim was not primarily to make sophists of them, but he wished to give the

layman a general education which he could use in life. His aim was therefore predominantly practical: the art and control of life."[5] However, despite somewhat greater promise than that of the atomists, the Sophist program is not altogether equivalent to modern positivism. If the program of Democritus and that of the Sophists could have been fused, the result would have amounted to a full-scale positivism.

Modern Positivism. Only in recent Western thought has it been possible to bring together the kinds of conceptual tendencies present in the ancient atomists with those present in the ancient Sophists. The tremendous gains of natural science in the last three centuries of the modern period increasingly make possible the conception of the complete reconstruction of thought on the basis of science and the extension of its procedures to society and civilization. Ruggiero justly speaks of a more or less latent positivism from the beginning of the seventeenth century on, reflecting the increasing success of science in the modern world.[6]

It is conventional to trace modern positivism to the writings of Francis Bacon. His *Novum Organum* appeared in 1620. It was an investigation of the imperfections of the sciences and the obstacles to knowledge that were located in the constitution of the human mind and the situation in which it finds itself. In the *Advancement of Learning* Bacon sketched the branches of knowledge to clarify the achievements and further problems of science. In the *New Atlantis* he portrayed the lot of humanity under the guidance of the new aristocracy of science, in which the domination of human being by human being is replaced by the domination of human being over nature.

The Early Positivistic Program. If a general positivistic program — the application of science to the regeneration of humanity — is presented by Bacon, a much more concrete, if more limited, program is contained in empiricism. The anti-

---

[4]Eduard Zeller, *Outlines of the History of Greek Philosophy*, 13th ed., rev. by Wilhelm Nestle and trans. L. R. Palmer (New York: Meridian Books, 1955).

[5]*Ibid.,* p. 94.
[6]Ruggiero, "Positivism," p. 261.

metaphysical tendencies of science are focused in the problem of constructing knowledge out of the data of experience without appeal to transcendent principles of any kind. Locke argued that "men, barely by the use of their natural faculties, may attain to all the knowledge they have, without the help of any innate impressions."[7] The manner in which this occurs is set down generally as follows: "The senses at first let in particular ideas, and furnish the yet empty cabinet; and the mind by degrees growing familiar with some of them, they are lodged in the memory, and names got to them. Afterwards the mind, proceeding farther, abstracts them, and by degrees learns the use of general names."[8]

The development of empiricist epistemology is a well-known story, of only incidental importance here. Through Locke, Berkeley, and Hume, the derivation of knowledge from experience and the consequences of this derivation were explored. It became clear that, when traditional ideas were put to the test of experience, an extensive liquidation occurred. Bishop Berkeley demonstrated that one could not justify the existence of a physical world on the basis of experience. The world could be reduced to ideas in the minds of human beings and God, a conclusion very agreeable to him. Hume in a famous argument showed that even the principle of causality could not stand the test of experience. "Let men once be fully persuaded of these two principles, *That there is nothing in any object, consider'd in itself, which can afford us a reason for drawing a conclusion beyond it; and, That even after the observation of the frequent or constant conjunction of objects, we have no reason to draw any inference concerning any object beyond those of which we had experience*. . . ."[9] When these principles are applied, it is soon discovered that we have no apparent grounds for accepting some very significant traditional ideas such as God, the self, the physical world, causality.

The significance of empiricism for positivism has been phrased with unusual cogency by a modern antipositivist:

the last bridge which still joined the new empiricism with the old metaphysics was broken, and the natural world was reduced to a complex of phenomenal data bound up with relations equally phenomenal; the corresponding subjective and mental world also was resolved into a bundle of sensations held together by empirical bonds of an associative nature. The mind, fortress of traditional metaphysics, was reduced to the level of nature and thus became, at least potentially, subject to the application of the same scientific methods which proved so fecund in the study of nature.[10]

In France Voltaire early in the eighteenth century had begun to popularize Newtonian science. The philosophy of Locke began to gain adherents. The ideal of progress of the individual and humankind received expression in Condorcet's *Esquisse d'un tableau historique des progrès de l'esprit humain* (1795). This, however, was more rationalistic than positivistic. Closer to the core of positivism was the utilitarianism of Helvétius in France and Bentham in England. The main epistemological theorists of the French Enlightenment were Condillac (1715–1780), a tutor and head of an abbey, and Helvétius (1715–1771), who was farmer-general.

Condillac attempted, by deductive rather than inductive means, to establish the principle that everything in consciousness consists in transformations of simple sensations. Memory is treated as an after-effect of sensation. Abstraction consists in singling out one sensation from others. All analysis proceeds by the assignment of signs to sensory elements discovered by analytical differentiation, and by the use of speech to combine and analyze signs, thus developing a calculus of signs. Helvétius adopted Condillac's doctrine of the transformation of sensation. He tried to apply the theory to the development of our faculties through experience and external influence. He argued that

[7] John Locke, *Selections*, ed. Sterling P. Lamprecht (New York: Scribner's, 1928), p. 96.
[8] *Ibid.*, p. 99.
[9] David Hume, *Selections*, ed. Charles W. Hendel (New York: Scribner's, 1927), p. 43.

[10] Ruggiero, "Positivism," p. 262.

even self-love is acquired. We do not feel love unless we first feel pleasure and pain. This is a datum of nature. Pleasure and pain arouse and sharpen attention and determine our actions. What will attract our attention depends on education — which includes everything in the environment and circumstances that influences personal development.

English Utilitarianism. In England Jeremy Bentham (1748–1832) developed a most influential form of positivistic utilitarianism. In Bentham's theory, all ethics, thought, and psychology rest on the fundamental principle that pleasure is preferable to pain. Only prejudice was thought to stand in the way of recognition of the principle; people do, in fact, follow it regardless of what they say. The greatest happiness of the greatest number is *utility*. In his most important work, *Introduction to the Principles of Morals and Legislation* (1789), Bentham argued that not only are feelings of happiness preferred above others, but some importance must be attached to the certainty, strength or intensity, and "purity" of pleasure as well as to the "fecundity" of any given pleasure. The principle of utility was employed as a device for measuring motives. Those motives are good that lead to a harmony of the individual's interests with others; bad motives lead to a separation of interests. On this basis, the older teleological and natural-law conceptions were submitted to radical criticisms as metaphysical constructs; the principle of utility was offered in place of them. Bentham and his followers also advocated an extensive reform of administration and law (finding a foremost advocate in John Austin) on the basis of utilitarian principles. It was argued, for example, that the aim of criminal law is to prevent crime. It is more important for a punishment to be certain than severe. Furthermore, the punishment must fit the crime. For, if a whole series of crimes of different seriousness are subject to the same penalty, not only will juries tend to refuse conviction when they think a given penalty excessive, but the criminal will be encouraged always to commit the more serious of the offenses. The basic principle for testing any given law or administrative act is a calculus of pleasures and pains.

Positivism and Social Reform. The critical point for social science in the development of empiricism was aptly put by Ruggiero: the mind reduced to the level of nature became subject to the application of scientific methods. One irreplaceable component of early sociology was its positivism, which consisted in the fulfillment of the scientific program made possible by the "naturalization" of mind and society.

This property of empiricism led it inevitably down the road toward reform. Locke's researches led him toward the theory of the state and civil society. Berkeley's led him to a theory of *Social Physics* and the concept of human love as a unifying force in society (moral attraction), binding people together in a lawful manner as a sort of social gravitation. Voltaire and the Encyclopedists visualized reconstruction in many social areas. Bentham and the utilitarians were led toward the reconstruction of administration and law.

The latter part of the eighteenth century saw the success of the American Revolution. Many of the American revolutionaries were trained in the doctrines of the eighteenth-century rationalists and empiricists. The linkage of rationalism, empiricism, and reform was also apparent in France. It is not surprising under such circumstances that the social reaction following the French Revolution, the eleven months of Robespierre's Reign of Terror, and the dictatorship of Napoleon should take the form of a reaction to empiricism, which was blamed for these events. But however intense the reaction following the Revolution, basic social tendencies remained. The program of social reform on the basis of science was pressed forward again, now by socialist-reformers.

Comte Henri de Saint-Simon (1760–1825), for example, is often called the father of French socialism. He was one of the first writers on a new style of social reform. He entered the army at the age of seventeen, fought with the French expeditionary forces under de Grasse in the American army, and was present at the surrender of Cornwallis at Yorktown. He did not take part in the French Revolution, but made a fortune speculating in confiscated church estates. He was in prison during Robespierre's Terror. Later he devoted himself to the problem of social reform. His *Introduction to the Scientific Work of the Nineteenth Century* was published in 1807. Other works include *The Reorganization of European Society* (1814), *The Industrial System* (1821–1822), *Political Catechism for Industrialists* (1822), *New Christianity* (1825). Saint-Simon proposed the scientific reorganization of society and the promotion of science, since, he believed, progress depended on it. In the new society, idlers would be punished, and people would be paid according to the wealth they produced. The industrial class, the only useful one, would prosper. The new political state would be confined to the maintenance and protection of the industrial organization. In time the national states of Europe would disappear. A new religion would give people a sense of unity in the world. Until they parted company, Comte was a disciple, secretary, and friend of Saint-Simon and was thoroughly familiar with these proposals.

That Saint-Simon did not represent an isolated phenomenon is shown by the fact that a school quickly gathered in his name, and he influenced such diverse persons as Proudhon, Marx, Owen, Blanc, John Stuart Mill, and Rodbertus. Robert Owen (1771–1858), the son of an iron monger and a successful industrialist, may be taken to illustrate parallel social ferment in England. William Godwin, with his belief in the perfectibility of human nature, was one of the inspirations of Owen. Owen's ideas were expressed in his essays, *A New View of Society* (1813–1814). Eventually he tried to carry out his theories of the effect of environment and education on character by forming model communities, organized on a cooperative model. Several attempts to put the theories into practice were tried. Other social reformers with schemes for social betterment included Charles Fourier (1772–1837), Étienne Cabet (1788–1856), Louis Blanc (1811–1882), and Pierre Joseph Proudhon (1809–1865).

Idealistic Organicism and Social Conservatism. Social reformism and utopia-building were the early nineteenth-century counterpart of the liberal and revolutionary movements of the eighteenth century. The conservative reaction to the course of events, on the other hand, may be seen in such persons as Burke, de Maistre, and de Bonald. Edmund Burke (1729–1797), who was born in Ireland and studied law, practiced as a journalist for a time in London. He gained fame as a Whig member of the British parliament. In 1775 he pleaded for a liberal policy toward the American colonies. The course of the French Revolution increasingly was a source of alarm to Burke, who eventually expressed a conservative reaction in *Reflections on the French Revolution* (1790) and *An Appeal from the New to the Old Whigs* (1791). He argued that society and the state are not created by conscious reason in the form of a contract; they emerge as an organic growth. Traditions and customs are ancient and important; they embody a wisdom more profound than reason. Institutions must be adapted to new situations, but the changes must be organic and from within, not violent and from without. Religion is the necessary basis of social stability. The hierarchy of society is a natural order difficult to improve. The doctrine of progress is dangerous.

Joseph de Maistre (1753–1821) was an *émigré* Savoyard noble and Sardinian ambassador to Russia. His reaction to the Revolution appears in his *Considerations on France* (1796) and *The Essay on the Generating Principle of Political Constitutions and Other Human Institutions* (1814). The idea that individuals rationally and voluntarily create society and government was rejected. These are thought rather to be products of natural organic growth. In fact, intelligence, religiousness, and sociability are human faculties dependent on life in society. Society is presupposed for the development of the highest elements of the individual. Language, for example, was not invented by individuals or groups of people, but was of divine origin. It was, however, a capacity that could emerge only in society. Individual reason and experience must be justified in terms of the collective historical experience of humankind. Social structure can be modified; it cannot be created or destroyed.

Louis de Bonald (1754–1840), a noble of the French court, had at first welcomed the Revolution. Its excesses, however, gave him pause, and he was eventually forced to flee to Heidelberg. There he wrote *The Theory of Political and Religious Authority* (1796). Later he added his *Analysis of the Natural Laws of the Social Order* (1800), *Primitive Legislation Considered by the Sole Light of Reason* (1802), and *Philosophical Demonstration of the Constitutive Principles of Society* (1830). De Bonald agrees with de Maistre that society does not originate in agreement like a trading group. It is divine in origin and a product of nature. Individuals do not create society; society creates the social individual. Like de Maistre, he believed the origins of language can reveal much about society. Words are necessary to make thinking and reasoning possible. But people could not have invented language itself; hence, it too must be of divine origin. The laws of society may best be studied among people who have preserved primitive revelation. Society necessarily rests on tradition and is most stable when hierarchical in structure. The professions (like the medieval guild) should be organized as corporations which are natural social institutions.

GIOVANNI BATTISTA VICO ANTICIPATES THE SOCIOLOGICAL SYNTHESIS

Vico (1668–1744), an Italian jurist and philologist, combined rationalistic ideas of human nature and natural law with the notion that myth plays an essential role in the formation and preservation of human groupings. He worked these into a theory of society that anticipated by one hundred years the notions of Comte, with, to be sure, some modifications.[11]

Vico was influenced by the natural law theorists (especially Selden and Pufendorf) and drew from them the idea that human beings' essential properties are their consciousness and reason,

GIAMBATTISTA VICO

Historical Picture Service, Chicago

which permit them to create their culture. However, Vico preferred an organismic model of society closer to that of Plato and Tacitus to the mechanistic notions of the enlightenment theorists. He was also intrigued by the prospect of employing inductive methods, as advocated by Bacon in *Novum organum*, to establish a new science of society.

Vico selected as much from the humanistic as from the emerging scientific perspective and, although dreaming of a science of society and culture, placed it on a different foundation from sciences of the physical world or nature. God, Vico argued, created nature, hence only God can understand it; human beings created society and culture, hence they are quite capable of understanding them fully. The same principles of human nature operate universally, but time and

---

[11]Vico's ideas were contained in *The New Science*, first published in Italian in 1725, trans. Thomas G. Bergin and Max H. Fisch (Ithaca, New York: Cornell University Press, 1948). See also *The Autobiography of Giambattista Vico*, first published in Italian 1726–1729, trans. Max H. Fisch and Thomas G. Bergin (Ithaca, N.Y.: Cornell University Press, 1944).

circumstance vary. To understand human society and culture, account must be taken of the historical conditions under which its formations appear. Vico assumed, along with such rationalists as Hobbes, that human beings originally lived like beasts in the field. Their natural inclinations and needs led them to form families, and natural events that they did not understand, such as lightning and thunder, frightened them into taking refuge in caves, giving birth to the oldest of all institutions, religion and matrimony. "Moral virtue began, as it must, from impulse. For the giants, enchained under the mountains by the frightful religion of the thunderbolts, learned to check their bestial habit of wandering wild through the great forest of the earth, and acquired the contrary custom of remaining hidden and settled in their fields. Hence they later became the founders of the nations and the lords of the first commonwealths."[12] People had, in short, conscious reasons for creating institutions and forming into communities or nations.

The fundamental institutions of a nation are marriage, religion, and burial customs. The three great ages in any given nation in terms of the manner in which its members account for themselves and their world are the age of gods, the age of heroes, and the age of peoples. In the communities born in the age of gods, when people lived in patriarchal families bound by blood ties and ruled over by powerful individuals who combined the roles of king and priest, refugees collected about them. Gradually the kinships developed into aristocracies, the age of heroes. Aristocracies in time collected plebians who grew strong enough to rebel and initiate an age of peoples. Transformations in theology, myth, and literature accompanied the movement through these cycles. The cycle terminates in the collapse of the popular state, making it ripe for a new monarchy, for conquest from the outside, or for a period of extended destruction until "the few survivors in the midst of an abundance of the things necessary for life naturally become sociable and, returning to the primi-

tive simplicity of the first world of peoples, are again religious, truthful, and faithful."[13]

Vico visualized his new science as bringing to a close the endless cyclical development and collapse of separate nations. He intended the new science to play a role as the common intellectual discipline for humankind, supporting Christianity as the one true religion for all people everywhere. Vico's writings had little effect in the eighteenth century. They did receive some recognition, particularly in literary circles, in the nineteenth century and had some influence on Marx and Engels, and on such late members of the first major school of sociology as Arnold Toynbee and Pitirim Sorokin. However, Vico's influence was eclipsed by August Comte, who independently combined the program for the scientific reorganization of society proposed by enlightenment thinkers with an organismic conception of society adapted from ancient and modern conservatives. Comte did not share Vico's intentions of salvaging and generalizing Christianity, aiming instead to replace it with the new science of society. Comte's formula was more positivistic than Vico's and, infused with the doctrine of progress, it was more fully adapted to the needs of the nineteenth-century mind than Vico's.

THE COMTEAN SYNTHESIS

The positivistic program of the reorganization of society on the basis of science was anchored in liberal and reformist circles. The idealistic program with its organic conceptions of society and history was anchored in conservative strata, opposed to planned social change. In taking over the socially conservative, idealistic-organismic concept of society and subordinating the positive method to it, Auguste Comte (1798–1857) may be seen to have been providing a conservative answer to socialism.[14] Comte was a success not because of a

---

[12]Vico, *The New Science*, p. 128.

[13]*Ibid.*, p. 381.
[14]Comte's first major work was *Cours de philosophie positive*, 6 vols. (Paris: 1830–1842), which was freely translated

AUGUSTE COMTE

Brown Brothers

freakish combination of intellectual and social elements but because his epoch had a need for precisely this combination. His simultaneous idealistic and conservative definition of subject matter is evident in his treatment of social phenomena. According to Comte, ideas govern the world or throw it into chaos. Social mechanisms rest on opinion. "The great political and moral crisis that societies are now undergoing is

shown by a rigid analysis to arise out of intellectual anarchy. While stability in fundamental maxims is the first condition of genuine social order, we are suffering under an utter disagreement which may be called universal."[15] However, Comte does not proceed from this point to an analysis of public opinion as one might think, but to a classification of the sciences as a first step in the institution of an intellectual, moral, and social order. A beginning of order in society is thus made by setting one's house in order.

The field of social order or structure was described by Comte as *social statics*.[16] Society was conceived as an organic whole analyzable into three elements: the individual, the family, and society. In his study of the individual the phrenologist Gall was followed, chiefly, it seems, because Comte thought Gall had proved basic social behavior to be biologically inherent. (It may be noted that the conservatives de Bonald and de Maistre had thought this.) While society is anchored in human nature, Comte does not agree that the individual is the simplest unit of society. The organs of society are institutions. The family is the smallest potentially self-sufficient unit — a sort of suborganic whole; it is the basic social unit. Other social forms arise out of it, be they tribes or nations. This permits the assertion of the organic wholeness of humankind: "the whole human race might be conceived of as the gradual development of a single family."[17] With the conservatives, the family is seen as a control institution arising out of the ordered and disciplined satisfaction of sex. Comte seems to feel that the family has undergone some deterioration, for he argues wistfully that the society of the future ought to have families founded on "the natural subordination of woman."[18] Only in this way can women be kept in "a state of perpetual infancy."

The real unit of sociological analysis is society. It is superior to the individual organism. It includes

and condensed, with Comte's approval, by Harriet Martineau and published as *The Positive Philosophy of Auguste Comte,* 2 vols. (London: J. Chapman, 1853). The quotations in the present work are from this translation. Comte's other major work was *Système de politique positive, ou traité de sociologie, instituant la religion de l'humanité,* 4 vols. (Paris: 1851–1854), trans. John Henry Bridges as *System of Positive Polity,* 4 vols. (London: Longmans, Green, 1875–1877).

[15]Comte, *Positive Philosophy,* I, 3.
[16]*Ibid.,* II, Chapter 5.
[17]*Ibid.,* I, 145.
[18]*Ibid.,* p. 134.

"the whole of the human species, and chiefly the whole of the white race."[19] The structure of society, its complexity and integration, rests on the division of labor. Because this source of its strength can, in the case of overspecialization, become a weakness, it is important to maintain the idea of the whole and a feeling of common interconnection. The most important of all the properties of society, beyond cooperation and division of labor, are its basic subordination and tendency toward government. Subordination is both material and social, and arises out of the natural differences of individuals. Individuals must be subordinate to those above them. Such subordination is the basis for a "natural" tendency toward government, which arises because of the greater fitness, by nature, of some people to command. Comte had great admiration for the Indian caste system, which seemed to him a paradigm of social stability.

One of the most important properties of the modern conservative-idealistic formula is its reception of the principle of development. This was its answer to the social-critical conception of progress. Conservatism, too, could accept development; in fact, it was its true heir! Progress was broken out of the revolutionary context and reset at the very core of the conservative position. In the course of this conversion it suffered a sea-change, for it became the principle of immanent development; it is inevitable; it can only be spurred on or checked by such things as climate, race, social boredom, or population density. The conservative content of this *coup* is clear only when the stages of progress are set down. Humankind, it is said, has developed from a theological, through a metaphysical, toward a positivistic stage. The metaphysical stage of social development is identified with the period of the French Revolution and the philosophy of rationalism. Metaphysical philosophy to Comte meant the ideas of social contract and natural rights; it referred to rationalism and Deism.

However, the real ingenuity in the converted progress formula is seen in the idea that each stage

has made its permanent contribution to social and intellectual development. Even the primitive theological period produced a permanent speculative class, a system of common opinions to control individual eccentricity, and hence the substratum of government. The primitives developed a leisure class that is the precondition of intellectual progress. A value is even found for the metaphysical period, which is said to have familiarized people with the idea of regularities or laws in social affairs, thus paving the way for science. The conservative argument maintains that the philosophy of revolution has made its contribution to progress and has been surpassed. In the same manner various institutions are vindicated: slavery inculcated (along with militarism) habits of regularity and discipline; industry is a major pacifying and civilizing influence of humanity; ancient astrology was a step toward science. Conservatism thus receives and surmounts the dangerous principle of change.

Comte had a stormy emotional nature, which, spurred by a stormy marriage, led to severe nervous crises. At one time in a letter to Stuart Mill he said he thought his sanity was in danger. About this time he fell deeply in love with a young woman, who died within a year. His love for her seems to have been central to the later synthesis of his ideas in *System of Positive Polity*. Comte prepared himself for this work by the practice of "cerebral hygiene," abstaining from reading anything he disagreed with, thus excluding all disturbing thoughts and insuring the unity and harmony of his ideas. He proposed a new religion of humanity, and saw himself as high priest of it. He conceived of the most elaborate and minute systematization of life. The functions of the sociological priesthood that would rule the new society were to exercise systematic direction over education. Domestic life, however, was to be left in the hands of women in their three roles as moral guardians, as daughter, wife and mother in accordance with his theory of the brain, each corresponding to three altruistic instincts of veneration, attachment, and benevolence.

In the religion of the new society Humanity be-

[19]*Ibid.*, p. 137.

comes the object of worship. Humanity includes all dead, living, or future beings who have labored for the blessedness of human beings. A calendar was drawn up in which each day of each month was named after heroes who had furthered the development of Humanity. The caste of priests in charge of education will not only have encyclopedic wisdom, but they will be poets and physicians as well. Every animal kind will be conceived as a human species whose growth was stunted. In the new religion, world space is the great medium and the earth the great fetish. The great medium, the great fetish, and the great being — space, the world, and humankind — are the positivistic trinity. In the sociocracy no one will have rights, only duties. The ruling power in external affairs will reside with the captains of industry, but they will be so rich they will feel no greed. They will conduct industrial life in such a way as to make family life possible as the basis of blessedness. Men are in charge of rational life, and women are in charge of feeling.

JOHN STUART MILL: ENGLISH CONFIRMATION OF THE COMTEAN POSITION

John Stuart Mill (1806–1873), English logician, economist, and political scientist, is not routinely included in the list of founders of sociology, but he was a correspondent of Comte and one of the first intellectuals of Britain to welcome Comtean sociology to the circle of what he called the moral sciences. As a matter of fact, Mill was acquainted with Vico's writings as well, but did not attribute to them the same importance as Comte's. Mill, like Vico and Comte, became convinced that deductions from human nature, the position of enlightenment social reformers, were not sufficient to account for human interpersonal conduct. He devoted Book VI of his *A System of Logic* (1843) to the logic of the moral sciences with studies ranging from psychology to sociology.

Mill's positivism is clear and unambiguous. Only by the extension and generalization of the

JOHN STUART MILL

Brown Brothers

methods of the physical sciences can the backward state of the moral sciences be repaired.[20] However, the best model for sociology is astronomy rather than physics or chemistry.[21] Although Mill believed sociology cannot hope to attain the same exactness as astronomy, sociology must rest on laws of individual psychology that can be established only by experiment and observation.[22] The empirical laws of human nature, Mill believed, are merely approximate generalizations. The universal laws of importance to sociology concern the formation of social character which cannot be as-

[20]John Stuart Mill, *A System of Logic* (New York: Harper, 1846), p. 519.
[21]*Ibid.*, p. 528.
[22]*Ibid.*, p. 532.

certained by observations and experiment, but must be studied deductively.[23]

However, although preliminary thereto, the laws of psychology and principles of ethology (social character) are not sufficient to account for sociological phenomena, which must be examined in the context of the society in which the phenomena occur. Sociology must discover empirical generalizations about tendencies.

States of society are like different constitutions or different ages in the physical frame; they are conditions not of one or a few organs or functions, but of the whole organism. Accordingly, the information which we possess respecting past ages, and respecting the various states of society now existing in different regions of the earth, does, when duly analyzed, exhibit such uniformities.[24]

In connection with his argument that the purpose of sociology was to establish laws of changes in social organisms by means of historical methods, Mill noted that Vico was the first to make the attempt to discover such laws through an analytical study of history. He added, however, that while Vico "conceived the phenomena of human society as revolving in an orbit; as going through periodically the same series of changes" later students "have universally adopted the idea of a trajectory or progress, in lieu of an orbit or cycle."[25]

Mill not only preferred Comte's laws of progress to Vico's stages of social cycles, but felt that Comte had given the best description so far of the proper method of sociology as an inverse deductive or historical method. "He looks upon the social science as essentially consisting of generalizations from history, verified, not originally suggested, by deduction from the laws of human nature."[26]

Mill concluded his review of the logic of the social sciences in Comtean terms:

We are justified in concluding, that the order of human progression in all respects will be a corollary deducible from the order of progression in the intellectual convictions of mankind, that is, from the law of the successive transformations of religion and science. The question remains, whether this law can be determined; at first from history as an empirical law, then converted into a scientific theorem by deducing it *a priori* from the principles of human nature. . . . The investigation which I have thus endeavored to characterize, has been systematically attempted, up to the present time, by M. Comte alone.[27]

Some twenty years after Mill's review of Comte in his *Logic,* after Spencer developed his own sociology and differentiated his views from those of Comte, Mill returned to the problems of positivism and Comtean sociology. In his examination *August Comte and Positivism*, Mill restated his general conviction of the value of sociology, finding Comte, however, to be "sadly at fault" in appreciating the manner in which circumstances in conjunction with psychological laws could produce diversity of character. Moreover, Mill dissociated himself from Comte's sociocracy: "Others may laugh, but we could far rather weep at this melancholy decadence of a great intellect."[28]

SPENCER'S REFORMULATION

Comte was born in France on the heels of the French Revolution, and was reared in an atmosphere torn by the extremes of socialism and conservative reactionism. In fact, he received much of his intellectual stimulation from one of the first of the French socialists. Herbert Spencer (1820–1903) was born in England in quite a different atmosphere, living through one of its freest and most optimistic periods. Spencer's father educated the boy outside the school system, and Spencer grew up as a confirmed individualist. The religious and political attitudes of his family encouraged

[23]*Ibid.,* p. 542.
[24]*Ibid.,* pp. 574–575.
[25]*Ibid.,* p. 575.
[26]*Ibid.,* p. 563.

[27]*Ibid.,* p. 586.
[28]John Stuart Mill, "August Comte and Positivism," *Westminster Review*, 83 (1865; reprint ed., Ann Arbor: Ann Arbor Paperback, 1961), pp. 67, 199.

HERBERT SPENCER

Brown Brothers

critical suspicion of all attempts at social legislation and state interference. Spencer was raised on Adam Smith's moral philosophy. He was fascinated by Lyell's *Geology,* and was impressed by its theory of natural development. In Spencer's first important work, *Social Statics* (1850),[29] he conceived social development by analogy with organic development, and he never gave up the idea. The form of positivism developed by Bentham was transmitted to Spencer by way of Mill. He worked

[29]Since the original publication dates of Spencer's chief works are given in the exposition, a full bibliographical note will not be attempted here. Quotations have been taken from the following editions: *Social Statics* and *The Man Versus the State* (New York: D. Appleton, 1904); *First Principles of a New System of Philosophy* (New York: DeWitt Revolving Fund, 1958); *The Study of Sociology* (New York: D. Appleton, 1929).

his way through some of its problems in his *Principles of Psychology* (1855).

There is little doubt that Spencer's fusion of positivism and organicism again operates in an essentially conservative manner. It is also clear that Comte and Spencer arrived at this requirement in quite different ways. Comte came to sociology from the standpoint of a profoundly unsettled personal emotional life and developed a message for an unsettled social order, the intellectual life of which was pulled between socialistic utopias and the conservative emphasis on tradition. In Comte's personal life he performed for himself a settling action in his "cerebral hygiene" like the one he wished to perform for society with his sociocracy. Comte, to be sure, did contemplate social legislation, a new society, and a new religion, but they were all in the interest of a traditionalistic, authoritarian social order, organized into permanent castes, with women back in permanent subordination in the home.

The impression Spencer conveys is very different; there are certainly no equivalent signs of inner torment. He seems to have been a man satisfied with himself and with his time and social order. He apparently feared that the educational reformers might be right; he felt he must by all means refute public education. The empiricists, in emphasizing the origin of all individual thought in experience, underlined the importance of education. They argued that since everything we know comes from the environment, by proper education (manipulation of the environment) any kind of society can be developed. We may be one generation away from utopia, but we are one generation away from barbarism as well. Spencer could not accept the idea that a society he liked so well could be disposed of so easily. The idea that a social order can be changed in a generation by education must at all costs be rejected. This was the basic thesis of his psychology: it is impossible to explain individual consciousness in terms of the individual's experiences alone. Spencer feared the social consequences if one could. Mental development, he asserted, takes place slowly. Modifications due to the environment gradually lead to the establishment of new forms. In the case of the individual mind, the experience of the race must be taken into account. Tradition, the structure of the mind, the manner in which ideas are associated, the form of development of the feelings and instincts, and hereditary tendencies are all important. Such was Spencer's answer to all who would change the world by education.

The concept of evolution[30] that came so handily into use in the *Principles of Psychology* (1st ed., 1855) was broadened in *Progress: Its Law and Cause* (1857), and was given general form in *First Principles* (1862): "Evolution is an integration of matter and concomitant dissipation of motion; during which the matter passes from an indefinite, incoherent homogeneity to a definite, coherent heterogeneity; and during which the retained motion undergoes a parallel transformation."[31] This formula was believed to apply to the universe, to the evolution of the earth, and to the development of biological forms, the human mind, and human society.

Society for Spencer was an entity formed of distinct units characterized by a relatively permanent arrangement in some specific area. The arrangement of the various parts of society are analogous to the arrangement of the parts of the living body. Among the basic properties of society as an organism are the facts that: (1) society undergoes growth; (2) in the course of its growth, its parts become unlike (that is, there is a structural differentiation); (3) the functions of society are reciprocal, mutually independent, and interrelated; (4) like an ordinary organism, the society may be viewed as a nation of units; and (5) the whole may be destroyed without at once destroying the life of the parts. There are, however, some contrasts between the ordinary living organism and society: (1) whereas the social organism is a discrete whole, the biological organism is a concrete whole; the units of the social organism are free and may even be widely dispersed; (2) the agencies of cooperation

are more important for society; these are the languages of emotion and intelligence, which create a living whole of the social aggregate; however, (3) while consciousness in the individual organism is concentrated in a small part, in society it is diffused, as are capacities for happiness and misery.

In his study of the problems of social growth and social structure, Spencer traced out more detailed comparisons. Like living bodies, societies begin as small units — germs — and grow to great size. They grow in aggregates of varying degrees. There is both an enlargement of groups and the fusion of groups of groups. Integration is discernible in the formation of masses and the increasing coherence of the parts of the mass. Growth as an increase of mass is accompanied by an increase in structure. As growth occurs from simple to compound and doubly compound, the unlikeness of parts increases. As the unlikeness of parts becomes greater, owing to the development of coordinating agencies, there is an increase in independence of unlike parts. Differentiation proceeds from general to specific. Moreover, the organic in animals and in societies is based on the same principle. There are, in both cases, instruments for conveying nutriment to its parts and bringing out waste products. There are regulative activities. In both societal and organic forms, in the most primitive of units there is no subdifferentiation of specialized functions.[32]

Just as in the case of growth there is a specialization of structure, so, too, there is a specialization of function. In little developed aggregates, actions are very little interdependent and the various parts of the social organism may easily exchange functions. With the advance of organization, however, every part comes to have a very special function which it performs in a relatively inelastic and irreplaceable manner.

Social differentiation begins with broad contrasts at first, showing the effects, respectively, of the primary external and then of internal conditions of society. Thus, for example, in the early stages of society the masters are warriors carrying

[30]Darwin, in *The Origin of Species* (1859), mentioned Spencer as one of his predecessors.
[31]Spencer, *First Principles*, p. 394.

[32]*Ibid.*, Sections 228–232.

on defensive and offensive activities, representing the societal agency in direct response to external conditions. At the same time the slaves carry on the internal activities of subsistence, serving first the masters, then themselves. The external and internal systems have been differentiated. A distributing system operates between the two and ties them together. In the simplest of social orders there is no distributing system, for the two original classes are in contact; in time, however, industries are localized and devices for transfer of goods appear. As society grows, new functional and industrial classes appear.

In all developed societies, thus, there are three systems of organs, even though in the simplest of societies at least one of these has little distinctness. (1) The *sustaining* system represents that organization of parts carrying on elimination in a living body, productive industries in society. In large societies built of smaller ones, industrial structures may extend without reference to political divisions. (2) The *distributing* system is required as a special integration of parts whenever the various parts of society are no longer in close contact. It is required by the division of labor. It appears between the original systems, and carries out that essential function of transfer among interdependent parts. (3) The origin of the *regulating* system is found in wars between societies, when the governmental-military organization comes into being. The subordination of local governing centers to the general governing center accompanies cooperation of components of the compound aggregate in its conflict with other aggregates. As in the individual organism, this takes the form of the appearance of a dominant center over subordinate centers, with an increase in the size and complexity of the dominant center.

Spencer suggested that societies may be arranged either in terms of their composition (as simple, compound, double-compound, etc.) or in terms of the dominance of a kind of system (predominantly military or predominantly industrial). The militant society is one where the external system predominates; the industrial society is one where the internal system dominates. In the mili-

tant type of society there is strong centralized control, an identity of the command for war and peace, a hierarchical ordering of authority. Religion in this society tends to be militant, and the ecclesiastical order is like the military. Even the sustaining system is a militarylike ordering. All life is subject to discipline. The individual is subordinated to the whole, and life is compulsorily coordinated. In the industrial society commerce has more importance than war; there is a development of free political institutions; freedom extends to the religious and industrial structures. The ideas of the relation between citizen and state are transformed. It becomes a duty to resist an unpopular government. Society is conceived as the instrument of individual action. Cooperation becomes voluntary.

The specific parts of society, the "organs" of the social organism are *institutions*. There are six types: domestic, ceremonial, political, ecclesiastical, professional, and industrial. Paralleling the general development of societal energy and structure from incoherence to coherence and from diffuseness to specificity has been a development of institutions. The *family*, for example, developed from a primitive state, where it barely served the need of sheer perpetuation of the race, to the free family of the present, in which there is a conciliation of the needs of young and old alike and a maximum of individual freedom. In form it evolved through promiscuity, polyandry, and polygyny, to monogamy. *Ceremonial* institutions compass the whole body of custom. Ceremony was the most primitive form of social control, regulating interhuman conduct before the appearance of institutions of control. Rites of the grave, for example, were attempts to propitiate the ghost and anticipated the rise of religion. Ceremonies include mutilations, trophies, presents, visits, obeisances, titles. The trend in evolution is toward replacement of ceremonies by more definite institutions. *Political* institutions also represent an evolution of structures from primitive anarchism through various types of domination by one or a few persons, to modern democratic and parliamentary structures. Especially important are the processes by which political institutions take over the functions of control. In turn, this is a product of conquest and the rapid evolution of political institutions which occurs with war and the emergence of a dominant class. *Religious* institutions originate in the rational misunderstanding of primitive people: their interpretations of phenomena like shadows, dreams, and reflections as real persons. Their terror of these ghosts is the motive power of religion. Religion represents a gradual evolution of such primitive ideas and sentiments beginning in ancestor worship. The *professions,* which originally function in the defense of tribal life, later serve national life. They represent the products of the specialization and differentiation of original social organization. *Economic* institutions, too, have gone through a slow evolution from primitive slavery through serfdom to free labor and contract.

In the social organism, structure is adapted to activity. The outer (regulating) and inner (sustaining) systems are increased or diminished by activities. Where societies descend from one another in a series, a type is established which undergoes development, maturity, and decay. When it resists metamorphosis, a society will tend to revert to an earlier state. Of especial importance is the transformation of militant into industrial society. When industry is not checked by war, noncoercive regulating systems become more important. However, it is quite possible for an industrial society to become more militant.

WARD AND THE INTRODUCTION OF SOCIOLOGICAL ORGANICISM IN AMERICA

Lester F. Ward (1841–1913), the first systematic sociologist in America, brought out his first and in some ways his most important study in 1883 between the publication of the first and last volumes of Spencer's *Principles of Sociology.* He added five additional major volumes to this statement.[33] Ward

LESTER WARD

Brown Brothers

brought the various ideas of Comte and Spencer into a peculiar synthesis of his own.

Ward divided his sociological ideas into those concerning the *genesis* of social structures and functions and those concerning social *telesis*—the application of social science for social improve-

[33]Ward's major works are: *Dynamic Sociology,* 2 vols. (New York: D. Appleton, 1883; 2d. ed., 1897); *The Psychic Fac-*

tors of Civilization (Boston: Ginn, 1893; 2d. ed., 1906); *Outlines of Sociology* (New York: Macmillan, 1898); *Pure Sociology* (New York: Macmillan, 1903; 2d. ed., 1925); and *Applied Sociology* (Boston: Ginn, 1906). For details on Ward's personal life, see Emily Palmer Cape, *Lester F. Ward* (New York: G. P. Putnam, 1922). A general sketch of Ward's work may be found in Harry Elmer Barnes, "Lester Frank Ward: The Reconstruction of Society by Social Science," in Barnes, ed., *An Introduction to the History of Sociology* (Chicago: University of Chicago Press, 1948), pp. 173–190. See also Samuel Chugerman, *Lester F. Ward: The American Aristotle* (Durham, N.C.: Duke University Press, 1939).

ment. The extensive organicism of his theory may be seen even in the very choice of terms that characterize the nature and development of social structure. Social development is "sympodial"; it develops like those plants that after growing to some degree give off a branch or sympode. Such social development displays creative synthesis; that is, each combination represents something new in nature. Ward's particular term was taken from Wilhelm Wundt, but he was clearly referring to what modern students describe as "emergence." (This is the theory that there are, so to speak, "leaps" in nature, points at which new syntheses occur with properties not explainable in terms of their components.) Any such new synthesis represents the working together of antithetical forces of nature. Ward describes it with the term *synergy*. It is crucial to his concept of the spontaneous development of society. In this development, socio-organic forces follow the principle of least resistance of the law of parsimony.

Life itself originated by the creative synthesis of chemical compounds in the process of "zooism," of which mind itself was an emergent product. "Awareness" was an irreducible new element, characterized by the capacity to distinguish pleasure and pain. Feeling and desire, the dynamic elements of mind, had an earlier origin than intellect, a directive faculty.

Spencer and Comte had established the division of sociology into social statics and social dynamics. Ward took these over. *Social statics* was taken as dealing with equilibration and the formation of social structure. Synergy is the most important principle in the formation of successful structure, which emerges in the processes of collision, conflict, antagonism, and opposition, eventually to collaboration, cooperation, and organization. Synergistic development occurs through "social karyokinesis" which, like fertilization in biology, is evident in the amalgamation and synthesis of different social groups.

Social dynamics deals with social process. Three basic principles are operative in it: difference of potential, innovation, and conation. In the contact of different cultures, the development of social

sports or mutations and social effort are operative. The basic social forces involved in the process are ontogenetic or preservative, phylogenetic or reproductive, and sociogenetic or spiritual. The theory of "gynecocracy" explains the peculiar primacy of these forces, for the female sex was original in nature and in human society.

Social telesis refers to the conscious control and direction of social development by the human mind. It is immensely superior to the operation of the blind forces of nature. The telic (purposive) control of social forces is characteristic of human social life. The state was created as the primary agent of conscious manipulation of the social process. It cannot, however, operate with any degree of precision until there is a general diffusion of basic knowledge. A general system of education, thus, is a basic prerequisite for the full realization of social telesis.

In a way it is perhaps too bad that the publication of *Dynamic Sociology* occurred before the appearance of Volume II of Spencer's *Principles of Sociology*. Inasmuch as Spencer had great influence on Ward's initial formulations, the major part of Spencer's investigations of institutions and structure were not a part of this influence. Moreover, Ward never changed in essentials the scheme of *Dynamic Sociology*.

For Ward, as for Comte and Spencer, "society" was the object of sociological analysis. However, he did no better job than his colleagues in formulating the peculiar properties of a society. Comte treated society as equivalent to humanity, but there is obviously no such entity which operates as a single working social unit. Humanity includes the living as well as the dead and people whose activities will never have any effect on the activities of others. Spencer realized that it was necessary to be more specific than this. He defined a society as a plurality of people occupying a specific territory and between whom various common features obtain. This definition of Spencer's, however, does not differentiate "society" and "the state." Ward's concept of society was even vaguer. He assumed that society is some kind of entity organized in accord with the principles of "synergy" and "equilibrium." But this was also, from Ward's position, true of any group.

The principles of synergy and equilibrium are of less value for the study of institutions than examination of a series of specifically delimited forms. At bottom, institutions are conceived by Ward as constructive equilibria of antagonistic forces. They are ultimately products of human wants. The social classes are three in number: producers, accessories to production, and parasites. Ward's entire discussion of structure is dominated by his reformist interests. This may be illustrated by the following: ". . . long before history began the earth was decked with costly temples, and within them a well-fed and comfortably clothed priesthood sat enjoying, all unearned, the luxuries vouchsafed by toil and credulity. . . . When we consider the universality of this hierarchic system, it presents one of the most extensive drains which are made upon the productive industry of the world."[34]

Ward did far more than simply repeat Comte and Spencer and add new biological and botanical terms to the analysis. Both Comte and Spencer in different ways elevate the value of the "organic" above the artificial. Comte, to be sure, dreams of a utopian society to be established, but it is thoroughly organic in character: castelike, authoritarian, and fixed. Spencer at all times elevates the organic property of society into a principle opposed to social legislation. "Thus admitting that for the fanatic some wild anticipation is needful as a stimulus, and recognizing the usefulness of his delusion as adapted to his particular nature and his particular function, the man of the higher type must be content with greatly moderated expectations, while he perseveres with undiminished efforts. He has to see how comparatively little can be done, and yet to find it worth while to do that little: so uniting philanthropic energy with philosophic calm."[35] How different this counsel of utmost caution in instituting any social change is from the impetuous revisionism of Ward. Spencer's list of in-

terdicted activities for the state—which should remain merely a joint stock company for the mutual protection of individuals—was famous: commercial regulation, state religious establishments, charitable activities, state education, colonization, sanitation, coinage of money, postal service, provision of lighthouses, and improvement of harbors.[36] For Ward, by contrast, the whole meaning of civilization lies in the triumph of the artificial over the natural. He wants neither the conservative utopia of Comte nor the rugged individualism of Spencer. His principle was "meliorism," the improvement of social conditions through the application of scientific intelligence. "There is one form of government that is stronger than autocracy or aristocracy or democracy, or even plutocracy, and that is sociocracy. The individual has reigned long enough. The day has come for society to take its affairs into its own hands and shape its own destinies."[37] Sociocracy is not considered to be identical with socialism. It is argued that, while individualism creates artificial inequalities, socialism seeks to create others. Sociocracy, however, recognizes natural inequalities and abolishes artificial ones. Whereas individualism confers benefits on those who obtain them by power, cunning, intelligence, or position, socialism would confer benefits on all equally. But sociocracy would confer benefits strictly in proportion to merit, determined in terms of equality of opportunity. In contrast to his conservative European colleagues, Ward was beginning to disintegrate the conservative synthesis and restore the combination of liberalism and positivism of the eighteenth-century rationalists.

POSITIVISTIC ELEMENTS IN THE SOCIOLOGY OF THE FOUNDERS OF POSITIVISTIC ORGANICISM

Positivism, the view that the methods which had proved their worth in the physical sciences were

[34]Ward, *Dynamic Sociology,* I, 589.
[35]Spencer, *The Study of Sociology,* p. 403.

[36]Ward, *Social Statics,* pp. 206ff.
[37]Ward, *Psychic Factors in Civilization,* p. 323.

appropriate to the study of social phenomena, was inseparably built into Comte's sociology. Sociology was, in fact, Comte's substitute for metaphysical philosophy, traditional common sense, and theology. Sociological knowledge is not in principle different from other forms of scientific knowledge; it is merely more complex and less general. Moreover, Comte argued, the more general knowledge of the physical sciences is essential as a foundation for biological and, eventually, sociological knowledge. Comte's classification of the sciences with sociology at the apex expressed these notions.

As sociology assumes its place in the hierarchy of sciences, Comte maintains, its means of investigation must be partly peculiar to it ("direct") and partly "indirect," or arising from sociology's relation to the other sciences. According to Comte, the three direct methods of sociology are observation, experiment, and comparison. To be effective, *observation* must be guided by theory:

> No real observation of any kind of phenomena is possible, except in as far as it is first directed, and finally interpreted, by some theory. . . .
> Scientifically speaking, all isolated, empirical observation is idle, and even radically uncertain. . . . science can use only those observations which are connected, at least hypothetically, with some law.[38]

Experimentation, the second of the methods, has only incidental application to social science materials:

> If direct experimentation had become too difficult amidst the complexities of biology, it may well be considered impossible in social science. Any artificial disturbance of any social element must affect all the rest, according to the laws both of co-existence and succession.[39]

Since everything in society is related to everything else, it follows that to change one thing, whether for experimental purposes or not, is to change everything. Since one cannot know everything, experiment can yield no knowledge; it can only render the world more irrational. However, Comte opines, the situation is not completely hopeless, for one can always observe pathological states of society, using them as a kind of spontaneous experiment.

It is on *comparison* that sociology must rely for its successes. In part, it is possible to compare contemporary with primitive society. "By this method, the different states of evolution may all be observed at once."[40] However, the truly significant comparisons are always historical:

> The historical comparison of the consecutive states of humanity is not only the chief scientific device of the new political philosophy. Its . . . development constitutes the substratum of the science, in whatever is essential to it.[41]

Herbert Spencer shared Comte's positivism. He assumed that scientific knowledge is the highest form of knowledge available. Its peculiarities lie in the rejection of metaphysical pretenses and in rigidly confining itself to the demonstration of the laws of phenomena.

> Ultimate Scientific Ideas . . . are all representative of realities that cannot be comprehended. After no matter how great a progress in the colligation of facts and the establishment of generalizations ever wider and wider . . . the fundamental truth remains as much beyond reach as ever. . . . The man of science sees himself in the midst of perpetual changes, of which he can discover neither the beginning nor the end.
> Supposing him in every case able to resolve the appearances, properties, and movements of things into manifestations of Force in Space and Time, he still finds that Force, Space and Time pass all understanding.[42]

Unknown causes work known effects, which we call phenomena, and between these phenomena

---

[38]Comte, *Positive Philosophy,* II, p. 97.
[39]*Ibid.,* p. 100.

[40]*Ibid.,* p. 103.
[41]*Ibid.,* p. 105.
[42]Spencer, *First Principles,* pp. 78–79.

likenesses and differences may be discovered. Space and time are the "modes of cohesion" under which such manifestations invariably appear. The manifestations themselves are perceived as forms of matter and motion:

> Over and over again it has been shown in various ways, that the deepest truths we can reach are simply statements of the widest uniformities in our experience of the relations of Matter, Motion, and Force; and that Matter, Motion, and Force are but symbols of the Unknown Reality. A Power of which the nature remains forever inconceivable, and to which no limits in Time or Space can be imagined, works in us certain effects. These effects have certain likenesses of kind, the most general of which we class together under the names of Matter, Motion and Force; and between these effects there are likenesses of connection, the most constant of which we class as laws of the highest certainty.[43]

Among the most general of such laws is evolution, representing an integration of matter and dissipation of motion.[44] Spencer believed that the change from incoherent homogeneity to coherent heterogeneity is at work throughout the universe:

> . . . there is habitually a passage from homogeneity to heterogeneity, along with the passage from diffusion to concentration. While the matter composing the Solar System has been assuming a denser form, it has changed from unity to variety of distribution. Solidification of the Earth has been accompanied by a progress from comparative uniformity to extreme multiformity. In the course of its advance from a germ to a mass of relatively great bulk, every plant and animal also advances from simplicity to complexity. The increase of a society in numbers and consolidation has for its concomitant an increased heterogeneity both of its political and industrial organization. And the like holds of all super-organic products—Language, Science, Art, and Literature.[45]

Thus the same laws obtain within all classes of phenomena, each science merely establishing them in its particular sphere. The method by which sociologists do this for social phenomena is ultimately comparative:

> By making due use not so much of that which past and present witnesses intend to tell us, as of what they tell us by implication, it is possible to collect data for inductions respecting social structures and functions in their origin and development: the obstacles which arise in the disentangling of such data in the case of any particular society, being mostly surmountable by the help of the comparative method.[46]

Lester Ward, who was a scientist in his own right as well as a careful reader of Comte and Spencer, agreed with them in the location of social science knowledge in a context of the physical sciences. He rested his case for sociology on the comparative method:

> It is the function of methodology in social science to classify social phenomena in such a manner that the groups may be brought under uniform laws and treated by exact methods. Sociology then becomes an exact science. In doing this, too, it will be found that we have passed from chaos to cosmos. Human history presents a chaos. The only science that can convert the milky way of history into a definite social universe is sociology, and this can only be done by the use of an appropriate method, by using the data furnished by all the special social sciences, including the great scientific trunks of psychology, biology, and cosmology, and generalizing and coördinating the facts and groups of facts until unity is attained.[47]

One need never doubt the basic positivism of the founders of sociology.

SUMMARY

Sociology became manifest first as a new point of view within traditional philosophy. The conceptual resources at its disposal were as deep and as rich as

[43]*Ibid.*, pp. 548–49.
[44]*Ibid.*, p. 289.
[45]*Ibid.*, pp. 535–536.

[46]Spencer, *The Study of Sociology*, pp. 101–102.
[47]Ward, *Pure Sociology*, p. 62.

Western philosophy itself. At the same time, there was no doubt about the novelty of the new point of view, fusing as it did tendencies in Western thought that had hitherto been opposed. The characterization of this point of view as "positivistic organicism" immediately calls attention to the potential conflict within it.

Organicism is that tendency in thought which constructs its picture of the world on an organic model. An organismic metaphysics refers to the attempt to explain the world, or reality, or the universe, as a kind of organism. This organismic tendency is anchored in the idealistic philosophies of the West. Plato and Aristotle, for example, advocated a kind of transcendent idealism, conceiving true reality to be a kind of living world beyond this world. Modern forms of idealism tend to relocate reality at the very core of experience. The philosopher Berkeley, for instance, thought that reality was as it was experienced to be, a subjective structure whose objective properties were sustained by the mind of God. A position somewhere between the subjective idealism of Berkeley and the transcendent idealism of the ancient Greeks was developed by Hegel, for whom reality represented the processes of history and the development of civilization through time. The development of civilization was conceived as the maturation of an objective mind. Finally, an irrational idealism or an idealism of the will was developed by Nietzsche and Schopenhauer, who went so far as to conceive the very law of gravitation as a kind of hungry will force.

Positivism is that movement in thought which attempts to explain the world exclusively in terms of experience or what experience eventually reduces to—facts, forces, energies, or something of the sort. The strong naturalism we tend to identify as positivistic was present in the Greek world in various ways in the atomists and the Sophists, but they were never able to bring it to full expression. Positivism has only come into its own with the rise of science. In the modern world it is almost synonymous with the attempt to make the procedures of science the norm of all effective thought.

Thus the true beginnings of modern positivism trace to the *Novum Organum* (1620) and other writings of Francis Bacon, with the proposal to extend science to every area of social and personal experience. Further developments of a positivistic empiricist spirit appear in the work of the British empiricists (Locke, Berkeley, and Hume) and the French and English utilitarians (Condillac, Helvétius, Voltaire, Bentham, and John Stuart Mill).

These philosophical points of view, idealism and positivism, have tended to have a characteristic social anchorage. Idealism has almost always been associated with philosophies of social conservatism. In the ancient world Plato and Aristotle were conservatives. In the modern world both the objective idealists and the irrational idealists were conservative. Hegel, for example, thought the state was the march of God through the world; and Nietzsche and Schopenhauer were even opposed to science itself. The positivists, on the other hand, both in the ancient and modern world tended to line up on the side of social reform. The Sophists were feared by Plato and Aristotle for this reason. In the modern world a whole series of reformist programs have been begun in the name of science from the time of Bacon's *New Atlantis*.

Following the events of the French Revolution in the closing days of the eighteenth century, the linkage of idealism with social reaction became particularly strong, as manifest in the writings of Edmund Burke, Joseph de Maistre, and Louis de Bonald. Meanwhile, the positivistic program became linked to the programs of scientific socialism, as may be seen in the works of Saint-Simon, Proudhon, Marx, Owen, Blanc, John Stuart Mill, and others.

It was under these circumstances that sociology made its appearance. It was dramatic as a spark across the positive-negative intellectual and social poles of the time. The fact that its contradictions were not seized upon as representing an impossible confusion testifies to the social need for such a new discipline. The world was unwilling to abandon either the idealistic and conservative image of society or the program of science. The Comtean synthesis of these two intellectual and social ten-dencies was so significant that the new point of view spread, was copied, and soon became an in-dependent discipline.

The three great original founders of sociology adapted the synthesis of organicism and positivism to the social and intellectual environments of their respective countries: Comte for France, Spencer for England, and Lester F. Ward for the United States. In this adaptation different features of the point of view were emphasized. In the case of Ward, there is indication of a tendency for the synthesis to come apart at the seams. There was al-ready little doubt that the inner tensions of these opposed modes of thought were going to become the dramatic element in the evolution of positivis-tic organicism.

V

The Classical Period of Positivistic Organicism

Every school of thought that manages to survive must first go through a pioneering or heroic phase. Comte, Spencer, Ward, and their immediate associates did their work well, and positivistic organicism went on to higher things. Before it could reach its full richness, however, this first school of sociology had to adapt itself to the changing requirements of its milieu. For a while, it was strongly deflected toward pure biological organicism, reflecting the powerful claims of nineteenth-century biology on the times. For sociology, however, this was a dead end, and the new field had to shake itself free of such influences to find its proper field.

EXTREME BIO-ORGANICISTS

The organismic theory of society has ancient origins in idealistic philosophy. The biological form of idealistic theory, on the other hand, is a rela-

tively modern phenomenon, a product of the imitation of the splendid gains of nineteenth-century biology. Pitirim Sorokin, who has given some thought to the matter, quite correctly argues that the organic conception of society has everywhere been most popular among philosophers.[1] He distinguishes three types of organicism: (1) philosophical, conceiving society as a super- or trans-individual reality; (2) psychosocial, conceiving society as a superindividual organism of ideas, representations, minds, and volitions; and (3) bio-organismic, conceiving society as like a biological organism in its nature, functions, origin, development, and variations. Sorokin is also quite correct in his assertion that organismic theories of one sort or other have been held by ancient Hindu, Chinese, Greek, and Roman writers. The dramatic development in biology culminating in the work of Darwin led to the special development in the latter

[1]Pitirim Sorokin, *Contemporary Sociological Theories* (New York: Harper, 1928).

part of the nineteenth century of a new series of bio-organismic theories.[2]

Paul von Lilienfeld (1829–1903), a Russian of German stock who had a place in the aristocracy and had held a number of political offices, seems to have arrived at his organicism independently of Spencer. His biological theories were elaborated in three books written between 1870 and 1900.[3] Society was conceived to be a living organism composed of smaller ones. The nervous system of the individual and society is argued to be similar. There is an intercellular substance binding the social organism together. There were three stages of social evolution from savagery through barbarism to civilization and every individual recapitulates these stages. Lilienfeld invented the term *social pathology* to refer to the study of maladjustments of society — disorders of industry, politics, justice, which operate in society like insanity, disease, and paralysis in the individual. The chief source of contemporary social pathology was seen to be the conflict between science and religion, which social science should mediate.

Albert Schäffle (1831–1903), who taught as an economist at Tübingen and Vienna, shows in his work[4] the influences of Spencer, Lilienfeld, and Darwin. The divisions of sociology were presented as social morphology, social physiology, and social psychology, which study individuals, national positions, social tissues and organs, and the mental life of society. His five types of social tissue homologous to biological tissue include somewhat direct organic comparisons such as settlements, buildings, and roads; protective tissues like the epidermal tissues of the body, including clothing, roofs, safes, the army, police; economic arrangements like nourishing tissues of the body; technical social structures for the application of social power (army, police) like the muscular tissues; and psychosocial tissues similar to the nerves, compassing all institutions concerned with intellectual and authoritative activity, the school, the state, science, and the church. The social organs are made up of the social tissues. For Schäffle, group life was the unit of conflict, mutual aid, and survival. In Small's estimate, "Schäffle even elaborates some biological parallels more minutely than Spencer does. . . . The difference, as I see it, reduces to this: Spencer does not succeed in making his interpretation of society . . . more than an *organization of mechanisms.* Schäffle's central conception of society is of an *organization of work.*"[5]

---

[2] A review of the bio-organismic group can be found in Albion Small, *General Sociology* (Chicago: University of Chicago Press, 1905, 1925), pp. 109–167; Pitirim Sorokin, *Contemporary Sociological Theories,* pp. 194–208; Harry Elmer Barnes and Howard Becker, *Social Thought from Lore to Science* (2d. ed., Washington, D.C.: Harren Press, 1952), pp. 664–691; and E. Kilzer and E. J. Ross, *Western Social Thought* (Milwaukee: Bruce, 1954), pp. 340–347.

The older form of biosociology is today primarily a historical curiosity. Under the influence of the new science of animal behavior ethology — see Irenäus Eibl-Eibesfeldt and Wolfgang Wickler, "Ethology," *International Encyclopedia of the Social Sciences* (New York: Crowell Collier and Macmillan, 1968), V, 186–192 — a new interest in sociobiology has taken its place. Typical works include: David P. Barash, *Sociobiology and Behavior* (New York: Elsevier, 1977); Daniel G. Freedman, *Human Sociobiology: A Holistic Approach* (New York: The Free Press, 1979); Davydd J. Greenwood, *Nature, Culture and Human History* (New York: Harper & Row, 1977); Marshall D. Sahlins, *The Use and Abuse of Biology* (Ann Arbor: University of Michigan Press, 1976); Lionel Tiger, *Optimism: The Biology of Hope* (New York: Simon and Schuster, 1979); Edward O. Wilson, *On Human Nature* (Cambridge: Harvard University Press, 1978) and *Sociobiology: The New Synthesis* (Cambridge: Belknap Press, 1975); Arthur L. Caplan, ed., *The Sociobiology Debate* (New York: Harper & Row, 1978); Pierre L. Vanden Berghe, *Man in Society: A Biosocial View* (New York: Elsevier, 1975).

[3] None of Lilienfeld's works are available in English translation. The three books referred to here are: *Gedanken über die Socialwissenschaft der Zukunft* ["Thoughts on the Social Science of the Future"] (Mitau: 1873–1881); *La Pathologie sociale* ["Social Pathology"] (Paris: 1896); and *Zur Vertheidigung der organischen Methode in der Sociologie* ["In Defense of the Organic Method in Sociology"] (Berlin: 1898).

[4] English translations are not available for Schäffle's major sociological works: *Bau und Leben des socialen Körpers* ["Structure and Life of the Social Body"], 4 vols. (Tübingen: 1875–1878) and *Gesammelte Aufsätze* ["Collected Works"] (Tübingen: 1885–1886).

[5] Albion Small, *General Sociology,* p. 167.

Alfred Fouillée (1838–1912), the French philosopher, has special interest among the bio-organicists. In his main works,[6] he makes the unique attempt to combine the ideas of social contract and organism. The doctrines of contract theory had been anchored in circles holding a mechanical conception of the state. Social-contract theory had implemented the notion of society as a purely rational arrangement for instrumental purposes. Fouillée's fusion thus has special interest. For Fouillée, society was a "contractual organism." It had both natural and artificial causes. The psychological character of social organization rests on the spontaneous attraction of people for one another, resting on sympathy. This becomes the basis of sociability. Society and the organism have five characteristics in common: concurrence of dissimilar parts; a functional distribution of members; organic subunits; spontaneity of movement; and the property of growth and decay. Society emerges as a new organism when people meet in assembly and when in their thinking they symbolize society as an independent form. Society arises because it has been thought and desired. It is born of an idea and is thus a contractual organism.

Another French scholar, René Worms (1869–1926), developed the bio-organismic thesis in a number of works.[7] Society was conceived to be an enduring aggregation of living beings, exercising activity in common. In both the organism and society, external structures vary in time and are irregular in form; internal structures undergo constant change through assimilation and integration, dissimilation and disintegration; there is a coordinated differentiation of parts; and both have power of reproduction. Detailed analogies are traced with regard to structure, function, evolution, and pathology.

There were many other extreme bio-organicists such as Jacques Novicow (1849–1912), the Russian industrialist from Odessa, Guillaume de Greef (1842–1924), the first sociologist of the University of Brussels, and the Scottish philosopher J. S. McKenzie (1860–1935). But it would serve no particular value to trace the views of these and others. Small put the matter very compactly. *"Not merely in sociology, but in every department of knowledge, the organic concept is the most distinctive modern note. . . .* The most intimate and complex and constructive coherence of elements that we discover, previous to our study of society, is the coworking of part with part in vital phenomena. About a generation ago, men who wanted to understand the social reality more precisely began to make systematic use of ascertained vital relationships as provisional symbols of societary relationships."[8] The bio-organismic school retained strong affinities with the positivistic point of view. It sustained, in fact, strong "reductionistic" tendencies, and despite the occasional admission that there is no complete identity between the individual and social organism, it assumes that, by and large, the laws of society are merely a special application of the laws of biology.

Bio-organicism has disappeared rather completely. When one asks what permanent residue of findings it left to sociology, it is remarkably difficult to come up with anything. In the perspective of the present, its importance lies at a semi-ideological rather than conceptual level. During the time when sociology was emerging, biology underwent spectacular development — it was the

[6]Fouillée's main sociological works, none of which are available in English translation, are: *La Science sociale contemporaine* ["Contemporary Social Science"] (Paris: 1880); *La Psychologie des idées-forces* ["The Psychology of Ideal Forces"], 2 vols. (Paris: 1893); and *Le Mouvement positiviste et la conception sociologique du monde* ["The Positivist Movement and the Sociological Conception of the World"] (Paris: 1896).

[7]René Worms' sociological works, none of which are available in English translation, include: *Organicisme et société* ["Organicism and Society"] (Paris: Giard & Brière, 1896); *Philosophie des sciences sociales* ["Philosophy of the Social Sciences"], 3 vols. (Paris: Giard & Brière, 1903–1907); *Les Principes biologiques de l'évolution sociale* ["The Biological Principles of Social Evolution"] (Paris: Giard & Brière, 1910); and *La Sociologie* (Paris: Giard, 1921; 2d. rev. ed., 1926).

[8]Albion Small, *General Sociology*, pp. 74–75. This was Small's statement of the case in 1905. (Italics in the original.)

bright new star in the nineteenth-century firmament. Bio-organicism in sociology represented an attempt to link the fortunes of the two disciplines. It was made plausible by the older "organicism" which sociology had derived from its idealistic components. Bio-organicism actually served the function of "protecting" the new field of sociology by camouflaging it. Among prevailing nineteenth-century trends, it added a protective armor around the discipline until it became strong enough to fend for itself. In time, the grotesque analogies to which it led became offensive and it was dismissed as the "big animal" theory of society.

THE CLASSIC PHASE OF POSITIVISTIC ORGANICISM

There has been a somewhat unfortunate tendency to define the organismic theory in such narrow terms as to obscure the extent of its theoretical assemblage of ideas. For example, in many works "organicism" is confined to the persons sketched in the previous section. Comte, Spencer, and Ward are treated as a sort of preorganismic type of theorist and the organismic school proper is dismissed as if it terminated with Worms, de Greef, and Novicow. However, this is to shift attention away from precisely those organicists who left the most decisive mark on sociology. The organismic framework is shared not only by Comte, Spencer, and Ward but also by such persons as Tönnies and Durkheim. Both of the latter thinkers restyled and developed organismic ideas in a manner that gave them long-range importance for sociology, having influences into the present.

Ferdinand Tönnies. Ferdinand Tönnies (1855–1936) was born on a farm in Eiderstedt on the coast of Schleswig-Holstein. He received his doctor's degree from the University of Tübingen in 1877, and became a lecturer at the University of Kiel in 1881, where he remained until ousted by the Nazis in 1933. The most influential of Tönnies' works was his *Gemeinschaft und Gesellschaft* (1887),

FERDINAND TÖNNIES

Courtesy of the Ferdinand Tönnies Institute, New University, Kiel

translated into English as *Community and Society;* it is the only one of his works generally appreciated in America, although in his later works he applied the influential concepts first developed in *Community and Society* to various social phenomena, among which might be singled out his study of folkways and mores in *Die Sitte* ["Custom"] and of public opinion in *Kritik der öffentlichen Meinung* ["Critique of Public Opinion"].[9] Among empirical studies

[9]Only two of Tönnies' books are presently available in English translation: *Gemeinschaft und Gesellschaft* (Leipzig: 1887; Berlin: K. Curtius, 1926) has been translated by Charles P. Loomis and published, first, as *Fundamental Concepts of Sociology* (New York: American Book Company, 1940) and, later, as *Community and Society* (East Lansing, Mich.: Michigan State University Press, 1957); and *Thomas Hobbes Leben und Lehre* (Stuttgart: F. From-

conducted by Tönnies was the review of the social situation of the longshoremen in Hamburg and other ports after the strike in Hamburg, the study of relationships between socioeconomic conditions and ideological phenomena in Schleswig-Holstein, and the study of cyclical changes in marriage rates and the sex ratio.

Tönnies divided sociology into three disciplines: (1) pure sociology, (2) applied sociology, and (3) empirical sociology. *Pure* or general sociology aspires to develop a system of concepts of "normal" or ideal types essential for the description and understanding of empirical phenomena. *Applied* sociology consists in the application of these concepts to contemporary and historical phenomena. As with Comte, sociology is the study of history. This discipline studies society dynamically and developmentally. *Empirical* sociology pro-

ceeds by inductive empirical methods utilizing the concepts of pure sociology as basic orientation devices. In his own work, Tönnies approached these areas by way of the *Gemeinschaft-Gesellschaft* dichotomy which he made famous.

All the facts of society and social relationship are viewed by Tönnies as products of the human will. "Social relationship or bond implies interdependence, and it means that the will of the one person influences that of the other, either furthering or impeding, or both. . . . The collective will can remain the same for an indefinite period, but it can also from time to time undergo change by renewed acts. . . . Such a collective person consists of single persons."[10]

The organismic core of Tonnies' thought could not be more clearly formulated. All interaction is at bottom the expression of acts of will. The result of acts of will is the development of a collective will. This collective will is very like a person. Fundamental to Tönnies' whole view is the concept of different types of will.

The simplest way of approaching the problems of Tönnies' sociology is through the interrelationships involved in exchange or barter. When we barter, two objects are involved in such a way that each is a means to the other considered as an end. An act of barter or exchange consists in carrying out an interrelationship in such terms. One can imagine an entire system of social life in which all acts are carried out in this manner. In contrast, there are situations in which one's motives to satisfy one's aims and desires take the form of satisfying those of another person or of groups. Such a volition, of this latter type, rests not on a calculation of means and the appropriateness of means to ends; rather, it is unconditional, like the love of a mother for an infant. Such unconditional relationships are not necessarily positive. Between man and woman, love may turn to hate, which becomes a kind of inverted love. Thus we have two kinds of social relationship, resting on two types of human willing. In the first case, we can speak of a

---

mann, 1925), the third revised edition of a study first published in 1896, has been translated and published under the title *The Elements of Law, Natural and Political* (Cambridge, England: The University Press, 1928). Important works which are not available in English include: *Die Sitte* (Frankfurt am Main: Rütten & Loening, 1909); *Marx: Leben und Lehre* ["The Life and Teachings of Marx"] (Jena: E. Lichtenstein, 1921); *Kritik der öffentlichen Meinung* (Berlin: J. Springer, 1922); *Soziologische Studien und Kritiken* ["Sociological Studies and Critiques"] (Jena: G. Fischer, 1925–1926); and *Einführung in die Soziologie* ["Introduction to Sociology"] (Stuttgart: F. Enke, 1931). An excellent review of Tönnies' sociology is Rudolf Heberle's "The Sociological System of Ferdinand Tönnies: 'Community' and 'Society' ", in Harry Elmer Barnes, ed., *An Introduction to the History of Sociology* (Chicago: University of Chicago Press, 1948), pp. 227–248. A Tönnies revival has been led by Werner J. Cahnman. See Werner J. Cahnman and Rudolf Heberle, *Ferdinand Toennies on Sociology: Pre, Applied, and Empirical* (Chicago: University of Chicago Press, 1971). And Werner J. Cahnman, ed., *Ferdinand Tönnies, A New Evaluation* (Leiden: E. J. Brill, 1973). Among reprints of Tönnies' work and new translations in the 1970s are: *Custom: An Essay on Social Codes,* trans. A. Farrel Borenstein (Chicago: H. Regnery, 1971); *Community and Association,* trans. Charles P. Loomis (London: Routledge & Kegan Paul, 1974); *Karl Marx: His Life and Teaching,* trans. Charles P. Loomis and Ingeborg Paulus (East Lansing: Michigan State University Press, 1974); *On Social Ideas and Ideologies,* trans. E. G. Jacoby (New York: Harper & Row, 1974).

---

[10]Tönnies, *Fundamental Concepts of Sociology,* pp. 9–10.

THE CLASSIC PHASE OF POSITIVISTIC ORGANICISM

rational will *(Kürwille)*, in the second, of a natural will *(Wesenwille)*.[11]

The simplest and most general unit of social life is the *social relationship*. Sociology as a special science is interested in the products of social life. These social products result from human thinking and exist only for human thinking. Social relationship is the most elementary of these things. Social relationships cannot be other than the embodiments of one of the two fundamental forms of the human will — *Kürwille* or *Wesenwille*. One total complex of social relationships (society) may differ from another as a result of the type of will predominant in it. In terms of the kind of will involved, two ideal types (also called "normal concepts") of society are possible. A society or total complex of social relationships which embodies the rational will is called a *Gesellschaft;* a complex embodying the natural will is a *Gemeinschaft*. A collective has the character of a *Gemeinschaft* insofar as its members think of the grouping as a gift of nature created by a supernatural will. On the other hand, to the degree that consciousness of authority arises from class relationships, the collective tends to assume the characteristics of a *Gesellschaft*.

Social entities of lesser scope than the entire society may be characterized in similar terms. The corporation is a social body or union. It can emerge from natural relationships, as does the kinship group, the gens, or the clan. Common relation to the soil tends to associate people, and the neighborhood may be the product of such an association. On the other hand, in the development of the state — the mightiest of all corporate bodies — or in the development of the characteristic corporations of capitalistic, middle-class society, the original qualities of the *Gemeinschaft* may be lost.

Tönnies thus distinguishes three main types of social units: social relationships, groups, and societies. All of these units are characterized by their volitional components. However, the manner in which these volitional components differentiate

total societies has attracted greatest interest, for from this base Tönnies developed his famous contrast of societal types, tracing out multiple lines of contrast through such things as the dominant social relationship, theory of personality, central corporate group, and many others. The accompanying table shows some of the more interesting contrasts which Tönnies developed — or, in some instances, summarized from his predecessors — to compare *Gemeinschaft* and *Gesellschaft* societal types.

Tönnies believed that the mentality basic to the *Gemeinschaft* is characteristic of the woman, and operates through sentiment. The mentality basic to the *Gesellschaft* is characteristic of the man, and operates through intention. The first appears through the mind and consciousness, the second through calculation and conscious behavior. Moreover, the same contrast appears between youth and old age, and the common people and educated classes. The *Gemeinschaft*, thus, is typical of the woman, the young, the masses. The *Gesellschaft* is typical of the man, of old age, and of the educated classes.

It has already been observed that having developed the contrast between the *Gemeinschaft* and the *Gesellschaft,* Tönnies applied it to the societal subunits — social relationships and social corporations or groups. In the case of the corporation, the social body is thought of as a person possessing a rational will to which it can give validity through functionaries. But in any case, all three categories of social entity *(Wesenheiten)* were thought to be determined primarily either by *Wesenwillen* or *Kürwillen*. The same scheme was applied to social norms and values. The main classes of norms distinguished by Tönnies are order, law, and morality. The kinds of social will by which they are created are *gemeinschaftliche* (including unanimity or concord, custom, or religion, the last based on faith in supernatural powers) or *gesellschaftliche*, based on convention, legislation, or public opinion. *Order* is the most general and complex of norms, based primarily on concord or convention. *Law* is the complex of norms enforced by judicial decision; it is created by either custom or intentional

---

[11]In making this contrast, Tönnies seems to have had Wilhelm Wundt's contrast between *Zweckwille* and *Triebwille* partly in mind.

Social Characteristic	Societal Type	
	GEMEINSCHAFT	GESELLSCHAFT
DOMINANT SOCIAL RELATIONSHIP	Fellowship Kinship Neighborliness	Exchange Rational calculation
CENTRAL INSTITUTIONS	Family law Extended kin group	State Capitalistic economy
THE INDIVIDUAL IN THE SOCIAL ORDER	Self	Person
CHARACTERISTIC FORM OF WEALTH	Land	Money
TYPE OF LAW	Family Law	Law of contracts
ORDERING OF INSTITUTIONS	Family life Rural village life Town life	City life Rational life Cosmopolitan life
TYPE OF SOCIAL CONTROL	Concord Folkways and mores Religion	Convention Legislation Public opinion

"legislation." *Morality* is the complex of these norms the interpretation and application of which are the work of an imaginary judge (God or conscience); the norms of morality are sanctioned either by religion or public opinion.

The public opinion of a country or nation is an expression of group will and not, as popularly conceived, a conglomeration of contradictory views. Public opinion as politically valid opinion must be distinguished from local or apolitical opinion. Public opinion can be more or less fixed, fluid, or gaseous, depending on the issues involved.

The idea of developing conceptions of contrasting types of society was by no means new in Tönnies' day. There is no value in reviewing early forms, for dualistic constructions of human society are as old as mythology. Tönnies himself was familiar with a number of them. The eighteenth-century rationalists had advanced the idea of the

origin of society in a contract and the rational agreements this implied. An extreme form of the rationalistic and contractual conception of society was expressed by Thomas Hobbes, with whom Tönnies was thoroughly familiar. The opponents of eighteenth-century rationalistic conceptions, among them the romantic conservatives of the nineteenth century, developed organic conceptions of the state. Tönnies specifically intended in his typology to represent the Hobbesian concept of society in the *Gesellschaft,* the romantic concept in the *Gemeinschaft.*

A somewhat similar set of ideas was familiar to Tönnies from Henry Sumner Maine. In his *Ancient Law,*[12] Maine traced, by means of the law, the development of ancient society. On the basis of the

[12]Henry Sumner Maine, *Ancient Law* (London: 1861). References here are to the 1906 edition (New York: Henry Holt).

evidence of Roman law, Maine advanced the patriarchal theory of society — the idea that in antiquity society was organized into households in which the eldest male was supreme, having dominion extending to life and death over his children and slaves. Maine believed that one can trace, in Roman legal development, the gradual decline in the authority of the father. Thus, for example, first the son was freed from the father's influence — a phenomenon attributable to the Roman army and civil administration, which required that the state receive the primary loyalty of its servants. Under later systems even the woman gradually achieved freedom. In ancient society, thus, Maine urges, the individual's life chances were fixed by his status in the family. The patriarchal origin of society allowed little room for the idea of contract. In its earliest form one family could contract with another only in the most ceremonious of manners. But in time contractual relationships spread to wider and wider spheres. "If then we employ Status . . . to signify these personal conditions only . . . we may say that the movement of the progressive societies has hitherto been a movement *from Status to Contract.*" [13]

These distinctions, too, were taken up into Tönnies' typology. Moreover, he was not only familiar with Wundt's contrast of mentalities in *Zweckwille* and *Triebwille* and Hegel's conception of the development of history as the evolution of the human spirit from the ancient world, in which only one (the despot) is free, to modern situations, where all are free, but with the contrast of societal types employed by Comte and Spencer. Comte believed that society evolved through three major types: theological, metaphysical, and positivistic. The metaphysical, corresponding to the eighteenth century, was little more than a transitional type. Spencer, on the other hand, reduced the major types to two: religious-militaristic and modern industrial-peaceable. All these and many other conceptions of contrasting social types were familiar to Tönnies. However, he did far more than merely summarize. He pulled together all the

main ideas into a systematic form. He developed the notion of an underlying integral mentality. He systematized the contrasts. He identified them with social development. The organismic character of the system is all-pervasive, but this is not its only important property. So long as one employs simply an over-all conception of society, organismic or not, made up of little-differentiated parts, analysis cannot proceed far. But a dichotomous typology made up of carefully itemized elements can, however crude, at least serve as a device for comparative review. It is for this reason that all modern societal typologies — such as Durkheim's distinction between "mechanical" and "organic" solidarity, Park's "sacred–secular" distinction, Redfield's "folk–secular" distinction — take Tönnies' conceptualizations as a starting point.

Émile Durkheim. The very utility of Tönnies' formulations for later sociological purposes seems to have obscured the anchorage of his ideas in organicism. The same appears to be true of the theories of Durkheim. Émile Benoît-Smullyan invented the term *agelicism* to epitomize Durkheim's theories:

> By "agelicism" we mean the general sociological doctrine which maintains the reality *sui generis* or the causal priority of the social group *qua* group. Agelicism in its modern form was introduced into the stream of French social thought by de Bonald and de Maistre, who maintained that the social group precedes and constitutes the individual, that it is the source of culture and all the higher values, and that social states and changes are not produced by, and cannot be directly affected or modified by, the desires and volitions of individuals. [14]

Quibbles over terminology have no interest here. By agelicism Benoît-Smullyan means precisely the "organismic thesis" in social science, no more, no less. The importance of Benoît-Smullyan's statement lies in its correct relocation of Durkheim's thought at the very core of the organismic school.

---

[13]*Ibid.,* p. 165. (Italics in the original.)

[14]Émile Benoît-Smullyan, "The Sociologism of Émile Durkheim and His School," in Barnes, *An Introduction to the History of Sociology,* p. 499.

ÉMILE DURKHEIM

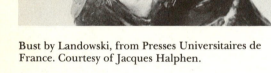

Bust by Landowski, from Presses Universitaires de France. Courtesy of Jacques Halphen.

Émile Durkheim (1855–1917), the son of a Jewish rabbi, entered the École Normale Supérieure of Paris in 1879, and after three years' study there began to teach philosophy. It is significant for his organicism that one of the works which aroused his interest in sociology was Schäffle's *Structure and Life of the Social Body.* In 1885 and 1886 he studied in Germany. In 1887, he inaugurated the first course in social science to be offered in France at the University of Bordeaux.

Durkheim's first book, his doctoral dissertation on *The Division of Labor in Society,* was published in 1893.[15] Because of his familiarity with Comte,

Spencer, Schäffle, Tönnies, Wundt, Alfred Espinas, and Evgeni de Roberty, Durkheim was in a position to ask precise questions. Taking (in *The Division of Labor*) the fact of social solidarity as the essential property of society, he divided societies into two primary types in a manner suggestive of Tönnies: those in which social solidarity was *mechanical,* or dominated by a collective consciousness; and those in which it was *organic,* or characterized

George Simpson as *The Division of Labor in Society* (Glencoe, Ill.: The Free Press, 1947); *Les Règles de la méthode sociologique* (Paris: F. Alcan, 1895) has been translated by Sarah A. Solovay and John H. Mueller as *The Rules of Sociological Method* (Chicago: University of Chicago Press, 1938; Glencoe, Ill.: The Free Press, 1950); *Le Suicide* (Paris: F. Alcan, 1897) has been translated by John A. Spaulding and George Simpson as *Suicide* (Glencoe, Ill.: The Free Press, 1951); *Les Formes élémentaires de la vie religieuse* (Paris: F. Alcan, 1912; 2d. ed., 1925) has been translated by Joseph Ward Swain as *The Elementary Forms of the Religious Life* (New York: Macmillan, 1915; Glencoe, Ill.: The Free Press, 1954); *Éducation et sociologie* (Paris: F. Alcan, 1922) has been translated by S. D. Fox as *Education and Sociology* (Glencoe, Ill.: The Free Press, 1956); *Sociologie et philosophie* (Paris: F. Alcan, 1924) has been translated by D. F. Pocock as *Sociology and Philosophy* (Glencoe, Ill.: The Free Press, 1953); and *Leçons de sociologie* (Paris: Presses Universitaires de France, 1950) has been translated by Cornelia Brookfield as *Professional Ethics and Civic Morals* (London: Routledge & Kegan Paul, 1957); *Socialism and Saint-Simon,* trans. Charlotte Sattler, introduction by Alvin Gouldner (Yellow Springs, Ohio: Antioch Press, 1958 and New York: Macmillan, 1962); *Moral Education: A Study in the Sociology of Education,* trans. Everett K. Wilson and Herman Schurer (Glencoe: The Free Press, 1961); *Primitive Classification,* trans. Rodney Needham (Chicago: University of Chicago Press, 1963); *The Evolution of Educational Thought: Lectures on the Formation and Development of Secondary Education in France,* trans. Peter Collins (London: Routledge & Kegan Paul, 1977). For evaluations and bibliography see: Yosh Nandan, *The Durkheim School: A Bibliography* (Westport, Conn.: Greenwood Press, 1977); Talcott Parsons, "Durkheim," *International Encyclopedia of the Social Sciences* (New York: Crowell Collier and Macmillan, 1968), IV, 311–320; Harry Alpert, *Émile Durkheim and His Sociology* (New York: Columbia University Press, 1939); Steven Lukes, *Émile Durkheim: His Life and Work* (London: Allen Lane, 1973); Robert Nisbet, *The Sociology of Émile Durkheim* (New York: Oxford, 1974); Anthony Giddens, *Émile Durkheim* (New York: Penguin Books, 1979).

[15]Almost all of Durkheim's major sociological writings have been translated into English: *De la Division du travail social* (Paris: F. Alcan, 1893) has been translated by

by specialization, division of labor, and interdependence. Durkheim devoted thought both to the problem of how a transformation of social solidarity occurs and how one is to determine its state or degree. He believed that as population grows in size, more complex societies develop. The division of labor was thought to be in direct ratio to the volume and density of society. Moreover, social growth in part takes place by condensation of societies. Such formations require greater division of labor.

The manner in which one is to determine the state of social solidarity led Durkheim to pick up from Maine and Tönnies the idea of the value of law for social analysis. In primitive society, Durkheim believed, solidarity is mechanical, for people are little differentiated and are held together by friendliness, neighborliness, and kinship as if by an external force. At this stage the law of the people will be dominated by *repressive* sanctions. The chief purpose of the law will be to satisfy an outraged collective sentiment. However, when society becomes more complex and its solidarity rests on a differentiation of people, one can no longer afford the luxury of simply giving vent to one's rage. A new motive enters the law — the restoration of the social system to a workable state and the repair, insofar as possible, of any damage done to the injured parties. Law becomes *restitutive* rather than repressive. Thus the law becomes a major index to this most crucial of all social facts — social solidarity.

The drive for a precision of concepts evident in *The Division of Labor* was continued in *The Rules of Sociological Method* (1895). Social solidarity had been conceived as the ensemble of beliefs and sentiments common to the average members of a particular society. This set of beliefs was thought to form a system and have a life of its own. In this further study, Durkheim set out both to give a more precise statement of the nature of sociological facts and to establish the criterion of method. One result was the achievement of one of the best statements of positivistic method to his time. The other achievement was to analyze social solidarity into its component elements. The data of sociology

were said to be *social facts*. These are any "ways of acting" capable of "exercising an external constraint on the individual"; they are, moreover, "general throughout" a given society. Societies may be most simply viewed, for Durkheim, as integral complexes of such social facts. The society has a "collective consciousness" which creates values and imposes them as imperative ideals on the individual.

One novel extension of these ideas occurred in Durkheim's study, *Suicide* (1897). He divided suicides into three types: (1) *altruistic* (where the suicide occurs in the interest of a group, as, for example, a war hero); (2) *egoistic* (due to a defect in social organization and search for an escape from the group); and (3) *anomic,* where social adjustment is disrupted (by economic changes such as sudden wealth, economic depression, the rise or fall of a social class). The idea of *anomie* is introduced as a strict counterpart of the idea of social solidarity. Just as social solidarity is a state of collective ideological integration, anomie is a state of confusion, insecurity, "normlessness." The collective representations are in a state of decay.

Another form of the elaboration and extension of these ideas came in *The Elementary Forms of the Religious Life* (1912). Collective representations are again taken as the starting point for analysis. In general, in a manner strongly suggestive of the old empiricists who attempted to derive every basic idea from the data of experience, Durkheim attempts to derive every major social form from the collective representations. Asking, in such manner, what is the object of religious sentiment and the source of its institutions, Durkheim discovers that it cannot be other than the social group itself. The world is divided into the sacred and the profane; the sacred consists of the collective representations of the group itself. Religious representations are those aspects of the collective representations expressing the collective realities. Religious rites are a manner of acting arising in the midst of the assembled group, destined to excite and maintain certain mental states in this group. Religious phenomena are of two classes, dogmas and rites, deriving their force from the social substance or the group within which they are obligatory. From this starting point, Durkheim proposes a sociology of knowledge. Moral facts have a kind of duality. They inspire respect and a feeling of obligation, but we must assume the content of morality is good even if it does not correspond to personal desires. The moral rule cannot emanate from the individual, since no act is moral which has as its exclusive end the conservation and self-development of the individual. The moral fact can only represent a value higher than the self. This higher moral fact is God, which is only society conceived symbolically. Thus religion and the moral life have the same origin.

Durkheim argued that thought depends on language and language depends on society. Thus society produces the basic instrumentality of thought. Moreover, he argues, the fundamental categories of cognition are merely the transformed and refined categories of society itself. The ultimate origins of the concept of "time" are found in the rhythms of group life; the idea of "space" is supplied by the territory occupied by society; the idea of "causality" is supplied by the control which a group exercises over its members.

During the course of his development, Durkheim's underlying organicism grew ever more pronounced:

> Around 1898, Durkheim entered on a new and distinct phase of his work. It is characterized, in the first place, by a more idealistic conception of the social group, with more emphasis on "collective representations" and less on the internal social milieu; and, in the second place, by adventurous speculation concerning the social origin of morals, values, religion, and knowledge. The social group is successively endowed by Durkheim with the characteristics of hyperspirituality, personality, creativity, and transcendence.[16]

But here again the basic organicism of Durkheim's work tends to be forgotten in the face of the fact that his ideas had great utility in later sociology. Durkheim and Tönnies illustrate the conceptual precision possible within the organismic framework.

Positivistic Aspects of the Theories of Tönnies and Durkheim. As positivistic organicism was being brought to its classical stage in the works of Tönnies and Durkheim, the first signs of possible tension between its positivism and its organicism began to appear. All the original exponents of positivistic organicism subscribed to the comparative method. However, this method operated so loosely that a variety of partly contradictory conclusions could be drawn from the same facts. For example, conflicting constructions were made of the evolutionary sequences of societies and social institutions.

Under these circumstances both Tönnies and Durkheim began to employ statistical material in their interpretations of social phenomena. In his study of suicide, Durkheim made extensive use of official statistics; in his study of institutions, he drew upon field data of ethnographers. Tönnies undertook a survey of the socioeconomic situation of longshoremen and sailors at various north German ports, investigated the relation between moral and socioeconomic conditions in Schleswig-Holstein, studied statistical and other materials collected in the provincial prisons, as well as suicide and marriage rates.[17]

The methodological crisis that was beginning to loom for positivistic organicism not only drove its classic representatives on to the employment of new methodological devices, but forced upon them a new level of methodological self-consciousness. The most impressive attempt to salvage positivistic methods was made by Durkheim in *The Rules of Sociological Method.* Durkheim urged that, while there is a distinction between natural and social science, the methods of natural science are applicable to the social field. Social facts are ways of acting and feeling. The criteria for judging whether given items are to be classified as "social fact" are whether they are capable of exercising

---

[16]Benoît-Smullyan, "The Sociologism of Émile Durkheim and His School," p. 510.

[17]See Rudolf Heberle, "The Sociological System of Ferdinand Tönnies," pp. 230 ff.

constraint over the individual. Durkheim sought to lay down the rules for the observation of social facts. There are, he believed, two types of social facts: normal and pathological. Those facts which are most generally distributed are "normal," others are "pathological."

> A social fact can . . . be called normal for a given social species only in relation to a given phase of its development. . . . we must also take special care to consider them at the corresponding phase of their evolution.[18]

Moreover, Durkheim argues, since a social fact can be construed as normal or abnormal only in relation to a given social species, one branch of sociology must be devoted to the creation and classification of social types. There are rules for the explanation of social facts and rules for establishing sociological proofs. Most of John Stuart Mill's methods, he believed, were not applicable. One can explain a social fact only by following its complete development through all social species. Moreover, societies must be compared at the same period of development, and the sociologist must avoid preconceptions and distinguish between normal and pathological conditions.

Somewhat more clearly than Durkheim, Tönnies glimpsed the potential tension between positivism and organicism:

> As human beings we are able to produce only inorganic things from organic materials, dividing and recombining them. In the same way things are also made into a unity through scientific manipulation and are a unity in our concepts. Naive interpretation or attitudes and artistic imagination, folk belief, and inspired poetry lend life to the phenomena. This creative element is also apparent in the fictions of science. But science also reduces the living to the dead in order to grasp its relations and conditions. It transforms all conditions and forces into movements and interprets all movements as quantities of labor performed, i.e., expended energy, in order to comprehend processes as similar and commensurable.

This last is true to the same extent that the assumed units are realities, and the possibility for thought is unlimited. Thus understanding, as an end, is attained and therewith other objectives.

> However, the tendencies and inevitableness of organic growth and decay cannot be understood through mechanical means. In the organic world the concept itself is a living reality, changing and developing as does the idea of the individual being. When science enters this realm it changes its own nature and develops from a logical and rational to an intuitive and dialectic interpretation; it becomes philosophy. However, the present study does not deal with genus and species, i.e., in regard to human beings it is not concerned with race, people, or tribe as biological units. Instead, we have in mind their sociological interpretation, which sees human relationships and associations as living organisms or, in contrast, mechanical constructions.[19]

This passage is noteworthy, not only for its confusion between things and the thought about things ("in the organic world the concept itself is a living reality, changing and developing as does the idea of the individual being" — presumably the concept of a man, like an actual man, gets up in the morning, puts on its pants, shaves, and in other ways prepares for a busy day), but for its treatment of science as analysis, analysis as dismemberment, and dismemberment as the destruction of life. Hence, when science deals with living and spiritual matters, we are told, it ceases to have the form of natural science: "it changes its own nature and develops from a logical and rational to an intuitive and dialectic interpretation."

There is little doubt that Tönnies was inclined toward a break with methodological positivism. The same inclination was evident in his handling of "types."

> In living, the organism proves its fitness for life, i.e., the appropriate (correct, good) condition, organization, and order of its focuses or parts. The form, as a whole, is constituted of its elements, which, in relation to it, are of a material character and maintain and propagate themselves through this very relation-

---

[18]Durkheim, *The Rules of Sociological Method,* p. 57.

[19]Tönnies, *Community and Society,* pp. 36–37.

ship. For the whole as a lasting form, each of its parts will always represent a more transitory modification of itself which expresses its nature in a more or less complete manner.

The intuitive and purely intellectual understanding of such a whole can be made easier and more readily grasped through classification by types, each of which is conceived as comprising the characteristic of all examples of the respective groups before their differentiation was made. Thus the types are more nearly perfect than the individuals because they embody also those forces and latent capacities which have withered away through lack of use. But they are also more imperfect, in that they lack the qualities which have been developed to a higher degree in reality.[20]

It is clear that, with other of his colleagues and predecessors, Tönnies retains the view that comparison is the proper method of sociology. Methodologically, the formation of types is the device by which comparisons in the social sciences are made precise. Tönnies, like Durkheim, was thus attempting to tighten up the comparative method inherited by the school from Comte, Spencer, and Ward. However, in his new emphasis on intuition and in assigning types an ontological status such that "types are more nearly perfect than . . . individuals," he is again on the threshold of a radical break with positivism.

Robert Redfield. One of the most able exponents of the classic phase of positivistic organicism in the contemporary period was Robert Redfield (1897–1958). Born in Chicago, he was associated most of his academic life with the Department of Anthropology of the University of Chicago. He received his doctorate in 1928, becoming instructor in anthropology in 1927, and professor in 1934. For some years (1934–1946) he served as Dean of the Division of Social Sciences and later chaired the Department of Anthropology. He was a research associate in charge of ethnological field work for Yucatan and Guatemala for the Carnegie Corporation between 1930 and 1947. Among his

[20]*Ibid.,* pp. 172, 173.

ROBERT REDFIELD

Courtesy of the University of Chicago

major works are *The Folk Culture of Yucatan* (1941), *The Primitive World and Its Transformations* (1953), and *The Little Community* (1955).[21]

Redfield observed that he and a number of

[21]For a complete bibliography, see Fay-Cooper Cole and Fred Eggan, "Robert Redfield," *American Anthropologist,* 61 (August 1959), 652–662. Redfield's best-known works are: *Tepoztlan: A Mexican Village* (Chicago: University of Chicago Press, 1930); *Chan Kom, A Maya Village,* written in collaboration with Alfonso Villa R. (Washington, D.C.: Carnegie Institution of Washington Publication No. 448, 1934); *The Folk Culture of Yucatan* (Chicago: University of Chicago Press, 1941); *A Village That Chose Progress: Chan Kom Revisited* (Chicago: University of Chicago Press, 1950); *The Primitive World and Its Transformations* (Ithaca, N.Y.: Cornell University Press, 1953); *The Little Community* (Chicago: University of Chicago Press, 1955); and *Peasant Society and Culture* (Chicago: University of Chicago Press, 1956).

other social scientists received their introduction to the main stream of sociological ideas from Robert E. Park at the same time.[22] The contrast between what Redfield and some of Park's other students did with this heritage is instructive; their works represent the best and worst possible uses that can be made of societal typologies. One of Redfield's contemporaries reduces ideas designed to deal with the richness of entire societies to the barren contrast between response to the new and response to the old. Even the fact that there are dozens of different ways of responding to the new and the old is ignored. The oversimplified formula that results is advanced as sufficient to account for the differences between entire societies. Next, the *Gemeinschaft-Gesellschaft* typology (or, as it is variously designated, "sacred-secular" or "folk-secular") has been divided into subtypes and these into so many sub-subtypes that it is difficult even to find examples of all of them, indicating the extent to which a great sociological tradition may degenerate into empty verbalisms.

Moreover, the startling suggestion has even been advanced that one can construct a *"Gemeinschaft–Gesellschaft* continuum."[23] *Continuum* is a pertinent concept in geometry and the theory of functions. A straight line may be said to be continuous when between any two points on it there is a third and whenever the line is separated into two pieces there is always an extreme point on one of the pieces that may be taken to define the separation. But the idea that these properties obtain between such complex, multidimensional phenomena as societies is pseudo-science. Quite in keeping with this surrealistic atmosphere, some individuals making this kind of use of the type have argued that they wish to use a typological method to determine how far their types deviate from reality.

Redfield's studies are in refreshing contrast to this. With his first study of the Mexican village of

Tepoztlan on the plateau of South Central Mexico, Redfield showed his capacity to use the societal typology of classical positivistic organicism as a skillful tool in field research. Tepoztlan, he felt, was typical of the peoples intermediate between "folk" and "demos." They had even developed an intermediate type of literature in the ballad form known as *corrido*.[24] The *corrido* is no longer the folk song of a truly primitive people, but lies on the threshold of news, public opinion, or propaganda. The folk culture producing these forms is neither Indian nor Spanish but a transitional type.

The fusion of elements from these two sources was traced through the material culture, the organization of community and village, the rhythms of social life, and religion. In its peculiar adjustment to its intermediate situation, the community finds its symbolic self-consciousness in songs known as *alabanzas* and *corridos:* the traditional, sacred, ritualistic songs on the one hand and the ephemeral, secular, and historical songs on the other. The *alabanzas* are songs of celebration of the *santos;* the *corridos* recount the exploits of the military heroes, the *veteranos*. The *santos* are local patron saints still found in every rural hamlet like the *barrios* of Tepoztlan. Each has its *santo,* represented by a particular effigy. While the *santo* tends to become a sacred effigy, the *veterano* also tends to become a symbol rather than a particular person. Both are symbols of the ideals and wishes of the ideologically as well as economically self-sufficient group.

The sharpest cultural differences in Mexico, Redfield observed, are not between one region and another, but between the city people *(los correctos)* and the country people *(los tontos)*. *Los tontos,* even despite the revolutions that have swept Mexico, tend to live in the mental world of folk culture. However, *los correctos* develop an intelligentsia who live in two worlds. A developing group consciousness is produced by the conflict between these elements, becoming most acute in individuals who, coming to live in the city, look back on the world of the folk. The frontier of change is thus located between *los correctos* and *los tontos.* The diffusion of

[22]Redfield, *The Little Community,* p. 143.
[23]It would be unfair to single out for illustration any one individual among those who have made this proposal. The issue is one of the adequate or inadequate use of ideas and not one of personalities.

[24]Redfield, *Tepoztlan: A Mexican Village,* p. 8.

city traits from their origin in the *plaza* comes into conflict with the traditions of the *barrios*. It is *los correctos* who promote the carnival with its secularized commercial aspects; but in the end, *los tontos* control the religious *fiestas* commemorating *santos*. In fact, the nearer a birth occurs to the *plaza*, the less the proportion of merely ritualistic and expressive behavior that attends the occasion. While the difference between *los correctos* and *los tontos* increases in times of disorder, it is always decreased in times of peace, showing the constant quiet erosion of the old ways.

Between *Tepoztlan* (1930) and *The Folk Culture of Yucatan* (1941), a considerable increase in conceptual subtlety and empirical skill is evident. Conceptually, the characteristics of isolated communities are grouped into a "type." These are: isolation, cultural homogeneity, organization of conventional understandings into a single unit, adjustment to local environment, predominantly personal character of social relations, relative importance of familial institutions, relative importance of sacred sanctions, development of ritual expression of belief and attitude, and a tendency for the behavior of the individual to involve his familial or local group. These traits were quite consciously derived from Maine, Durkheim, and Tönnies.[25]

Such a careful construction of types was made the basis for the development of a number of hypotheses: (1) primitive and peasant societies have characteristics of the first type; (2) when such societies come into contact with urbanized society, they tend to change in the direction of the opposite of these characters; (3) there is some natural or interdependent relation among various of these characters in that change with regard to some of them tends to bring about change in others.

This is no empty verbalism, but responsible social science. The major cultural contrast in Yucatan was found between the Spanish area of the northeast, particularly the city of Merida, and the Indian hinterland of the southwest. A comparative study of four communities was carried out along

the lines of contrasting culture: a tribal village (Tusik), a peasant village (Chan Kom), a town (Dzitas), and a city (Merida). These communities were progressively less isolated and homogeneous, progressively less traditionally organized; they were also more individualized and secular. Disorganization, individualization, and secularization were found not simply to be directly caused by the city but interrelated with mobility and heterogeneity and with one another. Lines of division already appear between the tribe and the peasant village. In the former (Tusik), people were most economically independent of the city. They were hostile to the national government and suspicious of the ways of the urbanite. But in Chan Kom the government was accepted and the ways of the urbanite had prestige. In general, the principles of tension were represented by race and class. Spanish and Indian cultures were concentrated in the extremes. The nearer one approached Tusik, the more completely an isolated Indian culture was manifest, while the city tended to supplant the original racial and cultural differences with a series of classes. Similar contrasts were found in every major area of life.

The less isolated and more heterogeneous societies were found to be more secular, individualistic, and disorganized. In the city, division of labor becomes more complex, less sexually defined, less cooperative, and more specialized. The stability of the elementary family declines with a decline in patriarchal and matriarchal authority; a disappearance of family customs occurs, a reduction in the strength of conventions of respect takes place, more unconventionality toward relatives is manifest, and a restriction in the application of kinship terms is evident. The pagan elements of religion give way. The symbols of saints and of God are most venerated in the remotest community. A secularization of Catholicism, turning it into a formal church, self-consciously organized and maintaining itself in competition with other interest groups, occurs. The festivals cease to be holy days, becoming holidays. The secularization of medicine and magic shifts healing functions from male shaman-priests to curers.

[25]Redfield, *The Folk Culture of Yucatan*, p. 343.

Magic increases in the city, perhaps as a product of increased individual insecurity.

In a series of studies in the 1950s,[26] Redfield developed his ideas into a general theory of civilization, quite in the manner of the classical representatives of positivistic organicism. He takes the world historical event in the development of humankind to be the emergence of the city. The urban revolution created a new type of person, a new type of outlook. Prior to this, each little group was largely self-contained, self-supported, without writing, composed of one kind of people, with a strong sense of group solidarity, preliterate, precivilized, and morally ordered. The most striking property of preliterate society was a predominance of the moral order over the technical order.

In civilization the moral order becomes small before the expansion of the technical order. In fact, the later histories of folk societies already show the influence of civilization. The developing city requires a wider area of production, it extends its influence by creating new cities, taxation is imposed on a tribal people, sending them on the road toward peasanthood, moneylenders make their appearance, the institutionalized resident stranger appears, local authority is transformed by the presence of alien political power, migratory professional entertainers appear, destroying the autonomy of local cultural life, literacy grows, and in many additional ways a society appears that is transitional between the isolated community and the city.

The city makes worldwide and conspicuous the self-conscious struggle to maintain a traditional ethos. Traditional morality is attacked and broken down. The moral order becomes managed by an elite or functional class. The family declines before the public hearth. Religion is on the way to creating citizens. Literacy produces speculative thinkers, and skepticism is not uncommon. Proletariats, internal and external, appear. The technical order extends its influence to all areas.

[26]Redfield, *The Primitive World and Its Transformations, The Little Community,* and *Peasant Society and Culture.*

In such fashion, with suggestions drawn from Maine, Tönnies, Durkheim, Sumner, Toynbee, Ogburn, and many others, Redfield advanced a special theory, first, of peasant society as a type between the isolated tribe and the city and, second, of civilization, the most dramatic events of which are formed in terms of the tense interplay of technique and moral order. Redfield developed a type of world-historical culture-lag theory. In contrast to such persons as Toynbee, Sorokin, and Spengler — who clearly influenced his thinking — Redfield never abandoned the positivistic aspects of positivistic organicism. His theories thus remain within the framework of the classic tradition.

SUMMARY

Positivistic organicism, the first school of sociological thought, was established by a series of great pioneering minds in Europe and America. It weathered the hazards that face every new discipline, and adapted itself to the changing intellectual milieu of the late nineteenth century.

The most important intellectual development in the last half of the century was the rise to popularity of biological theory. Sociological organicism, to be sure, was of a prebiological type, drawn from idealistic philosophy. But the rise to popularity of biological theories led to a penetration of biological forms of organicism in sociology. Lilienfeld pursued biological analogies at great length, arguing for the existence of a social nervous system, an intercellular substance binding the social organism together, and inventing the term *social pathology.* Schäffle distinguished five types of social tissue thought to be homologous to biological tissue. Fouillée attempted to synthesize mechanical and organismic theories of society in his strange conception of society as a contractual organism. René Worms drew out detailed analogies of structure, function, evolution, and pathology between society and biological organisms.

The overdrawn analogies of the extreme bio-organicists almost inevitably fell into disrepute as thinkers with clearer heads and a keener sense of humor appeared on the scene. The mechanical spinning of analogies can never take the place of science. Nevertheless, bio-organicism served sociology well. It camouflaged the new discipline, tied it in with a dominant nineteenth-century trend, and gave it the opportunity to find its proper field. By the time sociologists were ready to reject the "big animal" theory of society, sociology had come to stay.

Positivistic organicism was brought to its classical stage of development by a series of imaginative scholars, numbering in the early period Henry Sumner Maine, Ferdinand Tönnies, and Émile Durkheim, and in the modern period, Robert Redfield.

These thinkers developed the idea that the core of society is formed by a peculiar psychology, will (Tönnies), mentality (Durkheim), philosophical outlook (Redfield). Accepting total society as a primary object of analysis, the classic theorists developed a conception of contrasting types: societies based on status in contrast to those based on contract (Maine); societies characterized by mechanical solidarity in contrast to those based on organic solidarity (Durkheim); *Gemeinschaft* and *Gesellschaft* (Tönnies); folk society and secular society (Redfield).

In terms of such concepts the classic members of the school not only developed tools for the institutional analysis of actual societies, but laid the foundation for general theories of social and civilizational change.

VI

The Transformation and Eventual
Disintegration of Positivistic Organicism

From the very beginning, positivistic organicism was stricken with an inner conflict. Its organismic view of society tended to make it nonpositivistic; its positivism of method tended to make it antiorganismic. Whenever its members were not united to fight external enemies, their relations tended quickly to degenerate into civil war.

The dissatisfaction with the early view of society was already manifest in the speed with which sociologists accepted biological organicism. But the claims of science are not to be satisfied with mere figures of speech. Another position was current among the romantics and irrational idealists of the nineteenth century, who viewed society as a manifestation of emotion and will rather than reason. While this appeared to accord with the facts, it was also linked to strong antirational and antiscientific sentiments.

The early sociologists were by no means ready to abandon their positivism, for this appeared to them as the foundation of their claim to science. However, if the antiscientific and antipositivistic features of irrational idealism could once be eliminated, the view was available for a new kind of theoretical construction.

VOLUNTARISTIC POSITIVISM

Among the types of idealistic philosophy developed in the nineteenth century, irrational idealism was a not unimportant form. It is "idealistic" in the sense that it, too, models the world, society, history, and civilization on the analogy with human psychology. It is "irrational" in the special sense that it gives primacy in its picture of the world to the feeling-life of human beings, to the impulses or the will and not to their reason.

Initially, irrational idealism was in no shape to supply a foundation for a movement in sociological theory. In emphasizing the importance of emotion and will at the expense of reason, the irrational idealists often felt called upon to treat reason as relatively superficial. Science was dismissed as a shallow affair, dealing with superficialities, while a true analysis penetrated "deeply" into human feeling. This point of view appears in the works of Schopenhauer and Nietzsche, who had great influence on nineteenth- and early twentieth-century thought.

Gaetano Mosca. A number of personal and intellectual factors combined to press the Italian political scientist Gaetano Mosca (1858–1941) toward a fusion of positivism and irrational idealism. Mosca was born in Sicily, where during his youth the introduction of representative government had aggravated local political problems. As a result, Mosca developed an early suspicion of democratic government and parliamentary institutions, one of the major political and social products of enlightenment rationalism.[1] Also during his student days (he took the law degree in 1881) he came under the influence of the French critic and historian Hippolyte Taine (1828–1893).

Taine, who early made a reputation as a critic of art and literature, increasingly found his interest shifting to history, eventually centering on the French Revolution and origins of contemporary France. He was shocked by human folly and brutality, becoming convinced that human beings most of the time were fundamentally savage, vicious, violent, physically diseased, and mentally disordered. Taine attributed the French Revolution to reaction to the decadence of the ruling class under the monarchy, which he broke down into clergy, nobility, and crown; he attributed the properties of French civilization during the period of the flowering of the monarchy to the traits of the French aristocracy. Mosca early conceived the project of carrying through an analysis of Italian society armed with Taine's methods and theories.

Mosca completed and published his *Elements of Political Science* in 1896.[2] An empirical political science, in Mosca's view, must be based "upon the study of the facts of society and those facts can only be found in the history of the various nations."[3] Mosca believed there were severe limitations to the theories of sociopolitical phenomena current in his day: climatic theories, for example, rest on selec-

tive data; anthropological theories reason from primitive to advanced societies without taking into account the effects of level of civilization; racial doctrines fail when they ignore the rise and fall of particular ethnic groups; evolutionary theories overlook the frequent decline of social types. A scientific sociology requires fresh and unbiased study of historical social fact, avoiding the selection of only the evidence that confirms assumptions.

All societies, from the most primitive to the most advanced, Mosca argues, possess two classes: the rulers and the ruled.

> The first class, always the less numerous, performs all political functions, monopolizes power and enjoys the advantages that power brings, whereas the second, the more numerous class, is directed and controlled by the first, in a manner that is now more or less legal, now more or less arbitrary and violent, and supplies the first . . . with material means of subsistence and with the instrumentalities that are essential to the vitality of the political organism.[4]

Mosca cut the ground from beneath the usual classifications of governments with the view that all are aristocracies though, to be sure, of different types: military, priestly, hereditary, land based, money based, even merit based. Governments do not operate on the basis of forms alone, but by means of a "political formula" — a combination of theories and principles — and ethical standards accepted by the ruled. The basis for the ascendency of a given ruling class is supplied by the social forces (human factors of social significance, money, land, military power, religion, science, etc.) the class controls. Such social forces also determine the level of civilization of the given society. The stability of a given society rests on the ratio of the number and strength of the social forces a given ruling class is able effectively to bring under balanced control (a notion Mosca took over from Montesquieu).

Limits on the employment of social forces and their balanced employment in any given case is determined by the "juridical defense" — the

---

[1] This antagonism appears in Mosca's first major work, *Teorica dei governi e governo parlamentare* [On the Theory of Governments and Parliamentary Government] (Milan: Giuffrè, 1884).

[2] *Elementi di scienza politica*, 1896, translated by Hannah D. Kahn and edited and revised by Arthur Livingston, *The Ruling Class* (New York: McGraw-Hill, 1939).

[3] *Ibid.*, p. 41.

[4] *Ibid.*, p. 50.

habits, customs, morals, institutions, and the constitution. A social grouping with a shared combination of social forces and culture of sufficient integration to press for a political structure of its own is described by Mosca as a social type. Myths of race rather than race itself and religion have been particularly important in the formation of social types. Each social type maintains a distinctive ruling class and expresses its character in a unique political formula. A particular civilization lasts only as long as its distinctive social type remains intact. Social type and political formula have powerful formative influence on one another.

In contrast to his early skepticism about parliamentary institutions, in his later reflections Mosca became convinced that a representative system of government is able to comprise the largest social units and the highest levels of civilization.

Vilfredo Pareto. Before he made his acquaintance with Mosca's theories, Vilfredo Pareto (1848–1923) had begun to work out his own fusion of irrational idealism and positivism, making this form of theoretical orientation available for social science.[5] His methodology was a form of extreme

VILFREDO PARETO

Courtesy of the University of Lausanne

positivism. He argued that sociology must become a logico-experimental science based on observation and experiment to the exclusion of all reasoning and speculation going beyond the observed facts. The propositions of sociology should include nothing beyond a description of the facts and their uniformities. So rigorously did Pareto argue his case that his favorite illustrations of the sins against a logico-experimental method were taken from positivists like Comte and Spencer. For example, in his discussion of the rationalization of nonlogi-

---

[5]Pareto's chief sociological work, *Trattato di sociologia generale* (Florence: G. Barbéra, 1916; 2d ed., 1923), is available in an English translation by Andrew Bongiorno and Arthur Livingston, edited by Arthur Livingston, under the title *The Mind and Society*, 4 vols. (New York: Harcourt, Brace, 1935). Other of Pareto's works available in English include *Sociological Writings* selected and introduced by S. E. Finer (New York: Praeger, 1966); *The Rise and Fall of Elites*, introduction by Hans Zetterberg (Totowa, N.J.: Bedminster Press, 1968); *Manual of Political Economy*, trans. Ann S. Schwier (New York: A. M. Kelly, 1971). For studies of Pareto see: Georges H. Bousquet, *The Works of Vilfredo Pareto* (Minneapolis, Minn.: Sociological Press, 1928); Pitirim A. Sorokin, *Contemporary Sociological Theories* (New York: Harper, 1928); L. J. Henderson, *Pareto's General Sociology: A Physiologist's Interpretation* (Cambridge, Mass.: Harvard University Press, 1936); George C. Homans and Charles P. Curtis, *An Introduction to Pareto* (New York: Knopf, 1934); Franz Borkenau, *Pareto* (New York: Wiley, 1936); Talcott Parsons, *The Structure of Social Action* (New York: McGraw Hill, 1937); the articles by Maurice Allais and Talcott Parsons, "Pareto," *The International Encyclopedia of the Social Sciences*

(New York: Crowell Collier and Macmillan, 1968), XI, 399–416; Norberto Bobbio, *On Mosca and Pareto* (Geneva: Librairie Droz, 1972); Warren J. Samuels, *Pareto on Policy* (New York: Elsevier, 1974).

cal conduct in *The Mind and Society*, Pareto uses Comte and Spencer to illustrate pseudoscience:

> In his *Lectures on Positive Philosophy* . . . Comte seems to be decidedly inclined to ascribe the predominance to logical conduct. He sees in positive philosophy . . . "the one solid basis for that social reorganization which is to terminate the critical state in which civilized nations have been living for so long a time."
>
> After quoting Comte's dictum that ideas govern and upset the world, Herbert Spencer advances a theory that non-logical actions alone influence society. "Ideas do not govern and overthrow the world: the world is governed or overthrown by feelings, to which ideas serve only as guides. . . ."
>
> Then a curious thing happens: Comte and Spencer reverse positions reciprocally! In his *System of Positive Polity* . . . Comte decides to allow sentiment to prevail. . . . Comte becomes a prophet. The battle of ideas is over. He imagines he has won a complete victory. So now he begins proclaiming dogma, pronouncing *ex cathedra,* and it is only natural that nothing but sentiments, should now be left on the field — his own sentiments of course.
>
> Spencer, on the other hand, after admitting, even too sweepingly, the influence of non-logical actions, eliminates them altogether. . . . Says he: "Our postulate must be that primitive ideas are natural, and, under the conditions in which they occur, rational."[6]

Among Pareto's special arguments for positivism were: that sociology must operate with conceptions of mutual dependence, functional relationship, regularities, uniformities, and correlations in space and time, and quantitative measurements; it must exclude ideas of one-sided dependence, cause and effect, uniqueness and irregularity, and qualities. In this manner sociology will be able to obtain formulas that approximate the complexities of social reality more closely.

A society for Pareto is a system of forces in equilibrium. A number of types of factors are ultimately involved in this system: physical (such as soil, climate, flora, fauna, geography), external (other societies with which it may come into con-

tact), and internal (including race, sentiments and feelings, ideologies). Pareto was particularly interested in the study of the internal factors. Internally — as a system of behavior — the character of society is determined by the properties of the actions and the individuals who act. Since these individuals are illogical, illogical factors lie at the core of society. Quite an extensive part of Pareto's treatise is devoted to the task of showing that the explanations ordinarily given to explain human conduct do not in any way touch its essence.

The most fundamental classification of actions for establishing sociology as a science is that between logical and nonlogical types of action. It was Pareto's belief that almost the whole of human effort that has gone into the explanation of conduct is misguided. Most of the theological, philosophical, and even scientific explanations of human conduct have tended to ignore its nonlogical elements. Examples to prove this are found in the works of Aristotle and Plato, Polybius, Fustel de Coulange, Comte, and Spencer.

The starting point of a logico-experimental sociology appears in the recurrent features of action (*residues*) rather than the variable elements (*derivations*) they display. The residues are nonlogical constancies; they are manifestations of sentiments. For all intents and purposes, Pareto's residues are identical with what Schopenhauer and Nietzsche describe as "manifestations of the will." The residues are thought to be the real forces underlying the social equilibrium. They are grouped into six classes: (1) residues of combination, (2) residues of persistence of aggregates, (3) residues of manifestations of sentiments through external acts, (4) residues of sociability, (5) residues of individual integrity, and (6) sex residues.

Residues of *combinations* are sentiments expressed by the combining of things. The taking of signs in dreams as indications of luck, the astrological casting of horoscopes, the multiple forms of magic and prophecy, the belief that good is associated with progress, democracy, and universal suffrage, all are examples. There is often no logical reason for the combination; in fact, oppo-

[6]Pareto, *The Mind and Society*, I, pp. 188, 189, 191.

sites are often the preferred components. The residue of *persistence of aggregates* refers to the tendency of aggregates once formed to persist. The survival of all customs even beyond the conditions of their appearance is characteristic. The cult of the family is an example. The residue of *manifestation of sentiments in external acts* is illustrated by all phenomena such as religious exaltation and political agitation. The residues of *sociability* are basic to the drive to be like everyone else. Such residues are manifested in style, fashion, and standardization of all sorts. Pity, cruelty, and neophobia appear to be sentiments bound up with sociability. The residues of *integrity of personality* refer to the drive to preserve one's self against any thing tending to upset it or detract from it. Such residues cause us to resent every attack on ourselves or on our group, social status, or society. Finally, in connection with the *sex* residue, it is observed that various residues often enter into combination, as in the union of asceticism with the sex residue.

Of special interest for Pareto's sociology is the relation of the derivations to the residues. Derivations consist in the ways people dissimulate and explain their acts. Derivations are of various kinds: (1) *simple affirmation* — statements of real or imaginary facts; (2) *authority* — the pseudo-explanation of events by citing the authority of the past, of tradition and custom, or of the Divine Will; (3) *accord with sentiments or principles* — derivations which attempt justifications of conduct on the basis of the presumed fact that it is for the benefit of others; and (4) *verbal proofs* — consisting in using terms not in accordance with the facts, allegories, metaphors, and so on. The derivations correspond closely to what students often prefer to describe as "ideologies." They are pseudo-reasons for conduct.

The stability of society depends not on the derivations but the state and distribution of the residues. The derivations may be useful as instruments in the service of the residues, but they cannot take their place. Of the residues, the first two are of greatest importance for society. The residues are not equally distributed among individ-

uals and social classes. There are individuals and groups with strong residues of combination, others with strong residues of the persistence of aggregates. Two principal social types of persons and of social classes rest on these residues. The social type concentrating the residue of combinations are the *speculators;* those concentrating the residue of persistence of aggregates are the *rentiers.* To the first class belong combiners, entrepreneurs, schemers, inventors of all types. They are also the reformers, sentimentalists, and radicals. The second type represents the conservatives, persons with a strong sense of duty and a narrow determined will. In democratic and plutocratic governments the speculators are usually dominant. They are clever at combining. They are full of trickery and usually succeed in deceiving the masses. They are corrupt. Eventually they will be succeeded by the *rentiers.* But history is the graveyard of aristocracies, and if the *rentiers* are in the saddle, they are easily penetrated by the ingenious, subtle combiners from below. If the latter penetrate too deeply, the result is a wholesale weakening of the position of the *rentiers.*

Thus, history typically shows a "circulation of the elite." In any situation composed predominantly of a ruling group resting on residues of combination, the situation rapidly arrives in which the person of force is the only answer to the need for social stability. The lions oust the foxes. Once in power, however, it is easy for the elite, resting on residues of persistence, to maintain power by combinations of force and trickery. In such fashion the foxes penetrate the conservative circles and weaken the unity of the conservative elite. There is an upper and lower class in every society showing a difference in distribution of the residues. There is also a circulation of individuals from upper to lower classes and vice versa. Although the intensity of circulation varies from society to society and in a given society over a period of time, it is nonetheless inevitable that any aristocracy is destined some day to disappear. All of the devices of an aristocracy to maintain its position — including the elevation of dangerous leaders from the lower to the upper classes, the use of bribery, corruption, imprisonment, and extermination — will not prevail in the long run. Pareto's voluntarism adds new dimensions to organicism.[7]

Sigmund Freud. If one were to locate the sociological formulations springing from Freudianism, they could not be more accurately placed than as a form of sociological theory which fused voluntaristic organicism and positivism very similar to Pareto's theory. Sigmund Freud (1856–1939) was a thoroughgoing positivist by training and inclination. He assumed that, fundamentally, mental life is structured by underlying forces that always produce the same effects under the same conditions. Even his method of analysis was typical of his positivistic orientation: he observed the events of everyday life, taking careful note of slips, errors, and omissions of all sorts. He assumed that these are not accidental but rather the result of constant causal agencies. Constant forces are assumed to distort systematically in characteristic ways the little doings of everyday life. This was the burden of argument in *The Psychopathology of Everyday Life*.[8] Similarly, Freud assumes that

SIGMUND FREUD

New York Psychoanalytic Institute, Abraham A. Brill Library.

dreams are produced by constant features of human nature and that even the very content of the dream is capable of interpretation in terms of constant forces. So, for example, the mechanisms of distortion of dream content are thought to result from displacement, dramatizations, symbolization, and secondary elaboration.

Freud's affinities with the irrationalistic idealism of Schopenhauer and Nietzsche were as fundamental as were Pareto's. He, too, maintained that more basic than human beings' rationality (their "derivations," according to Pareto) is their emotional and instinctive life (their "will," their "residues" — Pareto). Freud did not work out the basic

---

[7]Certain aspects of Pareto's organicism will be explored further in Chapter XX.

[8]Translated by A. A. Brill from *Psychopathologie des Alltagslebens* (Berlin: S. Karger, 1904) and included in A. A. Brill, translator and editor, *The Basic Writings of Sigmund Freud* (New York: Modern Library, 1938). Those works of Freud that have special relevance for sociology are readily available in various editions; cited here are only the particular editions of translations that were consulted for the present discussion: *Totem und Tabu* (Leipzig: H. Heller, 1913), translated by James Strachey as *Totem and Taboo* (New York: W. W. Norton, 1952); *Massenpsychologie und Ich-analyse* (Leipzig: Internationaler Psychoanalytischer Verlag, 1921), translated by James Strachey as *Group Psychology and the Analysis of the Ego* (London: Hogarth Press, 1948); *Die Zukunft einer Illusion* (Vienna: Internationaler Psychoanalytischer Verlag, 1927), translated by W. D. Robson-Scott as *The Future of an Illusion* (Garden City, N.Y.: Doubleday, 1957); *Das Unbehagen in der Kultur* (Vienna: Internationaler Psychoanalytischer Verlag, 1930), translated by Joan Riviere as *Civilization and Its Discontents* (London: Hogarth Press, 1946); although the first two parts of *Der Mann Moses und die monotheistische Religion* appeared in

German in *Imago*, 23 (1937), the first edition of the book in its entirety was the translation by Katherine Jones, *Moses and Monotheism* (London: Hogarth Press, 1939).

drives in the same way as Schopenhauer or Nietzsche or Pareto. In the first form of his theory, the psychology of the individual was divided into a conscious, an unconscious — containing the more basic factors of emotional life, strongly sexual (libidinous) in nature — with a censoring mechanism operating between the two spheres. Later Freud conceived the central elements of the personality to consist of the id, the ego, and the superego, the id taking over many of the phenomena of the original unconscious and the superego taking over many of the functions of the former censor. Still later, Freud conceived the individual's emotional life to consist of life and death instincts. One institution, the family, was conceived by Freud to be absolutely essential to the development of personality. The libidinous impulses of human beings even in an infantile state were crucial to the stylization of behavior. Freud assumed that each new social achievement by the individual corresponded to the molding of the libidinous impulses as the infant passes through states from auto-eroticism through oral and anal eroticism to hetero-eroticism. Of particularly profound importance were the later stages of libidinous molding. In the course of development the child tends to anchor its love impulses on the parent of the opposite sex. This takes the form of the Oedipus model in the boy, the Electra model in the girl. For full normal development the child will have to transfer its sex interests to some member of the opposite sex other than the parent. If this final transfer fails, there is a tendency for the individual to regress to some previous stage of libidinous development.

The difference between Freud and other irrational idealists is clear enough. Schopenhauer and Nietzsche find the locus of the individuals' voluntaristic life in the will, particularly in the will to power. Pareto found it in the residues of combinations and persistence of aggregates. Freud found the sex drive particularly important. From all appearances, he had less reason than they to move out to a general theory of society, but precisely this step was taken — the attempt to develop a Freudian theory of society.

A general theory of primitive society and explanation of the origins of social structure and morals was projected in *Totem and Taboo* (1913). Taboo customs were identified by Freud with the manifestations of the symptoms of compulsive neurosis, in their lack of apparent motivation, their enforcement through an inner need, their capacity for displacement, and in the causation of ceremonial actions emanating from the forbidden.

A peculiar system of taboos characterizes totemism, which Freud takes to be the oldest form of religion and social structure. Totemism displays taboos on the killing and eating of the totem animal and on sexual intercourse with totem companions of the other sex. Freud assumes that this system of taboos arose in the following way. There was an original unstructured primitive horde under a primal father, who was envied and feared by his sons. The ancient father-beast monopolized the sexual services of all the women for himself. The sons banded together and killed him. They were then seized by guilt and remorse, and in their anxiety they substituted a symbol (a totem animal) for the primal father, making it taboo to kill and eat the totem. They denied themselves intercourse with the women of the horde (originating clan exogamy). In ceremonies once a year the totem animal was killed and eaten — ceremonial reenactment of the ancient crime. The structure of ancient society thus is determined as a racial form of the Oedipus drama.

In *Moses and Monotheism* (1939), Freud analyzes the origins of Christianity and Judaism along the broad lines laid down in *Totem and Taboo*. He sets forth and defends the hypothesis that Moses was originally an Egyptian, transformed by myth into a Jew. Moses is assumed to have been a noble Egyptian, accepting the monotheism of the Pharaoh-dreamer Ikhnaton. However, when the regime of Ikhnaton fell, Moses, who was a protector of the Jews, led them out of Egypt. In this new sect the custom of circumcision was taken over, and the Levites were the original, partly Egyptian practitioners of the new cult. However, in the course of the difficulties of leading the people out of Egypt, Moses was murdered. This operated to fix monotheism on the Jews in much the same manner that the murder of the primal father fixed totemism on the primitives. Later the triumph of Christianity represented a renewed victory of the Amon priests over the God of Ikhnaton after an interval of a millennium. "The great deed and misdeed of primal times, the murder of the father, was brought home to the Jews, for fate decreed that they should repeat it on the person of Moses . . . an eminent father substitute."[9] The murder of Christ was a repetition of the same theme and, for Freud, the reason for the profundity of Christianity.

In *Civilization and Its Discontents* (1930), Freud presented the individual's instinctive life as standing in the sharpest antagonism with civilization. The ordinary person's relation to religion, for example, is conceived as a duplicate of the relation to the family. "The ordinary man cannot imagine this Providence in any other form but that of a greatly exalted father, for only such a one could understand the needs of the sons of men, or be softened by their prayers and placated by the signs of their remorse. The whole thing is so patently infantile, so incongruous with reality, that to one whose attitude to humanity is friendly, it is painful to think that the great majority of mortals will never be able to rise above this view of life."[10] By its very nature civilization imposes privations on people. People cannot tolerate the degree of privation society imposes; they cannot help becoming neurotic. So long as society remained at the level of the primitive family, with its direct controls and gratifications, we were relatively safe. But "civilized society is perpetually menaced with disintegration through this primal hostility of men towards one another."[11] There is no escape. The civilized human being is inevitably frustrated, hostile, and neurotic.

In *Group Psychology and the Analysis of the Ego* (1921), Freud attempted to explain crowd psychology. The typical crowd was treated as an organized group with a leader, such as the Christian church with Christ as its head or an army with its commander. The relation between the members of the group and the leader was visualized as being like that between a patient and hypnotist, or lover and beloved. Older theories of the crowd, such as those of Le Bon, saw the physical contact and common stimulation of the group as the context generating leadership. Freud's formulation reverses this order.

In *The Future of an Illusion* and *Civilization and Its Discontents*, Freud attempted to go beyond the mere tension of the individual with society to the analysis of culture. The source of religion is taken as fear of the unknown. The primitive god-father was a product of this fear. The task of the gods is to exorcise the terrors of nature, reconcile people to the cruelty of fate, particularly death, and make amends for the suffering imposed by communal life. Religion is an instance of the "omnipotence of thought," for it is an illusion, a wish-fulfillment, a mass delusion comparable to the personal delusions of the neurotic. The struggle of the individual's nature against culture is inevitable. Nature and culture are menacing powers to which people must adjust. To accept society, it is necessary for people to recognize their limitations and accept social aims. Restrictions are placed on sex, the drive for power and aggression. Human beings submit to society, and their own superegos function as censors. Because impulses for aggression arise, the superego and culture brush aside the ego's claim for happiness. The price of progress is a sense of guilt.

The limitations of a Freudian theory of society are not difficult to locate. Primitive society, the great religions of the world, modern civilization — all are modeled after a narrow conception of the family drama. To make the basic arguments plausible, mythological reconstructions of human history, often on the basis of disputed authorities, were presented.[12] Arbitrary decisions were made,

---

[9]Freud, *Moses and Monotheism*, p. 143.
[10]Freud, *Civilization and Its Discontents*, p. 22.
[11]*Ibid.*, p. 86.

[12]For example, in his study of *Totem and Taboo*, Freud relied on anthropological authorities who had been rejected by their colleagues. Similarly, in the study of *Moses*

such as treating the crowd and the organized group as identical — a practice that no sociologist will accept. Further unacceptable assumptions were made, such as the existence of racial memories (without which the primitive taboo ceremonial, as Freud presents it, could not be maintained).

Some of the one-time associates of Freud also showed some inclination to develop a voluntaristic positivism. Alfred Adler made his point of attack on psychological problems through organ inferiority. He noted that any defect or weakness — a missing limb, poor motor ability, ugliness — places people in positions where they must either fight for a place in life or give up. The process set in motion by reaction to inferiority leads to compensation or even overcompensation. Inferiority feeling, overcompensation, and lust for power were made the basic categories for analysis of individual and social events.

Carl Gustav Jung, who was also at one time an associate of Freud, was closer to Freud's own position. Libido, a general sexual energy according to Freud, was subject to repression, transformation, and sublimation. Jung broadened the idea still more to include all psychic energy, in fact, all energy in animals and human beings responsible for biological and social evolution itself. Jung also contributed to the study of personality by his typology of introvert (a personality inwardly oriented, self-occupied, thoughtful) in contrast to the extrovert (an outgoing type of personality, objective, oriented toward action). Moreover, even in the early days, Otto Rank and Hanns Sachs suggested the application of psychoanalysis to mythology, religion, ethnology, and linguistics.[13]

Among repeated attempts to explain social phenomena on the basis of the voluntaristic positivism of Freud, some stand out. Harold D. Lasswell in *Psychopathology and Politics*[14] tried to trace the influence of infantile experience on political careers. Politicians were divided into agitators, administrators, theorists, and people of political convictions. A series of case histories was examined to discover the experimental foundation of each type. Typical findings were that early forms of animosity were compensated for by love of humanity and that feelings of uncertainty tended to produce an exaggerated vehemence in the assertion of principles. Franz Alexander and Hugo Staub in *The Criminal, the Judge, and the Public*[15] proposed nothing less than the reform of criminological procedure by the use of psychoanalytic concepts. They urged that when individuals find themselves neglected or abused by society, any protest against cultural impositions tends to be violent. Social justice is always felt repressively. When it breaks down, antisocial forms of individual protest are likely to take criminal form. Responsibility for crime commonly associated with free will has been shown by psychology to be determined by behavior lying in the unconscious id. Hence a new classification of criminals is needed in which the normal are distinguished from neurotic and acute. One must isolate, for example, neurotics who may commit criminal acts to secure the punishment demanded by the superego from inclinations of a criminal type arising out of the id.

A parallel trend to that of the Freudian forms of voluntaristic positivism appears in the ethnological school of culture configurationism. Its

and Monotheism, reliance was placed on questionable research. This is not responsible social science but poetic license.

[13]Otto Rank and Hanns Sachs, "The Significance of Psychoanalysis for the Mental Sciences," *The Psychoanalytic Review*, 2 (1915), pp. 297–326, 428–457; 3 (1916), pp. 69–89, 189–214, 318–335. Other early extensions of psychoanalysis to social phenomena include Karl Abraham, *Dreams and Myths*, tr. by William A. White (New York: The Journal of Nervous and Mental Disease Pub-

lishing Co., 1913); Oskar Pfister, *Some Applications of Psycho-analysis* (London: George Allen and Unwin, 1923); and Géza Róheim, *Social Anthropology* (New York: Boni and Liveright, 1926).

[14]Harold D. Laswell, *Psychopathology and Politics* (Chicago: University of Chicago Press, 1930).

[15]Franz Alexander and Hugo Staub, *The Criminal, the Judge, and the Public*, trans. Gregory Zilboorg (New York: Macmillan, 1931).

roots extend back to linguists and philosophers like Moritz Lazarus and Heymann Steinthal, who developed a form of the folk-soul notion taken from Hegel. In modern times the doctrine has been revived by Ruth Benedict in *Patterns of Culture*,[16] though her specific inspirations were found in Nietzsche (the concepts of Apollonian and Dionysian mentality) and the Gestalt psychology conception of "wholes." For Benedict a culture is like an individual, displaying a more or less consistent pattern of thought and action. In each culture, characteristic purposes appear which at least in their peculiar assemblage are not shared by any other. All items of behavior tend to assume contours with reference to these. This cultural-psychological whole is no mere sum of its special parts; it determines the parts in their relation and nature. Using Nietzsche's Apollonian and Dionysian types, Benedict analyzed three tribal groups — the Zuni of the Pueblos, the Dobuans of Northwestern Melanesia and the Kwakiutl of the Northwest Coast — to illustrate psychocultural forms.

A similar type of analysis appears in the work of Margaret Mead,[17] in whose work the conception of psychocultural wholes is shifted back toward a more distinctly Freudian type of explanation. The road back to Freud becomes still more clearly marked in modern students such as Abram Kardiner, Karen Horney, and Erich Fromm. Voluntaristic positivism seems by no means to have played itself out as a trend.

THE SEPARATION OF ORGANICISM FROM POSITIVISM

In reviewing the various formations of positivistic organicism, one must never lose sight of the fact that they contain opposed principles. Positivism

[16]Ruth Benedict, *Patterns of Culture* (Boston: Houghton Mifflin, 1934).
[17]See, for example, her *Sex and Temperament in Three Primitive Societies* (New York: William Morrow, 1935).

attempts to maintain knowledge on the level of experience; organicism at every point tends to exceed the limits positivism would impose. If one once denies the organic analogy, all the special claims of the point of view disappear; and if one once takes one's positivism seriously, the organic analogy must go.

The maintenance of a condition in which one accepts two antagonistic principles at the same time can only be explained by the presence of reasons good enough to cause one to overlook all the contradictions inherent in the principles. These reasons have already been identified. The exponents of early sociology wished to realize two major objectives in their discipline: (1) to maintain a position of unshakable social conservatism (which was secured by their particular interpretation of organicism) and (2) to remain scientific (which was secured by way of their positivism). Voluntaristic positivism had the same essential requirements. The moment one was willing to accept modification and tolerate a liberal social outlook (as in the case of Lester Ward), the formula of positivistic organicism tended to fall to pieces. The same was true for Alfred Fouillée, with the barbarism arising from his attempt to fuse the ideas of social contract (anchored in liberalism) with organicism and his outlandish proposal of a "contractual organism" to account for society. As in the case of Ward, the formula was breaking down.

Positivistic organicism thus was maintained not by its inner composition but by the presence of a set of external requirements imposed on sociology. The first form of sociological theory contains a set of internal contradictions precisely because it was socially responsible. But it follows that the moment the external situation changes, and the forces which led to the simultaneous acceptance of positivism and organicism are no longer present, positivistic organicism should decline. When the decline sets in, there are two major possibilities: the development of organicism relatively unmodified by positivism or vice versa. The first possibility may be illustrated by three interesting persons: Oswald Spengler, Arnold Toynbee, and Pitirim Sorokin.

OSWALD SPENGLER

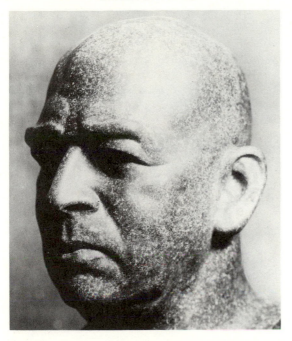

Professor Fritz Behn's bust of Oswald Spengler, author of *The Decline of the West*. Courtesy of Alfred A. Knopf, Inc.

Oswald Spengler. Oswald Spengler's *Decline of the West*[18] appeared at the turning point of four years of war, July 1918. It fitted the growing general mood, and the large and rather turgid work became a best seller. It was significant that the author was not a recognized scholar but a simple high school teacher (*Oberlehrer*), a fact accentuating his appeal.

The keynote of the work is found in an unrestricted, aggressive organicism, with a powerful antipositivistic bias. No ideal is more dear to the positivist than the mathematical analysis of experience; no notion is more savagely attacked by Spengler. "The means whereby to identify dead forms is Mathematical Law. The means whereby to understand living forms is Analogy. By these means we are enabled to distinguish polarity and periodicity in the world."[19] This distinction between mathematical law and analogy corresponds to a distinction drawn between the world as history and the world as nature and between the appropriate methods for understanding the one and the other. Nature is organic, civilization is mechanical; the one is represented by picture and symbol, the other by formula and system; the one is in the domain of chronology, the other in mathematical number; to the one applies the concept of causality, a logic of space, to the other, destiny, the logic of time. Only chronology and the idea of destiny are sufficient for ordering the facts of society, culture, and history as living things. The positivistic method is adapted only to superficialities, to surfaces, to evidence of the world of the senses. The true aim of cultural historical study is to penetrate to the living core or soul of phenomena where "imagination seeks comprehension of the living existence of the world in relation to . . . life."[20]

The unrestricted organicism of Spengler's view appears over and again. What diaries and autobiographies are to an individual, historical research and every kind of psychological comparison and analysis of alien peoples, times, and customs, are to the soul of culture. Only by such means do we discover, for example, that Indian culture has a perfectly ahistorical soul, expressed in Brahma Nirvana. Hence we learn the implications of the fact that there is no pure Indian astronomy, no calendar, no history. And while the Indian forgot

---

[18]The first volume of *Der Untergang des Abenlandes* was published in 1918 (Vienna: Braumüller); not until 1922–23 were both volumes published together (Munich: C. H. Beck). The book was translated by Charles Francis Atkinson as *Decline of the West* (New York: Alfred A. Knopf, 1926).

[19]Spengler, *Decline of the West*, I, p. 4.
[20]*Ibid.*, p. 8.

everything, the Egyptian forgot nothing, for the Egyptian's soul was historical in texture and impelled by primitive worship of the past and future of the world.

In developing his theory, Spengler draws sharp distinctions between culture (the organic living entity) and civilization (the dead external shell and monuments of a one-time living culture). The two phenomena, organic growth and death, are expressed in the peasantry, bound to the soil and lying outside history, and in the urban citizenry, the agents of history and civilization. History and society represent "the drama of a *number* of mighty cultures, each springing with primitive strength from the soil of a mother-region to which it remains firmly bound throughout its whole life-cycle; each stamping its material, its mankind, in *its own* image; each has *its own* idea, *its own* passions, *its own* life, will and feeling, *its own* death. . . . Here the Cultures, peoples, languages, truths, gods, landscapes bloom and age as the oaks and the stone-pines, the blossoms, twigs, and leaves. . . . Each culture has its own new possibilities of self expression which arise, ripen, decay, and never return."[21]

The ideological mood to which Spengler's argument is addressed is very different from that of early sociology. Not conservativism and science, but reactionary regression and antiscientific bias are its properties. While it was a German schoolteacher's rebellion against the doom to which the authorities, including the scientists, seemed to be leading his society, the rural mysticism present in it corresponded to the universal disillusionment following World War I. The world of the twentieth century has shown repeated preoccupation with the problem of the "death of civilization." In all such studies, a semireligious tone is maintained and an antipositivism is discernible. Toynbee's work is a famous example.

Arnold Toynbee. A less extreme form of organicism of the same general type as Spengler's is

ARNOLD TOYNBEE

Courtesy of Oxford University Press. Copyright by Philippe Halsman.

found in the work of the English historian, Arnold Toynbee (1889–1975). Toynbee argues, in *A Study of History*,[22] that if we explore the distribution of social facts in space and time — for example, those represented by English history — the conclusion is inescapable that we are dealing with a developing whole. His arguments at this point are not dissimilar from those by which Spengler set up cul-

[22]Arnold J. Toynbee, *A Study of History*, 10 vols. (New York: Oxford University Press, 1934–54). Oxford University Press has also published an excellent two-volume abridgment of the entire work by D. C. Somervell; the first of these, covering Volumes 1–6 of the original, was published in 1947, the second, covering Volumes 7–10, was published in 1957; both bear the same title as the original. References here are to the first of Somervell's abridgments.

ture as a unit of study. He claims "that the intelligible unit of historical study is neither a nation state nor (at the other end of the scale) humankind as a whole but a certain grouping of humanity which we have called a society."[23] Not only does analysis prove the existence of a unit that one may designate as Western European Society but also that there are at least four other living societies of the same species today: (a) an Orthodox Christian Society in Southeastern Europe and Russia; (b) an Islamic Society with its focus in the arid zone from North Africa to the Middle East and from the Atlantic to the outer face of the Great Wall of China; (c) a Hindu Society in India; and (d) a Far Eastern Society in the subtropical and temperate regions between the arid zones and the Pacific.

We know that Western European society developed out of the Greco-Roman world, and we can ask about the pertinent characteristics of Hellenic society just prior to its decline. There were three: (1) it developed a universal state; (2) when the Roman Empire fell there was a kind of interregnum during which there was a tremendous expansion of the Christian Church; moreover, (3) during this same period there were extensive movements of peoples both in the form of an internal and external proletariat. "The Church, a survival from the dying society, became the womb from which in due course the new one was born."[24] The fact that our society arose out of a previous one and that there were characteristic factors that signaled its decline opens up two possibilities. We should be able to study the factors in the growth, expansion, and death of a society. We are also able to build up a picture of the total array of such societies that have historically appeared. We are even able to develop information on various fossil societies of the parent society from which the living specimens are derived. In all, according to Toynbee, we are able to discover nineteen societies: the Western, the Orthodox, the Iranic, the Arabic (the last two now united in the Islamic), the Hindu, the Far Eastern,

the Hellenic, the Syriac, the Indic, the Sinic, the Minoan, the Sumeric, the Hittite, the Babylonic, the Egyptiac, the Andean, the Mexic, the Yucatec, and the Mayan. Moreover, it is useful to divide Orthodox Christian Society into the Orthodox-Byzantine and Orthodox-Russian and the Far Eastern into a Chinese and a Korean-Japanese Society. These societies, twenty-one in all, are all species of a single genus. It is customary to describe them as civilizations to distinguish them from primitive societies as a special genus. About 650 primitive societies are registered, most of which are alive today.

There are three different methods for studying such phenomena. The first is the ascertainment and recording of "facts"; the second is the elucidation, through a comparative study of the facts ascertained, of general "laws"; the third is the artistic recreation of the facts in the form of "fiction." Toynbee points out that it is usually assumed that the technique of ascertaining and recording facts is the method of history, the elucidation and formulation of general laws is the technique of science, and the use of fiction is the technique of drama. He feels, however, that this is a mistake: these methods are not to be kept in watertight compartments. To be sure, history does not concern itself with everything. "It leaves alone the facts of social life in primitive societies, from which anthropology elucidates its 'laws'; and it hands over to biography the facts of individual lives; . . . but besides recording facts, history also has recourse to fiction and makes use of laws. . . . History, like the drama and novel, grew out of mythology."[25] Thus it is clear that Toynbee, while not a rabid antipositivist in quite the same sense as Spengler, adds methods to his procedure, like fiction, which the positivists cannot tolerate.

Toynbee's whole treatment of civilization as a genus of society is characterized by a thoroughgoing organicism. He rejects the idea that primitive societies and civilizations differ because of the presence or absence of institutions in some which are

[23]Toynbee, *A Study of History*, I, 11.
[24]*Ibid.*, p. 13.

[25]*Ibid.*, p. 44.

not found in others, or because of a difference in the division of labor between them. They differ, he maintains, because of the quality of their inner subjective life. *Mimesis,* or imitation, is treated as a generic feature of all social life, operating both in primitive societies and in civilizations, in every activity "from the imitation of the style of film stars by their humbler sisters upwards." It operates differently in the two species of society. In primitive societies mimesis is directed toward the past. In such a society custom rules and the society remains static. On the other hand, in societies in process of civilization, mimesis is directed toward creative personalities who command a following because they are pioneers.

Primitive societies are compared by Toynbee to a people asleep on a mountain ledge with a precipice below and a mountain above. Civilizations are like the companions of the sleepers who have started to climb. Toynbee maintains that this contrast between active and passive societies was anticipated by the Chinese conceptions of *yang* and *yin*. What launched society in the movement from a *yin* (passive) to a *yang* (active) state? The attempt to account for the movement from primitive society to civilization on the basis of race and environment fails to deal accurately with a living thing. We are far better off, he suggests, in looking for the starting point of civilization in an encounter between two superhuman personalities. A society is confronted in the course of its life by a succession of problems. Each problem is a challenge to undergo an ordeal. The personal ordeals of Job and Faust represent, in the intuitive language of fiction, "the infinitely multiple ordeal of mankind." The same idea of an encounter of superhuman forces is portrayed in the Book of Genesis, and the New Testament. The expulsion of Adam and Eve from Eden follows the encounter between Yahweh and the Serpent. In the New Testament the passion of Christ is nothing less than Humanity's Redemption. The story opens with a perfect state of *yin*. Faust is perfect in Knowledge, Job is perfect in goodness and prosperity, Adam and Eve are perfect in innocence. The Virgins (Gretchen, etc.) are perfect in purity and beauty. In the astrologer's universe the sun is the perfect orb, and the *yin* state is complete in its peace before it is ready to pass into a *yang* state.

Into this perfect *yin* state some factor is intrusive, the Serpent in Genesis, Satan in the Book of Job, Mephistopheles in Faust, Loki in Scandinavian mythology, the divine lovers in the virgin myths. Some factor intrudes, serving as a stimulus of a kind best calculated to evoke potent creative variations.

When a civilization arising as the successful response to a challenge begins to lose its creative force, a differentiation occurs. The ailing civilization disintegrates into a dominant minority, which rules with increasing oppressiveness but no longer leads, and a proletariat (internal and external) which responds to this challenge by becoming conscious that it has a soul of its own and by making up its mind to save its soul alive. A conflict between these two wills continues, while the declining civilization verges toward its fall until, when it is *in articulo mortis*, the proletariat at length breaks free from what was once its spiritual home but has now become a prison-house and finally a "city of destruction." When this occurs the result is the genesis of an affiliated civilization.

When society has suffered its breakdown and the "creative minority" has ceased to be creative, becoming merely "dominant," a creator is called upon to play the part of a conqueror who replies to a challenge with a victorious response; in a disintegrating civilization, he is called upon to play the part of a savior. "The savior-archaist will try to reconstruct an imaginary past; the savior-futurist will attempt a leap into an imagined future. The savior who points the way to detachment will present himself as a philosopher taking cover behind the mask of a king; the savior who points the way to transfiguration will appear as a god incarnate in a man."[26]

Pitirim Sorokin. The most brilliant recent sociological exponent of a purified organicism was

[26]*Ibid.,* p. 534.

PITIRIM SOROKIN

Courtesy of L. P. Sorokin

professor of sociology at Harvard, where he continued to develop the sociological theory which will be our concern here.[27]

The core of original theory around which Sorokin's work is constructed consists of a form of idealistic organicism, and is most systematically expressed in *Social and Cultural Dynamics* (1937–1941) and *Society, Culture, and Personality* (1947). For him, the basic facts of sociology are "mentalistic in nature" and can only be understood in terms of "man's sociocultural universe as a whole."[28] This is true not only for "a minor phenomenon such as suicide," but for the cause of crime, revolution, war, and practically all sociocultural phenomena. Sorokin takes his stand on a platform of superorganic mentalistic wholes.

One of the surest indications of the serious critique of positivism that is intended by Sorokin is the relativization of truth as ordinarily understood. There are at least three distinct systems of

Pitirim A. Sorokin (1889–1968). He was born in a village of northeastern Russia, studied at the University of St. Petersburg, and had entered upon a career of teaching and research at the time of the outbreak of the Revolution. By 1914 he had published a major monograph on crime and punishment, and a system of sociology by 1919. He served as secretary to Alexander Kerensky in 1917, and was later arrested by the Communists, sentenced to death, but had the sentence commuted to exile. At the University of Minnesota, where he came after two years in Czechoslovakia, he completed *Social Mobility* (1927), which was long the undisputed major work in this field, and *Contemporary Sociological Theories* (1928), perhaps the finest single systematic study of sociological theory that America has produced. In 1930, he became

[27]Sorokin's two Russian works referred to above are not available in English translation: *Prestuplenie i kara, podvig i nagrada* ["Crime and Punishment, Meritorious Deeds and Rewards"] (St. Petersburg: 1914) and *Sistema sotsiologii* ["System of Sociology"] (Petrograd: 1920). Sorokin's principal writings in English are: *Social Mobility* (New York: Harper, 1927); *Contemporary Sociological Theories* (New York: Harper, 1928); *Social and Cultural Dynamics*, 4 vols. (New York: American Book Company, 1937–1941); *Sociocultural Causality, Space, Time* (Durham, N.C.: Duke University Press, 1943); *Society, Culture, and Personality* (New York: Harper, 1947); *Social Philosophies in an Age of Crisis* (Boston: Beacon Press, 1950); and *Fads and Foibles in Modern Sociology* (Chicago: Henry Regnery, 1956). This is only a small sampling of Sorokin's writing. In addition to many scientific papers Sorokin published more than thirty substantial volumes. Most have been translated into many languages. For example, *Contemporary Sociological Theories* was translated into eleven major languages, and *The Crisis of Our Age* into eight. At the time of his death there were forty-two translations of Sorokin's published works. There have been many reviews of Sorokin's work; particularly interesting is Philip J. Allen, ed., *Pitirim A. Sorokin in Review* (Durham, N.C.: Duke University Press, 1963). For Sorokin's own appraisal of his career his last autobiographical account is best, *A Long Journey* (New Haven, Conn.: College and University Press, 1963).

[28]Sorokin, *Society, Culture, and Personality*, p. 5.

truth, cognition, and knowledge.[29] *Ideational* truth is revealed by the grace of God through his prophets or oracles. It is absolutistic, nonutilitarian, and nonpragmatic. *Idealistic* truth represents a synthesis of sensory and supersensory forms. The role of the sense organs in verifying sensory truth is recognized, but supersensory truth coming from God is also accepted. *Sensate* truth finds the only true value to be sensory, and cognition is derived only through the sense organs. It denies supersensory reality altogether. It favors the study of the sensory world in its physical, chemical, and biological relations.

In *Social and Cultural Dynamics*, where these topics were treated extensively, Sorokin made a case for the existence of a kind of truth rising above and replacing all of these. He urged that each of the three main systems of truth and reality may be either entirely true, entirely false, or partly true or false. For this reason, the only adequate system of truth will embrace all three. Furthermore, one must recognize that the truths of intuition are the most profound of all. "All great religions explicitly declare that they are the *corpus* of the revealed, super-rational, superempirical, supersensory truth granted by grace of the Absolute to charismatically gifted persons — prophets, saints, mystics, oracles. . . . The experience of these instruments is always super-rational or mystic."[30]

Integral truth is not identical with any of the three forms of truth, but embraces all of them. In this three-dimensional aspect of the truth — of faith, of reason, and of the senses — the integral truth is nearer to the absolute truth than any one-sided truth of one of these three forms. "The empirico-sensory aspect of it is given by the truth of the senses; the rational aspect, by the truth of reason; the super-rational aspect by the truth of faith."[31] Thus it seems that Sorokin has not moved into the circle of positivism after all. He is, by his own admission, extraordinarily close to the Absolute.

Sorokin's particular type of organicism is most evident in his conception of the great supersystems. These are all said to be products of intuition, the initiator of all original conceptions in religion, ethics, philosophy, aesthetics, and even mathematical logic and scientific thought. No group, however, is encyclopedically creative. The central achievement of Greece was in the fine arts and philosophy, that of Rome in the creation of a political empire, a military system, and a system of law; the Hebrews in religion, ethics, and literature; medieval society expressed its creativity in organization and the development of Christianity; the Western World is creative in science, technology, philosophy, and the fine arts. It is precisely at this point that Sorokin both identifies his thought with — and distinguishes it from — that of Danilevsky, Spengler, Toynbee, and F. S. Northrop. They claim a great culture is creative in only one field. Sorokin sees them creative not in all but a few.[32]

A new system of meanings takes form first as a mere mental conception. "It must first somehow be objectified through vehicles and then socialized through becoming known to other human beings. If the conception of an ideological system may be compared to the conception of an organism, its objectification may be likened to the birth of an organism."[33] Some of the systems so invented and for which vehicles are found and socialization secured grow into great supersystems. If a petty system possesses three characteristics, it may evolve into a great system: (1) it must contain the potentialities of unfolding into a vast system, meaningfully and practically important; (2) as a minor ideological system, it must correspond to some genuine *need on the part of a given population;* and, finally, (3) to be durable, a minor system must be related to some *"perennial reality and value."* In order for a system to grow, ideas must be developed as they are exchanged in meaningful interaction; quantitative and qualitative accumulation of meanings, vehicles, and processes must

[29]*Ibid.*, p. 607 f.
[30]Sorokin, *Social and Cultural Dynamics*, IV, 758.
[31]*Ibid.*, pp. 762–763.

[32]Sorokin, *Society, Culture, and Personality*, p. 548.
[33]*Ibid.*, p. 555.

occur; there must be attacks by other ideological systems and survival of the given one; there must be cross-fertilization and merging of congenial minor systems; and, while unfolding under attacks and becoming more generalized and spontaneous, the great systems must be stimulated by good luck and incidental genius.

Some great supersystems have emerged that have integrated the vast majority of cultural elements of a time. These most vast of all supersystems are based upon the most "general of all the ontological principles, namely, *the one defining the ultimate nature of reality and value*. Ontologically there are no more all-embracing concepts than the three following definitions of the ultimate nature of reality and value: (a) true reality and true value are sensory — the major premise of the sensate supersystems. (b) True reality and value consist in a supersensory, super-rational God, Brahman, Atman, Tao, or its equivalent — the major premise of the ideational supersystem. (c) True reality and value are an infinite manifold, partly supersensory and super-rational, partly rational, and partly sensory — the premise of the idealistic supersystem."[34]

Around one of these three central definitions of reality and conception of value, in true organismic fashion, all or most of the other phenomena of culture are arranged: religion, arts, the state, politics, philosophy, criticism — in fact, all the aspects of human society and culture. Moreover, again like organisms, a supersystem may decline. This may occur chiefly quantitatively without loss of quality, it may occur qualitatively and not, at first, quantitatively, it may decline in both respects simultaneously, and it may become petrified. The three great supersystems have tended to alternate successively between sensate and ideational forms. The idealistic supersystem is conceived of as an intermediate type.

Unquestionably Sorokin's four-volume *Social and Cultural Dynamics* remains his *magnum opus*. He was aided in this work by a grant from the Harvard Committee for Research in the Social Sciences of $10,000 which he used to employ foreign, particularly Russian, specialists in the history of painting, sculpture, architecture, music, literature, science, philosophy, economics, religion, ethics, law, wars, and revolutions who systematically compiled quantitative data which Sorokin organized in tables in support of his hypotheses. While few directors of research projects ever used funds more economically and obtained so much for them, it is also true that Sorokin managed to give some sort of academic support and supply an invaluable base for able foreign scholars who were then able to make their way in American academic circles.[35] However, at the very time Sorokin was bringing his major life work to a conclusion, rather uncomfortable developments were in the making which Sorokin met with characteristic adaptability and luck.

In 1941 Sorokin was 52 years old and since 1929 had chaired a department he had built into one of the strongest in the country. It was inevitable that able younger scholars would cast envious eyes at his throne. Meanwhile, Talcott Parsons, his younger colleague, at the age of 39 had established a reputation as a translator of Max Weber and with *The Structure of Social Action* had won a reputation as a major theorist in his own right. Parsons, who viewed himself as Sorokin's heir apparent, did not leave matters to chance but teamed up with dissidents in other social science departments to place pressure on older members of their departments.

Sorokin resigned from his position at Harvard. The sociology department was merged with abnormal and social psychology and cultural anthropology to form the Department of Social Relations in 1942 under the direction of Parsons. Hence, at the very height of his reputation and scholarship and simultaneously with the completion of his greatest work, Sorokin found himself isolated and powerless. Meanwhile, Talcott Parsons became secretary of the American Sociological Association, from which position he managed

[34]*Ibid.*, p. 590.

[35]Pitirim Sorokin, *A Long Journey* (New Haven, Conn.: College and University Press, 1963, p. 245.

for many years to prevent Sorokin from being nominated for the presidency of the society.[36]

From 1942 to 1946 Sorokin was engaged in various projects that were a natural outgrowth of *Social and Cultural Dynamics*. In 1946, about the time he was beginning to grow restive under the limitations that resulted from the power move by his colleagues, Sorokin received the unsolicited offer of $20,000 from Eli Lilly, head of the biggest drug corporation in America and president of the Lilly Endowment, to assist him in his researches in the moral and mental regeneration of contemporary humanity. In his autobiography Sorokin represented Lilly's support as providential.

> Throughout my life I have often experienced this sort of "luck" from unanticipated sources in the moments of my urgent, sometimes even desperate need. In this sense I can repeat Gandhi's remark: "When every hope is gone I find that help arrives somehow, from I know not where."[37]

At a time when most scholars' careers are over Sorokin launched upon major researches in altruistic and creative love. His career was to follow the pattern of the founder of sociology, August Comte, whose intellectual endeavors, too, divide into a theoretical and practical phase. Though well aware of the cynicism of his sophisticated colleagues about his "foolish research project," Sorokin was quite undismayed.

> While many a modern sociologist and psychologist viewed the phenomena of hatred, crime, war, and mental disorders as legitimate objects for scientific study, they quite illogically stigmatized as theological preaching or non-scientific speculation any investigation of the phenomena of love, friendship, heroic deeds, and creative genius. This patently unscientific position of many of my colleagues is merely a manifestation of the prevalent concentration on the nega-

tive, pathological, and subhuman phenomena typical of the disintegrating phase of our sensate culture.[38]

He set to work with a will, finished a volume on *Reconstruction of Humanity* by 1948 and so impressed Lilly that the philanthropist advanced another hundred thousand dollars to be paid at the rate of twenty-thousand a year for the next five years to continue the work. The Harvard Research Center in Creative Altruism was founded in 1949 and supported by the Lilly endowment for the next ten years, whereupon an additional twenty-five thousand was advanced to finance continued work and publication of the Proceedings of the First International Congress for Comparative Study of Civilization at Salzburg in 1961, of which Sorokin was president.[39]

Just as Comte's work on the reconstruction of humanity resulted in a loss of the support of many of his more scientific-minded colleagues, so, too, did Sorokin's work in his Center in Creative Altruism. But Sorokin, like Comte, gained a new, wider, and more popular audience. Eventually in the 1960s a campaign was launched among the lay members of the American Sociological Association to force the officials of the society to place his name on the presidency ballot. When this succeeded, Sorokin was elected by a large majority. Moreover, in the 1960s Sorokin turned his attention once more to the general field of sociological theory which he had not touched since his classic text in

---

[36]George Vold, who was on the nominating committee of the association, reported that on at least one occasion, Parsons took the floor to passionately oppose the proposal to place Sorokin's name on the ballot.

[37]Sorokin, *A Long Journey*, p. 277.

[38]*Ibid.*, p. 277.

[39]Among major works produced in the course of this project were Sorokin's *Reconstruction of Humanity* (Boston: Beacon Press, 1948); *Altruistic Love: A Study of American Good Neighbors and Christian Saints* (Boston: Beacon Press, 1950); *Social Philosophies in an Age of Crisis* (Boston: Beacon Press, 1950); *Explorations in Altruistic Love and Behavior* (symposium) (Boston: Beacon Press, 1950); *S.O.S.: The Meaning of Our Crisis* (Boston: Beacon Press, 1951); *The Ways of Power and Love* (Boston: Beacon Press, 1954); *Forms and Techniques of Altruistic and Spiritual Growth* (symposium) (Boston: Beacon Press, 1954); *The American Sex Revolution* (Boston: Porter Sargent, 1957); *Power and Morality*, with Walter A. Lunden (Boston: Porter Sargent, 1959).

1928. The result was *Sociological Theories of Today*[40] in which he scrapped the classifications presented in his earlier work, substituting in their place a classification based on the distinction between holistic (which he calls systemic) and elementaristic (which he calls nominalistic-singularistic) theories.

In the last phase of his work in the 1960s Sorokin was experimenting with the ideas that American and Soviet societies were beginning to show convergent features and that his own theories of society, which he described as *integralism,* represented a new and higher synthesis than any of the three supersystems (sensate, idealistic, and ideate). Sorokin was, in short, beginning to move back somewhat closer to the classical synthesis of organicism, but he did not get around to accepting either its positivism or its doctrine of progress. Nevertheless, it is not unfair to characterize him as the last of the great pioneers of sociology.

THE SEPARATION OF POSITIVISM FROM ORGANICISM

As the examples of Spengler, Toynbee, and Sorokin indicate, once the formula of organismic-positivism disintegrated, organicism was free to go its way unhindered. One inevitable result was that organicism turned upon positivism itself. Spengler launched a frontal attack on science. Toynbee introduced alongside the ordinary methods of scholarship the methods of intuitive mythology as more appropriate to the cultural historian. Sorokin relativized truth in its ordinary sense, turning it into an ideology and setting up a new system of truth, integral truth, beyond all others.

But this is only one possibility flowing from the divorce. Positivism was free to go its own way as well. The result was, eventually, the development of an active movement known as "technocracy." It sought to synthesize the principles found in the writings of various engineers, economists, and students of science. The basic arguments of the technocrats centered in the conception that social phenomena are measurable and hence laws of social control can be deduced from these measurements. It was argued, with principles drawn from Veblen, that the phenomenon of machine production has made it impossible any longer to measure values in terms of a single commodity like gold. The engineers have destroyed the price system. The expansion of credit under the capitalistic system was said to have so disturbed the relative claims of capital and labor that capitalism had in fact already collapsed. Finally, the economic processes of the social order are too complex to be understood and controlled by politicians. The engineers and scientists are the only legitimate agents of control in modern society. In its milder and more methodological forms, the development appears as "operationalism," but whenever its social claims are developed in unimpeded fashion, it inclines toward technocracy.

Outstanding American representatives of this development in recent sociology were Stuart S. Dodd, William Catton, Jr., and George A. Lundberg. Dodd's *Dimensions of Society*[41] was neither a theory nor a method (which it claims to be) but a system of notation. It is of no interest here except as an example of the danger always facing pure positivism of degenerating into an empty formula.

George Lundberg. The able and influential positivist George A. Lundberg (1895–1966), was professor of sociology at the University of Washington for a number of years. The works embodying his position most fully are *Foundations of Sociology* and *Can Science Save Us?*[42]

The central category in Lundberg's theory is "adjustment." Sociology is conceived of as dealing with communicable techniques of adjustment de-

---

[40]Pitirim Sorokin, *Sociological Theories of Today* (New York: Harper & Row, 1966).

[41]Stuart S. Dodd, *Dimensions of Society* (New York: Macmillan, 1942).

[42]George Lundberg, *Foundations of Sociology* (New York: Macmillan, 1939); *Can Science Save Us?* (New York: Longmans, Green, 1947).

GEORGE LUNDBERG

Photograph by James O. Sneddon, Office of Public Information, University of Washington, Seattle. Courtesy of George Lundberg.

veloped by groups in relation to each other and their environment. Science itself is an adjustive technique and, as such, a subject of sociology. Adjustment represents the state of experience that terminates an imbalance or tension. It is a state of equilibrium. It is also the state of maximum probability in any organism or social situation. As such it is normal. When tensions are formulated verbally they take the form of a question. Scientific questions are hypotheses. A verified hypothesis is a "law" or equilibrium in thought — the mind in a state of rest.

Lundberg not only makes a concerted attempt to avoid the use of all terms such as "organic" or "spiritual" or "mental," but conceives the entire history of science as the expansion of the realms of the natural and physical at the expense of the mental and spiritual: "One by one 'spiritual' phenomena have become 'physical'. . . . The evolution of the concept of the 'soul' is especially relevant, because its final state of transition or translation by way of the 'mind' into purely 'physical' concepts is still underway."[43] The aggressive anti-organicism expressed here is typical.

On the other hand, Lundberg advocates an extreme positivistic operationalism of method. The data of science are the experiences of organisms or responses of organisms to environment. Symbols are also such responses. They are the data of communicable knowledge and science. All propositions or postulates regarding more ultimate "realities" than these are inferences, generalizations, or abstractions from such symbols. Extrapolations are merely new symbols. Any other statements are unverifiable phenomena. As far as science is concerned, all that exists is words; science is words about words. At the same time, Lundberg makes one vast metaphysical postulate: namely, that whatever it is that evokes our words or precipitates our responses exists. Behind the phenomenal world is the world of things in themselves.

Since the ultimate subject matter for study in Lundberg's view is responses or at least the words designating them, these responses come into central focus. Meanings are responses to words. Such phenomena as *"divisions, categories, classifications,* and *groupings* of phenomena of the universe are *words representing* differential responses of man."[44] Frames of reference and universes of discourse are "merely comprehensive ways of responding to large configurations of data."

A technology of word manipulation is presented as the solution to the most crucial of all human problems:

Personal, community, and international relations constantly reflect the tensions resulting from an inadequate symbolic system of communication. Whole

[43]Lundberg, *Foundations of Sociology,* p. 8.
[44]*Ibid.,* p. 25.

nations frequently fall upon each other with great ferocity because of word-systems or ideologies through which they attribute to each other characteristics, "motives," and behaviors entirely fantastic and demonstrably devoid of foundation in fact. Untold nervous energy, time, and natural resources are wasted in warfare upon or protection against entirely imaginary monsters conjured up by words. Widespread mental disorders result from constantly finding the world different from the word-maps upon which we rely for guidance to adjustments. Social problems cannot be solved as long as they are stated in terms as primitive and unrealistic as those which attributed diseases to demons and witches.[45]

The problem of the international world is due to words.

Furthermore, the backward state of sociology is due to words. The development in science attributed to Galileo, Newton, Lobachevski, and Einstein is attributed to their use of better symbol systems. In sociology we need "the selection of significant behavior — segments and . . . their representation by symbols which lend themselves to operational representation of relationships."[46] In the new order so created, all questions such as what an attitude really is will disappear. Like all other facts, theory will disappear into the words that designate it. The attitude will be defined as the behavior evoked by the particular test. And all such concepts as *racial, liberal, happiness, social status, intelligence* will vanish or become equally clear. It will be increasingly recognized that all phenomena of scientific concern consist of energy transformations in the physical cosmos manifest as various forms of motion.[47] Sociology is concerned with "the behaviors of those electron-proton configurations called societal groups, principally human groups."[48] These operate on the basis of the conversion of energy into human behavior — a conversion which "takes place through the well known metabolic process of the combustion of fuel, in this case called food."[49]

If we will do all these things, most of our problems will clear up, for "as a result of scientific knowledge, men will not want impossible or mutually exclusive things. They will not seek to increase foreign trade and at the same time establish more comprehensive and higher tariffs. They will not seek to reduce crime but at the same time maintain a crime-promoting penal system. They will not destroy the productive power of a nation and still expect it to be peaceful, prosperous, and democratic."[50]

All this and much more will be produced by a coherent system of symbols operationally defined. A coherent and consistent system of symbols

is important not only to science but also from the standpoint of mental health and practical social administration. A very large proportion of the population . . . are . . . carrying on a major part of their lives in an impersonal machine culture to which they adjust according to the assumptions and rules (word-systems) of science. Another important part of their lives (linguistic and otherwise), having to do with their social adjustments, is carried on according to vitalistic, animistic, primary-group assumptions . . . of a bygone age. . . . Our schizoid societal behavior resides largely . . . in the inadequate and inconsistent symbolic systems according to which we attempt to steer our course.[51]

Let no one say that Lundberg was a peddler of gloom who left humanity without hope. An equivalent amount of word magic has not been found in Anglo-Saxon countries since Merlin the Magician was active in King Arthur's courts. This, it must be noted, had nothing to do with Lundberg personally, but was a property of the popular semantics which he attempted to turn to sociological account. Sometimes the value of theorists for their time is the vigor with which they explore conceptual alternatives rather than the ultimate defensibility of

[45]*Ibid.*, p. 47.
[46]*Ibid.*, p. 58.
[47]*Ibid.*, p. 203.
[48]*Ibid.*, p. 204.

[49]*Ibid.*, p. 206.
[50]Lundberg, *Can Science Save Us?*, p. 29.
[51]Lundberg, *Foundations of Sociology*, pp. 76–77.

any one. Lundberg had one of the challenging minds of his generation. The forthrightness with which he has pursued a purified type of positivism forced a higher level of theoretical understanding upon his time.

SUMMARY

Positivistic organicism drew its original intellectual materials from two philosophic sources of profound significance in Western thought. Its organicism came originally from idealistic philosophy, which extends in an unbroken tradition back to classical Greece. Such idealistic philosophy tended to serve as an ideological bulwark to conservative sections of society. The other conceptual source was from empiricism, which had been evolving in the West since the seventeenth century. Empiricism increasingly carried out the naturalization first of knowledge, then of society, and paved the way for the demand for the fullest possible scientific analysis of society. It tended to become the philosophy of reform. One branch of it became the philosophy of the French Revolution. And in the opening days of the nineteenth century, it became a plank in the platform of scientific socialism.

Sociology arose in an atmosphere characterized by the conservative reaction to revolution. Sociology was supported by conservative groups. In fusing organicism to positivism, sociology proposed to convert the empiricist-positivistic tradition of the West to conservative ends. The early schools of sociology, as a result, have important ideological dimensions which were often only thinly disguised. Internally they found themselves faced with opposed principles which were difficult to reconcile. Even in the early days (as in the work of Ward), the formula of positivistic organicism tended to disintegrate.

The first major adaptation of positivistic organicism came with the rise to popularity of nineteenth-century biology. The new social science partly vindicated itself by assuming a bio-organismic form. This, however, did not persist for long. Meanwhile the possibilities of a concept formation in terms of the principles of positivistic organicisms were explored with unusual brilliance by Ferdinand Tönnies and Émile Durkheim. Many of the permanent gains for sociology made by its first theoretical form were due to them.

The second major adaptation of organicism came from the freeing of voluntaristic or irrational idealism from the strongly antiscientific bias it had assumed under the influence of Nietzsche and Schopenhauer. A voluntaristic positivism was explored by Pareto and in another way by Freud, the configurationists, and the neo-Freudians. The major additions to social theory by this form of positivism were due to the new perspectives on the emotional life of human beings developed by these schools.

The ideological atmosphere that sustained the fusion of organicism and positivism has passed away. The result has been the disintegration of the early theoretical formula. Under pure organicists such as Spengler, Toynbee, and Sorokin, organicism has been developed in an unrestricted manner, and radical modifications have been proposed for positivism. On the other hand, positivism, freed from the organismic context, has tended to transform itself into an antitheological, antispiritual, antiorganismic metaphysics of instruments. Its variations range from relatively mild operationalism to extreme forms of technocracy.

VII

The Foundations of Conflict Theory

The ideological requirements imposed on early sociology dictated that it be both scientific and conservative. Positivistic organicism was both. Its positivism pulled the teeth of anticonservative liberal and socialist programs, turning an instrument of reform into a weapon of defense. Meanwhile, the organic conception of society was almost foolproof. What should one add to a living whole? What organism needs two heads or a spare leg? What should one cut out of a living whole — its liver, or lungs, or stomach? Even change does not present any problems when it is identified with organic growth — artificially forced, reformist, or revolutionary change must give way before immanent change proceeding out of the inner nature of the social organism. To anyone concerned with issues in the present, there was counsel of patience. Ancient injustices often sustained important values: ancient theology nourished intellectuality, ancient excesses in leisure based on exploitation made independent thought possible, ancient war taught people discipline, even ancient slavery was a step in progress. By the same token, great good

must be contained in present injustices. When positivistic organicism was so brilliantly adjusted to the ideological atmosphere of nineteenth century, why was it ever given up?

It is unnecessary to remind the reader that sociology is not an ideology — a set of ideas defending a social position or promoting a program of social action. Sociology is a science — a set of ideas attempting to explain social life. Positivistic organicism was given up in part because it was seen to be ideological. Ideological factors may have a *causal* effect on inquiry, molding its direction and form. But the acceptability of a set of scientific ideas is determined by the application of the criteria of science.

By its very nature, science is a self-correcting enterprise. Hence, it did not matter, in one sense, where the science started. In the long run it was going to cast off its ideological moorings, for sociology is neither revolutionary nor reactionary, neither liberal nor conservative; it is a science — an objective enterprise in empirical knowledge. External requirements might incline sociology to fuse organicism and positivism; internal requirements, conformity to scientific and logical criteria, would determine the acceptability of the fusion.

The first result of the application of more exacting scientific standards to sociological propositions was a speed-up in the turnover of ideas. This only made matters worse, for no scientist needs to be told that if there are ten equally plausible explanations of a body of facts, any one is practically useless. The sure sign of a growing sense of crisis in sociology was an increased preoccupation with method. By the time of the classical stage of early organismic positivism, this preoccupation with method became increasingly apparent. Tönnies, for example, took his stand on the importance of "normal" concepts or "ideal types" for establishing sociological proofs. Durkheim devoted an entire book to the *Rules of Sociological Method*. Pareto addressed almost a quarter of his four-volume study of *The Mind and Society* to method. But anxiety was hardly confined to method. As the rival theories began to compete for acceptance, inadequacies in the content of early sociology were forced to attention.

WEAKNESSES OF POSITIVISTIC ORGANICISM

The most glaring of all content deficiencies in positivistic organicism was its apparent inability to handle the issues bound up with interhuman conflict. Comte feared social conflict so much that he dreamed of a castelike society organized in an authoritarian manner. So far as possible, Spencer assigned the major forms of social conflict to the militaristic societies of the past, predicting that the advance of industrial society would render war impossible. Tönnies located the more significant forms of conflict in the social type of which he most disapproved — the *Gesellschaft*. It is surprising even to find reference to conflict in Durkheim's work; when it occurs it is treated as a form of social sickness.

The one form of positivistic organicism that recognizes the role of conflict is the voluntaristic type. Pareto approves the forceful tactics of the conservative "lions" who do not hesitate to use the most ruthless means to keep themselves in power. Freud builds his picture of personality out of a tension between emotional and social life; he constructs his picture of the human being and culture in terms of further tensions and the dark inclinations of individuals as actors on the social stage. There is little doubt that part of the reason why voluntarism was introduced into positivistic theory was the attempt to account for conflict. But the evolution of voluntarism has tended — in the configurationists and neo-Freudians — to return to the more typical organismic model in which conflict has no place.

The failure to account for the facts of conflict turns up at every point. Positivistic organicism could hardly maintain its claims as a form of scientific theory in the face of this discrepancy. Every society has its conflicts. No society can survive without individuals who face up to them. In all societies some strata face conflicts more directly than others. Every society, for example, attempts to protect its young against conflict. One of the most universal meanings of "adulthood" or "maturity" is reception into the stratum of those who are expected to face up to the conflicts of the society in which they live. This is true even in our own society, where youth is protected from full admission to conflict situations, a fact that makes the act of growing up a "bitter pill." It is assumed that youth in its enthusiasm wishes to "make the world over." One of the paradoxes of maturity in our society is the forcing of the young into life situations with high ideals and no experience. By the time the young have acquired experience adequate for a realistic course of action, their ideals are often compromised. One sociologist has taken this fact to be the major clue to the understanding of the age differences in our society,[1] finding irresponsibility, the glamour pattern, and the cult of sports to be the result.

[1]Talcott Parsons, "Age and Sex in the Social Structure of the United States," in *Essays in Sociological Theory Pure and Applied*, 2d. ed. (Glencoe: Ill.: The Free Press. 1954).

In any case, once the idea was accepted that it was a legitimate objective to develop a social science to explain interhuman life, the most obvious difficulty of early sociology to the minds of mature students was its relatively complete failure to recognize and explain the facts of conflict. This also suggested a new grouping of the materials available in Western thought.

CONCEPTUAL SOURCES OF CONFLICT THEORY

If we adopt the notion that conflict and its resolution are a central fact of society, and search tradition for materials relevant to it, a great richness is available. Every society requires a minimum realism about its conflicts to survive. The analysis of society from the standpoint of its typical conflicts is neither new nor confined to the West. For objective "realism" Kautilya's *Arthashastra* has never been surpassed.[2] Han Fei Tzu in ancient China was the teacher of Li Ssû, the prime minister of Shih Huang Ti — the great dictator of the ancient state of Ch'n. He taught that the essence of society is power. People by themselves are cowardly and lazy. Fear of the law makes people good; fear of punishment puts them to work. In ruling the world one must act in accord with human nature, distributing rewards and punishments addressed to their likes and dislikes.

In classical Greece, Heraclitus (c. 544–484) of Ephesus, scion of a noble family with hereditary claims to the royal office of the sacrificial priest of the Eleusinian Demeter, was impressed by the instability of all things. He made conflict the law of the visible universe, conceiving everything as in process of transformation into its opposite. Strife is

the justice of the world, and war, which is common to all, is the father and king of all things. Heraclitus was not alone among the ancient Greeks to isolate conflict; the Sophists, who methodologically were strongly positivistic, also held conflict theories. Protagoras of Abdera (c. 481–411 B.C.) held a theory of knowledge resting on the Heraclitean doctrine of flux. Gorgias of Leontini (485?–?380 B.C.) recognized the manipulation of illusion as a means of controlling the minds of people. Callicles derived the concept of right from political strength, arguing that morals and law are the work of a majority of weak individuals who, through uniting, tame the natures of stronger individuals, who are like beasts of prey. Critias viewed the law as instruments for taming the beast in human beings, while religion operated through fear to keep them good. Thrasymachus of Chalcedon (c. 427 B.C.) argued that, nonsense aside, might makes right.

The conflict doctrines of the Sophists were transmitted on to Epicurus (342?–270 B.C.), who fused them with the conceptions of atomic structure of the atomists and the concept of eternal change of Heraclitus. Epicurus thought that in a wild state human beings were savage as beasts. The movement from savagery to civilization occurred in the course of the struggle with nature. The struggle with nature is followed by an interhuman struggle. The purpose of all laws is to secure society against injustice. The mass of people are deterred from harmful actions only by the fear of punishment.

Conflict Theories of Polybius. The fullest interpretation of society from the standpoint of conflict was advanced in antiquity by Polybius (c. 205–125 B.C.), the son of a statesman of the Achaean League and one of the thousand leading Achaeans who surrendered on demand of the Roman government in 167 B.C. and were interned in Italy as hostages for sixteen years. He imagined, like Plato, that a great catastrophe had destroyed all human communities, leaving only a few individuals. The impulse that causes impotent and defenseless animals to live in herds also works in

---

[2]Kautilya is identified by many scholars with Chanakya, the Brahman minister of the Maurya emperor Chandragupta, who reigned from about 321 to 296 B.C. The *Arthashastra*, long lost but recovered in 1909, deals with the art of government, including civil law and the science of warfare. Kautilya, *Arthashastra*, trans. R. Shamasastry (Mysore: Wesleyan Mission Press, 1923).

human beings, whose weakness leads them to form into communities with the strongest and bravest individuals as leaders. *Monarchy*, the rule of the strongest, is the first form of the human community. The virtue of this theory of the state, according to Polybius, is its concentration on essentials: power relations. The second step in the formation of society is the transition from the monarchy, which is based on force, to *kingship*, which is based on justice and legitimate authority. Kingship arises out of the sense of obligation on the part of the strong to keep the peace. This is the origin of the sentiment of justice, enforced on recalcitrant and unjust members, and sustained by the majority, who out of gratitude retain the ruler even when he grows old and fails in physical strength.

However, the descendants of the king often become haughty and overbearing, forgetting the need to sustain justice. The kingship turns into a *tyranny*. When the tyranny becomes unendurable, the most high-minded and noble of the subjects conspire to overthrow the monarchy, and they are supported by the people. But, alas, the *aristocracy* in turn becomes hereditary, forgets its lessons, loses its sense of mission, and gets to be unendurable. The *democracy* that replaces it will also work for a time. But people become used to liberty and equality; individuals and groups begin to conspire for influence. Demagogues appear, paying people out of their own pockets. It is time for the government to revert to a monarchy to restore law and order. The only way of bringing this cycle to an end is developing a kind of government combining the best elements of kingship, aristocracy, and democracy. Such a mixed constitution was designed by Lycurgus of Sparta. Such a one grew up gradually in Rome, where the consuls represented kingship, the senate aristocracy, and the people democracy. The state thus arises out of anarchy by the imposition of power which is stabilized by being made legitimate.[3]

Polybius has rather special importance among the early conflict theorists both because he collected so many of the previous ideas into his own theories and because he in turn transmitted his ideas to others. The later Epicurean school among the Romans added Polybius' doctrines to their own. Lucretius and Horace maintained that all things originate in conflict, and Livy sang the praises of Roman expansion, taking conflict as critical in the process of absorbing smaller states and, through the centralization of power, bringing the blessings of peace.

After the fall of Rome, conflict theories went into eclipse in the West, for the theologians of the medieval world found them inconsistent with their ideas. The one place where the conflict theory of society and the state continued to receive expression was in the Arab world.

Conflict Theories of Ibn Khaldun. Abu Zaid 'Abd-al-Rahman Ibn Khaldun was born in Tunis in 1332 of a family originating from Hadramaut of the agricultural region of southern Arabia. His family had played a leading part in the civil wars of the ninth century and members of the family for four centuries had occupied leading positions in the administration and army. Ibn Khaldun had much political experience in Spain and North Africa, serving in a variety of capacities, eventually as Chief Justice of the Malikite rite. He died in 1406 at the age of 74.

Ibn Khaldun has special interest to sociologists, for he was brought to the attention of the modern world by Ludwig Gumplowicz and treated with great respect by Franz Oppenheimer. Some per-

---

[3]For an outline of ancient Chinese conflict theory, see Fêng Yu-Lan, *A Short History of Chinese Philosophy*, ed. Derk Bodde (New York: Macmillan, 1948). The conflict doctrines in classical Greece are expounded in Milton C.

Nahm, *Selections from Early Greek Philosophy* (New York: F. S. Crofts, 1934); Eduard Zeller, *Outlines of the History of Greek Philosophy*, 13th ed., rev. by Wilhelm Nestle and trans. by L. R. Palmer (New York: Meridian Books, 1955); and J. B. Bury, *Ancient Greek Historians* (New York: Macmillan, 1909; Dover Publications, 1958), Chapter 6. For an analysis of Polybius, see Kurt von Fritz, *The Theory of Mixed Constitutions in Antiquity: A Critical Analysis of Polybius' Political Ideas* (New York: Columbia University Press, 1954).

sons have viewed him as the first true sociologist. Khaldun believed that social phenomena obey laws like those found in natural phenomena. He believed that they operate on masses and cannot be significantly modified by isolated individuals, maintaining, for example, that a reformer trying to rejuvenate a corrupt state will hardly achieve any success, for powerful social forces are against it. He thought that social laws can only be discovered by gathering a large number of facts and observing comparable cases. Both past and present events can supply such facts. Social laws operate the same way in the same kinds of structure. For example, the laws of nomadic behavior apply to Arabic Bedouins, Berbers, Turkomans, and Kurds indifferently. Moreover, societies change and evolve under contact of people or classes as a result of imitations and intermixtures.[4]

The core of Ibn Khaldun's sociology is found in his concept of "social solidarity" (*asabiyya*), the distinctive property of society. Human society originates out of necessity. Each individual in nature by himself or herself is hardly able to stay alive "unless he join with his fellow men, for he cannot, unaided, make the many tools needed. . . . Cooperation, however, secures both food and weapons, thus fulfilling God's will of preserving the species."[5] Ibn Khaldun was certain that no sooner do people band together and solve the problems of nature than

there arises the need of a restraining force to keep men off each other in view of their animal propensities for aggressiveness and oppression of others. Now the weapons with which they defend themselves against wild beasts cannot serve as a restraint, seeing that each man can make equal use of them. Nor can the restraint come from other than men, seeing that animals fall far short of men in their mental capacity. The restraint must therefore be constituted by one man, who wields power and authority with a firm hand and thus prevents anyone from attacking anyone else, *i.e.*, by a sovereign. Sovereignty is therefore peculiar to man, suited to his nature and indispensable to his existence. . . . The state is . . . to society as form is to matter, for the form by its nature preserves the matter and, as the philosophers have shown, the two are inseparable.[6]

The state and society emerge together as form and substance of the same thing. The really important phenomenon is *solidarity*, which is traced to its origins in kinship and blood ties, uniting smaller societies. But such blood ties mean nothing unless accompanied by neighborly contact and common life. These mutual interactions generate a solidarity as powerful as kinship. The relations between aliens, clients, patrons, slaves, and masters may all lead to wider solidarity. Social solidarity is strongest in tribal society, because of the nature of nomadic life. Nomads constantly require mutual assistance. Because the poverty of the desert frees them from ties to the land, to them all countries are equally good. They are more upright and self-reliant as a result of their way of life. One consequence of this is numerous conquests of populated empires by the smaller, more solidary tribes.

A state can be established only by conflict in which victory goes to the more cohesive and compact group. Similarly, a new religion can establish itself only by strife, but it will succeed only if it enlists the help of a powerful social solidarity. Once established, a religion can reinforce social solidar-

[4]The references to Ibn Khaldun's works here are from the translation by Charles Issawi, *An Arab Philosophy of History* (London: John Murray, 1950). An earlier edition of his writings is the translation by Duncan B. Macdonald, *A Selection from the Prolegomena of Ibn Khaldun* (Leiden: E. J. Brill, 1905). An American edition of his works, trans. Franz Rosenthal, is *The Muqaddimah: An Introduction to History*, 3 vols. (New York: Pantheon Books, 1958). See also Muhsin Mahdi, *Ibn Khaldûn's Philosophy of History* (London: George Allen and Unwin, 1957 and Chicago: University of Chicago Press, 1964); Walter J. Fischel, *Ibn Khaldun in Egypt: His Public Functions and His Historical Research (1382–1406): An Essay in Islamic Historiography* (Berkeley: University of California Press, 1967). A compact review is Muhsin Mahdi, "Ibn Khaldun" *International Encyclopedia of the Social Sciences* (New York: Crowell Collier and Macmillan, 1968) VII, 53–57.
[5]Khaldun, *An Arab Philosophy of History*, p. 100.

[6]*Ibid.*, p. 101.

ity, even replacing the cohesiveness of the tribe by centering emotion and thought in a common purpose. Religion is the most powerful cohesive force in a large sedentary people. The sweeping conquest of the Muslim Arabs in the seventh century was made possible by the fusion of tribal and religious solidarity. Tribal solidarity can solidify or weaken empires. It is easy to rule Egypt with its large sedentary population; it is almost impossible to rule Morocco because of the plurality of its tribes.

There must be some original basis of solidarity for a state to arise in the first place; but once established, its solidarity decreases. The presence of unquestioned authority leads to acquiescence and obedience by the subjects. In the early stages the state is cohesive; in time, change and decay set in. Sedentary life and luxurious living take their toll. Power is then concentrated in the hands of the rulers. A division and estrangement occur between ruler and subject. Growing luxury leads to heavier taxes. The state is ready for a change, and soon falls prey to internal or external aggression.

Machiavelli's Conflict Theory. However impressive the writings of Ibn Khaldun, they had no effect on Western European thought before the nineteenth century. When conflict as the key to the interpretation of social and political events was picked up again in the West after Roman times, it was in connection with work of French jurists and the Italian Niccolò Machiavelli (1469–1527), the son of a Florentine jurist. Machiavelli had served as a clerk at the time of the expulsion of the Medici in 1494, and in 1498 he became second chancellor of the republic, remaining in the post for fourteen years. He headed the correspondence bureau, went on diplomatic missions, and organized the Florentine militia. When the Medici returned to power in 1512, Machiavelli was first imprisoned, then exiled. He spent the rest of his life writing.[7]

His best-known work, *The Prince*, and his more profound *Discourses on the First Ten Books of Livy* were written from quite different points of view. The first is a handbook for dictators and the second the thoughtful statement of an Italian patriot dreaming of the unity of Italy. However, the theories of human nature and the state that inform them are the same. Human nature is basically evil. "Men are bad and ever ready to display their vicious nature, whenever they may find occasion for it."[8] In *The Prince*, this is interpreted to mean that the desire for conquest is most natural among human beings. They are good only when they are constrained. If the evil disposition is concealed for a time, it must be due to unknown reasons, and "we must assume that it lacked occasion to show itself." It is observed that "poverty and hunger make men industrious, and law makes men good."

Initially human beings were few in number, living dispersed like beasts. When the human race increased, people came into contact and the need for defense against one another was felt. By necessity, they "chose the strongest and most courageous from amongst themselves and placed him at their head, promising to obey him. Thence they began to know the good and the honest, and to distinguish them from the bad and vicious."[9] Machiavelli traces justice to the same source as Polybius — the attempt to constrain those who do injury to others. There is no difficulty so long as princes are wise and just. However, once sovereignty becomes nonelective, there is no guarantee against inferior stock. Excessive luxury in a prince is an occasion for envy of others. This leads to conspiracy. The fear this generates in the prince turns him into a tyrant. The rise of the conspirators against the tyrant establishes an aristocracy. It in turn is corrupted and replaced by de-

---

[7]Many editions are available in English of the two works of Machiavelli's with which we are chiefly concerned — *Il Principe* and *Discorsi sopra la prima deca di Tito Livio.* References here are to Luigi Ricci's translation "The Prince"

and Christian E. Detmold's translation "Discourses on the First Ten Books of Titus Livius"; both appear in a single volume: Niccolò Machiavelli, *The Prince and the Discourses,* ed. Max Lerner (New York: Modern Library, 1948).

[8]Machiavelli, *The Prince and the Discourses*, p. 117.

[9]*Ibid.*, p. 112.

mocracy, which in turn moves step by step toward anarchy, hurrying the day for a new dictatorship.

Machiavelli was not a systematic theorist, yet a clear plan was present in both *The Prince* and the *Discourses*. In the former work he brought under review all those properties of the political landscape which seemed to him to be either conditions or instruments of political activity. In the *Discourses*, these same properties assume a more general meaning, becoming the component forces, as he saw them, of political society. Among the forces at work on the state he discovers tradition, religion, popular ideology, social classes (at least the nobles and people), military institutions, and the person of the dictator. Machiavelli agrees with Polybius not only in viewing the state as a kind of equilibrium of forces, but also in his idea of a balance of forces as the source of a stable and durable state. Very probably he thought a unified state could be established only by the aggressive action of a dictator. However, only when the various forces are given recognition and the interests of prince, nobles, and people are all realized, will liberty be maximized.

Conflict Theories of Bodin.

Jean Bodin (1530–1596), the most powerful social and political writer in sixteenth-century France, and thought by many to be the most significant of the century, contributed much to the conflict theory of society and the state. Little is known of his family. It is thought that his father was a French lawyer, his mother a Spanish Jew. He knew Hebrew and was familiar with Jewish writing on the Old Testament. Trained for the law, he taught for twelve years at the University of Toulouse. He settled in Paris as an advocate, and later (1576) he was elected to the States-General at Blois. He also occupied the post of magistrate at Laon. His first book, *Method for the Easy Comprehension of History* (1566), dealt with problems of politics in general and with the foundation of the French constitution. Here he sought a means of studying history that would at the same time constitute a method of analyzing society. His solution was a theory of historical stages. In his next work, he turned to the study of the economic

conditions of France, *The Response of Jean Bodin to the Paradoxes of Malestroit* (1568). His great work, the *Six Books of the Commonwealth* appeared in 1576. His strange *De la Démonomanie des sorciers* ["On the Demonomania of Sorcerers"] was written in 1580 to defend magic and witchcraft against skeptics and to provide a practical manual for magistrates; Bodin was convinced that human beings live constantly under the influence of spiritual beings who work good and evil.[10]

At the time Bodin wrote, the French monarchy was weakened by the religious conflict between Catholic and Huguenot. Bodin supported the monarchy against such religious factions. The basis of society, he believed, lies in the family, founded on the inevitable association of man and woman and involving children, property, and rightful authority. Man is naturally the ruler of woman, because of woman's moral and intellectual inferiority. It would be a disaster to emancipate her. The family is the first and only "natural" form of society. The state is an association of families recognizing "sovereign power."

The formation of civil societies precedes the formation of the state. Families group around ad-

[10]The standard edition of Bodin's works is: Jean Bodin, *Œuvres philosophiques* (Paris: Presses Universitaires de France, 1951). The *Methodus ad facilem historiarum cognitionem* was translated by Beatrice Reynolds as *Method for the Easy Comprehension of History* (New York: Columbia University Press, 1945). An edition of *La Response de Jean Bodin aux paradoxes de M. de Malestroit* is the translation by George Albert Moore, *The Response of Jean Bodin to the Paradoxes of Malestroit* (Chevy Chase, Md.: The Country Dollar Press, 1946). *Les Six livres de la république* is available in an abridged translation by M. J. Tooley as *Six Books of the Commonwealth* (Oxford: B. Blackwell, 1955, reprinted 1967). There appears to be no available English translation of *De la Démonomanie des sorciers*. An excellent account of Bodin's work may be found in J. W. Allen, *A History of Political Thought in the Sixteenth Century*, 2d. ed. (London: Methuen, 1941). For recent evaluations of Bodin see: Julian H. Franklin, *Jean Bodin and the Sixteenth-Century Revolution in the Methodology of Law and History* (New York: Columbia University Press, 1963) and *Jean Bodin and the Rise of Absolutist Theory* (Cambridge: University Press, 1973); Preston T. King, *The Ideology of Order: A Comparative Analysis of Jean Bodin and Thomas Hobbes* (London: Allen & Unwin, 1974).

vantageous sites, being drawn to trade and cooperation for defense and common worship. A union follows among the loose associations, in which war and conquest play a part.

While the family precedes any form of complex social structure, the state arises from conquest. Many social phenomena, such as class distinctions, can ultimately be traced to the superiority–subordination relation of conquerors and conquered. A stable social structure consists in a process of continuing dissolution and reorganization in which conflict plays a part. The lack of conflict is fatal, as is evident in agriculturalists who lack fighting vigor. Discipline which is imposed by scanty natural resources is advantageous. Bodin also observes the trading cities are often located so as to be safe from attack; city dwellers are more adaptable than isolated peoples.

At the core of Bodin's thought there always appears the conception of *sovereign power* as the essence of civil society. Sovereignty, however, is never clearly separated by Bodin from legal prerogatives. Law is treated as the command of the sovereign. Customary law is valid only so long as sanctioned by the sovereign. Sovereignty has unlimited authority to make law.

Bodin was modern in far more ways than his anticipation of the contemporary problem of sovereignty. He broadened the trend already present in Machiavelli toward an empirical method. He attempted the systematic and critical use of historical materials. He proposed the systematic comparative study of law. He takes as accepted that a law of nature conditions all human relations and he does not identify such a law with the law common to all nations (*ius gentium*). Furthermore, in the course of reviewing historical materials he advanced many ideas necessary to a general sociology: he thought that every association of people involves subjection of some members to others; he conceived of humankind as organized in a series of associations from the family to the state; he thought nobility was a significant social and political institution; he believed that an individual's occupation is important for determining position in society and the state; he distinguished two types of

state — the commonwealth and the city; he wished to keep property inviolate against unjust seizure by political power; he formulated theories about the relation of law and custom; he conceived revolutions as changes in the location of authority.

Hobbes's Conflict Theory.   Bodin, in some respects, is more modern in spirit than his greater successor in conflict theory, Thomas Hobbes (1588–1679), who did his work in the face of conditions very similar to those that faced Bodin sixty years earlier. *De Cive* was written in 1642, *Leviathan* in 1651.[11] The English Puritans were as opposed to English tyranny as the Huguenots were to the French. Hobbes's political treatises were published in exile. In Paris he lived in close relation to the royalist colony and was identified, like Bodin, with the royalist cause in times of civil dissension. On the other hand, whereas Bodin borrowed much from other authors and from historical and contemporary events and arrived at inconsistent hypotheses, Hobbes carried through a deductively consistent argument from a basic set of premises about human nature.

Hobbes accepted a materialistic conception of humanity and nature and a rigorously empirical conception of knowledge. All thoughts of a human being begin with the senses and everything else is derived from this: memory, dreams, apparitions, or visions. Understanding and imagination work with these ultimate materials. They have no others. Language is important, for it consists of "named" sense materials. It must work with definitions.

The essence of the animal is found behavioristically in two kinds of motions: vital (like the course of the blood or breath) and animal (voluntary). Endeavor (or will) consists in the small beginnings of motion, which, directed toward something, is appetite or desire; directed away, it is

[11]The editions consulted here are: *De Cive, or The Citizen* (New York: Appleton-Century-Crofts, 1949) and *Leviathan* (New York: Macmillan, 1947). Other works of Hobbes which are of special interest are: *The History of the Civil Wars of England* (1679), *Behemoth* (1679), and *The Art of Rhetoric* (1681).

aversion.[12] All emotions reduce to these. Deliberation consists in the alteration in the individual of desire and aversion. The last appetite or aversion adhering to the action or omission of action is what is called the will.

On this basis Hobbes attacks the problems of the nature of society and the state. The mainspring of human action is formulated as follows: "In the first place, I put for a general inclination of all mankind a perpetual and restless desire of power after power, that ceaseth only in death." This operates in two ways, in king and subject alike. The desire for power is insatiable.

> Hence it is that kings, whose power is greatest, turn their endeavors to the assuring it at home by laws, or abroad by wars: and when that is done, there succeedeth a new desire; in some, of fame from new conquest; in others, of ease and sensual pleasure; in others, of admiration, or being flattered for excellence in some art, or other ability of mind. . . . Desire of ease, and sensual delight, disposeth men to obey a common power: because by such desires, a man doth abandon the protection that might be hoped for from his own industry and labor. Fear of death, and wounds, disposeth to the same; and for the same reason.[13]

The main forms of strife appear in the competition to gratify identical appetites, in fear lest each surpass the other in power and in craving for recognition and admiration. The natural relations of an individual to every other are competition, distrust, and the struggle for prestige. In a state of nature people are in a state of war, and life is "solitary, poor, nasty, brutish, and short." In the state of nature there is no distinction between right and wrong; there are no standards by which passions may be morally judged. There is no distinction between the just and unjust. Natural right means no more than the right to do anything that preserves one's existence.

The state originates in the need for self-preservation — the need to escape the natural

[12]Hobbes, *Leviathan*, p. 31.
[13]*Ibid.*, p. 64.

condition of war. The state is a real individual replacing the many. Every act of disobedience by a subject is unjust regardless of the grounds for the act. Nor can the sovereign set up grounds for violation of the contract by the subject. This would be an injustice by the sovereign, for it would violate the covenant. There is, moreover, no justification for resistance by the minority of the community on the grounds that it did not select the sovereign, who has entire power for prescribing laws as well as unrestricted power over property; who has the power to determine all controversies between subjects; sole authority to make war or peace, appoint magistrates, and distribute wealth, honors, and privileges. However, in the case of anarchy, when the sovereign can no longer protect the subject, one owes no obligation to the sovereign. Nor does one owe any obligation to the sovereign if captured in war or molested in a foreign country. Morality and justice are creations of the state. Even the church should be subordinated to the state.

CONFLICT THEORY ACQUIRES AN EMPIRICAL FOUNDATION

David Hume. The shift in conflict theory from a purely rational to an empirical foundation may be seen in the work of David Hume (1711–1776). Hume came from a well-to-do family, and was able to devote himself to the study of literature, philosophy, and law. He tried his hand at business. During a sojourn in France, he wrote *A Treatise of Human Nature* (1739–1740). His social and historical views appear primarily in the *Philosophical Essays* (1748), *Dialogues Concerning Natural Religion* (written about 1750 and published in 1779), and his *History of England* (6 vols., 1754–1763). Hume served for two years as secretary in France, where he became acquainted with Montesquieu and Helvétius. He brought Rousseau back to England, but they soon fell out. For a time Hume acted as under secretary of state for Scotland.

In his essay "On the First Principles of Government," Hume presents the picture of a state in remarkable contemporary terms. Nothing, he says, appears more surprising "than the easiness with which the many are governed by the few; and the implicit submission with which men resign their own sentiments and passions to those of their rulers. When we inquire by what means this wonder is effected, we soon find that, as force is always on the side of the government, the governed have nothing to support them but opinion."[14] Right is right to power and right to property. "When men act in a faction, they are apt, without shame or remorse, to neglect all the ties of honor and morality, in order to serve their party."[15] At the same time, nothing is more obstinate than a faction endowed with a sense of right. Opinion of right to property is fundamental (though not absolutely essential) to all government.

> Upon these three opinions, therefore, of public *interest*, of *right to power*, and of *right to property*, are all governments founded, and all authority of the few over the many. There are indeed other principles which add force to these, and determine, limit, or alter their operation: such as *self-interest, fear,* and *affection*.[16]

Thus, government is presented by Hume as a kind of complex equation in which force and public opinion are involved. The transition has been made by Hume to the concept of "legitimate power" as the critical phenomenon of the state, which rests basically on force.

The problem of the origin of government was handled in a common-sense and empirical-minded manner. Human beings, Hume thought, were born in a family, and are compelled to maintain society from necessity, from natural inclination, and from habit. In their further progress they are led to establish political society in order to establish justice, without which there can be no peace, safety, or mutual intercourse. Government prob-

ably began casually and imperfectly with the ascendancy of one person over multitudes during the states of war where superiority of courage and genius is most quickly seen and where concert is requisite, for the effects of disorder are sensibly felt. However, the transition to peacetime ascendancy must have been slow. "If the chieftain possessed as much equity as prudence and valor, he became, even during peace, the arbiter of all differences and could gradually, by a mixture of force and consent, establish his authority."[17] But the problems of force and freedom or authority, and liberty, are not solved all for one.

> In all governments, there is a perpetual intestine struggle, open or secret, between authority and liberty; and neither of them can ever absolutely prevail in the contrast. A great sacrifice of liberty must necessarily be made in every government; yet even the authority, which confines liberty, can never, and perhaps ought never, in any constitution, to become quite entire and uncontrollable.[18]

Hume insists that some combination of force and consent are operative in social structure. Since people are nearly equal in bodily force, mental powers, and faculties until cultivated by education, we must allow — if there ever was an original contract — that nothing but "their own consent could, at first, associate them together, and subject them to authority."[19]

Adam Ferguson's Conflict Theory. A member of the same circles of the Scottish Enlightenment, Adam Ferguson (1723–1816), a friend of Hume and an admirer of Montesquieu, tried to carry through the critical principles of Hume on the empirical foundations of Montesquieu. Ferguson was professor of psychology and moral philosophy at the University of Edinburgh. His ideas appear in *Institutes of Moral Philosophy* (1769), *Principles of Moral and Political Science* (1792), and particu-

[14]David Hume, *Essays: Moral, Political, and Literary*, ed. T. H. Green and T. H. Grose (London: Longmans, Green, 1907), 109–110.
[15]*Ibid.*, p. 110.
[16]*Ibid.*, p. 111.

[17]*Ibid.*, p. 113.
[18]*Ibid.*, p. 116.
[19]*Ibid.*, pp. 445–446.

larly in the greatest of his works, *An Essay on the History of Civil Society* (1766).[20] With Montesquieu he believed that external and unwilled elements determine social growth; natural causes rather than speculations of the philosophers determine the state. "No constitution is formed by concert, no government is copied from a plan."[21] With Hume and Bodin, Ferguson believed that humankind never lived in a kind of presocial individual state, but in groups. Also with Hume, he thought that while people are born in society, some of their important institutions originate in force. He believed that conflict in human communities is a genuine benefit and necessary concomitant to progress. "Without the rivalship of nations and the practice of war, civil society itself could scarcely have found an object or a form." In fact, we cannot even understand our fellows unless we have struggled ourselves: "he who has never struggled with his fellow creatures is a stranger to half the sentiments of mankind."[22] The various forms of strife and conflict appear in the competition of the economy as well as in politics; they appear in war and international relations. Economic prosperity is founded in political and military strife. Instinct and habit operating on their products create social forms. Natural right lies only in the right of individuals to use their own faculties. Out of the efforts of people to secure values arises the order and authority of society. The forms and powers of government are established by the incidents of struggle. Also like Hume, Ferguson believed that consent is a component in the institutions of government,[23] though it is only one component. He doubts that peace is the goal of society.

Turgot and Conflict Theory. In France, views essentially similar to those of Hume and Ferguson were developed by Anne Robert Jacques Turgot (1727–1781) under the influence of Montesquieu. Turgot had studied theology for a time, but instead of becoming an ecclesiastic he became a member of the French state bureaucracy, where he was concerned with problems of finance and taxation. In 1750, while holding an honorary office in the Sorbonne, he delivered his famous lecture *Tableau philosophique des progrès successifs de l'esprit humain.*[24] Later, under the influence of Quesnay, he wrote his *Réflexions sur la formation et la distribution des richesses* (1766).[25] Following Montesquieu, Turgot developed the conception of a plurality of influences on humankind (climate, custom, soil, etc.). He assumed, as a rationalist, that the human mind is everywhere the same. This casts into central focus the value for social science of comparative social and historical evidence, since every variety of barbarism and culture is to be found on earth and could be employed to reveal the laws of mind and society. Isolated nations, at present, show almost the same degree of barbarism as must once have characterized the human race. As culture develops, educational and religious institutions play an increasing role in fixing behavior. Migration and culture play a role in social change. However, without the effects of war and conflict in liquidating fixed customs, the human race would have remained in mediocrity.

[20]The works of Adam Ferguson include *An Essay on the History of Civil Society* (1767), (Philadelphia: Finley, 1819); *The Institutes of Moral Philosophy* (1769), (Basel: Decker, 1800); *The History and Progress and Termination of the Roman Republic* (1783), 3 vols. (Philadelphia: Wardle, 1841); *The Principles of Moral and Political Science* (1792) (New York: AMS Press, 1973). For evaluations of Ferguson, see William C. Lehmann, *Adam Ferguson and the Beginnings of Modern Sociology* (New York: Columbia University Press, 1930); David Kettler, *The Social and Political Thought of Adam Ferguson* (Columbus, Ohio: Ohio State University Press, 1965); William C. Lehmann "Adam Ferguson," in *The International Encyclopedia of the Social Sciences* (New York: Crowell Collier and Macmillan, 1968), V, 369–371.
[21]Ferguson, *Essay on the History of Civil Society,* p. 188.
[22]*Ibid.,* p. 36.

[23]Ferguson, *Principles of Moral and Political Science*, p. 244.
[24]Translated by McQuilkin DeGrange as *On the Progress of the Human Mind* (Hanover, N.H.: The Sociological Press, 1929).
[25]Translated as *Reflections on the Formation and Distribution of Wealth* (New York: Macmillan, 1898). See also *The Life and Writings of Turgot*, ed. W. Walker Stephens (London: Longmans, Green, 1895) and Douglas Dakin, *Turgot and the Ancien Régime in France* (London: Methuen, 1939).

Turgot believed that the relations between nomadic and sedentary-tillage peoples undergo typical sequences. Rulers holding agricultural peoples in subjection in turn reach a point where they become surrounded by barbarous tribes. When they become feeble, the barbarians, out of greed and ambition, attack. The barbarians in time adopt the culture of the conquered people, but as they become more domesticated, their fate is eventually the same as that of the rulers they supplanted. Conflict, the great liquidator, is the source of all real progress.

The Significance of Early Conflict Theories. This review of the highlights of the historical antecedents of conflict theory indicates the nature and richness of the material available to the new school of sociological theorists, and it supplies evidence of the sociological relevance of conflict theory.

The historical forms of conflict theory are not simple historical curiosities; they form a developing tradition. Polybius, for example, was familiar with various conflict interpretations in the Greek world. He synthesized these into his own. The Roman, particularly the Epicurean tradition, was in turn familiar with the views of Polybius. When conflict theory was vigorously advanced in the Renaissance world by Machiavelli, his preferred model was found in Polybius, though indeed he was also familiar with Latin authors in part also influenced by Polybius. From Machiavelli conflict tradition was passed on into the theories of seventeenth- and eighteenth-century students. Thus, the conflict theorists are no matter of historical curiosity; they constitute a fairly unified tradition. To be sure, the Chinese legalists and the Indian Kshatriya writers lie outside the Western traditions; they show that other societies, too, have had their "realists." Similarly, the theories of Ibn Khaldun, while influenced by the classical Greek discussions, perhaps even by Polybius, lie outside the developments in the West until the nineteenth century; not until they were introduced into Western discussions by Gumplowicz did they acquire interest for sociological conflict theory. Conflict theory is an ancient form which under-

went expansion and internal differentiation, supplying a rich tradition available to modern students. As one comes into recent times, conflict theory is given rationally coherent form (Hobbes) and made empirically and methodologically conscious (Bodin, Hume, Ferguson, and Turgot).

The social anchorage of its exponents is of special interest. Conflict theory is the creation of men of affairs. Heraclitus was the scion of a political and priestly family. The Sophists were displaced persons who had usually belonged to the ruling circles of their home cities. Plato, by contrast, as leader of a genteel sect, was passionately opposed to their views. Polybius was a statesman and political hostage. The Romans who adhered to a conflict interpretation of society were trained in the law and politically responsible. Machiavelli was an exiled politician; Bodin was a lawyer and magistrate, Hobbes a political secretary. Hume had served as a political secretary and ambassador, and Turgot was one of the more brilliant administrators of prerevolutionary France.

When sociology turned to the conflict theorists, it is evident that it was due to the appeal of the realistic analyses of mature men of affairs. However, before conflict theory emerged in sociology, it was to undergo rapid evolution in some of the near-by social sciences. In the course of this odyssey, conflict theory was considerably enriched.

CLASSICAL ECONOMICS AND THE EVOLUTION OF CONFLICT THEORY

In the seventeenth and eighteenth centuries the primary anchorage of conflict theory was in circles concerned with the problems of political science. However, in the eighteenth century some propositions central to conflict theory were adapted to the explanation of economic phenomena. Physiocracy, the product, was the first step toward modern economics. Important works of the physiocrats include Pierre Samuel Du Pont de Nemours' *De l'Origine et des progrès d'une science nouvelle* (1768), François Quesnay's *Le Droit naturel* (1765), Paul

Pierre Mercier de la Rivière's *L'Ordre naturel et essential des sociétés politiques* (1767),[26] and the works of Turgot.

Adam Smith. The physiocrats believed that there is a natural order in society which human beings can analyze rationally and control. The peculiar property of land is its capacity to produce an excess of value, forming a fund from which all classes of society live. Only the agricultural class can add new value; the other classes are all sterile and parasitical. All revenue for the support of government must come from the net produce of land. There should be a single tax, resting directly on land. The proprietors have a peculiar role in economic affairs. The advantages emerging from trade and commerce are of indirect value to agriculture, enabling the cultivators to concentrate on raising crops. For this reason the trades and commercial pursuits should be entirely free from obstruction of any kind in order best to serve agriculture. The duty of the state is to furnish instructions about the natural order, to protect it, to assist it by such things as roads, bridges, and harbors needed by the economy. In all other matters the state's activity should be curtailed. These ideas were taken over, expanded, and modified by Adam Smith, in *The Wealth of Nations* (1776), which traced the source of all value to labor and modified the idea of the agriculturalists as the sole productive class. The crucial ideas that emerged from Smith's reworking of physiocracy were: (1) that competition in economic affairs should be completely free: only in this manner could a maximum productivity be achieved; and (2) that the sphere of government should be correspondingly reduced; natural forces will reconcile the requirements of both individual and group.

> As every individual . . . endeavours as much as he can both to employ his capital in the support of domestic

ADAM SMITH

> industry, and so to direct that industry that its produce may be of the greatest value; every individual necessarily labours to render the annual revenue of the society as great as he can. He generally, indeed, neither intends to promote the public interest, nor knows how much he is promoting it. By preferring the support of domestic to that of foreign industry, he intends only his own security; and by directing that industry in such a manner as its produce may be of greatest value, he intends only his own gain, and he is in this, as in many other cases, led by an invisible hand to promote an end which was no part of his intention. Nor is it always the worse for the society that it was no part of it. By pursuing his own interest he frequently promotes that of the society more effectually than when he really intends to promote it.[27]

[26]"On the Origin and Progress of a New Science"; "Natural Law"; and "The Natural and Essential Order of Political Societies." None of these is readily available in English translation.

[27]Adam Smith, *The Wealth of Nations* (New York: Modern Library, 1937), p. 423.

Traditional conflict theory had made the state the central object of analysis, conceiving of it as the institution equilibrating the stress arising out of the conflicts of individuals or groups. The physiocrats shifted the focus: to them the most fundamental of all phenomena in human society is the struggle for the necessities of life. Even the conception of conflict as having positive value is not new; Turgot and Ferguson attributed positive effects to political conflict. In fact the positive functions of a form of conflict are formulated in terms of widest generality. Economic competition is the great agency of efficiency in the production of the basic necessities of life. The state is an institution resting on force but hardly productive in the manner of economic competition; like a great bird of prey, it tends to interfere with normal productive process. Between the physiocrats and Adam Smith the foundations of classical economics were laid. Moreover, Malthus soon showed that the conflict formula located at the heart of classical economics was capable of expansion.

Thomas Malthus. Thomas Robert Malthus (1766–1834), the son of a country gentleman, had been trained at Jesus College, Cambridge, and took holy orders. He became in 1805 professor of history and political economy at the East India Company's College at Haileybury. The first form of the *Essay on the Principle of Population* was printed in 1798, the second in 1803.[28] In these, the competition formula was rephrased in more general form.

One can, of course, look at competition positively as the basis for an increase in precision and competence. One can also look at it negatively, as the struggle for scarce value that everyone cannot have. Insofar as competition produces values, it is positive; but it loses this property the moment there is greater need for values than competition

can produce. This last is precisely Malthus' addition to the argument on the basis of demographic facts.

There is, according to Malthus, a constant tendency in all animated life to increase beyond the nourishment available to it. Nature scatters the seeds of life about in great abundance, but it is comparatively miserly in its provision of nourishment for them. In the plant and animal world, some balance is preserved by the fact that different life forms prey on each other. These same forces operate in human beings. The population has a constant tendency to increase beyond the means of subsistence. On the basis of statistical calculations available to him, Malthus urged that conservatively it may be assumed that the population, when unchecked, will tend to double itself every twenty-five years, or increase in a geometric ratio. Meanwhile the basic soil is being depleted. It is doubtful, he believed, whether the amount of subsistence can be doubled in any number of years. He predicted that in America the Indians would be driven farther into the country, until the whole race was exterminated. Under the best management, it is questionable whether the food supply can be increased faster than in an arithmetic ratio.

Taking the whole earth, instead of this island, emigration would of course be excluded; and supposing the present population equal to a thousand millions, the human species would increase as the numbers 1, 2, 4, 8, 32, 64, 128, 256, and subsistence as 1, 2, 3, 4, 5, 6, 7, 8, 9. In two centuries the population would be to the means of subsistence as 256 to 9; in three centuries as 4096 to 13, and in two thousand years the difference would be almost incalculable.

In this supposition no limits whatever are placed to the produce of the earth. It may increase for ever, and be greater than any assignable quantity; yet still the power of population being in every period so much superior, the increase of the human species can only be kept down to the level of the means of subsistence by the constant operation of the strong law of necessity, acting as a check upon the greater power.[29]

---

[28]References here are to the Macmillan edition of 1894, which contains both the first and second editions of the *Essay.* All of the quotations here are from Malthus' later version.

[29]*Ibid.,* p. 86.

The most general preventive check that can be conceived is rational abstinence from having children. If birth control did not produce vice, it would be just about the least evil that could arise from population. However, it is usual for a corruption of morals to result, particularly degrading the female character. There are clearly serious risks.

> When a general corruption of morals, with regard to sex, pervades all classes of society, its effects must necessarily be, to poison the springs of domestic happiness, to weaken conjugal and parental affection. . . .[30]

Moreover, a preventive check on population would operate most efficiently precisely on the most worthy elements of the population, while it increased unchecked on the part of the less worthy. Of course, it never increases quite unchecked:

> The positive checks to population are extremely various, and include every cause, whether arising from vice or misery, which in any degree contribute to shorten the natural duration of human life. Under this head therefore may be enumerated, all unwholesome occupations, severe labour and exposure to the seasons, extreme poverty, bad nursing of children, excesses of all kinds, the whole train of common diseases and epidemics, wars, pestilence, plague, and famine.[31]

Competition, as a central concern of economic theorists, has indeed been given a grim turn.

All competition in the end becomes a competition to survive. This inevitably drives wages down to that point where they are just sufficient to permit laborers to live and reproduce themselves. In other areas, also, Malthus introduces a grim note, calling into question any and all programs for reform, which are doomed unless the population growth is checked.

> . . . it seems evident, that no improved form of government, no plans of emigration, no benevolent in-

stitutions, and no degree or direction of national industry, can prevent the continued action of a great check to increase in some form or other; it follows, that we must submit to it as an inevitable law of nature. . . .[32]

The most important argument against Malthus is that he completely underestimated the gain in productivity made possible by the industrial revolution. For example, the United States in 1790 was only about 5 per cent urban. The ordinary American farm was able to raise only enough food for its own and perhaps one other family. At present the population is over 60 per cent urban, and farmers are able to produce enough for themselves and seventeen others. We are at the moment embarrassed by a tremendous farm surplus. However, it is by no means clear that this proportionate increase in productivity can continue indefinitely, and the argument may belong to the Malthusians in the long run. All this aside, however, the central concern here is with the sharp, hard turn given to the meaning of competition as a form of conflict central to economic behavior, and with the consequences of this conflict for the conduct of society, the standard of living, the condition of labor, and the social classes.

Malthus' conclusions were a very severe blow to the kind of rationalistic optimism of persons like Helvétius, Condorcet, and Godwin. But more important than this was the influence of Malthus on biology, and particularly on Darwin.

THE CONFLICT THEORY RECEIVES BIOLOGICAL SUPPORT

Great gains had been made in biology toward the end of the eighteenth century and in the early nineteenth century. The cell theory was established by Bichat, Schleiden, and Schwann. Embryology had been established by Karl Ernst von Baer (1792–1876). The evolutionary hypothesis

---

[30]*Ibid.*, p. 89.
[31]*Ibid.*, p. 89.

[32]*Ibid.*, p. 97.

had been advanced in various ways by such men as John Ray (1628–1705), Georges de Buffon (1707–1788), and Alexander von Humboldt (1769–1859). The effects of geographic factors on the distribution of flora and fauna had been studied by Carl Linnaeus (1707–1778). Attempts to state the mechanism of evolution began to make their appearance in the work of Étienne Geoffroy Saint-Hilaire (1772–1844), Erasmus Darwin (1731–1802), and Jean Baptiste Lamarck (1744–1829), but it was a conflict theory taken from classical economics, and particularly from Malthus, that provided the spur to nineteenth-century biology. Charles Darwin was led through the influence of Malthus to a restatement of the mechanism of evolution:

> In October, 1838, that is, fifteen months after I had begun my systematic inquiry, I happened to read for amusement, *Malthus on Population,* and being well prepared to appreciate the struggle for existence which everywhere goes on, from long continued observation of the habits of animals and plants, it at once struck me that under these circumstances favorable variations would tend to be preserved, and unfavorable ones to be destroyed. The result would be the formation of new species. Here, then, I had at last got a theory by which to work.[33]

Darwin took for granted the fact that variation occurs in all animal species. However, it was the idea of the struggle for existence and the survival of the fittest that provided the needed formula.

On a biological level, a parallel had been reached to the conception of the social benefits of struggle, conflict, and war. Conflict and the struggle to survive now appeared at the very heart of biological phenomena. A mechanism had been achieved that placed supreme importance on efficiency. All recourse to a teleological explanation of biological development became unnecessary. Thus an idea born in the sphere of politics migrated to

economics, was specialized in demography, and taken over and applied to biology. It was now ready to return to the field of general sociology, serving as the basis for one of the main types of conflict theory in modern times.

SUMMARY

Although positivistic organicism was adapted to the two main demands of the nineteenth century — its conservatism and the demand for the application of science to society — tension between these two sets of requirements could not be permanently avoided. If one actually did apply science to society, the results were certain to upset tradition; if one did not apply science to society, one could hardly pretend that the new discipline was a science. Moreover, the assemblage of information by the new discipline led to the rapid evolution of alternative ideas. This created the requirement for a dependable method. In various ways Tönnies, Durkheim, and Pareto all illustrate a growing concern with scientific standards.

The institution of more exacting standards, however, quickly revealed a major weakness of positivistic organicism — its apparent inability to handle issues of interhuman conflict. So glaring was this deficiency that the phenomena of social conflict became the point of gravity for reconstruction of the science.

Once conflict was accepted as a central fact of society, a rich intellectual tradition was available for its interpretation. Every society has its conflicts; every society has persons who face up to them. In classical Greece a series of thinkers from Heraclitus to the Sophists treated conflict as *a* primary, perhaps *the* primary, social fact. The best developed conflict theory of antiquity was that of Polybius, for whom it was the fundamental fact in the evolution of political institutions. In fact, he visualized the state as a kind of stabilized system of power. In the medieval Arabic world, Ibn Khaldun developed a

---

[33]Francis Darwin, *The Life and Letters of Charles Darwin* (New York: Appleton, 1887).

conflict theory of society based on the assumption that the struggles between the nomad and the tiller were fundamental to the evolution of civilization.

While Ibn Khaldun's ideas did not affect Western thought until the nineteenth century, Polybius' conceptions were transmitted directly to Niccolò Machiavelli, who found the origin of the state and its key institutions in the same place. These ideas were expanded by Jean Bodin, who became a harbinger of the modern theories of sovereignty. They were also transmitted to Thomas Hobbes, who developed them into a materialistic rationalism.

Modern conflict theory was pulled out of its rationalistic context and turned into an empirical investigation by David Hume and Adam Ferguson. In treating conflict as an empirical fact, Hume laid the foundations for the contemporary theory of the political party. Ferguson turned these ideas into a general account of political institutions and government, conceived as arising out of struggle. Parallel theories appeared in France in the works of Turgot.

The idea of universal competition taken from modern conflict theory became central to classical economics. Competition, in turn, was transformed from the central law of economic behavior by Thomas Malthus into a general competition to survive. It became the basis of his population theories. Conflict theory was now ready to migrate to biology, where, in the works of Darwin, it became the foundation for a reconstruction of biological science.

The theory of social conflict has had a richly colorful career in the West. At one time it had been turned into a very particular explanation of special events; at another it had been turned into a general examination of human affairs. A treasure of experience and insight was available to the new school of theory.

VIII

Major Conflict Ideologies of the Nineteenth Century: Marxism

If we compare the early conflict theorists with the thinkers who laid the foundations of the organismic view of society, some interesting similarities and contrasts are evident. The ancient intellectual was nearly always drawn from the upper social strata. This was almost inevitable, since except for unusual circumstances only these strata had access to the literary educations of their times. In their social-class positions, then, the predecessors of both schools were roughly equivalent.

However, among the founders of conflict theory there was a far greater preponderance of secular men of affairs than among the idealistic predecessors of positivistic organicism. Even in ancient China and India, Kautilya, Han Fei-Tzu, and Li Ssû were active men of affairs. And in the West, Heraclitus was from a political and priestly family, Polybius was the son of a statesman and a political hostage, Ibn Khaldun was a chief justice, diplomat, and administrator, Machiavelli was an exiled statesman and patriot, Jean Bodin was a practicing lawyer. By contrast, Plato was the leader of a semireligious genteel sect with only a tangential

(and inept) political experience, Aristotle was a tutor and school head, and in modern times the idealist has been much more likely to be a clergyman (Berkeley) or professor (Hegel) than an individual of affairs. The differences in social realism between conflict theory and a positivistic organicism are partly to be accounted for by the social roles of their founders.

In working closer to secular affairs, the conflict theorists of the past tended to develop ideas more immediately based on actual social experience and less "out of this world." However, such close involvement in actual affairs has its own risks. Individuals of affairs tend to be skeptical of abstract conceptualization, which appears to them to be speculative armchair philosophizing. Their thinking is likely to be dominated by the crises of the day. Much of their thought turns, automatically, to the task of getting the job done rather than pondering its meaning. It is not without significance in this connection that the thought of people of affairs frequently rises to the level of truly general formulations only when circumstances have isolated them from action. Polybius was a captive hostage, Machiavelli an exiled statesman, and Hobbes shared the exile of his royalistic sponsors.

Conflict theory tends to be only a step away from *ideology*, which may be defined as the organization of ideas for the promotion of social movements or for the defense of social institutions. An ideology is a system of ideas intended to serve practice rather than to promote the aims of understanding. It may, to be sure, raise the level of understanding, but this is not its primary function.

Three major forms of conflict ideology arose in the nineteenth century: Marxian socialism and two forms of social Darwinism. It is of great importance for the understanding of conflict theory to distinguish between ideology and scientific theory. For one thing, whatever their similarities, ideology and scientific theory are essentially different. For another thing, the major conflict ideologies of the nineteenth century raised a host of extremely vital problems that the social sciences eventually had to solve.

FROM ROMANTIC IDEALISM TO MARXIAN SOCIALISM

It was observed in tracing the backgrounds of positivism that nineteenth-century socialism was the true heir of the peculiar combination of scientific method and social reform of the eighteenth century. Sociology took over the scientific method, but set aside social reform. Indeed, in pressing science into the service of conservative social ends, sociology assumed the character of a conservative answer to socialism; for this reason it is not hard to understand the remarkably restricted influence that Marx had on early sociology. It is rare to find sociologists who even mention Marx or, for that matter, socialism — except, perhaps, to dissociate themselves from it, like Ward, for example. At the same time, to characterize socialism as combining scientific claims with social reform is insufficient to identify the peculiarities of Marxism, despite its

claims to being the "only scientific form of socialism." Therefore, we must characterize socialism more fully before differentiating Marxism.

Human society is not completely arbitrary, with unlimited possibilities of combining anything with anything. Societies are as incapable as people of eating their cake and having it too. Hence, basic institutional arrangements in one area have consequences for other areas of societal life. Whatever value there is in the "economic interpretation of society" lies here. It is a good point, but the Marxians rode it into the ground. The institutional possibilities are not so limited that only economic arrangements determine the rest. Nevertheless, it remains true that various other social arrangements tend to consolidate in a manner in which property and economy play a very significant role. In the feudal system, with its nobility, who claimed the right to bear arms and monopolized the games of war, and with its clergy and peasantry, the system of landed property held in hereditary entailment was critical. The basis for support of the bourgeoisie, who launched a series of revolutions against the feudal world, was found in economic institutions centering on private property. The revolutions that freed these new classes from the feudal system also had multiple influences on other than economic areas. The right to bear arms was secured; formal legal freedom of individuals was attained; and a class system replaced the system of estates. The new world created by the bourgeoisie extended formal legal freedom to the lower levels of society, tearing them out of systems of hereditary bondage, bringing them into dependence upon the new industries that were arising, and in which their fates were now determined by sale of their services on the labor market. The homeless and uprooted masses of modern times — the peculiarly modern proletariat — found no protection in "private property" but only exposure to the whims of the bourgeoisie. Insofar as it has advanced its own interests, the proletariat has found the point of gravity of its interests in socialized property. Whether private and socialized property should be considered to be absolutely antithetical — as some thinkers have assumed — is of no concern here. The only point of interest is that modern society has created groups quite without economic protection except for various types of transportation facilities — roads, is a structural development in the Western world. Among the kinds of property and services which have been socialized are: education; the postal and, at times, other communication systems; various types of transportation facilities—roads, bridges; and often other kinds of facilities. Unemployment insurance, old-age benefits, social security, all have appeared. Socialized medicine has many times been demanded and partly carried through. The common starting point in all systems of socialist ideology is their attempt to guarantee the economic security of all segments of society. In this lies their motive force, for proletarian groups have as undeniable claims as did the bourgeoisie in the feudal world. No modern nation has found it possible not to socialize some services and utilities. In England, France, Spain, the United States, and Germany, the common element of the socialistic argument has been found in the attempt to satisfy the needs of working groups. The differentiation of German-Marxian socialism from other types starts from this common base. Marxian socialism developed, first of all, against a background of German romanticism.

No mysterious dialectic of the spirit is necessary to see that for nearly every point in the rationalistic credo of the eighteenth-century intelligentsia, the conservative intellectuals of the nineteenth century tended to develop a counter point. The rationalists discovered the universal equivalence of human nature; the romantics discovered the genius of the particular race. The rationalists asserted cosmopolitanism as a principle of culture; the romantics discovered the national, the parochial, the bucolic. The rationalists conceived of history as the record of folly and error; the romantics discovered in history only profundity and depth. The rationalists found the essence of humanity in reason; the romantics found it in spirit.

Hegel and Romantic Idealism. In Hegel's great synthesis of the modern idealistic argument, the ego was located at the center of existence, credited with moral and aesthetic creativity. The ego and the moral or aesthetic world it creates appear as unified against a transpersonal psychic background. The processes of individual experience are paralleled in the process of nature.

Georg Wilhelm Friedrich Hegel (1770–1831), who advanced these ideas, was the son of a civil servant at Württemberg. Hegel received theological training at Tübingen. His philosophy was developed between 1793 and 1801, when he served as a private tutor. From 1808 to 1816 he edited a newspaper. In 1818 he was called to the University of Berlin, where he became a favorite of the government.

When mind is placed at the core of reality, change is transformed into an act of thought.[1]

---

[1] William Wallace, *Prolegomena to the Study of Hegel's Philosophy and Especially of His Logic,* 2d ed. (Oxford, England: The Clarendon Press, 1894, 1931). A complete bibliographical note on Hegel will not be attempted. The works of chief importance for the present discussion are: *The Philosophy of History,* trans. J. Sibree (New York: Dover Publications, 1956); *Science of Logic,* trans. H. W. Johnston and L. G. Struthers, 2 vols. (New York: Macmillan, 1929); *Hegel's Doctrine of Formal Logic,* trans. Henry S. Macran (Oxford, England: The Clarendon Press, 1912); *Hegel's Logic of World and Idea,* trans. Henry S. Macran (Oxford, England: The Clarendon Press, 1929); and *The Philosophy of Right,* trans. S. W. Dyde (London: George Bell, 1896). For a recent biography of Hegel see Franz Wiedmann, *Hegel: An Illustrated Biography,* trans. Joachim Neugroschel, (New York: Pegasus, 1968). The secondary literature on Hegel is enormous; the following is selected to illustrate evaluations of Hegel by American liberals (Hook), revolutionary Marxists (Lukács), existentialists (Heidegger), critical theorists (Lichtheim and Marcuse), and recent trends in Hegelian interpretation (O'Brien and Taylor): Martin Heidegger, *Hegel's Concept of Experience* (New York: Harper & Row, 1970); Sidney Hook, *From Hegel to Marx* (New York: Reynold & Hitchcock, 1936); Walter Arnold Kaufmann, *Hegel: Reinterpretation of Texts and Commentary* (Garden City, N.Y.: Doubleday, 1965) and *Hegel's Political Philosophy* (New York: Atherton Press, 1970); George Lichtheim, *From Marx to Hegel* (New York: Herder and Herder, 1971); Georg Lukács, *The Young Hegel,* trans. Rodney Livingstone (London: Merlin Press, 1975); Herbert Marcuse, *Reason and Revolution* (New York: Humanities Press, 1955); George Dennis O'Brien, *Hegel on*

Hegel was convinced that thought does not consist of eternally fixed forms; it is a process. As a process any particular idea cast up by thought (*thesis*) necessarily calls out its opposite (*antithesis*). Now thought must reconcile the conflict (*synthesis*). This process is dialectical. The way we think is also an expression of the innermost essence of existence. Every state of reality is a thesis which passes into its negation, or antithesis. The negation brings a new synthesis into being. Further development of the same process negates the negation, lifting thought to a higher unity. This dialectical evolution of concepts represents the self-development of existence. Every phenomenon points beyond itself to a greater whole. The appearance and synthesis of opposites, light and darkness, life and death, are conceived as the creative rhythm of the world of process. The innocence of childhood is canceled by unrest and doubts and synthesized in the adult character. The seed must perish for the plant to appear.[2]

The dialectical process has its first forms in nature in a first realization of the *logos* as a world-creating, world-ordering principle. Nature works its way up through a series of states from pure externality to inwardness of spirit. The most important stages are those from mechanism to the physical stage and on to the organism. The philosophy of the spirit also falls into three parts: the subjective mind, the spiritual life of the individual subject, and the objective mind. The last, the spiritual life displaced by the *logos* in social forms and institutions of history, covers the problems of law, morality, the ethical life of the family, and the state.

In Hegel's *Philosophy of Right,* he proposed to demonstrate the process by which the idea of the state was formed. The starting point for analysis was the will, conceived as pure intelligence — as eternal, universal, self-conscious, self-determining, as *Geist*. Freedom is the essence of the will. Freedom is the idea of the free will that wills the free will.[3] The absolute idea is only realized by the state. Law is the form of the will in which personality, property, and contract are realized. A living creature is a person so far as it freely wills to be so. An object determined by the will of a person becomes property. Human beings are slaves (property) only when they do not will to be free. The free will is also realized in subjective morality, which includes those aspects of self-determination in which the individual is affected by the consciousness of others. Purposes, responsibility, motive are manifestations of will at this level. The full relation of individual will to universal will occurs in customary morality or social ethics. The customs and habits of humankind express the working of universal cause at the same time that they embody individual choice.

The institutions embodying social ethics are the family, civil society, and the state. The family is a natural foundation for the order of reason which culminates in the state, but at the same time it represents such a foundation only in so far as it dissolves. However, the family has eternal reality in property, which destroys the family. Children grow up and establish property-holding families of their own. Thus the family unit breaks into a multitude of competing proprietors striving for their egoistic advantage. These groups prepare the way for civil society.[4]

Civil society rests on two principles: that individuals aim only at their private interests, and that individual interests are so related that the satisfaction of one depends on the satisfaction of the other. As a competition of egos, the civil community appears only to disappear in a "spectacle of excess, misery, and physical and social corrup-

Reason and History: A Contemporary Interpretation (Chicago: University of Chicago Press, 1975); Charles Taylor, *Hegel and Modern Society* (New York: Cambridge University Press, 1979)

[2]Harald Høffding, *A History of Modern Philosophy,* trans. B. E. Meyer (New York: Macmillan, 1935), II, 181.

[3]Hegel, *The Philosophy of Right*, Introduction, Section 27.
[4]*Ibid.,* Sections 177 and 182. An excellent summary of Hegel's importance for social theory is found in Herbert Marcuse, *Reason and Revolution* (New York: Oxford University Press, 1941); for his comments on the present issues, see pp. 200 ff.

tion."[5] This competition leads to the accumulation of wealth and the growing impoverishment of the working class.

> By generalizing the relations of men by way of their wants, and by generalizing the manner in which the means of meeting these wants are prepared and procured, large fortunes are amassed. On the other side, there occurs a repartition and limitation of the work of the individual laborer and, consequently, dependence and distress in the artisan class. . . .
>
> When a large number of people sink below the standard of living regarded as essential for the members of society, and lose that sense of right, rectitude, and honor which is derived from self-support, a pauper class arises, and wealth accumulates disproportionately in the hands of a few.[6]

Civil society is devoted to the satisfaction of economic needs. The satisfaction of economic needs requires the protection of property through the administration of justice and the protection of the general welfare by the police and the corporation. The administration of justice makes abstract right into law and introduces a conscious universal order into the contingent processes of society. The police represent the interest of the whole against social forces that are strong enough to disrupt the function of the civil process. The police, as a basic civil institution, are complemented by the corporation (conceived somewhat along the lines of the old guild system), which brings unity to competing economic interests and activities and champions the organized interests of civil society against the state.

The state is the highest of the ethical communities combining the essence of family and civil society. The state is the realized socioethical idea. Spirit reaches its greatest perfection here. The state is the progression of God in the world, and must be honored as semidivine. The idea of the state manifests itself as the constitution or internal public law, as external public law, and as world history. In each of these areas there is an unfolding of freedom. The basic property of a particular state is the political consciousness of a people. This consciousness determines the constitution. Three powers are indispensable to the state, the legislative, the administrative (including the judicial), and the monarchic. Monarchic power is highest, being the unifying force of the other two. The legislative power is conceived as an organ where prince, administration, and people have a role. The most popular element of the assembly, the people, are to be represented by the classes (*Stände*).

The final channel through which the state is revealed as the expression of the spirit is world history — the process of events in the unfolding of the universal spirit. The culture of a people, including its art, religion, and political institutions, expresses a stage in the self-realization of the absolute. Each age represents a level in the realization of the absolute spirit.

> The History of the World is the discipline of the uncontrolled natural will, bringing it into obedience to a Universal principle and conferring subjective freedom. The East knew and to the present day knows only that *One* is Free; the Greek and Roman world, that *some* are free; the German World knows that *All* are free. The first political form therefore which we observe in History, is *Despotism*, the second *Democracy* and *Aristocracy,* the third *Monarchy*.[7]

If one ignores all of the mystical aspects of Hegel's arguments, observing only their surface features, two general properties appear. The first of these is the tendency toward a rather complete organicism, which is present in every step. It is little wonder that Comte immediately recognized his kinship with Hegel. Comte's first work was well received by Hegel, and that Comte saw Hegel's point of view as a more metaphysical form of his own may be seen in his letter to his friend A. M. D'Eichtal in Berlin:

> Je suis bien aise d'avoir fait connaissance avec Hegel, et je regrette que votre extrait ne soit pas plus étendu;

---

[5] Hegel, *The Philosophy of Right,* Section 185.
[6] *Ibid.,* Sections 243 and 244.

[7] Hegel, *The Philosophy of History,* p. 104.

il est bien moins fort que Kant, mais c'est, sans aucun doute, un homme de mérite. Il me semble encore trop métaphysique; je n'aime point du tout son *esprit,* auquel il fait jouer un rôle si singulier. Mais je trouve, comme vous, un esprit positif dans les détails. . . .[8]

Hegel, thus, had a very direct effect upon the founding of sociology.

But the career of organicism and positivism in social theory has been traced. Interest here attaches primarily to the second major property of the idealism of Hegel and his predecessors. There is an almost pathological concern with conflict running through this school of idealists. Conflict, opposition, strife, the appearance of contradictions, appear over and over. There is conflict in the state, in civil society, in the family, between individuals, and within the individual. The most fundamental method of thought is a dialectic, the casting up and surmounting of oppositions. A whole series of stages appears in the dialectic of nature. The phenomena of art, literature, manners, institutions are to be understood as produced in the dialectic of history. All these forms of opposition, strife, or conflict are eventually transformed into a kind of debate of the Absolute with itself. In the end, all conflicts turn into a mere war of words.

KARL MARX

Brown Brothers

MARX AND ENGELS AS CONFLICT IDEOLOGISTS

With these ideas, much that was conceptually essential to Marxism was already present. Karl Marx (1818–1883) came as a student under the influence of Hegel, and with Bruno Bauer, Arnold Ruge, and Ludwig Feuerbach, he interpreted Hegelianism in a militant atheistic form. Failing to get a university position, Marx became a journalist, contributing to and later editing the *Rheinische Zeitung*, an organ of radical bourgeois opinion, established in 1842 and suppressed fifteen months later. In 1844 he embarked on the study of economics in Paris, continuing in Brussels after his expulsion. After a second attempt at political activity in 1848, cut short by the counter movement against the revolutionary action, Marx resumed his studies in London, continuing in them until his death.

Friedrich Engels (1820–1905) was Marx's closest friend and collaborator. He was born in Barmen of a prosperous commercial family. In 1842 he left Germany to take a position with a firm

[8]Émile Littré, *Auguste Comte et la philosophie positive*, 2d ed. (Paris: L. Hachette, 1864), p. 157. ["I am very much pleased to have made Hegel's acquaintance, and I regret that your excerpt was not more extensive; he is not nearly so strong as Kant, but without any doubt he is a man of merit. He still seems to me to be too metaphysical; I am not at all taken with his notion of *spirit*, to which he assigns such an extraordinary role. But I find, like you, a practical mind in the details . . ."]

in Manchester, England, and acquired a knowledge of *laissez-faire* economics. His friendship with Marx dates from their meeting in Paris in 1844, though they had met in 1842. In 1849 Engels took part, with Marx, in the republican insurrection in Baden. After 1850 he returned to England to engage in business, supporting Marx in his researches and the writing of *Das Kapital*.

The physiocrats and classical economists had come to the conclusion that there is one form of struggle at once universal and operating for human good: economic competition. Malthus had showed under what conditions this competition could turn into a grim downward spiral in which a good part of humankind is just able to stay alive. Hegel found a peculiarly ordered conflict of oppositions to be central to personality, society, the state, and humankind. Not without interest is the fact that Hegel had himself conceived the dialectic of civil society to be due to the egoistic struggle of each person to pursue his or her own good. Hegel had suggested that this inevitably sharpens the distinction between classes, separating the wealthy from those depressed in poverty. In the course of this, Hegel advanced another idea often attributed to Marx — that law and property are inseparable; in fact, the sharpening of the social classes goes on under the rule of law. By the time Marx and Engels wrote *The German Ideology* (1846), they were thoroughly familiar with and critically oriented toward both the Hegelian and *laissez-faire* ideas.[9]

The influence of Hegel was fundamental:

The great basic thought that the world is not to be comprehended as a complex of ready-made *things,* but as a complex of *processes,* in which things apparently stable no less than their mind-images in our heads, the concepts, go through an uninterrupted change of coming into being and passing away, in which, in spite of all seeming accidents and of all temporary retrogression, a progressive development asserts itself in the end — this great fundamental thought has, especially since the time of Hegel, so thoroughly permeated ordinary consciousness that in this generality it is scarcely ever contradicted[10]

It was not with Hegel's dialectical logic that Marx and Engels took issue, but rather with what they called the "idealist trammel" of his philosophy. Human beings distinguish themselves from animals, according to Marx and Engels, the moment they begin to produce their means of subsistence, a phenomenon determining their nature. "As individuals express their life, so they are. What they are . . . coincides with their production, both with what they produce and *how* they produce. The nature of individuals thus depends on the material conditions determining their production."[11] The break with the Hegelians was expressed in this assertion that the starting point of all understanding lies in the facts of material existence rather than in the spirit. They expressed the same point sarcastically: "Once upon a time an honest fellow had the idea that men were drowned in water only because they were possessed of the idea of gravity."[12] By contrast with this — and very close to the classical economists — Marx and Engels take the production of goods to stay alive as the basic social fact. "As soon as a need is satisfied . . . new needs are made; and this production of new needs is the first historical act."[13]

As with Hegel, the family is assumed to be the first and only natural human relationship. "The family which to begin with is the only social relationship, becomes later, when increased needs create new social relations and increased population new needs, a subordinate one."[14] The fact of human association creates language and con-

---

[9]Although the basic ideas contained in *The German Ideology* were more highly elaborated in the later writings of Marx and Engels, for present purposes this early formulation is adequate.

[10]Friedrich Engels, *Ludwig Feuerbach and the Outcome of German Classical Philosophy* (New York: International Publishers, 1941), p. 44. (*Ludwig Feuerbach* was written in 1886 and first published in 1888.)

[11]Karl Marx and Friedrich Engels, *The German Ideology* (New York: International Publishers, 1947), p. 7.

[12]*Ibid.*, p. 2.

[13]*Ibid.*, pp. 16–17.

[14]*Ibid.*, p. 17.

sciousness of a human type. "Man's consciousness of the necessity of associating with the individuals around him is the beginning of the consciousness that he is living in society at all."[15] There are, in this argument, echoes of the development from Fichte to Hegel — every development of consciousness is bound up with the appearance of some new distinctions and oppositions. "Division of labor only becomes truly such from the moment when a division of material and mental labor appears. From this moment onwards consciousness *can* really flatter itself that it is something other than consciousness of existing practice; that it is *really* conceiving something without conceiving something *real*."[16] Division of labor is correlated with a division of consciousness. With "the natural division of labor in the family and the separation of society into families opposed to one another, is given simultaneously the distribution . . . and unequal distribution . . . of its labor and its products."[17] There is a latent slavery already present in the family. An actual slavery quickly emerges. From this time on, society is divided into conflicting groups. Division of labor implies a contradiction between the interest of the separate individuals or individual family and the communal interest of all individuals. "This consolidation of what we ourselves produce into an objective power above us, growing out of our control, thwarting our expectations, bringing to naught our calculations, is one of the chief factors in the historical development up till now. And out of this very contradiction between the interest of the individual and that of the community the latter takes an independent form as the State, divorced from the real interests of individual and community."[18] Classes, determined by the division of labor, become the agents of the opposition. "It follows from this that all struggles within the State, the struggle between democracy, aristocracy, and monarchy, the struggle for the franchise, etc., are merely the illusory forms in which the real struggles of the different classes are fought out among one another."[19]

The Communist Manifesto. German workers living abroad had been organized into the League of the Just since 1836, with headquarters in London since 1840. In 1847 the League sent a representative to Brussels to learn more about Marx. The League later became the League of Communists, and held its first Congress in London in the summer of 1847. At the meeting of 1848, Marx and Engels prepared the *Communist Manifesto,* formulating a new program for the League. In this document, the ideas developed earlier were emphatically expressed. "The history of all human society past and present has been a history of class struggles."[20] It was urged further that the West was on the threshold of another revolution, for when modern bourgeois society arose out of the ruins of feudalism, it simplified class antagonisms, splitting society into two great hostile camps: the bourgeoisie and the proletariat.

The earlier class struggles under slavery and feudalism terminated either in the revolutionary reconstruction of society at large or in the ruin of the contending classes. Capitalism, which appeared with the opening of Asia and the discovery of America, replaced the guild system with the manufacturing system and supplanted hand power with steam power. The capitalist class has played the most recent revolutionary role in the world. It shattered feudal relationships, leaving no relation between individual and individual other than "crude self-interest and unfeeling 'cash payment.' "[21] It has drowned the most heavenly ecstasies of religious fervor, of chivalrous enthusiasm, of Philistine sentimentalism, in the icy water of egotistical calculation. It has resolved personal worth into exchange value, and in place of numberless indefeasible chartered freedoms, has set up that single, unconscionable freedom — free

[15]*Ibid.,* p. 20.
[16]*Ibid.*
[17]*Ibid.,* pp. 22–23.
[18]*Ibid.,* p. 20.

[19]*Ibid.,* p. 23.
[20]Karl Marx and Friedrich Engels, *The Communist Manifesto* (New York: International Publishers, 1930), p. 25.
[21]*Ibid.,* p. 28.

trade. "In a word, it has replaced exploitation veiled by religious and political illusions, by exploitation that is open, unashamed, direct and brutal."[22] On the other hand, the positive achievements of capitalism were more wonderful than the Egyptian pyramids, Roman aqueducts, or Gothic cathedrals.

Class conflict is taken as central to society. The conflict between the capitalists and the proletariat is central to our own society. All such conflicts assume the form of an increasing consolidation of the sides involved. The capitalist class has agglomerated population, centralized means of production, and has concentrated production in a few hands. The bourgeoisie has created more productive forces than all generations of previous history. But its own classes also are turning against one another. "More and more, society is splitting up into two great hostile camps, into two great classes directly facing each other: bourgeoisie and proletariat."[23]

Basic to the Marxian analysis is the conception of political power as an adjunct to class power and political struggles as a special form of class struggles. The administrative structure of the modern state is but a committee for managing the common affairs of the bourgeoisie. A number of general predictions are made about the future course of these conflicts. It is predicted that the middle class will disappear. Tradespeople, shopkeepers, handicrafters will sink into the proletariat because petty capital will not be able to compete with mass capital or more efficient methods of production. "Thus the proletariat is recruited from all classes of the population." Distinctions will be obliterated between the workers, and as conflicts become more frequent between the two classes, the workers will begin to form combinations. "The workers begin to form coalitions against the bourgeoisie, closing their ranks in order to maintain the rate of wages; they found durable associations which will be able to give them support whenever the struggle grows acute. . . . This struggle . . . turns . . . into a national

contest, a class struggle."[24] The proletarianization of sections of the bourgeoisie supplies the proletariat with elements of enlightenment and progress, increasing its revolutionary potential. When the class struggle nears the decisive hour, the process of dissolution within the bourgeoisie accelerates, providing leadership for the revolutionary class, the class that holds the future in its hands.

Marx's Political Activities, 1848–1872.
By the time Marx and Engels composed the *Communist Manifesto* they had joined the radical wing of the democratic movement that was stirring through Western Europe, which led to popular uprisings in 1848. However, the German middle-class liberals failed to take advantage of the alliance with urban workers and peasants that accompanied the movement to establish genuine parliamentary institutions. The leaders of the revolutionary uprising were forced into exile and the Prussian government took control of the "parliamentary program." Thereupon the alliance between the middle class, the peasants, and the urban workers fell apart. The stage was also set for later antagonism between liberalism and socialism.

Marx, who was forced into exile in England, moved permanently into the socialist camp and alternated between monitoring political events relevant to the radical cause and working on a general theory of socialism. While Marx was radicalized by the 1848 experience, he was also persuaded that the problems involved in revolution were more complicated than had appeared on the surface and deserved a deeper analysis. He also found his emerging system of socialism to be in competition with alternative systems of radical thought, such as the anarchism and syndicalism of Pierre Joseph Proudhon with its suspicion of private property and the state and its faith in direct, spontaneous mass action.

In 1864 the leaders of the British trade union movement decided to form an International Association. Marx came out of semiretirement from

---

[22]*Ibid.*
[23]*Ibid.*, p. 26.

[24]*Ibid.*, p. 32.

political activity to participate and in 1864 wrote the Inaugural Address of the International. He took care to embody the policies and aims of all interested groups, even his rivals the French Proudhonists as well as the liberal trade unionists and Marxists. His old antagonist, Proudhon (1809–1865) died the next year (1865) obviating possible conflicts between the Marxists and Proudhonists in successive congresses: Geneva (1866), Lausanne (1867), Brussels (1868), and Basel (1869). These congresses supplied a forum for the airing of the anticapitalist views and proposals of most nineteenth-century radicals: Fourierists, Cabetists, Considerationists, Proudhonists, and many others. However, the colorful rebel and exile from Czarist Russia, Mikhail Bakunin (1814–1876), who engaged in numerous conspiratorial schemes and intrigues, undertook to capture the International. He established an organization, the Alliance of Social Democracy, in Switzerland, and applied for corporate affiliation with the General Council of the International in London. After he was received into the International in 1869 a conflict broke out between him and Marx and Engels, who decided Bakunin had to go. The Hague Conference of 1872 was held for this purpose and Marx and Engels succeeded. Shortly after this, however, the International itself declined.

While the conflict between Bakunin and Marx was shaping up, France under Louis-Napoleon declared war on Prussia in 1870. Due to previous policies of the Emperor, France found herself without allies and in less than a month her armies were defeated. When Napoleon fell the republicans proclaimed a republic, but their ranks were divided and some of their members feared the revolutionaries among them would take over in the case of an election. Bismarck, however, refused to negotiate for peace except with a constitutionally elected government. After the French attempted to resume the struggle the German armies invaded Paris. The Paris revolutionaries demanded an election and the creation of a Commune. On October 31 of 1871 a revolution broke out in Paris led by Auguste Blanqui, a veteran rev-

olutionary. The revolution was suppressed brutally, though only after some difficulty.

Marx defended the Paris Commune in a pamphlet, *The Civil War in France,* as a major historical event and model state of the revolutionary proletariat. The effect of this pamphlet (three editions were sold in two months) was to shock gradualists within the First International, leading to major defections from the organization. Without question the pamphlet was a major element in the demise of the First International. After this experience, Marx devoted the rest of his life exclusively to research and writing. His *magnum opus, Capital,* left unfinished at his death, was the major product of this last period.

The Uniqueness of the Marx-Engels Synthesis. Although there has been an occasional tendency by some persons to play down Engels's contribution (in contrast to that of Marx) to what was to become the most influential tradition of scientific socialism in the nineteenth century, Engels appears to have been primarily responsible for some of its indispensable ingredients. Engels was drawn to the plight of the working classes before Marx (describing their circumstances in his native city as early as 1839). He belonged, with Marx, to the circle of Young Hegelians and before Marx, under the influence of Moses Hess, Engels was introduced to the works of Saint-Simon and Charles Fourier and transformed by them into a socialist. He also appears to have undertaken the study of the economists earlier than Marx. When Engels and Marx met in 1844, however, they found themselves in complete agreement and together made their departure from bourgeois-liberal to socialist-communist circles and co-authored *The Holy Family* (1845), *The German Ideology* (1845–1846) and *The Communist Manifesto* (1847). They shared the materialist conception of history which they applied to various cultural areas. However, through the course of their lifelong friendship, Engels took the lead in maintaining contact with actual working groups and various other socialist circles.

Marx unquestionably had the more impressive

theoretical ability of the two, a fact Engels generously acknowledged: "I could never have achieved what Marx did. Marx stood higher, saw farther, and had a broader and quicker grasp of the situation than all the rest of us. Marx was a genius; we others were at best talented."[25] Moreover, Engels not only gave financial assistance to Marx and his family, encouraged him in his writing, worked hand-in-hand with him in his contact with working and communist-socialist groups, but even assumed paternity of Marx's illegitimate son. After Marx's death Engels became his political as well as intellectual executor.

Among the ideas not original to them, but which Marx and Engels wove into a unique synthesis were: the humanistic tradition extending through eighteenth-century enlightenment thinkers; the thoughts of the young Hegel, Feuerbach, and the other young Hegelians who envisioned self-realization under conditions of freedom as the highest of values; the combination of the Jacobin tradition of radical revolution with components of chiliasm; the labor theory of value deriving from the classical economists, Adam Smith and Ricardo, and interpreted as a component in class formation and class exploitation, which could be remedied only by the socialization of property; the concept of alienation adapted from Hegel, but given a materialistic interpretation; the notion that working classes were the "chosen people" on whom the hope of progress and the self-realization of humankind rested — an idea held by the French scientific socialists.

The tradition of German historicism, which treated history as a whole with laws of its own, provided the matrix that held the Marx-Engels synthesis together. Their own approach which, in turn, became a major movement in this historicism, gave the tradition a "materialistic" thrust, locating the motor of history in human labor directed to survival in nature and implemented by science and technology. This, in turn, opened the way for a radical critique of all institutions and all spheres of culture.

Since, following Hegel's lead, historical development was conceived as lawful and following in regular states, Marxism held out the hope that no matter how dark things might look, once affairs had run their course they would inevitably move on to the next stage. At the same time, since the actual social relations of people (rather than abstracted thought) formed the running wheel of progress, the solution of problems was to be found in practice or, in Marxian jargon, praxis. The doctrine could thus be interpreted either as a counsel of stoicism or a spur to activism as deemed desirable from case to case. In this stress on practice, ideology inevitably prevailed over scientific requirements, for only after the fact could one determine whether society was ready for revolution. One could only be sure the times were ripe if one acted. If one failed, the times were not ripe.[26]

MARXISM

During Marx's lifetime he was relatively unknown outside radical circles and even in these circles only one of a number of socialists. Marx was surprised and delighted by the notoriety that resulted from his interpretation of the Paris Commune. The defeat of the Commune marked the end of the Jacobin democratic tradition of French labor and the decline of Paris as the center of revolutionary European democracy. Also, Marx's position on the Commune alienated nonrevolutionary elements in the labor unions and, as observed, was a component in the rapid decline of the First International.

---

[25]Engels, *Ludwig Feuerbach*, p. 292.

[26]Althusser distinguishes between the youthful and mature Marx. He has argued that in his early period, Marx was dominated by the humanistic ideology of Hegel and Feuerbach, but in his mature period he developed a rigorous science of society. Louis Althusser, *For Marx* (London: Allen, Lane, 1969). Other students dispute the idea that one can draw a sharp line between the youthful and mature Marx.

Thereafter Marx turned his attention almost exclusively to theoretical integration of his views. Finally, there is little question that in the last decade of his life, Marx was beginning to develop interest in the scientific study of processes he viewed as independent of human volition.[27] As this occurred, emphasis in his writings was shifted to historical necessity and away from activist interpretations of the role of classes in social progress.

Meanwhile, the period following 1870 marks a decline in liberalism and a period of improvement in the condition of West European labor. It was also a period of consolidation in the emerging social sciences and of increasing popularity of Darwinian biology. Beginning before Marx's death in 1883 and continuing until his own death in 1895, Engels undertook the consolidation of his and Marx's theories into a coherent body of doctrine. In time, a variety of editors, historians, and political leaders joined Engels in the process: Eduard Bernstein, Karl Kautsky, George V. Plekhanov, Franz Mehring, D. Ryazanov, Wilhelm Liebknecht, August Bebel, Jules Guesede and Victor Adler.

Marxism was conceived as the economic interpretation of history and named dialectical materialism. The essence of history was viewed as a series of changes in the social system resting on the relations of production active at the basis of the social system and on which all other institutions and ideas rise as a superstructure. The relations of production give rise to classes which find themselves in tension when those who own the means of production seek to exploit the producers and block progress in their special interests until overthrown by revolutionary activity of the producers. Progress is cyclical and has gone through four major phases — primitive communism, ancient slave production, feudalism, and capitalism — with a fifth stage of socialism which will result in the fulfillment of history.

Although capitalism represents the peak of development so far, has amassed great wealth, and has made brilliant contributions such as par-

liamentary democracy, it is torn by class conflicts which are becoming increasingly oppressive. These class conflicts will, in the long run, result in the impoverishment of the proletariat and the polarization and destruction of the middle class, which will be forced to choose between the forces of reaction and of the future. At the crucial time, the working classes, the repository of hope endowed with true class consciousness, will arise and in the name of all humankind free it from the twin evils of class and property. As a result of Engels's salvage operation, Marxism acquired a coherent world view "which simultaneously linked it to, and separated it from, the dominant ideology of 'bourgeois' radicalism and positivism."[28]

Second only to Engels in his role in the formation and spread of Marxism as a body of doctrine was Karl Kautsky (1854–1938), son of a Czech painter and Austrian actress who, in 1880, joined up with German socialists in exile in Zurich. In 1881 Kautsky visited Marx and Engels and in 1883, the year of Marx's death, founded a monthly periodical in Stuttgart called *Die Neue Zeit* devoted to the diffusion of Marxist thought. He published works of socialist students from all over the world and wrote hundreds of articles himself. From 1885 to 1890 he worked in London in close collaboration with Engels. His *Economic Doctrines of Karl Marx* (1887) promoted Marxism.

In various historical studies Kautsky applied the Marxist method. In 1891 he drafted the program of the German Social Democratic Party, which was the first major Marxist Party program, and he joined Engels as a major Marxist theoretician in the Second International, formed by socialist groups in 1889. In *Die Neue Zeit,* Marxism was institutionalized as the official ideology of the German Social Democratic Party.

Once Marxism became the official point of view of a political party, discrepancies were not long in making their appearance between the revolutionary formulas of the doctrine and the requirements of sociopolitical practice. Eduard

---

[27]George Lichtheim, *Marxism* (New York: Praeger, 1961), p. 236.

[28]*Ibid.*, p. 258.

Bernstein (1850–1932), one of the major proponents of Marxism, also became one of the first to urge its revision in the light of sociopolitical realities. From a lower middle-class Berlin family, Bernstein had become a bank employee. He joined the Social Democratic Party in 1872 and became one of its most active members. Like many socialists of the period, Bernstein was forced to move about from country to country until the German antisocialist laws were repealed (1890) and he was able to return to Germany (1891) without fear of arrest. Particularly as a result of his English experience (where he had been in contact with the Fabian society), Bernstein was disturbed by discrepancies between Marxist theory and social reality. He noted that the working class was not being impoverished, that capitalism was developing defenses against instability, that mass consumption was increasing, and a new middle class was arising. Bernstein even went so far as to call historical materialism into question. A polarization quickly developed between Kautsky, who was the spokesperson for orthodox Marxism and Bernstein, who headed up the revisionists.

The debate joined by Bernstein and Kautsky over revisionism and the challenge to orthodox Marxism spread to Marxist circles throughout Europe and led to radical reactions and, eventually, attempts to extend Marx's analysis to account for changes that had occurred since his death. Two were particularly important — analyses of the phenomenon of imperialism: Rudolf Hilferding's *Finance Capitalism* and Rosa Luxemburg's *The Accumulation of Capital*. Both treatises attempted to account for the "apparent" health of capitalism, despite Marx's predictions, as evidenced by the extension of capitalism to the sphere of precapitalist countries and the export of capital. However, once precapitalist countries had been absorbed into the system, Luxemburg argued, capitalism would, as Marx predicted, collapse. Hilferding, on the other hand, argued that capitalism had developed to a new stage, finance capitalism, with greater capacity to overcome economic crises. Nevertheless, Hilferding also believed capitalism would be overthrown and replaced by socialism in

the course of the political struggles of the working class.[29]

LENINISM

Marx and Engels were convinced that eventually the Czarist government in Russia would fall, but meanwhile they viewed Russia as the primary obstacle to the realization of social democracy in Western Europe. The period of the Second International (1889–1914) was also the time of the Franco-Russian alliance against Germany. At a time when Marxism was being institutionalized as the official ideology of the Social Democratic Party in Germany, Lenin saw the Czarist regime impeding European progress. To both Marx and Engels, Russian populism (*Narodnichestvo*), which pinned hopes for social reform on the peasantry, appeared to be retrogressive, a dead end. The Marxists and Populists (Narodniks) were divided over this issue.

Vladmir Ilyich Ulyanov (1870–1924), who shortly after 1900 began to call himself Lenin, was one of six children in a well-to-do, middle-class family. His father was a successful school teacher (mathematics and physics), school inspector, and director of the "people's schools." Lenin, an avid student and wide reader, was upset by his father's death in 1886 and by the execution of his elder brother Alexander (a research scholar with a promise of a brilliant career) for terrorist activity. Lenin was radicalized by the experience; he studied the Marxists; in 1895 he visited Georgii Plekhanov, the father of Russian Marxism, in Geneva, and met other Marxist leaders such as the son-in-law of Marx, Paul Lafargue, and Wilhelm Liebknecht.

[29]For a brief review of the revisionist-radical controversy, see Lichtheim, *Marxism*, pp. 278–324. Rudolf Hilferding's *Das Finanzkapital* (1910) has not been translated into English. Rosa Luxemburg's *The Accumulation of Capital* (1913) appears in English translation (London: Routledge & Kegan Paul, 1951).

V. I. LENIN

Brown Brothers

Lenin was arrested for his role in publishing an illegal newspaper in 1896. In 1897 he was released to make arrangements for a three-year period of exile in a Siberian village, where he lived in a peasant hut. He continued his reading and writing in prison and in exile, completing his first major work on *The Development of Capitalism in Russia* in 1899. Released from exile in 1900 but forbidden to reside in the capital, the university, or major industrial towns, he applied for permission to go abroad and soon was able to leave for Switzerland.

While in exile in Siberia Lenin had read Bernstein's book on *The Prerequisites of Socialism and the Tasks of Social Democracy* and was shocked by its proposals for modifying some of the basic tenets of Marxism. In voluntary exile in Switzerland he proposed to set up a newspaper to combat revisionism. Lenin's second major work, *What Is To*

Be Done?, was published in 1902. By this time he had begun to alienate some of his colleagues by his insistence on the need for a "dictatorship of the proletariat" in connection with framing an agrarian program. In 1903, largely on Lenin's insistence, a congress was called to create an All Russian Party. A basic division broke out during this conference between the majority (*bolsheviki*) and minority (*mensheviki*) over the philosophy and tactics of revolution. The mensheviks thought it essential to work with the laws of social change; the bolsheviks were activists convinced of the need for a dictatorship of the proletariat in the hands of a revolutionary elite. The dispute led to years of bitter infighting; so much so, in fact, that Lenin played virtually no role in the 1905 revolution since he was almost completely isolated from other revolutionaries. However, this isolation also had the unexpected result of leaving Lenin unscarred by their failures. During World War I, the German High Command decided that Lenin's presence as a troublemaker in Russia would be invaluable to the German cause. The German authorities arranged to ship him by sealed railway car through Germany to Finland, from which he could slip into Russia.

Lenin was not a first-rank thinker. His *Development of Capitalism in Russia* (1899) was a tract directed against the Russian populist tradition. *What Is To Be Done?* argued that the working class had to be organized for a revolutionary task, for left to its own devices it tended to be satisfied with minor improvements and reform. *Imperialism, the Highest Stage of Capitalism,* was an oversimplified rehash of ground better covered by Hilferding and Luxemburg, arguing that imperialism, in creating the objective conditions for world revolution, marks the doom of capitalism. Lenin, however, had the notion that there is a law of uneven development opening up the possibility of the later doctrine of socialism in one country. *The State and Revolution* is a forthright argument for a "dictatorship of the proletariat," a doctrine which found its authority in Marx's position on the Paris Commune of 1871.

However, while he was an indifferent intellectual, Lenin was a superb tactician, and with the single objective of obtaining power he was disciplined enough never to permit principle to stand in his way. He skillfully did whatever was necessary to seize and retain power and opened a new epoch: the employment of the peasantry of underdeveloped countries by professional revolutionaries who transform themselves into a new kind of elite. As the party became identical with the state, all other institutions were reorganized to conform to the needs of the ruling elite and the first major totalitarian system of modern times was born.

SUMMARY

Marxism was unique among the various types of socialism of the nineteenth century in that the starting point for its development was found in the romantic idealism of Fichte (who developed the dialectic of the moral experience), Schelling who developed a dialectic of artistic experience), and Hegel (who developed a spiritual dialectic of human history and civilization). These idealistic and romantic philosophers popularized the concept of human society as a single developing spiritual process in which every aspect was related to every other in an evolving whole. The dialectic which treats scientific method, logic, life growth, physical change, and innumerable other things as if they were identical, is outright mysticism. Similarly, the claim that Marxism was scientific because every phenomenon conceivable can be reduced to economics can only be explained as a failure to distinguish between metaphysics and scientific theory. Marxism was a form of utopian socialism, resting on the conviction that the destruction of the entire existing world was the prior step to its own realization.

There is little doubt that the sociopolitical events in nineteenth-century Germany gave the final reinforcement to the uniqueness of German socialism. The liberal movements expressed in the revolutionary stirrings of 1848 were accompanied by reform in other European states. In Germany they were largely suppressed, and the Prussian state entered upon an extreme program of suppression of both socialism and the labor movement while trying to pull the teeth of the revolutionary

argument by paternalistic state measures. Hence, in Germany more completely than anywhere else in Europe, the socialist program was not permitted to work within the existing order. Once one presses a force out of its normal sphere of manifestation, one does not destroy it; one merely forces it into a context where the ordinary limiting forces cannot react upon it. German socialism had profound ties with organismic romanticism in the first place. The political policy that outlawed it redoubled these properties. German socialism was forced to become utopian — its goals, frustrated in the present, could only lie in the future. It necessarily became revolutionary; being prevented from working within the society, it required bloody revolutions to clear space for action. As these forms became fixed, the hatred between orthodox old-line communists and revisionists such as Bernstein[30] was inevitable. It is noteworthy that when the program of suppression of the labor movement and socialism was abandoned in Germany and it became possible to work legally within the society, membership in old-line communist organizations rapidly declined.

One of the functions of extreme exaggeration of a point of view is its tendency to force into the open problems that might otherwise have passed unnoticed. Marxism was a socialistic conflict ideology. But in the passionate analysis of all problems into economically based class, class organization, class conflict, and in the attempt to reduce all phenomena — art, music, literature, philosophy, religion, the state, etc. — to forms dependent on economics, it played a major role in forcing these phenomena to the attention of the modern social scientist. In the long run these problems had to be faced if for no other reason than to answer the Marxians. The twentieth century has witnessed the emergence of a number of problems in some measure forced to attention by the Marxians: the problem of class, the problems of the sociology of music, art, culture, and knowledge, and the problem of the interrelation of economic and other social phenomena.

[30]Eduard Bernstein, *Evolutionary Socialism* (New York: Huebsch, 1909).

IX

Major Conflict Ideologies of the Nineteenth Century: Social Darwinism

Marxism represents a form of conflict ideology developed in the name of the proletariat. Social Darwinism represents a form of conflict ideology developed in the name of business groups of modern society. It is significant that Marxism was practically without influence on early sociology, making its effect only belatedly by indirect routes. Social Darwinism, on the other hand, lies close to the mainstream of sociological development.

As we have observed, the ideal of universal competition was made the foundation of economic life by the physiocrats and classical economists. The notion of competition was deepened into the concept of survival in the demographic reflections of Malthus. These notions formed one of the spurs to Darwinian biology — one of the outstanding scientific gains of the nineteenth century. So successful was biology that positivistic organicism for a time modeled itself on biology. Now it was time to make the return from biology to society.

SOCIAL DARWINISM: PHASE I

Darwin and Social Darwinism. Darwin was quite ready to apply his own theories to human beings. In such an extension, Malthus always seems to be in the background of his thinking. All creatures are in competition to survive. There must, Darwin argues, be a natural selection of the most fit. This is also true for human beings.

> The early progenitors of man must also have tended, like all other animals, to have increased beyond their means of subsistence. They must, therefore, occasionally have been exposed to a struggle for existence, and consequently to the rigid law of natural selection. Beneficial variations of all kinds will thus, either occasionally or habitually, have been preserved, and injurious ones eliminated.[1]

[1]Charles Darwin, *The Descent of Man* (New York: D. Appleton, 1880), p. 48.

CHARLES DARWIN

Brown Brothers

Implicit also in this passage is the idea that humankind has repeatedly found itself on a level of pure subsistence, at which time the laws of natural selection operate.

> Man in the rudest state in which he now exists is the most dominant animal that has ever appeared on this earth. He has spread more widely than any other highly organized form: and all others have yielded before him. He manifestly owes this immense superiority to his intellectual faculties, to his social habits, which lead him to aid and defend his fellows, and to his corporeal structure. The supreme importance of these characters has been proved by the final arbitrament of the battle for life. Through his powers of intellect, articulate language has been evolved; and on this his wonderful advancement has mainly depended. As Mr. Chauncy Wright remarks: "a psychological analysis of the faculty of language shows

that even the smallest proficiency in it might require more brain power than the greatest proficiency in any other direction." He has invented and is able to use various weapons, tools, traps, etc., with which he defends himself, kills or catches prey, and otherwise obtains food. He has made rafts or canoes for fishing or crossing over to neighboring fertile islands. He has discovered the art of making fire, by which hard and stringy roots can be rendered digestible, and poisonous roots or herbs innocuous. This discovery of fire, probably the greatest ever made by man excepting language, dates from before the dawn of history. These several inventions, by which man in the rudest state has become so preeminent, are the direct results of the development of his powers of observation, memory, curiosity, imagination, and reason. I cannot, therefore, understand how it is that Mr. Wallace maintains that "natural selection" could only have endowed the savage with a brain little superior to that of an ape.[2]

A subtle, but important, distinction is implied here. The laws of natural selection and survival of the fittest gave human beings their intelligence. But their intelligence made possible language, a complex social life, tools, and fire. Thus the whole area of culture would not be necessarily explainable in terms of natural selection directly but indirectly. It is incidentally worth noting that Darwin's estimate concerning what is peculiar to humankind has a remarkably modern sound.

Darwin is not altogether consistent about when and where one should not apply the principles of his biological theory. He does, it seems, think that a group with a solidary ethic has increased survival value.

> When two tribes of primeval man, living in the same country, come into competition, if . . . the one tribe included a great number of courageous, sympathetic, and faithful members, who were always ready to warn each other of danger, to aid and defend each other, this tribe would succeed better and conquer the other.[3]

[2]*Ibid.*, pp. 48–49.
[3]*Ibid.*, pp. 130–131.

However, Darwin approached the view that even for the primitive, bravery and moral sense may have been individually dysgenic:

> The bravest men, who were always willing to come to the front in war, and who freely risked their lives for others, would on the average perish in larger numbers than other men.[4]

Despite the interesting suggestion by some students that Darwin was not a "social Darwinist," by extending the point of view just noted to the problem of natural selection in civilized nations, Darwin comes to the usual conclusions.

> We civilized men . . . do our utmost to check the process of elimination; we build asylums for the imbecile, the maimed, and the sick; we institute poor-laws; and our medical men exert their utmost skill to save the life of everyone to the last moment. There is reason to believe that vaccination has preserved thousands, who from a weak constitution would formerly have succumbed to smallpox. Thus the weak members of civilized societies propagate their kind. No one who has attended to the breeding of domestic animals will doubt that this must be highly injurious to the race of man. It is surprising how soon a want of care, or care wrongly directed, leads to the degeneration of a domestic race; but excepting in the case of man himself, hardly any one is so ignorant as to allow his worst animals to breed.[5]

And worse, we not only keep the weak alive, but eliminate the fit:

> In every country in which a large standing army is kept up, the finest young men are taken by conscription or are enlisted. They are thus exposed to early death during war, are often tempted into vice, and are prevented from marrying during the prime of life. On the other hand, the shorter and feebler men, with poor constitutions, are left at home, and consequently have a much better chance of marrying and propagating their kind.

Nor is this the end.

[4]*Ibid.,* p. 130.
[5]*Ibid.,* pp. 133–134.

> The children of parents who are short-lived, and are therefore on an average deficient in health and vigor, come into their property sooner than other children and will be likely to marry earlier, and leave a larger number of offspring to inherit their inferior constitutions.[6]

Natural selection operating on individuals produced a superior animal. This superior animal creates a society tending to destroy its own biological superiority.

Spencer's Social Darwinism. Herbert Spencer has been treated as an organicist because of the primary structure of his sociological theory. His organicism goes back to a period before the appearance of Darwin's *Origin of Species*. The play back of Darwin's findings on Spencer is evident in his increased concern with conflict in his later works. Particularly as he turned attention to social issues, Spencer tended to welcome the conception of a natural process of conflict and survival which operates as a kind of biologically purifying process. Spencer gave a novel twist to social Darwinism, urging not that it does in fact operate in society but that it ought to!

> It seems hard that widows and orphans should be left to struggle for life or death. Nevertheless, when regarded not separately but in connexion with the interests of universal humanity, these harsh fatalities are seen to be full of beneficence — the same beneficence which brings to early graves the children of diseased parents, and singles out the intemperate and the debilitated as the victims of an epidemic.[7]

Spencer's attitude toward the poor-laws is typical of his approach to all meliorative legislation.

> By suspending the process of adaptation, a poor-law increases the distress to be borne at some future day; and here we shall find that it also increases the distress to be borne now. For be it remembered that of the

[6]*Ibid.,* pp. 134–135.
[7]Herbert Spencer, *Social Statics* and *The Man Versus the State* (New York: D. Appleton, 1908), p. 150.

sum taken in any year to support paupers, a large portion would otherwise have gone to support labourers employed in new reproductive works — land-drainage, machine-building, etc. An additional stock of commodities would by-and-by have been produced, and the number of those who go short would consequently have been diminished.[8]

Spencer was opposed to practically every form of state interference with private activity, justifying his opposition on the grounds of a social Darwinism. The list of his complaints includes state-supported education, sanitary supervision, regulation of housing conditions, state protection of the ignorant from medical quacks, tariffs, state banking, and government postal systems.

Spencer's theories were as agreeable to some business groups as Marx's were to some labor elements. Richard Hofstadter has assembled an interesting series of quotations to this effect from some of the business magnates of the time. James J. Hill, the railroad magnate, for example, argued that "the fortunes of railroad companies are determined by the law of the survival of the fittest." John D. Rockefeller took no less an occasion than a Sunday-school address to identify the survival of the fittest with the law of God. "The growth of a large business is merely a survival of the fittest. . . . The American Beauty rose can be produced in the splendor and fragrance which bring cheer to its beholder only by sacrificing the early buds which grow up around it. This is not an evil tendency in business. It is merely the working out of a law of nature and a law of God." Andrew Carnegie reports the reading of Darwin and Spencer to have been a source of great peace of mind. "I remember that light came as in a flood and all was clear. Not only had I got rid of theology and the supernatural, but I had found the truth of evolution. 'All is well since all grows better' became my motto, my true source of comfort. Man was not created with an instinct for his own degradation, but from the lower he had risen to the higher forms. Nor is there any conceivable end to his march to perfec-

tion. His face is turned to the light; he stands in the sun and looks upward."[9]

Sumner's Social Darwinism. A practical and applied social Darwinism appears also in the work of William Graham Sumner, described by Hofstadter as "the most vigorous and influential social Darwinist in America." Sumner (1840–1910) was the son of an immigrant English artisan. He was born in New Jersey, studied at Yale University, and spent three years at Geneva, Göttingen, and Oxford. He became a tutor in mathematics and Greek at Yale in 1866. As an ordained Protestant minister, he became assistant pastor at New York Church. In 1872 he was offered a professorship of political and social science at Yale, and remained in that position until his death. Sumner tied together the Protestant ethic, the doctrines of classical economics, and Darwinian natural selection.[10]

In his early essays, Sumner took a position with respect to economic and social issues that the original human situation was a struggle for existence. "The struggle of man to win his existence from nature is one which he begins with no advantages at all, but utterly naked and empty-handed. He has everything to conquer. Evidently it is only by his achievements that he can emancipate himself from the difficulties of his situation."[11]

---

[8]*Ibid.*, pp. 154–155.

[9]An excellent review of Spencer's social Darwinism is found in Richard Hofstadter's *Social Darwinism in American Thought*, rev. ed. (Boston: Beacon Press, 1955), pp. 31–50. The foregoing quotations, all from Hofstadter's book, were drawn originally from: James J. Hill, *Highways of Progress* (New York: Doubleday, Page, 1910), p. 126; Rockefeller was quoted in William J. Ghent, *Our Benevolent Feudalism* (New York: Macmillan, 1902), p. 29; and Andrew Carnegie, *Autobiography of Andrew Carnegie* (Boston: Houghton Mifflin, 1920).

[10]Sumner's most famous work, *Folkways* (Boston: Ginn, 1906; New York: Dover, 1960), will be discussed in the next chapter, where his more strictly sociological contribution is taken up. Sumner's many essays appeared in various editions; the references here, unless otherwise noted, are to *Essays of William Graham Sumner*, ed. Albert Galloway Keller and Maurice R. Davie, 2 vols. (New Haven, Conn.: Yale University Press, 1940).

[11]Sumner, *Essays*, I, 293.

WILLIAM GRAHAM SUMNER

Courtesy of Yale University, New Haven, Connecticut

Spencer conceived the ruthless elimination of widows and orphans as a first step by nature in maintaining the quality of the race. Sumner contemplates the elimination of the old in primitive society with equal equanimity: "The killing of old people by their children among savage tribes seems to us inexpressibly shocking, but this custom means something very different from the selfishness of the young; it testifies to the fact that the first liberty of all, the liberty to exist, becomes an unendurable burden to the savage man when he becomes old."[12]

In Sumner's thought it is only a step from the struggle for existence to the permanent importance of property for civilization. The first advance of humankind is the production of capital, increasing the fruitfulness of labor and making possible the advance of civilization. Primitive people withdrew from the competitive struggle, ceased to accumulate capital, and were reduced to permanent backwardness.[13] The captains of industry and capitalists are the great competitors of the present, the true creators of wealth and worth every cent they cost. "The captains of industry and the capitalists . . . if they are successful, win, in these days, great fortunes in a short time." There are, according to Sumner, "no earnings . . . more legitimate or for which greater services are rendered to the whole industrial body."[14] The burden of proof lies on those who affirm that our social situation needs radical regeneration. "The greatest folly of which a man can be capable" is "to sit down with a slate and pencil to plan out a new social world."[15] The impoverished have brought their situation on themselves.

At present, poverty is correlated with ignorance, vice, and misfortune — the slow and tedious processes which we have hitherto been invited to employ and trust, have aimed to abolish poverty by working against ignorance, vice, and misfortune. If we can abolish poverty by a device or contrivance introduced into the social organization, then we can divorce poverty from its correlation with ignorance, vice, and misfortune. We can let those things stand and yet escape their consequences.[16]

At the other end of the social scale are the millionaires who

are a product of natural selection, acting on the whole body of men to pick out those who can meet the requirement of certain work to be done. . . . They may fairly be regarded as the naturally selected agents of

[12]*Ibid.*

[13]Sumner, *The Challenge of Facts and Other Essays,* ed. by Albert Keller (New Haven, Conn.: Yale University Press, 1914), p. 40.
[14]Sumner, "The Absurd Effort to Make the World Over," *Essays,* I, 97.
[15]*Ibid.,* p. 106.
[16]Sumner, "The Abolition of Poverty," *Essays,* I, 108.

society for certain work. They get high wages and live in luxury, but the bargain is a good one for society. There is the most intense competition for their place and occupation. This assures us that all who are competent for this function will be employed in it, so that the cost of it will be reduced to the lowest terms. . . .[17]

The fundamental fact of all societies is a peculiar ratio of people to land. It is this ratio that determines the possibilities of human development and what human beings can attain by way of civilization. Standards of living reflect the type of resolution of the problem. A population of high intelligence, great social ambition, and self-respect will increase economic power and the average level of comfort, and it will *not* increase its numbers. When institutions have outlived their usefulness, they become an abuse. Wars and revolutions that overthrow them are a comparative good.

For Sumner the inequality of the social classes is normal. The "superstition of democracy" applies to the unusual case:

> Democracy itself, the pet superstition of the age, is only a phase of the all-compelling movement. If you have abundance of land and few men to share it, the men will all be equal. Each landholder will be his own tenant and his own laborer. Social classes disappear. Wages are high. The mass of men, apart from laziness, folly, and vice, are well off.[18]

The moment this condition does not exist, social classes appear and the competitive struggle sharpens. While within the society social distinctions grow tense, the state, as a whole, discovers a "manifest destiny" in the acquisition and holding of land.

> There is . . . some truth to be admitted in the doctrine of "manifest destiny," although the doctrine is, like most doctrines in politics, a glib and convenient means of giving an appearance of rationality to an exercise of superior force. The truth in the doctrine is

that an incompetent holder will not be able, as a matter of fact and in the long run, to maintain possession of territory when another nation which will develop it according to its capacity is ready to take it.[19]

It is rather startling to hear, about so indefatigable a defender of the status quo, that the Republican press and Republican alumni of Yale periodically urged his dismissal — a demand which became general when Sumner announced his opposition to the Spanish-American War.[20] It is a comfort to realize, however, that not all of Yale's alumni missed the point. "One old fashioned benefactor of Yale doubled his donation because Sumner's presence had convinced him 'that Yale College is a good and safe place for the keeping and use of property and the sustaining of civilization when endangered by ignorance, rascality, demagogues, repudiationists, rebels, copperheads, communists, butlers, strikers, protectionists, and fanatics of sundry roots and sizes.' "[21]

SOCIAL DARWINISM: PHASE II

Social Darwinism as illustrated by Sumner was primarily a defensive position — a vindication of the successful business groups of nineteenth-century European and American society and a defense of the status quo against all types of reform, whether internal or revolutionary. But there was no good reason why social Darwinism should not develop a "positive" program of its own as the strict counterpart of the activism of Marxism. Even before Darwin's great work on the origin of species, the foundations of racism were being laid — a position that could potentially claim Darwin's support.

Arthur de Gobineau. Count Joseph Arthur de Gobineau (1816–1882) was one of the upper-class

[17]Sumner, *The Challenge of Facts*, p. 90.
[18]Sumner, "Earth Hunger or the Philosophy of Land Grabbing," *Essays*, I, 185.

[19]*Ibid.*, p. 197.
[20]Hofstadter, *Social Darwinism in American Thought*, p. 64.
[21]*Ibid.*, p. 64.

Frenchmen disgusted with the political development of France. His essay on *The Inequality of Human Races* (1853–1857)[22] was dedicated to George V of Hanover, the blind German king who had just swept away the liberal constitution granted by his father to the people. The specific object of his anger was the revolution of 1848. He was one of the founders of a periodical to work for the establishment of a republic led by aristocrats. De Gobineau had been cabinet secretary, minister to Persia, and representative of the government on missions to Brazil and many European capitals.

The problem upsetting to de Gobineau was the disintegration of the aristocratic society he had known. He found race to be the key to history, and inequality of races sufficient to explain the entire enchainment of the destinies of peoples. He urged that "everything great, noble, and fruitful in the works of man on this earth, in science, art, and civilization, derives from a single starting point, it belongs to one family alone, the different branches of which have reigned in all the civilized countries of the universe."[23] The decline of aristocratic Europe was seen by de Gobineau to lie in the loss by the "Aryans" of their position of dominance.

H. S. Chamberlain. In the work of Houston Stewart Chamberlain and G. Vacher de Lapouge, the racialist position was shifted in the direction of Darwinism. There was also the development of a nationalistic cast to the doctrines, an emphasis on anti-Semitism, the establishment of the doctrines on a pseudo-quantitative foundation. Wagner's son-in-law, Houston Chamberlain (1855–1927), the son of Admiral William Charles Chamberlain, received a foreign education. He traveled extensively, and published several works. His most famous was *Foundations of the Nineteenth Century*,[24] a book with great influence on German thought. The Kaiser read two volumes of the work aloud to his sons; he had them distributed to army officers, and displayed in all libraries and bookshops in Germany.

Modern civilization was thought by Chamberlain to be derived from four sources: from Greek, Roman, Jewish, and Teutonic civilizations. It received poetry, art, and philosophy from the Greeks, statecraft, order, and the idea of citizenship from the Romans, Judaism and, indirectly, Christianity from the Jews. The fusion of these three traditions was the contribution of the Teutons. For Chamberlain, the Teutons included not only the Germanic tribes described by Tacitus, but the Celts and Slavs as well — all were descended from a presumed single pure stock. Mixture of blood between these subgroups prevented sterility, and accounts for German greatness. This race understands leadership, and gives unfaltering loyalty to it. The incidence of the leadership trait among the Italians and French — insofar as it is found in them at all — is due to the presence of Teutons among them. Chamberlain had little doubt that persons such as Louis XIV, Dante, Michelangelo, Marco Polo, and Jesus Christ were really Teutons.

Georges Vacher de Lapouge. The French anthropologist, Georges Vacher de Lapouge (1854–1936), in three works written at the turn of the century,[25] sharpened the Darwinian elements of

[22]De Gobineau, *Essai sur l'inégalité des races humains*, 4 vols. (Paris: 1853–1855; 2d ed., 1884). The first volume was translated by Adrian Collins and published as *The Inequality of Human Races* (New York: G. P. Putnam, 1915). A new edition with an introduction by Oscar Levy has been published: (Los Angeles: The Noontide Press, 1966 and New York: H. Fertig, 1967). Gobineau's *Selected Political Writings*, ed. Michael D. Biddiss (London: Cape, 1970). See also Maurice Lange, *Le Comte Arthur de Gobineau* (Strasbourg: Librairie Istra, 1924). For a critique, see Ruth Benedict, *Race: Science and Politics*, rev. ed. (New York: Viking, 1943), pp. 112 ff. See also R. Thenen, "Gobineau," *International Encyclopedia of the Social Sciences* (New York: Crowell Collier and Macmillan, 1968), VI, 193–194.
[23]De Gobineau, *The Inequality of Human Races*, pp. xiv–xv.

[24]H. S. Chamberlain, *Die Grundlagen des neunzehnten Jahrhunderts* (Munich: F. Bruckmann, 1900), translated by John Lees as *Foundations of the Nineteenth Century* (London: John Lane, 1911).
[25]Georges Vacher de Lapouge, *Les Sélections sociales* ["Social Selection"] (Paris: A. Fontemoing, 1896); *L'Aryen: son rôle social* ["The Aryan: His Role in Society"] (Paris: A. Fontemoing, 1899); *Race et milieu social* ["Race and So-

this type of racism and provided a pseudoquan-titative basis for it. Lapouge was too sophisticated to assume that there are any pure races. Traced back to the time of Christ, every person has no less than 18,000,000,000,000,000 ancestors. It was his opinion, however, that many incidental crossings would not appreciably alter the race. The popula-tion of Europe has three principal races: *Homo Europæus* or Aryan (tall of stature, blond, con-spicuously dolichocephalic); *Homo Alpinus* (of moderate stature, brown in pigmentation, and having a cephalic index of 85 and above as op-posed to the Aryan index of 76 and below); and *Homo contractus* or Mediterranean (of low stature, dark color, and cephalic index of about 78). Character and temperament were thought to be related to these traits. When the cranium is small, the race lacks energy. The brachycephalic race (that is, with a high cephalic index) is deficient in individuality and initiative. Intellectual power is correlated with the breadth of the anterior part of the brain. The Nordic or Aryan race are leaders in every creative activity.

As Lapouge saw it, education can work no long-run influence on temperament and charac-ter, hence on civilization. Selection argued on Darwin's principles represents the elimination of the unfit and survival of the fittest. Among human beings, natural selection is replaced by social selec-tion. In present society, such selection is primarily negative in its biological effects. Thus, the Aryan race is rapidly disappearing, and it will disappear altogether unless a natural aristocracy is created on the basis of the innate qualities of individuals and through greater procreation and organization of a new dominant racial caste.

There were many additional contributors to the fusion of racism, Darwinism, and nationalism, but these are sufficient to illustrate what was occur-ring. Such individuals provided the rationale for one type of social Darwinistic nationalism and im-perialism.

---

cial Milieu"] (Paris: M. Rivière, 1909). English transla-tions of these three works are not available.

Francis Galton. One form of social Darwinism, as we have seen, buttressed the imperialism and ex-pansionism subscribed to by a whole series of American statesmen and educators. A second form led to various programs of racial improve-ment as the only effective means of solving social problems. A more scholarly version of this second form than the master-race theories of Chamber-lain and Vacher de Lapouge was the work of Dar-win's cousin, Sir Francis Galton (1822–1911), who did much to inaugurate the eugenics movement. Galton was a grandson of Erasmus Darwin. He studied medicine at Birmingham Hospital and King's College, London, and in 1844 he graduated from Trinity College. His work on *Hereditary Genius* may serve to illustrate the tenor of Galton's books.[26]

Individuals differ from one another in bodily and psychological characteristics: stature, weight, health, energy, sensitivity, gregariousness, intelli-gence, and so on. Physical and mental characteris-tics differ according to typical frequency distri-butions. For example, if we grade the intelligence of one million individuals, we will find the greatest number of them concentrated in the group classified as mediocre and a great rarity of indi-viduals with commanding ability. There are fixed limits to educational development. Inheritance fixes these limits; talent and ability are inherited. Able fathers produce able children in much greater proportion than do others. Galton's study of English men of science, of genius, and Fellows of the Royal Society convinced him that families with two or more eminent men produce more fa-mous men of genius than families with only one. There is a rapid decrease in the frequency of noteworthiness as distance of kinship from emi-nent men increases. Abilities such as those of mathematician, musician, judge, and statesman

[26]Galton's principal works are: *Hereditary Genius* (Lon-don: 1869; 2d ed., 1892); *English Men of Science: Their Nature and Nurture* (London: 1874); *Inquiries into Human Faculty and Its Development* (London: 1883; 2d ed., 1907); *Natural Inheritance* (London: 1889); *Finger Prints* (Lon-don, 1892); and *Finger Print Directories* (London, 1895).

are inherited. Social hindrances cannot impede men of high ability from becoming eminent. Galton's study of twins, he thought, bore the same conclusion. There was no escaping the conclusion that nature prevails enormously over nurture when the differences of nurture do not exceed what is commonly found among persons of the same rank of society and in the same country.[27] What holds for individuals also holds for races. Just as upper and lower strata differ in regard to ability, the upper strata producing more men of genius and talent, so the races are unequal. This is to be judged by their ability to produce men of genius per given population number. The ancient Athenian Greeks produced one genius to 4,822 population. He argued that there were other groups that have not been able to produce a genius in their entire history.[28]

Karl Pearson. Karl Pearson (1857–1936) carried on Galton's work. Educated in mathematics at University College and at King's College, Cambridge, he was called to the bar in 1882, and later became an authority on eugenics. He was appointed Galton Professor of Eugenics at London University and Director of the Francis Galton Laboratory of National Eugenics. From 1902 until his death in 1936 he edited the journal *Biometrika*, and from 1925 on he was editor of *The Annals of Eugenics*. Quite apart from his great contributions to the science of statistics[29] was his development of the eugenic branch of social Darwinism. He believed that biological factors "are dominant in the

evolution of mankind; these and these alone, can throw light on the rise and fall of nations, on racial progress and national degeneracy."[30]

Like that of animals, human development rests on natural selection. Characteristics are variable and inherited. There is a selective death rate. The earlier a person dies, the fewer offspring that person leaves. Pearson was shocked by the differential fertility of present society, where the physically and mentally superior social classes have a lower rate of reproduction than inferior stock. He proposed that education should vary for different individuals and groups according to their ability.

Among the works in the United States which tremendously popularized the eugenics movement was Richard Dugdale's *The Jukes* (1877), a study of the descendants of a group of sisters who had lived in New York State in the eighteenth century, and which argued that disease, pauperism, and immorality are largely controlled by inheritance. Eugenics, in fact, grew with such rapidity that by 1915 it had reached the dimensions of a fad. The early eugenicists identified the "fit" with the upper classes, the "unfit" with the lower. They railed against multiplying morons. The poor were thought to be held down by biological deficiency rather than environmental conditions. Pearson set the tone for the eugenics movement by his estimate that nine-tenths of human capacity was determined by heredity. Henry Goddard studied successive generations of a family whom he called the Kallikaks, and concluded that feeble-mindedness is largely responsible for criminals, prostitutes, and drunkards. David Starr Jordan thought that poverty, dirt, and crime were due to poor human material, while Lewellys F. Barker, a distinguished physician, thought the birth and death of nations was due to the relative fertility of fit and unfit elements.

Lothrop Stoddard. Where this all leads is developed fully by Lothrop Stoddard (1883–1950), in his proposals for race building, "multiplication of

---

[27]Galton, *Inquiries into Human Faculty and Its Development.*
[28]Galton, *Hereditary Genius,* pp. 325–337.
[29]See his famous *Tables for Statisticians and Biometricians* (Cambridge, England: The University Press, 1914; 2d ed., 1924; 3d ed., 1945). Pearson's other principal writings are: *The Ethic of Free Thought* (London: 1883; 2d ed., London: A. and C. Black, 1901); *The Grammar of Science* (London: W. Scott, 1892; 3d ed., London: A. and C. Black, 1911; New York: Macmillan, 1911); *The Chances of Death* (London: E. Arnold, 1897); *National Life from the Standpoint of Science* (London: A. and C. Black, 1901; 2d ed., 1905); and *The Scope and Importance to the State of the Science of National Eugenics* (London: Dulau, 1909).

[30]Pearson, *The Scope and Importance,* p. 38.

superiors," and "elimination of inferiors" or "race cleansing."[31] These processes are termed "positive" and "negative" eugenics. The starting point is in race cleansing. This begins with the segregation of the insane and feeble-minded in public institutions, awakening society to the gravity of the situation, and tracing the relation between the "degenerate classes" and others "all the way from the unemployable 'casual laborer' right up to the 'tainted genius.' "[32] The eugenic ideal is that of "an ever-perfecting super-race." Not the "superman" of Nietzsche — "that brilliant yet baleful vision of a master *caste,* blooming like a gorgeous but parasitic orchid on a rotting trunk of servile degradation, but a super *race,* cleansing itself *throughout* by the elimination of its defects, and raising itself *throughout* by the cultivation of its qualities."[33] The neo-aristocracy so created will need a new philosophy more adequate than democracy. "Now I believe, *for the time being at any rate,* the new philosophy should be called 'Neo-Aristocracy'; because it involves first of all the disestablishment of the democratic *cult* and the rehabilitation of the discredited aristocratic idea."[34]

Nazism. The further full development and practical application of the kind of program indicated by Stoddard occurred in Germany, with beginnings before the date of his book (1922). Hitler outlined future German policy in *Mein Kampf.* National policy was to be based on racist theories, following Chamberlain. The Jews were held responsible for the national defeat. This became the core of National Socialism. In the Nazi program of 1920, citizenship and public office were proposed only for those of German blood, and everyone of alien blood was to be deported or eliminated. Upon Hitler's assumption of power in 1933, laws began to be passed to these various ends, and anti-Semitic persecutions began. In 1935, with the Nuremberg

Laws, full-scale actions began in earnest. All Jews were deprived of the right of citizenship, and marriages and extramarital relations between Jews and German non-Jews were prohibited. All Jewish children were removed from elementary schools. In 1936 the expropriation without recompense of Jewish property and banking accounts began and continued through 1937 — this measure aimed at eliminating Jews from trade and commerce. In 1938 outbursts against Jews became general, and mass arrests occurred in Berlin. Pogroms took place throughout Germany. By an edict, the Jews were assessed for all damage done during such outbreaks, plus a fine of a billion marks.

In 1939 the Jewish community in Berlin received orders from the police to produce daily the names of one hundred Jews who would receive two weeks' notice to leave the country. No provisions were made to finance the emigration. Racism in the Third Reich was beginning to spread to other areas. Alfred Rosenberg, editor-in-chief of official newspapers, pronounced the Christian Church to be a menace to true Nordics, and discovered racial antipathy of the Nordics in the decadent words of the Sermon on the Mount. This all terminated in the mass murders, the gas chambers, and the death factories of the concentration camps.

SUMMARY

The three major forms of conflict ideology, which must not be confused with conflict theory as a sociological school, were Marxian socialism and two forms of social Darwinism.

While Marxian socialism represented a conflict ideology advanced in the name of the proletariat, both forms of social Darwinism were developed as ideologies of the business groups of modern society. The first form of social Darwinism, already partly evident in the writings of Charles Darwin, conceived human society as a product of the struggle for existence and the survival of the fittest. In the works of Spencer, William Graham Sumner,

---

[31]Lothrop Stoddard, *The Revolt Against Civilization* (New York: Scribner's, 1922).
[32]*Ibid.,* p. 245.
[33]*Ibid.,* p. 262.
[34]*Ibid.,* p. 266.

and others, this led to the notion that the captains of modern industry represented the fittest members of society. It also led to the assumption that social welfare activities, in aiding the socially underprivileged, were destroying the biological potential of the race. The rich thus merited their wealth; the poor, by biological inferiority, deserved their fate.

Marxism was a conflict ideology projected in the names and interests of the proletariat. Social Darwinism was a conflict ideology projected in the name of the upper strata of bourgeois society. Marxism's external program was the worldwide union of the proletariat; social Darwinism's external program was imperialism ("manifest destiny," the "white man's burden"). Marxism's internal program was the overthrow of capitalistic society, the temporary dictatorship of the proletariat, and the withering away of the state. Social Darwinism's internal program was an active eugenic policy aimed at race improvement, mass sterilization, and the rooting out of socialism as if it were a genetic defect. It was left to the Germans to demonstrate fully the implications of consistent social Darwinism.

Just as Marxism left a residue of problems behind it for objective social science, so too did the ideological forms of social Darwinism. The problems of nationalism and imperialism were posed. The problems of racial and other minority groups were phrased. The possible relevance of individual differences to social conduct was formulated, and great strides were made in the study of individual differences. The fact was established that there are certain ultimate limits fixed for society in the nature of biological materials. As in the case of Marxism, these problems were posed for sociology — not solved.

X

Sociological Conflict Theories

Marxism and social Darwinism were ideologies — sets of ideas vindicating particular social positions and spurring particular action programs. Sociological conflict theory, though some of its propositions coincide with those appearing in the ideologies, is scientific, resting its hypotheses on the scientific standards of the discipline. Nevertheless, when sociologists began to turn to conflict theory in the late nineteenth century, the general ideological atmosphere that gave birth to positivistic organicism was still effective, as is evident in the fact that they found many more affinities with social Darwinism than with Marxism. If there had not been a predisposition toward one rather than the other ideology, we would expect equal receptivity or equal indifference.

The ideological atmosphere sustaining early sociology required a combination of conservatism and scientific method. However, positivistic organicism, though brilliantly adapted to both requirements, did not give stable results. It was a fluctuating compound, yielding to the whims of every student. Ultimately it could not satisfy the demand either for a conservative image of society or for a dependable method. It is not surprising, then, that a sober search for "realities" made its appearance.

Although positivistic organicism proved in the end to be inadequate, the need for scientific method and a conservative picture of society remained. Conflict theory was able to fulfill both needs. The sociological conflict theorists are, as a whole, even more positivistic than their organicist colleagues. They can afford to be: they have not had to close their eyes to whole blocks of empirical facts. While it is possible, as shown by Marxism and social Darwinism, to develop conflict theory into an aggressive ideology, it is by no means necessary. There is a milder ideological conclusion that may be drawn whenever one takes as the most obvious fact of society the occurrence of conflict. The normal task of on-going society can be seen as a constant movement toward what is variously called adjustment, stability, equilibrium, or the termination of conflict. Hence, bad as things sometimes seem, it is conservative wisdom not to make matters worse, nor to make the world over, nor to interfere with "the normal processes of society," but rather to leave well enough alone and keep whatever peace is possible. *Conflict sociology emerged as the second form of sociological theory precisely because while correcting positivistic organicism in a realistic manner it was conformable to the same ideological requirements.*

Walter Bagehot. The restylization of traditional conflict theory in Darwinian terms, with a theoretical rather than a practical (moralistic) intent, is presented by the work of Walter Bagehot (1826–1877), son of an English banker. Bagehot took his degree at London University in 1848, and was called to the bar in 1852. He entered his father's banking business, Stuckey and Company, for many years managing its London agency. Bagehot was also an underwriter at Lloyd's. He married the daughter of James Wilson, the first editor of the *Economist,* and began a long connection with the journal. His main books were *The English Constitution* (1867), *Physics and Politics* (1869), and *Lombard Street* (1873). For conflict theory, *Physics and Politics* was most important.[1] It attracted the favorable attention of Darwin. The subtitle, "Thoughts on the Application of the Principles of 'Natural Selection' and 'Inheritance' to Political Society," are a clue to Bagehot's theory of society, which rests on a fusion of biological and political considerations. He was familiar with Henry Sumner Maine's *Ancient Law,* and inclined to accept Maine's ideas about the original state of society.[2] Bagehot was also familiar with Darwin's theories, and was convinced that natural selection plays a part in the development of human society equivalent to its role in the evolution of animal species.

The peculiarity of our age to Bagehot is found in the rapidity of change: "by it everything is made 'an antiquity.' "[3] The function of science, by its

WALTER BAGEHOT

The British Museum, London

eternal prying and continuous recording, is to turn everything rapidly into an item of the past while thought moves restlessly on. This, for Bagehot, is in thematic contrast with past ages, which were marked by a stability based on unreflective habit. Prior to historical times, society was organized into patriarchal families; only the germs of the state were present in the patriarch. Behavior was automatic and arbitrary. Maine thought that the origins of political society occurred with the shift from the patriarchal family to local contiguity as a principle of organization. Bagehot saw this as superficial, for he thought Darwin's principle of natural selection was more adequate. "When once politics were begun, there was no difficulty in explaining why they lasted. Whatever may be said against the principle of 'natural selection' in other departments, there is no doubt of its predomi-

---

[1] References here are to: Walter Bagehot, *Physics and Politics,* introduction by Jacques Barzun (New York: Alfred A. Knopf, 1948).
[2] For a brief discussion of Maine, see Chapter V, pp. 98f.
[3] Bagehot, *Physics and Politics,* p. 4.

nance in early human history. The strongest killed out the weakest, as they could. And I need not pause to prove that any form of policy is more efficient than none."[4] The most fundamental of all problems for early political society was achieving order and obedience. This was obtained through the fusion of church and state. "To gain . . . obedience, the primary condition is the identity — not the union, but the sameness of — what we now call Church and State."[5] The object of such fusion was to create what may be called a "cake of custom." All the actions of life were to be submitted to a single rule for a single object — gradually creating the " 'hereditary drill' which science teaches us to be essential."[6] The early recorded history of the Aryan race shows that a king and a council were required to solve early conflicts. Rome and Sparta were "drilling" aristocracies, succeeding for this reason. This phenomenon of "drill" or discipline is a component in all societies and extends to the writers. "What writers are expected to write, they write; or else they do not write at all." While people vainly assume that they choose what they like, they are actually dominated by "received opinion" which prescribes what they ought to like; "or if their minds are too marked and oddly made to get into the mould, they give up reading altogether. . . . the principle of 'elimination,' the 'use and disuse' of organs . . . works here."[7]

This process of disciplining and customary consolidation of habits in terms of the social order gives rise to national character. "I believe that what we call national character arose in very much the same way. At first a sort of 'chance predominance' made a model, and then invincible attraction, the necessity which rules all but the strongest man to imitate what is before their eyes, and to be what they are expected to be, moulded men by that model. This is, I think, the very process by which new national characters are being made in our own time."[8]

Bagehot perceived the dynamics of society as the tension between customary behavior and intrusive elements which conflict with it.

> "Whoever speaks two languages is a rascal," says the saying, and it rightly represents the feeling of primitive communities when the sudden impact of new thoughts and new examples breaks down the compact despotism of the single consecrated code, and leaves pliant and impressible man — such as he then is — to follow his unpleasant will without distinct guidance by hereditary morality and hereditary religion. The old oligarchies wanted to keep their type perfect, and for that end they were right not to allow foreigners to touch it."[9]

From this theoretical base — a tension between customary and intrusive factors — Bagehot was in a position to present conflict as the central phenomenon in social development and structure.

> Three laws, or approximate laws, may . . . be laid down. . . . First. In every particular state of the world, those nations which are strongest tend to prevail over the others; and in certain marked peculiarities the strongest tend to be best.
>
> Secondly. Within every particular nation the type or types of character then and there most attractive tend to prevail; and the most attractive, though with exceptions, is what we call the best character.
>
> Thirdly. Neither of these competitions is in most historic conditions intensified by extrinsic forces, but in some conditions, such as those now prevailing in the most influential part of the world, both are so intensified.[10]

In developing the significance of conflict, Bagehot maintained that the "progress of the military art is the most conspicuous, I was about to say the most showy, fact in human history."[11] Taken as a whole, the fighting capacity of humankind has ever grown more immense. Military vices decline as military strength increases. For example, it is no longer true that living in cities makes people un-

[4]*Ibid.*, p. 26.
[5]*Ibid.*, p. 28.
[6]*Ibid.*, p. 29.
[7]*Ibid.*, p. 38.
[8]*Ibid.*, pp. 38–39.

[9]*Ibid.*, p. 42.
[10]*Ibid.*, p. 46.
[11]*Ibid.*, p. 48.

warlike and effeminate. The primitive could have withstood the attack of ancient civilized people in the past; the primitive in the present cannot withstand ours. In history the strongest nation always conquers the weaker, always prevailing over it. Every intellectual gain, so to speak, that a nation possessed was in the earliest times made use of — was invested and taken out in war. Moreover, conquest improved humankind by an intermixture of strength. Even civilization grows by coalescence of strengths and by the competition of strengths. The conflict of nations was at first a main force in their improvement.

Bagehot structures human history into three great ages: (1) the prehistorical age of custom, (2) the age of war and nation making, in which warfare and militarism were the primary constructive force, and (3) the age of discussion or science, which has built a social order open to the intrusive ideas of science. In the course of his elaboration of these themes, numerous stereotypes are disposed of. For example, he objects to the idea that progress is a general feature of history. The Greeks and Oriental nations knew nothing of the idea. A large part of humankind lived outside it. Bagehot also opposes the stereotype that humankind wants to be original. "At this very moment there are the most rigid Comtists teaching that we ought to be governed by a hierarchy — a combination of savants orthodox in science. Yet who can doubt that Comte would have been hanged by his own hierarchy?"[12] Nor is Bagehot sure that the academies are sources of original ideas. "The academies are asylums of the ideas and the tastes of the last age. . . . I have heard a most eminent man of science observe, 'by the time a man of science attains eminence on any subject, he becomes a nuisance upon it, because he is sure to retain errors which were in vogue when he was young, but which the new race have refuted.' "[13]

Bagehot's theoretical statement may serve as further illustration of the difference between conflict theory as a theoretical explanation and as the basis for a practical or applied program. Bagehot does not feel compelled to advocate the conquest of the world by the various English-speaking nations, nor does he seem unhappy if he cannot sterilize about three-quarters of humankind. He is certainly about as far removed from sentimental reformism as one can imagine, but he seems not to have felt obliged, for this reason, to embrace some special form of idiocy.

In Jacques Barzun's opinion, Bagehot explored two fundamental paradoxes of sociopolitical life. "The first was the *moral* paradox that the public good is not to be achieved by following the rules of private good. Now we face the *psychological* paradox that stability and change are equally necessary though diametrically opposed. But are men capable of being at once quiescent and active, habit ridden and original?"[14] Human nature is conceived as basically plastic. Training and "custom," or the "cake of custom," rigidify humanity's original flexibility. The plastic mind of a child can be molded into a merchant, barrister, butcher, baker, surgeon, or apothecary. Once make an apothecary, however, and that person will never again bake bread. Make a butcher, and that person will kill too extensively ever to be a surgeon. Acquired habit is the source of stability in professional and citizen. Bagehot maintains that good government rests on this stability. Paradoxically, the true source of the strength of English government is the stupidity of the population. All the way up to Parliament a few invaluable members think, but the best English people keep their minds in a state of decorous dullness. The stolid attention to business makes for steadiness, and once committed to free government it is effective there. If everyone were to do what he or she thinks is right in Parliament, there would be 657 amendments to every motion and no motion could be carried. "There never was an election without a party. You cannot get a child into an asylum without a combination. At such places you see 'Vote for Orphan A' upon a placard, and 'Vote for Orphan B (also an Idiot!!!)'

---

[12]*Ibid.*, p. 61.
[13]*Ibid.*, p. 63.

[14]From Barzun's introduction, *ibid.*, p. xiv.

upon a banner, and the party of each is busy about its placard and banner." But if the first need of government is order, arising as habit in the unthinking mass, the second requirement is "agitation." In the modern world, with its newspapers and speeches, the ideas of the few are pounded into the minds of the many.

Ludwig Gumplowicz. Ludwig Gumplowicz (1838–1909) was perhaps the most influential of the conflict theorists of his time. Son of a prominent family of Polish Jews in Cracow, he was educated and found a career in the Austro-Hungarian Empire. The powerful forms of anti-Semitism and multiple interethnic and interclass conflicts, and the political control of the Dual Monarchy, are thought to have been the most important influences on his sociology. Gumplowicz began his career as a journalist, later teaching law at the University of Graz. In 1909 he committed suicide. His most important books are *Rasse und Staat* (1875), *Philosophisches Staatsrecht* (1877), *Der Rassenkampf* (1883), and *Sozialphilosophie im Umriss* (1910).[15]

Gumplowicz worked with a narrow specific definition of the materials of sociology and a strongly positivistic conception of method. "The function of sociology consists in showing that universal laws apply to social phenomena; in pointing

LUDWIG GUMPLOWICZ

Courtesy of Frau Dr. Wanda Lanzer, Stockholm

out the peculiar effects produced by them in the social domain, and finally in formulating the special social laws."[16] Social phenomena consist in the operations of groups and aggregates of people. Sociology at bottom is always a study of groups and the interrelations of groups. The behavior of groups is orderly. "Social groups persist in their actual social condition and cannot be made to 'pass' into another without adequate social cause. . . . In other words, each alteration in the social condition of a group must always have a sufficient social cause."[17] Such a sufficient cause can only be found in the influence of other social groups. Intergroup causes and effects constitute a social event or process. "When two or more distinct (*heterogen*) groups

---

[15]Only one of Gumplowicz's works is available in English—*Grundriss der Sociologie* (Vienna: 1877; Innsbruck: Wagner, 1926), which was translated by Frederick W. Moore as *The Outlines of Sociology* (Philadelphia: American Academy of Political and Social Science, 1899). Irving L. Horowitz edited a new edition of *The Outlines* (New York: Arno Press, 1974). His other books are: *Rasse und Staat* ["Race and State"] (Vienna: 1875); *Philosophisches Staatsrecht* ["Philosophy of Constitutional Law"] (Vienna: 1877); *Der Rassenkampf* ["The Conflict of Races"] (Innsbruck: 1883); *Die sociologische Staatsidee* ["The Sociological Conception of the State"] (Graz: 1892); *Allgemeines Staatsrecht* ["General Constitutional Law"] (Innsbruck: 1897); *Soziologische Essays* ["Sociological Essays"] (Innsbruck: 1899); *Geschichte der Staatstheorien* ["History of Theories of the State"] (Innsbruck: 1905); and *Sozialphilosophie im Umriss* ["Social Philosophy in Outline"] (Innsbruck: 1910). See also *The Letters of Ludwig Gumplowicz to Lester F. Ward*, ed. Bernhard J. Stern (Leipzig: C. Hirschfeld, 1933).

[16]Gumplowicz, *The Outlines of Sociology*, pp. 82–83.
[17]*Ibid.*, p. 84.

come into contact, when each enters the sphere of the other's operations, a social process always ensues."[18] Social laws concern such process. "All social laws, indeed all universal laws as well, have one characteristic in common: they explain the becoming, but never the beginning, of things, the ultimate origin."[19] The question of ultimate origins of groups, strictly speaking, lies outside the sphere of sociological science.[20]

In explanation of social life, the antithesis of individual and group and the supposition that every individual is an active center of influence, are false leads. As a matter of fact, even what individuals think is a product of the influences to which they have been subject from childhood. The individual is like a prism that receives rays of influence from the surrounding social world and transmits them according to fixed laws. In their actions in the aggregate or the group, individuals have a sheeplike character.

Not only did Gumplowicz reject the notion that sociological science can fruitfully concern itself with the problem of social origins; he also rejected theories of society based on the assumption of rationalistic individualism. Gumplowicz's views were quite in accord with those of Bagehot, who was also suspicious of all theories of the total progress of humanity. Moreover, just as Bagehot's great emphasis on customary behavior led him to the counter principle of "agitation," so Gumplowicz's theory of the sheeplike character of individuals in assemblies requires — in order to explain the dynamics of a society — a variety of groups in conflict. He states:

If mankind is conceived to be a unit, the condition necessary for the action of opposing forces is by supposition absent. Besides, nowhere on earth, and at no time either in the present age or in remotest antiquity

has mankind been found to be a simple substance. It always consists in a countless number of distinct (*heterogen*) ethnical elements. Hence I was led to seek the starting point of sociological investigation in the hypothesis that there was originally an indefinitely large number of distinct (*heterogen*) ethnical elements; and it gives me satisfaction to note that good authorities consider the polygenetic hypothesis established.[21]

The polygenetic hypothesis—that humankind must have had a pluralistic origin—was argued at great length in *Der Rassenkampf*, where the attempt was made to reconcile it with Darwinism.

The natural tendency of people in aggregates is to mill about like sheep. In the simplest situations people must have lived in a herd or horde—"a group of men who are still dependent upon the simplest animal impulses, whose conditions of life and social constitution show no social change." Because sexual satisfaction was promiscuous, and biological paternity could not be recognized as such, the children were the mother's property. The family and the institution of property are both traced to intergroup conflict. Within a single promiscuous horde, wife-stealing would not have been possible. If a man wanted a woman for his own, he had to steal her from another group. In this way, marriage-by-capture and exogamy appeared, together with the father-family, with the woman as property of her lord. As the sovereignty of men was established, the overthrow of matriarchy was inevitable. These institutions, then, originated in intergroup conflict, but they were not the only ones. Rape was not only an occasion for early intertribal hostilities, but the plunder of property must also have been an incentive, just as it has always been and still is. Simple forms of irregular plunder must have occurred first; later expeditions led to the permanent subjection of the foreign horde and the acquisition of territory. The first form of property in land must have consisted of tracts for common use. Movable property must also have originated in conquest, at the time when

---

[18]*Ibid.*, p. 85.
[19]*Ibid.*
[20]Despite Gumplowicz's explicit rejection of the search for origins as a legitimate sociological task, the powerful currents of evolutionism and historicism of his day drew his work in their course, and his studies are permeated with the quest for origins.

[21]Gumplowicz, *The Outlines of Sociology*, p. 92.

one horde overpowered another and used its labor force. Some persons, the subjects, were excluded from enjoyment of goods produced by their own labor in favor of the ruling class.

The most striking social institution to emerge in the course of this pursuit of the women and property of another group was the *state*. The state was a social phenomenon obeying natural laws. The first step toward it was the subjection of one social group by another and the establishment of a sovereign minority in control. Numerical inferiority was supplemented by mental superiority and greater military discipline. The sovereign class required compulsory acquiescence of a subject class. Its objectives were defense against attacks, increase of power, and territory. The superior class also sought to make profitable use of the subject classes. In the organized control of a minority over a majority, the state was "not a union or community for securing the common weal, for realizing justice. . . . No state was ever founded with one of these ends in view."[22] States have only arisen in the subjection of one stock by another in the economic interest of the latter.

Once an order is established by force, a process of amalgamation gradually occurs. Labor must always be organized under compulsion. Training and discipline presuppose the state, which in the beginning demands untold sacrifices of life and health. Finally, in a rising civilization, even laborers become participants in material and moral possessions, and the whole interest of the subject class becomes devoted to expanding its privileges.

The origins of rank are in warfare, but the creation of classes does not stop here, for a complex of economic and historical facts continues to create a multitude of subclasses. The merchant comes as a guest, and he is permitted to come, for he has new things to sell. He is personally free, and knows how to maintain his freedom. He is identified with neither lords nor vassals, but soon becomes necessary to both. Such an intrusive autonomous middle class between the old classes introduces social stress

in the order. Basically, therefore, the classes have a twofold origin. "Some classes, the ruling, the peasant and the merchant classes . . . arose from the union . . . of different . . . ethnological elements. . . . There are others . . . the priesthood, large industry as contrasted with small, scholars, jurists, officials, and so forth, which arise from the others by a process of differentiation."[23]

Gumplowicz insists that individual conscience and morality have nothing to do with the social struggle. Individuals have a conscience; societies do not. The social struggle is carried on, not by individuals, but by societies. This is the basis for the establishment of a sharp distinction between *morals* and *right*. The social group is the source of opinions, feelings, and morals. At bottom, morality is nothing but the conviction implanted by the social group in the minds of its members of the propriety (*Statthaftigkeit*) of the manner of life imposed by it on them. Whereas morals are a product of the relations between the simple social group and the individual, rights are a product of the unions of different social elements. Rights never arise except in the union of societies, no matter how simple they may be; organized sovereignty is always presupposed. Morals, on the other hand, arise in the most primitive social element, in the simple aggregate or horde. This may be illustrated by some of the most fundamental rights. The rape of women from another tribe developed the first family right, the right of the man over his wife; also, by reducing the foreign element to servitude, the right of the lord over his slave was evolved; and from the resulting distinction between the lord, to whom the fruits of the soil belong, and the slave who cultivates the soil for a master, arose the right of property. Gumplowicz concludes: "Rights can arise only in the state and nowhere else for they are eminently political institutions . . . containing as it were a particle of political sovereignty."[24]

The concept of "inalienable human rights" rests on an unreasonable self-deification of man and an overestimation of the value of life as well as a mis-

---

[22]*Ibid.*, pp. 118–119.

[23]*Ibid.*, p. 134.
[24]*Ibid.*, p. 179.

conception of the basis and existence of the state. "This fancied freedom and equality is incompatible with the state and is a direct negation of it. But the only choice for men here below is between the state with its necessary servitude and inequality, and — anarchy."[25]

Gustav Ratzenhofer. Gustav Ratzenhofer (1842–1904) was influenced not only by Gumplowicz but by the same sociopolitical situation in the Dual Monarchy. Ratzenhofer was born in Vienna in 1842. The early death of his father, who was a clockmaker earning a modest income, forced the family into dire economic straits. This was the beginning of a series of difficulties that led Ratzenhofer to join the Austrian army. He became a lieutenant in 1864, and saw active service. After four years in an advanced military academy, he was promoted to the general staff in 1872 and placed in charge of the army archives, where he began systematic research and writing on military subjects. In 1898 he was made field marshal lieutenant and president of the military supreme court in Vienna. He retired from active service in 1901. Among his sociologically important works are *Wesen und Zweck der Politik* (1893), *Die sociologische Erkenntnis* (1898), and *Soziologie* (1907).[26]

Though Ratzenhofer has never been translated into English (except in fragments), he has rather special interest in the development of conflict theory, not only for his influence on Albion Small, the major early American student of

GUSTAV RATZENHOFER

Courtesy of the Photo Archives of the Austrian National Library, Vienna

conflict theory, but also because he presents a position midway between the individualistic conflict theory of classical economics and the social Darwinists and the collectivistic theory of Gumplowicz. For Ratzenhofer, the units of the social process are neither individuals nor groups but *interests*.

Interests arise on a biological foundation. Among the basic biological properties of life are: movement because of inner impulses; propagation; avoidance of alien conditions and growths; a tendency toward individualization; and capacity for perception.[27] These biological properties are also important to social structures, which operate under the same laws of life and death as the

---

[25]*Ibid.,* p. 180.
[26]Ratzenhofer's chief works, none of which has been translated into English, are: *Die Staatswehr* ["National Defense"] (Stuttgart: J. G. Cotta, 1881); *Wesen und Zweck der Politik* ["The Nature and Aim of Politics"] (Leipzig: F. A. Brockhaus, 1893); *Die sociologische Erkenntnis* ["Sociological Knowledge"] (Leipzig: F. A. Brockhaus, 1898; reprinted New York: Arno Press, 1975); and *Soziologie* (Leipzig: F. A. Brockhaus, 1907). A partial translation and paraphrase of important sections of *Wesen und Zweck der Politik* and *Die sociologische Erkenntnis* are contained in Albion Small, *General Sociology* (Chicago: University of Chicago Press, 1905), pp. 189–394.

[27]Ratzenhofer, *Die sociologische Erkenntnis,* pp. 108–112.

organism.[28] Nature thus outfits the individual with a number of basic drives. *Interests* may be defined as the social reconstitution of biological drives. Although the fate of the individual is drawn into and fulfilled in the stream of social development, it must never be forgotten that social development is possible only by means of the strivings of individual people. Individuals find self-fulfillment in society; society is produced by individuals seeking self-fulfillment. "The strivings of the individuals, in whom inherent interests are rooted, are either private (*rein subjektiv*) or public (*subjektiv im sozialen Wege*)."[29]

The social process is the product of interests which, depending on the circumstances, cause people to pull together or to pull apart. This may be seen in Ratzenhofer's eighteen-item outline of his theory of the social process:[30]

1. The preservation and propagation of humans is the basis for all association.
2. The individual's impulses of self-preservation and sex are modified by and adapted to the life conditions which he faces.
3. Every disposition in the individual is an imperative which he tends to obey without restriction.
4. When population presses against natural conditions, individuals and groups are forced into a struggle for existence.
5. Though men (like all creatures) would prefer to live and propagate at peace with others of the same species, the pressure of population on natural conditions gradually forces the interests of individuals and groups into a condition of absolute hostility toward others.
6. There are some advantages in common self-preservation by a number of persons; moreover, sex interests force people into association. Thus,

the first natural group is based on sex and kinship. However, the very success of the blood group in satisfying these interests permits population to increase and press against the food supply. Kin groups split and come, in time, to be different in culture and race. Contact between differentiated groups leads to flight or to battle. The conquest of one such group by another leads to more complex social formations, held together by common traditions and institutions of control, rather than by kinship.

7. Social structures arising from biological relationships are simple; those arising from conquest are complex.
8. The social process is a rhythm of *individualization* of structures by which new structures arise out of others already in existence, and of the *socialization* of structures already in existence.
9. *Differentiation,* or the impulse toward individualization, is limited only by the number of individuals. The limit of individualization is the atomization of society. *Socialization,* or the formation of a number of individuals into a collective unit, reaches its theoretical upper limit in the formation of all mankind into a single structure of *humanity.*
10. Differentiation frees men from social restraints, permitting free expression and satisfaction of inborn interests; socialization restrains men in order that they may achieve the cooperation necessary for securing natural or supposed interests.
11. For the social processes of socialization and differentiation, social necessity may be either *internal* (determined by the inborn capabilities of men) or *external* (determined by natural or social conditions).
12. The more men are spread out over the available space capable of sustaining life, the greater the social variations. Organization under such conditions increasingly assumes a formal and coercive character. Moreover, interests arising in other spheres tend to assume a political form.
13. The kinds of controls in the state depend upon the stage of social evolution. In the early stage of the formation of a state, controls are arbitrary and coercive; in time, customary and peaceable controls appear.
14. Conflicts consolidate social structures and create aggregations of power; culture and commerce, as

[28]*Ibid.,* p. 115.
[29]Ratzenhofer, *Soziologie,* p. 17.
[30]See *Die sociologische Erkenntnis,* pp. 244–250. A translation of this section appears in Small's *General Sociology,* pp. 189–199. What we present here are summaries of the main argument Ratzenhofer advances under each of his eighteen points. Much greater clarity is possible by freely rendering the main argument rather than translating the key sentences, which often contain terms and concepts which themselves need further explanation.

sources of social differentiation, tend to dissipate aggregations of power.

15. Social differentiation creates complicated social structures in superordination, coordination, and subordination.
16. As social structures grow more complicated, the occasions for war and violence are reduced, for every disturbance in a complicated social structure sets in motion the counter activity of many opposed interests.
17. The potential absolute hostility embedded in individuality tends to emerge whenever unlike social structures confront one another.
18. To the extent that the state resting on tradition (Ratzenhofer's "culture" state) takes the place of the state resting on force (the "conquest" state), differences among men in the satisfaction of interests tend to equalize.

In brief, biological requirements are the foundation of drives. When restyled by the presence of other persons, drives may be characterized as interests. Depending on the circumstances, interests may drive people into associations or cause them to differentiate within associations. The tribal horde resting on kinship was the first successful collaboration of human beings. However, its very efficiency permitted people to increase, caused them to differentiate into multiple tribal hordes, and eventually brought these hordes into group conflict. Thus, the principle of absolute hostility, which was kept under control so long as people lived in kin groups, broke out in the wars between kin-based groups. In time, the new structures tended to grow more peaceable. Interests, thus, are the basis for both association and dissociation of people. The peculiar intersection of interests with the conditions for their fulfillment gives them a constructive or destructive form in the given case. There is thus a rhythm of conflict and peace, during which people are pressed to form social structures of increasing comprehensiveness.

Conflict led people to form into the successively more comprehensive structures of (1) the horde and race, (2) the settled race, (3) the state as an exclusive society, (4) the hegemony with world control, and (5) the coalition and the balance of power and aggressive combination of states across state boundaries.[31] If by ethics one refers (as Ratzenhofer does) to the peaceable resolution of conflicts of interests rather than their resolution by further conflict, an ethical development accompanies each stage of social structure. These ethical stages are: (1) care of fellow beings, (2) community of interest, (3) political self-restraint for the sake of peace, (4) universal freedom, with equality of legal rights, (5) diplomacy between states, and (6) international peace.

Sumner as a Conflict Theorist. Ratzenhofer has a rather special interest, because he was a transitional figure between European conflict sociology and American, as represented by Sumner and Small. In fact, he had a distinct influence on both.

American forms of conflict theory are more individualistic than the European. Sumner, who developed a highly individualized form of conflict theory, has already been discussed as a social Darwinist. We have drawn a distinction between conflict *ideologies* — propaganda weapons in the interests of special class formations — and conflict *theory*; the term "social Darwinism" has been employed to refer to one of the major developments in conflict ideology. This terminology is used in the attempt to keep normative and empirical theory distinct. The ideological, social Darwinistic phase of Sumner's thought is found in the essays, written for the most part while he was still close to the ministry and under the influence of Spencer and Julius Lippert.[32] These essays display a most ardent apologist's enthusiasm for the middle class. Their very titles show propagandistic intent: "The Forgotten Man," "What the Social Classes Owe Each Other," "The Absurd Effort to Make the

---

[31]Ratzenhofer, *Wesen und Zweck der Politik*, I, Sec. 12.

[32]Julius Lippert (1839–1909) was an ardent proponent of social evolution. His *Kulturgeschichte der Menschheit in ihrem organischen Aufbau*, 2 vols. (Stuttgart: 1886–1887) has been translated and edited by George Peter Murdock and published as *The Evolution of Culture* (New York: Macmillan, 1931). His history of the priesthood, *Allgemeine Geschichte des Priesterthums* (Berlin: 1883–1884), and his history of the family, *Die Geschichte der familie* (Stuttgart: 1884), are not available in English translation.

World Over," "The Power and Beneficence of Capitalism." However, there is little doubt that Sumner was a conflict theorist as well as a conflict ideologist. Around 1893 he began to confine himself to sociology. His work thereafter displays a deepening sense of empirical responsibility, and he began with great energy a collection of comparative cultural materials on an immense scale. His plan for a comprehensive system of sociology was well under way at the time of his death; the first volume was drafted in rough form, and the notes were systematized. A. G. Keller completed this work, which appeared as the four volumes of *The Science of Society* in 1927.[33] The one major work Sumner completed was *Folkways* (1906), which was destined to become a classic. In this, the influence of Malthus, Spencer, Lippert, Gumplowicz, and Ratzenhofer is manifest.

However, before he came under the influence of the conflict theorists he was first influenced by the organic evolutionists, and his first attempts at a synthesis of sociology date from this earlier phase. *Folkways* was developed as an incident during the time when he was moving from the first to the second phase of his development. It is hard to say what might have happened had Sumner lived to bring out the synthesis he desired. As things stand, there are numerous incompletenesses and even contradictions between *Folkways* and the more ambitious *Science of Society* finished by Keller. For example, the conflict theorists were generally rather critical of unilinear evolutionism. It is significant that most of *Folkways* will stand even if unilinear evolutionism is abandoned; not so the work published later. The clearest statement of a conflict position appears in the former work. The argument is roughly as follows.

People act because they cannot help it to satisfy their needs. These are of four basic types: hunger,

sex, vanity, and fear of ghosts. (Some persons have assumed that W. I. Thomas got the four wishes here. There is no doubt that this statement in Sumner's account is closely modeled upon the theories of Ratzenhofer.) The most fundamental of all elements of the social process is the tendency of individuals to repeat actions that have been successful in satisfying recurrent needs. These are stereotyped as habits of individuals. When they arise out of the interhuman struggle for existence, they are social habits or customs.

Group habits have a special property: they arise in the minds and actions of the stronger members of the group, and are then imitated by others and spread by suggestion, which is at the base of mass phenomena. Invention and imitation are the second and third most important factors (after custom formation) of the social process. Inventions which are imitated are *folkways* (solutions to common problems which have become customary). Folkways are subject to a strain toward improvement and toward consistency. The formation of folkways is guided and checked by the principles of pleasure and pain. Moreover, there is an element of chance in human affairs. Those folkways thought to be right and true are enforced by fear of ghosts and powerful taboos. The differentiation of folkways into the general *folkways* and the *mores* is the next major element in the social process.

The folkways are the source of philosophy and ethics. They constitute the structure of roles, professions, classes, religions, and sects. They are the basis of group solidarity. They give rise to institutions, which consist of a concept and a structure. Institutions are simply collections of folkways and mores about a dominant interest — a formation that may occur gradually and unconsciously (*crescive* institutions) or consciously (*enacted* institutions). Laws are conscious regulation in areas of conduct originally covered by custom.

It may be seen that the social process ultimately is anchored in the relation of people to people and people to land — the person-land ratio. Sumner urged that for any given level of adjustment of people to land there is a specific appropriate arrangement of social institutions. The agents of so-

[33]William Graham Sumner and Albert Galloway Keller, *The Science of Society,* 4 vols. (New Haven, Conn.: Yale University Press, 1927). A recent edition of *Folkways* was brought out by Dover Publications (New York: 1959). For further bibliographical information on Sumner, see Footnote 10, Chapter IX.

cial development are not individuals but total groups. Only the fittest survive. One of the most significant of distinctions is between "we-groups" and "they-groups" or "in-groups" and "out-groups." The in-group is a peace group of an intimate type bearing strong ethnocentric attitudes of its own superiority. In the past, when any group was widespread it was because of its "survival value." Over time the tendency has been to expand the size of the peace group. Slavery, for example, was once universal. It taught people to "labor" and was only displaced when advanced technical development occurred. War has characterized all stages of the development process. It has been important as a source of social discipline, social stratification, government, and efficiency. Religion, with its origin in the fear of ghosts, has been a powerful source of social cohesiveness. But throughout, primary importance attaches to maintenance institutions, which form the basis of the institutional order.

Sumner, consciously or unconsciously, tried to reconcile the individualistic conflict position (derived from *laissez-faire* economics and Malthus) with the tradition of group conflict (derived from Gumplowicz). The distinctions between in- and out-group clearly follow Gumplowicz; the conception of an evolution of a peace group of ever increasing size comes from Ratzenhofer; and his location of ultimate importance in the achievement of stability — placing maintenance institutions at the heart of the institutional order — is a central phenomenon of conflict theory.

Albion Woodbury Small. Albion Woodbury Small (1854–1926) was perhaps the most balanced conflict theorist to appear on the early American scene. He was trained in theology at the Newton Theological School (1876–1879), and continued his studies in Germany at Leipzig and Berlin (1879–1881). There he came under the influence of the German social economists, Gustav Schmoller and Adolf Wagner. After teaching for some years at Colby College in Maine, Small attended Johns Hopkins University (1888–1889), coming in contact with the Adams school of historians, hot in

ALBION SMALL

Courtesy of Colby College, Waterville, Me.

the pursuit of theses based on the Teutonic and Aryan theories. Small worked out a conflict position of his own.

Small influenced sociology in a number of ways, for he brought to the field intellectual interests in history, political science, and economics. At Colby he introduced the second course in sociology to be given in the United States. (The first was Sumner's at Yale.) In 1892 he left Colby for the University of Chicago, and became chairman of the first graduate department of sociology in the world. In 1894, in collaboration with George E. Vincent, he produced the first textbook in sociology: *An Introduction to the Study of Society.*[34] He founded *The*

[34]Albion W. Small and George E. Vincent, *An Introduction to the Study of Society* (New York: American Book Company, 1894). Small's other books are: *General Sociology: An*

American Journal of Sociology in 1895 and remained its editor until his death. Small's publications reflect the variety of his interests: *General Sociology* (1905) was one of the most sophisticated reviews of theory in its time; *Adam Smith and Modern Sociology* (1907) and *The Cameralists* (1909) reflect his combined interests in economics and sociology, and *The Meaning of Social Science* (1910) and *Between Eras: From Capitalism to Democracy* (1924), in sociology and sociopolitical problems. *Origins of Sociology* (1924) was a sophisticated derivation of sociology from its nineteenth-century intellectual context. The theoretically most solid of all Small's work was *General Sociology,* where he gave fullest systematic expression to conflict sociology.

In the early *Introduction to the Study of Society,* the effort was made to delimit the field of sociology and present its main problems. The book outlined the field and development of sociology and described the evolution of society from an isolated agrarian form to modern metropolitan groups. Organic analogies were employed in the analysis of social structures and functions. The basis for a social psychology was tentatively sketched. In *Adam Smith and Modern Sociology* the attempt was made to free the field from the exclusive sphere of Comte. The beginnings of sociology were traced to Smith's theory of sympathy as developed in the *Theory of Moral Sentiments. The Wealth of Nations* was treated as a sociological study emphasizing economic process. "If one were to come upon *The Wealth of Nations* for the first time, with a knowledge of the general sociological way of looking at society, but with no knowledge of economic literature, there would be not the slightest difficulty nor hesitation

about classifying the book as an inquiry in a special field of sociology."[35]

In Small's view, sociology merely carried out the program of analysis implied in Adam Smith's moral philosophy. The tendency of the economists has been to exaggerate the significance of economic interests in isolation from other social interests of society. Sociology is a correction of this tendency. In *The Cameralists* Small examined the German analogue of British mercantilism. To him, cameralism was a forerunner of synthetic social science and an example of the exploitation of social science for guidance of social policy. Cameralism aimed at the subordination of everything in society to the problems of the state. *The Meaning of Social Science* attacked the kind of departmentalization of social science which leads to narrowness and incomplete analyses of social situations. Here Small maintained that the knowledge of society must be unified as well as specialized, for it is necessary to take account of the interaction of phases of social life upon one another. The aim of social science is to arrive at a valid appraisal of human values. In *Between Eras: From Capitalism to Democracy,* Small criticized conventional capitalism of his day from the point of view of nature and labor as the ultimate factors in productivity. He thought profit economics was ethically bankrupt, as evident in its waste, inefficiency, and injustice. The inheritance of immense fortunes was attacked, as was the conception of unlimited private property. In place of the profit economy, Small urged production for human service. Inheritance should be limited, and labor given a greater share in industrial enterprise and social policy.

Origins of Sociology traces the various phases of the development of social science in terms of the successive gains transmitted from field to field. From the Savigny–Thibaut controversy came a heightened concept of continuity in social and historical process; Eichhorn added the concept of the complexity of social and historical factors; Niebuhr advanced the scientific evaluation of historical

---

Exposition of the Main Development in Sociological Theory from Spencer to Ratzenhofer (Chicago: University of Chicago Press, 1905, 1925); *Adam Smith and Modern Sociology* (Chicago: University of Chicago Press, 1907); *The Cameralists: The Pioneers of German Social Polity* (Chicago: University of Chicago Press, 1909); *The Meaning of Social Science* (Chicago: University of Chicago Press, 1910); *Between Eras: From Capitalism to Democracy* (Kansas City, Mo.: Inter-collegiate Press, 1913); and *Origins of Sociology* (Chicago: University of Chicago Press, 1924).

[35]Small, *Adam Smith and Modern Sociology,* p. 1.

sources; Leopold von Ranke raised the level of adequacy in documentation of historical generalizations; the organization of source and archival material was improved by Pertz, Waitz, and the editors of the *Monumenta;* cameralism proposed objectivism in social science, as did the systematic economics of Smith and the classical school; Wilhelm Roscher promoted comparative economic history; Karl Menger advanced the psychological point of view in economics; Karl Knies advocated the study of ethical factors in economic science; and Schäffle and Schmoller promoted the ameliorative point of view in economic and political activity. These and other influences contributed finally to the rise of the sociological movement.

In *General Sociology* (1905), Small attempted both to summarize the main development of sociological theory and to present his own. Sociology, he thought, had gone through three major stages, represented respectively by Spencer, Schäffle, and Ratzenhofer. In his opinion, the ideas of Spencer, and Schäffle had served their purpose and had been by-passed. "We have . . . taken brief account of two conceptions which have been prominent in the history of sociological theory: the conception of social structure, and that of social functions. These concepts have been, in turn, centers for ambitious sociological systems. Those systems are no longer regarded as serious competitors for leadership in social theory. They have served their day. . . ."[36] The time had come, Small maintained, to drop analogical procedures and approach scientific precision. "We want an explanation, not of men's crystalline formations, not of their machineries, not of their institutional remains. We want an account of the intimate process of their lives, in terms that will assign their actual meaning and value to the chief and subordinate

factors concerned in the process. . . . No larger contribution to explanation in this spirit has been made than that of Ratzenhofer."[37] Small then took over the major bulk of Ratzenhofer's sociological theory, reformulating it wherever necessary to fit his own requirements. For our purposes, it is important to note the clear demand for positivism and realism.

For his own purposes, Small developed a framework of ideas around formulations very similar to those of Ratzenhofer. The central concept of the system is "social process." Society as interaction occurs against a background of conditions, ultimately those supplied by nature. At one level, human activity is devoted to the constant business of staying alive. Most of the goods produced by human economic activity are not in great supply. "Put an effective blockade around England for three months, and Westminster Hall and St. Paul's Cathedral would look like grinning skulls in a graveyard."[38] Life is an affair of adjustment to "material, matter-of-fact, inexorable nature." The various materialistic and mechanical theories of human history have attempted to find the secret of human development in the inevitable operations of nature. They are not completely wrong. They have merely overstated the absolute value of one fundamental factor. If nature represents one ultimate condition of the social process, biology is another. For Small, the same forces that reduced the universe from formless stardust to an organized system of process are still the undercurrents of every human life.

> Through the facts of food and sex, for example, we are indissolubly united, from the past and toward the future, with the ceaseless operation of the physical forces that have laid course after course in the structure of the worlds, and of the organic products upon the world. We may never unravel the methods of the physical forces that make the ultimate conditions of life, but we may know them as facts, and may make

---

[36]Small, *General Sociology*, p. 176. Small draws a distinction between subtypes of organismic positivism which was not found useful in the present account. In one basic respect, it is necessary to agree with Small: by this time positivistic organicism had seen its best days, and the future of sociological theory lay elsewhere.

[37]*Ibid.*, p. 188.
[38]*Ibid.*, p. 407.

somewhat appropriate accounts of them in our calculations of the possibilities of practical conduct.[39]

The requirements and possibilities of what will
occur in the social process are set by the properties
of the natural environment and biology. The social
process as a conflict and coordination of forces is
already established by environment and heredity.
As objects of scientific study, however, biology and
the natural environment are, according to Small,
the subject matter of other sciences. The social sciences have as their object of study the manifestation, operation, and causes of forces as they appear
in the social sphere. Here science requires an ultimate unit of study just as it does in other sciences.
The notion of interests serves the same purpose in
sociology as the notion of atoms in physical science.
They are the last elements to which we can reduce
the actions of human beings. *"Interests are the
simplest modes of motion which we can trace in the
conduct of human beings."*[40] The most basic of
interests — the health interest — is shared by
human beings with animals and plants. It is common to all forms of vital energy. It typifies all bodily organisms and has a specific content in a clover
plant, an oak tree, an insect, and a human being.
The biological study of human beings does not advance beyond the study of this interest. To the psychologist, however, the individual is interesting as
a center of knowing, feeling, and willing. To a
sociologist he begins to be interesting as knowing,
feeling, and willing *something*. Throughout, the
idea of "interest" provides the central clue. *"An
interest is an unsatisfied capacity, corresponding to an
unrealized condition, and it is predisposition to such
rearrangement as would tend to realize the indicated
condition.* . . . Human interests . . . are the ultimate
terms of calculation in sociology. *The whole life-
process, so far as we know it, whether viewed in its social
phase, is at last the process of developing, adjusting and
satisfying interests.* . . . We have several times named
the most general classes of interests which we find
serviceable in sociology, viz.: *health, wealth, sociabil-*

ity, knowledge, beauty, and *rightness."*[41] And sociology
becomes first of all a technique for detecting, classifying, criticizing, measuring, and correlating
human interests with reference to their past and
present manifestations and their indications for
the future.

A general property of conflict theory is its tendency either to ignore or to play down the importance of the individual. Bagehot derived the
stability of society in large measure from the
sheeplike behavior of the great mass of individuals. Gumplowicz not only agreed but added
ramifications of his own, maintaining that the individual is a prism of social influence, and that the
group rather than the individual thinks. One of
the special properties of Small's restylization of
conflict theory is its attempt to take the individual
into account. Small tried to accommodate insights
taken from Baldwin's *Social and Ethical Interpretations*, Cooley's *Human Nature and the Social Order*,
and Royce's *The World and the Individual*. In Small's
opinion, sociology has reached a stage where it
cannot get along without a concept of the individual, but has no completely adequate concept of
that individual.

> Today's sociology is still struggling with the prepos-
> terous initial fact of the individual. He is the only pos-
> sible social unit, and he is no longer a thinkable possi-
> bility. He is the only real presence, and he is never
> present. Whether we are near to resolution of the
> paradox or not, there is hardly more visible consensus
> about the relation of the individual to the whole than
> at any earlier period. Indeed, the minds of more
> people than ever before are puzzled by the seeming
> antinomy between the individual and the whole. . . .
> *the human individual is a variation of the sixfold interests,
> i.e., desires (subjective); and . . . the conditions of human
> satisfaction consists of variations of the sixfold interests, i.e.,
> wants (objective).*[42]

The sociologist, Small maintains, takes the individual for granted, and pursues the explanation of
associations. Everything that occurs in association

[39]*Ibid.*, p. 414.
[40]*Ibid.*, p. 426.

[41]*Ibid.*, pp. 433–435.
[42]*Ibid.*, pp. 443, 445.

is a function of elements in individuals in reaction to variable factors in the external conditions making up the individual's environment. Quite consistent with the idea that the basic property of people as moved by interests which are the same in all is Small's assertion that there is or can be an equality of people. One of the most fundamental problems, in view of the concept of common human nature, is how this human nature and society are differentiated. Small introduced a number of basic concepts to account for such variations. These include (1) spiritual environment, (2) contacts, (3) differentiation, (4) group, (5) conflict, and (6) social situation. One of the reasons why individuals and groups vary is that human beings respond to a milieu or spiritual environment. "Just as every portion of space has its physical atmosphere, so every portion of society has its thought-atmosphere. This mental envelope largely explains habit and custom, impulse and endeavor, power and limitation, with the society."[43] The basic incidents in the life of the human individual are contacts between individuals and with physical conditions. Contact is important in accounting for differences in kinds of character and of social life, since they are infinitely varied from case to case. The social process is varied, moreover, because as part of the world process it is a collection of historically distinct combinations. In the first instance, the interests are differentiated, and with this follows a corresponding differentiation of social structures and functions. The term "group" refers to any larger or smaller number of persons between whom relations are discovered such that they must be thought of together. A family, a mob, a picnic party, a trade union, a city precinct, a corporation, a state, a nation, all are illustrations. Individuals nowhere live in utter isolation. The moment they begin to adjust to a condition outside society, they die. It is critical to know to what groups a person belongs, the interests of the groups, and the means they use to promote their interests. Social life cannot be explained without this knowledge. Social life varies as an endless formation and destruction of groups. The social process is a perpetual action and reaction between group-based interests. "Conflict" is the basic and universal social process. Social life will be structured locally by whatever particular conflicts the individual faces. Finally, social variation is due to "social situation"; that is, to "any portion of experience brought to attention as a point in time or space at which a tension of social forces is present."[44]

The social process assumes a variety of forms in terms of spiritual environment or milieu, contacts, differentiation, groups, conflict, and social situation. The social process "*is a collection of occurrences, each of which has a meaning for every other, the whole of which constitutes some sort of becoming.*"[45] The social process always realizes some essential human interests. Some specific wants are present. When many persons are involved, there may be several classes of wants with relations between them. When these wants are realized, they leave a situation different from the one before the process occurred. "If we are justified in drawing any general conclusions . . . from human experience . . . it is safe to say that the social process tends to put an increasing proportion of individuals in possession of all the goods which have been discovered by the experience of humanity as a whole, and that all social programs should be thought out with a view to promotion of this tendency."[46] The concepts *social structure, social function,* and *social environment* have come into being for dealing with specialized aspects of the social process. *Social structure* is useful in accounting for the formation of elements in an activity. Whenever people act together some arrangement between persons emerges. Superiority and subordination, for example, are universal. Social structure refers to such instrumental arrangements. *Social function* refers to the various kinds of work done by any social group in the course of the social process. This is determined by group structure.

[44]*Ibid.*, p. 500.
[45]*Ibid.*, p. 513.
[46]*Ibid.*, p. 522.

[43]*Ibid.*, p. 486.

Herbert Spencer had divided institutions into six types: domestic, ceremonial, political, ecclesiastical, professional, and industrial. Every society, however primitive, has at least minute portions of these. But institutions, to Small, are only the shell of social activities. The analysis of them is preliminary to the study of actual working social arrangements and the social content they actually serve. According to Small, the ideas of "social forces" and "social ends" are also useful for analyzing the workings of the social process, but greatest interest attaches to his idea of "subjective environment." "Every individual begins to be a repository of feelings, notions, ideas, prejudices, beliefs, theories, purposes, so soon as he begins to be conscious."[47] Subjective environment refers to "a state of mind primarily in the individuals, and then diffused throughout the association, consisting first of perception that the group exists."[48] *Esprit de corps,* patriotism, ethnocentrism, all represent expressions of subjective environment.

Small sums up his whole position compactly. "The social fact is the incessant reaction between three chief factors: (1) nature; (2) individuals; (3) institutions, or modes of association between individuals. Each of these factors is composite, but at this point we may disregard that phase of the situation. *The social process is the incessant evolution of persons through the evolution of institutions, which evolve completer persons, who evolve completer institutions, and so on beyond any limit that we can fix.*"[49]

Franz Oppenheimer. The most prominent European conflict theorist of the recent past is Franz Oppenheimer (1864–1943). The son of a poor but liberal Jewish rabbi of Berlin, Oppenheimer had little chance under normal circumstances of becoming a professor. He studied medicine, and became a practicing physician in Berlin. His practice led him to an awareness of the correlation between the problems of disease and moral decline, between housing and ground rent. He began to read

[47]*Ibid.,* p. 544.
[48]*Ibid.,* p. 548.
[49]*Ibid.,* p. 552.

FRANZ OPPENHEIMER

Courtesy of the Johann Wolfgang Goethe Universität, Frankfurt am Main.

the socioeconomic literature on such problems. A high level of ability and personal courage is quite apparent in his actions. He became so interested in his studies that he abandoned medical practice, and supported his wife and child by writing articles. In 1909 be became *Privatdozent* of economics at the University of Berlin. As an unsalaried lecturer receiving only students' fees, he was still required to support himself by his publications. Oppenheimer was employed as economic adviser by the war office during World War I. In 1919 he became *Ordinarius* (the German equivalent of a full professor), teaching economic theory and sociology at the University of Frankfurt. Ill health caused him to retire in 1919. He took up residence in a rural settlement cooperative that he had founded before World War I. After 1933 he was guest lecturer in Paris, Palestine, and the United States. He died in Los Angeles in 1943.[50]

Society was conceived by Oppenheimer as an organism with an ascertainable "normal" state. This state is one organized and dominated by justice. Just as there are factors in human nature leading to conflict and mutual help, so there is a sense of justice originating in the pressure brought to bear on conflicting persons or groups by third persons or groups. Justice represents the limitation of the sphere of freedom of an individual made necessary in practice by the reciprocal interaction of individuals. Practically, justice always represents a limitation of the sphere of individual freedom. In every society deviations from the norm are due to social, economic, or political factors. Anthropology, history, psychology, and sociology study these factors.

Among the fundamental laws of sociology is that of systematic uniformity in the origin and development of state, the law, social classes, property,

monopoly, and surplus value. In working out this law, Oppenheimer distinguishes between economic and political means. Economic activity consists in the satisfaction of economic needs through economic means, which include some of the means of achieving a livelihood. Political means such as conquest and subjugation may also appear. Primitive economic inequality arose out of the employment of political means for economic ends: the ruling group introduced uniform institutionalization to make permanent their favorable situation, and the state and a system of law were thereby established. One of the first of such means was the introduction of a land monopoly—the first of all monopolies and basic to class stratification and surplus value. From a monopoly of land there developed a monopoly of tribute.

A second group of laws concerns the uniformity governing subjective evaluation of economic groups. The main one of concern to Oppenheimer states that satisfaction derived from consumption decreases with each additional unit of a given commodity until it reaches zero. Commodities are valued in terms of the last smallest unit in the available supply. Applied to the wages of the worker, "marginal utility" means that the amount of wage is determined by the value attached to the least useful worker whom it is necessary to employ in production.

The law of the ratio between quantity of emigrating rural population and the distribution of property arises in the following manner. The quantity of emigrating rural population is in direct proportion to the amount of land owned by the landed gentry and organized in estates. It is in inverse proportion to the land owned by peasants and worked by peasants in their families. When population is increasing, the profit rate of industrial products rises and that of agricultural products falls. This trend is compensated for by the immigration of the rural population to the city, intensifying competition and bringing prices of industrial products down. Meanwhile, the prices of rural products go up because of the increased demand for them. This is modified by peasant properties, however, for the surplus income

[50]Very little of Oppenheimer's work in German has been translated into English. *Der Staat* (Frankfurt am Main: Rütten & Loening, 1907; 4th ed., Stuttgart: G. Fischer, 1954) was translated by John M. Gitterman as *The State* (Indianapolis: Bobbs-Merrill, 1914; 2d American ed., New York: Vanguard Press, 1928). A new edition appeared in 1975 (New York: Free Life, 1975). Other sociologically important works, not available in translation, are: *Die Siedlungsgenossenschaft* ["The Communal Association"] (Leipzig: Duncker, 1896; 3d ed., Jena: G. Fischer, 1922); *System der Soziologie*, 4 vols. (Jena: G. Fischer, 1922–1933); and *Die Volkswirtschaftslehre der Gegenwart in Selbstdarstellung* ["The Self-Portrait of the Present System of Political Economy"] (Leipzig: F. Meiner, 1929). Biographical details may be found in *Mein Wissenschaftlicher Weg* ["My Scientific Course"] (Leipzig: F. Meiner, 1921). Reviews of Oppenheimer's theories and influence appear in Harry Elmer Barnes and Howard Becker, *Social Thought from Lore to Science*, 2d ed. (Washington, D.C.: Harren Press, 1952), pp. 712–726; and Paul Honigsheim, "The Sociological Doctrines of Franz Oppenheimer: An Agrarian Philosophy of History and Social Reform," in H. E. Barnes, ed., *An Introduction to the History of Sociology* (Chicago: University of Chicago Press, 1948), pp. 332–352. See also the entry on "Oppenheimer," by H.H. Gerth, *The International Encyclopedia of the Social Sciences* (New York: Crowell Collier and Macmillan, 1968), XI, 295–296.

created by the rise of the prices of primary products is distributed among the entire population. Also, one could expect rural workers to raise their demands for higher wages. But where there are larger estates, land monopolies are powerful enough to prevent a rise in the wages of the agricultural workers. Then the advantage in the decrease in prices of industrial products accrues to the holders of large estates.[51]

These laws explain the increase in supply of urban factory workers and the decline in wages of the group. They also account for emigration from countries where large estates are the predominant form of rural property. The lowest level of wages paid to the lowest type of agricultural worker determines the amount of existing supply of urban factory workers and is the cause of the excess of supply over demand. It is the cause of the low wages paid to the urban factory workers in industrial Europe and elsewhere. Thus, there are ultimate relations between political means and the absence of justice in the modern world. The low wage level of the agricultural workers on the feudal estates of eastern Europe is a product of the land monopoly. The land monopoly is the ultimate cause of the existence of a proletariat and the absence of justice in the world. And by the first group of Oppenheimer's laws, land monopolies were basically established by political means or force.

Oppenheimer's general sociology was an extension of the principles which he first developed in *The State*, a brilliant synthesis of European conflict sociology. In Oppenheimer's opinion, the conventional theories of the state from Plato to Rousseau and Karl Marx give no insight into its genesis, essence, or purpose. He maintains that "every state in history was or is *a state of classes*, a polity of superior and inferior social groups, based upon distinctions either of rank or of property."[52] The Marxian theory that the state arose by way of an internal differentiation of classes is a fairy tale. Oppenheimer maintains that at the time of the migration of barbarians (350–750 A.D.) in Europe, an able-bodied person was able to cultivate about twenty acres of land (at least one-third of which was uncultivated in any given year). What remained was sufficient to feed immense German families. Marxian theory holds that when the available space was fully taken up in the natural increase of families, a restructuring of families had to occur. But if we assume that it requires about twenty-five acres to support a family of five persons, Germany, with an agricultural area of about 84,000,000 acres, would still not have reached a stage where the differentiation of classes would begin. Thus Oppenheimer maintains that purely economic and demographic causes have not brought about the differentiation of classes and the growth of a propertyless laboring class. Hence, if it is true that the class state can arise only where all the fertile acreage has been completely taken up, then it follows from the historical fact that class states *have* arisen in territories where the population was not large enough to account for all the fertile acreage that this pre-emption of land must be *political*, rather than strictly economic. "Therefore the State, as a class-state, can have originated in no other way than through conquest and subjugation."[53] In its genesis and essence, the state is a social institution forced by a victorious group on a defeated group, and its original purpose was the economic exploitation of the vanquished by the victors.

The state develops in distinct stages. (1) There is first robbery, killing, and border fights, marked by killing of men, carrying off of women and children, looting of herds, and burning of dwellings. During this period, the differentiation of peasant and herder grows increasingly clear. (2) This gives

---

[51]This is no place to trace all the virtues and limitations of Oppenheimer's particular attempt to account for the influence of the rise of capitalism on the problems of agriculture, labor supply, and the like. Oppenheimer's arguments are outlined here merely to call attention to the fact that among the conflicts he thought to be central to the modern world are those between workers and capitalists. His basic theme is that the capitalists, both urban and rural, are usually exploiters.

[52]Oppenheimer, *The State*, p. 5.
[53]*Ibid.*, p. 14.

way to a second stage in which the peasants have accepted their fate and ceased resistance. The herders, having discovered that a fruit tree cut down will not bear and that a murdered peasant does not work, lets the tree stand and the peasant live. They kill a few peasants and burn enough fields to enforce wholesome respect and to break isolated resistance. Like the bee-keeper, they leave the bees enough honey to carry them through the winter. The herder has learned to "capitalize." The peasant has obtained a semblance of *right* to the bare necessities of life. It becomes wrong to kill unresisting people or strip them of everything. This is the germ of the process of external amalgamation out of which small hordes are formed into nations (3) A third stage arrives when the "surplus" obtained by the peasantry is regularly brought by the peasant to the tents of the herders as "tribute." The strains of the former method of taxation are mitigated. Fewer men are knocked on the head, fewer women violated, fewer farmhouses burned. The herders now have full time and energy free for the "extension of the works"—subjugating other peasants. (4) In the next stage there is the union on one territory of both ethnic groups. This is significant, since no jural definition of a state can be arrived at without the concept of a state territory. Such territorial union may be forced by foreign influence (strong hordes from the outside) or economic pressure. Perhaps it has become necessary for the conquering group to protect subjects by keeping a levy of young warriors in the neighborhood. At this stage, there is physical presence of the two groups in the same place, but not a single system of institutions. From particular centers the lords control their "subjects," mainly for the purpose of gathering their tribute, and pay no attention to them in other respects. They let them administer their affairs, carry on their religious worship, settle their disputes, and adjust their methods of internal economy in their own way. Their autochthonous constitution, their local officials, are, in fact, not interfered with. However, the logic of events quickly presses beyond this, for (5) quarrels arise between neighboring villages or classes which the lords

cannot permit, since service would be impaired. The lords assume the right to arbitrate. And, step by step, movement is toward a new internal unity, (6) the development of "nationality." In customs, habits, speech, and worship the groups begin to amalgamate. In almost all cases the master class picks the handsomest virgins from the subject races for concubines. A race of bastards develops, which is sometimes taken into the ruling class. With the blood of the masters in their veins, they become the born leaders of the subject race.

George Bryan Vold. The foremost conflict theorist in postwar North America, George Bryan Vold (1896–1968) was born at Platte, South Dakota. Vold took his M.A. degree at the University of Chicago (1924), and his Ph.D. degree at the University of Minnesota (1930). He was assistant professor of sociology at Macalester College from 1924 to 1927, joining the faculty at the University of Minnesota in 1927 and achieving full professor in 1937. In 1946–1947 he was with the United States Occupation Forces in Japan as a consultant on criminological problems for the occupation army. For years Vold taught a course in the sociology of conflict in the classic tradition of Albion Small. Many of his reflections have been embodied in *Theoretical Criminology,*[54] his most important publication. Uniquely among recent theorists, Vold formulated the problem of crime in a manner leading directly into conflict theory.

> If criminal behavior, by and large, is the normal behavior of normally responding individuals in situations defined as undesirable, illegal, and therefore criminal, then the basic problem is one of social and political organizations and the established values or definitions of what may, and may not, be permitted. Crime, in this sense, is political behavior and the criminal becomes in fact a member of a "minority group" without sufficient public support to dominate and control the police power of the state. Criminals often become involved in the serious business of poli-

[54]George B. Vold, *Theoretical Criminology* (New York: Oxford University Press, 1958).

GEORGE VOLD

Courtesy of George Vold

tics and the control of the police power of the state for their own protection. This is "pressure politics" in the interest of organized crime.[55]

The basic suppositions of conflict theory, according to Vold, are that the individual is a "group-involved being whose life is . . . a product of group associations." It is assumed, furthermore, that society is "a congeries of groups held together in a shifting but dynamic equilibrium of opposing group interests and efforts." The social process consists of the interaction of groups "in an immediate and dynamically maintained equilibrium." The end result is "a more or less continuous struggle to maintain, or to defend, the place of one's

own group in the interaction of groups." "Conflict is . . . one of the principal and essential social processes upon which the continuing on-going of society depends."[56]

The relative stability of conflicting group forces in uneasy equilibrium is social order or organization. The constantly changing adjustment of group interests of varying strength is the essence of society as a functional reality. Groups are formed where members have common interests and common needs that can be most effectively pursued through collective action. New groups, thus, are continually formed as new interests arise, while existing groups weaken and vanish. Whenever group interests overlap or encroach on one another, they become competitive. Conflict arises when they cannot be kept out of each other's territory. A group must be constantly alert to defend itself, for one of its basic objectives is to prevent displacement. Only where this possibility of displacement appears is there the risk of conflict between nations, races, religions, economic systems, labor unions, or any type of organization.

For the members of the group, participation in group activity and in its values and disvalues, makes the individual into a self-conscious person. Group identification and loyalty become intense psychological actualities, of a transrational nature. Conflict between groups tends to intensify these loyalties to highest degree, developing *esprit de corps* or morale. Individuals are most loyal to the group they have to die for. Patriotic feeling runs high in wartime, for example. The finest ideals of character are products of group conflict, where individuals serve the common purpose and not merely selfish ends. The consequences of group conflict are complete destruction of the other side, or flight of one's own, or some compromise between. Generally there is no compromise with a position of weakness. As a rule, the weak are overwhelmed, subjugated, and integrated with the victors in a subordinate capacity.

From this formulation of conflict, Vold ap-

[55]*Ibid.*, p. 202.

[56]*Ibid.*, p. 204.

proaches other sociological areas. Politics, for example, "as it flourishes in a democracy, is primarily a matter of finding practical compromises between antagonistic groups in the community at large." The law is a formula expressing a ratio of strength. "Thus the familiar cry, 'there ought to be a law,' . . . to suppress the undesirable is understandable as the natural recourse of one side or the other in a conflict situation."[57] And quite in accord with this modernized "might makes right" formula, Vold assures the reader that the law always asserts the dominant interests. The application to crime of this theory is direct. "The whole political process of law making, law breaking, and law enforcement becomes a direct reflection of . . . fundamental conflicts between interest groups and their . . . struggles for the control of the police power of the state."[58] The winners of the struggle decide "who is likely to be involved in violation of the law." The principle of compromise from positions of strength is said to operate at every stage of the conflict process from bargaining in the legislature to get the law passed, to bargaining between prosecution and defense in the conduct of the trial, to bargaining between prison official and inmate, parole and parole agent. From this standpoint, Vold urges, criminological theory is merely a special application of the general theory of conflict. There may, of course, be criminal behavior arising from defectiveness or abnormality or even impulsive irrational acts. Much "criminality" represents the normal, natural response of normal, natural human beings struggling in natural situations for the maintenance of the way of life to which they stand committed. The behavior of some individuals is incidental to the course of action required for the group to maintain its place in the struggle with other groups.

To phrase Vold's theory of crime in a sentence: so far as criminal acts do not arise from defectiveness, abnormality, or irrational impulse, so far, in short, as they are genuinely "social," they are best explained by conflict theory.

57 *Ibid.*, p. 208.
58 *Ibid.*, pp. 208–209.

Theoretical Criminology, if one may hazard a prediction, should live as a classic of contemporary conservatism. Superficially, it is a review of criminological theory; actually, the discussions of crime are merely illustrative material. The book represents a theoretical interpretation which quite obviously could apply to any area of social life. Classical conflict theory in Vold's formulation is reduced to an economical model: individuality is played down in a worthy tradition extending in Western thought from Polybius to Hobbes and in sociological conflict theory from Bagehot to Oppenheimer — the sheeplike character of the individual is emphasized. The primary flow of influence is from group to personality, not otherwise. The *social process* stands in contrast to the *socialization process*. Socialization is the molding of individuals into the image of the group, committing them to it, blowing up the thin bag of their egos with group pretensions and ethnocentrism until they find the highest of all individual values in their patriotic readiness to die for the group. It is noted that some kinds of crime represent, essentially, failures of socialization either because individuals are biologically defective, pathological, or socially substandard — impulsively unable to mold their actions to social requirements. These are among the least important forms of crime. The *social process* in contrast to the *socialization process* is the contact of groups — conceived of as an endlessly changing kaleidoscope of force-ratios. The laws are peace treaties intended to secure the permanent ascendancy of the victors in the social process, preferably in "hereditary" form, holding for all generations. In all these respects, *Theoretical Criminology* is a synthesis of the classic conflict tradition.

A good deal of crime is seen not as failure in the socialization process but as incidents of the *social process*. This is in accord with the view that individual behavior is primarily "sheeplike"; hence, if crime amounts to anything at all, it will be group behavior. It is argued, in fact, that crime is "minority group behavior." The evidence of a great number of students of crime and delinquency — Clifford Shaw and Henry McKay,

Sheldon and Eleanor Glueck, William F. Whyte, Solomon Kobrin, Frederic Thrasher, Herbert Asbury — is cited to the point that most crime is committed in association with others. Vold's theme is then expanded to include the "fact" that much criminal behavior is political in nature. It is maintained that a successful revolution makes criminals out of government officials previously in power; an unsuccessful revolution makes its leaders traitors and subject to exile or execution. Moreover, "murder, sabotage, seizure of private property, and many other offences against the ordinary criminal code are commonplace accompaniments of political rebellion."[59] Not quite as extreme, but of the same type, are the personal dishonesty, bribery, perjury, burglary, and theft occurring in the course of winning political elections and keeping political control. To this configuration belong all the incidents in the clash of interests of company management and labor unions. So, too, in this category are the "numerous kinds of crimes" which "result from the clashes incidental to the attempt to change, or to upset the caste system of racial segregation in various parts of the world, notably in the United States and in the Union of South Africa."[60]

It is only a step from the occurrence of all sorts of so-called crimes in connection with normal group process to the study of "The Organization of Criminals for Profit and Power." Vold observes that there is "general acceptance of the idea of crime as an organized business, conducted for business profit."[61] It is maintained that the incentive in normal society to earn a living, to improve one's profits, and to combine with others if profits are thereby increased, is the key to understanding the organization in the field of crime. Crime is transformed into syndicates or combinations only partly outside the law. A terminology for crime partnerships, groups, and institutional arrangements appear with teams, mobs, fixes, and fences. Profits are computed in some rational "pay-off."

The criminal syndicate may become a relatively stable business organization which organizes its rackets and pins down its flanks through political graft and corruption. Here as elsewhere, lucrative opportunities encourage rivals, teams, mobs, gangs, or syndicates, resulting in the lurid phenomena of underworld competition and gang war. Finally, the relations of underworld and upperworld tend to be integrated. "From the standpoint of the problem of control, organized crime seems to be more significantly affected by economic facts of supply and demand, and the fads and foibles in consumer habits, than by much legislation and sporadic attempts at formal control."[62]

Vold not only brings an extensive amount of evidence into an able synthesis in terms of group conflict, but in deliberate, carefully reasoned steps sets about to annihilate opposed interpretations. The idea that crime does not necessarily arise because of some atavistic throwback to an earlier evolutionary state, or because of mental or biological deficiency, or psychological abnormality, is not new. The idea that it is socially caused had received clear formulation by Gabriel Tarde among others. It has been generally recognized that the major modern heir to Tarde's approach is the late Edwin H. Sutherland's "differential association" theory of criminality. The common-sense element lying back of this view is that if criminality is not primarily caused by biological deficiency, psychological abnormality, or some other such thing, it must be "social" — specifically, it must be a special category of learned behavior. Since most learning takes place in association with others, Sutherland argues that criminal learning must be the product of "differential association": people learn to be thieves in much the same way that they learn to be Methodists or Roman Catholics. Since, however, not everyone who associates with criminals becomes a criminal, the attempt is made to tighten up the idea by adding that *frequency* and *consistency* of association are important. Systematic criminal be-

[59]*Ibid.*, pp. 214–215.
[60]*Ibid.*, p. 217.
[61]*Ibid.*, p. 220.

[62]*Ibid.*, p. 242.

havior occurs when criminality becomes a way of life like that of the professional thief, the circus grifter, the card sharp. A major application of these ideas was Sutherland's extension of the general theory to the special case of white collar crime.[63]

Vold's general argument against the "differential association" theory is that it is so general and nonspecific that it "reaches far into the margin of unreality."[64] Crime is a *mélange* of behavior, having in common only the fact that it is "in violation of the criminal law." The theory of differential association is undiscriminating. This fact should not obscure the significant point that, *at this very general level,* Vold and Sutherland agree on essentials. Most significant types of criminal behavior are of the same type as noncriminal behavior. The critical difference between the two thinkers emerges over Sutherland's *White Collar Crime.*

Barnes and Teeters, in *New Horizons in Criminology,*[65] described a large variety of commercial transactions of questionable ethics as "white collar crime," and placed them in the same context as racketeering and organized crime. Sutherland's interest in crimes of the well-to-do was lifelong. The full fruit of his theories appeared in the 1949 volume. He urged that the conception of the criminal as an economically underprivileged lower-class person is false. Even the robber barons of the early period — Ivar Kreuger, William Whitney, Samuel Insull, Albert B. Fall, Harry Sinclair — show that this is not the case. White collar criminality occurs as misrepresentation in financial statements of corporations, manipulations of the stock exchange, bribery of public officials, misleading advertising and selling, embezzlement and misuse of trust funds, dishonest bankruptcies. Evidences of a similar type were assembled by Marshall Clinard, in his study of the

black market,[66] for violations by reputable business people of the government's rationing and price control program in World War II. Sutherland made the most able analysis of the idea. Citing violations of the law on the part of seventy major American corporations, Sutherland argued that they should be treated as crimes, because they were recognized in the law as injurious to the public, there were legal sanctions against such violations, and the behavior involved was willful or intentional rather than accidental.

At first blush, the theories of Sutherland and Vold might seem to be identical: both treat crime as social, both treat criminal and noncriminal behavior as arising in the same way; both extend the conception of criminal behavior from acts of individuals to acts of complex organized groups. Sutherland extends his concept of crime to acts of corporations, and Vold to the incidents accompanying all group struggles and the organization paralleling and partly involving the upperworld by the underworld. Nevertheless, Vold finds Sutherland to be his most important opponent.

Vold's answer to Sutherland springs from the core of conflict theory. He argues: "There is an obvious and basic incongruity involved in the proposition that a community's leaders and more responsible elements are also its criminals."[67] Business leaders and corporation executives by and large play important roles in civic and community affairs. More often than not they constitute an important source of the imaginative leadership for community enterprise of all kinds. The very fact of reputable community standing is therefore one of the more confusing and inconsistent aspects of the concept of white collar crime. And quite succinctly to the point, he argues: "The label results in good part from the semantic device of calling all violations of law or regulations 'crime' and all the persons involved 'criminals.' "[68]

The peculiar properties of the conflict point of

[63]Edwin H. Sutherland, *White Collar Crime* (New York: Dryden, 1949).

[64]Vold, *Theoretical Criminology,* p. 199.

[65]Harry Elmer Barnes and Negley K. Teeters, *New Horizons in Criminology* (New York: Prentice-Hall, 1946; 2d ed., 1951).

[66]Marshall B. Clinard, *The Black Market: A Study of White Collar Crime* (New York: Rinehart, 1952).

[67]Vold, *Theoretical Criminology,* p. 253.

[68]*Ibid.,* p. 254.

view could hardly be more ingeniously contained in a single formula. The common property of crime is found originally in the fact that it is a violation of the law. But law is a formula expressing a force-ratio of dominant to minority group. Do then all violations of the law constitute crimes? To maintain this, it is said, is a semantic device. Violations of the law constitute crimes and the violators criminals only if they belong to the minority group. Two major arguments are assembled in defense of this. Eighty-five per cent of the law violations in America are traffic violations by average citizens, but this, it is said, does not make their violations crime nor make them criminals. The second major argument against treating violations of the law by "reputable sections of society" as crimes is the unassailable integrity of Robert A. Taft of Ohio. "It seems clear that the American effort at price control and rationing was something less than completely successful . . . because a large and influential portion of the population simply did not believe in or accept as valid any such conception of the proper role of government activity. Persons of the caliber and character of the late Senator Robert A. Taft of Ohio may not lightly be accused of having raised their voices in defense of crime and criminal practices."[69]

The clinching argument against Sutherland has special interest, since it sounds a basic theme in conflict theory as old as Sumner's "The Absurd Effort to Make the World Over." Vold argues that Sutherland "was not really seeking a reformation of criminological theory as much as he was urging a reformation in the mores and culture of America so that violation of laws regulating business transactions would be viewed as 'crime' rather than a misconduct of a less serious sort."[70] When is a given act a crime, since sometimes it is and sometimes it is not? It depends on whose ox is being gored.

Ralf Dahrendorf. George Vold was one of the last of the older generation (that is, pre–World War II)

[69]*Ibid.,* pp. 257–258.
[70]*Ibid.,* p. 259.

conflict theorists. His intellectual heritage extended through Small (with whom he had taken the M.A.) to Ratzenhofer and Gumplowicz. To this tradition, social life was group life and groups were always compositions of conflicting interests. The application of a conflict approach to the field of crime and delinquency by no means exhausted the explanatory power of the point of view; quite the contrary, this was only one illustration of an approach applicable to all other spheres. Vold had taught a course in conflict theory for many years and always intended to work up a theoretical monograph on conflict theory in general, a task he did not live to complete.

In the postwar period, conflict theory was revived by a new generation of theorists. This occurred in Europe before the United States and tended to take its point of departure from Marx, rather than from Gumplowicz, Ratzenhofer, Small, and their followers. Among the factors contributing to the popularity of a Marxian approach to conflict theory was its interpretation of fascism as the final stage of capitalism (hence as a fulfillment of the Marxian prediction of the ultimate hardening and downfall of the capitalistic system) and the prestige of the Soviet Union as one of the victorious allied powers that had overthrown Nazism. The memory of the Russian purges in the 1930s had faded, and the vitality of a power founded in revolution and on an official Marxian doctrine was apparently confirmed by events. Meanwhile, however, in the United States the Cold War and the persecutions by the House Un-American Committee and Senator Joseph McCarthy of democrats, intellectuals, liberals of both parties, and all others suspected of communist sympathies (which included anyone who had positive opinions about Marx even though he or she was not favorable toward Soviet Communism) made this type of conflict theory risky.

Ralf Dahrendorf as a young German sociologist pioneered the new type of conflict theory based, in part, on Marxism. Dahrendorf was born in Hamburg in 1929, the son of a Social Democratic Reichstag deputy at a time when Marxism was the official ideology of the Social Democratic Party. Dahrendorf senior was arrested when the Nazis came to power. In 1944 Ralf Dahrendorf was himself arrested by the Gestapo for anti-Nazi activities at school; he was sent to a concentration camp. After the war he earned his doctorate at Hamburg in philosophy and philology. For two years he studied at the University of London, where he also taught sociology, earning a Ph.D. Dahrendorf taught at the Universities of Saarbrücken, Hamburg, Tübingen, and Konstanz. He was research fellow at the Center for Advanced Study in the Behavioral Sciences at Palo Alto and held visiting appointments at a number of American universities. He was a major spokesperson for the new generation of German intellectuals and was appointed Chancellor of the London School of Economics.[71]

Dahrendorf's *Soziale Klassen und Klassenkonflikt in der Industriellen Gesellschaft* first appeared in a German edition in 1957. Two years later the author translated, revised, and expanded it. In his preface to the English edition on page xi and again on page 159 of the text, Dahrendorf set out the case for a conflict model of society in contrast to a consensus (or organismic) model. Recently, he argued that (in the immediate postwar period) sociology has been preoccupied with equilibrium in large social systems, which, while leading to interest in small social systems, has also resulted in the abandonment of other concerns.

> As a result, there is today a considerable need for reorienting sociological analysis to problems of change, conflict, and coercion in social structures, and especially in those of total societies. The interest in total societies, as well as in their historical dimension, is of course as old as sociology itself.[72]

And on page 159 he formulated the contrast as follows:

> It seems to me that two (meta-) theories can and must be distinguished in contemporary sociology. One of these, the *integration theory of society,* conceives of social structure in terms of a functionally integrated system held in equilibrium by certain patterned and recurrent processes. The other one, the *coercion theory of society,* views social structure as a form of organization held together by force and constraint and reaching continuously beyond itself in the sense of producing within itself the forces that maintain it in an unending process of change.[73]

Dahrendorf approached his task by way of a revisionist Marxism. He accepts as valid Marx's notion that class conflict is the key to social change, arguing that throughout his life Marx was dominated by his view of the importance of the French and industrial revolutions; that he traced conflicts back to patterns of social structure; and that he believed conflicts to be necessary outgrowths of social structure and, in particular, of capitalist society. Dahrendorf further argues that Marx assumed that in any given situation one particular conflict, operating on something like a two-class model, is dominant. In every conflict, one party attacks, the other defends.[74] All these notions Dahrendorf accepts. On the other hand, he rejects the notions, which he attributes to Marx, that in every society the dominant conflicts are always or only class conflicts; that class conflict inevitably results in revolutions; that classes are always manifest as conflict groups; that the determinants of social class are always found in private property; that there is a one-to-one correlation between class structure and social stratification; and that there is axiomatic identity between the managers or capitalists of industry and the highest ministers or civil servants of the state. Dahrendorf also observed that Marx had neglected the problem of the relation between individuals and classes.

---

[71]Ralf Dahrendorf's major works include *Class and Class Conflict in Industrial Society* (Stanford: Stanford University Press, 1959); *Essays in the Theory of Society* (Stanford: Stanford University Press, 1969); *Society and Democracy in Germany* (Garden City, New York: Doubleday, 1969).
[72]Dahrendorf, *Class and Class Conflict,* p. xi.

[73]*Ibid.,* p. 159.
[74]*Ibid.,* pp. 125–126.

Dahrendorf undertook to weld together a number of ideas adapted from Max Weber and Marx into a new form of conflict theory, or, as he phrases it, a coercion theory of social structure: that is, social structure is always a product of conflict. Authority is the probability that the commands by some in a given group will be obeyed by others. Domination is the possession of authority. Subjection is the duty to submit to domination. An association in which domination and subjection are found is said to be imperatively coordinated. The persons involved in this process possess latent interests. A plurality with a set of latent interests is a quasi-group. When latent interests are made articulate and conscious to their possessors they become manifest interests. A plurality sharing manifest interest is an interest group. Group conflict is the antagonism between interest groups. The extent of group conflict, its radicalness, its intensity, and the amount of violence associated with it are variable.[75]

In postcapitalist society structure is still a product of group conflict, but Marx's view of class conflict is inadequate because both capital and labor have undergone decomposition in the last hundred years,[76] and the intensity of industrial conflict has decreased. Furthermore, industrial and political conflict are no longer identical.[77] In both totalitarian and democratic societies the ruling class is increasingly "situational." Governments have tended to become mere switchboards of authority and decisions are made *through* rather than by them. The ruling class of a society is composed of four elements: the bureaucracy, governmental elite, majority party, and its favored veto groups. However, if the majority party is not in power, its favored veto groups are defense groups representing the interests of the subject class.[78]

Among the major criticisms made of Dahrendorf's book were that his retention of the term *class*

while dropping the notion that the great class conflicts of our time are between the bourgeoisie and proletariat does not make sense; his separation and confrontation of industrial and political class conflicts is mistaken; his application of conflict theory to the analysis of contemporary society and especially to its ruling classes is indefensible; and his analysis has not been grounded on large-scale inquiries of a practical kind.[79] Not without interest is the fact that much of this criticism originated in circles of orthodox Marxists. By treating coercion (or conflict) theory and consensus theory as inversions of one another and by opening the door to an employment of modified Marxian conceptions for this purpose, Dahrendorf pointed the way toward the sociological reappraisal of Marx whenever the prevailing mood in American society eased, and a renewed interest in the possibilities of conflict theory could again become possible. Dahrendorf's practice of employing Marxist revisionist ideas in the rehabilitation of conflict theory poses the question, is a Marxist sociology possible?

IS A MARXIST SOCIOLOGY POSSIBLE?

Beginning in the late 1880s and early 1890s, accompanying the development of Marxism into a doctrine (particularly by Engels and Kautsky) and its institutionalization as the official ideology of the German Social Democratic Party, an increasing number of social scientists began to take Marx's theories into account and, in some instances, to modify and extend them and subject them to examination: Ferdinand Tönnies, Ludwig Gumplowicz, Werner Sombart, Rudolf Stammler, Benedetto Croce, Vilfredo Pareto, Georges Sorel, and Max Weber among others treated various notions of Marx as hypotheses open to empirical investigation.

The exploration of ideas and themes of Marx-

[75]See Dahrendorf's summary, pp. 237–240. Many of these ideas were taken directly from Weber.
[76]*Ibid.*, p. 276.
[77]*Ibid.*, p. 277.
[78]*Ibid.*, p. 306.

[79]*Ibid.*, p. xii.

ism by scholars outside the circle was met half way by the revisionists from within Marxian ranks. Particularly in Austria-Hungary, Germany, and Russia, revisionists responded both to outside critics as well as to their own perceptions of problems in Marxian theory and discrepancies between theory and practice, with attempts to revise Marxist doctrine. Bernstein in Germany, Turgan-Baranowsky in Russia, and Max Adler and Karl Renner were among the revisionists. When some of the revisionists (such as Bernstein) began, in fact, to transform Marxism into an empirical social science indistinguishable from sociology, efforts got underway to purge the revisionists. As already observed, one of the major endeavors of Lenin was to counteract Bernstein's revisionism, although, ironically, no one transformed Marxism more radically than Lenin himself.

At stake in the threatened transformation of Marxism into a social science was the efficacy of Marxism as an ideology. The Marxian synthesis could not long survive the conversion of its individual notions into hypotheses to be tested, accepted, rejected, and modified. In such a process, ideological coherence of the doctrine would inevitably be set aside as irrelevant to the scientific task: to understand and explain the facts. Hence, anyone who wished to preserve the ideological effectiveness of Marxism as a program of revolution was quite correct in resisting its conversion into a social science. Lenin, of course, in fact revised Marxism, but not in the interests of turning it into a social science, but retooling it into a more effective ideology: conjoining the organizational abilities of professional revolutionaries with the restlessness of dissatisfied peasant masses for the purpose of the seizure of power in an underdeveloped country. Maoism performed a parallel function in China. With the success of the Lenin-Stalin brand of Communism in Russia, however, this version of Marxism ceased to be revolutionary and lived on as the legitimizing ideology of the totalitarian state. In this form, first Leninism and later Maoism became conservative ideologies legitimizing the social structures and, of course, the systems of domination these revolutions set up.

T. B. Bottomore, who wrote the entry on Marxist sociology for the *International Encyclopedia of the Social Sciences*, found himself at a loss when he contemplated the task of defining Marxist sociology. He perceptively observed:

> Betwixt Marxism and sociology, the place of Marxist sociology is variable and uncertain. In one sense, Marxist sociology could be regarded as the sociology of those thinkers (for example, Nikolai Bukharin and Max Adler) who, on other grounds, are Marxist in their general philosophical or political outlook. It would then be of the same kind as any other school of sociology — let us say Thomist or Hindu sociology — which is based directly upon a philosophical world view. But it would still be affected by, and would have to respond to, the findings of empirical social research; and at some stage Marxists would be led to consider, as has happened in recent years, whether in fact there can be a separate Marxist sociology any more than there can be a separate Marxist physics.[80]

In the 1960s and 1970s following the death of Stalin, revelations about abuses under his regime, the political and intellectual revolts in some countries dominated by the Soviet Union, and the rise of Maoism, created an atmosphere for an extensive revival of Marxist thought. In Bottomore's most recent evaluation: "Marxism no longer has the appearance, within the social sciences, of a body of thought which has long since been surpassed, or which can be set aside as a social doctrine expressing mainly value judgments and political aspirations."[81] In economics, Marxism has been the inspiration for one of the major theories of economic development. In anthropology, Bottomore maintains, it has inspired one of the major "structuralist" theories, spurring the study of political power and social class, economic and political structure, and large-scale historical prob-

[80]T. B. Bottomore, "Marxist Sociology," *International Encyclopedia of the Social Sciences* (New York: The Free Press, 1968), X, 51.
[81]T. B. Bottomore, "Marxism and Sociology" in *A History of Sociological Analysis,* ed. Tom Bottomore and Robert Nesbit (New York: Basic Books, 1978), p. 135.

lems.[82] In sociology, the revival of Marxist thought has brought with it a renewal of the conflict between ideology and social science theory. Henri Lefebvre, for example, though entitling his presentation of Marxist ideas for sociological consideration under the title *The Sociology of Marx,*[83] soon warns, "we shall not make a sociologist out of Marx. Anyone who ascribes such a thesis to us on the basis of the title of this little book either never opened it or is acting in bad faith . . . *Marx is not a sociologist, but there is a sociology in Marx.*"[84] He then outlines what he considers to be the main arguments of Marxism, considering its essential character to be dialectical analysis of social life as a whole and the "sociology in Marx" to be the implications of this analysis for particular institutions and processes. Lefebvre does not indicate what is to be done if such Marxian-derived "hypotheses," if one can call them that, are contradicted by social science findings. If one is a social scientist, however, the answer is clear — they must go. The collection of readings on *Marxism and Sociology*[85] by Peter Berger presents a diversity of positions on Marxism, varying from the idea that it is an antisociological ideology, to proposals for treating individual Marxist conceptions as if they were hypotheses like any other to be tested by the usual sociological methods, to suggestions for revising Marxism by the addition to it of social science notions such as the social psychology of G. H. Mead. Some sociologists in the postwar period — Norman Birnbaum can be taken as their prototype — have started out by subscribing to the idea that

Marxism, if only updated, is an alternative to other sterile traditions of contemporary sociology only to find themselves wrestling with the problem of having to deal with the conflict between the factual and theoretical components of the Marxian heritage. Sooner or later such persons have found themselves at a fork in the road: one direction leads to pure ideology (but this forks again for there is both a conservative and a revolutionary Marxian ideology); the other direction leads toward science from which ideological elements are progressively eliminated. Individuals who chose the fork that leads toward science experienced increasing disillusionment with Marxism much in the manner of American intellectuals such as Max Eastman and Sidney Hook in the 1930s and 1940s.

All of this adds up to the conclusion that there are both conservative and revolutionary Marxian ideologies, and there are Marxian-inspired problems in sociology, but not a Marxian sociology.

SUMMARY

No attempt has been made to cover all possible combinations of conflict theory. For example, Jacques Novicow (1849–1912) analyzed the concept of social conflict into four phases — physiological, economic, political, and intellectual. Benjamin Kidd (1858–1916) employed the idea to justify just about everything in the *status quo* as good because it has survived. Peter Kropotkin (1842–1921) introduced special considerations in his attempt to universalize mutual aid and cooperation to parallel universal conflict. And Thomas Henry Huxley (1825–1895) pursued social Darwinism into a series of social-ethical and cultural areas.

Generally the attempt has been made to trace conflict sociology as the second wave of sociological theory, arising in the same atmosphere as positivistic organicism. As the major failures of organicism became apparent, some modification of theory was inevitable. At the same time, the same general ideological demands that shaped positivistic organicsim from the outside remained.

[82]David Horowitz, ed., *Marx and Modern Economics* (London: MacGibbon, 1968); Louis Althusser and Etienne Balibar, *Reading Capital* (London: New Left Books, 1970); Maurice Godelier, *Perspectives in Marxist Anthropology* (Cambridge: Cambridge University Press, 1977); Perry Anderson, *Passages from Antiquity to Feudalism* (London: New Left Books, 1974).
[83]Henri Lefebvre, *Sociology de Marx* (Paris: Presses Universitaires de France, 1966), trans. Norbert Guterman, *The Sociology of Marx* (New York: Pantheon Books, 1968).
[84]*Ibid.,* p. 22.
[85]Peter L. Berger, ed., *Marxism and Sociology: Views from Eastern Europe* (New York: Meredith Corporation, 1969).

The first effect of the movement toward a new formation of theory was a return to the rich intellectual treasures of Western civilization. A stock of ideas was available, established by individuals of affairs of the past. In an atmosphere that demanded "realism," these were precisely the thinkers consulted. A brief sketch was made of the development of conflict theory in the West from the days of the Sophists, Epicureans, and Greek historians to the political writers from Machiavelli to Bodin and Hobbes, to the specialized form of economic conflict theory embodied in the works of the physiocrats and the classical economists.

It was noted that precisely because conflict theory comes from people who are close to actual affairs, re-enlistment in the social struggle is often invited. When this occurs, conflict theory is transformed into a conflict ideology and shaped to the special interests in the name of which it is designed. Two major forms of conflict ideology were sketched because of the number of problems they cast up for modern social science: Marxism and social Darwinism.

Conflict sociology, on the other hand, aspires to be an explanation rather than a social program. The development of modern sociological conflict theory has been traced from Walter Bagehot to George B. Vold and Ralf Dahrendorf. Dahrendorf pointed the way for the post-World War II generation of conflict theorists by developing a conflict position on the basis of a revisionist Marxism rather than on the foundation of works by Gumplowicz, Ratzenhofer, Small, and their followers. However, those Marxists who wish to retain the doctrine as an ideology of revolution have been highly critical of Dahrendorf's practice. This, in turn, suggests the question: Is a Marxist sociology possible?

There is, of course, no question that various propositions can be taken from the work of Marx and the Marxists, treated as hypotheses — when they assert empirical relations — and subjected to test. However, when this is done, Marxism ceases to be an intact structure, for its components are dismantled, accepted, rejected, or modified and replaced. From this point of view, the reaction by doctrinaire Marxists calls attention to the difference between conflict theory and revolutionary ideology. Marxism can be transformed into a sociological theory, but only by destroying its ideological properties in the process. Conflict theory, however, had properties which may be seen throughout to be such as to satisfy the ideological requirements imposed on early sociology. Conflict theory was more empirically positivistic even than organismic positivism. At the same time, in somewhat more subtle fashion, it did not violate the need for a conservative position. By and large, sociological conflict theory has found its lodestar in stability. Precisely because of its acceptance of the universality of conflict, the vindication of society is found in achieved order.

The sociological gains as one moves from organismic positivism to conflict theory are immense. The conception of society as a big tame animal is abandoned. Analysis shifts to infinitely variable relations of groups. Grand schemes of evolution drop away; a whole range of processes takes their place. One cuts below the surface of institutional formulas to the stabilities of custom and the factors that may disrupt it. The problem of the interrelation of economic and other institutions is posed and, above all, the interrelation of political and other institutions. The problem of social class is formulated as are the problems of "ideology," the "sociology of law," and "political sociology." Even the problem of the social shaping of the individual has made its appearance.

There can be no doubt about the significance of the conflict theory of sociology as a step toward mature science. The conflict theorists were more realistic than their organismic predecessors and colleagues. But if they were a bit less hysterical about it, most of the time they shared their conservatism. The ideological formula that sociological conflict theory supplied its adherents was precisely this — the paradox of maturity: "If you know enough to carry out a revolution, you know better."

PART III

SCIENTIFIC ELEMENTARISM

THE FIRST SCHOOLS of sociological theory rode the leading edge of a wave of collectivism and conservatism in the nineteenth century. Its proponents did not view themselves as conservatives, but as progressives, employing science to stabilize and strengthen society. To Comte, the Enlightenment, culminating in the French Revolution, was the metaphysical stage in human progress. While most later sociologists were not as extreme as Comte, they, too, generally found revolution repugnant. While the conflict theorists were more realistic than their organismic colleagues in recognizing the role played by force, war, revolution, and violence in human history, they largely neutralized it in their vision of conflict as the mechanism by which ever more comprehensive peace groups were formed. Both positivistic organicists and conflict theorists shared a holistic point of view. Sociology was not conceived as the study of individuals, but groups, communities, classes, societies, and humanity. Comte did not even consider the individual to be a component of society; society, he thought, was not composed of individuals, but institutions, the most basic of which was the family. The conflict theorists treated individuals as sociologically insignificant, except in their participation in groups. Still, in the postwar world when Dahrendorf undertook to revive conflict theory on a foundation of revisionist Marxism, he complained about the slight attention paid by Marx to the individual.

Sociology was largely the product of reflections of middle-class individuals and addressed the requirements of the contemporary nation-state the control of which was being removed from monarchs and aristocrats and placed into the hands of the public at large. The major task faced by the middle classes, who had greatly extended their share of control over the affairs of the nation, was to stabilize the new society and consolidate their position in its affairs. In this process France, England, and the United States took the lead and positivistic organicism, the first school of sociological theory, found its original home in these nations. At the same time in Germany and Eastern Europe, the middle classes were still largely excluded from power. The development of a national community was occurring more rapidly than the development of a state adapted to a broad foundation of social powers. This was quite possibly the major reason for the emergence of conflict theory in Eastern Europe. Just as France, England, and the United States were particularly well suited for the emergence of positivistic organicism, Germany, Austria-Hungary, and Poland were well suited for the emergence of conflict theory. Once they appeared, sociologists in both areas were enriched by the alternatives represented by positivistic organicism and conflict theory.

It was inevitable that sociology would sooner or later be pressed to the service of approaches to social life that placed the emphasis upon individuals and their activities rather than on the collective conceived as an entity. For one thing, the rationalist thinkers of the seventeenth and eighteenth centuries who carried out the critique of traditional society by contrasting outworn institutions with the requirements of a rational human nature and who welcomed science as the distinctive thought of contemporary humanity, were thoroughgoing individualists. They held a mechanistic, rather than an organic, conception of society, and believed that society should serve the development of individuality, rather than demanding the sacrifice of personality to the need for social order. The rationalistic view that society should be evaluated in terms of its contribution to the fulfillment of personality could be applied to the new community of the nation-state. If it failed to meet this test, the possibility of a return to an individualistic social outlook was present with consequences for the development of sociological theory.

There was another phenomenon that would sooner or later play a role in the rise of an individualistic or elementaristic social theory. There is a division of opinion, at least as old as Plato, on the status of abstract ideas in the Western world. Plato was convinced that abstract ideas have a reality of their own and that there must be some realm in which, for example, the idea of "horse" exists to permit us to recognize all the varied particular animals to which we spontaneously apply the term. Aristotle, however, argued that "horsiness" was, rather, a property found in all particular horses and had no existence apart from them. Plato was a realist believing that abstract ideas had a reality in their own right (*ante rem*) or before any particular thing exists; Aristotle was a nominalist believing the general property had existence only in particular objects (*in re*) with no independent reality. Aristotle's approach to the problem of abstraction was much closer to that of the contemporary scientist than Plato's.

The implication of the nominalism-realism distinction for sociology is clear. No one has ever seen a society or a community or humankind. This, of course, does not mean we have no idea about what we are talking about when we refer to these "entities." They are abstract ideas which are symbolized and reified — treated as if they were things in their own right. It is of particular interest in this connection that the notion by a collection of individuals in interaction that they constitute a "community" is often a reflection of the reactions of persons who see them from the outside as having things in common. Needless to say, there are practical consequences to such reification, naming, and treating of a complex process over time as if it were an entity in its own right. Reification is an important device for achieving desirable social objectives (of course, with the qualification that on occasion reification may also be quite frustrating); it serves to give boundaries and rigidity to what would otherwise be a fluid process.

However, as traditionally conceived, scientific methodology is fundamentally analytical. It solves its problems (including those which deal with complex events) by breaking them down into smaller units that can be studied in detail with the hope of eventually arriving at a more accurate understanding of interrelations. It then moves on to other combinations, assembling the various pieces of a complex puzzle into ever larger combinations. It is in the nature of the scientific attitude to be skeptical of popular reifications and to cut their components apart for intensive study.

Moreover, in every society there are individualists and collectivists, on the one hand, and nominalists and realists, on the other. Societies vary in the comparative importance they place upon the individual and upon the collective, though no society can give absolute importance to the individual without disintegrating as a society, or absolute importance to the collective without turning it into a prison. Moreover, over time in any given society there may be alteration in preference for or against greater opportunity for individual freedom and creativity versus social control. In the founding period of a community, for example, considerable scope tends to be permitted for individual innovation; this often is reduced as the community approaches maturity, when further individual creativity can become destructive. Also, communities sometimes reach a stage when rigid coercive control over the individual collapses into anarchism.

Within a given society, finally, there are uses for both realistic and nominalistic temperaments. This seems to be true even in science itself. The realistic mind seems to leap toward the higher syntheses; the nominalistic mind is inclined to dissolve all combinations into their components.

Until the last quarter of the nineteenth century, sociology was dominated by a realistic and collectivistic outlook. However, in the last quarter of the century, as a result of a series of disillusionments experienced by the same classes that had supported the rise and development of sociology, the times were ripe for the exploration of an individualistic or elementaristic sociology. The inclination remained, however, to leave sociology in the sphere of science. These tendencies were not confined to sociology but were aspects of a movement in philosophy, social science, and the humanities. Scholars renewed their contact with eighteenth-century traditions, and reanalyzed problems from an elementaristic point of view. Leading the way in this nominalistic movement was the Kantian revival. In all areas where neo-Kantianism became popular, it resulted in new analyses based on a distinction between form and content. The neo-Kantian revival was followed by a neo-Idealistic wave, which tended to play down a

---

Compass Points of Western Social Science

Methodology	The Nature of Social Reality	
	ELEMENTARISTIC	HOLISTIC
HUMANISTIC		
SCIENTIFIC	Neo-Kantianism Pluralistic Behaviorism Social-Action Theory Symbolic Interactionism	Positivistic Organicism Conflict Theory

formalistic approach to humanistic subject matter, placing emphasis on substance rather than form. In the United States pragmatism was among these new developments. At least four major movements in sociological theory reflect the elementaristic movement in Western thought around the turn of the century: neo-Kantian formalism; pluralistic behaviorism; social-action theory; and symbolic interactionism. It is possible to locate these movements in a model of the compass points (methodological and substantive) of Western social science thought that is an elaboration of the simpler chart that appears in Part II.

The period between 1890 and World War I was characterized by a rapid growth in elementaristic forms of social theory. Popular wars, as were World Wars I and II, usually engender an intensification of patriotic sentiment and an inclination toward holistic or collectivistic points of view.

During the Great Depression the overriding social problem was order in Western society, but the simultaneous economic crisis was accompanied by considerable exploration of conflict theory.

The period of the 1960s was distinguished by a resurgence of interest in all of the elementaristic positions, which have experienced new developments in the 1960s and 1970s.

As in the case of the first two schools of sociological theory, once established, elementaristic theories have become research traditions with, so to speak, lives of their own — that is, they may continue to appear and undergo development and revivals in the works of successive generations of scholars. Hence, as the first two schools of theory were traced in earlier chapters, the elementaristic theories have been reviewed as cultural traditions responsive to pressures both from inside the tradition and from the outside milieu.

XI

The Philosophical Foundations of Sociological Formalism

Organismic positivism and conflict sociology are the two oldest schools of sociological theory. They both drew deeply on ancient philosophic traditions in Western thought. Both brought a new integration, a new emphasis, and a new direction to the analysis of society. Their exponents cut out a territory from the established disciplines. Positivistic organicism laid down the outlines of the new synthesis, and conflict theory brought a density, specificity, and maturity of outlook. These schools established sociology as a recognized field of scientific endeavor. Two of their representatives, William Sumner and Albion Small, established, respectively, the first course and the first department of sociology in North America. Small collaborated in writing the first college sociology textbook.

Sociology was carried by the early schools to a stage where it was ready to be professionalized and institutionalized; the process was beginning. Besides the teaching of courses and the establishment of sociology departments in the colleges and universities, sociology was soon to have a professional society and two professional journals: in the United States, Small was active in establishing the *American Journal of Sociology;* in France, Durkheim played an equivalent role in connection with *L'Année sociologique.*

In all areas, professionalization and institutionalization have had sweeping effects. A new professional role has appeared. Materials have been integrated and interpreted for teaching purposes. Scholars are now systematically trained in sociology, and a wider public is being given some systematic instruction in it. Its journals serve as a platform for the expression of its ideas. Its societies serve as a meeting point for its members. The discipline as a whole begins to acquire a recognized prestige among others. It competes in university and college settings for the presentation of its own viewpoint and for student enrollment.

The phenomena of professionalization and institutionalization affect the intellectual structure of the discipline. Materials are accumulated specifically for teaching purposes. Teachers feel that they must present other points of view than their own as a part of their "responsibilities" toward their students and the field. The field must be justified in the context of other disciplines; at least equivalent standards must be established. Last but not least, the discipline cannot afford to be too imperialistic. Emphasis shifts from the enterprise of carving out new territories in the intellectual domain to holding and justifying the discipline and establishing boundaries around it. In sociology, the initial wave of this movement led to the development of a new school of sociological thought drawing upon different sources in the philosophic traditions of the West.

OLDER FORMS OF PHILOSOPHICAL RATIONALISM

Sociological formalism drew its primary inspiration from some special aspects of Western philosophical rationalism. Although the older forms of rationalism enter the picture only incidentally, they are significant for the understanding of those nineteenth-century forms which directly affected the social sciences. Groethuysen has called attention to the dual aspect of rationalism as explanation and action orientation. "Rationalism is a comprehensive expression applied to various theoretical and practical tendencies which aim to interpret the universe purely in terms of thought, or which aim to regulate individual and social life in accordance with the principles of reason and to eliminate as far as possible or to relegate to the background everything irrational."[1]

[1]B. Groethuysen, "Rationalism," *Encyclopaedia of the Social Sciences* (New York: Macmillan, 1931), XIII, 113. Especially useful studies of rationalism are: W. E. H. Lecky, *History of the Rise and Influence of the Spirit of Rationalism in Europe* (London: 1865; New York: G. Braziller, 1955); Wilhelm Dilthey, *Weltanschauung und Analyse des Menschen seit Renaissance und Reformation*, Vol. 2 of *Gesammelte Schriften*, 2d ed. Stuttgart: Teubner, 1957); Ernst Cassirer, *The Philosophy of the Enlightenment*, trans. Fritz C. A. Koelln and James P. Pettegrove (Princeton, N.J.: Princeton University Press, 1951); and A. W. Benn, *The History of English Rationalism in the Nineteenth Century* (London: Longmans, Green, 1906).

Rationalism, as idealism, declined in popularity during much of the twentieth century, though there are

In philosophy, rationalism promoted the conception of a world forming a coherent whole analyzable by reason; in science, it promoted the concept of a logical and mathematical universe; in human conduct, it led to the conception of self-evident principles regulating behavior. Any given form of rationalism involves a conception of reason and of the irrational, but there are different forms of rationalism, depending on whether the irrational is located in nature or human nature.

Greek rationalism conceived the irrational as manifest in the changeable world of sense. By contrast, the world of reason was populated by perfect, unchangeable forms. Aristotle directed his philosophy to the study of these permanent and unchangeable forms accessible to reason. His logic was intended to develop the relations between the forms, enabling the individual to achieve rational comprehension of them. Human and world reason were conceived as unified in divine reason. It was, however, not nearly as important as pure reason.

signs of return to some of its major tenets. The concept was not even discussed in the *International Encyclopedia of the Social Sciences* (published 1968) and no entry on rationalism appears in the index to Tom Bottomore and Robert Nisbet, eds., *A History of Sociological Analysis* (New York; Basic Books, 1978). There was a scarcity of recent items in the review of "Rationalism" by Bernard Williams in *The Encyclopedia of Philosophy* (New York: Crowell Collier and MacMillan, 1968), VII, 69–74, though he did note the examination of the influence of rationalism on science and the emergence of the doctrine of innate ideas among students of structural linguistics. Among studies of the influence of rationalism on science are: E. A. Burtt, *The Metaphysical Foundations of Modern Physical Science* (New York: Modern Library, 1949); Giorgio de Santilla and Edgar Zilsel, "The Development of Rationalism and Empiricism," *International Encyclopedia of Unified Science* (Chicago: University of Chicago Press, 1941) Vol. II; E. J. Dijksterhuis, *The Mechanization of the World Picture* (Oxford: Clarendon Press, 1961). Noam Chomsky and E. H. Lenneberg advance the idea that the deep structure of language is innate in J. A. Fodor and J. J. Katz, eds., *The Structure of Language* (Englewood Cliffs, N.J.: Prentice-Hall, 1964). In the 1970s there were some signs of a revival of interest in rationalism. See: Bruce Aune, *Rationalism, Empiricism, and Pragmatism* (New York: Random House, 1970) and Brand Blanchard, *Reason and Belief* (London: Allen & Unwin, 1974).

The nature of the divine thought involves certain problems; for while thought is held to be the most divine of things observed by us, the question how it must be situated in order to have that character involves difficulties. For if it thinks of nothing, what is there here of dignity? It is just like one who sleeps. And if it thinks, but this depends on something else, then . . . it cannot be the best substance, for it is through thinking that its value belongs to it.

Evidently, then, it thinks of that which is most divine and precious, and it does not change; for change would be change for the worse, and this would be already a movement.

Therefore it must be of itself that the divine thought thinks (since it is the most excellent of things), and its thinking is a thinking of thinking.[2]

The Greek forms of theoretical rationalism had little appeal for the Romans. What was of interest to them, however, was the fusion by the Stoics of rationalism and ethics. The school was founded by Zeno of Citium in Cyprus around 334–262 B.C. Of Semitic extraction, Zeno came to Athens in his twenty-second year and attached himself to the Cynic Crates. About 300 B.C. he became a teacher and philosopher. His studies were called Stoicism, from the *stoa,* or colonnaded porch, where the group met. The Stoics held that without knowledge true morality is impossible. They opposed the dualism of Plato, preferring the monistic materialism of Heraclitus and the atomists. They thought that dualism endangers the absolute rule of reason in human life, that everything obeys universal laws. Human beings by their reason are able to know these laws, and follow them consciously. In fact, through their rationality, human beings see themselves as part of the universe and pledged to work for the whole. They know they are related to all rational beings in nature. Rational beings are similar to them with equal rights under the same law of nature and reason. In Stoicism, cosmopolitanism takes the place of politics.

These Stoic doctrines, transmitted to the Romans, became an important basis for rational legal

action. As a city-state with dominion over an empire, Rome was placed in the position of having to legislate for the changing needs of a variety of peoples. Reason became for the Romans an instrument for the control of life. The theory that some moral and rational insights are basic to all human beings undergirded the idea of universal legislation as the basis of a political and social world order. These ideas were popularized by Cicero. With respect to the individual, the ideal arose of the wise person, guided by reason, with an independent and self-contained personality, preserving equanimity in the face of all the trials of the world.

In the medieval world, this doctrine went into eclipse. St. Augustine held that the instincts and will had independent existence and were not controlled by the intellect and reason. As a result of the fall, human beings were unable to carry out decisions on the basis of rational insight. Hence, because of the impotence of human reason, human beings needed divine grace. Human life and the world constituted a meaningful whole, not in terms of human reason but in terms of God's divine plan — a plan which could be known only through divine revelation. Thus the reason of antiquity was subordinated to a superrational, divinely inspired whole.

MODERN RATIONALISM

In the Renaissance, in place of the medieval notion of divine providence, the idea of "fortune" again appears from antiquity. The casual impudence of the Renaissance individual toward what was formerly piously regarded as divine providence is visible in Machiavelli's formulations:

> I certainly think that it is better to be impetuous than cautious, for Fortune is a woman, and it is necessary, if you wish to master her, to conquer her by force; and it can be seen that she lets herself be overcome by the bold rather than those who proceed coldly. And therefore, like a woman, she is always a friend to the

[2]Aristotle, *Metaphysics,* Book XII, Chapter 9.

young, because they are less cautious, fiercer, and master her with greater audacity.[3]

In the Renaissance individuals again were left to their own devices. They looked for security in the development of their individual reason as the means of escaping the tumult of life.

The Renaissance thinker was quite aware of the variety of things and events defying reduction to reason. There was an intensified sense of the individual, the particular, the unique. The problem of knowledge was reformulated. Its task was no longer one of reducing the variety of events to changeless forms but of discovering the rational principles for organizing and regulating the multiplicity of things. The ancient world was dominated by the dream of types, ideas, and forms. The new world was concerned with functions and laws. Not static conceptual classifications, but dynamic causal relations, typified the new. This was basic to the scientific rationalism of the seventeenth century, with its ideal of a mathematically understandable universe analyzable on the basis of a universal mathematical language. The ideal was formulated by Galileo. It was central to the philosophic systems of Descartes, Spinoza, and Leibnitz.

Parallel to this scientific rationalism was the rationalization of social life on the basis of self-evident, universal principles. The state was conceived as the instrument of reason in the control of individual arbitrariness and irrational instincts, just as, it was assumed, a person's mind is in control of his or her material body. In the state, the various domains of human life were to be regulated by definite principles on the basis of the decisions of a single sovereign will embodying the so-called *raison d'état*. Such an equation of rationalism and political absolutism soon declined, however, as the middle classes learned to shape life on the basis of their own foresight. The fundamental differences between the rationalism of the seventeenth century and that of the eighteenth were correlated

with a relocation of reason in individual activity and the fusion of the mental and the physical into a single unit. In the former period, reason was regarded as a compulsory force imposed from above, curbing the various irrational manifestations of individual life and coordinating them in such a way as to make social life possible; in the latter period, there was growing confidence in the rational endowments of every individual, endowments which could be developed through education and enlightenment. Of the contrast between the two centuries, Cassirer stated: "The difference in the mode of thinking does not mean a radical transformation; it amounts merely to a shifting of emphasis. This emphasis is constantly moving from the general to the particular, from principles to phenomena. But the basic assumption remains; that is the assumption that between the two realms of thought [the mental and the physical] there is no opposition, but rather complete correlation — except for Hume's skepticism which offers an entirely different approach."[4] Methodologically, the counterpart was a fusion of the logical and the empirical. Thus, the eighteenth century proposed to carry out an integration on three fronts: between the group and the individual; between the mental and physical in the individual; and between the logical and the empirical in the individual's methodology.

Descartes. The idea of a synthesis of logico-mathematical and empirical thought dominates the forms of rationalism important to the development of modern science since Galileo. Descartes, for instance, saw no inconsistency in applying the principle of doubt to knowledge as the device most quickly designed to uncover the immutable principles it contains. His aim was to arrive at those truths presented by the good sense found in all human beings. The mental operations giving certain knowledge were intuition and deduction — the direct perception of indubitable truths and the deduction of concepts from them.

[3]From Luigi Ricci's translation of *The Prince,* in Niccolò Machiavelli, *The Prince and The Discourses* (New York: Modern Library, 1948), p. 94.

[4]Ernst Cassirer, *The Philosophy of the Enlightenment,* p. 22.

One could, therefore, build an absolutely certain structure of thought. Descartes' development of analytical geometry occurred in response to his assumption that the world could be mathematized.

Descartes presented a rationalism quite different from that of the Greeks, who conceived the world of the senses to be irrational, over and against the world of thought. True, Descartes wanted to start with intuition and work with deduction, rather than rely on "the fluctuating testimony of the senses" or the "misleading judgment that proceeds from the blundering constructions of the imagination."[5] However, he posed no absolute antithesis between them; he did not conceive the purpose of reason to be the overcoming of the irrationality of the sensory world. Descartes could thus become a common starting point for either empiricism or further forms of rationalism. Later development in thought has a way of reclassifying its ancestors. In one respect, the philosophers who have come to be known as "empiricists" (Locke, Berkeley, and Hume) and those who are now thought of as "rationalists" (Descartes, Spinoza, Leibnitz) were similar: they both perceived a difference between logical and empirical knowledge, and both believed that these forms of knowledge would ultimately be brought into synthesis. They had different strategies for the solution of their problems, to be sure: the empiricists proposed to start with empirical facts and unify thought; the rationalists sought this unity by way of logical principles.

Both Descartes and Locke subscribed to the division of "primary" and "secondary" qualities. Descartes thought that sense knowledge was notoriously variable. He also thought that some forms of sense knowledge contain very real information about reality. Sense qualities were divided into "secondary," which to a large degree depend for their character on the mind itself, and "primary," which correspond directly to properties of nature. Our senses can deceive us about the smell or color of a thing, but they are very accurate about its extension and weight. It was not until the distinction between primary and secondary qualities collapsed that logical and empirical knowledge ended up in apparently irreconcilable spheres. Knowledge applying to reality had no certainty, and certain knowledge no application to reality. This was precisely what Immanuel Kant (1724–1804) thought had happened when Hume logically carried out the program of empiricism. He reported that Hume had awakened him from his dogmatic slumbers. To Kant, Hume's critique of the concepts of the "self," "God," and causality not only brought ethics and religion to a state of crisis but threatened the foundation of science itself.[6]

Kant's Rationalism. Kant's startled reaction to Hume can only be explained in terms of his rationalistic assumption. He had originally shared the idea of the ultimate unity of empirical and logical knowledge. The task of science was thought to be the attainment of knowledge at once logically certain and empirically accurate. Since the knowledge of science concerned causal laws, in Kant's view Hume had dissolved the very foundations of science itself by the acid of his wit. Kant's surprise at Hume's argument is a tribute to the clarity of his perception of the assumptions of rationalism and empiricism and his sensitivity to the critical state to which they had been brought. Kant's intellectual solidity appears in his formulations, which were made in such full awareness of the crisis that he became one of the main points of departure for many movements in modern thought.

By way of a series of distinctions, Kant proposed to save science from the skepticism of Hume. The first of these was the distinction between *synthetic* and *analytic* statements. A synthetic statement is any statement which adds some new item to the stock of knowledge about the world. It is a statement about the world, a statement of fact. Generally, there is only one way to arrive at a bit of

---

[5]René Descartes, *Selections* (New York: Scribner's, 1927), p. 46.

[6]Immanuel Kant, *Critique of Pure Reason,* trans. Norman Kemp Smith (New York: Macmillan, 1953).

factual knowledge; that is, to obtain it from experience. Synthetic knowledge is empirical knowledge. Analytic statements, on the other hand, do not require factual investigation. They are not statements arrived at in this manner. They are deduced from other statements already made. The conclusion of an Aristotelian syllogism is analytic. Such knowledge is not known after the fact (*a posteriori*) but before, or without appeal to facts (*a priori*). These two kinds of knowledge in terms of the manner in which they are known are as follows:

How Known?	Types of Knowledge	
	ANALYTIC	SYNTHETIC
A Priori A Posteriori	X	X

Kant did not invent this distinction. It is found in the writings of Hume and Leibnitz, and even suggested by some of Locke's arguments. Kant, however, sharpened the distinction and called it to attention. Furthermore, he posed his problems in terms of it.

Hume had shown that the causal knowledge of science is synthetic, and had presented the case for its being purely a posteriori. He denied logical necessity to the laws of science. Thus if science is to be saved from the skepticism of Hume, it is necessary to demonstrate, in addition to these categories of knowledge, the existence of a special type, a kind of scientific knowledge that is at once "synthetic," representing factual, but at the same time necessary knowledge. How can science be saved? By demonstrating that at least some synthetic knowledge is a priori possible.

Kant's second set of distinctions concerns the object of knowledge. We know that we have experience. We assume it refers to a real world. The world as experienced is called by Kant *phenomenon*. The thing in itself is the *noumenon*. Our knowledge

of the world, including all our scientific knowledge, is concerned with things as experienced. However much one might wish it, science does not apply to noumena, but only to phenomena. Kant made a tremendous concession to the empiricists: the identification of the objects of synthetic knowledge with phenomena.

But if knowledge of phenomena is synthetic and a posteriori, Hume's critique of causality holds. Kant therefore introduced a third set of distinctions. The knowledge of phenomena may be divided into two main types: *form* and *content*. Kant argued that the *forms* are fundamental, serving as conditions for anything becoming an object of knowledge in the first place. More simply, the forms are the missing *synthetic a priori*. The forms under which anything is known were assumed by Kant to be supplied by the faculty of knowledge itself. The content of experience is produced by external influences. Kant distinguished the activities of the mind into perceiving and conceiving. Perception, too, has its forms. When we perceive anything, it is in space and time. Location and duration characterize everything experienced. When all sense qualities are abstracted from things experienced, extension and succession remain. Space and time, then, are the fundamental forms of perception. Similarly the activity of conceiving and thinking may be analyzed. If we abstract every item of content from thought, something still remains in one's comprehension. Or, by reverse, whenever we understand anything, we do so by binding it together in certain relations, the most important of which are quantity and cause. By means of a judgment, a combining activity, we understand one phenomenon as cause or effect of another. The same form of synthesis may be employed, whatever the content.

There were for Kant three groups of forms. (1) *Forms of Perception*. Space is the form of all perception in the sphere of outer experience, time the form of all perception in the sphere of inner experience. They are forms, because every single experience presupposes them. (2) *Forms of Understanding*. Perception and conception are conjoint activities. Perception without conception is blind;

conception without perception is empty. In perception, a manifold is directly united into a whole. In conception, combination is consciously performed. Unity and self-identity of consciousness are the necessary conditions for conceiving any content. Only by the application of the causal conception can we apprehend such phenomena as the freezing of water, the transition from fluidity to solidity as an objective event. In all, Kant recognized twelve fundamental categories of conception. (3) A third type of form is found in the *Ideas of Reason,* which refer to the whole of the faculty of knowledge. Reason, in its narrow sense, refers to the faculty of knowledge in performing unconditioned syntheses. Perception fashions sensation into spatial and temporal form. Understanding arranges them into conceptual wholes in terms of such forms as quantity and causality. But reason demands an absolute beginning and limit to space and time, an absolute maximum to causal series. This is the continuation and consumption of the combining activity of perception and understanding. Concepts designating an absolute conclusion are *Ideas.* There are three such ideas: the Idea of the Soul, the Idea of the World, and the Idea of God. These ideas proceed from the nature of reason itself. No objective deduction of the Ideas is possible. They refer to an unconditioned ultimate. The Ideas have a subjective origin in the need of *Reason* for unity.

Kant was a child of the Enlightenment as much in his ethics as in his metaphysics and epistemology.[7] If Hume dominated his conception of scientific knowledge, Rousseau exercised an influence on his ethics. The problem of knowledge was solved, to Kant's satisfaction, by means of his forms. He attempted to solve the problem of ethics by the discovery of a law of right action in the human being's inner nature. From Rousseau he took over the idea of the dignity of the individual as a personal being. Following the pattern of his epistemology, he searched for the universally valid

element of ethical knowledge in a distinction between form and content. The moral law expresses itself as conscience. It consists of the injunction to act in such manner that one's action could be universally extended to every human being; moreover, it requires that each person be treated as an end, never as a means. An ethical action depends not on outer facts but on the inner will. Nothing is good in itself except the good will. Moral law, or duty, is not an anticipation of the goal of historical development, but, as a priori principles, prefigures experience. The ideal derived from experience and human need is that of a free society of human personalities.

Kant's central place in modern thought derives in part from his attempt to link two great traditions: the rationalistic and empirical. Kant yielded to the empirical criticism of concepts everything he thought it required. He made a tremendous sacrifice to empiricism when he restricted the application of reason to phenomena, in principle excluding it from analysis of the thing in itself. All this, however, was done in the name of science, to achieve that necessary knowledge he thought science required. In a similar way, Kant fused the principle of individual freedom from the eighteenth-century rationalistic tradition with the principle of order taken over from the conservative position. He performed the same type of synthesis in his socioethical philosophy as in his technical philosophy.

The idea of "freedom" was thrust into central focus. History was conceived as the development of the principle of freedom. Perhaps the entire history of the human race represents the fulfillment of nature's secret plan through the development of a system of government as the condition for the full realization of the nature of humanity. The central problem for humankind is that attainment of a universal system of law for civil society founded not on the relation of ruler to ruled, or force, but on interhuman relationship in which all individuals are ends in themselves. As free agents, human beings participate in a constitution on the basis of laws they helped to develop.

The ideas of the eighteenth-century contract

[7]Kant's ethical philosophy was expounded in the *Critique of Practical Reason,* trans. Lewis White Beck (Chicago: University of Chicago Press, 1949).

thinkers (particularly Rousseau) were reflected in Kant's notion that society rests on social contract. That was not, however, a historical fact but an ideal of reason, binding every law-giver to make laws in such ways that they express the united will of the entire people, compelling regard for all subjects so far as they wish to be citizens. Natural right has a different origin from the laws of nature; it arises from the noumenal world of the moral self, while the laws of nature apply only to the phenomenal world. Natural right is the contribution of the noumenal self acting in opposition to the principles of the sensory world. In this manner, Kant attempted to reconcile the problems of individual autonomy and freedom with the lawfulness and stability of society.

It is essential to keep these facts in mind if we are not to be faced with a solemn mystery in accounting for the unusual importance of Kant for later thought. After all, what had Kant done beside draw a distinction between form and content? In deriving ideas of form and content from two fundamentally different sources — form from the noumenal self and content from experience — he would seem to have created tremendous problems. The categories are contributions by the noumenal self to the world of phenomena. Yet they do not refer back to the noumena. If we try to make such an application, we fall into self-contradictions. Or again, when we turn to the problem of moral life, our first discovery is the contradictory requirements of the ethical and the scientific worlds. Morality requires freedom; science requires necessity. Our actions thus have two different constructions: scientifically as necessary and causal, ethically as free and "responsible." Does it really help us to ascribe these different characterizations to a phenomenal and noumenal world, respectively, since the problems then appear as a relation between the two spheres? Or, if we ask what new values the position makes possible, the most immediately obvious fact is the withdrawal of scientific thought permanently from the investigation of things in themselves. Science is saved, but is this not at the price of making it trivial? It does not take any great acumen to discover serious problems in the Kantian position. What would seem most in need of explanation is why science is so important.

The most important reason has already been stated. Kant's formulations were addressed to major problems of Western thought. He tried to reconcile the values of both the rationalists and the empiricists. Socially he tried to reconcile the theories of a free world with those of a lawful world. We do not solve Kant's problems by throwing out his solutions as shallow or inadequate. Kant had summarized these problems and sharpened them. Thus, good sense dictated that one start with Kant's formulations.

In the nineteenth century, Kant became one of the perennial starting points for new departures of thought: for absolute idealism, for irrational idealism, and even for extreme positivism. It was perhaps inevitable that when any given trend in thought broke down, a natural tendency was to return to Kant. Neo-Kantianism was also one of the ground movements in social science in the late nineteenth and early twentieth centuries.

NEO-KANTIANISM

Friedrich Albert Lange (1828–1875), philosopher and social reformer and foremost historian of materialism in the nineteenth century, founded the neo-Kantian movement.[8] He saw materialism as the most comprehensive explanation available of the physical world. At the same time he felt that it was basically deficient in its account of the human spirit. But this was no difficulty to be repaired by the arbitrary insertion of spiritual activity into the framework of materialism. "On the Atomic theory we explain today the laws of sound, of light, of heat, of chemical and physical changes in things in the widest sense, and yet Atomism is as little able today as in the time of Demokritos to explain even the simplest sensation of sound, light, heat, taste, and so on. In all the advances of science, in all the presentations of the notion of atoms, this chasm

[8]Friedrich Albert Lange, *The History of Materialism*, trans. E. C. Thomas (New York: Humanities Press, 1950).

has remained unnarrowed."[9] On the other hand, the question may be asked what reality a thing has other than that of the representation of a subject. There is no fundamental reason why dissolving the world into the facts of consciousness should be preferable to reducing consciousness to physical things. There must be a third reality transcending the physical and the psychical. This is found in poetry:

> Kant would not understand, what Plato before him would not understand, that the "intelligible world" is a world of poesy, and that precisely upon this fact rests its worth and nobleness. For poesy, in the high and comprehensive sense in which it must be taken, cannot be regarded as a capricious playing of talent and fancy with empty imagination for amusement, but it is a necessary offspring of the soul, arising from the deepest life-roots of the race, and a complete counterbalance to the pessimism which springs from an exclusive acquaintance with reality.[10]

Lange's analysis starts from Kant's division into the spheres of physical and psychical. He tries to solve their relation in a Kantian manner. Poetry provides the reconciliation of the creativity of the spirit and the determinism and skepticism produced by physical fact.

Among other early students developing the neo-Kantian point of view were Otto Liebmann (1840–1912) and Alois Riehl (1844–1924).[11] Drawing the distinction between subjective con-sciousness and objective knowledge of science, Liebmann tried to resolve their relation by distinguishing between the conception of space and time given in empirical intuition and a pure transcendental conception of space and time. But where was one to obtain the criteria of the transcendental conception of space and time? One cannot turn to consciousness, for it only gives the empirical conception. But the empirical conception is merely phenomenal and not real. By shifting one's point of view, Liebmann thought one could arrive at the teleological conception of thought passing from nature to "ethos."

For Liebmann, the Kantian dualism is located in the field of knowledge. Riehl locates it in being, and attempts a transition from the reality outside thought to consciousness. Starting with the fact of consciousness, Liebmann attempted to account for science. On the other hand, Cohen[12] did not take consciousness as the center of reference or reality; consciousness was treated rather as the pure form of modal reflection, establishing the possibility rather than the reality of the objects of thought. Thought is conceived by Cohen as a self-dependent production and a reality in itself. The mathematical science of nature is an illustration of the self-dependent production of thought. The quantitative reality of mathematics is spontaneously generated starting from infinitesimal calculus, which resolves the lacuna created in the antithesis of the continuous and discrete. The categories are integrated according to the inherent teleology of the mathematical science of nature.

This same idea is essentially continued by Ernst Cassirer, for whom the mathematical concept is an absolute a priori element in knowledge, expressing the rules of any possible scientific experience. This, Cassirer claims, supplants Kant's principle of pure apperception.[13] In its development

---

[9]*Ibid.*, p. 23.

[10]*Ibid.*, pp. 231–232.

[11]See Otto Liebmann, *Kant und die Epigonen* ["Kant and His Followers"] (Stuttgart: 1865) and *Zur Analysis der Wirklichkeit* ["On the Analysis of Reality"] (Strassburg: 1876). Riehl's chief work was *Der philosophische Kriticismus und seine Bedeutung für die positive Wissenschaft* ["Philosophical Criticism and Its Significance for Positive Science"], 3 vols. (Leipzig: 1876–1887; 3d ed., Leipzig: A. Kröner, 1924–1926); Part Three of this work (1887 edition) was translated by Arthur Fairbanks as *Introduction to the Theory of Science and Metaphysics* (London: 1894). For an excellent review, see Guido de Ruggiero, *Modern Philosophy,* translation of the first edition (1912) by A. Howard Hannay and R. G. Collingwood (New York: Macmillan, 1921).

[12]Hermann Cohen, *Logik der Reinen Erkenntnis* ["The Logic of Pure Knowledge"] (Berlin: B. Cassirer, 1902).

[13]Ernst Cassirer, *Substanzbegriff und Funktionsbegriff* (Berlin: B. Cassirer, 1910). A full bibliography of Cassirer's work will be presented in Chapter XV, where his importance for the sociological movement known as symbolic interactionism is taken up.

from Hermann Cohen to Ernst Cassirer, neo-Kantianism becomes the search for a mathematical concept to provide a regulative unity for the multiplicity displayed in experience. Mathematics becomes the universal science of form, containing the rule of all possible experience. The knowledge of natural science centers in number as an a priori form. Concepts such as substance and cause are constructions determined by a priori requirements of number. In these formulations the a priori and the scientific construction differ only in their degree of generality, insofar as the first is the more general law and includes the other.

The neo-Kantian philosophy of value starts from the subjectivity of consciousness and attempts to establish the objectivity of science by means of the concept of value. This is the essence of the theories of Windelband and Rickert, whom we have already had occasion to discuss. Accepting the traditional distinction of human psychological life into thought, will, and feeling, Windelband attempted to use the theory of values to unify the logical, ethical, and esthetic. Moral consciousness supplies the criteria for the universal valuations of philosophy. The central property of philosophy is its inquiry into the standards of thought, ethics, the will, and esthetics. The basic dualism in Windelband's thought is between ideal standard and empirical being, which is also a dualism between the immanent and transcendent.

Rickert accepts the doctrine of immediate experience, maintaining that being does not exist except as the content of consciousness. Immanent in consciousness is immediate reality as representation. The immanence of being, as found in consciousness, is that of the universal, the concept of formal logic in its representation. However, the objective of knowledge cannot be obtained from formal logic. All that is given in consciousness is the play of representations, and between representations there is no universal and necessary validity. To establish the objectivity of knowledge, it is necessary to get away from consciousness and to devise a transcendent standard that has required validity. The transcendent is not a content of consciousness; it is not being, for "to be" is to be in

consciousness. It is an "ought to be." This "ought" is the standard of logical valuations. The feeling of self-evidence is the only indication of its presence. Such self-evidence is the ultimate criterion of truth. In the further development of his ideas, Rickert abandons the abstract doctrine of "ought" and replaces it with "value," or the ideal, to which the doctrine of "ought" is a stepping stone.

This last form of neo-Kantianism was critically central to the neo-Kantian conception of history. Generally the form this took was somewhat as follows. History is conceived not as the field of mechanical interaction of forces but as a spiritual process. A dualism is then found between history as a spiritual process and science. History is the science of individualities, but these contain elements of human universality outside time. Historical development has no meaning without a priori conditions that surmount the temporal.

One of the most interesting phenomena of nineteenth-century thought was the movement beyond Kant in the early part of the century, then back to Kant in the later part of the century.

The reasons for the speed with which thought traveled beyond Kant are clear enough. The distinction between the phenomenal and noumenal world was used by Kant to salvage science, the ethical life of human beings, and their religious life. This was all well and good, but it was achieved only by tremendous concessions. Science was "saved" by confining it in principle to phenomena. The world of the really real, the noumena, was placed forever outside science. The ethical life of humanity was saved, but among other things it was permanently, so it seemed, deprived of the possibility of claiming a scientific foundation. And so with other formulations.

One trend in early nineteenth-century thought addressed to these problems posed by Kant, organismic idealism, leads from Johann Gottlieb Fichte (1762–1814) to Comte. Fichte's problem arose in the attempt to unite the self in its phenomenal and noumenal aspect. The moral personality of the individual is a noumenal fact belonging to the "kingdom of ends" not determined by phenomenal things. Does conscious moral experience have no relation to the noumenal self? Does not the "kingdom of ends" supply the very principles that structure the world of conscious ethical action? Fichte proposed the idea of the "ethical self" which imposes its forms on the phenomenal world of action. Ethically the self establishes ends to which action is a response. The ethical quality of humankind is revealed thus in response to a self-created world. Ethically the limits of the self are transcended and fully realized in society.

Friedrich Schelling (1775–1854) expanded a similar argument to account for the creative activity of the artist, and Hegel generalized the arguments of Fichte and Schelling to apply to all areas of experience. The essence of the individual and humankind is located in the human spirit, which has two spheres of manifestation: the conscious world of phenomena and the deeper, more profound, world of noumena. As with Kant, the idea is accepted that conscious life constantly presses against the limits of experience, and when it does, it is caught in contradictions (antinomies). But after all, the spirit of the individual and of humankind is "one." By this very process the spirit realizes itself ethically (in the manner of Fichte) and artistically (in the manner of Schelling). Human history is the history of progressive self-realization of the free spirit that constantly presses against the limits of its applicability, casting up antinomies and surmounting them in new syntheses. In the idea of history as the dialectical self-realization of the free spirit, Hegel tried to solve Kant's problem.

That this was not the only possible solution to the Kantian problems was shown by Schopenhauer and Nietzsche. They, too, started by accepting the distinction between the phenomenal world of experience and the noumenal world of what really exists. Morality belongs to the world of action, hence it is, as Kant said, a noumenal fact. The world of science, on the other hand, is concerned with the explanation of phenomenal events. This means, said Schopenhauer and Nietzsche, that human rationality and science are confined to relatively superficial aspects of reality. In the self on which action depends, emotional life is funda-

mental. The real essence of humanity is will. Anti-scientific movements were launched from this platform.

The reasons for the movement beyond Kant are thus clear enough. This hardly explains why there should be a return to formulations that had proved to be so unstable. The various forms of organismic idealism had been very important to the rise of the social sciences, but they had problems of their own. The absolute idealism of Hegel, for example, tended to turn into a kind of panlogism. It led to pantheistic religiosity and a mystic sense of wholeness. This is no way to arrive at the hard-headed hypotheses necessary to science. Nor did it help matters that the Marxians self-consciously took over the "dialectic" and turned it into a weapon of class struggle. Moreover, the other branch of the movement, voluntaristic idealism, by elevating human emotional life and will to the center of interpretation and reducing rationality (science) to mere instruments of the will, became paramount critics of science. Schopenhauer cynically offered his generation the self-negation of the orient. Nietzsche not only slashed away at science (including Darwinism, which he despised), but offered his world a race of amoral supermen. Under such circumstances it is clear why there should be some attempt to return to fundamentals.

But the battle cry, "Back to Kant!" was heard not only in philosophical circles. It formed one of the ground movements in the social sciences toward the end of the nineteenth century and in the early decades of the twentieth. It may be recalled that sociology itself had emerged as a new field with the daring fusion of apparently contradictory areas of nineteenth-century thought: organicism and positivism. The tension between these areas provides much of the motive power for the early development of sociology. But one can also say that the day of reckoning, while it may be postponed, must arrive. Sooner or later the new discipline must face up to the problem of how objective knowledge is to be achieved when its subject matter is defined "subjectively." Ideas, Comte had maintained, either rule the world or throw it into chaos. Not inconsistently with this, sociologists at a later date were to define the subject matter of sociology as collective representations (Durkheim), ideas and beliefs (Tarde), the imaginations people have of one another (Cooley), definitions of the situation (Thomas), consciousness of kind (Giddings), and so on. The moment sociological enterprise was not directed primarily toward extending its territories but justifying its existence and consolidating its method, the problems implicit in its origins had to be faced.

One product of this ferment was the emergence of conflict theory alongside of organismic positivism. Conflict theory added a sobering realism to sociological discussion. It rejected large-scale, loosely defined entities as units of analysis. It called various schemes of unilinear evolution into question. It exposed the value premises of progress theories. It showed organismic positivism to be superficial and biased. However, by supplying still new systems of explanation alongside those already competing for acceptance, it added to the babble of voices. Moreover, conflict theory was not easy for everyone to accept. Many persons shrink from a point of view placing conflict in central focus. There seems to be a sort of impiety about it. The function of conflict theory was primarily to call organismic positivism into serious question. The self-examination that resulted coincided with the professionalization of the field. Sociology could not continue forever to draw checks on an unbalanced account. Neo-Kantianism, representing a re-examination of the general trends of nineteenth-century thought, offered itself as one of the most direct means for the self-survey.

SUMMARY

Sociology was not invented by academic individuals. The early phases of the two oldest schools were the work of journalists and people of affairs. They were imaginative persons with capacities for synthesis, drawing material for their new points of view from wherever it could be found. They did their work well, establishing the field as an independent discipline.

The professionalization and institutionalization of sociology were accompanied by a heightened intellectual ferment. Material had to be organized for teaching purposes. Teachers had to be trained to deal with all points of view. A wide public had to be informed about the new field. Sociology had to be defined in ways that did not lead to endless boundary disputes with other disciplines. It had to develop standards if it was to achieve respectability in the family of sciences.

These new professional and institutional demands were felt both in the old disciplines and in the emergence of new schools of sociological theory. The professionalization of sociology coincided with the classic stage of positivistic organicism. A strong methodological consciousness was present in Tönnies and Durkheim. Similarly, in conflict theory, methodological and professional responsibility was a significant factor in the theories of Gumplowicz and Albion Small.

There were a number of reasons why the new intellectual ferment could not be confined to the old theories. For one thing, the number of alternatives had increased. When there are many possible explanations, one needs standards in order to choose among them. Moreover, in the social sciences, no one as yet had made full use of the rationalistic traditions of Western thought.

While rationalism has often been combined with idealism, there is no necessary connection between them. There are forms of materialistic rationalism and irrational forms of idealism. Rationalism as a philosophy has always promoted the conception of the world as a coherent whole, analyzable by reason. In science it promoted the concept of a logical and mathematical universe. In human conduct it led to the conception of self-evident principles which regulate behavior. Wherever rationalism appears it leads to the search for special forms, rules, or principles.

A significant form of rationalism was advanced by Immanuel Kant, intended to salvage empiricism from a skepticism that he thought would destroy it. Kant agreed with the empiricists that science aspires to a knowledge of phenomena. However, he disagreed with the apparent critical conclusion of Hume that if knowledge is confined to phenomena based only on experience, no general knowledge is defensible except on grounds of habit or prejudice. Kant argued that knowledge of phenomena is of two kinds: of *forms* which are a priori and certain, and of *contents* which are merely contingent.

Kant attempted to integrate the rationalistic and empirical traditions of the eighteenth century, to maintain science on an empirical level and still supply it with universal, rational concepts. In his theories of the social world, he tried to reconcile the ideas of a free and simultaneously lawful world.

But Kant made an unusually great sacrifice to empiricism. By confining science purely to experience and urging that every time knowledge aspires to extend beyond experience it breaks down into antinomic contradictions, Kant seemed to have saved science, but at the price of sacrificing everything that made science worth while. The repeated neo-Kantian movements of nineteenth-century thought constantly returned to the Kantian formulations and attempted to avoid these sacrifices. Among the major neo-Kantians was Lange, who found in poetry the reconciliation of the creativity of the spirit and the determinism of physical fact. Liebmann located the Kantian dualism in the field of knowledge, seeking to reconcile it in a teleological conception of thought. Other neo-Kantians like Riehl, Hermann Cohen, and Cassirer located it elsewhere. Windelband and Rickert attempted to establish the objectivity of science by means of the concept of value.

The multiplicity of partly conflicting theories in sociology, which by now had split into two major branches, each of which embraced a variety of alternatives, invited the institution of more precise methods. In fact, a growing methodological anxiety was discernible even in the older schools, as illustrated by Tönnies, Durkheim, and Gumplowicz. Moreover, sociology was being transformed into an academic subject. It was imperative that it find a limited definition of its subject matter. Under such circumstances it is hardly strange that many sociologists repeated the battle cry of the nineteenth century, "Back to Kant!" The rationalistic traditions of Western thought, particularly the Kantian, were explored by some sociologists in the effort to arrive at a more special and limited definition of the field.

Neo-Kantianism in sociology developed first with the attempt to find a special definition of subject matter for sociology in the same way that Kant had for epistemology. However, it appears to have been almost unavoidable that a neo-Kantian sociology should soon reach the stage when it would chafe against self-imposed limitations, as did the Kantians. As sociology grew restless under these limitations, one could anticipate that various expedients would be tried.

XII

The Neo-Kantian Branch of
Sociological Formalism

It could perhaps have been predicted that at the time sociology became established as an independent science some reaction would set in against the influence of ideological conservatism upon the theory of society. The effects of conservatism appear over and again. Society, not the individual, is made the unit of analysis. It is insisted that institutions, not persons, are the units of society. When individuals are considered at all, as in some of the conflict theories, their sheeplike character is emphasized. Again it is insisted that groups, not people, are the units of social analysis. Moreover, the central property of society is found in such things as stability, order, solidarity — the conservative values.

The liberal theory of society, on the other hand, places emphasis on the individual rather than the group. It is more concerned with opportunity than with solidarity. Kant had received the liberal theory of society from his eighteenth-century predecessors. Society for him was not an organic form but an ordered community of independent wills. "Freedom," not "stability," was the watchword.

History represents the development of the principle of freedom. At the same time, Kant attempted to formulate the principle of freedom in terms of the requirements of interhuman order. Hence, Kant suggested, one need not consider the external system of government as the antithesis or enemy of the individual. This external system may provide the very condition for the full realization of the nature of humanity. The central problem for humankind is the attainment of a universal system of law for civil society founded on the nature of humanity rather than on a rule of force. These conditions are applied only in a system of interhuman relationships in which all individuals are ends in themselves. As free agents, human beings participate in a constitution on the basis of laws they help to create. This is a long way from the conception of law as a peace treaty ceremonially confirming the dominance of one group over another. It is more subtle than the usual eighteenth-century rationalistic conception of society as a mere contractual agreement. It locates law in central position as the condition for an ordered liberal society. Kant provided the basis for a theory of jurisprudence very different from that of the conflict theorists.

Rudolf Stammler. For Rudolf Stammler (1856–1938), theoretical jurisprudence is concerned with the law as a set of rules formulating the means for achieving human aims; it inquires into the means by which human aims are realized and the justification of rules for achieving them.[1] Stammler's "critical" method is modeled on Kant's procedures; it draws a distinction between form and content and seeks to discover the pure forms of law irrespective of their particular content of matter. A distinction is also drawn between the concept of law and the idea of justice. "Law" sums up the ways in which means are related to ends in social volition; "justice" provides the criteria of just law.

There are two ways in which order is introduced in consciousness: perception and will. *Perception* forms sense impressions, in terms of categories, into objects in an order. The *will* orders materials in terms of a goal to be achieved in the future. Law is a form of volition in which we are concerned with means to bring about an end. A legal principle formulates an end to be achieved.

RUDOLF STAMMLER

Courtesy of the Archiv der Martin Luther Universität, Halle-Wittenberg

[1] Stammler's basic works are: *Wirtschaft und Recht nach der materialistischen Geschichtsauffassung* ["Economy and Law According to the Materialist Conception of History"] (Leipzig: Veit, 1896; 5th rev. ed., Berlin: W. de Gruyter, 1924); *Theorie der Rechtswissenschaft* (Halle: Waisenhaus, 1911; 2d ed., 1923); and *Lehrbuch der Rechtsphilosophie* ["Textbook in the Philosophy of Law"] (Berlin: W. de Gruyter, 1922). The present discussion follows *The Theory of Justice*, translated by Isaac Husik (New York: Macmillan, 1925 and New York: A.M. Kelly, 1969). For an evaluation of the place of Stammler in the theory of jurisprudence, see Morris Ginsberg, "Stammler's Philosophy of Law," in [no author], *Modern Theories of Law* (London: Oxford University Press, 1933). See also the renewed interest in Stammler indicated by publication of *Die Lehre von dem richtiger Rechte* (Bad Homburg: H. Gentner, 1964) and the translation of Max Weber's discussion of Stammler: Max Weber, *Max Weber, Critique of Stammler*, trans. Guy Oakes (New York: The Free Press, 1977).

Not all forms of will are legal. One form, which represents the ordering of means to achieve the ends of the individual personality, is "isolated volition" (*getrenntes Wollen*). This is the sphere of morals. Isolated volition is distinguished from the "binding will" (*verbindendes Wollen*), implying a social relationship in which one will makes use of the purposive acts of another as a means to its own ends. Society is a group of wills functioning as means and ends to each other. Through cooperative effort society attains common ends. Law as the binding will is concerned with the external form of the acts of people in social relationships.

Not every volition is right. The rightness of a volition is determined in two ways. (1) Some means may be essential to the achievement of a particular aim or end. If the end is willed, so too the means must be. (2) The claim to universal validity arises out of the idea of justice. Over and above the conditional validity of appropriate means is a criterion of unconditional validity. Justice rests on the harmony of all striving and endeavor, requiring us to subordinate the particular to the universal and to view all particular ends in terms of the maximum harmony possible for all ends.

It is the distinction between the particular and the binding will that locates morality. Morality is concerned with inner life and the expression of personality. Law, however, is concerned with the external relations of people and the binding character their wills have on each other. The ideal of justice applied to morality leads to the idea of the "pure will," requiring truthfulness and honesty with one's self and the principle of perfection. In the sphere of law, the idea of justice gives rise to the concept of the "pure community." A community has a pure will when its order is based on principles of universal validity. The principles of right law are *respect* (no act of will is subject to arbitrary control of another, and people remain ends in themselves) and *cooperation* (no person may be arbitrarily excluded from a community if he or she is legally a part of it).

A rule is a just law or right law or a law of nature when it passes certain tests. These tests are found in a volition purged of all subjective elements in the service of an ideal harmony represented by a community based on objective purposes. In such a community of free willing people, everyone is both bound and free, all persons are ends in themselves. Everyone is bound by respect for the purposes of others, but at the same time no one is subject to the caprice of another nor can anyone be arbitrarily excluded from the benefits arising from membership in society. Law is not derived from the state. Rather, the state is one type of legal order presupposing the notion of law in general. The obligations of international law do not rest on the existence of a league of states; they derive from the idea of justice. The ultimate appeal is always to the social ideal. "We obtain the formula of a *community of men willing freely*, as the final expression which comprehends in unitary fashion all possible pur-

poses of persons united under law. I call this *the social ideal*."[2] This is not an empirical issue:

> In undertaking to work out the universal principles which are to span the bridge between the idea of just law and its significance for specific legal questions, we must take notice of a two-fold danger and try to avoid it: (1) The principles must not be gathered at random from historical observation. . . . (2) We must keep out of the content of our principles everything that is merely empirical and pertains to the material. . . .[3]

This conception of society lies at the opposite end of the scale from Comte's. The true units of society are individuals. Society exists for them, not they for society. The dream of a castelike order has no place in this scheme.

There are both comparisons and contrasts with the conflict theorists. Like them, Stammler places great importance on the contrast between morality and law. However, while, for the conflict theorists, morality was the sphere of a peculiar type of group, the in-group or we-group, morality is here conceived as the sphere of personality. Furthermore, law is not peculiar to the conquest group, but to the external order of society. This realignment of distinctions introduces the individual as a genuine social agent in many capacities other than that of a sheeplike follower.

Such a rational and liberal model of society was taken over by Georg Simmel, the foremost sociological exponent of neo-Kantianism. Simmel goes beyond such general distinctions to develop a more detailed sociology.

Georg Simmel. Georg Simmel (1858–1918) was born in Berlin, the son of a chocolate manufacturer. After his father's death, a friend of the family and founder of an international musical publishing house was appointed Simmel's guardian. He left Simmel a considerable fortune, enabling him to live as an independent scholar. He entered the University of Berlin in 1876 at the age of

[2]Stammler, *The Theory of Justice*, p. 153.
[3]*Ibid.*, p. 158.

GEORG SIMMEL

From *Buch des Dankes an Georg Simmel,* ed. by Kurt Gassen and Michael Landmann, Duncker & Humblot, Berlin, 1958. Courtesy of the publishers.

eighteen, studying with such scholars as the historians Theodor Mommsen, Johann Droysen, Heinrich von Sybel, and Heinrich von Treitschke, the philosopher Eduard Zeller, the ethnologist Adolf Bastian, and the art historian Herman Grimm. He received his doctor's degree in 1881 with a dissertation of Kant's concept of matter. From 1885 to 1900 he was *Privatdozent* in philosophy, and for another fourteen years he was *ausserordentlicher Professor* in philosophy at Berlin. In 1914 he was called to Strassburg as full professor (*Ordinarius*).

The two main theories of society in the eighteenth and nineteenth centuries were the mechanical-atomistic (developing in the sixteenth and seventeenth centuries) and the organic. In the one theory, individuals were conceived as independent and self-sustaining units, and the community as a mechanical summation of them. (This appears very clearly in John Stuart Mill and is reflected in Stammler.) The organismic theory sees society as something distinct from and opposing the individual. It was already suggested by Rousseau; it was systematically developed by Hegel and Fichte. In the nineteenth-century historian Lorenz von Stein it was transmitted directly to sociology,[4] receiving typical expression in the idea of the *Volksgeist.* Theodore Abel very justly observes[5] that Tönnies' work can be conceived as an attempt to fuse the two concepts of society (organic and mechanical) into one formulation. Society as an organic group is represented in the *Gemeinschaft*; society as an association resting on interests is represented in the *Gesellschaft.* The organismic point of view was retained by Tönnies through the expedient, discussed earlier in Chapter V, of having these two societal forms spring forth as manifestations of different kinds of will, *Wesenwille* and *Kurwille.*

Simmel made a new approach to the problem of the nature of society, bringing forward the concepts "relation" and "function." He had the liberal's objection to the organic theory, particularly its frequent postulate of a group mind. Society seemed to him to be a function manifested in dynamic relations among individuals and in interactions between individual minds. Society exists wherever a number of individuals enter into reciprocal relationships. It is a process. There exist only relations and actions between individuals of whom it may be said that in interaction they form a unity.

This was all stated in thoroughgoing Kantian manner. Kant had tried to reconcile the epistemological requirements of rationalism and empiricism. Simmel attempts to reconcile the

[4] See especially von Stein's history of social agitation in France, *Geschichte der socialen Bewegung in Frankreich, von 1789 bis auf unsere Tage,* 3 vols. (Munich: Drei Masken Verlag, 1921).
[5] Theodore Abel, *Systematic Sociology in Germany* (New York: Columbia University Press, 1929), p. 14.

sociological requirements of the social theories of organicism and mechanism. Theoretically one of the most interesting of all Simmel's essays was the one in which he directly posed the Kantian question and discussed it in a manner paralleling Kant's procedure in the *Critique of Pure Reason:* "How Is Society Possible?"[6]

Kant's fundamental question in the *Critique of Pure Reason* was how is nature as the object of science possible? According to Simmel, Kant could propose an answer because "nature" was taken to be the *representation* of nature. Nature is the special way our intellect assembles, orders, and forms sense perceptions. Nature is a kind of cognition, a picture growing in and through our cognitive faculties. Simmel proposed the analogous question

for society: what are the a priori conditions making society possible? Here too there are individual elements always remaining in their discreteness (as in the case of nature as content) yet undergoing a synthesis into the unity of society through a process of consciousness which puts the individual existence of several elements into definite relationship through *forms*, in accord with definite laws.

There is, however, a difference between the unity of society and that of nature. While nature becomes a unity in the contemplation of the subject, societal unity is realized by its elements without further mediation. The societary connection is directly realized in the individual's experiences. Society does not acquire an objective unity through an outside observer. It does not need to. By its nature, it is a direct unity between observers. Society is my representation, posited in the activity of consciousness. The soul of another has for me the same reality as I have myself. Within consciousness, Simmel continues, one distinguishes between the fundamental character of the ego and the contents of consciousness. Thus the question "How is society possible?" has a different meaning from the question "How is nature possible?" The answer is given by an a priori residing in the elements themselves, while the a priori of nature rests in the observer.

When we discover the sociological apriorisms, Simmel continues, they will have the same double significance as those which make nature possible: they will more or less completely determine the actual process of sociation as functions of psychical occurrence and, on the other hand, serve as logical presuppositions of the perfect society. Specifically, then, the task is to investigate the conditions of "sociation"[7] as the conscious association of beings.

---

[6]Georg Simmel, "How Is Society Possible?", translated by Albion Small from "Exkurs über das Problem: Wie ist Gesellschaft möglich?" in *Soziologie* [see below], pp. 27–45, and appearing in *The American Journal of Sociology*, 16 (November 1910), 372–391. Simmel's main sociological works are: *Philosophie des Geldes* ["Philosophy of Money"] (Leipzig: Duncker & Humblot, 1900; 5th ed., 1930); *Kant* (Leipzig: Duncker & Humblot, 1904); *Soziologie* (Leipzig: Duncker & Humblot, 1908; 3d ed., 1923); *Hauptprobleme der Philosophie* ["Chief Problems of Philosophy"] (Leipzig: G. B. Göschen, 1910; 6th ed., Berlin: W. de Gruyter, 1927); *Philosophische Kultur: Gesammelte Essais* ["Social Philosophy of Culture: Collected Essays"] (Leipzig: Kröner, 1911; 2d enlarged ed., 1919); and *Grundfragen der Soziologie* ["Fundamental Problems of Sociology"] (Berlin: W. de Gruyter, 1917; 2d ed., 1920).

English translations of some of Simmel's essays, many of which were included by Simmel in *Soziologie*, were made by Albion Small and published in early issues of *The American Journal of Sociology*. Some of these have been reassembled and retranslated by Kurt Wolff and published, together with other selections from Simmel, in *The Sociology of Georg Simmel* (Glencoe, Ill.: The Free Press, 1950). Two other essays from *Soziologie* have appeared in English: *Conflict*, translated by Kurt Wolff, and *The Web of Group-Affiliations*, translated by Reinhard Bendix, published in a single volume with a foreword by Everett C. Hughes (Glencoe, Ill.: The Free Press, 1955). In the following discussion, some of the references will be made to Small's translations rather than to those of Kurt Wolff in order to call attention to the dates at which Simmel's work became generally available, through English translation, to American sociologists.

[7]The term "sociation" is Kurt Wolff's rendering of the German *"Vergesellschaftung."* The most literal translation would perhaps be "societalization," and Albion Small consistently translated the word as "socialization." Since the literal translation is awkward, and since the word "socialization" has come to have a more specific meaning in sociology, Wolff's practice has been followed and the word "sociation" will be used throughout this discussion.

The task is to discover the a priori effective conditions or forms of sociation.

The first discovery that is made is that sociation represents the intersection of two dominations. To enter into society is in some degree to be generalized. Yet all persons have in themselves a deep individuality, a nucleus that cannot be subjectively reproduced. From the complete singularity of personality, we form a picture of it that is not identical with its reality, but still is not a general type. Within a sphere which has any sort of community of calling or of interests, every member looks upon every other not in a purely empirical way but on the basis of an a priori which this sphere imposes on each consciousness having a part in it. From the common basis of life originate suppositions in terms of which people look at one another as through a veil. This does not conceal the peculiarity of individuality, but gives personality a new form. To enter into society, individuality must undergo a kind of generalization into a new form required by sociability. This generalization is always more and less than individuality. Thus every element of a group is not only a societary part, but also something else. With respect to certain sides of his or her personality, the individual is not an element of the group.

To be received into a group in any form, therefore, an individual must become at once more and less than an individual personality. The truth of this appears decisively in the fact that even the person who is shut out of the group — the stranger, the enemy, the criminal, the pauper — is simultaneously partly formed by the group. In the commerce of people in societary categories, people are confronted with each other in the character that belongs to each in the role for which he or she is responsible. The individual can enter society only by forgoing some individuality and exchanging it for the generality demanded by the role. At the one extreme are individuals giving up so little of their individuality that they can hardly function in

societal life; at the other are individuals in whom the whole tone of the total personality has disappeared, being merged into the function to such a degree that almost all traces of individuality have disappeared.

One of the most important sociological formations rests on the fact that the societary structures are composed of beings who are at the same time inside and outside them. Sociation brings individuals into a double situation. Individuals have their setting in the sociation and are at the same time in antithesis to it. The meaning of the a priori peculiar to society is revealed in the fact that between individual and society the "within" and "without" are not two determinations, but rather they are properties of a unitary social being. One may generalize this insight to society as a whole. Society may be conceived as a body of officials who have a definite ordering of positions, a preordination of performances which are detached from their personnel of a given moment. Within this series, all newcomers find unequivocally assigned places which, so to speak, waited for them and with which their energies harmonize. Individuals need not be aware of the a priori which creates the possibility of their belonging to a society. All persons, by virtue of their own qualities, are automatically referred to a determined position in their social milieu. These positions ideally belonging to them are also actually present in the social whole.

The a priori condition making society possible is found in the category of vocation (*Beruf*). To the individual, society begets and offers in itself a position which in content and outline differs from others, but which in principle may be filled by any person. It is therefore anonymous. At the same time, despite its generality, the particular position is grasped by the individual on the ground of an "inner call." Empirical society becomes possible only through the a priori category of *vocation*.

This is undoubtedly as amazing a piece of pure theoretical brilliance as modern sociological theory displays. Simmel's problem was identical with that of Stammler — to account for the problem of order while conceiving society as an association of independent persons. The phrasing of the Kan-

---

(See Wolff's introduction to *The Sociology of Georg Simmel*, pp. lxiii–lxiv.)

tian question was a device for exploring the inner nature of this order. In society both individual and group are surmounted. The idea of vocation is introduced at the point where the inner content of individual motivation, the "inner call," and the external requirements of interhuman action, the "position" or "office," are fused. The entire discussion is a brilliant anticipation of modern role theory. At the same time it permitted Simmel to develop a more special definition of sociology.

Simmel distinguished three problem areas of sociology: general sociology — the study of historical life from the standpoint of sociology; philosophical sociology — the study of the epistemological and metaphysical problems that border sociology; and formal or pure sociology. He found the true area of sociology in the study of societal forms. Pure sociology is compared to geometry. "Geometrical abstraction investigates only the spatial forms of bodies, although empirically, these forms are given merely as the forms of some material content. Similarly, if society is conceived as interaction among individuals, the description of the forms of this interaction is the task of the science of society in its strictest and most essential sense." Such societal forms "are conceived as constituting society . . . out of the mere sum of living men." And sociology, which isolates them "inductively and psychologically from the heterogeneity of . . . contents . . . proceeds like grammar, which isolates the pure forms of language from their contents." [8]

Simmel's analysis of "sociability" may illustrate formal sociology. In any human society one can, he believes, distinguish between form and content of interhuman action. The form and content of human interaction are separable: knowledge, for example, initially appears as a means in the struggle for existence, but it comes to be cultivated for its own sake autonomously, as happens in science. This is also true for law: the requirements of social life compel or legitimate some types of behavior simply because they meet these requirements; however, such requirements may then recede into

the background and the rule assume functional autonomy, remaining "law" regardless of the specific requirements that gave rise to it. Generalizing from such examples, Simmel continues:

> This complete turnover, from the determination of the forms by the materials of life to the determination of its materials by forms that have become supreme values, is perhaps most extensively at work in the numerous phenomena that we lump together under the category of *play*. Actual forces, needs, impulses of life produce the forms of our behavior that are suitable for play. These forms, however, become independent contents and stimuli within play itself or, rather, *as* play. There are, for instance, the hunt; the gain by ruse; the proving of physical and intellectual strength; competition; and the dependence on chance and on the favor of powers that cannot be influenced. All these forms are lifted out of the flux of life and freed of their material with its inherent gravity. . . . Here lies whatever may justify the analogy between art and play. In both art and play, forms that were originally developed by the realities of life, have created spheres that preserve their autonomy in the face of these realities. [9]

This process illustrates the separation of the form and content of societal existence. The forms may gain a kind of life of their own. The form exists, then, for its own sake and for the sake of the fascination due to liberation from the ties with content. This is true for the phenomenon of *sociability*, which Simmel defines as "the play-form of sociation." Sociability is the association of people for its own sake, not for loot (as hordes of bandits) or supernatural purposes (as a religious society) or for gain (economic association). Sociability is association for its own sake and for the delight in association without the restrictions of practical purposes. The conditions providing delight to the process of sociability are separate from the particular person involved. The character of the gathering is determined by personal qualities like amiability, refinement, and cordiality. Everything depends on the personalities of the participants,

[8] *The Sociology of Georg Simmel*, pp. 21–22.

[9] *Ibid.*, pp. 42–43.

not upon other interests. Tact is here of peculiar significance, for no external or immediate egotistic interest directs the self-regulation of the individual in the relation to others. Moreover, the individual possesses many attributes — wealth, social position, erudition, fame, exceptional capability, and merit — which are not permitted to play a part in sociability. One can, for this very reason, speak of "sociability thresholds." People enter the association as individuals with complex ideas, forces, and possibilities. They are capable of sociability only so far as they are able to neutralize these factors. The moment interaction is converted into an intentional form with objective content and purpose (to rise in the social scale, to make a sale, to obtain a job), sociability ceases. There are, thus, upper and lower limits to the individual's capacity for sociability — sociability thresholds which are passed either when individuals interact from motives of objective content and purpose or when their entirely personal and subjective aspects make themselves felt.

It is perhaps possible to find the positive formal motive of sociability which corresponds to its negative determination by limits and thresholds. In explaining law, Kant posited the axiom that each individual should possess freedom to the extent that it is compatible with the freedom of others. The same principle, says Simmel, may be applied to sociability. Each individual ought to have as much satisfaction of his or her sociability drive as is compatible with its satisfaction on the part of others. Therefore, as Kant's law is democratic, one sees here the democratic structure of all sociability. It is, however, a democracy that can be realized only within a given social stratum. Sociability between different strata can be inconsistent and painful. At the same time, the democracy of sociability even among social equals is only something played. It is an artificial world composed of individuals with no desire other than to create pure interaction with others. We do not enter sociability as full people but as people divested of various aims, goals, and intentions. In primitive society, sociable people did not have to be wrested from so many objective claims. The form appeared

more distinct in contrast with the individual's personal existence. Behavior at social gatherings was more ceremonial than it is today. As abstracted from sociation through art or play, sociability is the purest kind of interaction. It is the game in which one acts as if all people were equal. The game becomes a lie only when the sociable action and speech are mere instruments of intentions of a practical sort. Apparently Simmel would not have numbered himself among the followers of Dale Carnegie.

The connection between sociability and play explains why sociability covers all phenomena which are conventionally thought of as sociological playforms, particularly games as such. All forms of interaction in which people exchange or form parties are outside the framework. However, each of these areas may experience the penetration of sociability so that any one or all are played in the form of a game.

> . . . even where the game involves a monetary stake, it is not the money (after all, it could be acquired in many ways other than gambling) that is the specific characteristic of the game. To the person who really enjoys it, its attraction rather lies in the dynamics and hazards of the sociologically significant forms of activity themselves. The more profound, double sense of "social game" is that not only is the game played in a society . . . but that, with its help, people actually "play" society.[10]

Almost any area of social life may have its play form. In the sociology of sex, the play form of eroticism is flirtation. The erotic question in flirtation between the sexes and within a single sex is that of offer and acceptance or refusal (its objects are infinitely varied and by no means purely physiological). The nature of flirtation is to play up alternately allusive promise and allusive withdrawal: to attract the other, always stopping short of decision; to reject the other, but never deprive him or her of all hope. Behavior shifts back and forth between "yes" and "no," stopping at neither.

[10]*Ibid.*, p. 50.

Flirtation has the character of suspension, distance, ideality; and it is quite correct to speak of its "art," not merely of its "artifices." To develop as a form of sociability, flirtation must meet specific behavior on the part of the other. Flirtation unfolds its charms at the height of sociable civilization, leaving behind the reality of the erotic desire, consent, or refusal, becoming the interplay of the silhouettes of their serious import. As sociability plays with the forms of society, so flirtation plays with those of eroticism.

The full extent to which sociability abstracts the forms of interaction from their contents becomes evident in conversation, the most general thing people have in common. People talk seriously about some content they wish to communicate or come to an understanding about. At a social gathering, however, they talk for the sake of talking. Talk becomes its own purpose, and is fully realized in an "art of conversation," obeying its own laws. The topic of conversation is merely the medium of a lively exchange of speech, in which all the forms are recognized by the participants — quarrel, appeal to norms recognized by all, pacification by compromise, grateful acceptance of the new, covering up anything on which no understanding can be hoped. Talk presupposes two parties; it is two-way. Among all sociological phenomena, talk is the purest and most sublimated form of two-wayness. It is the fulfillment of a relation that wants to be nothing but a relation, in which the mere form of interaction becomes its self-sufficient content.

Another problem to which Simmel gave some thought was that of how one arrives at theories. A further illustration of his social forms and his conception of the method of arriving at them may be seen in his study of superiority and subordination. There are two steps in the analysis: (1) the bringing together of contents in which the form is manifest, and (2) the abstraction of the form. Simmel argues that we gain knowledge of the forms of sociation by bringing together actual historical manifestations. We must collect and exhibit the element of form which these historical manifestations have in common, abstracted from a variety of material (economical, ethical-ecclesiastical, social-political, and so on). Geometry has the advantage of finding within its field very simple figures to which the most complicated forms may be reduced. Truths respecting these simple figures are therefore widely applicable. From relatively few fundamental truths all possible arrangements of form may be interpreted. In the case of social forms, however, reduction to simple elements has not been made. "Social phenomena are too immeasurably complicated and the methods of analysis are too incomplete. . . . Long and patient labor will be necessary before we can understand the concrete historical forms of socialization [i.e., "sociation"] as the actual compounds of a few simple fundamental forms of human association."[11]

In developing the meaning of superiority and inferiority, Simmel maintains that it is one of the forms in which "society" comes into being. Despite appearances, it is by no means a one-sided relation. There is an often unnoticed but no less significant influence of inferior on superior, as well as the reverse. One of the basic sources of the differences in cases of superiority and inferiority is found in the relative amount of spontaneity which subordinates and superiors bring to bear on the total relation. At one extreme, absolute despotism, rulers attach to their edicts the threat of penalty or promise of reward. However, the inferior still has a claim on the superior — for example, the implied promise of protection. In law, there seems to be the connotation that the one who gives the law is unqualified superior. But as the Romans knew, the relation is always reciprocal. Where all spontaneity on the part of the subordinate is excluded, there is no longer sociation. The orator confronting the assembly or the teacher confronting the class seems to be the sole temporary superior. But the mass is not really passive, for it has a limiting and leading reaction. Even in hypnotism it has been suggested

[11]Georg Simmel, "Superiority and Subordination as Subject-Matter of Sociology," trans. Albion Small, *The American Journal of Sociology* (September and November 1896), 168.

that the hypnotized person exercises a not easily defined influence on the hypnotist.

Superiority may be exercised by an individual, a group, or an objective principle. The subordination of a group to a single person has consequences for the unification of a group — a generalization which holds even in the case where the group is opposed to the head. The transformation in the political life of a people may occur not merely in the case of a complete abolition of monarchy but in the gradual limitation of its power. The Christian religion is credited with attuning people's souls to peaceableness. In fact, it is a case of subordination to a divine principle. Unification may take the form of leveling or gradation. There is a considerable difference in the distribution of power in the two cases.

The imaginative charm with which Simmel explored his materials may be seen in his discussion of secrecy as a social form.[12] He pointed out that a precondition of relationship between people is that they know something about each other, whether it be between a buyer and seller, a teacher and student, or what not. One must, first of all, know with whom one must deal. In part, social relationships depend upon the completeness of knowledge of each other. At the same time, no one can know everything about the other. Various possibilities arise between people in terms of the limitations and aberrations to which our knowledge of each other is subject. Ordinarily we cherish only so much truth, so much science, as is useful for practical purposes.

In the relation between people, they may voluntarily reveal the truth about themselves or dissimulate and deceive each other. Sociological structures are differentiated by the measure of mendacity operative in them. This may vary from simple relations, in which a lie is relatively harmless, to complex relations, where it may be disastrous. Not only is there a relative permissibility of lying as between different types of relationship,

but various positive utilities reside in lying. For example, the lie may be useful in bringing about organization, stratification, and centralization of the group, bringing the physically less weak and intellectually less crafty under control. Simmel, who had a vein of old-fashioned socialism in his make-up, observes that, at the other extreme, when they reach a certain stage of development, wholesale and retail trade may arrive at a point where they can act in accordance with complete integrity in marketing their goods.

Without tracing all the additional ramifications, this is sufficient to illustrate the imagination and delicate surpise with which Simmel developed his sociological forms.

Not the least significant aspect of every school of thought is the manner in which it is able to receive the materials of alternative or opposed schools. Without attempting to do justice to the subtlety, range, and penetration of his discussion, it is interesting to note that Simmel received the concept of "conflict" into his system as a social form.

> . . . it must appear paradoxical to the ordinary mode of thinking to ask whether conflict itself, without reference to its consequences or its accompaniments, is not a form of socialization ["sociation"]. . . . If every reaction among men is a socialization, of course conflict must count as such. . . . The actually dissociating elements are the causes of the conflict — hatred and envy, want and desire. If, however, from these impulses conflict has once broken out, it is in reality the way to remove the dualism and to arrive at some form of unity, even if through the annihilation of one of the parties.[13]

In developing this theme, Simmel points out that, even in so organic a system as India with its caste system, the hierarchy of castes rests directly on their reciprocal repulsion. Competition is merely a formal relation of tension. Entirely apart from its results, it determines the form of the

[12]Simmel, "The Sociology of Secrecy and of Secret Societies," trans. Albion Small, *The American Journal of Sociology*, 11 (January 1906), 441–498.

[13]Simmel, "The Sociology of Conflict," trans. A. W. Small, *The American Journal of Sociology*, 9 (January 1904), 490.

group, reciprocal position, and distance of the elements. In the city, the whole internal organization of interhuman commerce rests on complicated gradations of antipathies, indifferences, and aversions. Antipathy protects us against typical dangers of city life: being smothered under its multiple impressions and shattered by the too extensive engagement of our sympathies. Erotic relationships are often woven out of love, respect, and contempt at once. Almost unavoidably an element of community weaves itself into a hostility. As a social form, conflict ranges in its manifestations all the way from the inner-subjective processes of personality to the affairs of great states.

The real cunning of Simmel's position is nowhere more clearly demonstrated than in the handling of conflict. By reducing it to one of a multiplicity of social forms, many of its decisive properties are transformed. While it is a form that can range in manifestation from inner-subjective spheres to international war, it can hardly function *solely* as a device to subordinate individuals to the group. The teeth have been pulled from the conservative position and its key idea pressed into the service of liberal ends.

At times Simmel turned his attention away from what he called "sociological forms" to factors or conditions affecting social forms. Such were his analyses of the "Persistence of Social Groups" and "The Number of Members"[14] as a determining factor in social forms. A few ideas from the latter essay may illustrate this kind of analysis.

Simmel asserts that some aspects of the form and inner life of a social group are determined by its numerical relationships. A very large number of people can form a unity only on the basis of a division of labor, but division of labor is not essential for a small group. A large group without structure

will tend to split into smaller segments. A previously calculated, mechanically working life system, regulated in every detail, can be applied only to a small circle, and cannot work on a large scale. A group organized on such a scheme will remain minute. It is not surprising, then, that there are such tightly organized group formations of an ecclesiastical sort which permit no application to large numbers. Again, an aristocratic body can have only a relatively narrow compass. When an aristocratic body gives way to democratic forms, centrifugal tendencies and fatal contradictions develop in its life principles.

Simmel did not carry out a systematic analysis on the basis of his *forms,* despite his obvious suggestion that this should be done. Raymond Aron quite accurately summed up this aspect of Simmel. "The reader becomes lost in an interminable succession, not so much of historical examples, as of theoretical cases and possible combinations. These dazzling exercises often seem like an elaborate game. The book (*Soziologie*) has thus brought its author many admirers, but few disciples."[15] Simmel achieved his results in part by the vague use of the concept "form." Abel has made a careful inventory of some of the main things included as forms: characterizations of complex situations (slavery, legal contests, exchange); characterizations of norms (law, custom, mores, honor); definitions of groups (family, secret society, political party); characterizations of social types (the stranger, the poor, the teacher, the middleman); characterizations of social relations (conflict, superiority–subordination); characterizations of social structures (hierarchy, stability, elasticity); and even generalizations about the social process.[16] This is to say nothing about the legitimacy of separating form from content in the first place — a point of especial importance, since most of Simmel's more brilliant analyses are secured by ignoring it.

[14]Simmel, "The Persistence of Social Groups," trans. Albion Small, *The American Journal of Sociology,* 3 (March and May 1898), 662–698, 829–836; 4 (July 1898), pp. 35–50; "The Number of Members as Determining the Sociological Form of the Group," trans. Albion Small, *The American Journal of Sociology,* 8 (July and September 1902), 1–46, 158–196.

[15]Raymond Aron, *German Sociology,* trans. Mary and Thomas Bottomore (Glencoe, Ill.: The Free Press, 1957), p. 6.
[16]Abel, *Systematic Sociology in Germany,* pp. 24–25.

However, all such criticism should not obscure the very significant point that Simmel developed a worthy liberal counterpart to the conservative theory of society of the two previous types of sociological theory. This is implicit in Aron's estimate. He had noted that Simmel made the reduction of the whole to its elements into a theoretical principle of his method. "Only those laws which regulate atomic movements are valid. A natural unity is defined by the reciprocal action of the parts. Thus sociology discovers individuals in the crowd."[17]

In this reduction of society to individual behaviors, Simmel stands sharply opposed both to organismic positivism and to conflict theory. This makes him a "sociologist of democracy."

> The dissolution of the idea of society as a real entity corresponds to a period in which the hostile classes are no longer united except by the fiction of one society. Crowds play a decisive role in democratic civilizations, and in the social sciences "the sociological spirit" expresses the individual's realization of the power of collectivities. . . . Simmel regarded crowds and institutions, not as superior beings, but as monstrous realities created blindly by men as a result of the collective life itself . . . . Simmel's sociology expresses a double antinomy, that between atomism and holism and that between individualism and the rule of the masses.[18]

Simmel stands in between worlds — perceiving a similar type of danger from the aristocratic society of the past and a society resting on mob action. In either case the individual is threatened.

Because Simmel was a contributor to L'Année sociologique, his ideas early came to the attention of French thinkers. Albion Small, as we have mentioned, translated many of Simmel's pieces and published them in The American Journal of Sociology, bringing them to the attention of the American audience. The imagination and charm they contained touched many minds. Moreover, they cor-

responded to the need both for a more professional definition of sociology and for one which avoided the extremes of conservative ideologies.

Célestin Bouglé. Célestin Bouglé (1870–1940) was perhaps the foremost sociologist in France to show Simmel's influence. He was professor of social philosophy at the University of Toulouse, later taking over Durkheim's position at the Sorbonne.

In a pleasant essay on the nature of sociology,[19] he invites us to imagine a little village, let us call it Saint-Pol, with all its ongoing social life: its people, its events, its institutions. What would the sociologist wish to know about it? What would be the object of his study? As with Simmel, Bouglé defines sociology as the study of social forms. He quickly adds, however, that sociology is no mere classification of empty categories. He closely approximates Simmel's suggestion that form and content should be separated.

The materials with which sociology works are to some considerable degree historical in nature. But Bouglé rejects the search for social origins as a vain task. He rejects also the historical task and the task

---

[17]Aron, *German Sociology,* p. 7.
[18]*Ibid.,* pp. 7–8.

[19]*Qu'est-ce que la sociologie?* ["What Is Sociology?"] (Paris: F. Alcan, 1907). Only one of Bouglé's books is available in English — *Leçons de sociologie sur l'évolution des valeurs* (Paris: A. Colin, 1922) — which was translated by Helen Stalker Sellars as *The Evolution of Values* (New York: Henry Holt, 1926). Also available in English is a lecture which Bouglé delivered at Columbia University, *The French Conception of "Culture Generale" and Its Influence upon Instruction* (New York: Bureau of Publications, Teachers College, Columbia University, 1938). Bouglé's principal works are: *Les Sciences sociales en allemagne* ["The Social Sciences in Germany"] (Paris: F. Alcan, 1896); *Les Idées égalitaires* (Paris: F. Alcan, 1899); *Essais sur le régime des castes* ["Essays on the Caste System"] (Paris: F. Alcan, 1908); *LaSociologie de Proudhon* (Paris: A. Colin, 1911); *Chez les prophètes socialistes* (Paris: F. Alcan, 1918); *Doctrine de Saint Simon* (Paris: M. Rivière, 1924); *Le Solidarisme* ["Solidarity"], 2d ed. (Paris: M. Giard, 1924); and *Humanisme, sociologie, philosophie* (Paris: Hermann, 1938). Recent translations of Bouglé's work include: *The Evolution of Values: Studies in Sociology with Special Application to Teaching,* trans. Helen S. Sellars (New York: A. M. Kelly, 1970) and *Essays on the Caste System,* trans. D. F. Pocock (Cambridge: University Press, 1971).

CÉLESTIN BOUGLÉ

Bibliothèque Nationale, Paris

of turning sociology into a philosophy of history. It aspires merely to be a science. As a science it must examine historical phenomena; how else could it judge the consequences of social forms? And in becoming a science, sociology inevitably passes over into the search not only for the consequences of the forms but their causes. "Il ne faudra pas sans doute qu'elle se contente de montrer les *conséquences* des formes sociales, il faudra encore qu'elle en découvre les *causes*."[20]

On occasion Bouglé was able to isolate a configuration and trace its various aspects through diverse situations with a learning and imagination at least equivalent to that of Simmel. Such was his book on the caste system (*Essais sur le régime des*

[20]Bouglé, *Qu'est-ce que la sociologie?*, pp. 22–23.

castes), which was so much in advance of the ordinary thinking on the subject of the time (1908) as still to be worth examining.

That caste was hereditary had been widely noted. Also, it was widely observed that race and military occupation were coupled in caste. But Bouglé was impressed by a phenomenon that had come to Simmel's attention where caste reigns: the different groups are repelled rather than attracted to one another. A man refuses to look for a wife outside the traditional circle. He refuses food from all except his own confreres. Contact with strangers is avoided as impure. While caste crumbles the societies it penetrates, it divides them into superimposed layers, and sets up groups separated by elementary repulsion. Thus Bouglé thought that the three elements of repulsion, hierarchy, and hereditary specialization were required to define caste completely. Where the system is found, the society is divided into a large number of hereditarily specialized groups, hierarchically superimposed and mutually opposed. In principle neither upstarts, hybrids, nor deserters of a profession are tolerated. Mixtures of blood, conquests of rank, and change of occupation are avoided.

Once we have isolated these three constituent elements of caste, we may inquire into the civilizations where caste is found to discover the social forms connected with caste. Many tendencies toward caste were present in occidental civilization: horror of misalliance, fear of impure contact. Statistics show that there are some occupations whose members willingly intermarry, others where intermarriage is rare. There are customs showing that different worlds do not mix; there are districts, cafés, schools frequented by exclusive categories of the population. There are villages where the same industry has been performed for centuries.

On the other hand, when the medieval clergy was described as a caste (Guizot), this was inaccurate. It was no hereditary stratum; its magistrates were celibates. The feudal system fell short of caste organization in many ways. The principle that land determines status is negative to the exclusive determination of status by birth. In systems of fiefs, a person might be a vassal to some, suzerain to others. Social rank ceases to be clearly defined. In the ancient world, one of the nearest approaches to caste was found among the Egyptians, who, according to Herodotus, were divided into several orders: priests, warriors, cowmen, herdsmen, merchants, interpreters, and river pilots. However, the priests and warriors alone enjoyed marks of distinction, special land, and exemption from taxes. All strata were riveted to the profession of their ancestors. When a priest died he was replaced by his son. A warrior did not have the right to practice an occupation other than that of arms. The extent of endogamous marriage is known in some cases. The coffins of thirty generations of priests attached to the Theban god Mentu show that nearly all belonged to two or three families, marrying among themselves or taking wives from the family of the priests of Ammon. One family of royal architects kept the post for several centuries under all Egyptian dynasties. On the other hand, during the hieroglyphic periods, a sort of bourgeois class appears with members not confined to any particular profession. In a famous anthem, a scribe tells of placing himself in the bureau of supplies and of becoming auctioneer, later tax collector, finally chief of bailiffs, master auctioneer, and director of the royal line. He was soon placed at the head of a village, then a city, and finally a province. He finished by being head of the occidental porte (the institution from which justice was administered). He enjoyed full honors, and possessed several fiefs, which were endowed his family and placed under his sons. Social stratification was not petrified; still the spirit of division and opposition was widespread in Egyptian society.

The full development of caste, however, takes place in the traditional system of India. The process of economic production remains relatively simple and so far as possible is allocated in the form of occupational tasks of local groups. Since even the professional group has subgroups, one may distinguish six castes of merchants, three of scribes, forty of peasants, twenty-four of journeymen, nine of shepherds and hunters, thirteen of liquor-makers, and so on. A caste may be distinguished by its members' abstaining from certain technical procedures, not using the same materials, not making the same products. From top to bottom of traditional Hindu society, plurality of occupations is prohibited in principle, change of occupation illicit. Functions are divided once and for all by birth. Heredity of profession is the rule.

Of all the castes, the Brahmans have the most varied profession, for they are not confined to sacred books but appear as plowmen, soldiers, merchants, and cooks. Their very superiority reserves to them more possibilities than for common mortals. Superiority implies purity. Purity excludes many modes of action. The doctrine of *ahimsa* prohibits wounding the smallest creature. The priest may not open the earth with a plow share. Most of the unusual trades of the Brahman are due to his right to practice different trades in time of distress. After the crisis is over, the Brahmans often retain the emergency profession. Thus the system of hereditary specialization admits more mobility than appears at first sight. However, mobility is collective rather than individual. Individuals do not leave the occupation of their ancestors; rather, groups detach themselves collectively. When groups change professions they depart clandestinely, or seek to justify themselves by some legend. How hard it is to move even then is shown by a group of weavers of Western Bengal. It took 30 per cent mortality in a trade under ruin by English imports before they decided to look for a new livelihood.

The traditional Hindu society is hierarchically organized with the pariahs at the bottom. They are permitted to cultivate the earth for their needs. They are obliged to hire themselves to other tribes. Their masters can beat them when they wish without their being able to demand reparation. A Nair meeting a pariah has a right to kill him. At the other end of the scale are the Brahmans, in principle sustaining themselves from alms. Their superiority is as uncontested as the absolute inferiority of the pariahs. Between these extremes is a multitude of castes ranked in terms of purity of blood, fidelity, abstinence from prohibited foods.

Practically, rank is determined by social distance from the Brahman caste. The key question is, will a Brahman accept gifts from a person of this caste?

Between the castes the principle of mutual repulsion holds. A self-respecting Hindu would die of thirst rather than drink from a glass served to a "mleccha" (foreigner). Much trouble was experienced in setting up a canalization of water in Calcutta: how could people of different castes be served by the same water pipe? Contacts with pariahs inspire horror. They have to carry bells to reveal their presence. Some persons are forced to go nearly naked for fear of being touched by flowing clothes. When two friends, daughters of a Gahapati and a Purohita, played in the gateway of a city, two Tshandal brothers appeared. When they were noticed, the children ran to save themselves and to wash their eyes. A stranger must not touch the food of a Hindu. At times a look is enough to contaminate it. If a pariah looks into the kitchen, all of the utensils must be smashed.

Meanwhile, the effects of endogamy tend to be redoubled by internal exogamy. Caste forms a narrow circle, and within it there are restrictions. In migrations of the Brahman caste, the caste is often divided into "gotras." Members of the same gotra cannot marry one another. The rules are complex, and vary with the castes. While there are breaches of the rules, a pure marriage can only be secured within the caste.

All in all, Bouglé thought that it was fortunate for sociological curiosity that the caste system triumphed in India over the forces that suppressed or thwarted it elsewhere. In this civilization it was realized in about as complete and pure a form as possible. It makes possible the observation of the characteristic properties in a more or less pure state. For those who wish it, India forms a kind of crucial experiment.

Bouglé's study of caste shows that he was at least as capable of carrying out a brilliantly articulated study of social forms as Simmel. However, he seems to have been as little inclined as Simmel to organize the existing body of sociological knowledge on the basis of forms. This task was clearly visualized by E. A. Ross.

EDWARD A. ROSS

Courtesy of the University of Wisconsin, Madison, Wisc.

E. A. Ross. Ross did not add anything new to the theory of social forms nor did his use of forms or formally conceived processes constitute the most significant of his theoretical contributions. He did, however, conceive the problem of utilizing forms as a device for the systematic presentation of sociological knowledge.

Edward Allsworth Ross (1866–1951) was born in Illinois. He received his doctorate at Johns Hopkins University in history, politics, and economics in 1891, and studied for a year at the University of Berlin. He taught economics at Indiana University and Cornell before going to Stanford University in 1893. There he was dismissed for his public stand on the use of Chinese labor in building the Central Pacific Railroad. From 1901 to 1906, Ross was professor of sociology at the University of Nebraska. He went to Wisconsin in 1906, where he remained until his retirement in 1937. With John L. Gillin, Ross built an effective department there that produced such notable students as Joyce O. Hertzler, Reuben Hill, D. E. Lindstrom, Lowry Nelson, and John Useem, among others. Ross published a total of twenty-nine books, the most useful for theoretical purposes being *Social Control* (appearing first as articles from 1896 to 1898) and *Social Psychology* (1908). From the standpoint of the attempt to systematize sociology by a review of basic social forms, the works of importance here are *The Principles of Sociology* and *New Age Sociology*.[21]

Ross had a journalist's nose for news and a sense of the current need. In the early decades of the twentieth century, the demand for a systematic sociology was widely felt. The evolutionary trends had fallen into disrepute and in the growing departments of sociology in the schools there was need for systematic coverage of the field. Simmel had indicated that one of the most direct ways of doing this was through an inventory of basic social forms. Small had introduced many of Simmel's discussions to the American public through translations in *The American Journal of Sociology*.

In *The Principles of Sociology*, Ross carried out a formalistic program. He divided the volume into five parts: Social Population, Social Forces, Social Processes, Social Products, and Sociological Principles. In this arrangement social population and social forces represented the raw materials of society. The social forces, for example, included the instincts, the interests resting on instincts, race, and geographic conditions affecting these. As Ross handled them, they were presupposed before anything really social was discussed. The sociological focus of the study was, therefore, in the social processes.

Ross did not come to the processes with any

refined concepts of form and content. In fact, he did not betray any philosophic sophistication. Simmel's forms and Small's processes seem to have been all one to him. Yet he was clearly interested in the processes as a kind of general or recurrent pattern of phenomena. The most fundamental of the social processes were treated as four in number: (1) association, (2) domination, (3) exploitation, and (4) opposition. Just as Simmel had examined the "form" in various contexts, so Ross examined these processes in the same manner. *Domination,* for example, was found to occur in parent over offspring, older over young, husband over wife, men over women, foremen over workers, one ally over the rest, and conquerors over conquered. *Exploitation* was found to be characteristic of the relations of parents and their offspring, of men and women, of the rich and the poor, of the intelligent and the ignorant, of priests and the laity, of the ruler and the ruled.

In addition to the four general processes, thirty-two others were isolated and discussed; they included such things as stimulation, personal competition, sex antagonism, class struggle, adaptation, cooperation, stratification, gradation, equalization, selection, individualization, commercialization, professionalization, and ossification.

The operation of the social processes was thought to produce various social products, such as uniformities, standards, groups, and institutions. Finally, a number of principles such as anticipation, stimulation, individualization, and balance were thought to be at work.

In Ross's last systematic statement, *New Age Sociology*, the same basic materials are present. The four fundamental processes are retained: association, communication, domination, and exploitation. The same subgroupings are presented of the remaining processes, which appear as conflict and adaptation, cooperation and organization, class and caste, processes involving society and the individual, those centering in occupation and social function, and finally those concerned with social repression and progress. Except for minor changes and additions, the general pattern is the same.

[21]E. A. Ross, *Social Control* (New York: Macmillan, 1901; Boston: Beacon Press, 1959); *Social Psychology* (New York: Macmillan, 1908, 1929); *Principles of Sociology* (New York: The Century Company, 1920; rev. ed., 1930); *New Age Sociology* (New York: D. Appleton-Century, 1940).

Ross stood astride two of the basic theories of sociology. His early and most creative phase was under the influence of that form of social behaviorism identified with Gabriel Tarde (to be discussed later). Two of his most important works, *Social Psychology* and *Social Control,* were produced under its influence. His actual theoretical contribution to sociological formalism was negligible, but he did much to popularize the view. In mid-career, Ross shifted perspective and devoted himself to carrying out the program implied in sociological formalism. Although there was some eclectic carry-over from his first position, it was too unconscious to lead to theoretically new formulations. A somewhat parallel phenomenon is observable in the textbook by Park and Burgess.

Robert E. Park and Ernest W. Burgess. Park and Burgess worked out their famous textbook, *Introduction to the Science of Sociology,*[22] at the University of Chicago in the shadow of the conflict tradition established by Small. Their statement represented a movement from conflict theory to formalism in somewhat the same manner that Ross's statement represented the movement from social behaviorism to formalism. Despite the fact that this work was perhaps the most famous sociological textbook to appear in the United States, both Park and Burgess are more significant for other things — Park for developing the studies of the city, race relations, and the immigrant press, Burgess for the study of the family.[23]

ROBERT E. PARK

From *American Sociology* by Howard W. Odum, Longmans, Green & Co., Inc., 1951. Courtesy of the publishers.

Robert Ezra Park (1864–1944) studied at the University of Michigan. For a time (1887–1898) he served as a journalist. He received his M.A. degree in philosophy at Harvard in 1899 under William James and Josiah Royce, and from there went to Berlin, where he studied under Windelband and Simmel. He was an assistant in philosophy at Harvard in 1905 and 1906. From 1905 to 1914 he was engaged in educational work, mostly with blacks. In 1914 he joined the faculty of the University of Chicago as a lecturer in sociology. He was professor of sociology at Chicago from 1923 to 1933, the time of his retirement.

[22]Robert E. Park and Ernest W. Burgess, *Introduction to the Science of Sociology* (Chicago: University of Chicago Press, 1921; 2d ed., 1924). References here are to the second edition.

[23]In addition to the *Introduction to the Science of Sociology,* Park's works include: *Old World Traits Transplanted,* with Herbert A. Miller (New York: Harper, 1921); *The Immigrant Press and Its Control* (New York: Harper, 1922); *The City,* with Ernest W. Burgess, Roderick D. McKenzie, and Louis Wirth (Chicago: University of Chicago Press, 1925); and *Race and Culture,* ed. Everett C. Hughes (Glencoe, Ill.: The Free Press, 1950). Burgess's other books include: *Predicting Success or Failure in Marriage,* with Leonard S. Cottrell, Jr. (New York: Prentice-Hall, 1939); *The Family: From Institution to Companionship* (New

York: American Book Company, 1945); and *Engagement and Marriage,* with Paul Wallin (Philadelphia: Lippincott, 1953).

ERNEST BURGESS

Courtesy of the University of Chicago

Ernest Watson Burgess (1886–1966) was born in Canada. He received his Ph.D. degree in sociology at Chicago under Small in 1913. He taught at Toledo University (1912–1913), the University of Kansas (1915–1916), and the University of Chicago from 1916 to his retirement in 1951.

With his background in philosophy and his training with and under two such notable neo-Kantians as Windelband and Simmel, one might have expected Park to carry forward the theoretical aspects of neo-Kantianism in sociology. Moreover, Park had been strongly influenced by James and Dewey and the tradition of sociology identified with Albion Small. The tradition of Windelband and Simmel remains, but is encrusted with many other things. Simmel and Windelband had played an important part in the differentia-

tion of sociology and history. Park and Burgess simply accepted this:

> Historically, sociology has had its origin in history. History has been and is the great mother science of all the social sciences. Of history it may be said nothing human is foreign to it. Anthropology, ethnology, folklore, and archaeology have grown up largely, if not wholly, to complete the task which history began and answer the questions which historical investigation first raised.[24]

Simmel had defined society (as content) as interaction. In essence, Park and Burgess accepted this definition:

> While it is true that society has this double aspect, the individual and the collective . . . the thing that distinguishes a mere collection of individuals from a society is not like-mindedness, but corporate action. We may apply the term social to any group of individuals which is capable of consistent action, that is to say, action, consciously or unconsciously, directed to a common end. This existence of a common end is perhaps all that can be legitimately included in the conception "organic" applied to society.[25]

With Windelband and Simmel it was argued that "history is the concrete, sociology is the abstract, science of human experience and human nature." The difference between sociology and the other social sciences is that they "are, to a greater or lesser extent, applications of principles which it is the business of sociology and of psychology to deal with explicitly."[26]

Park and Burgess seem primarily to have been responsible for introducing the distinction between realistic and nominalistic sociology. Moreover, they broke down the development of sociology into three periods:

1. The period of Comte and Spencer; sociology, conceived in the grand style, is a philosophy of history, a "science" of progress (evolution).

[24]Parks, *Introduction to the Science of Sociology*, pp. 42–43.
[25]*Ibid.*, p. 42.
[26]*Ibid.*, p. 43.

2. The period of the "schools"; sociological thought, dispersed among the various schools, is absorbed in an effort to define its point of view and to describe the kinds of facts that sociology must look for to answer the questions that sociology asks.
3. The period of investigation and research, the period which sociology is just now entering.[27]

Park and Burgess agree with both Simmel and Small that the common object of reference of sociology is found not in society as a structure but in the social group. Social process is taken as the general name for all changes in the life of the group. Sociology is said to be interested in "original nature" only insofar as it supplies the raw materials out of which individual personalities and social order are created. Out of these same materials every group is thought to create its own type of character which becomes a component part of the social structure. Under these circumstances, society becomes merely a kind of descriptive term. "Society now may be defined as the social heritage of *habit and sentiment, folkways and mores, technique and culture,* all of which are incident or necessary to collective human behavior."[28]

Park and Burgess built up a kind of sociological superstructure of elements taken from Le Bon, Cooley, Tarde, Small, Giddings, and many others. However, when all is said and done, their hearts belonged to Simmel, for the central integrating ideas of their sociological system were composed of processes, formally conceived. Actually, Park and Burgess presented two different approaches to social processes. In the first, the social processes were analyzed in terms of degree of involvement. Isolation, social contact, and social interaction were reviewed successively. This phase of the discussion terminated in an investigation of social forces which, in the long run, were identified with interests, sentiments, and attitudes. In effect, this amounted to a separation of form and content.

Once this review was completed, Park and

Burgess undertook a second systematization of materials. Rather than degree of involvement, the basis of systematization was now in terms of the amount of conflict and cooperation involved. The social processes were divided into four: competition, conflict, accommodation, and assimilation. In this context competition was conceived as a less social form of interaction, for it was identified with the biological struggle for existence. *Competition* was, in fact, conceived as interaction without social contact. It was viewed as the presocial struggle to survive that eventually initiates conflict, accommodation, and assimilation and hence creates sympathies, prejudices, and personal and moral relations. By contrast, *conflict* is a social process; it represents competition lifted to a conscious and social level. The authors summarize the interrelations among the social processes and their relation to social structure as follows:

Conflict is . . . to be identified with the political order and with conscious control. Accommodation, on the other hand, is associated with the social order that is fixed and established in custom and the mores.

Assimilation, as distinguished from accommodation, implies a more thoroughgoing transformation of the personality — a transformation which takes place gradually under the influence of social contacts of the most concrete and intimate sort.

Accommodation may be regarded, like religious conversion, as a kind of mutation. The wishes are the same but their organization is different. Assimilation takes place not so much as a result of the changes in organization as in the content, *i.e.,* the memories, of the personality. The individual units, as a result of intimate association, interpenetrate, so to speak, and come in this way into possession of a common experience and a common tradition. The permanence and solidarity of the group rest finally upon this body of common experience and tradition. It is the role of history to preserve this body of common experience and tradition, to criticize and reinterpret it in the light of new experience and changing conditions, and in this way to preserve the continuity of the social and political life.

The relation of social structures to the processes of competition, conflict, accommodation, and as-

[27]*Ibid.,* p. 44.
[28]*Ibid.,* p. 165.

similation may be represented schematically as follows:

Social Process	Social Order
Competition	The economic equilibrium
Conflict	The political order
Accommodation	Social organization
Assimilation	Personality and the cultural heritage[29]

Park and Burgess may not have added anything new to the theory of social forms or of formal processes, but their work belongs along with that of E. A. Ross among the major attempts in the early American period to systematize sociological knowledge from this point of view. Their *Introduction to the Science of Sociology* has been described as the most influential sociological textbook ever produced in America. It has even, on occasion, been listed among the four or five most important books of early American sociology. These judgments may be taken as indicative of the wide reading public to whom, through this work, the formalistic tradition was transmitted. To this day there are persons who do not feel they have covered the basic subject matter of sociology until they have discussed competition, conflict, accommodation, and assimilation.

Leopold von Wiese. Leopold von Wiese (1876–1969) was born in Glatz, Silesia. He received his doctorate from the University of Berlin. In 1915 he was appointed professor of economics at the School of Commerce in Cologne. (This school became the University of Cologne in 1919.) Except for the long interruption during the Nazi regime, von Wiese remained a professor of sociology at Cologne, where, among his other duties, he served as editor of the *Kölnische Zeitschrift für Soziologie.* After World War II, Wiese headed a revival of German sociology. His tradition at Cologne is presently being carried on by René König (1906–), who succeeded him in the department in 1949. His best known work is his *Allgemeine*

[29]*Ibid.,* p. 510.

LEOPOLD VON WIESE

Courtesy of Leopold von Wiese

Soziologie ["General Sociology"], published in two volumes in 1924 and 1929, and revised in 1933.[30]

[30]Leopold von Wiese, *Allgemeine Soziologie,* Vol. 1, *Beziehungslehre* (Munich: Duncker & Humblot, 1924); Vol. 2, *Gebildelehre* (Munich: Duncker & Humblot, 1929). The second revised edition, published in 1933 by Duncker & Humblot, was called *System der Allgemeine Soziologie. Allgemeine Soziologie* was translated, adapted, and amplified by Howard Becker and published as *Systematic Sociology on the Basis of the* Beziehungslehre *and* Gebildelehre *of Leopold von Wiese* (New York: John Wiley, 1932); this was later reissued with new title page and 1950 preface by the Normal Paul Press, 1148 St. Joseph Street, Gary, Indiana, 1950. Dr. Becker points out in a personal communication of December 1959 that an abridged version, stressing wherever possible those parts of the original treatise for which Wiese rather than Becker was primarily responsible, will shortly appear as:

Simmel formed the starting point of Wiese's reconstruction of sociology. One of the first changes worked in Simmel's scheme was the abandonment of the terminology of "forms" and the formulation in terms of relations. The formal character of relations, however, is made basic. "Sociology . . . must deal with interhuman relations without immediate reference to ends, norms, or purposes; it involves a wholly different kind of abstraction."[31]

The isolation of the relation from the things related is assumed as in the case of Simmel's separability of form and content.

> . . . The delimiting principle of sociology as a special social science is not based upon any of the purposes of sociation, as are all the other social sciences. Direction and rhythm of motion are often the same where the purposes in view are entirely different; contrariwise, efforts to achieve identical purposes may utilize social relations following widely discrepant paths. The sociologists therefore delimit according to *direction* (approach or avoidance) and *rhythm* of motion; economics, jurisprudence, linguistics, etc., delimit according to the *purposes* served by social relations.[32]

One tremendous advantage potentially offered by the concept of relations over that of forms is the fact that there is less danger of their reification. From ancient times, "forms" have been thought of as independently existing things with the power to act as independent causes. The concept of relation has been much less abused in this manner, for the idea of a relation existing independently of any items that are actually related is a bit absurd.

A second major difference between Wiese's formulation and Simmel's has been Wiese's strong positivism. After all, Simmel showed pronounced idealistic tendencies and intuitive proclivities. By contrast, Wiese insists that *"Our methodological starting point is the single human being as known to our naïve sense perception;* we began simply by observing what is 'given' in concrete behavior. . . . we do not begin with an abstraction, but with direct observation; the basis of the system here set forth is empirical."[33]

Strong positivistic inclinations also appear in the fascination with physical analogies.

> Relations as they occur in physical phenomena are based upon more or less rapid motion between magnitudes — upon interaction. In order to get a clear picture of such interaction and its effects, let us think of the magnitudes as molecules which are made up of atoms. A stream of energy flows between these molecules and produces relations. Many molecules must give up atoms in the process, but nevertheless do not disintegrate completely. The stream of energy carries the detached atoms to other molecules; these therefore change and grow through the combination of the new with their old atoms. At many places where a cluster of molecules forms, where a plural number of them accumulates, there results a structure or pattern of more or less definite configuration. Such structured clusters may be termed *plurality patterns.*[34]

Howard Becker, *Systematic Sociology as Based on Wiese* (New York: Dover Publications, 1960). Also available in English are a collection of articles and a lecture by von Wiese, translated by Franz H. Mueller, and published under the title *Sociology* (New York: Oskar Piest, 1941) and *Sociology: Its History and Main Problems* (Hanover, N.H.: The Sociological Press, 1928), a translation of *Soziologie: Geschichte und Hauptprobleme* (Berlin: W. de Gruyter, 1926). Other works of Wiese's, not available in English translation, are: *Die Weltwirtschaft als soziologisches Gebilde* ["The World Economy as a Sociological Structure"] (Jena: G. Fischer, 1923); *Gesellschaftliche Stände und Klassen* ["Societal Estates and Classes"] (Bern: A. Francke, 1950); and *Abhängigkeit und Selbstständigkeit im sozialen Leben* ["Dependence and Independence in Social Life"] (Cologne: Westdeutscher Verlag, 1951); *Philosophie und Soziologie* ["Philosophy and Sociology"] (Berlin: Duncker & Humblot, 1959); *Herbert Spencers Einführung in die Soziologie* ["Herbert Spencer's Introduction to Sociology"] (Köln: Westdeutscher Verlag, 1960); *Das Ich-Wir- Verhältnis* ["The I-We Relation"] (Berlin: Duncker & Humblot, 1962); *Der Mensch als Mitmensch* ["Man as Neighbor"] (Berne: Francke, 1964); *Die Philosophie der personlichen Fürwörter* ["The Philosophy of the Personal Pronoun"] (Tübingen: Mohr, 1965); and *Geschichte der Soziologie* ["The History of Sociology"] (Berlin: De Gruyter, 1971).
[31] von Wiese, *Systematic Sociology*, pp. 72–73.

[32] *Ibid.*, pp. 41–42.
[33] *Ibid.*, p. 21.
[34] *Ibid.*, pp. 25–26. Howard Becker points out in a personal communication that the term "plurality pattern" is his "somewhat arbitrary rendering of the German origi-

Before any mistakes are made, it should be noted that Wiese is talking about society, and not chemical transformation. Lundberg must be forgiven his tendency to clasp Wiese to his bosom and feel hurt when his love is unrequited.[35]

Nor does Wiese's positivism stop with physical figures of speech. The ideal method of analysis of social process is set forth in pseudo formulas:

Every social process implies a plurality of participants, sometimes quite large, but the simplest process takes place in an occurrence directly involving but two persons, and we shall here assume that this is what the formula indicates:

$$P = A \times S$$

That is, every social process is the result ("product") of a personal attitude (A) and a situation (S). In thus calling attention to the observable fact that in every social process both attitude and situation exert influence, there is no claim that both always exert it in the same degree.

Attitude and situation are composite factors. A is the resultant of (1) and socially relevant native equipment, or N (including, among other things, the temperamental attitudes described by Thomas); and (2) previous experiences, or E. The inherited *and* the experienced are to be taken into account. Therefore $A = N \times E$.

The situation, S, also yields two components: (1) the extrahuman environment, the physical basis, or B; and (2) the attitudes of the other participant in the process in question, or A_1. Here also one factor must not be disregarded for the sake of the other. Hence $S = B \times A_1$.

The factor A_1 offers the same possibility of separation into component elements. . . .

The various minor formulae used in analysis combine into the following major formula:

$$P = N \times E \times B \times (N \times E)_1.[36]$$

But, alas, all this quantification is only make-believe. It is almost with regret that von Wiese admits "all plurality patterns are intangible, incorporeal; they are nothing more than neuropsychic patterns — and nothing less!"[37] The situation, of course, is not as yet completely hopeless, for they could still be specific quantities of nervous energy — that is, if that has any meaning. But the problem, it seems, is worse even than that. "The strictly mechanistic task of measuring (or of stating numerically) the path of motion involved in interaction is only one stage and not the final goal of sociological knowledge, for that goal lies beyond the mechanistic. *The behavior of human beings, when all is said, is something qualitative.*"[38]

Over and beyond these discussions, von Wiese advanced the cause of formal sociology by bringing the entire field together as he perceived it. Sociology, the science of interhuman relations, is divided in two: the systematics of action patterns and the systematics of plurality patterns or social structures. Social relations are the basic elements of both divisions; they are of two types — common human relations and circumscribed relations. Relations, so far as delimited by the presence of social groups, are circumscribed. Common human social relations are studied as existent and as functional. They are sociative in three possible ways: associative, dissociative, or mixed. Social structures are divided into three main categories: crowds (patternings of lowest power), groups (patternings of intermediate power), and abstract collectivities (patternings of highest power). Sociation, the total social process, comprises all social relations: association or dissociation, circumscribed and common human. The two fundamental processes of association and dissociation may be divided into subprocesses, and these in turn into single processes subsuming concrete social actions. In the systematics of action patterns, all-inclusive and single processes are conceptually delimited and described; assigned places within the total system;

---

nal, *Gebilde*, for which 'structure' is not an exact equivalent. A perhaps more apt translation would be 'constellation,' for this makes it clear that the parts of the *Gebilde* are separately distinguishable, and when the definition of *Gebilde* is altered, may be viewed as parts of *other* constellations."

[35]See George Lundberg, *Foundations of Sociology* (New York: Macmillan, 1939), pp. 36, 87, 102, 111, 132, 248, 261, 267, 280, 281, 348, 371, 374.

[36]Wiese-Becker, *Systematic Sociology*, p. 73.

[37]*Ibid.*, p. 31.

[38]*Ibid.*, p. 52.

analyzed as objective or subjective phenomena; ranked; and compared with other action patterns. Wiese's actual procedure was far more of an armchair operation than his positivistic formulas would imply. It consisted in the patient collection of terms that seemed to have social import. This was followed by long conferences to assess the amounts of association they represent. Once this was done, the task for systematic sociology consisted in the assembly of the known sociological materials in tables. Whether von Wiese's followers in the school he established will manage to find their way back to empirical reality remains to be seen.

Hans Kelsen. Has the neo-Kantian brand of sociological formalism completely run its course in sociology proper? Certainly it is still alive in jurisprudence, supplying now as in the past a juridical theory of society. Hans Kelsen (1881–1973) is a primary representative of contemporary neo-Kantian jurisprudence. A native of Prague, he became lecturer (*Privatdozent*) at the University of Vienna in 1911. In 1919 he was appointed to the Chair of Public Law and Philosophy of Law at Vienna, and in 1930 he became Professor of International Law at the University of Cologne. Because his views were incompatible with the Nazi ideology, Kelsen was forced to leave Germany in 1933. For the next seven years, he divided his time between the University of Geneva and the University of Prague, where he taught international law and jurisprudence. In 1941 he was invited to Harvard University as research professor and lecturer on international law. From 1942 to 1952 he taught international law and jurisprudence at the University of California at Berkeley, where, since 1952, he has been University Professor Emeritus.[39]

[39]Hans Kelsen has written in both German and English. His main works with sociological import include: *Hauptprobleme der Staatsrechtslehre* ["Main Problems of Constitutional Law"] (Tübingen: J. C. B. Mohr, 1911); *Das Problem der Souveränität und die Theorie des Völkerrechts* ["The Problem of Sovereignty and the Theory of International Law"] (Tübingen: J. C. B. Mohr, 1920); *Allgemeine Staatslehre* ["General Political Science"] (Berlin: J.

HANS KELSEN

Photo by Paul Bishop. Courtesy of Hans Kelsen

Springer, 1925); *Probleme der Rechtsphilosophie* ["Problems of Legal Philosophy"] (Berlin: Rothschild, 1927); *The Legal Process and International Order* (London: Constable, 1935); *Law and Peace in International Relations* (Cambridge, Mass.: Harvard University Press, 1942); *Society and Nature: A Sociological Inquiry* (Chicago: University of Chicago Press, 1943); *Peace Through Law* (Chapel Hill, N.C.: University of North Carolina Press, 1944); *General Theory of Law and the State*, tr. by Anders Wedberg (Cambridge, Mass.: Harvard University Press, 1945); *The Law of the United Nations* (London: Stevens, 1950); and a collection of essays, *What Is Justice?* (Berkeley: University of California Press, 1957). Recent translations and republications include: *Essays in Legal and Moral Philosophy*, selected by Ota Weinberger, translated by Peter Heath (Boston: Reidel, 1974); *General Theory of Law and State*, trans. Anders Wedberg (New York: Russell & Russell, 1973); *Peace through Law* (New York: Garland Pub., 1973); *Society and Nature* (New York: Arno Press, 1974); *The Pure Theory of Law*, trans. Max Knight (Berkeley: Uni-

Kelsen's method is essentially Kantian, though he is critical of some features of Kant's legal theory. He believes that knowledge is no mere passive picture of the objective world. Knowledge creates its objects in terms of its inherent forms of the material presented to the senses. Law, as such a creation, is a product of a mental operation, but not one that belongs to the world of nature. Law belongs to the category of essence (*das Sollen*), not to the category of existence (*das Sein*). One essential property of law is the possibility that it will not be observed. A rule of law is a special kind of hypothetical proposition. If one defined set of factors occurs, another involving compulsion ought to follow as a matter of law, though not necessarily as a matter of experience. Law is an imperative in a hypothetical sense. Law is a branch of the normative rather than natural sciences. The legal rule is concerned with what positive law shall be, not with why positive law ought to be.

A law in the domain of natural science is an application of the principle of causality. It reveals certain events as the necessary consequence of others. The human-made law, on the other hand, lays down rules of right conduct. A norm cannot be explained by reference to the acts of existence. The question as to why a legal rule is established in fact is social-psychological and outside legal science. The question as to why a legal rule is binding is the proper study of jurisprudence.

A legal rule is binding only by reference to another, higher, legal rule. But must this legal rule then be based on another, and so on without end? There must, of course, be some stopping point. The regress from legal rule to legal rule must end

somewhere upon some ultimate proposition from which a legal system is traced. The initial hypothesis of a legal system is its fundamental norm (*die Grundnorm*). The reasons for accepting the fundamental rule are meta-legal. Jurists go back to the fundamental rule; they do not go beyond it. Thus, at the summit of every legal system there is a rule providing that the final legislative organ in the form it takes from time to time is to have the power of determining the process by which all other rules are maintained. The birth of a legal system is in this "hypothetical constitution." It is this hypothesis that transforms might into right, force into law.

Legal duty is the central and only essential property of a legal system. The essence of a compulsory ordering is that it binds those subject to it. The fact of being bound is expressed through the conception of duty. Every legal rule establishes a legal duty. Subjective right obtains only so far as it is laid down in objective law. A "person" is a bundle of legal duties and rights. The physical person is the personification of the total of legal rules applicable to one person. The juristic person is the personification of legal rules applicable to a plurality of persons.

The phenomenon of delegation from the fundamental hypothesis is essential for the relation between the pure objective fact of law and positive law. There is a descending process of delegation from the "constitution" to legislation, administration, judicial decisions, and private transactions. Legislation is only relatively law-creative; it applies the fundamental rule of law embodied in the constitution.

Once the distinction between the creation and application of law is clear, one may understand the distinction between private and public law in a new way. Kelsen rejects the idea that there is any principled difference. The very fact that the legal order protects a private interest shows that it is of public interest to do so. Any rule of criminal or administrative law can ultimately be traced to the individual person or persons in whose interest it has been created. The duty to observe certain conduct is grounded not in the will of one person but in agreement. The breach of legal duty thus

versity of California Press, 1967). Summaries of Kelsen's views may be found in J. Walter Jones, *Historical Introduction to the Theory of Law* (Oxford: Clarendon Press, 1940), pp. 222–234; and H. Lauterpacht, "Kelsen's Pure Science of Law," in [no author], *Modern Theories of Law* (London: Oxford University Press, 1933), pp. 105–138. Among biographical and critical works of Kelsen are Rudolf Aladar Métall, *Hans Kelsen: Leben und Werke* (Wien: Dutike, 1969); Ronald Moore, *Legal Norms and Legal Science: A Critical Study of Kelsen's Pure Theory of Law* (Honolulu: University Press of Hawaii, 1978).

created evokes compulsion not from the other party but from the state.

Moreover, just as private law and public law collapse and form one system, so too are the law and the state found to be identical. Negatively, this is seen in the fact that the other sciences cannot dispense with the legal conception of the state, but must assume it. The state assumed by sociology, for example, is a unity such as is posited by legal science. Positively, the state may be seen to be a normative ordering coextensive with the ordering of the legal system. Only by perceiving the state as *a system of norms* can it be seen as an authority, and the relation of the individual to the state can be seen as one of subordination. Moreover, the state can only be understood so far as duties issue from it, and individuals are bound to observe certain rules of conduct. The apparatus of compulsion, called the state, turns out to be simply the legal order. The legal norm is the rule through which the attribution of acts to the state occurs. It consists of the condition posited by law and the legal consequence. The power of the state is not its guns, ships, forts, prisons, and gallows; these are inanimate objects. They derive their significance from the human use made of them. This use results from the ideas dominating people. The state is a product of personification. Human thought finds it inconvenient to deal with the unity of the legal system except by a hypothetical device that embodies a multitude of abstract norms. The state is only the expression of the demand for logical completeness and inner consistency of a system of legal norms.

In somewhat the same fashion that Kelsen tends to fuse public and private law, there is a clear tendency to fuse the sovereignty of the individual state in the single unity of international law. Sovereignty is reduced to the expression of the unity and exclusiveness of the legal system. The assumption of such unity is essential for law as a science. But, asks Kelsen, do not the demands of that science press beyond the limits of the individual state? Kelsen's reasoning seems to run as follows. The sovereignty of the state implies that the legal order of the state is independent, self-existent, and

self-sufficient. When the exclusiveness of the individual sovereign state is necessarily asserted, other sovereign states exist only so far as recognized. However, so far as recognized, they are included within the legal order of the recognizing state. One must now either abandon the sovereignty of the state or accept the primacy of international law in which the legal system of the individual state is a partial legal order, deriving its validity by delegation from the fundamental rule of the world legal order. The world legal order is already in existence as a result of the existence of international law. The primacy of international law subordinates the state to a higher authority and deprives it of absolute superiority over the corporate entities within its territorial units.

Kelsen's objection to Kant arose from his view that Kant, as a personality rooted in Christianity, was led in his capacity as a legal philosopher to abandon his transcendental method, making his metaphysic of morals into a perfect expression of the classical natural-law doctrine. Kelsen's estimate is quite correct. Kelsen made the central point of his own position the break with natural-law doctrines. Natural law was, he thought, based on the assumption of a natural order with rules valid because they are not made by human authority, but are rather a product of God, nature, or reason. By rejecting natural law, Kelsen believed he was affirming the dignity and autonomy of human beings. The central concept in the pure science of law is the rejection of natural law. The foundation is located, as already noted, in the fundamental constitution that is placed in international law.

Kant had, indeed, drawn a distinction between the spheres of morality and causality. Kelsen, in effect, accuses Kant of having violated his own distinction, mistakenly assigning law to the realm of causality. Kelsen may thus claim to have carried out the original Kantian program.

Kelsen's criticism of Kant should not obscure his basic Kantianism. In both Kant and Kelsen, the liberal and rationalistic conception of society is maintained. Both men resist the idea of the absolute subordination of the individual to the group. Individual freedom is simultaneously limited and made possible by the group, which is merely another name for inter-individual behavior. Both men find their highest personal value in the dignity of the free personality.

In view of these agreements, Kelsen's accusation that Kant confused morality with causality may seem odd. But if one notes the frequency and passion of his rejection of the idea of a "natural" law, his accusation may have a simple explanation. The plastic eighteenth-century meaning of "natural" as "universal" permitted its application both to morality and to empirical regularities. To be sure, this ambiguity invites misunderstanding. While Kant nearly always kept it clear, his followers often did not. Kelsen, in fact, reasons like a "natural law" theorist of Kantian type. Like Kant, he dissolves the state into the law conceived as a binding interindividual arrangement. He sounds a Kantian note approximating the idea that nothing is ultimately good other than the good will. Kelsen thus places Kantian legal formalism and the sense of duty on the broadest possible base, such that the validity of every rule — every rule, eventually, of the human world — is derived from some other legal rule deriving eventually from a kind of "hypothetical constitution" of humankind. (This is Kelsen's counterpart to the Enlightenment's "reason.") In a sense, the Kantian formula, "so act that one's action can become a universal law," never received a more general formulation.

Kelsen has not stopped his reflections with these formulations, but has extended his analysis to sociology in his book *Society and Nature: A Sociological Inquiry* (1943). In this work he employs the dualism between society and nature and between normative order and the principle of causality in quite a new manner, to account for the evolution of people's conceptions of nature and society. Here Kelsen's argument is that primitive people were dominated by feeling and emotion rather than by rationality. The primitive person's concept of nature was also dominated by feeling, hence the initial form of the conception of nature was determined by evaluations establishing a normative order of human behavior. (This accounts for the lack of causal thinking and the dominance of

magic among primitives.) It also accounts for primitive people's lack of ego-consciousness and their belief that animals cannot be killed against their will, and that there are tongues in trees and spirits in running brooks. Autocratism, conservatism, and traditionalism rule among primitives, and, generally, primitive thought about everything is dominated by the principle of retribution — an idea appropriate to society — that applies to all things and all areas of natural events. Thunder and lightning, natural catastrophe, other natural events, all are given the form of retribution. This idea of retribution, Kelsen maintains, was still dominant in the religion and arts of the ancient Greeks.

Beginning with the Greeks, however, a new idea appeared, particularly in the doctrines of the atomists, of the existence of a principle of absolutely valid causality. The idea continued to grow in clarity until Hume performed the final act of shearing the last remnants of the idea of retribution from the concept. Kant completed the emancipation. The importance of the discovery of causality, however, tended to lead to its overemphasis and the reverse process of the incorporation of society into the order of nature.

Together with the emancipation of the law of causality from the principle of retribution occurred the divorce of the notions of nature and society. Nature appeared to be part of society when it was interpreted according to the principle of retribution.[40]

From this vantage point, Kelsen summed up the central point of his thought:

With the emancipation of causality from retribution and of the law of nature from the social norm, nature and society prove to be two entirely different systems. The idea of a system of norms regulating human behavior and constituting society as an order totally different from the laws of nature is possible without the fiction of freedom of will and therefore without contradiction to the principle of causality. . . .

[40]Kelsen, *Society and Nature*, p. 264. (Copyright 1943 by the University of Chicago.)

The idea of natural law . . . presumes a dualism within nature conceived as a universal society; the real, inadequate human society is contrasted with the ideal cosmic society. It is the antagonism of man and God, of the empirical and the transcendental. With the emancipation of the causal from the normative interpretation of nature . . . the antagonism of the empirical and the transcendental disappears from the sphere of science. Hence there is no longer room for a natural [law] behind or above a positive legal order.[41]

And with this formulation, Kelsen relinquishes to sociology all those aspects of human society in which it is a part of the order of nature. "After the complete emancipation of causality from retribution in the modern notion of law, society is — from the point of view of science — a part of nature."[42]

However comforting it may be to have a liberal image of society as a legally ordered plurality of independent wills, many problems are buried in neo-Kantian theory. By drawing the line between phenomena and noumena and making the former the sphere of science, the latter the sphere of morality — and incidentally, society — extraordinarily tough problems are posed for a science of society. Strictly speaking, a science of society seems to have been made impossible. Freedom, for example, belongs to action and morality; it does not belong, as does "causality," to phenomena. But if the thing of interest in society is its "freedom," does not the study of society lie outside science? If we study society causally, do we not miss precisely its most significant element? Kelsen is therefore very traditionally Kantian when he appropriates everything socially significant for jurisprudence, leaving to sociology the study of everything that does not matter.

Nor do our woes stop here. Kant had "saved" science on the basis of a distinction between form and content. But forms are mind-given. Clearly we do not discover a mind-given "form" by the

methods appropriate to the discovery of content. If the forms are really a priori, we need no experience to discover them. Not inductive study of facts, but mental inspection, is suggested as the proper method for this most important element. To the degree to which sociology seriously follows this lead, *it for the first time launches a fundamental attack on methodological positivism.* Since it represents the attempt to face up to the inner difficulties of neo-Kantian formalism, phenomenological formalism is more profound.

Carl Gustav Jung. Carl Gustav Jung (1875–1961) was the son of a clergyman and offspring of protestant theologians on both sides of his family. During his upbringing in Basel, Switzerland he developed interests in the sciences (biology, zoology, paleontology and medicine) and religion (occultism, mysticism, mythology, as well as traditional religion). His career in psychiatry began with systematic researches as assistant to Eugene Bleuler at Burghölzli, the psychiatric clinic of the University of Zurich. Shortly after completing his degree as doctor of medicine in 1902 he published his *Studies in Word Association* and coined the term *complexes* for groups of ideas in the unconscious. The work added a basic technology and concept to the emerging system of psychoanalysis.

His work was converging toward that of Freud and led to their contact in 1907 and to a brief collaboration between the two men. In 1909, Freud and Jung undertook a joint lecture tour through the United States and for four years (1909–1913) Jung was editor of the *Yearbook for Psychological Research* and president for a time of the International Psychoanalytic Society which Jung founded. After 1913 the paths of the two thinkers separated. Jung coined the term *analytical psychology* to distinguish his position from that of Freud. In 1913 Jung gave up his lectureship at the University of Zurich to devote himself to private practice, research, and travel. Jung studied primitive peoples in the southwest United States and in North and West Africa. He also undertook intensive studies of Asian culture, particularly Buddhism, Confucianism, Taoism, and Hinduism, twice travelling

[41]*Ibid.,* pp. 265–266.
[42]*Ibid.,* p. 266.

CARL GUSTAV JUNG

Brown Brothers

to India. His researches extended to Greek and other mythologies, patristics, Christian mysticism, gnosis, cabala, alchemy, and hermetic philosophy.[43]

While he was still associated with Freud and had not yet distinguished his position from psychoanalysis as analytical psychology, Jung had observed that psychoanalysis works backward like history but "just as the largest part of the past is so far removed that it is not reached by history, so too the greater part of the unconscious determinants is unreachable."[44] Historical interpretations, Jung commented, isolate the first element by postula-

tion, the second by historical analysis. The effect of such historical predetermination, in a sense, is to anticipate the future. With self-conscious reference to Kant's procedure, Jung remarked:

> In so far as to-morrow is already contained in to-day, and all the threads of the future are in place, so a more profound knowledge of the past might render possible a more or less far-reaching and certain knowledge of the future. Let us transfer this reasoning, as Kant has already done, to psychology.[45]

Jung made a number of characteristic shifts in the emerging psychoanalytic point of view. The *libido* had been visualized by Freud to consist primarily in sexuality. Jung thought of libido more as vital energy (somewhat like Bergson's *elan vital*) of which sexuality was only one important manifestation. He also conceived the psyche as a self-regulating system in which the conscious and unconscious are complementary, a different interpretation than Freud's idea of the tense suppression of unconscious by conscious. Moreover, in his concept of the unconscious, Jung drew a distinction between the personal and collective spheres, the first originating in individual development, and the second in the development of the race. The contributions of the development of the species to the unconscious was described by Jung as *subjective aptitudes*.

> There is no human experience, nor would experience be possible at all, without the intervention of a subjective aptitude. What is this subjective aptitude? Ultimately it consists in an innate psychic structure which allows man to have experiences of this kind. Thus the whole nature of man presupposes woman, both physically and spiritually. His system is tuned in to woman from the start, just as it is prepared for a quite definite world where there is water, light, air, salt, carbohydrates, etc. The form of the world into which he is born is already inborn in him as a virtual image.

---

[43]Jung's publications extend from 1902 to 1959 and appear in *The Collected Works of C. G. Jung*, G. Adler et al., trans. R. F. Hull, 17 vols. (Princeton: Princeton University Press, 1954–1971).

[44]C. G. Jung, *Psychology of the Unconscious*, trans. Beatrice

M. Hinkle (New York: Dodd, Mead and Company, 1947), p. 493.

[45]*Ibid.*

Likewise parents, wife, children, birth and death are inborn in him as virtual images, as psychic aptitudes. These *a priori* categories have by nature a collective character; they are images of parents, wife, and children in general, and are not individual predestinations.[46]

The deepest layers of the unconscious mind, Jung was convinced, were philogenetically determined predispositions. These, he felt, were more efficiently explored not in the dreams and fantasies of the individual but in art, literature, mythology, magic, and religion—particularly when these are approached comparatively, permitting an estimation of the presence of a common tendency or form capable of varied contentual determination. Jung described such forms as archetypes.

> Again and again I encounter the mistaken notion that an archetype is determined in regard to its content, in other words that it is a kind of unconscious idea (if such an expression be admissible). It is necessary to point out once more that archetypes are not determined as regards their content, but only as regards their form and then only to a very limited degree. A primordial image is determined as to its content only when it has become conscious and is therefore filled out with the material of conscious experience.[47]

Among such archetypes are those of the wholly good or wholly bad mother (the witch versus the mother goddess), the father (devil versus god), the man's archetypal image of the woman (anima), or woman's archetypal image of the man (animus), the archetypal image of the self (as bad, the shadow or virtuous, the wise old man).

One effect of Jung's analysis has been to give a far more positive value to the studies of the sociology of art, play, literature, knowledge, and culture than did the positivistic organicists.

CLAUDE LÉVI-STRAUSS

Henri Cartier-Bresson/Magnum Photos, Inc.

Alexander Goldenweiser and Claude Lévi-Strauss. Before turning to Claude Lévi-Strauss it is of interest to review briefly some ideas of an anthropologist who, though usually ignored, clearly anticipated Lévi-Strauss's point of view. Alexander Alexandrovich Goldenweiser (1880–1940) was born in Kiev, Russia, the son of a lawyer. He was educated in Kiev and at Harvard and Columbia where he earned the Ph.D. in 1910. He was the most cosmopolitan and theoretically most competent of the brilliant school that gathered around Franz Boas and, for a time, was considered to be Boas's most obvious heir-apparent at Columbia. However, because of a personal scandal at a time when Victorianism still reigned in American academic institutions, he never held a full-time permanent academic position (he obtained a Mexi-

[46] Jung, *Two Essays on Analytical Psychology, Collected Works,* VII, 190.
[47] Jung, "Psychological Aspects of the Mother Archetype," *Collected Works,* 9 (1):79.

can divorce from his first wife and, since such divorces were not recognized by New York State laws, he found himself charged with bigamy and thrown into jail when he remarried). He was hounded by the scandal the rest of his life. Goldenweiser was the primary architect of both the New School for Social Research and *The Encyclopedia of the Social Sciences*, institutions for which he has never received proper credit but for which others achieved fame.[48]

Even in the *International Encyclopedia of the Social Sciences* traces of the old rumors that haunted Goldenweiser in life appear in David French's essay:

> Goldenweiser was not at home in the world as he knew it. Sometimes he was irresponsible in his relations with publishers or with academic systems. He appears to have lacked a substantial theoretical basis for studying the regularities of human life; the writings of his contemporaries did not readily offer such a basis, and even had it been there, his personal anarchistic predilections might have militated against his finding it.[49]

Goldenweiser had a cosmopolitanism that made him at home, as Jacob Burkhardt would have said, wherever a cultivated person is found. Contrary to French, wherever Goldenweiser was, was home. He had the best qualities of a Renaissance humanist or eighteenth-century rationalist. In fact, it was the example of the encylopedists that had led him to envision the possibilities of *The Encyclopedia of the Social Sciences* and The New School for Social Research, two institutions of contemporary social science that Goldenweiser first planned and promoted. Rather than anarchistic, Goldenweiser was a humanistic and rationalistic individualist. It was from this point of view that he left his decisive mark on the two major anthropological controversies of the opening days of the twentieth century: totemism and the diffusion controversy. Totemism was being widely treated, as one would say today *structurally*, as a decisive phase in the evolution of culture. The diffusion controversy underestimated the creativity of humankind, and was tracing just about everything that was however remotely analogous to a single cultural origin in ancient Egypt.

In his "principle of limited possibilities" Goldenweiser dealt a decisive blow to naive diffusionism. He argued from the assumptions of his humanism and rationalism that the human constitution, both mental and physical, is about the same everywhere and human beings face an environment that is also more or less the same. If, then, they are to solve problems, such as crossing a stream without getting wet, a boat or raft or canoe will have to be big enough to carry a person without sinking but not too big to be paddled or rowed. There is no good reason, thus, to suppose that boats, rafts, and canoes have not been independently invented many times — for people around the world must often have wished to get to the other side of a body of water. However, the appearance of an identical design with a parallel meaning on the handle of a paddle in widely separated areas strongly suggests diffusion even if the parallelism seems to be widely separated. Goldenweiser had confronted the diffusion theory with the alternative possibilities of similarly constituted minds and bodies (as his eighteenth-century counterparts would have said, similar faculties and powers) and had stressed the creativity and adaptability of human beings.

Similarly, rationalistic suppositions were basic to Goldenweiser's critique of totemism, which was being conceived as a structural stage in the universal evolution of culture. Culture, to Goldenweiser, was the creation of individuals who found them-

[48]Goldenweiser's major works were "Totemism: An Analytical Study," *Journal of Mexican Folklore*, XXIII, 179–293; *Early Civilization: An Introduction to Anthropology* (New York: Knopf, 1922); *Robots or Gods: An Essay on Craft and the Mind* (New York: Knopf, 1931); *History, Psychology, and Culture* (New York: Knopf, 1933); "Loose Ends of Theory on the Individual, Pattern and Involution in Primitive Society," in *Essays in Anthropology* (Berkeley: University of California Press, 1936); *Anthropology: An Introduction to Primitive Culture* (New York: Crofts, 1937).
[49]David H. French, "Alexander Goldenweiser," *International Encyclopedia of the Social Sciences* (New York: Macmillan and the Free Press, 1968), VI, 197.

selves in endlessly varied situations. By a reanalysis of the materials of the students of totemism, Goldenweiser demonstrated that no single entity called "totemism" could be found in fact, but only a congeries of partially similar overlapping phenomena.

> All indications are that totemism is very old; its distribution . . . is world-wide if not universal; moreover it comprises a whole complex of features — social, religious, ceremonial, etc. A complex such as this cannot be picked up casually. When therefore one finds it in hundreds of tribes, this can only be explained by assuming that a certain congeniality exists between totemism and the many tribal cultures which have it. This being so, the very conditions favoring the borrowing of totemism from without would invite its development from within. It follows that many totemic tribes must be assumed to have developed it independently.[50]

Totemism, it follows, is not a stage in the universal evolution of culture but a category of similar cultural responses by similarly constituted minds to similar conditions. Such arguments, together with Goldenweiser's conviction that some traits are simple and basic and incapable of dismemberment or analysis except in psychological terms,[51] clarify the extent to which Goldenweiser's basic theoretical position was rationalistic.

The times were not ready for Goldenweiser's rationalistic approach to anthropological problems; moreover, he had made himself vulnerable by his offense against the Victorian mores of the American universities of the time. When he was arrested for bigamy and his academic career was in ruins, colleagues who visited him in jail were shocked not to find him downcast but in a state of ecstasy. Goldenweiser saw himself as similar to Marco Polo, John Bunyan, and Cervantes who also had found themselves in jail: he was composing *Robots or Gods,* a poetic essay on the nature of humanity.

The person who more than anyone else explored the rationalistic position in anthropology, which was more implicit than explicit in Goldenweiser's work, was Lévi-Strauss. Claude Lévi-Strauss (1908–   ), born in Brussels, studied law and philosophy at the University of Paris and belonged for a time to the Jean-Paul Sartre circle. He became professor of sociology at the University of São Paulo, Brazil leading several expeditions to central Brazil between 1935 and 1939. From 1942 to 1945 he taught at the New School for Social Research. He was cultural advisor to the French ambassador to the United States from 1946–1947. In 1950 he became director of studies at the École Pratique des Hautes Études at the University of Paris and was appointed to the chair of social anthropology at the College de France in 1959.[52]

Lévi-Strauss describes his theoretical approach as structuralism. Antecedents of his approach appear in the late nineteenth-century theories of psychology. Not only perception, but experience generally was theorized to rest on elementary experiences or sensations that occur in various combinations. Such elementary experience comprised both the physical qualities of objects and perceptions of people, including their intention and social relationships.[53] A second major form of structuralism, arising sometime after the decline of structuralism in psychology, appears in what is known as synchronic or structural linguistics of Ferdinande de Sassure.[54] De Sassure believed that the synchronic study of language (the study of language as a system) was antithetical to the diachronic study of language (its study historically). Later structuralists almost abandoned the historical study of language,

[52]Among Lévi-Strauss's major works are: *Les Structure élémentaires de la parenté* (1949); *Tristes Tropiques* (1955); *Anthropologie structurale* (1958); *Le Totémisme aujourd'hui* (1962); *Mythologiques* (4 vols.; 1964–1971); *Anthropologie structurale Deux* (1973); *La Voie des masques* (2 vols.; 1975).

[53]See Edward B. Tichener, *An Outline of Psychology* (New York: Macmillan, 1902), and Wilhelm Wundt, *Outlines of Psychology* (Leipzig: Engelmann, 1896).

[54]Ferdinand de Sassure, *Course in General Linguistics* (New York: Philosophical Library, 1959). First published as *Course de linguistique genérale* in 1916.

[50]Alexander Goldenweiser, *Anthropology* (New York: Crofts, 1937), p. 323.

[51]*Ibid.,* p. 472.

turning attention primarily to structure and form. A number of schools of structuralism emerged (in Switzerland, Denmark, and Russia) developing new methodologies for the studies of phonology and grammar. In the United States combinations of the historical and structural analyses of language were pursued by Franz Boas, Edward Sapir, and Leonard Bloomfield.[55]

The step from a structural psychology and structural linguistics to a structural ethnology was, perhaps, inevitable. In fact, as already noted, this was already present by implication in the work of Goldenweiser on totemism and the cultural diffusion controversy. In his first major book, Lévi-Strauss took this step.[56] Chapter seven of *The Elementary Structures of Kinship* was devoted to structures of the mind as revealed by psychological evidence. Adult thought, Lévi-Strauss argued, centers on structures processed out of the undifferentiated structures of childhood experience. Understanding of this enables the social scientist to "penetrate the nature of institutions" inasmuch as "the common capital of mental structure and institutional schemata are the initial resources"[57] upon which people rely in their social enterprises. The relational properties of kinship systems are the raw material for the creation of heterogeneous systems.

The study by Marcel Mauss (1872–1950) of *The Gift*[58] supplied Lévi-Strauss with one of his major clues to the role played by basic forms in the varieties of human cultural experience. The exchange of gifts, Mauss demonstrated, occurs in almost endless variations throughout all societies. Although gifts are, in theory, voluntary, disinterested, and spontaneous, they are, in fact, obligatory and interested. They establish obligations to give, receive, and repay and are inseparable from contexts of mutual aid, understanding, reciprocity, and community.[59] Lévi-Strauss generalized this rule and made it the cornerstone of his theory of kinship. The rule of incest, for example, renouncing sex with one's daughter or sister, has a positive counterpart in the claim on the daughter or sister of another. The incest prohibition, thus, constitutes a rule of reciprocity and exchange.[60]

In Lévi-Strauss's view all kinship institutions are methods of achieving integration between families in terms of three elementary structures (bilateral, patrilineal, and matrilateral) constructed, in any given case, into a cycle of exchange between the groups. Where residence and sex are based on the same sex line the result is a generalized exchange in contrast to the restricted exchange where they are separate.

Among the basic principles of structuralism as elaborated in his first major work and developed in later works were: the analysis of the relationships holding between social phenomena; their reduction to simple and elementary structures; the conception of social phenomena as "objectivated systems of ideas"; the recognition that such objectivated ideas are unconscious.

When interviewed about his ethnological assumptions and procedures, Lévi-Strauss stressed the Kantian character of his anthropological method. "Philosophically I find myself more and more Kantian, not so much because of the particular content of Kant's doctrine, but rather for the specific way of posing the problem of knowledge."[61] This may be illustrated by the manner in which Lévi-Strauss handled the problems of totemism in *The Savage Mind*. His observation follows the same lines as Goldenweiser. When one reviews

[55] Franz Boas, ed., *Handbook of American Indian Languages* (Washington: Govt. Printing Office, 1911), pp. 1–83; Edward A. Sapir, *Languages: An Introduction to the Study of Speech* (New York: Harcourt, 1921); Leonard Bloomfield, *Language* (New York: Holt, 1933, revised 1951).
[56] Claude Lévi-Strauss, *The Elementary Structures of Kinship* (Boston: Beacon Press, 1969). First published as *Les Structures Elémentaires de la parenté* (Paris: Plon, 1949).
[57] *Ibid.*, p. 95.
[58] Marcel Mauss, *The Gift*, trans. I. Cunnison (New York: The Free Press, 1954).
[59] *Ibid.*, p. 43.
[60] Lévi-Strauss, *Structures of Kinship*, p. 51.
[61] Claude Lévi-Strauss, an interview by A. Koun and F. Morin, *Psychology Today*, 5 (December 1972), 74.

the phenomena of totemism cross-culturally one is struck both by recurrent patterns and endless variations.

> These observations seem to make it possible to dispose of theories making use of the concepts of 'archetypes' or a 'collective unconscious'. It is only forms and not contents which can be common. If there are common contents the reason must be sought either in the objective properties of particular nature or artificial entities or in diffusion and borrowing, in either case, that is, outside the mind.[62]

The same mind-supplied form appears throughout the primitive world and accounts for the recurrent patterns in totemism. But as long as the situations to which the mind is responding vary, variations in content are to be expected. It may be noted, incidentally, that Lévi-Strauss seems to be trying to refute Jung; however, Jung was always careful to insist that by *archetypes* and the collective *unconscious* he meant forms, not content.

It was clearly Lévi-Strauss's purpose in *The Savage Mind* to reassert the basic similarity of the savage and the civilized (or perhaps better, scientific) mind, despite their apparent dissimilarities. The savage mind operates concretely; the scientific mind, abstractly. The savage mind approaches the world totally or holistically; the scientific mind, analytically.

> In order for *praxis* to be living thought, it is necessary first (in a logical and not a historical sense) for thought to exist: that is to say, its initial conditions must be given in the form of an objective structure of the psyche and brain without which there would be neither *praxis* nor thought.[63]
>
> The savage mind is logical in the same sense and the same fashion as ours, though as our own is only when it is applied to knowledge of a universe in which it recognizes physical and semantic properties simultaneously.[64]

Certainly the properties to which the savage mind has access are not the same as those which have commanded the attention of scientists. The physical world is approached from opposite ends in the two cases: one is supremely concrete, the other supremely abstract; one proceeds from the angle of sensible qualities and the other from that of formal properties . . . both, independently of each other . . . have led to two distinct though equally positive sciences: one which flowered in the neolithic period, whose theory of the sensible order provided the basis of the arts of civilization (agriculture, animal husbandry, pottery, weaving, conservation and preparation of food, etc.) and which continues to provide for our basic needs by these means; and another which places itself from the start at the level of intelligibility, and of which contemporary science is the fruit. . . . The entire process of human knowledge, thus assumes the character of a closed system.[65]

Throughout the whole range of human culture, past and present, in good Kantian form, Lévi-Strauss assumes the mind operates on the same principles, organizes its material according to the same limitations and requirements. The scientific mind appears only as a special case, extracting the form, the abstraction, and reorganizing the whole of human thought on its foundation.

Noam Chomsky. Avram Noam Chomsky has advanced a basically neo-Kantian rationalistic position in linguistics. He was born in Philadelphia in 1928 and earned the B.A., M.A. and Ph.D. at the University of Pennsylvania. He is presently Ferrari P. Ward Professor of Linguistics at the Massachusetts Institute of Technology.[66] In the 1960s

---

[62]Claude Lévi-Strauss, *The Savage Mind* (Chicago: The University of Chicago Press, 1966), p. 65.
[63]*Ibid.*, pp. 263–264.
[64]*Ibid.*, p. 268.

[65]*Ibid.*, p. 269.
[66]Among Chomsky's major writings are: *Syntactic Structures* (The Hague: Mouton, 1957); *Current Issues in Linguistic Theory* (The Hague: Mouton, 1964); *Aspects of the Theory of Syntax* (Cambridge, Mass.: MIT Press, 1965); *Cartesian Linguistics* (New York: Harper & Row, 1966); *Language and the Mind* (New York: Harcourt, Brace, Jovanovich, 1968); *American Power and the New Mandarins* (New York: Pantheon Books, 1969); *Problems of Knowledge and Freedom* (New York: Pantheon Books, 1971); *Studies on Semantics in Generative Grammar* (The Hague:

NOAM CHOMSKY

Wide World

and 1970s Chomsky emerged as a major radical social scientist. Chomsky, together with his teacher Zellig Harris,[67] is author of the most influential recent model of structural linguistics both in the United States and abroad.

Transformational-generative grammar is a technique for text and syntax analysis accounting for relations between sentences. Ambiguities in sentences deriving from different underlying phrases were clarified by this type of analysis. Superficially similar sentences were at times demonstrated to possess underlying differences. The analysis was able to integrate the productive relations between different forms of (active, passive, negative) sentences. Working beyond Harris, Chomsky elaborated a new model of language and the reconstruction of previous objectives. Originally, emphasis was placed on the analysis of the underlying "deep structure" of grammar relegating descriptive linguistics to the state of a "surface structure." Grammar was viewed as shaping phonology and the phonological output specified in in terms of distinctive features. Chomsky turned his program into a general attack on behavioristic and positivistic approaches to language. In the following passages of his *Reflection on Language* Chomsky explicates his rationalistic theories of transformational-generative grammar.

> Language is a mirror of mind in a deep and significant sense. It is a product of human intelligence, created anew in each individual by operations that lie far beyond the reach of will or consciousness.[68]

> Tracing the development of such ideas, we arrive at Kant's rather similar concept of the "conformity of objects to our mode of cognition." The mind provides the means for an analysis of data as experience, and provides as well a general schematism that delimits the cognitive structures developed on the basis of experience.[69]

> Each grammar is a theory of a particular language, specifying formal and semantic properties of an infinite array of sentences.[70]

> Let us define "universal grammar" (UG) as the system of principles, conditions, and rules that are elements or properties of all human languages not merely by accident but by necessity — of course, I mean biological, not logical, necessity. Thus UG can be taken as expressing "the essence of human language."[71]

> It is a reasonable surmise, I think, that there is no structure similar to UG in nonhuman organisms and

---

Mouton, 1972); *For Reasons of State* (New York: Pantheon Books, 1973); *Reflections on Language* (New York: Pantheon Books, 1975).
[67]Zellig S. Harris, *Methods in Structural Linguistics* (Chicago: University of Chicago Press, 1951).

[68]Noam Chomsky, *Reflections on Language* (New York: Pantheon Books, 1975), p. 4.
[69]*Ibid.*, p. 7.
[70]*Ibid.*, p. 13.
[71]*Ibid.*, p. 29.

that the capacity for free, appropriate, and creative use of language as an expression of thought, with the means provided by the language faculty, is also a distinctive feature of the human species, having no significant analogue elsewhere.[72]

Kant suggested that "the schematism of our understanding, in its application to appearances and their mere form, is an art concealed in the depths of the human soul, whose real modes of activity nature is hardly likely ever to allow us to discover, and to have open to our gaze . . . Perhaps this is true in some respects at least.[73]

Chomsky's neo-Kantian formalism has rejuvenated contemporary linguistics and stimulated activity in surrounding social sciences.

ETHOLOGY AND SOCIOBIOLOGY

The twentieth-century heirs of the rationalistic point of view, in contrast to their eighteenth-century counterparts, do not believe that the universal, innate faculties or relations or abilities that both empower and limit behavior and culture are directly accessible to consciousness. Since they are assumed to be inherited powers, potentialities, and limitations of the species, they are present, as Kant would say, from the moment the proper experience occurs to evoke them if only as a potentiality that may be developed. Antiempiricism is manifest in some of the recent neo-Kantians or, as they at times prefer to describe themselves, structuralists. One does not arrive at such prerequisites or forms of experience through empirical examination of the contents of experience, though one may do so by examining how the content is organized. Postulation and deduction are the more usual tools of the neo-Kantian. However, the possible existence of inherited or innate forms and predispositions become empirical subject matter for the biological sciences. There are some indications of con-

vergence between the recent forms of rationalism and the new branch of zoology called ethology, especially as incorporated in the new biological synthesis, sociobiology.

Although the scientific study of animal behavior has roots in the work of Darwin[74] and other nineteenth-century biologists, it was relatively undeveloped until Konrad Z. Lorenz founded modern ethology, when in the 1930s he began to systematically apply biological research methods to the analysis of animal behavior. Nikolaas Tinbergen wrote the first contemporary text in ethology and E. H. Hess and Irenäus Eibl-Eibesfeld have summarized its approach to behavior.[75] The most extensive application of ethological principles and interpretations to human social behavior have been made by sociobiologists Edward O. Wilson and David Barash and by sociologist Pierre van den Berghe.[76]

The object of ethology is to explain both the ontogenetic and phylogenetic components of behavior resulting in the reliable prediction of the behavior of a living system in any situation. Ethologists are primarily interested in the behavior of a species under natural conditions. Their basic method rests on the compiling of an *ethogram* (action catalogue) of the species — a description of behavior that is possible throughout the animal's life cycle. Even when ethologists extend this procedure

---

[72]*Ibid.*, p. 40.
[73]*Ibid.*, pp. 156–157.

[74]Charles Darwin, *The Expression of Emotions in Man and Animals* (1872); (reprint ed., Chicago: University of Chicago Press, 1965).
[75]Nikolaas Tinbergen, *The Study of Instinct* (Oxford: Clarendon, 1951); Echard H. Hess, "Ethology: An Approach Toward the Complete Analysis of Behavior," *New Directions in Psychology* (New York: Holt, 1962), pp. 157–266; Irenäus Eibl-Eibesfeldt, *Ethologie: Die Biologie des Verhantens*, V, 341–549 in *Handbuch der Biologie*, edited by Ludwig von Bertalanffy (Potsdam: Akademische Verlagsgesellschaft Athenaion, 1966). Translated as *Ethology, The Biology of Behavior* (New York: Holt, Rinehart & Winston, 1975).
[76]Edward O. Wilson, *Sociobiology: The New Synthesis* (Cambridge: Harvard University Press, 1975); Pierre L. van den Berghe, *Man in Society* (New York: Elsevier, 1975); David Barash, *Sociobiology and Behavior* (New York: Elsevier, 1977).

to aspects of human social behavior they avoid, in principle, any subjective interpretations and reflections about inaccessible psychic materials. Observation of the animal in its natural habitat is desirable, an objective most easily realized when the animal is tame but unconfined. In the comparison of wild with domesticated species, Lorenz observed, a deterioration of species preserving patterns occurs — a phenomenon important to human beings inasmuch as they first domesticated themselves before domesticating other creatures.[77]

A fundamental task of the ethologist is to ascertain what in behavior may be due to genetic preprogramming and what may be a product of learning. By the middle of the eighteenth century the maturation of instincts had been discovered. Information that is stored in the genes may guide learning in a manner favoring survival. But such preprogrammed behavior may only become manifest as the organism matures. Among the methods developed by ethologists for isolating learned from innate components of behavior is the deprivation experiment: withholding from the young organism information concerning givens of its natural environment, but not, of course, the stimulus for a given type of behavior. This may permit determination of "whence the organism has obtained the information underlying a given adaptedness of behavior."[78]

Sociobiology is a specialization of ethology concentrating on the innate and learned facts in social or intraspecific behavior. In the classic conception of evolution, species development was primarily a problem of individual survival. However, in social behavior sometimes the individual creature sacrifices itself for the group. This would seem to mean that in time all the altruists disappear, leaving only the egotists. The question this raises is how complex social communities sometimes require massive sacrifice of individuals for the community, as may occur in insect societies. The answer by the sociobiologists, summarized by Wilson, is that when genes basic to altruistic behavior are shared by two or more organisms because of common descent, and when the sacrificial act of one increases the joint contribution to the next generation, "the propensity to altruism will spread through the gene pool."[79] Wilson speaks in such cases of "inclusive fitness" rather than individual fitness: and feels that it applies after a fashion to human beings as well as to lower organisms. The human mind, he feels, is moved in part by "the intuitive calculus of blood ties and proportionate altruism."[80]

Van den Berghe accepted the view that human social cultural behavior is a product of the interplay of biogenetical and environmental factors. He believes that human beings have innate tendencies to maintain families and religion and transform biological propensities (to aggression, hierarchy, and territoriality) in the creation of dominance hierarchies and complex political systems. However, in view of the fact that the ethology of human behavior is still in its infancy and little is known for certain about the character of innate human propensities and powers, approaches such as van den Berghe's at best formulate a program for future research. Lorenz expressed a basic caution:

> In order correctly to appreciate how indispensable cultural rites and social norms really are, one must keep in mind that, as Arnold Gehlen has put it, man is by nature a being of culture. In other words, man's whole system of innate activities and reactions is phylogenetically so constructed, so "calculated" by evolution, as to *need* to be complemented by cultural tradition.[81]

The convergence of the ethobiologists and such neo-Kantians as Jung, Lévi-Strauss, and

[77]Konrad Lorenz, *Studies in Animal and Human Behavior* (London: Methuen, 1971), II, 193.
[78]Konrad Lorenz, *Evolution and the Modification of Behavior* (Chicago: University of Chicago Press, 1965), p. 84.
[79]Edward O. Wilson, *Sociobiology*, p. 4. See also Barash, *Sociobiology of Behavior*, p. 81.
[80]Wilson, *Sociobiology*, pp. 119–120.
[81]Konrad Lorenz, *On Aggression*, translated by Marjorie Kerr Wilson (New York: Harcourt, Brace & World, 1966), pp. 264–265; Arnold Gehlen, *Der Mench, seine Natur und seine Stellung in der Welt* (Berlin: Junker und Dürrhaupt, 1940).

Chomsky upon a common problem is seen clearly by Chomsky.

> The study of language falls naturally within human biology. . . . Given the role of language in human life and probably human evolution, and given its intimate relations to what I have been calling "common-sense understanding," it would not be very surprising to discover that other systems within cognitive capacity have something of the character of the language faculty and its products. . . . Furthermore, as a number of biologists have pointed out, something of the sort is to be expected on simple evolutionary grounds. Citing Lorenz, Gunther Stent points out that Darwinian considerations offer a "biological underpinning" to a kind of Kantian epistemology, but in addition, these considerations concerning the evolutionary origin of the brain explain "not only why our innate concepts match the world but also why these concepts no longer work so well when we attempt to fathom the world in its deepest scientific aspects."[82]

There have been, in short, fascinating recent developments in the neo-Kantian approaches to the social sciences that pose research problems that the ethologists and sociobiologists may be best equipped to solve.

SUMMARY

The two earliest schools of sociology were predominantly conservative in orientation. They were interested in groups rather than individuals. The values of stability, order, and solidarity repeatedly appeared as social objectives.

One could well have expected some change with the professionalization and institutionalization of sociology. Once the role of sociologists became established among the accepted academic positions, recruitment could take place purely in terms of the role itself rather than in terms of prevailing ideological atmospheres. Sooner or later, liberals would appear among the ranks of sociologists with the demand for a theory of society more suited to their requirements.

Neo-Kantianism was one of the first examples of a liberal theory of society in sociological circles. Kant had been heir to eighteenth-century liberalism. Society was not, for him, an organic form that swallowed up the individual, but an ordered community of independent wills. Kant shrank from the view that the external system of government had to be the antithesis of the individual. Rather, this system might provide the very condition for the full realization of the nature of humanity. Law was thrust into central position as the basis of an ordered liberal theory of society and the new school of sociological formalism developed ties with jurisprudence, as may be illustrated by the social theories of Rudolf Stammler.

The new school of sociological formalism came into its own with the theories of Georg Simmel. He even attempted to carry out a Kantian type of analysis directly in his study, "How Is Society Possible?" He tried to deduce the a priori condition making society possible as an entity in which the individual is simultaneously realized and surpassed. The concept of "calling" or "role" was thought to be this form. This was Simmel's only attempt to deduce a system of a priori forms. For the rest, he rejected the organismic concept of society, treating it merely as interaction analyzable into form and content. The systematic study of social forms was set down as the objective of sociological study. Simmel carried out many intuitively rich studies of forms such as sociability, coquetry, secrecy, superiority, and subordination and conflict.

The neo-Kantian position migrated to France, where it found its most imaginative exponent in Bouglé, who also posed the task of sociology in formalistic terms. Like Simmel, Bouglé had the capacity for unusually subtle analysis of social events as revealed in his study of *caste*. More than any other single study, this essay laid the basis for the modern theory of caste.

In America, neo-Kantian formalism found able exponents in E. A. Ross and Park and Burgess, who utilized a mechanism of forms as the founda-

[82]Chomsky, *Reflections on Language*, pp. 123–124.

tion for the most nearly systematic general sociology to be achieved at the time. The fullest development of neo-Kantian formalism was the work of Leopold von Wiese, who tried to integrate the entire field of sociology in formalistic terms. Though this enterprise was bolstered by elaborate positivistic analogies and pseudo-mathematical formulas, the actual procedure consisted in a patient collection of terms with apparent social importance. These terms were then consolidated in lists and assembled in tables in terms of the presumed type and amount of association they were thought to signify.

Meanwhile, so far as neo-Kantian formalism remains a vital position in the contemporary world, its ablest exponents are found not in sociology but in jurisprudence, as illustrated by Hans Kelsen; in psychiatry, illustrated by C. J. Jung; in anthropology, illustrated by Claude Lévi-Strauss; and in linguistics, illustrated by Noam Chomsky. The most recent neo-Kantian development — the search for underlying powers, faculties assumed to be innate and shaping the scope and limits in various areas of culture — has converged with new developments in the biological sciences represented by ethology and sociobiology. Pierre van den Berghe has already moved into the vacuum to formulate a sociological position from this point of view. As could be expected, a formulation that so directly challenges an assumption of the traditional liberal ideology (that human nature has unlimited plasticity) has been a major source of controversy — one of the symptoms of vitality in an area of theory.

The convergence of the neo-Kantian analysis of sociocultural experience and sociobiology has in it the potential to draw the social sciences together once more — if it proves to be true that there are genetically preprogrammed deep structures at the basis of human behavior, they could not be expected to operate in the field of any one social science, but across the social sciences. Moreover, not only would the social and biological sciences be drawn more closely together, but the methodology of the social sciences could well be enriched in the process.

XIII

The Conceptual Foundations
of Social Behaviorism

Social behaviorism was the rival school to formalism to arise in sociological theory at the time when sociology was undergoing professionalization and institutionalization. The term *social behaviorism* is borrowed from George Herbert Mead and applied to the whole school of which Mead occupied only one branch. The school worked with a behavioral definition of the materials of sociological science, in contrast to the structural definition of organismic positivism and conflict theory, on the one hand, and to the relational definition of the formalists, on the other. It attempted to devise new empirical methods of sociological study, avoiding both the methodological weaknesses of the early schools and the antiempirical tendencies in formalism. While this general characterization holds for the whole school, three separate branches of social behaviorism can be distinguished by their special analyses of social behavior and their special methodological emphases.

THE PROBLEM OF THE FORMALISTS

The demand for a delimited and precisely defined subject matter in sociology called forth sociological formalism. The new formula for sociology bore many interesting contrasts to organismic positivism and conflict theory. Organismic positivism claimed to be the general science of the social; formalism claimed to be a very special science. Organismic positivism found the basic units of sociological analysis in entire societies; formalism rejected such units as fictitious, finding its basic units in subjectively apprehended "forms." Organismic positivism advanced a conservative image of social phenomena; formalism was deeply rooted in the liberal traditions. Organismic positivism combined a conservative image of society with a positivism of method; formalism at first tried to fuse a liberal idea of society with a positivistic method in a manner which quickly proved to be unstable. The basic antipositivism of the formalists could not be permanently concealed. The clarification of its presence and implications in considerable measure accounted for the internal evolution of formalism and the transition from a neo-Kantian to a phenomenological form.

There were, in fact, two fundamental problems that quickly emerged to haunt the formalists. Neither has ever been satisfactorily solved. (1) The separation of form and content has not been adequately justified, and (2) sociological formalism shows the repeated tendency to turn into a nonempirical discipline. In any case, it modified early positivism without supplying a defensible substitute.

The dualisms of phenomena and noumena and form and content were critical to the Kantian synthesis of modern philosophic thought. No one remained happy with the distinctions for long. The attempt to solve the problems they created led to the mysticism and panlogism of Hegel. When the neo-Kantians developed a modified Kantianism, a half-dozen interpretations of form appeared. In neo-Kantian treatments, the form–content dualism was transposed from a metaphysical into a methodological type.

When Simmel applied the form–content dichotomy to sociological problems, it carried with it a host of new issues. Simmel himself recognized that the distinction between form and content had new significance when applied to social data, but he offered no solutions to the new issues he raised. To make matters worse, many of Simmel's most brilliant results were attained by ignoring the distinction between form and content, comparing a wide variety of different situations. But by implication, if one established the forms by inductive analysis of comparative events, the sociological forms were not of a different character from the contents of interhuman life. Simmel suggested that in contrast to the Kantian "forms" of "nature," which are imposed on nature as experienced by the observer, the "forms" of "society" are parts of the internal structure of the matters they shape. The forms of nature are imposed from the outside; the forms of society arise from within.[1]

But the implications of this difference were not explored. This means either that there is no methodological difference between form and content after all, or that both, though different from each other, are "subjective" and outside the "externalistic" procedures of natural science. In any case there is no doubt of the validity of Vierkandt's judgment: Simmel did not achieve a purely formal analysis.

To the degree that one retains the distinction between form and content and attempts to carry out a "pure" formal analysis, one's enterprise tends to turn in a nonempirical direction. If the fundamental forms are actually a priori, one need not analyze a wide variety of diverse experiences to discover them. Vierkandt again has a point: one does not discover "forms" in this manner, at least if one accepts the distinction in the Kantian manner. Vierkandt proposed phenomenology as the missing method that would make a "pure" sociology possible. Formal sociology was simultaneously transformed into a nonempirical discipline. But what is the status of findings made by use of the phenomenological method? If these are treated as hypotheses and solved by inductive study, there is no difference between phenomenological and inductive method after all. However, if one can do this, one has not truly applied the phenomenological method.

A series of tough problems is left over for both versions of formal sociology, neo-Kantian or phenomenological. It is no help to cast up a smoke screen over the issue, as von Wiese did in offering a schema of pseudomathematical formulas, or to bury them, as Gurvitch does, under an elaborate mechanism of depth levels of sociological analysis. Thus for all its splendid gains in elevating to paramount consideration the theory of social rela-

[1]There are shades of Dilthey in this argument. Dilthey had drawn the distinction between knowledge in the natural sciences, which is "external," and knowledge in the cultural sciences, which is "internal."

tions, formal sociology left a veritable mare's nest of new issues. The demand that gave rise to formal sociology remained unsatisfied. The process of professionalization was still going on, and the requirement of a precise definition of sociological subject matter only became more urgent.

NEO-IDEALISM

In the continued search for an adequate definition of sociological subject matter, some possibilities had been eliminated. Total organic units had proved to be too vague to serve precise analysis. Biologistic entities had led to the multiplication of analogies that began to appear a bit silly. Besides, with the downfall of evolutionism they lost much of their original appeal. Conflict definitions were uncomfortably close to social ideologies. Formalistic definitions of sociological subject matter were also proving to be inadequate. There was strong inclination to search Western thought for points of view allowing one to avoid relapsing into empty formalism or dilution into vague all-inclusive psychic entities of one sort or another.

Rudolf Hermann Lotze. Some forms of idealism were being developed that did not take anti-scientific form. Rudolf Hermann Lotze (1817–1881) was in the forefront of this development. He was born in the Bautzen district, from which Lessing and Fichte had come. He had studied philosophy, medicine, and physics under E. H. Weber, A. W. Volkmann, and Gustav Fechner, making firsthand acquaintance with scientific methods. He graduated as doctor of philosophy and medicine, and after working some years at Leipzig, he succeeded Johann Friedrich Herbart in his professorship at Göttingen. Important works include *Mikrokosmus* and *System der Philosophie.*[2]

[2]*Mikrokosmus: Ideen zur Naturgeschichte und Geschicte der Menschheit* (Leipzig: 1856–1864), translated by Elizabeth Hamilton and E. E. Constance Jones as *Microcosmus: An Essay Concerning Man and His Relation to the World* (4th ed.,

Lotze's training in philosophic idealism and scientific materialism bore fruit in his attempt to fuse them. Moreover, as a medical writer, he tried to maintain physiology as a mechanical science of nature. Natural forms appear in organisms as everywhere in nature. Organic life is not something higher than mechanics, but merely a particular way in which mechanical forces operate. However, mechanism is only one aspect of nature, and in *Microkosmus* Lotze attempted to develop a psychology that would harmonize with physiology, the history of culture, cosmology, and the philosophy of religion.

To Lotze, the spiritual was the highest aspect of humanity. He theorized that mechanical laws and causes are necessary for the realization of these highest spiritual ideals. A plurality of elements in reciprocal interaction is the foundation of a mechanical conception of nature. However, the mechanical conception of nature cannot encompass all aspects of nature, for it cannot go beyond a manifold of atoms in reciprocal action; it results in a pluralism. Beyond the relations of atoms are relations of elements and their interconnections. Thus, for Lotze, the concepts of causal relation and reciprocal action (basic to the mechanical conception of nature) lead to the idea of an original substance, or all-embracing principle, which he called the "ultimate postulate" or "ultimate fact of thought." This, he believed, was presupposed even in the simplest case of reciprocal action.

Lotze was an atomist, but he did not think of the

New York: Scribner's, 1897), *System der Philosophie* (Leipzig: 1874–1879) is not available in English translation. *Outlines of Psychology* has been translated by C.L. Herrick (New York: Arno Press, 1973). Also important is the republication of George Santayana's *Lotze's System of Philosophy* (Bloomington, Indiana: Indiana University Press, 1971). Studies of his work are contained in: G. Stanley Hall, *Founders of Modern Psychology* (New York: D. Appleton, 1912); E. E. Thomas, *Lotze's Theory of Reality* (New York: Longmans, Green, 1921); and Harald Høffding, *A History of Modern Philosophy*, trans. B. E. Meyer (New York: Macmillan, 1935), II, 516–524. See also John Passmore, *A Hundred Years of Philosophy* (New York: Penguin Books, 1978), pp. 49–51.

atoms as material. Extension and other sensory qualities in themselves result from the reciprocal action of atoms. The atoms must not possess such qualities. Like life, the sensory fact of extension emerges from the cooperation of points of force. The atoms must be conceived as starting points of the inner working of infinite primal being.

The mechanical conception of nature explains only the mutual relation of elements, not inner nature. To arrive at the notion of the inner nature of elements, we must conceive of these elements by analogy with our own inner nature. Atoms must be feeling beings in a more primitive form. We must assume that the elements of the universe are animated in various degrees. Inner states are bound together into a unity. Our own inner spiritual life is the only example known to us of the possibility of the preservation of unity in the midst of fluctuating states. Thus the world principle is to be conceived as absolute personality. Absolute being must be personal, for personality alone possesses inner independence and originality. Personal life involves resistance to be overcome and the faculty of suffering.

In summary, on such bases, Lotze developed a spiritualistic psychology. He argued that psychical phenomena must either be derived from a soul or explained by the cooperation of physical forces. But the second alternative is excluded by the fact that reciprocal action of physical forces cannot explain the unity of even the simplest expression of psychical life. There are areas in which the soul is influenced by physical events; outside these, it is determined by its own laws. The material organisms work in service of spiritual activities by supplying the material on which the soul exercises its force. Given the material, spiritual activities such as memory, thought, and aesthetic and moral feeling can operate. Despite all the unpromising aspects of Lotze's view, there is one aspect of basic importance for further development: the psychical and physical are being brought together in a way that particularly invites investigation. The basis is being laid for a scientific psychology. An idealistic philosophy and a wide-ranging scientific knowledge are being brought together.

Gustav Fechner.   This integration of idealism and science opened the way for a new departure in scientific psychology, which was as significant for psychology as positivistic organicism was for sociology. The potential was already evident in the work of Lotze. The actual transition to a quantitative psychology was made by Gustav Theodor Fechner (1801–1887). Fechner, born at Lausitz, also studied medicine and physics. In 1835 he became professor of physics. In 1839–1840 he contracted a disease of the eyes which eventually forced the abandonment of his professorship. His interests turned at this time to philosophy.[3]

Høffding compares Fechner to Kepler in the employment of bold, imaginative speculation which led to positive exact results. Fechner was led to the conviction that there is a definite quantitative relation between the mental and material. In working out the idea, he became the founder of psychophysics or experimental psychology.

Fechner's general theory is very similar to Lotze's. The mechanical and nonmechanical worlds must differ in degree rather than in kind, for the phenomena of mind and animation could not be derived from a purely mechanical world when this is conceived as the antithesis of mind. The consciousness of plants must be as much lower than that of animals as that of animals is below that of human beings. There is no good reason why the heavenly bodies should not also be animated. Lower souls may be related to higher ones, as are

---

[3]Fechner's best-known book is *Elemente der Psychophysik* ["Elements of Psychophysics"] (Leipzig: 1860). For Fechner's views on religion, see Gustav Fechner, *Religion of a Scientist*, ed. and trans. Walter Lowrie (New York: Pantheon Books, 1946). General accounts of his theories as set forth in such books as *Elemente der Psychophysik, Die drei Motive und Gründe des Glaubens* ["The Three Motives and Bases of Belief"] (Leipzig: 1863), *Über die physikalische und philosophische Atomenlehre* ["Concerning the Physical and Philosophical Doctrine of the Atom"] (Leipzig: 1864), and *Vorschule der Aesthetik* ["Introduction to Aesthetics"] (Leipzig: 1876), can be found in: Harald Høffding, *A History of Modern Philosophy*, Vol. 2; G. Stanley Hall, *Founders of Modern Psychology*; and John Theodore Merz, *A History of European Thought in the Nineteenth Century* (Edinburgh: 1896–1914), Vol. 2, Ch. 11.

ideas and motives to particular souls. All souls must be part of the highest embracing soul, whose life and reality are manifest in the causal law, the principle of interconnection and order in the world.

The program of a psychophysics is visualized. The difference between mental and material, Fechner reasoned, cannot be that between two beings. The material world is the outer, the spiritual the inner side of events. The difference between them is phenomenal, depending on the standpoint of the spectator. It is like the concave and convex side of the same circle. Consciousness is in reciprocal relation to external events. The sum total of physical energy at our disposal is sometimes used one way, sometimes another. Physical energy may be consumed when we do physical work or when we think. Both cannot be done equally well at the same time. There must be a mathematical-functional relation between the two sides of existence. The mental does not rise or fall in simple proportion to the material, but changes in the former correspond to proportional changes in the latter. The change in intensity of a mental state is determined by the relation between the change of energy in the corresponding material state and previously existing energy. (The intensity of a sensation equals a constant times the logarithm of a stimulus, or, symbolically, $S = K \log R$.)[4] Formulations had now been made which could be phrased as exact hypotheses subject to experimental test. Fechner found that the intensity of the sensation of a light does not increase as quickly as the intensity of a physical stimulus. Fechner called this "Weber's Law," after its discoverer. He tried experimentally to investigate the relation between activities of the mind and corresponding events of the brain. Serious laboratory testing had begun!

Eduard von Hartmann. A third member of this group was strongly influenced by Schopenhauer,

forming a transition between Schopenhauer and Freud. Eduard von Hartmann (1842–1906) was born in Berlin, the son of an army general. Though slated for a military career, he devoted his leisure to music, painting, and philosophy. When, in 1865, a knee infection forced his retirement from military service, he began to occupy himself with philosophizing and essay writing. His most famous book was his *Philosophie des Unbewussten* (1869); of nearly thirty additional works, *Phänomenologie des sittlichen Bewusstseins* (1879) is most important.[5]

Whereas Lotze and Fechner took the scientific mode of explanation as fundamental and attempted to establish their thought on a scientific basis, Hartmann partly represents a neo-romantic reaction. His aim was to show that scientific explanation is not sufficient. Beside the causes assumed by the mechanical conception of nature, we must assume a spiritual principle. Matter, to be sure, must be conceived as a system of atomic forces. But interconnection and coherence require an additional principle such as the striving of a will and the unconscious idea of an end. Force at bottom is a will. In organic growth an unconscious will is manifest, for the organism realizes an unconscious end. Between organic and instinctive action there is only a difference in quantity. Instinct is neither an automatic mechanism nor conscious reasoning but a manifestation of will. All mental life ultimately rests on feelings and motives produced by the unconscious.

> Conscious reasoning is only denying, criticizing, controlling, correcting, measuring, comparing, combining, classifying, inducing the general form from the

---

[4]This general concept is expressed in various formulas; see *Elemente der Psychophysik*, II, 96 ff.

[5]*Philosophie des Unbewussten* (Berlin: 1869) was translated by William Chatterton Coupland as *Philosophy of the Unconscious* (New York: Harcourt, Brace, 1931). *Phänomenologie des sittlichen Bewusstseins* ["Phenomenology of the Moral Consciousness"] (Berlin: 1879) is not available in English translation. Summaries of Hartmann's views are contained in Hall, *Founders of Modern Psychology*, pp. 181–243, and Høffding, *A History of Modern Philosophy*, II, 532–540.

particular, ordering the particular case according to
the general rule, but it is never creatively productive,
never inventive. Here man is entirely dependent on
the unconscious, and were he to lose the faculty by
which he receives inspiration from the unconscious,
he would lose the spring of his life, without which he
would drag out a monotonous existence entangled in
the dry schematism of the general and particular.
Hence the unconscious is *indispensable* to him, and
woe to the age which, in one-sided over-estimate of
the consciously reasoned, listens to the latter only,
and violently suppresses the unconscious.[6]

In the attack and defense that *Philosophy of the
Unconscious* called forth, Hartmann made many
concessions to his critics. He admitted that he had
underrated mechanical causes. He also provided
more place for the scientific method, though he
tended to limit it to the task of filling in gaps in his
theories and confirming the results his speculation
had turned up. In his ethical studies Hartmann
developed a peculiar type of pessimism and attempted to reconcile the philosophies of Hegel
and Schopenhauer by combining Hegel's "absolute
idea" with Schopenhauer's "will."

One effect of this continued evolution of
idealistic philosophy upon sociology has already
been noted. The modification of the antiscientific
aspects of early voluntaristic idealism made possible a major subdivision of the development of organismic positivism. However, the influence did
not stop here. New syntheses of idealism and scientific methodology were opening up the possibilities of a laboratory psychology. Hence, when
sociology began to search for a new definition of
subject matter in neo-Kantianism and found itself
with major problems on its hands, it tended to review the idealistic traditions which were themselves
undergoing change. The lesson of the Lotze-
Fechner school was that it was possible to have a
delimited idealistic definition of spiritual material
that was capable of scientific study.

6*Philosophy of the Unconscious*, II, 42.

NEO-HEGELIANISM

Neo-Hegelianism is actually a form of neo-
idealism, distinguished by its ties to Hegel. It was
perhaps crucial to the attempt by idealists such as
Lotze and Fechner to construct neo-idealism on
a realistic-scientific basis that the collapse of
Hegelianism had been so complete. In many respects, these thinkers were almost pre-Kantian in
attitude and inclination, bearing more similarities
to Spinoza and Leibnitz than to Hegel and his
school. But precisely this detachment from Hegelianism was a component in the attempt to
carry out their idealistic programs scientifically.

Once the fusion of idealism and scientific
method had been launched, the modern forms of
neo-idealism were able to make further contributions to the social sciences. This has already been
made apparent in the adaptation of various
philosophies of human unconscious life to the
needs of social science. For Schopenhauer and
Nietzsche, science was concerned only with relatively superficial aspects of human life. To
Nietzsche, the scientist was a paradigm of the
hated mass person. In Eduard von Hartmann's
interpretation of the significance of will for human
conduct, despite some of the suspicion of science
carried over from Schopenhauer and Nietzsche,
the position was gradually opened to the reception
of science. Under critical attack, Hartmann yielded
ground and provided space for scientific method.
By the time we reach the theories of Pareto and
Freud, all this has been reversed and theories of
the importance of the individual's unconscious life
are advanced on strongly positivistic grounds.

Once the integration of a scientific program and
idealistic theories of human psychic life had been
started by the school deriving from Lotze and
Fechner, the social sciences also received new ideas
from other idealistic schools, despite their antiscientific bias. This was true of the neo-Hegelian
movement.

Francis H. Bradley. The outstanding neo-
Hegelian in England was Francis Herbert Bradley

(1846–1924). Bradley studied at Oxford and lived in retirement as fellow of Merton College from 1876 to the end of his life. Philosophically, Bradley was convinced that true reality is spirit, which is one and identical with itself. One of the key problems to which Bradley addressed himself was the relation of this reality to the world of experience.[7] When the spirit is conceived as one and self-identical, there seems to be no way of getting to experience from it. Experience becomes a world of illusion, of mere appearance. Between the eternal and the temporal, between the absolute and the contingent, mediation is impossible. Hence Bradley turns the full force of his subtle dialectical criticisms on the concept of *relation* which had been employed to hold the two worlds together. Experience concerns finite things. Every finite thing, however, presents the contradictions that it is only finite in itself in relation to other things. Thus no object of experience is self-determined and self-contained, but is embedded in external relations. Every finite thing is self-transcendent, alienated, and passing away from itself toward another thing. The finite is mere appearance. Applied to persons, this means that no person is complete in himself or herself. Individuals are completed only in the process that transcends the self leading to the other. Bradley's work was important in discrediting individualistic forms of the English philosophy of experience. The ideological individualism associated with the hedonistic utilitarianism of Bentham and James Mill was sharply attacked. Only by integration of the individual into a larger whole can the true self be found. The problem of the self is being posed in modern form.

Josiah Royce. The single most important idealist in the United States was Josiah Royce (1855–1916). Although he was a neo-Hegelian, he developed a highly individualized form of the position. Born and educated in California, Royce came under the influence of Joseph Le Conte, a pupil of Agassiz. His thinking was determined primarily by Kant, Hegel, the Romantics, and Schopenhauer. He was a teacher at Harvard University for thirty-four years. The first full expression of his ideas was contained in *The World and the Individual.*[8]

Royce's basic problem concerned the nature of Being. He argued that in addition to the brute facts, experience also possesses ideal properties: meanings. The purpose embodied in any idea Royce conceived as its "internal meaning." The idea also has "external meaning." The idea resembles or corresponds to facts wholly beyond itself. In the conflict of the immediate and ideal aspect of experience, Being appears as that which we first regarded as real in advance of more special definitions. It is not a transient phenomenon. Being is something "Other" than the finite ideas which seek it, for ideas seek Being as that which when completely known will fullfill them and end their doubts. As a fragment, the idea looks elsewhere for the rest of itself. An idea seeking its Other, seeks only the expression of its own will in an empirical conscious life. The theory of Being requires us to view every fact of nature and of human life as a fragmentary glimpse of the Absolute life, as a revelation of the unity of the perfect whole. Science does not give us either a complete or adequate picture of reality, for it suggests that the ultimately real is material substance. When we deal with nature we deal with a realm of consciousness of which our own is a part and example.

The self, for Royce, is not a thing, but a meaning embodied in a conscious life. Its individuality implies the essential uniqueness of this life. Its unity transcends what we find presented in consciousness. The true individual self receives final

---

[7]Important works of Bradley's are: *Ethical Studies* (London: 1876); *The Principles of Logic* (London: 1883); and *Appearance and Reality* (London: 1893).

[8]Josiah Royce, *The World and the Individual,* 2 vols. (New York: Macmillan, 1900–1901). Royce's other principal works are: *Studies of Good and Evil* (New York: D. Appleton, 1898); *Outlines of Psychology* (New York: Macmillan, 1903); *The Philosophy of Loyalty* (New York: Macmillan, 1908); *The Problem of Christianity* (New York: Macmillan, 1913); *The Hope of the Great Community* (New York: Macmillan, 1916); and *Lectures on Modern Idealism* (New Haven, Conn.: Yale University Press, 1919).

expression in some form of consciousness different from that which we now possess. For each of us, the absolute self is God. However, we still retain our individuality and our distinction from one another just so far as our life spans extend. By the very nature of their social basis, people possess mutually contrasting life-plans, each one of which can reach its own fulfillment only by recognizing other life-plans as different from its own. The inclusion of the individual will in the divine will is the assurance of individual freedom. The problem of freedom is the final problem of individuality.

In Hegel's thought, the whole, the "concrete universal," tends to swallow up the individual. Royce rejected the idea that one must choose between the life of the whole and individual freedom, but insisted that neither could be had without the other. It is only in the development of the individual that the life of the whole can properly be expressed. In extension with these ideas, Royce believed that the individual is not a closed moral unity, nor are societies made up of these. Rather, social consciousness is a necessary condition of self-consciousness. These ideas were extended into the notion that the self is a community and the community a self. The universe itself was viewed as an ideal community. In all such respects Royce made a basic contribution to the reconceptualization of the relation of the self and the community.

Wilhelm Wundt. Wilhelm Wundt (1832–1920), who taught at the universities of Heidelberg, Zurich, and Leipzig, was a man of extraordinary encyclopedic knowledge who made contributions to a whole range of theoretical and experimental sciences. He is best known for contributions to the development of experimental psychology and folk psychology. In philosophy, he contributed to the shift from positivism through neo-Kantianism to greater emphasis upon totality and organic relations. Commenting on the influence of Wundt's *Ethik* (1886), Vierkandt sums it up as follows:

. . . He not only assailed utilitarianism but insisted upon the reality of a general will and supported Hegel in the precedence over the individual which he

gave to objective forms and institutions, such as the state. He considered psychology as more than a special discipline; to him it was the foundation of all knowledge of the intellectual and spiritual world and the intermediary between natural science and philosophy. His psychological views reflected the change from an atomistic and analytical conception to one which was more unified and organic. . . .[9]

Stimulated by Fechner and Ernst Heinrich Weber, Wundt established the Psychological Institute, from which stemmed the experimental trend in American psychology; G. Stanley Hall and James McKeen Cattell studied there.

Wundt's sociological thought is closely bound up with his psychological system. "Will," or "conation," was located at the center of his psychological interpretations as the synthesizing and integrating aspect of psychic life. This integrating power is found in the phenomenon of "apperception,"

[9]*Encyclopedia of the Social Sciences* (New York: Macmillan, 1931), XV, 506. Wilhelm Wundt's major works include: *Grundzüge der physiologischen Psychologie* (Leipzig: W. Engelmann, 1874; 6th ed., 1908–1911), the fifth revised edition (1902–1903) of which was translated by Edward B. Titchener as *Principles of Physiological Psychology* (New York: Macmillan, 1904); *Logik*, 2 vols. (Stuttgart: F. Enke, 1880–1883; 4th ed., 1919–1921); *Ethik* (Stuttgart: F. Enke, 1886; 4th ed., 1912), the second revised edition (1892) of which was translated by Edward B. Titchener, Julia H. Gulliver, and Margaret F. Washburn as *Ethics*, 3 vols. (New York: Macmillan, 1897–1901); *Grundriss der Psychologie* (Leipzig: 1896; 14th ed., Stuttgart: A. Kröner, 1920), of which three English translations have been made, the latest being Charles Hubbard Judd's translation of the 7th edition (1907), *Outlines of Psychology* (New York: G. E. Stechert, 1907); *Völkerpsychologie: Eine Untersuchung der Entwicklungsgesetze von Sprache, Mythus, und Sitte* ["Folk Psychology: An Investigation of the Developmental Laws of Speech, Myth, and Custom"], 10 vols. in 12 (Leipzig: W. Engelmann, 1900–1920); *Sprachgeschichte und Sprachpsychologie* ["The History and Psychology of Speech"] (Leipzig: W. Engelmann, 1901); *Allgemeine Geschichte der Philosophie* ["General History of Philosophy"] (Berlin: B. G. Teubner, 1909; 2d ed., 1913); and *Elemente der Völkerpsychologie* (Leipzig: A. Kröner, 1912), translated by Edward Leroy Schaub as *Elements of Folk Psychology* (New York: Macmillan, 1916). A summary of Wundt's earlier work appears in G. Stanley Hall, *Founders of Modern Psychology*.

which contrasts with perception: apperception adds a creative element to the external events that enter experience. This is the simplest example of the "creative synthesis" which functions throughout mental life.

Wundt draws a distinction between explanation in the natural and psychical realms. In interpreting natural phenomena, explanation is in terms of a hypothetical stable stratum. In the psychic realm, the real is directly experienced, no substratum beyond experience has any meaning. Causality has a different meaning in psychic process than in physical process. In natural events, cause and effect, action and reaction, are equal and opposite; in psychic events, there is transmutation and growth, and effects are greater than causes. While the causal principle operates differently in the psychical and the physical realms, it does not operate between them. There is rather a parallelism between the psychical and physical.

In more complex individual and social circumstances, the principle of creative synthesis is expressed in the "mutation of motives" and "heterogeneity of ends." Social forms are stable, but psychological motivation changes, and persisting forms are devoted to new purposes.

Wundt employed these ideas in the analysis of the problems of folk psychology, shifting the emphasis from the intellectual to emotional and intuitive factors. Human reaction to nature was conceived as an intuitive response described as "mythological apperception," the direct metaphorical grasp of natural events. The primitive apprehension of natural phenomena like lightning was not brought by reasoning into comparison with a snake but was apperceived as a snake. In parallel fashion, the primitive relation of individual and society was not one of reasoned receipt of society by the individual nor the rational projection of society by individuals. Rather, individuals were so closely determined by, and bound up with, their social setting as to be incapable of being understood without it. There is an unconscious functional relationship between individuals of a group so close that it is not possible to separate the elements from the psychological whole.

Three aspects of culture were thought by Wundt to be particularly subject to group penetration: language, myth, and custom. Wundt's *Völkerpsychologie* explored these areas. The first two volumes examined the problems of primitive languages. This was followed by a study of art, an examination of the history of human imagination. There followed three volumes on myth and religion, two on social organization, one on law, and a final volume on culture and history. Such materials were thought to have basic value for the study of psychology.

> Psychology needs the folk-psychological material comprised in certain social sciences not less urgently than the latter require a psychological foundation. As soon as psychology begins to exploit the sources which pour in upon it from the different spheres of psychic life, the contributions of psychology itself to the interpretation of individual facts, contributions derived from the broader contemplation of psychic life, will no longer remain unrecognized. For in one respect, at least, the most refined practical tact and the richest life-wisdom cannot come up to the achievements of scientific psychology. . . . The historian, linguist, and mythologist must operate with complex concepts. Only when a bridge has been built to span the gap between the individual mind and the psychic aspects of the social process does it become possible, by retracing one's steps, to apply folk-psychological conclusions to the scientific psychologist.[10]

In his briefer work, *The Elements of Folk Psychology*, Wundt described cultural areas that succeed each other in the history of culture. The evolution of the *Zeitgeist* is divided into four stages: (1) the period of primitive people, (2) the period of totemism, (3) the period of gods and heroes, and (4) the period of humanity. The first period was one more rudimentary than any now known among

[10]Translated from p. 29 of *Völkerpsychologie* (4th ed., Vol. 1) by Alexander Goldenweiser in "The Psychosociological Thought of Wilhelm Wundt," in Harry Elmer Barnes ed., *An Introduction to the History of Sociology* (Chicago: University of Chicago Press, 1948), p. 225, Footnote 9.

existing primitive peoples; it was arrived at by "psychological reconstruction." The totemic period was thought to be a stage of universal gentile society and the totemic complex. The age of heroes appears when human heroes replaced the totemic or deified animal of the totemic stage. The gods were introduced when social crises led to rationalization of experience. During this period of the age of gods and heroes, the state, property, and economic and social classes appeared. Moreover, individual personality was recognized and religion took on moral properties, becoming a social force. The stage of humanity arises with the great world empires and the development of a sense of mutual interdependence, humanity, and brotherhood.

The preservation and promotion of an idealistic point of view in Wundt's work is illustrated by his idea of the difference between psychic causality and physical causality. Psychic causality has effects which are never equal and opposite to causes. A perception, he argues, is never a mere sum of sensations. The significance of a perception is the synthesis of sensations. Psychical causality is creative, while physical causality is merely mechanical. Moreover, Wundt defended the parallelism of the psychic and physical. He argued that psychic processes cannot be derived from physical ones nor physical from psychic ones in the same causal sense in which we attempt to derive physical processes from other physical ones and psychic processes from other psychic ones. Such coexistence, of course, does not preclude the presence on the physical side of certain phenomena to which no psychic phenomenon corresponds, nor on the psychic side, of certain phenomena with reference to which no accompanying physical ones can either be demonstrated or conjectured, with any degree of probability.

The neo-Hegelians, who included not only Bradley and Royce and Wundt, but persons like Dilthey, had already begun to influence the sociologists. Dilthey and Wundt, for example, influenced Tönnies, Durkheim, and, to some degree, Simmel. But their primary importance for sociology was not here. As contributors to the idealistic traditions stemming from Hegel, they represent a restructuring of "holistic" forms of idealism. Even while carrying through brilliant criticisms, as did Bradley in England, of liberal individualism, the neo-Hegelians tended to modify Hegelianism to make a basic place for the problem of personality. Furthermore, the neo-Hegelians like Dilthey and Wundt advanced the study of cultural forms such as religion, myth, ethics, and language. Neo-Hegelianism also had a strong influence on that heavily "biologized" form of idealism known as pragmatism.

PRAGMATISM

Pragmatism does not represent a single unified body of philosophic ideas. Nevertheless it does not completely deserve the unfriendly estimate of Ruggiero: "Pragmatism was born in America, the country of 'business,' and is, par excellence, the philosophy of the business man." Fixing on the conception of the instrumental nature of ideas and truth — a view presented occasionally by Peirce, frequently by James, and constantly by John Dewey, Ruggiero argues: "Pragmatism is the logical conclusion and therefore the reductio ad absurdum of empiricism. If reality is sensation and the concept is merely the arbitrary abbreviation of sensible experience, the sole value of the concept will lie in its character as an arbitrary but convenient fiction." He continues: "That ideas should work is all very well, but in practice they always seem to be other people's ideas: if [philosophy] has any of its own it never gives them anything to do. Philosophy has vanished and we are on the brink of comedy, if not downright charlatanism." And so far as William James accepts the identification of truth and utility, Guido de Ruggiero asserts: "All the discordant tendencies of the pragmatist thesis are united in the personality of William James; a curious patchwork of good and evil, of seriousness and extravagance. But the strictly pragmatist basis of his thought represents a stage of decadence, a sterilization of a personality whose first appearance was far more complex and robust."[11] In view of the fact that James's concept of knowledge and truth was taken as the core of pragmatism in Italy, Ruggiero's reaction is understandable. After all, it was in this same land that Mussolini welcomed the designation "pragmatism" for his own political philosophy. The instrumental conception of knowledge and truth can easily degenerate into Machiavellian political expediency.

Bertrand Russell is strongly inclined to locate the core of pragmatism in the same place as Ruggiero, though recognizing greater diversities among the pragmatists. Russell tends to disapprove of it almost as much. Pragmatism, as it appears in James, he observes, is primarily a new definition of "truth." There were two other protagonists of pragmatism — F. C. S. Schiller and John Dewey. Schiller was of less importance than the other two. Between James and Dewey, there is a difference of emphasis. Dewey's outlook is scientific, and his arguments are largely derived from an examination of scientific method, but James is concerned primarily with religion and morals. According to Russell, James

> is prepared to advocate any doctrine which tends to make people virtuous and happy; if it does so, it is "true" in the sense in which he uses that word. The principle of pragmatism, according to James, was first enunciated by C. S. Peirce, who maintained that, in order to attain clearness in our thoughts of an object, we need only consider what conceivable effects of a practical kind the object may involve. . . . Ideas, we are told by James, become true in so far as they help us to get into satisfactory relations with other parts of our experience. . . . In a chapter on pragmatism and religion he reaps the harvest. "We cannot reject any hypothesis if consequences useful to life flow from it." "If the hypothesis of God works satisfactorily in the widest sense of the word, it is true." "We may well believe, on the proofs that religious experience affords, that higher powers exist and are at work to save the world on ideal lines similar to our own."[12]

One could hardly expect a first-rate logician like Russell to be other than shocked by the wholesale confusion of the requirements of action with the properties of thought. Moreover, even the friends of pragmatism have not always been altogether clear about what should be included in it. Horace Kallen states that it denotes an attitude of mind rather than a system of ideas. All such systems to which it is applied have in common certain fundamentals, such as plurality and diversity of things and thoughts, the primacy of change, movement and activity, the genuineness of novelty, and belief in immediate experience as the court of last resort in validating ideas. Kallen has also argued that in accounting for the differences between true and false, right and wrong, good and bad, beauty and ugliness, pragmatists employ the Darwinian notions of spontaneous variation and the struggle for survival.[13]

The vagueness of the statement of the nature of pragmatism by its proponents and the often contradictory estimates by its opponents, taken together with the powerful influence of pragmatism on American social science, are significant. Pragmatism was one of the many attempts to reconcile some of the premises of idealism with scientific method, and unite a spiritualistic and biological conception of human development. This is evident in both of its key figures, James and Dewey.

William James. William James (1842–1910) was the eldest of five children. When he was eighteen years old and his family was living in Newport, Rhode Island, he tried his hand at art. Tiring of this, he entered the Lawrence Scientific School of Harvard University, concentrating on chemistry and anatomy. He went on to study medicine at the Harvard Medical School. He interrupted his study to accompany Louis Agassiz in exploring the Amazon. His health failed, and he returned to study medicine for a term, then went on to Germany for

---

[11]Guido de Ruggiero, *Modern Philosophy*, 1st ed. trans. A. Howard Hannay and R. G. Collingwood (New York: Macmillan, 1921), pp. 252, 253, 254.
[12]Bertrand Russell, *A History of Western Philosophy* (Lon-

don: George Allen and Unwin, 1945; New York: Simon and Schuster, 1945), pp. 816–817.
[13]Horace M. Kallen, "Pragmatism," in *Encyclopaedia of the Social Sciences*, XII, 307.

WILLIAM JAMES

Harvard University Library, Cambridge, Mass.

courses with the physiologists Hermann Helmholtz and Claude Bernard and the pathologist Rudolf Virchow. While in Germany he suffered a nervous breakdown, during which he entertained thoughts of suicide. He returned home in 1868, took the M.D. degree, and lived in a state of semi-invalidism, experiencing a prolonged period of phobic panic relieved only when he read Renouvier on free will. The materialistic determinism of nineteenth-century science overwhelmed James with a sense of psychic oppression, and he resolved to make the first act of free will the abandonment of all determinism. In this personal drama there are comparisons with Max Weber's tragic sense of the disenchantment of the world. In 1872, James was appointed instructor in physiology at Harvard College, serving in this capacity until 1876. Around 1880 he began the researches that led to

the *Principles of Psychology* (1890), which was to establish the functional point of view in psychology. It also assimilated psychology to biology and treated intelligence as an instrument in the struggle to survive. While defending free will, James made use of the principles of psychophysics. With the completion of this work, he lost interest in psychology, and began to teach and write in ethics and religion, occupying himself with the existence of God, the immortality of the soul, free will and determinism, and the value of life. During these years James made increasing use of the "pragmatic rule" formulated by Peirce. The meaning of an idea, whether scientific, religious, philosophical, political-social, or personal, was to be found only in the experiential consequences to which it leads. Truth and error are identical with these consequences. This was applied to the study of religion, change, chance, freedom, variety, pluralism, and novelty. It was used against "monism" and the "block universe," against internal relations, against all finalities, completeness, and absolutes. In 1906, the Lowell Lectures were delivered in Boston. They were published as *Pragmatism: A New Name for Some Old Ways of Thinking.*[14]

The theoretical high point of James's thought may be found in the essay, "Does 'Consciousness' Exist?"[15] In it James denied that the subject–object relation is fundamental. The idea that in the occurrence of "knowing" there is a subject aware of an object or thing known had long been taken for granted. The knower was thought to be a mind or soul, the object was material or an essence or

[14]The most important works of William James for our purposes are: *Principles of Psychology*, 2 vols. (New York: Henry Holt, 1890); *The Will to Believe and Other Essays in Popular Philosophy* (New York: Longmans, Green, 1896); *Human Immortality* (Boston: Houghton Mifflin, 1898); *Talks to Teachers on Psychology and to Students on Some of Life's Ideals* (New York: Henry Holt, 1899); *Varieties of Religious Experience* (New York: Longmans, Green, 1902); *Pragmatism* (New York: Longmans, Green, 1907); *Essays in Radical Empiricism* (New York: Longmans, Green, 1912).
[15]First printed in the *Journal of Philosophy, Psychology and Scientific Methods*, 1 (September 1, 1904), 477–491; reprinted in *Essays in Radical Empiricism.*

another mind. A great deal of philosophy rested on this dualism of subject and object — the distinction of mind and matter, the contemplative ideal, and the traditional notion of "truth."[16]

James came to the conclusion that there is no "entity" to be called consciousness. Those who cling to the idea are hanging on to an echo, a faint rumor left behind by the disappearance of the soul from philosophy. There is no original being, contrasted with the being composing material objects, out of which thoughts of those objects are made. This does not mean that mind does not perform a function which can be called "being conscious." The primary stuff out of which everything is composed is "pure experience." Knowing is a peculiar sort of relation between two aspects of pure experience. The subject–object relation is derivative. A given portion of experience can in one context be knower, in another known. Pure experience is "the immediate flux of life which furnishes the material to our later reflection."[17]

At bottom, James was an idealist. The long road beginning with personal pathological reactions to the implications of materialistic determinism leads to the conception of a mentalistic proto-stuff of pure experience out of which both subject and object are mere differentiations. When one adds to this James's pragmatic rule, it is clear that he was anxious to procure a device that would permit him to accept mind as an independent reality. The rule in fact permitted him to accept anything that made him happy. Comte's mental hygiene was not nearly as effective. It is very doubtful whether even George Lundberg's semantic exorcism of mental ills has more utility as a device for self-confirmation. But in any case the conclusion is inescapable that pragmatism for James was a device for reconciling idealism with science.

John Dewey. The task of the reconciliation of idealism and science was ably carried forward by

John Dewey (1859–1952), also a New Englander. Dewey taught at the universities of Minnesota (1888–1889), Michigan (1889–1894), and Chicago (1894–1904). He first won fame as director of the School of Education at Chicago, where he established an experimental school and carried out the ideas of a new pedagogy, formulating principles that have revolutionized instruction and educational practice in America. For two years he lectured on education and philosophy at the University of Peking in China. The Turkish government engaged him to draw up a report on the organization of its national schools. After 1904, when he joined the department of philosophy at Columbia University, his influence began to penetrate philosophy.

Philosophically, Dewey's starting point was found in Hegel. He made, without any sense of conflict, the transition from German idealism to pragmatism under the influence of William James. From his neo-Hegelian starting point, Dewey retained to the end the sense of the central value of intelligence and the concept of mental activity as a process. There was a sort of parallel between Dewey's movement from neo-Hegelianism to pragmatism and Marx's transition from Hegel: Marx retained the Hegelian notions of process and development, but conceived them in terms of a thoroughgoing materialism; Dewey always retained the notions of intelligence and process, but "biologized" and "instrumentalized" them. The organism is constantly reconstructing the environment as well as being determined by it. Thought is an organ of response and instrument of behavior, not an entity in the older sense. James's pragmatic rule and Dewey's instrumentalism are cut from the same cloth. Similarly, Dewey conceives of the individual as in process of development. He was also impressed with the social process represented by the industrial revolution. A new curriculum was needed, adequate to the practice of the arts and discipline of industrial life. If they are to live in society, human beings must be studied as citizens, growing within a complex of interactions and relationships. Through education, individuals are made into images of their fel-

[16]See Russell's estimate, *History of Western Philosophy*, p. 812.
[17]It is easy to see why Russell describes James as an unconscious Berkeleian idealist, *ibid.*, p. 813.

lows in a process which, while reducing their uniqueness, extends the limits of possible development. Education is the instrument of social adjustment and of political and moral reconstruction, just as thought is the instrument of adjustment in the world.

In his *Logic*, the theoretically central point of Dewey's philosophy was expressed in his conception of inquiry. "Inquiry is the controlled or directed transformation of an indeterminate situation into one that is so determinate in its constituent distinctions and relations as to convert the elements of the original situation into a unified whole."[18] Russell not unfairly observes that inquiry, "as conceived by Dewey, is part of the general process of attempting to make the world more organic. 'Unified wholes' are to be the outcome of inquiries. Dewey's love of what is organic is due partly to biology, partly to the lingering influence of Hegel. Unless on the basis of an unconscious Hegelian metaphysic, I do not see why inquiry should be expected to result in 'unified wholes.' "[19]

But this conception of organic process and the equilibrium of organic wholes is more than the framework for understanding logic. It is the framework for understanding the individual, education, and the social process as well. Thought, the need for self-development, the need for invention, the need for social change, all start with some kind of indeterminate situation or disturbed equilibrium. Every element of thought, education, social innovation, invention, or act of legislation is conceived as called forth by the indeterminate situation and functioning to restore equilibrium. A process of adjustment of activity and results is carried through in all cases, terminating only when equilibrium is restored.

Thus a kind of biological Hegelianism is crucial to every aspect of Dewey's thought. His "instrumentalism" arises as a kind of generalization of Peirce's and James's pragmatic rule; everything is estimated exclusively in terms of its equilibrium-restoring functions. Science is particularly dear to Dewey, for in all its aspects it is viewed as the most efficient of all instruments. In Dewey, as in James, a reconciliation of idealism and science seems to have been a major motive for his theories.

BEHAVIORISM

Behaviorism was a naturalistic and positivistic movement in contemporary thought parallel to and influenced by pragmatism, but breaking with the idealistic tradition more completely than pragmatism. It attempted to preserve the empirical and experimental program of Wundt and his major American interpreter, Edward Bradford Tichener (1867–1927),[20] but broke even more sharply than the pragmatists with subjectivistic interpretations of the animal and human mind or psyche. Although John Watson was the first to explicitly formulate behaviorism, Pavlov anticipated it by at least a decade.

I. P. Pavlov. Ivan Petrovich Pavlov (1849–1936), Russian psychologist, graduated from the division of natural sciences of the University of St. Petersburg in 1875 and became a student of the Imperial Medico Surgical Academy. He graduated in 1879, having performed a number of original experiments and with eleven scientific publications to his credit. His doctoral thesis (published 1883) was on the "Efferent Nerves of the Heart." In 1884

[18]John Dewey, *Logic: The Theory of Inquiry* (New York: Henry Holt, 1938), pp. 104–105. Other works of Dewey's important to the present discussion are *Human Nature and Conduct* (New York: Henry Holt, 1922) and *Experience and Nature* (Chicago: Open Court Publishing Company, 1925).
[19]Russell, *History of Western Philosophy*, p. 823.

[20]Tichener maintained that psychology is a descriptive science addressed to the study of the normal adult human mind. He introduced the new German psychology to America, translating various works, including Wundt's *Ethics* and *Physiologische Psychologie*. He promoted the development of experimental psychology and directed analysis toward the problems of feeling, attention, and thought.

IVAN PAVLOV

Brown Brothers

he was given the rank of lecturer and awarded a fellowship for foreign travel. He used the opportunity to acquaint himself with the research traditions of laboratories in Leipzig and Breslau. In 1890 Pavlov became professor of pharmacology at the Academy and director of the physiological laboratory of the Institution of Experimental Medicine of St. Petersburg. From 1895 to 1924 Pavlov served as professor of physiology at the Academy. In 1925 he was made director of the Institute of Physiology of the Soviet Academy of Science.

For more than sixty years Pavlov continued his experiments. During the first sixteen years of his career his research was concerned with neural mechanisms in digestion and in blood circulation. In the 1890s he concentrated on mechanisms of digestion. After 1903 he turned his attention to the study of salivation. The core of Pavlov's research was directed at conditioned reflexes. In Western Europe and America, scientists considered reflexes as simply unconscious, automatic responses and did not give them major significance in the explanation of behavior. In Russia, however, the theory had been advanced that they were the basic units of behavior, whether simple or complex, conscious or unconscious.[21] At the time Pavlov turned his attention to the idea of reflex it was thought that reflexes were determined by measurable physical stimuli and mediated by the nervous system. Pavlov quickly came to the conclusion that reflexes, even of such things as glandular secretion, were potentially determined by more than measurable physical stimulation alone.

After some initial formulations concerning the role of the psyche in the function of the salivary glands, Pavlov found himself increasingly uncomfortable with ideas about the desires, feelings, and thoughts of experimental animals. By 1903 he had begun flatly to subscribe to an objective-physiological analysis of behavior.

> Vital phenomena that are termed psychic are distinguishable from pure physiological phenomena only in degree of complexity. Whether we call these phenomena psychical or complex-nervous is of little importance, as long as it is realized . . . that the naturalist approaches them only objectively, leaving aside the question of their essence.[22]

Pavlov's experimental investigations soon proved that the pairing of other stimuli with the unconditioned stimuli that produced a reflex action also resulted in an automatic response. Experimental study of such conditioned reflexes yielded a number of empirical generalizations or laws: (a) a conditioned stimulus not followed by the

[21]Ivan M. Sechenov, *Reflexes of the Brain* in Selected Works (McColl: State Publishing House for Biological and Medical Literature, 1928), pp. 263–336. First published in 1903.
[22]Ivan P. Pavlov, *Lectures on Conditioned Reflexes* (New York: International Publishers, 1928), pp. 59–60. First published in 1903. Extract translated by Gregory Razran.

unconditioned stimulus was gradually *extinguished*; (b) however when the unconditioned stimulus was again linked to the conditioned stimulus it resulted in *spontaneous* recovery; (c) conditioned stimuli were often *generalized* to similar stimuli; (d) alternate presentations of conditioned and unconditioned stimuli could result in *differentiation*; (e) conditioned reflexes could become the basis for additional conditioned reflexes in a kind of higher-order conditioning; (f) conditioned stimuli could be presented in a manner such that positional order determined the magnitude of the conditioned reflex in a manner described as *dynamic stereotype*; (g) when an extra stimulus is applied to an inhibited or partially inhibited conditioned stimuli it may be *disinhibited*. Confirming experiments of Pavlov's work run into the thousands, and American experimental psychologists attribute to Pavlov an influence second only to Freud[23] in the development of psychology.

Treating the formation of conditioned reflexes as the core of learning, Pavlov postulated a complex system of excitation and inhibition at the bottom of all conditioned-reflex manifestations. Modern electroencephalographic procedures have by and large confirmed Pavlov's hypotheses.[24] He also extended his analysis to human beings.[25] However, although Pavlov considered words as conditioned stimuli for human beings, he treated them as second order signals (or signals of signals) and essentially abstractions, introducing a new dimension in human behavior that was qualitatively different from that of animal behavior.

Pavlov even extended his researches to psychopathology, postulating that the conflict of excitation and inhibition was the general cause of psychopathic behavior. He believed the primary way to treat psychopathic disturbances was through protective inhibition. Pavlov also assumed that special forms of psychopathological neural action could occur and undertook to study them in unconditioned and conditioned behavior. He encouraged his students in the investigation of the relation between first and second order signal systems and drug and sleep therapy.

J. B. Watson. John Broadus Watson (1878–1958), born near Greenville, South Carolina, attended Furman University and earned the master's degree in 1899. He went on to study philosophy at the University of Chicago, but soon became interested in psychology. He had special interest and abilities in the laboratory study of animal behavior. His doctoral dissertation (1903) was on "Animal Education." Among Watson's early scientific publications were researches on the sensory determinants of maze learning in the rat (1907). He moved to Johns Hopkins in 1908, pursuing his studies on monkeys and birds. He continued his studies of birds on an island off the coast of Florida, where he skillfully adapted laboratory techniques to field study.

In a manner parallel to Pavlov's some ten years earlier, Watson came to the conclusion that the advance of psychology required, once and for all, the abandonment of an examination of states of mind, concepts, and values as objects of study and of introspection as a method. Behavior was the proper object of study; objective observation of behavior in response to controlled stimuli was the proven method. Human behavior, like animal behavior generally, can yield its properties to laboratory study. At the time he made these formulations in "Psychology as a Behaviorist Views It"[26] (1913),

---

[23]Gregory Razran, "Russian Physiologists' Psychology and American Experimental Psychology," *Psychological Bulletin*, 63, No. 1 (1965) 42–64.

[24]I. P. Pavlov, *Lectures on Conditioned Reflexes*, 2 vols. (New York: International Publishers, 1928–1941).

[25]I. P. Pavlov *Conditioned Reflexes: An Investigation of the Physiological Activity of the Cerebral Cortex* (New York: Dover, 1960).

[26]Published in *Psychological Review*, 20 (1913) 158–177. Among major works by Watson are *Animal Education* (Chicago: University of Chicago Press, 1903); "Kinaesthetic and Organic Sensations: Their Role in the Reactions of the White Rat to the Maze," *Psychological Review* Monograph Supplements, vol. 8, no. 33, Lancaster, Pa: Revue (1907); "Imitations in Monkeys," *Psychological Bulletin*, 5 (1908), 169–178; "The Behavior of Noddy

JOHN B. WATSON

The Ferdinand Hamburger, Jr. Archives, Johns
Hopkins University

Watson was unfamiliar with Pavlov's researches. A
year later, when he read various of Pavlov's papers
in German and French translation, Watson immediately made the conditioned reflex the cornerstone of behavioristic psychology.

and Sooty Terns," Carnegie Institution Publications, 103
(1908), 187–255; *Behavior: An Introduction to Comparative
Psychology* (New York: Holt, 1914); *Psychology From the
Standpoint of a Behaviorist* (Philadelphia: Lippincott,
1929); *Behaviorism* (Chicago: University of Chicago Press,
1962); John B. Watson and William McDougall, *The Bat-
tle of Behaviorism: An Exposition and an Exposure* (London:
Routledge, 1928); John B. Watson and Rosalie Watson,
Psychological Care of Infant and Child (London: Allen &
Unwin, 1928); "John Broadus Watson," in *A History of
Psychology, Autobiography* (Worcester, Mass.: Clark Uni-
versity Press, 1936).

In 1920 Watson's first wife divorced him for
adultery with Rosalie Rayner, his research assistant
during his work on child and infant behavior. She
became Watson's second wife and they published
their studies of the conditioning of a child to fear a
white rat by presenting the rat to the child simultaneously with loud noise. In 1928 the Watsons
published a book on child rearing. However, Watson's divorce resulted in the loss of his academic
position; it disrupted his research on child training, and led to his transfer to advertising — where
he enjoyed considerable success — and the shift of
his intellectual activity to popular writing. Watson's
writings were well received and unquestionably
helped create a favorable atmosphere for the rise
of psychology in America.

Watson remained opposed to all forms of
mentalism, making the reflex and conditioning
central to the formation of behavioral habits. He
viewed pleasure as arising in the erogenous zones
and thought as subvocal speech, conceptualizing it
as a series of muscle movements. In one of his
popular formulations in the mid-1920s he gave a
dramatic statement of his antihereditarianist environmentalism:

> Give me a dozen healthy infants, well-formed, and my
> own specific world to bring them up in and I'll
> guarantee to take any one at random and train him
> to become any type of specialist I might select —
> doctor, lawyer, artist, merchant-chief and, yes, even
> beggar-man and thief, regardless of his talents, pen-
> chants, tendencies, abilities, vocations, and the race of
> his ancestors.[27]

E. C. Tolman. At the very time that Watson's future as the foremost psychologist of America was
struck down by the permanent loss of his academic
position, Edward Chace Tolman (1886–1959) was
in the process of elaborating a system of "purposive behaviorism" directed against Watson's determination to eliminate from psychology everything
that smacked of mentalism.

[27]Watson, *Behaviorism*. Revised Edition. First published in
1925, p. 104.

E. C. TOLMAN

The New York Times

Tolman was born in Newton, Massachusetts and attended the Newton public schools, earning a B.S. in electrochemistry in 1911 from the Massachusetts Institute of Technology. He found himself drawn to philosophy and psychiatry and entered graduate school at Harvard in 1911, obtaining the doctorate in 1915. He was an instructor at Northwestern for three years before accepting an instructorship at the University of California. In the early 1920s Tolman expressed dissatisfaction with Watson's stimulus-response psychology and his inclination to ban all traces of the introspective analysis from psychology. In an early paper he proposed the development of a nonphysiological behaviorism, a more comprehensive approach to behavioral problems examining "the problems of motive, purpose, determining tendency and the

like" but without committing the mistakes of the "older subjectivistic formulation."[28]

Tolman avoided the reductionism of the average behavioral psychologists for an integrating schema receptive to motivation, perceptual, and emotional variables. He opposed extreme environmentalism and opened experimentation in behavioral genetics. He promoted the idea that the laws holding stimulus and response together were most fruitfully approached through "intervening variables" such as "cognitions," or "cognitive maps," "expectations," and "purposes." The effect of this approach was twofold: (1) it made a place in behavioristic psychology for many of the problems that had concerned the older introspective psychologists; (2) it provided room for a variety of interests of different specialists such as social, clinical, industrial, and learning psychologists.

In the 1950s, despite extreme shyness, Tolman led the opposition against the university regents during a controversy over loyalty oaths in the "Year of the Oath" (1949–1950) that was inspired by the Cold War mentality and McCarthyism. In the view of some, this act of moral courage saved academic freedom on the campus at a troubled time.

Clark L. Hull. Although Clark L. Hull (1884–1952) was only two years younger than Tolman, he came into the field somewhat later. He was born in a log cabin in New York State and received his early education in a country school. He took a job as a mining engineer and only after he became ill with poliomyelitis (which forced him to use a cane the rest of his life) did he continue his education.

[28]Edward C. Tolman, *Collected Papers in Psychology* (Berkeley: University of California Press, 1951), p. 8. The formulation appears in the first of the papers ("A New Formula for Behaviorism," 1922) collected by Tolman's colleagues and students. The papers were selected by Tolman himself to illustrate the development of his ideas. His first full statement of his position was published in 1932, *Purposive Behavior in Men and Animals* (Los Angeles: University of California Press, 1951). Tolman continued to develop his position throughout his life.

CLARK HULL

Yale University Archives, Yale University Library

He received the Ph.D. from the University of Wisconsin in 1918.

At Wisconsin, where Hull continued to work after earning the Ph.D., he developed the areas of measurement of achievement and the validation of tests, and conducted experiments in hypnosis. Hull moved to the Institute of Human Relations at Yale in 1929, at which time he began to formalize his theories of behavior.[29] Hull and his colleagues

formulated a set of learning principles expressed in logical and mathematical language in 1940. Three years later Hull translated his ideas into general language. He continued the rest of his life to work along the lines laid down in these formulations, applying them to selected examples of more complex individual behavior. The proposal to extend them to social and cultural problems and behavior remained unrealized at Hull's death.

Hull accepted the behaviorist propositions from Watson and Pavlov that the elementary unit of behavior was the response to a stimulus and that learning was the bonding of stimuli and responses and their formation into more complex patterns. Emotion, ideas, and motivations were accepted as descriptive properties of molar behavior. Although not particularly useful when analyzed per se, they are understandable as end points of consequences of basic stimulus-response units. Hull stressed the role in learning of events at the end of a behavior chain that can have an effect on the beginning of such a chain. Hull's reenforcement theory of learning rests on the function of success or rewards for behavior in strengthening the stimulus-response connection. Learning occurs when the response is rewarded and occurs more quickly the stronger the drive. Habit strength (the stimulus-response connection) is bound up with the survival needs (hunger, thirst, avoidance of pain, pursuit of sex) of the individual and species. Habits learned in one situation are generalized to others. To account for discrimination learning, Hull postulated the existence of an excitatory potential; that is, in a field of conflicting and alternative stimuli, one learns to respond to the rewarded alternative. Thus, in various ways, an attempt was made to extend analysis from the basic units of behavior to ever more complex units of molar behavior. Ultimately, Hull envisioned the creation of a system of quantitative explanations of social behavior. It seems incredible, he concluded, "that nature would create one set of primary sensory-

[29]For Hull's own account of his development see his *Autobiography*, IV, 143–162, in *History of Psychology in Autobiography* (Worcester, Mass.: Clark University Press, 1952). His first two major works were *Aptitude Testing* (New York: World, 1928) and *Hypnosis and Suggestibility* (New York: Appleton, 1933). His formal theory appears in *Mathematico-Deductive Theory of Rote Learning: A Study in Scientific Methodology* by Clark L. Hull et al. (New Haven: Yale University Press, 1940); *Principles of Behavior: An Introduction to Behavior Theory* (New York: Appleton,

1943); and *A Behavior System: An Introduction to Behavior Theory Concerning the Individual Organism* (New Haven: Yale University Press, 1952).

motor laws for the mediation of individual behavior and another set for the mediation of group behavior. Presumably, then, the laws which are derived for social behavior will be based for the most part on the same postulates as those which form the basis of individual behavior."[30]

In the long run, Hull envisioned the fusion of sociology and psychology on the basis of behavioristic theory.

SUMMARY

As its representatives experienced the crises that accompanied the conversion of sociology from a freelance, somewhat journalistic discipline into a professionalized academic area of study, they cast about among the systems of thought of the nineteenth century for a foundation. Formalistic theories of sociology arose as one product of this enterprise, with the attempt to establish pure sociology as the study of *a priori* social forms. Perceiving that the establishment of *a priori* forms was not an empirical task, one group of formalists turned to phenomenology as a base for the formalistic program. The risks presented by formalism gradually emerged into clear view: either one succeeded in maintaining the formalistic program but at the expense of being scientific, or one remained sociologically relevant and failed to develop consistent formalism. This is no way to establish a science.

Meanwhile, however, there was renewed activity among the idealistic-minded thinkers. The group stemming from Lotze attempted to establish idealistic hypotheses on the basis of scientific method. Although the neo-Hegelians were far more critical of science, they brought pungent criticisms to bear upon special aspects of current social theories. Against an overdrawn individualism they advocated the claims of institutions, and against mechanistic claims they advanced the cause of personality. At the same time, they

modified older forms of idealism by inserting the problem of personality. Finally, the pragmatists were attempting a solution to the problem on their own. William James came to pragmatism by way of reaction against the emotional implications of mechanism, and Dewey came to it by way of converting neo-Hegelianism into a practical program.

Parallel to the rise of American pragmatism, J. B. Watson's behaviorism arose as a less idealistic form of individualism in the ranks of psychologists. In its initial form it was antimentalistic, eschewing all traffic with ideas, thoughts, values, or purposes. However, most of the behaviorists, even Pavlov, one of the founders of the point of view, felt some need to come to terms with the uniqueness of human behavior. Pavlov thought that even though words were acquired like any other conditioning, they introduced a qualitatively new dimension that set human experience apart. Watson, to be sure, was inclined toward reductionism: reducing thought to verbal behavior. However, most of the American behaviorists either followed Pavlov's lead or, like Tolman, treated concepts, thought, and purposes at the very least as adequate descriptions of molar behavior at their level.

A whole series of closely related sociological theories took shape along the lines suggested by these philosophical movements. There were fluid transitions between them. They often borrowed not only from each other but from a variety of the idealistic and pragmatic trends. There were, however, some properties common to them all which united them into one general movement in sociological theory: (1) they sought a definition of sociological subject matter in terms of idealistic theories; (2) they avoided as far as possible the assumption of large-scale social units (total societies, humanity, civilization) as units of sociological analysis; they were, in one terminology, strongly "nominalistic"; (3) they had as one foremost problem the development of a theory of social persons; and (4) they brought the problem of sociological method under review.

Once the movement in elementaristic social theory that responded to idealistic and pragmatic trends in Western philosophy got under way, the time was ripe for behavioristic social theory.

[30]Clark L. Hull, *A Behavior System: An Introduction to Behavior Theory Concerning the Individual Organism* (New Haven: Yale University Press, 1952), p. 355.

XIV

From Pluralistic Behaviorism to Behavioristic Social Theory

The school of social behaviorism covers a remarkably varied and fertile development of ideas, characterized by both theoretical and methodological ferment. At its core was a behavioristic concept of sociological subject matter, distinguishing it from positivistic organicism, conflict theory, and sociological formalism, with their structural and relational approaches. Its philosophic origins were in neo-idealism and related trends. While it retained a strong methodological positivism that separated it from sociological formalism, it recognized that the older methods were inadequate.

Social behaviorism was manifest in a series of closely equivalent but distinct and parallel forms. The oldest of these was pluralistic behaviorism. The school originally took shape in the works of Gabriel Tarde, whose position has at times been called "imitation–suggestion"; Franklin Giddings later gave it the more appropriate name of pluralistic behaviorism; and since World War II, "social exchange theory" has been the designation of this approach to explaining interpersonal behavior from an elementaristic perspective. Many recent behavioristic sociologists take as a metaphor for social life as a whole the trade-offs made in the marketplace by individuals who appear to be equals.

Although there is no question of the right of people to describe their activities in any language they please, some problems have emerged for persons who have employed the term *exchange theory* to define a special school of sociological thought. Richard M. Emerson, who considers himself to be an exchange theorist, felt compelled when invited to review exchange theory to state: "We must understand that it is not a theory at all. It is a frame of reference within which many theories — some micro and some more macro — can speak to one another, whether in argument or in mutual support."[1] So-called exchange theory, Emerson

[1] Richard M. Emerson, "Social Exchange Theory," *Annual Review of Sociology,* ed. Alex Inkeles, James Coleman, and Neil Smelser (Palo Alto, Calif.: Annual Reviews, 1976), II, 336. For Emerson's contributions to exchange theory see "Power-dependency Relations," *American*

maintained, is a "frame of reference that takes the movement of valued things (resources) through social processes as its focus. As I see it, its scope is defined by an assumption: that a resource will continue to flow only if there is a valued return contingent upon it. Psychologists call this contingent return *reinforcement* — economists simply call this reciprocally contingent flow *exchange.*"[2]

Emerson's admission that exchange theory is not a theory at all is also implied by Harry C. Bredemeier in his amusing and ironic review of exchange theory. As Bredemeier sees the matter, not only does exchange theory make strange bedfellows out of such sociological rivals as George Homans and Talcott Parsons, but even places B. F. Skinner (one of the mentors of some of the exchange theorists) and his pigeons on common ground.

> Skinner wants a pigeon to do something — peck a round dot. The pigeon wants some food, as well as a lot of other things I shall come to. Under certain conditions, each gets what he or it wants. The emphasis is usually put on how Skinner gets what he wants, but it is essential to realize that one of the conditions under which Skinner gets rewarded by the pigeon is that Skinner does what the pigeon requires him to do — all of it. There is food at the end of those pecks, a reasonably warm and dry cage, no cats lunging, ample water, and on and on. Moreover, Skinner does not ask the pigeon to sing "The Star Spangled Banner," and he does not try to pay off the pigeon with dollar bills or cheese.[3]

Sociological Review 27 (1962), 30–40; "A Psychological Basis for Social Exchange," in J. Berger, J. Zeldich, Jr., and B. Anderson, *Sociological Theories in Progress,* Vol. 2 (Boston: Houghton Mifflin, 1967); "Role Theory and Diminishing Utility in Group Problem Solving," *Pacific Sociological Review,* 1 (1969), 110–115.
[2]Emerson, "Social Exchange Theory," p. 339.
[3]Harry C. Bredemeier, "Exchange Theory," in Tom Bottomore and Robert Nesbit, eds., *A History of Sociological Analysis* (New York: Basic Books, 1978), p. 421. The irony results from confusing perspectives of different scope: like concluding that since both are human there is no difference between men and women. Exchange is not a theory but rather a practice that is differently interpreted by different theories.

Not only is exchange theory not a theory, it is also not a distinctive perspective. Most of the core group of individuals who call themselves "exchange theorists" are actually recent recruits to behavioristic sociology with no common academic background. As the older group of social behaviorists, particularly of the Giddings tradition, have died off they have left no major followers. However, a new generation of individuals is beginning to fill the vacuum left by their departure. This new generation has at its disposal developments in the behavioristic tradition that have occurred since the original pluralistic behaviorists were students. The new behavioristic sociologists are elementarists and positivists, with even stronger preferences for quantitative data and both laboratory and mathematical analysis of data than their pluralistic behavioral predecessors. Moreover, it is quite clear that if sociologists had not made a new assault on sociological problems from a contemporary behavioristic point of view, the behavioristic psychologists would eventually have done so. This was on Clark Hull's agenda at the time of his death. B. F. Skinner has already presented a major approach to sociological problems from this point of view. Skinner not only has had strong influence on the new behavioristic sociologists, but can, not unfairly, be viewed as a major founding member of this most recent version of behavioristic sociology.[4] It is useful to review developments in social behaviorism in sequence, starting with pluralistic behaviorism.

PLURALISTIC BEHAVIORISM

Gabriel Tarde. The new importance in sociology represented by the imitation-suggestion school is well illustrated by the fact that Gabriel Tarde is

[4]Exchange is neither a theory nor a perspective but an aspect of social life that must be taken into account by any theory. Exchange is explained in different ways by different theories and assigned varying significance in the whole of social life by the different theories.

GABRIEL TARDE

Bibliothèque Nationale, Paris

often considered to be the founder of social psychology. Tarde (1843–1904) was born at Sarlat in southern France. He studied in Paris and became a judge in his native town, where he made quantitative analyses of the cases that came before him, thus acquiring a reputation for his study of criminality. He opposed the ideas of Cesare Lombroso (1836–1909), who held that criminality is inherited and who had started a school of the biological explanation of crime. This work prepared Tarde for his position as head of the Bureau of Statistics of the Ministry of Justice in Paris. He also lectured at the École des Sciences Politiques until his retirement in 1900, when he became professor of modern philosophy at the Collège de France.[5]

[5]Tarde's two chief works in criminology are *La Criminalité comparée* ["Comparative Criminality"] (Paris: F. Alcan,

The idea of imitation for which Tarde is famous was not original with him. Hume had employed it in his essay on national character, and Bagehot had accounted for social stability in terms of it. It was also elaborated independently by William James and Josiah Royce. However, Tarde's particular use of the idea was quite new, for by means of it he fused a scientific demand for methodological precision with an idealistic definition of sociological subject matter.

Every science, he argued, deals with a variety of phenomena among which there are repetitions. It is the task of science to isolate and explain these repetitions. This is not done all at once. At first, science seizes upon bold ideas of apparent repetitions in phenomena; but these large-scale reg-

1886; 8th ed., 1924) and *La Philosophie pénale* (Lyon: A. Storck, 1890; 4th rev. ed., 1903); the first of these is not available in English, but a translation of the fourth edition of the second was made by Rapelje Howell, *Penal Philosophy* (Boston: Little, Brown, 1912). Two other books of Tarde's which are available in English translation are: *Les Lois de l'imitation* (Paris: F. Alcan, 1890; 2d rev. ed., 1895; 4th rev. ed., 1904), the second edition of which was translated by Elsie Clews Parsons as *The Laws of Imitation* (New York: Henry Holt, 1903); and *Les Lois sociales* (Paris: F. Alcan, 1898; 6th ed., 1910), the first editon of which was translated by Howard C. Warren as *Social Laws* (New York: Macmillan, 1899). Some of Tarde's other important works, not available in English, are: *La Logique sociale* (Paris: F. Alcan, 1895); *L'Opposition universelle* (Paris: F. Alcan, 1897); *Études de psychologie sociale* ["Studies on Social Psychology"] (Paris: Giard & Brière, 1898); *L'Opinion et la foule* ["Opinion and the Mob"] (Paris: F. Alcan, 1901; 4th ed., 1922); and *Psychologie économique*, 2 vols. (Paris: F. Alcan, 1902). Excellent reviews of Tarde's work are found in two books by Michael M. Davis, *Gabriel Tarde* (New York: Columbia University Press, 1906) and *Psychological Interpretation of Society* (New York: Columbia University Press, 1909). Interest has been reviving in Tarde in the late 1960s and 1970s. See: *On Communication and Social Influence*, edited with an introduction by Terry N. Clark (Chicago: University of Chicago Press, 1969); *Penal Philosophy*, with an editorial preface by Edward Lindsey and an introduction by Robert H. Gault (Montclaire, N.J.: Patterson Smith, 1968); *Social Laws* (New York: Arno Press, 1974); *Underground Man*, translated by Cloudesley Brereton with a preface by H. G. Wells (Westport, Conn.: Hyperion Press, 1974).

ularities are only apparent, and must be abandoned in time for the genuine subject matter of the science.

The special phenomena sociology studies are "beliefs or desires under the different names of dogmas, sentiment, laws, wants, customs, morals, etc."[6]

Psychology studies their interrelations in the single mind; sociology studies their relations between minds. The methods by which these are studied are archaeology and statistics — the latter proper to sociology, the former to history. The task of the archaeologists is to trace out the remote, almost imperceptible analogies in form, style, situation, language, legend, dress — in anything that is the vehicle of the transmission of human beliefs and desires. Statistics consists in the enumeration of acts which are as much alike as possible, but, because statistics deals with the outer manifestations of beliefs and desires, it cannot always arrive accurately at judgments of intensity. Nevertheless, in the long run the hope of sociological science lies in the analysis of the psychological quantities of belief and desire. Wants once initiated tend to spread in a geometric fashion, displaying a curve characterized by a slow start, a rapid expansion, and gradual leveling. Statistical curves representing development are among the most accurate items of sociological information we possess.

While the method of sociology is archaeological and statistical and the ultimate subject matter of the science consists of beliefs and desires, the specific object of interest is the interpsychic patterns of manifestation and transmission of beliefs and desires. These are three in number: *repetition* (imitation), *opposition,* and *adaptation.*[7] An aspect of Tarde's idealism is manifest in this triad, which reflects Hegel's dialectic of thesis, antithesis, and synthesis. Of these processes, the first, repetition (imitation), accounts for the transmission, constancy, and spread of social forms; the third,

adaptation (invention), is the final source of all progress and development. Inventions are any new thoughts or actions that reach expression. They arise in the minds of gifted individuals or in the conflict of imitation and existing practices. Once an invention is made, it spreads in a geometric manner from its source, opposed at every step by existing ways of doing things.

The source of all new events is in new individual ideas and inventions. Imitation is the socializing process by which an invention is spread, socially accepted, and shared. A number of factors play on invention. There is always some difficulty in combining ideas into an invention and there is always a differential ability for this task. Moreover, social conditions may favor or check mental alertness and the expression of ability. Imitation is affected by the tendency of an invention to spread from an initial center in geometric progression. Physical and biological influences (including race characteristics) may play a role in imitation, for imitations are refracted by their media. The social influences affecting imitation and invention are both logical and extralogical. The reception of an invention is determined in part by its agreement or disagreement with inventions already accepted. Logical factors operate when an individual imitates an invention because he thinks it is more useful or efficient. But sometimes ideas are imitated before means. Imitation typically proceeds from socially superior to socially inferior. Societies and periods differ in their imitation patterns, and periods in which the past has prestige (custom imitation) alternate with periods of fashion imitation, in which the novel and foreign have prestige.

In understanding the phenomena of *opposition* in society, students have moved from the large-scale apparent similarities to the actual empirical recurrences. Early students saw opposition in terms of mythical struggles between good and evil. Later the idea of conflict of races and nations came into view. Eventually the economists perceived the oppositions of competition. The sociologists, finally, perceived the oppositions in individuals themselves, present whenever they hesitate or experience a conflict over whether to imitate a new

[6] See *Social Laws,* and *The Laws of Imitation,* p. 28.
[7] Tarde devoted a book to each of these: *Les Lois de l'imitation* treats repetition, *L'Opposition universelle* treats opposition, and adaptation is taken up in *La Logique sociale.*

invention. The main types of opposition are war, competition, and discussion, and they have appeared roughly in this sequence.

In understanding *adaptation,* the first form of thought was the perception of the development of history as the integration of nation to nation, making of world history a teleological unit. But as with opposition, so here increasing precision eventually locates adaptation in the mind of the individual inventor.

The fundamental units of society for Tarde are always beliefs and desires, and the fundamental social processes repetition, opposition, and adaptation. A society is a group of persons. The only original institution was the family, which transmuted the ideas and beliefs of animal society into forms that made more complex social organization and development possible. The family was the source of all moral obligation, the source of language, worship, and art, the original political institution, the agency of social control. All specialized institutions, such as religion and the state, arose by invention within the framework of the family, and by the imitation and spread of the invention. Initially, inventions gave rise to a nobility which monopolized the advantages of the invention. Such a nobility became the point from which imitation waves could radiate. In time, the nobility was superseded by cities as the locus of inventions and source of imitation. These in turn were replaced by nations.

In *L'Opinion et la foule,* Tarde moved farther into the field of collective behavior. A "crowd" was defined as a plurality of persons gathered together in a given place and time and unified by emotion, belief, and action. The physical and mental factors associated with their contiguity account for crowd action. A "public" is a number of persons with sufficient unity of belief and emotion to act in concerted fashion, but separated from each other in time and space. For Tarde, the public is a product of modern agencies of mass communications: the printing press and the newspaper. Since the public is not in actual contiguity, it is more possible for the members of a public to deliberate. The public mind is the product of opinion produced by the impact of the printed word and gossip.

There are echoes of Bagehot in Tarde's conception of social change in terms of the alternation of epochs of custom imitation with epochs of fashion imitation. The same notions were applied to economics, leading to an anticipation of institutional economics. Custom and fashion were treated as fundamental to the study of economic development. The economics of the primitive family rested on custom imitation. It was bound by traditional forms. The spread of new consumption desires shattered the economic monopoly of the primitive family. But fashions tended to become customs, and these, in turn, were transformed into corporations, which were followed, in their turn, by a new period of fashion imitation. The two types of economic epoch differ; the one produces for use, the other for sale. We are living in a period of fashion imitation.

The properties of the school that merit the description of "social behaviorism" are already evident. While an "idealistic" definition of sociological subject matter is retained (beliefs and desires), the notion that the ultimate units of study are total societies is abandoned (as a prescientific analogy. Distinctions between form and content are avoided — the position is quite distinct from sociological formalism. However, like formalism, it is the vehicle for a more "liberal" conception of society. This has as a consequence the emergence of the problem of the individual personality as an area of sociological study. But in contrast to formalism, the school does not call the positivistic tradition of sociology into question. Rather, it sees the hope of sociology to lie, in part, in the development of statistical method. Like formalism, pluralistic behaviorism separates itself, despite Tarde's borrowings from Walter Bagehot, from conflict theory. Conflict is not located between groups, and certainly it is not turned into a social form. Conflict is located as the conflict of ideas in the individual mind.

Gustave Le Bon. Tarde had extended his ideas of suggestion-imitation to the problems of crowd psychology and the formation of publics. The ability of the theory to isolate new problems was already clear. Le Bon's importance lay in developing

GUSTAVE LE BON

A. Harlingue, Archives Photographiques de l'Histoire, Paris

and popularizing these extensions.[8] Gustave Le Bon (1841–1931), who for a time practiced medicine, found his primary work in the study of crowd psychology.[9] In addition to having practiced

medicine and written on physiology and hygiene, Le Bon was employed by the French government as an archaeologist and paleographer in the Orient, and served as editor of *Bibliothèque de philosophie scientifique.*

Whatever difficulties were later to be revealed in the principle of imitation as developed by Tarde, it was superior to any so far advanced in simultaneously doing justice to the individual and the group, for it apparently did not require the reduction of one to the other. In France, however, another strong tradition was represented by Durkheim. Hegel had viewed world history as the evolution or progress of the human spirit under the successive leaderships of the genius of one or another world power. The absolute in the form of an immanent principle of development determined the course of world history. Comte, as has been noted, was not too greatly removed from this view. He was led, in later life, to a mystically religious attitude toward society. These ideas were brought to more specific form by Moritz Lazarus (1824–1903) and Heymann Steinthal (1823–1899), who linked simpler theories to the problems of a scientific psychology. They proposed that the study of the problems of cultural history and "objective mind" should comprise the historical development of the folk mind in general and the folk minds of particular peoples. The folk community was assumed to be the fundamental communal group, with all other forms of social structures developing from it. Within the folk community, a people expressed its peculiar imagination in its art and literature; it expressed its emotion in its religion; it expressed its judgment in its codes of conduct. These notions were transmitted on to Tönnies and Durkheim. In addition to Tarde, it was

---

[8]Also important in the field is Scipio Sighele (1868–1913), whose chief work is *La Folla delinquente* ["The Delinquent Mob"] (Turin: 1891; rev. ed., 1895).

[9]A full bibliographical note on Gustave Le Bon will not be attempted. His work in crowd psychology is well represented by the following four works: *Les Lois psychologiques de l'evolution des peuples* (Paris: F. Alcan, 1894), translated into English (translator not identified) as *The Psychology of Peoples: Its Influence on Their Evolution* (New York: Macmillan, 1898; G. E. Stechert, 1912; references here are to the latter edition); *Psychologie des foules* (Paris: F. Alcan, 1895), translated into English (translator not identified) as *The Crowd* (New York: Macmillan, 1896, and later editions); *Psychologie du socialisme*

(Paris: F. Alcan, 1898), translated into English (translator not identified) as *The Psychology of Socialism* (New York: Macmillan, 1899); *La Révolution française et la psychologie des révolutions* (Paris: E. Flammarion, 1912), translated by Bernard Miall as *The Psychology of Revolution* (New York: G. P. Putnam, 1913). Unavailable in English translation are Le Bon's works on archaeology, such as *La Civilisation des Arabes* ["Arabic Civilization"] (Paris: 1884) and *Les Civilisations de l'Inde* ["Indian Civilizations"] (Paris: 1887).

Durkheim, a terminal point in this tradition, who most influenced Le Bon. Durkheim, the opponent of all forms of social nominalism, was at the other extreme of the sociological scale from Tarde, stressing the group rather than the individual in the social process. The point of emphasis for Durkheim was not ideas and beliefs invented in the individual mind and transmitted by imitation until slowed by conflict with others, but a special kind of belief, "collective representations," marked by "exteriority" and "constraint." "Collective representations" constituted a reality *sui generis* and the essential reality of society is found in its solidarity. Before he was done, Durkheim attempted to derive all other social phenomena, including science and religion, from the collective psychology of the group.

But this is merely a review to isolate the influences playing on Le Bon, who fused three primary elements in his sociological interpretations: (1) Tarde's conceptions of imitation and suggestion as basic social processes, (2) Durkheim's conception of collective mentality and the importance of group factors in social life, and (3) a racial mysticism with an antidemocratic bias.

Le Bon's racial mysticism is most fully apparent in *The Psychology of Peoples*. He takes inequality as the fundamental social fact:

> . . . people found it easy to persuade themselves that . . . inequalities were merely the outcome of differences of education, that all men are born equally intelligent and good, and that the sole responsibility for their perversion lies with the institutions they live under. This being the case, the remedy was simple in the extreme: all that had to be done was to reform the institutions and to give every man an identical education. It is in this way that institutions and education have ended by becoming the great panaceas of modern democrats, the means of remedying inequalities which clash with the important principles that are the only divinities that survive today.[10]

Le Bon's whole object was to blast this democratic "myth" by describing the psychological characteristics which constitute the soul of races, and to show how the history of a people and its civilization are determined by these characteristics. Only in this way, Le Bon thought, could one smash democracy and socialism.

The moral and intellectual characters of a people, for Le Bon, form the soul of a people, an inheritance from its ancestors and a motive for its conduct. The national character, he maintains, is due to simple psychological causes. Individuals are products not merely of their immediate parents but also of their race.

To make this argument apply, of course, it is necessary to assume the inheritance of ideas and other acquired characteristics. This Le Bon did not hesitate to do. A community of sentiments, ideas, beliefs, and interests, created by slow, hereditary accumulations, gives a high degree of identity and fixity to the mental constitution of a people. It was the cause of the greatness of Rome in ancient times, and at the present day it is the source of the greatness of England. A race is thought to possess psychological characteristics almost as fixed as its physical characteristics. There are basic inequalities among races and within any given race; the more a race approaches civilization, the greater the inequality within it. The effect of civilization is to differentiate both individuals and races. Peoples are not progressing toward equality but toward inequality. The formation of a race is due to interbreeding continued during centuries, and to a similar existence under identical conditions until the agglomeration has acquired common sentiments, common interests, and common beliefs.

While Le Bon's *Psychology of Peoples* illustrates his acceptance of a mystical biology and antidemocratic racialism, his attempt to fuse Durkheim's and Tarde's theories appears in his study of the crowd. He argues that "men are ruled by ideas, sentiments, and customs — matters which are of the essence of ourselves. Institutions and laws are the outward manifestations of our character. . . . Being its outcome institutions and laws cannot change that character."[11] However,

[10]Le Bon, *The Psychology of Peoples*, pp. xiv–xv.

[11]Le Bon, *The Crowd*, p. vi.

while the complex of traits received by heredity constitutes the genius of a race, when people are assembled in a crowd for purposes of observation or action, new psychological characteristics appear, in addition to and differing from racial characteristics. Crowds have always played a part in the life of peoples, but never more important than at present. The present epoch is one of these critical moments in which human thought is undergoing transformation. Two fundamental factors are at the base of it: the destruction of the religious, political, and social beliefs in which all the elements of our civilization are rooted, and the creation of entirely new conditions of existence as a product of modern scientific and industrial discoveries. We have entered upon an era of crowds. This follows from the fact that the popular classes are entering political life and transforming the governing class. It follows from the growth of the masses in power. Civilizations are created and directed by a small intellectual aristocracy, never by crowds. Crowds are powerful only for destruction. Their rule is always tantamount to a barbarian phase of civilization.

A crowd is a gathering of people. Under certain circumstances the sentiments and ideas of the persons in the gathering take the same direction, and "conscious personality vanishes." The psychological crowd appears, forming "a single being, and is subject to the law of the mental unity of crowds." Certain conditions are necessary for predisposing individuals to subordinate themselves to the crowd mind. These are as follows: (1) the individual forming part of the crowd feels a sentiment of invisible power; (2) contagion is felt; (3) a suggestibility results. Conscious personality vanishes as discernment is lost. All feelings and thought are hypothetically determined. Intellectually the crowd is always inferior to the individual, but morally it may be good or evil, cowardly or heroic, more than is possible for any individual. Everything depends on its local bent.

Le Bon's scorn of crowds appears in the terms he successively applies to them: impulsive, mobile, irritable, suggestible, credulous, ingenuous, prone to exaggeration, intolerant, dictatorial, conserva-

tive, capable of entertaining contradictory ideas, characterized by inferior reasoning powers, possessed of an abnormally sensitive imagination, religiously tenacious of a conviction, and likely to hold fundamental convictions with great firmness while exchanging superficial opinions with amazing alacrity.[12]

The successful leaders of crowds are rhetoricians, agitators, or fanatics obsessed with an idea and dogmatic in method. The procedure of influence is reiteration rather than analysis. An idea once accepted spreads with great rapidity by contagion and imitation. Leaders of crowds maintain their control by prestige (which may have a variety of derivations). They operate by oratory, verbal extravagance, and vagueness. Crowds may be heterogeneous or homogeneous. They may be criminal crowds, criminal juries, electoral crowds, or parliamentary assemblies; as crowds, they are always the same.

In *The Psychology of Revolution*, Le Bon brought together and applied many of the ideas present in the *Psychology of Peoples* and *The Crowd*. The problems projected in *The Crowd* are fulfilled in Le Bon's theory of revolution. Crowd action is by no means identical with revolution. "The multitude is . . . the agent of a revolution; but not its point of departure. The crowd represents an amorphous being which can do nothing, and will do nothing, without a head to lead it. It will quickly exceed the impulse once received, but it never creates it."[13] Revolutions are those changes which "transform the destinies of the people."[14] Revolution is the more general problem of which the crowd is an incident.

Governments are futile in the face of a true revolution, representing a change in the soul of a people. The more stable the institutions of a people are in normal times, the more violent its

---

[12]See Harry Elmer Barnes, "The Psychosociological Theories of Gustave Le Bon," in Barnes, ed., *An Introduction to the History of Sociology* (Chicago: University of Chicago Press, 1948), esp. pp. 489–490.

[13]Le Bon, *The Psychology of Revolution*, p. 24.

[14]*Ibid.*, p. 25.

revolutions are likely to be. In a revolution, the people follow the dictates of their leaders. Most of the people are relatively peaceably inclined, but not all. The conception of the people as a mystic entity endowed with all powers and virtues is the creation of demagogues intent on manipulation. This popular entity is conceived as a superior personality, never having to answer for its actions and never making a mistake. The people may kill, burn, ravage, commit the most frightful cruelties, glorify its hero today and throw him into the gutter tomorrow. Actually, Le Bon argues, this mysterious fetish breaks down into two categories. The first includes peasants, traders, and workers who need tranquillity and order to exercise their callings. The second category, which plays a capital part in all national disturbances, consists of a subversive social residue dominated by a criminal mentality. Degenerates of alcoholism and poverty, thieves, beggars, destitute "casuals," indifferent workers without employment — these constitute the dangerous bulk of the armies of insurrection.[15]

Le Bon was in terror of socialism and syndicalism. Science and industry were seen as having precipitated the growth of cities, concentration of population, improvement of communication, and the extension of suffrage. All such democratizing factors and agencies opened the era of crowds. Because of their emotionality and susceptibility to suggestion, they are instruments in the hands of leaders with prestige and a readiness to utilize affirmation, repetition, contagion, and imitation in molding and directing them. One of the prime dangers of modern society is the exploitation of crowds by selfish demagogues.

The somewhat more "liberal" conception of society noted in Tarde's work also appears in Le Bon. Society is not a great organism, any part of which may not be interfered with without disaster; society is a strategy of collective actions. Once this is granted, however, Le Bon is immediately in arms with passionate defenses against inferior races, mobs, popular publics, democracy, and

socialism. A sultry ideological atmosphere surrounds most of his work. Nevertheless, the general fact remains: the whole area of collective behavior has been discovered by sociology.

James Mark Baldwin. The imitation–suggestion theory founded by Tarde was extended to the interpretations of a whole series of institutions and social processes. Tarde also indicated the manner in which it could be used to analyze the problems of the crowd and the public. Le Bon further developed its implications for the crowd, extending its application to social revolution and other catastrophic social change. Baldwin's importance lay in the extension of the ideas of imitation and suggestion to the problems of the personality and the relation between self and society.

James Mark Baldwin (1861–1934), who is best known as editor and chief author of the *Dictionary of Philosophy and Psychology*, helped bring about the shift in the social sciences in America away from biological organicism and evolution toward a more psychological analysis of society.[16] Baldwin was influenced not only by Tarde but by the Hegelians (particularly Josiah Royce) and the pragmatists (particularly James).

Personality study at this period was partly adapted to prevailing evolutionary doctrines. One could study the mind of the child, the primitive human being, and the animal as evolutionary products. G. Stanley Hall and Baldwin proposed to use the recapitulation doctrine, made significant by the evolutionists, for this purpose. From this point of view, the psychological development of the individual represents a recapitulation of the evolutionary development of the race. At the same time, the imitation-suggestion point of view tended

---

[15]*Ibid.*, p. 70.

[16]James Mark Baldwin, ed., *Dictionary of Philosophy and Psychology* (New York: Macmillan, 1901–1905; corr. ed., 1925; reprinted, 1940). The other works of Baldwin with which we are concerned in the present discussion are: *The Mental Development in the Child and the Race* (New York: Macmillan, 1895; 3d rev. ed., 1906) and *The Story of the Mind* (New York: D. Appleton, 1898; 5th ed., 1912).

JAMES MARK BALDWIN

Courtesy of Mrs. Philip M. Stimson

to focus primary interest upon the environmental determination of mental life rather than on hereditary elements. In Baldwin's case, a particularly happy fusion of these two traditions occurred: the recapitulation doctrine made the mind of the child an object of major interest, and the imitation-suggestion mechanism focused attention on the factors involved in learned behavior. *The Mental Development in the Child and the Race* is a landmark in the sociological study of personality. In one of those brilliant flashes that mark a basic turn of thought, the fusion of the imitation-suggestion idea with that of recapitulation carried out the shift of interest from the historical development of the mind to the development of individual self. "The relations of individual development to race development are so intimate — the two are so identical in fact — that no topic in the one can be treated with great clearness without assuming results in the other."[17]

For all intents and purposes, one can forget about the mentality of the race, and concentrate on the more immediately observable phenomena present at first hand.

In carrying out the project of examining the development of the mentality of the child, Baldwin finds the central processes to lie in various forms of "suggestion." These were developed at length in *The Mental Development in the Child and the Race,*[18] and compactly summarized in *The Story of the Mind* in the little series of volumes quaintly described as "The Library of Useful Stories."[19]

Suggestion refers to "the fact that all sorts of hints from without disturb and modify the beliefs and actions of the individual."[20] Suggestion represents all the processes which mold psychic life. Baldwin distinguished a number of types: (1) *physiological* — the molding of behavior on the basis of environmental influence below the level of consciousness; (2) *subconscious adult suggestion* — the adult counterpart of the physiological suggestion in infants; (3) *tune suggestion* — an example of adult subconscious suggestion in which a tune heard some time previously may take possession of consciousness, serving as the counterpart of a whole series of similar types of suggestion; (4) *normal auto-suggestion* — in which individuals may consciously or unconsciously set up suggestions operating on themselves (as in falling asleep in putting the baby to sleep); (5) *inhibitory suggestion* — a phenomenon present at all levels of nervous action in which inhibitory suggestions tend to suppress, check, or inhibit movement; (6) *pain suggestion* — a suggestion of a negative sort operating at all levels of mental development to suppress movement; (7) *control suggestion* — covering all cases of any kind of restraint placed on the move-

[17]Baldwin, *The Mental Development in the Child and the Race* (1906 edition), p. viii.
[18]Pp. 104–169.
[19]Baldwin, *The Story of the Mind* (1910 edition), pp. 148–166.
[20]*Ibid.,* p. 148.

ments of the body short of those coming from voluntary intention; (8) *contrary suggestion* — representing a special class of exaggerated instances of control suggestion, again operating at all levels of mental development and manifest in refined forms in the behavior of people of ascetic temperament with self-imposed duties of self-denial; and finally (9) *hypnotic suggestion* — referring to all instances of hypnotism. Baldwin was inclined to accept the theory that hypnosis is a special application of the principles of suggestion under deliberate manipulation.

For Baldwin, the two processes of suggestion and imitation sum up the plastic relations between individual and environment. Suggestion is the process of being acted on and imitation the response to suggestion. By locating these processes centrally to psychological development, emphasis is shifted away from all forms of hereditary determination (despite the recapitulation idea) of mental life; various psychological activities such as adaptation, consciousness, emotional expression, attitude formation, memory, recognition, imagination, and thought are seen as special emergents. Individual development consists in forming habits and adapting and modifying them. The essential property of habit is found in the tendency of an organism to continue processes proved beneficial. A habit maintains advantageous stimulations by the organism's own movements. Accommodation, on the other hand, is adaptation to more complex conditions of stimulation by the performance of more complex functions.

Continued accommodation is possible only because of habit, which conserves the past response and solidifies the structure for new accommodations. Moreover, the copy becomes, by transference from the world to the mind, capable of revival in memory. Hence accommodation may take on a conscious basis in volition. Volition is a kind of persistent imitative suggestion arising when a copy is linked with other copies in thought and action. The residue of motive is bound up with attention. The final coordination of all motor elements is volition or choice. Imitation is the integrating principle between habit and accommodation.

In applying the suggestion–imitation formula to the development of selfhood in the child, Baldwin came to the conclusion that personality emerges in stages or "epochs of functional differentiation."

> First, the epoch of the rudimentary sense processes, the pleasure and pain process, and simple motor adaptation, called for convenience the "affective epoch": second, the epoch of presentation, memory, imitation, defensive action, instinct, which passes by gradations into, third, the epoch of complex presentation, complex motor coordination, of conquest, of offensive action, and rudimentary volition. These, the second and third together, I should characterize, on the side of consciousness, as the "epoch of objective reference": and, finally, the epoch of thought, reflection, self-assertion, social organization, union of forces, cooperation; the "epoch of subjective reference," which in human history merges into the "social and ethical epoch."[21]

There are four very distinct phases of children's experience of persons not themselves, all subsequent to their purely *affective*, or pleasure-pain, epoch. First, persons are simply *objects*, parts of the material environment; second, persons are very peculiar objects, very interesting, very active, very arbitrary, very portentous of pleasure or pain. If objects with these properties are *projects*, then persons at this stage may be called *personal projects*. They have certain peculiarities later seen to be the attributes of personality. Third, children's own actions issuing from themselves, largely by imitation in response to the requirements of this "projective" environment, having their own organisms as their center and their own consciousnesses as their theatre, give them light on themselves as *subjects*. Fourth, this self-knowledge is reflected upon other persons to illuminate them as also subjects, and they to children then become *ejects* or social fellows.[22]

Analogically, Baldwin treated the suggestion–imitation formulas that link the individual mind to society as "social heredity" and the process of in-

[21]*Ibid.*, p. 16.
[22]*Ibid.*, p. 18.

teradjustment of persons as "social selection." Socially, the person fit for social life "must be born to learn," for in society learning is the essential need. People receive their personalities and constitute a social organization in terms of their plasticity. Plasticity is the means of their progress. So they grow into the social organization, take their places in the work of the world, and lay deep the sense of values, upon the basis of which their own contributions to the wealth of the world are brought out. They participate in and help constitute a milieu in which each member of society gives and gets the same set of social suggestions. Out of this give and take, in all the interchange of suggestions, an obscure sense of social understanding grows up about ourselves generally — a *Zeitgeist,* an atmosphere, a taste, or in minor matters, a style. The continuity of society is found in the processes of imitation or "social heredity." The innovating or inventive aspects of social process are found in genius.

The interrelation between self and society was nowhere more delicately summed up by Baldwin than in the concluding paragraphs of his *Mental Development,* where he suggests that the antithesis between the self and the world is not valid.

> The self is realized by taking in "copies" from the world, and the world is enabled to set higher copies only through the constant reactions of the individual self upon it. Morally I am as much a part of society as physically I am a part of the world's fauna; and as my body gets its best explanation from the point of view of its place in a zoological scale, so morally I occupy a place in the social order; and an important factor in the understanding of me is the understanding of it.[23]

The rich potential lying in the pluralistic behavioral branch of social behaviorism is dramatically revealed in Baldwin's perceptive studies. It is perhaps not unfair to say that for the first time *the study of the social person* has come into its own as a recognized branch of sociology. The conflict

theorists, particularly Gumplowicz and Small, had perceived the area, but hardly invested it with full standing. Their failure to do so was inevitable: the very emphasis on the more or less complete domination of the individual by the group led to a deemphasis on the individual.

Franklin Henry Giddings. Franklin Henry Giddings (1855–1931) was the son of a Congregational minister of Connecticut. He attended Union College, Schenectady, for the study of engineering. His education was interrupted for teaching, but he completed his degree in 1877. For the next ten years Giddings worked as a journalist. He succeeded Woodrow Wilson at Bryn Mawr College in 1888, teaching political science, economics, and the principles of charity and correction. He introduced a graduate course in sociology at Columbia University, and in 1894 he took over the newly established chair in sociology there. He was one of the founders of *The Annals of the American Academy of Political and Social Science,* and third president of the American Sociological Society.

Giddings's writings extend over a thirty-year period, and reflect a variety of influences.[24] From Comte, he drew his general picture of the main stages of the development of civilization and was, without doubt, influenced by Comte's positivism. From Darwin and Spencer, he took over a naturalistic form of evolutionism. He was strongly influenced by Ward's concept of the use of sociology for social reform. The notion of "sympathy" was taken from Adam Smith, and "social constraint" from Durkheim and Sumner. Other elements of his thought were garnered from John Stuart Mill and Karl Pearson. However, the real core of his sociology, the ultimate conception of its

---

[23]Baldwin, *The Mental Development in the Child and the Race,* pp. 87–88.

[24]Among Giddings's more important works are: *The Principles of Sociology* (New York: Macmillan, 1896, 1926); *The Elements of Sociology* (New York: Macmillan, 1898, 1916); *Inductive Sociology* (New York: Macmillan, 1901); *Studies in the Theory of Human Society* (New York: Macmillan, 1922); *The Scientific Study of Human Society* (Chapel Hill, N.C.: University of North Carolina Press, 1924); and the posthumous *Civilization and Society,* ed. Howard W. Odum (New York: Henry Holt, 1932).

FRANKLIN H. GIDDINGS

The Columbiana Collection, Columbia University

nature and basic units, shows the primary influence of Tarde (possibly reinforced by Ross). Like Tarde, he was interested in the small-scale repetitions of personal acts in interaction. He was convinced that these could be — and ultimately had to be — analyzed statistically.

> Like acts by detached individuals may be competitive, or they may fall into combinations, as when animals in a pack follow the same quarry or beat off a common enemy. When it is often enough repeated, combined action becomes habitual group action.
>
> Whether they are dissimilar or similar, rivalistic or combined, simultaneous or not, equal or unequal, pluralistic reactions to a common stimulation make a strictly individualistic struggle for existence impossible. Above all is this true of the human struggle for achievement. It is a pluralistic struggle.

> Pluralistic behavior, in distinction from individual behavior, has its own conditions, forms, and laws.
>
> Always the character of pluralistic reactions . . . is determined by two variables, namely, (1) the strength of the stimulation, and (2) the similarity (or dissimilarity) of the reacting mechanisms.
>
> Pluralistic behavior is the subject-matter of the psychology of society, otherwise called sociology, a science statistical in method, which attempts, first, to factorize pluralistic behavior, and second, to explain its genesis, integration, differentiation, and functioning by accounting for them in terms of the variables (1) stimulation, and (2) the resemblance (more or less) to one another or reacting mechanisms.[25]

There is an essential identity between Tarde's and Giddings's formulations. Tarde was interested in repetitive and similar overt behaviors. He believed that they expressed inner beliefs and desires. Giddings states that pluralistic action is determined by the strength of stimulation. Tarde believed that a transmitted pattern of behavior is a ray of imitation reflecting the character of its transmitting medium. The second basic variable determining the character of pluralistic action, according to Giddings, was the nature of the reacting mechanisms. Just about everything that Tarde thought important is repeated except for the notion of imitation itself. Of Tarde's idea Giddings stated:

> Tarde examined imitation and all that can be shown to proceed from it with thoroughness and penetration. He gave to the world a precise and characteristic meaning, that of the action at a distance of one mind upon another, whether consciously willed or not willed, passive or active. If it were possible to demonstrate that society is but a tissue of imitations defined as intermental actions, it would be difficult to add much of interest or value to Tarde's argument.[26]

It may be gathered from this that Giddings thought Tarde produced the single most satisfactory system of sociology outside his own: that his

[25]Giddings, *Studies in the Theory of Human Society,* pp. 251–252.
[26]*Ibid.,* p. 116.

principles of "consciousness of kind" and "like-mindedness" were conceived as a direct substitute for Tarde's principle.

Giddings's substitutes for imitation ("like-mindedness" and "consciousness of kind"), except for a shift of emphasis, have quite the same effects as Tarde's principle. Imitation as the central principle of social life casts the primary emphasis upon interhuman action. Giddings's principles play down this interaction and emphasize parallel response to parallel stimuli. Consciousness of kind as the basis of society may be viewed simply as a special form of the similarity of stimulus coming from like individuals. "Combining with and supplementing like-response to stimulation, the consciousness of kind converts a merely instinctive cooperation into concerted action."[27]

When imitation occurs, it is as a kind of second-level principle leading to complex social forms. When an audience springs to its feet at the cry of fire, its initial action, Giddings argues, is not imitation. Example and imitation enter as complicating factors the instant that movement toward the door begins. A cool and fearless person may even prevent a panic. Intermental action is interstimulation and response. Like-mindedness, complicated by intermental action, may become competition or may become concerted volition. It may become solidarity. Unlike-response differentiates and individualizes; it may disintegrate.[28]

Thus Tarde emphasized the transformation of behavior in society; Giddings reversed the emphasis, and treated society largely as a product of pre-social individual similarity. It is not surprising that Giddings found himself in sharp disagreement with Baldwin's argument that *ego* and *alter* represent parallel differentiations from suggestive-imitative life. Consciousness of kind, rather, was argued to be the true source of personality. "The rise of this consciousness marks a distinct stage in the evolution of the mind of the many. Also, *it converts mere gregariousness into society;* and it trans-

forms further the already twice amended and doubly amplified natural ego."[29]

In *Inductive Sociology* (1901), Giddings distinguished five forms of the consciousness of kind: (1) organic sympathy, (2) perception of resemblance, (3) reflective sympathy, (4) affection, and (5) desire. The nature of the particular form of like-mindedness determines all that is essential to the society, social organization, institution, or social class. The key to social life is the formation of like-response. Four like-responses are fundamental: appreciation, utilization, characterization, and socialization. On the basis of such like-response types, four fundamental types of character arise in society: the forceful, the convivial, the austere, and the rationally conscious. The four types of mind correlated with these are the ideo-motor, the ideo-emotional, the dogmatic-emotional, and the critical-intellectual. There are three primary classes: vitality classes, personality classes, and social classes. High-vitality classes have high birth rates and low death rates (rural land-owning), medium-vitality classes fall in between (business and professional), low-vitality classes have a high birth rate and high death rate (workers in the cities). Personality classes divided into genius, talented, normally endowed, and defectives. Social classes are determined by contribution to social life. The true natural aristocracy consists of philanthropists with a highly developed consciousness of kind. The pseudo-social class is composed of congenital and habitual paupers with a degenerate sense of the consciousness of kind.

Giddings was a careful student of Mill, and in his *Inductive Sociology* he followed Mill's discussion. He argued that Mill's methods of agreement and difference establish conditions and causes.[30] This,

[27]*Ibid.*, p. 117.
[28]*Ibid.*, p. 116.

[29]*Ibid.*, p. 163.
[30]John Stuart Mill's inductive logic was a major attempt to generalize scientific procedure to all areas of experience. In trying to clarify the steps of a scientific proof, he outlined a number of procedures, of which the *method of agreement* and *method of difference* were most important. If we are interested, say, in high morale and wish to discover the causes of it, there are, Mill thought, two basic ways to proceed: comparing cases of high morale with

for Giddings, was preliminary to sociological study proper, which depended upon comparative and historical methods. The aim of sociological method is to determine whether a given fact belongs to a given class, and this is a product of historical method. Statistics show what is truly common to social phenomena. In fact, "standard deviation is the key to an understanding of all phenomena of evolution — variations and artificial selection." Moreover, "a coefficient of correlation is always equivalent to a generalization of law."

Such ideas developed in the *Inductive Sociology* were reformulated in a more temperate form in *The Scientific Study of Human Society* (1924). Here he argued that the scientific study of social facts requires the exercise of greatest care, becoming precise only in terms of measurement. He thought that the classification of social facts proceeds dichotomously in terms of the character inherent in them. Sociological study is eventually concerned with complex and variable phenomena (pluralistic behavior), and since it cannot be exhaustive it must utilize samples. Whereas statistics studies factors distributively, the statistical method may be legitimately supplemented by the case method, which studies factors in combination. Casual groups of persons anywhere are rich sources of sociological data. Newspaper items, families, college classes, all may be analyzed. One's discoveries include habits, reactions, consciousness of kind, reactions to the mores, and social interests. Among other things, such detailed study proves the existence of social

---

one another or comparing cases of high morale with cases of low morale. In the first comparison, we would employ the method of difference: we would try to match instances of high morale in such a manner that they would differ item by item in every single respect except for those items causally related to high morale. On the other hand, in the comparison of cases of high morale with those of low morale, we would pursue the method of agreement: we would match the cases of high and low morale item by item for agreement in order to discover the facts which when present bring about high morale but which when absent do not. In attempting to develop experimental designs for field research, Giddings's students also went back to Mill.

telesis, the presence of purpose in human social affairs. Basic methods of measurement include averages, gradings, ratios, percentiles, modes, and coefficients of correlation.

The inconsistencies and errors in Giddings's methodological arguments are far less important than his influence. He made Columbia a center from which radiated the demand for a more rigorous, quantitatively anchored method.

E. A. Ross. It has already been necessary to examine Ross in connection with sociological formalism. The same journalistic sense that led him to turn to sociological formalism, which seemed to offer itself as the most plausible basis for systematizing sociology, had led him at an earlier period to the traditions of Tarde. There is little doubt that the period of Ross's sociology under the influence of Tarde was his richest; why did he ever abandon it? In the first decade of the twentieth century, a number of powerful individual voices commanded the field. Lester Ward, after his retirement from government, taught at Brown University, advocating a form of positivistic organicism, modified somewhat by the conflict theorists; Albion Small at Chicago was building a powerful department and teaching a form of conflict theory; Cooley was developing a branch of social behaviorism somewhat distinct from Tarde's at Michigan; and Giddings at Columbia developed a position similar to that of Tarde. Social behaviorism was the theory of the younger set. At a later period, Ross turned as naturally to Simmel as at this period he turned to Tarde. In the opinion of most students, Ross's two greatest books were done under Tarde's influence — *Social Control* (1901) and *Social Psychology* (1908).[31]

The evidences of Tarde's influence on Ross are many. They include (1) Ross's objection to taking too large units for comparative analysis, (2) his treatment of the historical method and statistical method as essentially complementary, and (3) his

---

[31] For bibliographical information on Ross, see Chapter XII, Footnote 21.

insistence on the importance of a statistical treatment of social phenomena. At this stage, his concept of society is that of Tarde.

> "Society" is, of course, a kind of fiction. There is nothing to it, after all, but people affecting one another in various ways. The thesis of this book is that from the interactions of individuals and generations there emerges a kind of collective mind evincing itself in living ideals, conventions, dogmas, institutions, and religious sentiments which are more or less happily adapted to the task of safeguarding the collective welfare from the ravages of egoism.[32]

Ross took over from Tarde, with little change, the concept of the nature and importance of imitation as well as the proposition that contrasting forms of imitation were manifest in epochs of custom and fashion imitation.

If one conceives of society as a plurality of interacting individuals, as is characteristic of social behaviorism, a series of special subareas leap into prominence. Some of these have been noted: the field of collective behavior emerged in the work of Le Bon and Tarde; the field of personality appeared with Baldwin. In Ross's work still another area of sociological study came into its own — the problem of social control. It is a peculiarity of the theory of social control that it poses anew the problem of the relation of the individual and society. Ross observed that the relation of the individual to society varies, among other things, with the degree of social complexity. The study of social control is the examination of the manner in which the interests of the individual and those of society are combined and ordered.

Had Ross been more of a theorist, there is little doubt that the entire topic would have been considerably more developed. As it was, a latent typology was already present in *Social Control*, a typology designed to sharpen the sorts of social conditions which affect social control. The distinction was drawn between a "natural society" and a

"class-based society." A natural society is the social order appearing when basic human impulses are able to work themselves out without interference. *"Sympathy, sociability, the sense of justice,* and *resentment* are competent, under favorable circumstances, to work out by themselves a true, *natural order,* that is to say, an order without design or art."*[33]

Such a natural order as a "freely competitive society" has been approximated in the societies formed in the American West during the gold rush. Persons coming to the frontiers from various cultural backgrounds worked out a society on the basis of differential abilities and a foundation of natural dependability, trust, and fairness. At the other extreme are "class-based societies" oriented toward the established interests of a particular group. "When the . . . center of such inhibition is a class living at the expense of the rest of the community, we no longer have social control in the true sense, but *class control.* This may be defined as *the exercise of power by a parasitic class in its own interest."*[34]

Presumably the problem of social control displays its full possibilities in societies lying between these extremes — situations in which interhuman adjustment is spontaneous and unforced and situations in which control is arbitrary and coercive. Social control represents the manner in which social phenomena are ordered in the interest of society. It emerges as an issue only when society becomes more complex than the freely established order. The idea implicit in Ross's discussion seems to be that, the moment institutionalization takes place, ordering of the relations of the individuals to others cannot any longer occur spontaneously, and the problem of the regulation of the actions of the individual with respect to institutions appears. The state represents precisely a specialized institution for this purpose. "The state is, in theory at least, a channel and not a source of control. It is supposed to be a device by which social power is

---

[32]E. A. Ross, *Social Control* (New York: Macmillan, 1928), p. 293.

[33]*Ibid.,* p. 41.
[34]*Ibid.,* p. 256.

collected, transmitted, and applied *so as to do* work. But as a matter of fact, the state, when it becomes paternal and develops on the administrative side, is able in a measure to guide the society it professes to obey."[35] In the background of social control is the problem of the relations between the interests of some and the interests of all. This may be seen in the "three laws of social control." (1) Social power is concentrated or diffused in proportion as people do or do not feel themselves in need of guidance or protection.[36] (2) The greater the ascendancy of the few, the more possible it is for social control to affect the course of the social movement.[37] (3) The more distinct, knit together, and self-conscious the influential minority, the more likely is social control to be colored with class selfishness.[38] The risk in the relation of individual and society is that the interests of some achieve ascendancy over the interests of all. In a democratic society, moneyed interests tend to dominate. In fact, the state itself, developed to oppose private interests, creates officials and may become a locus of social power.

The topic of social control is divided into the grounds of control, the means of control, and the system of control. The basic psychological materials of importance for control are sympathy, the sense of justice, sociability, and resentment. These produce the *ego* and *alter,* the sense of justice and equity, the concept of fair play. By themselves, they are sufficient to produce a natural order in which social control is not a specialized fact. The means of control include public opinion, law, belief, social suggestions (including education), custom, religion, personal ideals, ceremony, art, personality, enlightenment, illusion, social evaluation, the ethics of survival, and the ethics of elites. Finally, the problem of systems of control raises the question of the place of social control in the social order. Chiefly, in this section, Ross was occupied

with the socioethical problem of the most desirable system of control. For him, this was the simplest and most spontaneous system possible.

Ross's *Social Psychology* was both less original and better organized than *Social Control.* It was built around the processes of suggestion–imitation and organized its subject matter into conventionality and custom imitation. It took over Tarde's laws that imitation spreads from upper to lower classes, from city to country, and other issues. Among the problems particularly interesting to Ross in this work was the part played by suggestibility in the transfer of ideas, habits, and attitudes from one group to another. The basic anchorage of Ross's interest was in the distributional uniformities of attitudes, ideas, and habits in society rather than in personality.

Ross was a strong voice in the popularization of the pluralistic behavioral branch of social behaviorism. The *Social Psychology,* moreover, not only introduced the ideas of Tarde and Le Bon to the general American audience, but represented the first complete volume in America devoted to collective behavior. Furthermore, from Tarde he derived and transmitted a strong conviction that the future of sociology rested largely upon the development of an adequate statistical method. Though Ross did little to advance such a method, with Giddings he was one of the main persons to popularize it and dramatize its necessity.

However, Ross also illustrates the dilemma that members of the school found themselves in, once they accepted a more liberal conception of society. The organismic positivists and conflict theorists had little trouble accounting for individuals, who were considered to be socialized only to the degree that they were subordinate to the group or society. But once society is conceived as a structure of pluralistic behavior, there is no such easy solution. For this very reason, collective behavior, social control, and the sociology of personality make their appearance. Although Tarde is relatively liberal, Le Bon advocates passionate conservatism. Although Baldwin is primarily liberal, Giddings is primarily conservative. Ross has strong liberal tendencies overlaid with conservatism, as shown pre-

---

[35]*Ibid.,* p. 82.
[36]*Ibid.,* p. 78.
[37]*Ibid.,* p. 85.
[38]*Ibid.,* p. 86.

cisely by his concern with the problem of how society controls the individual.

Meanwhile, pluralistic behaviorism continued to develop in the work of the students of Giddings, two of whom will be reviewed here.[39]

W. F. Ogburn and M. F. Nimkoff. William Fielding Ogburn (1886–1959) earned his doctorate at Columbia University in 1912. He taught sociology at Reed College from 1912 to 1917, and after war service with the government he returned to academic work. He joined the faculty of the University of Chicago in 1927, staying until his retirement in 1952. From 1920–1926, he edited the *Journal of the American Statistical Association*. The most striking of all Ogburn's work was his *Social Change*.[40] Here he developed for the first time the most original and influential of his ideas, one which he continued to elaborate throughout his life.

Ogburn can be approached most simply as developing some aspects of the ideas of the pluralistic behaviorist school. This school generally tended to emphasize social influence rather than biology in the explanation of social events. Significantly, the starting point of Ogburn's analysis was a complaint against the overemphasis on biological factors in

WILLIAM F. OGBURN

United Press International Photo

accounting for social events. More important than biology was humanity's "social heritage" — a term preferred by Baldwin and other members of the school. "The social heritage . . . is not solely the product of human association occurring at a particular period . . . but is a certain surviving product over a very long period of time."[41]

Culture is conceived as the accumulated products of human society, and includes material objects as well as social institutions and social ways. Cultural change is the change in these products. The fundamental factor in cultural change is the accumulation of cultural forms which result from invention and discovery. The basic elements of the social process are invention, diffusion, and

---

[39]Among the important students of Giddings were J. P. Lichtenberger, J. E. Gillin, W. F. Ogburn, H. W. Odum, F. S. Chapin, F. H. Hankins, Hugh S. Carter, C. E. Gehlke, Stuart A. Rice, Elbridge Sibley, Warren S. Thompson, Malcolm M. Willey, and Julian Woodard. By and large, they all remained true to the tenets of pluralistic behaviorism.

[40]W. F. Ogburn, *Social Change with Respect to Culture and Original Nature* (New York: B. W. Huebsch, 1922; Viking, 1927; rev. ed., Viking, 1950); references here are to the two Viking editions. Other important writings of Ogburn and his collaborators are: *The Social Sciences and Their Interrelations*, with Alexander Goldenweiser (Boston: Houghton Mifflin, 1927); *The Economic Development of Post-War France*, with William Jaffe (New York: Columbia University Press, 1929); *Sociology*, with Meyer F. Nimkoff (Boston: Houghton Mifflin, 1940; 3d ed., 1958); *The Social Effects of Aviation*, with Jean L. Adams and S. G. Gilfillan (Boston: Houghton Mifflin, 1946); *Technology and the Changing Family*, with Meyer F. Nimkoff (Boston: Houghton Mifflin, 1955).

[41]Ogburn, *Social Change* (1927 edition), p. 43.

adaptation of cultural elements. This all takes place in a context made up of humanity's accumulated culture or social heritage. There is practically nothing in this that was not stated by Tarde and others of the school. Tarde had located the poles of the social process in repetition and invention. In imitation, conflict, and adaptation, he located the basic model of the spread, reception, and resistance to social influence.

What was new in Ogburn's account was the emphasis on the difference between material culture and adaptive culture. The real sources of progressive change were found in material invention — tools, weapons, and technical processes. Adaptive culture refers to the rest of human social and institutional life, which is "adapted" to this material base. Many things may interfere with the adjustment of this "adaptive" culture to the material base. (1) Those who have vested interests "derive a differential advantage under existing conditions and . . . offer resistance to change."[42] (2) Anything upsetting tradition tends to occasion fear. "So the mores in a culture may embody a definite attitude for or against change."[43] (3) Slowness to change may be due to habit. "Conservatism is . . . an attribute of a people of a particular age and locality or . . . a trait of a special class of individuals."[44] And resistance to change may be due to (4) education or a variety of (5) social pressures or even (6) the wish to forget the unpleasant.

> Culture once in existence persists because it has utility. Forces that produce changes are the discovery of new cultural elements that have superior utility, in which case the old utilities tend to be replaced by the new. The slowness of culture to change lies in the difficulties of creating and adopting new ideas.[45]

A social problem is created by such lack of adjustment. "Material-culture changes force changes in other parts of culture such as social organization and customs, but these latter parts of culture do not change as quickly. They lag behind the material-culture changes, hence we are living in a period of maladjustment.[46]

Ogburn seems to have been quite unhappy with this statement of social change and account of social problems, for he immediately proceeded to develop another. Some problems arise, he argued, not from the lack of adjustment of the various parts of culture, but from the lack of adjustment between human nature and culture. The general argument is that human biology changes very slowly, while human culture changes quickly. "Man is the same biologically as he was in the late ice age, while his culture has suddenly become vastly different. The problem may be popularly expressed as that of cave men trying to live in a modern city. . . . Can we, being biologically the same as Cro-Magnon men, adjust ourselves to the sedentary life demanded of office workers?"[47] It seems emphatically not. It is claimed that a great many social problems such as war, crime, sexual aberrations, and disease "arise because of the inability or difficulty of the original nature of man to adapt itself to modern conditions and cultural standards." So also it is claimed that "much of our unhappiness, nervousness, and insanity is traceable to the same general causes."[48]

There are important discrepancies between the biological and cultural lag theories of social problems. There are, moreover, problems presented by the idea of *culture lag* — a term that remains meaningless until one has first decided what lags behind what. These difficulties throw significant light upon some aspects of pluralistic behaviorism. For one thing, the contrast between the implications of the two lag theories, the cultural and biological, dramatizes an issue faced by the pluralistic behaviorists. The theory of cultural lag, in posing the primacy of technology over the other aspects of culture, shows the remote penetration of modes

[42]*Ibid.*, p. 169.
[43]*Ibid.*, p. 173.
[44]*Ibid.*, pp. 173–174.
[45]*Ibid.*, p. 193.

[46]*Ibid.*, p. 196.
[47]*Ibid.*, p. 286.
[48]*Ibid.*, p. 287.

of thought characteristic of Marxism (with its contrast between "mode" and "relations" of production) or, perhaps, Veblen (with his implicit technocracy). The cultural lag theory finds the progressive element of society to lie in science and technology in a manner characteristic of many liberal positions. However, the biological lag theory spells out the precise opposite implication, in its assertion that the nature of human beings, having evolved much more slowly than their culture, finds many of humanity's most critical problems to derive from the contradictions between a stone-age biology and a twentieth-century culture. This affords a contradictory explanation of the same issues. While the first explanation of social problems attributes them to a deficient application of science, the second would view every gain of science as widening the gap between human nature and culture and driving humanity into crime, homosexuality, suicide, and insanity. Whereas the culture lag theory of social problems is semiliberal, the biological lag theory — treating human culture as the thin veneer over a fundamental savagery — is typically conservative. The uncertainty of self-identification by representatives of pluralistic behaviorism could hardly be more effectively dramatized. Meanwhile, however, Ogburn added still another area or perhaps the blurred outlines of two areas, to pluralistic behaviorism: a theory of social change and its account of social problems.

A new edition of Ogburn's *Social Change* was put out in 1950 with a supplementary chapter. The first edition had appeared in no less than ten printings from 1922 to 1938. In it, Ogburn had produced one of the most widely read and discussed books in the whole of American sociology. Because it has been so much copied, attacked, and defended, the present discussion has focused on the first edition.

It is significant that in the supplementary chapter to the 1950 edition, with the mature wisdom of a man looking back on the work of nearly thirty years, Ogburn was not dissatisfied. "On rereading the section on social evolution in *Social Change,* it is thought that the essential factors that explain social evolution are there to be found.

They are there set forth quite modestly, with apologies for the scarcity of evidence."[49]

Ogburn went on to repeat some of the main arguments of the original. Cultural evolution is explained by four factors: invention, accumulation, diffusion, and adjustment.[50] Invention is either mechanical or social, resulting from the operation of three factors: mental activity, demand, and the existence of other cultural elements. Accumulation occurs when more elements are added to the cultural base than are lost. Diffusion represents the spread of inventions. Adjustment is forced when an invention interacts with other cultural elements. The most general process of such adjustment appears with the lag between material and nonmaterial culture.

The most significant element in this restatement of his original position is the fact that Ogburn repeated only the first of his lag hypotheses: the theory of cultural lag. While he retained the biological lag theory in the 1950 edition and did not reject it, he did not emphasize it either. Whether unconsciously or by intention, Ogburn alone can answer, but he emphasized only the more liberal of his lag theories.

The shift within Ogburn's work to the more liberal position is perhaps in part related to the unusually fruitful collaboration he undertook with Meyer F. Nimkoff.

Meyer F. Nimkoff (1904–1965) received his A.B. degree at Boston University in 1925, taking his M.A. at Southern California in 1926, and his Ph.D. in 1928. He was a professor of sociology at Bucknell University. From 1950 until his death he chaired the sociology department of Florida State University. A major scholar in his own right, Nimkoff has written *The Family* and *Marriage and the Family,* as well as collaborated with Ogburn in *Sociology* and *Technology and the Changing Family.*

In Nimkoff's studies of the family, he argued that the inventions and discoveries of modern science and industry are the most important factors

---

[49]Ogburn, *Social Change* (1950 edition), p. 374.
[50]*Ibid.,* p. 377.

in social change and thereby also in understanding the patterns of contemporary family organization. The family reached its greatest strength in agricultural society, when plow technology was of central importance. The family's economic importance was foundational to its educational, protective, and state functions. The industrial revolution transferred many of these functions to industry and the state, bringing about compensatory forces that accent the affectional role of the family, explaining the family's increased preoccupation with happiness.[51]

It is evident from this that Nimkoff and Ogburn profoundly share the same perspective. Both are pluralistic behaviorists; both take cultural behavior as a primary point of attack on sociological issues; both are impressed by the lines of tension that may emerge between material and nonmaterial culture, the running edge of social change. The difference between the two men in part accounts for the unusual fertility of their collaboration. This difference may be seen between *The Social Effects of Aviation* and *Technology and the Changing Family*.

In *The Social Effects of Aviation,* the thesis is advanced that there is a time sequence between an invention and its social effects, and therefore we should be able to anticipate changes from an invention like aviation. Aviation is argued to parallel automobile transportation, which affected institutions, industries, customs, and personal values. The automobile revolutionized transportation, helped eliminate the use of horses and mules, transformed rail traffic, affected modern tank warfare, redistributed population, led to the centralized school and church, helped to centralize the modern government, transformed the structure of leisure, and changed the patterns of courtship.

A parallel set of transformations is anticipated from aviation. It is expected to increase the size, speed, and variety of aircraft. There will be greater safety and efficiency. The number of passenger miles of air travel will increase. It is possible that first-class domestic mail traveling over four hundred miles and all foreign first-class mail will go by air, leading to an extension of trunk lines and a network of local feeder lines. Air cargo will rise to around 300,000,000 ton miles. A specialization of airports will occur. Private flying will increase, particularly with the development of a low-priced helicopter. However, for some time most families will still prefer the automobile. While the growth of population will be little affected by aviation, the distribution of population will change with more use of sparsely inhabited and out-of-the-way localities. Purchasing a plane will help keep the family small and stimulate location of more families in suburbia or large plots of ground. Inland towns will increase in importance. They will also tend to be decentralized. Aviation will promote the consolidated church, aid missionary work, and administration, but also contribute to secularization and decline in religious sentiment. Aviation will promote the large-scale operations of professional criminals. It will increase opportunities for smuggling and disposal of stolen goods. While it will have little effect on prostitution, it will promote large gambling centers.

Ogburn's interests always tend to be occupied primarily in the development of material culture and from there to its effects. Ogburn and Nimkoff were quite conscious of this difference. They described this kind of study as "like that of a wheel, with the mechanical invention or scientific discovery at the hub and the influences upon society emanating outward like the spokes."[52] By contrast, Nimkoff's interests tend always to be in the social institutions, even when he discovers a large proportion of the forces playing upon them to originate in material culture. Here, again, Ogburn and Nimkoff phrased this very precisely in their joint study of *Technology and the Changing Family:* "In this book . . . a single institution, the family, has been chosen and upon it are recorded the influences

---

[51]M. F. Nimkoff, *The Family* (Boston: Houghton Mifflin, 1934); *Marriage and the Family* (Boston: Houghton Mifflin, 1947).

[52]Nimkoff, *Technology and the Changing Family*, p. iv.

coming from many different inventions and scientific discoveries."[53]

Among the recent changes in the family, the following were found most important: (1) the family ceases to be an economic institution, becoming a romantic and affectional structure; (2) the average age at marriage declines; (3) the trend is toward a smaller family; (4) the number of family functions declines; (5) there are more working wives; (6) the authority structure decays; (7) the accent shifts to the child; and (8) there is more disorganization.

A whole battery of factors, including such things as the use of contraceptives, the effects of the standard of living, the market for the purchase of goods, international relations and religious sanctions, causes these changes. These factors often operate in clusters. For example, "the city represents a cluster of factors, concerned with occupation, density, and ideologies that affect changes in the family."[54] The city, in turn, is said to have been caused by the application of nonhuman power to manufacture and transportation. These in turn were affected by the inventions of steam and steel. The family has also been affected by the invention of contraceptives. And finally, the family has been changed by ideologies regarding democracy, the welfare state, humanitarianism, and education, not so readily traceable to technology.

Ogburn was a man with a single great idea; Nimkoff has been a much more well-rounded sociologist. When they have teamed up, the effect has been to sheer away the more conservative aspects of Ogburn's thought and to convert pluralistic behaviorism into one of its general forms. The two major contemporary syntheses of pluralistic behaviorism, representing the classic phase of the doctrine, and in this respect comparable, for example, to the positions of Tönnies, Durkheim, and Redfield in positivistic organicism, are the works of F. Stuart Chapin on the one hand, and the joint work of Ogburn and Nimkoff on the other. Ogburn and Nimkoff's *Sociology*, first published in 1940 and revised in 1950 and again in 1958, is for this reason one of the most widely used and influential textbooks in North America.

When Ogburn and Nimkoff take the central clue to society to lie in culture, this could easily be misconceived, for this is no return to the tradition of positivistic organicism. They do not propose an organismic theory of society, and culture is not conceived as some kind of superorganic entity in its own right. Culture is merely a general term for learned behavior. "Behavior transmitted by learning from one generation to another is called culture."[55] This quite corresponds to Tarde's insistence that, at bottom, society always consists of individual acts, or Giddings's belief that it represents pluralistic behavior. The same original pattern for explanation of these cultural behaviors is proposed. They are either new (inventions) or repetitions of old acts (diffused patterns or imitations) which lead to readjustments (adaptations). "A culture consists of inventions, or culture traits, integrated into a system, with varying degrees of correlation between the parts."[56]

Quite in accordance with the tradition of pluralistic behaviorism, Ogburn and Nimkoff place the point of gravity in the interdetermination of social behavior. Biological and environmental factors are mere conditions and limitations of social life, not social life itself.[57] A trend present in pluralistic behaviorism since the days when Tarde rejected biological interpretations of crime is reaffirmed. This also emphasizes the liberal aspects of the particular sociological tradition.

Pluralistic behaviorism (Tarde, Le Bon, and Ross) made the discovery of collective behavior. It is significant that once they have developed their concept of cultural behavior and discussed its biological conditions and environmental limits, Ogburn and Nimkoff place the point of analysis of social life proper in the group, the crowd, and the public.[58] The crowd and public are treated as the

---

[53]*Ibid.*
[54]*Ibid.*, p. 257.

[55]Nimkoff, *Sociology* (1958 edition), p. 72.
[56]*Ibid.*, p. 73.
[57]*Ibid.*, Chapters 4 and 5.
[58]*Ibid.*, Chapters 6–9.

two polar types of group, characterized by irrational and rational behavior, respectively. They are, in a sense, the first integration of pluralistic behaviors into structural wholes.

Approached from this point, the social classes and, later, institutions arise as more complex and more stable patterns. In this fashion, by successive steps the Ogburn-Nimkoff analysis moves from cultural behavior toward the communities in which human social life is eventually integrated. But meanwhile, again in accord with the range of the pluralistic behavioral tradition and in contrast to both positivistic organicism and conflict theory, the social individual is given an acknowledged and significant place in sociology,[59] the chief changes in the treatment of the social individual from early pluralistic behaviorism being the incorporation of numerous insights from the symbolic interactionists (such as James, Cooley, Mead, and Dewey), who are still to be discussed.

F. Stuart Chapin. Another graduate of the sociology department at Columbia University, F. Stuart Chapin (1888–1974), developed a very complete system of theory out of the principles of pluralistic behaviorism. After receiving his doctorate in 1911, Chapin taught at Wellesley College (1911–1912), Smith College (1912–1922), and the University of Minnesota. His publications have spanned a period of almost fifty years.[60]

An important part of the Tarde-Ross-Giddings tradition was the conception of statistics as the true method of sociology and the demand for more exact measures of recording and scaling data. Chapin's *Field Work and Social Research* (1920) was one of the first books in American sociology to attempt to provide a systematic inventory of the

F. STUART CHAPIN

Courtesy of F. Stuart Chapin

methods of sociology. Sociology, he maintained, is an inductive discipline. This inductive method consisted, in his opinion, of four parts: a working hypothesis; the collection and recording of observational facts; the classification of them into series and sequences for comparative purposes; and generalization from classified facts to some formula or law which explains their relations.[61] There were, Chapin believed, three major methods of social research: the historical method, using documentary sources; field work, consisting of case work, sampling, and complete enumeration; and statistical analysis, consisting in tabulation and the employment of graphs, ratios, averages, indexes, correlation coefficients, and the like. The various

---

[59]*Ibid.*, Part IV, "Personality."

[60]Chapin's most important works are: *An Introduction to the Study of Social Evolution* (New York: Century Company, 1913; 2d rev. ed., 1925); *Field Work and Social Research* (New York: Century Company, 1920); *Cultural Change* (New York: Century Company, 1928); *Contemporary American Institutions* (New York: Harper, 1935); and *Experimental Designs in Sociological Research* (New York: Harper, 1947).

[61]*Field Work and Social Research*, p. 17.

types of field-work technique were thought to be appropriate to different types of social data: case work to the study of the individual; sampling to the study of the group; and complete enumeration to the study of the entire community.

Conceptions of the statistical method have come a long way since 1920, but *Field Work and Social Research* remains a landmark among the early attempts to press statistics systematically into the service of sociological method. The pluralistic behaviorists took the lead in the promotion of statistics.

Because the pluralistic behaviorists, including Chapin, were placing their faith in the development of statistical methods as the best way to establish a properly inductive sociology, their attention was increasingly directed to the task of devising more exact measures for recording and scaling social data. Their theories forced them to the position that social life consisted at bottom not of acts, which could be counted and partly quantified, but of attitudes, values, and beliefs, which could not. Hence, if the statistical method were to fulfill its promise, these data had to be quantified. The most notable of Chapin's efforts in this direction were his living-room scale of social status and his social participation scale. His social status scale may illustrate his work along these lines.

As early as 1928 Chapin had raised the question of the possibility of measuring social status.[62] The hypothesis was posed that relations of a quantitatively exact character obtain between various factors composing social status (culture, income, material possessions, and so on). Hence, we are able not only to measure these variables by special scales but we can use any one scale as an index to socioeconomic status as a whole. It was assumed that the items found in a living room should permit the construction of such an index of socioeconomic status. The scale was formed by assembling such items, dropping irrelevant ones, and assigning a system of weights to those retained. Rules for the use of the scale were carefully standardized. A few items taken from the 1933 version of the scale[63] are illustrative:

Schedule of Living Room Equipment

I. FIXED FEATURES
1. Floor _____
      Softwood, 1
      Hardwood, 2
      Composition, 3
      Stone, 4
2. Floor covering _____
      Composition, 1
      Carpet, 2
      Small rugs, 3
      Large rug, 4
      Oriental rug, 5
3. Wall covering _____
      Paper, 1
      Kalsomine, 2
      Plain paint, 3
      Decorative paint, 4
      Wooden panels, 5

However, as time went by, Chapin became increasingly convinced that the full potential of an inductive sociology would not be achieved by statistics alone, even when implemented by more exact scaling and measuring devices. Returning, as did Giddings, to the methods of agreement and difference as elaborated by John Stuart Mill, Chapin proposed the establishment of experimental designs under field conditions which would, in effect, approximate the kind of control achieved manually in the laboratory experiment. The aim of such experimental designs under field conditions was to provide the basis for testing causal hypotheses. Experimental design in the field proceeds by means of two groups — an experimental group and a control group. The key problem is securing

[62]F. Stuart Chapin, "A Quantitative Scale for Rating the Home and Social Environment of Middle Class Families in an Urban Community: A First Approximation to the Measurement of Socio-Economic Status," *Journal of Educational Psychology,* 19 (February 1928).

[63]F. Stuart Chapin, *The Measurement of Social Status by the Use of the Social Status Scale* (Minneapolis: University of Minnesota Press, 1933).

controlled observation. "Sometimes this control is achieved by identical individual matching; but more often it is approximated by equating frequency distributions on a given trait."[64] In two groups of persons, processes, or structures which have been made comparable in this fashion, the effect of varying factors is studied. Preferably only a single factor is varied at a time in the experimental group; the matching factor is not varied in the control group. Studies of both experimental group and control group are made before and after the experimental operation. Presumably differences between the experimental group and the control group will be causally related to the factor which has been varied. Three types of experimental designs are outlined:

1. *Cross-sectional design,* which makes controlled comparisons for a single date by procedures of selective control. . . .
2. A *projected design* of "before" and "after" study, in which an attempt is made to measure the effects of a social program or social force at some future date, thus following through the flow of events from a present date to some future date, by procedures of selective control. . . .
3. An *ex post facto design,* in which some present effect is traced backward to an assumed causal complex of factors or forces at a prior date, using for this purpose such records as are available. . . .[65]

Experimental Designs in Sociological Research is the methodological culminating point in Chapin's career.

In his two most important theoretical works, Chapin shows somewhat greater departures from the original formulations of Tarde, Giddings, and Ross than do Ogburn and Nimkoff. In *Cultural Change* (1928), for example, the attempt to include the ideas of other schools is evident. Cultural change is treated as "selectively accumulative in time, and cyclical or oscillatory in character." Moreover, the cycles "may be split up into cycles of

(1) material culture and (2) non-material culture." It is selectively accumulative because there is an "adding of new elements by invention borrowing," as well as a dropping of elements.

It is clear that the ideas of invention and imitation or diffusion are complemented in this account with the added idea of cultural cycles (an idea developed by various representations of the organismic schools). The cycles are of several types: those of first order relate to material culture and may be minor, small, and limited in time, like a business cycle or cycle of dependency in a city; or they may be major, like the rise and fall of the slave system of Rome, the manorial system of England, feudalism in France, or capitalism in modern Europe. Cycles of second order relate to nonmaterial culture and also may be of minor degree (like the rise of religious sects, or the growth of a type of governmental structure) or of major degree (illustrated by ancestor worship, the patriarchal family, or monarchical government). Cycles of third order refer to larger cultural compositions such as national culture or civilization, and vary from minor things like the rise and fall of dynasties or classes to major types like the rise of Hellenic, Mycenaean, or Hindu culture.

Chapin believed it to be possible to develop basic hypotheses to account for such cycles. Four were proposed: every cultural form has its own law of change; the law of each cultural form is cyclical and probably periodic; it is possible to express the law of its life cycle quantitatively; and when cycles or periods of a number of cultural forms are synchronous, there is produced a period of maturity of the cultural nation or a group in which the traits are located.

This cyclical notion also leads to the assumption that there is a period of equilibrium in every cyclical change. This led Chapin to the idea that there may be present devices — social regulators — which directly implement the equilibrium. On the level of material culture, there are the well-known regulators, the stock and produce exchanges and the Federal Reserve System of bank-note issue. On the level of nonmaterial culture, "we have as regulators of social change the various elements in the

[64]Chapin, *Experimental Designs in Sociological Research,* p. 35.
[65]*Ibid.,* pp. 32–33.

The Cycle of the Social Process[68]

Phase	Ascendant Pattern	Leadership Type	Popular Psychology
PHASE III: INTEGRATION	Manifest culture patterns (*i.e.,* open public, accepted patterns)	Administrators who consolidate	People are tired of social experiments
PHASE II: EXPERIMENTATION	Manifest patterns in process of formation	Innovators; experimental executives	People are anxious, looking for an answer to their problems
PHASE I: STABILITY INERTIA	Latent patterns fermenting	Titular leaders	People are complacent

system of social control such as custom, belief, public opinion, and education, as well as law."[66]

In general, Chapin's account of social change is characterized by the addition of many elements from other traditions than that of the Tarde-Giddings school. However, it is interesting that in the continuation of his thesis he discovers that underneath the phenomenon of selective cultural accumulation and cyclical manifestation is a more fundamental group reaction pattern. This group reaction pattern has three phases in response to any new situation.

> Phase I. The group reacts by an effort to enforce its mores. . . . But a lack of adjustment is soon felt and a shift to the second phase of the reaction pattern follows.
> Phase II. The group reacts by trying out different expedients. . . .
> Phase III. The group integrates its trial and error efforts into a stable plan. . . .[67]

At the most fundamental level of his theory of social and cultural change, the same elements as are present in Tarde's scheme of imitation, conflict, and adaptation are found. Chapin's societal reaction pattern starts the cycle with the conflict stage. In *Cultural Change,* Chapin lifts the theory of change of pluralistic behaviorism from Tarde to Ogburn to general form.

The societal reaction pattern, Chapin's point of closest affinity with the Tarde-Giddings tradition, formed the starting point for his approach to other areas — the problem of leadership, for instance. He suggested that the different phases of the societal reaction pattern required different types of leaders. In Phase I, titular or bureaucratic leaders were sufficient. But in Phase II, spontaneous natural and experimental leaders were required. In Phase III, great organizing, coordinating, consolidating, and selective leaders were needed. Culture patterns and popular psychology were also organized in terms of this schema.

In *Contemporary American Institutions,* Chapin's second major theoretical work, his affinities with the Tarde-Giddings tradition are made even more clear. He insists that sociology needs a small, concrete unit of investigation. This is a unit of individual behavior structure in terms of considerations of means–ends (that is, based on attitudes, ideas, and beliefs). To be sure, large-scale, unplanned forces may be generated as unplanned

[66]Chapin, *Cultural Change,* p. 222.
[67]*Ibid.* p. 228.

[68]Chapin, *Contemporary American Institutions,* abbreviated from the table on p. 299.

Nucleated Social Institutions[70]

Type Part	Family	Church	Government	Business
I. ATTITUDE AND BEHAVIOR PATTERNS	Affection Love Loyalty Respect	Reverence Loyalty Fear Devotion	Subordina-tion Cooperative-ness Fear Obedience	Workmanship Thrift Cooperation Loyalty
II. SYMBOLIC CULTURE TRAITS, "SYMBOLS"	Marriage Ring Crest Coat of arms Heirloom	Cross Ikon Shrine Altar	Flag Seal Emblem Anthem	Trademark Patent sign Emblem
III. UTILITARIAN CULTURE TRAITS (REAL PROPERTY)	Home Dwelling Furniture	Church edifice Cathedral Temple	Public building Public works	Shop Store Factory Office
IV. CODE OF ORAL OR WRITTEN SPECIFICATIONS	Marriage license Will Genealogy Mores	Creed Doctrine Bible Hymn	Charter Constitution Treaties Laws Ordinances	Contracts Licenses Franchises Articles of incorporation

consequences of individual behaviors. These too must ultimately be brought under study. Institutions arise through the stabilization of the elements of behavior. (1) Institutions arise out of the repeated grouping of individuals in the satisfaction of basic needs (sex, hunger, fear). (2) Reciprocating attitudes and conventionalized behavior pattern appear, embodying attitudes of affection, loyalty, cooperation, domination, subordination. (3) Cultural objects embodying symbolic values are invented (idols, crosses, rings, flags). (4) Cultural implements and objects facilitating the behavior associated with the institution are constructed (buildings and furniture). (5) The knowledge gained in such experience is either preserved in written documents or transmitted orally to new generations.[69]

Two kinds of institutions (stabilized social behavior patterns) arise: diffuse or cultural (like language, art, and so on), and nucleated. Nucleated institutions have four type parts, as shown in the table above. Chapin's development of the concept of institutions with a strongly empirical slant was quite in the tradition of Tarde and Giddings.

[69]*Ibid.*, p. 14.
[70]*Ibid.*, p. 16.

There were many other interesting aspects of Chapin's theories, including the development of a concept of latent and manifest functions (an idea that has recently become popular in other theories). He also developed a theory of the bureaucratic and professional personalities, which he tied to his theories of the societal reaction pattern and institutions. However, Chapin, like Ogburn and Nimkoff, represents the same kind of classical synthesis of the basic ideas of pluralistic behaviorism as Tönnies and Durkheim do for the theories of organismic positivism. He developed its method, its theory of social change, structure, leadership, and personality.

BEHAVIORISTIC SOCIOLOGY

B. F. Skinner. With the death of F. Stuart Chapin, one of the last members of the old Giddings school, the pluralistic behavioral branch of social behaviorism would seem to have come to an end. Meanwhile, however, behavioristic psychology had been undergoing extensive development. Its members had been observing a rigorous discipline in preserving the analysis of the actions of animals and human beings on a strictly behavioral level and developing a solid foundation of experimental evidence in support of their theories.

Sooner or later, as long as a behavioristically inclined school of sociology remained fruitful, one of the following alternatives could be expected: either pluralistic behaviorists among the sociologists would begin to draw inspiration from the behavioristic psychologists or the behavioristic psychologists would begin to move into sociology, quite possibly through social psychology. The older pluralistic behaviorists made little use of new developments in psychological behaviorism, despite the evident attractiveness of its scientism and rigorous empiricism. The reasons for that disinterest can probably be found in the inclination of professionals once established in their disciplines to remain within their boundaries. Major recombinations across disciplines tend to be made by

B. F. SKINNER

Courtesy of B. F. Skinner. Photo by Hans-Peter Biemann

newly trained novices in the field whose training programs may require them to work up minor as well as major programs of study.

By World War II, at a time when the older pluralistic behaviorists were nearing the close of their careers, a number of behavioristic psychologists had brought their theories to a point where extension of their principles to social and cultural problems and activities appeared to be the next major challenge. No one was more ready for this step (it was noted earlier that Clark Hull was also on this threshold at the time of his death) than B. F. Skinner.

Burrhus Frederic Skinner was born in Susquehanna, Pennsylvania in 1904. He earned the A.B. at Hamilton College in 1926, the M.A. in 1930, and the Ph.D. at Harvard in 1931. He was a research fellow and junior fellow at Harvard from 1931 to 1936. From 1936 to 1945 he was on the teaching staff of the University of Minnesota, conducting war research sponsored by General Mills during 1942 and 1943. Between 1945 and 1948 he chaired the psychology department at Indiana University. He became professor of psychology at Harvard in 1948 and remained there until his retirement as professor emeritus in 1974.

A pioneer of operant behavior, Skinner, who does not appear to have special theoretical abilities or interests, was an adept behavior tactician and a talented home mechanic fascinated by prospects of the control of the behavior of animals and human beings. He had at his disposal a body of experimentally established behavioral concepts: the notion that the stimulus-response arc was a basic building block of behavior; the idea established by Pavlov that new units of behavior could be built by substituting or adding conditioned to unconditioned stimuli; the idea that stimulus-response units could be consolidated (as Edward Thorndike[71] put it, "stamped in") when followed by a satisfying state of affairs (hence trial and error, or instrumental learning, was reenforced by what Thorndike called the "law of effect").

Taking a nontheoretical descriptive approach and viewing behavior as under the control of environmental consequences that positively or negatively (aversively) reenforce it, one may divide the controls into a number of basic types: reward, escape, avoidance, and punishment. The reenforcers may be primary or secondary (conditioned). Satisfying hunger by eating is a primary reenforcer; signaling the imminent appearance of food is a conditioned or secondary enforcer. Under the pressure of some primary reenforcer it is possible to build elaborate chains of behavior in which each step in the chain becomes a reenforcing stimulus for the chain as a whole. Such chains are typically built from their termination in a reverse sequence.

Reenforcement control may be applied in schedules that are continuous or intermittent, which, in turn, may be interval or ratio schedules. The slot machine, for example, is designed to pay off in accordance with the principles of a variable ratio. Motivation or drive is argued to be largely a product of schedules of reenforcement. Highly motivated individuals are able to sustain high ratio requirements without apparent strain.

In his first major study Skinner suggested that human equivalents of the same types of results obtained by experimental psychologists in the study of other animals could also be obtained from the study of humans.[72] Human behavior, in short, arises and is maintained by operant conditioning. In every life sphere, behavior is learned and stabilized on the basis of trial and error, imitation, and instruction. Both imitation and willingness to follow instruction are explainable in reenforcement terms. Skinner maintains that language, the most significant human skill, arises on the basis of differential reenforcement, which builds a basic repertoire of words and expressions, imitation, and instruction. Even creativity (originating when reenforcement is provided to the search for a novel response), emotional response, religion, and mental illness (disordered or undesirable behavior intensified because of its reenforcing consequences) are believed to result from operant conditioning. This approach, in Skinner's view, opens up an unlimited vista in the prediction, modification, and control of behavior, suggesting drastic modification of current educational practice. It

[71]Edward L. Thorndike, *Animal Intelligence* (New York: Macmillan, 1911).

[72]Among major books by B. F. Skinner are: *The Behavior of Organisms: An Experimental Analysis* (New York: Appleton-Century-Crofts, 1938); *Walden Two* (New York: Macmillan, 1948); *Science and Human Behavior* (New York: Macmillan, 1953); *Verbal Behavior* (New York: Appleton-Century-Crofts, 1957); *Schedules of Reinforcement*, with Charles B. Verster (New York: Appleton-Century-Crofts, 1957); *The Technology of Teaching* (New York: Appleton-Century-Crofts, 1968): *Contingencies of Reinforcement: A Theoretical Analysis* (New York: Appleton-Century-Crofts, 1969); *Beyond Freedom and Dignity* (New York: Knopf, 1971).

has, in fact, led to the development of programmed instruction, the wide use of "teaching machines," and a burgeoning practice of behavior therapy.

Skinner's practical ingenuity led him to develop the Skinner Box, an instrument to trace changes in animal behavior. He was also inclined to extend his talents and interest in control to humans and invented both the Air Crib, a mechanical baby tender, and a teaching machine. But he gave full expression to his fantasies of human behavioral control in his utopian novel *Walden Two*.

Walden Two presents a utopian community experiment conducted by a renegade behavioral psychologist named Frazier. It is a self-sufficient community, employing the latest scientific principles and technologies. Everyone works for the community and receives pay in the form of credits against the collective. The cooking, serving, and consuming of food takes place in collective messes. The community is under the direction and control of six planners who make policies, review the managers, and keep track of events in the community as a whole. Each serves for ten years, receiving a number of credits for service. Administration is in the hands of managers in charge of such divisions and services as Food, Health, Play, Arts, Dentistry, Dairy, various industries, Supply, Labor, Nursery School, Advanced Education and the like. Such managers are specialists with long service in the community and are more like civil servants than elected officials. In fact, no democracy is permitted in Walden Two.

Special care is devoted to socialization and education. Infant care occurs in aquariumlike pens or boxes, clearly modeled after Skinner's baby tender. All education rests on the principles of operant conditioning. Ethical training is completed by the age of six.

Operant conditioning has eliminated sex as a problem in *Walden Two*. Early marriage is advocated. Girls are encouraged to marry by the age of fifteen or sixteen with the hope that their child rearing (four children being desirable) will be completed by the age of twenty-two or twenty-three, freeing women for affairs of the community for the rest of their lives. On the drawing boards is the possible elimination of the family altogether (experience in the outside world testifying to the increasing irrelevance and frailty of the institution). Food preparation, child rearing, and education have already been removed from its sphere. Similarly, religion has been virtually abandoned except for a communal code and some ceremonial observance designed as much to confuse the world outside on the position of Walden Two as to take up any residual emotional slack that the elimination of traditional religion may have left.

Freedom, responsibility, dignity, and autonomy have no place in Walden Two. Bravery means nothing, since operant conditioning has made everyone equally brave, and most of the emotions, especially the negative ones — ambition, envy, jealousy, spite, and anger — have been removed by proper reenforcement schedules. However, inasmuch as there are still many Walden Two members whose pre-Walden personal histories may have left them with reenforcement schedules that permit inappropriate emotions or negative ideas, the full realization of the ideal of Walden Two will have to wait until a complete self-trained generation takes over.

Since part of its conditioning includes the permanent attachment to the culture of Walden Two itself, closing the arc, the community will henceforth remain immune to outside influence and will no longer be subject to change, except from within by its own scientists and with the approval of its own planners. Until then, even the founder, Frazier, was forced to admit that he was inclined to the Walden Two experiment by an inappropriate sentiment, the wish for power over people, to play God.

Walden Two is a watered-down version of Aldous Huxley's *Brave New World*, though not written as an ironic humanistic critique of major trends in contemporary society, but as a serious intention to realize a positively reenforced social life. *Walden Two* was critically reviewed by Joseph Wood Krutch, professor of English, editor, art critic, writer, and naturalist. Krutch describes it as an *ignoble* utopia.

> Walden Two is a utopian community created by an experimental psychologist named Frazier who has learned the techniques for controlling thought with precision and who has conditioned his subjects to be happy, obedient and incapable of antisocial behavior. Universal benevolence and large tolerance of individual differences reign — not because it is assumed, as the founders of such utopias generally do assume, that they are natural to all innocent men uncorrupted by society — but because an experimental scientist, having at last mastered the "scientific ability to control men's thoughts with precision," has caused them to think benevolently and tolerantly. . . . whereas Plato's *Republic* and More's *Utopia* are noble absurdities, *Walden Two* is an ignoble one . . . the first two ask men to be more than human, while the second urges them to be less.[73]

Skinner and his fellow behaviorists, in Krutch's view, were "cheerful mechanists" asking from many not reasoned behavior but automatism; they were advancing a modernized and mechanized version of the ideal of cloistered virtue.

The observations of Krutch and of other critics of *Walden Two* apparently rankled (or perhaps Skinner would prefer, represented an aversive reenforcment that lasted for twenty years) and Skinner's motivation remained high (or had been subjected to an unusually effective variable ratio reenforcement schedule), for twenty years later he returned to all the ideas on which he had been challenged in *Walden Two* and defended them vigorously.

All the most severe problems of our age, Skinner argues, arise from the persistence of prescientific notions of humanity including: character, personality, the autonomous individual, the pursuit of freedom, the positive evaluation of dignity, and the tendency to distribute praise and blame. The primary task of contemporary human beings, in Skinner's view, is the application of the available technology of behavioral control. This means the transformation of all behavior problems into contingencies of reenforcement. The ultimate source of good and bad is traced to evolutionary selection: "Things are good (positively reinforcing) or bad (negatively reinforcing) . . . because of the contingencies of survival under which the species evolved."[74] All conditioned reenforcers derive their power from personal enforcers, and hence are anchored in the evolution of the species. This is important to keep in mind since from birth the child is responding more to a social than to a natural environment.

> A child . . . begins at once to acquire a repertoire of behavior under the contingencies of reinforcement to which he is exposed as an individual. Most of these contingencies are arranged by other people. They are, in fact, what is called a culture . . . .
>
> The social contingencies, or the behaviors they generate, are the "ideas" of a culture; the reinforcers that appear in the contingencies are its "values."[75]

Our task, according to Skinner, is to strip away the functions previously assigned to the autonomous individual and transfer them to the controlling environment. We must see the self as a repertoire of behavior appropriate to its controlling environment and, once and for all, abolish "the inner man, the homunculus, the possessing demon, the man defended by the literatures of freedom and dignity."[76]

George C. Homans. George Caspar Homans (1910–   ) was born in Boston. He earned the A.B. at Harvard College in 1932 in English literature, but found himself unemployed when a prospective job in journalism with William Allen White of the Emporia, Kansas, *Gazette* failed because of the Depression.[77] He entered the famous

---

[73]Joseph Wood Krutch, *The Measure of Man* (New York: Grosset & Dunlap, 1953), pp. 57, 58 and 59.

[74]Skinner, *Beyond Freedom and Dignity,* p. 99.

[75]*Ibid.,* p. 121.

[76]*Ibid.,* p. 191.

[77]An autobiographical statement appears in the collection of Homans's essays, George Caspar Homans, *Sentiments and Activities* (New York: The Free Press, 1962), pp. 1–49.

GEORGE C. HOMANS

Harvard University News Office

seminar (Fall 1932) of Lawrence Joseph Henderson at Harvard on Vilfredo Pareto, and started on the course that would both bring him into sociology and thrust him to the center of an emerging school of sociological theory that came to be known as structure-functionalism. Homans reports that as a self-satisfied Bostonian from a wealthy family, he was drawn by Pareto's anti-Marxism. In Henderson's seminar he became close friends with Bernard DeVoto, Crane Brinton, and Joseph Schumpeter. With Charles P. Curtis he wrote *An Introduction to Pareto*. This, in turn, was a major factor in Homans's admission to the newly established Society of Fellows, formed by John Livingstone Lowes in cooperation with President Lowell and Alfred North Whitehead to explore the possibility of graduate training more adequate than that of the Ph.D. This experience brought

Homans in direct contact with the new work in industrial sociology being developed by Elton Mayo, Wallace Donham, Fritz Roethlisberger, and others and the work of functional anthropologists such as A. R. Radcliffe-Brown, Bronislaw Malinowski, and W. Lloyd Warner. Durkheim's works were popular in these circles.

Homans's increasing involvement with functionalism provided him with the interpretative framework for approaching the world of his English ancestors. His study of *English Villagers in the Thirteenth Century* was based on a functionalistic point of view. He was a fellow from 1934 to 1948. He became an instructor in 1939, remaining until 1941 when he completed his study of *English Villagers*. From 1941 to 1945 he served in the United States Navy. He rejoined the Harvard staff in 1946, moving full time into sociology, and becoming a full professor in 1953. In 1950 he completed a classic of the emerging functionalistic theory, *The Human Group*.[78]

Homans demonstrated a dramatic change of theoretical position after writing *The Human Group*, which may be accounted for by time he spent at Cambridge University obtaining an M.A. in English in 1955. Homans himself explained the shift as a result of his readings in experimental psychology and in the logic of scientific method, and his preference (inherited from his puritan ancestors) for individualism. All of these factors led to an in-

[78]Homans's major prewar works were *An Introduction to Pareto*, written with Charles P. Curtis, Jr. (New York: Knopf, 1934), and *English Villagers of the Thirteenth Century* (Cambridge, Mass.: Harvard University Press, 1941). *The Human Group* (New York: Harcourt Brace, 1950) will be discussed in Chapter XX on macrofunctionalism. Homans's major contributions to behavioristic sociology include: "Social Behavior as Exchange," *The American Journal of Sociology*, 62 (May 1959), 595–606; *Social Behavior: Its Elementary Forms* (New York: Harcourt, Brace & World, Inc., 1961); *Sentiments and Activities* (Glencoe, Ill.: The Free Press, 1962); "Bringing Men Back In," *American Sociological Review*, 29 (December 1964), 809–818; *The Nature of Social Science* (New York: Harcourt, Brace & World, 1967); *Social Behavior: Its Elementary Forms*, rev. ed. (New York: Harcourt, Brace, Jovanovich, 1974).

creasing dissatisfaction with the functionalism of Durkheim and Talcott Parsons from the early 1950s on. What seemed like a radical reorganization of his point of view appears to have come about gradually by way of a series of small changes that eventually added up to a new departure. However it was spurred, Homans's essay on "Social Behavior as Exchange" was the first sketch of his behavioristic phase.

In this article, written for a special issue of the *American Journal of Sociology* in honor of Georg Simmel, Homans suggested that Simmel was the ancestor of postwar small-group research, which he took to be the growing edge of a scientific sociology. Homans urged that the tasks of small-group research were to integrate laboratory experiments with quantified field work, and to reduce the propositions established in small-group research to a more basic and general set which, he opined, would be discovered ultimately to be psychological. He stated emphatically: "I hold myself to be an 'ultimate psychological reductionist.'"[79] The value of this position can be seen by adopting the view "that interaction between persons is an exchange of goods, material and non-material."[80] Moreover, a special virtue of the exchange theory is that it will "bring sociology closer to economics,"[81] the oldest, most advanced, and most practical of the sciences of humanity. Sustaining economic exchange theory, in turn, is the behavioral psychology of Skinner as illustrated in his study of pigeons. In his social exchange with pigeons, Skinner proved that by reenforcing the behavior he was anxious to produce (such as enacting a parody of table tennis) with corn (the paradigm of value), Skinner was able to train his birds to perform bizarre stunts. Homans, in turn, treats the social exchange between Skinner and his pigeons as the paradigm of all social exchange. Homans, thus, bears direct responsibility for Bredemeier's reaction quoted above.

Armed with his behavioristic theory of social life drawn from instrumental psychology and generalizing it to human economic exchange, Homans lost no time in attacking the central premise of those branches of small-group theory deriving from Kurt Lewin and the gestalt psychologists: the notion that small group behavior occurs in fields in which properties of the field (such as cohesiveness and solidarity, which operated as restorative or equilibrating mechanisms) are the cause of behavior. "I shall not, as structure-functional sociologists do, use an assumed equilibrium as a means of explaining, or trying to explain, why other features of a social system should be what they are."[82] Rather, Homans argues, the parties to a social exchange approach it with a variety of interests or values (behavioral reenforcers or the equivalents of a pigeon's corn) such as material and nonmaterial rewards (enjoyment of power and receiving esteem and pay). Group equilibrium is reduced to a condition of "distributive justice" when the rewards and costs to all parties to the exchange are in rough balance. "Distributive justice," he concludes, "may be one of the conditions of group equilibrium."

To illustrate the application of his exchange paradigm of behavioristic sociology to general problems of social structure, Homans reviewed Peter Blau's study of *The Dynamics of Bureaucracy*.[83] Blau studied the behavior of sixteen agents in a federal law-enforcement agency who investigated firms and prepared reports on their compliance with the law, with particular interest in discovering consultations between agents in preference to admitting possible incompetence to their supervisors. The interrelations that were found between agents were said to arise as trade-offs or exchanges of recognition and esteem in return for help in which the more competent agents were centers of the most brisk interaction. The lesson Homans drew from this is that if the behavioristic theory and

[79]Homans, *Sentiments and Activities*, p. 279.
[80]*Ibid.*
[81]*Ibid.*, p. 280.

[82]*Ibid.*, p. 284.
[83]Peter M. Blau, *The Dynamics of Bureaucracy* (Chicago: University of Chicago Press, 1955).

economic exchange paradigm are capable of extension to activities of individuals in a federal bureaucracy, they presumably can also apply to any area of social life whatsoever.

In the first edition of *Social Behavior: Its Elementary Forms*, Homans indicated, without elaborating on the point, his realization that he was on a course that would bring him into conflict with his colleague Talcott Parsons. "Much modern sociological theory seems to me to possess every virtue except that of explaining anything." He then footnoted to Parsons in that connection.[84] And, indicating that he proposed to explain social life by the reduction of its principles to those of behavioral psychology he made explicit in a footnote his rejection of Durkheim's antireductionism.[85] He developed at length his debt to Skinnerian psychology and his belief that market behavior, as described in elementary economic theory, was the best of all possible paradigms for the extension of behavioral psychology into a general explanation of human social life. He formulated the five fundamental principles of social life from a behaviorist point of view:

1. The more often an activity has been rewarded in the past the more likely it is to occur in a similar stimulus situation in the present.
2. Other persons tend to repeat behaviors one rewards.
3. Individuals tend to repeat activities that are most rewarded.
4. An individual may grow surfeited with an excessively rewarded activity.
5. An individual tends to get angry when he is inadequately rewarded, especially if others are adequately rewarded.[86]

Homans also developed at some length the idea that the economic exchange paradigm of behavioral psychology was applicable, when appropriately modified, to many other areas of social life

(political, administrative, general, social). Finally he suggested that institutions differ from elementary social behavior only in being more complex and indirect or roundabout. Homans speculated that when institutions generate tensions with elementary social behavior, civilization may be heading for trouble.

With the publication of the 1961 edition of *The Human Group*, Homans's behavioristic sociology was essentially complete. Much of his activity in the 1960s consisted of sharpening his criticism against such functionalists as Durkheim and Parsons, and elaborating his methodological principles. This work appears in a series of statements from his autobiographical introduction to his essays in *Sentiments and Realities*, through the Walter Ames lectures at the University of Washington in 1965, published as *The Nature of Social Science* in 1967, and his introduction, "The Sociological Relevance of Behaviorism," to *Behavioral Sociology*.[87]

Homans's basic criticism of Durkheim is that in treating society as a reality sui generis and proposing to explain one social fact by another as if the social represented an emergent new reality, he never uncovers the underlying psychological and historical realities of social life.[88] His basic criticism of Parsons is that he endlessly elaborates a conceptual scheme consisting of definitions of words and rarely, if ever, states propositions capable of empirical test.[89]

There are, Homans urges, four types of explanation prevalent in sociology: explaining institutions by other institutions (structural explanations, which are no explanation at all); explaining institutions filling a vital need (functional explanations, which somehow never manage to get down to specifics and in practice are a failure); explaining institutions as the end products of historical development (historical explanations); and ex-

[84]Homans, *Social Behavior*, p. 10.
[85]*Ibid*., p. 12.
[86]Paraphrased from *Human Behavior*, pp. 53, 54, 55, and 75.

[87]Homans, "The Sociological Relevance of Behaviorism," in Robert L. Burgess and Don Bushell, Jr., eds., *Behavioral Sociology: The Experimental Analysis of Social Process* (New York: Columbia University Press, 1969), pp. 1–24.
[88]*Ibid*., pp. 17–20.
[89]*Ibid*., p. 5.

plaining institutions by the characteristics of human behavior and the circumstances in which it occurs (psychological explanation). In practice, Homans argues, historical explanations ultimately rest on psychological explanations, which alone supply the basic generalizations of all the social sciences.[90]

Although Homans grants that from time to time sociologists will make empirical discoveries, the true task of sociology is not analytic (the basic propositions of social science have already been established by behavioral psychology), but synthetic, displaying the relevance of behavioral psychology for human society. Among the illustrations of behavioral psychology are the following propositions:

> If an action has been rewarded (reinforced), the probability that it will be repeated increases. This I call the *success* proposition. The greater the value of the reward, relative to some alternative, the greater is the probability that the action will be performed. This I call the *value* proposition. If in the past the occurrence of particular stimuli has been the occasion on which a person's action has been rewarded, then the more similar the present stimuli are to those of the past, the more likely the person is to perform the action now. This I call the *stimulus* proposition. A person whose action has often been rewarded, under particular stimuli, in the past, but is not rewarded, under similar stimuli, in the present, is likely to perform acts of aggression. This I call the *frustration-aggression* proposition.[91]

What cannot be explained by behavioral psychology, in Homans's opinion, cannot be explained by any other psychology. Moreover, behavioral psychology comprises a theory of rational behavior, by assuming that all people act to increase their values. To those who oppose this as psychological reductionism, Homans argues, the burden of proof is on those who urge emergence upon us.

Peter M. Blau. The only reason for including Peter Michael Blau (1918–   ) in a discussion of developments in behavioristic sociology is the unfortunate inclusion by Homans himself of Blau's early formulation as an important contribution to "exchange theory." Blau's 1958 work on the behavior of agents in a federal bureaucracy had been cited by Homans as a striking example of the manner in which social activities that appear remote from economics can be fitted to the economic paradigm of behavioral sociology. After Homans's dramatic theoretical reorientation from the functionalist position to which he had contributed so effectively, to his fully elaborated behavioristic model in 1961, it was inevitable that some persons would be drawn to the point of view. By 1962 Richard M. Emerson, who had run experimental studies on the influence processes of small groups for his Ph.D. dissertation, reinterpreted his findings in exchange terms.[92] And in 1964 Peter Blau joined the development of exchange theory.[93]

Blau's *Exchange and Power in Social Life*, although still viewed in some quarters as a "semiclassic in sociological theory,"[94] is, in fact, quite eclectic, treating Homans's behavioristic analysis as adequate for microsociology and resorting to structure-functional principles for problems of macrosociology. Seeing his problem as the derivation of the social process that governs complex structures of communities and societies "from the simpler processes that pervade the daily intercourse among individuals and their interpersonal relations," Blau cautions "two dangers must be avoided . . . the Scylla of abstract conceptions too remote from observable empirical reality and the Charybdis of reductionism that ignores emergent social and structural properties."[95] The figure of

---

[90]*Ibid.*, pp. 4–8.
[91]*Ibid.*, pp. 11–12. What he had earlier called the basic principles of social life have now been reduced to analytical propositions of psychology.

[92]Richard M. Emerson, "Power-Dependency Relations," *American Sociological Review*, 27 (1962).
[93]Peter M. Blau, *Exchange and Power in Social Life* (New York: Wiley, 1964).
[94]Margaret M. Poloma, *Contemporary Sociological Theory* (New York: Macmillan, 1979), p. 62.
[95]Blau, *Exchange and Power in Social Life*, pp. 2–3.

speech distracts attention from the reversal of principles when Blau moves from micro- to macrosociology. Peter Ekeh[96] was not quite accurate when he contrasted the theories of Homans and Blau as "individualistic behaviorist" versus "collectivistic structuralist." Blau straddles behaviorism and structure functionalism.

In Blau's view individuals are attracted to social life by its intrinsic and extrinsic rewards. To enter into exchange with others — the major process of elementary social life — behavior must be directed to values or ends only obtained by interaction and must adopt means directed to such values or ends. However, in the very process of interaction, this elementary competition is said to crystallize into a stratification system and a differentiation of power. The entire social game is then transformed by the appearance of power.

> Although complex social systems have their foundation in simpler ones, they have their own dynamics with emergent properties.[97]

> Some groups evolve as individuals with opportunities for social contact become increasingly attracted to each other. . . . These emergent groups often have diffuse boundaries . . .[98]

> Eventually, group norms to regulate and limit the exchange transactions emerge, including the fundamental and ubiquitous norm of reciprocity, which makes failure to discharge obligations subject to group sanctions.[99]

> Needs, however, do not remain constant. . . . The development of new needs . . . underlies the increasing consumer demand that is an essential element in an expanding economy. But emergent needs serve this function. . . . Religious and political ideals derive their driving force in large part from imbuing adherents with values that make the satisfaction of material wants comparatively unimportant. . . . By reducing material needs, revolutionary ideologies become a

source of independent strength and resistance to power.[100]

In such fashion, in Blau's account, properties, groups themselves, norms, and even needs, ideals, and values of complex society arise by a metamorphosis called emergence from microsociological behaviorial exchange. For all complex forms of social life the behaviorism of Homans is abandoned and problems are analyzed in structure-functionalist terms in essentially a Parsonian manner. Blau cites Parsons almost as much as Homans. Moreover, Blau's functionalism is modified with a conflict perspective in much the same manner as Lewis Coser and Seymour Martin Lipsit, to whom he also frequently refers. Blau is, indeed, a rare breeder of theories: his theory seems to be a cross between a kangaroo and a hippopotamus.

THE FUTURE OF BEHAVIORISTIC SOCIOLOGY

When Homans named his new point of view exchange theory and cited Blau's work on a federal bureaucracy as an illustration of the manner in which complex social behavior — which was apparently remote from the world of animal experimentation and elementary economic behavior — could be analyzed in terms of the exchange paradigm, he opened a door he could hardly have expected Blau not to enter. Blau, however, delivered Homans's point of view into the hands of his enemies. It is quite possible that in the process Blau set the development of behavioristic sociology back by at least a decade. Even Emerson, who was perhaps the first new recruit to Homans's point of view, when reviewing exchange theory for the *Annual Review of Sociology* in 1976, felt it essential to do battle with Blau's heritage and was moved to deny that exchange theory was even a theory. Rather surprisingly, it did not seem to occur to Emerson that Blau had saddled the point of view

[96]Peter P. Ekeh, *Social Exchange Theory: The Two Traditions* (Cambridge: Harvard University Press, 1974).
[97]*Ibid*., p. 20.
[98]*Ibid*., p. 33.
[99]*Ibid*., p. 92.

[100]*Ibid*., pp. 120–121.

with a fatal contradiction: elementaristic behaviorism and holistic structure-functionalism will no more mix without separating than oil and water. The way to theoretical consistency is to pursue each of these theories in isolation from the other and somewhere down the line subject to empirical investigation contradictory explanations that will clearly develop of the same event.

It is quite possible that behavioral sociologists will never be able to shake free from the contradictions that have developed around their proposals, but this does not mean a behavioristic sociology will fail to develop. There may be some significance in the fact that in the volume on *Behavioral Sociology*, edited by Burgess and Bushell in 1969, a large number of the contributors were not sociologists. And in the 1970s Skinner returned to the task of applying behavioral psychology to human social life. Also, in recent years, behavioral psychiatry has been enjoying growing popularity. Hence, if the sociologists do not continue with the development of a behavioristic sociology a variety of other social science professionals can be expected to do so. Furthermore, of all of the current points of view behavioristic sociology is unquestionably most receptive to statistical and experimental methodologies. And in the long run, it is the explanations that can withstand empirical test that will prevail.

SUMMARY

The pluralistic behavioral branch of social behaviorism contributed richly to the development of sociology. It was the bearer of strong empirical tendencies and a number of persons trained in its tenets contributed to the development of statistics and general sociological methodology. Its adherents were perhaps more centrally responsible than any other school for establishing social psychology as a special subdiscipline. Its members contributed to the theory of institutions, social change, social control, and personality, to say nothing of the field of criminology, in which Tarde

was an important voice. In the works of Chapin on the one hand and those of Ogburn and Nimkoff on the other, pluralistic behaviorism was brought to its classical synthesis in a manner comparable to the classic stage of positivistic organicism in the works of Tönnies, Durkheim, and Redfield.

Perhaps the best critique of the suggestion–imitation school was the very course of its development. Its central formulas — imitation and pluralistic behavior — were too facile. It was able to do so much because it was so vaguely defined. For the same reason, the moment intensive analysis was turned on this central point of the theory, it tended to fall apart. When the concept of imitation is used so vaguely as to make it almost synonymous with social interaction, it will indeed "seem" to explain all forms of interaction until one examines it more closely. The profound theoretical gains made by use of the imitation formula were not due to its explanatory power but to an incidental result of its use. The explanation of social interaction was at least made in terms of the things presented in social interaction without an appeal to outside materials (like climate, environment, heredity, race, and what not). Once the harvest of this kind of analysis had been reaped, the imitation formula left no positive theory. Giddings's formula of "like-mindedness" represents the reintroduction into analysis of materials lying outside the interaction proper — introducing preinteractional biological similarities as a factor in interaction. But this was no solution, either. Thus, it is not surprising that, by the time one reaches the work of Chapin, not too much remains of the suggestion–imitation school other than a set of definitions and a formal outline of procedure.

Imitation, upon analysis, turns out to conceal a host of problems. When imitation does in fact take place, it turns out to be a highly complex act and not a fundamental social fact at all. It is easy to imagine that "monkey see, monkey do." It is quite another thing to persuade a monkey to imitate. True imitation is learned and requires high intelligence. Suggestion, far from being identifiable with imitation, lies at the other end of the scale from imitation, presumably referring to various forms of subconscious social influence. It rarely involves repetition of the original act. The entire rich range of interhuman processes mediated by language is left out of account.

Similarly, Giddings's formula of pluralistic behavior resting on consciousness of kind assumes that social life is structured of externally similar acts. But interhuman life is not built out of unit acts like bricks, but out of complex interadjustments. Moreover, the theory assumes that these unit acts rest on attitudes and beliefs, the relation to which is not made clear. If this assumption is correct, it makes the statistical study resting on unit acts alone superficial. Thus, the quantification of unit acts as indices of attitudes and beliefs is not always easy to justify. In fact, the serious students of this tradition — from Bogardus to Chapin and on to Louis Guttman — have been much concerned with refining the processes of scale construction in order to justify the assumptions made by pluralistic behaviorism.

At the very time the sociological pluralistic behaviorists were vigorously advancing the cause of an empirical sociology the conditioned-reflex and instrumental learning psychologists were laying a new foundation of behavioristic psychology. If anything they were even more rigorous than their predecessors in attempting to account for behavior (including human behavior) without reference or with minimum reference to mentalistic states such as ideas, feelings, values, and the like. And about the time when the older pluralistic behaviorists in sociology were dying off without leaving immediate heirs, the behavioral psychologists were approaching the point of readiness for a major assault on human social behavior. B. F. Skinner has gone farthest among the psychologists in this direction; George Homans has gone farthest among sociologists. However, one apparent recruit to the point of view, Peter Blau, has tended to hollow out the distinctiveness of the behaviorist approach and return the position to the structure-functionalistic fold. As a result, the contemporary situation remains in doubt. It is not clear whether a major reintegration of the statistical and experimental programs will occur and be launched in the name of behavioristic sociology, postwar style. Meanwhile a major wave of antiscientism and antipositivism has swept the Western world.

It is evident that there were tensions buried in pluralistic behaviorism emerging between its theory and method. In a minor way, a drama similar to the tension between organicism and positivism was being played out within pluralistic behaviorism. Transformations were invited both in theory and method. These were brought about by other branches of social behaviorism. The antipositivism of the 1960s and 1970s has worked to the disadvantage of behavioristic social theory and to the advantage of other types of elementarism.

XV

Symbolic Interactionism

The second major branch of social behaviorism is named by its adherents "symbolic interactionism." Although its problems and general solutions to them run parallel to those of the suggestion–imitation or pluralistic behavioral theorists, there is a considerable difference of detail, and its intellectual foundations, too, are somewhat different. The suggestion–imitation school originally took shape in Europe, most directly under the influence of neo-idealistic philosophy and an idealistically inclined experimental psychology. Although it was influenced to some degree by pragmatism, this influence was secondary. The symbolic interaction school took shape in America, primarily under the influence of pragmatism, and, in fact, many of its early members classified themselves as pragmatists. For them, the neo-Hegelian philosophy and idealistic experimental psychology were secondary. In the early days of its appearance, the suggestion–imitation school was most directly characterized by the centrality given to the idea of *imitation*. Symbolic interactionism placed the accent on *attitude* and *meaning*. The point of gravity of

the suggestion–imitation school was in *mass* phenomena; symbolic interactionism found its point of gravity in the *self* or *personality*.

William James. It is convenient to trace symbolic interactionism to the work of William James. His brilliant *Principles of Psychology*[1] opened up new possibilities for re-examining the relations of individual and society. Although James had taken over and accepted the instinct theory current in his day, there were other aspects of his thought that tended to modify it, including his brilliant examination of *habit*.

Habit is of considerable importance, James observed, to a creature that is plastic. "*Plasticity* . . . means the possession of a structure weak enough

---

[1] *Principles of Psychology*, 2 vols. (New York: Henry Holt, 1890). The references here are to *Psychology* (Cleveland: World Publishing Co., 1948), which is James's own abridgment of the *Principles*; it was originally published by Henry Holt in 1892. For other writings of William James, see Chapter XIII, Footnote 14.

to yield to an influence, but strong enough not to yield all at once. Each relatively stable phase of equilibrium in such a structure is marked by what we may call a new set of habits."[2]

Among the influences of habit on behavior is the simplification of movement which makes behavior more accurate and diminishes fatigue. Moreover, habit reduces the need for conscious attention. In a creature capable of forming habits, the acquisition of a new nature is possible. " 'Habit a second nature! Habit is ten times nature,' the Duke of Wellington is said to have exclaimed; and the degree to which this is true no one probably can appreciate as well as one who is a veteran soldier himself. The daily drill and the years of discipline end by fashioning a man completely over again, as to most of the possibilities of his conduct."[3] Not only does the individual acquire a new nature through habit; habit also has the greatest importance for society.

> Habit is . . . the enormous fly-wheel of society, its most precious conservative agent. It alone is what keeps us all within the bounds of ordinance, and saves the children of fortune from the envious uprisings of the poor. It alone prevents the hardest and most repulsive walks of life from being deserted by those brought up to tread therein. It keeps the fisherman and the deck-hand at sea through the winter; it holds the miner in his darkness, and nails the countryman to his log-cabin and his lonely farm through all the months of snow; it protects us from invasion by the natives of the desert and the frozen zone. It dooms us all to fight out the battle of life upon the lines of our nurture or our early choice, and to make the best of a pursuit that disagrees, because there is no other for which we are fitted, and it is too late to begin again.[4]

James had discovered in habit a principle that would require the explanation of behavior in its own terms rather than through appeal to outside forces. In this way, it could operate in the same manner as imitation did for Tarde and his followers.

A second major event in James's psychology was his reconceptualization of "consciousness" as a process. "States of mind" become mere momentary incidents in a process: "(1) Every 'state' tends to be part of a personal consciousness. (2) Within each personal consciousness states are always changing. (3) Each personal consciousness is sensibly continuous. (4) It is interested in some parts of its object to the exclusion of others, and welcomes or rejects — chooses from among them, in a word — all the while."[5] No state, once gone, can ever return again. A permanently existing idea, which makes its appearance in consciousness periodically, "is as mythological an entity as the Jack of Spades." Consciousness is the stream of thought or subjective life. It is the halo of relations around an image. In this manner, James eliminated consciousness as a kind of metaphysical substance. Through reconsideration of the importance of habit and the reduction of consciousness to a process, James opened new possibilities for the reconceptualization of the self.

One of the peculiar properties of consciousness is the fact that it always to some degree involves an awareness of the person's self. The person thus appears in thought in two ways, "partly known and partly knower, partly object and partly subject. . . . For shortness we may call one the *Me* and the other the *I*. . . . I shall therefore treat successively of (A) the self as known, or the *me*, the 'empirical ego' as it is sometimes called; and of (B) the self as knower, or the *I*, the 'pure ego' of certain authors."[6]

The empirical self or *me* in its widest sense is the sum total of all the person can call his or hers. The "me" typically arouses feelings and emotions of self-appreciation and prompts actions of self-seeking and self-preservation. Its constituents include the material "me," the social "me," and the spiritual "me." The material "me" encompasses first of all the body and then successive circles of things associated with it, one's clothes, one's family, one's home up to and including all possessions. The social "me" is the recognition one gets from

[2]James, *Psychology*, p. 135.
[3]*Ibid.*, p. 142.
[4]*Ibid.*, p. 143.

[5]*Ibid.*, p. 152.
[6]*Ibid.*, p. 176.

others. People have as many social selves as there are individuals who recognize them and have images of them in mind. People have as many social selves as there are distinct groups about whose opinion they care. Particularly important is the social self which exists in the mind of a person one is in love with. One's fame, good and bad, and one's honor or dishonor are names for one's social selves. One of the strongest forces in life is "club opinion." The spiritual "me" refers to the collection of one's states of consciousness and psychic faculties. Next in importance after these constituents of the self are the feelings and emotions of self. These are of two sorts: self-complacency and self-dissatisfaction. The occasion for these is normally one's actual success or failure and the good or bad position one holds in the world. A person with a broadly empirical ego and powers that have uniformly brought success will rarely be visited by self-doubts. The emotions of self-satisfaction and abasement are of a primitive emotional species like pain and rage. On the basis of the constituents of the "me" and the self-emotions, self-seeking and self-preservation arise. The primitive form of such actions is biological self-preservation, but self-seeking carries beyond the biological person to social self-seeking. Because of this we are sensitive to the opinions even of persons about whom we otherwise care nothing.

The complexity of the structure of the empirical self often gives rise to the necessity of choice. A rivalry and conflict of the different "me's" appears. "Not that I would not, if I could, be both handsome and fat and well dressed, and a great athlete, and make a million a year, be a wit, a *bon-vivant*, and a lady-killer, as well as a philosopher, a philanthropist, statesman, warrior, and African explorer, as well as a 'tone-poet' and saint. But the thing is simply impossible." [7] Out of the complex of rival "me's" arises the paradox of a person shamed to death because he or she is only the second publicist or the second oarsman or oarsworman in the world. Self-esteem, in fact, is a fraction of

which pretensions form the denominator and success the numerator:

$$\text{Self-esteem} = \frac{\text{Success}}{\text{Pretensions}}$$

Such a fraction may be increased either by diminishing the denominator or by increasing the numerator. Among the ways of handling the ratio are the range of phenomena varying from a frantic extension of striving to ascetic withdrawal of self-expectation.

Fairly unanimous opinion arranges the different selves of a person in a hierarchical scale with the bodily "me" at the bottom, the spiritual "me" at the top, and the extracorporeal material selves and various social selves between. But they are all important. A certain amount of bodily selfishness is required as a basis for all the other selves. In each kind of "me" — material, social, and spiritual — people distinguish between the immediate and actual and the remote and potential. One may forgo bodily enjoyment in the present for potential health later, abandon a dollar for the sake of a hundred, or make an enemy of a person in one's immediate presence for the sake of a wider circle of friends. Of all the potential selves, the potential social "me" is most interesting because of the apparent paradoxes to which it leads, as when for motives of honor and conscience one braves the condemnation of family, club and "set," or when as Protestant, one turns Catholic, or as Catholic, freethinker. The impulse to pray, James maintains, is a necessary consequence of the fact that the innermost social self tends to evolve standards which it can find approximated only in an ideal world. The progress of the social self is the substitution of higher tribunals of self-judgment for lower ones.

The self as knower, the "I" or pure ego, is a much more difficult subject of inquiry. It is that which at any moment is conscious; the "me" is only one of the things it is conscious of. One spontaneously conceives the "I" to be always the same. "This has led most philosophers to postulate behind the passing state of consciousness a permanent Substance or Agent whose modification or act it is.

[7] *Ibid.*, p. 186.

Divisions of The Empirical Self[8]

	Material	Social	Spiritual
SELF-SEEKING	Bodily Appetites and Instincts. Love of Adornment, Foppery, Acquisitiveness, Constructiveness. Love of Home, etc.	Desire to Please, Be Noticed, Admired, etc. Sociability, Emulation, Envy, Love, Pursuit of Honor, Ambition, etc.	Intellectual, Moral and Religious Aspirations, Conscientiousness.
SELF-ESTIMATION	Personal Vanity, Modesty, etc. Pride of Wealth, Fear of Poverty.	Social and Family Pride, Vainglory, Snobbery, Humility, Shame, etc.	Sense of Moral or Mental Superiority, Purity, etc. Sense of Inferiority or of Guilt.

This Agent is the thinker; the 'state' is only its instrument or means. 'Soul,' 'transcendental Ego,' 'Spirit,' are so many names for this more permanent sort of Thinker." [9]

But James argues that various inconsistencies arise when one presupposes a unity behind the passing thought. If one assumes the existence of a stream of consciousness, things that are known together are like single pulses of that stream. The function of the supposed soul, ego, or spirit is that of a combining medium. But we never experience this; we assume it. If we stick to what we experience we have only passing states. The sense of the sameness of the self of personal identity does not require a metaphysical self. It refers to certain comparable characteristics of experience from time to time. It arises out of a resemblance of conscious states. We need no substantial identity in the thinker to account for resemblances in the various states of consciousness. Yesterday's and today's states of consciousness have no substantial identity, for when the one is here, the other is irrevocably dead and gone. But they have a *functional* identity, for both know the same objects. States of consciousness are all that psychology needs to work with. "Metaphysics or theology may prove the Soul to exist; but for psychology the hypothesis of such a substantial principle of unity is superfluous." [10]

The identity found by the "I" in its "me" is only a loosely constructed thing, an identity, on the whole, just like that which any outside observer might find in the same assemblage of facts. "We often say of a man 'he is so changed one would not know him'; and so does a man, less often, speak of himself. These changes in the *Me,* recognized by the *I,* or by the outside observers, may be grave or slight." [11] Such mutations of self divide into alterations of memory and alterations in the present bodily and spiritual self. Alterations in memory include the loss of memory — normal with advanc-

[8]*Ibid.,* p. 195.
[9]*Ibid.,* p. 196.
[10]*Ibid.,* p. 203.
[11]*Ibid.,* p. 205.

ing years — and false memories. Alterations in the present self include such things as insane delusions, alternating selves, the mediumship of the spiritualistic séance, and possession by supernatural beings. In various ways, the ratio between the "I" and "me" is transformed.

> The consciousness of Self involves a stream of thought, each part of which as "I" can remember those which went before, know the things they knew, and care paramountly for certain ones among them as "Me," and *appropriate to these* the rest. This Me is an empirical aggregate of things objectively known. The *I* which knows them cannot itself be an aggregate; neither for psychological purposes need it be an unchanging metaphysical entity like the Soul. . . . It is a *thought,* at each moment different from that of the last moment, but *appropriative* of the latter. . . .[12]

Such was the challenging manner in which James struck out the lines for a new analysis of the social self.

Charles Horton Cooley. The sociological extension of these ideas was begun by Charles Horton Cooley (1864–1929), the son of the distinguished jurist Thomas M. Cooley. He did his undergraduate work in engineering at the University of Michigan and worked for a short time as a surveyor. After some time spent in travel and study in Europe, he took his Ph.D. in economics, with a minor in sociology. He began teaching at the University of Michigan in 1892, and remained there for the rest of his life. In comparison with some of his contemporaries in sociology, he wrote very little, but his books were carefully written and have had a lasting influence.[13]

The imaginations people have of one another,

Cooley maintained, "are the solid facts of society." Society is a mental phenomenon, a relation between personal ideas. "Society exists in my mind as the contact and reciprocal influence of certain ideas named 'I,' Thomas, Henry, Susan, Bridget, and so on. It exists in your mind as a similar group, and so in every mind." [14]

In a basic sense in this formulation Cooley applied to society the kind of approach that James had applied to the self. It is not surprising, then, that Cooley's conception of the self corresponds very closely to what James called the social self. "The personality of a friend, as it lives in my mind . . . is simply a group or system of thoughts associated with the symbols that stand for him." [15] Similarly, a person's own self represents some of his or her ideas — a notion that would be meaningless without the basic distinction introduced by James between the "I" and the "me." The social self is a core of ideas adhering to the self words "I," "me," "mine," "myself." The self consists of those things individuals conceive as belonging peculiarly to them. The core of the self is formed by an instinctive self-feeling. Imagination and habit, operating on instinctive self-feeling, create the social self. "Imagination cooperating with instinctive self-feeling has already created a social 'I' and this has become a principal object of interest and endeavor." [16] Moreover, "habit has the same fixing and consolidating action in the growth of the self that it has elsewhere, but is not its distinctive characteristic." [17]

Cooley's famous "looking-glass self" was his particular form of what James had described as the social self. Even the elements had been developed in more detail by James. The general argument, of course, is that the social self arises reflectively in terms of the reaction to the opinions of others on the self. "A self-idea of this sort seems to have three principal elements: the imagination of our

---

[12]*Ibid.,* p. 215.

[13]Cooley's books are: *Personal Competition* (New York: Macmillan, 1899); *Human Nature and the Social Order* (New York: Scribner's, 1902; rev. ed., 1922); *Social Organization* (New York: Scribner's, 1909); *Social Process* (New York: Scribner's, 1918); and the posthumous *Sociological Theory and Social Research,* introduction and notes by Robert Cooley Angell (New York: Henry Holt, 1930).

[14]Cooley, *Human Nature and the Social Order,* p. 84. (References are to the first edition of 1902.)

[15]*Ibid.,* p. 81.

[16]*Ibid.,* p. 167.

[17]*Ibid.,* p. 155.

CHARLES HORTON COOLEY

University of Michigan, Ann Arbor, Mich.

appearance to the other person; the imagination of his judgment of that appearance, and some sort of self-feeling, such as pride or mortification." [18]

If the only claim for Cooley's importance lay in the "looking-glass self," he would hardly deserve the place he holds in the development of sociology, for the idea was only a neat restatement of James's "social self." But Cooley went beyond the "looking-glass self" to develop a general theory of society, expanding this type of social behaviorism to the explanation of groups and social organization. Cooley's foremost contribution to the theory of groups was the reevaluation of what have been called since Cooley "primary groups." William Graham Sumner had drawn a distinction between the "in-group" and the "out-group." The conflict sociologists, such as Gumplowicz, had drawn the distinction between the prestate type of social group, characterized by a moral unity, in contrast to the social order originating in war and conquest and leading to the emergence of the state and a legal order. Tönnies had distinguished between the *Gemeinschaft* and *Gesellschaft*. There were many anticipations of Cooley's analysis. Cooley brought these conceptualizations of the group into relation with the concept of the social self, recast in terms of the needs of social behaviorism. Primary groups are "characterized by intimate face-to-face association and cooperation." Their chief properties include: (1) face-to-face association, (2) unspecified nature of associations, (3) relative permanence, (4) a small number of persons involved, and (5) relative intimacy of participants. Characteristic examples of the primary group are the family, the old-fashioned neighborhood, the play group of children, the group of elders. In such primary groups, there is an intimate fusion of individuality and group. The primary group is "fundamental in forming social nature and ideals of the individual." [19]

It is in such groups that individuals get their earliest and most basic experiences of social unity. They are the source of the individual's ideals, which derive from the moral unity of the group itself. A subordination of the interests of the individual to the group occurs here, supplanting individual egoism and greed. The ideal of a moral whole may be analyzed into the principles of "loyalty, lawfulness, and freedom." Such principles are fundamental, in turn, to the ideals of good faith, service, kindness, and justice. Democracy and Christianity are extensions of primary-group ideals to wider society.

Ideals such as those which make up the reflexive self and are produced by the primary group constitute the unity and structure of the social mind. *Social organization* is this unity and structure. It is partly coextensive with public con-

[18]*Ibid.*, p. 152.

[19]Cooley, *Social Organization*, pp. 23 ff.

sciousness or public opinion, representing "a mutual understanding of one another's points of view on the part of individuals or groups concerned as naturally results from discussion." [20] The social mind constantly forms itself into wholes, consciously and unconsciously represented by fashions, traditions, institutions, and so on, which spread and generate more varied structures of differentiated thought symbols. Such structures of the social mind constitute types. "Any fairly distinct and durable detail of this structure may be called a social type; this being a convenient term to use when we wish to break up the whole into parts, for analysis or description. Thus there are types of personality, of political structure, of religion, of classes, of the family, of art, of language. . . ." [21]

This analysis into types was extended to institutions, which Cooley conceived as fixed phases of the public mind; to various special institutions such as the family; to the problems of public opinion; and to the social classes, which he conceived as formed on the basis of two fundamental principles: *caste* (the distribution of social functions and privileges on the basis of inheritance) and *competition* (the distribution of functions and privileges on the basis of comparative efficiency). These were the distinctions which Ralph Linton renamed "ascription" and "achievement."

The implications of his social behaviorism are kept unwaveringly in mind by Cooley: the task, as he sees it, is to explain social events by principles applying to their internal structure, not by some *deus ex machina* from the outside. In striking contrast to the pluralistic behaviorists ranging from Le Bon, through Giddings, and even at times to Ross and Ogburn, Cooley is never tempted to explain social events by the physical environment or heredity or race. Thus, when Galton's *Hereditary Genius* came into Cooley's hands, he refused to be deceived by its statistics, and cut directly to its explanatory principles. Cooley pointed out that one had no right to explain the frequent unusual people in notable families on the basis of hereditary factors alone so long as their social situations were distinctively advantageous.

The symbolic interactionists, as already illustrated by James and Cooley, were establishing a more precise definition of the ultimate materials of sociology. For Tarde these were acts of invention or imitation; for Giddings they were externally similar acts by a plurality of persons. Both wings of pluralistic behaviorism — the Tardean and the Giddings branches — stated that the ultimate subject matter of sociology consisted of ideas and beliefs. Among the more sensitive members of the school, there is evidence of an uneasy feeling that between the external act and the idea or belief there may be numerous problems. Tarde, for example, cautioned that by merely counting external acts one might well lose sight of important problems of intensity. Chapin showed a strong impulse to pry apart the externally similar pluralistic behaviors and carry out an analysis in terms of *latent* and *manifest* patterns. His scale construction, too, reflects some sense of the problems that might be involved in the transition from internal beliefs to external acts.

However, with James and Cooley, the order is reversed: not external acts, but ideas and beliefs are the facts of sociology. As Cooley put it, "the imaginations people have of one another are the solid facts of society." But by putting the emphasis here, Cooley brought to light the potential tensions between the definition of subject matter by the social behaviorists and sociological method. Cooley was not against statistics. He had observed that under proper circumstances statistics could be most revealing. But everything, he insisted, depended on the "interpretation." Sometimes, he opined, the only thing exact in a statistical account is the mathematical operation involved.

If the imaginations people have of one another are the ultimate facts of society, it follows that sociological method will produce results only if it concerns them. Some form of introspection is most directly implied as proper sociological method. Cooley saw this and proposed "systematic autobiography" as the fundamental method of

[20]*Ibid.*, p. 10.
[21]*Ibid.*, p. 22.

sociology. The underlying tension in social behaviorism between its definition of content and its method has become manifest.

W. I. Thomas. William Isaac Thomas (1863–1947) gave a characteristic restylization to symbolic interactionism. Thomas graduated from the University of Tennessee in 1884 and taught English and modern languages there. In 1888 and 1889, he studied in Berlin and Göttingen, coming under the influence of the folk psychology of Lazarus and Steinthal. From 1889 to 1895, he taught English and sociology at Oberlin College. He joined the new faculty in sociology at Chicago in 1895 taking his doctorate under Small. He remained at Chicago until 1918 when, for personal reasons, he retired. In 1923, he resumed lecturing, this time at the New School for Social Research. From 1930 to 1936, he went yearly to Sweden in connection with the Institute of Social Science at the University of Stockholm. He lectured at Harvard (1936–1937). Until 1939, he lived in New Haven and then moved to Berkeley, California, where he lived until his death in 1947.

The strong influence of the pragmatic tradition, which had one of its main centers in Chicago, is manifest in *Social Origins* (1909).[22] There Thomas argued that the sociologist is interested in those human activities demonstrating conscious control, in which people produce language, forms of government, religion, and art. The object of central interest to the sociologist is precisely the phenomena of *attention* — "the mental attitude which takes note of the outside world and manip-

W. I. THOMAS

From *American Sociology* by Howard W. Odum, Longmans, Green & Co., Inc., 1951

ulates it."[23] Attention is produced by a crisis, however small, which may be due to a disturbance of habit or the result of an incident or suggestion. By the time of *The Polish Peasant* (1918–1920), these ideas had undergone considerable development. The purpose of sociology was conceived as one of tracing the dependence of individuals on social life and culture and of culture and social life on the individual. The subject matter of interest consists of attitudes and values, processes of consciousness determined by objective conditions, pre-existing attitudes, and definitions of the situation.[24]

[22]William I. Thomas, ed., *Source Book for Social Origins* (Chicago: University of Chicago Press, 1909). Thomas' other books are: *Sex and Society* (Chicago: University of Chicago Press, 1907); *The Polish Peasant in Europe and America*, with Florian Znaniecki, 5 vols. (Chicago: University of Chicago Press, 1918–1920); *The Unadjusted Girl* (Boston: Little, Brown, 1923); *The Child in America*, with Dorothy Swaine Thomas (New York: Alfred A. Knopf, 1928); and *Primitive Behavior* (New York: McGraw-Hill, 1937). Thomas was also the chief author of *Old World Traits Transplanted* (New York: Harper, 1921), published under the names of Robert E. Park and Herbert A. Miller.

[23]Thomas, *Source Book for Social Origins*, p. 17.
[24]Thomas, see *The Polish Peasant*, I, Methodological Note.

Some further shift was evident in *The Unadjusted Girl* (1923), when attitude and value were reduced to secondary importance and the "definition of the situation" became the central object of study in sociology. "Preliminary to any self-determined act of behavior there is always a ... *definition of the situation* ... gradually a whole life-policy and the personality of the individual himself follow from a series of such definitions." Some of the most interesting of interhuman facts flow from different definitions of the situation. There is "always a rivalry between the spontaneous definitions of the situation made by the member of an organized society and the definitions which his society has provided for him." [25]

It is occasionally suggested that W. I. Thomas was influenced in these ideas by Ratzenhofer. The suggestion may be attributable to an apparent similarity between Thomas's concept of "attitudes" and Ratzenhofer's "interests"; and there is a further point of similarity in Thomas's typology of "the four wishes": the desire for new experience, the desire for security, the desire for response, and the desire for recognition. This typology was clearly modeled on the six interests advanced by Ratzenhofer and Small. [26] Beside such derivations

of Thomas's views must be placed the influence of European neo-idealism and the obvious strong ties with pragmatism. William James had dramatized the program of judging an idea in terms of its "consequences" without insisting upon too exacting an inquiry into its intrinsic truth. Although for James this seems to have been partly a device for accepting ideas that his professional standards otherwise would seem to reject, it involved a principle that could represent pure gain from a sociological point of view. If sociologists once accept ideas as components of interhuman conduct, they must also examine those ideas which they know on logical or scientific grounds to be untrue if they are held by the human subjects, for they may enter as factors in the conduct of those subjects. Sociologists may not believe in magic. This, however, is no excuse for ignoring those factors in a people's conduct determined by their ideas of magic. (There is all the difference in the world between this approach and the acceptance of magic as true because it seems to have good social effects.) The importance of ideas for conduct was advanced by James and echoed by Cooley. Thomas' notions of "definition of the situation" and "attitude" — and his earlier concept of "attention" — were various forms in which he accepted this principle and founded his sociology on it. The similarity with Cooley is evident.

Again, Thomas's idea that "attention" is elicited by crises (be they as small as the mere upsetting of a habit) and that it functions to restore conduct to stability is a direct parallel of the ideas advanced by Dewey's argument that thinking is aroused by an indeterminate situation and has the function of restoring behavior to equilibrium. Similarly, the great emphasis on situation in *The Polish Peasant* is

---

[25] Thomas, *The Unadjusted Girl*, p. 42.

[26] Thomas and Znaniecki were writing at a time when instinct theories of behavior were being scrapped. The habit of mind associated with instinct theories inclined social scientists to speak as if the various presumed organic motors of conduct (instincts, desires, wishes, interests, or drives) were the direct and primary causes of behavior, even while the alternative notion was gaining ground that these were, at best, secondary causes of conduct. The new idea was that the organic motor was not the cause of conduct in its raw form but only in the form it assumed as a product of experience. When Small classified the interests into six, he did so as a matter of convenience; the actual interests were assumed to be almost innumerable. Thomas seems to have been doing the same thing when he renamed the interests "wishes" and reclassified them into four. That the thought of the wishes largely as a convenient classification seems indicated by the fact that he was inclined to phrase the classification somewhat differently in different places. Moreover, at the very time when other sociologists were taking up his classification, he tended to drop it almost alone, using the notion of "definition of the situation" almost alone to carry out analyses that at one time he would have carried out on the basis of the four wishes. The "four wishes" are, perhaps, best viewed as a transitional phase in modern social theory during a time when the instinct theory of conduct was being abandoned.

comparable to Dewey's lifelong insistence on its importance in individual and social life.

Finally, Thomas's statement of the problem of sociology as one of tracing the influence of society and culture on the individual and the individual on society and culture parallels Cooley's theory and practice. For Cooley, too, had this problem in mind when he traced the effect of the primary group on the rise of the self and when he traced the effects of personal ideas upon social organization, institutions, and public opinion.

At every critical point Thomas's affinities are with the pragmatists and symbolic interactionists.

Theoretically, the most significant work of Thomas was that done in collaboration with Znaniecki; in fact, it was the greatest contribution of both to the symbolic interactionist point of view.[27] The framework for analysis was provided by the transformations in personality and social structure in the Polish peasant community in the course of its movement to America.

> . . . the Polish peasant community has developed during many centuries complicated systems of beliefs and rules of behavior sufficient to control social life under ordinary circumstances, and the cohesion of the group and the persistence of its membership are strong enough to withstand passively the influence of eventual extraordinary occurrences, although there is no adequate method of meeting them. And if the crisis is too serious and the old unity or prosperity of the group breaks down, this is usually treated at first as a result of superior forces against which no fight is possible.
>
> But when, owing to the breakdown of the isolation of the group and its contact with a more complex and fluid world, the social evolution becomes more rapid and the crises more frequent and varied, there is no time for the same gradual, empirical, unmethodical elaboration of approximately adequate means of control, and no crisis can be passively borne, but every one must be met in a more or less adequate way, for

they are too various and frequent not to imperil social life unless controlled in time.[28]

These paragraphs illustrate that, in the last analysis, the study of the Polish peasant was intended as an examination of social disorganization and a consideration of the materials necessary for rational social policy. But meanwhile the study served as a vehicle for the examination of the interrelation of personality and social order. "There are two fundamental practical problems which have constituted the center of attention of reflective social practice in all times. These are (1) the problem of the dependence of the individual upon social organization and culture, and (2) the problem of the dependence of social organization and culture upon the individual." [29]

The social theory necessary to solve these problems takes as the most fundamental data "the objective cultural elements of social life and the subjective characteristics of the members of the social group. . . . For these data we shall use now . . . the terms 'social values' and 'attitudes.' " [30] *Attitudes* represent "a process of individual consciousness which determines real or possible activity of the individual in the social world." [31] *Values* are the objects in the world to which attitudes are addressed. The consequences for behavior of the attitudinal pursuit of values are quite objective.

> Rules and actions, taken . . . with regard to the attitudes provoked by them, are quite analogous to any other values — economic, artistic, scientific, religious. . . . The rules of behavior, and the actions viewed as conforming or not conforming with these rules, constitute with regard to their objective significance a certain number of more or less connected and harmonious systems which can be generally called *social institutions,* and the totality of institutions found in a concrete social group constitutes the *social organization* of this group.[32]

---

[27]Znaniecki's contributions to social-action theory and functionalism will be discussed in Chapters XVIII and XX.

[28]Thomas, *The Polish Peasant,* I, p. 2.
[29]*Ibid.,* p. 20.
[30]*Ibid.,* pp. 20–21.
[31]*Ibid.,* p. 22.
[32]*Ibid.,* pp. 32–33.

In specific cases, the individuals' attitudes and values in their objective manifestation — constituting the social institutions and social organization — are always embodied in practical situations. The *situation* is the set of values and attitudes with which the individual or the group has to deal in a process of *activity* and with regard to which this activity is planned and its results appreciated. Every concrete activity consists in the solution of a situation which involves three kinds of data: (1) the objective conditions under which the individual or society has to act and which at the given moment affect the conscious status of the individual or the group; (2) the pre-existing attitudes of the individual or the group; and (3) the "definition of the situation" by the individual or group as a more or less clear conception of the conditions of consciousness and of attitudes. Individuals develop their attitudes and make their selection of the values that a situation offers on the basis of a general pattern of wishes. These wishes include: (1) the desire for new experience (art, adventure); (2) the desire for recognition (sexual response and general social appreciation, secured by devices ranging from display of ornament to the demonstration of worth through scientific attainment); (3) the desire for mastery (ownership, domestic tyranny, political despotism, based on the instinct of hate, but capable of being sublimated to laudable ambition); (4) the desire for security (exemplified negatively by the wretchedness of the individual in perpetual solitude or under social taboo).[33]

From this theoretical base, Thomas and Znaniecki developed a theory of personality that viewed personality as manifesting itself, as a whole, only in the course of its total life.[34] This evolution, however, tends toward stabilization and hence the concept of type may be applied to social personalities. Personality arises along *"typical lines of genesis* of a series of events in which attitudes [develop] from other attitudes." Such lines of

genesis are dependent in part on the milieu in which the individual lives. Society imposes a frame of activities on the individual, the family, education, career, marriage. Extensive uniformities of development are found in connection with temperament and character. Temperament and character work together in a life organization, with the sphere of experience of individuals consisting of a limited number of selected and organized groups of social values that play a predominant part in their lives as causes and effects of their organized attitudes. *Temperament* refers to an original group of individual attitudes existing independently of any social influences. *Character* is the set of organized and fixed groups of attitudes developed by social influences operating upon the temperamental base.

Individuals are thus products of interaction. In order to become social personalities in any domain, individuals must not only learn the social meanings which objects possess but also learn how to adapt themselves to the demands which society puts upon them. Since meanings imply conscious thought, they must do this by conscious reflection, not by mere instinctive adaptation of reflexes. The stabilized activity arrived at in this manner becomes habitual and is thus dropped below the level of consciousness once again.

Depending on the nature of the attitudes involved in the character and in the schemes of life organization, as well as on the way they are unified and systematized, three types of life organization are developed. The set of attitudes constituting the character may be such as practically to exclude the development of any new attitudes of an individual. Such individuals' attitudes have attained so great a fixity that they are accessible only to a certain class of influences — those constituting the most permanent part of their social milieu. These may be called "Philistines." Their opposites are "Bohemians," whose possibilities of personal development are not closed, simply because their characters remain unformed. Some of their temperamental attitudes are in their primary form, others may have become intellectualized but remain unrelated to one another and consequently do not

[33]*Ibid.*, p. 73.
[34]See Volume III of *The Polish Peasant,* "Life Record of an Immigrant."

form a stable set. The individuals remain open to any and all influences. Opposed to both these types are people whose characters are settled and organized in a manner requiring inner development. This is the type of the "creative individual." In these various personality types the fundamental wishes — desire for new experience, for response, for security, for recognition — enter in varying degrees. It was Thomas's and Znaniecki's judgment that the development of the modern world, particularly the forces bringing the primary group rapidly into contact with the outside world with its new and rival schemes, tends to shatter the old organization, increasing the numbers of Philistines and Bohemians.

Just as from personal ideas Cooley moved his analysis either to the self or to social organization and institutions, so the concepts of attitude and definition of the situation were used by Thomas and Znaniecki. Particularly in the theory of social personality they made important advances beyond Cooley — this quite apart from the monumental assemblage of firsthand materials and the isolation of the case history and life history as major techniques and tools in sociological research.

W. I. Thomas's own life appears to have been a somewhat painful proof of his own theories. Following personal difficulties in which Thomas lost his job at the University of Chicago, a marked change is discernible in his intellectual activity. The academic community was the only one he had remaining. The possible direction of Thomas's thought, had it not been for his personal difficulties, appears in *Old World Traits Transplanted* (1921). The general intention seemed to have been to rise beyond the confines of a single minority group toward more general formulations. In later works, Thomas seemed to be inclined to drop any idea that his academic colleagues brought under critical review. The ideas of personality, the four wishes, were all largely withdrawn until little was left except the notion of "definition of the situation." Thomas even became very defensive about his use of the case history. *Primitive Behavior* was a return to the period of the *Source Book for Social*

Origins. Thomas's fullest synthesis of symbolic interactionism remains the theoretical sections of the *Polish Peasant.*

At the time Thomas and Znaniecki achieved their major synthesis of symbolic interactionism, it was quite clear to both of them that their definition of sociological materials was such as to require special methods of study. How does one quantify definitions of the situation? What measurements apply to life organization? What are the weights to be assigned to temperament in contrast to character in a specific Bohemian personality? Thomas and Znaniecki advocated the life history, the detailed personal narrative, and the exhaustive study of the individual case as the methods appropriate to their materials. They made major firsthand assemblages. Having demonstrated the emancipation of sociology from dependency for its materials upon history, the *Polish Peasant* deserved the great acclaim it received. Inevitably, with the development of methodological sophistication it became clear that the case or life history is only a technique and not a self-sufficient method, but this does not obscure the importance of its development or its consistency as a technique with the particular definition of sociological subject matter of symbolic interactionism.

G. H. Mead. However, even while these developments were occurring, George Herbert Mead (1863–1931) was transforming the inner structure of the theory of symbolic interactionism, moving it to a higher level of theoretical sophistication. George Herbert Mead had been an associate of John Dewey at Michigan and continued his association at Chicago. Philosophically, he was a pragmatist. Mead had studied under Royce and was familiar with the idealist theory of personality. He was also familiar with the work of Tarde, Baldwin, and his friend Cooley. He had studied in Germany, where he became impressed by Wundt's theories of language and the gesture. From 1900 on, Mead's influence began to spread throughout the United States from his course in social psychology at the University of Chicago. Although he published many articles, he was never able to

GEORGE H. MEAD

Courtesy of David Miller, University of Texas

bring his ideas together into a book that satisfied him. Many of his students, out of personal devotion and a feeling for the value of the material Mead was presenting, had stenographic transcripts made of some of his lectures, and these transcripts, together with lecture notes, were carefully assembled into four volumes which were published posthumously.[35]

In arriving at his own peculiar interpretation of the self, Mead had the representatives of three dif-

ferent traditions in mind. Wundt was the heir of a German idealistic tradition which he salvaged for social science by means of his psychophysical parallelism. On the other hand, J. B. Watson represented the attempt to account for sociopsychological phenomena in purely behavioristic terms. Finally, Mead shared the pragmatism of James and Dewey. Mead made three types of criticisms of the previous theories of the self: (1) either they presupposed the mind as antecedently existing to account for mental phenomena (Wundt); (2) or they failed to account for specifically mental phenomena (Watson); and (3) they failed to isolate the mechanism by which mind and the self appeared (James and Dewey).

In his third criticism, Mead seems to have had Williams James particularly in mind. Mead was impressed by James's famous 1904 article "Does Consciousness Exist?", which had made a new attack on the problem of mind. In this brilliant formulation, James had brought the traditional subject–object and mind–matter dichotomies under critical review, indicating that they may not be ultimate realities but derivations from a more fundamental reality. Mead observed: "There has been of late in philosophy a growing recognition of the importance of James's insistence that a great deal has been placed in consciousness that must be returned to the so-called objective world."[36]

The properties of Mead's social psychology may be seen as arising out of a generalization of the procedure by which James brought the notion of consciousness under critical review, while at the same time attempting to be as behavioristic as Watson and using Wundt's mechanism of language to account for the inner restructuring of experience into self and other. Just as James had taken pure experience as a starting point, treating subject and object as distinctions arising within it, so Mead proposed to start analysis with an observable activity, the dynamic, on-going social process, and the social acts which are its component elements, and

[35]*The Philosophy of the Present,* ed. Arthur E. Murphy (Chicago: Open Court Publishing Co., 1932); *Mind, Self, and Society,* ed. Charles W. Morris (Chicago: University of Chicago Press, 1934); *Movements of Thought in the Nineteenth Century,* ed. Merritt H. Moore (Chicago: University of Chicago Press, 1936); and *The Philosophy of the Act,* ed. Charles W. Morris (Chicago: University of Chicago Press, 1938).

[36]Mead, *Mind, Self, and Society,* p. 4 (Copyright 1934 by the University of Chicago.)

then to treat the mind and society as arising as discriminations within this process. Mead thus proposed to surmount both the mentalism of the introspectionists and the narrow form of behaviorism represented by Watson. "The problem that presents itself as crucial for human psychology concerns the field that is opened up by introspection; this field apparently could not be dealt with by a purely objective psychology which only studied conduct as it takes place for the observer."[37]

It has been pointed out that Thomas and Znaniecki had taken *attitudes* as the central object of analysis in *The Polish Peasant*. It is not impossible that Thomas was partly influenced in this choice by what his brilliant colleague was doing in his course in social psychology. In any case, for Mead as for Thomas and Znaniecki, analysis centers in attitudes. "Present results . . . suggest the organization of the act in terms of attitudes. There is an organization of the various parts of the nervous system that are going to be responsible for acts, an organization which represents not only that which is immediately taking place, but also the later stages that are to take place."[38] However, in Mead's analysis, "attitudes" were given far more precise significance, for attitudes have the simultaneous character of representing both introspective states and the starting point of the act. "We can find in that sense in the beginning of the act just those characters which we assign to 'horse' as an idea, or if you like, as a concept."[39]

Mead devoted considerable space to the discussion of psychophysical parallelism. The importance of this approach of Wundt's to psychological problems was the attempt to do justice simultaneously to the introspectively revealed states of consciousness and external behavior. The entire importance of Mead's own position lay in his giving equal weight to both kinds of factors without requiring a schema of two irreconcilable phenomena to do it. Mead started out with

Wundt's form of psychophysical parallelism and from it took the element that was to provide the mechanisms for the rise of the self within ongoing activity. Wundt set out to show the parallelism between what goes on in the body and what goes on in the mind. In trying to find what was common to these two fields — what, in the psychical experience, could be referred to in physical terms — Wundt isolated a very valuable conception of the *gesture* as that which later becomes a symbol but which is to be found in its earlier states as a part of a social act. The gesture is that part of the social act which serves as a stimulus to other forms involved in the same social act.

Following Wundt, Mead took the gesture as the transitional link to language from action, and also as the phenomenon establishing the continuities of human and infrahuman social life. The gesture mediates the development of language as the basic mechanism permitting the rise of the self in the course of ongoing social activity. Social life represents the interaction of creatures of the same type. Social insects and other nonhuman creatures, such as herding animals, and humans all have social life. Social interaction implies that the actions of one creature are in part the basis of the action of another. The "gesture" is any phase or aspect of the action of a creature which may serve to the other creatures party to the social act as a sign for the action as a whole. Baring of teeth, for example, accompanies the fighting of a creature: in the preparatory phase of attack, a dog bares its teeth and another responds to this as a sign of the attack about to begin. This phase of the action has become a sign (gesture) for the course of action that may follow. The sign has "meaning"; its meaning is precisely the potential occurrence. Gestures are the means by which nonhuman social action is possible.

But human social life is carried on not in terms of gestures but in terms of *language*. Language is a special transformation of the gestures essential to the conduct of more complex forms of social life. The gesture is an aspect of action that is taken as a sign of the course of action. If one could once isolate a class of gestures that could serve as common

[37]*Ibid.*, p. 8.
[38]*Ibid.*, p. 11.
[39]*Ibid.*, p. 12.

signs both to maker and perceiver, one would have a class of gestures making language possible. Verbal gestures represent such a class of common signs, which, being heard by the maker as well as the other parties to the social act, can serve as a common sign to all parties to the social act. The mutually understood gesture is a *significant symbol*. The continuities between gestures and language are established. In language, the gesture has been converted into a significant symbol. "Meaning" is located, in the same fashion, in the sign function of the significant symbol with respect to the future course of the social act. Language, moreover, operating with common signs on the basis of logical rules, makes possible a degree of integrated, precise, and differentiated yet plastic social behavior quite impossible to any creatures without language. In precision and integration, only the complex instinctive patterns of behavior among the social insects present any comparisons. But such instinctively produced social behaviors cannot show plasticity and variation.

> Gestures become significant symbols when they implicitly arouse in an individual making them the same responses which they explicitly arouse . . . in other individuals, the individuals to whom they are addressed. . . . Only in terms of gestures as significant symbols is the existence of mind or intelligence possible; for only in terms of gestures which are significant symbols can thinking — which is simply an internalized or implicit conversation of the individual with himself by means of gestures — take place.[40]

In communication, individual and society interpenetrate to an unusual degree. "We are more or less unconsciously seeing ourselves as others see us. We are unconsciously addressing ourselves as others address us. . . . We are calling out in the other person something we are calling out in ourselves, so that unconsciously we take over these attitudes. We are unconsciously putting ourselves in the place of others and acting as others act. . . ."[41] Society, in terms of language, pene-

trates to the innermost recesses of thought itself. "Meaning arises and lies within the field of the relation between the gesture of a given human organism and the subsequent behavior of this organism. . . . Meaning is thus a development of something objectively there as a relation between certain phases of the social act."[42]

Meaning is not fundamentally a state of consciousness or a set of organized relations. Meaning is accounted for in terms of symbols at the most complex stage of their development. Intelligence is essentially the ability to solve the problems of present behavior in terms of its possible future consequences as implicated on the basis of past experience. It involves both memory and foresight. Meaning and mind have their origins in the social act and are made possible — in fact, necessitated — by language. Intelligence is the utilization of these instruments. The units of this process are attitudes, representing the beginning, or potential, initiation of some social act in which, along with others, the individual is involved or implicated. Thus, mind arises in the social process only when that process as a whole enters into the experience of any one individual. When this occurs, the individual becomes self-conscious and has a mind. It is by means of reflexiveness, the turning back of the experience of the individual upon himself or herself, that the whole social process is thus brought into the experience of the individuals involved in it. Reflexiveness is the essential condition, within the social process, for the development of mind.

The reflexive property that human social experience acquires as a product of the use of language is critical for Mead's account of the rise of the self. The very definition of the self rests on this quality. A self is possible only to a creature that can be an object to itself, a characteristic possible only in society and by means of language. The underlying process producing the self consists in *role taking*, which is present whenever significant symbols are used. One learns a significant symbol when one shares a sign referring to a common course of ex-

---

[40]*Ibid.*, p. 47.
[41]*Ibid.*, pp. 68–69.

[42]*Ibid.*, pp. 75–76.

perience with someone else. Through the significant symbol, one is inevitably in the position of having taken the role of another. Every item of language carries with it some of the social matrix. Society penetrates individuals with every term they employ or acquire. Some aspect of society enters into people with every different person with whom they associate. Or, by reverse, they have to become a slightly different thing to each new person. There are as many selves, in one sense, as there are persons with whom one associates, and a multivaried personality is normal. While ordinarily people are unified selves in the community to which they belong, at times the different requirements of social life may lead to the actual splitting up of the self and breakup of personality.

Role taking is the basic process and the genesis of the self as one kind of unity of the social experience of the individual. The early stages of organization of social experience in terms of roles is evident in the imaginary companions which many children produce in the early stages of the formation of the self. It is a way of organizing responses called forth by others in the self. Play — at being mother, teacher, police officer, fire fighter — consists in taking various different roles. Children utilize their own experiences to build a self. These are exercises in the more complex forms of role taking that the social environment demands. In contrast to play, the organized game requires that the child take up a very specific role which reflects in its structure the roles of everyone else in the game in specific relationship to it. To perform the game role properly, the child must be able to take the role of everyone else within the game. The organization involved is put in the form of the rules of the game. But it is critical that the attitudes of all the others involved in the game be internalized. "The organized community or social group which gives to the individual his unity of self may be called 'the generalized other.' The attitude of the generalized other is the attitude of the whole community."[43]

Through the generalized other, the community exercises control over the conduct of its individual members. The two stages in the development of the self are thus (1) the organization of the particular attitudes of other individuals toward one's self and (2) the organization of the social attitudes of the generalized other toward one's self. The self reaches full development by organizing individual attitudes and generalizing them, becoming an individual reflection of the general systematic social pattern of group behavior in which all others are involved.

Mead followed James's terminology of "I" and "me" in accounting for the structure of the self. The self does not consist simply of a bare organization of social attitudes. It consists of an "I" which is aware of the social "me." The "I" is not a "me" and cannot become a "me." The "I" is the principle of action; the "I" reacts to the self that arises through the attitude of others. The "I" of the moment is present in the memory of the "me" of the next. The "I" is the response of the organism to the attitudes of the others, the "me" is the organized set of attitudes of others which one assumes himself or herself.

> . . . the "I" is always something different from what the situation itself calls for. So there is always that distinction, if you like, between the "I" and the "me." The "I" both calls out the "me" and responds to it. Taken together they constitute a personality as it appears in social experience. The self is essentially a social process going on with these two distinguishable phases. If it did not have these two phases there could not be conscious responsibility, and there would be nothing novel in experience.[44]

Just as the self arises as one kind of organization, so *society* appears as another:

> There are what I have termed "generalized social attitudes" which make an organized self possible. In the community there are certain ways of acting under situations which are essentially identical. . . . There

[43]*Ibid.*, p. 154.

[44]*Ibid.*, p. 178.

are . . . whole series of such common responses in the community in which we live, and such responses are what we term "institutions." . . . Thus the institutions of society are organized forms of group or social activity — forms so organized that the individual members of society can act adequately and socially by taking the attitude of others toward these activities.[45]

Institutions are for society the counterpart of what the "me" is to the self.

One of the most daring of Mead's analyses appears in *Movements of Thought in the Nineteenth Century,* in which he attempted to make the transition from the social psychology of the self to the processes of intellectual history. This study bears the same relation to Mead's work that Freud's studies of *Totem and Taboo, Civilization and Its Discontents, The Future of an Illusion,* and *Moses and Monotheism,* bear to psychoanalysis. The movement from eighteenth-century rationalism and revolution to nineteenth-century romanticism is treated by Mead as though it were a direct parallel to the stages in the development of the self. The romantic discovery of the past, for example, represents a reflexive discovery of the self. Lest this seem strange, it should be recalled that Cooley treated social organization as a kind of organized public opinion and institutions as fixed phases of the public mind. It is a perfectly logical extension of such ideas to conceive the emergence of total patterns of intellectual life in Mead's terms. The scientific acceptability of this, of course, is quite another story.

The concept of *role* emerged in central focus in Mead's work as the point of fusion for personality and social structure, moving discussion to an essentially new level of efficiency. This had been brilliantly anticipated by Simmel's splendid essay in Kantian vein, "How Is Society Possible?", in which the concept of "vocation" seemed the proper integrating point between self and society. But this was, for Simmel, a fragment in his thought; it did not arise, as for Mead, as a logical derivation from more basic propositions.

[45]*Ibid.,* pp. 260–262.

ERNST CASSIRER

The Columbiana Collection, Columbia University

Ernst Cassirer. Ernst Cassirer (1874–1945) was born in Breslau and educated in several German universities. From 1919 to 1934 he taught at Hamburg, and he was professor of philosophy at the University of Göteborg in Sweden when he was called to Yale University in 1940. His first work to appear in English translation was *Substance and Function* (1923); after publication of his second work in English, *An Essay on Man,* and through his teaching at Yale and Columbia, his work has become increasingly well known and translated into English.[46] The special interest of Cassirer for our

[46]*Substanzbegriff und Funktionsbegriff* (Berlin: B. Cassirer, 1910) was translated by William Curtis Swabey and Marie Collins Swabey as *Substance and Function* (New York: Dover Publications, 1923, 1953). The three volumes of *Philosophie der symbolischen Formen* were published

purposes lies in the illustration his work provides of the independent development, out of neo-Kantianism and neo-idealism, of ideas that partly parallel and partly complement symbolic interactionism as it arose in America.

Human life, Cassirer maintains, is distinguished by a new method of adaptation to the environment, based on the use of the "symbolic system." "This new acquisition transforms the whole of human life. As compared with the other animals

man lives not merely in a broader reality; he lives, so to speak, in a new *dimension* of reality."[47] This proposition is directly parallel to Mead, who would also agree that "language, myth, art, and religion" are parts of the symbolic universe human beings respond to. Cassirer continues: "Physical reality seems to recede in proportion as man's symbolic activity advances. . . . Man does not live in a world of hard facts, or according to his immediate needs and desires. He lives rather in the midst of imaginary emotions, in hopes and fears, in illusions and disillusions, in his fantasies and dreams."[48]

The whole development of human culture is dependent upon symbolic behavior; thus, for Cassirer as for Mead, the differentiation of animal reaction from human response rests on the emergence of language. As Cassirer sees it, speech arises on a substratum of the "language of the emotions." Koehler stated that chimpanzees achieve a considerable degree of expression by means of gestures: rage, terror, despair, grief, pleading, desire, playfulness, and pleasure. Human language requires something more. "The difference between *propositional language* and *emotional language* is the real landmark between the human and the animal world."[49]

A distinction may make the transition clear:

> We must carefully distinguish between *signs* and *symbols*. That we find rather complex systems of signs and signals in animal behavior seems to be an ascertained fact. . . . The famous experiments of Pavlov prove only that animals can easily be trained to react not merely to direct stimuli but to all sorts of mediate or representative stimuli. . . . Symbols — in the proper sense of this term — cannot be reduced to mere signals. Signals and symbols belong to two different universes of discourse: a signal is a part of the physical world of being; a symbol is a part of the human world of meaning. Signals are "operators"; symbols are "designators."[50]

---

between 1923 and 1929 (Berlin: B. Cassirer): Vol. 1, *Die Sprache* (1923); Vol. 2, *Das mythische Denken* (1925); Vol. 3, *Phänomenologie der Erkenntnis* (1929). This work has been translated by Ralph Manheim as *The Philosophy of Symbolic Forms* (New Haven, Conn.: Yale University Press, 1953–1957); the English titles of the three volumes are *Language, Mythical Thought,* and *The Phenomenology of Knowledge.* Cassirer's *Sprache und Mythos: ein Beitrag zum Problem der Götternamen* (Leipzig: B. G. Teubner, 1925) has been translated by Susanne K. Langer as *Language and Myth* (New York: Harper, 1946). *Die Philosophie der Aufklärung* (Tübingen: J. C. B. Mohr, 1932) was translated by Fritz C. A. Koelln and James P. Pettegrove as *The Philosophy of the Enlightenment* (Princeton, N.J.: Princeton University Press, 1951). Cassirer's works in English include: *An Essay on Man: An Introduction to a Philosophy of Human Culture* (New Haven, Conn.: Yale University Press, 1944) and *The Myth of the State* (Yale University Press, 1946). For a review of Cassirer's work, see Paul A. Schilpp (ed.), *The Philosophy of Ernst Cassirer* (Evanston, Ill.: Library of Living Philosophers, 1949). New translations of Cassirer appeared through the 1960s and 1970s including: *The Logic of the Humanities,* trans. Clarence Smith Horne (New Haven: Yale University Press, 1961); *The Question of Jean-Jacques Rousseau,* trans. Peter Gay (Bloomington, Indiana: Indiana University Press, 1963); *The Problem of Knowledge, Philosophy, Science, and History since Hegel,* trans. William Woglom and Charles W. Hendel (New Haven: Yale University Press, 1966); *The Platonic Renaissance in England,* trans. James P. Pettegrove (New York: Gordian Press, 1970); *The Individual and Cosmos in the Renaissance,* trans. Mario Domandi (Philadelphia: University of Pennsylvania Press, 1972); *Symbol, Myth and Culture: Essays and Lectures of Ernst Cassirer,* ed. Donald Philip Verene (New Haven: Yale University Press, 1979). For recent estimates of Cassirer see Paul Arthur Schilpp, "Cassirer," *International Encyclopedia of the Social Sciences* II, 331–333; Seymour W. Itzkoff, *Ernst Cassirer: Philosopher of Culture* (Boston: Twayne Publishers, 1977); David R. Lipton, *Ernst Cassirer: The Dilemma of a Liberal Intellectual in Germany, 1914–1933* (Toronto: University of Toronto Press, 1978).

[47]Cassirer, *An Essay on Man,* p. 24.
[48]*Ibid.,* p. 25.
[49]*Ibid.,* p. 30.
[50]*Ibid.,* pp. 31–32.

On the basis of this difference, the human being is released from the immediate stimulus. Psychologists do not hesitate to speak of a creative or constructive imagination in animals. But this imagination is of a human type. The animal possesses a practical imagination and intelligence, whereas human beings alone have developed *symbolic imagination and intelligence*. Symbolism adds universal applicability and versatility. It makes possible relational thought. The very awareness of relations is a specific feature of human consciousness. Geometry is the classical example of the turning point in human intellectual life. Even in elementary geometry we are not concerned with the apprehension of concrete individual figures. Confirming evidences for this power of abstraction are found in research on the psychopathology of language. Loss or impairment of speech caused by brain injury is never an isolated phenomenon. Such a defect tends to alter the whole character of the individual. Patients suffering from aphasia, for example, not only lose the use of words but undergo changes of personality. They may be able to perform outward tasks in a perfectly normal way but are at a complete loss in the solution of problems requiring theoretic or reflective activity. "Having lost their grip on universals, they stick to the immediate facts, to concrete situations. Such patients are unable to perform any task which can be executed only by means of a comprehension of the abstract."[51]

William James opposed the idea of the primacy of the separation of subject and object and suggested that they are differentiated out of something more primitive, "pure experience." Mead also opposed the opposition of mind and matter current in the psychologies of his day. He proposed "on-going activity" as a prior context. Wundt, who had himself employed a psychophysical parallelism, was nevertheless used as a starting point for Mead's analysis. Cassirer took a similar road, also beginning with Wundt, though he selected other elements of Wundt's thought than those which were central for Mead. He stated:

> It would not be possible to speak of a discovery of the subjective in myth if the widespread view that the concepts of the I and the soul were the *beginning* of all mythical thinking were justified. Ever since Tylor in his fundamental work advocated this theory of the animistic origin of myth formation, it seems to have been accepted more and more as the secure empirical core and empirical rule of research in mythology. Wundt's approach to myth from the standpoint of ethnic psychology is entirely built on this theory; he, too, sees all mythical concepts and ideas essentially as variants of the idea of the soul, which thus becomes the empirical *presupposition* rather than the specific *aim* of the mythical world view.[52]

Cassirer's fundamental argument is similar to that of James and Mead. Just as James had taken "pure experience" as his starting point and Mead the "on-going social process," so Cassirer utilizes "mythical thinking" as a kind of matrix out of which the soul, the "I," and the self are differentiated. "A glance at the development of the various symbolic forms shows us that their essential achievement is not that they copy the outward world in the inward world or that they simply project a finished inner world outward, but rather that the two factors of 'inside' and 'outside,' of 'I' and 'reality' are *determined* and delimited from one another only in these symbolic forms and through their mediation."[53] The crucial property of every symbolic form is found in the fact that it does not have the limit between "I" and "reality" as pre-existent; rather each symbolic form creates such limits. While metaphysics and "rational psychology" have treated the concept of the soul as a possession, taking it as a substance, mythical consciousness operates the opposite way. "The concept of the soul may just as well be called the end as the beginning of mythical thinking."[54] The soul

---

[51]*Ibid.*, p. 41.

[52]Cassirer, *Mythical Thought* (Vol. 2 of *The Philosophy of Symbolic Forms*), p. 155.
[53]*Ibid.*, pp. 155–156.
[54]*Ibid.*, p. 156.

and the "I" do not arise in mythical thinking all at once. Only gradually and by all manner of detours does the new category of the "I," the idea of the person and the personality, grow from the mythical category of the soul. Within mythical consciousness, a separation begins to occur between the objective and subjective, between the world of the "I" and the world of things.

The first form of thinking is thus represented by the magical world view. For originally in the world of mythical ideas, precisely in its most immediate forms, there is a close connection with "the world of efficacy." That is, in this world of proto-thought, the world and the "I," subject and object, the subjective and objective, are blurred. "Thus, in the magical world view the I exerts almost unlimited sway over reality: it takes all reality back into itself."[55]

The soul is the first mythical form in which the "I" is apprehended. Inevitably, since the soul arises as the first differentiation of the "I" in primitive mythical consciousness, it is seen as a kind of demonic being. The personal self is conceived only vaguely at this stage. As we go back to the more primitive levels of mythical thinking, the sharpness, clarity, and definiteness of the subjective and personal existence diminish. Primitive thinking is actually characterized by the peculiarly fluid and fugitive character of its intuition and concept of personal existence. There is as yet no soul which is seen as an independent unitary substance separate from the body; the soul is life itself, immanent in the body and necessarily attached to it. Inevitably people's spittle, their excrement, their nails, cuttings of their hair remain in a sense vehicles of their lives and souls, and it may be a part of magical lore to collect these to control the soul.

Cassirer's formula for the emergence of the self is similar to that of James and Mead, though his starting point and appeal to Wundt are made on different grounds. For Cassirer, materials are found in the entire field of mythology and magic. Typically the materials of Egyptian mythology contained in the Book of the Dead are employed to trace the evolution of the self from the primitive magico-ethical principle of demonic possession to a more complex concept of the self as an ethical autonomy. "If the intuition of the I is to be freed from this confinement, if the I is to be apprehended in ideal freedom as an ideal unity, a new approach is needed. The decisive turn occurs when the accent of the soul concept shifts — when the soul ceases to be considered as the mere vehicle or cause of vital phenomena and is taken rather as the subject of the ethical consciousness."[56] The Book of the Dead mirrors the progress from the mythical to the ethical self. Human beings rise from magic to religion, from the fear of demons to the worship of gods, and this apotheosis is not so much outward as inward. Now people apprehend not only the world but themselves, in new spiritual form. Continuation of this process makes possible the apprehension of the personality in its contemporary sense.

Furthermore, it is not the self alone that gradually arises through mythical forms to consciousness, but the community as well. Mythical consciousness and religious feeling, according to this analysis, embrace an even more fundamental contrast. For more basic than a contrast between subject and object is a contrast between the "I" and the "thou." "Subjectivity" has its correlate not in some external thing, but rather in a "thou" or "he" or "she," from which on the one hand it distinguishes itself, but with which on the other hand it groups itself. Thus is formed the true antithesis which the "I" requires in order to find and define itself. For here, again, the individual feeling and consciousness of self stand not only at the beginning but at the end of the process of development. In the earliest stages to which we can trace back this development, we find the feeling of *self* immediately fused with a definite mythical-religious feeling of *community*. The "I" feels and knows itself only as a member of a community, grouped with others into the unity of a family, a tribe, a social organism.

[55]*Ibid.*, p. 157.

[56]*Ibid.*, p. 166.

"Only in and through this social organism does it possess itself; every manifestation of its own personal existence and life is linked, as though by invisible magic ties, with the life of the totality around it."[57]

Just as the self is apprehended only by stages through a series of mythical conceptions, each becoming more differentiated, precise, and rational, so in the progressive apprehension of community there are stages which take the form of a mystic feeling of the unity of all life in one community, mythical class formation, and totemism. Here, again, it may be noted that, in contrast to Mead, Cassirer opens up the approach to these issues through mythology and ethnographic studies of primitives. Mythical-religious consciousness follows not from the empirical content of the social form but is one of the most important prior factors in the feeling of community and social life. The linkage between religion and community was original. The orgiastic cults of the world merely restored people to that sense of magical identity with things lying at the deepest level of the mythic consciousness of community. In none of these cults do individuals stop at the mere contemplation of the natural process; they are impelled to burst through the barrier that separates them from the universe of living things, to intensify the life feeling in themselves to the point of liberating themselves from their generic or individual *particularity*. This liberation is achieved in wild, orgiastic dances which restore human identity with the original source of life. The mythical narrative is an outward reflection of this inner process. In the cult of Dionysus, for instance, this process can be seen in the form of the cult which gives rise to the story of Dionysus-Zagreus, who is overpowered by the Titans, torn to pieces, and devoured, so that the one divine being is broken into the multiplicity of forms.

Thus, starting with mythic consciousness as the proto-reality, language, art, religion, and science are all seen by Cassirer as activities differentiating

these materials. Human culture is the process of humanity's progressive self-liberation. Language, art, religion, science, are various phases in this process. In each, human beings discover a new power to build up a world of their own, an "ideal" world. Philosophy cannot give up its search for a fundamental unity in this ideal world. At the same time, it must not confound this unity with simplicity nor overlook the tensions and frictions between the various powers of humanity, which cannot be reduced to a common denominator. They incline in different directions and obey different rules. Nevertheless, they do not denote discord, for these functions complete and complement one another. Each one opens a new horizon and shows us a new aspect of humanity.

Jean Piaget. The psychologist Jean Piaget (1896–   ) was born in Neuchâtel, Switzerland, and educated at the University of Neuchâtel, where he took his Ph.D in zoology in 1918. His biological studies led to an early interest in the structure and processes of the human mind, and in 1918 he went to Zurich to study psychology. Shortly afterwards, he went to Paris, where he worked with Théodore Simon, co-author of the Binet-Simon intelligence tests. In 1921, Piaget returned to Switzerland, where he began his connection with the Institut des Sciences de l'Éducation, now an associate institute of the University of Geneva for the scientific study of the child and the training of teachers; Piaget was made its co-director in 1933. In 1926, Piaget became a professor of philosophy at the University of Neuchâtel; in 1929, professor of psychology at the University of Geneva; and in 1937, professor of general psychology at Lausanne University. Piaget has been a prolific writer, and his books have been very quickly translated into English. They include: *The Language and Thought of the Child* (1923), *Judgment and Reasoning in the Child* (1924), *The Child's Conception of the World* (1926), *The Child's Conception of Physical Causality* (1927), *The Moral Judgment of the Child* (1932), *The Origins of Intelligence in Children* (1935), *The Construction of Reality in the Child* (1937), *Play, Dreams and Imitation in Childhood* (1945), *The Psychology of Intelligence*

[57]*Ibid.,* p. 175.

JEAN PIAGET

University of Geneva and Jean Piaget

(1947), *The Child's Conception of Space* (1948), and *The Child's Conception of Number* (1950).[58] The 1960s and 1970s brought reissues of all these volumes together with new translations from Piaget and evidence of Piaget's increasing attention to general problems of psychology, the social sciences, and education. Without attempting completeness these may be illustrated by: *The Child's Conception of Geometry*, trans. E. A. Lunzer (London: Routledge & Kegan Paul, 1960); *The Child's Conception of Number*, trans. C. Gattegno and F. M.

Dodson (London: Routledge & Kegan Paul, 1961); *Psychology and Epistemology: Toward A Theory of Knowledge,* trans. Arnold Rosin (New York: Viking, 1971); *Main Trends in Interdisciplinary Research* (New York: Harper & Row, 1973); *Main Trends in Psychology* (New York: Harper & Row, 1973); *The Principles of Genetic Epistemology,* trans. Wolfe Mays (New York: Basic Books, 1973); and *To Understand is to Invent,* trans. George-Anne Roberts (New York: Grossman, 1973).

There seems to be little evidence that Cassirer, Mead, and Piaget ever had much direct influence on one another. This makes all the more interesting their convergence on a common point of view. Symbolic interactionism appears independently in a number of forms as a kind of common solution to problems presented by the sociological tradition. Because of the sheer volume of Piaget's studies, it would be impossible to examine them all. Two will be reviewed here because of their parallels to American forms of symbolic interactionism.

Mead had found the game to be of particular importance for the formation of both the self and the social order. Piaget makes a similar case for the significance of games in *The Moral Judgment of the Child*:[59]

> Children's games constitute the most admirable social institutions. . . . If we wish to gain any understanding of child morality, it is obviously with the analysis of such facts as these that we must begin. All morality consists in a system of rules, and the essence of all morality is to be sought for in the respect which the individual acquires for these rules.[60]

The simplest social games contain rules elaborated by children themselves. Little boys who are beginning to play are gradually trained by the older ones in respect for the rules. The game permits the study of the process of socialization; the practice of the rules and the way children of dif-

[58]The dates given in parentheses are those of the original French publication, not of the translations. Because Piaget's output has been so enormous, and because it is difficult to single out a few titles as more significant than the others, a complete bibliographical footnote will not be attempted here.

[59]Jean Piaget, *The Moral Judgment of the Child* (New York: Harcourt, Brace, 1932), translated by Marjorie Gabain from *Le Jugement moral chez l'enfant* (Paris: F. Alcan, 1932).

[60]*Ibid.,* p. 1.

ferent ages apply them; consciousness of rules and the ideas which children of different ages form of them as something obligatory and sacred or as something subject to personal choice; the heteronomy or autonomy of the rules.

Piaget found that the rules of children's games such as those of marbles constitute a social reality independent of individuals (in Durkheim's sense) and transmitted, like language, from one generation to another. This set of customs is more or less plastic, for individual innovations, just as in the case of language, succeed only when they meet a general need and when they are collectively sanctioned as conforming to the spirit of the game. Piaget maintains that when children are studied in terms of their use and awareness of the rules of their games, four stages may be distinguished. In the first stage the rules are used habitually and without awareness. This may be described as a purely *motor* stage. So far as it enters awareness at all, use of rules may result in the formation of ritualistic schemas. The second, *egocentric,* stage begins when the child receives examples of codified rules from the outside world. Sometime between the ages of two and five children start to imitate such examples even though they continue to play by themselves or to play with others without trying to win. Between the ages of seven and eight, an incipient *cooperative* stage begins, in which each tries to win and all concern themselves with the question of mutual control and unification of the rules, even though there is considerable discrepancy in the children's information about the rules. Finally, between eleven and twelve appears the stage of *codification of the rules,* during which every detail of procedure in the game becomes fixed and children gain an awareness of the rules of reasoning that will enable them to apply the rules to any situation that may arise.

The child's emerging *consciousness* of the rules, though elusive in detail, is clear enough on the whole. It develops through three general stages, not completely identical with the practice of the rules. During the first stage, the rules are not yet coercive because they are purely motor or received unconsciously. This is followed by a stage in which the rules are regarded as sacred and untouchable, emanating from adults. Every suggested alteration appears as a transgression. Finally, the rule is looked on as a law resting on mutual consent — a law that must be respected if one is to be loyal but which one may alter by enlisting general opinion on one's side.

In the course of trying to understand the game and adapt themselves to it, children bring order into their behavior, which becomes schematized and ritualized. Particularly important is the fact that symbolism is grafted on the child's motor schemas. These symbols are initially enacted in play rather than thought out, and they imply a certain amount of imagination. Both rites and symbols lie in the conditions of preverbal intelligence. Two fundamental kinds of moral judgment already make their appearance during the second and third type of consciousness of the rules. Correlated with the egocentric practice of the rules is a feeling of respect for elders, corresponding to a theoretical judgment which turns a rule into something mystical and transcendental. To the rational practice of rules, there corresponds a theoretical judgment which attributes to the rules an autonomous character.

In connection with his derivation of morality from the practices in children's games, Piaget brought under review the socioethical theories of three modern thinkers: (1) Durkheim, who treated society as something standing above individuals and as the source from which all authority emanates; (2) M. Bovet, who derived morality from interindividual relations;[61] (3) James Mark Baldwin, who derived the ethical self as an emergent from interactive Life. All these theories, according to Piaget, express part of the truth, with Baldwin perhaps closest to a comprehensive view. Piaget's own conclusion[62] was that the morality prescribed by society for the individual was not homogeneous. Society is not a single thing. Society is the sum of social relations, among which two

[61]Piaget, "Les Conditions de l'obligation de la conscience," *L'Année psychologique,* 1912.
[62]Piaget, *The Moral Judgment of the Child,* pp. 402 ff.

types may be distinguished: relations of *constraint* and relations of *cooperation*. Relations of constraint come from the outside as a system of rules with obligatory content; relations of cooperation arise in the consciousness of ideal norms. From the outside, the child's world tends primarily to be structured on the basis of ties of authority and unilateral respect; from within, however, relations of cooperation arise between equals, expressing an equilibrium limit rather than a static system. Externally, experience is under the constraint of duty; internally, experience is ordered by spontaneous pursuit of the good and autonomous rationality, which are the fruits of reciprocity.

If one accepts from Mead's type of analysis the idea that capacity to take roles is essential to the social efficacy of the individual and that such roles form a common point of approach for personality and social structure, then the affinities of Mead's and Piaget's analyses are clear. For Mead's roles are codified in "the rules of the game," which were the object of analysis for Piaget. The rules, the learning of which Piaget was interested in, define role behaviors and the development of the "moral life" of the child from moral realism to moral democracy — this last, a close parallel to Mead's conception of the movement from the particular to the generalized other. It also parallels Cooley's concept of democracy as the extension of the ideals of the primary group. The two analyses are complementary. To Mead's theory of role-consolidation and development of the self, Piaget adds new perspectives on the ethical evolution of the self.

Piaget also turned his attention to the problem, so central to Mead's analysis, of language. Here, again, Piaget's treatment is an extension of symbolic interactionism with reference to the imitation–suggestion school. Piaget's latest discussion of these problems appears in *Play, Dreams and Imitation in Childhood*.[63] The focus of this study is on the symbolic function of the mind. The symbolic function is considered as a mechanism common to the various systems of representation — both verbal and nonverbal — and as a mechanism whose existence is a prerequisite for conceptual interaction between individuals and consequently for the acquisition of collective meaning. Piaget is clearly aware of the danger of circularity in deriving language from social interaction and social interaction from language. He adds that he in no way disputes the social nature of collective meanings but shows that it implies cooperation and reciprocity. "The social fact is for us a fact to be explained, not to be invoked as an extra-psychological factor. Hence it seems to us that the study of the symbolic function must cover all the initial forms of representation, from imitation and ludic or oneric symbols to verbal schemas and elementary pre-conceptual structures."[64]

The problem posed by Piaget is identical with Mead's attempt to make the transition from the "gesture" to the "significant symbol." Piaget believes that in play and imitation it is possible to trace the transition from sensory-motor assimilation and accommodation to the sort of mental assimilation and accommodation which characterizes the beginnings of representation. Representation begins when there is simultaneous differentiation and coordination between "signifiers" and "signified." The first differentiation between these is provided by imitation and the mental image derived from it. These images extend accommodation to external objects. The meanings of the symbols originate in assimilation, the dominating factor in play. At the sensory-motor level, an image develops that is capable of going beyond the immediate present. Assimilation and accommodation finally come together in a combination made necessary by this advance beyond the immediate present. The constitution of the symbolic function is a product of the union between actual or mental imitation and an absent model and the "meanings" provided by the various forms of assimilation. Thus language, a system of collective signs, be-

[63]Jean Piaget, *Play, Dreams and Imitation in Childhood* (New York: W. W. Norton, 1951), translated by C. Gattegno and F. M. Hodgson from *La Formation du symbols chez l'enfant* (Neuchâtel: Delachaux & Niestlé, 1945).

[64]*Ibid.*, p. 4.

comes possible and acquires the set of individual symbols through which the sensory-motor schemas can be transformed into concepts or may integrate new concepts. The symbol results from prerepresentational schematism. The ego inevitably follows as a symbolically integrated structure. The various forms of representation may interact. There is representation when an absent model is imitated in symbolic play, in imagination, and even in dreams. The system of concepts and logical relations, both in their intuitive and operational forms, implies representation.

Basic to all Piaget's explanations is a conception of the individual life process. This has two major aspects or phases: the assimilation of objects to individual activity, on the one hand, and the accommodation of activity to the object world on the other. The two processes of assimilation and accommodation are polar phases of the total life process. They are not always in equilibrium and may even operate in partial autonomy from one another. One of the fundamental facts of the life process is the establishment of an equilibrium between assimilation and accommodation. The first phase of individual development is described by Piaget as one of sensory-motor adjustment. Sensory-motor adjustment consists in the development of an assimilating activity which tends to incorporate external objects in its schemas while at the same time accommodating the schemas to the external world. This is the first and basic form of life adjustment. Imitation is not taken as an original form of activity but as secondary, including a component of intelligence. Imitation appears when the subject's schemas of action are modified without use of the external world that modified it. Imitation is a continuation of the effort at accommodation. The linkage of imitation with representation arises in the fact that representation involves the image of an object. Representation is a kind of interiorized imitation. This corresponds to Mead's idea of thinking as internalization of the social process. Representation appears as a phase of the continuation of the effort at accommodation.

On the other hand, every act of intelligence represents an equilibrium between assimilation and accommodation, and while imitation is a continuation of accommodation for its own sake, it may be said roughly that play is essentially assimilation, or the primacy of assimilation over accommodation. Play is functional, or reproductional, assimilation. Primitive play begins by being almost identical with the set of sensory-motor behaviors of which it is only one pole. With the interiorization of schemas, play becomes more distinct from adaptive behavior (intelligence). In contrast to objective thought, which seeks to adapt itself to external reality, imaginative play symbolically transposes things to the child's activity without rules or limitations. Thus, in the early stages of representation the property of the symbol as a "signifier" is a continuation of imitation. What the symbol signifies may vary from adequate adaptation to free satisfaction. With the socialization of the child, play acquires rules or gradually adapts symbolic imagination to reality in the form of constructions which are still spontaneous but which imitate reality.

For Piaget, imitation, symbolic play, and cognitive representation demonstrate the progressive establishment of equilibrium between assimilation and accommodation on a new basis. There is an equilibrium at the stage of sensory-motor adjustment level, but only assimilation and accommodation are involved. Representation, however, goes beyond the present, extending the field of adaptation in space and time. It evokes what lies outside the immediate perceptual field. The collective institution of language is the main factor in both the formation and socialization of representations. The "signifier," for Piaget, is a product of accommodation continued as imitation, that is, as images of interiorized imitations. The "signified" is the product of assimilation which, by integrating the object in earlier schemas, provides it with a meaning. Thus, representation involves a double interplay of assimilations and accommodations, past and present, tending toward equilibrium. The process is slow, occupying the whole of childhood.

HANS GERTH

Courtesy of the University of Wisconsin, Madison, Wisconsin

Hans Gerth and C. Wright Mills. The work of two very vigorous theorists may indicate the continued development of symbolic interactionism and the way in which it can be adapted to special purposes. Hans Gerth (1908–1978) was a social psychologist and political sociologist at the University of Wisconsin, where for some years he taught a famous course in social stratification. He was born in Kassel, Germany, and educated at Heidelberg under Karl Mannheim. Later, he studied at London and Frankfurt, where he took his Ph.D. in 1933. After coming to the United States as a refugee, he became one of the primary translators of Max Weber (*From Max Weber: Essays in Sociology; The Religion of China; Ancient Judaism*). C. Wright Mills (1916–1962) took his Ph.D. at the University of Wisconsin

in 1941 under Hans Gerth and Howard Becker. He has made significant contributions to the study of social stratification in such works as *The New Men of Power; The Puerto Rican Journey; White Collar: The American Middle Classes;* and *The Power Elite.* Mills was professor of sociology at Columbia University from 1946 until his death.

The unusual talents of Hans Gerth and C. Wright Mills were linked in their joint study, *Character and Social Structure,*[65] their most complete theoretical statement. Gerth and Mills trace their affinities primarily to Mead and Freud. "Behaviorism's most fruitful outcome was George Mead's work, especially his daring effort to anchor personal consciousness itself in the social process. Mead's concept of the generalized other, and Freud's super-ego — their closest point of contact — enable us to link the private and the public, the innermost acts of the individual with the widest kinds of social-historical phenomena."[66]

In both views they find serious limitations: they feel that Mead had neither an adequate theory of emotions and motives nor a dynamic theory of the affective life of human beings; on the other hand, Freud's notion of the personality tends, they think, to be socially inflexible. Furthermore, neither Freud nor Mead presents a conception of social structure relevant to social-psychological problems. However, the authors think, when properly integrated, Freud and Mead provide a model of character structure and the most fruitful set of ideas available in modern social science adequate for the treatment of social structure as developed by Marx, Sombart, Weber, and Mannheim.

To Gerth and Mills, the primary requirements for an adequate theory of symbolic interactionism include: the integration and systematization of Mead and Freud; the development of an adequate

---

[65]Hans Gerth and C. Wright Mills, *Character and Social Structure: The Psychology of Social Institutions* (New York: Harcourt, Brace, 1953; London: Routledge and Kegan Paul, 1953). Mills's books will be discussed in Chapter XVIII.

[66]*Ibid.,* p. xvi.

theory of motivation; and the development of a social-psychologically relevant conception of social structure.

The two fundamental concepts by which Gerth and Mills unite personality and social structure are drawn from Mead: *role* and *institution*. "Role" is taken to refer to units of behavior which by their occurrence stand out as regularities and which are oriented to the conduct of other actors. "Institutions" are taken as organizations of roles carrying different degrees of authority, one or more of which serves to maintain the entire system of roles.[67] Human beings, as persons, are composed of the roles they perform and the effects of these roles on them. Society, as social structure, is composed of roles, variously combined.

The integration and systematization of Mead and Freud constitute Gerth's and Mills's concept of *character*. A character is a psychic structure formed on a foundation of organic potential. A psychic structure is an integration of perception, emotion, and impulse. Inner feelings become emotions by being linked to socially recognized gestures of which people are aware and which they relate to themselves. For sensation to become perception, certain meanings must be added. For impulses to become purposes, the objects so specified must be defined and learned.

Language is important for all these transformations, for it is through language that experience is composed in terms of the expectations of others. Character arises when, in the course of social experience through language, the organic materials of the individual are stylized into roles. And with roles, everything necessary for the concepts of institution and social structure is at hand.

Before turning to Gerth's and Mills's concept of social structure, it is worthy of note that in their conception of character they have actually taken precious little from Freud. Of such conceptions as the unconscious, conscious, censor, id, superego, ego, repression, sublimation, autoeroticism, narcissism, Oedipus complex, Electra complex, dream symbolism, they make practically no use. Rather,

the materials formed by social roles into character are conceived in pre-Freudian terms. The materials for behavior are conceived originally to break down into sensation, feeling, and impulse, which by language are transformed into perception, emotion, and purpose. Freud actually receives little more than lip service.

Just as Mead is primarily important for the Gerth and Mills concept of character, so is he central to their view of social structure. For Marx, Sombart, Weber, and Mannheim seem to have as little to do with their idea of social structure as Freud did for their idea of personality. Institutions are clusters of roles anchored in an authoritative role. The parental authority of the head of a household, for example, rests on awards and punishments emanating from this role and maintaining the entire role pattern. Institutions are in turn classified in terms of objective function, and the two ideas of institutional *order* and *sphere* are introduced. An "institutional order" consists of all institutions in the social structure which have similar consequences and ends or which serve similar objective functions. The following institutional orders form the skeleton structure of the total society.

1. The *political* order consists of those institutions within which men acquire, wield, or influence the distribution of power and authority within social structures.
2. The *economic* order is made up of those establishments by which men organize labor, resources, and technical implements in order to produce and distribute goods and services.
3. The *military* order is composed of institutions in which men organize legitimate violence and supervise its use.
4. The *kinship* order is made up of institutions which regulate and facilitate legitimate sexual intercourse, procreation, and the early rearing of children.
5. The *religious* order is composed of those institutions in which men organize and supervise the collective worship of God or deities, usually at regular occasions and at fixed places.[68]

[67]*Ibid.*, pp. 10 ff.

[68]*Ibid.*, p. 26.

The institutional orders, however, are not sufficient to characterize social structure completely, for there are several "spheres" of social conduct which characterize all institutional orders, such as technology, symbols, status, and education. *Symbols* include the signs, emblems, ceremonies, language, music which sustain the order. *Technology* includes tools, apparatus, machines, instruments, and physical devices. *Status* consists of agencies for and means of distributing prestige, deference, or honor. And the *educational* sphere includes activities concerned with the transmission of skills and values to persons who have not yet acquired them.

The picture of social structure that emerges is one characterized by nine institutional orders interlaced by four spheres. People, for example, may be teachers, with their behavior thus forming part of the educational *sphere*; at the same time, since they make their living by teaching, their behavior forms a part of the economic *order*. In view of such institutional overlap, it sometimes requires considerable ingenuity to decide just what institutional affiliation a given item of behavior has. One must assume that, at least under some conditions, orders and spheres may change places and become spheres and orders to each other.

Despite the economical formulation given by Gerth and Mills to the concepts of character and social structure, their greatest innovations in symbolic interactionism do not lie here. The conception of roles, after all, and of their importance for the formation of personality has been basic to symbolic interactionism from the outset. Furthermore, the conception of roles as the unit elements of institutions is not new either, having been formulated by Mead. Even the idea of institutions as authoritatively instituted role groupings is not new; it was formulated by Znaniecki. The idea of institutional systems is at least as old as Herbert Spencer, and the distinction between orders and spheres was drawn by Max Weber. The contribution of Gerth and Mills at this level is primarily one of unusual compactness of formulation.

On the other hand, there is not the slightest doubt that their sociology of *motivation* represents a distinctly new addition to symbolic interactionism. Motivation, they argue, is equilibrium-restoring behavior and has three forms: physio-chemical, emotional, and social:

> At the level of the *organism,* we might assume that "all organic processes are initiated by the need to restore a physio-chemical equilibrium which is experienced as health." In terms of the *psychic structure* we might assume that "psychological processes are initiated by the need to restore an emotional equilibrium which is experienced as pleasure." In terms of the *person,* we might assume that conduct is motivated by the *expectations* of others, which are internalized from the roles which the persons enact. . . . Motivation thus has to do with the balance of self-image with the appraisals of others.[69]

For Freud, the psychic structure may be socially molded, but it is not the ideal subject of social modification. Sublimation implies that role-conditioned forms of psychic drives are epiphenomena of the basic drives. To Gerth and Mills, this argument is bad metaphysics, for the biological person has no more reality than the psychic person. Hence it is only on the level of the person that we can hope to deal with understandable motives. The question of understandable intentions or motives calls attention to the role of language in interpersonal conduct.

Gerth and Mills introduce here their most original conception—"vocabularies of motive." Motives, they observe, are usually thought of as subjective springs of actions lying in the psychic structure of the organism. However, they urge, since persons ascribe motives to themselves and others, motives may be considered "as the terms which persons typically use in their interpersonal relations."[70] Sociologically, they continue, a motive is a term in a vocabulary which appears to the actor and to the observer to be an adequate reason for his or her conduct. "Conceived in this way," they insist, "motives are acceptable justifications

[69]*Ibid.,* p. 112.
[70]*Ibid.,* pp. 114–115.

C. WRIGHT MILLS

Photograph by Yaroslava. Courtesy of C. Wright Mills

for present, future, or past programs of conduct."[71] Nor is this the end of the matter. "When a person confesses or imputes motives, he is not usually trying to describe his social conduct, he is . . . usually trying to influence others."[72] Vocabularies of motive, they maintain, have histories as their institutional contexts change. While the motives accompanying the institutional conduct of war are not the causes of war, they promote continued participation in warfare.

Examine the shift from the laissez faire to the monopolistic phase of modern capitalism. The profit

motive of individual gain may be widely espoused and accepted by business men during a relatively prosperous and free economic era. . . . Now, if a man finds himself unable to engage in business conduct without joining a "liberal" business organization and proclaiming its public-spirited vocabulary, it follows that this particular vocabulary of motives is an important reinforcing feature of his social conduct.[73]

Thus, according to Gerth and Mills, symbolic interactionism requires for its completion an adequate theory of motivation. Such an adequate theory of motivation, it seems, takes its stand on the assumption that people are going to do what they would do anyway. Motivation consists of specialized vocabularies, systems of terms and phrases, that have instrumental value for self-justification and deceit. To be sure, we are warned that we "must abandon the notion that merely because vocabularies of motives are acceptable they are necessarily deceptive shams."[74] This way of putting the case suggests, however, that most of the time they are. While it is suggested that various vocabularies of motive are integrated with different levels of psychic structure and that unconscious motives refer to unverbalized conduct, it is difficult to escape the view that, for Gerth and Mills, "vocabularies of motive" are at bottom always social strategies. "No one vocabulary of motives is accepted by everyone, so the alert individual must use one or the other tentatively, until he finds the way to integrate his conduct with others, to win them as allies of his act."[75] Presumably for this purpose one might find such handbooks as Dale Carnegie's *How to Win Friends and Influence People* extremely helpful.

SUMMARY

The conceptual foundations of symbolic interactionism are found primarily in pragmatism, al-

[71]*Ibid.*, p. 115.
[72]*Ibid.*, p. 117.

[73]*Ibid.*, p. 118.
[74]*Ibid.*, p. 119.
[75]*Ibid.*, p. 122.

though strong additional influence comes from neo-idealism, both in its older and in its neo-Hegelian version. In America the primary lines of development extend from William James, through Cooley and W. I. Thomas, to George Herbert Mead. From Mead, in turn, symbolic interactionism has had influence upon almost every contemporary sociologist. The continued evolution of its theoretical structure is evident in the work of Gerth and Mills.

Though symbolic interactionism has found its strongest development in America, it represents a structural trend in sociological thought. Two very significant Europeans illustrate this: Piaget and Cassirer.

Symbolic interactionism achieved a more precise definition of sociological subject matter than pluralistic behaviorism. It opened up the problem of the linguistic structuring of interhuman behavior. It developed more adequate theories of personality and made major strides toward the linkage of personality and social structure. It is also of interest to observe, incidentally, that its picture of society was far more uniformly "liberal" than was true for pluralistic behaviorism. This is true not only for James, Cooley, Thomas, and Mead, with their Jeffersonian ideal of a small-town democracy, but also for Piaget and Cassirer, who preserve sociopolitical conceptions of an Enlightenment model.

Moreover, closely related to the more theoretically consistent notions of sociological subject matter, the members of this branch of social behaviorism brought statistical methods under serious question as solely adequate to sociology, preferring some sort of comparative case method or even, as in the case of Cooley, systematic autobiography (introspection).

XVI

Further Developments in Symbolic Interactionism

In 1978 in an essay for *A History of Sociological Analysis*, Bernice Fisher and Anselm Strauss ask, "What is interactionism?"[1] They observe that it is a difficult question to answer definitively: sometimes persons both inside and outside the Chicago tradition are called interactionists; sometimes they are called symbolic interactionists; and sometimes they are called the Chicago school or Chicago tradition. To compound the confusion, Fisher and Strauss explain, when the Society for the Study of Symbolic Interactionism was formed some interactionists entered, but some symbolic interactionists stayed out. In the development of their argument, it appears that Fisher and Strauss wish to reserve the term *interactionism* for the theory advocated by persons trained at the University of Chicago in the generation of W. I. Thomas, Robert E. Park, and George H. Mead. However, even that

criterion is not absolute, since they omit Ernest Burgess and Louis Wirth. Fisher and Strauss believed the essence of interactionism to be the possession of a liberal social philosophy or ideology: faith in progress, belief that social change yields to rational control, and the conviction that individuals are creative and collective action is effective despite the limitations of institutions.[2] However, although both W. F. Ogburn and Samuel Stauffer were liberals in this sense and taught at Chicago, they also are not included in the circles of interactionism and symbolic interactionism.

The ambiguities in the Fisher-Strauss account appear to arise from two sources: (1) the application of mixed criteria for determining who does and who does not ascribe to the theory; and (2) vacillation as to the purpose of their essay. They waiver between writing the intellectual history of the Chicago department and rendering an account of the internal development of the department's

[1]Bernice M. Fisher and Anselm L. Strauss, "Interactionism," in *A History of Sociological Analysis,* ed. Tom Bottomore and Robert Nisbet (New York: Basic Books, 1978), p. 457.

[2]*Ibid.,* pp. 462–463.

single most vigorous theoretical tradition. What they describe as the essence of interactionism is the ideology of twentieth-century American liberalism, an ideology by no means confined to symbolic interactionists. Moreover, they do not seem to recognize that rarely, if ever, do all members of an academic department hold identical theoretical positions. The natural inclination in a collegiate body for members to find niches of their own leads to the distribution of the members over the intellectual space available to them. It is difficult to find an academic department without dissidents. Furthermore, a developing system of explanations rarely remains the exclusive property for long of a single academic department. Once they read each other's publications, persons at different universities see convergences in their respective formulations and team up or make brilliant use of each other's ideas. Fisher and Strauss appear to have ignored the possibility of the dispersion of interactionist theory to other locations that was suggested by Manford Kuhn in his posthumously published essay, "Major Trends in Symbolic Interactionism in the Past Twenty-five Years."[3] Kuhn made a strong case for the existence of at least two basic schools of symbolic interactionism: one at Iowa, and at Chicago. Kuhn viewed himself as a symbolic interactionist although he had graduated from the University of Wisconsin and had spent no time at Chicago.

In the original review of symbolic interactionism in the first edition of *Nature and Types,* which was completed and published in 1960, a view similar to that of Kuhn was presented: symbolic interactionism was seen to be a system of social theory characterized by elementarism, with its conception of the centrality of meaning in the analysis of social interaction and its special concern with language, role-taking, the self, and mind (which in the classical tradition was a euphemism for culture). To the degree to which thinkers made these ideas central to their analyses they were

treated as symbolic interactionists whether they had spent some time at Chicago (like David Riesman) or not (like Hans Gerth and C. Wright Mills). Students of symbolic interactionism have generally accepted this interpretation without complaint.

For a time after World War II, American sociologists (and to some extent world sociologists under the powerful influence of American sociology) were hypnotized by the magnetic spell of structure-functionalism. Although symbolic interactionists were at work, no one presented the position as a major alternative to the establishment point of view. However, by the early 1960s increasing restiveness with structure-functionalism was manifest. Just as the behavioristic sociologists began to press their case at this time, the symbolic interactionists, too, were stirred to renewed activity. Since the views of Kenneth Burke played a role in the formulations of the younger recruits to the position, he must be added to the shapers of the recent developments in symbolic interactionism.

Kenneth Burke. Kenneth Duva Burke, who was born in 1897 in Pittsburgh, Pennsylvania, never spent more than a year as a student in college; he attended Ohio State University for a semester in 1916 and enrolled at Columbia (1916–1917) but soon left to devote himself to writing. In 1918 he joined the circle of avant-garde writers in Greenwich Village. Among them were Malcolm Cowley, Mathew Josephson, Slater Brown, Hart Crane, and Gorham B. Munson. He married for the first time in 1919 and joined the editorial board of *The Dial* in 1921, remaining until it ceased publication in 1929. Meanwhile he bought a farm near Andover, New Jersey, which remains his permanent home. In 1926 he was research worker for the Laura Spellman Rockefeller Memorial Foundation. In 1927 he became music critic for *The Dial* and from 1933 to 1936 was music critic for *The Nation.* During the 1920s and 1930s Burke wrote short stories, critical essays, and a novel. His larger works on philosophy, sociology, and criticism began with *Permanence and Change* in 1935.

Burke opened a new career as a university lec-

[3]Manford Kuhn, "Major Trends in Symbolic Interactionism in the Past Twenty-five Years," *The Sociological Quarterly*, 5 (Winter 1964), 61–84.

KENNETH BURKE

Courtesy of the University of California Press

turer with a course in criticism at the New School for Social Research in 1937. He was summer lecturer at the University of Chicago in 1938, and again in 1949–1950. Intermittently Burke served as professor of criticism at Bennington College, Vermont. In 1949 he was a member of the Princeton Institute of Advanced Studies; in 1957, Fellow at the Center for Advanced Study in the Behavioral Sciences. In 1964–1965 he was appointed Regents Professor, University of California, Santa Barbara. In 1967 he was a lecturer at Harvard University.

In 1971 Kenneth Burke was invited to give the Heinz Werner Lectures which were published as *Dramatism and Development.*[4] In these lectures

Burke traced the evolution of his ideas. In his first book of criticism, *Counter Statement,* he explored the property of literary form in arousing and fulfilling expectations in an audience and treated the problem of "identity" as explainable as a crisis of expectations. At this period Burke was radical in his sympathies and raised serious questions about social and political trends in the society. In *Permanence and Change* Burke extended to human relations in general the notion that a "perspective of incongruity" is of value in the study of form. In view of the fact that some terms seem spontaneously to evoke others, Burke tried the experiment of confronting terms with their antitheses. He was delighted when meanings tended to explode in the process and ever after, whether analyzing literature or life, used this device to generate unexpected properties of any matter under consideration. In *Attitudes Toward History* Burke carried his emerging theory and methodology one step further: he advanced a theory of human relations based on a perspective of incongruity. In *Philosophy of Literary Form* he added an additional tool to the analysis of literature and life by suggesting that they were dominated by "equations," linkages between the key terms in the sphere of concern. Hitler's *Mein Kampf,* for example, was taken to be a set of "equational devices" in the Nazi rhetoric of anti-Semitism.[5]

In his next book, *A Grammar of Motives,* Burke gave the name *dramatism* to his notion that life and literature must be based on the equation that "things move, persons act."[6] Analysis can best proceed by study of the cycle of terms implicit in the

[4]Kenneth Burke, *Dramatism and Development* (Worcester, Mass.: Clark University Press, 1972). Burke's books most important to the social scientist include: *Permanence and Change; An Anatomy of Purpose* (first published 1935) (New York: Bobbs-Merrill, 1965); *Attitudes Toward History* (first published 1937) (Boston: Beacon Press, 1961); *A Grammar of Motives* (first published 1945) (New York: G. Braziller, 1955); *A Rhetoric of Motives* (first published 1950) (New York: G. Braziller, 1955); *The Rhetoric of Religion: Studies in Logology* (Boston: Beacon Press, 1961). For a good review of Burke's life and work see Armin Paul Frank, *Kenneth Burke* (New York: Twayne, 1960).

[5]Burke, *Dramatism and Development,* p. 20.

[6]*Ibid.,* p. 21.

act, and these are revealed most clearly in the notions central to the construction and criticism of the drama: act, scene, agent, agency, and purpose. George Herbert Mead convinced Burke that it might be a good idea to add a sixth term, *attitude*, to this pentad. These terms, Burke insists, can be taken in various combinations or "ratios" permitting the analysis of any conceivable aesthetic or nonaesthetic event. *A Rhetoric of Motives* made two important additions to this scheme: (1) the indispensability of mystery in human affairs — a phenomenon obscured by naturalism; (2) that in addition to the need to consider the role of persuasion in art and life, there is also a need to take account of "identification."

The Rhetoric of Religion, Burke informs us, was motivated by his "hankering after a cosmic perspective on human affairs."[7] As he set about to work out the cycle of terms implicit in the idea of order, he became impressed with the pressure for sacrifice in human congregations and the need to have scapegoats, to victimize. Finally, Burke maintains, no matter where one looks in human affairs one sooner or later becomes aware of a pressure toward an "entelechical, summational, culminative, or paradigmatic version of what is implied." He suggests that "archetypes" or "prototypes" may be "mythic ways of formulating entelechical implications . . . by translating them into terms of a vaguely hypothetical past."[8]

In Burke's own review, his thinking was in continuous evolution. *Permanence and Change* (1935) was a major synthesis, marking a point about half way from his starting point as an artist and critic to that of social scientist and social philosopher. *Permanence and Change* began to attract social scientists by its unexpected discoveries and illuminations, despite the fact that it was untidy and lacked a clear developing structure. It is the picture of a mind in process, struggling with ambiguities toward some sort of understanding. Its most basic assumptions often appear belatedly and where one

would least expect them. However, this is not the place to trace the details of an act of clarification as it emerges, but to sum up its primary message to students of sociological theory.

Burke is an elementarist. The basic reality underlying the experience of human beings is thought to be their psychosomatic structure, which exists prior to any historical events. Historically, and in the present, in art and in life, people can only do and be what their psychic constitution permits. From this point of view, all human history and all human art can be thought of as exploring the potentiality of human nature.

In a manner that calls upon a long series of thinkers, including August Comte and Sir James Frazer, Burke conceives of the cultural history of humanity as divided into a number of periods or "orders of rationalization": magic, through religion, to science. Each period had its strengths and its weaknesses. The scientific epoch, too, has limitations and in various ways violates human needs. Hence, Burke envisions a fourth stage, the poetic, with many affinities between magic and poetry.

Changes from one cultural period to another result from the fact that the primary orientation of any given period only satisfies some of the interests of the universal nature of humanity. The primary orientation frustrates other potentialities and the frustration initiates a search for a more adequate vehicle of self-realization. The dominant outlook of an epoch may be visualized as a group psychosis or cycle of rationalizations for one perspective. And while it has built-in frustrations, which send people on the search for alternative points of view, one must also recognize that some individuals are so out of key with the dominant perspective that they are in danger of being locked into asylums. In Burke's view, psychotherapy achieves its results by the progressive misnaming of a patient's syndrome, an activity that approximates "exorcism by misnomer." Then the patient's superego rebuilds his or her personality, by its socialization in terms of the group psychosis.

The essential element of all learning is substitution or transference, which establishes compulsive linkages. Such linkages characterize every occupa-

[7]*Ibid.,* p. 29.
[8]*Ibid.,* pp. 43–44.

tion. A world view is a culture comprised of such compulsive linkages. Whether the results be occupation or preoccupation the result is self-fulfilling, setting the terms for the approach to new situations. However, every capacity acquired through training also brings with it various trained incapacities as well.

If learning consists of establishing the compulsive linkages of terms, social change and sociocultural analysis consists in breaking them up and discovering their limits. This may occur spontaneously, as when one point of view arises in contest with another, or it may be a self-conscious instrument of research as represented by Burke's "perspective by incongruity." Every speech-act is poetic, suggestive, and magical, conveying the attitude of the speaker in an ideal community, enticing the audience to react correspondingly. By confronting the perspective involved in a speech-act with alternative formulations, limits come into view, and alternatives become visible.

> Let us not only discuss a nation as though it were an individual, but also an individual as though he were a nation, depicitng massive events trivially, and altering the scale of weeds in a photograph until they become a sublime and towering forest — shifting from the animal, the vegetable, the physical, the mental, "irresponsibly" applying to one category the terms habitual to another, as when Whitehead discerns mere habit in the laws of atomic behavior — or like a kind of professorial E. E. Cummings who, had he called man an ape, would then study apes to understand Aristotle. "Let us do this?" Everywhere in our systems for forcing inferences, it is being done.[9]

Whereas *Permanence and Change* represented a halfway house on the way to his mature position, *Grammar of Motives* marked Burke's arrival. For the rest of his career Burke has continued to round out his "dramatism" as he named his position in this work. We have Burke's own summary of his beliefs in his essay on "Dramatism" in the *International Encyclopedia of the Social Sciences.*[10]

In a manner that echoes Hegel's distinction between gravity and spirit, Burke observes that natural things move, but human beings act. Action is motion based on meaning and resting on humanity's unique character (the species being), the "intrinsic involvement with 'symbolicity' as a necessary part of his nature."[11] Dramatism assumes that the direct route to understanding human relations and motivations is through inquiry into the function of cycles of terms. The term *Act* itself is a center (a "god-term") from which a whole universe of supplementary terms is derived. A philosophy of language and "symbolicity," in Burke's view, provides the basis for a general understanding of human beings and society.

One may illustrate this by the unavoidable imputation of motives that takes place whenever action is considered. To be an act there must be a scene, an agent, a means or agency, a purpose, and an attitude. The analysis of an action or a work of art then consists in the consideration of various ratios between the terms: act-scene, purpose-agency, agent-act, and so on. Burke insists that dramatism is no mere metaphor "but a fixed form that helps us discover what the implications of the terms 'act' and 'person' really are."[12] Any study of human relations inevitably becomes dramatistic and although the use of mechanical models by scientifically inclined social scientists seems to exempt them, their freedom from dramatism is illusory. In fact, "mechanical models might best be analyzed, not as downright anti-dramatistic, but as fragments of the dramatistic."[13] However, since, scientific analyses tend toward specialization, a dramatistic analysis of humanity is more comprehensive — "not strictly 'scientific,' but philosophical."[14]

Dramatism, Burke maintains, considers the negative to be an important linguistic invention, but in contrast to Henri Bergson who concentrated on the propositional negative, dramatistic analysis

---

[9]Burke, *Permanence and Change*, p. 122.
[10]*International Encyclopedia of the Social Sciences* (New York: The Free Press, 1968), VII, 445–451.

[11]*Ibid.,* p. 447.
[12]*Ibid.,* p. 418.
[13]*Ibid.,* p. 449.
[14]*Ibid.,* p. 450.

centers on the hortatory negative (Thou shalt not). When applied to the idea of order, a polar term, the principle of negativity conjures up the notion of disorder. These ideas of order and disorder, in turn, evoke obedience and disobedience, faith and reason, temptations of the senses, and imagination.

This series of positive and negative terms, according to Burke, defines the area of indeterminance we call the will, where one can say yes or no to a "thou shalt not." Ontologically (from the standpoint of reality), action is a function of the will; but logologically (from the standpoint of the logic of words), the will is derivable from the idea of an act. From the idea of will, in turn, are derived the ideas of grace (the intrinsic ability to make proper choices) and sacrifice (a choice involving the mortification of some desire). The sacrificial principle, thus, is intrinsic to the nature of order. Dramatistic analysis is said to show how the negative principle of guilt implicit in the nature of order combines with the principles of thoroughness (or perfection) and substitution, in such manner that the sacrificial principle of victimage ("scapegoating") is intrinsic to the human congregation. "Dramatism . . . asks not how the sacrificial motives revealed in the institutions of magic and religion may be eliminated, in a scientific culture, but what new forms they may take."[15] Moreover, vicarious victimage extends the range of these manifestations to include: Hitlerite genocide, the symbolic "cleansing" in wars, uprisings, and heated political campaigns, social exclusiveness, "beatnik" art, rabid partisanship in sports, the excessive pollution of air and streams and even the "bulldozer mentality" that rips into the natural environment without qualms threatening to destroy the ecological balance of nature.

A dramatistic view of human motives . . . culminates in the ironic admonition that perversions of the sacrificial principle (purgation by scapegoat, congregation by segregation) are the constant temptation of human societies, whose orders are built by a kind of animal exceptionally adept in the ways of symbolic action.[16]

Burke's dramatistic sociology erases the distinction between literature and life. Literature, to be sure, always takes its materials from life and human social life is always symbolically mediated and implemented; however, most people in most societies have carefully drawn the distinction between fiction and fact, even while recognizing that the idealizations of the artist may alter or deepen understanding of social life. In contrast to Mead's sociology, which, although centered on symbolically mediated action and reaction, still placed the ultimate stress on behavior, Burke's sociology emphasizes that everything dissolves into an interaction of symbols. It is little wonder that Burke's formulations often have a kind of magical aura, for he was, without question, on the road back to magic.

Herbert Blumer. Although George Herbert Mead was destined to become the patron saint of symbolic interactionism, it was only by accident that Mead's influence was introduced directly into the University of Chicago sociology department. W. I. Thomas's resignation, forced by scandal in his personal life, left a vacuum in the sociology department, particularly in the area of social psychology where Thomas had been teaching. Ellsworth Faris (1874–1953) had been a missionary and professor of philosophy before completing graduate work in philosophy and psychology under John Dewey, George Mead, and James Angell. After completing the Ph.D in 1914, Faris taught sociology at Iowa, Chicago, and again at Iowa. He happened to deliver a lecture at Chicago around the time of Thomas's resignation which impressed his audience with his familiarity with the Dewey-Mead tradition. As a result of the lecture, Faris was invited to join the department, which he later chaired in 1925. By 1926 he was also editor of the

---

[15]*Ibid.*, p. 451.

[16]*Ibid.*, p. 451.

HERBERT BLUMER

Courtesy of Herbert Blumer, University of California, Berkeley

American Journal of Sociology. It was Faris who first introduced the Meadian tradition into the Chicago sociology department. Henceforth, all Chicago students received direct indoctrination into Meadian theory whether they took courses in the philosophy department under Mead or not.

However, although Faris provided the introduction, it was Herbert Blumer who became the major sponsor of the Meadian point of view in the Chicago department. Born in St. Louis in 1900, Herbert Blumer was educated at the University of Missouri, earning the A.B. in 1921 and the A.M. in 1922. He went on to take his Ph.D at the University of Chicago in 1927. Blumer became instructor in sociology at Chicago in 1925, was associate professor from 1931 to 1947, and professor from 1947 to 1952. He accepted a position as professor of sociology at the University of California, Berkeley,

between 1952 and 1975, where he chaired the department. Blumer was a leading proponent of Mead-based social theory at both Chicago and Berkeley. He claims credit for having invented the term *symbolic interactionism,* which has become the primary designation for this branch of social theory.[17]

As founder of the orthodox branch of symbolic interactionism, Blumer has remained close to the original position of Mead. Humans act on the basis of meaning; meanings arise out of social interaction; language mediates this process and through its use individuals are forced to take the attitude and role of the other and, hence, also to treat themselves as objects — a process giving rise to selfhood. However, individuals remain actors as well as objects, selecting, regrouping, and transforming meanings in the light of the situation in which they find themselves. Human groups are joint actions. Culture is how people behave in the course of their joint actions. Collective action, the special domain of sociological concern, involves no new principles of interpretation: a corporation, an army, or even a nation, "needs to construct its action through an interpretation of what is happening in its area of operation."[18] Finally, whether newly formed or long-established, groups as joint actions arise out of a background of previous action.

In his straightforward codification of Mead for teaching purposes, Blumer continually stressed the creative spontaneity of the self and the reducibility of all social processes, however complex, to meaningful interpersonal behavior. Blumer saw his major contribution to symbolic interactionism as the elaboration of its methodology and defense of the symbolic interactionist point of view against alternative explanations.

With "depressing frequency," Blumer states, methodology is viewed as "synonymous with the study of advanced quantitative procedures. . . . Such conceptions are a travesty on methodol-

---

[17]Herbert Blumer, *Symbolic Interactionism: Perspective and Method* (Englewood Cliffs, N.J.: Prentice-Hall, 1969).
[18]*Ibid.,* p. 16.

ogy."[19] A full-bodied methodology involves (1) a prior picture of the world, (2) a problem, (3) exploration of data and instruments for describing the problematic situation, (4) determination of relations between data, (5) an interpretation of findings, and (6) the use of concepts.[20] This picture of methodology is similar to that of John Dewey in his *Logic* though no reference was made to this source.

> . . . much of present-day methodology in the social and psychological sciences is inadequate and misguided. The overwhelming bulk of what passes today as methodology is made up of such preoccupation as the following: the devising and use of sophisticated research techniques, usually of an advanced statistical character; the construction of logical and mathematical models, all too frequently guided by a criterion of elegance; the elaboration of formal schemes on how to construct concepts and theories; valiant application of imported schemes, such as input-output analysis, systems analysis, and stochastic analysis; studious conformity to the canons of research design; and the promotion of a particular procedure, such as survey research, as *the* method of scientific study.[21]

In place of all this, Blumer urges, there is one and only one way to study social life, by firsthand acquaintance with what people express individually and collectively. If one does not get acquainted with social life firsthand, one will unavoidably import some alien picture into one's interpretations. Firsthand study has two phases: exploration and instruction. The guiding maxim of exploration is to use any ethically allowable procedure that provides the best picture of what is going on: direct observation, interviewing, listening to conversations, reading letters and diaries, securing life histories, examining public records, and even arranging for group discussions and counting items of interest.[22] Inspection means "an intensive focused examination of the empirical content of whatever analytical elements are used for purposes of analysis."[23] On the basis of inspection the meanings will emerge. When one has established its meanings one has obtained the most important thing there is to know about social life.

In Blumer's view, symbolic interactionism is opposed not only to the dominant trends in current methodology but to many modern theories as well. It opposes: entity theories of society;[24] the reduction of society to some limited set of relations such as a complementarity of expectations like Parsons;[25] to behaviorist theories which treat individuals primarily as responding organisms;[26] to views which maintain that common values hold society together rather than a complementarity of values, interests, and expectations;[27] and to dominant theories of socialization as internalization of norms and social control as external constraints, and social change and social disorganization as a breakdown of structure.[28] From a symbolic interaction point of view the essence of socialization is the capacity to take roles successfully; social control is self-control; social change is a continuous and indigenous process, and social disorganization is inability to mobilize action effectively in the face of a given situation.

From the standpoint of Blumer's orthodox version, symbolic interactionism offers the major hope for the solution of sociology's major current problems.

Manford Kuhn. Kenneth Burke viewed the dramatistic study of the act as a high or central point of interest and he liked to visualize alternative modes of study represented by the scientific and poetic-humanistic analyses of conduct as slopes. In terms of this metaphor, the approach of Manford Kuhn to conduct was down the scientific slope.

[19]*Ibid.*, p. 24.
[20]*Ibid.*, pp. 24–25.
[21]*Ibid.*, pp. 26–27.
[22]*Ibid.*, p. 41.

[23]*Ibid.*, p. 43.
[24]*Ibid.*, p. 57.
[25]*Ibid.*, pp. 67–68.
[26]*Ibid.*, pp. 72–73.
[27]*Ibid.*, p. 76.
[28]*Ibid.*, p. 77.

Manford H. Kuhn (1911–1963) was born in Kennard, Indiana. He was stricken by polio at the age of seventeen and crippled for life, though he never permitted his disability to influence his optimism and good nature. He was deeply religious and moral, and a libertarian and strong civil rights activist in the American Society of Friends and American Civil Liberties Union. Kuhn completed his undergraduate work at Earlham College, earning the A.B. in sociology and economics in 1931. He began graduate work in sociology at the University of Wisconsin shortly after the discipline separated from economics, where it had thrived under the tutelage of the institutional economist John R. Commons, who had been promoting a methodologically responsible version of social action theory. Kuhn earned the M.A. at Wisconsin in 1934 and the Ph.D. in 1941. He began teaching at Wisconsin as an instructor between 1937 and 1942. In 1946 he went to the State University of Iowa as assistant professor and reached full professor in 1956.

In a review of major trends in symbolic interactionism[29] Kuhn observed that although Mead postulated ongoing activity as the context existing prior to the self, when he came to deal with the self in its own terms, he distinguished between the self as "I," an unpredictable principle of action, and the self as "Me," a determinable object. The self as "Me" displays the influence of the generalized other of the groups within which an individual acts — at least those groups with which an individual identifies and takes as a reference in his or her various self-estimates. This distinction, Kuhn felt, was the essential source of two major types of symbolic interactionism: those presupposing determinacy and those presupposing indeterminacy.[30]

Kuhn traced his own adoption of symbolic interactionism to the immediate postwar period with his employment of the term *self theory* for his attempts to codify the conceptions of this branch of interaction and submit them to empirical test.[31] He differentiated his enterprise from the orthodoxy of Blumer, which he located in the indeterminacy tradition. The contrast between the Blumer and Kuhn versions of symbolic interactions was epitomized by Jerome Manis and Bernard Meltzer as follows:

> Blumer has continued to lead what can properly be called "the Chicago school" of symbolic interactionism. Stressing the processual character of human behavior and the need for "sympathetic introspection" in the study of human behavior . . . Kuhn's "Self Theory," based at the State University of Iowa has sought to "operationalize" symbolic interactionism by reconceptualizing the self in structural terms, by abandoning such "nonempirical" concepts as Mead's "I," and by developing paper and pencil measures of the self.[32]

In the 1950s Kuhn was systematically expanding the scope of symbolic interaction theory, directing his doctoral students to such problems as: the relations between the self and social structure, the self and syndromes of mental-emotional disturbance, the self and prejudice, the self and systems of objects, role taking and the self, role taking and the communication system.[33] He identified such researches with the determinate model of symbolic interactionism and summarized their importance as "demonstrating to some degree, at least, that the key ideas of symbolic interactionism

---

[29]Manford H. Kuhn, "Major Trends in Symbolic Interactionism in the Past Twenty-Five Years," *The Sociological Quarterly*, 5 (Winter 1964), 61–84. Reprinted in *Symbolic Interactionism: A Reader in Social Psychology*, ed. Jerome G. Manis and Bernard N. Meltzer (Boston: Allyn and Bacon, 1967), pp. 46–67.

[30]Kuhn, *Symbolic Interactionism*, p. 50.

[31]*Ibid.*, p. 55.

[32]Manis and Meltzer, *Symbolic Interactionism*, p. vi. For contrasts in the methods of the two traditions, see: Howard S. Becker and Blanche Geer, "Participant Observation and Interviewing: A Comparison" and Manford H. Kuhn and Thomas S. McPartland, "An Empirical Investigation of Self-Attitudes" in *Symbolic Interactionism*, pp. 109–133.

[33]See his review of unpublished dissertations at Iowa in *Symbolic Interactionism*, pp. 55–56.

could be operationalized and utilized successfully in empirical research."[34]

The most significant example of Kuhn's attempt to extend the symbolic interaction perspective to new areas, however, was his study with Hickman of the social psychology of economic behavior.[35] The book presents an interesting contrast to the exchange theories, which treated elementary market behavior as a fundamental paradigm of social life as a whole. Hickman and Kuhn proposed to direct self theory to the solution of a number of problems in the economic sphere that, in their estimation, resist explanation in terms of rational profit making: managerial motivation, the feasibility of making interpersonal comparisons of utility or satisfaction, and the question of whether economic freedom and planning are compatible. The real basis of managerial motivation is found, they believe, in managerial reference groups (which, however, do correspond in part to a rational profit-making model); interpersonal comparisons of utility or satisfaction are not universal events in the marketplace, but are substructured as events in smaller reference groups, although between reference groups there are no valid comparisons; finally, democratic freedom can be made compatible with planning only if the economic planners extend their reference group to include the entire population. They are not compatible if planners impose the technical scheme of a small elite on the great mass.

For a year before his death, Kuhn was engaged in establishing at Iowa — under a grant from the National Institute of Mental Health — a graduate training program in social psychology. If he had not died the year before it was to go into operation, the whole development of symbolic interaction since the early 1960s might well have been different.

Hugh Dalziel Duncan. If one were to describe Kuhn as exploring the scientific left of symbolic interactionism, Hugh Dalziel Duncan (1909–1970) would have to be described as exploring its humanistic right. Born in B'ness, Scotland, the son of a grocery chain executive, Duncan received the B.A. in 1931 from Drake University. He did his graduate work at the University of Chicago, earning the M.A. in 1933 and the Ph.D. in 1948. He was copywriter for an advertising agency in Chicago during 1931 and 1932 and in 1933 and 1934 worked at Hull House. He taught school in Des Moines, Iowa for two years, served in the army as a captain, and began writing in 1946, undertaking part-time teaching at the University of Chicago. To finance his writing he organized a real estate syndicate to buy a golf course in Olympia Field, Illinois and in 1953 managed the development of a subdivision. He was visiting professor at a number of schools and a professional lecturer before becoming professor of sociology and English at Southern Illinois University at Carbondale in 1965, where he remained until his death.[36]

The most important event in Duncan's life was his encounter at Chicago with Kenneth Burke. William Rueckert, who made a collection of responses to Burke, observed:

> Once Mr. Duncan discovered Burke (when he was lecturing at the University of Chicago) he became a convert and true disciple. He has written more about Burke, used him more completely, and absorbed him more profoundly than anyone else I know of. All of his many books have been about or have been applications of Burke and have been parts of a life-long attempt to develop a methodology and working model (in the scientific sense of theoretical construct) from Burke for the study of society.[37]

[34]Ibid., p. 56.
[35]C. Addison Hickman and Manford H. Kuhn, *Individuals, Groups, and Economic Behavior* (New York: Dryden Press, 1956).

[36]Among Duncan's major works are: *Language and Literature in Society* (Chicago: University of Chicago Press, 1953); *Communication and Social Order* (New York: Bedminster, 1962); *The Rise of Chicago as a Literary Center* (New York: Bedminster, 1964); *Culture and Democracy* (New York: Bedminster, 1965); *Symbols in Society* (New York: Oxford, 1968); *Symbols and Social Theory* (New York: Oxford, 1969).
[37]William H. Rueckert, ed., *Critical Responses to Kenneth Burke* (Minneapolis: University of Minnesota Press, 1969), p. 260.

Anyone who has read his Burke and this book, *Communication and Social Order,* knows how difficult and futile it is to separate the Burke from the Duncan. Hugh Duncan has simply ingested Burke and taken him into his own system, organically. He illustrates a kind of total and beneficent reception of Burke that would be hard to find elsewhere.[38]

In the last two of his books, *Symbols in Society* and *Symbols and Social Theory,* there is some indication that Duncan was at last ready to codify Burke into a form suitable to his needs in preparation for moving out on his own. In *Symbols in Society* Duncan argues that symbols create and sustain social integration because: symbolic integration is achieved through naming; honorable means give power by endowing actions with dignity, radiance, and glory; symbolic action becomes social by identification with principles of social order; symbols are kept pure through victimage or sacrifice; purgation through tragic victimage is not the only kind of purification, for the comic victim stands beside the tragic victim. He insists that in the present world two great dramatic forms are struggling for world audiences: communism — a tragic drama — and democracy — a comic drama of argument, bickering, disputation, insult, beseechment, and prayer.[39]

In such reformulations, Burke's ideas, musings, and speculations are ever present. However, even more than with Burke, one is left unsure of whether one is dealing with a tautology or the gross oversimplification of common observation. Symbolic integration is achieved through naming? Not necessarily. Of course, sometimes symbolic integration is promoted by naming, but not always. The battle of the sexes does not come to an end in those societies where the woman upon marriage takes the husband's name. Honorable names do not always give dignity, but may be defiled by application to disreputable persons or enterprises. The notion that symbolic action becomes social by identification with principles of social order is a strange combination of awkwardness and redundancy. Symbolic action is already social. How could it become social by some added operation? And what does one do with the curious implication that what is important is identification with the principles of social order rather than with the social order itself?

On a number of occasions Duncan has insisted that it was his lifelong objective to transform the thought of Burke designed for the study of literature into a model adequate for the study of society. Burke, of course, thought he had already done this. Duncan evidently felt this objective was realized in *Symbols in Society* and, although he did not formulate his view on the nature of theoretical models, the organization of his book reveals his conception of the ideal character of such a model. The three main sections of his book are on axiomatic propositions, theoretical propositions, and methodological propositions. Of his position and his axioms Duncan says:

> We assume in this book that how we communicate determines how we socialize. The twelve axioms which follow are really assumptions. Without them it would be impossible to create the theoretical and methodological propositions which come later. Axioms cannot be tested, nor can they be demonstrated to be true or false. They are more like the rules of a game which we agree to so we can play together.[40]

A sample of Duncan's axioms follows:

1. "Society arises in, and continues to exist through, the communication of significant symbols."[41] Presumably this includes the language of the ants and bees.
3. "Emotions, as well as thought and will, are learned in communication."[42] And poor Darwin thought emotions in men and animals were biologically based.
5. "From a sociological view motives must be un-

---

[38]*Ibid.,* p. 357.
[39]*Ibid.,* pp. 23–25.

[40]Duncan, *Symbols in Society,* p. 43.
[41]*Ibid.,* p. 44.
[42]*Ibid.,* p. 48.

derstood as man's need for order in his social relationship."[43] For example, a man with motives for murder?

10. "The expression of hierarchy is best conceived through forms of drama which are both comic and tragic."[44] And there are few things more comic and tragic at the same time, for example, than a federal bureaucracy.

The somewhat whimsical comments were added to illustrate selections of Duncan's axioms to indicate that the statements were anything but axiomatic, that is, elementary definitions of relations incapable of further analysis, hence to be taken as givens for purposes of argument.

Duncan follows his review of axiomatic propositions with a chapter on theoretical propositions. In an introductory paragraph, Duncan states that his theoretical propositions are based on a sociodramatic model of human relationship; that the structure of a model is determined by its function and its function by the structure; that the sociodramatic model is designed to analyze action and passion and not thought. The following are typical propositions.

12. "The general public ("They") is a symbolization of the whole community."[45] That is, except in those cases where "they" refer to others in contrast to ourselves.

16. "Principles of social order are grounded in ultimate principles of order which serve as the final audience in social address."[46] And when you talk to principles in contrast to principals, they listen.

20. "Disorder in society originates in disorder in communication."[47] What a peaceful world it would be without so many carping critics.

21. "Social disorder and counter-order arise in guilt which originates in disobedience of those whose commandments are believed necessary

to social order."[48] Theoretical proposition 21 should get in touch with theoretical proposition 20. Perhaps they would form good audiences for one another as it seems do principles.

Duncan's introduction to his methodological propositions is brief. "Methodological propositions are supposed to demonstrate how we know what we know . . . The test of these propositions is simple. Do they tell us anything about concrete human acts in society?"[49] A few typical methodological principles are:

1. "All statements about the structure and function of the symbolic act must be demonstrated to exist in the symbolic context of the act."[50]

2. "Sociological explanations of symbols must be grounded in the analysis of social drama as a drama of hierarchy."[51]

25. "Basic functions in society must be dramatized before they can be communicated as actions."[52]

26. "Authorities must create and sustain ways of making, distributing, and consuming food, clothing, and shelter, according to beliefs in the right of superiors, inferiors, and equals to share in these services."[53]

There is no discernible difference between Duncan's axioms, theories, and methodological propositions. About the best one can say is that Duncan was of the conviction that whenever one adds the term *must* to a statement it becomes a methodological proposition.

Duncan was inspired by what he considered to be his success in *Symbols in Society* to undertake a book on social theory in which he identified dramatistic sociology as its major hope. In this work Duncan dwelt much on the mysteries in human affairs and where he was not commenting

---

[43]*Ibid.*, p. 49.
[44]*Ibid.*, p. 59.
[45]*Ibid.*, p. 93.
[46]*Ibid.*, p. 110.
[47]*Ibid.*, p. 130.

[48]*Ibid.*, p. 135.
[49]*Ibid.*, p. 151.
[50]*Ibid.*, p. 151.
[51]*Ibid.*, p. 155.
[52]*Ibid.*, p. 199.
[53]*Ibid.*, p. 206.

on them, he was formulating little mysteries of his own. He said, for example:

> In a life dominated by conflict between saving and spending, we save in order to go into debt.[54]

> The mysteries of rules are personified in the figure of umpires . . . We watch them in awe . . . . In the dignification of the umpire we dignify the game.[55]

> As social beings we enjoy being hated. . . . We even enjoy hating ourselves.[56]

> Mystery is the obverse expression of the disrelationship among classes, while guilt is the reverse expression. Between mystery and guilt there is embarrassment and shame.[57]

Duncan's summary statement of the nature and promise of dramatistic sociology was as follows:

> When we use the mystifications of art, science, and religion as a typology of social experience and ask: Where and when in society are art, science, and religion used, in what kinds of acts, enacted in what kinds of roles, in what communicative forms, and to achieve what kind of order in social relationships? Our abstractions become *sociological* abstractions, formed by a theory of action as *action in society*. This theory, now developing in American sociology, is based in the view that symbolic action in society must be thought of as dramatic action, as against religious thought of action as ritual, or scientific thought of action as equilibrium.[58]

There is nothing wrong with analyzing social life in terms of the categories used by students of the drama and, vice versa, in visualizing comic and tragic dramas as idealized portrayals from everyday life. This has been done repeatedly at least since Aristotle. One can describe this practice, if one wishes, as a new form of theory. Which of us does not occasionally view our hobby horse as the dashing stallion of a White Knight? However, to enscone this simple and straightforward notion in language of mystification and ambiguity is to depart from the sphere of theory (the clarification of ideas) for some muddy netherworld. In reviewing *Symbols and Social Theory* for the *American Journal of Sociology*, I quoted the passage from page 287 and undertook, humorously, to drive Duncan into the open where he would be forced to clarify his ideas.

> When Duncan puts his case in this manner, he has a right to be mystified. As far as I can make any sense of this, he appears to be saying that when we apply mystifications to themselves, the mystery is compounded and we become truly sociological. Perhaps in his next book Duncan will explore the logic of mystification. One wonders whether two mystifications, mystifying to the same mystification, are mystifying to each other.
>
> Since Duncan feels that only a dramatistic model is appropriate to true sociology, it is unfair to sum up *Symbols and Social Theory* in other than analogical terms. The volume impresses me as a virtuoso performance by a tone-deaf, self-taught country musician laboriously picking out tunes on a swinette.[59]

Unfortunately Duncan passed away before he could accept the challenge to clarify his arguments. Duncan's importance lies in his transmission of the thought of Kenneth Burke, which he had absorbed so completely that it was present to some degree in every statement. Burke's thought, for its part, had been enriched by careful reading of many of the masterpieces of Western thought and enlivened by a variety of nonstandard devices of philosophical analysis: taking puns seriously; confronting all arguments with their negations (perspective by incongruity); exploring possible new connections through the enthusiastic use of analogies; displacing vocabularies to ever more distant spheres from the area of their origin and

---

[54]Duncan, *Symbols and Social Theory*, pp. 265–266.
[55]*Ibid.*, p. 266.
[56]*Ibid.*, p. 267.
[57]*Ibid.*, p. 267.
[58]*Ibid.*, p. 287.

[59]Don Martindale, *The American Journal of Sociology*, 76 (September 1970), 359–60. (Editorial Note: A swinette is a mythological instrument appearing occasionally in American folk humor. It is generally defined as six strings stretched across a pig's ass — you pick it with your teeth.)

the like. Hence, even without Burke's extensive research and analytical tricks a rich humus of possibilities had been churned up for Duncan to develop. Despite the inadequate theoretical and methodological framework into which he tried to force them, the aphorisms of *Symbols and Society* remain an evocation of the work of Kenneth Burke. Unfortunately, Duncan all too often confuses rather than clarifies Burke's insights.

TOWARD AN IDEOLOGICALLY COMMITTED SYMBOLIC INTERACTIONISM

Although there has been a general discernible drift across the history of the discipline away from ideological involvement in the sociopolitical currents of the day, the fact that sociology is relatively close to everyday life constantly holds out the temptation to sociologists to become involved. There is rarely a time when some voice is not raised with cries of betrayal when sociologists are not politicizing their fields, not simply taking part in affairs as citizens apart from their social science roles. From time to time the chorus takes up the lament of the individual vocalist.

There is, to be sure, some tendency in relatively quiet times for sociologists to make peace with what has been variously called "city hall," "the business and political elite," "the establishment" or the leaders and policymakers of the major institutions: government, business, and, at times, religion. Nor need such accommodation to the establishment be conspiratorial in intent. Social scientists may be genuinely patriotic and ethnocentrically proud of their societies and anxious to do their best to make them work. Sociologists are not only flattered when their aid is solicited, but they obtain honors and prestige and, even, a minor share in the rewards of power when they receive grants or contracts for research. Inevitably, avenues are opened that draw social scientists into the "power structure."

However, as this happens, those social scientists who for ideological reasons are alienated from the establishment, or those who seek but fail to obtain patronage and are envious of their more fortunate colleagues may give voice to their dissatisfaction and denounce conservatives in and outside the profession. They may issue calls for reform. At such times the profession as a whole may become polarized between the "Old Guard" and the "Young Turks." Since the establishment of American sociology in the universities in the first two decades of the twentieth century, stirring calls to action in quasi-revolutionary tracts have been issued at least every twenty years: Lynd's *Knowledge for What* in 1939; Mills's *Sociological Imagination* in 1959; and Lee's *Sociology for Whom?* in 1979.[60]

Except for the Korean War, the period from the end of World War II to the 1960s had been relatively peaceable. The country was anxious to settle down after the upset of the Great Depression and the war years. The rush to the suburbs was under way, the colleges were expanding, sociology was growing in popularity. The international Cold War and domestic McCarthyism discouraged social criticism in the 1950s. Displaying a rare spirit of unity, American sociologists overwhelmingly subscribed to a structure-functionalist point of view. Persons who were becoming more critical of the establishment both within and outside sociology, like Sorokin[61] and C. Wright Mills, were treated as outsiders, renegades, and outlaws. However, as both McCarthyism and the Cold War eased and the mood of the country shifted sufficiently in a liberal direction to permit the election of John F. Kennedy, the first Catholic President, the door was opened not only for a rapid expansion of symbolic interactionism, but for a new generation of scholars ready to respond to new demands for ideological commitment. Three persons have been chosen to illustrate this trend in symbolic interactionist ranks.

[60]Robert S. Lynd, *Knowledge for What* (Princeton: Princeton University Press, 1939); C. Wright Mills, *The Sociological Imagination* (New York: Oxford, 1959); Alfred McClung Lee, *Sociology for Whom?* (New York: Oxford, 1979).
[61]Pitirim A. Sorokin, *Fads and Foibles in Modern Sociology and Related Sciences* (Chicago: Henry Regnery, 1956).

Erving Goffman. Erving Goffman was born in Manville, Alberta, Canada in 1922. He earned the A.B. at the University of Toronto in 1944, the M.A. at the University of Chicago in 1949, and the Ph.D. in 1953. He was a member of the Shetland field research at the University of Edinburgh (Scotland) from 1949 to 1951 and visiting scientist of the National Institute of Mental Health from 1954 to 1957. He joined the department of sociology at the University of California at Berkeley as assistant professor in 1958, rising to full professor by 1962. In 1968 he became Benjamin Franklin professor of anthropology and sociology at the University of Pennsylvania, Philadelphia.

Goffman completed his studies at a time when Blumer's version of Mead's social thought was most influential and when the work of Kenneth Burke was popular in interactionist circles. He shows the influence of both traditions. He brought to symbolic interactionism an unusually strong sense of embattled, anarchistic individualism.[62] In his first book, *The Presentation of Self in Everyday Life,* Goffman took over the dramatistic model of society suggested by Burke and Duncan, but carried the analogy a step further and worked it out in a manner Burke never intended. Social life is conceived as composed of performances in which various routines, or patterns of activity, are enacted. In any individual roles of the routine only a few formal, idealized elements are involved. A performance occurs in two regions: front and back stage. The front stage performance before the audience is possible in large measure because both actor and audience conspire to save the show. The impression management may, to be sure, fail because of accidents, self-consciousness, or lack of dramaturgical direction, in which case discrepancies between the real and the social self may be unexpectedly revealed. Seen from this point of view, social life is an affair of collective deceit and illusion. The real individual who sustains the pretense is rather pathetic.

> Whether the character that is being presented is sober or carefree, of high station or low, the individual who performs the character will be seen for what he largely is, a solitary player involved in a harried concern for his production. Behind many masks and many characters, each performer tends to wear a single look, a naked unsocialized look, a look of concentration, a look of one who is privately engaged in a difficult, treacherous task.[63]

There is, in Goffman's view, a basic dialect of self-presentation in everyday life. As performers, individuals are busy maintaining impressions, seemingly living up to the standards in terms of which they are judged. In the process they are conveying the impression that they are living in a moral world. As performers individuals are "merchants of morality." However, the very act of merchandizing morality creates distance from its substance. The real concern is with merchandizing. "The very obligation and profitability of appearing always in a steady moral light, of being a socialized character, forces one to be the sort of person who is practiced in the ways of the stage."[64]

If one were to phrase in Meadian terms Goffman's transformation of symbolic interactionism in his version of the dramatistic tradition, he no longer locates the traditional problem of selfhood in an internal dialectic between the "I," the principle of action, and the "me," the internalized standards of the community or "conscience." The dialectic is between the private and

---

[62]Goffman's major works include: *The Presentation of Self in Everyday Life* (New York: Doubleday Anchor, 1959); *Asylums: Essays on the Social Situation of Mental Patients and Other Inmates* (New York: Doubleday Anchor, 1961); *Encounters: Two Studies on the Sociology of Interaction* (Indianapolis: Bobbs-Merrill, 1961); *Behavior in Public Places: Notes on the Social Organization of Gatherings* (Glencoe, Ill.: The Free Press, 1963); *Stigma: Notes on the Management of Spoiled Identity* (Englewood Cliffs, N.J.: Prentice-Hall, 1963); *Relations in Public* (New York: Harper Colophon Books, 1971); *Frame Analysis: An Essay on the Organization of Experience* (New York: Harper Colophon Books, 1974).

[63]Goffman, *The Presentation of Self in Everyday Life,* p. 235.
[64]*Ibid.,* p. 251.

public self in which the real self is a naked, unsocialized, and unsocializable expediency.

In a series of essays completed around 1960 and collected in *Asylums,* Goffman applied the same general type of analysis appearing in *Presentations of Self* to institutions and the inmates of mental hospitals. Total institutions were defined as places of residence and work of large numbers of similarly situated individuals who were cut off from the wider society and for a time led an enclosed, formally administered round of life. Denizens of total institutions include mental hospital patients, TB patients, cloistered monks and nuns, military recruits, and incarcerated prisoners of all types. *Total institution* was Goffman's term for a specialized kind of community; however, he carefully avoids the use of the term *community* — possibly because it had a positive connotation he wished to avoid. As Goffman sees it, total institutions, through a series of humiliations and degradation ceremonies, strip away the individual's (patient's, novice's, recruit's) sense of dignity and worth and reduce him or her to complete dependency on the hierarchical powers of the institution. In the moral career of the mental patient, he reviewed what he considered to be the contingencies that transform an individual into a mental patient. In Goffman's view, accident plays a major role in the making of a mental patient. Because of some offence, an individual no different from any others on the street finds himself or herself facing both family and public servants who operate like a "funnel of betrayal" to incarcerate him or her; once in the mental hospital, he or she experiences complete deracination. However, once again, suddenly and unexpectedly the mental patient may find him- or herself stripped down to real self, but with the unusual opportunity to reveal it publicly.

In the usual cycle of adult socialization one expects to find alienation and mortification followed by a new set of beliefs about the world and a new way of conceiving of selves . . . The moral career of the mental patient has unique interest, however; it can illustrate the possibility that in casting off the raiments of the old self — or in having this cover torn away — the person need not seek a new robe and a new audience before which to cower. Instead he can learn, at least for a time, to practice before all groups the amoral arts of shamelessness.[65]

In "The Underlife of a Public Institution" Goffman describes multiple ways in which mental patients cope with the mental institution and work the system to their advantage. In *Stigma* Goffman considers at length the presentations of self by a variety of persons including the blind, members of minority groups, ex-mental patients, ex-convicts, women, obese persons, dwarfs, and even childless married couples who engage in impression management to deal with their "spoiled identities." In *Encounters* Goffman examines impression management in temporary or nonenduring face-to-face groups. He elaborates the concept of role distance, to characterize the potential separateness between individuals and their putative roles, a separation essential to all of the more cynical forms of impression management. In *Behavior in Public Places* he examined contact in streets, parks, restaurants, theatres, shops, dance halls, and meeting halls to explore impression management in such transitory situations. However, over and again Goffman returns to his primary interest, the stigmatized, the alienated, and the disadvantaged.

Finally, in *Frame Analysis*, where he turns back to the analysis of fraud, deceit, con games and shows of various kinds,[66] Goffman indicates that he was seeking a general theoretical statement of his position.

Goffman cited William James, W. I. Thomas, and Alfred Schutz as sources of his basic conceptionalization of elementary intersubjective life. A *strip* is a slice from the stream of ongoing activity. Frame analysis is such a strip cut from the flow characterized by "definitions of a situation" and made according to "principles of organization which govern events . . . and our subjective involvement in them."[67] The basic idea here is that the flow of intersubjective experience is not undif-

[65]Goffman, *Asylums*, p. 169.
[66]Goffman, *Frame Analysis*, p. 14.
[67]*Ibid.*, p. 10.

ferentiated but is organized, characterized, and identified by its participants in terms of shared-definitions or, as Alfred Schutz argued, "typifications." They form a basic stock of experience in terms of which any given group does its business. They constitute its shared or common culture.[68]

A set of frames (Goffman's elementary forms of social life) established in everyday experience is viewed as basic — presumably they are the most shared intersubjective forms of the group — and supplying the building blocks of larger patterns of social life. They can, Goffman thinks, be used for fun, deception, experiment, rehearsal, dream, fantasy, ritual, demonstration, analysis, and charity.[69] The basic devices by which they are employed for other than their original function are *keying* (utilizing a set of conventions originating in one area of life to give meaning to activity in another) and *fabrication* (the deliberate use of basic frames for deceit). As a result of keying, complex frames may be viewed as layered or laminated. When basic frames are fabricated the fabricators may also be viewed as operators and deceivers and those taken in as dupes, marks, pigeons, suckers, butts, victims, or gulls.[70] Fabrications, of course, are subject to discrediting. However, it must be remembered that fabrications may be benign as well as malignant[71] and sometimes we not only fabricate others but fabricate (that is, deceive) ourselves.[72]

In his frame analysis, Goffman no longer takes the drama as the sole basic model for social life. Theatrical frames are viewed as a special complex type which he differentiates into stage, movie, and novelistic types.[73] He also discusses what he calls structural issues in fabrications, out-of-frame analysis and, while defining mental illness as a special kind of out-of-frame behavior, indicates that a frame perspective permits all of us "to generate crazy behavior and to see that it is not all that crazy."[74]

While frames have been substituted for the theatrical role as the basic units of social life, Goffman restores in his analysis a parallel to his contrast between front and back stage — an idealized reality versus a more grubby real reality. What the individual does in everyday life is done in relation to cultural requirements established for the given role. Everyday life while real enough in itself, often seems to be a laminated adumbration of a pattern or model that is a typification of quite uncertain status. "(A famous face who models a famous-name dress provides in her movements a keying, a mock-up, of an everyday person walking about in everyday dress, something, in short, modeled *after* actual wearings; but obviously she is also a model *for* everyday appearance-while-dressed, which appearance is, as it were, always a bridesmaid but never a bride)."[75] Ordinary life is "an imitation of the properties, a gesture at the exemplary forms, and the primal realization of these ideals belongs more to make-believe than to reality." And in all this the self "is not an entity half-concealed behind events, but a changeable formula for managing oneself during them."[76]

It is perhaps significant that Goffman has often been heralded as "one of the greatest writers alive." This can only mean that many share his view that our civilization is largely an ever changing panorama of fabrication in which the most basic stratification is between the deceivers and the deceived and the self in the end always remains, as Goffman phrased it in his first book, an amoral merchant of morality ever intent on the pillage of others or the avoidance of their pillage of him or her. Goffman transformed paranoia and schizophrenia into the norms of contemporary life.

Howard S. Becker. With his conviction that society is a conspiracy, his identification with the crushed, the cast off, the defiled, and the stigmatized; and

---

[68]*Ibid.,* p. 26.
[69]*Ibid.,* p. 560.
[70]*Ibid.,* p. 83.
[71]*Ibid.,* p. 14.
[72]*Ibid.,* p. 116.
[73]*Ibid.,* pp. 124ff.

[74]*Ibid.,* p. 246.
[75]*Ibid.,* p. 562.
[76]*Ibid.,* p. 573.

HOWARD S. BECKER

Tom Mayer, Center for Urban Affairs, Northwestern University

mantle of liberal reformer descended, rather, on his Chicago colleague.

Howard Saul Becker was born in Chicago in 1928. He completed his education at the University of Chicago, earning the A.B. in 1946, the M.A. in 1949, and the Ph.D. in 1951. He was instructor in sociology at Chicago from 1952 to 1953, Ford Foundation Fellow at the University of Illinois from 1953 to 1955, resident sociologist for Community Studies, Inc., in Missouri from 1955 to 1960, associate professor at Stanford from 1962 to 1965, and professor of sociology at Northwestern University from 1965.[77] Although there was little that was new in Becker's development of the symbolic interactionist tradition, he codified it in a rather simplistic theory of victimage.[78]

Deviance, Becker insists, is created by society in the first place because it is the infraction of social rules that constitutes deviance. No rules; no deviance. Deviance is also a consequence of the actions of others who effectively apply the label "deviant" to an individual who breaks or is alleged to have broken the rules. Some are accused of

his inclination to employ disreputable forms of social life like the con game as paradigms for the whole of social life, Goffman brilliantly designed his work to serve as a source for all persons eager to criticize the establishment but lacking the imagination to invent their own strategies. He quickly developed into the philosopher of the libertarians and radical social critics of the 1960s. However, Goffman's descriptions appear to have been too close to his own point of view to permit him to accept the role of cult priest or leader of social protest movements which could, in turn, crystallize into a new system of conventional and institutional constraints. Goffman's anarchism was basic. Terminologically he kept moving constantly, seeking neologisms that would permit him again and again to restate the same basic message. The

[77]Becker's major publications include: Howard S. Becker, et al., *Boys in White* (Chicago: University of Chicago Press, 1961); *Outsiders: Studies in the Sociology of Deviance* (New York: The Free Press, 1963); "Whose Side Are We On?" in *Sociological Work* (Aldine, 1970), pp. 123–39.

[78]Kenneth Burke's encounters with religious and political writing convinced him that the ultimate high dramas (in religion and politics) of social life were victimage and sacrifice, which were especially cathartic for the social group when the pure and innocent were sacrificed. Goffman took the position that social life victimized just about everyone, doing a particularly good job on the poor, minority group members, the mentally ill, and the deformed. Meanwhile, students of crime and delinquency who had been influenced by symbolic interactionist tradition such as Frank Tannebaum in *Crime and the Community* (New York: McGraw Hill, 1951), and, particularly, E. M. Lemert in *Social Pathology* (New York: McGraw-Hill, 1951) had observed that technically crime consists in breaking the law, and criminals and delinquents may be confirmed in their deviance by the successful fixing of labels on them. In "Societal Reactions to Deviance: Problems of Theory and Method," *Social Problems*, 9 (Winter 1962), 247–256, John Kitsuse formulates a position almost identical with Becker's.

Types of Deviant Behavior[a]

	Obedient Behavior	Rule-breaking Behavior
PERCEIVED AS DEVIANT	Falsely accused	Pure deviant
NOT PERCEIVED AS DEVIANT	Conforming	Secret deviant

[a]Becker, *Outsiders,* p. 20.

breaking the rules when they have not; others break the rules, but their infractions are undetected or ignored. The rules themselves are the creation of special groups. The powerful impose their rules on the weak; majorities on minorities, native American Protestants on foreign-born non-Protestants, whites on blacks, and men on women. One can set up a table of types.

In terms of the perception of deviance and type of behavior, conforming or deviant, Becker distinguished four behavior types: (1) conformers, (2) persons with "bum raps," that is falsely accused of rule-breaking behavior, (3) secret deviants, rule breakers who have not been apprehended, and (4) pure deviants, who break the rules and get caught at it. People can, of course, break a rule unintentionally, but if individuals are committed to the standard culture they usually avoid such behavior thereafter. On the other hand, many persons may wish to break the rules, but avoid doing so because of the consequences for their careers. One theory of deviance[79] traces its source to various techniques of neutralization, by which the consequences of delinquency are played down or neutralized, sacrificing the demands of the wider society to those of the delinquent pair, gang, club, or friendship clique. Hence, of considerable importance are those contingencies that either firm up the commitment of an individual to the wider society or shift his or her loyalties to a delinquent subgroup.

A turning point in an individual's movement into a delinquent career is getting caught and being publicly labeled as a deviant. Branding as "fairy," "dope fiend," "nut," "lunatic," or "crook," often marks formal and permanent entry into a deviant group while building walls of prejudice that prevent an individual's rejoining the square world. The label acts as a self-fulfilling prophecy. The process is completed by the deviant subgroup, which rationalizes deviancy, building self-justifying ideologies that sustain it. Eventually deviants learn how to carry on their deviant activity with a minimum of self-doubt.

In the last chapter of *Outsiders* Becker expressed his conviction, following Herbert Blumer,[80] that in studying deviance it is necessary to "take the viewpoint of at least one of the groups involved"— either of the deviants or of the rule enforcers.[81] He

[79]Gresham M. Sykes and David Matza, "Techniques of Neutralization: A Theory of Delinquency," *American Sociological Review,* 22 (December 1957), 667–669.

[80]"To try to catch the interpretative process by remaining aloof as a so-called objective observer and refusing to take the role of the acting unit is to risk the worst kind of subjectivism . . ." Herbert Blumer, "Society as Symbolic Interaction" in Arnold Rose, *Human Behavior and Social Processes* (Boston: Houghton Mifflin, 1962), p. 188.

[81]Becker, *Outsiders,* p. 172.

asks, "Whose viewpoint shall we present?"[82] He states that there are strategic and moral considerations raised by the question of whether we "expose the depravity of deviants or we expose the depravity of those who enforce rules on them."[83] Strategically, he urges, we should take the point of view of the deviant, since this point of view is usually the least well known. However, we do not really know the perspective of the law enforcers and they are not easy to study. It is also possible that the deviant actually represents the liberalism of the community in an extreme form. Becker suggests ultimately that we should treat deviancy as we do pornographic words—as mere words that some see as good, others as bad.

> We ought to see it simply as a kind of behavior some disapprove of and others value, studying the processes by which either or both perspectives are built up and maintained. Perhaps the best surety against either extreme is close contact with the people we study.[84]

In his paper, "Whose Side Are We On?" Becker repeated at some length these same arguments, coming to the same conclusions.

In an essay entitled "The Sociologist as Partisan,"[85] Alvin Gouldner argued that Becker was a spokesperson for such men as Howard Brotz, Donald Cressey, John Kitsuse, Raymond Mack, David Matza, Sheldon Messinger, Ned Polsky, and Albert J. Reiss, and therefore his position had to be taken seriously. All these persons, in Gouldner's view, go slumming in their sociology and are

> at home in the world of hip, drug addicts, jazz musicians, cab drivers, prostitutes, night people, drifters, grifters and skidders: the 'cool world'. Their

identifications are with deviant rather than respectable society.[86]

Although these sociologists resent, for example, the legal straitjackets placed on drug addicts and the degradations of the mental hospital, they make no commitment to the perspectives they have assumed while developing a metaphysics of the underdog. They join the rule breakers or rule enforcers from case to case, in the end manifesting "the devotional promiscuity of sacred prostitution."[87] While rejecting the myth of a value-neutral sociology "Becker . . . creates a new myth, the myth of the sentiment-free social scientist."[88] Despite their apparent underdog sympathies, Gouldner argues, Becker and his associates are actually the agents of the elites of the current welfare establishment. Gouldner correctly calls attention to Becker's belief that sociology is unavoidably partisan. He disagrees with Becker only in his view that sociology should be radical rather than liberal.

Thomas Szasz. A psychiatrist and educator who was born in Budapest, Hungary, in 1920, came to the United States in 1938, and was naturalized in 1944, Thomas Stephen Szasz provides further evidence that an individual does not have to be trained in the Chicago sociology tradition to become a symbolic interactionist. He received the A.B. at the University of Cincinnati in 1941 and his M.D. from the University of Cincinnati's College of Medicine in 1944. Subsequently, he served his psychiatric residence at the University of Chicago Clinics (1946–1948) and underwent psychoanalytic training at the Chicago Institute for Psychoanalysis (1947–1950). He received his certification in psychiatry from the American Board of Psychiatry and Neurology in 1951, and became a staff member of the Chicago Institute for Psychoanalysis. Since 1956, Szasz has been professor of psychiatry at the Upstate Medical Center of the State University of New York in Syracuse. We

[82]*Ibid.*, p. 174.
[83]*Ibid.*, p. 175.
[84]*Ibid.*, p. 176.
[85]Alvin Gouldner, "The Sociologist as Partisan," *The American Sociologist* (May 1968), reprinted in Alvin Gouldner, *For Sociology* (New York: Basic Books, 1973), pp. 27–68.

[86]Gouldner, *"The Sociologist as Partisan,"* p. 29.
[87]*Ibid.*, p. 31.
[88]*Ibid.*, p. 33.

THOMAS SZASZ

Courtesy of Doubleday. Photo by Gabor Szilasi

will consider only a few of his astonishing production of books in what follows.[89] In addition to his prolific writing, Szasz has also produced a considerable number of meetings and addresses in his efforts to mount and lead a crusade against involuntary hospitalization, a crusade which he has sought to institutionalize in the American Association for the Abolition of Involuntary Mental Hospitalization, which he has founded and directed.

Szasz made clear in *The Myth of Mental Illness* his

indebtedness to George Herbert Mead, indicating that his study was based on Mead's game model of social life in which the mind and self are visualized as social products and language communication differentiates human from general animal behavior.[90] The spirit of the game and the belief that it is worth playing were seen as responses to the generalized other of the organized group. From this standpoint there is no more crucial question than what sort of behavior does the individual (including the hysteric and mentally ill individual) consider worth playing well and winning? The demands placed on individuals in the processes of growing up, developing sophistication, or getting treated by psychoanalysis share in common attempts to teach or persuade individuals that the games they are playing are not the same as those of others around them.[91] Psychiatrists in their roles as theoretical scientists, applied scientists, and social manipulators are experts in game-playing behavior, engineers sorting out players according to the kinds of games they are playing or ought to play, and busybodies seeking to persuade people to desist from some games and play others.[92]

Mental illness, Szasz believes, is a myth, and psychiatrists are not really treating a disease but, at best, seeking to deal with personal, social, and ethical problems in living.[93] The myth of mental illness is scientifically crippling (representing a false definition of problems in living) and is morally reprehensible, encouraging abandonment of personal responsibility by assigning to a presumed external source (illness) the blame for antisocial attitudes.[94]

What is misnamed mental illness arises because of poor upbringing which, for example, may leave the individual's life empty with no recourse other than neurosis or delinquency as a means of fulfillment. Being mentally ill or psychotic may be the only game left for the individual.[95] Interpreted as

[89]Among his major books of interest here are: *The Myth of Mental Illness* (New York: Harper & Row, 1961); *Law, Liberty and Psychiatry* (New York: Collier, 1963); *The Ethics of Psychoanalysis* (New York: Dell Publishing Co., 1965); *Psychiatric Justice* (New York: Collier, 1965); *Ideology and Insanity* (New York: Doubleday, 1970; *The Manufacture of Madness* (New York: Dell Publishing Co., 1970).

[90]Szasz, *The Myth of Mental Illness*, p. 223.
[91]*Ibid.*, p. 240.
[92]*Ibid.*, p. 292.
[93]*Ibid.*, p. 296.
[94]*Ibid.*, p. 297.
[95]*Ibid.*, p. 258.

a game, hysteria is characterized by the aims of dominance and control of others. Typical strategies are coercion of others through one's presumed disability and illness. Typical tactics are lies and deceit; they are a significant part of the game of hysteria.[96] Mental illness may be considered a form of indirect communication, employing the iconic images of body language. In fact, the language of illness as of social deviance generally, "constitutes the last and perhaps the firmest bastion on the grounds of which unsatisfied and 'regressed' man can make a stand and claim his share of human 'love'."[97]

The game model of human behavior, Szasz maintained, is ideal for unifying psychology, sociology, and ethics. This is an important consideration in view of the fact that contemporary psychiatric practices, particularly those involving legal actions and involuntary patients, "appear to serve a function analogous to that served by the medieval witchcraft trials."[98] Not only does the game model of human behavior permit us to see that malingering, the Ganser syndrome, and hysteria all include violations of the rules to the individual's advantage, but it also gives us the opportunity to understand why the phenomenon miscalled mental illness occurs so frequently. Cultural conditions are changing so rapidly that everyone experiences difficulty in adapting games learned in childhood to later conditions. Anomie, which is similar to the psychiatrists' object loss and anxiety depression, is a crisis of ego identity linked to modern humanity's loss of the "games" learned early in life.[99] Individuals may be unable to forget old rules and because of their inappropriateness to their present situation go on a strike against living (malingering, hysteria, dependency reactions and the like) or superimpose old goals and rules on new games (developing a neurotic character structure) or come to the conclusion that in the end no game can be won and hence no game is worth playing (depression).

Undoubtedly, *The Myth of Mental Illness* will stand as a classic in the extension of the symbolic interactionist perspective to the phenomenon of mental illness. In it, Szasz laid down his own basic life-game; in his later works he extended his doctrines further afield, giving them increasingly more dogmatic and stereotyped form. He became an intensifyingly shrill extreme civil libertarian, denouncing his fellow psychiatrists as the primary agents of a therapeutic welfare state, who in the name of mental health were attempting to enslave human beings. Szasz became one of the major leaders and ideologists in the campaign of de-institutionalization, even forming an association to promote the case of abolishing involuntary hospitalization. By the 1970s increasing numbers of Szasz's contemporaries no longer found his games interesting and moved on to others.

THE MOVEMENT TOWARD INSTITUTIONALIZATION

As early as 1932 the distinctiveness of the movement that would be named *symbolic interactionism* was noted by Fay Karpf in a book with a foreword by Ellsworth Faris, the major spokesperson for the point of view in sociology at the time. Karpf had described the movement as "interaction social psychology."

Interaction social psychology may be said to be a synthesis of the currents of thought represented by instinct psychology and psychological sociology. . . . It began to take form in an atmosphere of protest against biological determinism and *laissez-faire* doctrine in human affairs. It has incorporated instead as practical social motives an intense interest in education and in the scientific control of human conduct. It took its departure from the orthodox position of the instinct theory of human conduct, in the first place, through a broader social interpretation of the evolutionary process as it bears on human development; but gradually it has been building up its position

---

[96]*Ibid.*, p. 278.
[97]*Ibid.*, p. 301.
[98]*Ibid.*, p. 304.
[99]*Ibid.*, p. 308.

through the direct functional analysis of the processes and mechanisms of personal growth and social action.[100]

Although work in symbolic interactionism continued throughout the 1930s, 1940s, and 1950s, even its exponents did not seem to realize that it was more than simply an interpretation of social-psychological problems; it was potentially a complete system of sociology. The review of symbolic interaction in the first edition of *Nature and Types* dramatized its potential for wider significance as a theory. Not long after the appearance of *Nature and Types* in 1960 Arnold Rose edited a volume on symbolic interactionism. In 1963 when Manford Kuhn delivered an address before the Midwest Sociological Society on "Major Trends in Symbolic Interactionism in the Past Twenty-Five Years," he clearly wished to define his own operations at Iowa as a major branch of the symbolic interactionist tradition. In the course of his defense of this proposal he made a significant observation.

> If one were to arrogate to oneself the privilege of deciding these issues and others raised essentially by the ambiguities in symbolic interaction orientation, one could sharply narrow the task surveying the major trends in this theory in the past twenty-five years. This, however, I deem to be neither proper nor useful. Similarly, if symbolic interactionists had their own professional organization, their own journal or journals, their own pontifical leader or tight-knit little clique of leaders clearly assigned the role of determining the "correct" view among competing doctrinal differences, the survey of the fruits of orthodoxy might be simple. Instead, however, we have none of these things, and for the most part we wish none of them. But the consequences are that there is a welter of partial orientations which bear varying relationships to the general point of view.[101]

Not only did Kuhn manage to establish the Iowa school as a subbranch of symbolic interactionism,

but, as seen above, other subbranches have flourished: the dramatistic version of symbolic interactionism has continued to develop; and an activistic or "relevant" version of symbolic interactionism made its appearance, some members of which have cast their lot with welfare-state liberalism, others with a crusading antiwelfare-state civil libertarianism. Kuhn's death at the time the Iowa operation was about to go into high gear left this branch somewhat in disarray; and Blumer's retirement left orthodox symbolic interactionism in a similar state. By the end of the 1960s symbolic interactionism was suddenly without a major leader and ready for reorganization. The individual who more than any other assumed the mantle of leadership was Gregory P. Stone.

Gregory P. Stone. Gregory Prentice Stone was born in Olean, New York, in 1921. He earned the B.A. at Hobart College in 1942, a certification in Turkish area language in 1944, the M.A. at the University of Chicago in 1952, and the Ph.D. in 1959. He was instructor at the University of Illinois (1948–1949), assistant professor at Michigan State University (1949–1955), instructor at the University of Minnesota (1955–1959), assistant professor at Washington University, St. Louis (1959–1960), and permanent member of the Minnesota sociology department after 1961.[102]

The most comprehensive integration of Stone's version of symbolic interaction to date is his

---

[100]Fay Berger Karpf, *American Social Psychology: Its Origins, Development and European Background* (New York: McGraw-Hill, 1932), p. 420.

[101]Kuhn, *Symbolic Interactionism*, p. 51.

[102]Among Gregory P. Stone's major writings include: *Herman Schmalenbach on Society and Experience*, translated and edited with an introduction with Gunther Lüschen (Chicago: University of Chicago Press, 1977); *Being Urban: A Social Psychological View of City Life,* with David A. Karp and William C. Yoels (Lexington, Mass.: D. C. Heath, 1977); *Games, Sport and Power*, ed. Gregory P. Stone (New Brunswick, N.Y.: Transaction Books, 1972); *Social Psychology Through Symbolic Interactionism*, ed. Gregory P. Stone and Harvey A. Farberman (Waltham, Mass.: Ginn-Blaisdell, 1970); *Community in Disaster*, with William Form, Sigmund Nosow, and Charles Westie (New York: Harper, 1958). He also has many original essays breaking new ground, particularly in the areas of the sociology of clothing and the sociology of sports.

essay on "Appearance and the Self."[103] Observing that George H. Mead had maintained that the self is established, maintained, and altered through communication, Stone proposed to supplement the Meadian theory of the self by considering the role of appearance in social action and self formation. This, Stone urged, requires the demonstration of four theses: (1) that every transaction breaks down into appearance and discourse, (2) that appearance is as important as discourse, (3) that the study of appearance expands the scope of symbolic interaction theory, and (4) that appearance is important at every stage in the development of the self.[104]

The self and its transactions, Stone argues, depend upon meaning; however, meaning is a variable (which in any given situation varies from sense to nonsense). Hence, there must be guarantees of meaning beyond the meaning itself. Such guarantee of a context of meaningfulness, he suggests, is supplied by appearance. We not only possess vocabularies which establish gender, for example, but the anchorage of them is distinctive appearance. People also dress differently for parties than for work. Appearance is normally communicated by nonverbal gestures such as clothing, grooming, and the like. "Appearance and discourse are in fact dialectic processes going on whenever people converse or correspond.[105]

An individual's management of his or her own appearance is a *program,* its interpretation by others is a *review.* When program and review coincide, meaning is established. The establishment of such meaning may be broken down into ascertainment of identity, value, mood, and attitude.[106] Identity, which is intrinsically associated with arrivals and departures in social life, is normally com-

municated by clothing which, in turn, is translated by four types of words: (1) universal words designating such things as age, gender, community; (2) names and nicknames; (3) titles; and (4) relational categories such as customer, movie-goer, jazz fan, and the like.[107] When one rises or falls in the world, undertakes a new or loses an old occupation, changes of appearance and title normally accompany and signal the transformation.

As identity serves to place the individual, value and mode, representing appraisal and appreciation, qualify the identity. Stone maintains that his studies of responses to clothing and appearance revealed such references to value and mood as (1) consensual goals like wealth, prestige, and power, (2) achievement, (3) norms or rules regulating the pursuit of consensual goals, and (4) moral precepts referring to valued behavior (cleanliness, politeness, thriftiness, and the like.[108] Following Burke, Stone urged that attitudes serve to activate identity processes: "Appearance *substitutes* for past and present action and, at the same time, conveys an *incipience. . . .* the doffing of dress, signaling that an act is done (and another act about to begin), the donning of dress, signaling the initiation of a new act, and the wearing of dress, signaling that action is going on."[109]

Appearance, representing response mobilized by clothes, takes four forms: placement (identity); appraisal (value); appreciation (mood); and anticipation (attitude). And since appearance is central to the presentation of self, it is essential to examine its forms in the course of the rise of selfhood. Mead isolated three stages in the rise of the self: the preplay stage, the stage of play, and the stage of the game, the form of all later socialization. In the preplay stage communication is largely in the form of conversations of gestures. At this time, usually the mother invests the child with what she considers appropriate to it as an infant and a young child with a gender. In the play stage of development real communication begins, though it is

[103]Gregory P. Stone, "Appearance and the Self," in *Human Behavior and Social Processes,* ed. Arnold M. Rose (Boston: Houghton Mifflin, 1962), pp. 88–110, reprinted in *Social Psychology Through Symbolic Interactionism,* ed. Gregory P. Stone and Harvey A. Farberman (Waltham, Mass.: Ginn–Blaisdel, 1970), pp. 394–414.
[104]*Ibid.,* p. 395.
[105]*Ibid.,* p. 397.
[106]*Ibid.,* p. 398.

[107]*Ibid.,* p. 399.
[108]*Ibid.,* p. 402.
[109]*Ibid.,* p. 402.

Discourse and Appearance in the Early Establishment of the Self[a]

Stages of Early Socialization	Discursive Process	Type of Discourse	Apparent Processes	Types of Appearance
Preplay	1. Parental representation of infant babbling as verbal symbols (Cooley, Markey) 2. Progressive curtailment of whole body movement by parental intervention (Latif)	Conversation of gestures (Mead) Prototaxis (Sullivan) Signal communication or designation as in "ma-ma"	Investiture	Representation as infant, young child, and gender
Play	Identification with discrete differentiated others as in role playing (Mead) 1. Anticipatory socialization 2. Fantastic socialization	Egocentric speech (Piaget) Parataxis (Sullivan)	Dressing out	Misrepresentation of the self Costume
Game	Generalization and consolidation of other roles Taking the role of the "generalized other" or "team"	Socialized speech (Piaget) Syntaxis (Sullivan)	Dressing in	Representation of peer-group affiliation Uniform

[a]Stone, "Appearance and the Self," p. 414.

still dominated by a child's egocentric employment. A characteristic of play is the child's trying on of various costumes and roles in a process Stone describes as dressing out. The child's appearance is a misrepresentation of the self in the costumes of play. At the stage of the game, the child is fully socialized and he or she is in the process of assimilating appearance to those of the peer group or "dressing-in," professing the uniform of his or her age grade. As Stone summarizes his argument: "We have attempted to show . . . that the self is established, maintained, and altered in social transactions as much by the communication of appearance as by discourse."[110]

[110]*Ibid.*, pp. 413–414.

In this seminal essay, Stone outlined a program of research that he has followed periodically ever since.[111] Stone has also developed a program of research in the sociology of play and sport, which he visualized in connection with spectacles and ritual.[112] Stone's importance for symbolic interaction does not end with his original writings. At the University of Minnesota he has drawn an able group of students into his sphere and is one of the major persons training the new generation of symbolic interactionists.[113] Furthermore, he has been catholic in his writing and teaching, drawing together influences from all the subbranches of the symbolic interactionist tradition (not only from the founders of the positions — Faris and Blumer — but also from the exponents — Burke, Whorf, Goffman, and Kuhn).[114] He has employed a wide spectrum of methodological techniques in the solution of problems and has refused for himself and his students to confine his methods to participant observation and systematic introspection alone.

Finally, Stone has been one of the most active and committed participants in the Society for the Study of Symbolic Interaction, of which he was co-founder and first president. His was the primary enterprise that led to the establishment of *Symbolic Interaction*, the official journal of the society, Volume 1 of which appeared in the Fall of 1977. The possibility envisioned by Manford Kuhn has been brought to pass; symbolic interactionism may have finally acquired "their own professional organization, their own journal or journals, their own pontifical leader or tight-knit little clique of leaders clearly assigned the role of determining the 'correct' view among competing doctrinal differences."[115] At least, there has already been complaint by Fisher and Strauss.

> The impetus for its formation seems to have come primarily from several men and women whose avowed intellectual positions are grounded in the writing of Mead. Among those invited to join the society were some who stem rather less from Mead than from other Chicagoans like Everett C. Hughes and the early sociologists, Robert E. Park and W. I. Thomas. A substantial proportion of interactionists have remained outside the society, and perhaps a paraphrased comment by one represents a not unusual stance: "They seem too sectarian, there is much more to sociology than Meadian social psychology. And I don't like the term 'symbolic' interactionism anyhow."[116]

This, of course, is a poor description of the first president of the SSSI, but since he has been succeeded in the presidency and a new editor of the journal has been installed, Stone, himself, has been somewhat distressed by some trends in the society toward a narrow parochial orthodoxy.[117]

[111]This may be seen in "Sex and Age as Universes of Appearance," in *Social Psychology Through Symbolic Interactionism*, ed. Stone and Farberman, pp. 227–237; "The Circumstances and Situation of Social Status," *Ibid.*, pp. 250–259; and in "Personal Act," *Symbolic Interactionism*, 1 (Fall 1977), 2–19.

[112]See "The Play of Little Children," *Quest*, 4 (April 1965), 123–131, revised in *Social Psychology Through Symbolic Interactionism*, pp. 545–553; "Halloween and the Mass Child," *The American Culture*, ed. Hennig Cohen (Boston: Houghton Mifflin, 1968), pp. 257–265; "Ritual As Game: Playing to Become a Sanema," with Gladys I. Stone, *Quest*, Monograph 26, *Learning to Play* (Summer 1976), 28–47; "American Sports: Play and Display," *Chicago Review*, 9 (Fall 1955), 83–100, revised in *The Sociology of Sport*, ed. Eric Dunning (London: Frank Cass, 1971), pp. 47–65.

[113]Among Stone's doctoral students are several who hold promise of becoming the next generation of symbolic interactionists. They include William Burch, Harvey Farberman, Richard Travisano, David Franks, and Stanley Yoels. David Maine, who worked with Stone on a postdoctoral fellowship, has been an active member of this cohort.

[114]The influence of Burke, Goffman, and Whorf on Stone is evident in the paper done with Lea Hagoel on motivation, "Uber den Umgang Mit Motiven" ["On the Scope of Motives"] *Kölner Zeitschrift für Soziologie und Sozialpsychologie*, vol. 20 (1978), 30–66.

[115]Kuhn, *Symbolic Interactionism*, p. 51.

[116]Fisher and Strauss, "Interactionism," pp. 457–458.

[117]In the early seventies Stone and a number of his students at Minnesota were unhappy with the national society and the situation of sociology in the United States. Encouraged by David Maine, Stone applied for a social problems grant from the ASA, which together with funds from Minnesota and Iowa, subsidized a seminar at Stone's home and at the University of Minnesota in June

SUMMARY

Among the major developments in American sociological theory in the 1960s and 1970s has been the expansion and differentiation of symbolic interactionism. Its humanistic perspective has been developed by Burke, its methodological sophistication has been greatly enhanced by Kuhn, and its liberal ideological program has drawn the

applause of civil libertarians, won the approval of liberal government sponsors of the welfare state, and won the scorn and the contempt of radicals who wish to see the underprivileged rise in revolt rather than turn into meek charges of paternalism.

A decade and a half of rapid growth currently appears to be climaxing in the emergence of a new generation of symbolic interactionists and in the founding of an official society and journal. Symbolic interactionism has evolved into an establishment institution. One cannot help wonder whether all this was foreseen in Kuhn's crystal ball.

---

of 1974. In addition to Maine the meeting was attended by Herbert Blumer (University of California, Berkeley), Carl J. Couch (University of Iowa), and Norman Denzin (the University of Northern Illinois). They constituted a Committee for the Study of Symbolic Interactionism chaired by Stone and Harvey Farberman. In the spring of 1975 a consortium was held at Iowa sponsored by the Universities of Minnesota and Iowa. Hence from the beginning the emerging society united the former Chicago and Iowa branches into a common effort. Norman Denzin brought in Northern Illinois and Clark McPhail, who became recording secretary, extended its influence to the University of South Carolina. The society incorporated as the Society for the Study of Symbolic Interaction (with 100 to 150 members) in 1976 and in the spring of 1976 held a consortium at the University of Missouri. By this time the society began to hold meetings on ASA sites and Nelson Foote brought its influence to Hunter College of the City College of New York. Two persons played a major role in launching the official journal of the society. The first was James Haidos, Professor of Sociology at Metropolitan Community College of the Twin Cities and President of the Institute for the Study of Science and Society. Through Haidos's influence the ISSS gave a grant to the SSSI insuring publication of its journal for at least two years. The second instrumental person was James Graham, a graduate student at Minnesota, who found a reasonable publisher in Arkansas and assisted in the design of the cover of the journal. At the time of writing (1980) the SSSI has grown from its initial 100 to more than 600 members and Anselm Strauss has been elected president, representing some further neutralization of forces initially in partial opposition to the association.

Interest in symbolic interactionism extends to Japan, since back in the salad days of American sociology the

If I may be permitted a brief look at the crystal ball, I would see in it for the next twenty-five years of symbolic interaction theory an accelerated development of research techniques on the one hand, and a coalescing of most of the separate subtheories under consideration in this paper, on the other. I have a basic confidence that symbolic interactionism will hold its own and gain against the competition of such major theories as psychoanalysis, the learning theories, and field theory. The reason I am confident is that I believe that of these major theories only symbolic interactionism is logically consistent with the basic propositions of the social sciences: the psychic unity of man (Boas); the extreme cultural variability of man; the creativity of man; the continual socializability and modifiability of man; the ability of man to feed back complex correctives to his behavior without engaging in trial and error, or conditioning, learning.[118]

---

first Japanese scholar ever to take a Ph.D. in the United States in sociology and philosophy studied with Dewey and Mead in the Chicago department. Periodic seminars had been held in Tokyo on Mead. When the Japanese learned of the formation of the Society for the Study of Symbolic Interaction they formed an active Japanese branch. The Fourth G. H. Mead Seminar was held under the joint sponsorship of the JSSSI and the KKK (Kodo Kagakuka Kyokai, The Society of Behavioral Sciences) on October 30, 1977.

[118]Kuhn, *Symbolic Interactionism*, p. 62.

XVII

The Social-Action Branch of Social Behaviorism

Social-action theory, the third significant branch of social behaviorism, was an independent response to the same problems that gave rise to pluralistic behaviorism and symbolic interactionism. It represented a special theoretical solution to the general problems of the school. For their analysis of personality, social structure, and collective behavior, the pluralistic behavioral branch found their starting points in such notions as imitation, innovation, suggestion, diffusion, conflict of innovations, and consciousness of kind; the symbolic interactionist branch took attitudes, mutual expectations, language viewed as an interbehavioral mechanism, and social roles as critical to their approach to the same issues. There were many links between these two branches: Baldwin was influenced by James; Cooley was influenced by Baldwin; Chapin was in part influenced by Cooley; Piaget stood astride the traditions and was influenced by Baldwin. But despite such influences across boundaries, the properties of the two branches remain quite distinct.

Reciprocal influences also characterize social-action theory. Gerth and Mills, for example, were as much influenced by it as some other symbolic interactionists were by pluralistic behaviorism. But the unit of analysis of social-action theory — *meaningful social action* — is distinct, as are a series of related concepts. This branch of social behaviorism has worked out its problems in a theoretically distinctive manner. Its outstanding figure is Max Weber.

Max Weber. Max Weber (1864–1920) was the son of a middle-class German liberal who was prominent in the politics of the National Liberal Party in the Bismarck era. Max Weber studied law and was appointed *Privatdozent* at the University of Berlin. In 1893, he became professor of economics at the University of Freiburg, moving from there to the chair of economics at Heidelberg, where he succeeded the famous economist Karl Knies. In 1900, he suffered a nervous breakdown and for many years lived as a private scholar in a state of semi-

MAX WEBER

Painting by Otto Neumann. Courtesy of the
Kurpfälzisches Museum of the city of Heidelberg

invalidism in Heidelberg. During World War I, he
resumed teaching duties.[1]

[1]The first fairly complete editions of Weber's works were
published shortly after his death: *Gesammelte Aufsätze zur
Religionsoziologie* ["Collected Works in the Sociology of
Religion"], 3 vols. (Tübingen: J. C. B. Mohr, 1920–
1921); *Gesammelte politische Schriften* ["Collected Political
Writings"] (Munich: Drei Masken Verlag, 1921); *Gesammelte Aufsätze zur Wissenschaftslehre* ["Collected Works
on Scientific Theory"] (Tübingen: J. C. B. Mohr, 1922);
Wirtschaft und Gesellschaft ["Economy and Society"], 2
vols. (Tübingen: J. C. B. Mohr, 1922); *Wirtschaftsgeschichte* ["Economic History"] (Munich: Duncker &
Humblot, 1924); *Gesammelte Aufsätze zur Soziologie und
Sozialpolitik* ["Collected Works in Sociology and Social
Politics"] (Tübingen: J. C. B. Mohr, 1924); and *Gesammelte Aufsätze zur Sozial- und Wirtschaftsgeschichte* ["Collected Works in Social and Economic History"] (Tübingen: J. C. B. Mohr, 1924).

Weber's works are gradually finding their way into English translation. Because in many instances a given book
in English translates only a section from a larger work,
and because a single book in English may translate material from more than one of Weber's German works, to
present a complete correlation of English translations
with German originals would take up more space than we
can here allow. The following English translations are
listed in the order of their appearance in America:
General Economic History, trans. Frank H. Knight from
Wirtschaftsgeschichte (New York: Greenberg, 1927; reissued by The Free Press, 1950); *The Protestant Ethic and the
Spirit of Capitalism*, trans. Talcott Parsons from parts of
GAzW, GpS, and *WuG* (New York: Scribner's, 1930,
1958); *From Max Weber: Essays in Sociology*, trans. and ed.
Hans Gerth and C. Wright Mills (New York: Oxford
University Press, 1946); *The Theory of Social and Economic
Organization*, trans. A. M. Henderson and Talcott Par-
sons from *WuG* (New York: Oxford University Press,
1947); *The Methodology of the Social Sciences*, trans. Edward
A. Shils and Henry A. Finch from *GAzW* (Glencoe, Ill.:
The Free Press, 1949); *The Religion of China*, trans. Hans
Gerth from *GAzR* (Glencoe, Ill.: The Free Press, 1951);
Ancient Judaism, trans. Hans Gerth and Don Martindale
from *GAzR* (Glencoe, Ill.: The Free Press, 1951); *Max
Weber on Law in Economy and Society*, trans. Edward A.
Shils and Max Rheinstein from *WuG* (Cambridge, Mass.:
Harvard University Press, 1954); *The City*, trans. Don
Martindale and Gertrud Neuwirth from *WuG* (Glencoe,
Ill.: The Free Press, 1958); *The Religion of India*, trans.
Hanz Gerth and Don Martindale from *GAzR* (Glencoe,
Ill.: The Free Press, 1958); and *The Rational and Social
Foundations of Music*, trans. Don Martindale, Johannes
Riedel, and Gertrud Neuwirth from *WuG* (Carbondale,
Ill.: Southern Illinois University Press, 1958); *The Sociol-
ogy of Religion*, trans. Ephraim Fischoff (London: Me-
thuen, 1965); *Max Weber on Law and Economy*, trans. Max
Rheinstein (New York: Simon and Schuster, 1967); *Econ-
omy and Society: An Outline of Interpretive Sociology*, trans.
Ephraim Fischoff and others (New York: Bedminister
Press, 1968 and Berkeley: University of California Press,
1968); *Max Weber on Universities: The Power of the State and
Dignity of the Academic Calling in Imperial Germany*, trans.
Edward Shils (Chicago: University of Chicago Press,
1974); *Max Weber: The Interpretation of Social Reality*, trans.
J. E. T. Eldridge (New York: Scribner's, 1975); *Roscher
and Knies: The Logical Problem of Historical Economics*,
trans. Guy Oakes (New York: The Free Press, 1975); *The
Agrarian Sociology of Ancient Civilization*, trans. R. I. Frank
(Atlantic Highlands, N.J.: Humanities Press, 1976);
Critique of Stammler, trans. Guy Oakes (New York: The
Free Press, 1977). The secondary literature on Weber is
enormous. Still among the best introductions to Weber
are the intellectual biography and selections of *From Max
Weber* by Hans Gerth and C. Wright Mills; Reinhard
Bendix's *Max Weber: An Intellectual Portrait*, revised

Weber tried to synthesize the Kantian and neo-Kantian, and idealistic and neo-idealistic traditions in Germany. A simplified model may be set up for considering the problems with which he wrestled and the kind of decision he won from them by contrasting a neo-idealist and a neo-Kantian: Dilthey and Rickert. In reaction to what he thought were crass oversimplifications of the positivists (like Comte), Dilthey, the neo-idealist, objected to the use of the instruments proper to the physical sciences in the domain of the cultural sciences. Dilthey sharpened the distinction between the physical and the cultural sciences. He argued that human thought in each has a distinct form, a distinct method. The physical sciences deal with *facts*; the cultural sciences with *meanings*. In the physical sciences, thought takes the form of *explanation*; in the cultural sciences, it takes the form of *understanding*. Explanation establishes causal laws and approaches its object from the outside, or externally; understanding links meaning with meaning and grasps its object immediately in acts of intuition. The objectives of explanation and interpretation differentiate the physical and the cultural sciences from one another. The method of explanation in natural science is experiment; the method of understanding in the cultural sciences consists in interpretation by means of ideal types or configurations of meaning.

Rickert, as a neo-Kantian, was quite opposed to Dilthey's conceptions and he drew his distinctions in a very different way. To a Kantian, the realm of science is the explanation of phenomena — and it does not matter whether the phenomena concern the individual or the physical world. Phenomena are phenomena and science is science. Dilthey was making introspective psychology into a science different in kind from physics. The way in which all science explains is by establishing causal laws among phenomena, and psychology is no different except for its historical recency. It has not reached

the same stage of precision as physics. Rickert thus returns psychology — in fact all the social sciences — to science. Rickert, however, introduced distinctions along a new dimension. The real contrast, he believes, is between history and science. Science is the analysis of nature in terms of causal laws; history is the analysis of nature as a pattern of unique events. While the critical concepts of science are *laws*, the critical conceptions of history are unique *configurations of value*.

These arguments were developed in great variety and detail and advanced by a variety of persons besides Dilthey and Rickert, but this simplified picture may show the conceptual task Weber tackled. If one were to assume that Dilthey and Rickert both have a point, how could one bring their ideas together? Weber's answer may be approached most simply in terms of a tabular comparison of Dilthey and Rickert. (See page 378.)

One of the chief differences between Dilthey as a neo-idealist and Rickert as a neo-Kantian is Dilthey's idea that the cultural and social sciences deal with a *differentiated* content, as contrasted with Rickert's belief that science deals with phenomena which are not so differentiated. On the other hand, as a neo-idealist, Dilthey believes that the cultural sciences deal with the human spirit, which is in constant process of change and development. This process of change and development — a characteristic of the content of the cultural sciences — is perceived by Rickert not as a property of content, but as a distinction in method. Nature is all of one piece, but nature may be studied as science or as history, requiring a different formation of concepts in each case.

The neo-idealists were concerned with the world as a field for action; the neo-Kantians were dealing with the world as an object of knowledge. Weber was influenced by these ideas. Practically, the science of the world as a field for action is politics, the theory and art of bringing to pass irrevocable action changes. Social change is a unique process of development which is understood both as history and as science. Science achieves its full explanatory power only by becoming value-free and independent of our preferences. This very

paperback ed. (New York: Doubleday, 1962); Marianne Weber, *Max Weber: Ein Lebensbild* (Tübingen: J. C. B. Mohr, 1926) trans. Harry Zohn, *Max Weber: A Biography* (New York: Wiley, 1975).

Dilthey (Neo-idealist)		Rickert (Neo-Kantian)	
DISCIPLINE	APPROPRIATE TYPE OF KNOWLEDGE	DISCIPLINE	APPROPRIATE TYPE OF KNOWLEDGE
Cultural Science	Intuitive, meaningful	History	Unique determinations with respect to values
Natural Science	Causal-law explanations	Science	Causal-law explanations

freedom from one of the immediate properties of action makes science indispensable for action. Ideas from both Dilthey and Rickert were fused in this account.

The neo-Kantian influence of thinkers like Rickert is seen in Weber's idea that reality is ultimately not reducible to a system of laws. No body of laws can exhaust a science of culture. Nor can one ever hope to achieve complete predictability, since prediction is successful only within limited or closed systems. Moreover, relation to values is fundamentally necessary to apprehension of the unique. At the same time, this clear neo-Kantianism is modified. The idealists thought of the development of the human spirit as a genuinely creative *process*. Even the values change. Weber agrees that the objective of history can never be founded on a universal system of values. Historical change moves toward unknown ends, always permitting new activities and revealing new spiritual possibilities.

Neo-Kantianism was modified by Weber in still another way. He was not ready to view phenomena as identical simply because of the fact that they are phenomena, whether in the natural or cultural sciences. With the idealists, Weber held that the role of cultural sciences is to apprehend "meanings." An objective in the cultural sciences is to "understand" a process having to do with the special kind of evidence associated with the grasp of meaningful relations. Meaningful relations are such as obtain between motives and acts and between means

and ends. These appear in our own actions, and interpretive sociology must grasp them in the behavior of others as well as in the behavior of ourselves. It has been penetratingly observed that at this point Weber reverses Durkheim's formula, which, in its crass positivism, treats social facts as things. Interpretive sociology treats the historical world not as a collection of objects but as a process of development of human lives.[2]

At the same time, this broad concession to the neo-idealists was again modified: Weber was not willing to argue that science is in principle different in the cultural and the natural sciences, such that method in the first is immediate, in the second mediate. Intuition, he insisted, has the same role in the cultural sciences as it does in the natural sciences. There is no more immediate apprehension of objects in the cultural sciences than in the natural. And again, as a concession to the neo-Kantians, the role of science in the field of cultural data is only completed when causal connections are established. Weber's synthesis of the neo-idealist and neo-Kantian positions is summarized in the scheme of possible disciplines shown on page 379.

Weber's Methodology. It is unfortunate that Weber never developed his methodology apart from the

[2]See Raymond Aron, *German Sociology*, trans. Mary and Thomas Bottomore (Glencoe, Ill.: The Free Press, 1957), p. 76.

Weber's Scheme of Possible Disciplines

Discipline	Kind of Data Studied (item on top being primary)	Type of Explanation Employed	Nature of Resultant Explanation
CULTURAL HISTORY	*Meanings,* factual conditions	Meaningful interpretations, causal explanation	Unique sequences of cultural development
CULTURAL SCIENCE	*Meanings,* factual conditions	Meaningful interpretations, causal explanations	Causal laws of cultural phenomena
NATURAL SCIENCE	*Facts,* explored by meanings	Causal explanations	Laws of natural phenomena
NATURAL HISTORY	*Facts,* explored by meanings	Meaningful interpretations, causal explanation	Unique sequences of physical development

theoretical and philosophical issues that have just been reviewed. This has not promoted the clear isolation of theoretical and philosophical issues from methodological issues. It is partly the reason for the numerous conflicting interpretations that have arisen in connection with Weber's method of the ideal type.

The methodological problems of early sociology, including those which Weber faced, were in considerable measure a product of the conditions of sociology's origin. The science arose as an attempt to apply various theories derived from philosophy to empirical social materials taken from history. Although many early sociologists paid lip service to laboratory experimentation as the ideal method of science, none of them was able to see quite how it could be employed, and some thought it would be an abomination if it were. These same early sociologists could not rely upon the statistical method, for it had not yet been developed. Under the circumstances, sociological method took its only possible form: it employed a *comparative* method, based on historical data. Its historical data were soon amplified by others from ethnography.

However, two circumstances almost guaranteed the abuse of the early forms of the comparative method. Because of the sultry ideological atmosphere of early sociology, it was a foregone conclusion that early sociologists would be inclined to employ historical and ethnographic materials merely to illustrate conclusions which they had already reached in advance. The early unilinear evolutionists, for example, usually assumed that their own societies represented the high point of social evolution, and that some one of the primitive groups described by the ethnographers represented approximately the point from which every society had started. Their task, as they saw it, consisted in arranging available ethnographic and historical evidence in a series between these points. Facts were ripped from a variety of social contexts and strung together like beads on a chain.

The second circumstance that encouraged the abuse of the early comparative method was the lack of standards, other than those supplied by common sense, for deciding what constituted a legitimate comparison. The standards of common sense have a rough workability in their sphere. However, once thought moves outside the sphere of common experience, the standards of common sense are inadequate. A science tends quickly to move beyond such spheres, whereupon its growth assumes the form of a spiral of theoretical refinement and increasing methodological precision.

When these two circumstances — the ideological atmosphere and the lack of any but common-sense standards for comparison — both operated together, early sociology began to develop such an array of conflicting explanations of the same things as to bring the whole science into question. In the search for a solution to the problem of standards, the relation between science and history had to be re-examined.

Dilthey and Rickert, as we have seen, took different positions on this relationship. Weber pursued a course somewhere between the two. With Dilthey, he accepted meanings and values as basic subject matter of sociology. With Rickert, he viewed science as science, whether it deals with mental, social, or physical phenomena. In opposition to Dilthey, he did not believe that the isolation of the meanings of social events put sociology in a differ-

ent class from those disciplines which establish causal laws. In opposition to Rickert, he did not place science and history in opposite camps, leaving sociology the character of a purely formal science. Rather, Weber accepted the traditional situation of sociology as a scientific discipline, working with materials from history. He believed that a properly developed *typological* procedure was the primary device for increasing the methodological precision of sociology.

The problem for comparative method is to get cases that can actually be compared. Weber's solution was the "ideal type." As he conceived them, "ideal types" are hypothetically concrete individuals (personalities, social situations, changes, revolutions, institutions, classes, and so on), constructed out of their relevant components by the researcher for the purpose of instituting precise comparisons. Thus, for example, the ideal types of "church" and "sect" represent two idealized types of arrangement of the critical elements of religious institutions which may help the student in the analysis of the rise of Protestantism; "Protestantism" and "Christianity" themselves are ideal types. Ideal types are not general or abstract concepts, but hypothetical individuals; as hypothetical individuals, ideal types consist of a selection of items which could appear in reality. To this extent, they are like stereotypes. But stereotypes are evaluative concepts, designed to close rather than to open analysis. Finally, ideal types are not averages, which are arithmetic computations appropriate only to the analysis of quantitative variations along a single dimension.[3]

As "hypothetical individuals," ideal types do not come ready made, but must be framed by the researcher. This has led some students to strange conclusions about the scientific process. It has been

[3]For Weber's views on the ideal type, see *The Methodology of the Social Sciences,* pp. 89 ff. For a review of Weber's study and a comparison of his views with those of recent American sociologists, see Don Martindale, "Sociological Theory and the Ideal Type," in *Symposium on Sociological Theory,* ed. Llewellyn Gross (Evanston, Ill.: Row, Peterson, 1959), pp. 57–91.

argued that ideal types are "if . . . then" propositions. However, since ideal types are imaginary individuals, the argument really makes no more sense than to maintain that if wishes were horses, beggars would ride. Even more startling is the suggestion that we compare actual individuals with the (admittedly imaginary) ideal typical individuals to see how much they deviate from them. This is nothing but a form of intellectual acrobatics, for actual individuals ought to deviate from the ideal type just as much as one made them deviate in the first place.

Weber had little interest in such mental gymnastics. To him, the framing of ideal types was an incident in the attempt to understand the empirical world. If that world presented itself to the student in tidy packages, ready for generalization, the framing of types would be unnecessary. However, the world usually presents the individual case as a tangle of incidents appearing in varying degrees of relief. Thought moves against the problems of the actual world with its puny tools and surmounts its obstacles more like a patient mountain climber than a spectacular trapeze artist entertaining an audience.

The ideal type is a strategy in empirical explanation. It is framed in terms of the scientific knowledge available to researchers at the time of their studies and in terms of the empirical situations they are trying to understand. The moment understanding is won, an ideal type has lost its utility, except, perhaps, as a pedagogical device for the instruction of untried scientists or as a diagnostic instrument for practitioners.

There are two criteria for constructing an ideal type: objective possibility and adequate causation. An item to be included in an ideal type is acceptable only if it does not violate the existing scientific knowledge already in the possession of the researcher. The elements of a type must be, in this sense, "objectively possible." Furthermore, the whole purpose of the type is to isolate configurations of facts which have causal influence on the course of social events. The causal relevance of any single item can vary from zero to one hundred per cent. Any item included in a type is subject to the test of adequate causation: that is, it should be causally relevant to the result. For example, if we are studying the sociology of religion and if we find it expedient to set up types of religion, we ought to include as an item of a given religious type its theodicy only if theodicy is causally relevant to socioreligious behavior.

Once a type has been formulated — and no social or natural science is without them — it should permit us to compare various kinds of situations more precisely than we could without it. If the ideal type does not do this, it should be eliminated. Moreover, we do not play games with nature. We compare different empirical configurations, not empirical configurations and types. When a new level of understanding is gained, the type has done its work. Further understanding may then suggest the formation of new types. However, any single ideal type is destined to be scrapped.

Weber's Applied Sociology. One whole block of Weber's studies may perhaps best be described as applied sociology, or the employment of sociology for the purposes of understanding the historical world or solving problems that lie in the present.

It was Weber's view that Western capitalistic civilization is unique. It has properties not duplicated by any other civilization. One of the thematic elements holding all of Weber's sociological researches together was the problem of the nature, causes, and effects of *rationality* as one of the most fundamental respects in which our civilization is distinct.[4] Only in the West, for example, has science, the most rational mode of thought, become the norm of all thought. Although partial anticipations have appeared elsewhere, something was always lacking. Precise knowledge and refined observation appeared in India, China, Babylonia, and Egypt. But Babylonian astronomy lacks a mathematical foundation, Indian geometry lacks the rational proof, medicine was developed in India but without a biochemical foundation, and a

[4] See Weber's introduction to *The Protestant Ethic and the Spirit of Capitalism.*

rational chemistry was absent everywhere except in the West.

Fully developed historical scholarship appeared only in the West. China had no historical method like that of Thucydides. Indian political thought had no systematic method or rational concepts. Nor did a rational jurisprudence develop elsewhere as it did in the West under the influence of Roman law and a series of special economic and political conditions.

The contrast even extends to the arts. Musical sensitivity has been highly developed by other peoples. Polyphonic music is widely diffused over the earth. But the rational tone intervals, while calculated and known elsewhere, do not appear outside the West in systems of rational harmonious music in the forms of counterpoint and harmony with the formation of tone material on the basis of three triads with the harmonic third. Also peculiar to the West are chromatics and enharmonics interpreted in terms of harmony, the orchestra built around the string quartet, the system of notation, and a music possible only with print.

In architecture, only in the West had the pointed arch and cross-arched vault been rationally employed for distributing pressure and roofing many kinds of spaces. The arch has been employed as a constructive principle in great monumental buildings and made into the foundation of a style. This is parallel to the use of perspective as a rational device for representation in painting.

While printing appears in China, only in the West does a literature designed only for print appear. In the universities, meanwhile, the rational, systematic, and specialized pursuit of science is unique. The Western state is the only political association with a rational, written constitution, rationally ordered law, and a government bound by rational laws and administered by trained officials.

Capitalism, with its pursuit of profit by means of continuous, rational, capitalistic enterprise, is peculiar to the West. Capitalism is a form of economic action resting on expectation of profit by utilization of opportunities for exchange and formally peaceful chances for profit. Various elements of capitalism have appeared outside the West in many forms and places: capitalistic acquisition, with rational pursuit of profits resting on calculations in terms of capital; the conduct of activity in terms of balances with the ascertainment of profit and loss; the capitalistic entrepreneur. But the Occident not only developed these to a greater quantitative extent but added numerous additional properties, such as the rational capitalistic organization of free labor, rational industrial organization attuned to a regular market, rational bookkeeping, legal separation of corporate and personal property, and the integration of science into its service.

An extensive number of Weber's studies in applied sociology had these problems in view. They include his studies of the agrarian history of the ancient world, the study of the condition of the worker in large-scale industry, his study of trading companies in the Middle Ages, the decline of the ancient world, the agrarian problems of East Germany, the Protestant ethic and the psychology of capitalism, the rational and social foundations of music.

Weber's Pure or Theoretical Sociology. As in his applied sociology, in his pure sociology Weber had the neo-Kantian formalists and the neo-idealists in mind. He borrowed something from each, and arrived at a unique formulation of his own. With the neo-Kantians, Weber was convinced that sociology required a precise formulation as a scientific discipline. With the idealists, he was convinced that the field must be defined in terms of content rather than forms. In contrast to the neo-Kantians, Weber insists that sociology must study not mere forms but *social action* itself. He agrees, however, that the unit of analysis, once determined, is subject to genuine scientific study by the same methods in all science. With the idealists, Weber agrees that sociology deals with "meanings," but he does not agree that these require a nonscientific procedure. Weber's own formulation brings both issues together. "Sociology (in the sense in which this highly ambiguous word is used here) is a science which attempts the interpretive understanding of social action in order thereby to arrive at a causal explanation of its course and effects." Like the idealist, one "interprets," but it is with the aim of arriving at causal knowledge, which the neo-Kantians had maintained to be essential to science. This appears again in the concept of action. "Action is social in so far as, by virtue of the subjective meaning attached to it by the acting individual (or individuals), it takes account of the behavior of others and is thereby oriented in its course."[5]

This is certainly unambiguous enough. Weber assumes that the subjectively intended meaning present in an action is a causal component of it. Sociology is concerned with action only so far as it possesses meanings. Such meanings may be of two types, either (1) the actually existing meaning in the concrete case or (2) a theoretically conceived pure type attributed to the hypothetical actors. Meaning does not necessarily refer to an objectively correct meaning or one true in a metaphysical sense. The meaning is the one held by actors in situations and not the meaning the situation may have to a scientist or a metaphysician. (Cooley's "ideas that people have of one another" and Thomas's "definitions of the situation" are parallel.)

Two fundamental questions about such meanings were of concern to Weber. First, one must recognize the fact that meaningful behavior blurs off into nonmeaningful forms. Many types of traditional behavior are so habitual as to be almost meaningless. On the other hand, many magical experiences are so personal as hardly to be communicable. Weber perceived this problem as one for interpretation. To the degree that behavior is rational (in a logical or scientific sense or according to logical or scientific standards), it is understandable directly without further ado. Beyond this, empathic understanding (sympathetic understanding of behavior on the basis of one's own) is of great assistance in explaining conduct. One does

not have to have been Caesar to understand Caesar. Empathic understanding, however, was not for Weber, as it was for the neo-idealists, the true method of cultural science; rather, he viewed the employment of sympathetic empathy, the "method of *Verstehen*," as only of secondary significance. Weber's actual procedure consisted primarily in the construction of typologies of behavior and the institution of comparative study on the basis of such typologies.

Weber's second question about meaning is of greater significance, for it concerns the causal importance of meaning: to what extent does meaning cause conduct? One must recognize the existence of a range of experience in which meaning is variably present. To be devoid of meaning is not identical with being lifeless or nonhuman. An artifact like a machine can be understood only in terms of its meaning for human action. A thing is devoid of meaning only if it cannot be related to action in the role of means or ends. A category of facts devoid of meaning but important for explaining action includes various psychophysical phenomena such as fatigue, habit, euphoria, etc. Understanding may be of a direct type, as when we understand the meaning of a proposition such as two plus two equals four when we hear or read it, or it may be explanatory, as when we understand why an actor performs a given act in terms of his motive. Understanding in terms of motive consists in placing the act in a more inclusive context of activity, as when we understand people's actions when they work on sheets of paper in making out their income tax. Furthermore, modern psychologists isolate types of behavior in which the motives are unconscious and not known to the actor.

The study of human behavior shows that meaning is only one of the causal components of action. In some behavior, meaning is prominent; in other behavior, meaning is at best only marginally present. Sometimes isolation of the meaningful element of conduct is difficult. The conscious motives may well conceal, even from actors themselves, the real motives which constitute the driving force of their actions. Many life situations which appear superficially to be very similar must

[5]Weber, *The Theory of Social and Economic Organization*, p. 88.

sometimes be understood or interpreted very differently in terms of the meanings involved.

In view of these facts, Weber maintains, *Verstehen* is never a complete method in itself. Verification of subjective interpretation by comparison with the concrete course of events is indispensable. Unfortunately, this type of verification is feasible with relative accuracy only in cases susceptible to psychological experimentation. The approaches to a satisfactory degree of accuracy are exceedingly various, even in the limited number of cases of mass phenomena which can be statistically described and unambiguously interpreted. For the rest, there remains only the possibility of comparing the largest possible number of historical or contemporary cases which, while otherwise similar, differ in the one decisive point of their relation to the particular motive or factor being investigated. Interpretation of behavior in terms of motives varies in degree. A motive is a complex of subjective meaning which seems to the actors themselves or to the observers an adequate ground for the conduct in question. An adequate explanation of behavior on the level of meaning refers to the subjective interpretation of a course of conduct so far as, according to the habitual modes of thought and feeling of ordinary persons, it is satisfactorily explained. A correct causal interpretation of a concrete course of action is arrived at when the overt action and motives have both been correctly apprehended and at the same time their relation has become meaningfully comprehensible. An explanation of conduct in terms of everyday motives is "adequate on the level of meaning." It represents a common-sense explanation of conduct which may or may not coincide with the causally adequate explanation of conduct to which the sociologist or psychologist as scientist aspires.

Throughout his analyses Weber thus assumes that subjectively intended meaning is a causal component in conduct. This is his most general hypothesis. It includes all others. Weber carefully located sociology in terms of its concern with meaning. Comparative psychology is useful in distinguishing between mechanical and instinctive factors in conduct, on the one hand, and mean-

ings, on the other. But while helpful in differentiating animal and human behavior, it is not sociology. Similarly, the proposals of the Austrian economist and sociologist Othmar Spann to investigate all social phenomena in terms of their objective purpose and function is treated as presociological, for true sociology is concerned with subjectively intended meanings. So, too, for Weber, all analyses of nonmeaningful uniformities such as Gresham's law are nonsociological. Specifically, sociology is concerned with social action (which also includes failure to act and passive acquiescence in action). Action is nonsocial if it is oriented solely to the behavior of inanimate objects. Subjective attitudes constitute social action only so far as they are oriented to the behavior of others. Thus, the crowd studies by Le Bon are largely outside the sphere of social action; they are "actions conditioned by crowds." Similarly, Tarde's imitations are at best borderline social actions. But throughout all analysis, sociology is never to be confused with history, for it is a generalizing science, seeking abstract concepts, and not simply the causal analysis and explanation of individual actions. Conscious interhuman behavior is the unwaveringly conceived object of study.

In his assumption that subjectively intended meanings are a causal component of conduct, Weber was by no means unique. Comparable assumptions are made by all other members of other branches of social behaviorism. Tarde thought the real causes of social regularities were "beliefs" and "desires," which were seen as the mainsprings of imitation. In his "will to believe," William James had insisted that a belief has consequences even if its truth is unknown. Thomas abstracted a socially relevant orientation from James's proposition in his insistence that one could not adequately account for social events except in terms of the "definitions of the situation" of the parties involved. Cooley had treated "the imaginations people have of one another" as the solid facts of society, and Mead sharply opposed the behaviorism of Watson on the grounds that it left out of account the role of "attitude" and "meaning." Thus, in assuming that meaning is a causal component of behavior, Weber shared a basic supposition with other representatives of social behaviorism. In fact, this assumption is one of the generally distinguishing properties of the school. Because he clarified the issue, Weber has often been singled out as somehow or other a pure subjectivist—a charge which is paralleled by the idea that Weber had no other idea of method than *Verstehen* or empathy. If Weber is objectionable on this score, so too is every other member of the social-behaviorist school.

The basic device by means of which Weber made the transition from social action to general social life was a typology of action. Action was classified into four types in terms of the arrangement of its inner conscious components. Action is *zweckrational* ("rationally purposeful") when it is addressed to a situation with a plurality of means and ends in which actors are free to choose their means purely in terms of efficiency; action is *wert-rational* ("rational in terms of values") when the means are chosen for their efficiency but the ends are fixed in advance; action is *affective* when emotional factors determine the means and ends of action; and action is *traditional* when both means and ends are fixed by custom.

It is perhaps unfortunate that Weber chose to express his basic analysis of meaningful action in the form of a typology. A meaning is a consciously perceived relation between means and ends. Such a meaning may be organized in a number of ways: by efficiency, by advance fixing of the ends and means (as in religiously correct goals and religiously proper means to reach them), by the presence of emotion, or by the determination of tradition and custom. However, though tending to obscure his analytical framework, Weber's action typology is of tremendous importance for another reason. Weber was strongly nominalistic. To him, only individuals and individual actions exist. Any regularities in interhuman conduct represent no more than the stabilization of behavior in terms of rationality, ethical fixity, emotionality, or habit. To be sure, behavior will always display an admixture, for people are not merely rational or emotional; they are both, and the question is often one of de-

termining which will be paramount. But only individual acts exist; there are no new superindividual entities. A *way* of acting is not a new *thing*.

Some of the most theoretically exciting problems of Weber's sociology were buried in his typology. It is evident that the various different ways of stabilizing or regularizing meaningful conduct are in tension. Rationalization can make its way, often, only by breaking down traditional patterns of conduct; a fixity of ends may promote a vast rationalization within some areas of life (as the Protestant sects promoted the rational psychology of capitalism); affective behavior almost always yields the social field to other types of action, becoming generally relevant only during mob actions and periods of revolution. The possible tension between these different modes of stabilizing meaningful action compare to the tension between Bagehot's "cake of custom" and the agitational and disrupting influences of modern science and war; between Tarde's imitation and disrupting innovations; between Sumner's stabilizing folkways and mores and innovating incidents; between W. I. Thomas's habitual solutions to social problems and crises. Throughout Weber's empirical studies there is an amazing array of empirical judgments concerning just what did or did not, in the given case, stabilize conduct on a rational, ethical, affective, or traditional model. Undoubtedly had he lived to carry out the program of a pure sociology, the analysis of issues such as those just raised would have been one of the most fundamental of his theoretical problems.

The next major theoretical step in Weber's sociology was the introduction of the concept of *social relation*. This is the fundamental concept for making the transition from individual acts to patterns of behavior. It is the critical concept by which one moves eventually from social action either to the social person or to social groups, institutions, and communities.

The concept *social relationship* is used to denote the behavior of a plurality of actors insofar as, in its meaningful content, the action of each takes account of that of the others and is oriented by this. The social relationship consists in the existence of a probability that there will be, in some meaningfully understandable sense, a course of social action. There must be a minimum of mutual orientation of action, though the content of action be most varied. The meaning involved is either the actual one or of a theoretically conceived pure type. The meaning need not be the same for all parties. The social relationship may be temporary or permanent. The moment there is no longer a chance that certain kinds of behaviors will occur, no "relation" can be said to exist. By "the United States government" we mean that some people act in certain ways. We need not reify this action. If people did not act this way, there would be no United States. Weber needed the concept of social relation to account for the recurrence of social action. For example, *A* dominates *B*, who is subordinate to *A*. This action of domination and subordination may occur between *A* and *B* in many different areas of their lives on many occasions. For analytical convenience, we may wish to isolate the arrangement or form of the action without reference to the varied occasions and content of the social actions between *A* and *B*. We "abstract" this arrangement and with a new economy of thought say that a dominance–subordination relation holds between *A* and *B*. Weber needed the concept of social relationship in order to make the transition from his concept of social action to that of social structure.

Just as from his concept of social action Weber turned to a typology of social actions resting on empirically observed regularities, so he turned directly from his concept of social relationship to categories of empirical uniformities in social practice. He distinguished: (1) usage — an actual uniformity of social relations; (2) custom — usage resting on long familiarity or habit; (3) rational usage — when the uniformity is determined by the rational actions of actors under similar conditions; (4) fashion — a usage determined by the presence of novelty in the corresponding behavior; (5) convention — usage springing from desires for social prestige, usage determined by normative patterns; and (6) law — usage determined by the presence of designated enforcing authorities.

These are empirically observed categories of social relations.

Weber's concept of social relationship and his distinctions between empirical uniformities of social relationship were used in defining a "legitimate order," an added notion required to isolate the group. Action involving social relationships may be oriented by the actors to a belief (*Vorstellung* in the existence of a "legitimate order." The probability that action will be so oriented is called the "validity" (*Geltung*) of the order in question. The legitimacy of such an order may be guaranteed from disinterested motives, for emotional reasons, because of rational belief in the absolute validity of the order as an expression of ultimate values, for religious reasons, or because of self-interest. Such a system of order is conventional if it is guaranteed by the fact that deviation will result in relatively general and significant reactions of disapproval. Such an order is called *law* when conformity is upheld by sanction of physical means in the hands of people designated to perform the function. The idea of legitimate order is needed to account for patterns of social relationship of an extensive sort. "Validity" of such an order is the probability of its being upheld. As in Weber's definition of social relationship, this is a sop to his fear of reification. Basically important is the manner in which the order is upheld—whether by moral disapproval (convention) or by legally constituted authorities (law). A significant feature of the analysis of legitimate orders is the way that it ties in with the problem of meaning. The bases of legitimacy of an order are said to lie in tradition, rational belief in an absolute value, emotional certainty, or its establishment in a manner accepted as legal.

Having developed the case for extensive systems of social relations as integrated in conventional and legal orders, Weber turned to specific problems of social relationship such as conflict and solidarity and open and closed relationships, all of which are critically important for understanding the organized group. A social relationship is treated as conflicting so far as the action embodying it is determined by the intention of carrying the actor's will against the opposition of others. Conflicting relationships vary from relatively peaceable forms like competition (formally peaceful attempts to gain control over opportunities desired by others) to bloody forms of conflict. Social relationships are communal so far as the orientation of action is based on the subjective feeling of the parties that they belong together. This kind of relationship varies from relatively rational associations (market exchange) to communal relationships of great intensity. Social relationships, whether communal or associative, are open to outsiders to the degree that, in terms of the subjective meaning, the social action relevant to the order is available to them. There are many degrees of openness and closure.

It has been noted that no theoretical bridge has been provided explicitly by Weber between the concepts of legitimate order and conflicting, solidary, open, and closed relationships. The discussion of these four kinds of relationship presupposes the operation of legitimate orders. Thus, generally, it may be supposed that conflict and solidarity represent subsidiary forms of social relation occurring within the framework of conventional and legal orders. A competitive social relationship, for example, represents a regulated conflict. The regulation is provided either by a conventional or a legal order.

With the substructuring of social relationships and their formation into solidary systems with comparative closure, the problems of representation and responsibility become crucial. And these ideas form the final transition for Weber to the concept of the *corporate group* and its types. A social relationship which is either closed or limits the admission of outsiders by rules, is a "corporate group" (*Verband*) so far as its order is enforced by the action of specific individuals whose regular function this is, that is, a chief or head (*Leiter*) and usually also an administrative staff. Corporate groups may be self-governing or subject to the law of other groups. The types of order in corporate groups may be established by voluntary agreement or by imposition and acquiescence. The systems of order governing action in corporate groups may be administrative or regulative. The types of organization of corporate groups, including the voluntary association and compulsory association, are organizations of power and imperative control.

Just as in Weber's thought the transition is made from social action to the far reaches of social structure, so there are transitions from social action to the characteristics of culture, social change, and socially relevant forms of individually manifest behaviors ("callings"). In this case, a complex block of social changes characteristic of modern Western culture are traced to a transformed subjective interpretation of the meaning of everyday action.

The concept of "calling" or "vocation" served Weber in the same manner that the concept of "role" served symbolic interactionism — as the point of contact between personality structure and social structure. Vocation represents a peculiar accentuation and development of individual abilities relevant to social structure in a specific way. Two of Weber's most brilliant studies of social roles are his "Politics as a Vocation" and "Science as a Vocation."[6]

Weber found it fruitful to analyze a vocation (role): (1) historically; (2) distributively and statistically — and in terms of its integration with other social roles and the sources of recruitment into it; and (3) intrinsically, in terms of the inner psychological requirements of the role itself.

Scattered throughout Weber's work are many other studies of social roles. Such was his study of the Brahman, the Chinese literati, the Junker, and the scriptural prophet. However, this is only part of the story. Weber's analysis moves as easily and challengingly in the field of social structure as in the area of the formation of the social person. The more purely sociological studies occur in the course of his studies in three great subdisciplines of sociology that trace their contemporary forms primarily to him — the sociology of religion, political sociology, and the sociology of law.

[6]Both of these were originally speeches delivered at Munich University in 1918. They appear in *From Max Weber: Essays in Sociology*, pp. 127–156.

Weber's political sociology contains some of his most interesting analyses of social structure and change. His discussion of the legitimation of power belongs here. He developed a typology paralleling the fundamental modes of stabilizing social action. Power may be legitimized *rationally*, on the basis of the belief in the legality of the rules; it may be legitimized *charismatically,* when it is thought to rest on the magical or other personal properties of an individual; or it may be legitimized *traditionally,* claiming to rest on immemorial custom. The forms of legitimation of authority may be further subdivided in various ways which are critical for the discrimination of various kinds of states and other structures of power.

Various modes of administration also are possible. Of particular interest among them was Weber's study of bureaucracy. Modern officialdom rests on the principle of fixed official jurisdictional areas ordered by rules, laws, or regulations. Authority to give commands is distributed in a stable manner, delimited in terms of the rules affecting the means placed at the disposal of officials. Methodical provision is made for the regular and continuous fulfillment of these duties and the exercise of the corresponding rights. Generally only persons with proper qualifications are employed. The bureaucratic type of administration, articulated in such terms, is critically important to all modern types of large-scale social structure: the modern state, ecclesiastical institutions, great banks and other large commercial enterprises, even modern hospitals and labor unions.

To the area of political sociology also belong Weber's studies of class, status, and party. *Class* was defined objectively in economic terms by Weber as consisting of a plurality of persons sharing a common component in their life chances, consisting of opportunities for the possession of goods and income as represented by the conditions of the commodity and labor markets. Multiple forms of class organization, class consciousness, and class action, as well as class struggle, are possible in terms of this economic component in people's life chances. Weber defined *status groups*, by contrast, as communities consisting in a plurality of persons whose life fate is determined by a specific positive or negative social estimation of honor. Status honor is normally expressed in a style of life expected of all those belonging to the circle. It is decisively manifest in the sharing of table and marriage community but it may organize and distribute a great range of items of deportment. Among the most significant of events in modern social life is the interplay of class and status. *Caste* was treated by Weber, in terms strongly suggesting the extension of the brilliant discussion by Bouglé, as a ritualistically closed, magically tabooed class and status situation in which the entire community is sealed into mutually antagonistic endogamously closed groups, the ranks of which are determined by social distance from the Brahman caste. *Parties* were treated as pluralities organized purely for the acquisition of power. Parties may exist in a social club as well as a state. As against the actions of classes and status groups (which tend to traditionalize conduct), the actions of parties always mean a societalization (a tendency toward the rationalization of social action). Party actions are always directed toward a goal in a planned manner. Parties may represent interests determined through class or status position and they may recruit their following from one or the other (although they need not be exclusively recruited from one or the other). They may represent ephemeral or enduring structures. Their means of attaining power may be varied, ranging from the use of outright violence to bribery or canvassing for votes.

Also belonging in considerable measure to Weber's political sociology was his theory of *social change*, though, to be sure, it was much broader than this. Social change finds its point of focus in the conflict of three general principles: traditionalism, rationality, and charisma. Much of the evolution of human social structures has been played out in terms of the tension between traditionalization and the disruptive influence of rationalization. But both of these principles have frequently appeared in tension with the charismatic principle — the following of some individual because of his or her presumed magical or supernatural or other purely personal properties and powers (Jesus, Buddha, Confucius, Alexander the Great, Napoleon, Joseph Smith, Hitler). Charisma, in turn, by its highly personal nature must be transformed (routinized) into a rational or traditional form if the movement and structures it establishes are not to perish.

In the opinion of some sociologists, Max Weber was the greatest social scientist of the first half of the twentieth century. Certainly Weber formed the starting point for the careers of many major contemporary sociologists; among leading social scientists who took their point of departure in considerable measure from Weber are Karl Mannheim, Hans Speier, Hans Gerth, Talcott Parsons, Robert Merton, C. Wright Mills. There have been many others. A full appreciation of the richness of Weber's work can be gained only through a knowledge of his empirical studies, in which the theoretical and methodological concepts described here were combined with a truly extraordinary scholarship to bring historical data into a new and sharper focus.* Many of the significant trends in contemporary social science are continuations of work begun by Max Weber. Among these are stratification theory, the study of bureaucracy and large-scale organization, the study of legitimate authority, the sociology of law, the sociology of politics, the sociology of religion, and the sociology of music.

Thorstein Veblen. Thorstein B. Veblen (1857–1929) quite independently developed some aspects of a social-action theory. Veblen was born in Wisconsin and graduated from Carleton College in 1880. He studied at Johns Hopkins and at Yale and Cornell universities. In 1893, he was appointed reader in political economy at the University of Chicago, becoming instructor and assistant professor. He was associate professor of economics at Stanford University from 1906 to 1909, lecturer

*See Reinhard Bendix's *Max Weber: An Intellectual Portrait* (Garden City, N.Y.: Doubleday, 1960). Since it contains simplified paraphrases of many of Weber's works, it should make an ideal introduction to Weber for undergraduates.

THORSTEIN VEBLEN

Kay Harris, New York

in economics at the University of Missouri from 1911 to 1918, and lecturer in the New School for Social Research beginning in 1918. For ten years he was managing editor of *The Journal of Political Economy*. He died at Menlo Park, California, August 3, 1929.[7]

[7]Thorstein Veblen's works with major sociological import are: *The Theory of the Leisure Class* (New York: Macmillan, 1899); *The Theory of Business Enterprise* (New York: Scribner's, 1904); *The Instinct of Workmanship* (New York: Macmillan, 1914); *Imperial Germany and the Industrial Revolution* (New York: MacMillan, 1915); *The Higher Learning in America* (New York: B. W. Huebsch, 1918); *The Place of Science in Modern Civilization* (New York: B. W. Huebsch, 1919); *The Engineers and the Price System* (New York: B. W. Huebsch, 1921); *Absentee Ownership and Business Enterprise in Recent Times* (New York: B. W. Huebsch, 1923); and the posthumously published *Essays in Our Changing Order*, ed. Leon Ardzrooni (New York: Viking, 1934).

Veblen's approach to social-action theory was anchored in his peculiar cultural and intellectual interests. Born the son of Norwegian immigrants in a Wisconsin farm community, he was brought up in an atmosphere where the Norwegian language, religious organization, and social customs prevailed — in tension with the Americanizing influences of town and city. There was also tension between the midwestern farmers and eastern capitalists. His early reading was dominated by Herbert Spencer, but his interests were broad and he was also influenced by Hume, Kant, and the nineteenth-century idealists. When he studied classical economics, he brought to the study a special grouping of interests. The formal framework for Veblen's thought was provided by the evolutionary hypothesis, which he seems to have derived originally from Spencer. Unlike Spencer, he was critically oriented toward current economic activity — a position which is understandable in the light of his cultural background. He was also critically oriented toward classical economic theory, which he held responsible for economic tensions. The general project carried through all Veblen's works was an evolutionary presentation and institutional criticism of the existing economic system and its sustaining theories.

Just as Veblen subscribed to an evolutionary construction for his developmental studies, he subscribed to an instinct theory in his analysis of behavior. People are assumed to be moved by an instinct for practical efficiency and by the desire to emulate and surpass. But neither evolutionism nor instinct theory touches the real basis of Veblen's thought, for one can dispense with both and still say everything he wished to say.

Veblen actually held a type of social-action theory. The units into which his analysis ultimately resolves are interindividual actions. These actions embody human purposes, intentions, and aims. There are, for Veblen, two fundamental types: predatory and constructive. Veblen's concept of social action was not as rich as Weber's: his types were not complete and somewhat different, but he approached analysis the same way and applied his analysis to the same kinds of problems.

Weber wished to explain the tremendous growth of rationality in all spheres of Occidental life. Rationality, particularly scientific rationality, was of central interest to Veblen. Weber, in his interest in the reconstruction of economic theory on more adequate grounds, reviewed the traditional concept of social classes, examined the factors frustrating full achievement of rationality, and investigated the interrelations among institutions. All these problems were of concern to Veblen as well. Both thinkers were suspicious of all tendencies to reify abstractions. Both wished to promote a value-free science.

In Veblen's view, human nature is developed by selective necessity. In their own apprehension, human beings are a center of impulsive teleological activity. In every act, they seek the accomplishment of some specific end. Thus, by nature, human beings have a taste for effective work and a distaste for useless effort. Action is guided by a sense of merit, serviceability, or efficiency, and a sense of the demerit in futility, waste, and incapacity. This attitude or propensity is called the *instinct of workmanship*. Wherever comparison of persons with respect to efficiency occurs, the instinct of workmanship issues into an emulative comparison of persons. The extent to which this occurs is related to the temperament of the population. Where such a comparison is habitual, visible success becomes an end sought for its own utility and as a basis for esteem. Esteem is gained and dispraise is avoided by making one's efficiency manifest. The result is that the instinct of workmanship works out in an emulative demonstration of force. So far as tangible evidence of prowess such as trophies finds a place in people's habits of thought as an essential feature of the paraphernalia of life, aggression may in fact become the accredited form of action. Booty may serve as prima facie evidence of success. An invidious distinction arises then between exploit and acquisition, on the one hand, and industrial employment, on the other. Labor then acquires a character of irksomeness by virtue of the indignity imputed to it.[8]

---

[8]For Veblen's own summary of these views, see his introduction to *The Theory of the Leisure Class.*

A surprising number of the basic elements of social-action theory are contained here. Veblen's "instinct of workmanship" corresponds with Weber's *zweckrational* (rational-purposeful) type of social action. Although Weber locates tension between rational and both affective and traditional types of action while Veblen locates it between the instinct of workmanship and the instinct of aggression, the differences are more apparent than real. Even though he does not formally incorporate it into his theories, Veblen looked upon the instinct of efficiency as the great rationalizer in human affairs, disrupting traditional and outmoded solutions to problems of all sorts. Similarly, while Weber did not isolate "aggressive social action" as one of his types (it is contained by implication in others), one of the problems of constant interest to him was the multiple points of intersection between the two ways of making a living: peaceable, by economic activities; or exploitative, by politics and war. Veblen's suggestion that rationalizing social actions (the instinct of workmanship) find some social environments more favorable than others compares in some measure to Weber's discussion of the social atmosphere produced by inner-worldly ascetic Protestantism. (Veblen, incidentally, like Weber himself, was in some measure a product of the Protestant ethic). Similarly the interplay between life styles of status groups (Veblen's "invidious distinctions") and class and party was a common problem for both men.

According to Veblen, the emergence of a leisure class coincided with the beginnings of ownership. The earliest form of ownership was that of women by the able-bodied men in the community and began with the seizure of female captives in the cultural stage of lower barbarism. The extension of the practice led to slavery. Ownership of women in turn was extended to ownership of the products of their industry, an ownership of things as well as people. While the normal aim of acquisition and accumulation was consumption of the goods acquired, a new aim now appeared — ownership for reasons of emulation. Ownership is transformed into an institution unrelated to subsistence, and the incentive becomes invidious — to secure the distinctions attaching to wealth. Wealth has now become intrinsically honorable, conferring honor on its possessor. It is imposed upon people whether they will or no, for only individuals with aberrant temperaments can maintain their self-esteem in the long run when faced with the disesteem of their fellows. Thus, when possession of property becomes the basis of popular esteem, it becomes a prerequisite of complacency or self-respect. The end sought by accumulation is to rank high in pecuniary strength in comparison with the rest of the community. In the nature of the case, the desire for wealth can hardly be satisfied in the individual instance.[9] Furthermore, wealth also confers power, which becomes another motive for accumulation. Relative success is tested by an invidious pecuniary comparison with others as the conventional goal of action.

If undisturbed by other elements, even this pecuniary struggle would tend to make people industrious and frugal. Where people live by their labor — at least among the lower classes — they take emulative pride in a reputation for efficiency in work. Things tend to be otherwise in the superior pecuniary class, which, while also having incentives to diligence and thrift, find their action overshadowed by pure demands of pecuniary emulation. Wealth and power must be put in evidence, for esteem is awarded only on the basis of evidence.

One of the most direct ways of proving one's wealth and power is by conspicuous display of leisure. It becomes the conventional mark of superior pecuniary achievement and the conventional index of reputability. In theory, at least, the leisure class has existed from the beginning of

---

[9]Veblen assumes that the desire for wealth, like other socially reconstructed drives, has no "natural" limits. The desires for food and for sex satisfaction have built-in limits at the point of physiological satiation. At this point, still more food or sexual activity may not only cease to be utilities, but they may become positive disutilities. However, the desire for wealth has no built-in satiation point, and it may become more inflamed the more it is appeased.

predatory culture. Taking on new and fuller meaning with each stage of pecuniary culture, it early assumed the form of conspicuous exemption from all useful employment. Government and war as predatory activities became the monopoly of the leisure class. These activities reveal the nature of the leisure class most characteristically, for they are the precise opposite of gainful industry. The chase and sport are the pure exercise of the predatory impulse; they are typical. Abstention from labor is honorific and meritorious, the prerequisite of decency. Labor becomes disreputable in the eyes of the community, morally impossible to the noble and incompatible with a worthy life.

Around the leisured class a secondary, pseudo-leisured class appears, abjectly poor, living a life of precarious want and discomfort but morally unable to stoop to gainful pursuit — the decayed gentleman and lady who have "seen better days."

Meanwhile, "leisure" connotes the nonproductive consumption of time. A whole cluster of symbols advertise the leisure class: trophies, systems of rank, titles, degrees and insignia, heraldic devices, medals, and honorary decoration. The criteria of past performances of leisure take the form of quasi-scholarly accomplishments and a knowledge of processes and incidents not conducive to furtherance of human life — knowledge of dead languages; occult science; correct spelling, syntax, and prosody; the forms of domestic music, equipage, of games, sports and fancy bred horses.

One incidental function of manners is the demonstration of the amount of time spent in learning them. Manners are symbolic and conventionalized survivals representing former acts of dominance or personal service expressive of status relations. In the last analysis, manners are vouchers of a life of leisure. Refined tastes, manners, habits of life are useful evidence of gentility, for good breeding requires time, application, and expenses and cannot be compassed by those whose time and energy are taken up with work. The conspicuous leisure which is made manifest in decorum grows into a laborious drill in deportment and an education in taste and discrimination.

The development of the concept of the leisure class formed the central object of Veblen's early work. But having once established its central property, he proceeded to trace its manifestations through practically every area of life. Thus, for example, the leisure class manifests itself through endless variants of conspicuous consumption. The noble becomes a connoisseur of creditable viands of various degrees of merit, of manly beverages and trinkets, of seemly apparel and architecture, of weapons, games, dancers, and narcotics, of all objects addressed to a cultivated aesthetic faculty. High-bred manners and ways of living are items in conformity with the norm of conspicuous leisure and consumption. A pecuniary standard of taste comes to dominate all features of life to a point where the domestic life of most classes is relatively shabby compared to the éclat of the portion of their lives carried on before the eyes of others. People tend to screen their private lives from observation. They lower the birth rate of the class to meet the requirements of reputable expenditure. A lowered birth rate is one of the prices of a standard of living resting on conspicuous waste. The high standards of pecuniary decency among the superior classes is transmitted to the scholarly classes, which as a result spends a large proportion of its substance in conspicuous waste. The resulting pecuniary canons of taste are everywhere evident. Prescriptive expensiveness is manifest even in objects not observable to outsiders, such as articles of underclothing, some articles of food, kitchen utensils, and household apparatus one would expect to be designed for service rather than evidence. The canons of expensiveness have penetrated the deepest levels of taste. In the end, a beautiful object which is not expensive is not accounted beautiful. Veblen maintains that the standards of the leisure class penetrate the very structure of higher learning itself to such a degree that many of its peculiar features are traceable to the leisure-class scheme of life.

If money making is accepted as the criterion of success, then the more successful the technology, the more it becomes possible for the processes of invidious comparisons and conspicuous consumption to operate. But the significance of money making goes further; this was merely the starting point of Veblen's thought. Money making also leads to the cultivation of a type of rationality epitomized in modern accounting. It leads to a peculiar psychology and philosophy of human behavior. The classical economists, in Veblen's view, were nothing more than formulators of a money-determined philosophy of behavior; they were led to ignore other institutional factors. Money making promotes and obstructs the process of making a living. It leads to the production of raw materials, their transformation into usable goods, their transport and distribution. It leads, as well, to a series of bargains, in which individuals seek to take as much as they can for themselves from others.

Industrial efficiency requires division of labor and exchange. The capitalistic economy is the most productive people have so far designed. Its devices, such as business accounting, are adequate to its needs. Industry requires capital and credit, the capitalist and banker. The recurrent crises and depressions which reduce the flow of goods are due to business rather than industry; there are no technological reasons for them. Business enterprises are run for profit rather than for need, and the alternation of prosperity and depression are the result.

Thus, the theme of the tension between the instinct of workmanship and the consequences of pecuniary emulation is expanded by Veblen into the contrast between the productive and predatory aspects of modern capitalism — the productiveness of industry and the predatory modes of procedure of business and finance. The phenomena of industrial crisis and depression are treated in terms of the interrelation between the predatory and productive phases of economy. These are the main themes of *The Theory of Business Enterprise* (1904).

Veblen's *The Instinct of Workmanship* (1914) represents his fullest treatment of the positive elements in his thought. Humanity's most profound impulse, the instinct of workmanship, is to create rather than to destroy. The most significant of all aspects of human civilization has been the devel-

opment of technology from the New Stone Age to modern machine industry. Technology is the manifestation of the instinct of workmanship.

Veblen's concept of technology led him toward a form of technocracy. Even by training, businesspeople are incapable of understanding the engineers. Technology becomes increasingly a matter of applied science. The graduates of engineering schools know how to make things, organize production, increase output. Less and less are businesspeople even able to talk their language. The engineers talk in terms of physical science, businesspeople in terms of natural rights and ownership. The engineers cannot understand why pecuniary interests should curtail production. Veblen saw the task of modern society to be one of setting the engineers free in a process that will create a new system of institutions.

Veblen is significant in a number of respects. In the first place, it is important to clear up the curious contradiction in treating Veblen as one of the most creative minds produced by twentieth-century America and at the same time providing neither a clear institutional nor a clear theoretical place for him. From the beginning, Veblen's economics was more than an analysis of economic phenomena; it comprehended higher learning, science and civilization, political economy, and stratification. Even his interests in economic phenomena included many issues that fell outside the sphere of traditional economics. He tended to be classified as an economist by the sociologists and as a sociologist by the economists. His proper field, it appears, is sociology; it is high time sociologists claimed him for their own.

The reason why Veblen's theoretical importance tended to be obscured was the general sociological rather than specifically economic nature of his theories. Economists thought of his work as tangential to the main business of economics. And as long as sociologists have treated him as an economist, they have not — and frequently still do not — look at Veblen's work as a type of sociological theory. Hence, one of America's most original theorists is at times denied recognition as a theorist. However, as the preceding review has tried to show, Veblen was developing a form of social-action theory which in many points bears comparison with that of Max Weber. This is particularly interesting inasmuch as the framing of social-action theory by Weber in Germany and by Veblen and other institutional economists in America was going on independently. Similar solutions to similar problems were being elaborated in different parts of the Western world.

John R. Commons. John Rogers Commons (1862–1945) illustrates the emergence of social-action theory in still another form. Born in Hollandsburg, Ohio, he studied at Oberlin College and Johns Hopkins, later teaching at Wesleyan University, Oberlin, the University of Indiana, Syracuse University, and the University of Wisconsin. He did basic work in value and distribution, the history of economic thought, public utilities, immigration, housing, labor legislation, social insurance, trade unionism, industrial government, labor history, monopoly prices, index numbers, business cycles, tariffs, civil service and administration, municipal government, and proportional representation. He worked with and for a variety of public bodies and foundations. With Richard T. Ely, who brought him to the University of Wisconsin in 1904, he prepared the *Documentary History of American Industry* (1909–1911) in eleven volumes; the two men can be said to have created the field of American labor history.[10]

Social-action theory seems to have been a logical

JOHN R. COMMONS

Courtesy of the University of Wisconsin, Madison, Wisconsin

step for persons who were both impressed by and at the same time critical of classical economics. Among the most obvious characteristics of the classical theory of capitalism were: its conceptualization of economic phenomena in terms of rational individual behavior; its opposition to the reification of patterns of economic action and to reification generally (the classical economists persistently opposed treating the state as an entity above and superior to people, insisting on treating it as the ways people act); its interpretation of economic activity primarily from the standpoint of production and the market (these being the spheres in which rationalization is carried through).

If one accepts the general analysis of economic life in terms of these ideas and at the same time is

---

[10]Commons' most original works containing his general sociological as well as specifically economic theories are: *Races and Immigrants in America* (New York: Macmillan, 1907); *History of Labor in the United States,* by Commons and others, 4 vols. (New York: Macmillan, 1918–1935); *Industrial Government* (New York: Macmillan, 1921); *The Legal Foundations of Capitalism* (New York: Macmillan, 1924); *Institutional Economics: Its Place in Political Economy* (New York: Macmillan, 1934); and the posthumously published *The Economics of Collective Action*, with a biographical sketch by Selig Perlman, manuscript edited, introduction, and supplementary essay by Kenneth H. Parsons (New York: Macmillan, 1950).

critically oriented toward it, there are definite lines along which such opposition tends to develop. One may accept the idea that rational individual action is significant but explore the economic relevance of various types of nonrational economic behavior as well. One may go along with the classical economists in their reluctance to reify patterns of individual action but complete the study and modify the classical economic picture by a fuller analysis of noneconomic social actions. One may accept the idea that technological, productive, and exchange institutions are important but also explore economic and social factors represented by consumption processes. This is precisely what seems to have happened in the studies of the institutional economists, including Weber. They accept the concept of rational social action as a starting point but expand the concept of social action to include nonrational types. They are reluctant to reify institutions but still examine other than economic relational complexes. Accepting the importance of production, they examine the influences of consumption and noneconomic processes as well.

It is interesting to note the parallel between the American institutional economists and Max Weber in this respect. The classical economic concept of *capitalism* was reduced by Weber to an ideal type. To rational social action, he added a number of additional types. He explored the bearing of religion, politics, and other institutional complexes on the economic. He added the idea of status group (a consumption-oriented stratum) to class (a market-based stratum). He examined the interrelations between economy and law. Weber, of course, was trained in law and economics.

Veblen, as has been noted, developed a social-action theory out of classical economics, pragmatism, and neo-idealism. His most influential teacher at Carleton had been the classical economic theorist John Bates Clark. Some things taken from classical economics were always retained by Veblen — his admiration for scientific technology, production, and the manifestations of rational social action based on the instinct of workmanship. For Veblen this was the basic constructive force of human society. But Veblen modified the concept of action of classical economics by locating, along with rational social action, actions resting on emulation. Countering the productive forces are those predatory modes of achieving power that rest on exploitation. Modifying the constructive effects of scientific technology are the destructive effects of the conspicuous consumption patterns of the leisure class. Veblen's starting point is parallel to Weber's and he rises to his concept of the leisure class by a process not unlike those leading to Weber's concept of status group.

There is no need to multiply examples, but it is relevant to note that a close affinity exists between social behaviorism generally and institutional economic analysis. Tarde was anchored not in the social-action but suggestion–imitation school. Nevertheless, when he turned to economic phenomena, he tended to develop some economic interpretations quite parallel to those of the institutionalists. Tarde's invention and imitation could, on occasion, operate somewhat like Weber's contrast between rational and traditional social actions. The total patterns of economy, for Tarde, were determined by the properties of the epochs of custom or fashion imitation. Moreover, in the nature of the case, Tarde's principle of imitation brought consumption patterns more completely under analysis than was true for the classical economists.

John R. Commons also expanded into fields outside the classical economic framework and rose theoretically to a general theory of social action. Commons' opposition to reification is evident in his very definition of economic institutions as "collective action in control of individual action." Characteristically, the actions of working people became as important as the establishment of capitalistic structures. He observed them forming trade unions, cooperative buying clubs, cooperative workshops. His attitude toward the workers is stated compactly by Selig Perlman: "As self-determining beings, the workers and their movements were to set their *own* objectives, their *own* values, and were entitled to claim from the intellectuals expert aid in the road they should take to attain the goals set by leaders risen in their midst."[11] The degree to which Commons subscribed fundamentally to a social-action theory is brought out by Kenneth Parsons: "Commons devoted his life to devising and using methods of investigation and understanding which explicitly recognize that human activity is volitional."[12]

Commons conceived social life as based on judgments and actions of persons. Social events rest upon the human will, individually and collectively. Critically central is his conception of social relationships. He proceeded from a postulate of the economy as a social organization, rather than as a mechanism or organism. As a social organization, the economy is the way participants act. Organization is achieved through the stabilization and regularization of activity. Activity is regularized or controlled in a society of citizens (persons with legally recognized wills of their own) by the working rules which define the limits within which individuals may exercise their own wills.

Individuals are not self-sufficient, independent entities; they are what they are through their participation in the institutions or going concerns of which they are members. Commons noted the way in which membership in labor unions lifted workers from a level of fear and servility to a new dignity, commensurate with the rights of economic citizenship, and he formulated his conception of an institution as "collective action in control, liberation, and expansion of individual action."

Although Commons ended up with the main essentials of a general theory of social action, he did not arrive at them all at once. Shortly after going to Wisconsin in 1905, he was called in by the state to study the problem of industrial accidents. Working conditions were hazardous and legal liability for accidents followed the common-law rule of negligence. Where accidents were held by the courts to be due to corporation negligence, the usual recourse for the police and courts was to arrest and often imprison the foreman or superintendent. The persons of the stockholders were beyond the reach of the law. Relations between industry and labor were particularly bitter over these affairs. Commons proposed the elimination of criminal prosecutions for accident liability and the substitution of accident compensation commensurate with the injury as a penalty on the company. He also helped employers form their own mutual insurance company, by which the benefits of safe employment would accrue to the employers responsible for safety improvements. The insight gained in helping draft a public utility law for Wisconsin about 1910 led Commons to a study of the economic principles followed by the courts. The result was *The Legal Foundations of Capitalism* (1924). Here again the parallel with Weber is direct, for Weber was led in somewhat similar manner to a study of law and his work on a sociology of law.

The understanding of economic action could not be complete without an understanding of its ties with legal action. Commons observed that out of economic transactions come practices which serve as guides to the courts in their resolution of economic conflicts brought to it.

> A transaction occurs at a point of time. But transactions flow one into another over a period of time, and this flow is a process. The courts have fully developed the notion of this process in the concept of a "going concern," which they have taken over from the customs of business and which is none other than a technological process of production and consumption of physical things and a business process of buying and selling, borrowing and lending, commanding and obeying, according to shop rules or working rules or laws of the land.[13]

Commons was led to the concept of economic and legal activity as forming an interrelated working whole. He formulated a theory of the in-

---

[11]Commons, *The Economics of Collective Action*, p. 3.
[12]*Ibid.*, p. 13.

[13]Commons, *The Legal Foundations of Capitalism*, p. 8. Quoted from the 1957 edition (Madison, Wisc.: Wisconsin University Press, 1957).

terrelations between group customs and the common law, of the rise of new social classes, and of their struggle for recognition. He showed how in the struggle around the "rent bargain," the English barons had reduced the King of England from theoretical owner to a mere recipient of a land tax fixed by collective bargaining between their representatives and his. Similarly, through their participation in the piepowder courts at the fairs, English merchants were able to impose the customs of their group upon the presiding judges. From this beginning, in a process extending over several centuries through judges increasingly appreciative of the growing importance of the merchants of the Commonwealth and through a continuous custom making, adapted to changing conditions, by that merchant class, came the law merchant. The unremitting activity of the merchant class, the willingness of the judges to absorb pressures from below, and ultimately a judicial sifting of these merchant customs and the selective acceptance of some of them finally resulted in the incorporation of the law merchant in the common law. The basic mechanism by which this was accomplished was the expansion of the meaning of *property* from the mere physical object to embrace the incorporeal and the intangible forms.

By 1924, Commons had worked beyond the traditional conception of exchange through an exhaustive analysis of social relations. The concept of social action had been broken out of its framework in classical economics and conceived in a wider social framework and expanded to include customary actions in addition to rational ones.

The concept of "transaction" increasingly came into central focus in Commons's thought and found expression in his *Institutional Economics* (1934). Transactions were distinguished into three types in terms of the kind of issue and social relations involved: bargaining, rationing, and managing. Commons' analysis of rationing transactions was a pioneer work, which showed the fundamental differences in social organization implied by the adoption of price and production rationing in the place of the usual (market) bargaining relations. With the outbreak of the war and the neces-

sity for curbing the exercise of individual choices and bargaining through a system of rationing, Commons's analyses were of value for the administration of price controls. (Again this type of analysis is directly paralleled by those of Max Weber.)

In his last book, *The Economics of Collective Action,* all the essentials of Commons's theory of social action are assembled. His very definition of the field parallels Weber's. "The early nineteenth century economists patterned their work upon the materialistic sciences of physics and chemistry, instead of on a volitional science of the human will as developed by the courts."[14] Paralleling the emphasis on subjectively intended meaning is Commons' emphasis on will:

> The human will is the "will in action." Whether one is earning a living, getting rich, or avoiding a loss, one is always confronted with alternatives in every choice of action taken. It is not merely a choice between one act, or direction, and another; it is a choice between alternative objects, and also a choice as to degrees of power or control exerted in the alternative actually chosen in the performance. . . .[15]

The degrees of power or control in individual action are reckoned by the courts in terms of performance, forbearance, and avoidance. The kinds of collective action may be conceived in terms of the types of pressure, influence, or sanctions that may be used: moral power, economic power, or physical power. A church, for example, exercises moral power. A labor union exercises economic power. Political bodies like a state attempt to monopolize the exercise of legitimate physical force (sovereignty). The tie between the various forms of power is found in the fact that the sanctions of sovereignty establish property.

Commons operated with a typology of transactions which partly paralleled Weber's typology of social action. Three types of transactions were distinguished. Besides voluntary exchange of physical

[14]Commons, *The Economics of Collective Action*, p. 36.
[15]*Ibid.*, p. 43.

commodities by individuals, there are *rationing* transactions by the "policy-makers" of the organization (boards of directors of corporations or similar directors of labor unions and administrative political governments) in laying down working rules; *managerial* transactions between superiors and inferiors (mainly wage earners and salary earners in the production of wealth); and *bargaining* transactions on the markets, transferring ownerships of corporeal property and the new kinds of incorporeal and intangible property of bonds and stocks of corporations.

A transaction for Commons is a two-sided relation of wills, or joint action, which issues in an agreed upon performance to be executed according to working rules. Commons's concept of institutions is parallel to Weber's notion of relation. An institution is collective action in control, liberation, and expansion of individual action. Moreover, one need not and should not reify organization. The point of gravity lies in transactions and working rules, in the problems of organization, and in the way collective action becomes organized into going concerns. Such forms of collective action are not something different from what people do. The organization of activity is simply the more stabilized aspect of activity. The form is a part of the process. Such an institution as the "state" is simply "the collective action of politicians." In fact there are three predominant kinds of collective action in the twentieth century — "corporations, labor unions, and political parties." Their interplay creates the destiny of modern humanity. They are manifest in units or "going concerns," which perform the same function in Commons's thought as "corporate groups" did in Weber's.

This summary of Commons's ideas hardly gives a full idea of his great sociological relevance. *The Legal Foundations of Capitalism* is a brilliant major contribution to the sociology of law. His studies of the immigrant and labor are major substantive studies of their kind. The full richness of his theory has only been suggested. It is perhaps unfortunate that Commons has been classed as an institutional economist rather than a sociologist and

thus been insulated from full influence on American sociology.

Robert M. MacIver. Robert Morrison MacIver (1882–1970), one of the foremost contemporary social-action theorists in America, was born in Stornoway, Scotland. He was educated at the Nicholson Institution of Stornoway and attended Edinburgh University, receiving his M.A. in 1903, his D. Phil. in 1915. In 1907 he became lecturer in political science in Aberdeen University and in 1915 was made professor of political science at the University of Toronto. During World War I he was vice-chairman of the Dominion of Canada Labor Board. He taught at Barnard College in 1927 and became a member of the Columbia University faculty in 1929, where he remained until his retirement in 1950. He was a Fellow of the American Philosophical Society, a Trustee of the Russell Sage Foundation, and has been President of the American Sociological Society.

As early as 1917, in *Community*, MacIver had developed the main essentials of his position.[16] He consciously perceived his affinities with the social behaviorists. His only real disagreement with Gabriel Tarde and E. A. Ross was that he thought they defined "social facts" too broadly. MacIver's own definition centers in interhuman acts in which conscious willing is present. *"Whenever living beings enter into, or maintain willed relations with one another, there society exists.* All such willed relations are the primary social facts, and their consequences are secondary social facts. . . . Society is present *in a greater or less degree"* wherever such conscious willing is found.[17]

Social facts consist in the relation of wills to one another. Social facts are grouped into two great

---

[16]Robert M. MacIver, *Community: A Sociological Study* was first published in 1917 (London: Macmillan), and was subsequently printed in 1920, 1924, 1927, 1928 (first American edition), 1931, and 1936; the references here are to Macmillan's English edition of 1927. The other two books of interest in the present discussion are: *Society: A Textbook of Sociology* (New York: Farrar & Rinehart, 1937) and *Social Causation* (Boston: Ginn, 1942).

[17]MacIver, *Community*, p. 4.

ROBERT MACIVER

The Columbiana Collection, Columbia University

classes: social relations, which represent interaction of wills; and social institutions, which are the general forms of such relations. Sociology as a science is devoted to the discovery of the laws holding between social facts (wills in interrelation). Social laws are a unique kind within the cosmos. The laws of the inanimate world state invariable concomitance or sequence while the laws of living facts are unstable, relative, and changeable. The keynote to the vital is its teleological nature. Among the properties of life is its urge to increase in knowledge of itself. The teleological law becomes clearer as life develops. The task of sociology is "the discovery and formulation of the laws we have called free — as well as of those secondary laws which reveal the immediate interrelations of men's purposes."[18]

[18]*Ibid.,* p. 21.

MacIver is very critical of the value of statistics for social research. Such statistics as totals, averages, and ratios are not social facts to MacIver's mind; to be of any use to sociological analysis, they must be interpreted. In their zeal for measurement, he thinks, some sociologists tend to overlook the fact that measurement touches only certain quantitative aspects of things. The most vital of sociological data we can often rate and grade but hardly quantify. MacIver's own method has consisted in imaginative reconstruction, a form of comparative method.

In *Community,* largely following Tönnies' distinction between *Gemeinschaft* and *Gesellschaft,* MacIver was primarily concerned with developing the contrast between community as a complete system of social life based on territory and *associations* which promote specific interests. In *Society* (1937), he examined the concept of social structure in some detail, with particular attention to norms. Various social institutions such as the family, the community, social class and caste, ethnic groups, crowds, and political associations were analyzed in detail. Throughout, MacIver was particularly interested in developing his analysis from the standpoint of the fundamental role of subjective interpretation in social life. The degree to which the conceptions of "wills in relationship" and "forms of relation" are preserved may be seen from MacIver's own table of social structure, shown on the following page.

MacIver brought the theoretical core of his social-action theory to its fullest precision in *Social Causation* (1942), where he maintains that the fundamental task of all science is to determine causes. This is as true for social as for physical science. However, he argues, there are a number of distinct levels of causal analysis and two types of noncausal analysis. He distinguishes the problems posed by these different levels of analysis as modes of the question "Why?":

(1) The Why of invariant order is directed to the physical nexus. It represents universal causality.
(2) The Why of organic function is directed to the biological nexus and represents the causality of organic being.

Schematic View of the Social Structure*

A Groupings or Organizations (persons in relationships)	B Forms or Systems (modes or conditions of interpersonal relations)
I. *Inclusive territorial unities* Generic type: *Community* Specific types: Tribe Nation Neighborhood Village City	I. *Folkways and mores* Specific types: Custom Ceremony Ritual Creed Fashion
II. *Interest-conscious unities without definite organization* Generic type (a): *Social class* Specific types: Caste Elite Competitive class Corporate class Generic type (b): *Crowd* Specific types: Like-interest crowd Common-interest crowd	II. *Institutions* Generic type (a): Established *conditions* of social relations Example: Property Generic type (b): Established *modes* of social relations Example: Marriage Specific types under (a) and (b): Political Economic Religious Familial Educational *Note.* Types under B-I and B-II need not be mutually exclusive.
III. *Interest-conscious unities with definite organization* Generic type: *Association* Specific type (a): *Primary group* Varieties: Family Play group Club Specific type (b): *Large-scale association* Varieties: State Church Economic corporation, etc.	III. *Functional systems* Generic type (a): *Institutional complex* Generic type (b): *Interest complex* *Note.* Under III-b we include the two great orders of *culture* and *civilization*. These should be regarded not as parts but as foundations of the social structure.

*From R. M. MacIver, *Society: A Textbook of Sociology* (New York: Farrar & Rinehart, 1937), p. 144.

(3) The Why of psychological behavior is directed to the psychological nexus and represents the causality of conscious being.

(4) The Why of social conjecture is directed to the social nexus and also forms a part of the causality of conscious being.

(5) The Why of inference is a non-causal type, directed to the logical nexus.

(6) The Why of obligation is also of a non-causal nexus, directed to normative nexes.[19]

The task for a scientist is to identify, first, the proper causal mode. Next, "we identify the situation or type of situation in which the phenomenon occurs, as against a comparable situation or type of situation from which it is absent, and engage ourselves to discover how the phenomenon is related to the differential organizations of the situation containing it."[20]

Scientific study has two major steps: identifying the causal level of the phenomenon in question, and instituting comparative study. The first task, the identification of level, occurs for sociology when we recognize the "teleological aspects of social phenomena." There is, MacIver observes, a school of social scientists who refuse to admit that there are significant differences of subject matter characteristic of the social sciences. There are other scientists who recognize the differences between physical and social subject matter but who deny that such differences require differential methods or approaches. To such scientists, the lack of exact quantification in the social sciences seems evidence solely of their backwardness. But, MacIver insists, we as human beings are immersed in the strivings, purposes, and goals that constitute the peculiar dynamics of this area of reality. The chain of social causation "needs mind for its existence." There is no point in applying to social systems the causal formula of classical mechanics. "On the other hand we have the advantage that some of the factors . . . in social causation . . . *understandable as causes,* are validated as causal by our own experience."[21]

Once the identification of causal level has been completed we are ready for the verification process. In social affairs we have only very limited power of experimentation. We are compelled to resort to comparison of cases and particularly the device of imaginative reconstruction. In our everyday relations we apply it continually in the assessment of the behavior of our fellows. In fact, we could hardly carry on any kind of human existence, and we certainly could not enter into effective relations with others, if we did not reconstruct, from overt but often subtle evidences, the hidden system of thoughts, attitudes, desires, motivations that lie behind them.

The task of the sociologist is to establish causal laws in the "realm of conscious being" — not an easy task. In this realm, the sociologist encounters every type of law. The nexus of invariant law is everywhere. So, too, is the nexus of organic life. Within human organic life, the nexus of consciousness is manifest and within that the social. "Consequently, when the social scientist pursues *his x* to its specific causal nexus, he is embarrassed by the discovery that his causal factors belong to all the diverse orders of being." In a series of emergent levels of reality sociologists find their special problem. "Always we are confronted with diverse factors that belong to different dynamic orders and are incomparable and scientifically intractable as such."[22]

Thus, while sociology is concerned with the psychological and social realms, which emerge out of the biological and physical, the latter continue to have causal effects on sociological events. Within the general psychological nexus, three subforms of psychological nexus must be distinguished: objective, motivation, and design. In psychological activity, according to MacIver, we encounter for the first time the relation of means and ends, the emergence into consciousness of the relation of

[19]MacIver, *Social Causation,* paraphrased from pp. 12–23.

[20]*Ibid.,* p. 251.

[21]*Ibid.,* pp. 263–264.

[22]*Ibid.,* p. 270.

organs and functions. As this realm of activity becomes socially articulated, two interdependent systems of order become distinct — the system of apparatus or means, and the system of values or ends. These are designated as the technological order and the cultural order. The social order itself is the scheme of relationships between social beings.

All these orders, systems and realms form the factors selectively unified in the processes of individual and group behavior. In every conscious act they enter into "dynamic conjuncture." Their unity in experience is provided by some conscious decision, with or without calculation, representing a "dynamic assessment of a situation."

All conscious behavior presents a twofold process of selective organization. On the one hand, the value system of individuals, their active cultural complex, their personalities, are focused in a particular direction, toward a particular goal. On the other hand, certain aspects of external reality are selectively related to the controlling valuation. From mere externals, human values may transform elements of external reality into instruments.

The social facts of interest to sociologists are those arising out of the individual and collective dynamic assessments. These give rise to events of three main types: (1) *distributive* phenomena, directly expressive of like or converging assessments of a number of people as they issue in separate activities of a like nature, and constituting an aggregate or ratio of the same order, such as a crime rate or opinion trend; (2) *collective* phenomena, directly expressing convergent assessments of a number of people, and issuing in conjoint action, such as legal enactments or organizational policy; (3) *conjunctural* phenomena, arising from variant assessments and activities of interdependent individuals and groups, and resulting in unpurposed results such as the business cycle, or the capitalistic system.

Thus, for MacIver, every social fact represents a product, directly or indirectly, of individual meanings and decisions. The components of a social fact represent all those phenomena from the diverse spheres and realms of being which are fused by the meaning or dynamic assessment in

the particular case. In MacIver's own formulation, a conscious action develops a dynamic relation of particularized aspects of various systems. These comprise:

1. A set of objectives (including conscious drives) arising within a particular cultural complex and finding particular expression in the process of dynamic assessment.
2. A set of techniques, derived from the apparatus of civilization, and applied to the specific objectives.
3. A set of social relations, organized conformably to the particular objectives and constituting an agency if not a goal of action.
4. A set of biophysical conditions relevant to the particular action.[23]

How closely MacIver's scheme of social-action theory follows those of other representatives hardly needs to be pointed out. Like Commons, Weber, and Veblen, MacIver is concerned with meaningful action. "Dynamic assessments" are like Commons' acts of will" or Weber's "subjectively intended meaning." Even MacIver's "imaginative reconstruction" parallels Weber's discussion of the "ideal type." Like Weber, MacIver also made basic contributions to political sociology.

SUMMARY

Social-action theory was the third significant branch of social behaviorism. It arose in Germany as a parallel response to the forces which led to pluralistic behaviorism in France (which spread and developed further in North America) and to symbolic interactionism in North America. The founder of social-action theory was Max Weber.

Weber attempted to synthesize the twin traditions of neo-Kantianism and neo-idealism. He defined his subject matter in ways bearing similarities to Dilthey, but maintained the scientific character of the science with Rickert. Weber avoided a purely formal definition of the subject

---

[23]*Ibid.*, condensed from pp. 330–331.

matter of sociology. At the same time, he retained the strong nominalistic epistemology and liberalism of the neo-Kantians.

"Meaningful social action" was the ultimate object matter of sociology, according to Weber. A typology of rational, evaluative, affectional, and traditional types of action was proposed for social analysis. Relations were isolated as the patterns that may be discerned in recurrent actions. They formed the transitional concept to social structure. A social structure at bottom consists only of a complex pattern of social relations. Social structures are formed into various kinds and integrated in communities. A pattern of social relations stabilized in the individual life is a "calling," the parallel concept in Weber's theories to "role" in symbolic interactionism.

In North America a number of developments, largely independent of Weber, among social scientists describing themselves as "institutional economists" parallel the social-action theories of Weber. The two most important examples are Veblen and Commons. Veblen advanced the concepts of *conspicuous consumption* and *the instinct of*

workmanship, which operated in a manner parallel to Weber's typology. Commons' theory of "transactions," in terms of which he analyzed economic, political, and administrative behavior, was even closer to Weber. A parallelism in other respects appears in the fact that Commons, like Weber, was led toward the development of a sociology of law, a brilliant example of which was *The Legal Foundations of Capitalism*.

However, American developments of social-action theory were by no means confined to economists who had studied abroad. MacIver broke with positivistic organicism to establish sociology on a liberal and neo-idealistic foundation. Numerous comparisons to Weber's sociology appear throughout MacIver's works. In his most theoretical book, *Social Causation,* the definition of sociology as the study of "individual and collective dynamic assessments" is similar to Weber's "meaningful social actions." Even the method of imaginative reconstruction proposed by MacIver for comparative study is similar to Weber's use of ideal types. Finally, like Weber, MacIver went on to develop a political sociology.

XVIII

Further Developments in Social-Action Theory

Social-action theory has not yet had any decisive historians. Perhaps when they appear they will explain the unusually fitful character of its development. One of the reasons for this irregular development may be the fact that for so many years Max Weber operated outside the universities as an independent scholar. Apparently the existence of an established plant and the constant meeting of teacher and student are an almost irreplaceable element in the continuity of a school. The generation of scholars trained by a single teacher may serve to transmit the ideas of a school and preserve them until their properties can be explored. A significant contribution is made to the continuity of a school even by those individuals who do not particularly advance it, but who form a context against which new developments can responsibly emerge.

The establishment of a tradition in considerable measure based upon Max Weber was under way in the work of Karl Mannheim during the days of the Weimar Republic, but it was cut short by the rise of Nazism and Mannheim's emigration to England.

The precipitous events leading up to World War II shifted Mannheim's interests to the problem of saving Western civilization from the forces he thought would destroy it.

Meanwhile, only gradually in the 1930s (through the work of Talcott Parsons) and more rapidly since World War II (largely through the work of Mannheim's former students) has Max Weber been generally introduced to American sociology. The development of social-action theory continues to have an erratic career.

Karl Mannheim. Karl Mannheim (1893–1947) was born of a Hungarian father and a German mother. He studied at Budapest, Freiburg, Paris, and Heidelberg. He was strongly influenced by Marxism (Karl Marx and György Lukács), neo-Kantianism (having taken courses with Heinrich Rickert), phenomenology (he was familiar with Max Scheler and a student of Edmund Husserl), and finally Max Weber, who more than anyone else provided him with his basic integrating framework. Mannheim, in fact, was the primary

KARL MANNHEIM

Courtesy of Mrs. Julia Pilisansky and the London School of Economics and Political Science

intellectual heir of the Max Weber tradition in Germany under the Weimar Republic, and was in the process of developing one of the fullest statements ever made of a sociology of knowledge, as indicated by *Ideology and Utopia* (1929) and his article, "Wissenssoziologie" (1931),[1] when the political events of 1933 forced him into English exile, where he became a professor at the University of London. He now turned his talents to the diagnosis and solution of the problems of European social history. His views appear in *Man and Society in an Age of Reconstruction* (1940) and *Diagnosis of Our Time* (1943). Devoted students have since got

out the incompleted fragments of his earlier works.[2]

While Mannheim's immersion in social-action theory was profound, the only part of that theory that he worked into a unified new form was its sociology of knowledge. His original contributions developed on the basis of social-action theory. His rejection of all "organismic," "conflict," and "formal" definitions of social reality locates him in the category of social behaviorism. With Weber, he conceived society as a network of meaningful individual acts. Also with Weber, he worked with polar concepts of traditionalism and rationality, analyzing the composition of inter-individual actions. With the Marxians, Mannheim was convinced that class-based actions are among the most significant in modern times. With Weber and partly opposed to the Marxians, he was not willing to conceive the ideas associated with class-based actions as merely epiphenomenal, as a kind of superstructure. Mannheim was familiar with Weber's study of the role of the Protestant ethic on the rise of capitalism; the kind of relation it presupposed between ideas and social structures was also basic to his own interpretations.

For Mannheim, knowledge has the function of adapting human beings to their environment. But because the environment is not always the same, knowledge cannot be expected to be the same or always to operate in quite the same way. Mann-

---

[1] In Alfred Vierkandt, ed., *Handwörterbuch der Soziologie* (Stuttgart: F. Enke, 1931), pp. 659–680.

[2] Mannheim's chief works are: *Ideology and Utopia* (New York: Harcourt, Brace, 1936), trans. Louis Wirth and Edward Shils from *Ideologie und Utopie* (Bonn: F. Cohen, 1929), "Wissensoziologie," *loc. cit.*, and a special introduction by Mannheim; *Man and Society in an Age of Reconstruction* (New York: Harcourt, Brace, 1940), trans. Edward A. Shils from *Mensch und Gesellschaft in Zeitalter des Umbaus* (Leiden: A. W. Sijthoff, 1935); *Diagnosis of Our Time* (New York: Oxford University Press, 1944); *Freedom, Power, and Democratic Planning* (New York: Oxford University Press, 1950); *Essays on the Sociology of Knowledge*, ed. Paul Kecskemeti (New York: Oxford University Press, 1952); *Essays on Sociology and Social Psychology*, ed. Paul Kecskemeti (New York: Oxford University Press, 1953); and *Essays on the Sociology of Culture*, ed. Ernest Manheim and Paul Kecskemeti (New York: Oxford University Press, 1956).

heim takes as established the fact that the social environment of the modern individual is organized into various classes. The most important aspect of history is the competition for political and economic power by the various classes. As an adaptive instrument, knowledge is class organized.

The treatment of knowledge as class-based perspectives raises two critical problems: is knowledge true? is it merely relative? Mannheim was of the view that there is one type of theoretical knowledge which rests on the criteria of science, and hence has nothing to do with class perspective. This knowledge, however, is special and limited. All the rest of our knowledge (popular, traditional, religious, philosophical, and qualitatively scientific) is class-based, having purely practical validity.

Since the great bulk of human knowledge is class-based, it must be relative to its particular perspective. Apparently it can never claim general validity. But Mannheim was not willing to go this far. There could, he argued, be a genuine qualitative knowledge of social affairs which was of general validity. He called his position "relationism" rather than relativism. He maintained that unanimity and the broader point of view represented by intellectuals coming from different social strata made true knowledge possible. His critics, however, have been unconvinced, pointing out that if all knowledge is true only for a perspective, then unanimity itself will make no difference. Moreover, a perspective that synthesizes other perspectives merely multiplies the alternatives. The truth is no synthesis of lies. Mannheim's perspectivism, if consistent, applies also to his own views, making them true only for a perspective as well. His relationism degenerates into a relativism after all.

While there are theoretical problems unsolved in Mannheim's formulation, there is no doubt about the skill with which he isolated and characterized the ideological perspectives of some of the major political and economic classes of modern history. Tracing ideological analysis to Marx, Mannheim went beyond Marx in drawing a distinction between two major types of ideology. An ideology is a set of ideas that function in the promotion and defense of interests. It is akin to fiction or perhaps to what Marx called "false consciousness" — a state of mind which falsifies everything coming within its sphere. Such sets of ideas either defend patterns of interest strategically placed in the given social order, in which case they are "ideologies," or they promote the interests of underprivileged groups of the given society and locate their social objectives in the future, in which case they are "utopias." Four major examples of utopian mentality were developed by Mannheim in *Ideology and Utopia:* (1) the orgiastic chiliasm of the Anabaptists, (2) the liberal-humanitarian idea, (3) the conservative idea, and (4) the socialist-communist utopia.

(1) At the threshold of modern times, among the Hussites, the followers of Thomas Münzer, and the Anabaptists, the ferment of change was manifest. Among these oppressed peasant strata of medieval society, the dream of a new and better world took the form of "chiliasm," the belief that the millennium was at hand. This belief rose to great intensity, leading to predictions of a second coming of Christ and the intense expectation of the immediate advent of the millennial kingdom. Some of these groups prophesied the actual date, and their members sold their holdings for anything they could get, purchased ascension robes, and walked out into the hills in prayer, awaiting the appointed hour. The peculiar properties of the chiliastic mentality, according to Mannheim, lie in this kind of detachment of social aspiration from both past and future, leading to the heightened ecstatic anticipation of social and personal self-realization in the immediate present.

(2) The liberal-humanitarian idea is the utopia of the modern bourgeoisie. In contrast to the chiliast, the liberal does not sever all relationships with historical existence. His positive acceptance of culture gives the liberal an ethical approach to human affairs. The liberal conception of unilinear progress has two sources. One source is Western capitalism. The bourgeois ideal of reason was intended to bridge the gap between the imperfection of things as they occurred in a state of nature and the requirements of reason. The other source of

the idea of progress is found in German pietism. The ebbing away of chiliasm left in its stead a mood of waiting and anticipation. In all these respects, the liberal-humanitarian idea is the utopia of the rising bourgeois stratum of modern times.

(3) While the liberal always tends toward theorizing, the conservative does not. The conservative mentality is a structure in harmony with a reality which it has temporarily mastered. It does not reflect on the historical process. The conservative mentality comes to consciousness only when goaded by opposing theories; it discovers its idea ex post facto. The original conservative social classes, in fact, did not succeed in developing a theoretical interpretation of their position. This interpretation was achieved by a body of ideologists who attached themselves to the conservatives. These are represented, for Mannheim, by the conservative romantics, particularly Hegel. Hegel set up a conservative counterpart to the liberal idea. To the conservatives, the liberal ideas of the Enlightenment were something vaporous, mere opinion. Conservatism was presented as resting on no merely formal norms but as manifest in the concrete content of the prevailing laws of the state. In the objectification of culture, art, and science, spirituality unfolds itself and the idea expresses itself in tangible fullness.

(4) The anchorage of the socialist-communist utopia was neither in the dispossessed peasants, the rising liberal members of the bourgeoisie, nor the power elite, but in the proletarian groups of modern society. Their utopia took form, in the first instance, in the attempt to radicalize the liberal idea or to overcome anarchism in a most extreme form. Its conservative antagonist was considered only secondarily; communism fights revisionism more energetically than it fights conservatism. As it took shape, it increasingly envisioned the possibility of pitched battles that would sweep away the structure of existing society, followed by a withering away of the state and a new classless social order.

Scattered throughout Mannheim's writings, there were many rich additional observations on these and other ideological formations.

It has been noted that the advent of national socialism and World War II shifted Mannheim's attention away from the systematic development of such ideas to the diagnosis of the crises of our civilization and their cure. In the course of this practical reflection, some of his theories of social change and social structure were brought partly into order.[3] Mannheim increasingly visualized the problem of our age as that of finding a workable solution to social life between the extremes of a planless *laissez-faire* democracy and the totalitarian organization of society. History, he thought, has displayed three kinds of order. "Three essential historical stages can be distinguished here: (1) man at the stage of horde solidarity, (2) man at the stage of individual competition, (3) man at the stage of super-individual group solidarity."[4]

The task of bringing order into the social world eventually falls, according to Mannheim, on the society's elites. Modern democratic-liberal societies, on the other hand, are still in the second historical stage. "Cultural life in modern, liberal mass-society is rule mainly by the laws peculiar to an unregulated social order, whereas in a dictatorially governed mass society it is the institutions which have the greatest influence on social life."[5] The most critical question, then, is what is happening to the elites of democratic society. "We may distinguish the following main types of elites: the political, the organizing, the intellectual, the artistic, the moral, and the religious."[6] It was Mannheim's thesis that the crisis of liberal-democratic society is due to the presence of forces tending to destroy both the reality and the prestige of elite groups. These forces are: (1) the growing number of elite groups and the consequent diminution of their power, (2) the destruction of the exclusiveness of the elite groups, (3) the change in the principle of selection of these elites, and (4) the change

[3]See particularly *Man and Society in an Age of Reconstruction, Diagnosis of Our Time,* and *Freedom, Power, and Democratic Planning.*
[4]*Man and Society in an Age of Reconstruction,* p. 68.
[5]*Ibid.,* p. 81.
[6]*Ibid.,* pp. 82–83.

in the internal composition of the elites. The fundamental task is to rally the elite groups and achieve a planned social order while avoiding the negative values both of *laissez-faire* anarchism and dictatorial absolutism. Planning, Mannheim seems to agree with Weber, means among other things the extension of rational bureaucratic organization to new areas of life. However, such an extension presents a danger, for once the work of passive democratization by bureaucracy is carried through, the possibility of absolutism is at hand. "But this can only happen if there is no power greater than bureaucracy, for the problem of the democratic constitution of a planned society mainly consists in avoiding bureaucratic absolutism."[7] There were times when Max Weber had envisioned the future of Western civilization in terms of an increased tension between charisma and bureaucratization. There are more than echoes of the Weber position in Mannheim's final theory of social structure and change.

FELLOW TRAVELERS

There is little doubt about the imaginative challenge contained in social-action theory. It is perhaps not surprising, for this reason, that a number of the major contemporary sociologists worked for a time as fellow travelers with social-action theory before moving on toward a new theory of their own. At least three of them made contributions to social-action theory before leaving it. They deserve discussion in the present chapter, even though the full discussion of their work remains for later chapters. These are Florian Znaniecki, Talcott Parsons, and Robert K. Merton.

Florian Znaniecki. Florian Znaniecki (1882–1958) was born to a well-to-do Polish family in Russian-dominated territory. After being dismissed from the University of Warsaw for his active support of

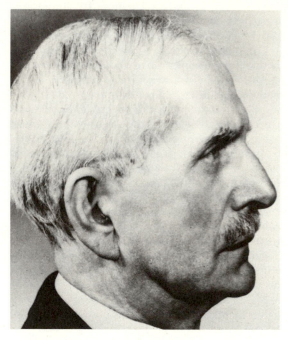

FLORIAN ZNANIECKI

Courtesy of Mrs. Florian Znaniecki

Polish nationalism, he went abroad to study at the University of Geneva (1905) and from there to Zurich and the Sorbonne, finally completing his Ph.D. at the University of Cracow in 1910. Between 1910 and 1914, while at work helping Poles to migrate, he became acquainted with W. I. Thomas, and he was invited to join Thomas at the University of Chicago in 1914, where the famous collaboration on *The Polish Peasant* began. Znaniecki taught at Columbia University (1916–1917) and Chicago (1917–1919). In 1920 he became professor of philosophy at the new University of Poznań after Poland received her independence. He was instrumental in getting sociology established in the university and he founded the Polish Institute of Sociology. In 1929 he established a Polish sociological review. He remained at

Poznan until 1939. With the outbreak of World War II and conquest of Poland, he was invited to America once again to teach at Columbia University. In 1941 he became professor of sociology at the University of Illinois, where he remained until his retirement in 1951. He was president of the American Sociological Society in 1955.

Znaniecki has already been treated in connection with *The Polish Peasant*.[8] Znaniecki's work on this great classic made him a contributor to the development of the symbolic-interactionist branch of social behaviorism. Znaniecki also contributed something to social-action theory, though his eventual theoretical significance lies elsewhere.

With other members of the social-action school, Znaniecki finds that social and cultural data possess a special property. "This essential character of cultural data we call the *humanistic coefficient,* because such data, as objects of the student's theoretic reflection, already belong to somebody else's active experience and are such as this active experience makes them."[9] Not only does Znaniecki define the field by something corresponding to Commons' "act of will," Weber's "meaning," and MacIver's "dynamic assessment," but he argues at one period that the smallest units into which social material may be analyzed are social actions.[10] Eventually Znaniecki was to drop social actions as the primary units for the analysis of social and cultural life, with the result that his later work belongs to another branch of sociological theory. But in his earlier work, he developed a unique analysis of the elements of social action.

The objects of social action are "values"—meaningful objects with a partly sensory, partly spiritual character. These values have a positive or negative axiological significance. Most values are organized into cultural systems and constructed and maintained by active tendencies. Such tendencies are empirically determinable by the values achieved. When not active, a tendency is potential — it is an "attitude." Action breaks down into: (1) the humanistic coefficient (meanings), (2) primary social values or the social object (people), (3) secondary social values (things), (4) the method, and (5) the social result or reaction. The method makes use of social instruments, the means utilized by the social agent to influence the object. The social method as a whole is the manner in which the social instrument is utilized. The social reaction is the action of the social object, which may not coincide with the intentions of the agent. To illustrate these concepts, let us say that a father believes he ought to discipline his son for some misbehavior — experimenting with cigarettes, for example. These ideas are the humanistic coefficient. The father is the social agent. The son is the primary social value or social object. The various objects and rewards made available by the social relation between father and son are secondary social values. The father's social method of disciplining his son could consist, for instance, in the use of his hand as a social instrument for the application of force to the seat of his son's pants, or it could be the exercise of his power not to grant the son's allowance until he perceived the error of his ways. The social reaction is the change brought about in the son's behavior.

Znaniecki's contribution to social-action theory is more important than this relatively conventional analysis (of social action into ideas, means, ends, and other persons) would suggest. In a manner quite in the spirit of Weber, Znaniecki suggested in his analysis of the component elements of vocations that one of the most fruitful approaches to the problems of the sociology of knowledge is the examination of the social role of the person of knowledge. According to Znaniecki, individual specialization in any kind of cultural activity is socially conditioned. The concept of social role was

---

[8] In addition to *The Polish Peasant,* which has already been discussed in Chapter XV, Znaniecki's important works include: *The Laws of Social Psychology* (Chicago: University of Chicago Press, 1925) ; *The Method of Sociology* (New York: Farrar & Rinehart, 1934); *Social Actions* (New York: Farrar & Rinehart, 1936); *The Social Role of the Man of Knowledge* (New York: Columbia University Press, 1940); and *Cultural Sciences: Their Origin and Development* (Urbana, Ill.: University of Illinois Press, 1952).
[9] Znaniecki, *The Method of Sociology,* p. 37.
[10] Znaniecki, *Social Actions* (1936), Chapter 1, and particularly pp. 33 ff.

developed to designate this kind of phenomenon. A social role assumes the existence of a complex of values between the person performing the role, the social person, and others in the social circle. The person is an object of positive value to his or her circle. The person is conceived as an organic and psychosocial entity or "self." He or she is the kind of person the circle needs if he or she has the qualities required by the role. In the social circle, the person has a status, role-based rights, and social functions related to the role requirements.

So long as the average knowledge of the ordinary person is adequate to social requirements, the intellectual role does not emerge as a specialized one. But even in the primitive world, the technically excellent person tended to be consulted in times of difficulty. In addition to the technical expert in general social matters, one of the earliest advisors was the priest, who was supposed to possess direct or indirect control over the magico-religious forces of the community. His role was perhaps more differentiated in primitive circles than the technical advisor, who — like Odysseus — might be old and traveled.

The role of technological advisors may be specialized in terms of theoretical and practical requirements. Their task is that of diagnosis. When diagnosis of the problem has been made, the problem remains of carrying out a plan. The technological specialists in diagnosis and planning foreshadow the role of the scientist. Regardless of how they achieve their position (inheritance, election, appointment, force), they can maintain it only so long as their diagnosis and plan are attended by success.

In modern times, there has been continuous evolution of the social role of the technological expert. It has been separated from the role of the technological leader, who makes the decisions about practical applications. A phase of the work of experts may be technological experiment. They may even be expected to invent alternatives to the patterns of action or advancement of the leader's plan. (Modern captains of industry maintain laboratories for such purpose). A specifically modern

development is the emergence of independent inventors (becoming a recognizable role only in the second half of the nineteenth century). Their role is a lonely one. They are often destined to be laughed at and have their visions viewed as curiosities.

The other types of intellectual roles trace ultimately back to that of the priest. Further evolution of the priestly role leads to the sages, the intellectual leaders of the conservative order. They are thought to be wiser than others. Their function is to rationalize the tendencies of their party, to prove by scientific arguments its rightness. Beginnings of differentiation in the role of the cultural person of knowledge lead to the appearance of the social technologist. Machiavelli's *The Prince* is perhaps the first consistent work in pure cultural technology.

On a tribal level, there are two possible origins of sacred schools: secret associations and individual medicine men (shamans, wizards, magicians). The invention of writing to transmit sacred and secret knowledge was probably the work of such schools, where it served the interests of training in sacred ritual. The lore of such schools is usually claimed to be derived from a divine source; it is knowledge about divine or mysterious things and is usually concerned with description of a sacred text.

The social role of religious scholars is performed within the sacred school, where their task is to perpetuate the sacred law. The secularization of schools and scholars develops out of conflicts and internal schisms which are due to contacts and rivalry with outside sacred schools. A distinction between sacred and secular truth comes to be made. Sacred schools must either isolate themselves or adopt secular criteria of truth. The second process was important in the rise of the Western universities. Theological faculties, on the other hand, isolated themselves.

The rivalry between schools casts significance on fighters for truth who are interested in the logical victory for the system in which they believe. Znaniecki explains the scholar's low estimation of empirical evidence on historical grounds. Empirical evidence was appealed to for thousands of years as a criterion of truth before secular scholarship developed. The tendency to discredit empirical evidence was a phase of the creation of the standard of rational evidence. Scholars prepared the way for a scientific standardization of empirical data as materials for inductive theory. Among additional types, specialists in eclectic and historical knowledge appear, rejected by all schools because of their failure to adapt their inner evaluations to the school's requirements but valued because they provide materials for the busy fighters for truth.

In this manner Znaniecki added to the growing body of studies of specific roles, a project required by the dynamic development of all branches of social behaviorism.

Talcott Parsons. Talcott Parsons (1902–1979) is another of those persons whose work belongs in part to social-action theory. Parsons graduated from Amherst College in 1924 and studied under Hobhouse, Ginsberg, and Malinowski at the London School of Economics (1924–1925). He spent one year at Heidelberg University (1925–1926). After a year of teaching at Amherst College, he received his doctorate from Heidelberg University in 1927. From 1927 to 1931, Parsons taught in the economics department at Harvard University. In 1931, he began to teach in sociology, and became professor of sociology in 1944. In 1946, he chaired the new Department of Social Relations. In 1949 he was president of the American Sociological Society. Parsons continued to work after retirement from Harvard until his death from a stroke in Munich on May 8, 1979.

It will be necessary to examine the more important phase of Parsons' theoretical work in another connection, but for a time, it is clear, he was under the influence of social-action theory. Parsons' Ph.D. thesis was based in part on the work of Max Weber. In his translation of *The Protestant Ethic*, he did much to introduce Max Weber's sociology to the American audience. Parsons' first

TALCOTT PARSONS

Courtesy of *The Harvard Crimson*, Cambridge, Mass.

book, *The Structure of Social Action*, rested on social-action theory.[11] It was only later that he

[11] Parsons' major works include: *The Structure of Social Action* (New York: McGraw-Hill, 1937; Glencoe, Ill.: The Free Press, 1949); *Essays in Sociological Theory, Pure and Applied* (Glencoe, Ill.: The Free Press, 1949; rev. ed., 1954); *The Social System* (Glencoe, Ill.: The Free Press, 1951); *Toward a General Theory of Action*, with Edward A. Shils and others (Cambridge, Mass.: Harvard University Press, 1951); *Working Papers in the Theory of Action*, with Robert F. Bales and Edward A. Shils (Glencoe, Ill.: The Free Press, 1953); *Family, Socialization and Interaction Process*, with Robert F. Bales and others (Glencoe, Ill.: The Free Press, 1955); and *Economy and Society*, with Neil J. Smelser (Glencoe, Ill.: The Free Press, 1956); *Theories of Society* (2 vols.), co-edited with Edward Shils, Kaspar D. Naegle, and Jesse R. Pitts (New York: The Free Press, 1961); *Social Structure and Personality* (New York: The

changed his theoretical approach. In his preface, Parsons had made his intentions quite clear: he intended "a study in social *theory,* not *theories.*" His aim was to present "a *single* body of systematic theoretical reasoning the development of which can be traced through a critical analysis of the writings of this group [the selected persons considered in the study] . . . they have all, in different respects, made important contributions to this single coherent body of theory. . . . This body of theory, the 'theory of social action' is not simply a group of concepts with their logical interrelations. It is a theory of empirical science the concepts of which refer to something beyond themselves."[12]

Part I of Parsons' study was a presentation of what Parsons describes as the "positivistic theory of action." The entire work was conceived in polemical opposition to positivism. The principle features of the positivistic theory of action as listed by Parsons are: (1) the emphasis upon rationality; (2) the identification of rationality with the procedures of modern science; (3) the analysis of elements in terms of an "atomism" of unit acts (that is, the treatment of unit acts as the atoms or analytical units of social events); (4) the treatment of ends (goals of action) as given and as if they varied randomly in relation to the actor; (5) the treatment of irrationality as a lack of knowledge. The entire burden of Parsons' argument is to develop the "voluntaristic theory of social action," which corrects the limitations of the positivistic theory of action. Parsons' procedure is to conduct an elaborate

critique of several social thinkers in order to show that various concepts emerged in their systems which, when synthesized, form the "voluntaristic theory." Part II of his study is described as "the emergence of a voluntaristic theory of action from the positivistic tradition"; here Parsons analyzes some features of the work of Alfred Marshall, Vilfredo Pareto, and Émile Durkheim. Part III of the study examines "the emergence of a voluntaristic theory of action from the idealistic tradition," and consists primarily in an analysis of some features of the thought of Max Weber. In Part IV, Parsons brings the "voluntaristic theory of action" together.

According to Parsons, the starting point for the modern theory of action was the idea of the intrinsic rationality of action. This concept supposed that action consists of "ends," "means," and "conditions." Rationality of action consisted in a scientifically determinable relation of means to the conditions of the situation. Parsons maintains that two positivistic positions (a rationalistic and antirationalistic) tended to alter the place of rationality in action. The one erased the distinction between ends, means, and conditions of action making it a process of adaptation to the situation. The other tradition of positivism eliminated rationality altogether.

Parsons maintains that Marshall took a step away from the positivistic theories of actions by refusing to accept the independence of wants. Moreover, he refused to accept the idea that the concrete actions of economic life are solely explainable as means to the satisfaction of wants — they are also exercises of faculties helping in the development of character. Pareto's contribution to voluntarism, according to Parsons, centers in his introduction of the concepts of "residues" and "nonlogical action." Pareto proved that ultimate ends of action belong to a nonlogical category and that logical action is intermediate to them. Moreover, Parsons insists, Pareto proved that values are not exhausted by the kinds classical economics could accept. Durkheim's contribution is conceived to be the presentation of a fuller understanding of the nonnatural normative element of

---

Free Press, 1964); *Societies: Evolutionary and Comparative Perspectives* (Englewood Cliffs, N.J.: Prentice-Hall, 1966); *Sociological Theory and Modern Society* (New York: The Free Press, 1967); *American Sociology* (New York: Basic Books, 1968); *Politics and Social Structure* (New York: The Free Press, 1969); *The System of Modern Societies* (Englewood Cliffs, N.J.: Prentice-Hall, 1971); *The American University*, coauthored with Gerald M. Platt and in collaboration with Neil J. Smelser (Cambridge, Mass.: Harvard University Press, 1973); *Social Systems and the Evolution of Action Theory* (New York: The Free Press, 1977); *Action Theory and the Human Condition* (New York: The Free Press, 1979).

[12]Parsons, *The Structure of Social Action*, p. v.

action. The decisive step in Durkheim's analysis was the distinction of social constraint from naturalistic causation. The social milieu constitutes a set of conditions beyond the control of a given concrete individual, but not beyond the control of human agency in general. In fact, from this point of view its most conspicuous aspect turns out to be a system of normative rules backed by sanctions. Finally, Max Weber was seen as giving full appreciation to the value element of action in that he advanced a theory of the role of value elements in the form of a combination of religious interests in their relation to systems of metaphysical ideas.[13] Weber's ghost must have winced at this.

Parsons' general argument was that these four writers, taken together, have managed to discover the main elements for a new theory of action. When these are synthesized, the result is a new departure in theory. "This generalized system of theoretical categories common to the writers here treated is, taken as a total system, a *new* development of theory and is not simply taken over from the traditions on which they built."[14]

The elements for this new generalized system of action are four in number: (1) heredity and environment, as the ultimate conditions of action; (2) means and ends; (3) ultimate values; and (4) zeal or "effort" — the "name for the relating factor between the normative and the conditional elements of action."[15] The product of this laborious analysis, covering over seven hundred pages on Pareto, Durkheim, Marshall, and Weber, bears a close similarity to the findings of another great Western thinker in search of science:

> We have stated, then, what is the nature of the science we are searching for, and what is the mark which our search and our whole investigation must reach.
>
> Evidently we have to acquire knowledge of the original causes (for we say we know each thing only when we think we recognize its first cause), and causes are spoken of in four senses. In one of these we mean

the substance, i.e., the essence (for the "why" is reducible finally to the definition, and the ultimate "why" is a cause and principle); in another the matter or substratum, in a third the source of the change, and in the fourth the cause opposed to this, the purpose and the good (for this is the end of all generation and change).[16]

If it were not for the independent value of the review of such basic thinkers as Durkheim, Pareto, Marshall, and Weber, it could well be questioned whether it is worth seven hundred pages of turgid analysis to discover Aristotle's doctrine of the four causes.

Despite consorting with organicists like Durkheim and Pareto at this stage, Parsons genuinely belongs in the social-action school. He accepts the idea that the ultimate units of social life are meaningful social actions. He even accepts Weber's nominalism (rejecting it later), when he agrees that structures are "as if" entities, representing economies of analysis.

With tremendous daring, Parsons argues that the value of this system may be demonstrated by the fact that it makes analytical laws in sociology possible. In fact, he urges, there already exists one such law of wide scope and great importance:

> The law may be tentatively formulated as follows: "In any concrete system of action a process of change so far as it is at all explicable in terms of those elements of action formulated in terms of the intrinsic means-ends relationship can proceed only in the direction of approach toward the realization of the rational norms conceived as binding on the actors in the system." That is, more briefly, such a process of action can proceed only in the direction of an increase in the value of the property of rationality.[17]

This analytical law discovered by action theory is comparable, according to Parsons, to the second law of thermodynamics.

Parsons seems to be saying that the fundamental law of sociology discovered by social-action

[13]*Ibid.*, p. 715.
[14]*Ibid.*, p. 720.
[15]*Ibid.*, p. 719.

[16]Aristotle, *Metaphysics,* Book I, Sec. 3.
[17]Parsons, *The Structure of Social Action,* p. 751.

theory is a tautology — at least the statement that "so far as it is at all explicable" in terms of the action scheme, the action "can proceed only in the direction of approach toward the realization of rational norms," seems to say that the more rational an action becomes the more understandable it is. If it was Parsons' intention with delicate irony to take this method of telling us that all laws to which social-action theory can aspire are tautologies, one would have to agree that sociology is indeed intrinsically different from physical science. But some uncertainty is caused by Parsons' further suggestion that the law of rational tendencies in social action is like the second law of thermodynamics. This would mean that all social actions move in fact in the direction of increasing rationality. In this second interpretation of the "law of rationalization," one would have to agree, again, that sociology is a special kind of science: one which formulates empirically false generalizations as laws.

But these uncertainties arise, perhaps, because Parsons, while beginning his career in action theory, was on his way to other things. His concern with Durkheim and Pareto is symptomatic, for they are not social-action theorists at all but two types of organismic positivists. The minor ambiguities that have been found in Parsons' formulation of social-action theory are not important in themselves but for what they signify — a deep dissatisfaction with social-action theory.

Robert K. Merton. Among the recent sociological theorists whose work belongs in part to social-action theory is Robert Merton (1910–   ). Merton was born in Philadelphia and received his A.B. at Temple University in 1931. His M.A. and Ph.D. were taken at Harvard University (1932, 1936). He began his teaching career as assistant in sociology at Harvard in 1934 and became instructor in 1936. In 1939 he went to Tulane as associate professor and served as professor and chaired the department in 1940 and 1941. Since 1941 he has been on the faculty of Columbia University, becoming associate professor in 1944, and full professor in 1947. He has been Associate Director of the

The Columbiana Collection, Columbia University

Bureau of Applied Social Research and has been President of the American Sociological Society.

Merton's original affinities with social-action theory appear in his first book, *Science, Technology and Society in Seventeenth Century England.*[18] In this and a series of related articles, reprinted in *Social Theory and Social Structure,* Merton implicitly accepted the social-action framework from Weber and continued along the lines of analysis set down

[18]Published as Vol. 4, Pt. 2 of *Osiris,* "Studies in the History and Philosophy of Science" (Bruges [Belgium]: The Saint Catherine Press, 1938). Major works of Merton's are: *Mass Persuasion,* with the assistance of Marjorie Fiske and Alberta Curtis (New York: Harper, 1946); *Social Theory and Social Structure* (Glencoe, Ill.: The Free Press, 1949; rev. ed., 1957); and *Continuities in Social Research,* with Paul F. Lazarsfeld and others (Glencoe, Ill.: The Free Press, 1950).

by Weber in *The Protestant Ethic and the Spirit of Capitalism.*

Weber had developed hypotheses concerning the relation between early ascetic Protestantism and capitalism and had suggested that this same ascetic Protestantism helped motivate and canalize the activities of people in the direction of experimental science. Merton set out to examine and verify the hypothesis. The general argument and mode of verification is typified by Merton's own statement that even a cursory examination of the writings of members of the British Royal Society discloses that certain elements of the Protestant ethic had pervaded the realm of scientific endeavour and had left their indelible stamp upon the attitudes of scientists toward their work. Discussions of the why and wherefore of science were found to bear a point-to-point correlation with the Puritan teachings on the same subject. Religion was not, and perhaps could not be, compartmentalized and delimited. Thus, in Boyle's highly commended apologia for science, *Some Considerations Touching the Usefulness of Experimental Natural Philosophy* (1664), it is maintained that the study of nature is to the greater glory of God and the good of humanity. This motif recurs constantly. The juxtaposition of the spiritual and the material is characteristic. The culture rested securely on a substratum of utilitarian norms which constituted the measuring rod of the desirability of various activities. The definition of action designed for the greater glory of God was tenuous and vague, but utilitarian standards could easily be applied. The spirit of seventeenth-century English science was traced to the Protestant ethic.

That Merton has been receptive to other branches of social behaviorism as well as the social-action branch may be seen by his interpretation of W. I. Thomas's "definition of the situation" as a "self-fulfilling prophecy."[19] Thomas, following William James and Charles Peirce, had noted that ideas, even if false (like magic), still have conse-

quences for action. In Thomas's formulation, "definitions of the situation" became basic facts of social actions. Merton's reconceptualization of "definitions of the situation" as self-fulfilling prophecies shows his receptivity to the idea. As a stable financial structure, a bank rests on interlocking definitions of the situation. But if the depositors define the situation otherwise and start a run on the bank, they are in danger of producing the very result they fear — the failure of the bank. The self-fulfilling prophecy is a false definition of the situation evoking a new behavior which makes the originally false conception come true. Such self-fulfilling prophecies go far toward explaining race and ethnic conflict: for example, blacks are often excluded from the unions on the grounds that they are strike breakers, forcing them to become strike breakers to get jobs. The principle operates throughout social life.

Still other positive responses by Merton to one or another branch of social behaviorism are shown by his interest in various social roles, such as the technical expert, adviser, and bureaucrat, and by his attempt to expand the conception of the "generalized other" of Mead into the concept of a "reference group" — that group which individuals take as the basis for their own comparative self-judgments and which may be not at all equivalent to the group in which they actually find themselves. "Reference group" is to "generalized other" what "self-fulfilling prophecy" is to "definition of the situation."

However, despite such obviously close ties with social behaviorism, Merton feels that his own most progressive and original theory belongs to the development of functionalism. Serious discussion of Merton must be postponed for that context.

NEW RECRUITS

It is an interesting fact which invites explanation that, while some of the most able of the older generation of sociologists who began their careers in social-action theory have abandoned the posi-

[19]Merton, *Social Theory and Social Structure* (1949 edition), p. 179.

tion, the generation of theorists now coming into their prime numbers some extremely vigorous exponents of the theory. They have not developed or tried to develop well-rounded social-action theories, but have carried out unusually penetrating criticisms of American society in social-action terms.

William H. Whyte, Jr. William H. Whyte, Jr. (1917–   ) is a social scientist by avocation rather than vocation. A graduate of Princeton (1939), he worked for a time for the Vick Chemical Company (1939–1941). He was a writer for *Fortune* magazine (1946–1951), and since 1951 one of its editors. In 1952 he published *Is Anybody Listening?*, a collection of articles on communication. In 1953 he won the Benjamin Franklin Award for the best magazine article on United States life. The study of importance here is *The Organization Man.*[20]

The Organization Man is a study of the ideology, the social ethos, of the new middle class, the corporation men, the junior executives, the doctor headed for the corporate clinic, the physics Ph.D. in a government laboratory, the intellectual on a foundation-sponsored team project, the engineering graduate in the huge drafting room, the young apprentice in a Wall Street law factory. These strata form the first and second echelons of social and institutional leadership in American society. Their values form the central point of references for the values of America.

[20]William H. Whyte, *The Organization Man* (New York: Simon and Schuster, 1956). William H. Whyte's *Is Anybody Listening? How and Why United States Business Fumbles When It Talks to Human Beings* (New York: Simon and Schuster, 1952) also rested on social action presuppositions. In the 1960s Whyte began to shift his interests to problems of ecology and urban planning. His basic assumptions as to the nature of social life remain the same and his movement into these areas indicates the flexibility of this form of social theory. Among major studies by Whyte are *Cluster Development* (New York: American Conservation Association, 1964); *The Last Landscape* (Garden City, N.Y.: Doubleday, 1962); and *Open Space Action. Report to the Outdoor Recreation Resources Review Commission* (Washington, D.C.: U.S. Government Printing Office, 1962).

WILLIAM H. WHYTE, JR.

Photo by Bernard Newman. Courtesy of William H. Whyte, Jr.

The problems studied by Whyte were brought into focus by social-action theorists. It was Weber who opened up both the study of the bearing of the Protestant ethic on the development of capitalism and the modern trend toward bureaucratic rationalization of almost every area of life. The single most significant trend in America, Whyte feels, is the development of big organization both in politics (the civil service corporation) and in business (the large corporation). Emerging from them is a managerial hierarchy that may dominate the whole of American life. Historically, on the other hand, we are a people who adhere to the Protestant ethic. Our ethical heritage is in tension with the realities of the present. More than any other people, Americans have publicly worshipped individualism. The observation of how basic this individualism is to the nature of American life extends back to de Tocqueville over a hundred years ago.

The norms of the corporation are described by Whyte as a social ethic, a contemporary body of thought making morally legitimate the pressures of society against the individual — pressures which violate every aspect of individuality in the older sense. Its major propositions are reduced by Whyte to three: the belief that the group is a source of creativity, the belief in belongingness as the ultimate need of the individual, and a faith in the application of science to achieve this belongingness. As Whyte sums this up:

> Man exists as a unit of society. Of himself, he is isolated, meaningless; only as he collaborates with others does he become worth while, for by sublimating himself in the group, he helps produce a whole which is greater than the sum of its parts. There should be, then, no conflict between man and society. What we think are conflicts are misunderstandings, breakdowns in communication. By applying the methods of science to human relations we can eliminate these obstacles to consensus and create an equilibrium in which society's needs and the needs of the individual are one and the same.[21]

This, Whyte observes, is a utopian faith. It coincides with none of the types of mentality outlined by Mannheim. The social ethic as described by Whyte is a new kind of conservatism unique to modern people.

The decline of the Protestant ethic and the rise of the triad of ideas — scientism, belongingness, and togetherness — are the crucial ideas in terms of which Whyte traces the social history of the typical member of the new middle class: his training, his very neuroses, the new methods of personality testing, the bureaucratization of the scientist, his image in fiction, and his life in New Suburbia (the organization man's home).

The Organization Man is one of the outstanding books of contemporary social science.

[21]Whyte, *The Organization Man*, p. 7.

DAVID RIESMAN

Courtesy Harvard University News Office

David Riesman. A second penetrating critic of modern American society belonging primarily in the social-action school is David Riesman (1909–   ). He took his A.B. degree at Harvard in 1931, becoming a law clerk to Justice Brandeis after graduation (1935–1936). He was professor of law at the University of Buffalo from 1937 to 1942, and deputy assistant district attorney of the New York Court. During World War II he worked with the Sperry Gyroscope Company, afterward becoming professor of social sciences first at the University of Chicago and since 1958 at Harvard.

There is no evidence that Riesman had very extensive acquaintance with Max Weber. He was, however, quite familiar with people strongly influenced by Weber, such as Erich Fromm. From such students, Riesman took over a number of concepts central to social-action theory and transformed them into tools for the analysis of American society and character. The best of these studies are *The Lonely Crowd* and *Faces in the Crowd*.[22]

Weber had analyzed social acts into rational, evaluative, affective, and traditionalistic. He had suggested that both character structure and social structure are capable of analysis on the basis of this typology. He even indicated that a given type of action may predominate in a single role (or calling) or in a personality. In the study of *The Protestant Ethic and the Spirit of Capitalism,* Weber had demonstrated the unusual place played by evaluative social actions derived from Protestantism, both in personalities and in social change. The socioreligious ends of typical Protestants force a peculiar rationalism on life, together with personal responsibility for their own social and economic destinies. The inner-worldly asceticism of such persons was important both to the rise of capitalism (Weber) and the rise of science (Merton).

Unfamiliarity with the full range of social-action theory occasionally leads Riesman to some rather bizarre hypotheses, such as the derivation of personality structures resting on an inner-worldly asceticism (Riesman's "inner-directed" personalities)

from population growth. "The society of transitional population growth develops in its typical members a social character whose conformity is insured by their tendency to acquire early in life an internalized set of goals. These I shall term *inner-directed* people and the society in which they live *a society dependent on inner-direction.*"[23] It is hard to say whether this is worse as sociology or demography. The two other types of personality (also derived from population) are *tradition-directed* and *other-directed*.[24]

In a "tradition-directed" society (Tönnies' *Gemeinschaft*), social change is minimal. Conformity is assured by inculcating the young with automatic obedience to tradition in a role defined from birth. Obedience is taught by the clan, age, and sex group.

In an "inner-directed" society, a new pattern of conformity resting on internalized controls appears. The parent is in control rather than the extended family. The inner-directed type of person has special attitudes toward work, the self, leisure, and history. The concept of inner-direction is central to goals such as wealth, fame, goodness, and achievement. This is a personality driven by the Protestant ethic.

The "other-directed" personality is a cause and consequence of contemporary industrial society and the rise of the new middle class. There is a preoccupation with consumption rather than production, a concern for the "human factor" in productive spheres, a weakening of parental control over children, and a new set of attitudes toward work, consumption, sex, politics, and the self. Interpersonal relations loom large, for the point of social control lies outside rather than inside the individual.

Tradition-direction is a primitive condition, appropriate to Redfield's "folk society." The important part of Riesman's typology is equivalent to the contrast introduced by Whyte between the Protestant ethic and the social ethic. In fact, their aims

---

[22]*The Lonely Crowd* was written by Riesman in collaboration with Reuel Denney and Nathan Glazer (New Haven, Conn.: Yale University Press, 1950); *Faces in the Crowd* was written in collaboration with Nathan Glazer (New Haven, Conn.: Yale University Press, 1952). Other works of Riesman's are: *Thorstein Veblen: A Critical Interpretation* (New York: Scribner's, 1953); *Individualism Reconsidered and Other Essays* (Glencoe, Ill.: The Free Press, 1954); and *Constraint and Variety in American Education* (Lincoln, Neb.: University of Nebraska Press, 1956). Typical of his extension of the social-action perspective to a wide range of problems in higher education are various of Riesman's works with other scholars: with Joseph Gusfield and Zelda Gamson, *Academic Values and Mass Education* (Garden City, N.Y.: Doubleday, 1970); with Vere A. Stadtman, *Academic Transformation* (New York: McGraw-Hill, 1973); with Seymour Martin Lipset, *Education and Politics at Harvard* (New York: McGraw Hill, 1975); with Christopher Jencks, *The Academic Revolution* (Chicago: The University of Chicago Press, 1977); and with Gerald Grant, *The Perpetual Dream* (Chicago: The University of Chicago Press, 1978).

[23]Riesman, *The Lonely Crowd,* p. 9.
[24]For a compact discussion of these types, see *Faces in the Crowd*, pp. 5–6.

are identical — the critical examination of contemporary American society and culture. However, while Whyte carries out a controlled study of the organization man proper, the point of gravity in Riesman's analysis is in general middle-class institutions, leisure patterns, and culture.

The inner-directed individuals of the nineteenth century are seen to be on the decline. Their places are being taken by other-directed individuals. This change affects all basic institutions. For example, the parental role changes with the shift from bringing up children to "bringing up father." Similarly, the roles of teacher and of peer group are transformed.

The entire problem may be epitomized, according to Riesman, in the altered meaning and function of leisure. Inner-directed people pursued their hobbies by themselves and used their leisure as a phase of their own personality development. Other-directed people have far greater leisure at their disposal, but find themselves trapped in a lonely crowd of others like themselves, desperately trying to have fun. Parallel changes are found in every area of middle-class American life. The political individualist disappears, being replaced by the team of policy writers and the opinion poll. The newspapers and magazines are no longer the stages of the rugged individualist, but run on the basis of anonymous findings of market research. Even work, the field of salvation proper for the old inner-directed types, becomes confounded with leisure, while leisure has become arduous.

While Riesman has used only relatively superficial features of social-action theory, there is no doubt about the imagination with which middle-class American social life and culture are integrated in terms of his typology of societal and personality types.

C. Wright Mills. Although Whyte and Riesman are not primarily sociologists, the new recruits to social-action theory are not confined to non-sociologists. C. Wright Mills was well trained in the Max Weber tradition in the course of his work with Hans Gerth, and his contribution, in collaboration with Gerth, to symbolic interactionism has already

been discussed. In the books to be considered here—*White Collar* and *The Power Elite*—Mills's use of social-action theory represents a more or less direct extension of the theories of Max Weber.[25]

White Collar is an attack on the same problems as *Organization Man* and *The Lonely Crowd*. However, it does not approach these problems from the standpoint of the composition, structure, and inner motivations of the crucial social roles or from the standpoint of typical personality structure and leisure patterns. Mills's study is more traditionally sociological. He attacks the issues by way of class analysis. In a burning satirical style, reminiscent of Veblen, Mills traces the contours of that mindless monster, the new middle class. Even if the middle class has a history, it is a "history without events; whatever common interests they have do not lead to unity; whatever future they have will not be of their own making."[26]

Compared to the old hierarchies, the new white collar pyramids are youthful and feminine bureaucracies, freshly scrubbed like a Lux-girl picture of the American way of life. These white-collar masses, however, are managed by people more like the old middle classes with their independence and spirit of free enterprise. In phrases reminiscent of Weber's essay on bureaucracy, Mills describes the situation of the new white-collar persons. They follow clearly defined lines of authority, all related to the purpose of the enterprise. Their power is located in the office. All relations within the enterprise are impersonal, formal, and hierarchical. Expectations are calculated and enforced by governing rules and explicit sanctions. Appointment is by examination and on the basis of trained competence. They are vocationally secure,

[25] Works by Mills which have not been previously noted (see Footnote 65, Chapter XV; and Footnote 1, Chapter XVII) are: *The New Men of Power*, with the assistance of Helen Schneider (New York: Harcourt, Brace, 1948); *The Puerto Rican Journey* (New York: Harper, 1950); *White Collar* (New York: Oxford University Press, 1951); *The Power Elite* (New York: Oxford University Press, 1956); and *The Sociological Imagination* (New York: Oxford University Press, 1959).

[26] Mills, *White Collar*, p. ix.

with life tenure and regularized promotion schemes.

The phenomena that create these automatons — industrialism, corporateness, and bureaucracy — also, according to Mills, penetrate the old social classes. Even the formerly free professions yield to the process, as illustrated by the doctor, lawyer, and professor, whom Mills describes in scathing stereotypes. Once through medical school, the young doctors face the hospital, which they find contains departments, hierarchies, and grades. The main qualification comes to be "personality" — adaptability to the organization. And if the doctor as medical bureaucrat appears as the prototype of modernity, the lawyer is no better off. Young graduate lawyers face bureaucratic incorporation in a law factory. Their best hope is to become businesspersons and proprietors in their own right. They may also then "become the . . . general manager of a factory of law, with forty lawyers trained by Harvard, Yale, Columbia, and two hundred clerks, secretaries, and investigators to assist him."[27] Most lawyers will never make it. And as for the modern professor, Mills's scorn is boundless. The professionalization of knowledge has narrowed the grasp of the individual professor. In fact, "like the pharmacist who sells packaged drugs with more authority than the ordinary storekeeper, the professor sells packaged knowledge with better effect than the layman. He brings to the market the prestige of his university position. . . . This halo of disinterestedness has more than once been turned to the interests of companies who purchase the professor's knowledge and the name of his university."[28] Throughout, Mills sees the victory of "the technician over the intellectual."[29]

All this might seem to be enough to drive promising young men and women out of the professions were it not for the fact that Mills's contempt is even greater for other middle-class types, such as sales personnel. "Salesgirls in large de-partment stores of big cities often attempt to borrow prestige from customers, but in the big store of strangers, the attempt often fails, and, in fact, sometimes boomerangs into a feeling of powerless depression. The hatred of customers . . . is one result."[30]

America itself becomes a great salesroom. "The personality market, the most decisive effect and symptom of the great salesroom, underlies the all-pervasive distrust and self-alienation so characteristic of metropolitan people. . . . Men are estranged from one another as each secretly tries to make an instrument of the other, and in time a full circle is made: one makes an instrument of himself, and is estranged from it also."[31]

In Kafka-like terms Mills sums up his conception of the white collar worker as like an item in an enormous file. Smaller hierarchies fit into larger ones. A formal order is expressed by titles expressing diminishing gradations of status and rank. Personal life and leisure are distorted by the vain attempt to rid one's self of the tensions this mindless existence generates. "Urban masses look forward to vacations not 'just for the change,' and not only for a 'rest'. . . . on vacation one can *buy* the feeling, even if only for a short time, of higher status."[32] In fact, "like those natives who starve until whales are tossed upon the beach, and then gorge, white-collar workers may suffer long privation of status until the month-end or year-end, and then splurge in an orgy of prestige gratification and consumption."[33]

Concentrating, as it does, only selectively upon some of the middle classes (for example, the clergy is never mentioned) and then concentrating only upon the negative and extreme aspects of middle-class roles, *White Collar* creates a kind of Frankenstein monster. However, the aim of *White Collar* seems to have been more to satirize and caricature than to develop an objective sociological picture. As one middle-class position after another is sav-

[27]*Ibid.*, p. 123.
[28]*Ibid.*, p. 133.
[29]*Ibid.*, p. 10.

[30]*Ibid.*, p. 173.
[31]*Ibid.*, pp. 187–188.
[32]*Ibid.*, p. 257.
[33]*Ibid.*, p. 258.

agely run through, no positive social value is seen in any middle-class role.

The limitations of *White Collar* make of *The Power Elite* an essentially greater book, though for some reason the reviews were more negative.

In his analysis of political institutions, Weber developed his theory of class, status group, and political party. Political parties, Weber had indicated, live in a house of power. They represent the association of those whose common ultimate aspiration is to gain and hold power. The operation of this objective may lead to the cutting of all other lines of association, be they class, status, ethnic association, or any of a plurality of institutional anchorages.

It is Mills's thesis that at the top of the structure of American society there is a "power elite . . . composed of men whose positions enable them to transcend the ordinary environments of ordinary men."[34] They are the persons in command of the major hierarchies and organizations: the big corporations, the state, the military establishment. Major national power, Mills asserts, now lies in the economic, political, and military domain. The economy, once scattered in small productive units, is now "dominated by two or three hundred giant corporations, administratively and politically interrelated, which together hold the keys to economic decisions."[35] The political order has become a centralized executive establishment, and the military order has become the largest and most expensive feature of government, which, "although well versed in smiling public relations, now has all the grim and clumsy efficiency of a sprawling bureaucratic domain."[36]

There is, Mills observes, a tendency for the consolidation of both the power and prestige of the power elite:

. . . one feature of these hierarchies of corporation, state, and military establishment is that their top positions are increasingly interchangeable. One result of

this is the accumulative nature of prestige. Claims for prestige, for example, may be initially based on military roles, then expressed in and augmented by an educational institution run by corporate executives, and cashed in, finally, in the political order, where, for General Eisenhower and those he represents, power and prestige finally meet at the very peak.[37]

According to Mills, the power elite grows at the expense of the destruction of local society and its strata. It is more and more completely represented by the metropolitan "four hundred." And even the metropolitan four hundred changes in composition, assuming the cheap tinsel brilliance of the world of the professional celebrity. "Both the metropolitan 400 and the institutional elite must now compete with and borrow prestige from these professionals in the world of the celebrity."[38] The professional celebrity (male or female) is a product of the star system. Ironically, they are celebrated because they are displayed as celebrities. The star of the silver screen has displaced the golden debutante.

The corporate rich, the war lords, the political directorate, all are at the top of a mass society, which they manipulate by advertising and propaganda. The *public* is transformed into a *mass* which, for Mills, means that (1) fewer people express opinions than receive them, (2) communications are so organized that the individual receiving opinions is unable to answer back immediately with any effect, (3) opinion is controlled by the authorities who dominate the channels of communication, (4) the mass has no institutions for developing autonomous opinions. "In a mass society, the dominant type of communication is the formal media, and the publics become mere *media markets*: all those exposed to the contents of given mass media."[39]

Meanwhile, the power elite at the top are characterized by a peculiar moral ethos. "The higher immorality is a systematic feature of the American

[34]Mills, *The Power Elite*, p. 3.
[35]*Ibid.*, p. 7.
[36]*Ibid.*

[37]*Ibid.*, p. 10.
[38]*Ibid.*, p. 71.
[39]*Ibid.*, p. 304.

elite; its general acceptance is an essential feature of the mass society."[40] This involves a weakening of older values and an organization of irresponsibility. The higher circles in America today contain, on the one hand, the laughing, erotic, dazzling glamor of the professional celebrity, and on the other, the prestige aura of power, authority, might, and wealth. "These two pinnacles are not unrelated. . . . The professionals, in the main, are either glossy little animals or frivolous clowns; the men of power, in the main, rarely seem to be models of representative men. . . . America — a conservative country without any conservative ideology — appears now before the world a naked and arbitrary power, as, in the name of realism, its men of decision enforce their often crackpot definitions upon world reality. The second-rate mind is in command of the ponderously spoken platitude."[41]

Whether at bottom the entire social world — or perhaps only the United States — is only pure, cold, expedient, moral-less, cynical, and ruthless power, as Mills seems to indicate, is open to question, but the signal service performed by him in posing once again the central significance of the problem of the sociology of power is not to be denied. This is true, even though — as in *White Collar* — *The Power Elite* substitutes deeply etched caricatures for objective analysis. Despite its apparently overdrawn concept of a conspiracy at the top, *The Power Elite* is one of the most significant studies of our time.

EXPANSION AND CONSOLIDATION OF SOCIAL-ACTION THEORY

Two thinkers who showed considerable potential for expanding the social-action point of view at the time of the first edition of *Nature and Types* were Hans Gerth and C. Wright Mills. Neither made any further contribution to this branch of theory;

[40]*Ibid.*, p. 343.
[41]*Ibid.*, p. 360.

Gerth's attention was absorbed with other things until his death in 1978 and Mills's interest shifted to semipolitical pamphleteering and an increasing interest in a form of left-wing romanticism with Marxist overtones until his untimely death in 1962. Meanwhile, however, other persons were working in this branch of theory to expand and consolidate it throughout the 1960s and 1970s.

H. Stuart Hughes. Henry Stuart Hughes, who was born in New York City in 1916, received the A.B. from Amherst College in 1937, and earned the M.A. at Harvard in 1938, the Ph.D. in 1940. He taught history at Brown University before enlisting in the army as a private in 1941. By 1944 he was Chief of the Research and Analysis Branch of the Office of Strategic Services in the Mediterranean Theater. He was relieved from active duty as a Lieutenant Colonel in 1946 and became Chief of the State Department's Division of Research for Europe from 1946 to 1948. He joined Harvard as an assistant professor in 1948. After serving as associate professor from 1952 to 1955 at Stanford, he became professor and head of the history department there for one year. He then returned to Harvard as a professor from 1957 to 1975. Since 1975 he has been professor of history at the University of California, San Diego.[42]

According to Hughes, the essence of history is change, which must, at least in part, be a result of conscious mental activity. Somewhere, somehow, sometime, someone must have decided to do something new or cease from doing something that had been done for most human changes to occur. Any discussion about vast impersonal forces

[42]H. Stuart Hughes' major writings included *An Essay for Your Times* (New York: Knopf, 1950); *Oswald Spengler: A Critical Estimate* (New York: Scribner's, 1952); *The United States and Italy* (Cambridge, Mass.: Harvard University Press, 1953); *Consciousness and Society* (New York: Knopf, 1958); *Contemporary Europe: A History* (Englewood Cliffs, N.J.: Prentice-Hall, 1961); *An Approach to Peace* (New York: Atheneum, 1962); *History As Art and Science* (New York: Harper & Row, 1964); *The Obstructed Path* (New York: Harper & Row, 1968); *The Sea Change* (New York: Harper & Row, 1975).

H. STUART HUGHES

Courtesy of Harvard University News Office

is an abstraction. Although the outcome of a large number of choices may be statistically predictable, most persons are convinced that in a metaphysical and ethical sense, choice is possible. Hence there is a sense in which Benedetto Croce was right in his insistence that history is necessarily the story of freedom.[43] This, of course, is not to deny that the repetitive, the irrational, and the quasi-instinctual play no role and may not, in fact, be the substratum of history, but they cannot be the subject matter of history itself. And, if one views humanity's conscious ideas and thoughts as mere ideologies or rationalizations of such unconscious forces, as in various ways thinkers like Freud and Pareto were inclined to do, it follows that

rationalizations are the primary subject matter of intellectual history.

There are both dangers and opportunities, however, in intellectual history: the most persistent error is the inclination of historians to write about what they do not understand, that is, what they have not internalized and thought through themselves. However hazardous, historians must seek to understand their materials from the standpoint of their creators. Such a task carries with it the risk that historians will see clear designs in their materials which are, in fact, impositions of their own points of view. At the same time, in resisting doing such violence to their materials, and "descrying an immanent reason in history,"[44] they can easily fall into the converse fallacy of seeing intellectual history as intrinsically irrational.

When intellectual historians can avoid these dangers and concentrate on the objective of characterizing an intellectual milieu or ascertaining the "spirit of the times," they will discover that this is at once the most rewarding and baffling of their tasks. "The discovery of the spirit of the times is at once a technical near-impossibility and the intellectual historian's highest achievement."[45]

Just as ideas are the primary subject matter of history, individuals are the ultimate units of historical study. Ideas, like "trends," "movements," or "currents" of thought are merely human constructions.[46] This elementaristic notion (taking the individual as the basic unit of society and human history) was typical of the eighteenth-century Enlightenment thinkers and Hughes confides, "I still fall most naturally into a 'rationalistic' way of thought." The base line of his study is "the Enlightenment of the eighteenth century. My own position is quite consciously 'eighteenth century.' "[47] However, Hughes also confesses that he has "more than a little tolerance for the intuitive approach — and with it, to a conviction of the deci-

[43]Hughes, *Consciousness and Society,* p. 5.

[44]*Ibid.,* p. 7.
[45]*Ibid.,* p. 8.
[46]*Ibid.,* p. 23.
[47]*Ibid.,* pp. 26, 27.

sive role of spiritual motivations,"[48] and of the insufficience of the merely naturalistic explanation of human conduct.

Consciousness and Society was Hughes's study of transformations in European social thought from 1890 to 1930. In it he took a point of view close to the center of the social-action perspective and examined the body of thought that was shaping the point of view of the governing elites of the Western world.[49] According to Hughes, the major intellectual events in the decade of the 1890s included: a revolt against positivism; the critique of Marxism; the rediscovery of the unconscious, accompanied by the search for a new definition of reality; and the elaboration of neo-idealistic and neo-Machiavellian approaches to society and social history. Hughes saw Max Weber as the great central figure in this development, holding the positivist and idealistic trends together into a provisional balance.

In Hughes's view, the generation of thinkers of the 1890s undertook the accommodation to a new concept of reality, in which something like a return to rationalism occurred. There was a difference, however, for reality could no longer be conceived as rational and forming a coherent whole. The natural world was seen as approachable only through conventional fictions. However, though Vico said society was understandable by human beings directly since it was their artifact, it was no longer sustained by unquestioned myths. The new point of view was epitomized in a quotation from Croce.

> We no longer believe . . . , like the Greeks, in happiness of life on earth; we no longer believe, like the Christians, in happiness in an other-worldly life; we no longer believe, like the optimistic philosophers of the last century, in a happy future for the human race . . . We no longer believe in anything of that, and *what we have alone retained is the consciousness of ourselves, and the need to make that consciousness ever clearer and more evident,* a need for whose satisfaction we turn to science and to art.[50]

The new point of view originated in a revolt against positivism but retained a positivist faith in the procedures of exact science; it revived idealistic thinking but rejected belief in eternal spiritual values. And although it found clearest expression in pragmatism, pragmatism tended to degenerate in practice into mundane instrumentalism. The generation that developed this point of view tried to walk the razor's edge between the errors of rationalism and positivism, on the one hand, and the errors of emotionalism and unreason on the other. Henri Bergson and Georges Sorel eventually succumbed to social mysticism. Freud, after a lifetime of unsophisticated faith in mechanistic thinking, toward the end of his life indulged in unchecked speculation. Croce's old-fashioned conception of reason was eventually surpassed. Only Max Weber, central to the entire generation, held the uneasy synthesis in some kind of tense balance.

> Max Weber had been acutely aware of the danger. In his effort to transcend the positivist-idealist polemic, he had striven for formulations that would keep together the sphere of logic and the sphere of value. In so doing, he alone invariably held to the central understanding of his whole generation. He alone never wavered in his insistence that both reason and illogic were essential to the comprehension of the human world. While reality, he implied, was dominated by unreason, it was only through rational treatment that it could be made comprehensible. Yet Weber's intellectual coherence had been acquired at the price of a psychic tension that was almost too much for the human mind to bear.[51]

[48]*Ibid.,* p. 30.

[49]This type of intellectual history he contrasts to retrospective cultural anthropology, or the study of popular ideas and practices, and a study of the aspirations of ruling minorities and their opponents. It is a type of approach sometimes described as ethico-politico by Croce, whom Hughes follows. *Consciousness and Society,* pp. 10–11.

[50]Hughes, *Consciousness and Society,* pp. 428–429. Quoted from Mario Corsi, *Le origini del pensiero di Benedetto Croce* (Florence, 1951), p. 201.

[51]Hughes, *Consciousness and Society,* p. 431.

In *Consciousness and Society* Hughes not only undertook the history of recent social thought from a social-action point of view, a task that he resumed in *The Sea Change,* but he also established his own version of the attempt to tread the line between science and art, which he applied to his own craft in *History as Art and Science.*

John Kenneth Galbraith. If in H. Stuart Hughes social action-theory has found its major postwar intellectual historian, in John Kenneth Galbraith it has found its major institutional economist-sociologist in the style of such early twentieth-century figures as John R. Commons and Thorstein Veblen.

John Kenneth Galbraith was born in 1908 in Iona Station, Canada, a rural Scottish Canadian colony. In 1932 he graduated with a B.S. from the Ontario Agricultural College, then a branch of the University of Toronto. He studied agricultural economics at the University of California, Berkeley, taught in a branch of the University of California, and completed the Ph.D. in economics in 1934. He taught for a short time at Harvard and from 1934 to 1941 became a peripatetic scholar and researcher in and out of government and academic institutions in the United States and abroad. From 1941 to 1943 he was Deputy Administrator of the Office of Price Administration. In 1943 he joined the editorial board of *Fortune.* In 1949 he returned to Harvard, which became his home base for the rest of his academic career. He served in a number of presidential administrations, was an active campaigner and speech writer for John F. Kennedy, and was appointed Ambassador to India (1961–1963). He worked in the campaigns of Senator Eugene McCarthy and Senator George McGovern, supporting their stand against the war in Asia.[52] As were many other

JOHN KENNETH GALBRAITH

social-action theorists, Galbraith was raised in an atmosphere of ascetic Protestantism, preserving its work discipline and moralistic tone in secular contests. Gambs observed that "none of Calvin's followers ever worked much harder," his tone is "un-

---

[52]Among Galbraith's major books are: *American Capitalism: The Concept of Countervailing Power* (Cambridge, Mass.: Riverside Press, 1952); *A Theory of Price Control* (Cambridge, Mass.: Harvard University Press, 1952); *The Great Crash, 1929* (Boston: Houghton Mifflin, 1955); *The Affluent Society* (Boston: Houghton Mifflin, 1958); *The Liberal Hour* (Boston: Houghton Mifflin,

1960); *The New Industrial State* (Boston: Houghton Mifflin, 1968); *Ambassador's Journal: A Personal Account of the Kennedy Years* (Boston: Houghton Mifflin, 1969); *A Contemporary Guide to Economics, Peace and Laughter* (Boston: Houghton Mifflin, 1971); *Economics and Public Purpose* (Boston: Houghton Mifflin, 1973); *The Age of Uncertainty* (Boston: Houghton Mifflin, 1977). Among books on Galbraith are: Charles H. Hession, *John Kenneth Galbraith and His Critics* (New York: New American Library, 1972); Myron E. Sharpe, *John Kenneth Galbraith and the Lower Economics* (White Plains: International Arts and Science Press, 1973); John S. Gambs, *John Kenneth Galbraith* (Boston: Twayne, 1975).

failingly formal" and when present his righteousness is "like a sledgehammer."[53] However, he is thoroughly urbane, something of a performer, a master of the put-on, a constant individualist, and although confessing to being a liberal democrat and reformer, often speaks of the liberals in the third person—reserving the right to differentiate himself from liberalist myths and illusions. He began his life as an agrarian economist in the midst of the Great Depression which, together with the study of Keynes, Berle, Means, and Veblen early moved him toward heterodox economics. His work as a price administrator in World War II acquainted him firsthand with federal bureaucracies and left him with a lifelong concern over the problem of inflation and the possible role of wage and price fixing in its control. He has had a lifetime of alternating experience in highest governmental and academic circles and is therefore familiar with a large number of contemporary power figures, in contrast to Veblen, who was something of a recluse and with whom he is most often compared.

He is a man with unusual powers of self-expression, with a lucid, ironic, witty, playful style, equally at ease in a world of scholars, bureaucrats, and politicians. Galbraith early began to perfect his skills in testing ideas against experience and experience against ideas, cutting through rationalization and mythology to the core of ideas and events. Gambs reports that he writes constantly, even composing paragraphs in his head while apparently listening to conversations that bore him. Ideas that occur to the ordinary person but slip away or are dismissed, in Galbraith result in an essay, an address, or a letter to the editor. He follows up notions far afield and reads in psychology, history, sociology, and political science. However, though widely read, his scholarship is erratic and superficial. He states that Marshall, Veblen, and Marx have influenced him most in economics, but except for Gardiner Means he makes little reference to the heterodox economists with whom he is aligned. He has confessed to Gambs that he knows

little about John Dewey who "bears approximately the same relationship to holistic economics in the United States as Bentham bore to standard theory."[54] However, Gambs added that Galbraith could have learned his pragmatism vicariously from Veblen, who was a devoted Deweyite.

Galbraith's writing ranges from political satires and romances (like *The McLandress Dimension* and *The Triumph: A Novel of Modern Diplomacy*) through political pamphlets or tracts (*How to Get Out of Vietnam; How to Control the Military; Who Needs the Democrats and What It Takes to Be Needed*) and memoirs and travel books (*The Scotch Ambassador's Journal: A Personal Account of the Kennedy Years; A China Passage*), a work in art history and culture (*Indian Painting* with Randhawa), light pieces in economic history (*The Great Crash, 1929; The Age of Uncertainty*) to his work on economic theory. Although Galbraith himself considers his work on economic theory to be the heart and soul of his intellectual activity, his periodic excursions into areas peripheral to his central interest seem to rest both on temperament and conviction. Economic activity cannot be separated from the rest of life, nor, in the long run, understood without reference to it; the ties between economic and political power are particularly close. He is, unquestionably, the most able working pragmatist in America today, convinced that theory cannot be separated from practice, nor understanding from reform. The range of his writings does not mean that he is a dilettante who disperses his energies: the whole of life is his classroom and the "lessons" must be extracted from all experience. He continually revises and recasts, opening up new areas, arriving at more comprehensive synthesis. Given enough time, Galbraith will unquestionably develop a general theory of social science in much the same manner as he has developed his economic doctrine into a systematic statement of heterodox economic theory.

Capitalism: The Concept of Countervailing Power described the decline of the competitive model of

---

[53]Gambs, *Galbraith*, p. 23.

[54]*Ibid.*, p. 38.

the economy traceable to Adam Smith. In standard economic theory the competitive model has been superseded by the belief in imperfect competition and the conviction that depression can only be remedied by Keynesian remedies. Moreover, Galbraith adds, a new kind of equilibrating force has tended to appear. Whenever unusual power develops in the hands of an economic group, a countervailing force tends to arise to prevent individuals and groups from being wiped out. In *A Theory of Price Control,* appearing in the same year as *American Capitalism* (1952), Galbraith argued that the prices of oligopolies are easiest to control by wage and price regulation; in the more complicated competitive market modest rationing may be necessary. In any case, Keynesian remedies are useless for controlling inflation. *The Great Crash, 1929* (1955) deals with the greed and speculative mania that gripped Americans of all classes in the 1920s and the arrogance and stupidity of politicians, economists, and others in response to it. Galbraith offers the hypothesis that without the crash there might not have been a Great Depression, or at least it might have been far less severe and more easily absorbed. In the same year, 1955, Galbraith published *Economics and the Art of Controversy*, in which he deals with the psychology of economic reform, examining New Deal reforms that were accepted almost without question while others were enduring sources of controversy.

The Affluent Society (1958), which argues that the basic states of technology, capital, and the quality of the population are such as to make a decent level of living potentially available to all, mounts a basic attack on the "conventional wisdom" (that is, rationalizations or ideology) of standard economic theory. When the giant firm assumes control of production, it no longer makes sense to visualize production as responding to wants. Rather, advertising manipulates and manages wants, which leads to the dangers of installment buying and inflation. Moreover, the standard notions of how to curb inflation are inappropriate to the giant firm: fiscal and tax policy is largely irrelevant and the restriction of government spending is mainly a rhetorical

exercise. Contemporary productivity creates unemployment, hence, it makes no sense to condemn those on whom the burden falls. It is time to realize that more and more aspects of work are becoming artistic, scientific, and service-oriented in nature. *The Affluent Society* heralds the creation of a new class. Sociologists following up on Galbraith's suggestions have increasingly spoken of a postindustrial society marked by the expansion of service, professional, and artistic activities. In *The New Industrial State* Galbraith turned full attention to the giant corporation with its "technostructure" — a managing bureaucracy of professional scientists and specialists — and its role in such industrial problems as growth, alienation, bureaucracy, and the military-industrial complex. The giant corporation is argued to be so powerful, with so many resources at its disposal as to render itself immune from the traditional market mechanisms. Furthermore, symbiosis develops between the bureaucracies of government and business. The priorities of the firm determine those of the wider society.

In the preface to *Economics and the Public Purpose*, Galbraith announced his goal to bring the market sector of the economy, and therewith the whole economic system, into focus. In order to do so it would be essential to deal also with the highly organized sector of the economy that he had examined in *The New Industrial State*.[55] He opened his discussion with some old themes: economics (the discipline and standard economic theory) is the ideology of the organized sector of the economy, (the technostructure or planning system) serving the goals of those with power in the system; economics is also a surrogate for reality for legislators, civil servants, television commentators, professional prophets, and the like; in addition, standard economic theory has been rendered irrelevant to actual economic life except as an ideology. However, although this approach establishes continuities with his earlier economic work, to some extent it disguises the degree to which Galbraith

[55]Galbraith, *Economics and the Public Purpose*, p. xiii.

reorganized and extended his point of view. In *Economics and the Public Purpose*, after twenty-five years of criticism and harassment of standard economic theory. Galbraith has, in a brilliant strategic move, ceased to reject it and rather encircled and reduced it to a reasonably adequate interpretation of a subpart of his own explanation of the economic system.

There are, in fact, two economic systems. The giant corporation or planning system has enormous resources, is administered by committees of specialists, controls its own markets (administering prices rather than setting them in response to market forces), reduces its board of directors and stockholders to rubber stamping the decisions of management, secures adequate prophets to quiet its stockholders and creditors, utilizes its own capital in considerable measure for expansion, and has close ties with the bureaucracies of government (in fact, there is considerable migration between the bureaucracies of government and business that is most notorious in the military-industrial complex). The market system, on the other hand, is the contemporary descendent of the preindustrial world of small businesses, entrepreneurs, professions, service workers, and the like. In the United States one thousand manufacturing, merchandizing, transportation, power, and financial corporations produce approximately half of all the goods and services not provided by the state. The two largest industrial corporations, General Motors and Exxon, have combined revenues far exceeding those of California and New York. Making up the rest of the economy are around twelve million smaller firms, including three million farmers whose total sales are less than those of the four largest industrial corporations.[56] And although the market system also departs somewhat from the neo-classical model of the economy (for example, intervention by the state is far more extensive than this model suggests) it does lack control over its markets and displays many of the egalitarian tendencies postulated in the neo-

classical system. To be sure, the market system was modified by the rise of the planning system which, for example, transformed women into cryptoservants confined and subordinated to the household, administering all the new equipment and services required as the traditional servant class vanished. In the process such professions as physicians, priests, schoolmasters, concubines, and prostitutes — once members of the household — arose as independent entrepreneurs in the market system.

Galbraith sees the modern labor union as largely confined to the planning system, though a few minor labor unions appear in the market system. Through the planning system, wage and other benefits won by labor are simply passed on in higher prices to the consumer. Much of the time the technostructure and the labor unions are in symbiotic relationship. By contrast in the market system, the exploitation of labor and self-exploitation are the rule. Where labor unions appear they have quite different results than in the big unions of the planning system.

The two systems even deal with different branches of government: the technostructure normally does its business quietly without fanfare with the bureaucracy; the market system must deal in a blaze of publicity with the weak embattled legislature. Public policy and the policy of the technostructure are usually identical.

Among the new areas Galbraith explored in *Economics and the Public Purpose* are the conversion of women into cryptoservants as a product of the rise of the planning system and the extension of the planning system into the areas of international production and trade via the multinational corporation. Galbraith is convinced that the Marxian analysis of multinational corporate expansion (usually described as imperialism), as a product of the drive for profits occurring primarily in the underdeveloped world, is wrong. He sees it as a natural extension of the technostructure in its drive for survival (control over its resources and its markets) and for growth.

Galbraith locates many of the instabilities of the present economy in the disequilibrium between

[56] Galbraith, *Economics and the Public Purpose*, p. 43.

the planning and the market system. The real source of inflation, the single major economic problem, is the planning system. All traditional policies of inflation control such as reduction of government spending, taxation, and management of fiscal policy are impotent to control the giant firm. It is in position to pass on its costs, be they from labor contract, tax increases, or whatever, in its administered prices. It is largely immune from fiscal policies intended to make investment funds less accessible. It is able to expand out of its own resources. In the long run strains arising from operations of the planning system are passed on to the market system, which has no alternative but to adapt in an ever more embattled fashion.

On the basis of this analysis of the economic system Galbraith develops a general theory of reform. Three major types of proposals compose it: (1) to transform the tax system, employing it particularly to control earnings of individuals in the technostructure; (2) to move toward the democratization of government, seeking to place the bureaucracy under more effective control of the legislature and making the legislators more responsive to forces from the market system; (3) to move toward forthright (effective rather than the current fragmentary and inefficient) socialization of those areas of the market system that perform essential public services (health, housing, transportation) but are weak, and those areas of the planning system (the military-industrial complex) that have virtually destroyed all countervailing forces that could control them.

SUMMARY

A common problem and a set of general solutions characterize all branches of social behaviorism. Generally, they all took their initial shape during the period from 1890 to 1910. This was precisely the period of the academic institutionalization of sociology. Sociology was faced during these critical years with dropping its claims to be a kind of universal science and defending a specific definition

of its tasks. During the same period, another model for the new field was being provided by sociological formalism — a model that was unsatisfactory to those sociologists who believed that an adequate definition of their field must include reference not simply to forms but to social content. Hence, an appeal was made to traditions other than the neo-Kantian and phenomenological. Various branches of the neo-Hegelian, neo-idealistic, and pragmatic philosophies were invoked for a new approach to social matters.

With the excesses of organicism before their eyes, the sociologists who were seeking a specialized definition of sociology could hardly accept the existence of large-scale, ill-defined social entities with vast and vaguely-defined powers. The founders of social behaviorism shared with the formalists a deep suspicion of reification.

The theorists of the new schools of social behaviorism all shared a profound concern for providing sociology with an adequate method. This was in reaction to the formalists as well as the organicists. The formalists, after all, were tending to define sociology in terms that would have turned it into a kind of introspective product. But the social behaviorists were interested in establishing sociology as an empirical science. Significantly, every branch of social behaviorism made some contribution to sociological method. The suggestion–imitation school under Tarde, Ross, and Giddings made active demands for the construction of sociology as a statistical science. Persons trained under these men were to be among the most active sociologists in advancing the employment of statistics and attempting to construct scales for the underlying social materials. Some members of the symbolic interaction school were foremost among those promoting the use of case-history and life-history materials. This was of tremendous importance in advancing the assemblage of firsthand data by sociology. Finally, sociological method was a common preoccupation of all social-action theorists, and they made fundamental contributions to it. Weber's ideal type may illustrate both the preoccupation with method by social-action theorists and the attempt to construct devices to make the comparative method more precise.

Among the conjoint and common products of all the branches of social behaviorism were: (1) the introduction of the social person as an object of sociological study, and (2) the establishment of social psychology as one of the fundamental branches of sociology. Were it only for these effects, social behaviorism would have left its permanent mark on sociology.

Although all three branches of social behaviorism contributed to this study of the social person, special consequences were brought about by each branch. The suggestion–imitation theory is of particular importance in calling attention to the problems of invention and diffusion of social items. Uniform patterns of equivalent behavior were of particular interest. Thus, with this branch, fads, fashions, crazes, social movements, crowds, mobs, and publics came into their own as objects of sociological study. Inevitably the phenomena of invention of all kinds assumed special significance and the mechanisms of communication, both technical and social, came under review. The methodological significance of the school in leading eventually to such things as the public opinion survey and the attempts to scale social-psychological materials, as well as to utilize statistical devices for study, have already been commented on.

All three branches of social behaviorism show a parallelism and trend toward the development of full systems of sociology. But symbolic interactionism and social-action theory do not account for collective behavior as well as the suggestion–imitation school, which, for its part was less competent to develop a theory of social persons and a concept of social structure. But in the development of the theory of social persons, symbolic interactionism outruns the other trends. When the very topic of social persons is mentioned the names of symbolic interactionists spring to mind: James, Cooley, Thomas, and, above all, Mead. Baldwin, of course, deserves mention, but, then, he was strongly influenced by William James. Among the concepts brought to greater refinement and transmitted on to the sociological tradition by the symbolic interactionists were the concept of language as a fundamental social mechanism, the concepts of the stylization of personality by primary groups and by play and game situations, the concept of roles, and the concept of the self as formed in terms of social structure.

Social-action theory, too, took account of collective behavior and developed a concept of social persons (as seen in its elevation of the concepts of "calling" and "vocation" and in such studies as those of the technical expert, bureaucrat, intellectual, scientist), but it excelled the other branches of social behaviorism in its account of social structure and social change. Various of its members brought the processes of social change involved in the growth of patterns of rationalization in Western social structure under serious review. The relation between religious values and economic and scientific behavior were examined. The problems presented by modern bureaucratization in all areas of life were clarified. The structural anchorage of leadership in relation to legitimate order was explored in the forms of legalistic, traditional, and charismatic leaders. The sociology of law and political sociology, as well as the sociology of religion and the study of social stratification, were established as special subdisciplines of sociology.

Among major developments in social-action theory in the post-World War II period have been the transformation of its perspectives by David Riesman into a general sociology of education, the applications by H. Stuart Hughes of its point of view to European history and to developments in recent intellectual history, and the emergence in John Kenneth Galbraith of an outstanding heir to the traditions of Max Weber, John R. Commons, and Thorstein Veblen.

Taken all together a rather amazing array of the progressive trends in modern sociology have been the work of the social behaviorists.

The general position has been taken throughout this study that perhaps the best of all criticisms of any school of sociological theory is the full presentation of its varieties. It is assumed that a theory continues to "develop" — which means also that older forms of the theory are rejected — only if some of its basic problems remain unsolved. The abandonment of a theory usually means that a temporary stalemate has been reached. The suggestion–imitation branch of social behaviorism, for example, took the phenomena of suggestion and imitation as fundamental social processes. But further analysis showed them to be neither original nor fundamental. Imitation, when it occurs, is a highly complex and rather special learned product. Suggestion, assumed to be fundamental, was the attempt to construe social life on the model of a kind of primitive herding tendency. The abandonment of them as the sole or fundamental social processes was inevitable.

Symbolic interactionism, on the other hand, while giving powerful and exciting insights into the role of language in socialization, isolating a basis in behavior for the notion of meaning, and presenting interesting insights into the social structuring of the self and the roles that integrate self and social structure, has given only a very partial and restricted interpretation to the nature of symbolic mechanisms and a quite inadequate account of social structure. In view of the promotion by symbolic interactionism in its early days of the use of case and life histories and of personal documents of all kinds, the frequent charge that symbolic interactionism has no adequate research base and the lamentations over the fact that "George Mead has not been made researchable" are beside the point.

The deficiencies in the social-action branch of social behaviorism lie primarily in the failure to provide genuine theoretical transitions from the fundamental concept of social action to social structure — the area where the position has displayed its greatest power. Fundamentally, a typology such as the one that Weber used to make the transition is no substitute for theory construction.

Perhaps the difficulties noted in the various branches of social behaviorism are by no means fundamental. Any one of them may yet find its Aristotle who will bring it to full form. Perhaps a new formulation will appear, having as its base, not any one branch of social behaviorism, but social behaviorism as a whole. This last is suggested by work such as that of Gerth and Mills, who clearly started with social-action theory but later, in their formulations, made a new start on the basis of symbolic interactionism, relying on social-action theory for the explanation of social structure. Even Merton, before his departure from social behaviorism, showed a strong inclination to use elements from various branches of the theory: social action from Max Weber, definition of the situation (self-fulfilling prophecy) from W. I. Thomas, the generalized other (in the modified form of reference group) from G. H. Mead, and homophily from Giddings ("consciousness of kind").

On the other hand, the trend is clearly afoot by many of the most sensitive of the former adherents of social behaviorism to abandon the school altogether and to launch a new development in theory construction. At the same time, some of the most vigorous young social scientists in North America have made brilliant use of social-action theory.

PART IV

HUMANISTIC HOLISM

THE FIRST TWO SCHOOLS of sociological theory, positivistic organicism and conflict theory, were forms of scientific holism. Toward the end of the nineteenth and in the early twentieth century until World War I, four schools of scientific elementarism took shape: neo-Kantian formalism, pluralistic behaviorism, symbolic interactionism, and social-action theory. The scientific component of the early sociological synthesis of humanistic subject matter and scientific method was the more stable of its constituents.

But it was perhaps to be expected that sooner or later the humanists would react to the sociologists who assumed that since the materials of history include human thoughts and feelings, manifestations of the human spirit, they deserve special treatment. In accord with his positivism, Comte reduced history to the overt happenings in human behavior. The presumed human spirit behind behavior was ignored.[1] Sociology's task was to analyze social and cultural events with the methods of the natural sciences and the principles of succession, coexistence, and cause, thereby establishing the general laws of social evolution.[2] Comte's arguments were reenforced by John Stuart Mill, who always hoped to improve the state of the social sciences by application of the methods of natural science. In fact, Mill thought it possible to deduce the successive states of consciousness from the physiological functions of the brain. Such deduction was the first step in establishing the natural laws of human pluralities.[3] The sociology of Comte and Mill had a direct influence on the historical writings of Henry Thomas Buckle. Sociological positivism was beginning to invade the sphere of historical writing.

At the same period that Comte was introducing his French contemporaries to the possibilities of a new science based on a combination of an organismic theory of society and positivism, the French historian Jules Michelet (1798–1874) in *Oeuvres choisiers de Vico* was popularizing an alternative combination of organicism and humanistic methodology. Giovanni Battista Vico (1688–1744), Italian jurist and philosopher, set forth a philosophy of history in *The New Science* (1725). To Vico it was a "truth beyond all question . . ."

that the world of civil society has certainly been made by men, and that its principles are therefore to be found within the modifications of our own human mind. Whoever reflects on this cannot but marvel that the philosophers should have bent all their energies to the study of the world of nature, which, since God made it, He alone knows; and that they should have neglected the study of the world of nations, or civil world which, since men had made it, men could come to know.[4]

Human beings can understand themselves and the whole of human culture which they have created, but not by the application of methods designed for the study of nature. The inductive study of culture must be undertaken on its own terms as a product of encounters of mind and nature at different times and places. Each age has its own problems. Responses to these problems reflect the level of rationality achieved in the culture of the time. Each culture is a macrocosm of the transformations that occur in individuals as they pass through life stages from birth to death. Each age has its own needs, its own institutions. To understand the problems and institutions of people of another age one must enter sympathetically into the kind of world they assumed. In the earliest stage, for example, the family formed the nucleus of society and religion was humanity's way of accounting for the fearful unknown. This age of the gods in time was transformed into an age of heroes, the age of religion into the age of poetry. The fundamental tools of the new science are philological, applying to the cultural products of

[1]Auguste Comte, *System de politique positive*, 4 vols., trans. John Henry Bridges (London: Longmans, Green, 1975–1977), I, 9.
[2]*Ibid.*, IV, 17.
[3]See John Stuart Mill, *A System of Logic* (London: Longmans, Green, 1949), pp. 529–532.

[4]Giovanni Battista Vico, *The New Science,* trans. Thomas Goodard Bergin and Max Harold Fisch (Ithaca: Cornell University Press, 1970), pp. 52–53.

human beings, above all to their literary culture, their myths, poetry, theology, philosophy, in fact, to any literary products in which human beings undertake to account for themselves, their society, their history, their world.[5]

The influence of Vico was primarily confined to circles of historians and students of aesthetics and literature. Only when positivistic sociology showed signs of invading their areas, did the humanists mount a counterattack on its influence from a point of view based on or similar to that of Vico. A major attempt to combat positivism by means of a reconstructed historicism was undertaken by Johann Droysen (1808–1884), who in 1852 developed a course at the University of Berlin on the "Methodology and Encyclopedia of the Historical Sciences," which proposed to study history, as he put it, on an historical foundation.[6] Droysen drew a sharp distinction[7] between the natural and the historical sciences and argued that the spheres of history and of science are distinct: history deals with moral judgments and other manifestations of the spirit which largely elude statistics and causal study. However, Droysen admitted statistical and causal methods are appropriate for the study of things, a line of argument followed by Dilthey.

Wilhelm Dilthey (1833–1911), German philosopher, historian, and literary critic, became one of the primary spokespersons in the nineteenth century for the humanistic opposition to positivism in the sphere of the humanities. Positivism, Dilthey believed, was not new, but the culmination in recent times of the materialistic explanation of

events extending through d'Alembert and Hobbes to Comte. The peculiarity of the materialistic philosophy of history is found in its attempts to explain spiritual events in terms of categories developed to explain things. A basic distinction must be drawn between the natural and cultural sciences (*Geisteswissenschaften*). In the natural sciences we seek to explain by analysis from the outside; in the cultural sciences, of which history is the queen, we understand our materials from within, for we are in a position to grasp directly the thoughts, feelings, and desires at the core of human action. To be sure, we are only inside our own experience but we have empathic understanding of the behavior and experiences of others. We are able in some measure to relive or re-experience the experience of others in our own minds. There are, of course, limits to the extent of empathy with the experience of others and errors are possible in interpreting what goes on in the mind of another. In a manner that would have delighted Vico, Dilthey declared that the poets had taught him more about the world than many of the philosophers.

> The systems of Schelling, Hegel, and Schleiermacher, were but logical and metaphysical translations of a *Lebens-und Weltansicht* of a Lessing, a Schiller, and a Herder. The poet is interpreter of a state of mind which permeates a generation and crystalizes it into a system. A system lives or dies, not according to reasons of logic, but by virtue of the duration of that state of mind which has originated it.[8]

Dilthey turned much of his attention to the development of working rules for the interpretation of written texts, the method of hermeneutics which arose in patristic times from the needs of scriptural exegesis and underwent extensive development during the controversies of the Reformation and Counter Reformation. He also developed a typology of world views (the most basic being naturalism, the idealism of freedom, and objective idealism) which inform complete synthe-

[5]In the nineteenth century Vico's alternative to positivistic organicism influenced such persons as Goethe, Mazzini, Coleridge, Taine, and even to some extent Marx and Engels. In the twentieth century he had influence on Croce, Gentile, Collingwood, Joyce, Yeats, Trotsky, Toynbee, Pareto, Sorel, and Sorokin among others.

[6]Johann Gustav Droysen, *Grundries der Historik*, trans. E. B. Andrews as *Outline of the Principles of History* (Boston: Ginn, 1893).

[7]Johann Gustav Droysen, "Zur Characteristik der europaischen Krisis," in *Politische Schriften*, ed. Felix Gilbert (Munich: 1933), pp. 307–342.

[8]William Kluback, *Wilhelm Dilthey's Philosophy of History* (New York: Columbia University Press, 1956), p. 75.

ses of culture (customs, institutions, ideas, schools of art, and religious and philosophical systems). In the sphere of culture, Dilthey opposed the separation of fact and value as an operation that destroyed the special character of cultural materials. At the same time, having abandoned the enlightenment position, which treated rationality as a universal measure of progress, Dilthey was left with no standards for comparatively estimating the significance of various world views. Dilthey's humanism, thus, led to cultural relativism.

Toward the end of the nineteenth century, Tolstoy added a new dimension to the humanistic criticism of sociology. In 1887 Isabel Hapgood made a collection of Tolstoy's essays which at the time were circulating in Russia in manuscript form. In one of them Tolstoy made a point quite different from the usual humanistic complaint that sociologists, in treating social and cultural phenomena as things, were ignoring values — Tolstoy observed that despite all their pretense of scientific objectivity the sociologists were actually making value judgments. The sociologists, in Tolstoy's view (he primarily had Comte and Spencer in mind) in the name of experimental, positive science, were providing a new justification for exploitation by "all persons who have freed themselves from toil." The position of sociology was that

> Only sociology, founded on biology, founded on all the positive sciences, can give us the law of humanity. Humanity, or human communities, are the organisms already prepared, or still in process of formation, and which are subservient to the laws of the evolution of organisms.[9]

This organismic doctrine, founded on experimental positivistic science, was, in Tolstoy's view, the most recent justification of idleness and cruelty. Fifteen years later, Tolstoy was still railing at the rationalization of inequality and exploitation implied in the organismic view of society that as-

sumed, however bad it might appear from the outside, everything present in the social organism was an indispensable part of the whole and required for its proper functioning. In an essay on "The Restoration of Hell" Tolstoy had Beelzebub, chief of the devils, review reports on the state of the contemporary world from his cohorts. One reported that to distract human beings from spiritual things he invented sociology.

> I have devised for them . . . sociology, which consists in studying how former people lived badly. So instead of trying to live better themselves according to the teaching of Jesus, they think they need only study the lives of former people, and from that they will be able to deduce general laws of life, and that to live well they need only conform their life to the laws they thus devise.[10]

In Tolstoy's view, sociology was the latest form of philistinism whose only novelty lay in its claim to a scientific foundation. Nietzsche came to a similar conclusion from a different point of view. He described Comte as the shrewdest of the Jesuits who was undertaking to lead people back to traditional Christianity by the dubious route of science.

The target of the humanistic critique of sociology was positivistic organicism. By the time humanist critics got around to calling attention to the ideological implications if not intent in the organismic conception of society, the shining armor of social science was starting to become bespattered. The humanistic critics played a role in the evolution of sociology. Conflict theorists, for example, who offered a holistic approach to society alternative to the organismic approach, had the methodological critique of the humanists in mind when they called for more rigorous positivism and taking into account the realities of social conflicts, revolution, and war — the real facts of society. The humanistic critique was also a component in the development of positivistic organicism in the classic works of Tönnies and Durkheim. Both showed

---

[9]Leo Tolstoy, *What To Do?* trans. Isabel F. Hapgood (New York: Thomas Y. Crowell, 1887), p. 169.

[10]Leo Tolstoy, *On Life*, trans. Aylmer Maude (London: Humphrey Milford, 1934), p. 326.

a new sensitivity to methodological problems and their methodological writings appear, in part, to have been an answer to the humanists.

The early humanistic critique of sociology reached a climax at the same time the elementaristic forms of social theory began to offer alternatives to sociological holism. The elementarists were also responding to the humanist critics when they abandoned the organismic theory of society, in fact, when they abandoned holism altogether. Moreover, many of the elementarists virtually renounced the use of historical materials again in some measure in response to neo-Kantian and neo-idealistic criticism. All of the elementarists recognized the need to make adaptations in scientific methods to accommodate them to the peculiarities of social and cultural materials. The elementarists also showed a refined sensibility to the problem of values in social science. In the case of the social-action theorists, particularly Max Weber, the attempt was made to take over insights by the humanists and reset them in a revised positivistic framework. While still retaining the classical combination of a humanistic subject matter and scientific method, the elementaristic social theorists of the turn of the century made many adjustments to the prevailing humanistic critique of positivism.

As sociologists began to modify the positivistic tradition of sociology, a combination of holism and humanism was beginning to appear as a shadow on the distant horizon. For this combination to appear, however, social conditions favoring a return to holistic points of view had to be simultaneously accompanied by disillusionment with science and technology at least as applied to society.

Both conditions, a return to holistic approaches to society and a simultaneous sense of uneasiness over the applications of science to human affairs and culture, accompanied the major social crises of the twentieth century, particularly the world wars and worldwide depression. During these great collective crises elementaristic points of view with their concern for individuals appeared trivial and insignificant. At the same time, the confident predictions by some early sociologists that in an or-

ganically relativised world with a complex division of labor, major wars would become impossible, proved to be stunningly mistaken. The gigantic technical-industrial apparatus of modern society was also capable of organizing and launching the violent destruction of people and natural resources on an unimaginable scale. The twentieth-century heirs of positivistic organicism such as Spengler, Toynbee, and Sorokin, broke with progress doctrines, developed relativised models of sociocultural holism, and sounded a new note of antipositivism. In their works positivistic organicism was disintegrating.

In the 1920s it soon became clear that the Russian Revolution was transforming Marxism into the ideology of a party dictatorship. The Stalinists launched a form of political terrorism that made that of the Czars look like humanitarian liberalism. Furthermore, outside Russia, in the official Marxism of the German Social Democratic Party, the tradition of revisionist Marxism begun by Engels and developed in the prewar period was continuing. While the rhetoric was revolutionary in practice, Marxism was becoming indistinguishable from positivistic sociology. In response to this, a small group of German intellectuals attempted to retain the chiliastic revolutionary program of Marxism by freeing it from all temptations to positivism. They formed the Frankfurt Institute for Social Research, which developed as a relatively isolated cult in Europe and in exile in America until after World War II, when its members were invited to return to Frankfurt and assume leadership in restoring continuity in the German sociological tradition.

In the 1930s Talcott Parsons, who was eventually to emerge as the key figure in an American version of holistic social theory, reviewed a number of major thinkers in the interest of a new departure in social theory. Whatever else may be said, Parsons' instincts were sound: the times were ripe for change. While in *The Structure of Social Action* he integrated the ideas of Pareto, Marshall, Weber, and Durkheim in an elementaristic perspective, he was, possibly at this time unconsciously, laying the foundation for a transition to

---

Compass Points of Western Social Science

The Nature of Social Theory

METHODS	ELEMENTARISTIC	HOLISTIC
Humanistic	Social-Action Theory* Symbolic Interactionism*	Macrofunctionalism Critical Theory of the Frankfurt School and Reflexive Social Theory
Scientific	Neo-Kantianism Behavioristic Sociology Social-Action Theory Symbolic Interactionism	Positivistic Organicism Conflict Theory Microfunctionalism

*The original social-action theorists and symbolic interactionists (for example, Max Weber and George Herbert Mead) took their point of departure from materials that classically belonged to the humanists (meaningful social action, ideas, interpretations) but reinterpreted them in a scientific-positivistic framework. Under the influence of the recent upsurge of antipositivism some social-action theorists (for example H. Stuart Hughes, some students of Weber) and some symbolic interactionists (those belonging to the traditions of Herbert Blumer and Kenneth Burke) have tended to shift these positions toward the humanistic pole.

---

holism. Parsons also carried through a strong critique of positivism in *The Structure*; he was moving in the direction of a holistic humanism. As structure-functionalism took shape under the joint guidance of Parsons and Merton, it had strong humanistic leanings. However, the United States was not yet ready for this combination. Science had increased in prestige during World War II. The preoccupation of American social scientists with quantitative procedures was at an all-time high. And in the postwar period structure-functionalism developed two major forms: macrofunctionalism (which always retained some elements of an anti-positivistic humanism) and microfunctionalism (which was strictly positivistic in its methodology). On occasion Parsons clarified his latent antipositivism with the startling observation that the chief reason for empirical research was to eliminate possibilities not requiring further conceptual elabora-

tion. Merton for many years indicated that he intended to work out a methodology of paradigms, with the implication that only this type of methodology was fully appropriate to the structure-functionalistic theory. Also over the years, positivistic-minded methodologists who sought to recast Parsons' ideas into operational form usually threw up their hands in despair, for they were not amenable to precise formulation. In time it became conventional to insist that Parsons had not developed a theory, but a series of categories and a perspective.

It is possible to locate on the chart introduced in Part III the critical theory of the Frankfurt School and the two forms of structure-functionalism in terms of their humanistic and scientific components. A comment is in order on an important difference between the two major components (holism-elementarism, and humanism-science) that have been employed to identify substantive and methodological peculiarities of the theories. Figuratively they were described as compass points of western thought.

Although this is a convenient figure of speech, it should not be permitted to obscure an important difference between the so-called dimensions of social theory. Social holism and social elementarism are mutually exclusive conceptualizations of the nature of social reality. One cannot without self-contradiction be a social holist and a social elementarist at the same time. Humanism and science, by contrast, are programs of interpretation, areas of interest, and procedures (or methods) which developed over time to implement theories. Humanism developed originally as a human-centered (in contrast to the God-centered program of the theologians) study of people, meanings, and culture; science arose as the study of the physical world.

There has been some tendency to treat humanism and science as mutually exclusive: humanism has sometimes been visualized, because of its interest in values, ideas, the spirit, and mind, as a kind of polar opposite of science, with its interest in facts, things, physical relations, matter, behavior, and even the human body. Whenever this has been done the perennial mind-body, spirit-matter problem of the philosophers has reemerged to haunt the social theorist.

In actual practice the programs, areas of interest, and methods of humanism and science have always interpenetrated one another. And if there is a lesson at all in the insights of such founders of elementaristic positions as Max Weber and George Herbert Mead, it lies in the wisdom of setting aside the mind-body dichotomy and recognizing that there is no absolute difference between the subject matter studied and the methods employed by humanism and science, even though, at some point irreducible differences may arise between them.

This is important to keep in mind in view of the strong tide of antipositivism which arose among the philosophers even before the social sciences showed the full effects of logical positivism. A strong antipositivism began to manifest itself among social theorists only in the late 1960s and 1970s. As this has occurred there has been a tendency to shift methodological preferences in a more humanistic direction. Some of the differences which appear in the various charts of social theory (in the introductory sections to Parts III and IV and in the final chapter) should be interpreted as the tracing of shifts in the location of theories in response to the rise and decline of logical positivism in the twentieth century.

XIX

The Nature and Origins of Sociological Functionalism

Despite the tremendous sociological gains made by the various branches of social behaviorism, many prominent sociologists seem to feel that it is no final answer. The ranks of social behaviorism have been decimated, and by persons who made significant contributions to it.

Why is social behaviorism being abandoned? It is too early to be sure. Often if children who run away from home knew why, they would realize that they need not go. The reasons why a scientific change is made often become fully clear only when the change has been successful. Defining precisely what is wrong is an aspect of establishing a new solution. One may, at best, hazard some rough guesses.

The three main branches of social behaviorism — pluralistic behaviorism, symbolic interactionism, and social-action theory — presented quite independent solutions to the same set of problems. Their points of strength are quite different. Theoretically the weakest and methodologically the strongest branch of social behaviorism is the pluralistic behavioral branch. Its

members strongly promoted and helped to develop modern sociological statistics. They have been very busy developing various kinds of scales for measuring sociologically significant items. In part, their method could be so widely applied because their theory was so inexact. The precise definition of the object to be studied revealed it to be unmeasurable by existing instruments. By assuming that overt, countable behaviors are an accurate index to inner beliefs and desires, measurement and statistics could be advanced with no embarrassing questions asked. As the school evolved, its theories tended more and more to become a mere set of definitions.

The second major branch of social behaviorism — symbolic interactionism — was strong (theoretically) precisely where pluralistic behaviorism was weak. But unfortunately it was weak (methodologically) where pluralistic behaviorism was strong. There is no doubt that its conceptualization of sociological subject matter as consisting in "attitudes," "roles," "language as a social mechanism," "the looking-glass self," "the generalized other," "reference groups," "life organization," and so on, was a tremendous improvement in subtlety and precision over the conceptions of pluralistic behaviorism. To be sure, its methods showed some development — from the mere proposal of systematic autobiography of Cooley to the attempt to set down standards for case and life histories of Thomas and Znaniecki. Nevertheless, there were areas of theory left relatively undeveloped (large-scale social organization, for example), and its methods were eventually brought under severe attack. One of the sure signals that a given person is ready to depart from the ranks of this branch of social behaviorism is the announcement that "it is a shame that no one has made George Herbert Mead (or Cooley, or Thomas, etc.) researchable."

The third branch of social behaviorism, social-action theory, has suffered from a number of difficulties. The partial failure to visualize the full range of the school has not promoted its detachment from the powerful personality of Max Weber. For example, though J. R. Commons was a fundamental contributor to social-action theory, and though he also did much to develop social science methods, he has had few sociological followers. Furthermore, since Weber had a strong personal tendency to retain ideas "in solution" until they were fully matured, hesitating to define them formally, the only indication of many of his most vital conceptions is contained in his types. When the abstract concept is buried in the type, it stands in the way of clear conceptualization of ideas and helps to blur the lines between concept and methodological device. Finally, the cloud under which the comparative method has fallen has not encouraged the frank projection of theory on its basis. Thus, with some irony, though half a dozen new subdivisions of contemporary sociology take their point of departure in large measure from social-action theory, particularly Weber's, the theory itself tends to be abandoned.

When one takes the three branches as a whole, the weaker their theory, the stronger their method; the stronger their theory, the weaker their method. It is little wonder that there are de-

sertions from the ranks. These desertions are almost universally made in the name of sociological functionalism.

THE MEANING OF FUNCTIONALISM

One of the major reference points in social science discussions of "functionalism" is Horace Kallen's article in the *Encyclopaedia of the Social Sciences*.[1] He traces it to a movement in late nineteenth-century philosophy under the influence of Darwinism on the biological and social sciences. Its distinguishing properties are found to be in its concern with relations and activities rather than substances. Characteristic notions identifying functionalism are: transformation, dynamic patterns, and process, growth, expansion, emergence.

According to Kallen, activity or function in the past had been treated as a dependent variable or faculty of a fixed structure or form. Now all this was reversed and function was regarded as the independent variable while form or structure was demoted to second place. To illustrate this notion with an extreme example, whereas in the past it was assumed that a man had a pair of legs (structure) and he walked, now it is assumed that a man walks (function) and this activity produces a pair of legs.

Functionalism, Kallen continues, has influenced every discipline. In psychology, it led to the substitution of the stream of consciousness for states of mind; in logic, it replaced the "laws of thought" with the "theory of scientific method"; in philosophy, it led to the rise of instrumentalism and pragmatism. Functionalism came to be conceived as a going process and as a means to an end. However, to Kallen the real animus of functionalism is the conception of function without purpose. In this form it is said to be a component in the

---

[1] *Encyclopaedia of the Social Sciences* (New York: Macmillan, 1931), VI, 523–524.

thought of Bergson,[2] Dreisch,[3] and Marx, the basic feature of Gestalt psychology, and distinguishing property of social reform and innovating movements exalting functionalism such as guild socialism, syndicalism, communism, and fascism, as well as the theoretical ideal of Bergson's *élan vital* and the dialectical materialism of Marx. A manifestation of the same movement appears in pluralism in political theory, institutionalism in economics, functionalism in anthropology (a functionalism which sees religion, the arts, and the sciences reduced to specific habits, materials, meanings, and activities within the context of a cultural situation), and functional architecture, in which form arises out of the uses for which it is intended and reenforces those uses.

One may conclude from this review that *functionalism* in the many senses of the term here given is completely meaningless, for it has been applied to just about every new departure, however slight, in thought or experience since the mid-nineteenth century. The real synonyms of the term when so used are *contemporary* or *modern*. Clearly, so long as the term *function* is used in this vague sense, it is useless for designating any particular departure in social theory. If one is to understand sociological functionalism, this vague, overgeneralized formulation of the meaning of functionalism must be made more precise.

There are a number of possible meanings of *function* that could be employed for serious sociological theory construction. Among the more important of these are: (1) function in a mathematical sense, (2) function as useful activity, (3) function as appropriate activity, and (4) function as system-determined and system-sustaining activity.

(1) A function in mathematics is a variable whose values are determined by those of one or more other variables. If x and y are two variables, and if to each value of x corresponds one and only one value of y, y may be said to be a single-valued function of x: $y = f(x)$. In this expression, x is the independent and y the dependent variable. If more than one value of y corresponds to a value of x, the variable y is a many-valued function of x. Historically, the theory of functions goes back to the publication of Descartes' work on analytical geometry (1637). The evolution of the theory of functions is central to the development of mathematics.

Although the needs of a positivistic sociology would be brilliantly met if one were able to express all social relations as mathematical functions, even the most daring positivist has not been willing to go this far. What tentative gestures have been made in this direction have not been very successful, producing mere empty notations (Stuart Dodd) or metaphysical oversimplifications of social relations (G. K. Zipf) or make-believe and pseudosimple social arrangements (Nicolas Rashevsky) or speculative structures (Norbert Weiner). The work of most of the recent functionalists has been at the opposite pole from this meaning.

(2) The term *function* has often been used to mean *useful activity*; in fact, it is sometimes used even for *activity*. This usage is reflected in popular speech. Public and institutional ceremonies and activities (Fourth of July fireworks, Veterans' Day parades, the church socials or picnics, the annual outing of the Royal Order of Moose, the city and county picnic) are said to be *functions*. In this sense, the term *function* is useless for sociological analysis, for it would encompass every activity of people in one manner or other.

The term has more bite to it, however, when it is conceived as "*useful* activity": the germs of a theory of interhuman activity have been introduced. Two subforms of "functional" theory become distinguishable at this point. A function may be conceived not merely as a useful activity but as (a) "need fulfillment" or (b) "purpose realization." In the first sense, functional analysis of social life is the proposal to analyze all activities (functions) in

[2]Henri Bergson (1859–1941) was a French philosopher who devoted himself to the substitution of durational for nontemporal values and the values of motion and change for static values in the interpretation of events.
[3]H. Dreisch was a German biologist-philosopher, whose work *Der Vitalismus als Geschichte und als Lehre* (Leipzig: 1905) had an important influence on Gestalt psychology.

terms of a system of presumed needs. In the second sense, a theory of social life is proposed by which activities are to be interpreted in terms of their instrumental value in achieving purposes. In the first sense, one occasionally hears Sumner called a functionalist because the starting point of his analysis was the assumption of the rise of customary regularities (folkways) as stable solutions to needs. Or, at times, the proposal is made to treat Freud as a functionalist because individual and social behavior were conceived to arise in the fulfillment of powerful unconscious needs. The first usage has led to proposals to reduce sociology to psychology. In the second sense, analyses of human activity in terms of means and ends, as well as all "instrumental" analyses of activity, have been claimed to be "functional." The conflicts over a "teleological" interpretation of social conduct emerge repeatedly over this usage. Apart from these issues, it is highly doubtful whether the use of the concept *function* in either or both senses warrants description of the theorist as a functionalist.

(3) The third usage treats function as "appropriate activity," a concept by no means identical with "useful activity." An activity can be quite useful either in fulfilling a need or in implementing a purpose without being "appropriate." A distorted craving for recognition may, in the opinion of a psychiatrist, drive the individual to megalomania. There is no doubt in the psychiatrist's mind about the relation between need and activity. When he describes this as a "functional disorder," he is judging its appropriateness with respect to otherwise "normal" operations of the system of behavior. There are analogies in biology where a functional disease is a morbid change in the function of an organ without a structural transformation in the tissues involved. Instrumental activity is also occasionally judged in terms of appropriateness. Businesspeople's purposes may be all too clear when they drive themselves at (note the judgment of appropriateness) a "killing" pace.

Repeated cases have arisen in sociology of conceptions of functionalism which rest on the idea of "appropriate activity." For example, Robert Mer-

ton distinguishes between latent and manifest functions.[4] In the context, it is strongly suggested that a manifest function is somehow like the "manifest content" of Freudian dream analysis — the apparent, surface content of the dream in contrast to its hidden meanings to the dreamer. This would seem to make of the manifest function the conscious, overt one; the latent function the hidden, secret one. Examples are given of the manifest functions of the elected public officials in contrast to the nonofficial activities of the ward heelers, fixers, and bosses. But there is nothing unconscious or unintentional about the activities of a political boss — quite the contrary. It is usually difficult to find an activity that is not quite cold-bloodedly intended. The latent-manifest distinction actually refers to judgments of appropriateness.

(4) The fourth major meaning of function is that of a "system-determined and system-maintaining activity." The critical property of this position is the view that social life is fundamentally incorporated in systems. In these systems, any item is to be judged in terms of its determination by the system and its place in maintaining the system. This is clearly a more inclusive meaning than either the second or the third. In fact, these meanings are sometimes taken up into the fourth.

Putting aside the mathematical conception of function, which the theorists calling themselves sociological functionalists do, the other three notions are utilized in various combinations. This has not been any great boon to precision. The critical questions are which concept of *function* and what manner of use constitute grounds for interpreting functionalism as a special departure in sociological theory.

The conception of function as "useful activity" in both of its subforms ("need fulfillment" and "purpose realization") is very widely distributed. Probably there is no sociologist who does not view the various items of social practice, customs, social

---

[4]Robert Merton, *Social Theory and Social Structure* (Glencoe, Ill.: The Free Press, 1949, 1957).

roles, institutions, and social organization as satisfying needs and realizing purposes. Functionalism cannot mean this, for in applying to all sociologists it would discriminate none. For example, it would not discriminate functionalism from social behaviorism. There are ways of reducing structures to needs and assigning instrumental purposes to them that involve various kinds of errors, but that is another matter.

Clearly it is only when "function" is used in the third sense (as "appropriate activity") and in the fourth (as "system-determined and system determining") activity that one has moved into the sphere of a special system of theory. The properties of sociological functionalism can be seen most directly in terms of their ties with organicism.

SOCIOLOGICAL FUNCTIONALISM AND SOCIOLOGICAL ORGANICISM

Sociological functionalism departs from social behaviorism in an essential manner. Social behaviorism was haunted by the fear of reification. In all of its major branches, it arose in polemical opposition to entities whch seemed to it to be hypostatized abstractions. Tarde announced his conviction that a new science begins by assuming the existence of large-scale "apparent" regularities, but can genuinely advance only with the discovery of the real, small-scale repetitions. Tarde was always opposed to Durkheim, who seemed to him to believe in the reality of fictions. Max Weber was never more insistent than in his view that relations and structures represent no more than the probabilities of the occurrence of specific social actions. A state, for example, was treated as no more than a way people act. When they no longer act that way the state does not exist. The programs of the pragmatists and symbolic interactionists also began with a strong reaction against all metaphysical entities. This was nowhere clearer than in William James's rejection of both subject and object and of consciousness as an entity in his essay "Does Con-

sciousness Exist?". Thus, in two fundamental points, functionalism represents a departure from social behaviorism: (1) in its concept of the primacy of a system, and (2) in its idea that all units (such as those of the social behaviorists) are only secondarily relevant, and then from the standpoint of the system in which they are found.

The present interpretation, it may be noted, stands in direct contrast to the formulation of Kingsley Davis in his presidential address to the American Sociological Association in 1959:

> For more than thirty years now "functional analysis" has been debated among sociologists and anthropologists. Perhaps the time has come for the debate to be either settled or abandoned. My view is that it should be abandoned, because it rests on the false assumption that there is a special method or body of theory called functional analysis which can be distinguished from other methods or theories *within* sociology and social anthropology.[5]

To be sure, Davis does correctly touch the theoretical core of functionalism:

> Turning from the sheer variety of conceptions to the traits most frequently cited as characterizing functional analysis, we find that functionalism is most commonly said to *do* two things: to relate the parts of society to the whole, and to relate one part to another.[6]

However, this formulation is not quite precise, for it is in its view of the causal priority of the whole over the part that functionalism begins to be distinct as a special theory. Hence, when Davis assumes that there is no school of functionalism because every sociologist is a functionalist, an injustice is done both to the actual varieties of theory in contemporary sociology and to the theoretical distinctness of functionalism.

In fact, functionalism represents a radical break

[5]Kingsley Davis, "The Myth of Functional Analysis as a Special Method in Sociology and Anthropology," *American Sociological Review*, 24 (December 1959), 757.
[6]*Ibid.*, p. 758.

with social behaviorism, treating as primary precisely a kind of item which social behaviorism had rejected as reification, and automatically tending to move sociological functionalism back to ideas against which social behaviorism was a reaction. This brings functionalism close to organicism. Such was Albion Small's considered judgment after his review of two early organicists, Spencer and Schäffle:

> Spencer does not succeed in making his interpretation of society . . . as more than an *organization of mechanisms*. Schäffle's central conception of society is of an *organization of work*. Of course, mechanism implies work, and work implies mechanism. Moreover, language has grown up in such connection with the working processes of life that we cannot talk of mechanism without talking of work, and *vice versa*. For that reason, the ideas of mechanism, structure, and work (function) are in both of these systems, as certainly as they are in either. They have different degrees of importance in the two systems. The relative prominence of *structure* in the one system, and the relative importance of *function* in the other, give them the rank, respectively, of a first step and a second step in approach to adequate analysis of human association.[7]

Small was convinced that these theories and concepts had done their work, and while they had left a permanent residue, they had been surpassed. Social functions themselves require a sphere of relations by which they may be approximately explained. Functions are aspects of processes, not parts of mechanisms. To know social functions it is necessary to become acquainted with the social processes within which they are incidents. Hence, Small thought that while "social structure" and "social functions" had been conceptual centers for ambitious sociological systems, these systems were not serious competitors for leadership in social theory. They had had their day, and social theorists could not now be fully equipped without thinking through the problems which those systems tried to solve. However, "the concepts 'social structure' and 'social function,' or some substitute which we cannot imagine, will always be indispensable in analysis of the social reality. The principal deposit of permanent value left by the two types of sociological theory developed around the two notions 'structure' and 'function,' consists of the two conceptions, as elementary terms in more adequate explanation."[8]

These comments of Small made in 1905 already tie the basic problems of functionalism at the turn of the century to organicism. It is significant that the estimate by Nicholas Timasheff fifty years later also traces functionalism primarily to the organicists.[9] He notes that the conception of the integration of parts into wholes and of the interdependence of the different elements of society appeared in Comte's *consensus universalis*, in Spencer's integration compensating for differentiation, in Cooley's organic theory, and in Pareto's conception of society as equilibrium. He notes moreover that the estimate of a social item in terms of its contribution to the whole was characteristic of Durkheim and W. I. Thomas.

The organic type of system is the primary model of functional interpretation. To link nonorganicists like Cooley or Thomas with functionalism is not unjust, for they were strongly influenced by organicism. However, they were not functionalists. The true founders of functionalism were the positivistic organicists.

What is really in need of explanation more than the ties of functionalism with positivistic organicism is the extreme shyness of contemporary functionalists in admitting their ancestry. One would think — so sensitive are they to genealogical questions — that their forebears way back were all cattle rustlers. In fact, it seems they will admit influences from biology, from psychology, from cultural anthropology — anything but their own field.

---

[7]Albion W. Small, *General Sociology* (Chicago: University of Chicago Press, 1905), pp. 167–168.

[8]*Ibid.*, p. 176.
[9]See Nicholas S. Timasheff, *Sociological Theory: Its Nature and Growth*, rev. ed. (New York: Random House, 1957), pp. 221–223.

Of course, this is not actually difficult to explain. Organicism of the older type fell into disrepute. The functionalists are understandably reluctant to commit the same errors. But these are not best avoided by ignoring the tradition. There were, after all, creative possibilities in the organismic point of view in both its biological and non-biological forms. The peculiar tensions arising in the conjunction of organismic theory and positivistic method were important in the very establishment of the science. The functionalistic return to the organismic point of view is itself proof that its creative potential has not been exhausted. In ancient mythologies there sometimes appears the figure of a strange giant who gains his strength from contact with the earth. He is almost unbeatable by normal types of hand-to-hand combat, for when he is hurled to earth he gains strength from the contact and comes back with redoubled energy. In sociology, the organic point of view seems to have some of this property; cast down in the form of positivistic organicism, it arises with redoubled vigor in the form of functionalism.

In the long run, if functionalistic sociological theory is to succeed where other theories have failed, it will not be by ignoring its origins but by facing up to them, extracting the positive values and meeting the criticisms that brought organicism into disrepute.

It is quite unnecessary here to review the anticipations of functionalism contained in organicism. An entire chapter has been devoted to the tracing of the development and forms of organicism. Every one of them has important relevance for functionalism.

There are, however, two points to be noted: (1) in functionalism, sociology has seen the first school of theory that is not derived from some philosophic current: (2) functionalism has some peculiarities that set it off from older types of organicism. With respect to the first point, the fact that sociology has reached a point of development in which new movements can take their points of departure within it without particular reference to outside currents of thought may be most significant. A kind of critical density of collective experience has been built up to a point where the discipline can show the properties of autonomous development. This observation, to be sure, is speculative, but it may be the surest indication we have of the approaching maturity of the science.

The second point is less speculative and of more relevance to theory formation. The fundamental explanatory model of functionalism is that of the organic system. This was the organizing conception of sociology in the first place. But if functionalism involved merely a return to the organic model, without adding anything new, it would have to be dismissed as an unprogressive tendency. However, as far as one can tell, this is not the case.

Organicism, indeed, worked with the concept of the organic system, but it was dominated by the conception of large-scale, total organic structure. For Comte, no less a structure was conceived as forming an organic system than "humanity" or, as he put it, "chiefly the white race." Spencer conceived of "society" as his unit. This, too, was the unit of analysis for Durkheim. These are large-scale systems with a vengeance.

Functionalism represents a departure from this kind of organicism in three ways: (1) the concept of "organic system" is generalized (without commitment in advance to the acceptance of only one type or only of vast total forms); (2) the concept of "system" is given explicit central theoretical status, becoming the point from which all analyses of structure and process are made; (3) the critical system is not identified with historical society.

SOCIOLOGICAL FUNCTIONALISM AND PSYCHOLOGICAL CONFIGURATIONISM

While there has been some reluctance on the part of sociological functionalists to recognize their ties with sociological organicism, there has been frequent explicit recognition of their ties with psychological configurationism.

The organismic basis of Gestalt and configuration theory in psychology has long been made explicit. Raymond Wheeler, for example, frankly takes this as its crucial element. In fact, psychology, he believes, tends to be ultimately either mechanistic or organismic. The last two periods in the history of psychology dominated by the mechanistic pattern occurred roughly from 1710 to 1790 and from 1830 to 1910. Accordingly, the last two organismic periods occurred between 1790 and 1830 and from 1910 to the present. Prior to the twentieth century, periods of organismic thought have been vitalistic in nature, and certain of the organismic trends within this century have been vitalistic.[10]

Mechanistic theories, whether in psychology or elsewhere, locate their fundamental and derived elements in quite a different manner from organismic ones. Mechanistic theories usually prefer an atomic pattern. An element, a particle, an individual thing, or a unit is taken as fundamental. Organismic theories, on the other hand, locate what is essential not in parts or elements, but in systems, patterns, or wholes. The part or element is secondary and derived from the whole. Organismic types of theories are not confined to psychology and sociology but turn up even in physical science in the idea of systems of positively and negatively charged particles or systems of energy obeying laws of equilibrium; they appear in biology where the basic fact is conceived as the organism as a whole, not the cell.

The problems posed by mechanism and organicism in psychology were quite distinct. The atomists needed mechanisms or expedients to put the parts together. Hence, there is emphasis upon such concepts as bonds, attractions, repulsions, affinities, sociations, contacts. Scientific laws pertain to the mechanisms by which complexes are formed; otherwise laws are merely statistical.

While organicism visualizes the parts as being in relation with one another and as possessing form and order, nevertheless these parts are reduced in importance. The *whole* with its parts in interrelation in time and space becomes the primary fact. There were many anticipations of this organismic concept of continuity over time, and unity in time and space: Wundt's concept of apperception, Fechner's search for a systematic relationship between mind and body, James's shift of emphasis from states of mind to the "stream of consciousness," the British concept of "conation," Ehrenfels' work on "Gestaltqualitäten," and Dilthey's work on psychological wholes are all frequently cited as anticipations of the rise of the recent forms of the organismic point of view in psychology.

In America, the shift to functionalistic psychology was strongly advanced by William James. His treatment of consciousness, the will, the emotions, and memory all moved in this direction. As already noted, in his treatment of consciousness he proposed to substitute the concept of process or "stream of consciousness" for the old notions of mind as a substance and of consciousness as states. In his treatment of the will, he was convinced that mechanistic statements are inadequate. While he drops the "soul," he retains the will as a group of integrating functions in experience. His treatment of emotions (paralleling those of Carl Lange) rejected the idea that emotions exist apart from bodily, physiological changes; rather, they are a product of such changes. In James's formulation, we see a bear, we run, and are afraid, or we lose our fortune, we weep, and are sorry. Memory, too, was treated neither as a fixed faculty nor as a miscellaneous property of separate items but as a general property of brain structure.[11]

Functional psychology in America is often traced to the paper by John Dewey in 1896 on *The Reflex Arc Concept in Psychology*. Dewey criticized the division of the reflex arc into stimulus and response, maintaining that the minimal unit that

[10]Raymond H. Wheeler, "Gestalt Psychology," in *The Encyclopedia of Psychology*, ed. Philip Lawrence Harriman (New York: Philosophical Library, 1946), p. 239. The two opposed ways of explaining the phenomena of life are "mechanism" and "vitalism." Mechanism offers a physicochemical explanation of life, whereas vitalism maintains that there is a fundamental difference between animate and inanimate matter.

[11]For a summary of James's theories, see Gardner Murphy, *An Historical Introduction to Modern Psychology* (New York: Harcourt, Brace, 1929), pp. 207–223.

could profitably be considered in isolation, if one were to analyze behavior, was the entire reflex, the key to which is its function. Functionalism, as the new developments in psychology were called, found its distinctiveness in dealing with operations rather than elements. It considered consciousness to be a biologically adaptive activity. It was concerned with interrelations in all spheres of behavior and adaptation.[12]

Of all the movements toward functionalism in psychology, the Gestaltist has proven to be the most significant to sociology. It had its beginnings in Max Wertheimer's theories and research carried on at Frankfurt am Main in 1912. In the early nineteenth century, Joseph Plateau had invented the stroboscope, permitting the projection of a series of different pictures on the eye, each picture being slightly different from the previous one. Wertheimer reduced the experiments to two pictures each with a single line, the first vertical, the second sloping. By varying the length of the blank interval between the pictures, he could study the conditions under which the illusion of movement arises. When the interval was 1/5 of a second or longer, the observer saw first one line, then another. When the interval was as short as 1/13 of a second the two lines appeared to stand side by side. Between these limits, the observer had the impression of a single line moving from one position to another. Since there was no justification for this in the objective stimuli, Wertheimer theorized that the experience represented one that could not be reduced to simpler terms. It was similar to, and yet it was not, an elementary sensation. It was a phenomenon sui generis which he called the *phi-phenomenon*.[13]

Beginning with this important discovery, Wertheimer, Köhler,[14] and Koffka[15] developed the early forms of the Gestalt position. The earliest researches of the school (particularly those of Köhler and Koffka) were directed to the phenomena of perception in opposition to associationistic psychology. In experiments with chickens, for example, the creatures were taught to peck at feed on a gray rather than on a white or black background. If the same chickens were then placed in a new situation where the gray on which they had learned to eat represented the darkest of three colors, the chickens responded not to the original color to which they had been conditioned but to the medium color. The perceptual situation formed a whole, a *Gestalt*.

Among the most famous of the studies by members of the school were those carried out on chimpanzees by Köhler when he was isolated at Teneriffe during World War I. The apes were presented with all sorts of situations — bananas just out of reach outside the cage but with sticks available so that the creature could spear them or paw them in; bananas outside the cage but to which a string within their reach was attached; fruit suspended from the ceiling but with boxes that could be piled up to reach it. In contrast to the random trial-and-error behavior of rats, studied by American psychologists, in which the successes were gradually learned, the problem solving under these conditions had a different form. Initially, there was often some trial behavior on the part of the chimpanzees. When this did not succeed the chimpanzee seemed to give up and ignore the banana just outside reach. However, sometimes the creature behaved for all the world as if he suddenly had an idea, as when without hesitation the creature picked up a stick and speared an inaccessible fruit. Solutions were remembered and used without the need for relearning. Insight and goal-directed behavior appeared as responses within a whole situation. The contrast between the experimental trends among German and American psychologists led Bertrand Russell to the famous quip that rats studied by German psychologists had been observed to sit down and think and evolve the answer out of their inner consciousness while rats studied by American psychologists had

[12]J. C. Flügel, *A Hundred Years of Psychology, 1833–1933* (New York: Macmillan, 1933), pp. 230–231.
[13]*Ibid.*, pp. 241–242.
[14]Wolfgang Köhler, *The Mentality of Apes*, trans. Ella Winter (New York: Harcourt, Brace, 1925); *Gestalt Psychology* (New York: Liveright, 1929).
[15]Kurt Koffka, *Principles of Gestalt Psychology* (New York: Harcourt, Brace, 1935).

been noted to rush about with great bustle and pep, finally achieving the desired results by chance.

Among the most impressive results of Köhler's experiments were those in which the chimpanzees learned to pile several boxes on top of one another in order to reach a suspended fruit. And perhaps the most striking case of all was the instance of one creature chewing the end of one of two small sticks and fitting it to another to actually make an instrument capable of reaching the banana beyond the reach of either one. In the animal's conscious experience, the elements of the situation were rearranged. A configuration appeared, organizing the elements of the situation as means and ends. Insight in these simple cases is the perception of the possibility of a new arrangement.

The concept of organic wholes is preserved throughout Gestalt theory. Koffka argues that "the term *Gestalt* is a short name for a category of thought comparable to other general categories like substance, causality, function." The essence of the problems faced by Gestalt theory are found in: "first, the problem of the relation between a whole and its parts; and, second, the problem of harmony, adaptation or teleological perfection of certain morphological structures and types of behavior."[16] Koffka believed that the role of Gestalt theory has in part been the restoration of organic conceptions in biology. In psychology, Gestaltists theorized that the main properties of systems are the movement toward coherence and integration, called the "law of *Prägnanz.*" This means that in any behavioral system the best possible equilibrium will be achieved; the actual organization will be as good as the conditions allow with respect to closure, articulation, and consistency of the particular behaviors and of the total behavioral field. The chief content of Gestalt theory is the idea of the relation of parts and wholes involving the recognition of intrinsic real dynamic whole-properties which, it is argued, may legitimately be called meaningful. Gestalt theory generally is the attempt to find coherent functional wholes within phenomena and to treat them as primary realities and to understand the behavior of these wholes, as well as their parts, from the whole rather than from the parts.

Gestalt theory by no means exhausted the organismic tendency in modern psychology. Dewey, who has already been examined, pulled together the unsystematic functionalistic elements in William James. His *Human Nature and Conduct* approached the field of social psychology from the standpoint of the concept of "habit," explored so brilliantly in William James's *Principles of Psychology.* In Dewey's treatment, habit assumes the form of a central behavioral function. "Habits," he said, "may be profitably compared to physiological functions, like breathing, digesting."[17] Habits were even proposed as the reference point for problems of morality. "To get a rational basis for moral discussion we must begin with recognizing that functions and habits are ways of using and incorporating the environment in which the latter has its say as surely as the former."[18] As the functional form in which both the individual and the environment are involved, habits are inevitably social. This fact has been obscured by a metaphysical tradition of individual free will and responsibility. Close analysis shows the very will itself to represent merely the manifestation of habit, for habits are "demands for certain kinds of activity; and they constitute the self. In any intelligible sense of the word will, they *are* the will. They form our effective desires and they furnish us with our working capacities."[19]

To date, sociological functionalism has not gone outside the social sciences to philosophy for firsthand inspiration. This, however, does not mean that the traditions of Western thought have been without influence upon it. As a development out of positivistic organicism in sociology and functional and Gestalt psychology, sociological

[16]Kurt Koffka, "Gestalt," in the *Encyclopædia of the Social Sciences,* VI, 642.

[17]John Dewey, *Human Nature and Conduct* (New York: Henry Holt, 1922), p. 14.
[18]*Ibid.,* p. 15.
[19]*Ibid.,* p. 25.

functionalism draws its inspiration indirectly from idealistic philosophy of the nineteenth century and to some lesser extent from nineteenth-century biology.

It is precisely the older and more traditional forms of idealism that come into question, not so much the scientifically modified forms or those types restyled under the influence of Kantianism. Sociological functionalism responds indirectly to those philosophic traditions and directly to those social science traditions in which organismic models of thought are paramount. Social behaviorism, too, in all its branches drew something from idealism, but it was a very different type of thing — the kind of thing the functionalists denounce as atomistic, mechanistic, or elementaristic.

The attention in some detail to the Gestalt sources of sociological functionalism is in part necessary because one of the major branches of the theory proceeded directly from it.

SOCIOLOGICAL AND ANTHROPOLOGICAL FUNCTIONALISM

The rather curious phenomenon already observed of an unwillingness on the part of sociological functionalists to admit their sociological origins, even while they have freely admitted influence from some types of psychology, is also manifest in their relations to anthropology. A number of the sociological functionalists quite frankly trace their origins to anthropology. This has its ironic twist, inasmuch as anthropological functionalism was developed in considerable measure under the influence of sociology.

Functionalism would seem in advance to be a much more "natural" position for anthropology than for sociology. The two critical properties of functionalism as a system of social theory are the analysis of interhuman behavior from the standpoint of the primacy of interbehavioral systems and the study of various elements or incidents as system-determined.

One can easily understand Albion Small's sage

judgment that this is very good as a provisional starting point for sociological analysis of modern society. But to Small, modern society is enormously complex. What is impressive about it is not its character as a system but its infinitely varied encounters. Any group, he agrees, is a system, but he is never inclined to treat it as an ultimate fact, for social life is the phenomenon of the endless establishment and destruction of groups. Hence, Small's judgment was that once we have made the important first step possible with functionalism, it is time to get down to business.

The case would seem offhand to be somewhat different for the anthropologists, dealing with numerous relatively isolated, often preliterate tribes that have frequently occupied the same river valley or island or mountain plateau for centuries. The natural unit of study is the tribal community which is often almost completely closed culturally and socially. If ever the conception of the primacy of the system were relevant, it would seem to be here. It would also seem plausible to consider the single most significant aspect of any "part" the degree to which it is system-determined and system-sustaining. Yet, this point of view was rather slow to develop in ethnology.

One could not touch ideological motives more directly than in the speed with which the functionalistic point of view emerged in early sociology (in the form of organicism) and the slowness of its appearance in ethnology, where it would seem more natural. In early sociology, organicism corresponded directly to conservative needs. It found society to be a delicately adjusted system, not something fools should be permitted to tamper with, but something even angels fear to touch.

The speed with which modern functionalists rush to their own defense when there has been no attack, denying that functionalism has any conservative ideological implications, is fairly direct testimony of their sensitivity to the conservative implications of organicism. Sociological functionalism as a maiden branch of theory has made its debut with pronouncements of its virginal character and with excited defenses of its honor.

By contrast, the functionalistic theory made its way very slowly in ethnology because there were no ideological reasons making it desirable. Western scholars studying contemporary preliterate tribes were under no obligation in presenting their researches to prove that "order" was after all the natural state of social affairs. They could be frankly curious in an uncommitted manner. The emergence of anthropological functionalism thus waited for a sociologist like Durkheim, infused with organismic suppositions, to take the ethnographic materials collected by others (as he did with the ethnographic reports on Australia) and subject them to functionalistic analysis. The rich suggestiveness of his analysis was something of a shock to the anthropologists of his day. One was not supposed to come to brilliant interpretative conclusions without ever having been near the field. In some measure this was possible only because in this area the kinds of questions asked by the organicists were relatively new. (This, of course, is not to underestimate Durkheim's brilliance.) In this connection, it is incidentally clear that Radcliffe-Brown drew the correct conclusion as to why Durkheim was able to make as much of a contribution as he did. Radcliffe-Brown quite appropriately took Durkheim as the starting point for his functionalism.

Prior to the influence of Durkheim, ethnology was concerned with the common properties of humanity (psychic unity of humankind) or with the evolutionary search for origins, rather than the analysis of integral organismic units. Moreover, when the evolutionary hypothesis was shattered, it was replaced by diffusionism, which tended to concentrate study on the migration of traits and trait complexes from some place of invention, rather than on the "functional integration of elements" in a tribal community.

There were, of course, anticipations of functionalism, found for example in the works of J. J. Bachofen and Fustel de Coulange. It is not surprising that so sensitive a student as Boas should have appreciated some aspects of functionalism. In 1887 he opposed the usual practice of museum exhibits of a synoptic form. He ar-

gued that when a specimen is isolated it becomes impossible to understand its meaning. A rattle may be a musical instrument or a ritualistic object. A people's productions have to be studied as a whole if informing styles are to be discerned.[20] Boas insisted that before equating phenomena, we must first be sure of their comparability, which can be determined only from their context.

In deriving his concept from Durkheim, A. R. Radcliffe-Brown (1881–1955) frankly acknowledged the relation between functionalism and organicism:

> The concept of function applied to human societies is based on an analogy between social life and organic life. The recognition of the analogy and of some of its implications is not new. In the nineteenth century the analogy, the concept of function, and the word itself appear frequently in social philosophy and sociology. So far as I know the first systematic formulation of the concept as applying to the strictly scientific study of society was that of Émile Durkheim in 1895.[21]

In Radcliffe-Brown's conception, Durkheim defined the function of social institutions as the satisfaction of the needs of the social organism. Radcliffe-Brown believed that one must avoid teleological interpretations. Hence, he suggested that for the term "needs" the phrase "necessary conditions of existence" should be substituted. The concept of function applied to social science involves the assumption that there are necessary conditions of existence for human societies which are discoverable by scientific study.

By further elaboration of the organic analogy, Radcliffe-Brown developed the meaning of function to refer to "the life of an organism . . . conceived as the *functioning* of its structure. . . . Through the continuity of the functioning . . . the continuity of . . . structure is preserved. If we consider any recurrent part . . . its *function* is the part it plays in, the contributions it makes to, the life of

[20]See Robert H. Lowie, *The History of Ethnological Theory* (New York: Farrar & Rinehart, 1937), p. 142.
[21]A. R. Radcliffe-Brown, *Structure and Function in Primitive Society* (Glencoe, Ill.: The Free Press, 1952), p. 178.

A. R. RADCLIFFE-BROWN

Royal Anthropological Institute, London

the organism as a whole. . . . the function of a re-current physiological process is . . . a corre-spondence between it and the needs . . . of the or-ganism."[22] Radcliffe-Brown believed that there were three questions raised by organic systems: morphology (the study of structure), physiology (the study of function), and evolution (or devel-opment). All three questions, he thought, apply to social life. We can recognize the existence of a so-cial structure; individuals as the essential units are connected by a definite set of social relations in an integrated whole. The continuity of structure is maintained by the process of social life. The social life of the community is the *functioning* of the social structure.

There is, however, a difficulty involved in the application of the functional point of view to soci-ety. An animal organism can be seen as a structural unit. In human society, however, social structure as a whole can only be observed in its functioning. Hence social morphology cannot be established independently of a social physiology. Moreover, an animal organism does not change its structural type in the course of its life. But a society may change its structural type without any breach of continuity. Throughout, the function of any unit or partial activity is the contribution which a partial activity makes to the total activity. We can further distinguish in the social organism the equivalent to biological health and disease. "The Greeks of the fifth century B.C. thought that one might apply the same notion to society, to the city-state, distin-guishing conditions of *eunomia*, good order, social health, from *dysnomia*, disorder, social ill health."[23] At all times it brings the problems of interrelations into central focus.

Among contemporary ethnologists, the most important single functionalist besides Radcliffe-Brown was Bronislaw Malinowski (1884–1942). In his most general statement, Malinowski identifies functionalism with the study of interrelations. The functional conception of culture, he maintains, is critical to theory and method. To study details de-tached from their setting must inevitably stultify theory, field work, and practical handling alike.[24] Culture, for Malinowski, is the social heritage of humanity, comprising all inherited artifacts, goods, technical processes, ideal habits, and values. Even social organization cannot really be under-stood except as a part of culture. Culture does not in any way contradict the psychological nature of social reality. The ultimate medium of culture is the individual mind and social organization. "Culture is a reality *sui generis* and must be studied as such. . . . Culture is a well organized unity di-

[22]*Ibid.*, p. 179.

[23]*Ibid.*, p. 182
[24]Bronislaw Malinowski, *The Dynamics of Culture Change* (New Haven, Conn.: Yale University Press, 1945), p. 41.

BRONISLAW MALINOWSKI

Courtesy of the Harvard University News Office, Cambridge, Mass.

vided into two fundamental aspects — a body of artifacts and a system of customs."[25]

Malinowski was opposed quite explicitly to both evolutionary and diffusionist interpretations of culture. Evolutionary interpretations, he argued, rest on the concept of survivals and attempt to reconstruct the past. Diffusionism attempts to reconstruct the history of culture by tracing out its diffusion on the basis of imitation or taking over of artifacts. To both of these views, he opposed the functionalist theory.

The primary concern of functional anthropology is with the function of institutions, customs, imple-

ments, and ideas. It holds that the cultural process is subject to laws and that the laws are to be found in the function of the real elements of culture. The atomizing or isolating treatment of cultural traits is regarded as sterile, because the significance of culture consists in the relation between its elements, and the existence of accidental or fortuitous culture complexes is not admitted.[26]

The foundations for a functional theory of culture were laid down by Malinowski as follows: (1) it is accepted, first of all, as an axiom that human beings have needs for food, reproduction, shelter, etc.; (2) it is assumed that human drives are physiological but restructured by acquired habit; (3) culture is conceived as a conditioning apparatus which through training in skills and norms amalgamates nature with nurture; (4) it is taken as fundamental that human beings never deal with their difficulties alone; they organize into families, communities, tribes, with authority and leadership culturally defined; (5) the symbolism of language is a component in all technology and social organization; (6) cultural satisfaction of primary biological needs imposes secondary imperatives on human beings; (7) the functional theory postulates that the system of production, distribution, and consumption must be carried on even in the most primitive of communities.[27]

The real units of culture are *institutions,* which are sets of activities organized around some need. They are groups of people united for the pursuit of an activity by means of a material endowment and a technical outfit. They are organized on a definite legal or customary charter; linguistically formulated in myth, legend, rule, and maxim; and trained or prepared for the carrying out of its task.[28]

In the analysis of any item, say the construction of a seagoing craft, there are certain stable elements of form determined by the nature of the activity to which the craft is instrumental. Variations, however, occur within the limits imposed by the

[25]Bronislaw Malinowski, "Culture," in the *Encyclopædia of the Social Sciences,* IV, 623.

[26]*Ibid.,* p. 625
[27]Malinowski, *The Dynamics of Culture Change,* pp. 42–44.
[28]*Ibid.,* p. 50.

primary function, which causes the primary characteristics of an artifact to remain stable. The form of cultural objects is determined by direct bodily needs on the one hand and by instrumental uses on the other. The cultural mode of satisfaction of biological needs creates new conditions and thus imposes new cultural imperatives. Thus, sooner or later the act of "placing an object, custom, or idea, within its natural setting, brings us to an institution, that is to an organized, purposeful system of human effort and achievement."[29] Among illustrations of functional analysis of various cultural items, magic, myth, sorcery, and play are typical. Magic, for example, is explained as a functional product of human needs, arising whenever there is an unbridgeable gap between people's knowledge and their powers of practical control and under circumstances in which they are forced to continue their activity. Magical practices and beliefs reassure the individual and permit life to continue. Religion, too, is explained as due to deep although derived needs of the individual and of the community. Primitive religion is largely concerned with sanctifying the crises of human life: birth, puberty, marriage, death. Sorcery is interpreted as a normally conservative force used at times for intimidation but usually for the enforcement of customary law or the wishes of those in power. Play, games, sports, and art are conceived as devices which tear people out of their ordinary rut, mitigating the strain and discipline of workaday life and restoring them to full capacity for routine work. And, finally, culture itself is an instrumental reality which came into existence to satisfy the needs of human beings in a manner surpassing any direct adaptation to the environment.

Robert Lowie, who was an anthropological social behaviorist, was distinctly annoyed by Malinowski's functionalism:

In messianic mood Malinowski is forever engaged in two favorite pastimes. Either he is battering down wide open doors; or he is petulantly deriding work

that does not personally attract him. In the same spirit, Malinowski thumbs his nose at technology, flouts distribution studies, sneers at reconstruction of the past. The only worthy aim is to study "the part which is played by any one factor of a culture within the general scheme." In short, Malinowski's functionalism treats each culture as a closed system except insofar as its elements respond to vital biological urges.[30]

Firth has recently brought anthropological functionalism under review. Firth thinks that Malinowski's functionalism was superior to that of Radcliffe-Brown in treating the individual. He had two major objections to the latter's formulation: (1) there was, he thought, a residual teleological element in it; and (2) Radcliffe-Brown had suggested that a social system may display functional unity or a tendency toward functional integration.[31]

If Radcliffe-Brown's functionalism is inferior to Malinowski's, it must surely be for reasons other than those given by Firth. He differs from Malinowski, most certainly, in a more frank acknowledgment of the organismic origins of functionalism, in recognizing the tendency of functional analysis to become teleological, and in proposing the functional integration of social systems as a "working hypothesis." Malinowski does none of these things. His functionalism has, thus, a much more dogmatic cast. If one accepts the grounds given, Radcliffe-Brown's functionalism is to be treated as inferior because of its greater theoretical honesty. But however this may be, both Radcliffe-Brown and Malinowski gave recognition to that trend in ethnology which cuts itself loose from evolutionism and diffusionism in their pure forms and elevates the problem of system integration and the study of interrelations into primary focus.

Ruth Benedict's *Patterns of Culture* rests frankly on functional grounds. The significance of cultural

[29]*Ibid.*, p. 51.

[30]Lowie, *The History of Ethnological Theory*, pp. 234–235.
[31]Raymond Firth, "Function," in *Yearbook of Anthropology*, ed. William L. Thomas, Jr. and Jean S. Stewart (New York: Werner Gren Foundation for Anthropological Research, 1955), p. 240.

behavior is not exhausted when it is seen to be so-cial, human-made, and variable. A culture is con-ceived to be a more or less consistent pattern of thought and action with characteristic purposes. "This integration of culture is not in the least mys-tical. It is the same process by which a style in art comes into being and persists."[32] This necessity for functional studies of culture is traced by Benedict to Malinowski, with clear recognition of its or-ganismic properties. "Malinowski . . . criticizes the usual diffusion studies as post-mortem dissections of organisms."[33] And confirmation of the value of functional analysis is found in the theories of Wilhelm Stern, who insisted that the undivided totality of the person must be the point of depar-ture for psychological study. He criticizes atomistic studies, which he finds have been almost universal in introspective and experimental psychology, and he substitutes investigation into the configurations of personality. Gestalt psychology is felt by Ben-edict to have done some of the most striking work in "justifying the importance of this point of de-parture from the whole rather than from its parts,"[34] and Wilhelm Dilthey is also cited as jus-tifying functional analyses of philosophical sys-tems. "He sees them as great expressions of the variety of life, moods, *Lebensstimmungen,* integrated attitudes the fundamental categories of which cannot be resolved into one another."[35] Finally, Oswald Spengler is treated as particularly valuable for promoting the idea "that these cultural configurations have, like an organism, a span of life they cannot overpass."[36]

Benedict's inventory of the sources and justifications of her functionalistic approach to culture have been reviewed to reenforce a point that has already been made. The reluctance of sociological functionalists to admit their ties with organismic social theory on the one hand and idealistic philosophy on the other cannot be ac-cepted as long as they continue to trace their affinities only or primarily to anthropology. Radcliffe-Brown frankly made his point of de-parture from Durkheim and extolled the virtues of the organismic hypothesis, which was the core of functionalism for him. Malinowski works directly out of Radcliffe-Brown. Benedict lists a whole series of organismic social theorists and idealistic philosophers as the sources of her functionalism: Dilthey, Nietzsche, Spengler. Incidentally, she also frankly recognizes the ties with Gestalt or configu-ration psychology as well. And once again the or-ganismic hypothesis is brought forward.

It is of no particular value to trace any further here the forms of anthropological functionalism.[37] There is little doubt that powerful functionalistic themes run through the "culture and personality" studies.[38] Murdock, in a somewhat defensive man-ner, has insisted that functionalism genuinely traces to Sumner and Keller.[39] This, of course, is correct only insofar as Sumner and Keller share the tradition of organismic positivism. To this ex-tent, they belong among the persons who fore-shadow contemporary functionalism. The only mis-take is to single them out as if they were exclusive sources.

. . . William Graham Sumner . . . foreshadows functionalism. . . . He insisted on what is now a com-monplace . . . that culture is adaptive, satisfying indi-vidual and societal needs and altering over time in re-sponse to changing conditions of life. He was the first to promulgate explicitly the doctrine of cultural rel-ativity, shocking his contemporaries by asserting that

[32]Ruth Benedict, *Patterns of Culture* (Boston: Houghton Mifflin, 1934), p. 47.
[33]*Ibid.,* p. 50.
[34]*Ibid.,* p. 51.
[35]*Ibid.,* p. 52.
[36]*Ibid.,* p. 53.

[37]Some others may be found in Walter Buckley, "Structural-Functional Analysis in Modern Sociology," in *Modern Sociological Theory,* ed. Howard Becker and Alvin Boskoff (New York: Dryden, 1957), pp. 236–259.
[38]See, for example, Abram Kardiner, Ralph Linton, Cora du Bois, and James West, *The Psychological Frontiers of So-ciety* (New York: Columbia University Press, 1945).
[39]George Peter Murdock, *Social Structure* (New York: Macmillan, 1949), pp. x, 10, 126, 198, and "Sociology and Anthropology," in *For a Science of Social Man,* ed. John Gillin (New York: Macmillan, 1954), p. 16.

even slavery, cannibalism, and infanticide are adaptive and socially justifiable in societies that normally practice them.[40]

To be sure, the same could be said about Comte.

SUMMARY

Social behaviorism has tended to re-enact a drama similar to that of positivistic organicism. From the very beginning, positivistic organicism was saddled with a problem: it attempted to combine an idealistic definition of society with a positivism of method. The tensions that emerged between these two factors forced the rapid internal evolution of the school. In the end the attempt to reconcile them broke down, and positivistic organicism fell apart into its separate components.

Conflict theory preserved the positivism of the first school of sociology, but varied its definition of social reality. The formal school of sociology varied both the definition of social reality and the positivism of its method. The reasons why these were abandoned by many sociologists have been traced.

Social behaviorism did not accept the old organismic definition of society, but in reaction to the formalists, it returned to a more idealistic position. At the same time, there was a powerful tendency to establish sociology on a more positivistic foun-

dation. Social behaviorism was thus saddled with a special form of the same tensions that had characterized positivistic organicism. The tense interplay of these factors was at the basis of the rapid evolution of both theory and method. The more precise one made the theory, the more difficult the methodological problem tended to become. There is little doubt that these new tensions have been some of the components in the movement of many former members of one or another branch of social behaviorism into functionalism.

At least four major conceptions of function must be distinguished to understand modern discussions: function in a mathematical sense, function as useful activity, function as appropriate activity, and function as system-determined and system-sustaining activity. Only the last of these provides uniqueness to functionalism as a type of sociological theory.

In the simplest terms, the difference between social behaviorism and sociological functionalism is that the former was a type of social nominalism, the latter a modern form of social realism. As it is sometimes expressed, social behaviorism is a form of social atomism; sociological functionalism is a form of social organicism. The key ideas of functionalism are the concept of the primacy of system and the idea that all units of the system are only secondarily relevant.

The origins of sociological functionalism are threefold: from early sociology, from the functionalistic branch of psychology, and from social anthropology. It is a pleasant irony that contemporary sociological functionalists have gone to anthropology to discover their own origins.

[40]Murdock, "Sociology and Anthropology," *loc. cit.*

XX

Macrofunctionalism in Contemporary Sociology

Two major schools of sociological functionalism are in process of development at the present time. Since all the essentials of functionalism are manifest in both, it is rather inappropriate to expend the term *functionalism* on only one. For want of better terms they will be described here as *macrofunctionalism* and *microfunctionalism*. This distinction is made purely in terms of the size of the unit chosen as the basic type of system for the branch of the theory in question. The macrofunctionalists basically presume the existence of relatively large-scale systems, the microfunctionalists of fairly small-scale systems. The first branch of functionalistic theory had its origins primarily in sociological organicism (though its exponents are often more inclined to trace their origins to anthropology); the second branch of functionalism had its origins primarily in Gestalt psychology. The employment by the macrofunctionalists of relatively large-scale systems as the basic referents of its theory is in part understandable in terms of its origins. The organismic sociological theory from which it derives had been anchored in the study of entire societies conceived as superorganisms. The relatively small-scale systems assumed by microfunctionalism (often designated as "group dynamics") are also partly understandable in terms of its derivations. The original systems assumed by Gestalt theory consisted of such things as acts of perception within a perceptual situation and acts of judgment within specific empirical context. As they develop, the macrofunctionalists tend to direct analysis toward smaller, less inclusive systems, whereas the microfunctionalists tend to expand analysis to embrace larger, more inclusive systems. Whether the two schemes of functionalism can ever be brought together in a single formulation waits to be seen.

Since functionalism is anchored so deeply in organicism, practically every item said to be peculiar to functionalism has been anticipated by the organicists. Functionalism at best represents merely a regrouping of and re-emphasis upon ideas that were already present. This is one of the reasons why the moment a functionalistic program is formulated it tends to look like either an old error or something that has always been known.

Theoretically, interest attaches in functionalism not to some presumed special "functional method" but to its characteristic ideas.[1] When functionalism is taken to mean "interrelation," it has to be dismissed as a special theory. If there were no more to functionalism than this, every school of sociological thought would have to be described as functionalistic. So long as functionalism is taken to mean "teleological analysis," it has to be dismissed as questionable metaphysics or as a mere shorthand or economy of statement for ideas that could be re-expressed in more exact form. Functionalism reaches its distinctive subject matter when it takes the organism-like *system* as its peculiar object of study and conceives of this as the primary subject matter of sociological analysis, studying all other items as system-determined and system-maintaining.

Because the ideas distinctive to functionalism are those which bring it closest to organicism, special importance attaches to the criteria by which one draws the line between organicism and functionalism. To be sure, organicism has largely declined as a distinctive form of sociological theory; functionalism has taken its place. A purely terminological distinction is of no value for theory. Besides, Arnold Toynbee, Pitirim Sorokin, and Oswald Spengler are clearly organicists. Sorokin, at least, does not describe himself as a functionalist. (It is noteworthy, however, that modern functionalists find support among these three — as Ruth Benedict did from Spengler.)

The position is taken here that so far as the organic system serves as the model of theory, the organicists and functionalists are identical. However, the distinctive property of the positivistic organicists was that their supersensory organisms represented actual historical configurations: it is our own society which is "sensate" for Sorokin; it is Western civilization that is in process of organic decline for Spengler.

The transition from positivistic organicism to functionalism is made when the theoretical explanations of the sociologist turn from social criticism of actual historical societies or civilizations, conceived as organisms, to abstract formulation and the development of the concept of system as an explanatory principle of theory. It goes without saying that the transition from positivistic organicism to functionalism is rather fluid. Functionalism is a program of theory construction; positivistic organicism was a program of action. The anticipations of functionalism among the organicists are taken to represent those ideas that aided in the abstraction, analysis, and description of components of the idea of organic system. (Of course, if anyone wished to take organicism and functionalism to represent the applied and theoretical aspects of the same enterprise, there could hardly be much dispute.) Positivistic organicism left to functionalism (and sociology generally) a whole general heritage of concepts, including "structure," "social organization," "social order," and "function" itself, as well as a great number of detailed analyses of structures and the activities they sustain. But over and beyond this heritage, certain sociologists contributed to the abstraction and precision of the concept of organic system itself. Some of these (like Durkheim) have already been noted.

Vilfredo Pareto. Since the organismic positivists as a whole are the ancestors of sociological functionalism, there is a high level of arbitrariness in isolating one—as Radcliffe-Brown does in Durkheim, Murdock does in Sumner, Benedict does in Spengler — and treating him as the precursor of sociological functionalism. Tönnies, or Schäffle, or any of dozens of others could serve equally well.

The case is different, however, for the sociological functionalists proper. They are the persons who isolated and gave abstract formulation to the critical concept of organic system, mak-

---

[1]Carl G. Hempel once and for all disposes of the so-called functional method in "The Logic of Functional Analysis," in *Symposium on Sociological Theory*, ed. Llewellyn Gross (Evanston, Ill.: Row, Peterson, 1959), pp. 271–310.

ing it a unit of sociological analysis. They proposed to analyze all other elements in terms of their system unit. Pareto was a voluntaristic organicist. At the same time, he is a transitional figure between organicism and sociological functionalism. He clearly perceived and gave abstract formulation to the concept of system. The form of a society, according to Pareto, is determined by all the elements acting upon it and which society, in turn, reacts upon. A reciprocal determination arises, among such elements as: soil, climate, flora, fauna; geological, mineralogical, and other similar conditions; elements external to a given society at a given time, such as the influences of other societies upon it and the effects of the previous situation within it; and internal elements like race, proclivities, interests, aptitudes for thought and observation, state of knowledge, and so on.[2] But however few or many the elements, Pareto maintains that they form a system. By "the social system" he means that state which a society takes both at a specified moment and in the successive transformations which it undergoes within a period of time. The real state of the system is determined by its conditions, which are of such a nature that if some modification in its form is introduced artificially a reaction will take place tending to restore the changing form to its original state. If that were not the case, the form, with its normal changes, would not be determined but would be a mere matter of chance.[3] More specifically, "equilibrium" is defined as some state X such that, if subjected to some artificial modification different from those it usually undergoes, a reaction at once occurs tending to restore it to its real, normal state.

Quite in accord with the conception of the primacy of the complex whole, Pareto maintains that we cannot simplify a society or one of its subparts beyond a certain point without falling into error:

The economic system is made up of certain molecules set in motion by tastes and subject to ties (checks) in the form of obstacles to the acquisition of economic values. The social system is much more complicated, and even if we try to simplify it as far as we possibly can without falling into serious errors, we at least have to think of it as made up of certain molecules harboring residues, derivations, interests, and proclivities, and which perform, subject to numerous ties, logical and non-logical actions. In the economic system the non-logical element is relegated entirely to tastes and disregarded, since tastes are taken as data of fact. One might wonder whether the same thing might not be done for the social system, whether we might not relegate the non-logical element to the residues, then take the residues as data of fact and proceed to examine the logical conduct that originates in the residues.[4]

But, Pareto maintains, residues are not, like tastes, merely sources of conduct. They function throughout the whole course of conduct, developing from the source. Thus, a science based on the hypothesis that logical inferences are drawn from certain given residues would yield a type of social phenomenon having little or no contact with reality. Society is a prelogical phenomenon. Individuals, the molecules of the social system, are possessed of certain sentiments manifested by residues. These sentiments, and not the rationalizations of them, determine the forms of social life.

Pareto clearly adheres to the concept of society implied by the organicists, identifying it with actual society, but his abstract formulation of the concept of equilibrium is a movement in the direction of functionalism.

Florian Znaniecki. While Sumner and a number of other early sociologists tended to make the idea of system primary and the implicit cause of all other social phenomena, and while Pareto brought the idea into a sharper formulation in the notion of equilibrium, Znaniecki abstracted and generalized the concept of system itself. Znaniecki, to be sure, made contributions to more than one branch of social behaviorism (symbolic interac-

[2]Vilfredo Pareto, *The Mind and Society,* trans. Andrew Bongiorno and Arthur Livingston (New York: Harcourt, Brace, 1935), Vol. 4, *The General Form of Society,* p. 1433.
[3]*Ibid.,* p. 1453.

[4]*Ibid.,* p. 1442. Pareto's concepts of *residue* and *derivation* have already been discussed. (See pp. 112–114.)

tionism with Thomas and social-action theory), but he found his peculiar identification in functionalism.

Znaniecki maintains that the scientific problem of selecting relevant from irrelevant factors is solved by the "principle of a closed system." As Znaniecki sees it, the idea of a closed system guides the physicist and the astronomer, the chemist and the geologist, the biologist and the philologist, the economist and the art student, in the choice and determination of their respective data. Reality is constituted by innumerable and various *closed systems,* "each of which is composed of a limited number of elements more intimately inter-related with one another than with any objects which do not belong to the system, and each possessing a specific internal structure which isolates it in certain respects from external influences."[5] Once he isolated the idea, Znaniecki retained it as his central theoretical principle, only renaming the idea in defense against critics.

A term has been used . . . to denote . . . systems, the term "closed systems." It was applied particularly to mechanical and thermodynamic systems. Years ago we borrowed this term and tried to apply it to social systems; but this application was misunderstood by social scientists, since closed system . . . means a system isolated from external influence. . . . this is obviously not true of a living organism . . . nor yet . . . of a cultural system. We shall adopt, therefore, a *limited system* to denote any combination of particular interdependent components with an inner order of its own.[6]

The first important contribution Znaniecki made to functionalism was the generalization of this notion. The system of concern to sociologists is not — as is still true for Pareto — "society." Society may, indeed, be a system. But the distinctive property of Znaniecki's view is the concept of the *plurality* of systems. In fact, Znaniecki maintains, one of the problems to be determined is whether the given system is included in others and itself includes others. The sun and planets may be viewed as a system or as an element of a wider sidereal system. Critical to his theory is the idea that every empirical object is either a system or an element in a system or both.

The first task of the scientist is to circumscribe the system in question and determine the elements belonging to it. For this purpose, special tests are often necessary. This task of circumscription partly overlaps with that of description. If the system as circumscribed at the outset proves to be too comprehensive, the scientist will need to break it up into smaller systems or else group many objects into larger units which behave in like respects. Moreover, we are interested in the relation to the system of any object chosen for study; we are not interested in its total unique qualities. The system itself provides standards of selection. "A system is relatively isolated from external influences owing to its structure, *i.e.* to the total combination of forces which keep its elements connected in a way none of them are connected with any outside objects."[7]

The central task of analysis is to move from detailed causal relations within the system to the increasingly inclusive picture of more comprehensive changes. After two changes within the same system or two interacting systems have been causally connected, we can try to formulate the connection in terms of *functional dependence.* The functional relationship is not a substitute for the causal relationship, but merely a more exact and more certain kind of causal relationship.[8]

The transition was made by Znaniecki from social-action theory to sociological functionalism by way of subsuming the concept of social action under the concept of system. In this manner the entire approach to social process proposed by

[5]Florian Znaniecki, *The Method of Sociology* (New York: Farrar & Rinehart, 1934), p. 12. (Znaniecki's major works are listed in Footnote 8, Chapter XVIII.)
[6]Florian Znaniecki, *Cultural Sciences: Their Origin and Development* (Urbana, Ill.: University of Illinois Press, 1952), pp. 163–164.

[7]Znaniecki, *The Method of Sociology,* p. 16.
[8]*Ibid.,* pp. 20–21.

Znaniecki is dominated by the concept system. In his *Laws of Social Psychology,* it is proposed to establish general laws regarding (1) interrelations between the elements of the system and (2) transformations to new systems due to outside factors. Social action, conceived as a system, has a situation, a tendency, other parties to the social act, goals, instruments, and methods. In terms of these elements, Znaniecki thought it was possible to establish a whole series of laws. A few illustrations may reveal the continuous domination of the discussion by the idea of system:

1. When activity continues to turn up negative values, a desire for stability arises in the given line of behavior.
2. When activity continues to turn up positive values, a desire for new experience arises in the given line of behavior.
3. When social action resting on positive tendencies meets unexpected negative values, the positive tendency tends to turn into a negative one.
4. If a social action resting on a tendency meets with unexpected positive values, the tendency becomes positive.
5. If an action is socially represented by a negative reaction of an individual or group not the original object of the action, the original positive tendency becomes anti-social.
6. If an action is socially sublimated by a positive social reaction on the part of an individual or group not the original object of the action, the original tendency becomes a conformist one.
7. If the object of a social action becomes inaccessible, the tendency becomes idealistic.
8. If the object of a social action becomes more accessible, the tendency becomes more sensual and less idealistic.
9. If, during a system of actions, new social objects are substituted for the original ones, the tendency is generalized.
10. When a contrast of situation makes goals self-contradictory, the tendency ceases to be directed toward achievement, changing into sentimental valuation.
11. If the psychological conflict between a present and virtual action is solved by accommodating the virtual situation to the present situation, the present tendency becomes rationalistic.

12. If in an action the situation becomes egocentric through introduction of the reflected self, the tendency becomes self-seeking.[9]

It may be seen that Znaniecki in part carried out the program of theory construction he proposed. The laws of social psychology are codified as laws of system integration and system transformation. He suggests the reformulation of the whole field of social action in terms of systems. The suggestion was also made that personality systems are one type of system among others. In all this, Znaniecki made extensive movements in the direction of a functionalistic theory. Znaniecki argued that previous to his own discussion, sociology had been variously conceived as (1) the theory of social actions, (2) the theory of social relations, (3) the theory of social persons, and (4) the theory of social groups. From Znaniecki's standpoint, these disciplines lose their independence and become merely branches of social theory.

> It is . . . high time for the sociologists to drop the superannuated claims of making a "synthetic" or "fundamental" science of societies and culture, and to realize that whatever positive scientific results they can show to their credit have been achieved only by concentrating on those kinds of specific data we have characterized . . . as social actions, social relations, social persons, and social groups.
>
> The logical reasons for uniting these data within the domain of one science and separating this domain from those of other sciences is founded on the fact that all of them as cultural systems have an essential *similarity of composition,* while they differ in composition from all other cultural systems — technical, economic, religious, linguistic.[10]

Znaniecki's attempt to reconstruct social theory on the basis of his functionalism may also be seen with respect to the study of the social role of the person of knowledge. The study was partly influenced by social behaviorism, and has been dis-

[9]See Florian Znaniecki, *The Laws of Social Psychology* (Chicago: University of Chicago Press, 1925), pp. 112–270.
[10]Znaniecki, *The Method of Sociology,* p. 130.

cussed as such in Chapter XVIII. At the same time, the study treats culture as a *system* of knowledge, the participation in which is determined by people's activities in social systems. The social role is conceived as linking cultural and social systems. "In sociology a conceptual framework for dealing with these problems has been gradually developing in the course of monographic investigations. In recent years the term 'social role' has been used by many sociologists to denote the phenomena in question."[11] Role is treated as a complex of values relating the person performing the role ("social person") and a number of other persons ("the social circle"). The person is conceived as an organic psychological entity (a "self"). The self is a system incorporated in a more comprehensive system. In terms of the social circle, the person is required to display the kinds of qualities the social circle needs. Thus, in the social circle the person possesses status. He or she has rights tied in with his or her role and performs a function, a requirement of the role. Hence, social roles are a class of social system linking two others — "social circles" and "culture." Znaniecki thus was inclined to remove the concept of role from symbolic interactionism, reinterpreting it in functionalistic terms.

Robert K. Merton. Merton's initial contributions to sociology were made in the social-action branch of social behaviorism — most completely in the extension of Weber's analysis of the Protestant ethic to the development of rational models of behavior under the influence of the inner-worldly asceticism of Protestantism. In his own original theorizing, Merton has abandoned the framework of social behaviorism for what he views as the more promising functionalistic theory. "Functional analysis is at once the most promising and possibly the least codified of contemporary approaches to problems of sociological interpretation. Having developed on many intellectual fronts at the same time, it has grown in shreds and patches rather than in depth. The accomplishments of functional analysis are

sufficient to suggest that its larger promise will ultimately be fulfilled. . . ."[12]

It is interesting to note that the persons from whom Merton explicitly derives functional analysis are primarily anthropologists: Radcliffe-Brown, Malinowski and Clyde Kluckhohn. The theory was approached by way of a distinction between five different meanings of the term function:

(1) Function as public occasion or gathering.
(2) Function as occupation.
(3) Function as activities assigned to the incumbent of a social status, e.g., to the occupant of an office.
(4) Mathematical function.
(5) Functions as biological or social procedures which help maintain the system.[13]

It is Merton's preference for the fifth of these meanings that ties his treatment most closely to those of the anthropologists and moves him into the circle of functionalistic theory proper. In his continued discussion, however, Merton indicates that over and beyond these five meanings there are still others. He notes that the term is frequently used alternatively with "purpose," "motive," "design," "primary concern," and "aim." It is a mistake, he feels, to confuse functions with subjective feelings. Social functions have *observable objective consequences.* The *motives* for entering into marriage, for example, should not be equated with functions. Nor are the reasons advanced by people for their behavior the same as the observed consequences of their behavior. One could not ask for a more direct rejection of social-action theory of Weber's type. Essentially, Merton has retained two basic meanings of "function": (1) as an organic type of system; (2) as the consequences of any design, aim, purpose within an organic type of system.

[11]Florian Znaniecki, *The Social Role of the Man of Knowledge* (New York: Columbia University Press, 1940), p. 13.

[12]Robert K. Merton, *Social Theory and Social Structure* (Glencoe, Ill.: The Free Press, 1949), p. 21. References here to this work are all to the first edition of 1949. Merton's major works are listed in Footnote 18, Chapter XVIII.
[13]*Ibid.,* p. 23.

Merton took his own point of departure from what he called the "prevailing postulates" of functional analysis. He assumes that other functionalists believe that "standardized social activities or cultural items are functional for the *entire* social or cultural system; second that *all* such social and cultural items fulfill sociological functions; and third, that these items are consequently *indispensable.*"[14] Although Merton has selected quotations from Radcliffe-Brown and Malinowski to "prove" the generality of these as "prevailing postulates of functional analysis," his assumption hardly holds in an unqualified sense for Sumner or Pareto and decidedly not for Znaniecki. As against these "postulates," Merton makes a number of points: (a) functional unity is not a postulate beyond the reach of empirical test, and degree of integration is an empirical variable; (b) social usages and incidents may be functional for some groups and dysfunctional for others, and the notion that they are functional for the entire society must therefore be modified; (c) the postulate of universal functionalism must be modified, for persisting cultural forms have a net balance of functional consequences for the entire society, or a unit or subgroup of it; (d) the postulate that an item is functionally indispensable must also be modified, for the same item may have multiple functions and the same function may be fulfilled by alternative items; one substitutes the concept of functional alternatives or substitutes; (c) the nature of a particular item must be spelled out for the particular case, and functional analysis calls for a specification of the social units served by functions, for some items may have variable functions, some consequences of which are dysfunctional.

Merton emphatically denies that functional analysis is "ideological." Although this denial is implicit in his criticism of the "postulates of functionalism," he developed his position explicitly in a "paradigm" for functional sociological analysis. In Merton's view, functional analysis primarily applies to standardized items (such as so-

cial roles, institutions, social process, cultural items, social norms, group organization). It operates with some concept of motivation of individuals in social systems. It works with an idea of multiple consequences and a net balance of items. It distinguishes between motives and objective consequences, utilizing two main concepts: *manifest functions* as objective consequences, contributing to the adjustment or adaptation of the system, which are intended and recognized by participants in the system; and *latent functions* as consequences which are neither intended nor recognized. An item may be functional in a "society," but a given item may be functional for some units, dysfunctional for others. A series of units may be affected by an item: status, subgroups, larger systems, cultural systems. Functional analysis works with the assumption that there are foundational requirements of the system under observation. It also requires a knowledge of mechanisms through which the function operates (such as role-segmentation, insulation of institutional demands, hierarchic order of values, social division of labor, ritual and ceremonial enactments). A range of possible variation must be taken into account with respect to any given item in terms of functional equivalents or substitutes. The range of variation in an item which can fulfill designated functions is limited by the structural context of the item. And, finally, functional analysis must also cover dysfunctions, which imply strain, stress, and tension on a structural level, and which account for dynamics and change.

The descriptive protocol for functional analysis should include the location of the participants in the pattern provided by social structure, the alternative modes of behavior which are excluded by emphasis on the observed pattern, the emotional and cognitive meanings attached by participants to the pattern, a distinction between motivations for participating in the pattern and objective behavior involved in the pattern, and regularities of behavior not recognized by the participants but associated with the central pattern.

In terms of the previous discussion it may be noted that the additions made by Merton to func-

---

[14]*Ibid.,* p. 27.

tional analyses are basically two in number, though they have partial anticipations. (1) To the concept of function Merton added the concept of dysfunction. The anticipations of this concept, of course, are clear enough. Durkheim had believed that not only may a given society display a degree of "solidarity," but quite the opposite, a degree of *anomie*. The same idea was picked up by Radcliffe-Brown in his distinction between a social condition of order and health, or *eunomia,* in contrast to a condition of social ill-health, or *dysnomia*. Merton's *dysfunction* extends this concept to the unit of the functional system.

It should be observed that the concept of *dysfunctions* carries with it rather special risks. When any unit, activity, structure, or organization is described as "dysfunctional," such a description can easily take the form of an implicit value judgment unless the system is specified. When primitives make a canoe they employ the technology at their disposal. It will prove to be seaworthy only if the materials and technical processes of its construction are "adequate" for this purpose. Canoe making may be attended by a good deal of specialized magic, without which primitives would not even consider launching their canoe. In terms of improving its sailability — say, by adding a kind of magical leak-proofing — the magic attendant on canoe-making is quite "dysfunctional." However, there is nothing dysfunctional about its psychological function of reassurance in the face of uncertainty attendant upon putting out to sea in a cockle shell.

It may be noted, too, that when the term *dysfunctional* is introduced, the meaning of *function* tends to shift — even if ever so slightly — toward the meaning of *appropriate*.

(2) Merton's second major addition to the theory of sociological functionalism was the distinction contained in the concepts of *manifest* and *latent* function. Here, again, there are direct anticipations in sociology. In his study of social institutions, F. Stuart Chapin had treated one of the decisive properties of institutions as the appearance, organization, and integration of formal structures. He indicated, however, that this does not mean that informal behavior loses its importance. In fact, though the institutionalization of formal problems introduces efficiencies, new needs develop that the formal patterns cannot or will not absorb. Moreover, the complex of informal patterns may become integrated into a complex of their own. In Chapin's own illustration, the folkways of drinking are expressed by a demand for liquors. When (as in the case of the prohibition amendment) liquor is prohibited, a network of relations among politics, crime, and vice arises in the fulfillment of the demands related to the folkways surrounding drinking. There is, thus, a fundamental distinction between formal and informal relations and *manifest* and *latent* functions. "The formalism of creed and doctrine, although a check on freedom, was not designed to suppress personal initiative. Thus the essence of the latent pattern is not its anti-social nor yet its ethical significance, but lies rather in the fact that it is a configuration of segments of behaviors undirected by the separate purposes of the individuals who contribute to its formation."[15]

Merton, however, took the distinction not from Chapin but from Freud, who initially introduced it to refer to manifest and latent dream content, anchored in conscious and unconscious motivation. Moreover, Merton gave the distinction a quite different interpretation from that of Chapin and closer to that of Freud. *Manifest functions* are those objective consequences contributing to the adjustment or adaptation of the system which are intended and recognized by the participants in the system; *latent functions,* correlatively, are those which are neither intended nor recognized.[16]

As a major illustration of the value of a distinction between manifest and latent functions for sociological analysis, Merton cited bossism and machine politics. To understand the role of bossism and the machine in political behavior, we must look at two types of sociological variables. (1) The *structural context* of politics makes it practically

[15]F. Stuart Chapin, *Contemporary American Institutions* (New York: Harper, 1935), p. 47.
[16]Merton, *Social Theory and Social Structure,* p. 51.

impossible for morally approved structures to fulfill essential social functions; the way is thus left open for the political machines. (2) Moreover, these are *subgroups* whose distinctive needs are left unsatisfied except for the latent functions which the machine in fact fulfills.

Functional deficiencies of the official structure lead to alternative unofficial structures which satisfy existing needs more efficiently. Deprived social classes are satisfied by the political machine more adequately than by the official structure. For a second group, business (both big and small), the political boss serves the function of providing privileges which entail immediate economic gain. The demand for special privileges is built into the structure of society and the boss fulfills diverse functions for this second subgroup of business-seeking-privilege. The political machine also provides channels of social mobility for persons otherwise excluded from the conventional avenues of personal advancement. The machine mediates the needs of "illegitimate business," which often differs only in degree from legitimate business. "To seek social change, without due recognition of the manifest and latent functions performed by the social organization undergoing change, is to indulge in social ritual rather than social engineering."[17]

In actual fact, Merton quite violates his definitions of manifest and latent function as conscious and unconscious, intended and unintended consequences respectively. In the first place, it must be noted that this formulation again tends to draw Merton's concept of function into the framework of "purposiveness." But, beyond this, the examples simply do not fit the definition. It is rather curious to assume that incumbents in the office intend their actions (manifest functions of politics) while the political bosses do not (latent functions of the boss) or that officials are conscious of their actions, the political bosses are not.

Perhaps the single most significant example of a functional analysis is Merton's study of "Social Structure and Anomie."[18] In this study he proposed to analyze the social and cultural sources of deviant behavior. His aim more specifically was to examine the manner in which social structures exert a definite pressure upon certain persons in society to engage in nonconformist rather than conformist conduct. Social and cultural structures, Merton indicates, define certain goals and objectives as legitimate. In addition, they determine and regulate acceptable modes of reaching these goals. In our society, there is an exceptionally strong emphasis upon specific goals, without a corresponding emphasis on institutional procedures. When this process reaches its extreme form, demoralization or a state of "anomie" develops. Contemporary American culture is an extreme type in which great emphasis upon success goals occurs without equivalent emphasis upon the institutional means of achieving these goals. American culture enjoins the acceptance of three cultural axioms: "First, all should strive for the same lofty goals since these are open to all; second, present seeming failure is but a way-station to ultimate success; and third, genuine failure consists only in lessening or withdrawal of ambition."[19]

In the acceptance of these success goals and the prescribed means to them, Merton considers five possible types of adaptation, as illustrated on the following page. In a stable society, the majority of people both *conform* to cultural goals and accept the legitimate institutional means for achieving them. However, where there is unusual emphasis upon success goals without equal emphasis on the means for achieving them, the situation tends to change. Many individuals may accept the success goals, but not the institutionalized means; under such circumstances, the line between business-like striving and shady practice may grow quite vague. In America, in the course of the accumulation of their fortunes, the Robber Barons often employed *innovations* in this sense which were institutionally questionable. A *ritualistic* adaptation, by contrast, accepts the institutional means for achieving social

---

[17]*Ibid.*, p. 80.

[18]*Ibid.*, pp. 125–149.
[19]*Ibid.*, p. 132.

A Typology of Modes of Individual Adaptation[20]

Modes of Adaptation	Cultural Goals	Institutional Means
I. Conformity	+	+
II. Innovation	+	−
III. Ritualism	−	+
IV. Retreatism	−	−
V. Rebellion	±	±

goals in the given society but avoids psychological strains by rejecting the social goals a society may prescribe. For example, in some sections of American society where one's social status depends on achievement, a highly competitive struggle may ensue. By permanently lowering the level of one's aspirations, one may seek to allay the anxieties which such striving produces. Many lower-middle-class Americans have had recourse to this kind of conduct. *Retreatism* is a type of adaptation to social life that rejects both social goals and the means for achieving them. It is said to typify the activities of many psychotics, artists, pariahs, vagabonds, tramps, chronic drunkards and drug addicts. *Rebellion*, while superficially similar to retreatism, is quite different, for it is characterized by a combination of rejection and acceptance both of social goals and the institutional means for achieving them. The revolutionary who would both set up a new society and a new set of institutional means for achieving the goals of the new society epitomizes the rebel in pure form.

As an example of functional analysis, this essay by Merton represents a general improvement over Durkheim's assignment of anomie as a state of "social ill-health" to society. It isolates specific features of society in their possible combination (ends and means) as a basis for the location of adaptation

possibilities. It may, incidentally, be noted that David Riesman's typology (in *The Lonely Crowd*) of personality types (inner-directed and other-directed people) is surpassed by this more precise schematization of types of personality adaptation. At the same time, in this example of functional analysis the fundamental unit — the system forming the basis for estimates of the functional significance of items — is no less than American society itself. This is fully developed functionalism, in which the system determines the elements.

George C. Homans. The wave of theory construction in a functionalistic vein signaled by the publication of Merton's essay in 1949 was followed by the appearance of George Homans's *The Human Group*[21] in 1950 — one of the major examples of functionalistic theory construction. (For a discussion of the developments of Homans's career see Chapter XIV, pp. 310–314.) Because of its thoroughness, if for no other reason, Homans's work will undoubtedly remain for some time as one of the most effective statements of the functionalistic theory. Early in the book he sets down the rules for theory construction and included among them — almost menacingly — is the precept: "Once you have started to talk, do not stop until you have finished."[22]

Essentially the book accomplishes two tasks: (1) the development of a general functionalistic theory of sociology, and (2) the illustration of the theory by the analysis of a series of concrete cases in terms of it: (a) The Bank Wiring Observation Room from F. J. Roethlisberger and William J. Dickson's *Management and the Worker*; (b) the Norton Street Gang from William Foote Whyte's *Street Corner Society*; (c) The Family in Tikopia from Raymond Firth's *We, The Tikopia*; (d) The Social Disintegration of Hilltown from D. L. Hatch's

[20]*Ibid.*, p. 133.

[21]George C. Homans, *The Human Group* (New York: Harcourt, Brace, 1950). For other major works by Homans, see Footnote 78, Chapter XIV.

[22]Homans, *The Human Group*, p. 17. This and the following quotations are used with the permission of Harcourt, Brace & Company and Routledge & Kegan Paul.

Changes in the Structure and Function of a Rural New England Community Since 1900; (e) The Social Conflict in an Electrical Equipment Company from C. M. Arensberg and D. Macgregor, *Determination of Morale in an Industrial Company.*

With the considered ease of a man who has thought through his task and is sure of himself, Homans shows no sense of urgency in advancing his theory but carefully presents the social situation described between members of the bank-wiring team studied in the Western Electric researches. Homans then "induces" his theory from this study. This done, he carefully illustrates ("tests") it in a series of extended examinations of the remaining empirical cases. Thus, the basic theory is not broached until well into the first quarter of the book.

The distinctive property of functional analysis is the utilization of some concept of system as primary for sociological analysis. The first requirement of a comprehensible analysis is the clear definition of the system presumed. Nothing will render a functional analysis ambiguous more quickly or completely than uncertainty as to just what, in the particular case, constitutes the system. Once one has isolated the system, the next task is to identify its components. And once the components have been identified, the relation between these components becomes primary. Merton had insisted that functionalism could work with units (systems) less than total societies. He did not, however, identify these. Furthermore, in the most highly imaginative case of functional analysis he conducted ("Social Structure and Anomie"), he said nothing explicitly about the system under consideration or its elements. By implication, the system is considered to be American society, and its component elements for the particular study were (1) success goals and (2) institutional means to successes. Homans was quite clear about the system under consideration and its elements. Merton was quite understandably lyrical in his introduction to the study: "despite my occasional disagreement with certain details in the book . . . I should like to express this considered judgment: not since Simmel's pioneering analyses of almost half a century

ago has any single work contributed so much to a sociological theory of the structure, processes, and functions of small groups as George Homans's *The Human Group.*"[23]

The system with which he is concerned is identified by Homans as the group, which he does not hesitate to expand to comprise the whole of the city of Hilltown. He is equally clear about the elements into which such a system is analyzable: (1) *activity* — what the members of the group do as members; (2) *interaction* — the relation of the activity of one member of the group to that of another; (3) *sentiment* — the sum of the feelings of group members with respect to the group; and (4) *norms* — the code of behavior adopted consciously or unconsciously by the group. It may be noted that these are quite remarkably like the elements which Znaniecki thought characterized a social system — tendency, attitude, value, social instrument, social method, social reaction.

In his consideration of the manner in which these form a system, Homans closely follows the division suggested by Pareto in his concept of external in contrast to internal system. The group is defined as a plurality of people in interaction. The activities, interactions, and sentiments of the members, together with mutual relations of these elements when the group is active, constitute a social system. If one were to arrange various organized wholes, from a thermodynamic system like hot coffee in a thermos bottle to the system of the human body, in a scale of their "organicity," social systems would come somewhere in between.[24] The group as a social system first forms an external system, determined by the needs of the group and the conditions of the environment. The environment is broken down into three main aspects: physical, technical, and social. The external system represents the group so far as it is conditioned by the environment, and it is called external because it is conditioned by the environment. It is a system because the elements of behavior are mutually dependent. The external system, plus another set of

[23]*Ibid.*, p. xxiii.
[24]*Ibid.*, p. 87.

relations called the *internal* system, make up the total social system.

Homans is not only quite explicit about his system unit — the group (and community) as a social system made up of (a) an external and (b) an internal system — and his units of analysis for the study of systems, — activity, sentiment, interaction, norms; he is also clear that there is a series of relations of mutual dependence between the elements of the external system.

(1) Between sentiment and activity: both motives and associated activities persist, both continuously recreated, but if either side of the relationship is changed, the other will be affected. For example, if one has just eaten and his hunger (sentiment) is appeased, he is not likely to go down to the restaurant and order a meal (activity).

(2) Between activity and interaction: if the scheme of activities is changed, the scheme of interaction will also change and vice versa.

(3) Taken as a whole, the elements form a pyramid of interaction. Whatever changes occur in the scheme of activities of a group, the scheme of interaction between the leaders of various levels and their followers tend to keep the same general pyramidal form. For instance, military units tend to keep their same non-commissioned officers when they are on a field problem or at home base.[25]

The model for developing these ideas is a specific subgroup in a modern factory. It may be noted that in all such cases the task of a specialized group in the factory is fixed by its place in the factory production schedule as a whole. It makes complete sense to speak of the output of the group as if it were a more or less fixed requirement placed on the group — it often is precisely that.

It may be noted, however, that there are some risks involved in conceiving the "external system" of all groups in terms of the situation of a subgroup in a factory. The concept of external system is extended to other groups which do not fit into such a tightly organized scheme imposed by an outside source. A primitive family, among the Tikopia for example, does not have clear-cut externally imposed production requirements; its relations to the external environment are much more various and plastic. Nothing could be more absurd than to treat it as if it were a kind of cog in a cosmic social machine. While the subunit of a factory has to maintain a given level of externally required output, the precise counterpart of this simply does not occur in a street corner gang of young men during a depression who hang around the streets, bowling alleys, and settlement houses because they have nothing else to do. To treat such a gang as maintaining a level of output in bowling scores is not a little farfetched.

Homans maintains that on the basis of the external system an internal system appears. The "external system" represents the behavior of a group so far as that behavior represents one possible answer to the question: how does the group survive in its particular environment? By contrast, the "internal system" represents the elaboration of group behavior that simultaneously arises out of the external system and reacts upon it. "We call the system 'internal' because it is not directly conditioned by the environment and we speak of it as an 'elaboration' because it includes forms of behavior not included under the heading of the external system."[26]

The further interrelations between the various elements of the group as a social system produce effects that create the internal system. There seem to be two general processes: (a) integration of the specifically social system and (b) differentiation of its subcomponents.

The integration of the specifically social system arises in the further interrelations of the basic variables.

(1) Mutual dependence of interaction and sentiment: persons who interact frequently with one another tend to like one another. [This apparently holds in all cases except those where the individuals grow to hate one another.]

---

[25] *Ibid.*, pp. 99–104. (Paraphrased)

[26] *Ibid.*, p. 109.

(1a) If the frequency of interaction between two or more persons increases, the degree of liking for one another will increase and vice versa. [Except, again, where absence makes the heart grow fonder.]

(1b) A decrease in the frequency of interaction between the members of a group and outsiders, accompanied by an increase in the strength of their negative sentiments toward outsiders, will increase the frequency of interaction and the strength of positive sentiments among group members.

(2) Mutual dependence between sentiment and activity: persons who feel sentiments of liking for one another will express those sentiments in activities over and above any activities of the external system, and these activities may further strengthen the sentiments of liking.

(3) Mutual dependence of activity and interaction: much of social activity — dances, parties — is enjoyed less for the sake of the activity itself, which may be trivial, than for the possibilities of social interaction it affords.

(4) Standardization as a product of interrelation: the more frequently persons interact with one another, the more alike in some respects their activities and sentiments tend to become.[27]

The integration of a specifically social (internal) system is evident in the appearance of a new item or element in the schema of social systems, norms. A norm is an idea in the minds of the members of a group concerning what one ought to do under given circumstances. Norms are one of the most important parts of the culture of the group, emerging from activities and playing back on them. The members of a group are often more nearly alike in the norms they hold than in their overt behavior.

The integration of the specifically social products of interaction and the formation of a normatively integrated scheme is the first distinctive process in the emergence of the internal system. Differentiation within the group is the second. Here, again, the end result (the formation of subgroups within the larger group) is derived by Homans from the relation between the basic elements of action.

(1) Mutual dependency of interaction and sentiment: the more frequently persons interact, the stronger their sentiments of friendship for one another are likely to be [except for contrary cases].

(2) Sentiment and activity: persons who feel sentiments of liking for one another will express those sentiments in activities after work [at times, at least].

(3) Activity and interaction: persons who interact with one another frequently are often more like one another in their activities than they are like persons with whom they interact less frequently.[28]

These are all general relations already adduced to account for the appearance of an integrated internal system over and beyond the external system. It is Homans's view that they continue to operate to differentiate the subgroup. Moreover, a great deal of the behavior of the internal system is expressive or symbolic. The behavior of a clique is expressive of its identity. The cliques are subject to a social ranking, as are the individuals within them. Social ranking is primarily based on the relation between cliques. But it applies also to persons not tied in with the cliques, who are typically down-graded because they are not members.

In all this, there is a reaction of the internal system back upon the external system. Homans introduces the concept of *feedback* — taken from the property of electrical circuits arranged in such a way that current at a certain point in the circuit is partly fed back by an appropriate hookup into an earlier point in the circuit, an arrangement which permits the circuit to build up more rapidly to its full load and carry that load without fluctuations. Feedback and build-up go on continuously. In the social system, Homans maintains, one of the distinctive properties is the feedback of the internal into the external system, with the process of build-up going on continuously. "Beneficent or vicious circles — 'spirals' would be a better word — are

[27]*Ibid.*, pp. 111–120. (Paraphrased)

[28]*Ibid.*, pp. 132–135. (Paraphrased)

characteristic of all organic phenomena. We can say that the feedback of the internal system may be either favorable or unfavorable to the group, making its action or the environment more or less effective, provided we have adopted a definite basis for judgment."[29]

With these notions Homans's functionalistic theory is essentially complete, the rest of his study consisting primarily in the application of these ideas to a variety of groups such as a street corner gang and a primitive family. Homans's study of a New England city, "Hilltown," concerns a negative "spiral"; here he applies his "feedback" principle, tracing a process of disintegration which begins in a less favorable socioeconomic situation (in the external system) and which leads to a declining system of interaction; he tries to demonstrate the "negative feedback" from a weakening internal system into the external system. Economic opportunities were reduced; population decline (after 1890); schism appeared in the church; social life weakened; norms became less binding; the boys turned to petty theft, the girls to prostitution; a state of anomie prevailed.

Homans's study of an electrical equipment company, on the other hand, presents more serious problems, for it represents a case of conflict, not one of a declining spiral from external system to internal system and back to external system. There is neither a decline of external system nor a lack of intensity in the various subgroups. In this case, a series of increasingly irreconcilable discrepancies arose between design engineers and supervisors. As the two groups worked at cross-purposes, without clear lines of authority, the situation became explosive. Conflict arose because there was no coordinating structure that could consistently operate. The role of leadership is found in supplying such decisive coordination.

The ties of functionalism with organicism are testified to, once again, as Homans turned his analysis from the small group, considered as an organic system, to the problems of the birth of civilization in the manner of Spengler, Toynbee, and Sorokin. Human beings remained at the level of the comparatively small group, he argues — the tribe, village, small group, in which members have firsthand knowledge of all the others — for many millennia before written history. Such small groups have survived and produced a surplus of goods and have made morale, leadership, and cooperation between increasingly larger groups possible. Civilization, in Homans's view, was erected on the foundation of such small groups.

> In our view, and here we are following Toynbee . . . ancient Egypt and Mesopotamia were civilizations. So were classical India and China . . . so is our own Western civilization. . . . These societies on the grand scale have had many characteristics in common. At its height, each has been inventive: it has devised and used a more powerful technology than any at the command of the tribes coming before and after it. Each has been coterminous geographically with a communications network . . . Each . . . developed new formal organizations, in law, government, warfare, and religion. . . . almost every one of the civilizations has worked out and adopted a single body of values and beliefs.[30]

But, alas, after thriving for a time each civilization has collapsed. Homans suggests why. "Our own theory, in its main lines, would run as follows. At the level of the tribe or group, society has always found itself able to cohere. We infer, therefore, that a civilization, if it is in turn to maintain itself, must preserve at least a few of the characteristics of the group. . . . Civilizations have failed in failing to solve this problem."[31] Psychiatry, Homans argues, proves that membership in a group sustains people, enabling them to maintain their equilibrium under the ordinary shocks of life. If they leave a group under stress they may develop disorders of thought, feeling, and behavior. Their thinking will be obsessive and unrealistic, anxious, negativistic, and their behavior will be compulsive. This is particularly important at the time of the

[29]*Ibid.*, pp. 153–154.

[30]*Ibid.*, p. 455.
[31]*Ibid.*, p. 456.

death of a civilization. There is a net increase in the number of isolated individuals lacking the old feeling of belongingness. "Each of the sociologists—Durkheim, Le Bon, Figgis, Brooks Adams—who began, just before World War I, to point out the signs of decay in our society, used the same metaphor. They said that society was becoming a dust heap of individuals without links to one another."[32]

Thus, as civilization advances, a process like that in the Electrical Equipment Company or Hilltown occurs. The technical and economic adaptation of society to its environment changes. Since the internal system is continuous with the external, the relations between groups in society are disturbed and a negative spiral downward begins. The circulation of elites and rise of the most effective leaders may be involved. Able people devote their skills to making money, intrigue, using force, or exploiting the increasing antagonisms between groups. Effective communication flows naturally toward the leader, but when these events occur the communication channels are disrupted, transmitting inaccurate information. No one is responsible for paying attention to the whole. The small group controls persons who threaten to depart. Groups divide; society splits into warring camps, difficulties of communication appear, the spontaneous control by groups disappears in favor of control by force imposed by the central power. Society is in a complete state of anomie.

Throughout Homans's work it is assumed that society is organized into systems. These are not simply small groups. They may be large groups, communities, societies, or entire civilizations. It is assumed, however, that they are all systems of the same type and identical laws apply within them.

Every system has two subsystems: the external and internal. The model for this is the subgroup of a modern factory, where the distinction makes some sense. The extension of the pattern to all systems up to and including civilization represents the attempt to model the social universe after the

pattern of the factory subgroup. This results in curious distortions of judgment, such as treating the bowling scores of the Norton Street gang like a factory output. A tantalizing sense of duplication adheres to the entire discussion. It reminds one of those medieval theories which treated the personality as a small man inside the big man, with the former behaving in an identical manner to the latter. Even if one accepts the rather strained assumption that the whole of the social world operates like a factory subgroup, the theory is subject to radical modification. If one does not admit that there are two systems, but sticks to the only one that is sometimes apparent, matters are worse.

The proposal to isolate the various elements of the system is a decided advance, but the difficulty with using such elements as "tendency," "sentiment," "activity," and "interaction" is that they do not appear to be distinct. Activity is not one thing and interaction another. The activity is interaction. The same mysterious sense of duplication appears here. If activity and interaction are merely two ways of describing the same thing, what possible meaning can adhere to a set of principles describing their interrelation? A good number of the presumed principles obtaining between the variables are gratuitous or tautological. At the same time, to the extent that the theory rests on indistinct variables and nonexistent systems, it is metaphysically irrefutable.

These shortcomings, however, should not obscure the clear gain in theoretical precision involved in any attempt to define more precisely the properties of the system and the nature and mode of operation of its elements. Homans's work is a significant step forward. Ironically, this very demand for clarity seems to have led Homans to abandon functionalism for behavioristic sociology.

Talcott Parsons. The rapid evolution of functionalistic theory is shown by the appearance, the next year after Homans's study, of Talcott Parsons' first full-scale systematic venture into functionalistic theory construction with *The Social System* (1951). As noted earlier, Parsons' first work on sociology was social behavioristic. The degree to

[32]*Ibid.*, p. 457.

which he departed from this early social behaviorism is in part indicated by the attack on *The Social System* by C. Wright Mills, one of the most vigorous of the contemporary social behaviorists. Unfortunately, Mills confined his attack primarily to quoting abstract and often clumsy statements and translating them into simpler language.

> Is grand theory, as represented in *The Social System,* merely verbiage or is it also profound? My answer to this question is: it is only 50 per cent verbiage; 40 per cent is well-known textbook sociology. The other 10 per cent, as Parsons might say, I am willing to leave open for your own empirical investigations. My own investigations suggest that the remaining 10 per cent is of possible—although rather vague—ideological use.[33]

In the present discussion, the attempt is made to demonstrate both the fact that the materials of *The Social System* represent an internal development in Parsons' own outlook and a stage in the formulation of contemporary functionalism.

Parsons, to be sure, had already broached the problem of functionalist theory construction in the early forties and again in an address to the annual meeting of the American Sociological Society (1947) on "The Position of Sociological Theory," where he had urged the advisability of developing a "structural-functional theory." Such a theory would analyze action into cognitive, goal-directed, and affective elements. It would, moreover, complete itself by "an analysis of the functional prerequisites of the social system," which must somehow provide for the "minimum biological and psychological needs of a sufficient proportion of its component members." On a more strictly social level, two functional prerequisites were found. "One lies in the problem of order . . . the second focus is on the adequacy of motivation. The system can only function if a sufficient proportion of its members perform the essential social roles with an adequate degree of effectiveness." Moreover, Par-

sons urged, the structure of social systems needs to be studied. One aspect of this is found in "institutions," the second in "differentiation." The most promising lead in solving these problems is thought to lie in the "demonstration of the existence of certain invariant points of reference about which differentiated structures focus."[34]

However, it is in *The Social System* that Parsons undertakes a major program of functionalistic theory construction. This program was frankly based on Pareto. "The title, *The Social System,* goes back, more than to any other source, to the insistence of the late Professor L. J. Henderson on the extreme importance of the concept of system in scientific theory, and his clear realization that the attempt to delineate the social system as a system was the most important contribution of Pareto's great work. This book therefore is an attempt to carry out Pareto's intention, using . . . the 'structural-functional' level of analysis."[35]

In this work Parsons took a definite step away from the conception of "social action" as a kind of atomic unit out of which societies are composed and treated action itself as a system. A social system was conceived as a new whole composed of a plurality of interacting persons "motivated in terms of a tendency to the 'optimization of gratification' and whose relation to their situations, including each other, is defined and mediated in terms of a system of culturally structured and shared symbols."[36] A social system is one of three ways in which social action is structured. The other two are the personality systems of the individual actors and cultural systems.

The action system of the individual has two basic aspects: gratificational and orientational. The "gratificational" is called by Parsons "cathectic," the "orientational" is called "cognitive." That is, human action is thought by Parsons to display both

---

[33]C. Wright Mills, *The Sociological Imagination* (New York: Oxford University Press, 1959), p. 49.

[34]Talcott Parsons, *Essays in Sociological Theory, Pure and Applied* (Glencoe, Ill.: The Free Press, 1949), pp. 6, 7. Parsons' major works are cited in Footnote 11, Chapter XVIII.

[35]Talcott Parsons, *The Social System* (Glencoe, Ill.: The Free Press, 1951), p. vii.

[36]*Ibid.,* pp. 5–6.

desires and ideas. The objects that may satisfy needs are many; for example, there are numerous items that can satisfy hunger. "Cognitive mapping has alternatives of judgment or interpretation as to what objects are or what they 'mean.' There must be ordered selection among such alternatives. The term 'evaluation' will be given to this process of ordered selection."[37] That is, action is to be analyzed into desires, ideas, and values or norms. An action system containing these elements is one of three types: (a) a social system, (b) a personality system, or (c) a cultural system.

A society is the sociologically decisive type of social system according to Parsons. As he phrases it in his own inimitable language:

> Because empirical organization of the system is a fundamental focus, the norm, as it were, must be the conception of an empirically self-subsistent social system. If we add the consideration of duration sufficiently long to transcend the life span of the normal human individual, recruitment by biological reproduction and socialization of the oncoming generation become essential aspects of such a social system. A social system of this type, which meets all the essential functional prerequisites of long term persistence from within its own resources will be called a *society*. It is not essential to the concept of a society that it should not be in any way empirically interdependent with other societies, but only that it should contain all the structural and functional fundamentals of an independently subsisting system. Any other social system will be called a "partial" social system.[38]

In other words, society is a large-scale, persistent, self-sufficient system of social interaction which must train its own members since it lasts longer than the individual.

If the fundamental unit of Homans's analysis is the group, the basic unit of Parsons' analysis is the society. The society is conceived as a system of interaction and the relations between the actors represent its structure. Its dependent subunits are "status-roles." Participation by actors in the social system means that they are "located" relative to other actors. This is their "status." In this position they do various things, and what they do is called their "role." There are two other possible units of society: The *actor*, who, as member of the social system, represents a bundle of statuses and roles; and the social *act*. However, the system is superior to its units. The collectivity as a composite unit "cuts across the individual actor as a composite unit." Thus, "status-role" is the proper unit of the social system rather than the actor or the action.

The functional prerequisites of social systems are the things needed if it is to remain stable. An action system may be centered in personality, society, or culture. Thus, the minimum conditions of stability or orderly development of a social system may be represented in terms of the following:

I. Functional prerequisites with respect to the individual: the minimum needs of the majority of the actors must be met.
II. Functional prerequisites with respect to the society: a minimum control over potentially disruptive behavior must be maintained.
III. Functional prerequisites with respect to culture: the social system is made possible by language and culture; hence, there must be sufficient cultural resources to internalize a level of personality adequate for a social system.[39]

According to Parsons, an action system brings motivational and symbolic elements into an ordered system. This order is normative and either instrumental or intrinsic. The norms are critical to *roles,* which organize the expectations of the individual in relation to a particular interaction context and govern interaction with one or more "alters" in complementary roles. The roles are critical to *institutions,* which are role integrates of strategic structural significance in the social system. A collectivity is the organization of a series of institutions. The degree to which normative patterns as role integrates are institutionalized varies from

---

[37]*Ibid.,* p. 7.
[38]*Ibid.,* p. 19.

[39]*Ibid.,* pp. 26–27. (Paraphrased)

complete integration to anomie. Throughout, the normative ordering of need satisfaction is the basic phenomenon of the dynamics of social systems.

The parallels between Homans's account and Parsons' are fundamental. Homans analyzes his basic systems (groups) into sentiments, activity, and interaction. These arose in response to the external environment. The interrelation between these elements led to the development of a new element, the "norms," which formed the integration point of the internal system. Parsons analyzes his basic systems (societies) into status-roles. But the individuals who act in these status-roles have ideas and beliefs which are normatively ordered. In fact, the normative ordering of ideas and beliefs is already the critical aspect of status-roles. They are as central for Parsons' "society" as they were for Homans' "internal system." As the elements of integration, the distinctively "social" elements of the social system, norms are equally basic for Parsons and Homans.

Just as Homans found in the norms the point of integration of the internal system, but went on to account for differentiation within the internal system (the formation of subgroups), so Parsons, at the precisely equivalent place in his analysis, states that "the next step is to begin to lay the groundwork for dealing systematically with the differentiation of roles."[40] Parsons carries out this phase of analysis somewhat differently from Homans. Parsons has treated as the distinctive features of action the presence of ideas, desires, and values; or, as he phrases it, the organization of action-orientations consists "of the three modes of motivational orientation, cognitive, cathectic and evaluative." Parsons proposes that role differentiation occurs in terms of the relative predominance of one or another mode over the others. Moreover, just as there are types of role differentiation, so there are types of institutionalization relative to the social system. The central institutions are critical to the pattern. These are *relational* institutions. In terms of collective integration, the functional problem in social systems is the regulation of interests, giving rise to *regulative* institutions. *Cultural* institutions, the third type, pattern cultural orientations. Relational institutions define reciprocal role-expectations, regulative institutions define the legitimate means to be employed in the pursuit of interests, and cultural institutions define obligations with regard to cultural patterns. Relational institutions, in Parsons' theory the most fundamental of all, lie at the very core of society.

Parsons' most unique contribution to sociological functionalism appears at this point in his conception of what he calls the "pattern-alternatives of value-orientations." These represent the possibilities in which the normative elements of relational institutions are defined. As he states the case: "It should again be emphasized that we are here dealing with the foci for the patterning of relational institutions."[41]

In any given action, Parsons maintains, the actor aims at optimum gratification. However, no action system can be organized or integrated without the renunciation of some gratifications. One cannot realistically want everything, one has to be neutral about some things. "The polarity of affectivity-neutrality formulates the patterning out of action with respect to this basic alternative."[42] Secondly, individuals face a choice of pursuing interests private to themselves or shared with others. The one alternative may be called "self-orientation," the other, "collectivity-orientation."[43] Thirdly, the given action may be determined either by ideas or feeling. "The primacy of cognitive values then may be said to imply a *universalistic* standard of role-expectation, while that of appreciative values implies a *particularistic* standard."[44] Moreover, in any action there are alternatives with respect to the properties of social objects. "There is one dilemma which is of the most generalized significance. . . . With respect to characteristics of the object it is that of the focus on

[40]*Ibid.*, p. 46.

[41]*Ibid.*, p. 59.
[42]*Ibid.*, p. 60.
[43]*Ibid.*
[44]*Ibid.*, p. 62.

its qualities or attributes as distinguished from focus on its performances."[45] In other words, one may value the other party to the social action on the basis of what that person is (ascription) or what that person does (achievement). There remains, according to Parsons, one further action alternative — that which defines the scope of ego's interest in the object. One possibility open to the actor is the definition of the role "as orienting to the social object in *specific* terms" in contrast to orientation in a "*diffuse*" mode.[46]

The five "pattern variables," as Parsons calls these dichotomies, may be grouped in various ways. When this is done, "their permutations and combinations should yield a system of types of possible role-expectation pattern, on the relational level, namely defining the pattern of orientation to the actors in the role relationship. This system will consist of thirty-two types, which may in turn be grouped into a number of more fundamental ones."[47]

It is useful to summarize Parsons' argument:

    I. Parsons breaks with the social-action branch of social behaviorism, reducing social action to the status of a dependent unit of one of three kinds of system.

    II. The fundamental elements of action are conceived to be ideas, desires, and values (cathectic, cognitive, and evaluative orientation).

    III. Action as a system is differentiated into three subsystems: personality, social system, culture.

    IV. A social system is, if total rather than partial, a society.
        a. It is a large-scale, persistent, independent system of social action.
        b. The primary units into which it is analyzed are role-statuses: positions plus the activities appropriate to them.
        c. The functional prerequisites of a society are those minimum requirements with respect to individuals, social systems, and culture without which the society could not exist.

        d. Institutions are large-order units formed out of status-roles when they are integrated and standardized.
        e. A collectivity is formed around a core of central institutions.

    V. Social norms form the central element in status-roles and institutions.

    VI. Institutions are of three types: relational (defining reciprocal role expectations); regulative (defining legitimate means to values); and cultural (defining cultural requirements).
        a. Of these, relational institutions are most critical for establishing the character of a society.

    VII. Pattern alternatives of value orientation define relational role-expectation patterns. There are five of these pairs:
        a. Affectivity vs. Affective Neutrality
        b. Self-Orientation vs. Collectivity-Orientation
        c. Universalism vs. Particularism
        d. Achievement vs. Ascription
        e. Specificity vs. Diffuseness

Parsons' most original contribution to functionalistic social theory appears in his proposal to generate possible societies by counting the permutations and combinations of what he calls the "pattern alternatives of value orientation in role-expectation problems."

Parsons assumes that social structure is made up of institutions, institutions of roles, and roles of mutual expectations. This is not new, having been encountered many times before (Znaniecki, Mead, Gerth and Mills, Merton, and so on). He has assumed that the actions which compose roles are analyzable into ideas, emotions, and values. This idea, too, is not new. It has been actively promoted in sociology by Gerth and Mills, W. I. Thomas, Znaniecki, and many others. The idea is as old as medieval psychology — in fact, as old as Aristotle.

Many times in human history the various elements of action have been conceived dichotomously. It has been observed that the scope of sympathies may be very general or very specific; one may be emotionally engaged over an issue or quite lukewarm or even neutral. So far as one's actions may involve others, one may be selfish or unselfish, egoistic or altruistic. In short one's ideas, feelings, or values and the presence or absence of

[45]*Ibid.*, p. 63.
[46]*Ibid.*, pp. 65–66.
[47]*Ibid.*, p. 47.

others in an act have at various times been categorized dichotomously.

Parsons' novelty consists in treating five of such dichotomous categorizations of action as (1) exhaustive and as (2) defining a society — or at least defining relational-expectations or roles, which in turn define a society. If one grants this, Parsons is quite correct. By counting the permutations and combinations of this system of dichotomies, one will have established a system of possible societies. There are two fundamental points at which this scheme may break down. Either these dichotomous classifications are not exhaustive and/or they are insufficient to define a society.

However, that the full originality of Parsons' formulation is by no means exhausted by these interesting proposals appears when the resulting theoretical scheme is used to assess empirical uniformities. The scheme permits the discovery of how limited reality is, for "in certain crucial areas of social structure we do not find that empirically observable structures cover anything like the whole range of theoretically possible variability."[48] It seems, however, that the barrenness of reality can serve some value. At least it can save us the necessity of investigating all this theory. The existence of such clusterings as we find, in fact, "serves a two-fold purpose for the sociologist. On the one hand it justifies his short-cutting investigation of the *whole* range of structural possibilities and concentrating on a fraction of them."[49] Even more, it may aid in the formulation of laws showing why the theory doesn't apply. "It can serve as a highly important lead into the formulation, and hence testing, of fundamental dynamic generalization, of laws of social process, since the explanation of *why* the logically possible range of variability is empirically restricted can be found only in terms of such laws."[50]

The application to fact of this theoretically generated system turns up a surprise. "From a purely taxonomic point of view any considerable prominence of kinship in social structures generally would seem highly problematical."[51] This strongly suggests to Parsons a kind of conflict of facts with theory. "The fact that kinship looms large in every known society means that a great many other logically possible permutations of the structural elements have either been eliminated or relegated to secondary positions in the social structure."[52]

This formulation of functionalistic theory by no means represents Parsons' final statement of the theory. He has continued to advance the analysis and it will be useful to return later to some other phases of his formulations.

Marion J. Levy. The sudden ferment in functionalistic sociological theory continued, and a year after the appearance of Parsons' *The Social System,* Marion Levy brought out *The Structure of Society.*[53] Marion J. Levy was born in Galveston, Texas, in 1918. He received his A.B. degree at Harvard in 1939, and his Ph.D. degree in 1947. He has been on the staff at Princeton since 1947. In *The Structure of Society,* Levy attempted to synthesize structural-functional analysis. His formulation has interest for its attempt to bring the views of Merton and Parsons together. Levy conceives a "function" as a condition or state of affairs resulting from the operation of a structure through time. A "structure" is conceived as a pattern or observed uniformity of action. A "functional requisite" is defined as a generalized condition necessary for the maintenance of the unit with which it is associated, given the level of generalization of the definition of the unit and the setting of the unit. A "structural requisite" is defined as a pattern of action necessary for the continued existence of the unit with which it is associated.

In addition to functional and structural requisites, Levy also defines functional and structural prerequisites. A "functional prerequisite" is con-

[48]*Ibid.,* p. 152.
[49]*Ibid.*
[50]*Ibid.*

[51]*Ibid.,* p. 153.
[52]*Ibid.,* pp. 153–154.
[53]Marion J. Levy, *The Structure of Society* (Princeton, N.J.: Princeton University Press, 1952).

MARION J. LEVY

Courtesy of Marion J. Levy

ceived as a function that must pre-exist if a given unit in its setting is to come into being. A "structural prerequisite" is conceived as a structure that must pre-exist if a given unit is to come into existence in its setting.

Still further the concepts of *eufunction, dysfunction, eustructure,* and *dysstructure* were added. A *eufunction* is a condition or state of affairs resulting from the operation of a structure of a given unit through time which increases or maintains adaptation or adjustment to the unit's setting, thus making for the persistence of the unit, as defined, of which the structure concerned is a part. A *dysfunction* is a condition, or state of affairs, that results from the operation of a structure of a given unit through time and which lessens the adaptation or adjustment to the unit's setting, making for

a lack of persistence of the unit of which the structure concerned is a part or aspect. A *eustructure* is a structure the operation of which results in eufunctions. A *dysstructure* is a structure the operation of which results in dysfunctions.

To these distinctions, that between manifest and latent function and structure is added. A factor is "manifest" if it is intended and recognized by participants in the system. A factor is "latent" if it is neither intended nor recognized. Also, functions may be intended but unrecognized, and unintended but recognized.

A concrete structure is a pattern that defines the character of units which are in theory capable of physical separation from other units of which they are parts. Patterns defining the character of membership units are of this type. Analytical structures are patterned aspects of action that are not even theoretically capable of concrete separation from other patterned aspects of action.

Institutions are a particular type of normative pattern, conformity to which is generally expected and failure to conform to which is generally met with moral indignation of those persons involved in the same general social system. There are different degrees of institutionalization, and differences in conformity and the degree to which conformity is expected. There are also differences in sanctioning and in the degree to which failure to conform is met with moral indignation. Crucial and strategic institutions are defined by the fact that they are structural requisites of the system in which they appear. An institution is strategic to the degree to which it is the institutionalized form of all or a portion of structural requisites, and the pattern concerned may be altered without destroying the structural requisite involved. A tradition is an institution the perpetuation of which is institutionalized.

A society is a system of action in operation which involves a plurality of individuals recruited at least in part by the sexual reproduction of members of the plurality, at least in theory self-sufficient for the action of the plurality, and capable of existing longer than the life span of an individual of the type involved. The members of society are the plurality of interacting individuals involved in the system and acting in terms of the system. Individuals are better or more poorly integrated as members of society to the degree that they accept and orient their actions without conflict to the structures in general but particularly to the crucial and strategic institutions of that society. The four conditions that may terminate a society are (a) biological extinction or dispersion of the members, (b) apathy of the members, (c) the war of all against all, and (d) absorption of the society into another. A social change is any alteration which occurs in a system of action of a given type which is not subject to explanation solely in terms of heredity of that species and its environment. A culture is the system of action of a society considered apart from its operation.

A given function is a requisite of any society if in its absence the relationship between the unit under discussion and its setting in the most general terms can be shown to be such that one or some combination of the four conditions for the termination of a society would result. Among the functional requisites of any society are:

(1) Provision for an adequate physiological relationship to the setting for the sexual requirement. Maintaining a sufficient number and sufficient kinds of members for the adequate functioning of society.

(2) Role differentiation and role assignment. A role is any position differentiated in terms of a given social structure, whether the position be institutionalized or not.

(3) Communication. Communication is the activity or process by which ideas and/or feeling states are conveyed.

(4) Shared cognitive orientations.

(5) A shared set of goals.

(6) A regulation of the choice of means.

(7) Regulation of affective expression.

(8) Adequate socialization. There is adequate socialization if there is a sufficient number of adequately socialized individuals for the structural requisites of the society to operate.

(9) Effective control of disruptive behavior.

(10) Adequate institutionalization. Institutionalization is adequate if its conformity and sanction aspects are carried sufficiently far to permit the persistence of the minimal normative structures involved in other functional requisites.

It may be noted that Levy has brought the formulations of Merton and Parsons together with unusual compactness. The definitions of function, dysfunction, and latent and manifest function are all directly equivalent to those of Merton. The analysis of society, institution, and of the functional prerequisites of society are quite in the tradition of Parsons. Other than the attempt to fill in the blanks and work the ideas together, no basic innovations are attempted. Thus, so far as critical considerations apply to the functionalistic theories of Merton and Parsons, they would seem to apply to this formulation as well.

Not the least interesting of the novelties is Levy's conception of the field:

> Structural-functional analysis is not something new. . . . It has a pedigree that stretches indefinitely far back . . . The only "new" aspect of it is its formidable new name, "structural-functional analysis." Simply speaking, it consists of nothing more complicated than phrasing empirical questions in one of the following several forms or some combination of them: (1) What observable uniformities . . . may be discovered in the phenomena studied? (2) What conditions . . . may be discovered? or (3) When processes . . . may be discovered to take place in terms of observable uniformities, what resultant conditions may be discovered?[54]

This is rather startling in view of the evident purpose Levy had in mind of synthesizing, by way of a uniform vocabulary, the positions of Merton and Parsons. This statement denies that sociological functionalism is a special movement in sociological theory. This is hardly the position of either Parsons or Merton or any of the functionalists reviewed. Sociological functionalism, it seems, sometimes has to be protected against its friends.

For the reasons developed above (see pp. 443

---

[54]*Ibid.*, p. 27.

ff.), the conceptions — as I interpret them — of *function* as the effects of the operation of a structure, *eufunction* as those functions which increase or maintain adaptation or adjustment, and *dysfunction* as those which do not, are neither very enlightening nor do they constitute a distinctive theory. If one considers the activities of the human body, they may be grouped into two types: those internal to the operation of the body, on the one hand, and overt behavior, such as walking, on the other. The heart beats, the blood pulses through the arteries and veins, the lungs alternately expand and contract, oxygen is absorbed, carbon dioxide is released, and so on. Each one of these events may be conceived as making for adaptation or adjustment. But if one once starts walking, the entire system is thrown off balance. The pulse increases, the breath comes a bit faster, and so on. Presumably, in Levy's terms, the operations of heart, lungs, blood, etc., are "eufunctions" but walking is not. If one is correct in assuming that Levy intends his distinctions to be exhaustive, whatever is not a eufunction is a dysfunction, and walking, in this context, is transferred to the field of pathology. It is not suggested that Levy intends this, but it calls attention to the consequences of a simplistic conception of function. Moreover, it is related to a basic deficiency in this version of functionalism — the failure consistently to isolate the system forming the fundamental unit of analysis. In view of this, the elaborate mechanical baggage of terms (eufunction, dysfunction; eustructure, dysstructure) is rather beside the point — or perhaps "dysfunctional"?

The Parsonians. Parsons' first full statement of a functionalistic position was reviewed earlier. However, it was not his final statement, for he has continued to develop his theories. Further, he has formed the center of a very active school. In the interesting study, *Working Papers in the Theory of Action*,[55] Robert F. Bales and Edward Shils joined

[55]Talcott Parsons, Robert F. Bales, and Edward A. Shils, *Working Papers in the Theory of Action* (Glencoe, Ill.: The Free Press, 1953).

ROBERT F. BALES

Harvard University News Office

their talents to those of Parsons in the development of functionalistic theory. Robert F. Bales was born in Ellington, Missouri, in 1916. He received a B.S. degree from the University of Oregon in 1938, and a Ph.D. degree in 1945 from Harvard, where he has continued to teach.

A Macrofunctionalist Theory of Personality. The problem of developing a macrofunctionalistic theory of personality was broached by Parsons in a paper on "The Superego and the Theory of Social Systems." He proposed linking the theories of Freud and Durkheim, utilizing as the link between them the interaction of two or more persons considered as a system. This, he suggests, corrects both Freud and Durkheim. Freud failed to consider the fact that the individual's interactions with others form a system; Durkheim failed to see that the social system consisted in the interaction of personalities. Two interacting persons, Parsons suggests, are objects to each other cognitively and emotionally. The third way which persons orient themselves to an object is by evaluations, which constitute the normative aspect of action — the integration of the conceptual and emotional into a system over time.

The only way in which a stable mutually oriented system of interaction on the human level can arise is on the basis of a common culture, consisting of shared symbols, the meanings of which are mutually understood. This symbol system is important in the socialization of the child. The elements of common culture have significance for all the modes of orientation of action.

Only when a sufficiently developed cognitive reference system and a system of expressive symbolism have been internalized is the foundation laid for the development of the superego. Culture is a system of generalized symbols and meanings. In order for its integration with the emotional life of an individual, which constitutes internalization, to occur, the individual's own affective organizations must be generalized at a high order. The mechanism by which this occurs is through emotional communication with others, sensitizing the individual to the attitudes of others. It is not only the superego which is internalized; also internalized are the systems of cognitive categorizations of the object world and the system of expressive symbolism.

To summarize Parsons' general argument:

I. Social interaction is a system analyzable into three kinds of elements: (a) ideas, (b) emotions and drives, and (3) values and norms.
II. Human culture consists, in part, of the system of common symbols with common meanings that make interaction possible.
   A. If interaction is complete, it must involve all three types of elements.
   B. Culture must consist of symbol systems adequate to all three categories of elements. These are:
     1. A cognitive reference system.
     2. A common moral standard.
     3. A system of expressive symbolism.

III. Socialization consists in the structuring of individual behavior on the basis of the symbol systems of common culture.
IV. Freud had already perceived that socialization represents the structuring of individual personality on the basis of the internalization of cultural norms.
V. A complete theory of personality requires the recognition that under the influence of common culture something more than common moral standards are internalized. Such a complete theory establishes the following links:

Cultural Objects	Internalized Subject and Social Objects
1. Cognitive reference system	Internalized self-object images
2. Cultural moral standards	Superego
3. Expressive symbolism	Symbolically organized affect

In brief, Parsons believes that the functionalistic theory of personality represents a modified form of Freudianism. His analysis differs from the Freudian theory primarily in the fact that it contemplates the formation of personality not only on the basis of the internalization of common moral standards, which Freud himself had originally seen as providing the personality with a superego, but it involves as well the internalization from the culture of concepts of self and symbols for emotional expression. (Freud, I suspect, would retort that he always said personality is made up of an *ego* and *id* as well as a *superego*.)

It is significant that Parsons turns to Freud rather than to one or any of the branches of social behaviorism for a theory of personality adequate for functionalism.

A Functionalistic Theory of Symbolism. In another of the papers, Parsons proposes the development of a functionalistic theory of symbolism. He feels that there has been a failure to develop "a coherent treatment of the *content* as distinguished from the meanings of expressive symbolism."[56] Parsons ar-

---

[56]*Ibid.,* p. 31.

gues that a symbol always has both cognitive and expressive meanings. The former primarily refers to the situational object, the latter to the actor's own motivations or intentions.

Cognitive symbolism involves the actor as knower. Expressive symbolism involves the actor as a motivated agent. Expressive symbols mediate the action of the actor and others in a social situation.

A plurality of actors in an interactive situation are mutually interdependent for gratification. "We may now introduce another generalization or postulate. This is that two or more objects which are cathected with the same *quality* of cathectic significance, which in expressive terms have the same order of meaning for the ego, will tend to become symbolically associated with each other."[57] Moreover, insofar as one's own preference is an expression of one's motivation, it becomes susceptible to interpretation by oneself and the others in the social act as an expressive sign or symbol of one's motivation. However, "it must not be forgotten that when we speak of communication here there is always a cognitive component, but the distinctive feature of expressive symbolism is its communication of 'affect' or of 'feeling.' "[58] There remains only one further point. "A set of expressive signs or symbols . . . comes to be organized as a system. As such, a principal condition of its serving the communicative function in either its cognitive or its expressive aspects is necessarily that the interacting actors are oriented to conformity with normative standards. The 'conventions' of the symbolic system must be observed if there is to be effective communication, just as in the case of language."[59]

Reduced to its simplest terms, Parsons argues: (1) that functionalism requires a new theory of symbolism; (2) such a theory of symbolism must take account of the fact that human interaction requires a "language of emotions" as well as a "language of ideas"; (3) such a language of emotions permits the communication of motives and emotions ("It is crucial that *what* is communicated is not only *understanding of motives* in the cognitive sense, but is *mutuality of affective meanings.*");[60] (4) for full use as a communicative device, this "language of emotions" must rest upon symbolic conventions.

This particular paper seems intended to take over the Freudian system of emotional symbolism into functionalistic theory. Parsons appears to contemplate the possibility that there are two quite distinct sets of symbols: one for ideas, one for emotions. The latter are formed into distinct systems, and based on distinct linguistic conventions. At least this seems to be the implication of a statement such as the following: "This organization of expressive symbols, according to appreciative standards on a cultural level, is not merely 'external' to the actor but becomes, by 'internalization,' a constitutive part of his own personality structure."[61] To anyone brought up in the belief that the communication and "expression" of ideas are merely different uses of ordinary language, this seems rather mysterious. Perhaps before long we can expect from Parsons a dictionary of the emotions, a grammar of the emotions, and a logic of the emotions.

The Dimensions of Action-Space. In the joint paper on "The Dimensions of Action-Space," Parsons and Bales took a major step toward demonstrating the identity of their two brands of functionalism and went a step further in developing Parsons' concept of pattern variables. Bales has for some time made studies of small groups, some of the results of which were published in *Interaction Process Analysis.*[62] The fundamental theoretical ideas of the joint paper are summarized by Bales and Parsons:

> The essential approach was to think of the small group as a functioning social system. It was held that

[57]*Ibid.*, p. 36.
[58]*Ibid.*, p. 38.
[59]*Ibid.*

[60]*Ibid.*
[61]*Ibid.*, p. 39.
[62]Robert F. Bales, *Interaction Process Analysis* (Reading, Mass.: Addison-Wesley Press, 1950).

such a system would have four main "functional problems," which were described, respectively, as those of *adaptation* to conditions of the external situation, of *instrumental* control over parts of the situation in the performance of goal oriented tasks, of the management and *expression* of sentiments and tensions of the members, and of preserving the social *integration* of members with each other as a solidary collectivity.[63]

Meanwhile, Parsons, in collaboration with Edward Shils,[64] developed the scheme of pattern variables reviewed earlier. These were conceived of as "dilemmas" in choice situations. Two of them (affective expression versus affective neutrality, and specificity versus diffuseness) are here said to concern the dilemmas actors face in deciding how their *attitudes toward objects shall be organized.* Furthermore, a second set of dilemmas (those of universalism versus particularism and of ascribed quality versus performance) represent dilemmas actors face in deciding how *objects themselves shall be organized* in relation to each other and in relation to the motivational interests of the actors. Parsons and Bales maintain that the fifth pattern variable, that of self-orientation versus collectivity-orientation is not paired with any other, and does not as such belong either to the attitudinal classification or to object categorization. This is because it is concerned with problems internal to the system of interaction rather than with problems internal to each act.[65]

These further comments on the pattern variables have an extremely deceptive property. In the actions of ordinary mortals, one is not faced with a dilemma whether to be or not to be emotionally involved. As a matter of fact one *is* or one *is not* emotionally involved. There may be a series of dilemmas in action occurring over alternative goals: whether to marry or pursue a career, whether to pursue one career rather than another, whether to lie and protect a friend or tell the truth and expose him or her. But to describe the pattern variables — the dichotomous classifications of various properties of the means, ends, or norms of action — as "dilemmas of action choice" is surrealism. Ordinary mortals sometimes have conflicts in their choices, but Parsons and Bales have problems as to whether to choose to choose.

It is the argument of Parsons and Bales that their "two sets of categories, or paradigms," though independently arrived at, may be brought together into a single formulation. They argue that the basic conception underlying both original schemes is that of a process described by comparison with a hypothetical system in a state of moving equilibrium. New elements are being added, either by perception and cognition, by personalities, or by a change in the situation. If the system is to regain equilibrium, there must be a process of adjustment to the disturbance.

Thus, it is maintained that the two schemes may be fused forthwith and the pattern variables conceived as dimensions of a four-dimensional space. "The suggestion was first made by [Robert R.] Bush that what we have here are the *dimensions of a four-dimensional* space in the mathematical sense of that term. We would like to assume from here on that this interpretation is correct and attempt to develop the implications of this assumption for the nature of the variables involved and of the theoretical system in which they belong."[66] Thus, Bales's "four functional problems" and Parsons' "pattern variables" are now fused and conceived as dimensions of space. Any activity is treated as a change of location in such a social space. The unit of observation for such change of location is taken to be the behavioral role. "This is the unit of observation in the interaction process but it is *not* the unit or particle of the *system* of action in the theoretical sense."[67] Where the system being

[63]Parsons, Bales, and Shils, *Working Papers in the Theory of Action,* p. 64.
[64]See especially Talcott Parsons and Edward A. Shils, eds., *Toward a General Theory of Action* (Cambridge, Mass.: Harvard University Press, 1951).
[65]Parsons, Bales, and Shils, *Working Papers in the Theory of Action,* p. 66.

[66]*Ibid.,* p. 85.
[67]*Ibid.,* p. 87

studied is a system of social interaction, the unit is a role; if it is a personality system, it is a need-disposition.

Action now is conceived as a change of location on the dimensions of action-space. However, since we are dealing with systems in equilibrium, a tendency toward constancy or "inertia" must be assumed. The maintenance of a system is attributed to "boundaries" of the theoretical action-space. Three of these are particularly important:

I. The first is involved in the conception of the goal attainment of a system unit-act.
II. The second boundary condition concerns the dimension of tension, which may decline to a zero point.
III. The third boundary-feature of the system is assimilation to the environment.[68]

Parsons and Bales urge that the disintegration of a boundary-maintaining system represents disappearance of differences between internal states and the environment. This is death in the biological sense. Corresponding to the reification of dichotomous classification of the elements of action is the reification of functional prerequisites.

It becomes increasingly clear, with the conception of the pattern variables as dimensions of action-space, the conception of motivation as a change of location on these coordinates, and the conception of actions as a part of boundary-maintaining systems, that the model of classical mechanics is basic to the argument. This is made quite explicit. The laws of equilibrium in social systems are expressed as:

1. *The Principle of Inertia:* A given process of action will continue unchanged in rate and direction unless impeded or deflected by opposing motivational forces.
2. *The Principle of Action and Reaction*: If, in a system of action, there is a change in the *direction* of a process, it will tend to be balanced by a *complementary change which is equal in motivational force and opposite in direction.*

3. *The Principle of Effort*: Any change in the rate of an action process is directly proportional to the *magnitude* of the motivational force applied or withdrawn.
4. *The Principle of System-Integration*: Any *pattern* element (*mode of organization* of components) within a *system* of action will tend to be confirmed in its place within the system or to be eliminated from the system (extinguished) as a function of its contribution to the integrative balance of the system.[69]

This seems to be nothing less than a return to the social physics of Berkeley.

The same fusion of Bales's "functional problems" and of the Shils-Parsons "pattern variables" into dimensions of action-space forms the theoretical foundation of the paper by all three of these authors, "Phase Movement in Relation to Motivation, Symbol Formation, and Role Structure," in which they investigate motivation and related problems. The whole elaborate baggage of concepts is developed to trace the changing nature of the motivation of an act. The extensively elaborate account that results bears a direct similarity to the very simple one with which John Dewey had acquainted the world at least half a century earlier. He had stated that some tension situation always represents the beginning of an act. If the tension cannot be ignored, or if it grows worse, it leads to the institution of a problem, the location of the conditions causing the tension, and the developing of a plan of action to clear it up. When the plan is tried out, it either solves the problem or leads to a new plan. When the tension is resolved, the organism is in a state of satisfaction. One's emotions have gone through a series of stages. Initially one was at rest. Some tension disturbed the peace. A solution was sought and found. One returns to a state of rest. The identical argument seems to be contained in the Parsons-Bales-Shils study of phase movement in relation to motivation. The three authors conclude that the processes accompanying motivation are a clockwise movement through the dimensions of action-space.

[68]*Ibid.*, pp. 91–92. (Paraphrased)

[69]*Ibid.*, pp. 102–103.

Recent Achievements. Two other works of Parsons and the Parsonians have had major importance for later developments in his theory. In 1956, two years before he was to complete his Ph.D. at Harvard, Neil Joseph Smelser joined Parsons in the application of his emerging functional theory to the economy in *Economy and Society*.[70] And in 1961 Edward Shils, Kaspar D. Naegele, and Jesse R. Pitts joined Parsons in editing a two-volume *Theories of Society*, which traced the rise of sociological theory and its fulfillment in functionalism.[71] In *Economy and Society*, Parsons and Smelser made major strides in developing the basic scheme of analysis they would later apply to all problems. In this work they undertook to integrate economic and social theory into that single analytical framework. "A social system," they urged, "is the system generated by any process of *interaction* . . . between two or more actors: The actor is either a concrete human individual . . . or a collectivity."[72] Only a sector of behavior or role is involved in interaction. "A society is the theoretically limiting case of the social system which, in its sub-systems, comprises *all* important roles of the persons and collectivities composing its population."[73] In a technical note Parsons explains that

the basis for his analysis had been laid in the *Working Papers,* in the course of which he fused his scheme of pattern variables (also reducing them from five to four) with Bales's concept of four phase movements in the dynamics of an act.[74] The result, he argued, was to clarify the fact that any action system has four functional imperatives, as illustrated in Figure 20.1 below.

FIGURE 20.1 *The Functional Imperatives of a System of Action**

A	Adaptive Instrumental Object Manipulation	G	Instrumental-Expressive Consummatory Performance and Gratification
L	Latent-Receptive Meaning Integration and Energy Regulation Tension build-up and drain-off	I	Integrative-Expressive Sign Manipulation

KEY

1. A—Adaptation
2. G—Goal Gratification
3. I—Integration
4. L—Latent-Pattern Maintenance and Tension Management

*Adapted from Figure 2, p. 182, in Parsons, Bales, and Shils, *Working Papers.* The above figure deals with the "functional imperatives" aspect of the system of action; that in the *Working Papers* deals with the "phase movement" aspect.

Source: Parsons and Smelser, *Economy and Society,* p. 19.

Since the economy is, by definition, also a social system, it must have the same structure. The chief task faced by the authors in displaying this was to search economic theory and research for the terms that fit into the proper boxes. The product of Parsons' and Smelser's enterprise is as follows in Figure 20.2.

[70]Neil Joseph Smelser was born in Kahoka, Missouri in 1930. He earned the B.A. at Harvard in 1952 and the Ph.D. in 1958. Although he continued to work sporadically with Parsons for the rest of Parsons's life, Smelser has had a distinguished career of his own. He became a member of the faculty of the University of California, Berkeley, in 1958 and professor of sociology in 1962 with service as an administrator in that institution and as an editor and author in the profession. Among his major works are: *Economy and Society* with Talcott Parsons (Glencoe, Ill.: The Free Press, 1956); *Theory of Collective Behavior* (New York: The Free Press, 1963); *The Sociology of Economic Life* (Englewood Cliffs, N.J.: Prentice-Hall, 1963); *Essays in Sociological Explanation* (Englewood Cliffs, N.J.: Prentice-Hall, 1968); *Sociological Theory: A Contemporary View* (New York: General Learning Press, 1971).

[71]Talcott Parsons, Edward Shils, Kaspar D. Naegele, and Jesse R. Pitts, *Theories of Society: Foundations of Modern Sociological Theory,* 2 vols. (New York: The Free Press, 1961).

[72]Parsons and Smelser, *Economy and Society,* p. 8.

[73]*Ibid.,* p. 9.

[74]*Ibid.,* pp. 33f.

FIGURE 20.2 *Functional Differentiation of the Economy as a System*

A	G
Capitalization and Investment Subsystem	Production Subsystem— including Distribution and Sales
Economic Commitments: Physical, Cultural and Motivational Resources	Organizational Subsystem: Entrepreneurial Function
L	I

Source: Parsons and Smelser, *Economy and Society,* p. 44.

And, of course, what applies to a subsystem of society must also apply to a society, as in Figure 20.3.

FIGURE 20.3 *Functional Differentiation of Society as a System*

A	G
The Economy	The Polity
Socialization	Societal Community
L	I

Source: Parsons and Smelser, *Economy and Society,* adapted from p. 53.

At the time of *Economy and Society,* Parsons had not yet named the Integrative Subsystem of the society the societal community nor the subsystem for pattern maintenance socialization; however, he had already envisioned the activity within the society of any of its subsystems as a series of boundary interchanges. This appears in Figure 20.4.

Most of the work in *Economy and Society* consisted in fitting economic terminology into the system. On the basis of this carpentry the authors concluded that economic theory is a special case of the general theory of social systems, with inputs and outputs over its boundaries, and that many of its problems can only be solved when it is seen not to be "an 'island' of theoretical specificity totally alone in an uncharted 'sea' of theoretical indeterminacy."[75]

In *Economy and Society,* the Parsonians developed functionalism into an instrument that was apparently able to swallow social sciences in a single gulp. In *Theories of Society*, they presented functionalism as the culmination of sociological thought. In the epilogue, Edward Shils[76] undertook the establishment of its ideological credentials, a task for which he was fitted both by his work with Parsons on the development of functionalism in *The Working Papers* and his work as one of the coeditors of *Theories of Society.* In addition, he was motivated by his own deep personal commitment to transforming alienated intellectuals into supporters of the pluralistic society, utilizing their skills and science to defeat extremism of the right or left.

By the late 1930s, Shils argues, sociology was still in a state of disarray: in the United States there was a mass of disconnected particular inquiries and most other nations did not even have this

[75]*Ibid.,* p. 308.

[76]Edward Shils, who was born in 1911, earned the B.A. from Pennsylvania in 1931 and is professor of macrosociology, intellectuals and higher education, and history of sociology and social thought at Chicago. He was cotranslator of Max Weber's *Methodology of the Social Sciences* and Karl Mannheim's *Ideology and Utopia.* Among his major books are: *The Torment of Secrecy: The Background and Consequences of American Security Policies* (Glencoe, Ill.: The Free Press, 1956); *The Intellectual Between Tradition and Modernity: The Indian Situation* (The Hague: Mouton & Co., 1961); *Criteria for Scientific Development: Public Policy and National Goals,* a selection of articles from Minerva, edited by Edward Shils (Cambridge, Mass.: The M.I.T. Press, 1968).

FIGURE 20.4 *Boundary Interchanges Between the Primary Subsystems of a Society**

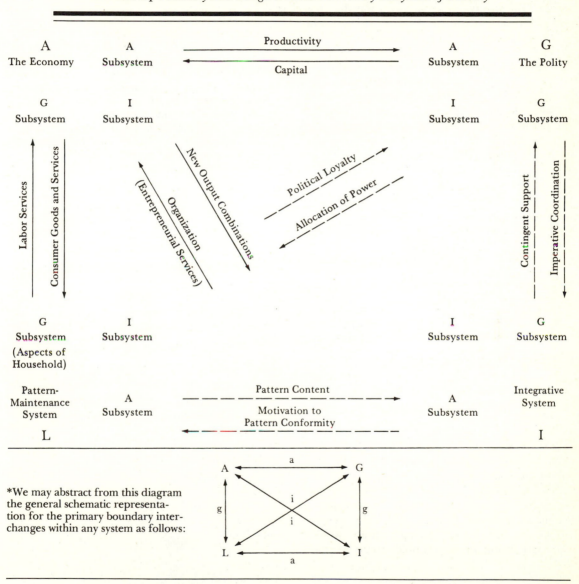

*We may abstract from this diagram the general schematic representation for the primary boundary interchanges within any system as follows:

Source: Parsons and Smelser, *Economy and Society,* p. 68.

achievement; in France and Germany practically nothing had been done since Durkheim and Weber. *"The Structure of Social Action* was the turning point. It was this work that brought the greatest of the partial traditions into a measure of unity."[77]

Sociology, in Shils's opinion, arrived in the nick of time for alienated intellectuals who roamed the Western world. As a substitute or complement of Marxism, sociology "has come into its present estate because its own development bears a rough correspondence to the development of the consciousness of mankind in its moral progress."[78]

Unfortunately, there are negative tendencies in contemporary society that have also had effects on sociology. And there are oppositional trends sponsored by people who may have started out with the intention of improving things but ended up doing more harm than good.

> It is still a proud boast of some sociologists that sociology is an "oppositional" science. Some of those who take pride in the oppositional character of sociology are former or quasi-Marxists . . . After first focusing attention on the miserable, the homeless, the parentless, the insulted, and the injured, sociologists later generalized this particular condition into one which was put forward as representative of all of modern society. . . . There is often an overtone to the effect that those in authority have acted wrongly. . . . The result is an outlook that radically distrusts the inherited order of society. . . .[79]

By contrast, "The sociological theory that grows from the theory of action is simply a more forward part of a widespread consensual collectivity . . . that is self-interpretive and has its correlate in the practice of collective self-control."[80] Among the beneficent effects of functionalism have been the salvage of youth. "Lively young men and women who have been, or who would otherwise have been, drawn to Marxism have turned to sociology."[81] This works as follows:

> The content of a human life flows outward into other minds and lives through the medium of sociology. The "larger mind" is extended and deepened through the program of the sociology that moves in the direction of the theory of action. The oppositional impetus and the drive toward a critical assessment existed earlier. They still exist and will necessarily always exist, from the very nature of sociological analysis, as long as sociology continues. The consensual impetus to sociological inquiry is, however, something new in the world, and a positive addition to the moral progress of the race.[82]

Structure-functional social theory, Shils leaves no doubt, is the theology of conventional liberalism.

THE SCHOLASTIC SYNTHESIS

Thirty years after the appearance of *The Structure of Social Action* a second, paperback edition was published with a new introduction by Parsons that addressed the comments and criticisms that had been made of his work. Attention had been called to the fact that he had an unusual conception of empirical work (for example, that he treated the *Structure*, basically a review of the theories of others, as an empirical work). Parsons reiterated his conviction that it was empirical, but admitted that it was also theoretical.[83] He agreed that he had justly been accused of developing a form of "grand theory" and retorted, "of course, why not?"[84] It had been observed that Parsons' theory had gone through a number of phases. He conceded that this was correct and even undertook to describe them himself:

[77]Edward Shils, "The Calling of Sociology," in *Theories of Society*, p. 1406.
[78]*Ibid.*, p. 1410.
[79]*Ibid.*, pp. 1422–1423.
[80]*Ibid.*, p. 1420.

[81]*Ibid.*, p. 1423.
[82]*Ibid.*, p. 1430.
[83]Talcott Parsons, *The Structure of Social Action* (New York: The Free Press, 1968), I, vi–vii.
[84]This criticism had been made by C. Wright Mills. For Parsons' reaction, see *The Structure of Social Action*, p. iv.

It would be *most* unlikely and incongruous if any such generalized theoretical scheme should, as first formulated for a particular purpose, prove or claim to be definitive. . . . It may be useful to distinguish three phases in this development in the thirty years since the publication of the *Structure*. The first may be thought of as the phase of "structural-functional" theory. . . . With respect to the conception of "action" in the narrower sense, the theory became more Durkheimian than Weberian, thus giving rise to Martindale's allegation that I had abandoned the whole Weber position, which surely was not the case . . . I came to attribute great importance to the convergence of Durkheim and Freud in the understanding of the internalization of cultural norms and social objects as part of personality. . . . The second major phase of development in general theory after the *Structure* . . . departed from the Paretan conception and economic theory was abstract and partial relative to a theory of the social system as a whole. . . . it proceeded to show that the economy is a clearly and precisely definable *subsystem* of society. . . . It was probably fair to criticize my theoretical work in its "structural-functional" phase for not adequately accounting for the problems of political structure and process. . . . The third main phase of my "post-Structure" theoretical development has come to center in [cultural and psychological systems]. Its keynote is a return to Weberian as distinct from Durkheimian interests. . . .[85]

This formulation, written when Parsons was sixty-five years of age and when the Vietnam War, the generation crisis, and countercultural revolt were tearing American morale to tatters, sounds as if Parsons were contemplating a return to Weberian elementarism. He did, in fact, thereafter spend increasing amounts of time on problems of socialization (particularly education, religion, and health) and personality. However, his commitment to functionalistic modes of analysis was too deep to be reversed.

Parsons was essentially a scholastic, moved by a passion for order and the search for God. No cloistered monk or inner-worldly ascetic nurtured

on the Protestant ethic ever worked harder or more continuously. He possessed an idealistic conception of the world: the central fact in human action was value, hence when one explored any area of social experience one was best advised to review the major thinkers and interpreters of this area. When one did so — as he reviewed Marshall, Pareto, Durkheim, and Weber in the *Structure* — one was engaging in empirical research. On occasion, Parsons suggested that a reason for conducting actual empirical research, presumably in the field or laboratory, was to discover which of the theoretical possibilities did not apply. Some persons have drawn a distinction between Parsons' essays — assumed to be empirical — and his theoretical formulations. In his "essays," Parsons was primarily reviewing and criticizing the ideas of others and formulating his own interpretations of what they discussed; the empirical material was usually supplied by the persons under discussion. In his theoretical formulations, Parsons was primarily occupied with formalizing his ideas and fitting them into his various paradigms. There is little question that Parsons viewed his essays as empirical research, preliminary and foundational to his theoretical integration. They are usually empirical in the same sense as the *Structure*. Parsons' empirical research was actually a less abstract conceptualization. The analysis of human activity in terms of actor and situation, means and ends, and values and norms has ancient roots in Western thought. It was taken for granted in the pragmatic traditions popular at the time Parsons was a student. It is astonishing that it required such detailed analysis empirically grounded to confirm Marshall, Pareto, Durkheim, and Weber in order to discover that social action involves (1) a subject-actor, (2) a situation, (3) symbols, and (4) rules, norms, and values. It is even more astonishing that Parsons would view this as a new departure in theory. This can only be explained by the hypothesis that Parsons' passion for order took the form of a search for a set of categories with apparent applicability to an unlimited variety of thinkers and situations. The basic categories in terms of which he proposed to analyze social action seemed to qualify.

[85]*Ibid.,* pp. x–xiii.

In general, whenever in the course of his reading and essay writing after the *Structure* Parsons encountered a striking formulation with extensive applicability to his own scheme, he tended to take it over and make it a part of his emerging system of concepts: such were his discoveries of the notion of system; the concept of society as a complete social system; the dichotomies by which Tönnies contrasted *Gemeinschaft* and *Gesellschaft,* which Parsons renamed pattern variables; the four phases of group activity as analyzed by Bales; Merton's typology of structural factors in deviance, which became the starting point for Parsons' own paradigms of deviance and social control; the concept of the economy as the paradigm societal subsystem; the so-called cybernetic principle by which systems high in meaning but low in energy were said to control systems low in meaning but high in energy.

Somewhere along the line Parsons developed the intuitive certainty that the truth was four-square. Hence he was unhappy with any analysis of a social component until he had raised or reduced its elements to four. He initially developed five pattern variables, but decreased them to four. He adopted from Sorokin the idea that human social life was manifest in three systems: society, personality, and culture. He added a fourth, the biological organism. He took over from Freud the notion that personality had three structures: id, superego, and ego; he added identity.

By 1960 Parsons had emerged as a dominant figure in American and Western sociology. By this time he had already examined in his essays most of the themes he would deal with over the next nineteen years. However, he would continue to work up essays, republish essays in book form, occasionally undertake some extension or reorganization of his ideas, and periodically sum up his notions in abstract paradigmatic form. But by 1960 there was growing concern with the apparent difficulty of adequately accounting for change and power in structure-functional terms. C. Wright Mills had made a slashing attack on Parsons for advancing an empty, pretentious form of "grand theory." Sociologists were beginning to examine the ideological dimensions of Parsons' theory.[86] Parsons' strategy for handling accusations of "global theorizing" and "ideological bias" was to meet them head on, pointing to the size of his audience as evidence that he was on the right track. He recognized that the problems of explaining power (particularly in view of the rise of interest in the conflict sociologies and the sociology of power) and social change were potentially more serious.

Parsons took up the problems of social change and comparative society in *Societies: Evolutionary and Comparative Perspectives* (1966) and *The System of Modern Societies* (1971). Parsons returned to the classical sociologists, particularly Spencer, for guidance and revitalization of the evolutionary hypothesis. To this he added the law of cybernetic hierarchy, which presumably accounted for the direction social change must inevitably take: systems high in meaning or information but low in energy dominate and give direction to systems high in energy but low in meaning or information.[87] Cultural systems, according to this law, provide the direction of social change and those with highest ca-

---

[86] In *The Social Theories of Talcott Parsons,* ed. Max Black (Englewood Cliffs, N.J.: Prentice-Hall, 1961), a number of major scholars critically reviewed Parsons' theories. Chandeler Morse was critical of what he saw as Parsons' inclination "to regard power as an interesting side-phenomenon rather than a central feature of social systems" (p. 151). Alfred Baldwin concluded his review of Parsons' treatment of personality with the observation that "he has so impoverished the personality that it cannot function effectively, even in his theory and for his problems" (p. 190). Urie Bronfenbrenner concluded after reviewing Parsons' theory of identification that, when reduced to plain English, it had nothing that had not been previously expressed "in the writings of such diverse theorists as G. H. Mead, Piaget, Sullivan, Werner, Cottrell, Heider, and Newcomb" (p. 213). Andrew Hacker concluded that an outmoded ideological bias did, indeed, underlie Parsons' formulations. "The ideology underlying Parsons' political theory is a worthy one in many respects. But liberalism of the eighteenth and nineteenth centuries no longer has the structural basis which gave it its strength" (p. 309).

[87] Talcott Parsons, *Societies: Evolutionary and Comparative Perspectives* (Englewood Cliffs, N.J.: Prentice-Hall, 1966), p. 28.

FIGURE 20.5 *Subsystems of Action*

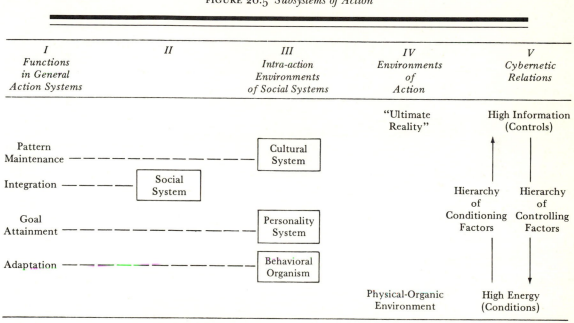

I *Functions in General Action Systems*	II	III *Intra-action Environments of Social Systems*	IV *Environments of Action*	V *Cybernetic Relations*

Source: Talcott Parsons, *Politics and Social Structure* (New York: Free Press, 1969), p. 32.

pacity for generalized adaptation prevail. The three major stages in social evolution from primitive through intermediate to modern societies were marked by the development of writing, moving societies from the primitive to the intermediate stage, and the development of law, moving societies from the intermediate to the contemporary stage.

For dealing with problems of comparative sociology Parsons found he needed only to dust off the pattern variables once again, since they had been primarily derived as comparative components of Tönnies *Gemeinschaft-Gesellschaft*. *Gemeinschaft* had been visualized as placing central value on particular relations and qualitative position in traditional social hierarchies; *Gesellschaft* was visualized as stressing universal standards of judgment and performance. However, if these were recombined the typology could be expanded.

Pattern Variable Combination and Societal Type

Universalism plus Performance	Society in the United States
Particularism plus Quality	Latin American Society
Universalism plus Quality	German Society
Particularism plus Performance	Classical China

Parsons' critics maintained that he did not have an adequate political sociology or achieve a realistic treatment of the problem of power. His response was to adapt the same basic approach to the polity as he had applied to the economy, dividing it into subsystems and visualizing its relation to the rest of society in terms of a series of inputs and outputs. Parsons treated power as the equivalent of money as a medium of exchange in the hierarchy of control. And since the subsystems of the societal community and socialization were assumed to be similar in structure, Parsons envisioned commitments in the sphere of socialization and influence in the societal community as similar in function to money and power. He described them as categories of power and summarized them in the following table in *Politics and Social Structure* (1969).

During the 1960s Parsons' major concern was the development of his theories of power and social change. During the 1970s he turned his attention to various problems of socialization, with special emphasis upon education, health institutions, personality, and religion. In a series of studies culminating in *Action Theory and the Human Condition* (1978) Parsons undertook to round out his

FIGURE 20.6 *The Categories of Social Structure*

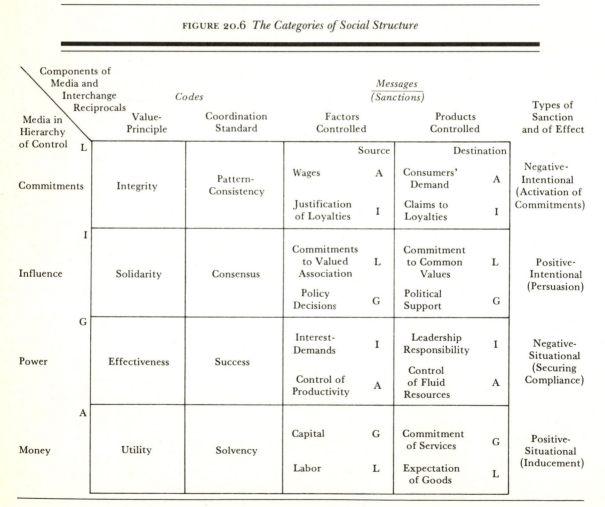

Components of Media and Interchange Reciprocals / Media in Hierarchy of Control	Codes		Messages (Sanctions)		Types of Sanction and of Effect
	Value-Principle	Coordination Standard	Factors Controlled	Products Controlled	
L			Source	Destination	
Commitments	Integrity	Pattern-Consistency	Wages A Justification of Loyalties I	Consumers' Demand A Claims to Loyalties I	Negative-Intentional (Activation of Commitments)
I					
Influence	Solidarity	Consensus	Commitments to Valued Association L Policy Decisions G	Commitment to Common Values L Political Support G	Positive-Intentional (Persuasion)
G					
Power	Effectiveness	Success	Interest-Demands I Control of Productivity A	Leadership Responsibility I Control of Fluid Resources A	Negative-Situational (Securing Compliance)
A					
Money	Utility	Solvency	Capital G Labor L	Commitment of Services G Expectation of Goods L	Positive-Situational (Inducement)

Source: Talcott Parsons, *Politics and Social Structure* (New York: The Free Press, 1969), p. 403.

conception of personality. Fully spelled out the personality has, in Parson's view, sixteen subdivisions. (See Figure 20.7 below.)

While Parsons was clearly in his last book seeking to round out his theory of humanity, it is also clear that he had at last found his way to God. There was a tone of suppressed excitement with which he announced that there was a system higher than the action system that served as the ultimate source of meaning, value, and order. He describes it as the telic system. The ultimate paradigm that summarizes all others is the *Structure of the Human Condition as a System*, illustrated in Figure 20.8. The

input from the action system to the telic system is faith, from which it receives grace.

Talcott Parsons was, unquestionably, one of the most interesting figures of postwar sociology. No one better qualifies as the pope of contemporary social science, who was a working priest as well, an administrative head who built his own cathedral and wrote his own *Summa Sociologica*. No doubt Parsons dreamed that for the next few centuries the multitudes would worship in the temple and the scholarly elite would study his lessons in the temple archives. There was some internal evidence in his last work, in which he completed the *steeple*

FIGURE 20.7 *Symbolic Components of Human Personality as a System of Meanings*

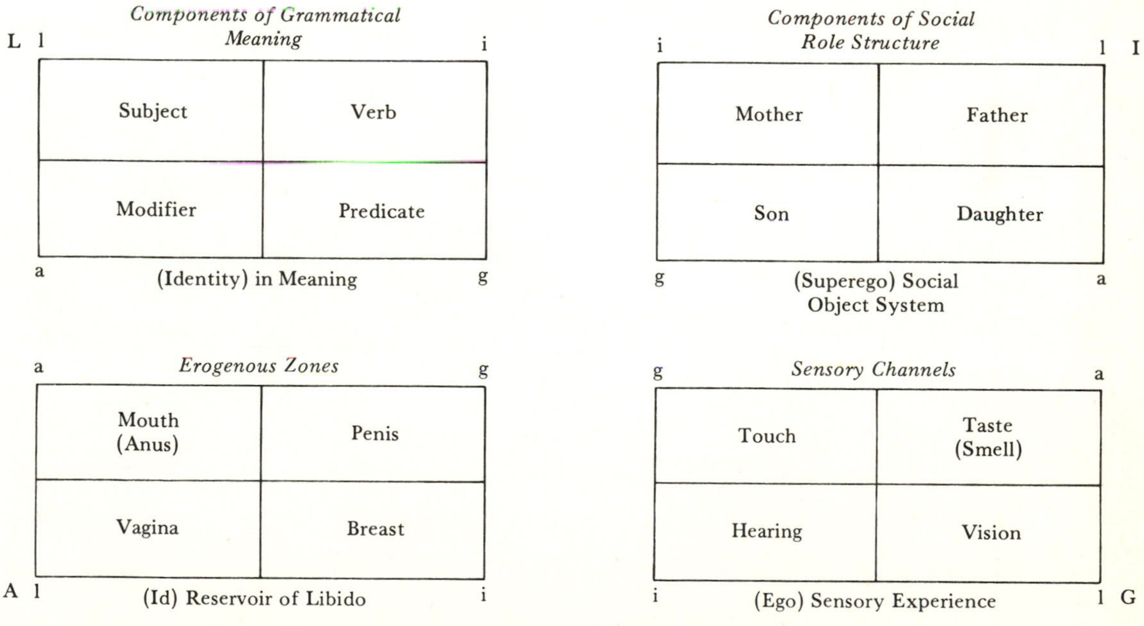

The words in parentheses under each of the four sets are the ones previously used to identify the functional subsystems of the personality within the structural paradigm of the general system of action. The L designation is taken from Erikson, the others from Freud. How these concepts are to be related to those presented here remains to be worked out.

Source: Talcott Parsons, *Action Theory and the Human Condition* (New York: The Free Press, 1979), p. 414.

of the central tower, that Parsons felt close to God — in his terminology "The Ultimate Ground of Meaning."

However, these are not times favorable to the spread of faith. Parsons' endless labors in the works of Western thought and of his contem-poraries, his reifications, his chipping them to fit and fusing them into blocks of fours endlessly re-duplicating the same basic patterns is, at best, the creation of an object of contemplation, not of use. Parsons formed a metaphysical holding company or, perhaps in a better image, constructed a gothic

FIGURE 20.8 *Structure of the Human Condition as System*

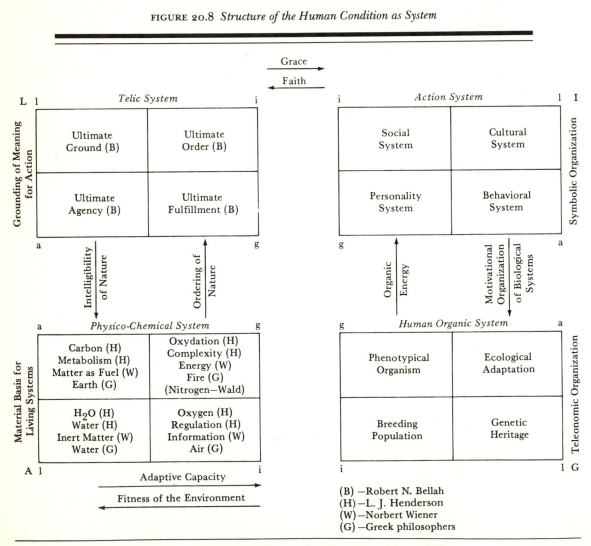

Source: Parsons, *Action Theory and the Human Condition,* p. 382.

cathedral out of ice. When the sun comes out it may well melt and run away.

But, who knows, perhaps in the very futility of Parsons' vision lies the true source of his insight into the human condition and of his fascination for us, for with the poet we suspect that

> The cloud-capp'd towers, the gorgeous palaces,
> The solemn temples, the great globe itself,
> Yea, all which it inherit, shall dissolve,
> And like this insubstantial pageant faded,
> Leave not a rack behind.

SUMMARY

The two major subschools of functionalism today are macro- and microfunctionalism. The chief difference between them lies in the size of the organic unit they take to be fundamental. The macrofunctionalists focus on large-scale social systems, the microfunctionalists on the small group.

The deepest roots of macrofunctionalism are found in positivistic organicism. The transition to macrofunctionalism was made possible by the abstraction and generalization of the concept of *system*. The performance of this task was the work of Pareto and Znaniecki. Pareto developed the concept of an external and internal system, and Znaniecki developed the concept of a closed system. The general features of macrofunctionalism have evolved rapidly in the works of Robert Merton, Talcott Parsons, George Homans, Marion Levy, and the Parsonians, including Shils and Bales.

XXI

Microfunctionalism: Group Dynamics

The form of functionalistic sociological theory that has just been sketched has been called macrofunctionalism to distinguish it from the second branch of the theory. Functionalism is characterized by its conception of the primacy of system. It is therefore appropriate to describe the subtypes of functionalism in terms of the kind of system isolated. Historically, the predecessors of the macrofunctionalists were the positivistic organicists. Society in almost all cases represented their primary unit of analysis. The macrofunctionalists attempt repeatedly to give an exact definition of "society" (as, for example, a total, independent, self-sufficient system, persisting for time periods longer than the individual life). There is little question that, in terms of their derivations and emphasis, the macrofunctionalists rest their case on the large-scale social system (typically the society). At the same time, with the increasing attempts to generalize the concept of system (beginning seriously with the work of Florian Znaniecki) and with the application of the concept to a wide variety of social phenomena at different levels of complexity, the macrofunctionalists tend to narrow the compass of their critical systems. Still, even though criticizing the anthropologists for working with systems of too large a scale, Robert Merton tended to take the society-sized unit as his analytical model. And Talcott Parsons, in *The Social System,* took society as his unitary system, although he later fused his idea of systems with Bales's smaller units. Starting with societies as their unitary system, the macrofunctionalists tend to extend analysis downward to include less inclusive systems.

The microfunctionalists, on the other hand, seem to be in process of working out a general functional sociological theory from the opposite direction. The origins of this branch of functionalism were in Gestalt psychology, which, as has been noted, originated in the reassertion of teleological explanations in human psychology against the mechanistic theories of the associationists. Against associationistic atomism (or as some prefer, "elementarism"), it asserted the presence of design in consciousness — an idea quickly broadened to include the concept of totality. The

496

problems that soon came under investigation were those involved in the relationship between various kinds of psychological wholes and their parts and the problem of the adaptation of behavior to structures.

The starting point of the position can be traced to the work of Christian von Ehrenfels, who called attention to the fact that a melody is instantly recognized though transposed into a different key. He postulated a *Gestaltqualität* to account for this phenomenon, suggesting that order arises from a spontaneous process that forms functional wholes. The physical environment affects the organism through the senses. The resulting impressions are organized into distributions within the organism. Subjected to stresses, they are released by a form of energy within the distribution. Relations of closure, articulation, and consistency characterize these wholes.

The importance of the early formulations by Ehrenfels is due to the clarity with which the concept of system was perceived and formulated. From these beginnings the Gestalt psychologists soon came to protest against the exclusively neurological explanation of learning. A configurational interpretation of learning was brilliantly advanced in Köhler's theories and experiments with chimpanzees. Step by step, it moved toward a general organismic conception of human nature. It found analogical parallels between physical systems of energy (like the gravitational system) and organismic systems and developed the principle of the dynamics of energy systems. Whereas macrofunctionalists have tended to come to grips with the basic properties of systems under the more or less vague idea of "functional prerequisites," the Gestaltists early attempted an exact formulation.

I. *The Principle of Field Properties.* The units studied by science are systems in which parts are conjoined into something more than the qualities of the parts, which acquire their character through a field of properties. Relation of parts has the properties of a gradient in an organism.

II. *The Principle of Conditioned Action.* The movement of any body within a system is determined by the system as a whole, like an object in a gravitational system or the cell in a multi-cellular organism.

III. *The Principle of Differentiation.* Living systems are generated in undifferentiated cells. Growth occurs through a differentiation of parts as structure is specialized into organs.

IV. *The Principle of Unitary Evolution.* Differentiation is not an additive process. The whole is primary.

V. *The Principle of Least Action.* Energy is redistributed in a system by way of the shortest distance from high to low potential.

VI. *The Principle of Maximum Work.* When a system of energy is in equilibrium its maximum energy is distributed within the field as potential energy. When the balance is disturbed the energy is converted into kinetic energy exerted to restore the balance.

VII. *The Principle of Reciprocal Unitary Reaction.* The whole integrates its elements into a harmonious and complete system. When the unit member retains some autonomy in the exercise of its special differentiated function this is in accordance with impulse emanating from the whole.[1]

As Albert Levine has pointed out, the Gestaltists view every system of energy as in constant alternation from quiescence to activity, balance to disequilibrium and back. And nature itself is conceived as an energy system.

In a situation where the macrofunctionalists were appealing to Gestalt theory for support, it is little surprising that Gestaltists should develop their own brand of sociological functionalism. The charismatic leader who led the Gestaltists into the promised land was Kurt Lewin.

Kurt Lewin. Kurt Lewin (1890–1947), a German Gestalt psychologist, and his associates Ronald Lippitt and R. K. White, demonstrated the possibility of extending the Gestalt point of view into social situations in a series of studies, conducted at the University of Iowa Child Welfare Research Station, of the effect of democratic, authoritarian,

[1]Paraphrased from the very clear summary of Albert J. Levine, *Current Psychologies* (Cambridge, Mass.: Science-Art Publishers, 1940), pp. 94–99.

KURT LEWIN

Courtesy of Gertrud Weiss Lewin

and laissez-faire types of leaders upon groups. In 1945, Lewin formed the Research Center for Group Dynamics at the Massachusetts Institute of Technology. After Lewin's death, Dorwin Cartwright, the present director of the Research Center, carried on the work with the assistance of Ronald Lippitt and others. In 1948 the Center was moved to the University of Michigan. The Center has actively pursued the functionalistic sociology originally shaped in Lewin's work.[2]

[2]Kurt Lewin's major works are: *A Dynamic Theory of Personality: Selected Papers*, trans. Donald K. Adams and Karl E. Zener (New York: McGraw-Hill, 1935); *Principles of Topological Psychology*, trans. Fritz Heider and Grace M. Heider (New York: McGraw-Hill, 1936); *The Conceptual Representation and the Measurement of Psychological Forces* (Durham, N.C.: Duke University Press, 1938); *Resolving Social Conflicts: Selected Papers on Group Dynamics, 1935–*

The steps by which Lewin made the transition from Gestalt psychology to a microfunctionalistic sociology are quite logical. Gestalt psychology had continually expanded its investigations until it was ready to develop a theory of personality. When Lewin took this step, he found that it almost automatically raised the question of the bearing of the social and cultural milieu (field) on the person. When his field theory of personality was followed by the study of the effects of leader types on group atmospheres, the link to a general theory of groups had been provided. With the founding of the Research Center for Group Dynamics, the very name confirmed the transition. The fundamental objectives of the center were phrased as advancing knowledge and formulating theories about the forces underlying group life, affecting the relations between groups, and acting on personality and individual adjustment. Lewin's studies of personality and topological psychology preceded his elaboration of a theory of general sociological functionalism. In fact, since they form a natural bridge to his sociology, they are of basic interest.

Gestalt theory, which originated with the notion of perception as an act determined by the perceptual field, was fruitfully extended to learning, now conceived as the dynamic reorganization and instituting of a new order in behavior. The next logical step was the conception of personality as a dynamic energy system, at any moment moving toward a state of equilibrium, but undergoing change in time. Lewin was led to this conception in the course of the study of the effects of unfinished tasks and satiation on behavior. The perception of an object or event can cause the formation of a definite tense psychical system which did not previously exist in that form. Such an experience produces an intention or awakens a desire which did not exist previously. An already existing state of tension, on the other hand, may go back to a purpose or need or a half-finished activity directed toward a certain object or event experienced as an

1946, ed. Gertrud Weiss Lewin (New York: Harper, 1948); and *Field Theory in Social Science: Selected Theoretical Papers*, ed. Dorwin Cartwright (New York: Harper, 1951).

attraction or repulsion. Such objects are said to possess "valence." Valences of this kind operate simultaneously with other experiences as field forces. They steer the psychical processes, particularly the action mechanism, or "motorium." Certain activities are caused in part by imbalances leading to satiation processes or the carrying out of intentions and hence the reduction of tensions in the basic system involved to an equilibrium at a lower level of tension. Such phenomena permit an understanding of the fact that every single everyday experience of the past may influence the present psychical life, though this influence may be so mild as to approach zero. Individual psychic experiences, actions, emotions, purposes, wishes, hopes are imbedded in definite psychical structures, spheres of personality, and whole processes. Such belonging to definite psychical systems is characteristic of the basic psychological tensions and energies. The ego or self may be viewed as one system or complex of systems, a functional part-region of the psychical totality. "The psychical totality which is Mr. X is at least different from that of Mr. R and from that of the child Q. This difference, which constitutes the individuality (*Eigenart*) of the persons involved . . . is probably evident in some way as always the same special, characteristic individuality, in each of its processes, parts and expressions."[3]

The formation of definite psychical systems is related to the ontogenetic development of the mind. The tendency to equilibrium, the dynamic firmness of boundaries and relative segregation of psychical systems, come into central focus in personality study. The psychical processes may often be deduced from the tendency to equilibrium. The transition from a state of rest to motion is due to disturbance of the equilibrium. The process of reestablishment of a new state ensues. The process is a movement toward equilibrium for the system as a whole. Part processes may proceed in opposite directions. A state of equilibrium does not mean that the system is without tension. Systems can come to equilibrium in a state of tension. An unfinished task does not cripple the whole motorium but remains a special tension system that may operate in experience for a long time. There are systems of considerable functional firmness in the psyche. In the adult there are, as a rule, a great number of relatively separate tension systems. They form reservoirs of energy for action. Without their considerable independence, ordered action would be impossible.

The formation of personality thus represents the constant evolution of a psychical system toward equilibrium under many sorts of interruptions and disturbances. The difference between the adult and child personality lies in the formation of complex, relatively independent tension systems in the psychic structure of the adult. These provide various kinds of tendencies toward action that define individuality in the particular case.

In arriving at his theory of personality, Lewin did not concentrate on intelligence but on will and need. His original experimental subjects were mentally retarded children in Berlin, including samples of morons and imbeciles from age two to six. Control experiments were performed on normal children. Experiments concerned the problems of satiation, unsatisfied need, and substitute action. Satiation represents the transfer of a positive valence to a negative or neutral one. Interrupted tasks produce tension systems. Release of tension may occur through resumption of the task or substitution of psychologically equivalent action.

Individuals were found to differ in the degree of differentiation of psychic material, differences in tension systems, and differences in psychic content. From childhood on, the individuals are subject to differentiation in their psychical regions and in their life spheres (family, friendships, profession). The child displays fewer psychic substructures and is more a unitary system. The subsystems are developed differentially as between people. They may be many and closely knit or few and loosely integrated. In extreme cases, they may take the form of split personality. Structures are also differentiated in terms of their rigidity and

[3]Lewin, *A Dynamic Theory of Personality*, p. 56.

plasticity: they may be elastic, hard, brittle, or fluid. Such properties determine the individual's capacity for adaptation. Tension is present in need satisfaction. Individuals differ in their tension systems. Some tensions change slowly, others rapidly, and the state of tension is a general persistent quality of the individual. Finally, goals, ideas, and meanings of the individual's life rest on cultural forms of the environment. This aspect of personality is most influenced by culture.

The differences between macro- and microfunctionalism are well illustrated by the very different stages at which the problem of personality is raised. It turns up only relatively late for the macrofunctionalists, who work to it from the problem of society. For the microfunctionalists, on the other hand, it is raised early, serving as a step toward a general sociological theory.

For Lewin, "topology" provided the means for formulating the general principles of *fields*, considered in abstraction from any applications, but providing a theory general enough to be applied to ever more encompassing fields.[4] Topology is a branch of geometry which deals with problems of continuity rather than size or shape. A circle is not the same as an oval or of any variety of figures with closed lines. It is, however, similar with respect to closure. It is different if there is a hole punched in it. Or, again, a closed sphere with a hole in it is topologically different from one with two holes in it. Topological space is a set of objects or points with definite relation to one another. A rectangle is a space with a set of points organized in a certain structure. The peculiarities of topological space lie in the following: it deals with open sets (sets without limits); it includes the ideas of the surroundings of a point; it comprises the idea of "region" (an area with points), which may be open or closed. A "cut" is some division of a region. A "manifold" is a smooth surface without singularities. Space may be divided into subwholes which structure it, and so on.

Lewin believed that the first prerequisite for a scientific representation of the psychological field is the finding of a geometry adequate to represent the spatial relations of psychological facts. Perhaps for psychology, as for physical space, more than one geometry might be found useful. There is, Lewin felt, at least one geometry which permits a mathematical interpretation of terms like *approach* and *withdrawal* without being psychologically meaningless. Such a geometry is found in the "hodological space," a finitely structured space, whose parts are composed of certain units or regions. Direction and distance are defined by paths that can be coordinated to psychological locomotion. Such a geometry, Lewin thought, permits an adequate representation of the step-by-step character of most psychological processes. It also permits one to ascribe different psychological directions to locomotions in the same physical direction if the goal of those locomotions is different, a fact particularly important for the problem of roundabout routes. The hodological space furthermore permits the description of the structure relations within persons as well as in their psychological environment. The degree of differentiation within the person and the presence of the peripheral and central layers can thus be defined. Hodological space may also be used to describe the structure of groups and their changes.[5]

Behavior is conceived as a function of the person and his or her environment. The totality of facts determining people's behavior are conceived topologically as their psychological life-space. The relations between persons and their situations are perceived as positions with spatial properties. Behavior is expressed in terms of the topological notions of region, correctedness, separateness, and boundaries. Within life-space, some regions are forbidden, some are free. Forbidden regions are separated by boundaries which are as solid as the discipline supporting them. Lewin translated many familiar ideas into the analogical framework of his topological psychology. The *role* of an individual is translated into a psychological position.

[4]See his *Principles of Topological Psychology*.

[5]See *Field Theory in Social Science*, pp. 25–26.

Activity in connection with roles is translated into locomotion in relation to position. *Attitudes* are treated as tendencies toward locomotion of varying force. *Goals* are conceived as "force fields," distributed in "regions," with "boundaries" representing barriers, difficulties, or aversions. *Frustration* is treated as an overlapping of two or more force fields. *Fear* has the same dimensions as aversion, being a force away from a field. Fear is usually related to a psychological future. *Power* is the possibility of inducing forces of a certain magnitude in another person. *Values* have positive or negative valence. They induce force fields in individuals.[6] It is not difficult to see that when topological concepts were developed on the basis of such elastic analogies Lewin would indeed find it easy to apply his "hodological space" to behavior, to personality, and to groups.

By 1935 Lewin had begun to expand his field theory into sociological form. This is apparent in his study of the "Psycho-Sociological Problems of a Minority Group,"[7] a study of the effects of marginality on the Jews. The transition to a sociology was made simply by expanding the conception of what may constitute the behavior field or background. Pointing out that judgment, understanding, and perception are impossible except against a background which determines the meaning of an event, Lewin reasoned that general properties of the background may have more or less permanent effects on personality. Children growing up in a family group often respond to it as their most basic background. Instability in the background of children may lead to instability in adults; children who lack clarity about their belongingness to a group may never be completely certain. Individuals belong to many groups — say, upper middle class, merchant, member of a small family, member of a specific church, of special clubs, etc. During the course of their lives, the groups to which people belong are not all equally dominant at the same time.

There are persons whose whole life-situation is characterized by uncertainty about their belonging, as a result of their standing near the margin of groups. This is true of the nouveaux riches or of other persons crossing the boundaries of social classes. It is typical of members of religious or national minority groups everywhere when they try to enter the main group. Typically, persons crossing the boundary between groups are borderline, belonging to both new and old. "It is for example one of the greatest theoretical and practical difficulties of the Jewish problem that Jewish people are often, in a high degree, uncertain of their relation to the Jewish group."[8] Among minorities there are single individuals or sections of the main group who see their chief hope in crossing the line that separates them from others. One speaks, thus, of "assimilation." Since the Jews live in Diaspora, the Jewish group is numerically a small minority in all nations. The character of the group is further determined by the strength of the boundary separating it from other groups. In the period of the ghetto, there were clear strong boundaries between Jewish and other groups. The Jews had to live in restricted territories. One of the important facts of social life is the amount of "space of free movement." The boundaries of the ghetto imposed a strict limitation on the very bodily locomotion of the Jews, in addition to limiting social locomotion.

During the period of the ghetto, the following traits characterized the Jewish group. It was compact, spacially and socially, representing a closed region which rarely included foreign sections. Belonging to the group was clearly marked. A yellow badge was imposed from without. The boundary between the Jewish group and other groups was strong, almost impassable. The space of free movement was very limited, creating a state of high tension for the individual and the group. Such isolated groups are usually extremely conservative, even retarded, and this conservatism preserves the group intact.

---

[6]*Ibid.,* pp. 39–41.
[7]Reprinted in Lewin, *Resolving Social Conflicts,* pp. 145 ff.

[8]*Ibid.,* p. 148.

In contrast to this was the situation of the Jewish group in Germany before World War I. The Jewish group was no longer compact. Jews were not compelled to live in special districts, and where they did, the group could contain foreign elements. The boundary between Jewish and other groups was no longer a boundary by law; it had lost much of its strength and concreteness. It was passable for some individuals. The space of free movement for social action had expanded. Some restrictions remained, but the possibilities were greater. There were pronounced tendencies toward progressivism and radicalism. The weakening of the boundary of the group involved more points of contact with others, and devices for maintaining separate identity (yellow badge) disappeared. With the increasing space of free movement, the tension under which the group lived decreased.

With the intermingling of Jewish and non-Jewish groups, Jewish people have more often to face the pressures against the Jews as individuals. Two kinds of forces play on them: those coming from their own wishes and hopes and those socially induced. The very nearness of the goal of assimilation with the outside creates strong forces in its direction. Multiple forms of conflict situations emerge, creating tensions which lead to restlessness, unbalanced behavior, overemphasis in one direction or another. "Indeed the Jews are commonly characterized as being restless. The most productive type of restlessness is over-exertion in work. Some of the best work of Jewish people in the last century was partly due to this over-activity."[9] This restlessness is not an inborn trait of Jews but a result of their situation. It is notably absent from the Jews in Palestine. The conflict is especially severe for young members of well-to-do families.

If one is going to expand the concepts of life-situation, space of free movement, boundaries, and location to account for the total relations of minority groups to the outside world and their bearing upon the problems of individual behavior,

there is no good reason why the same concepts should not be extended to the general problems of personality and culture. Lewin does not hesitate to examine the social psychological differences between the United States and Germany. His attack on the problems was quite reasonably made by way of education, whose processes, he thought, depend to a high degree on the spirit of the larger social body in which the persons are living. Any change in the political, economic, or social structure of this larger group, like the nation, deeply affects not only the organization of education, but its whole spirit and technique as well. The concept of life-space has been broadened to include the "general cultural atmosphere." And Lewin is not at all of the opinion "that such general characteristics as 'freedom,' 'authority,' and 'social atmosphere' are too vague and too delicate to be grasped through any really strict concepts."[10] In fact, Lewin finds that between the United States ("freedom") and Germany ("authoritarian") there is such a general difference in social atmospheres manifest in the amount of free space of movement and structure. Generally, the educational situation in the United States as compared to Germany seems to Lewin to be characterized by regions of very different degrees of freedom and sharply determined boundaries of these regions. The educational atmosphere in German institutions, as well as in German homes, is more homogeneous, lacking regions of such high degree of freedom, and having less strictly defined limits than are found in a similar institution or home life in the United States. Totalitarian Germany tended to increase the homogeneity in education. The structure of education in the two countries was taken as an expression of the cultures as a whole. The aim of socialization was very different. In America Lewin found a quite exceptional emphasis upon personal achievement. The result, however, is not the elimination of homogeneity in America but the creation of a rather special kind of social difference.

Lewin found that the average "social distance"

---

[9]*Ibid.*, p. 156.

[10]*Ibid.*, p. 5.

between individuals seems to be smaller in the United States so far as surface or "peripheral" regions of the personality are concerned. People meet easily and invite visitors home, for the American feels less need for privacy in certain regions of life. It is possible even to find the office door of the president of a college open all day. In America only the central regions of personality tend to be separated between persons.

By contrast, Lewin finds that in Germany, although the surface layer of personality is open to others, there is a hard boundary not far below the surface. If, however, one ever penetrates this sort of shell all the inner layers of personality may be open. The personality of the American for Lewin has open surface layers but a relatively inaccessible hard core and the personality of the average German has a hard surface but no particularly special boundaries within.

The great homogeneity — on surface levels — in America is explained in terms of this difference. In America there can be relatively close relations between persons without a deep personal friendship. At the same time, for this reason, there is less danger of personal friction. Moreover, since the peripheral layers of personality include what one may call "motoric" or "executive" elements, such a person is an action type. Thus, the American emphasizes achievement more than status. Lewin finds affinity between such ideologies as German idealism and American pragmatism and the characteristics of other areas of life in Germany and America.

The experimental traditions in which Gestalt psychology was anchored were of great importance for the development of a sociology from such beginnings, for if the first thought was how to extend the conceptions of system and system-determined social areas, the second was how to prove one's extensions experimentally. Lewin and Lippitt urge that it is possible to investigate experimentally such fundamental sociopsychological problems as group ideology, group conflicts and their spontaneous substructuring, the stability of spontaneous group structures versus authoritarian structure, minority problems, renegades and scapegoats, and double loyalty conflicts. To do so, "one has to create a set up where group life might be studied under rather free but well defined conditions. Instead of utilizing the groups in schools, clubs, factories, one should create groups experimentally because only in this way the factors influencing group life will not be left to chance but will be in the hands of the experimenter."[11] Thus, the wave of modern experimental studies by microfunctionalists was begun by Lewin and Lippitt in their study of group atmosphere.

In this instance, two experimental mask-making clubs of ten- and eleven-year-olds were formed, using children who had little initial relation to one another. The attempt was made to create a total group atmosphere and study its effects. In the experimentally-created authoritarian group, all policy was determined by the leader, techniques for attaining the goal were dictated by the leader one at a time, authority was autocratic, and the leader praised and criticized individual activities and remained aloof and impersonal. In the experimentally-created democratic group, all policy was determined by the group (encouraged by the leader), perspective and explanation were given in general and advice given when needed, individuals were free to work with whomever they chose, and the leader attempted to praise and criticize the group as a whole.

The experimental results of the study were: (1) the appearance of a higher state of tension in the autocratic group, with more social interaction, less stable group structure, more ascendency, and the development of scapegoats; (2) the appearance of more cooperative behavior in the democratic group, more objectivity, more constructive suggestions and objective criticism; (3) the appearance of more primary-group feeling in the democratic group and a stronger feeling of group property and group goals.

That Lewin had made full transition to sociol-

---

[11] Kurt Lewin and Ronald Lippitt, "An Experimental Approach to the Study of Autocracy and Democracy: A Preliminary Note," *Sociometry*, 1 (January–April 1938), 292.

ogy was clear to him by 1939. "I am persuaded that it is possible to undertake experiments in sociology which have as much right to be called scientific experiments as those in physics and chemistry."[12] Moreover, the focus of study has become the group. The experimental task will consist in creating groups and social climates or styles of living. "The sociologist I hope will therefore forgive him when he cannot avoid handling also the so-called sociological problems of groups and group life."[13] Such groups are sociological wholes; "the unity of these sociological wholes can be defined operationally in the same way as a unity of any other dynamic whole, namely, by the interdependence of its parts."[14]

Lewin's interest in the group became increasingly more absorbing. The social group came to be viewed as a fundamental determinant of life-space. The essence of the group was found in the interdependence of its parts. It represents a dynamic whole such that a change in the state of any subpart changes the state of all other subparts. The degree of interdependence of the subparts varies from a loose "mass" to a compact unit, determined, among other factors, by size, organization, and intimacy of the group. A group may be a part of a more inclusive group, like a family in a community. The individual usually is a member of overlapping groups. The importance of any one of these groups may vary from person to person. For Lewin, the group is the ground on which people stand, determining their readiness to fight or to submit and other important characteristics of their behavior. Upon it rests much of their general security. If people are not clear about their belongingness, or if they are not well established within their group, their life-space will show the characteristics of an unstable ground.

The group is also a means to individuals. From early childhood individuals are accustomed to using a group relation as a means to achieving various physical and social goals. The prestige people acquire through belonging to a group (family, university, club, etc.) is one of the important vehicles to further achievement. Outsiders treat them as a part of this group.

It follows, also, that the change in the circumstances of individuals is to a great extent directly due to a change in the situation of the group of which they are a part. An attack upon their group, a rise or decline of their group, means an attack upon them, a rise or decline of their position. It teaches them ideas and goals which are group derived.

For individuals, the group is a part of the life-space in which they move about. To reach or maintain a certain group status is one of the vital goals of individuals. Their status in the group, the amount of space of free movement within it, and similar group properties are important in determining the life-space of individuals.

Belonging to a group, however, does not mean that individuals lose their identities within it. They have their personal goals, and they need sufficient space of free movement in the group to pursue them. For individuals, the problem becomes how to satisfy their individual needs without losing membership and status in the group. If the space of free movement of individuals in the group is too small, individuals will be unhappy. Intense frustration may force them to leave the group — it may even destroy the group. The adjustment of the individual to the group rests on the character of the group, the position of the individual within it, and the character of the person.

By this period Lewin's shift to sociology was complete. The group was established as the fundamental "system" in this branch of sociological functionalism.

SOME PRIMARY AREAS OF STUDY BY THE MICROFUNCTIONALISTS

If there were no more to Lewin than his elaborate and often overdrawn physical analogies, he could be dismissed without too much concern. His work,

[12]Kurt Lewin, "Experiments in Social Space," *Harvard Educational Review,* 9 (1939), 21–32. Reprinted in *Resolving Social Conflicts,* from which the quotation here is taken (p. 71).
[13]*Ibid.,* p. 72.
[14]*Ibid.,* p. 73.

however, has become the starting point for much research. His extended analogies permitted Lewin to weave together an elaborate set of ideas on various levels of precision from psychology, sociology, and common sense. The analogies themselves frequently suggested new problems and areas of inquiry. And when these ideas were appended to a talent for experimental manipulation, promising leads were opened. Moreover, the establishment of the Research Center for Group Dynamics, the success in getting funds, and the luck and skill in assembling a talented group of dedicated young people has given to microfunctionalism a combination of the properties of a crusade and a gold rush. The clear proof that there was gold in the hills of small-group research led many students outside the immediate circle of the original group-dynamics program to join the trend.

The type of research situation suggested by Lewin proved to be so manipulable that research students applying it have far outrun the developments of systematic theory. In one of the most interesting anthologies of studies by the microfunctionalists, Dorwin Cartwright and Alvin Zander say:

> No statement is available which systematically summarizes the results of these various investigations, nor is there easily at hand a collection of the more significant articles which describe the methods and findings of research on group dynamics. . . . The preparation of an integrative summary seemed to us to be premature. To achieve theoretical consistency at the present time, we should have to omit important findings which do not as yet fit readily into a single theory and we should have to present large segments of theory for which adequate empirical testing has not yet been provided.[15]

Although Cartwright and Zander, in assembling the outstanding products of microfunctionalism, decline the opportunity to theorize, the very categories found most convenient for summarizing the research studies indicate the primary pattern of thought.

Among the main sections of the book there is: (1) a section on the formation of groups and development of group cohesiveness; (2) a section on group pressures and standards; (3) a section on group goals and group locomotion toward them; (4) a section on group structure; and (5) a section on group leadership. In terms of its origins and development, the research of microfunctionalism rests directly on its most fundamental concept: the primacy of the organic-type system. The fundamental organic-type system which they select as their central object of study is the *group*. Thus, Cartwright and Zander could hardly have chosen a more fundamental organization of the research materials than one beginning with the formation of the group and the development of its unifying properties, followed by a series of analyses of group characteristics, structure, movement, and order of the group.

Group Cohesiveness. The ultimate affinity of microfunctionalists with macrofunctionalism and sociological organicism appears in the fact that they have all been preoccupied with the property of "groupness." They even tend to use the same analogies and distinguish between "healthy" and "unhealthy" group states.

And just as Durkheim long ago made the kind and state of "solidarity" the central point of approach to society conceived as an organic system, so the microfunctionalists have been preoccupied with "cohesiveness." They even talk about it in the same way.

> What do we mean intuitively when we speak of the cohesiveness of a group? A number of meanings quickly come to mind. We think, for example, of a group that has a strong feeling of "we-ness," meaning that the members are more likely to talk in terms of "we" than "I." We think, too, of a group where everyone is friendly or where loyalty to fellow members is high. A cohesive group might be characterized as one in which the members all work together for a common goal, or where everyone is ready to take responsibility for group chores.[16]

---

[15]Dorwin Cartwright and Alvin Zander, eds., *Group Dynamics* (Evanston, Ill.: Row, Peterson, 1953), p. x.

[16]*Ibid.*, pp. 73–74.

No macrofunctionalist or organicist could object to this. The varied studies of the microfunctionalists bear on the nature of cohesiveness, the factors associated with it, and its role in group formation.

If one takes as the most significant property of functionalism the conception of the primacy of some kind of system, and if one takes as the most critically defining property of microfunctionalism the conception of the group as the decisive system, there are hardly more important questions than those referring to the property of the group as a group (cohesiveness), the forces strengthening or weakening it, the limits of group formation with the breakdown of the group into splinter groups. By far the great majority of the experimental studies of the microfunctionalists have been on these themes — the oldest and most traditional subject matter of sociology. However, the conception of groups as systems is by no means, despite some claims, an exclusive discovery of microfunctionalistic theory.

The properties of functionalism as a distinctive formation in sociological theory fully appear with the revival of the second organismic thesis of the primacy of the whole over the parts.

The Primacy of the Whole over the Parts. The group conceived as the fundamental system of social life has been the primary object of analysis by microfunctionalism. Quite in organismic vein is the preoccupation with group-maintaining and group-restoring processes, the determination of the parts by the whole:

> Some groups consciously and deliberately set out to exert pressures for uniformity of behavior and attitude among their members. We expect them to do so when we join them. Thus churches, political parties, character building agencies, school clubs, and others are eager to influence the membership to behave in accordance with certain norms, and everyone grants them the privilege of trying to do so.[17]

According to the microfunctionalists, two kinds of effects are produced by uniformities among members: uniformities may help the group to accomplish its purposes, and they may help the group maintain itself as a group. As with group cohesiveness, an ardently pursued experimental program has been carried out by the microfunctionalists.

Lewin had conceived the group as constituting a kind of action-space. Consistent with this analogy, motion becomes a change of position on a hypothetical set of coordinates. The group-dynamics students have retained these analogies. Thus, Cartwright and Zander ask:

> What do we mean when, in everyday language, we assert that a group does or does not "get somewhere" or "accomplish something"? These terms seem to imply that a group can be said to have a location, that it may change its location from time to time, and that certain locations are preferred by all or some segment of the members to other locations. . . . With these concepts we may ask concerning any group at any given time (a) whether, or to what degree, it has a goal; (b) whether it has more than one goal, and, if so, whether these goals are compatible or conflicting; (c) whether as a result of some group activity group locomotion has occurred; and (d) whether any given locomotion was toward or away from the group's goals.[18]

Four concepts of group goals are developed: (1) group goals as a composite of similar individual goals, (2) group goals as individual goals for the group, (3) group goals as dependent upon a particular interrelation among motivational systems of several individuals, and (4) group goals as an inducing agent.

The microfunctionalists have also continued the study of group structure. It is maintained that an adequate description of any group will reveal that it has not one structure but several, and any particular individual has one or more positions in each of these structures. The structure of a group consists in distinguishable parts or portions and their arrangement with respect to one another. Three kinds of factors produce stable differentiations within groups: (1) requirements for efficient

---

[17]*Ibid.*, pp. 137–138.

[18]*Ibid.*, pp. 306–307.

group performance, (2) the abilities and motivations of individuals, and (3) physical and social characteristics of the group's environment. The structure of the group may be informal or highly formalized.

THE MOVEMENT TOWARD MACROFUNCTIONALISM

The microfunctionalists fall into three subgroups, one headed by Bales, one guided by Cartwright and Zander, and the third headed up by Leon Festinger, Henry W. Riecken, and Stanley Schachter. There are some evidences that all these subgroups are moving toward a liaison with macrofunctionalism. The combined work of Parsons and Bales has already been discussed in Chapter XX. An interesting example of the movement from the laboratory and the small ad hoc group to the field is portrayed in the study by Festinger, Riecken, and Schachter, *When Prophecy Fails*.[19]

Leon Festinger was born in New York in 1919. After taking his B.S. degree at City College, he went to the State University of Iowa, where he came under the influence of Kurt Lewin. He received his Ph.D. in psychology in 1942 and worked as psychologist at the Psychopathic Hospital in Iowa from 1940 to 1942. Between 1942 and 1951, Festinger taught at Iowa, the University of Rochester, the Massachusetts Institute of Technology (where he was program director of the Research Center for Group Dynamics), and the University of Michigan. From 1951 to 1955 he was professor of psychology at the University of Minnesota, and since 1955, professor at Stanford University. Henry Riecken was born in Brooklyn in 1917, receiving his A.B. degree at Harvard in 1939 and his Ph.D. in 1950. He was lecturer in social psychology at Harvard from 1950 to 1954, and was professor of sociology at the University of

[19]Leon Festinger, Henry W. Riecken, and Stanley Schachter, *When Prophecy Fails* (Minneapolis: University of Minnesota Press, 1956). Copyright 1956 by the University of Minnesota.

LEON FESTINGER

Courtesy of Stanford University *News and Publications Services*

Minnesota from 1954 to 1958. Stanley Schachter was born in New York City in 1922. He received his M.A. and Ph.D. degrees at Michigan in 1950. He was at the University of Minnesota 1949–1961. Thus, while forming one of the subbranches of microfunctionalism, these three young men are well acquainted at first hand with the other two branches. Riecken has been associated with Bales and Festinger, and Schachter with Cartwright and Zander. *When Prophecy Fails* thus potentially has significance not only as a liaison point between micro- and macrofunctionalism but as a transfer point in the movement of the small-group theorists into general sociology.

The object of study for these social scientists was the reaction of a social group to unfulfilled prophecies and the failure of messiahs to appear according to prediction. At times, the most immediate response to a disappointed expectation is the attempt to reaffirm it. The authors set down five conditions for such a response: the belief must be deeply held; the person must be committed to it; the belief must be sufficiently precise for events to contradict it; the disconfirming evidence should be recognized; and the individual must have social support.[20]

Major examples in American experience of successive readjustment to a fervently held prophecy were provided by the Anabaptists, particularly the Millerites. When the end of the world and second coming of Christ had been predicted, the Millerites sold their New England farms, purchased ascension robes, and went out in prayer on the appointed hour to meet their maker. At first they simply refused to accept the fact that the end of the world did not come, and in an abortive way they changed the date. But these dates also passed and, alas, the movement eventually disintegrated.

When the investigators read in the newspapers of a midwestern town that a suburban housewife, on the basis of messages received from the planet "Clarion," had predicted the town's destruction by a flood, they seized upon this as an opportunity to study the response to an unfulfilled prophecy. They immediately called upon the woman, and discovered her to be a neurotic, suffering from a long preoccupation with the exotic, and in contact with several other such marginal individuals with a few gullible hangers-on.

The skill of the investigators in handling small-group situations could not be more clearly demonstrated than in their success in creating the semblance of a social movement out of these marginal neurotics and their handful of fellow travelers. For one thing, the very fact that investigators with intelligence and training were interviewing, apparently in all seriousness, the two main spirits of the prophecy (a Mrs. Keech and a Dr. Armstrong) tended to act as an authenticating sounding board for them. Furthermore, the requirements of having observers "inside" the

movement clearly helped provide a nucleus of clientele for the "movement."

> We have already reported the difficulty our observer experienced in arousing Dr. Armstrong's interest in him; all his efforts to stimulate an invitation to the "advanced" group meetings were having no success. Time was passing. . . . We therefore decided upon a stratagem suggested to us by Dr. Armstrong's inquiry to our observer as to whether he had ever had any "psychic experiences." We decided to equip our representative with an "experience" with the supernatural.[21]

This worked so well that the investigators decided to repeat the trick.

> Forewarned by his difficulties in approaching the Armstrongs through the medium of the elementary Seekers, we decided to arm our female observer with a "psychic experience." . . . Mrs. Armstrong's reaction . . . was enthusiastic. She welcomed the observer warmly, and at once began to enlighten her visitor about the protectors from outer space.[22]

The presence of an attentive set of investigators, apparently taking all this seriously, on the one hand, and the presence within the group of a number of participant-observers, actively contributing to the mutual self-deception of this little group and providing a solid core for its continued activity, had their effect. The investigators succeeded so well that they managed to persuade the rest of the community that the prophets were a genuine menace.

> On December 24 . . . as they caroled and waited for a spaceman to visit, they were ringed about by a crowd of some 200 unruly spectators, and . . . the police were flooded with complaints against Mrs. Keech ranging from disturbing the peace to contributing to the delinquency of minors. . . . A warrant was sworn out making specific charges against Mrs. Keech and Dr. Armstrong. . . . The police themselves seem to have

[20]*Ibid.*, p. 4.

[21]*Ibid.*, p. 239.
[22]*Ibid.*, p. 240.

been reluctant to set legal machinery into motion. They telephoned Mrs. Keech's husband to inform him of the warrant and warned him that, unless the meetings and gatherings at his home were at once brought to an end, they would serve the warrant. Furthermore, they strongly hinted that, once legal action began, the community could try to commit Mrs. Keech to a mental hospital.[23]

Dr. Armstrong, it seems was no easy dupe, for

within minutes of receiving the warning from the police in Lake City on December 26, the Armstrongs had packed their bags, tumbled their two younger children into the car, and were on the road back to Collegeville.[24]

In the end the investigators were quite disappointed with their prophets from outer space:

While circumstances combined to pull the steadfast adherents apart, the group failed to win a single new convert. . . . Their ideas were not without popular appeal. . . . Had they been more effective, disconfirmation might have portended the beginning, not the end.[25]

To be sure, the hypotheses of *When Prophecy Fails* are almost platitudinous. When people are committed to a course of action on the basis of a powerful set of beliefs, even in the face of the demonstration of their error, they will often rationalize fanatically rather than give up their beliefs. The single most interesting thing about the study — apart from the demonstration of the unusual skill of the investigators in manipulating people in small-group situations — is the almost complete absence of any reference to the ancient sociological studies bearing on the problem. The problem of group illusion is one of the oldest in the sociology of knowledge. No reference or use was made of any of the numerous studies. Even the special problem coming into focus in this study

had been described by Karl Mannheim as a peculiar ideological type — *chiliasm*. No reference appears either to Mannheim or to other students of the chiliastic mentality.

Similarly, no consideration whatever was given to the many sociological factors that have bearing on the potential or lack of potential for a social movement. The class and status anchorage of such ideology was ignored. One of the things that made Mannheim's study so fruitful was his perception of the fact that the chiliasm of the European Anabaptists was anchored in the frustrated hopes of peasants, trapped between the middle ages and the modern world, and lacking the institutions to make their aspirations manifest; here, at least, was a class and status situation that the chiliastic mentality could articulate. No consideration was given to equivalent social anchorage in *When Prophecy Fails*. Moreover, the failure of the group to win new converts is attributed exclusively to the ineptness of Mrs. Keech and Dr. Armstrong. Even the obvious role of a powerful, organized, modern urban world in preventing such a possibility is admitted only indirectly. Yet a single threat from the police could send Dr. Armstrong scampering from the scene.

All these considerations indicate how important for microfunctionalism the book, *When Prophecy Fails*, really is. It illustrates profoundly the kind of sociological problems that must be faced the moment this branch of sociological theory ceases to deal with purely ad hoc groups.

SUMMARY

It is difficult to escape the impression that with sociological functionalism the field has come full circle. The concept of organicism has been refurbished and upholstered with new analogies and terminology, but returned to a central place as the key to the understanding of interhuman life. To be sure, the concept of organic system has been given more abstract formulation and its properties

[23]*Ibid.*, p. 230.
[24]*Ibid.*, pp. 231–232.
[25]*Ibid.*, pp. 232–233.

have been drawn out in somewhat more detail. That is to be expected.

The similarities between sociological functionalism and positivistic organicism do not stop here. A strong movement back toward greater positivism of method is apparent throughout functionalism. The traditionalism is strongest precisely among the groups that have presented the most cultic and exclusive character — the microfunctionalists. In the first place, they have been preoccupied with the most traditional of sociological themes: the unity of the group mentality, its morale, the nature of the "group will," as Tönnies would say, or as Durkheim would put it, "solidarity." The microfunctionalists call this "cohesiveness" and have devoted the larger block of their studies to it. Furthermore, the similarities do not stop here, for the microfunctionalists have actively promoted a program of experimentalism, thus restoring a positivism of method to an organicism of theory.

Sorokin has described the group-dynamics section of the microfunctionalists as having a "discoverer's complex" and of being "new Columbuses."[26] The only thing wrong with the statement is that it is sometimes a bit tactless to say some sorts of truths in public. In any case, the irritation his characterization has caused is a bit hard to understand. Once Sorokin made the matter public, one would expect the members of the cult to welcome the opportunity to return to the general scientific community, frankly basing their researches on traditional grounds.[27]

[26]See Pitirim Sorokin, *Fads and Foibles in Modern Sociology* (Chicago: Henry Regnery, 1956).
[27]It should be noted that not all adherents of the group-dynamics movement have ignored their sociological origins. Bales and his associates, for example, are quite self-consciously identified with traditional sociology, as can be seen in such works as A. P. Hare, E. F. Borgatta, and R. F. Bales, eds., *Small Groups: Studies in Social Interaction* (New York: Alfred A. Knopf, 1955) and Edgar F. Borgatta and Henry J. Meyer, eds., *Sociological Theory: Present-Day Sociology from the Past* (New York: Alfred A. Knopf, 1956).

A question perhaps even more difficult to answer is whether there are ideological grounds for the shift to functionalism. It will be recalled that positivistic organicism was powerfully affected by ideological currents. It was the conservative answer to socialism. The conflict theorists (in contrast to the conflict ideologists, who were either relatively extreme reactionaries or extreme radicals) were largely conservative. Sociological formalism, by contrast, promoted a frankly liberal "Enlightenment" model of society. Some branches of the social behaviorists were uncertain: the pluralistic behaviorists seem to have experienced considerable frustration as they wavered between a relatively liberal and relatively conservative point of view. Some, like Giddings, were consistently conservative; others, like Ross, wavered. Ogburn even invented two interpretations of social problems, one for each mood. On the other hand, the symbolic-interactionist and social-action branches of social behaviorism were fairly consistently liberal.

As one moves from school to school in the development of sociology, ideological factors decline in importance. But even so, it is not at all clear that the latest development in sociological theory is completely free from any ideological coloration whatsoever. The excited protests by some of the functionalists concerning their inviolability suggests that they protest too much. Moreover, there are two major reasons for wondering whether sociological functionalism does not have some residual "conservative" significance. Organicism has almost always been acceptable to the conservatives. The very topics that have occupied the forefront of functionalist research are of a kind usually dear to the conservative: "morale," "cohesiveness," "solidarity," how groups control their deviates, why this is to be expected, and so on. Furthermore, the very dates of the steep rise of interest in functionalism among sociological theorists also suggest that it may have some ideological import. It arose after 1940 and with particular speed after World War II. Moreover, its ranks have been increasingly swelled by deserters from social behaviorism — an evidently liberal position. The rise of sociological functionalism thus coincided with the return of the Republican Party to power, the return to religion, the rise of McCarthyism, and other typical manifestations of a postwar conservative reaction. Whether these are just accidental correlations or not, it is certainly true that ideological factors are now far less important for the structure of sociological theory than was once the case.

Sociological functionalism is in a very real sense a new name for an old trend. It is distinctive in being the first major departure in sociological theory that did not draw its inspiration directly from philosophy. The organismic and idealistic philosophy that influenced it did so directly through the social sciences. In order of importance these were, despite a reluctance to admit it: (1) positivistic organicism in sociology, (2) functionalistic and Gestalt psychology, and (3) functionalistic anthropology.

Four basic meanings of functionalism have been outlined here: the mathematical conception, function as useful activity for need fulfillment and/or purpose implementation, function as appropriate activity, and function as system-produced and system-maintaining activity. The first meaning of functionalism is specifically set aside as an objective by all schools. The second meaning of function appears universally and is insufficient to define a functionalistic program. Modern forms of functionalist sociological theory are primarily built out of combinations of the third and fourth meanings: function as appropriate activity (as in the distinctions between function and dysfunction, eunomia and anomie, and manifest and latent functions) and function as system-produced and system-maintaining activity.

The mere use of some variety of the concept "function" thus is distinguished from the advocacy of a brand of functionalist sociological theory. Such a theory is characterized as the interpretation of social interaction from the standpoint of functions in the two senses noted above. There are many differences among individuals and between the two subbranches, but two major theoretical propositions hold all branches of functionalist

theory together: (1) the fundamental unit of interpretation of interhuman life is an organic-type system; (2) the parts, elements, aspects, or phases of this organic-type system are in a functional relation to the whole, both determining the whole and being determined by the whole.

Two major subschools of modern functionalist sociological theory are distinguished as: the macrofunctionalists (comprising such persons as Znaniecki, Merton, Parsons, Homans, Shils, Levy) and the microfunctionalists (comprising such persons as Lewin, Bales, Cartwright, Zander, Schachter, Festinger, and numerous others). The macrofunctionalists focus primarily on large-scale systems and work out of the traditions of sociology and anthropology. Their tendency has been to extend the concept "system" downward, from presumed unities as large as the society and civilization to the group. The microfunctionalists have worked their way up from the *Gestalten* of perception and behavior through personality to the group. This latter movement represents the evolution of Gestalt psychology into a full-fledged sociology.

The two movements have drawn more closely together than some members of either seem to realize. As microfunctionalism has tended to develop its terminology concerning the systems of interest to it from topological psychology, preferring such expressions as "field," "valence," "boundaries," "sector," "tension system," and so forth, the macrofunctionalists have been showing inclinations to meet them half way. And at least Parsons, Bales, and Shils have begun to conceive dichotomous distinctions applying to action alternatives as "dimensions of action-space." Motivation is increasingly conceived as a movement or locomotion. The term *boundaries* has become ever more important. The events in a social system have even been represented in terms of classical mechanics.

Two events in 1961 marked a new stage in the development of structure-functionalism in postwar sociology: (1) the two-volume *Theories of Society* presented selections from the history of sociological thought on the assumption that they climaxed in functionalism; (2) a major symposium, edited by Max Black on *The Theories of Talcott Parsons,* brought much of Parsons' theory to that time under critical review. In the first of these two works, in his epilogue, Shils certified the credentials of functionalism as a liberal ideology. Parsons and Merton at Harvard and Columbia were still the dominant figures in the functionalistic movement. However, a number of former students of both men were established in major West Coast schools, making them, too, strongholds of functional analysis and potential rivals for leadership of the movement where residual problems had been partly identified in the Black volume.

Although a large number of the sociologists who would inevitably dominate much of American sociology in the 1960s and 1970s began their work within the functionalistic framework, they usually confined their study to particular problems within it and, particularly after completing their degrees and getting established in the field, were no longer inclined to remain as zealous followers of Parsons in all the new developments of his thought. Through the natural dynamics of the individual careers of second- and third-generation students, functionalism has tended to spread out in a number of different directions, gradually losing its overall coherence. Macro- and microfunctionalism already showed by 1960 some inclination to separate despite other tendencies toward convergence (for example, when Parsons and Shils found common cause with Bales). Moreover, the changed social milieu of the 1960s favored a revival of conflict theories of sociology and some functionalists began to explore possible liaisons between conflict theory and functionalism.[28]

During that period, however, there was also some tendency to reintegrate the entire functionalism movement and to provide it with a sounder scientific foundation than the Mertonians and Parsonites had provided. This movement rallied under the banner of general systems theory.[29] However, Parsons, Merton, and their students have not joined the movement toward a general systems theory and numerous other developments in theory have placed their rival form of functionalism in partial eclipse. It is quite possible, however, that general systems theory may some day form the starting point for a revived functionalism in sociology.

Social Structure," in Peter M. Blau. ed., *Approaches to the Study of Social Structure* (New York: The Free Press, 1975). Lewis Coser illustrates another approach by taking Simmel's notion of conflict as a social form and seeking to effect a combination of conflict theory and structure-functionalism. See Lewis A. Coser, *The Functions of Social Conflict* (New York: The Free Press, 1956) and *Continuities in the Study of Social Conflict* (New York: The Free Press, 1967). Coser's work on the fusion of Simmel, conflict theory, and functionalism, bears comparison to Homans's *The Human Group.* Coser's formulations are almost step-by-step the converse of Homans's. In Dahrendorf's first and most famous book, *Class and Class Conflict in Industrial Society* (Stanford, Calif.: Stanford University Press, 1959), he takes conflict propositions from Marx, and in a manner roughly parallel to Coser, works them out in a framework of functionalistic theory. In later work, however, such as *Essays in the Theory of Society* (Stanford, Calif.: Stanford University Press, 1968), Dahrendorf moved toward a more pure conflict perspective. In his theory of stratification, Gerhard E. Lenski also tried to combine conflict and structure-functional theory. See *Power and Privilege: A Theory of Social Stratification* (New York: McGraw-Hill, 1966).

[29]An able summary of the case for such a theory and its incorporation of both macro- and microfunctionalism into a more general systems framework was made by F. Kenneth Berrien who traced its sources to "von Bertalanffy, a theoretical biologist (1950), who was subsequently joined by Boulding, an economist (1956); J. G. Miller, a psychiatrist and psychologist (1955); Ashby, a bacteriologist (1958); Rapoport, a mathematician (1956); and a growing list of persons representing a diversity of formal training and academic affiliations." F. Kenneth Berrien, *General and Social Systems* (New Brunswick, N.J.: Rutgers University Press, 1968), p. 5.

---

[28]Peter Blau illustrates some of the ways in which structure-functionalism has been combined with other views. Blau is, in fact, an eclectic accepting a behavioristic point of view for elementary social interaction and a functionalistic position for groups and classes. He utilizes the notion of emergence to account for the appearance of autonomous structure out of elementary exchange. See Peter M. Blau, *Exchange and Power in Social Life* (Chicago: John Wiley & Sons, 1964) and "Parameters of

XXII

Critical Theory or Reflexive Sociology: The Left Hegelian Movement in Twentieth-Century Social Science

The development of Marxism into an orthodoxy, already begun by Engels with Marx's approval while he was still alive, was a factor in its usefulness as the official ideology of the German labor movement but also invited the conversion of Marxism into a positivistic discipline. As did sociology, for example, Marxism subscribed to an evolutionary theory of social change. Social scientists were encouraged to treat the propositions of Marxism, like those of sociology, as hypotheses subject to test. Inevitably this would mean that such propositions were subject to modification or even rejection[1] and Marxism would be dismantled.

If Marxism disappeared into social science it would, of course, lose its properties as an effective revolutionary ideology. Moreover, adaptations of Marxism to the needs of the labor movement meant that Marxist practice would be altered to meet the requirements not of bringing about a revolution, but increasing the efficiency of groups working within the system. The revolutionary Marxists felt the need to resist both tendencies in Marxism.

Lenin's version of revolutionary Marxism proved to be most successful. Lenin rejected the quietistic notion that the materialist theory of history implied that change was not possible until the times were ripe, whereupon it became inevitable. He also discarded the idea that the peasants were not material for revolution and the notion that the laboring class was necessarily revolutionary. Nor did Lenin permit himself to be put off by the idea that true revolution was possible only in the advanced Western nations and not in a backward nation like Russia. In Lenin's view a revolutionary elite had to initiate the dictatorship of the proletariat; once the Bolshevik coup succeeded, he reorganized his strategy to the preservation of the

---

[1]Second International Marxism, as it is sometimes called, was developed not only in the later works of Engels, but in the works of Eduard Bernstein (1850–1932), Karl Kautsky (1854–1938), George V. Plekhanov (1856–1918), Max Adler (1873–1973), Otto Bauer (1881–1938), and Rudolf Hilferding (1877–1943) among others.

gains in the Soviet Union at all costs. Leninism-Stalinism was quickly converted into the doctrinaire support of a system of bureaucratic statism, a new orthodoxy.

Three other persons in addition to Lenin illustrate the attempts in the twentieth century to "rescue" Marxism from conversion into a positivistic science or the sustaining dogma of a non-revolutionary labor movement: Karl Korsch (1886–1961), Antonio Gramsci (1890–1937), and Georg Lukács (1885–1971). They found themselves in tension with Leninism-Stalinism in their efforts to recover the revolutionary zeal of Marx at the time he was making his departure from the ranks of the Young Hegelians. Korsch, Gramsci, and Lukács form major reference points for understanding the contemporary return journey from Marx to Hegel.[2]

Karl Korsch, a German professor of philosophy and an active Communist Party member in the 1920s was alarmed by the potential for Marxism to turn into one more positivistic sociological theory. He pointed to the fact that in his early formulations, Marx, while fresh under the influence of Hegel (whose ideas he never completely abandoned), intended his doctrine to be one of revolutionary practice. Marxism, Korsch insisted, should recover its character as a movement for political and economic change based on the analysis of social life in terms of the changing rela-

tion between society and nature. Korsch came into conflict with the emerging Bolshevik orthodoxy and found himself expelled from the German Communist Party (1926). His work was condemned as idealistic and revisionist. Korsch remained in touch with radical groups until his exile to the United States, and after 1933 gradually changed his views, coming in the end to view Marxism as a philosophy of the working-class movement. Korsch's early work helped force a reevaluation of the Hegelian origins of Marxism.

Antonio Gramsci, born of a middle-class family of Sardinia, was a hunchback, possibly because of a spine injury from being dropped as an infant. Though very bright, he was sickly and because of tragedies that impoverished his family, was dependent on the winning of scholarships to attend the university. He managed to obtain a scholarship at the University of Turin where he became active in young socialist circles and completed three years at the university before becoming engaged (1915) in political work full time. He was active as an editor and writer for left-wing journals and a labor organizer. A co-founder of the Italian Communist Party, he was a delegate (in 1922) to the Comintern's executive committee in Moscow. In 1925 Gramsci was elected to the Chamber of Deputies of the Italian Parliament, but shortly after his maiden speech was arrested, though still legally covered by parliamentary immunity. After a number of attempts to frame evidence against him, he was eventually sentenced to twenty years, four months, and five days. He was imprisoned until his death in 1937.

After imprisonment for more than two years (in February 1929) Gramsci was finally granted what he needed to work in his cell. He set upon a task that became life itself: to examine the formation of intellectual groups in nineteenth-century Italian history, to review the theory of history and historiography, and to explore Americanism and Fordism. He completed thirty-two notebooks of sketches, thoughts, and reflections, amounting to around four thousand typewritten quarto pages. His central purpose was to ascertain what was

---

[2]This is the title of a series of studies of this movement by George Lichtheim, *From Marx to Hegel* (New York: The Seabury Press, 1974). Among works of interest in this connection are Karl Korsch, *Marxismus und Philosophie* (1923), English translation (London: New Left Books, 1970) and *Karl Marx* (London: Chapman & Hall, 1938). For Antonio Gramsci's views, see *The Study of Philosophy and of Historical Materialism, The Modern Prince and Other Writings* (London: Lawrence and Wishart, 1957) and *Selection From the Prison Notebooks*, trans. Lynne Lowner (New York: Harper and Row, 1973). For George Lukács, see *History and Class Consciousness* (Cambridge, Mass.: MIT Press, 1971); *Lenin: A Study of the Unity of His Thoughts* (Cambridge, Mass.: MIT Press, 1971); and *Marxism and Human Liberation*, ed. E. San Juan, Jr. (New York: Dell, 1973).

necessary to guarantee a new stable proletarian-based social order.[3]

His examination of Italian history and of the theories of Croce convinced Gramsci that ideology (*Weltanschauung*) was the key both to social change and stable social order. The insecure course of the Italian Risorgimento of the nineteenth century was a product of its comparative lack of popular acceptance, hence legitimacy. After the unification of Italy, Bendetto Croce was its first great bourgeois-democratic theorist. Croce's criticism of current Marxism was directed against a rudely mechanistic or positivistic and evolutionary version of that doctrine. Croce had a point in centering attention on the active politico-ethical element in human history. However, Croce dealt with human beings, in general, metaphysical entities, and did not come to grips with human beings as social creatures whose thoughts and personalities are products of their interaction with other human beings and with nature. Crocean historicism, thus, remains theological and speculative. Only the philosophy of praxis (Gramsci's term for Marxism) can liberate humanity from such traces of the transcendent.

The special task, to Gramsci, if the proletariat is to emerge as the stable core of a new order, is to win over the other exploited classes, especially the peasants, to its point of view. But this, in turn, requires the emergence of a new stratum of intellectuals who will undermine and supplant the current bourgeois *Weltanschauung*. Croce, in part, showed the way, when he inadvertently called attention to the Hegelian elements of Marxism at the time it still retained the character of a revolutionary doctrine.

Just as the philosophy of praxis was the translation of Hegelianism into true historicist language, so today the philosophy of Croce is . . . the retranslation into speculative language of the realist historicism developed by the philosophy of praxis.[4]

The task is to create a new proletarian *Weltanschauung* which will penetrate the minds of the governed, undermine popular consent to the reigning point of view, and lay the foundation for a new state in which the proletariat will be the dominant and ruling class. The task for the philosophy of praxis is not, as in Russia, violent revolution. The actual condition in the West has passed beyond the stage where a new order can be created in this manner. What is required is a "war of positions," that is, a battle for people's minds in which the moral and intellectual legitimacy of the bourgeois is replaced in the popular mind by the moral and intellectual outlook of the proletariat.

This will be accomplished only when intellectuals associated with the working classes win over the traditional intellectuals to socialism. Then the "fortress" (culture/dominance) can pass into the hands of the working class, followed by occupancy of the front line or "trench" (political dominance), and the hegemony of the proletariat. The "collective intellectual" of the working class is the revolutionary party which Gramsci calls the "Modern Prince."

The Modern Prince must be, and cannot fail to be, the protagonist and organizer of intellectual and moral reform — that is, he proposes the terrain for a further development of the collective, national-popular will towards the construction of a superior, all-embracing form of modern civilization. These two fundamental points: formation of a collective national-popular will (of which the Modern Prince is both expression and creator), and intellectual and moral reform, should constitute the structure of the work.[5]

Georg Lukács, born of a wealthy Jewish banking family in Budapest of the Austro-Hungarian

[3] For an excellent review of the central ideas in Gramsci's prison notebooks, see Giuseppe Fiori, *Antonio Gramsci: Life of a Revolutionary*, trans. Tom Nairn (London: NLB, 1970), pp. 235–258.

[4] Quoted by Fiori, *Antonio Gramsci*, p. 241.
[5] Gramsci, quoted by Fiori, *Antonio Gramsci*, p. 245.

monarchy, was interested in European literature, and early displayed talent for criticism. He studied in Berlin and Heidelberg, remaining until 1916, and coming under the influence of Max Weber and Georg Simmel. He developed an interest, for a time, in the neo-Kantian and phenomenological schools. His early publications were on literature. He was reoriented to politics by World War I and the Russian Revolution and upon returning to Budapest became active in the Hungarian revolution. Around 1916 he discovered Hegel, becoming convinced that his philosophy offered solutions to the neo-Kantian and positivistic problems (which treated values as extrascientific and the sphere of phenomena as the only legitimate object of science).

In 1919 Lukács moved to Vienna and became editor of the official Communist Party journal. The publication in 1923 of a collection of his essays brought him into conflict with the Hungarian Communist Party. Lukács eventually recanted, denouncing his work on *History and Class Consciousness,* as an unintended error. He supported the Leninist-Stalinist position, lived in Moscow, and even managed to survive the great purge of 1936–1938. In his later work Lukács became increasingly doctrinaire and dogmatic.

As a student of Nietzsche, among others, Lukács became convinced that Western bourgeois civilization was bankrupt. His acquaintance with the neo-idealism of Dilthey, the neo-Kantians, and the phenomenologists did not satisfy him that they had the answers. However, he agreed with the revisionist Marxists that Marx had to be brought up-to-date, but increasingly perceived revisionism as the emasculation of Marxism, as the conversion of Marxism into a positive science. He was most excited by Rosa Luxemburg, insisting "Rosa Luxemburg, alone, among Marx's disciples, has made a real advance on his life's work in both the content and method of his economic doctrines."[6] Lenin,[7]

he added, "has developed the *practical essence* of Marxism to a pitch of clarity and concreteness never before achieved."

In proposing to examine the essence of revolutionary Marxism, Lukács insisted, it is advisable to heed "Marx's warning not to treat Hegel as a 'dead dog.' . . . He is a more profitable and potent thinker than many people imagine. . . . a greater knowledge of Hegel's writings is utterly indispensable."[8] Marx, in his view, adopted the progressive part of the Hegelian method, the dialectic, radically transforming all phenomena of society and socialized human beings into historical phenomena. The aim was to understand society as a whole. "The category of totality . . . determines not only the object of knowledge, but also the subject."[9]

The whole system of Marxism, as Lukács viewed it, stands or falls with the principle that revolution is the product of a point of view dominated by the category of totality. The bearer of this point of view is the proletariat. However, it requires the work of an intellectual elite to articulate this point of view and to undermine the competing point of view of the bourgeoisie, substituting the true consciousness of the proletariat for the false consciousness of the liberal middle classes. The disruption of the totalizing point of view splits theory and practice and renders Marxism impotent in the face of social change. Marx's great concrete discovery of the "truth as subject," by contrast, unified theory and practice. "The scientific superiority of the standpoint of class (as against that of the individual) . . ." arises from the fact that *only the class can actively penetrate the reality of society and transform it in its entirety. . . .* The proletariat as the subject of thought in society destroys at one blow the dilemma of impotence: the dilemma created by the pure laws with their fatalism and by the ethics of pure intentions."[10]

Although Lukács was forced to recant *History*

[6]Preface to the first edition of *History and Class Consciousness,* trans. Rodney Livingstone (Cambridge, Mass.: MIT Press, 1971), p. xli.
[7]*Ibid.,* p. xlii.

[8]*Ibid.,* pp. xliv and xlv.
[9]*Ibid.,* p. 28.
[10]*Ibid.,* p. 39.

and Class Consciousness in order to remain within the communist fold, his formulations were important for the sociology of Karl Mannheim — who was led by Lukács's formulations to counter with the development of his theories of ideology and utopia — and for the sociologists of the Frankfurt School and Institute for Social Research.

THE FRANKFURT SCHOOL AND INSTITUTE OF SOCIAL RESEARCH

With so many crosscurrents in postwar Germany of the 1920s — the conviction by many that Western civilization was declining, the disappointment by others that Marxist hope for reconstruction seemed to be frustrated by the split between a bolshevized German Community Party (KPD) and a nonrevolutionary Socialist Party — it was perhaps inevitable that some left-wing intellectuals would dream of the possibility of pursuing their theoretical reflections and researches with some freedom from outside pressures. Martin Jay, in his brilliant history of the Frankfurt School attributes the idea of establishing an institution for this purpose to Felix J. Weil in 1922.[11] The son of a German-born grain merchant who had earned a fortune exporting grain to Europe from Argentina, Felix Weil began to utilize his family's private wealth to support various radical ventures. An independently endowed institute was visualized as a means of freeing researchers from the pressures of university life. Felix's father agreed to set up an endowment amounting to around $30,000 a year (at a time when it required only about $50.00 a month to support an unmarried assistant at the Institute). It was also thought prudent to seek affiliation with the University of Frankfurt (itself only established in 1914) although the Institute was intellectually and financially independent. The Institute was officially created (February 3, 1923) on decree of the Education Ministry. A building was constructed to house it (officially opened June 22, 1924). It eventually published its own house organ, initially depending on *Grünberg's Archiv*, later publishing the *Zeitschrift für Socialforschung*.[12] It quickly became a center for radical thought and sponsored a vigorous program of research into the socioeconomic problems of bourgeois society.

Kurt Weil, who retained control of the Gesellschaft für Sozial Research, the institute's financial and administrative body, proposed Kurt Albert Gerlach as the Institute's first director. However, in 1922 Gerlach died suddenly of an attack of diabetes, leaving a library of eight thousand volumes to Weil who presented them to the Institute. Carl Grünberg served as Gerlach's replacement. Through the 1920s the *Archiv* reflected Grünberg's interest and stressed the history of the labor movement. Grünberg's health was seriously impaired by a stroke in 1927, leading him to decide to step down. In 1930, at the age of 35, Max Horkheimer assumed directorship of the Institute.

By the time Horkheimer took over directorship of the Institute it had become increasingly clear that the climate for left-wing studies in Germany was growing bad. Explorations were underway to make contact with left-wing students in Geneva, Paris, and London in the interest of launching a Europeanwide study of the proletariat. In 1931 the Institute's endowment was quietly transferred to Holland as a neutral center for disbursement for contemplated new research. On January 30, 1933 with the Nazi assumption of power, the days of the Institute in Germany were numbered. It was closed down in March for tendencies hostile to the state and its library (sixty thousand volumes) was seized by the government. The *Zeitschrift*'s Leipzig

[11]Martin Jay, *The Dialectical Imagination: A History of the Frankfurt School and the Institute of Social Research 1923–1950* (Boston: Little Brown, 1973), p. 5. This review of the history of the Institute follows Jay.

[12]Carl Grünberg, who was persuaded to leave his post as professor of law and political science at the University of Vienna to come to Frankfurt and serve as the Institute's director, had edited since 1910 the *Archiv für Geschicte des Socialismus und der Arbeiterbewegung*, known popularly as *Grünberg's Archiv*. It became the official house organ of the Institute until replaced by the *Zeitschrift*.

publisher could no longer risk continuing publication, which was taken over by Librairie Felix Alcan in Paris until 1940 when this, too, became impossible with the fall of France. Only the fortunate transfer of the Institute's endowment to Holland saved it from financial confiscation.

Horkheimer and other Institute scholars were among the first German professors to lose their jobs under the Nazis. Just before the seizure of the Institute Horkheimer managed to slip across the border to Switzerland, but limited academic opportunities and the growth of fascism in Switzerland convinced him that Geneva was not the best place for the Institute. Negotiations to establish the Institute at the London School of Economics (Winter of 1934) fell through, and there were only limited scholarly opportunities in England in any case. The French intellectual establishment as always was hostile to outsiders. In May, 1934, Horkheimer made his first trip to the United States to explore with the president of Columbia University, Nicholas Murray Butler, the possibility of affiliation of the Institute with Columbia. Butler was receptive and even offered the Institute a home in one of its buildings.

> And so the International Institute for Social Research, as revolutionary and Marxist as it had appeared in Frankfurt in the twenties, came to settle in the center of the capitalist world, New York City. Marcuse came in July, Lowenthal in August, Pollock in September, and Wittfogel soon after. Fromm had been in the United States since 1932 . . . These men were among the first to arrive of that wave of Central European refugee intellectuals who so enriched American cultural life in the decades that followed.[13]

Although the Institute began to offer lectures in the Extension Division of Columbia in 1936, and, in time, developed a variety of seminars, its major activities centered on theory and research. Meanwhile the decision to continue to publish the *Zeitschrift* in Paris and in German militated against any major impact of its theory and research on American thought. The pages of the *Zeitschrift* were opened to some American scholars (Margaret Mead, Charles Beard, and Harold Lasswell, for example), but, by and large, the American intellectual world was largely unaware even of the Institute's existence. Meanwhile, in its concern to maintain its ties with German culture, the Institute aided many younger scholars as well as some older scholars such as Ferdinand Tönnies. According to Jay, the Institute extended support to around 200 émigrés including such persons as Fritz Sternberg, Hans Mayer, Ernst Bloch, Paul Lazarsfeld, Fritz Karsen, Gerhard Mayer, and A. R. L. Gurland. In the decade after its establishment at Columbia $200,000 was distributed to 116 doctoral candidates and 14 post-doctoral candidates.[14]

In the 1940s a number of things made the future role of the Institute at Columbia uncertain. A vicious battle broke out between the theoretical (headed up by Robert S. Lynd and Robert MacIver) wings of the Columbia department. The empiricists won, representing a triumph of positivism that made the Institute's antipositivists uneasy. A number of prominent Institute members entered military and governmental service. Finally, a circulatory illness required Horkheimer to move to California's more benign climate (1941). Meanwhile the Institute's finances had been drained by its members' research on authority and the family and its extensive assistance to refugees. However, the empiricists of the Columbia department, particularly Paul Lazarsfeld in his role as director of the newly formed Bureau of Applied Social Research, sought to tighten the ties of the Institute to Columbia. In 1946, however, Horkheimer was again inclined to move the Institute. He explored the possibilities for institutional affiliation in California but in 1946 he received an invitation from members of the Frankfurt community to rejoin the university.

Over the next two years negotiations to return

---

[13]Jay, *The Dialectical Imagination*, p. 39.

[14]Jay, *Dialectical Imagination*, pp. 114–115.

the Institute to Frankfurt, reestablishing continuities of German social science culture and restoring some of the university's former eminence, were conducted with growing enthusiasm and with the encouragement of occupation officials such as John J. McCloy, the High Commissioner. On July 13, 1949, Horkheimer's professorship was restored and the Institute, with its endowment and library, was welcomed home. Not all the Institute's members returned to Frankfurt. In addition to reorganizing the Institute in 1950 Horkheimer became dean of the philosophy department and the following year was chosen as rector of the University.

Max Horkheimer. Max Horkheimer (1895–1973) was born in Stuttgart of a prominent Jewish family. His initial interest was in Gestalt psychology, but he shifted to philosophy under the influence of Hans Cornelius with whom he took the doctorate with a thesis on Kant in 1922. His habilitation thesis was also on Kant. Horkheimer gave his first lecture in 1925 as *Privatdozent* on Kant and Hegel. In the 1920s Horkheimer developed close ties with members of the Institute, sharing their radical inclinations so completely that he was the inevitable choice for director in 1930. Horkheimer's personality dominated the Institute throughout its American sojourn, its return to Frankfurt, and to the time of his retirement in 1958. He lived quietly in Switzerland until his death in 1973.

Events of the 1920s and 1930s had forced Horkheimer and his associates on a course that eventually led from revolutionary Marxism back toward radical Hegelianism: revolutionary Marxists such as the young Lukács and Korsch had been forced either to recant or be driven out of the Communist parties of their respective countries; Russian Communism was turning into a form of bureaucratic domination; the proletariat was proving to be far less revolutionary than Marxist theory had postulated; the collapse of parliamentary institutions in Italy and Germany had opened the way, in fascism, to a new devastating form of caesarism; forces for new savage barbarism were

MAX HORKHEIMER

German Information Center

being unleashed. In view of these developments Horkheimer in the 1930s began to pull together the strands of what he called critical philosophy.[15] One can find all of the major components of critical theory by its primary architect in the collection of his essays from the 1930s and 1940s.

Among what Horkheimer views as the major myths of the contemporary Western world are the belief that science is the major instrument for realization of the just society and that positivism, the treatment of social and cultural phenomena as

[15]Among the major works of Horkheimer available in English are: *Critical Theory, Selected Essays* (New York: Seabury Press, 1972); *Eclipse of Reason* (New York: Oxford, 1947); *Dialectic of Enlightenment,* with Theodor W. Adorno (New York: Seabury Press, 1972).

things, is a desirable orientation to social issues. Science, positivism, and in fact, even theory in the traditional sense established by Descartes and practiced everywhere in the pursuit of the specialized sciences, organizes experience in the light of questions arising out of present-day society. The result, in the network of disciplines, is the development of information useful in particular circumstances for the largest possible number of purposes.[16] However, all this scientific effort mirrors an economy filled with contradictions and dominated by monopolies, while on a world scale, human society is disorganized and chaotic. Western society is richer than any previous one, but is unable to eliminate human wretchedness.[17] Even science is in crisis, a crisis inseparable from the general crisis and reflecting the contradictions of society. The Western approach to science results in a view of reason useful only for purposes of everyday life, but useless for dealing with the big problems. "The result is the avoidance of any theoretical consideration of society as a whole."[18]

However, Horkheimer argues, social reality, that is, human beings acting in history, has a structure which if properly grasped may transform and revolutionize all cultural relationships. But this cannot be achieved by the simple recording of events, the method of old-style science. It requires the rehabilitation of philosophy in its old-fashioned prescience sense and, even, the rehabilitation of metaphysics. More than the objective of the metaphysician to arrive at a unified view of ultimate reality in the effort to make every item of personal life depend on insight into the ultimate ground of things must be realized. There are contradictions in social reality and the old metaphysical struggle between the established and disestablished appeared in the conflict between idealism and materialism. The idealists were spokespeople for the status quo. Today, however, the struggle for a better order of things has been cut loose from

its old supernatural justification. The theory appropriate to the struggle today is materialism.[19]

The task of critical theory is to hasten the developments of a society without injustice. This may lead the theorist into opposition even with views prevailing among the proletariat.[20] Every part of critical theory presupposes a criticism of the existing order. It has for its object human beings as producers of their own historical being. It is not concerned only with goals imposed by existent ways of life, but with people in all their potentialities. It is, thus, not only the heir of German idealism, but of philosophy itself.[21]

In the failure of the proletariat to fulfill the revolutionary potential once assigned to it by socialist thinkers, Horkheimer and, through him the Institute, had sponsored studies of the working classes, with particular attention to socialization in the family in its apparent role in generating authoritarian or antiauthoritarian points of view. The critical theorist concluded that in the bourgeois golden age there had been a fruitful interaction between the family and society and the authority of the father was based on his role in society, while society, in turn, was reenforced by the indispensable education for authority which occurred in the patriarchal family. "The family was the 'germ cell' of bourgeois culture and it was, like the authority in it, a living reality."[22] However, Horkheimer observes, this type of family is everywhere in decline and the forces for disruption of the family are more strongly felt than the forces for unity. Inasmuch as it still fosters human relations determined by the woman, the present-day family is a source of strength to resist the total dehumanization of the world and contains an element of antiauthoritarianism. However, there is no longer a question of a private existence with its own satisfactions and values; the family is tending

---

[16]Horkheimer, *Critical Theory*, pp. 244ff.
[17]*Ibid.*, p. 8.
[18]*Ibid.*, p. 4.

[19]*Ibid.*, p. 22.
[20]*Ibid.*, p. 221.
[21]*Ibid.*, p. 245.
[22]*Ibid.*, p. 128.

to become available purely for sexual satisfaction and is also a source of multiple anxieties.[23]

While the status of the working classes and the family calls attention to the need for critical theory, a similar message appears in the tensions manifest in the modern arts. Art is knowledge no less than science and the state of the arts reveal contradictory forces in much the same manner as the dissolution of the family, the transformation of personal life into leisure, and leisure into routines supervised in the last detail — the pleasures of the ball park, the movie, the best seller, and the radio have brought about the disappearance of inner life.[24] Criticism in art has been replaced either by actual hatred of the arts or the wisdom of obedience. The opposition of individual and society, of private and social existence, which gave seriousness to the pastimes of art, have become obsolete.[25] Popularity has been detached from the specific content and truth of artistic production. In the democratic countries the arts are no longer in the hands of the educated, but are in those of the amusement industry.[26] Horkheimer quotes John Dewey with approval: "Indifference to response of the immediate audience is a necessary trait of all artists that have something new to say."[27]

Theodor W. Adorno. Theodor Wiesengrund Adorno (1903–1969), born in Frankfurt, was the youngest son of a Jewish wine merchant and a talented woman who had pursued a successful career in singing until her marriage. Under his mother's influence Adorno took up piano and studied composition at an early age. He became friends with Horkheimer in 1922 when they met in a seminar on Husserl directed by Cornelius. At the time both men were interested in Gestalt psychology as well as philosophy. In 1924 Adorno earned the doctorate under the direction of Cornelius, with a dis-

[23]*Ibid.*, p. 124.
[24]*Ibid.*, p. 277.
[25]*Ibid.*, p. 289.
[26]*Ibid.*, p. 290.
[27]*Ibid.*, p. 290.

THEODOR ADORNO

German Information Center

sertation on Husserl's phenomenology. In the same year, at the Frankfurt Festival of the Universal German Music Society, Adorno met Alban Berg (one of the major students of Arnold Schönberg, who was developing the twelve-tone system of music). Adorno returned with Berg to Vienna, joining the Schönberg circle, and studying composition with Berg for the next three years.

Although Adorno renewed his friendship with Horkheimer upon his return to Germany, he pursued his own researches in aesthetics and music, remaining outside the Institute circle. Nor did he immediately follow the Institute to America, but for much of the 1930s pursued his career in London and Oxford. Only in 1936 was Horkheimer able to persuade Adorno to become a half-time member of the Institute. Adorno made his first visit to New York in June of 1937 and completed his negotiations when Paul Lazarsfeld's Princeton Office of Radio Research offered him a half-time position as head of a music study (in 1938).

For the rest of his life Adorno remained with the Institute, following Horkheimer to California in 1941, and accompanying the Institute back to Frankfurt in 1949. When Horkheimer retired from the directorship in 1957, Adorno was the natural choice to succeed him. He died in 1969 of a heart attack during the difficult period of the student revolt which had the Institute (now a part of the establishment) as one of its targets.

All his life, Adorno was interested in music and it formed a major preoccupation of his written work.[28] Throughout his musical writings Adorno preserves: a Hegelian point of view; cultural elitism, the conviction that the arts reflect the state of society, displaying both its progressive and retrogressive components; and the notion that the mission of the creative artist is to press on toward a fuller realization of humanity's spiritual potential. In *The Rational and Social Foundations of Music*,[29] Max Weber had traced the rise of the Western scale system, and the movement of the principle of tonality (sum of melodic and harmonic relations

between the tones of a scale, musical system, or key) to the center of musical composition in Western polyphonic music. Weber had viewed this development in the arts as a parallel to the extension of the principle of rationality in other life spheres such as architecture, science, technology, and the like. Adorno reinterprets this development in a framework of idealistic philosophy. Music, he believed, originated in the rhythms and rituals of everyday life, being emancipated from its purely functional significance and subjected to special development in the course of ever higher self-realization of human spiritual potential. In polyphonic music a high point was realized in the musical consciousness of bourgeois society of high capitalism. It is the least representative of the aesthetic forms. At its best the music of a period expresses both the unity and dissonance of the times. Richard Strauss, in Adorno's view, was the last meaningful "bourgeois" composer; however, the fact that in his compositions all negation tends to vanish indicates that the tradition in which he worked had reached its end.

Adorno's interest during the 1930s and 1940s centered in the music of Schönberg and Stravinsky. Schönberg's twelve-tone (or atonal) music treated all musical intervals as of equal value and undertook to establish rules of musical compositions (such as the banning of repetition of any one note until all twelve had been sounded). Schönberg eliminated tonality and created a style of composition that stressed an interval of a fourth (rather than the usual interval of a third). He visualized his music as recovering the dissonance of contemporary society and hence expressing everything that was progressive in contemporary life. By contrast, Adorno interpreted the work of Stravinsky, whose music stressed premodern primitive rhythms and prebourgeois tonal forms, such as the dance, as neoclassical "objectivism" and, even, as the musical correlate of fascism.

Opera, in Adorno's view, had lost its appeal to upper middle-class audiences in preference to concerts, which provided them with a sense of subjective intensity. Folk music, he thought, was no longer a living form but, as all popular culture, an

[28]Among Adorno's major works are: *Alban Berg: Der Meister des kleinsten Ubergangs* [Alban Berg: Master of the Nuance] (Vienna: Osterreichicher Bundesverlag, 1968); *The Authoritarian Personality*, with Else Frenkel-Brunswik, Daniel J. Levinson, and R. Nevitt Sanford (New York: Harper, 1950); *Dialektik der Aufklärung* [Dialectic of the Enlightenment] with Max Horkheimer (Amsterdam: Querido, 1944), trans. John Cumming (New York: Herder and Herder, 1972); *Negative Dialektik* [Negative Dialectics] (Frankfurt: Suhrkamp, 1966); *Philosophie der neuen Musik* [The Philosophy of Contemporary Music] (Frankfurt: Suhrkamp, 1973); *Aspekte der Hegelschen Philosophie* [Aspects of Hegelian Philosophy] (Berlin: Suhrkamp, 1957); *Aufsätze zur Gesellschaft/teorie* [Essays on Societal Theory] (Frankfurt: Suhrkamp, 1970); *Dissonanzen. Einleitung in die Musiksoziologie* [Dissonance: An Introduction to the Sociology of Music] (Frankfurt: Suhrkamp, 1973).
[29]Max Weber, *The Rational and Social Foundations of Music*, trans. Don Martindale, Johannes Riedel, and Gertrud Neuwirth (Carbondale, Ill.: The Southern Illinois University Press, 1958).

artifact of commercial manipulation; and jazz, despite its suggestion of sexual liberation, was characterized as a capitulation to the status quo.[30]

When health reasons forced Horkheimer's relocation in 1941 to California, Adorno accompanied him. They found a thriving exile community which included, among others, Arnold Schönberg and Thomas Mann. At the time Adorno was working on his *Philosophy of Modern Music*, Thomas Mann decided to revive the Faust story (in which a bargain is struck with the devil for the soul in return for knowledge and power) as a symbol for the rise and fall of Germany. Mann's device of using a composer's life and works as a vehicle for his updated version of the Faust legend (in *Doctor Faustus*) was facilitated by the loan of Adorno's manuscript. Mann's use of Adorno's material had the later unfortunate consequence of being the source of Schönberg's accusations that Mann had plagiarized.[31] For his part, Adorno had grown critical of atonal music, which he thought was hardening into a series of artistic dogmas.

In the 1940s Adorno was not only bringing his theories of music into synthesis, but with Horkheimer took part in the completion of the second great research project of the Institute after their *Studies on Authority and the Family*.[32] In his

preface to *The Authoritarian Personality*, Horkheimer reported that the concept of *authoritarian personality* which grew out of the studies on authority and the family was advanced as a link between psychological disposition and political leanings. The notion led the Institute to publish, in 1939, suggestions for comprehensive research on anti-Semitism. This formed the agenda of a conference on religious and racial prejudice sponsored by the American Jewish Committee in May, 1944, to which a group of American scholars had been invited. At the conclusion of the conference a research program was outlined to review and develop solutions to the problems of anti-Semitism. The research was jointly undertaken by the Berkeley Public Opinion Study and the Institute of Social Research.[33]

The general hypothesis explored in *The Authoritarian Personality* was that the political, economic, and social attitudes and convictions of individuals form a pattern expressive of deep trends in their personalities. Such an organized body of ideals, values, and opinions concerning human beings and society constitutes an ideology. The method of study proposed for examining the connection between personality and individual ideology was by questionnaires and clinical techniques:

---

[30]See Martin Jay's *Dialectical Imagination*, pp. 182ff, for a full review of Adorno's treatment of music.

[31]See Jay's review, *Dialectical Imagination*, pp. 194ff.

[32]By the end of the 1920s it had become increasingly clear that Lenin had a point when he scoffed at the revolutionary potential of workers and insisted the development of a revolutionary consciousness was a responsibility of an intellectual elite, a party that spoke in the name of the workers. However, the Leninist-Stalinist dictatorship of the proletariat did not wither away, but consolidated its position and developed a form of bureaucratic domination. Meanwhile it was everywhere evident that the socialist parties often spouted revolutionary rhetoric, but the workers, in fact, shrank from revolutionary action. One of the problems Horkheimer placed in top priority when he took over the Institute in 1930 was to explore the mentality of the working classes and to enlist the aid of psychoanalysis in explaining such things as the ready acceptance by German workers of fascism. Erich Fromm joined the Institute as director of the project, several thousand questionnaires were

distributed to workers exploring their views on such things as education, technology, war, politics and state power. Interviews, which were taken down in full, were later to be analyzed by psychoanalytic techniques. The questionnaire procedure developed in the course of this study was incorporated in the *Studies on Authority and the Family*. These ideas and methodology also had influence on the Institute's *Studies in Prejudice*.

[33]Max Horkheimer, T. W. Adorno, Else Frenkel-Brunswik, Daniel J. Levinson, and R. Nevitt Sanford, *The Authoritarian Personality* (New York: Harper, 1950), p. xi. Other volumes in the *Studies in Prejudice*, ed. Max Horkheimer and Samuel H. Flowerman, include: *Dynamics of Prejudice: A Psychological and Sociological Study of Veterans,* by Bruno Bettelheim and Morris Janowitz; *Anti-Semitism and Emotional Disorder: A Psychoanalytical Interpretation,* by Nathan W. Ackerman and Marie Jahoda; *Rehearsal for Destruction: A Study of Political Anti-Semitism in Imperial Germany,* by Paul W. Massing; and *Prophets of Deceit: A Study of the Techniques of the American Agitator,* by Leo Lowenthal and Norbert Guterman.

factual questions, opinion-attitude scales to obtain quantitative estimates of such ideological trends (as anti-Semitism, ethnocentrism, and political conservatism), interviews, and thematic apperception tests. In short, in addition to using the types of techniques employed in the earlier *Studies on Authority and the Family,* the researchers made extensive use of American quantitative techniques.

The authors concluded that there was a close correspondence between an individual's outlook and his or her approach to a wide variety of life spheres ranging from intimate family and sexual relationships to economic and political problems. They claimed to have isolated both authoritarian and democratic personalities. On the one hand, "a basically hierarchical, authoritarian, exploitive parent-child relationship is apt to carry over into a power-oriented, exploitively dependent attitude toward one's sex partner and one's God and may well culminate in a political philosophy and social outlook which has no room for anything but a desperate clinging to what appears to be strong"; on the other hand, there is a pattern characterized "chiefly by affectionate, basically equalitarian, and permissive interpersonal relationship."[34] The first personality complex was associated with a readiness for prejudice and a seed bed of fascism. Although the two types stand in sharp contrast, there are many variations between them which merge into one another. The more authoritarian the individual the less he or she is subject to appeals to reason. "For the fascist potential to change, . . . there must be an increase in people's capacity to see themselves and to be themselves,"[35] a result that cannot be achieved by manipulation. Behavior responds to needs and the combination of an individual's hopes and fears. "Thus, we need not suppose that appeal to emotion belongs to those who strive in the direction of fascism, while democratic propaganda must limit itself to reason and restraint. If fear and destructiveness are the major emotional sources of fascism, *eros* belongs mainly to democracy."[36]

With some irony, in the same decade (the 1940s) that Adorno and Horkheimer were involved in the researches on prejudice and making a place for American quantitative research techniques (the epitome of positivism) in the Institute's program, they were bringing their versions of critical theory as radical versions of neo-Hegelianism into synthesis. A central component of critical theory was opposition to positivism in all its forms. In the *Dialectic of Enlightenment*[37] Horkheimer and Adorno envision the contemporary world as the product and betrayal of the very Enlightenment which set out to disenchant the world, dissolving myth, substituting knowledge for fancy, but which, in the process, created myths of its own and resulted in new forms of domination. "Mythology itself set off the unending process of enlightenment in which ever and again, with the inevitability of necessity, every specific theoretic view succumbs to the destructive criticism that it is only a belief — until even the very notions of spirit, of truth, and, indeed, enlightenment itself, have become animistic magic."[38] Only what can be verified as evidentiary propositions is taken as truth; the achievements of great thinkers are degraded as a kind of stock of superannuated clichés which can no longer be distinguished from truth naturalized as a cultural commodity.[39]

The objective social tendency of the age is incarnate in the hidden subjective purposes of company directors, foremost among whom are the most powerful sectors of industry — steel, petroleum, electricity, and chemicals. However, the economic productivity they make possible, while supplying the conditions for a world of greater justice, also allows for the disproportionate superiority of the administrators of the rest of the population and results in a culture in which ev-

---

[34]Adorno et al., *The Authoritarian Personality,* p. 971.
[35]*Ibid.,* p. 975.
[36]*Ibid.,* p. 976.

[37]The original edition by Max Horkheimer and Theodor W. Adorno, *Dialektik der Aufklärung* (Amsterdam: Querido, 1944), references in the following material are to the translation by John Cumming (New York: Seabury, 1973 and New York: Herder and Herder, 1972).
[38]Horkheimer and Adorno, *Dialectic of Enlightenment,* p. 11.
[39]*Ibid.,* pp. 40f.

erything has the same stamp and individuality vanishes.

> In the culture industry the individual is an illusion not merely because of the standardization of the means of production. He is tolerated only so long as his complete identification with the generality is unquestioned. Pseudo individuality is rife: from the standardized jazz improvizations to the exceptional film star whose hair curls over her eye to demonstrate her originality.[40]

The stronger the cultural industry becomes, the more summarily it deals with consumer needs: producing them, disciplining them, even frustrating them at will.

Anti-Semitism reveals the same properties in political spheres as in the cultural industry. It supplies an approved outlet for the anger of the repressed masses and is an obvious asset to the ruling clique: a diversion, a cheap means of corruption, and an intimidating example. "Anti-Semitic behavior is generated in situations where blinded men robbed of their subjectivity are set loose as subjects."[41] In the world of mass series production, stereotypes replace individual categories and judgment is based on blind subsumption.[42] Anti-Semitism is "ticket thinking," a product of industrialization and its advertising machine. The loss of subjective experience by modern people leaves them with unordered emotions that are remobilized by the ticket of the political party. In the case of the murder of the Jews by the Fascists, for example, the Jews had so long ago, under the leveling forces of late industrial society, lost their character as bearers of a special alien religion that individuals persecuted as Jews had first to be located by means of complex questionnaires.[43]

> The fact that anti-Semitism tends to occur only as part of an interchangeable program, is sure hope that it will die out one day. Jews are being murdered at a

time when the Fascist leaders could just as easily replace the anti-Semitic plank in their platform by some other just as workers can be moved from one wholly rationalized production center to another.[44]

The *Dialectic of Enlightenment* depicts the Enlightenment as an antimythological program that created its own myths and, in freeing people from old forms of subjection, paved the way for newer forms of mass deception. In *Eclipse of Reason* Horkheimer explored the same themes in the spheres of science and philosophy.

Erich W. Fromm. Erich W. Fromm (1900–1980), who was born in Frankfurt, was raised in a religious home and strongly influenced as a youth by messianic Judaism, spent his adolescence in the atmosphere of World War I, and came to manhood during the ferment of the 1920s. He was a member of the Freies Jüdisches Lehrhaus, a close friend of the members of the Institute for Social Research. He studied at the universities of Heidelberg, Frankfurt, and Munich, and obtained psychoanalytic training at the Berlin Psychoanalytic Institute. He was analyzed in 1926, receiving instructions from Theodor Reich, and set up in clinical practice. In addition to being affected by the dissident Freudianism of Reich, Fromm was influenced by Marx and early came to the conclusion that psychoanalysis could supply the link between the materialistic base of society and its ideological superstructure. This idea made Fromm the ideal director for the Institute's *Studies on Authority and the Family,* which undertook to explain the failure of the working classes to live up to the revolutionary ideals to which they paid lip service. Fromm drew upon clinical practice and his psychoanalytic training in developing questionnaires that would guide the gathering of interview material for intensive analysis.

Fromm was also responsive to the revival of theories of a matriarchal stage in human society, a notion that had been advanced by J. J. Bachhofen in the nineteenth century and which

---

[40]*Ibid.*, p. 154.
[41]*Ibid.*, p. 171.
[42]*Ibid.*, p. 201.
[43]*Ibid.*, p. 206.

[44]*Ibid.*, p. 207.

ERICH FROMM

United Press International Photo

had influenced Henry Louis Morgan, the anthropologist, and, through him, Marx and Engels. Fromm was also impressed by Robert Briffault's *The Mothers,* especially by the idea that altruistic sentiments derive from maternal feelings, an interpretation that offered a nonsexual derivation of love in contrast to the orthodox view of Freud. Sex, in contrast to maternal feeling, is often coupled with hate and violence.

Although a central figure in the Institute's researches in the 1930s Fromm's free-ranging receptivity to currents of thought outside the interests acceptable to Horkheimer brought him into tension with the Institute. Hence, although he played a role in the integration of psychoanalytic doctrines in critical theory, by 1939 Fromm had broken with the Institute. However, in *Escape From*

Freedom, published in 1941, Fromm was still close to critical theory.

Postulating an original state of unity of human beings and nature, Fromm maintained that the more human beings become individuals, the greater their need to engage in spontaneous activity and productive work. If they do not find outlets for creativity, they will be inclined to seek security by destroying their freedom and the integrity of the self.[45] The emergence of modern individuality from the unity of the middle ages occurred by stages marked by the Renaissance, the Reformation, and the rise of capitalistic society. However, the economic system arising as a means to a better life tends to turn into an end, with negative consequences for individuality: "The subordination of the individual as a means to economic ends is based on the peculiarities of the capitalistic mode of production, which makes the accumulation of capital the purpose and aim of economic activity."[46] Under the monopolistic phase of capitalism, individuality is curtailed and the individual frustrated by gigantic forces in a manner similar to the condition of the individual in the fifteenth and sixteenth centuries. What is true in the economic sphere is paralleled in the political sphere where the voter is confronted by major parties. Contemporary humanity's alienation prepares them for fascism, the readiness to abandon individual selfhood and to submit to new forms of authority.[47] There are three major mechanisms of escape from the contemporary feeling of helplessness: authoritarianism, destructiveness, and automaton conformity. Authoritarianism and sado-masochism were powerful in lower middle-class German society, and supplied the motivational core of the Nazi movement. These same forces are also present in the democratic societies. "Only if man masters society and subordinates the economic machine to the purposes of human happiness and

[45]Erich Fromm, *Escape From Freedom* (New York: Holt, Rinehart and Winston, 1941), p. 23.
[46]*Ibid.,* p. 111.
[47]See *ibid.,* pp. 134–135.

only if he actively participates in the social process, can he overcome what now drives him into despair — his aloneness and his feeling of powerlessness."[48]

In an appendix to *Escape From Freedom,* Fromm argues that the theoretically distinctive feature of his interpretation of social process is found in the concept of social character — a nucleus of personality most members of a group developed as a result of basic experiences and a mode of life common to the group. This view, he urges, differentiates his views from the "psychologism" of Freud, the "economism" of Marxists, and the "idealism" of Max Weber. It is not psychological forces alone, nor economic forces alone, nor ideals and cultural traditions alone, but their *interaction* which are the central mechanism of the social process. Ideologies and culture are accepted and become influential only when rooted in the social character which, in turn, is molded by the mode of existence of a given society.[49]

After *Escape From Freedom* Fromm put increasing distance between himself and critical theory. By the time of *Man For Himself* he had begun to place stress on human nature in a manner that suggests the Enlightenment thinkers. Also, like them, he proposed to unite science and ethics: "I shall attempt to show that the character structure of the mature and integrated personality, the productive character, constitutes the source and the basis of virtue and that vice, in the last analysis, is indifference to one's own self and self-mutilation."[50] Neither a good nor evil outcome of the sociohistorical process is preordained, everything depends on man's "ability to take himself, his life and happiness seriously; on his willingness to face his and his society's moral problem. It rests upon his courage to be himself and to be for himself."[51]

[48]*Ibid.,* p. 276.
[49]*Ibid.,* p. 296.
[50]Erich Fromm, *Man For Himself* (New York: Rinehart, 1947), p. 7.
[51]*Ibid.,* p. 250.

FRANZ NEUMANN

Warman, Columbia University

Franz Neumann. In Franz Neumann (1900–1954) the Institute gained its most able interpreter of fascism. He was born of Jewish parents in the border area of German Poland, entering military service late in World War I and participating in the Soldiers' Councils which were formed immediately after the war. Neumann studied labor law in Frankfurt and settled in Berlin as a labor lawyer in 1927. He also taught at the Hochschule für Politick and acted as legal advisor to the Social Democratic Party. He was arrested and deprived of German citizenship when the Nazis came to power, but escaped within a month to London.

Neumann retrained himself in political science under Harold Laski at the London School of Economics, migrating to the United States and joining the Institute for Social Research in 1936. He contributed to the *Zeitschrift* a series of essays on law, which Horkheimer and Adorno found consistent with their critical theory. He also began work on the problem of fascism. After the entry of America into the war, Neumann joined the Office of Strategic Services of the State Department as an expert on Germany. After the war, when a professorship of political science became available at Columbia, he left the State Department. In 1954 during a summer vacation in Switzerland he was killed in an automobile accident.

Neumann brought to his analysis of the rise of fascism in Germany the talents of a lawyer and political scientist and the experience of a practicing labor lawyer and active politician. He posed the question as to why the Weimar Republic in Germany collapsed into fascism against a background of the success and failure of the imperial system in Germany. So long as the imperial system was able to expand on the basis of successful war and imperialistic policies, imperial Germany was able to satisfy the primary needs of the people. The army, bureaucracy, industry, and the big agrarians ruled, but not absolutely, for they were bound by law. Because of material advantages to the population as a whole the authority was not seriously challenged. However, when Germany lost World War I the imperial government abdicated and expansionist policies were checked; imperial Germany fell apart. The Weimar Republic had to rebuild an impoverished and exhausted country with polarized class antagonisms. In attempting to do so, it sought to integrate the heritage of the past with parliamentary democracy and pluralistic collectivism (incorporating powerful social and economic organizations directly into the political system). What it actually produced were sharpened antagonisms, the breakdown of voluntary collaboration, the destruction of parliamentary institutions, the suspension of political liberties, the growth of a ruling bureaucracy, and the renaissance of the army as a major political force.

The Weimar Republic could possibly have rebuilt Germany with foreign assistance, but this was denied. The system could have operated if the ruling groups made voluntary concessions under compulsion of the state. German industry, however, did not permit this and the state increasingly sided with it. The country was not ripe for the transformation into a socialist state. This left only a return to imperialist expansion. But imperialistic ventures could not be organized within democratic traditions and a return to the monarchy was out of the question. Moreover, an industrial society that has passed through a democratic phase cannot exclude the masses from consideration.

> Expansionism therefore took the form of National Socialism, a totalitarian dictatorship that has been able to transform some of its victims into supporters and to organize the entire country into an armed camp under iron discipline.[52]

National Socialism, Neumann argued, "has no theory of society."[53] Thought of any kind "whether positivist or pragmatic, whether idealist or not" is suppressed because it must inevitably have "critical and revolutionary impact."[54] Its so-called nonrational concept, "blood, community, folk" are devices for hiding the real constellation of power and the manipulation of power. Law, he argued, did not exist and Germany had no state. Rather, it had four semi-independent powers.

> It is doubtful whether National Socialism possesses a unified coercive machinery, unless we accept the leadership theory as a true doctrine. The party is independent of the state in matters pertaining to the police and youth, but everywhere else the state stands above the party. The army is sovereign in many fields; the bureaucracy is uncontrolled; and industry has managed to conquer many positions . . . the whole of the society is organized in four solid, centralized groups, each operating under the leadership principle, each with a legislative, administrative, and judicial power of its own.[55]

[52]Franz Neumann, *Behemoth: The Structure and Practice of National Socialism* (New York: Oxford, 1944), p. 34.
[53]*Ibid.*, p. 462.
[54]*Ibid.*, p. 464.
[55]*Ibid.*, p. 468.

Not only did National Socialism represent a form of society in which ruling groups controlled the rest of the population directly, without mediation by the state, but there were deep antagonisms within the ruling classes. There were no common loyalties. What bound them together was profit, power, and fear of the oppressed masses. There were, Neumann believed, flaws and breaks in the system and many hierarchies in the army, civil service, and industry were falling to pieces. Nevertheless, he believed, "even the military defeat of Germany will not lead to an automatic collapse of the regime. It can only be overthrown by conscious political action of the oppressed masses, which will utilize the breaks in the system."[56]

Herbert Marcuse. Herbert Marcuse (1898–1979) was closer to the center of critical theory than either Fromm or Neumann and when he chose to remain in the United States after the return of the Institute to Frankfurt, was the major representative of critical theory in America.

Marcuse was born in Berlin in 1898 of a well-to-do Jewish family, sharing its concern for liberal causes and social reform. He resigned from the Social Democratic Party in 1919 following the assassination of Rosa Luxemburg. His early interests were in the phenomenology of Husserl and Heidegger (from whom he acquired a deep hostility to technology); he studied with them at the University of Freiburg where he obtained the Ph.D. He was estranged from Heidegger in 1932 when Heidegger made temporary peace with the Nazis. He joined the Institute for Social Research in 1933, was assigned to the Geneva office, and was among the first members of the Institute to migrate to the United States, remaining in the Institute from 1934 to 1942. Marcuse's *Reason and Revolution*, in which he stressed the revolutionary implications of Hegel's employment of the idea of

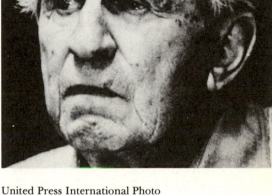

HERBERT MARCUSE

United Press International Photo

alienation and dialectical reasoning in his youthful writings, was the first book to be published in English by a major Institute figure.

In 1942 Marcuse accompanied Neumann to Washington, D.C. as analyst and later chief of the central European Branch of the Office of Strategic Services of the Department of State. Marcuse remained in the government for a time for lack of options, after Neumann's departure for Columbia University. From 1950 to 1952 he was senior fellow in the Russian Institute of Columbia. During 1952 through 1954 he was senior fellow of the Russian Research Center of Harvard University. From 1954 to 1965 he was professor of political and social philosophy at Brandeis University and from 1965 to his retirement was professor of philosophy at the University of California, San Diego

[56]*Ibid.,* p. 476. For an account of the tensions arising in Institute circles due to the publication of Neumann's study of National Socialism in 1942, see Jay, *The Dialectical Imagination,* pp. 160ff.

(La Jolla). He returned to Switzerland after retirement until his death in 1979.[57]

Marcuse's essays in the 1930s[58] were directed to all the major themes of critical theory at the time. He saw fascism as an outcome of liberalism; he approached all problems from the standpoint of left or radical Hegelianism; he accepted the Marxian critique of capitalism; he was convinced of the need to develop a more adequate psychology (to explain the failure of the working class in fulfilling its revolutionary mission) and looked to Freud for this purpose; he was suspicious of all forms of positivism. During this same time he was carrying out the research that resulted in *Reason and Revolution*, possibly his most important book, a classic of critical theory. *Reason and Revolution* integrated critical theory as of the early 1940s.

Philosophical knowledge, according to Marcuse's interpretation of Hegel, aims only at the essentials that have a bearing on humanity's destiny and their world.

> The sole object of philosophy is the world in its true form, the world as reason. Reason, again, comes into its own only with the development of mankind. Philosophic truth, therefore, is quite definitely concerned with man's existence; it is his innermost prod and goal.[59]

Hegel and Marcuse visualized the world of human beings as the world of mind, arising in and struggling for autonomy and freedom within nature. Such a process of growth and becoming, they believe, is only possible if in some sense mind differentiates itself against what it is not (the principle of negativity), penetrates it, and becomes something fuller and more comprehensive by incorporating the negation into a new synthesis.

> A philosophic system is true only if it includes the negative state and the positive, and reproduces the process of becoming false and then returning to the truth. As a system of this kind, the dialectic is the true method of philosophy. It shows that the object with which it deals exists in a state of 'negativity,' which the object, through the pressures of its own existence, throws off in the process of regaining its truth.[60]

The world of human beings develops in a series of integrations of opposites.

> In the first stage, the subject and its object take the form of consciousness and its concepts; in the second stage, they appear as the individual in conflict with other individuals; and in the final stage they appear as the nation.[61]

Language is the medium in which the first integration between subject and object takes place and is also the first actual community in the sense that it is objective and shared by all individuals. It is also the first medium of individuality and the first lever of appropriation. By means of language individuals can take conscious positions against their fellows.

> The labor process is responsible for various types of integration, conditioning all the subsequent forms of community that correspond to these types: the family, civil society, and the state . . . This transition from family to nation corresponds roughly to the transition from 'a state of nature' to a state of civil society.[62]

In his doctrine of the role of labor in the rise of society, Marcuse maintained, the young Hegel

[57]Marcuse's major books include: *Reason and Revolution: Hegel and the Rise of Social Theory* (New York: Oxford, 1941); *Eros and Civilization: A Philosophical Inquiry Into Freud* (Boston: Beacon Press, 1955); *Soviet Marxism: A Critical Analysis* (New York: Columbia University Press, 1958); *One-Dimensional Man: Studies in the Ideology of Advanced Industrial Society* (Boston: Beacon Press, 1964); *Negations, Essays in Critical Theory* (Boston: Beacon Press, 1968); *An Essay on Liberation* (Boston: Beacon Press, 1969).
[58]Herbert Marcuse, *Negations: Essays in Critical Theory*, trans. Jeremy J. Shapiro (Boston: Beacon Press, 1969).
[59]Marcuse, *Reason and Revolution*, p. 99.

[60]*Ibid.*, pp. 100–101.
[61]*Ibid.*, p. 74.
[62]*Ibid.*, pp. 75, 76.

anticipated the radical interpretations later made by Marx, who was not familiar with Hegel's early writings.

> In 1844 Marx sharpened the basic concepts of his own theory through a critical analysis of Hegel's *Phenomenology of Mind*. He described the 'alienation' of labor in the terms of Hegel's discussion of master and servant. Marx was not familiar with the stages of Hegel's philosophy prior to the *Phenomenology*, but he nevertheless caught the critical impact of Hegel's analysis.[63]

The labor process, Marcuse argues, is fundamental to the Marxian analysis of capitalism and its genesis is the ground on which theory and practice operate in capitalist society.[64] Marxian economics leaves no room for philosophy, psychology, or sociology. "According to Marx, the correct theory is the consciousness of a practice that aims at changing the world."[65] The concrete conditions for realizing the truth may vary, but truth remains the same and practice follows truth. "This absolutism of truth completes the philosophical heritage of the Marxian theory and once for all separates dialectical theory from the subsequent forms of positivism and relativism."[66]

Having linked Hegelianism and Marxism as radical critiques of capitalistic society, Marcuse turned the final chapters of *Reason and Revolution* to a critique of positivism and the analysis of fascism as the extreme antithesis of everything that Hegelianism stands for. Marcuse gave a number of the basic themes of critical theory strong philosophic underpinning in *Reason and Revolution*. In *Eros and Civilization* Marcuse undertook a similar task with respect to Freudian psychology, that is, its reinterpretation in a manner that fitted it to the requirements of critical theory.

Freud had come to essentially conservative conclusions in his review of the interrelation between the demands of the instincts (the pleasure and aggressive impulses, Eros and Thanatos) and the requirements of society and culture (the reality principle). Culture and the instincts were not only in tension justifying an authoritarian social order, but a self-destructive one. Eros must be controlled if a society is to exist; but the effect of repression may also be to weaken Eros in its function of binding the members of society together. When this occurs the destructive instincts are unleashed and civilization itself is threatened.[67] The answer, suggested by dissident Freudian Theodor Reich as early as the 1920s, is to find a way to expand the sphere of Eros, which would strengthen the pleasure principle in its ability to bind people together.

Marcuse reexamined the repressive forces operating on the pleasure principle, arguing that they arise not only from the requirements of biological survival, but for social reasons. They result in "surplus repression" of Eros, that is, repression over and beyond the biological requirements. This, in turn, may weaken the performance principle (Marcuse's name for the reality principle) which in mythology finds its archetype in Prometheus. Even in mythology there were counter images to the demands of Prometheus in the Orphic-Narcissistic images, epitomizing the reduction of pleasure, protesting against the repressions of procreative sexuality. When, during the counterculture revolts Marcuse became the hero of the student rebels, they transformed his arguments into the political slogan "make love, not war."

In *One-Dimensional Man*, the third of the books in which Marcuse updated and integrated critical theory, he turned to the problems of the rise of mass culture as a repressive force and to the castrating influence of positivism. In the guise of affluence and liberty, technological rationality has become the major instrument of social domination. The price of better living with more and more gadgets is ever greater alienation; the individual has become the willing subject

---

[63]*Ibid.*, p. 115.
[64]*Ibid.*, p. 320.
[65]*Ibid.*, p. 321.
[66]*Ibid.*, p. 322.

[67]Marcuse, *Eros and Civilization*, pp. 73ff.

of technological domination. "People recognize themselves in their commodities; they find their soul in their automobile, hi-fi set, split-level home, kitchen equipment. . . . there is only one dimension, and it is everywhere and in all forms."[68] Moreover, what applies to contemporary mass culture is also everywhere characteristic of the positivistic mode of thought, even including linguistic analysis. The only answer to the one-dimensional mentality of contemporary human beings, in Marcuse's view, is a return to the negative or dialectical thinking.

> In the equation Reason = Truth = Reality, which joins the subjective and objective world into one antagonistic unity, Reason is the subversive power, the "power of the negative" that establishes, as theoretical and practical Reason, the truth for men and things — that is, the conditions in which men and things become what they really are.[69]

NEW RECRUITS

Critical theory was shaped by the milieu in which it evolved: the unsettled conditions of the Weimar Republic; the rise of fascism forcing the Institute into exile; the war years; the unexpected role of the Institute in reestablishing the continuities of German intellectual culture, bridging the hiatus created by the Nazi and war years; the emergence of the Institute for Social Research as an establishment institution. The effect of location and milieu is illustrated by the very different receptions of such major members of the original Institute cadre, Adorno and Marcuse, during the postwar period and the student revolt. Marcuse was an outsider to the main stream of American philosophy and social science, and the postwar milieu in America seems to have played a role in the integration of utopian and anarchistic elements in Marcuse's works which, for the first time, were

popularly received. Adorno, on the other hand, inherited the directorship of the Institute, and found himself a major establishment figure in postwar German social science. Adorno was the major figure in the positivism controversy that raged in the 1960s. During the student revolt in America Marcuse became the hero of the New Left. In Germany the Institute for Social Research, as an establishment institution, was a target of militant student demonstrators. The building in which the Institute was located on the Frankfurt campus was repeatedly occupied. Adorno's classroom was invaded in April of 1969 by student militants. Three young women bared their breasts, showered Adorno with flowers and kisses, and declared him dead "as an institution."[70] The original cadre of the Frankfurt school of revolutionary Marxian socialists had found themselves trapped between the monstrosities of Stalinism and the boredom of an atomized affluent society with a pop culture and pop sociology in the place once occupied by religion.[71] From this perspective capitalism and socialism were merely alternative ways of producing the industrial and technocratic society of the later twentieth century. The radical Marxism of the 1920s left members of the Institute with no place to go.

> Hence Horkheimer's disillusioned return to liberalism, Adorno's revival of idealist metaphysics (plain for all to see in his *Negative Dialectic* of 1966), and Marcuse's attempt to combine the politics of anarchism with the philosophy of the early German Romantics — a curious hybrid, more remarkable for his personal sincerity than for its illumination of the problems of contemporary society.[72]

The response by student militants incidentally dramatized the extent to which the members of the

---

[68]Marcuse, *One-dimensional Man*, pp. 9, 11.
[69]*Ibid.*, p. 123.

[70]See Martin Jay, "The Permanent Exile of Theodor W. Adorno," *Mid-stream*, 15 (December 1969), 66–67.
[71]See George Lichtheim, *From Marx to Hegel* (New York: Seabury, 1971), p. viii.
[72]*Ibid.*, p. 170. Lichtheim characterizes *One-dimensional Man* as an ideology of pure rebellion against technological rationality in every form (p. 174).

original cadre were either being pressed back into the framework of liberalism or toward anarchistic utopianism. However, even apart from this, members of the original Frankfurt school were retiring or dying off raising the question: What would happen to critical theory in the process?

Jürgen Habermas. Jürgen Habermas, born in 1929, studied at the universities of Göttingen, Zurich, and Bonn. He was research fellow and professor at the universities of Frankfurt am Main, Marburg, and Heidelberg before accepting his present position as director of the Max Planck Institut in Starnberg.[73]

In the first edition of the group of essays published under the title *Theory and Practice* (first collected in 1963), Habermas examined such questions as, "The Classical Doctrine of Politics in Relation to Social Philosophy," "Natural Law and Revolution," "Hegel's Critique of the French Revolution," "Labor and Interaction: Remarks on Hegel's Jena Philosophy of Mind," "On Hegel's Political Writings," "Marxism as Critique," and "On Theory and Praxis in Our Scientific Civilization." There could be little doubt that Habermas was systematically returning to the historical sources of every basic idea and problem in critical theory. Meanwhile, the ancient conflict of critical theory with positivism had taken a new turn. In 1961 the German Sociological Association in Tübingen had set up a session on the logic of the social sciences to which it invited Karl Popper to present his views. Adorno was requested to reply to the discussion. Ralf Dahrendorf had the task of summarizing the discussion. The only conflict between critical theory and positivism had been thrust to the center of social scientific and philo-

sophical discussion in Germany, opening a controversy that raged through the 1960s. After 1963 Jürgen Habermas and Hans Albert emerged as the major spokespersons for critical theory and positivism, respectively.[74] In the opinion of Lichtheim, Habermas is "the most original and distinguished of the present generation of West Germany philosophers,"[75] and is not only the heir of the Frankfurt school of critical theory but has "both assimilated and transcended the heritage of the Institut für Sozialforschung and its surviving members. . . . in an intellectual synthesis which serves the original purpose of the 'critical theory,' while freeing it from the dead weight of the German metaphysical tradition . . . without lapsing into positivist scientism, whether linguistic or structuralist."[76]

In the fourth edition of his essays on theory and practice, Habermas added a new introduction epitomizing their aim and detailing developments in his own work since the first edition. His object, he observes, was to present "historical materialism . . . as a theory of society conceived with a practical intent which avoids the complementary weakness both of traditional politics and of modern social philosophy; it thus unites the claim to a scientific character with a theoretical structure referring to praxis."[77] In later investigations, he indicates, he has undertaken to further clarify (1) the empirical aspects of the relation between science, politics, and public opinion in advanced capitalistic social systems; (2) the epistemological aspects of the relation between knowledge and interest; and (3) the methodological aspects of a social theory capable of serving as social critique. However, such investigations of the interaction between science, politics, and public opinion must remain unsatisfactory so long as the theory of advanced capitalism has not

---

[73]Among Habermas's major works are: *Knowledge and Human Interests,* trans. J. Shapiro (Boston: Beacon Press, 1971); *Kultur und Kritik* (Frankfurt am Main: Suhrkamp Verlag, 1973); *Legitimation Crisis,* English trans. T. McCarthy (Boston: Beacon Press, 1975); *Philosophisch-politische Profile* (Frankfurt am Main: Suhrkamp Verlag, 1971); *Theory and Practice*, trans. J. Viertel (Boston: Beacon Press, 1971); *Toward a Rational Society,* trans. by J. Schapiro (Boston: Beacon Press, 1970).

[74]Theodor W. Adorno, Hans Albert, Ralf Dahrendorf, Jürgen Habermas, Harald Pilot, and Karl R. Popper, *The Positivist Dispute in German Sociology*, trans. Glyn Adey and David Frisby (London: Heinemann, 1976).

[75]Lichtheim, *From Marx to Hegel,* p. 130.

[76]*Ibid.*, pp. 174–175.

[77]Habermas, *Theory and Praxis,* p. 3.

yet been adequately worked out.[78] The basic problems this involve are: (1) Why does legitimation become a major problem under conditions of advanced capitalism? (2) Can the new potential for conflict and apathy endanger the entire system of advanced capitalism? and (3) Does the wage-labor relation which is not extensively mediated politically still make possible the formation of class consciousness? These problems appear to form not only the agenda for Habermas's continuing research but for the research program of the Max Planck Institut of which he is director. Among Habermas's own most original theoretical reflections are his attempts at formulating a linguistic foundation for the philosophy of historical materialism and a reanalysis of the problems of labor and instrumental reason found in the left Hegelian and Marxian traditions.[79]

Alvin Gouldner. Alvin Gouldner, who earned the Ph.D. at Columbia in 1953, is Max Weber Research Professor of Social Theory at Washington University, St. Louis. Gouldner, who first made his mark in American sociology as a functionalist, has become one of its major critics. His first work, *Patterns of Industrial Bureaucracy,* although presumably "seen in the light of Max Weber's theory of bureaucracy,"[80] does not actually subscribe to Weber's brand of social-action theory, which examines various alternative forms of administration as strategies, but treats bureaucracy as a social system in which bureaucratic roles operate as tension-reduction and tension-diversion devices in the interacting whole. Gouldner, however, does not seem to have rested easily under the mantle of functionalism to which he eventually assigned the ideological functions of the bringing of peace and ceremonial administration of order — in short, the

ALVIN GOULDNER

Courtesy of Washington University, St. Louis, Missouri

conservation of the status quo. Gouldner also emerged as a major critic of the positivistic tradition in sociology with his presidential address at the annual meeting of the Society for the Study of Social Problems.[81]

At the time of the height of the student uprisings and so-called counterculture revolt, Gouldner launched a frontal attack on American sociology

---

[78]*Ibid.,* p. 7.
[79]For a full treatment and a clarifying review see Jürgen Habermas, *Knowledge and Human Interests* and *Legitimation Crisis,* and the introduction to the latter by Thomas McCarthy, pp. viiff.
[80]Alvin W. Gouldner, *Patterns of Industrial Bureaucracy* (Glencoe, Ill.: The Free Press, 1954), p. 9.

[81]Alvin Gouldner, "Anti-Minotaur: The Myth of a Value-free Sociology," *Social Problems,* 9 (Winter 1962), 199–212. Among Gouldner's major books are: *Enter Plato* (New York: Harper, 1966); *The Coming Crisis of Western Sociology* (New York: Basic Books, 1970); *For Sociology* (New York: Basic Books, 1973); *The Dialectic of Technology* (New York: Seabury, 1976); *The Future of Intellectuals and the Rise of the New Class* (New York: Seabury, 1979).

leaving no doubt that he had made the cause of the student rebels, on the one hand, and the critical theorists, on the other, his own.

> It will be impossible either to emancipate men from the old society or to build a humane new one, without beginning, here and now, the construction of a total counter-culture, including new social theories; and it is impossible to do this without a critique of the social theories dominant today. . . . That theory has had an effect upon the emerging New Left, whatever the attitude toward it, is evidenced, among other things, by the role of the "Frankfurt school of critical sociology" — including Jürgen Habermas, Theodor Adorno, and Max Horkheimer — which has been said to be "as important as any single event" in the political revitalization of the *Sozialisticher Deutscher Studentbund* from 1961–1965. Also, there is the international responsiveness of the new radicals to the work of another member of that school, Herbert Marcuse, whose practical importance was backhandedly acknowledged by recent Soviet critiques of his theory.[82]

He based his criticism of American sociology on the platform: "A critique of sociology will be superficial unless the discipline is seen as the flawed product of a flawed society."[83]

The significance of *The Coming Crisis* lies in its attempt to demolish American sociology. Gouldner is undoubtedly the most gifted railer, relentless fault finder, and venomous critic of contemporary sociology. There were actually few criticisms of contemporary sociology in *The Coming Crises* that were new; many had been made from both inside and outside the discipline for a decade or more. Gouldner had unquestionably ransacked the arsenal of the critical theorists and had made a large number of their devices his own. Moreover, to all the standard criticisms, Gouldner added devices of his own.

"I do not intend," he said, "to focus on sociology as a science, or on its 'method,' . . . it will not be to its *methods* of study to which I will look for an un-

derstanding of its character, but rather to its assumptions about man and society."[84] Every theory, he maintains, contains two elements: its explicit formulations and its background assumptions. "Social theories . . . contain a charge of surplus meanings derived . . . from their background assumptions, and these may congenially resonate the compatible background assumptions of their hearers or may generate a painful dissonance."[85] Every theory is said to be produced by or, at least is responsive to, a group. The author is, in essence, merely the "emblem" of a shadow group. A theory thus is conventional and an expression of real activities and initiatives of an "infra structure" which shapes both the ideas and shadow group whose tacit collaboration eventuates in the theatrical performance.[86] "In a way, every theory is a discrete obituary or celebration for some social system."[87] Domain assumptions concerning humanity and society are not only built into substantive social theory but also into methodology, and every theory and method eulogizes a social reality. For example, "the conventional methodologies of social research often premise and foster a deepgoing authoritarianism, a readiness to lie to and manipulate people: they betray a bureaucratic numbness."[88] The basic function of high science methodologies is to widen the gap between what sociologists are studying and their personal realities: "The more rigorous the methodology, the more dimwitted the sociologist; the more reliable his information about the social world, the less insightful his knowledge about himself."[89] Gouldner opines, "It is my strong but undocumented impression that when some sociologists change their work interests, problems, or styles, they also change mistresses or wives."[90] By way of illustration the infrastructure of the conservative so-

---

[82]Gouldner, *The Coming Crisis,* p. 5.
[83]*Ibid.,* p. 14.

[84]*Ibid.,* pp. 27, 28.
[85]*Ibid.,* p. 29.
[86]*Ibid.,* pp. 46–47.
[87]*Ibid.,* p. 47.
[88]*Ibid.,* p. 50.
[89]*Ibid.,* p. 56.
[90]*Ibid.,* p. 57.

ciological theory of Talcott Parsons is said to have antecedents going all the way back to Plato: "The image of Academic Sociology that emerges is, in its dominant form, of a marriage between an octogenarian dowager and a young stud, between an ancient infrastructure and modern science."[91]

Among the findings Gouldner claims to have made by applying this method of analysis to American sociology is that Western sociology is approaching a crisis. This is said to be manifest in (1) moves toward rapprochement between functionalism and Marxism; (2) an alienation of some of the young sociologists from functionalism; (3) a tendency of expression of individual alienation to take group or collective form; (4) increasing technical criticism of functionalism; (5) the development of some alternatives to functionalism by such persons as Goffman, Garfinkle, and Homans; (6) the appearance of middle-range and problem research on freedom and equality. Three forces are said to contribute to this coming crisis: (1) the appearance of new infrastructure; (2) the development of conflicts and divergences within functionalism; and (3) the development of the welfare state which has increased the resources available to functionalism.[92]

Gouldner describes his version of critical theory as reflexive sociology. About the best that one can say about his critical methodology is that he has reinvented the ad hominem and rediscovered Francis Bacon's idols (erroneous forms of reasoning) and transformed them into the critical apparatus of reflexive sociology. A person's biography may have causal effect upon his or her thought, but what he or she thinks must be judged true or false on the basis of the criteria of logic and empirical method. The same is true with respect to the relation between a theory and the so-called domain assumptions with which it may or may not resonate. Gouldner seems to be attempting to raise the ad hominem to the status of a general philosophical principle.

Gouldner's formulation of the positive content of reflexive sociology in *The Coming Crisis* is a form of Left Hegelianism:

> The historical mission of a Reflexive Sociology is to foster a critical awareness of the character of contemporary liberalism, of its hold upon the university and upon American sociology, as well as of the dialectic between Welfare and Warfare policies, and of the liberal sociologist's role as market researcher on the behalf of both. Reflexive Sociology premises that the character of any sociology is affected by its political praxis and that further development of sociology now requires its liberation from the political praxis of liberalism.[93]

Gouldner's methods of criticism, his ad hominems and various forms of guilt by association which rarely meet ideas head on in the open, but which undermine and denigrate them on the basis of their presumed implications, were calculated to evoke outrage. Gouldner used a collection of his essays in *For Sociology* as a means of answering his many critics. His critics had pressed him to develop his own views. So far as he did so the fundamental Hegelianism of his position became more apparent. Normal sociology, he argued, cannot liberate because it lacks reflexiveness, avoiding activism with a stress on the instrumental and useful. It is externalizing. The normal sociologist operates as follows:

> Interested in something, he . . . mounts a 'research' and, in precisely that invidious sense, he 'commits' a social science. . . . Higher and prior to research there is *reflection*. The sociologist should first conduct a dialogue with himself and with others to see what he already knows. . . . And there is absolutely no case on record in the history of sociology in which a sociologist is known to have systematically pondered the meaning of 'is.'[94]

This, of course, is pure Hegel of a relatively primitive sort.

[91]*Ibid.*, p. 413.
[92]See *ibid.*, p. 410.

[93]*Ibid.*, p. 502.
[94]Gouldner, *For Sociology*, p. 110.

In *The Dialectic of Ideology and Technology* Gouldner gives his own twist to the argument Marcuse had advanced in *One-dimensional Man*. Gouldner wishes to restore ideology to its rightful place at the core of sociology. "Ideology is not some arcane condition that sociology outgrows in its maturity. It remains, rather, a boundary wall that is manned, watched, and recurrently repaired."[95] Technology, including consumerism, productivity, and science, stresses enjoyment while repressing ideological creativity. Mass conduct is governed not by belief even in the rightness of the technology, but only by sheer gratification. This becomes clear at the moment when wars and depressions occur and the gratification level falls.

> We then see that it is not science and technology, nor even their continued development that suffices to maintain the morale and loyalty of the modern citizens. There remains an abiding need for a justificatory ideology. Growing rationalization, technological hardware, the scientization of bureaucracy, do not circumvent this need. They never did.[96]

Gouldner looks to reflexive or critical theory to supply the ideological ingredient necessary to the continuing progress of society, an ingredient which will serve as a moral force binding society together, an ingredient vanishing from both the capitalist and socialist countries.

In *The Future of the Intellectuals and the Rise of the New Class* Gouldner continued his progress toward full Hegelianism. He replaces Marx's notion of the accumulation of capital with the accumulation of culture. He no longer looks to the worker to serve as the vehicle of human liberation, but finds that the hope of humankind rests with a new expanded class of intellectuals. If unified by its reverence for intellectual culture, Gouldner is convinced, the new class will displace the corporate elite of the Trilateral Commissions and the party bosses of the Soviet Union. Norman Birnbaum, in a sage review of *The Future of the Intellectuals* observes:

Professor Gouldner retains the form of Marxism, but ignores its historical content. Must the old class have a successor? It may have several, struggling endlessly with one another in a world polycentric at best, chaotic at worst. The proletariat having failed, there is no warrant for supposing that another class will come forward to unify society, much less redeem it. Professor Gouldner's high hopes for the new class rest largely on his conviction that it shares a common culture with an emphasis on critical thinking.[97]

The appeal of Gouldner's book, Birnbaum observes, lies in its theological tension; between the search for a new eschatology and fear that the world may continue as it is.

SUMMARY

The Hegelian finds the essence of human society in the state of the human spirit that provides it with its character. Human history is the self-realization of the spirit. The mind of any single individual is only an incident and moment in the mind of humankind, for it is the collective mind that is the concrete universal. The true individuals of history are societies or states. The collective spirit of humankind grows by a dialectical process, by pushing out to what is not mind, by negations, which are overcome in a new synthesis marking a higher stage in the spiral achievement of freedom and autonomy. Hegelianism, which is a type of holism or collectivism, has both a conservative and a radical form. Its conservative form takes the view that anything that has happened in human history was an inevitable product of the spirit, and that despite the injustices of the present it is still the best of all possible worlds. Its radical form (which Hegel himself held as a young man and to which the Left Hegelians returned after Hegel's death) holds that whatever has been achieved in human history must be viewed simply as the starting point for change; it must be negated, overcome, and in-

[95]Gouldner, *The Dialectic of Ideology*, p. 10.
[96]*Ibid.*, p. 246.

[97]Norman Birnbaum, *New York Times Book Review*, April 15, 1979, p. 3.

corporated into a more comprehensive synthesis. The truth lies only in the whole, or in approximations following repeated negations.

Messianic elements in Marx's personality responded to the radical interpretation of Hegel, contributing to his emergence as the most effective and influential of the Left Hegelians. He restated Hegel's idealistic collectivism in material terms: it was not thought, but work which was the mainspring of human development; the essential vehicle of progress was not ideas, but organized groups of society, classes which carried on the historical process; not the self-realization of the spirit, but the fulfillment of humanity represented the goal of history.

However, Marxism in time was being converted into a utopian ideology, on the one hand, and a program of social science on the other. Lenin and other revolutionary Marxists saw the necessity to resist both tendencies if Marxism was to retain its revolutionary potential. However, with the triumph of Leninism and its conversion into a new orthodoxy by Stalin, Soviet Marxism was transformed into a justification for the bureaucratic absolutism of a party — a transformation which soon brought it into conflict with other versions of Marxism. Those seeking to restore the revolutionary core of Marxism found themselves vigorously opposed: Lukács was forced to recant; Korsch was kicked out of the German communist party; and Gramsci, in Italy, was imprisoned by the Fascists until his death. In response to exile, the rising tides of prejudice, and the triumph of Central European fascism, the Frankfurt school undertook to interpret the times and keep alive its hope for the future. Within these circles the step-by-step return from revolutionary Marxism to Left Hegelianism took place.

The Frankfurt school formed the institutional base for research that in the long run would have major influence on the development of contemporary thought quite out of proportion to the number of scholars involved. In addition to the studies that have been reviewed in the present chapter are many others which, for lack of space, it has been necessary to pass over. Particularly significant were Walter Benjamin's studies in aesthetics, Leo Lowenthal's studies on the sociology of literature, and Karl Wittfogel's studies of oriental despotism.

Finally, the Left Hegelianism of the Frankfurt school (or, as they preferred to call it, Critical Theory, and as Gouldner would describe it, Reflexive Sociology) took the lead in the restoration of German social science culture after World War II, on the one hand, and emerged as the philosophy of the New Left, on the other.

PART V

HUMANISTIC ELEMENTARISM

As LONG AS HOLISM and elementarism, on the one hand, and humanism and science, on the other, describe the main compass points of Western thought, whenever any group of individuals loses confidence simultaneously in both holism and science, the only alternative left for them is to explore the theoretical possibilities of a humanistic elementarism. In the 1960s both science and holism were being extensively questioned but usually not by the same persons.

C. Wright Mills, for example, had originally favored a form of scientific elementarism. However, by the time he wrote the *Sociological Imagination* he was vigorously attacking positivism, describing science as "a false and pretentious messiah." In his pamphleteering writings in the early 1960s Mills was moving closer to revolutionary Marxism and toward a combination of humanism and holism. Alvin Gouldner, who began his career as a macrofunctionalist, also became one of the major antipositivists in America in the 1960s. However, Gouldner, showing no inclination to break with holism, simply substituted a radical for a conservative form of holism. By the time he published *Coming Crisis,* Gouldner was developing a position similar to that of the critical theorists of the Frankfurt School.

The 1960s were characterized by a general dissatisfaction with holism that was manifest in the expansion of all branches of elementarism. However, most elementarists remained methodologically scientific or positivistic. For example, Homans completed his break with structure-functionalism by the early 1960s. He was reacting to the humanistic as well as holistic components of functionalism and became more positivistic in his behavioristic sociology.

At the same time, however, critical theory, which had become a major component in German establishment sociology, was mired in a dispute over positivism. This tended to exacerbate the positivism-antipositivism dispute in England and America. The critical theorists, however, were violently opposed to all forms of elementarism, and traced the major problems of the contemporary world to the Enlightenment. This denun-

ciation placed the rationalistic individualism of the Enlightenment under a cloud. The most significant enemy, according to the critical theorists, was liberalism. This was the fundamental message of Herbert Marcuse, who was the leading representative of critical theory left in the United States when other members of the Frankfurt Institute for Social Research accepted the invitation of the German authorities to return to Germany. When the liberal establishment in the United States got bogged down in the Vietnam War, with all its attendant generational conflicts, teach-ins, antiwar demonstrations, and the like, Marcuse emerged as the hero of the New Left. Marcuse systematized opposition to the establishment and popularized antipositivism. However, he remained suspicious of elementarism.

The countercultural revolts proved to be evanescent and did not outlive the end of the Vietnam War. They left no radical social movement in their wake. By the 1970s the young persons who had participated in the revolts were growing older and were trying to settle into jobs and careers. However, they were doing so in a world that provided little confidence in the establishment: the shocking display of illegality in high places during the Watergate scandal; the revelations of illegal activities by the FBI and CIA; the recession and inflation; the energy crisis. The 1970s did not present a milieu favorable to the development of holistic theories of society.

During the 1960s there was much talk of anomie, alienation, and the loss of community. However, the decade was activistic and thousands of communes of varying duration were a product of the search for a more adequate community. The large majority of these experiments were poorly planned, short-lived, and disillusioning. In the 1970s the collapse of the communes was itself a component in the distinctive mood of social resignation and self-preoccupation or egotism that many students of contemporary culture see as the signature of the decade. The 1970s has been described as the "me" decade, the prevailing mood as narcissistic. In a widely acclaimed volume, Christopher Lasch summed up a decade of reflection about the outlook of contemporary Americans in the 1970s as follows:

> The new narcissist is haunted not by guilt but by anxiety . . . Superficially relaxed and tolerant, he finds little use for dogmas of racial and ethnic purity but at the same time forfeits the security of group loyalties and regards everyone as a rival for the favors conferred by a paternalistic state. His sexual attitudes are permissive rather than puritanical, even though his emancipation from ancient taboos brings him no sexual peace. Fiercely competitive in his demand for approval and acclaim, he distrusts competition because he associates it unconsciously with an unbridled urge to destroy. Hence he repudiates the competitive ideologies that flourished at an earlier stage of capitalist development and distrusts even their limited expression in sports and games. He extols cooperation and teamwork while harboring deeply antisocial impulses. He praises respect for rules and regulations in the secret belief that they do not apply to himself. Acquisitive in the sense that his cravings have no limits, he does not accumulate goods and provisions against the future, in the manner of the acquisitive individualist of nineteenth-century political economy, but demands immediate gratification and lives in a state of restless, perpetually unsatisfied desire.[1]

Lasch has the following to say about the causes of contemporary humanity's narcissism and the prospects for an alternative to it:

> In a dying culture, narcissism appears to embody — in the guise of personal "growth" and "awareness" — the highest attainment of spiritual enlightenment. The custodians of culture hope, at bottom, merely to survive its collapse. The will to build a better society, however, survives, along with the traditions of localism, self-help, and community action that only need the vision of a new society, a decent society, to give them new vigor.[2]

Lasch is fundamentally a conservative sociocultural holist seeing no hope in the individual, but only in a new society and culture which, it seems, will resemble the Gemeinshaft of the past.

Early in the 1970s C. M. Turnbull, the anthropologist, spent two years in the mountain valleys of northern Uganda with a tribe of former nomadic hunters and gatherers called the Iks. When the government established a national park, the Iks were forced to give up hunting and gathering and became tillers on the hillsides. Although compelled to live together in small villages the tribespeople remained socially and psychologically isolated: ill-tempered and loveless, abandoning their elders and their children as soon as they can walk to forage for themselves, defecating on each other's doorsteps, and laughing at each other's misfortunes.[3] Turnbull interpreted the Iks as a paradigm for what contemporary human beings are becoming. Turnbull, like Lasch, had a Hobbesian conception of humanity: the view that, left to themselves human beings are fundamentally selfish. Turnbull's message, too, is basically conservative; only a return to traditional culture can prevent contemporary humanity from engaging in a war of each against all.

In one of the short essays in *The Lives of a Cell*, Lewis Thomas examined the Iks, called attention to the assumptions about human nature taken for granted by Turnbull, and suggested a different appraisal of the individual and the collective.

> I do not believe that the Iks are representative of isolated, revealed man, unobscured by social habits. I believe their behavior is something extra, something laid on. This unremitting, compulsive repellance is a kind of complicated ritual. They must have learned to act this way; they copied it somehow.
>
> I have a theory then. The Iks have gone crazy.
>
> The solitary Ik, isolated in the ruins of an exploded culture has built a new defense for himself. If you live in an unworkable society you can make up one of your own, and this is what the Iks have done. Each Ik has become a group, a one-man tribe on its own, a constituency.

[1]Christopher Lasch, *The Culture of Narcissism* (New York: W. W. Norton, 1978), p. xvi.
[2]*Ibid.*, p. 235.

[3]C. M. Turnbull, *The Mountain People* (New York: Simon and Schuster, 1972).

Now everything falls into place. This is why they do seem, after all, vaguely familiar to all of us. We've seen them before. This is precisely the way groups of one size or another, ranging from committees to nations, behave. It is, of course, this aspect of humanity that has lagged behind the rest of evolution, and this is why the Ik seems so primitive. In his absolute selfishness, his incapacity to give anything away no matter what, he is a successful committee. When he stands at the door of his hut, shouting insults at his neighbors in a loud harangue, he is city addressing another city.

Cities have all the Ik characteristics. They defecate on doorsteps, in rivers and lakes, their own or anyone else's. They leave rubbish. They detest all neighboring cities, give nothing away. They even build institutions for deserting elders out of sight. Nations are the most Iklike of all. No wonder the Iks seem familiar. For total greed, rapacity, heartlessness, and irresponsibility there is nothing to match a nation. Nations, by law, are solitary, self-centered, withdrawn into themselves. There is no such thing as affection between nations, and certainly no nation ever loved another. They bawl insults from their doorsteps, defecate into whole oceans, snatch all the food, survive by detestation, take joy in the bad luck of others, celebrate the death of others, live for the death of others.[4]

Already by the nineteenth century, as illustrated by Dostoyevsky's *Notes From the Underground* (1864), sensitive observers had noted the emergence of amoral individualism at the heart of contemporary society. Nietzsche and Kierkegaard delved further into the properties of the new mass human beings, attributing their psychology to their existential predicament, and began to explore individual alternatives to a society that had such consequences. Kierkegaard and Nietzsche were the forerunners of the existentialists, who would note the increasing prevalence of Iklike and

narcissistic personality traits in the contemporary mass world and, at the same time, deplore all inclinations to shift moral responsibility from the individual to the group. Edmund Husserl, meanwhile, laid the foundations of phenomenology which, though originally conceived as a more adequate form of empiricism, eventually became the methodological counterpart of existentialism.

Max Scheler, Alfred Vierkandt, and, somewhat belatedly, Georges Gurvitch undertook the first moves toward a phenomenological sociology. They took their point of departure from the forms of social theory current at the time, specifically from neo-Kantian formalism. For this reason, in the first edition of *Nature and Types* phenomenological sociology was discussed in connection with formalism.

However, the mood that became manifest in the 1960s and 1970s opened the way toward a new approach to phenomenological sociology, now conceived as the sociology of everyday life. The work of Alfred Schutz, who had taught part-time at the New School for Social Research, provided the basis for this new approach. In Schutz's own life work he had employed phenomenology to illumine the social-action theory of Max Weber. Schutz's students, however, proposed to develop it as an independent social theory in its own right. Finally, in the 1970s, phenomenological sociology was officially recognized by the national association, and moves have been underway to form a society of phenomenological sociologists, with their own newsletter and journal.

The phenomenological sociologists, one branch of whom calls themselves ethnomethodologists, have continued a trend toward antipositivism present in Husserl's own later writings (Husserl's first version of phenomenology was quite positivistic in spirit and intent). The notion of a creative, morally responsible individualism is the mainspring of the humanistic elementarism of phenomenological sociology.

[4]Lewis Thomas, *The Lives of a Cell* (New York: Bantam Books, 1975), pp. 128–129.

XXIII

Humanistic Elementarism: The Foundation of Existentialism and Phenomenology

The first school of sociological theory, positivistic organicism, linked an organismic theory of society with the methodology of science. The founders were well aware that since the Renaissance and Reformation, Christianity had been losing its unquestioned binding power in Western society. They also knew that the Enlightenment thinkers — even when not agnostics, such as the Deists — as spokespeople for individual rationalism were accomplishing the liquidation of religion's traditional role in everyday conduct. They were also convinced that some substitute for religion had to be found, to supply cohesiveness to human affairs. This task they assigned to sociology. In Augustinian terms the sociologists were substituting the City of Humanity for the City of God, human society for the church, and sociologists for priests as ideologists and norm givers.

Although it is conventional in some quarters these days to see Hegelian philosophy as an antithesis to sociology, it, too, was holistic (taking a given system of culture sustained by civil society and the state to be the "concrete universal," the true individual in the historical process) and rationalistic.

The appeal of this combination of holism and rationalism-scientism lay in its apparent capacity to solve major philosophical and social problems: philosophically it seemed to overcome the apparent gap between fact and value; practically it both assigned to the community the integrating function lost by the decline of the traditional religions and overcame tendencies toward anarchistic individualism.

However, the conflict over the place of values in interpersonal experience was not about to disappear. In France, the home of Comteian sociology, dissension arose between the sociologists and scientific socialists. In Germany, the home of Hegelianism, a division appeared between the right and left Hegelians, and later between the objective Idealists and Marxians. Moreover, both philosophically and practically, attempts to return to an individualistic (or elementaristic) position took a new form in the postrevolutionary world, that is in the world of nation-states.

INDIVIDUALISM IN A WORLD OF NATION-STATES

Descartes, who is generally recognized as the thinker who made the definitive step into modern philosophy, was an individualist and rationalist. He assumed society to be a collection of rational individuals. To build an appropriate system of explanation of human beings and their world, Descartes proposed to doubt everything until he arrived at self-evident premises and then to proceed with an interpretation of humanity, the world, and God step-by-step with the same certainty as mathematical demonstration. In applying this method he quickly arrived at the proposition that one could doubt everything except that one was doubting: "I think, therefore, I am."

However, Descartes's program of rebuilding knowledge developed difficulties that plagued his successors until Kant, at the end of this first wave of Western philosophizing, proposed to reexamine the entire problem of knowledge to determine whether there are any intrinsic limitations. Kant concluded that scientific knowledge, which deals with phenomena, cannot, in principle, go beyond phenomena to the things assumed to be behind them without falling into self-contradiction. The world of things-in-themselves, which includes the individual, however, has its own requirements, which contradict those of the phenomenal world. In the phenomenal world everything obeys necessary laws; but in moral and ethical actions, we assume human beings have genuine choices and we hold them accountable for their actions (punish them, for example, when they commit crimes). Behavior was being divided into contradictory spheres.

Hegel had advanced his holistic theory in some measure to eliminate the contradiction between Kant's theory of scientific exploration and his theory of moral conduct. In the process, Hegel defined the society or social group as the unit of social reality and understood reason to refer not to the individual mind but to the collective mentality of the group. This seemed to offer the promise of a unified program of knowledge once more. Hegel

ARTHUR SCHOPENHAUER

Brown Brothers

quickly won acclaim, becoming the most popular philosopher in Germany in the early nineteenth century, but the individual was now left in an ambiguous position. The individual was now less real than the groups to which he belonged.

Arthur Schopenhauer. Arthur Schopenhauer (1788–1860) was born in Danzig, the son of a prosperous merchant and a popular novelist. He inherited a fortune that permitted him to study at Göttingen and Berlin under Fichte. He earned his doctorate in 1813. Although possessing considerable ability, Schopenhauer was egotistical, brooding, and pessimistic, unable to form enduring friendships with men or women. In a familiar story, he once deliberately scheduled his lectures at the same hour as Hegel's and left in rage when his classroom was nearly empty. He eventually settled permanently in Frankfurt. Only in the last ten years of his life, when changes in the social milieu made his theories more attractive, did he become popular.

In the *World As Will and Idea*[1] Schopenhauer preserved an individualistic point of view while accepting Kant's distinction between the world as experienced phenomena and the world of things-in-themselves (noumena), without attempting to overcome the distinction (as Hegel did) by postulating a collective mind. Phenomena are ideas; the subject (noumenon) which has ideas is emotional and passionate. Time, space, causality, and all the other forms of phenomena and all their varied content are clear, incisive, and rational; but below this superficial level of experience is always the blind yearning and suffering of the subject, the will. Consciousness, with all its apparent rationality, is ultimately nothing other than an instrument of the will which strives to protect the individual and propagate the species. So long as experience remains at a conscious level, only aesthetic experience and philosophical contemplation — rare gifts of the especially talented and then only sporadically effective — can provide relief from the endless pressure of the will. Social development, progress, hope for a historical future that will be better than the present are all illusory. Only denial and extinction of the will (as in the nirvana of the Eastern religions) will finally release one from its torments.

Schopenhauer, thus, preserved an elementaristic interpretation of social life, but with a considerable difference in stress from the eighteenth-century rationalists. Human nature was conceived as basically evil and human beings typified by their passion rather than by their reason. Schopenhauer had influence on such persons as Hartmann, Nietzsche, Wagner, Tolstoy, Freud, and Thomas Mann.

[1]Arthur Schopenhauer, *The World As Will and Idea*, trans. R. B. Haldane and J. Kemp (New York: Doubleday, 1961). Other works include: *On the Will in Nature* (1836); *The Two Main Problems of Ethics* (1841); and *Parega and Paralipomena* (1851).

SÖREN KIERKEGAARD

Brown Brothers

Sören Kierkegaard. Sören Kierkegaard (1813–1855) was born in Denmark of elderly parents (his father was fifty-six, his mother forty-five at the time of his birth) in an authoritarian, gloomy, pietistic household. He was a sickly child with a weak constitution. His father took over his education, placing almost exclusive stress on religion, granting the youth a minimum of time for play and exercise, and dressing him in old-fashioned clothes. Added to Kierkegaard's natural shyness and minor physical deformity, his father's authoritarian training and policies denied to him the possibility of a normal childhood. In response to his father's wishes Kierkegaard chose to study theology when entering the university at the age of seventeen.

For a time, under the libertarian influence of the university and the aesthetic atmosphere of the capital city of Copenhagen, Kierkegaard indulged himself to the full in the intellectual and aesthetic advantages of the university and the city: enjoying the opera, theatre, restaurants, purchasing many books, reading widely in aesthetics, literature, and philosophy. He became estranged from his father and developed serious doubts about religion. A series of blows culminating in the deathbed confession of his own blasphemy by his father, which he laid as a curse on his son, marked a turning point in Kierkegaard's life. He fell in love with a young woman, but could not bring himself to marry her. He plunged into a fever of intellectual activity, writing under a variety of pseudonyms as well as under his own name.

The events of Kierkegaard's life transformed him into an intense individualist in tension with both the conventional, unreflective Christianity of the habitual churchgoer and the abstract holistic theology of popular Hegelianism. Against both the depersonalized conformity of the unthinking churchgoer and the abstract, deindividualized, reason of the philosophers, Kierkegaard counterposed the concrete situation of individuals, with their doubts, uncertainties, anxieties, and passions. The search for Christian truth must renounce both, beginning with an act of faith by the individual progressing through a series of choices from aesthetic to scientific, from scientific to ethical, from ethical to religious points of view. The motive for the search arises out of deep feelings of despair. Collectivism, whether in fact or in theory, was anathema to Kierkegaard.

> The secret of the deceit which suits the world which wants to be deceived consists partly in forming a coterie and all that goes with that, in joining one or another of those societies for mutual admiration, whose members support one another with tongue and pen in the pursuit of worldly advantage . . . A crowd . . . in its very concept is the untruth, by reason of the fact that it renders the individual completely impenitent and irresponsible . . . "The individual is the category through which, in a religious respect, this age, all history, the human race as a whole, must pass. . . . If I were to desire an inscription for my tombstone, I should desire none other than "That Individual."[2]

Jacob Burckhardt.

Jacob Burckhardt. Jacob Burckhardt (1818–1897) was born in Basel of a prominent family of professors and pastors. He grew up beside the cathedral where his father was minister. He studied at Berlin and Bonn, completing his apprenticeship under the historian Ranke. When he returned to Basel in 1843 he worked part-time on the staff of the *Basel Journal*, an organ of the civic administration. Because of political troubles in Switzerland in 1846 Burckhardt found it expedient to go to Italy to study, returning in 1848. Again, five years later, Burckhardt was in self-exile for a time in Italy. However, most of his time was spent in Basel, and he declined Ranke's chair at Berlin when it was offered to him. When Nietzsche arrived at Basel in 1868 as professor of classics, he and Burckhardt became close friends sharing a common appreciation of Schopenhauer.

Like so many sensitive persons in the nineteenth century, Burckhardt had lost his faith in traditional Christianity. At the same time, though apprenticed to the most important historian of Germany at a time when Hegelian traditions were strong, Burckhardt did not find Hegelian holism to be an adequate substitute for religion. If anything his individualism was strengthened by his resistance to collectivistic trends in both thought and social life.

> Hegel, in the introduction to his *Philosophy of History* tells us that the only idea which is "given" in philosophy is the simple idea of reason, the idea that the world is rationally ordered: hence the history of the

[2] Walter Kaufmann, *Existentialism From Dostoyevsky to Sartre* (New York: Meridian Books, 1956), pp. 87–88, 93, 98, 99. Among Kierkegaard's works of special interest to sociologists are: *The Concept of Dread*, trans. Walter Lowrie (Princeton: Princeton University Press, 1944); *Either/Or* (New York: Doubleday, 1959); *The Journals of Sören Kierkegaard*, trans. Alexander Dru (New York: Oxford, 1938); *The Present Age*, trans. Alexander Dru and Walter Lowrie (New York: Oxford, 1940).

world is a rational process, and the conclusion yielded by world history *must* [sic!] be that it was the rational, inevitable march of the world spirit — all of which, far from being "given," should first have been proved.[3]

He was suspicious not only of philosophers (like Hegel) but of theologians and socialists who write history to make a point. Burckhardt took his own stand on a type of individualism, modeled after that of Schopenhauer.[4]

We, however, shall start out from the one point accessible to us, the one eternal centre of all things — man, suffering, striving, doing, as he is and was and ever shall be. Hence our study will, in a certain sense, be pathological in kind.

The philosophers of history regard the past as a contrast to and preliminary stage of our own time as the full development. We shall study the *recurrent, constant,* and *typical* as echoing in us and intelligible through us.[5]

The central phenomena of history, from Burckhardt's point of view, is the rise of a power, justified in its own time, which synthesizes the various forms of social life (political organization, privileged classes, a religion closely knit with secular life, group processes, a complete code of manners, and a distinctive conception of law). As a

rule, in the face of such historical forces the contemporary individual feels utterly helpless and usually falls into the bondage of aggressor or defender. Few are able to obtain an Archimedian point of view outside events and to detach themselves in spirit from the cultural synthesis of their times. Yet it is precisely the achievement of such an Archimedian point to which Burckhardt aspired. As a student of Schopenhauer he was convinced that there are only two possible attitudes toward the times: to treat the world as idea, as an object of artistic contemplation, living *in* but not *of* it or to treat the world as will and ravaged by its endless torments to seek nirvana. In his own life and theory Burckhardt proposed the first alternative: "While, as men of a definite epoch, we must inevitably pay our passive tribute to historical life, we must at the same time approach it in a spirit of contemplation."[6]

In envisioning the task of the historian as the evaluation of the spiritual synthesis of an epoch, Burckhardt's history became a kind of historical sociology closer to the typological sociology of Max Weber than to any of the other major nineteenth-century historians. With special frequency he went to the artists, writers, and poets rather than to the usual historical sources for clues to the distinctive meaning of an epoch. The major forces of history as he saw them were the state, religion, and culture (in its broadest sense including the arts). An important characteristic of an epoch depended on which of these forces played the major role in initiating the civilizational synthesis. In evaluating the nineteenth century in these terms Burckhardt was unusually sensitive to its potentialities. He was convinced that the growth of state power in all spheres would eventually result in an extensive loss of civil liberties and that the democrats were sacrificing liberalism for paternalistic control. He believed that socialism, in the end, would terminate the democratic tendency and that, in any case, political and military machines were being developed that would be available as instruments for

---

[3]Jacob Burckhardt, *Force and Freedom: Reflections on History,* ed. James Hastings Nichols (New York: Pantheon Books, 1943), p. 80.
[4]Jacob Burckhardt's major works include: *Gesamtausgabe,* 14 vols. (Stuttgart: Deutsche Verlags-Anstant, 1929–1934); *The Age of Constantine the Great,* first published as *Die Zeit Constatin's des Grossen* (1853) (New York: Pantheon, 1949); *Der Cicerone: Eine Einleitung zum Genuss der Kunstwerke Italiens* [The Cicerone: An Introduction to the Enjoyment of Italian Art] (Leipzig: Kröner, 1925); *The Civilization of the Renaissance in Italy,* first published as *Die Kultur der Renaissance in Italien,* 1860 (London: Phaidon, 1955); *Griechische Kulturgeschichte* [The Cultural History of Greece], 4 vols. (Basel: Schwabe, 1956–1957); *Force and Freedom: Reflections on History* (New York: Pantheon, 1943); *Judgments on History and Historians,* trans. Harry Zohn (Boston: Beacon, 1958).
[5]Burckhardt, *Force and Freedom: Reflections on History,* pp. 81–82.

[6]*Ibid.,* p. 85.

political adventurers ruthless enough to seize and exploit them by force. The growth of nationalism and militarism suggested to Burckhardt that Europe was entering upon an era of wars in which Germany would have to contend with Russia. He believed the political and economic revolution would have disastrous effects on the arts, scholarship, and education. It seemed to him that the social basis for higher culture was disintegrating and a new type of philistinism was appearing. He anticipated that anti-Semitism would become an ideological weapon and with the recession of liberal Protestantism only the conservative churches would offer major resistance to the new (totalitarian) tendencies. Burckhardt never forgot that only individuals make history and only they invent new forms; hence, he placed special stress on great individuals and, in a manner anticipating Weber's conception of charismatic leadership, argued that sometimes they are essential to strike out new solutions of humanity's spiritual impasses.

Friedrich Nietzsche. Friedrich Wilhelm Nietzsche (1844–1900) was the son of a protestant pastor. Under the influence of the Hellenist scholar Friedrich Ritschl at Leipzig and Bonn he was emancipated from Lutheranism, but all his life he was in search of something to supply ultimate meaning to life. As professor of Greek at Basel from 1869–1879 he became friends with Jacob Burckhardt, Franz Overbeck, an historian of Christianity, and the paleontologist Rütimeyer. He developed a close friendship with Richard Wagner. After 1879, Nietzsche spent his summers in the Engadine and winters at the Riviera of Genoa or Nice. In January, 1889, while at Turin, he lost his sanity and spent his last years in an asylum.

Nietzsche's thought,[7] in the view of Charles

FRIEDRICH NIETZSCHE

Brown Brothers

Andler,[8] has alternated between periods of imaginative vision and analysis: (1) a Wagnerian period (1869–1876); (2) a period of intellectual evolutionism (1876–1881); (3) a period of lyrical affirmation (1882–1885); and (4) a period of reflections on cultural decadence and renaissance (1885–1888). In his Wagnerian period Nietzsche maintained that the highest point in Hellenic culture was reached when Greek tragedy, evolving from the primitive dithyramb, fused the Apollonian vision of the Ionian philosopher and the ecstasy of Dionysius, god of death and resurrec-

[7]Friedrich Nietzsche's complete works appear in the *Musarion* edition of *Gesammelte Werke*, 23 vols. (Leipzig, 1920–1929). There are three collected editions in English: (1) *The Complete Works*, ed. Dr. Oscar Levy; (2) *The Philosophy of Nietzsche* (a Modern Library giant) which includes five of his most important works; (3) *The Portable Nietzsche,* selected and edited by Walter Kaufmann (New York: Viking, 1954).

[8]Charles Andler, *Nietzsche, sa vie et sa pensee* [The Life and Thought of Nietzsche] 6 vols. (Paris, 1920–1931). For a brief overview see Charles Andler, "Nietzsche," *Encyclopaedia of the Social Sciences* (New York: Macmillan, 1931) XI, 373–375.

tion. In the work of Schopenhauer and music of Wagner, this spirit is reborn. Wagner performed a similar fusion for the present. Nietzsche was convinced at the time that the philosopher, the saint, and the creative artist represent three types of human greatness revealed in culture. As he reflected on the means to fulfill this vision of culture, the synthesis disintegrated under Nietzsche's analysis: science seemed to him to have destroyed belief in geniuses, heroes, and saints and the new evolutionism supplied biological and evolutionary foundations for individual and social morality, which have their roots in the will to power. Nietzsche decided that trust had to be placed in reason and the creation of a society of free spirits. The state had to be deprived of its functions of justice and war; nationalistic bourgeois culture and the multiplicity of national cultures had to be replaced by a pan-European society. In this formulation, the powerful influence of Burckhardt was everywhere present and Nietzsche's arguments amount to a restatement of Burckhardt's position and attitudes.

In a visionary period between 1882 and 1885 in *Thus Spoke Zarathustra*, a gospel written in poetic prose, the prophet Zarathustra teaches two mysteries, "eternal recurrence" and the "superman." Zarathustra proclaims the downfall of present-day conventional values and the birth of a new era, with a new morality, and vistas of unsuspected human greatness.

To Nietzsche's last period belong brilliant statements of the implications of the waning of traditional religious faith (the "death of God"), analyses of the ethics of democracy, interpretations of traditional Christianity and Judaism as slave moralities or moralities of humility, and analyses of the role of resentment by the masses in democratic and socialistic societies. Nietzsche argued that a race of blonde beasts had set in motion all that was progressive in Western society; that a master race had created a warlike ethics in contrast to the slave morality of serfs and servants. Nietzsche now argued that Christianity, with ethics of humility and equalitarian revolt, had ruined the Renaissance and continues to spread its rot

through socialism and neo-romanticism. It even corrupted the great art of Wagner. This will continue unless a new race of supermen is established. Such arguments had enough superficial similarity to some of those of the National Socialist Party of Hitler's Germany to lead to some minor attempts to use Nietzsche for totalitarian purposes. However, these moves were quickly abandoned, for anyone who took the trouble to examine Nietzsche discovered that he was advocating an extreme form of responsible individualism and the Nazi program involved a form of regimentation of the kind Nietzsche most despised.

The basic theme running through both the synthetic and analytical phases of Nietzsche's thought was the conviction that new scope had to be found for individuals against all the forces tending to destroy them. In his last period he had come to the conclusion that neither the combination of Schopenhauer and Wagner nor the Apollonian vision of history as a work of art by Burckhardt were sufficient, but a new, more positive basis of individualism had to be found. He epitomized this in his concepts of eternal recurrence (which gave absolute value to the present moment by assimilating it to eternity) and the variation that only a new superior form of individuality (the superman) could cope with it.

INTUITIONISM AND PHENOMENOLOGY

The first edition of *Nature and Types* made note of the influences of individualistic critics of social thought and social life on nineteenth-century social science. The holistic traditions, positivistic organicism and conflict theory, assumed a voluntaristic form, in part, in accommodation to these critics. Moreover, the individualistic critics were in some measure responsible for the rise of neo-Kantian and neo-Idealistic forms of elementarism. Phenomenological sociology, in the first edition, was treated as a special departure from neo-Kantianism.

When, in reaction to the holistic trends, social

philosophers returned for inspiration to the elementarists, or individualists of the eighteenth century, Kant was a logical reference point, for at the end of the first great wave of recent Western philosophical development he had tried to map the boundaries of all of its major divisions. Kant had located the *Critique of Pure Reason* in the center of his interpretations, establishing the natural limits of scientific thinking and placing metaphysics and ethics, in principle, outside its boundaries. The *Critique of Practical Reason* systematized, from an elementaristic point of view, the problem of morality and ethics, and the *Critique of Judgment* performed a similar operation for the problems of taste and aesthetics. However, the order in which Kant found it convenient to review the major divisions of thought, beginning with the place of science does not mean that "pure reason" — that is, rational scientific knowledge of phenomena — is more important than practical reason — judgments of morality and ethics. Although some of the neo-Kantians were inclined to take the *Critique of Pure Reason* as a basis for their own reflection, others worked primarily from the *Critique of Practical Reason* or *The Critique of Judgment*. These groups of neo-Kantians divided over the question whether, in an age of science, all other philosophical issues should be subordinated to the critical examination of the foundation of knowledge or whether the problems of the morality of religion were of greater importance than the problems of science. This second position was taken by Cassirer in his statement in the *Encyclopaedia of the Social Sciences*. Still other students noted that in the *Critique of Judgment*, Kant developed formulations that appear to mediate the problems of the other two critiques. They were inclined to interpret Kant as locating the problem of ends and purposes (teleology) at the core of religion, science, and art. In such fashion, the neo-Kantians differentiated into subgroups.

However different in their interpretations and specific areas of interest, common to the neo-Kantians was an antipathy to preoccupation with philosophical systems and a stress on rationalism and on empirical methods. Whether they were primarily interested in religion, in value, or in knowledge, the neo-Kantians were inclined to review a specific body of experience or phenomena and to approach it by way of distinctions between form and content. They conceived their fundamental task as discovering the basic forms that organized diverse contents.

It was perhaps inevitable that some scholars would break with the rationalistic-scientific bias of the neo-Kantians as well as with their search for forms which eclipsed content in importance (this last was a major component in the development of neo-Idealism). At present, however, we will trace the modification of neo-Kantian approaches in the various forms of psychologism, which led eventually to intuitionism and to phenomenology.

Charles Renouvier. Charles Renouvier (1815–1903) was the founder of a theory, based on the study of Kant, known as "phenomenalism" or "neo-criticism."[9] Reality, he held, is the fact of consciousness and the system of relations between the facts of consciousness. Renouvier thought in this manner to eliminate the noumena, thus reversing the usual attempt to reduce phenomena to noumena.

Whereas for Kant the categories were brought to experience by the subject, for Renouvier they were already present in phenomena as the most general relations. Number, for instance, was thought to be the relation of plurality to quantitative unity. Similarly, Dauriac[10] applied the notion of contingency to the Kantian categories, treating them not as necessary but conditional. Renouvier attempted to solve the antinomies of pure reason on the basis of phenomenal relations. For example, the antinomy of the finite and infinite is approached from the point of view that an actual infinite is impossible. The world is internally finite,

[9]See Charles Renouvier, *Essais de critique générale. Premier essai: Traité de logique générale* ["Essays in General Criticism. First Essay: Treatise on General Logic"] 2d ed. (Paris: 1875).
[10]Lionel Dauriac, "Essai sur les catégories," *L'Année philosophique, 1900* (Paris: F. Alcan, 1901), pp. 29–63.

with a definite measurable size beyond which there is nothing. However, it cannot actually be measured by the beings who are a part of it, for they can only investigate relations less than the whole — relations subordinate to other relations. Ruggiero not unfairly observes that the contradiction which Kant had tried to avoid with his distinction between noumena and phenomena has obscurely crept back, now appearing as a contradiction of method.

Renouvier gradually abandoned his phenomenalism. Organic forms increasingly appeared to him to be genuine individualities, not mere aggregates. In the study of personality, he came to recognize that the individual possesses a unifying power he had originally denied to it. There is a connection between volitional acts and personality, making it impossible to view the self as a mere aggregate of sensations. Increasingly he saw the presence of freedom as the thing that binds a being in countless relations to other beings. Eventually, in *The New Monadology,* he conceived the person as the center of spontaneity, a representative power endowed with the faculty of producing representations.[11]

Franz Brentano. Franz Brentano (1838–1917), who was trained as a priest and tried, rather unsuccessfully, to combine the roles of priest and philosopher, is considered by Herbert Spiegelberg to be one of the forerunners of phenomenology.[12] After seven years teaching at the University of Würtzburg, Brentano resigned from the priesthood, thus losing his university position. He was appointed, in 1864, to a full professorship at the University of Vienna, but six years later, when he decided to marry, again lost his position. He continued teaching for fifteen more years as an unsalaried lecturer, but in 1895 when the permanent appointment he had been led to expect was denied, he retired from teaching. He spent the rest of his life as a private scholar in Italy and Switzerland. Some of his students, including Alexius Meinong, Carl Stumpf, and Edmund Husserl, became brilliant successes.

Brentano's training centered on Aristotle and the scholastics, of whom he was critical. He conceived the period in Western philosophy from Bacon through Descartes, Locke, and Leibnitz as a high point, and developments from Kant through the Idealists as a decline. He responded warmly to the British empiricism, and carried on an extensive correspondence with John Stuart Mill. He liked Auguste Comte, despite Comte's atheism, though he did not accept Comte's rejection of either metaphysics or psychology.[13] His studies of Mill were a component in his view that the reconstruction of philosophy could only be accomplished through the empirical analysis of experience and the founding of a more adequate science of psychology. He approached experience in the spirit of Descartes, convinced that analysis would reveal necessary empirical relationships. He divided psychology into descriptive and genetic; descriptive psychology, resting on the intuitive examination of phenomena to establish general or structural relationships was defined as independent of and logically prior to genetic psychology.

Brentano thought the immediate awareness of feelings was self-evident and infallible in contrast to the unreliability of introspection or self-observation. The most basic problem of psychology is to distinguish psychological from physical phenomena. The peculiarity of psychological phenomena is found in their *intentionality;* psychological phenomena always refer to an object. "In the representation . . . something is repre-

[11]Charles Renouvier and L. Prat, *La Nouvelle monadologie* (Paris: A. Colin, 1899). See Ruggiero's summary of Renouvier's position in *Modern Philosophy,* trans. A. Howard Hannay and R. G. Collingwood (New York: Macmillan, 1921), pp. 141–147.

[12]Herbert Spiegelberg, *The Phenomenological Movement* (The Hague: Martinus Nijhoff, 1976), pp. 25–50. Among Brentano's major works are: *Psychologie vom empirischen Standpunkt* [Psychology from an Empirical Point of View] (1874), and *Vom Ursprung sittlicher Erkenntnis* [The Origins of Customary Knowledge] (1889).

[13]*August Comte und die positive Philosophie in die vier Phases der Philosophie* [August Comte and Positivism in the Four Phases of Philosophy] (Leipzig: Meiner, 1962), pp. 99f.

sented, in the judgment something is acknowledged or rejected, in desiring it is desired. . . . No physical phenomena shows anything like it. And thus we can define psychical phenomena by saying that they are such phenomena as contain objects in themselves by way of intention."[14] Psychological phenomena always consist in acts referring to objects. Such acts fall into three groups: representations, judgments, and states of feeling or desire. Of these three, representations are primary, providing the foundation for judgment and emotional response. One can conceive of a being without judgment and love, equipped only with representations, but the reverse is not conceivable.

Brentano resolved to his own satisfaction the puzzle of time by treating it as the way phenomena are referred to when they are represented. The present mode is stated directly, the past and future only indirectly by reference to the present. He treated belief in standards of right and wrong analogously to the notion of self-evidence. Theoretical judgments and ethical judgments, he thought, are parallel in that they are founded on representation and are either positive or negative. Valid thinking, according to logical norms, has a natural superiority. Similarly, right is experienced as self-evidently preferable to wrong. "Everyone experiences the difference between the one and the other kind of judging; here, as anywhere else, the final elucidation can consist only in pointing to this experience, just as in the case of any other concept."[15]

Carl Stumpf. Carl Stumpf (1848–1936), the first of Brentano's students to achieve major success, at the age of twenty-five was Brentano's successor at Würtzburg. He taught successively at Prague, Halle (where he was joined by Husserl, sent on from Vienna by Brentano), Munich, and Berlin. Stumpf, in Spiegelberg's opinion, not only used

the term *phenomenology* before Husserl but played a major role in the introduction of phenomenological methods into psychology, where they had influence on the gestaltists and the field theorists: Wolfgang Köhler, Max Wertheimer, Kurt Koffka, and Kurt Lewin. He also became friends with and had some influence on William James.[16]

Phenomenology, to Stumpf, was the study of primary and secondary phenomena: the contents of immediate experience given to the senses (primary) and images of these in memory (secondary). Phenomena do not include mental contents formed by the mind (concepts, values or constructs, and relations). The study of phenomena is a neutral science and inasmuch as no concepts can be built without the material supplied by phenomena, phenomenology is a fundamental stage in the discipline of every established science. Stumpf believed that there was considerable value in the employment of experimental techniques in the services of phenomenological description. He distinguished between dependent (inseparable even in imagination) and independent parts of experience and maintained that phenomenological analysis revealed (in contrast to Hume) not only linkages but feeling states, and argued that structural laws not based on induction were discoverable among phenomena.

As in the case of his teacher Brentano, Stumpf was positivistic and sought to establish psychology as a fundamental scientific discipline. His work signals the break of phenomenological psychology from general philosophy.

Henri Bergson. Henri Louis Bergson (1859–1941) was born in Paris. He was admitted to the École normale in 1879 where he earned the doctorate in 1889. After holding various professorships in provincial lycées, he became *maître de conferences* at

---

[14]Quoted by Spiegelberg, *The Phenomenological Movement*, pp. 39–40.
[15]Brentano, *Vom Ursprung sittlicher Erkenntnis*, Par. 26, quoted by Spiegelberg, *The Phenomenological Movement*, p. 46.

[16]Among Stumpf's major works are: *Tonpsychologie* [The Psychology of Music] (1883); *Erscheinung und psychische Funktionen* [Appearance and Psychic Functions] (1906); *Selbstdarsellung* [Self-Presentation] (1924); *Erkenntnisleher* [Theory of Knowledge], 2 vols., ed. Felix Stumpf (Leipzig: Johan Ambrosius Barth, 1939).

HENRI BERGSON

Brown Brothers

the École normale superieure in 1897 and a member of the College de France in 1901. In 1918 Bergson gave up teaching to devote himself to political and international affairs. He was head of a mission to America and, in the 1920s, President of the Committee of Intellectual Cooperation.

Bergson marks a further stage in elementaristic reaction to nineteenth-century holism and system building. His object was to justify the belief that values, freedom, and creativity are the central characteristics of individual experience, which, in turn, is the central reality of human social life. In contrast to Brentano and Stumpf, who took their point of departure from the empiricists, particularly Hume, in their attempts to establish a more adequate scientific psychology, Bergson worked from Kant's formulations. His point of attack was the problem of time, which emerges as the central

issue whenever one takes the individual experience, which always occurs only in special time and circumstances, as the starting point for analysis. In Western thought since Plato, ultimate reality had been envisioned as timeless essence. When one deals with the individual, however, time is inseparable from the reality.

In *Time and Free Will: An Essay on the Immediate Data of Consciousness,*[17] which he developed and wrote between 1883 and 1887 and first published in French in 1889, Bergson established the basic position he was to continue to apply to various areas throughout the rest of his life. As did Schopenhauer, Bergson began with the Kantian distinction between the *Critique of Pure Reason* (the phenomenal knowledge of science) and the *Critique of Practical Reason* (the sphere of actual moral conduct); however, he handled the problem differently. He considered immediate experience as the primary reality and viewed the rational interpretation of it as a special departure within and from it. The world of the concept, of reason, and of science is one of fixed forms, magnitudes, and quantities. Immediate experience, on the other hand, is a flux, a process which continually casts up new forms; it is spontaneous and rarely predictable in advance.

Bergson abandoned the distinction between pure and practical reason, substituting for them the contrast between concepts and a more fundamental mental activity, intuition. Kant's distinction between perception (apprehension of the descriptive properties of phenomena) and conception was subject to reconstruction. The two basic forms of perception for Kant were space and time. However, Bergson maintained that they are different. In immediate experience time is apprehended in intuition. Conceptualization is essentially a reorganization of experience on the model of space. The idea of a homogeneous, measurable time, the abstract time of mathematics

[17]Henri Bergson, *Time and Free Will: An Essay on the Immediate Data of Consciousness,* trans. F. L. Pogson (New York: Harper, 1960).

and physics and, to some extent, language and common sense, is an artificial construct formed by the reorganization of the realm of pure duration.

There is a strong antipositivistic component in Bergson's formulation. Bergsonianism became synonymous with the apotheosis of intuition and the depreciation of concepts, and with the proposal that cultural progress is only possible by disregarding general theories and universal systems, and considering rather a closer adaptation to the true nature of things as apprehended intuition. Bergson believed the most essential component in human social life to be spontaneous creativity, which lies at the base of all movement and change.

Edmund Husserl. The phenomenalism of Renouvier took its point of departure from Kant. So also did the phenomenology of Edmund Husserl (1859–1938). Renouvier attempted to dispose of the noumena by taking phenomena as ultimate. But he was led step by step from this position, through his interest in living being, personality, and individual consciousness, eventually to an idealistic position reminiscent of that of Leibnitz. Husserl, too, seems to have had Kant in mind when he advanced his formulations. He did not, however, as did Renouvier, attempt the reduction of all reality to phenomena, but rather took the intuition of phenomena as fundamental to the approach to any and all forms of reality.[18]

Husserl assumed that there is a real external world which can be known. Experience, which must be consulted for access to this world, consists of both objects and essential objects or essences. The sense qualities of an object consist of its essences. Corresponding to these are cognitive relationships. The existence and meaning of objects are independent of the subject and act of cognition. These, existence and meaning, yield themselves in special modes of experience. All knowl-

EDMUND HUSSERL

Historical Picture Service, Chicago

edge is based on experience in which objects are presented. The central problem of Husserl's epistemology is the investigation of how objects are known by immanent inspection, since they are known only when they become part of pure consciousness. His method is that of phenomenological reduction.[19]

Like Renouvier, the starting point for Husserl's position is the assumption that understanding may operate with phenomena without need to appeal to an "unknowable." Kant's fundamental error, according to Husserl, was his assumption that the

[18]Edmund Husserl, *Ideen zu einer reinen Phänomenologie und phänomenologischen Philosophie* (Halle: Niemeyer, 1913); trans. W. R. Boyce Gibson as *Ideas: General Introduction to Pure Phenomenology* (New York: Macmillan, 1931).

[19]For an excellent analysis of Husserl's phenomenology, see E. Parl Welch, *The Philosophy of Edmund Husserl* (New York: Columbia University Press, 1941), especially pp. 203–204.

only objects of experience and cognition are those of a sensory character. Instead, it was Husserl's opinion that there are many kinds of experience. Phenomena are not, as for Kant, constructions of consciousness; they are essences (Greek "eidos") forming the content of pure consciousness.

Husserl's aim was to establish phenomenology as an "eidetic" science, as the theory of the essentiality of the transcendentally purified consciousness. His method is a special kind of "reduction" as a refined analysis of the properties of conscious experience. Husserl believed that there are two kinds of experience: natural and eidetic. The content of knowledge consists of natural objects and their intrinsic phenomenal essentiality.

There is an important difference between the naturalistic and the phenomenological attitude. As natural human creatures, we will, judge, and feel. We are aware of the world in space and time as a becoming without end. We are aware of our selves and others in a world of nature and events. The phenomenological method consists in the analysis of experience to discriminate within it its various properties. It involves an eventual reduction of experience to pure consciousness and its correlates. The method assumes that every experience has essences accessible to intuitive apprehension. Husserl's ultimate objective was the investigation of pure consciousness and its correlative realm of eidetic being. To arrive at this, it is necessary that the world of objects and the "I" as a psychophysical organism be "put aside" or "bracketed" for the purpose of gaining an intuitive vision of the pure sphere of transcendental subjectivity.

The first step in the application of the phenomenological method of reduction is the differentiation of the natural and eidetic realms. The second major step is distinguishing between "immanent" and "transcendent" essences. Transcendent essences include such essences as "thing," "spatial shape," "movement," "color of a thing," and "quality of character." The transcendent essences are required for knowledge of the physical objects of nature. The second act of bracketing holds the transcendent essences apart from analysis and moves on to the immanent essences of pure consciousness. Within the world of immanent essence one may arrive, by further successive acts of bracketing, at a pure ego.

George Santayana. On the American scene, an analysis very similar to Husserl's was developed by George Santayana (1863–1952), who also argued that the complex world of ordinary existence involves many inferential elements. "Existence . . . not being included in any immediate datum, is a fact always open to doubt."[20] One may, however, by "a difficult suspension of judgment" deprive "a given image of all adventitious significance, when it is taken neither for the manifestation of a substance nor for an idea in a mind nor for an event in a world, but simply if a color for that color and if music for that music." When this is done, "scepticism at last has touched bottom, and my doubt has found honorable rest in the absolutely indubitable. Whatever essence I find and note, that essence and no other is established before me. I cannot be mistaken about it, since I now have no object of intent other than the object of intuition."[21]

Husserl and Santayana are not altogether similar, for Husserl seems to feel that for every phenomenon that can be known there is some corresponding essence, while Santayana suggests that one rises from essence to existence by a leap of imagination. The leap is taken when one hypostatizes an essence into a fact, locating it in relations not given within it. This rests not on essence, but on animal faith. The existence of things and one's self is not founded on reasons, but on action. It is a faith which does no "violence to a sceptical analysis of experience; on the contrary, it takes advantage of that analysis to interpret this volatile experience as all animals do and must, as a set of symbols for existences that cannot enter experience."[22]

Each essence has a character distinguishing it from all others. It has an inalienable individuality which renders the essence a universal. However,

[20]George Santayana, *Scepticism and Animal Faith* (New York: Scribner's, 1923), pp. 39–40.
[21]*Ibid.*, p. 74.
[22]*Ibid.*, p. 106.

GEORGE SANTAYANA

United Press International Photo

essences do not exist. The realm of matter is the second realm of being. It is the field of action. It is essentially dynamic. The existence of this realm is a matter of animal faith. The third realm of being is the realm of truth, of things seen under the form of eternity. Beyond this is the realm of the spirit.[23]

TOWARD SYNTHESIS

In the long run, theory and method cannot remain separate. When reactions to nineteenth-century

holism led to a reconceptualization of the problems and place of the individual in society, it forced reconsideration of the methods by which social life is most effectively studied. The group of thinkers from Schopenhauer to Nietzsche who illustrated the rediscovery of the individual brought into focus a whole series of properties which had earlier been treated as marginal: the individual's irrationally negative sentiments (capacity for envy, spite, jealousy), frequent lack of courage, creativity, capacity for faith. The methodological counterpart to this new emphasis on the individual varied from a restructured psychology to serve as a foundational discipline to all humanistic and behavioral studies, through a new empiricism and phenomenological analysis, to intuitionism. It was perhaps inevitable that the new substantive theories of the individual that came to be designated as existentialism should be joined to the series of methodological procedures centering on phenomenology.

However, it should be noted that there is considerable ambiguity as to precisely what is or is not to be included in both existentialism and phenomenology. Existentialism has been described as a religious search for meaning, but few collections of existentialists would eliminate such atheists as Heidegger and Sartre while including Kierkegaard and Jaspers. Moreover, in his preface to his history of the phenomenological movement, Spiegelberg maintains:

> Among the many misconceptions which this book is meant to rectify is the idea that there is such a thing as a system or school called "Phenomenology" with a solid body of teachings which would permit one to give a precise answer to the question "What is phenomenology?"[24]

In Spiegelberg's view phenomenology and existentialism were antagonistic in Germany, but almost identical in France.[25] So far as existentialism

---

[23]Santayana develops these ideas not only in *Scepticism and Animal Faith* but also in *The Realm of Essence* (1927), *The Realm of Matter* (1930), *The Realm of Truth* (1938), and *The Realm of Spirit* (1940), all published by Charles Scribner's Sons, New York.

[24]Spiegelberg, *History of the Phenomenological Movement*, p. xxvii.
[25]*Ibid.*, II, 408f.

and phenomenology lack clearly defined central characteristics there will inevitably be confusion, not only as to whom is or is not to be included in each, but what membership is to be assigned to the areas of their overlap.

Much of the ambiguity concerning existentialism, phenomenology, and their interrelation can be eliminated if one realizes that they are both elementaristic reactions against holist theories of society and collectivistic social trends. The chief difference between them is that existentialism is concerned with substantive problems of the nature of individuals and their predicament; phenomenology (along with psychologism, that is, the consideration of psychology as a foundational discipline of others, and intuitionism, the view that intuition is a more fundamental methodology than either conceptualization or the analysis of immediate experience) is chiefly preoccupied with methodological problems. It was only natural that these two branches of elementarism should join forces. Moreover, Spiegelberg's observation about the phenomenologists applies equally to the existentialists: that they are too individualistic to form organized schools.[26] Nevertheless, there is an elective affinity between existential theories of the contemporary individual and the methodologies of the phenomenologists, though, of course, existential theories can be developed by nonphenomenological methods and phenomenological methods, when they prove to be trustworthy, can be applied to nonexistential theories. By joining the forces of existentialism and phenomenology, thinkers opened the prospect of developing a fully constituted body of theory and a research tradition, which neither could hope to achieve alone. In varying ways both traditions are combined in the works of Jaspers, Heidegger, and Sartre, who will be presented as illustrative of the many thinkers in the combined movement.

Karl Jaspers. Karl Jaspers (1893–1969) was born at Oldenberg in 1883, the son of a bank manager.

[26]*Ibid.*, I, 22.

KARL JASPERS

German Information Center

His initial interest was in law, which he pursued at Heidelberg and Munich. He later shifted to medicine, which he studied at Berlin, Göttingen, and Heidelberg. Work as a scientific assistant in the psychiatric clinic in Heidelberg before World War I marked another shift of interest to psychiatry and psychology on the way to philosophy. Jaspers was appointed to the chair of philosophy at Heidelberg in 1921. During the National Socialist regime Jaspers, who was married to a Jewish woman, went into voluntary retirement, returning to teaching only in 1945 with the end of World War II. However, he soon left Germany to become professor of philosophy at Basel. He remained in Switzerland until his death.

Already in his *Psychology of World-Views* (1919), Jaspers had conceived Kierkegaard and Nietzsche as joint prophets of the dilemma of the contemporary individual and had formulated the major themes of existentialism.[27] A review of his basic existentialist philosophy appears in his *Way to Wisdom*. As in other of his writings, Jaspers made the underlying Kantian structure of his thought apparent. Fundamentally he accepts the Kantian distinction between the world of concern to science, phenomena, and the world of things-in-themselves. Empirical existence is the sphere of science.

> Fundamentally we can express the reality of the world as the *phenomenality* of empirical existence. Everything we have said thus far: that there is an element of suspension in all modes of reality; that world systems represent merely relative perspectives; that knowledge has the character of interpretation; that being is manifested in the dichotomy of subject and object — our whole characterization of the knowledge to which man can attain — implies that objects are mere appearances; no being that we know is being in itself and as a whole. The phenomenality of the empirical world was made fully clear by Kant.[28]

This phenomenal world, bounded by existence and transcendence, is the proper sphere of enlightened thought. It is the sphere of science, which was itself one of the finest products of the Enlightenment. Jaspers does not agree with those existentialists who see science as an enemy.

In opposition to these beliefs we are certain that today there can be no integrity, reason, or human dignity without a true scientific attitude, where tradition and situation make this attitude possible. Where science is lost man falls into the twilight of vaguely edifying sentiments, of fanatical decisions arrived at in self-willed blindness. Barriers are erected, man is led into new prisons.[29]

However, Jaspers was opposed to all who treat science as the norm of all knowledge and who seek to give philosophy an exact scientific foundation.

> They seized upon questions which, they claimed, were reserved for philosophy because they concern all the sciences; namely, logic, epistemology, phenomenology. In an effort to refurbish its reputation, philosophy became a servile imitator, a handmaiden to the sciences. It proceeded to establish in theory the validity of scientific knowledge, which was not questioned anyhow.... Today many thinkers regard symbolic logic as the whole of philosophy.[30]

The identification of modern science and modern philosophy is catastrophic.[31] Marx's absolute, for example, "originated in a conception of philosophy as total, systematic knowledge; but at the same time his doctrine is presented as a result of modern science, from which it does not follow."[32] It is, in fact, a new kind of fanaticism which invokes not faith but modern science and, in fact, runs directly counter to the scientific spirit. Whenever science seeks to take over the sphere of values the results are disastrous.

> In his debunking psychology Freud naturalized and trivialized the sublime insights of Kierkegaard and Nietzsche. A barren, hateful Weltanschauung masked by humanitarian forms was indeed appropriate to an age whose hypocrisy it pitilessly dissected, but Freud failed to see that this world was not the whole world.[33]

[27]Among Karl Jaspers' major works are: *Philosophie* (Heidelberg-Berlin: Springer-Verlag, 1948); *Von der Wahrheit* [On Truth] (Munich: R. Piper, 1948); *Der Philosophische Glaube* [Philosophical Belief] (1948), English trans. Ralph Manheim (New York: Philosophical Library, 1949); *Die geistige Situation der Zeit*, English edition, *Man in the Modern Age* (London: Routledge and Kegan Paul, 1934); *Von Ursprung und Ziel der Geschichte*, English edition, *The Origin and Goal of History* (London: Routledge and Kegan Paul, 1949); *Vom Europäischen Geist* (1947), English edition, *The European Spirit* (London: S.C.M. Press, 1948); *Allgemein Psychopathologie* [General Psychopathology] 5th ed. (Heidelberg-Berlin: Springer Verlag, 1949); *Way to Wisdom*, trans. Ralph Manheim (New Haven: Yale University Press, 1954).
[28]Jaspers, *Way to Wisdom*, p. 79.

[29]*Ibid.*, p. 91.
[30]*Ibid.*, pp. 148–149.
[31]*Ibid.*, p. 153.
[32]*Ibid.*, p. 155.
[33]*Ibid.*, p. 190.

As did Kant in the *Critique of Pure Reason,* Jaspers wished to keep science pure, but to confine it strictly to its appropriate sphere. He argued that a pure science, moreover, requires a pure philosophy. "Science left to itself as mere science becomes homeless. The intellect is a whore, said Nicholas of Cusa, for it can prostitute itself to anything. Science is a whore, said Lenin, for it sells itself to any class interest."[34] The motives for philosophy, according to Jaspers, are wonder (expressed by Plato), doubt (expressed by Descartes) and a sense of forsakenness (expressed by Epicurus and the Stoics). It searches for knowledge, certainty, and the realization of self. In his characterization of our times as an age of unprecedented ruin, which call for the reconstruction of philosophy, Jaspers takes the same basic view as Kierkegaard and Nietzsche.

> In all past history there was a self-evident bond between man and man, in stable communities, in institutions, and in universal ideas. Even the isolated individual was in a sense sustained in his isolation. The most visible sign of today's disintegration is that more and more men do not understand one another, and they meet and scatter, that they are indifferent to one another, that there is no longer any reliable community or loyalty.[35]

It is the human state that is the starting point for philosophy, a state that also recalls the formulations of Kierkegaard and Nietzsche.

> We are always in situations. Situations change, opportunities arise. If they are missed they never return. I myself can work to change the situation. But there are situations which remain essentially the same even if their momentary aspect changes and their shattering force is obscured: I must die, I must suffer, I must struggle, I am subject to chance, I involve myself inexorably in guilt. We call these fundamental situations of our existence ultimate situations . . . to ultimate situations we react either by obfuscations or,

if we really apprehend them, by despair and rebirth: we become ourselves by change in our consciousness of being.[36]

Martin Heidegger. Martin Heidegger (1889–1976), born in a Roman Catholic family of Messkirch, Baden, the Black Forest, was initially trained as a Jesuit seminarian in the Thomist tradition, but later was affected by the neo-Kantian tradition, to which he was exposed in an academic department of philosophy under the supervision of Heinrich Rickert. He traced his own interest in the problem of Being to the reading of Franz Brentano's essay *On the Manifold Meanings of Being in Aristotle* (1862). His habilitation thesis was on "Die Kategorien-und Bedeutungslehre des Duns Scotus" [Dun Scotus on the Science of Categories and Meanings] (1915). In 1916 Heidegger came under the influence of Husserl, becoming convinced that phenomenology offers the possibility of the reconstruction of philosophy. In 1923 Heidegger was appointed professor of philosophy at the University of Marburg. In 1927 he published what many scholars feel is his greatest book *"Being" and "Time."* In 1929 he was appointed as Husserl's successor to the chair of Philosophy in Freiburg. Under the National Socialist regime in 1933 Heidegger was elected Rector of Freiburg University, giving and later publishing an address on the position of the German universities in which he urged support of the new regime. For the rest of his life, Heidegger was under a cloud because of his support of the Nazis. In 1934 he resigned as Rector, though he remained as professor of philosophy. He claimed to have repudiated his support of the Nazis, but his critics have argued that evidence for this is ambiguous. In 1945 he was dismissed from his position for his alleged sympathies with and support of the Nazis.[37]

[34]*Ibid.,* p. 158.
[35]*Ibid.,* p. 25.
[36]*Ibid.,* pp. 19–20.
[37]Heidegger's major works include: *Sein und Zeit* [Being and Time], first published in *Jahrbuch für Philosophie und phanomenologische Forschung,* Vol. VII (1927); *Kant und das Problem der Metaphysik* [Kant and the Problem of Metaphysics] (Bonn: Verlag Fred. Cohen, 1929); *Was ist*

MARTIN HEIDEGGER

United Press International Photo

If one accepts the invitation that had repeatedly been extended to *Western* thinkers since Descartes, an invitation also vigorously renewed by Husserl in his phenomenology, to analyze reality, Kierkegaard and Nitzsche had a point: the first thing one must take into account before one starts to philosophize is that one is "there" present at some particular time and place. However, Heidegger did not proceed at the task of analysis in quite the same man-

ner as Husserl, who bracketed the natural attitude in his hurry to locate the transcendental subject. Heidegger, rather, focused attention on this very natural attitude and criticized the traditional procedure by which Western thinkers carried out their empirical analyses. As they undertook their analyses they assumed that there were two entities, mind and matter, subject and object. Basic to their method was their consideration of the subject as an observer, which posed the problems of how a spiritual subject could have knowledge of a material object or how a material object could influence a spiritual subject. And, still worse, they assumed a distinction between observation and action, and had difficulty deciding how to reconcile fact and value. In contrast to this tradition was Brentano's interpretation that when an individual wakes up to consciousness, he or she becomes aware of the self only as an incidental result of the fact that consciousness is always consciousness of something, it is *intentional*. What one is aware of is always located in a context of intentions.

Being-in-the-world, which, Heidegger maintains, is characteristic of human existence, means to be immersed in it as an actor responding to and being responded to by others, that is, to be concerned or have care about them. The problem of thought emerges out of action; the problems of meaning, significance, and value, arise out of concern. There are three aspects of concern with things that are authentic (based on an individual's relation to things in terms of the whole structure of what he or she really is) or inauthentic (based on an individual's particularistic concern to such an extent that he or she fails to respond to his or her full potentialities). The three aspects of authentic concern toward things are the discovery of the self as already in the world (*Befindlichkeit*), understanding (*Verstehen*), and discourse (*Rede*); the corresponding inauthentic forms are ambiguity (*Zeideutigkeit*), curiosity (*Neugier*), and prattle (*Gerede*).[38]

Metaphysik? [What is Metaphysics?] (Bonn: Verlag Fred. Cohen, 1930); *Die Selbstbehauptung des deutschen Universität* [The Self-Reliance of the German University] (Breslau: Verlag Korn, 1933); *Einführung in die Metaphysik* [Introduction to Metaphysics] (Tübingen: Niemeyer Verlag, 1953). See also Werner Brock, *Introduction to Existence and Being* (Chicago: Regnery, 1952), which contains translations of some of Heidegger's major essays.

[38]See Thomas Langan, *The Meaning of Heidegger* (New York: Columbia University Press, 1959), pp. 22ff.

In relation to the question of how one discovers the authentic self, Heidegger analyzed the problem of anxiety phenomenologically and introduced his concept of the role of Nothing and the importance of extreme situations, above all the individual's death, in the discovery of authenticity. The fundamental mode of "Human Existence" is to live in the future, in anticipation, and to be characterized by *care*, which takes the form of a rootless anxiety, a sense of alienation, and an attendant feeling of guilt. In contrast to a genuine fear of a real danger, this anxiety and guilt are not aroused by something that is done, but by what is not done, by the failure to realize one's potentialities about Nothing. And always in the end there is the anticipation, however suppressed, of that ultimate situation, death.

Only by thrusting the ultimate situation before one's consciousness, recognizing one's mortality and developing a sense of guilt over the failure to realize one's potentialities, can one develop the resoluteness to face the future with confidence. Heidegger proposed that this object — the attainment of authentic being, the origination of the individual in terms of Being as a whole — was most effectively advanced by returning to the past, particularly the early Greek philosophers, and dedicating thought to the realization of Being. As Heidegger was making his way to God, he visualized science as one of the major obstacles in his path.

> Though today two seemingly different conceptions of science seem to combat one another — science as technical, practical, professional knowledge and science as cultural value per se — both are moving along the same downgrade of misinterpretation and emasculation of the spirit. They differ only in this: in the present situation the technical, practical conception of science as specialization can at least lay claim to rank and clear consistency, while the reactionary interpretation of science as cultural value, now making its reappearance, seeks to conceal the impotence of the spirit behind an unconscious lie.[39]

[39]Martin Heidegger, *An Introduction to Metaphysics,* trans. Ralph Manheim (New York: Doubleday, 1961), pp. 39–40.

JEAN-PAUL SARTRE

Brown Brothers

Jean-Paul Sartre. Jean-Paul Sartre (1905–1980) was born in Paris to a French middle-class family. His mother was Protestant, his father Catholic. At the age of two he lost his father, a naval officer who died in French Indochina. Sartre was brought up by his mother and maternal grandparents. He was a weak, sensitive child. When he was eleven his mother remarried and the family went to live in La Rochelle, where he spent most of his lycée years. His family eventually moved back to Paris where Sartre prepared for the baccalaureate, which he passed in 1922. He passed the aggregation (the exam qualifying an individual for admission to the circle of French professors who teach in lycées and universities) in 1929. After military service (as an army nurse because of defective vision), he was appointed professor of philosophy at the lycée of Le Havre where he served for two years (1931–

1932). He was offered a grant to study with Husserl in Berlin under whom he learned the phenomenological method. Sartre returned to Le Havre and from there went to Läon and finally to the Lycée Pasteur in Paris (1937–1939). He was drafted in 1939 and taken prisoner in Lorraine in June 1940. Since he was not a member of the regular corps he was liberated a year later. Back in Paris he taught at the Lycée Pasteur and Lycée Condorcet (1942–1944), engaging actively in the Resistance movement. He terminated his teaching career at the end of the war, devoting himself thereafter exclusively to writing and political activity.

Sartre's first novel, *La Nausée* (translated as *The Diary of Antoine Roquentin*), is an extensive examination of the alienation, dismay, and sudden sense of a loss of meaning — the nausea ("a sweetish sort of disgust") experienced by an individual the first time he faces up to the contingency and brute indifference of existence to human purposes, hopes, and interpretations. The stuffy middle-class world with its stereotyped inanities and pompous individuals who accept them without question is the epitome of bad faith, or as Heidegger would call it, inauthenticity. Through his hero, Sartre explores the phenomenology of perception, the nature of freedom, and the problems of thought, memory, and art. Although basically a philosophical novel. *La Nausée* expressed so vividly the experience of a large number of sensitive contemporaries, that it became popular. With it Sartre emerged as a major contemporary philosopher. *La Nausée* belongs among the classics of existential literature along with Dostoyevsky's *Notes from Underground* (1864), Rainer Maria Rilke's prose work, *The Notes of Malte Laurids Brigge* (1910), and the works of Franz Kafka, such as *The Trial* and *The Castle* (which were left unfinished at his death in 1924 and only published posthumously).

Being and Nothingness (appearing in France as *L'Être et le Néant* in 1943) is a study of the human condition, including such problems as love, hate, sex, anguish, bad faith, and the original choice of Being by which real individuals make of themselves what they are. Descartes, Sartre believed, was wrong in suggesting conscious doubt was the prerequisite of thought about existence. Prior to such self-consciousness is a prereflective consciousness which undercuts the philosophies of realism and idealism, and rejects the Kantian doctrine of a noumenal world behind phenomena. Sartre then distinguishes between unconscious Being (Being-in-itself) and conscious Being (Being-for-itself).

Sartre locates the critical property of Being-for-itself in the presence of Nothingness, that is, in its movement toward what is not or toward "nothing." Although this is revealed most strikingly in anguish, it is a general property of Being-for-itself and not confined to extreme situations such as contemplation of one's death. Humans are the beings who are what they are not and who are not what they are; bad faith is manifest in the instant any person for whatever reason accepts what he or she "is" in the fleeing moment for the "is" of Being-in-itself.

For-itself as Nothingness, as a pursuit of Being in the form of selflessness, involves possibility, value, and temporality. These are all inseparable from the for-itself as an internal negation of Being-in-itself. Knowledge is the bridge between them. The study of Being-for-others and concrete personal relations reveals that the For-itself has an outside, and while never connected with the In-itself, is nevertheless in the midst of it.

In connection with his discussion of how we can be in the midst of the In-itself without losing our freedom, Sartre develops his ideas of freedom and facticity. An individual's basic relation to Being is present in the desire either to appropriate it through action and possession or to become one with it; everything depends on the individual's original choice of Being, a choice he or she cannot avoid, for even not to choose is a choice, that is, to accept things as they are and in this sense make them one's own. This question leads Sartre to propose the need for an existential psychoanalysis.

In summing up his position on the place of consciousness in and against the great inner background of existence within which it appears, Sartre adduces the compelling imagery of a hole at the heart of being and employs, for clarification, a device used by science writers to explain the principle of the conservation of energy to the layperson.

> The For-itself, in fact, is nothing but the pure nihilation of the In-itself; it is like a hole of being at the heart of Being. One may be reminded here of that convenient fiction by which certain popularizers are accustomed to illustrate the principle of the conservation of energy. If, they say, a single one of the atoms which constitute the universe were annihilated, there would result a catastrophe which would extend to the entire universe, and this would be, in particular, the end of the Earth and of the solar system. This metaphor can be of use to us here. The For-itself is like a tiny nihilation which has its origin at the heart of Being; and this nihilation is sufficient to cause a total upheaval to happen to the In-itself. This upheaval is the world.[40]

In her study of Sartre, Iris Murdoch had described him as "profoundly and self-consciously contemporary and having the "style of the age." She urged:

> He is a thinker who stands full in the way of three post-Hegelian movements of thought: the Marxist, the existentialist and the phenomenological. He has felt the impact of each and brought to each his own modifications. He uses the analytical tools of the Marxists and shares their urgent passion for action, but without accepting a theological view of the Dialectic. He remains at heart a liberal social democrat. He takes from Kierkegaard the picture of man as a lonely anguished being in an ambiguous world, but he rejects the hidden Kierkegaardian God. He uses the methods and terminology of Husserl but lacks Husserl's dogmatism and his Platonic aspirations.[41]

However, by involving himself in so many contemporary controversies Sartre also aroused much opposition and found his version of existentialism

under attack as subjective and ultraindividualistic, as preoccupied with negative and disgusting phases of human existence, and as amoral. Sartre undertook to answer his critics.

Sartre's atheistic individualism automatically alienated all persons who were searching for a new religious interpretation of human existence and who treated some form of the human collective as a primary social reality. "Atheistic existentialism," he said, "states that if God does not exist, there is at least one being in whom existence precedes essence, a being who exists before he can be defined by any concept, and that being is man."[42] Sartre classed Jaspers and Gabriel Marcel as religious and himself and Heidegger as atheistic existentialists. However, both Jaspers and Heidegger, in response to Sartre's formulations, denied that they were existentialists.

Sartre's rejection of holism included not only all forms of historicism (both Hegelian and Marxian), but also all religious views of a proper end of human beings (that is, toward which their whole development moves) and both classical sociology and fascism.

> The existentialist will never consider man as an end because he is always in the making. Nor should he believe that there is a mankind to which we might set up a cult in the manner of Auguste Comte. The cult of mankind ends in the self-enclosed humanism of Comte, and, let it be said, of fascism. This kind of humanism we can do without.[43]

Far from advocating quietism and irresponsibility, Sartre argues, existentialism believes human beings to be both free and responsible in the ultimate sense. They are "condemned to be free." Man "carries the weight of the world on his shoulders, he is responsible for the world and for himself as a way of being."[44] Human beings find themselves alone and without help, engaged in the

---

[40]Jean-Paul Sartre, *Being and Nothingness*, trans. Hazel E. Barnes (New York: Philosophical Library, 1956), pp. 617–618.

[41]Iris Murdoch, *Sartre, Romantic Rationalist* (New Haven: Yale University Press, 1953), p. vii.

[42]Jean-Paul Sartre, *Existentialism and Human Emotions* (New York: Philosophical Library, 1957), p. 15.

[43]*Ibid.*, p. 50.

[44]*Ibid.*, p. 52.

world for which they alone are responsible, unable to shunt responsibility for even an instant. "Someone will say, 'I did not ask to be born.' This is a naive way of throwing greater emphasis on our facticity. . . . Yet I find an absolute responsibility for the fact that my facticity (here the fact of my birth) is directly inapprehensible and even inconceivable, for this fact of my birth never appears as a brute fact but always across a projective reconstruction of my for-itself. I am ashamed of being born or I am astonished at it or I rejoice over it, or in attempting to get rid of my life I affirm that I live and I assume life is bad. Thus, in a certain sense I *choose* being born."[45]

And in his defense of his version of existentialism Sartre again insisted on the need for an existential psychoanalysis that will attack the problems of choice and responsibility rather than those of sex adaptation and force. However, Sartre has not convinced his critics that he has provided for a common interpersonal world. At the conclusion of a sensitive study of Sartre, Wilfred Desan observes:

> The most striking argument against Sartre is the fact that other authors using the same *method* come to *different* results. For Heidegger, for instance, *Dasein* (human reality) implies a *Mitsein*. That is, I am conscious of my finitude and of my contingency, but this consciousness (Heidegger calls it the act of authenticity), while it is an act of individuality, also arouses my fellow-brother at the same time; we walk toward death in a spirit of decision and communion. . . . For Gabriel Marcel, love and communion are the enriching values of life. He accepts the limitation of human reality, but sees in friendship the compensation for this restriction.[46]

THE PHENOMENOLOGICAL METHOD

In the final chapter of his two-volume history of the phenomenological movement, Spiegelberg tried to set down the essentials of its method. He envisioned it as a protest against reductionism.[47] Phenomenology is seen as a revolt against all philosophy that proceeds on the basis of accepted beliefs and theories. It proposes to enrich knowledge by a return to phenomena. Among the obstacles to such a procedure are the principles, particularly espoused by the positivists, of simplicity and economy and, traditionally epitomized by Occam's razor, the principle that entities ought not to be multiplied beyond necessity. One might assume that Husserl's proposal to bracket preconceived notions (since once they have cluttered up one's mental horizon they are not easily removed), and to attend only to what is there in experience, is a contemporary version of Occam's razor, but Spiegelberg argues that this is not so. Occam's razor, in his view, had "better be called the positivist's bulldozer." By contrast, "phenomenology stands for a kind of rebellion against the trend in modern science which begins with simplifying abstractions and ends with a minimum vocabulary of scientific concepts."[48] Not only does phenomenology seek to work from a full picture of reality, but it is opposed to the positivistic preference for working with sense data.

The phenomenological program that rallied under Husserl's battle cry "to the things themselves" comprises seven steps in all, the first three of which are shared by *all* who call themselves phenomenologists, the rest shared by variable subgroups of phenomenologists. They are:

1. investigating particular phenomena;
2. investigating general essences;
3. apprehending essential relationships among essences;
4. watching modes of appearing;
5. watching the constitution of phenomena in consciousness;
6. suspending belief in the existence of phenomena;
7. interpreting the meaning of phenomena.[49]

[45]*Ibid.*, pp. 57–58.
[46]Wilfred Desan, *The Tragic Finale* (New York: Harper, 1960), p. 187.
[47]Spiegelberg, *The Phenomenological Movement*, II, 656ff. The present section follows Spiegelberg.
[48]*Ibid.*, p. 658.
[49]See *ibid.*, p. 659.

Investigating particular phenomena, usually called phenomenological description, comprises three operations: the intuitive grasp of the phenomena, their analytical examination, and their description. Phenomenological intuiting is said to be "one of the most demanding operations, which requires utter concentration. . . . Nevertheless there is little that the beginning phenomenologist can be given by way of precise instructions beyond such metaphoric phrases as 'opening his eyes,' 'keeping them open,' 'not getting blinded,' and 'looking and listening.' "[50] Phenomenological analysis "comprises the distinguishing of constituents of the phenomena as well as the exploration of their relations to and connections with adjacent phenomena."[51] Phenomenological description "is primary predication" and "is based on a classification of the phenomena" and "presupposes a framework of class names."[52] Describing involves some selectivity and hence already presupposes some attention to essences; nevertheless, intuiting, analyzing, and describing particulars in their full concreteness are the common program of all members of the phenomenological movement.

The second step in the phenomenological method is the investigation of general essences (Eidetic Intuiting). General essences "are conceived of as phenomena sui generis that differ from particulars."[53] Examples include the consciousness of goodness in general. They are discovered by "ejective intuiting," that is, arriving at general types on a basis of particular examinations such as lining up particulars in a continuous series based on the order of their similarities.

The third step in the phenomenological method, apprehending essential relationships, consists in the discovery of relationships or connections between essences. These are said to be of two types: relationships within a single essence and relationships between several essences. Internal relations are discovered by free mental variations, that is, the mental attempt to eliminate certain components or replace them by others. Such imaginative experiments determine whether the structure designated by the general name is affected or unaffected by the operation. The same procedure is employed to establish relations between several essences.

Watching modes of appearing, the fourth step in phenomenological analysis, consists in exploring not only what appears, but the way it appears. There are three different senses of appearance that a study of modes of givenness must distinguish: the aspect of an object from which we know the object as a whole, the appearance of the object that is perspectively deformed, the degrees of clarity and distinctness in the appearance of an object.

Exploring the constitution of phenomena in consciousness is the study of how it takes shape in the mind. This may occur spontaneously or result from attempts to "integrate unrelated phenomena." As a matter of fact, "this integration follows structural 'laws.' There is a definite affinity between them and the laws of 'good gestalt.' "[54]

Suspension of belief in existence, which Spiegelberg lists as the sixth method of phenomenology, is Husserl's procedure of the suspension of belief — reduction or bracketing. Husserl had associated the original meaning of reduction with the mathematical operation of bracketing; this was a metaphor for holding attention in abeyance from some aspects of phenomena while heeding others. In Spiegelberg's view bracketing is not as essential as Husserl thought but while "a distinct aid to all the steps . . . is still not indispensable."[55]

The final step in phenomenological procedure, hermeneutics, "is an attempt to interpret the 'sense' of certain phenomena. . . . In fact, the whole study of intentional structures consisted largely in an interpretative analysis and description of the meaning of our conscious acts. . . . The goal of 'hermeneutic phenomenology' . . . is the discovery of meanings which are not immediately manifest to our intuiting, analyzing and describing . . . an

[50]*Ibid.*, pp. 659–660.
[51]*Ibid.*, pp. 669–670.
[52]*Ibid.*, p. 673.
[53]*Ibid.*, p. 677.
[54]*Ibid.*, p. 689.
[55]*Ibid.*, p. 693.

unveiling of hidden meanings, or at most of an intuitive verification of anticipations about the less accessible layers of phenomena, layers which can be uncovered, although they are not immediately manifest."[56]

SUMMARY

The most significant social development in the Western world in the nineteenth century was the rise of the nation as the distinctive community and the state as the sovereign political institution of contemporary humanity. The two dominant trends in the sociopolitical institutions of the nation-state were the movements toward mass democracy and socialism. The most distinctive event in the social thought of the nineteenth century was the rise of positivistic organicism, a linkage of scientific and rationalistic methodology with holistic theories of society.

Throughout the nineteenth century there were elementaristic reactions to the new forms of collectivism. We examined Schopenhauer, Kierkegaard, Jacob Burckhardt, and Nietzsche, not as exclusive, but as dramatic spokespeople for elementaristic approaches to humanity, society, and culture. Such thinkers brought the collectivistic trends in nineteenth-century society and thought under critical review: they called attention to the erosion of institutions that had formerly supplied Western people with values. They envisioned a new era of cultural leveling. Moreover, they presented a view of the individual quite different from that of their eighteenth-century rationalistic counterparts: they were less impressed by the rationality of human beings than by their emotional drives and their capacity for faith, for creativity, and even for depravity.

While there is little doubt that these elementaristic critics were a major inspiration for the neo-Kantian movements in recent times (which revived elementaristic approaches to social life and encouraged methodological innovations appropri-

ate to such elementaristic perspectives), they also prepared the way for more radical methodological unrest. Several thinkers made proposals for the development of psychology into a general tool of the sciences: for the cultivation of intuition as a more basic and more powerful tool than reason (Brentano and Stumpf), at least in human affairs (Bergson) and for an analysis of phenomena in a manner more fundamental than either Kant or Hegel (Renouvier, Santayana, and Husserl).

The reflections of the psychologists, intuitionists, and phenomenologists were primarily methodological in import. It followed that the substantive trends in social interpretation could potentially find a natural affinity with the new methodological trends. In retrospect, the connection seems virtually foreordained between the methodological activity that resulted in phenomenology and the social judgments of the individualistic critics of collectivism. In any case, existentialism and phenomenology fused.

Jaspers, Heidegger, and Sartre illustrate some of the major variations of the combined phenomenology-existentialism. None of them was prepared to agree with Husserl in his inclination toward Platonic idealism and his search for the pure transcendental self (perhaps soul?). Their reliance was rather on descriptive phenomenology. However, they shared the view that contemporary society and culture are profoundly alienating (in fact, they provided one of the most important approaches to problems of anomie and alienation as an alternative to those of the Marxist critical theorists) and moved toward restoration of an elementaristic perspective. They all agreed that contemporary human beings are experiencing a crisis of values. Jaspers was the most religiously oriented of the three, Sartre the most atheistic, Heidegger somewhere in between although in his later writings, he moved more in the direction of Jaspers than Sartre.

Without any question the way was opened toward a fuller exploitation of phenomenological-existentialist approaches in sociology — a development that has become pronounced in the 1960s and 1970s.

[56]*Ibid.*, p. 695.

XXIV

Phenomenological Sociology and Ethnomethodology

In the neo-Kantian program for knowledge and science, the search for the general, the objective, and the universal sooner or later became a search for the formal. From its sources in Kant, this formalism had been derived from a twofold distinction: (1) one that separated phenomena from the thing in itself, rejecting the latter as an object of cognition, and (2) from a distinction between the form and content of phenomena, with forms seen as objective and universal, representing the mind-supplied universal element of knowledge. Things were different for phenomenology.

The procedure of the two approaches was distinct. The point of departure in the analysis of the objective aspects of scientific knowledge for Kant was made through the question: how is nature a priori possible? Simmel, as was seen, paraphrased this in his neo-Kantian sociology with the question: what are the a priori conditions that make society possible? In the Kantian framework there is only one possible answer: forms. Husserl had Kant in mind when he insisted that phenomena are the object of immediate experience and the data of

cognition. He maintained that Kant's error was to assume that only objects of experience and cognition can be of a sensory character. He maintained that phenomena as essences are the contents of pure consciousness. He argued that the objects of ordinary experience are constituted as "essences" which are objects of immediate intuition. Every object, whether factual, actual, natural, imaginary, or essential, is at least a potential object of some kind of experience. Whenever something is experienced, it is experienced by virtue of the fact that it is in some relation to consciousness and the ego. The two basic subdivisions of experience are the natural and eidetic, referring respectively to the natural world of events and to the essences directly intuited. Husserl was interested in the second, for in the last analysis all meaning assigned to the natural is derived from its relation to the essences. To analyze the latter, Husserl proposed a special method of bracketing or reduction: a progressively focused and controlled concentration of attention on experience to reveal the levels in depth it displays. For our purposes, the thing of interest in this is *the possibility it offered for an alternative to sociological formalism in which directly intuited essences are assumed to supply the element of generality in social life.*

The first stage in the rise of a phenomenological sociology was represented by the employment of phenomenological language to designate the general components of social life in a manner that, at least superficially, avoided the Kantian distinctions between noumena and phenomena, on the one hand, and form and content, on the other. A second stage in the rise of a phenomenological sociology occurred when phenomenological sociology followed the lead of the persons who sought to combine phenomenology and existentialism. Husserl was initially interested in developing a rigorous methodology of philosophy. Far from making the everyday world a primary object of study, he set it aside, bracketed it, and directed his attention to the discovery of essences. By contrast, existentialists like Jaspers, Heidegger, and Sartre, had made the existential self the very center of analysis, which, of course, meant that they had more use for a descriptive than for a pure phenomenology. The rise of the phenomenology of everyday life represents the second stage in phenomenological sociology. In the 1970s, efforts at the full institutionalization of a phenomenological sociology began.

PHENOMENOLOGICAL ALTERNATIVES TO FORMALISM

Three persons are presented here to illustrate contributions to the pioneering stage in the development of a phenomenological sociology: Alfred Vierkandt, Max Scheler, and Georges Gurvitch. To Vierkandt, a phenomenological approach offered the possibility of isolating constants in interindividual experience without the necessity for recourse to instinct theory (which was being discredited at the time) or without a relapse into contentless formalism. Vierkandt's intuitions were sound: in the long run scholars would explore a

phenomenological sociology (and psychology) because of insecurity about the presuppositions of other types of elementaristic theory. Scheler and Gurvitch, in his phenomenological phase, had other considerations: Scheler had become dissatisfied with neo-Kantianism (both because of his personal antirationalism and his experience of the neo-Kantian method as a straitjacket imposed on his perceptionism) and he found new inspiration in the work of Husserl and Bergson; Gurvitch, who left Russia in 1920 and spent five years in the Russian Institute at the University of Prague, became friends with Max Scheler and undertook an extensive study of Husserl's work and the intuitionism of Bergson as a result of his influence. Scheler brought his considerable talents for phenomenological description to bear on the enrichment of interpersonal sentiments (his study of sympathy and resentment are classics of their kind); Gurvitch, during his phenomenological phase, explored the possibility of isolating a series of depth levels of interpersonal experience by means of a phenomenological approach.

Alfred Vierkandt. Alfred Vierkandt (1867–1953) had made his reputation in his study of culture history and ethnology, *Naturvölker und Kulturvölker* (1896) and in the study of cultural change, *Stetigkeit im Kulturwandel* (1908), before he undertook the fusion of the formalistic tradition in sociology with Husserl's phenomenology.[1] In his earlier

[1]None of Vierkandt's major sociological works are available in English translation, including: *Naturvölker und Kulturvölker* ["Natural Peoples and Cultural Peoples"] (Leipzig: Duncker & Humblot, 1896); *Die Stetigkeit im Kulturwandel* ["The Order in Cultural Change"] (Leipzig: Duncker & Humblot, 1908); *Gesellschaftslehre: Hauptprobleme der philosophischen Soziologie* ["The Study of Society: Main Problems of Philosophical Sociology"] (Stuttgart: F. Enke, 1923, 2d rev. ed., 1928; New York: Arno Press, 1975); and *Kleine Gesellschaftslehre* ["Small Studies of Society"] (Stuttgart: F. Enke, 1949). A review of Vierkandt's sociology appears in Theodore Abel's *Systematic Sociology in Germany* (New York: Columbia University Press, 1929), pp. 59–79. Vierkandt's *Staat und Gesellschaft in der Gegenwart: eine Einfuhrung in das Staatsbürgerliche Denken und die politische Bewegung unserer Zeit* [State and So-

ALFRED VIERKANDT

Photo by Schatzmann & Muster, Berlin. Courtesy of Martha Vierkandt.

work, Vierkandt anticipated Clark Wissler's concept of "culture area" and Ogburn's conception of "cultural lag." In this early stage, sociology had been conceived as the generalizations of ethnological and historical materials. However, under the growing demand to make sociology into a special science, Vierkandt rejected this historical approach to sociological problems and the use of historical materials, and in his *Gesellschaftslehre* (1923) he proposed a form of sociological formalism. The object of his study, Vierkandt maintained, was to examine the last forms, powers or forces, and facts of societal life which reveal the

patterns free of all historical change but which emerge from the character of society. Though this scientific goal had been established by Simmel and Tönnies, Vierkandt believed it was not obtainable in Simmel's terms. It becomes fully attainable only through the development of phenomenology, which permits us in a quite new manner to isolate the final a priori circumstances that make society possible.[2]

Vierkandt objected to the lack of precision in the concept of sociology which was characteristic of a whole series of disciplines applying to human groups, their life, spiritual activity, products, and culture. Like Simmel, he wished to confine the term *sociology* to the study of the peculiarities of the group and the theory of social interaction and its products. Also like Simmel, Vierkandt did not stop here, but insisted that the sociologist is interested in the innermost actualities of societary facts, and not simply the objective external manifestations of interaction. Precisely for this reason, sociology is different from naturalistic investigation. Human beings live in a world of biological and cultural relations but also in a world of social relations, a realm with qualities of its own and different from those of the cultural and biological spheres. These qualities are *mental states,* emerging in the process of living together. Thus, while studying interaction, formal sociology is not behavioristic. And it is not attempting to isolate behaviors, but rather the mental states presupposed by these behaviors. Similarly, the investigation of products of interaction has no concern for their external manifestations but only for their utility in the isolation of the ultimate unchangeable aspects. Only when the interplay of the forces of interaction is the object of study, rather than the totality of the cultural complex, is the investigation sociological. The relation of formal sociology to the cultural sciences and practical life is similar to the relation between mathematics and physics or technology.[3]

Vierkandt thought the systematization of social

ciety in the Present: An Introduction to the Civic Thought and Political Movements of Our Time] was also published (Leipzig: Quelle und Meyer, 1961).

[2]Vierkandt, *Gesellschaftslehre,* Foreword, p. 1. (References are to the 1923 edition.)
[3]*Ibid.,* p. 18.

phenomena to be the primary task of sociology. This could be achieved by reducing social phenomena to their ultimate a priori forms. Simmel, he felt, had failed in this by burdening his writing with too many examples and displaying too much fascination with concrete social content. Domination is a social form, but any concrete manifestation of domination (as between social classes, for example) is historical. Simmel remained at this level and did not develop sociology into a true theory of pure forms or categories. This task, Vierkandt believed, was made possible only by the newly developed phenomenological method. This is applicable to sociological problems, because societal life is directly given in experience as all mental life.[4] Thus, the argument develops that, through the phenomenological method, and through it alone, is a true formal sociology possible.

The phenomenological method consists in controlled examination of the process of awareness itself. It requires the focus of attention on aspects of conscious experience and not upon external manifestations. It represents a kind of "immanent reflection" and concentration upon the inherent meaning of things as given. The phenomenological method attempts, through the analysis of experience, to uncover certain fundamental social dispositions assumed to lie at the foundation of common life. These fundamental dispositions or essences are discoverable only through this method of progressive discrimination and reduction. Among other things, it may indicate that apparently similar experiential processes are intrinsically different. "Shame," for instance, differs from "fear of undesirable consequences." If one attends only to externals, such a distinction will never be discovered. In fact, this was the mistake made by Simmel. Through the inductive review of historical events, one may discover the basis for historically determined individual differences, but not irreducible essences. No inductive procedure of inference involving either repeated

observation or the consideration of various cases is required. Potentially, the insight may be gained in a single act of intuition. Simmel's procedure is a relatively crass kind of induction, destined to fail because it attempts to arrive at the form by mistaken methods. The dispositions discovered by phenomenology, on the other hand, are essences, a priori properties of interhuman mental life.

Examples of phenomenological analysis are found in the disposition of *self-respect*, which simultaneously calls forth a deep inner sense of superiority and instills respect. It displays the presence of an inner bond expressed as submission to the values of the group. At times it is manifest as a will to power for the purposes of achieving distinction and of being recognized as better than others. When satisfied, it is the source of the feeling of dignity. Frustrated, it becomes the source of the feeling of hurt and shame.

The phenomenological study of *submission*[5] shows that it is not due to fear or other ulterior motives but may imply a voluntary inner surrender. It is accompanied by psychological states such as timidity, embarrassment, and a feeling of the need for contact with the superior personality. Characteristic attitudes associated with it are adoration, devotion, and respect. But its course is a kind of participation in the greatness of the other, an instinct which manifests itself in the cult of power, the desire to follow the leader, the feeling of duty and blind submission to an inner command.

The general issues to which Vierkandt addressed his sociology were: (1) the historical character of human mental life, (2) the nature of society, (3) the power of the environment, (4) relations as fundamental categories of sociological thought, and (5) the concept of social wholes. Human nature is not universal; there are only particular historically influenced configurations. The possibility of historical influences on the individual is due to the plastic conditions affecting the innate dispositions. Society is a group of people, so

[4]*Ibid.*, p. 15.

[5]*Ibid.*, pp. 68–87.

far as they are the bearers of inwardly established interrelations. The social relations that hold in society are among the powerful forces molding, controlling, and conditioning the expression of the dispositions.

Society,[6] in fact, is easily defined, since individuals are not enclosed within themselves but participate in the life of other people and derive self-awareness as well as ideals, affections, and desires from others. Social life implies at least a minimum of reciprocity. The internal bond is the fundamental characteristic of society. The community is its ideal form. Only in community do social dispositions flourish. In no case is society to be assumed to be an organism. The inner character of societal materials bears the imprint of the forms of relations which must be presupposed from the outset.

Within this framework, sociological analysis was thought to begin with the phenomenological investigation of the innate dispositions or instincts. In addition to the two referred to — the dispositions of self-respect and of submission — Vierkandt examines the parental drive and the dispositions of struggle, sympathy, imitation, expressiveness, and sociability. Probably the single most important source for the materials of these particular discussions was William McDougall's *Introduction to Social Psychology* (1908). Vierkandt also made use of discussions by William James, James Mark Baldwin, Gabriel Tarde, Karl Groos, and Simmel.

After completing this phase of his study, Vierkandt turned his attention to fundamental societal relations. The general formula for this phase of the study was provided by Tönnies' typology of *Gemeinschaft* and *Gesellschaft*, representing, respectively, a relatively compact and a relatively loose form of interhuman life. An understanding of both was said to be essential to the comprehension of human affairs. *Gemeinschaft* was the original form of society, *Gesellschaft* a later dissolution of the early form. The most important historical forms of the *Gemeinschaft* were the family, the sib

[6]*Ibid.*, pp. 560–562.

and locality groups, the men's club, the status group, class, political party, and the cultural unities of folk, lineage, nation, and the state. Vierkandt completed his study with the examination of collective phenomena of the group, such as morale, collective consciousness, and group self-consciousness.

The phenomenological study of social relations also concentrates on mental process, or "inner" life. All social relations affect the inner life of the participating individuals. Social relations are sought not only for external advantage but in the anticipation of inner experience. One may enter into a social relation with others for external reasons or for inner stimulation or some combination of both. This is most clearly the case in the establishment of union (*Gemeinschaft*) with others; one expects sympathetic response. But relations of dominance, mutual recognition, and conflict also offer inner satisfaction. This is a product of the specific qualities of experience each relation offers. *Gemeinschaft* offers, in the surrender to the whole, an enhanced and expanded sense of self; conflict affords the pleasure of achievement and exhilaration due to the exertion of one's powers. The inner bond in human intercourse is fundamental. It is most pronounced in primary-group relations, resting on awareness of the mutual benefit of the union and presupposing like-mindedness and we-feeling. In other social relations, the basis of the inner bond is found in the regulation of the activities present in all the relations. The inner bond is here expressed in the mutual recognition of norms. Regulation results from the demands of the group, imposed on inborn motives. Regulation originates in the primary group, where the dependence of the individual or the group most quickly leads to the acceptance of discipline. Moreover, the *Gemeinschaft* prevails in three other fundamental relations: those based on agreement (keeping of agreements or contracts), those based on dominance, and those based on conflict (the recognition that the conflict takes place according to rules, presupposing a moral community). Therefore, there is an inner bond or degree of *Gemeinschaft* in all social relations.

According to Vierkandt, not only does phenomenological sociology give the first adequate account of the innate dispositions out of which society is constructed, and the *only* adequate account of social relations, but it makes possible, for the first time, the full understanding of the group. The group is thought to be more than the mere sum of individuals composing it. Moreover, it develops new properties in its individual members. It creates a set of external forms which act as a constraining force on them. Such forces emerge from the group as a whole. The group possesses a spirit of its own that forces the individual to think, feel, and act in a definite way. The group is self-conscious and manifests a life-urge and life-organization, acting like a person.[7]

For the adequate explanation of the group, we need a new theory of social wholes. Gestalt theory is an instance of this new theory. The external and constraining force exercised by the group is explained by the fact that the members at any time may divide into actors and spectators. The spectators watch and control the behavior of the actors. The group is in reality the spectators. Its will is their will. Conformity of the actors is due to the change of roles to which every group is subject. The individual is actor at one time and spectator at others. The actor is at other times a spectator, in which role he or she controls the actors. The group spirit embodies the ideas, attitudes, and values shaped by all. It is external to each, for it is not a product of the individual mind but results from the interaction between the individuals and their circumstances. Group self-consciousness is the awareness of each individual of the inner bond uniting him or her to others. Each member is conscious of belonging to a whole of which he or she is a part. It is a consciousness of common elements. The life-urge of the group is a product of each member's desire to maintain intact the group to which he or she belongs. The objectivity of the group is the constancy of functions of collective representations, which are independent of any

particular individual and appear as a uniform, causal, and purposeful system.

Thus, the phenomenological method, the method of pure sociology, discovers the essences of society, social behavior, and social relations. It is not to be confused with the inductive-empirical approach to social materials, although the latter may consist in the specialized research that applies the principles and discoveries of the phenomenological method. In fact, the inductive-empirical and phenomenological methods are not simple alternatives, for the latter is more profound, establishing results more basic than the former. The phenomenological method, in contrast to induction, may arrive at judgments of absolute certainty and finality. Through use of this method, one discovers the ultimate, a priori facts of social life, the inborn but plastic dispositions. These dispositions — to fondle, to help, to fight, to sympathize, to imitate, to receive suggestions, to be sociable, to trust, and so on — are the a priori preconditions of human society, and social life is reducible to the development of them. Because they are inborn, they are discoverable directly — if only one has the proper method. As original qualities of mental experience, they are susceptible only to phenomenological analysis, which discovers them and reduces all other qualities of experience to them.

The adherence by phenomenologists to the Enlightenment model of society is nowhere more completely shown than in the treatment of society and the group. They are not treated as external coercive structures. While they may exercise a "constraint" over the individual, it is a constraint exercised by one aspect of a person's mind over others.

Max Scheler. The chief importance of Max Scheler (1874–1928) for modern sociology is his popularization of the sociology of knowledge (*Wissenssoziologie*). Theoretically, however, he belongs to the phenomenological branch of sociological formalism and deserves consideration here from that standpoint. Scheler was a student of Dilthey and Simmel and became professor of

[7]*Ibid.*, pp. 241–242.

MAX SCHELER

Courtesy of the Universität zu Köln

Fundamental to all aspects of Scheler's thought was the distinction characteristic of the phenomenologists between the realm of ideal value — essence — and the realm of existential fact. While they partly parallel one another, they must not be identified.[9] Real existence consists in factual relationships changing in time; the realm of values is a sphere of timelessly valid, intuited meanings. This metaphysical distinction is essential to the contrast between cultural sociology and the sociology of real factors. Cultural data are "ideal," existing in the realm of ideas and values. Real factors are part of changing events in time. Cultural data are defined by ideal goals or intentions; real data form an impulse structure around such things as sex, hunger, and striving for power. It is wrong to assume that real factors such as race, political power, and economic production exclusively determine meanings. It is also wrong to assume that external events of experience consist in the unfolding of spiritualistic and personalistic ideas. Ideas do not become concrete and actualized unless bound up in some fashion in collective tenden-

sociology and philosophy at the University of Cologne, thus having many-sided contact with the formalists, for at Cologne he was a colleague of von Wiese.[8]

[8]Among Scheler's works translated into English are: *Man's Place in Nature*, trans. Hans Meyerhoff (Boston: Beacon Press, 1961); *The Nature of Sympathy*, trans. Peter Heath with introduction by Werner Stark (London: Routledge & Kegan Paul, 1958); *On the Eternal in Man*, trans. Bernard Noble (London: Student Christian Movement Press, 1960); *Philosophical Perspectives*, trans. Oscar A. Haac (Boston: Beacon Press, 1958); *Resentment*, trans. William W. Holdheim and edited with introduction by Lewis A. Coser (New York: Free Press of Glencoe, 1961). Other major works include: *Schriften zur Soziologie und Weltanschauungslehre* ["Writings in Sociology and Philosophy"], 3 vols. (Leipzig: P. Reinhold, 1923–1924); *Versuche zu einer Soziologie des Wissens* ["Essays Toward a Sociology of Knowledge"] (Munich: Duncker & Humblot, 1924); *Die Wissensformen und die Gesellschaft* ["Forms of Knowledge and Society"] (Leipzig: Neue-Geist Verlag, 1926); and *Bildung und Wissen* ["Culture and Knowledge"] (Frankfurt am Main: G. Schulte-Bulmke, 1947). His collected works have now been edited by Maria Scheler, *Gesammelte Werke* (Bern: Francke, 1954).

For reviews of Scheler's work, see: John Raphael Staude, *Max Scheler, 1874–1928: An Intellectual Portrait* (New York: The Free Press, 1967). Howard Becker and Helmut Otto Dahlke, "Max Scheler's Sociology of Knowledge," *Philosophy and Phenomenological Research*, 2 (March 1942), 309–322; H. O. Dahlke, "The Sociology of Knowledge," in H. E. Barnes, Howard Becker, and Frances Bennett Becker, eds., *Contemporary Social Theory* (New York: D. Appleton-Century, 1940), pp. 64–92; Robert Merton, "The Sociology of Knowledge," *Isis*, 27 (November 1937), 493–503, reprinted in *Social Theory and Social Structure* (Rev. ed.; Glencoe, Ill: The Free Press, 1957); and Maurice Mandelbaum, *The Problem of Historical Knowledge* (New York: Liveright, 1938), pp. 147ff.

[9]Scheler, *Die Wissensformen und die Gesellschaft*, pp. 347–348.

cies and incorporated in institutional structures. The peculiar problem of historical knowledge for Scheler is the explanation of how these two realms are jointly effective.

The goal of cultural sociology is the apprehension of the ideal — the object matters of the artist, musician, and scientist who address themselves to the comprehension of ideal ends. Cultural sociology studies religion, philosophy, scientific thought, and art. Empirical sociology, on the other hand, is directed to the study of the drives which produce changes in actuality. There is a sort of selective affinity between the *real* basis of society and the ideal. Real factors encourage or discourage the exploration of ideal values. Hence, a fundamental task is the discovery of the successive ways in which real and ideal factors interact. There is a sequence of stages of integration of these realms from domination of blood and kinship, to influence by political structure, to determination by economic facts. This sequence of stages is substituted for Comte's theological, metaphysical, and positivistic stages in the development of human mentality.

Scheler was able, on occasion, to display great virtuosity in the conduct of phenomenological analysis, as in his qualitative differentiation of apparently similar feeling states in the study of *The Nature of Sympathy*. A series of feeling states normally identified as "sympathy" is discriminated into subunits. One may, for example, isolate *sympathy*, or emotional solidarity (*Miteinanderfühlen*), from other forms. This is identified as the immediate sharing of the same emotion with someone, as when persons participate in a common joy or grief. *Mimpathy*, or emotional imitation (*Nachfühlen*), is very distinct, inasmuch as the feeling does not arise from the same base. Both these forms, in turn, are distinguished from *propathy*, or emotional participation (*Mitgefühl*), found in cases where one participates in another's emotional state. However, this in turn is not automatic, like *emotional contagion* (*Gefühlsansteckung*), but more conscious. These are distinguishable from *empathy*, or emotional introjection (*Einfühlung*), and *unipathy*, or emotional identification (*Einsfühlung*). In this last type of formation one sees the basis for the

ecstasies of the mystery cults in which worshipers feel themselves to be one with the god.

But despite such analyses, the major trend in Scheler's thinking was away from the elaboration of distinctions in the realm of essences and toward the comprehension of sociohistorical meaning complexes, the problem that cast the sociology of knowledge into focus. History as the fusion of vitalistic and normative spheres reveals the intrusion of norms into otherwise undirected organismic events. Mind affects events both by guiding and directing, restraining and releasing, dispositional impulses. This interaction of vital and normative events is mediated by an elite, a small number of persons taking the lead in the fusion of ideal and factual events. They grasp the phenomenological essences. Their insights in turn are diffused by imitation through the masses. History thus is a product of the drive structure of the leaders of society and its ethos. The essence of a culture becomes conscious in its elite.

Cultural sociology stands in contrast to real sociology in that it deals with ideal factors (deriving from goals and aspirations) rather than real factors (resting on drives). Ideal factors have an influence on cultural development when they are anchored in interests and incorporated in institutional forms; otherwise, they remain epiphenomenal.

There are a number of forms of knowledge, the most basic of which are the fundamental cultural axioms of the group, which form the climate of opinion. The most fundamental of all the tasks of the sociology of knowledge is to isolate these basic suppositions and their transformations. Such basic cultural suppositions constitute an organic growth more fundamental than any body of mere theories. They are possibly transformed by the mixture of races, languages, and cultures.

Once this fundamental task has been accomplished, the sociology of knowledge analyzes more superficial forms of knowledge resting on these: technological information, scientific and mathematical knowledge, philosophical knowledge, mystic knowledge, religious knowledge, folk wisdom, and legendary knowledge. The more technical and rational the form of knowledge, the more rapid its rate of change. Each type of knowledge has its own peculiar rate.

The sociological character of forms of knowledge (of thought, intuition, and cognition) is unquestionable, according to Scheler. Nevertheless, neither the content nor the objective validity of knowledge is determined by social structures. Knowledge per se consists of a realm of essences. From this realm of essences, one or another set is selected. Hence, the different types of knowledge are tied up with the particular forms of groups. Plato's theory of ideas, for example, was the ideal counterpart of the Platonic academy. Every type of social movement or structure has forms of knowledge peculiarly appropriate to it. The *Gemeinschaft*, as a type of society, has a traditionally defined fund of knowledge. Far from being concerned with discovery or the extension of knowledge, even the effort to test traditional knowledge is a blasphemy. The prevailing mode of thought is one of demonstration rather than testing, and the methods of thought are ontological and dogmatic. Thought is realistic rather than nominalistic, and its categories are organismic.

Between ideas and institutional forms, for Scheler there was a relation of selective affinity, a parallelism or structural identity. The rise of modern industrial civilization of a *Gesellschaft* type, for example, was related to a new individualism in contrast to the old collectivism; a principle of competition rather than cooperation became central to the ethos, and scientific and technical knowledge rather than a treasure house of wisdom became the objective; a movement to science in place of theology and philosophy occurred.

Georges Gurvitch. Georges Gurvitch (1894–1965), a Russian sociologist, became a naturalized citizen of France in 1928. He was appointed to a chair of sociology at the Sorbonne in 1949. He was founder and first director of the Centre d'Études Sociologiques, established after World War II under the auspices of the Centre Nationale de la Recherche Scientifique, and he was editor of the *Cahiers internationaux de sociologie*. During the war years (1940–1945), Gurvitch taught at the New

GEORGES GURVITCH

United Press International Photo

School for Social Research and other colleges in North America. Among the major influences on Gurvitch are the phenomenology of Scheler and sociometry.[10]

[10]Gurvitch's chief sociological works include: *L'Idée du droit social* ["The Concept of Social Justice"] (Paris: Sirey, 1931); *Morale théorique et science des moeurs* ["Theoretical Ethics and the Science of the Mores"] (Paris: F. Alcan, 1937; 2d rev. ed., Paris: Presses Universitaires de France, 1948); *Essais de sociologie* (Paris: Sirey, 1938); *Éléments de sociologie juridique* ["Elements of Sociological Jurisprudence"] (Paris: Aubier, 1940); *Industrialisation et technocratie* ["Industrialization and Technology"] (Paris: A. Colin, 1949); *La Vocation actuelle de la sociologie* ["The Real Vocation of Sociology"] (Paris: Presses Universitaires de France, 1950; 2d ed., 1957); and *Déterminismes sociaux et liberté humaine* ["Social Determinisms and Human Liberty"] (Paris: Presses Universitaires de France, 1955). During the war years, Gurvitch published two books in

In Gurvitch's view, the sociological positivism of Comte had two basic features: the attempt to build a positive science of social facts and the conception of sociology as a total science or science of sciences. After Comte, sociological positivism renounced the identification of sociology with philosophy and with a theory of progress. It tended to become social naturalism, reducing sociology to a kind of mechanics, a theory of energy, geography, demography, and biology. Only organicism (Spencer and Schäffle) took account of the problem of societal regulation. Social psychologism (Lester Ward and Tarde) began to react against mechanical naturalism. Sociological formalism and American behaviorism (Simmel, von Wiese) limited sociology to the study of pure forms, excluding from sociology all study of spiritual content. More promising were the various kinds of recognition of the role of organization and control in human affairs (Sumner, and particularly E. A. Ross). Cooley, with his analysis of the organic wholeness of society, was particularly valuable for a fully developed sociology. The self and social unit are abstract forms of this organic unity. Another basic contribution to sociological development occurred with Max Weber, who helped give logical precision to the problem of the sociology of spiritual meaning. Durkheim began to divide social reality into distinct levels: (1) on the surface social reality consists of a geographic demographic unity; (2) underneath this Durkheim located reestablished collective behaviors; (3) a third level was found in symbols corresponding to institutions; (4) below symbols are collective values, ideas, and ideals symbolized by symbols; (5) finally we arrive at the deepest level of social reality, states of the collective mind, collective representations, collective memory, collective feeling, tendency, aspiration, and volition. It was on the basis of these distinctions that Durkheim distinguished various branches of sociology, including (1) social morphology, the study of the social surface; (2) social physiology, studying institutions, symbols, values, and ideas; (3) collective psychology; and (4) general sociology, studying the integration of all levels. In various ways, especially through Durkheim, the sociology of spiritual materials was developed. Particularly important for this were Wilhelm Dilthey, Max Scheler, and Karl Mannheim. The discussion of social symbols and noetic collective mentality was advanced by Ernst Cassirer, Lucien Lévy-Bruhl, and George Herbert Mead. Finally, Robert MacIver and Pitirim Sorokin and the philosopher, Elijah Jordan, have focused attention on the relation between social reality and spiritual meaning. In such fashion Gurvitch conceives the relation of the sociological tradition to his own theoretical position. Actually, most of such attributions are secondary reflections arising out of the extensions of the phenomenological point of view. They are interesting indications of the manner in which a modern phenomenologist organizes the whole field of theory.

The real final core of sociology is to be found in the study of the noetic mind or of the human spirit. Only the phenomenological method, Husserl's reduction, or Bergson's "method of inversion," is appropriate. What is needed is the immanent downward reduction of experience through successive stages toward whatever is most directly experienced as social reality.[11] The various levels of social reality correspond in part to those attributed to Durkheim. (1) The surface of social reality is made up of individuals and directly perceptible things, such as the demographic and geographic facts of society, including buildings, means of communication, and so forth. This material surface is social only to the extent that it is transformed and organized by collective human actions

English: *Sociology of Law* (New York: Philosophical Library, 1942) and *The Bill of Social Rights* (New York: International Universities Press, 1946). *The Spectrum of Social Time* has been translated by M. Korenbaum and P. Bosserman (Dordrecht, Holland: D. Reidel and Sons, 1964). For a study of Gurvitch's sociology see Phillip Bosserman, *Dialectical Sociology: An Analysis of the Sociology of Georges Gurvitch* (Boston: Porter Sargent, 1968).

[11]Gurvitch, *Déterminismes sociaux et liberté humaine,* pp. 103–104.

and penetrated by symbols and values given by the mind. It is a sort of external manifestation of human spiritual life. (2) The next level of social reality is made up of organizations, superstructures, or collective conducts, hierarchized and centralized according to prefixed patterns. (3) Below this is a level of patterns of standardized images and collective conducts. They need not — as with the second level — be rigged or prefixed. They may be flexible, ranging from rites and traditions to changing fashions. However, a sharp distinction must be drawn between technical or economic patterns and symbolic-cultural patterns linked to spiritual values. The latter form a part of the noetic or spiritual realm. (4) Beneath these patterns lie unorganized collective conducts. Their spontaneity is limited by standardization. They are habitual conducts. (5) Beneath these in turn is a layer of social reality constituted by social symbols. Without them, organization, cultural patterns, and collective conduct are impossible, since they guide such patterns. Such symbols are neither simple expressive signs nor illusions. The symbols mediate between appearances and things in themselves. Social symbols are inadequate expressions of the spiritual realm adapted to concrete social situations. Social symbols are simultaneously conditioned by social reality and the spirit. They can take varied forms. They are not necessarily connected with patterns and not necessarily standardized and generalized, for they may be images valid for a unique behavior. (6) Below the level of symbols are collective behaviors, which innovate, disrupt old patterns, and create new ones. These innovating social behaviors are unforeseeable. But they are manifest in times of revolution, epochs of reform, religious disturbance, and war. They conceal some symbols, weaken or change others, and create new symbols. (7) Below creative and unforeseeable social conduct is a real level of values and collective ideas which inspire this unforeseeable conduct and serve as the spiritual basis of symbols. Only at this level of social reality do we encounter the spiritual realm proper, the realm of values and ideas which are irreducible to acts which realize them and to states of the collective

mind which grasp them. At various epochs and in different cultural spheres they appear and vanish. The study of the particularization of spiritual values defines the framework of the sociology of the noetic mind. (8) Spiritual values and ideas particularized with reference to social epochs and structure must be grasped, tested, and experienced. Thus, one must assume the existence of collective mentalities aspiring toward such values and ideas, enlightening itself with them. This is the deepest level of social reality — the level of the collective mind — the collective psyche which displays itself at every level of social reality. It may be studied in a state of greater or less detachment from its content. The study of the human spirit or noetic mind is the study of cultural patterns, social symbols, and collective spiritual values and ideas in their functional relations with social structures and concrete historical situations of society. Only a sociological method interpreting inner meanings, or *"verstehen,"* is appropriate to this type of study.[12]

An interesting question is why Gurvitch abandoned the phenomenological perspective that he promoted imaginatively in his work until sometime in the mid-fifties. In his *Essais de sociologie,* Gurvitch had argued that the only way to find objective criteria for distinguishing between different forms of sociability is the method of inversion or phenomenological reduction, which consists in digging ever deeper into the superimposed levels of social reality.[13] And in his *Sociology of Law* he asserted:

> The best approach to problems of the sociology of the noetic mind (or of human spirit) and to the determination of its exact place among the various sociological disciplines, would seem to be via the levels — or depth — analysis of social reality. This type of analysis is inspired by the "method of inversion" (Bergson) or "phenomenological reduction" (Husserl), i.e., an immanent downward reduction through successive

[12]*Ibid.,* pp. 99–161. For a brief statement, see *Sociology of Law,* pp. 33–40.
[13]Gurvitch, *Essais de sociologie,* p. 21f.

stages towards whatever is most directly experienced in social reality.[14]

Gurvitch's phenomenological period clearly accompanied his exile from Russia, which suggests that the appeal of phenomenology arose from its anticollectivism, its stress on individual potentiality, freedom, and responsibility despite the irrationalities in the world that confronts an individual.[15] He began to abandon his phenomenological position at the time he was appointed at the Sorbonne to the chair once occupied by Émile Durkheim. There is no reason to doubt Phillip Bosserman's description of Gurvitch after his return to France from America, in the estimate of many, as the most important sociologist in postwar France.

> The fundamental roots for Gurvitch's view of social reality are found in works of the "founders" of sociology. He pays particular attention to Saint-Simon, Proudhon, Comte, Marx and Spencer . . . He saw society as a real entity in movement, in which the collective efforts, both spiritual and material, were something different from the individual participants with whom they interacted and interpenetrated. . . . The

real precursers of Gurvitch's thought are Émile Durkheim and certain of his disciples.[16]

Upon returning to France, Gurvitch abandoned an elementaristic for a holistic point of view. Sociology became, for him, the study of total social phenomena conceived as a unit determining its parts. One can accept Bosserman's summary:

> The total social phenomena have a primacy over all their particular levels. These various levels making up each total phenomenon have not only a methodological primacy over the astructural, structural and structured sectors, but an *ontological* one. . . . Ontology is the ultimate reference. . . . The various social phenomena are related dynamically and dialectically. Hence, all separations between them are relative. The existential fact is their wholeness; they are *total social phenomena*, united in a complex web which is social reality.[17]

> Three processes hold for sociology, since causality reveals precious little: (1) functional correlation, (2) tendency toward regularity, and (3) the direct integration in the whole.[18]

Gurvitch's total sociology in his last phase bears considerable similarity to Pitirim Sorokin's integral sociology in his last phase; both men were on their way toward an organicism that suggests the founders of sociology, with increasing reservations about the exclusive value of positivistic methods. Perhaps some day Gurvitch will find the sensitive biographer who will explore the reasons for this change of theoretical perspective.[19]

---

[14]Georges Gurvitch, *Sociology of Law* (London: Kegan Paul, 1947), p. 33.

[15]Phillip Bosserman, Gurvitch's student, was apparently oblivious to the intriguing problem of the role of Gurvitch's existential situation on his thought. In 1920, despite an appointment to teach at the University of Petrograd, Gurvitch left Russia never to return, with his sole luggage consisting of his notes for books. One can only assume that there was an urgency in his departure indicating that it was not completely voluntary. Bosserman's summary of these events is hardly satisfactory: "He felt obligated to leave Russia when all hope vanished that a truly pluralistic state based on decentralized democratic principles could become reality. He also disagreed with the decision to draw up a peace treaty with Germany" (Bosserman, *Dialectical Sociology*, p. 13). Gurvitch's actual behavior suggests, rather, that this was a traumatic career break, a flight from his homeland under circumstances that led him to rush into the arms of Scheler and Husserl, whom, along with Bergson, he continued to follow until he returned to France in 1945 after his American sojourn.

[16]Bosserman, *Dialectical Sociology*, pp. 93–94.
[17]*Ibid.*, p. 140.
[18]*Ibid.*, p. 244.
[19]Gurvitch obviously took his role as France's foremost sociologist seriously, and, among other things, became actively involved in French political concerns. In the summer of 1962 an attack was made on his life when his apartment was bombed, but Gurvitch and his wife escaped serious injury. One cannot help wonder whether his shift to holism at this period (when functionalistic holism was popular in America and Marxian holism was popular in France) did not have some of the properties of the behavior of the intellectual who was seen by his as-

THE PHENOMENOLOGY OF EVERYDAY LIFE AND ETHNOMETHODOLOGY

The pioneering phase of phenomenological sociology consisted of early attempts to develop new methods (particularly by Husserl and Bergson) for the task of solving problems raised by neo-Kantian sociology, that is, identifying basic psychological components of interpersonal life without reduction to contentless formalism. The approach was elementaristic. The essential subject matter of sociology was meaningful interaction. (Gurvitch, in his phenomenological phase, would probably have described it as the study of the interpersonal aspects of the noetic mind.) This early development occurred largely before the fusion of phenomenology and existentialism which took place in the 1920s.[20]

The joining of phenomenology and existentialism was primarily the work of Jaspers and Heidegger in the 1920s. In his *General Psychopathology* (1913) Jaspers had taken over a distinction introduced by Wilhelm Dilthey between comprehending and explaining (*Verstehende* and *Erklärende*) psychopathology as a device to describe a variety of abnormal personalities. Comprehending psychology tries to understand interrelations; explaining psychology tries to provide causal explanations. In this study Jaspers treated descriptive phenomenology as an important (though not exclusive) tool of investigation. In Jaspers' second book on the *Psychology of World-Views* he tried to penetrate the core of possible world-views, in search of the key ideas at the basis of an individual's self-conceptions and decisions. The work was sensitive to the individual's condition and situations which press home upon him or her the finitude of human life: chance, conflict, suffering, and, eventually, death. In *Man in the Modern World* (1931) Jaspers carried through a diagnosis of the times.

Between the time of Jaspers' *Psychology of World-Views* and his penetrating analysis of alienation in *Man in the Modern Age*, Heidegger's *Sein und Zeit* (1927) appeared. In the words of J. H. Heinemann,

> Instead of moving in mere possibilities like Jaspers, he chose one possibility and drew, with extraordinary forming power and penetration, pictures of unauthentic and authentic existence which were a true expression of the inarticulate longings of the time. He stole the existentialist show from Jaspers, just as Sartre did with Marcel in France. That he himself as a person assimilated the principle merely intellectually and not existentially, has unfortunately been proved by his utter human failure in the existential trial of the Third Reich, whereas Jaspers passed this examination with high honors and gained enormously in stature.[21]

---

sociates marching in the front ranks when the Bastille was stormed. When asked what he was doing in the mob, he was said to have replied: "I have to be here, I'm their leader."

[20]Gurvitch, to be sure, continued his work in the pioneer phase of phenomenological sociology well beyond the period when the connection to existentialism changed the course of phenomenological sociology. However, he adopted a phenomenological point of view before the marriage of phenomenology and existentialism. Husserl had borrowed the idea of bracketing from mathematics, and transformed it into a device to legitimize the abandonment of concerns of everyday life in his search for the pure transcendental ego in and by itself. Gurvitch took this figure of speech and retooled it, turning it into a kind of geological image. When he eventually found it desirable to accommodate his sociology to various forms of holism, Gurvitch dropped the phenomenological justification for his depth level analysis and "discovered" that numerous other sociologists, without phenomenological background, had also used a similar figure of speech. He then advanced his dialectical analysis of total social life in a manner comparable to Sorokin in the latter's integral sociology.

[21]F. H. Heinemann, *Existentialism and the Modern Predicament* (New York: Harper, 1953), p. 87. Heinemann refers to the fact that when Heidegger was made rector of the University of Freiburg under the Third Reich he gave a speech defending the objectives of the regime and, though he resigned the rectorship a year later, the evidence is not clear that he ever, as was claimed later, repudiated his address. Jaspers, by contrast, withdrew from public life at Heidelberg into voluntary exile in his own home and until the end of the Third Reich turned all his efforts to private research and scholarship.

The linkage between phenomenology and existentialism made by Jaspers and Heidegger not only reversed the thrust of Husserl's original analysis (Husserl had bracketed existence in the interest of getting ahead on the structure of mind; the existentialism of Jaspers and Heidegger made the predicament of human beings in everyday life the primary focus of analysis), but captured center stage. Husserl would have been either less or more than human if he had not experienced this development with dismay: the loss of control over a movement of which he was founder. Spiegelberg states that when, upon his retirement in 1929, Husserl designated Heidegger as his successor at Freiburg it was with the hope that it would lead to closer cooperation between them.

> It was only after Heidegger's return from Marburg to Freiburg that Husserl became fully aware of the divergence between his own and Heidegger's conceptions of phenomenology . . . The full realization of this fact was by far the severest personal disappointment in Husserl's philosophical career. Also it soon led to a personal estrangement . . . Heidegger's involvement . . . in the Nazi regime . . . added to Husserl's bitterness.[22]

In 1929 Husserl gave a series of lectures at the Sorbonne (first published in French as *Cartesian Meditations*) in which he presented phenomenology as a form of neo-Cartesianism and tried to answer the charge of solipsism (the notion that the self is the only object of verifiable knowledge) to which his phenomenology was thought by many to be open. He sought to show, in Spiegelberg's words, "how the transcendental ego constitutes other egos as equal partners in an intersubjective community, which in turn forms the foundation for the objective, i.e, the intersubjective world."[23] Moreover, in lectures given at Prague and Vienna in 1935 and his last major work, *The Crisis of the European Sciences and Transcendental Phenomenology*, Husserl was seeking not only to establish a phenomenological foundation for the human community, but to accommodate phenomenology to the growing disillusionment with science and positivism and the new concern with the predicament of individuals in their everyday concerns which were being brought into focus by existentialism.

By the *Crisis of the European Sciences*, Husserl refers to the growing dismay of many contemporaries in the face of a collapse of self-understanding, accompanied by both a breakdown of technical-scientific explanation and a failure in practical orientations to the world. The source of this breakdown was later traced to scientific objectivism or positivism, the notion that the ultimate reality of the self and the world can be adequately grasped by the objective sciences. The answer to this crisis was to start over by means of a careful analysis of everyday, prescientific life. This required a new kind of phenomenological reduction, not one which brackets existence, as in *Ideen*, but one which brackets everything originating in scientific theories and philosophic conceptualizations. It is a return to the everyday life-world.[24] Husserl now saw all the sciences, all special disciplines as having their origin in the subjective realm of everyday life, which provides the starting conditions for the possibility of any experience whatsoever. Husserl's enterprise, at this point, has a Kantian sound. From Joseph Kockelmans's summary, Husserl's approach appears as a deepened Kantianism in which the distinction between pure and practical reason has been eliminated and reduction within the everyday experience of the life-world is in search of structural components, a priori, of morality as well as other forms of knowledge.

---

[22]Spiegelberg, *The Phenomenological Movement*, I, 154.
[23]*Ibid.*, I, 158.

[24]The *Crisis* was unfinished at the time of Husserl's death. He did not use the concept *life-world* in the first sections which were published, but did so extensively in his notes. The concept was first referred to by L. Landgrebe who had made a study of the Husserl archives. L. Landgrebe, "World as a Phenomenological Problem," *Philosophy and Phenomenological Research*, 1 (1940), 38–58.

The reduction teaches us that the truth of the world cannot be found in its entirety in the world determined by the sciences. The pre-scientific world opens up the possibility for the explication of certain general structures which are given in our original experience, namely the structures of the *Lebenswelt*. In our pursuit of these structures we encounter an unconditional, general a priori. . . .

We can already conclude from Kant's *Kritik der reinen Vernunft* that we cannot uncover the ground of all beings by means of our theoretically objectifying, scientific knowledge. Phenomenology adds to this that the ground of all beings cannot be reached by means of postulates of practical reason either. . . . The process of uncovering the ground of all beings cannot start from a position which defines man as rational subject only. The point of departure for such a venture is man in his full concreteness (which includes his thinking, striving, and his moral activities as well as his sensory-bodily being) and also the way in which this concrete man uncovers the richness of the world in its intuitive fullness. Only if we choose this as a starting point can we hope to uncover a really true world.[25]

There is much similarity between what Husserl was doing in his last unfinished work and what the existentialists, particularly his student Heidegger, had done. Husserl's *Crisis* is perhaps best interpreted as an attempt not to accommodate his and Heidegger's versions of phenomenology, but to perform an encircling movement against the existential threat. The existentialists' aim was the explanation of human beings and their world. Husserl appears, rather, to have used the concept of the life-world (his version of the existential predicament) as a starting point for a more radical attempt to develop a general unified phenomenological approach to all the disciplines, remaining more positivistic in orientation. Whatever his intentions in *The Crisis*, Husserl eventually joined the ranks of those who placed everyday life in the forefront of analysis, bracketing scientific theories and philosophic conceptions. This development became a catalyst for transforming phenomenology into an antipositivistic program.

Alfred Schutz. Alfred Schutz (1899–1959) was born in Vienna. He served in the Austria-Hungary army during World War I and studied law and social science in Vienna with Hans Kelsen, Ludwig von Mises, Friedrich von Wieser, and Othmar Spann. As a student he became interested in the works of Husserl and Max Weber. His publication of *Der sinnhafte Aufbau der sozialen Welt* (1932, translated as *The Phenomenology of the Social World,* 1967) brought him into direct contact with Husserl. They became close friends; Schutz visited with Husserl frequently; and the two men corresponded until Husserl's death. Husserl invited Schutz to become his assistant at Freiburg, an invitation Schutz was unable to accept. In the face of the impending Nazi occupation of Austria in 1938, Schutz emigrated to Paris and a year later made his way to the United States, where he joined Alvin Johnson's University in Exile at the New School for Social Research. Thereafter, Schutz divided his time between academic work and a full-time business position. He became close friends with various of Husserl's students such as Dorian Cairns, Aron Gurwitsch, Marvin Farber, and Felix Kaufman. With Farber he established the International Phenomenological Society and joined the editorial board of *Philosophy and Phenomenological Research* when it was established in 1941. He died in New York in 1959.[26]

---

[25]Joseph J. Kockelmans, *Edmund Husserl's Phenomenological Psychology* (Pittsburgh, Pa.: Duquesne University Press, 1967), pp. 273–274.

[26]Schutz's writings include: *Der Sinnhafte Aufbau der sozialen Welt* (Vienna: Springer, 1932); *The Phenomenology of the Social World,* trans. George Walsh and Fredrick Lehnert (Evanston, Ill.: Northwestern University Press, 1967); *Collected Papers I: The Problem of Social Reality,* ed. Maurice Nathanson (The Hague: Nijhoff, 1962); *Collected Papers II: Studies in Social Theory,* ed. Arvid Brodersen (The Hague: Nijhoff, 1964); *Collected Papers III: Studies in Phenomenological Philosophy,* ed. Ilse Schutz, with an introduction by Aron Gurwitsch (The Hague: Nijhoff, 1964); *Reflections on the Problem of Relevance,* ed. Richard

ALFRED SCHUTZ

The New York Times

Alfred Schutz was the major architect of a re-founded phenomenological sociology which focused on the problem of everyday life (or the sociology of the life-world). In Helmut Wagner's words, Schutz was a man with a single objective, the development of phenomenological sociology.[27] In his first book, which may some day be viewed as a classic of phenomenological sociology,[28] Schutz undertook to clarify Weber's ideas by means of

Husserl's phenomenology, with some help from the theories of Georg Simmel, H. Bergson, William James, and Max Scheler. He presented all of his basic concerns and themes in this volume. In his later writings he elucidated, extended and, at times, modified the positions, stands, and problems in his first work. In his later period he also made extensive use of the writings of John Dewey, George H. Mead, Charles Cooley, and W. I. Thomas. In Wagner's estimation:

> Schutz's critique of Weber did not result in the refutation of any of the latter's basic postulates. Rather, it amounted to clarifications, to the exposure of hidden meanings, to the development of individual concepts beyond the point at which Weber had broken off his analysis, and to the establishment of the different meanings some concepts assumed when used in different contexts. In this sense, Schutz simply developed Weberian conceptions in the direction indicated by Weber himself.[29]

Max Weber had defined the task of sociology as the science that attempts the interpretative understanding of social action in order to arrive at a causal explanation of its course and effects.[30] The focus of analysis was the concept of meaning (which could be the actual existing meaning of a concrete actor in a given case or a theoretically conceived pure type) and the social behavior in which it was embodied. He suggested a fourfold typology of meaningful social actions as a basic tool for analysis: rational personal, evaluative, traditional, and affective. In this typology, fully rational action has privileged status, not because it is the most valuable or frequent in actual social life, but because it is mutually the most understandable. It therefore serves as a measuring rod of other types of social action, which in varying degrees are matters of unthinking habit (traditional social actions),

M. Zaner (New Haven, Conn.: Yale University Press, 1970); *Alfred Schutz: On Phenomenology and Social Relations*, ed. Helmut R. Wagner (Chicago: University of Chicago Press, 1970).

[27]Wagner, *Alfred Schutz*, p. 3.
[28]*Der Sinnhafte Aufbau der sozialen Welt* (1932) was the only book published in Schutz's lifetime.

[29]Wagner, *Alfred Schutz*, pp. 10–11.
[30]See "The Fundamental Concepts of Sociology," *Max Weber: The Theory of Social and Economic Organization*, trans. A. M. Henderson and Talcott Parsons (New York: Oxford University Press, 1947), pp. 87f.

or emotion (affective social actions), or ethical commitments.

Weber used the concept *social relationship* (taken in the sense of the existence of the possibility that there will be a social action in a meaningfully understandable sense) as a means of generalizing his sociology to the problems of institutions. He extended his theory of social relationships with ideas of: modes of orientation of social action (usage, custom, fashion, and law); types of legitimate order (disinterested, evaluative, affectual, and rational-legal); openness and closure; and representation and responsibility. Weber capped his statement of basic concepts with a review of the types of corporate groups, types of order in corporate groups, and the problems of power, authority, and imperative control.

Weber never abandoned his basic position that the primary reality to which sociology as a science was addressed was meaningful interpersonal conduct and the fundamental method by which it was analyzable and understood was by ideal-typical constructs.

Schutz believed that Weber's sociology began analysis with the natural attitude of the world of daily life or the life-world. From the outset, the world of daily life into which we are born is not private, but intersubjective, common to all. Individuals have not a theoretical, but a practical interest in it. In this shared world at any moment a stock of knowledge is at hand which supplies schemes of interpretation of past and present and determines anticipations of things to come. The knowledge of the person who acts and thinks, to be sure, is usually inaccurate, only partially clear, and not at all free from contradictions. Moreover, it is taken for granted that the social world is different for each culture and society, though certain features are common to all social worlds because of similarities in the human condition.

Schutz points out that this taken-for-granted world consists in shared ideas, a common system of typifications and relevances. Any given in-group centers on a common myth. The myth is a product (social construction) of the persons who hold and

who are constantly changing it. This is the deeper reason why Max Weber could say that the existence of a marriage or a state means nothing other than the probability or chance that the participating individuals will act in a specific way. This does not mean that any individual can transform the whole of social life simply by nonaction, but it does mean that in the moment any considerable number begin to think otherwise, the common foundation of in-group stability has begun to collapse.

Only a small part of one's knowledge of the world originates in personal experience. The great part is derived. Individuals are taught how to define the environment and, even, how typical constructs have to be formed in accordance with the system of relevances of the in-group. The typifying medium par excellence is the vocabulary and syntax of everyday language. Language as a scheme of interpretation and expression does not merely consist of symbols and the rules of syntax (which can be translated) but also a variety of connotations, including a fringe or aura ultimately unique to the in-group. Only when one has written love letters in a language, when one knows how to pray and curse in it and can express every shade of feeling appropriate to the situation, does one have full command over it. Systems of relevance, that is, schemes of value order, are either intrinsic (self-established) or imposed (by forces outside one's control). Domains of relevance are ordered in particular groups and at particular times. But they are also endlessly changing.

The factual world of experience, for its part, is a typical one from the outset. As used in everyday life, language is a treasure house of preconstituted types, each bearing an open horizon of unexplored typical contents. All forms of recognition and identification, even of real objects of the outer world, are based on a generalized knowledge of the type of these objects or of the typical style in which they manifest themselves. What sociologists call "system," "status," "role expectation," "situation," and "institution," are experienced by the individual as a network of typifications — typifications of individuals of their courses of action-patterns, their motives, goals, and the sociocultural products of their actions. Knowledge of these typifications and of their appropriate use is an inseparable element of the sociocultural heritage.

This system of relevances and typifications determines which facts have to be treated as substantially — that is typically — equal. Such a system transforms unique acts of unique humans into typical actions of typical social roles, originating in typical motives, and bringing about typical results. The system functions both as a scheme of interpretation and of orientation for each member of the group. The chance of success in human interaction is enhanced when the scheme of typification is standardized.

It is against this background of a discussion of the natural attitude toward the life-world that Schutz takes up Weber's problems of social action: the understanding of action and motivation; the meaning of rational conduct; the inevitability of anticipating, projecting, and planning. If intention, anticipation, and projecting make a difference in conduct, the conclusion is unavoidable that one who lives in a social world is a free being.

In following Weber's lead, Schutz avoided Husserl's problem of solipsism. If we retain the natural attitude as people among people, the existence of others is no more questionable to us than the existence of an outer world. And, as a matter of fact, among the objects we experience in the vivid present are other people's behavior and thoughts. Schutz observes, "This experience of the other's stream of consciousness in vivid simultaneity I propose to call the *general thesis of the alter ego's existence.*"[31]

Individuals in the natural world understand the world by interpreting their own lived experiences of it. And, in fact, the Thou who confronts one is a fellowperson discovered by explicating one's own consciousness. Ironically, far from being trapped in a solipsistic isolation, one experiences the other directly, one can find one's self only in an act of

reflection after the fact. A Thou-orientation is a pure mode in which one is aware of another human being as a person. Face-to-face relationships in which the partners are aware of each other are We-relationships. There are other, mediate relationships with contemporaries, in which the self of the other does not become accessible as a partner to a unity. These are segmental relationships. The other appears as a partial self best described as "They-orientation," which calls attention to the conscious experience of contemporaries apprehended only as anonymous processes.

A major feature of human life in the modern world is the extending reciprocal anonymity of partners. More and more people are aware that their life-world as a whole is neither fully understandable by themselves nor by any of their fellow-people. Yet there is assumed to be a stock of knowledge theoretically available to everyone, built up by practical experience, science, and technology as warranted insights. It is not integrated, but consists of juxtaposed coherent systems. Schutz envisions three ideal types of access to the common stock of knowledge: that of the expert (whose knowledge is restricted to a limited field but therein is clear and distinct), that of the person on the street (with a working knowledge of many fields, which are not necessarily coherent with one another), and that of the well-informed citizen (who is somewhere between the person on the street and the expert).

In Schutz's view sociology and the other social sciences begin with the life-world, and proceed from it by developing fundamental hypotheses which define fields of research and provide the regulative principles for building up a system of ideal types. In the process they automatically start upon a course which would transcend the life-world. But Schutz raises the question: should we want to do so?

> If the social world as object of our scientific research is but a typical construction, why bother with this intellectual game? Our scientific activity and, particularly, that which deals with the social world, is also performed within a certain means-ends relation, namely,

---

[31]Schutz, *On Phenomenology and Social Relations*, p. 167.

in order to acquire knowledge for mastering the world, the real world, not the one created by the grace of the scientist. We want to find out what happens in the real world and not in the fantasies of a few sophisticated eccentrics.

There are a few arguments for quieting such an interlocutor. First of all, the construction of the scientific world is not an arbitrary act of the scientist which he can perform at his own discretion:

1. There are the historical boundaries of the realm of his science which each scientist has inherited from his ancestors as a stock of approved propositions.
2. The postulate of adequacy requires that the typical construction be compatible with the totality of both our daily life and our scientific experience.[32]

Berger and Luckmann. The extent to which Schutz's phenomenology of the life-world was destined to become the core of a revived phenomenological sociology may be illustrated by its use by Berger and Luckmann to refurbish the sociology of knowledge.

Peter L. Berger was born in Vienna and came to the United States in his late teens. He earned a master's and a doctor's degree in sociology from the New School for Social Research. He has taught in Germany, the University of North Carolina, the Hartford Seminary, and the New School for Social Research. Thomas Luckmann taught at Hobart College and the New School for Social Research before accepting a chair of sociology in the University of Frankfurt.

The sociology of knowledge, according to Berger and Luckmann, must concern itself with everything that passes for "knowledge" in society, and hence with the social construction of reality. This insight is attributed to Alfred Schutz. "How is it possible that subjective meanings *become* objective facticities? . . . This inquiry, we maintain, is the task of the sociology of knowledge."[33]

This is accomplished, they say, by the phe-

nomenological analysis of everyday life, which contains numerous pre- and quasi-scientific interpretations of reality which are taken for granted and which must be described "within phenomenological brackets" on the assumption that "consciousness is always intentional." The reality of everyday life presupposes "an intersubjective world" with routines which continue without interruption so long as they are unproblematic. The everyday world is structured spatially and temporally and has a social dimension "by virtue of the fact that my manipulatory zone intersects with that of others." Moreover, the "temporal structure of everyday life confronts me as a facticity with which I must reckon." "Clock and calendar ensure that, indeed, I am a 'man of my time.' "

The reality of life is shared with others in important face-to-face situations. For in face-to-face situations the other is fully real. However, to discover myself, I must stop and turn my attention back upon myself "such reflection about myself is typically occasioned by the attitude toward me that *the other* exhibits." At such times I feel "the immediate, continuous and massively real presence of his expressivity." On the other hand, I apprehend the other by means of "typificatory schemes" which "ongoingly affect my interaction with him." The typificatory schemes in face-to-face situations are reciprocal and "enter into an ongoing 'negotiation' in the face-to-face situation." However, unfortunately, in these times the occasions for face-to-face negotiation decline and others must be faced as "mere contemporaries. Anonymity increases as I go from the former to the latter." In any case, the social reality of everyday life is apprehended "in a continuum of typifications, which are progressively anonymous as they are removed from the 'here and now.' " Social structure, incidentally, "is the sum total of these typifications and of the recurrent patterns of interaction established by means of them."[34]

Following these observations, which Berger and Luckmann presented under the rubric "The

[32]*Ibid.*, pp. 314–315.
[33]Peter L. Berger and Thomas Luckmann, *The Social Construction of Reality: A Treatise in the Sociology of Knowledge* (Garden City, N.Y.: Doubleday, 1966), p. 18.

[34]Paraphrased from Berger and Luckmann, *The Social Construction of Reality*, pp. 20–35.

Foundations of Knowledge in Everyday Life," they addressed themselves to two other topics, "Society as Objective Reality" (a discussion of institutionalization and legitimation) and "Society as Subjective Reality" (a review of socialization, primarily consisting of ideas taken over from Mead and translated into phenomenological jargon).

Institutionalization is the process other students speak of as the formation of social structure. It is made possible and necessary by human biological adaptability: "One may say that the biologically intrinsic world-openness of human existence is always, and indeed must be, transformed by social order into a relative world-closedness."[35] "Institutionalization occurs whenever there is a reciprocal typification of habitualized actions by types of actors."[36] Once formed, institutions are reified, that is, viewed as things. However, they must then be legitimized. "Legitimation as a process is best described as a 'second-order' objectivation of meaning. Legitimation produces new meanings that serve to integrate the meanings already attached to disparate institutional processes."[37] There is said to be a dialectical relationship between social institutions and the theories that rise to legitimate them. "What remains sociologically essential is the recognition that all symbolic universes and all legitimations are human products; their existence has its base in the lives of concrete individuals, and has no empirical status apart from these lives."[38]

Although there is very little in the Berger-Luckmann treatise that was not already present and with greater subtlety in the formulations of Alfred Schutz, there is considerable difference in the claims made for the respective formulations. Schutz claimed only to have undertaken to clarify some of the more cryptic formulations in Max Weber's explanations; Berger and Luckmann not only claim a new departure in theory, but an original solution to the problems of the sociology of knowledge. In fact, their major contribution seems to have been the codification of phenomenological language into a stereotyped jargon.

Harold Garfinkel. Harold Garfinkel was born in Newark, New Jersey, in 1929, educated at Newark, North Carolina, and Harvard, where he received the Ph.D. in 1952. He joined the faculty of the University of California in 1954, becoming professor in 1966. Garfinkel is presented here as the representative of an active group which has undertaken to convert Schutz's approach to sociology into a viable research program. In a collection of his essays, Garfinkel, who invented the term *ethnomethodology* to designate the phenomenology of everyday life, listed the major scholars whom he viewed as involved in this enterprise.

> Over the past ten years a group of increasing size has been doing ethnomethodological studies as day to day concerns: Egon Bittner, Aaron V. Cicourel, Lindsey Churchill, Craig MacAndrew, Michael Moerman, Edward Rose, Harvey Sacks, Emmanuel Schegloff, David Sudnow, D. Lawrence Wieder, and Don Zimmerman.[39]

Garfinkel, somewhat surprisingly, listed Talcott Parsons as his initial inspiration in addition to such phenomenologists as Alfred Schutz, Edmund Husserl, and Aron Gurwitsch. However, the most important influence of all was clearly Schutz, if one judges from the generous sprinkling of Schutzian terminology and distinctions in almost every passage of his work: *taken-for-granted, life-world, intentionality, ongoing, domain of relevance, practical activity, typification,* and the like.

Garfinkel claims that he got the idea for the term *ethnomethodology* while working in the Yale crosscultural area files through a section with such terms as *ethnobotany, ethnophysiology, ethnophysics,* and so forth. During the same period he reports he had been reviewing secretly made tapes of jury deliberations. The jurors were struggling toward a

[35]*Ibid.*, p. 51.
[36]*Ibid.*, p. 54.
[37]*Ibid.*, p. 92.
[38]*Ibid.*, p. 128.

[39]Harold Garfinkel, *Studies in Ethnomethodology* (Englewood Cliffs, N.J.: Prentice-Hall, 1967), p. viii.

decision in a hit-or-miss manner or, in Garfinkel's words, "they were doing their methodology in the 'now you see it, now you don't' fashion."[40] If one were to take Garfinkel seriously this would seem to mean that ethnomethodology refers to the more or less muddled manner in which persons in problematic collective situations arrive at a decision. However, sometime later Garfinkel identified the primary concerns of ethnomethodology to be with "materially grounded tasks of discovering the identifying issues of the problem of social order."[41] Ethnomethodology appears to be the study of social order.

Whatever the definition of ethnomethodology, the primary object of the phenomenological tradition stemming from Schutz is the direct examination or firsthand study of ongoing social life. Methodological procedures have shifted toward participant observation and the study of social events from the inside. Garfinkel's chief contribution has been the addition of confrontational ("experimental") gimmicks to the participant observer's repertoire. For example, students were asked not only to take special note of background expectations in their family homes but to "spend some fifteen minutes to an hour in their homes imagining they were boarders and acting out this assumption . . . to conduct themselves in a circumspect and polite fashion . . . avoid getting personal, to use formal address, to speak only when spoken to."[42] Some students refused to do this, a few tried but were unsuccessful (their families laughed at them), but those who completed the assignment found that their families were dismayed.

In the remaining four-fifths of the cases family members were stupefied. They vigorously sought to make the strange actions intelligible and to restore the situation to normal appearances. Reports were filled with accounts of astonishment, bewilderment, shock, anxiety, embarrassment, and anger, and with charges by various family members that the student was mean, inconsiderate, selfish, nasty, or impolite.[43]

It was perhaps inevitable that Garfinkel's ethnomethodology would evoke the censure of Alvin Gouldner. The publication of Garfinkel's collected essays coincided with the rise of the countercultural revolt of the 1960s at the time that Gouldner was moving from a structure-functionalist toward a neo-Hegelian position (that is, from a right- to a left-wing form of holism) and was negative to all forms of elementarism, whether conservative or liberal. In *The Coming Crisis of Western Sociology*, Gouldner correctly interprets Garfinkel's work within the phenomenological tradition of Alfred Schutz and as preoccupied with the problem of order in everyday life.

Garfinkel focuses on everyday life . . . rather than on critical events . . . He regards all people as being "practical theorists," collaboratively creating meanings and understandings of one another's activities . . . He seeks to communicate *their* sense of things, with an almost Nietzschean hostility to conceptualization and abstraction, and particularly by avoiding the conceptualizations conventional to normal sociology . . . He seems to be responding to a social world in which sex, drugs, religion, family, school, all are uncertain . . . a social world resting on tacit understandings that . . . are still fragile and rather readily eluded.

Garfinkel normally exposes these rules through game-like "demonstrations" of what happens when some men, without informing others of their intent, deliberately proceed to violate these tacit understandings . . . Garfinkel aims, primarily, at baring and unmasking the invisible commonplace by violating it in some manner until it betrays its presence . . . Garfinkel's is an attack upon the common sense of reality . . .

The cry of pain, then, is Garfinkel's triumphal moment; it is dramatic confirmation of the existence of certain tacit rules governing social interaction and of

[40]Harold Garfinkel, in Richard J. Hill and Kathleen Stones Crittenden, eds. *Proceedings of the Purdue Symposium on Ethnomethodology* (Fayetteville, Ind.: Purdue Research Foundation, 1968), p. 3.
[41]Giesla J. Hinkel, chairperson of the panel on "When Is Phenomenology Sociological?" (1976), in *The Annals of Phenomenological Sociology*, 2 (1977), 12.
[42]Garfinkel, *Studies in Ethnomethodology*, p. 47.
[43]*Ibid.*, p. 47.

their importance to the persons involved. That he feels free to inflict these costs on others, on his students, their families, friends, or passersby — and to encourage others to do so — is not, I would suggest, evidence of a dispassionate and detached attitude toward the social world, but of a readiness to use it in cruel ways.[44]

Gouldner arrived at his judgments of the sadism and cruelty of ethnomethodology by taking out of context the accounts of the social consequences of such experiments as having students behave like boarders in their own homes and interpreting the results of such experiments as a source of cynical satisfaction to Garfinkel. Garfinkel, in fact, reported, "There were no cases in which the situation was not restorable upon the student's explanation"[45] and admitted that the experience left elements of distress in most family members and students. This hardly suggests that Garfinkel was motivated by sadistic cruelty or by a wish comparable to the countercultural student rebels of the 1960s to trash society, wreck the establishment, and shatter the structure of everyday life (as Gouldner suggests), nor that he was really expressing amoral indifference to the distinction between "is" and "ought," as Kurt Wolff concluded from his review of the Garfinkel-Gouldner incident.[46]

In their essay on ethnomethodology for the McKinney-Tiryakian volume on *Theoretical Sociology*, Garfinkel and Harvey Sacks take note of the fact that sociologists other than phenomenologists have been interested in the formal structures of everyday activities. Garfinkel appears to have been trying to establish the right of ethnomethodologists to study the problem of everyday life without denigrating the findings of other brands of social theorists when he introduced his principle of "ethnomethodological indifference."

Ethnomethodological studies of formal structures are directed to the study of such phenomena, seeking to describe members' accounts of formal structures wherever and by whomever they are done, while abstaining from all judgments of their adequacy, value, importance, necessity, practicality, success, or consequentiality. We refer to this procedural policy as "ethnomethodological indifference."[47]

I would take this to mean that Garfinkel believes it to be the task of ethnomethodology to account for the order in practical activities from the standpoint of its participants, without either denigrating such accounts because they are not made by professional sociologists, nor rushing precipitously to judgments of the rightness or wrongness of the view of their activities by participants — who, of course, could turn out upon further study to be quite wrong in their convictions about the nature and causes of the order their conduct displays. Garfinkel's and Sacks's "principle of indifference" need not be read as an indifference to the distinction between fact and value of "is" and "ought" as Kurt Wolff insists. In any case, Garfinkel and the other ethnomethodologists have taken the analysis of everyday activities as a primary field of sociological study, and are innovatively seeking to extend the methodology of effective phenomenological study to its phenomena.

Robert Nisbet. Robert A. Nisbet, Albert Schweitzer Professor of the Humanities at Columbia University, member of the American Academy of Arts and Sciences and the American Philosophical Society, and former faculty member at the University of California, Berkeley and Riverside, has not officially classified himself as a phenomenological sociologist, but is best viewed as an idiosyncratic member of this school. In a variety of books,[48] Nis-

---

[44]Alvin W. Gouldner, *The Coming Crisis of Western Sociology* (New York: Basic Books, 1970), pp. 391, 392, 393.
[45]Garfinkel, *Studies in Ethnomethodology*, p. 48.
[46]Kurt Wolff, "Phenomenology and Sociology," in *A History of Sociological Analysis*, ed. Tom Bottomore and Robert Nisbet (New York: Basic Books, 1978), p. 539.

[47]Harold Garfinkel and Harvey Sacks, "On Formal Structures of Practical Actions," in *Theoretical Sociology: Perspectives and Developments*, ed. McKinney and Tiryakian (New York: Meredith, 1970), p. 345.
[48]Including, among others, *The Sociological Tradition* (New York: Basic Books, 1966); *Social Change and History* (New York: Oxford, 1969) and *Sociology As an Art Form* (New York: Oxford, 1976).

ROBERT NISBET

Courtesy Oxford University Press

bet has presented what appears to be a phenomenological conception of sociological activity within a framework of elitism and conservatism.

Nisbet has primarily devoted himself to the presentation of the ideas of others, and hence is perhaps best described as an intellectual historian or, perhaps he would prefer, an intellectual and cultural critic. In *The Sociological Tradition* he describes the period in the nineteenth century between 1830 and 1890 as a minor golden age: "Would anyone deny that the sociological ideas which emerged in the brief period between Tocqueville and Weber have been other than determinative of the way we, a century later, continue to see the social world about us?"[49] These ideas, he maintains, form the core of modern conservativism and are "the child of the Industrial and French revolutions."[50] They include: community, authority, status, the sacred, and alienation.[51] And while their authors (such as Tönnies, Simmel, Weber, and Durkheim) did not consider themselves to be conservative, "deep currents of conservatism" run through their writings.[52]

Nisbet stressed his conviction that the central ideas of sociology are artistic (or intuitive) creations resting on a moral basis. "The great sociologists never ceased to be moral philosophers. And never ceased to be artists."[53] Nisbet views himself as an artist second removed. "Our dependence upon these ideas and their makers is akin to the artist's dependence upon the artists who precede him."[54]

Nisbet argues the identity of art and science, conceiving each as a response to experience with "creative . . . utilization of intuition and . . . 'iconic imagination.'"[55] Art and science differ only in direction and emphasis of interest. "The artist's interest in form or style is the scientist's interest in structure or type."[56] Nisbet deplores the "crimes committed in the name of 'proof' or 'verification' or 'validation' in the classroom today."[57] He shudders to think how we would be impoverished if "Darwin had been checked by 'theory constructionists.'"[58] He urges:

The problems, insights, ideas, and forms which come to the artist and to the scientist seem to come as often from the unconscious as the conscious mind, from wide, eclectic, and unorganized reading, observing, or experiencing, from musing, browsing, and dreaming, from buried experiences, as from anything immediately and consciously in view.[59]

[49]Nisbet, *The Sociological Tradition*, p. 316.

[50]*Ibid.*, p. 11.
[51]*Ibid.*, p. 8.
[52]*Ibid.*, p. 17.
[53]*Ibid.*, p. 18.
[54]*Ibid.*, p. 20.
[55]Nisbet, *Sociology As an Art Form*, p. 9.
[56]*Ibid.*, p. 10.
[57]*Ibid.*, p. 16.
[58]*Ibid.*, p. 16.
[59]*Ibid.*, p. 19.

Nisbet's antagonism extends both to systematic theory and to all forms of positivistic methodology. Working on the principle that art abhors all systems Nisbet insists:

> For of all the Idols of the Mind or Profession regnant today the worst is that which Bacon might have placed among his Idols of the Theatre: the belief, first, that there really is something properly called theory in sociology, and second, that the aim of all sociological research should be that of adding to or advancing theory . . . Quite as fatal to creative thought as the passion for systems is the current consecration of what, for want of a better phrase, is known as 'theory construction.' This is at bottom no more than old-fashioned methodology in the social sciences dressed up in pretentious and faddish clothing.[60]

Art and science are said to have a common quest, "to understand reality."[61] The social conditions favorable to both are said to be similar.

> Great art and great science have commonly emerged in small, informal groups where a few like-minded individuals can stimulate one another in autonomous intimacy. Repeatedly in the history of thought we find that where the great individual, the titan, exists, there exist with him, often unsung and unheralded, a tiny few others almost as great.[62]

Nisbet identifies his own position — that growth in both art and science takes the form of the development of styles at the core of which is a theme or cluster of themes — with Thomas Kuhn's concept of paradigms and their role in scientific revolutions.[63] The themes, in turn, in both art and science, "have their origins in very ancient myth, ritual, metaphor, and other expressions of mankind's effort over countless millennia to convert chaos to order."[64] Sociology is said, first of all, to share a number of themes with the social sciences: the individual, freedom, and change. Moreover,

sociology had a number of additional themes peculiar to it: community, authority, status, the sacred, and alienation. Among the activities of the sociologists of the minor golden age of the nineteenth century, paramount was the painting of landscapes. The major sociological landscapes were: the masses, power, the desolation of factory production, and the anonymous metropolis. When not preoccupied with landscapes sociologists have painted portraits. Among the more important were: the bourgeois, the worker, the bureaucrat, and the intellectual. Sociologists were also engaged in the representations of motion including both panoramas (like evolution) and dioramas, like capitalism (Marx), democracy (Tocqueville), and rationalization (Max Weber). Finally, sociologists have been seeking to portray or represent the "rust of progress": loss of community, anomie, estrangement, and degeneration.

It is clear from these arguments and ideas that Nisbet is an individualistic adherent of phenomenological sociology, antipositivist, elitist, and conservative, locating the essential components of both science and art in iconic images arising in response to broad, directly intuited experience. Such iconic images serve as the power cells of cultural styles which thrive for a time until they run out of energy and are replaced by newer ones.

THE INSTITUTIONALIZATION OF PHENOMENOLOGY IN AMERICAN SOCIOLOGY

A milestone was passed in 1971 when Professor George Psathas wrote to William Sewell, then president of the American Sociological Association, to propose that a session be devoted to phenomenological sociology. It was Psathas's suggestion that a philosopher of the social sciences introduce the main issues accompanied by a commentary by a sociologist familiar with the phenomenological tradition. Richard Zaner, who had firsthand acquaintance with Alfred Schutz as his student and later as editor and translator of

[60]*Ibid.*, pp. 20, 21.
[61]*Ibid.*, p. 22.
[62]*Ibid.*, p. 25.
[63]*Ibid.*, pp. 30f.
[64]*Ibid.*, p. 31.

Schutz's manuscript (*Reflection on the Problem of Relevance*), was invited to present the issues. Kurt Wolff, who had run seminars on Schutz at Brandeis and who had translated and edited works of Georg Simmel and Karl Mannheim, was invited to discuss Zaner's remarks. Helmut Wager, who edited a volume on Schutz for the Heritage of Sociology Series of the University of Chicago Press, was invited to act as second discussant. At the same ASA meetings Psathas organized a second, more informal seminar session on phenomenological sociology, at which contact was made with Roger Jehenson who agreed to join the wider project of the publication of a volume of essays on phenomenological sociology. Around this core Psathas reported that he gradually recruited an additional series of scholars: Herbert Spiegelberg (whose workshops on phenomenology he had attended at Washington University, St. Louis), Fred Dallmayr (whom he had met at the meetings of the Society for Phenomenology and Existential Philosophy in 1970), Francis C. Waksler, Alex Blumenstiel, Egon Bittner, John O'Neill, and Peter Manning.

Also in the 1970s Myrtle Korenbaum, who had co-translated a study of a work dating from Georges Gurvitch's phenomenological period (*The Spectrum of Social Time*) took the initiative of establishing a Phenomenological Newsletter. A new series of sociological publications: *The Annals of Phenomenological Sociology*, Volume I, appeared in 1976; Volume II in 1977. After Korenbaum gave up editorship of the newsletter members of the department of sociology at the University of Oklahoma took it over.

The volume *Phenomenological Sociology*[65] was produced from the ASA session in 1971. The ASA session on which the volume was based marks the point at which professional sociologists in the United States formally acknowledged phenomenological sociology to a rightful place among their concerns. Since a concerted effort was made to assemble the best spokespeople in the United States and Canada to formulate the case for phenomenological sociology, the presentation of the issues has special interest.

Although the editor of *Phenomenological Sociology* indicates in his introduction that the purpose of the book is to present the reader relatively unsophisticated in phenomenology with an introduction to it and demonstration of its relevance, he also observes "phenomenology is philosophy, method, and approach. As such, phenomenology cannot easily be explicated, particularly when it is still developing and refuses to stand still."[66] He observes that it is a movement originated by Edmund Husserl that has affected sociology, psychology, and psychiatry without indicating in which ways. He then launched into a historical overview, not of phenomenology, but of thinkers who were interested in the same kinds of issues as phenomenology, including: Max Weber, Georg Simmel, Max Scheler, Karl Mannheim, William James, Charles Cooley, W. I. Thomas, and George Herbert Mead. "This overview," he said, "does not intend to 'claim' all these thinkers for phenomenological sociology but rather to show that a rich tradition exists in social theory for the treatment of issues phenomenology has also addressed."[67] The historical overview was concluded with reference to the contribution of Alfred Schutz who "remains distinctive and monumental, and no modern scholar can ignore his work and consider himself conversant with phenomenological social science."[68] Unfortunately, the editor did not choose to sum up Schutz's contribution,[69] but quite clearly took it for granted (Schutz might have loved that touch) that Schutz had established the understanding of the world of everyday life as the primary task of phenomenological sociology. Of course, such understanding has to be accomplished phenomenologically, the meaning of which the editor seems to "take for granted" is

---

[65]George Psathas, *Phenomenological Sociology: Issues and Applications*, edited by George Psathas (New York: John Wiley, 1973).

[66]Psathas, *Phenomenological Sociology*, p. 2.
[67]*Ibid.*, p. 3.
[68]*Ibid.*, p. 7.
[69]See *ibid.*, p. 8.

self-evident. The editor might have been more helpful to the naive reader if he had said simply that at its present stage, phenomenological sociology is an emerging discipline which proposes the phenomenological understanding of everyday social life. Had he then explained briefly what kinds of things were involved in phenomenological description, phenomenological explanation, and everyday life, the reader might have been in a position to decide to what extent such thinkers as Weber, Cooley, James, Mead, Thomas, and the like did or did not contribute to a phenomenological sociology. This approach might also have made clear the possible issues facing further development of a phenomenological sociology. However, the statement of the issues was left to the humanist and philosopher Richard M. Zaner.

Zaner accepts Gouldner's interpretation (in *The Coming Crisis of Western Sociology*) that society and contemporary sociology are in crisis. He also observes:

> I am . . . very impressed by Gouldner's call for a "reflexive sociology." . . . Gouldner's major points are (a) social science is not only a conception of the social world, but is also a *part* of it and (b) this implies that the sociologist must be reflexively cognizant of *himself* as a social being. . . . In its negative thrust, Gouldner's thesis is also twofold: (a) it involves a rejection of the subject/object dichotomy as a viable model for understanding "our social selves"; and (b) it denies the worth and even the possibility of "value-freedom" in social science.[70]

Gouldner, as observed above, had criticized Garfinkel and the ethnomethodologists when they caused some dismay by temporarily contradicting routine assumptions in day-to-day conduct during an experiment. Gouldner had accused the ethnomethodologists of cruelty and sadism and of contributing to the crisis of contemporary society. Zaner, however, disagrees with this interpretation.

The fact of "taken for grantedness" itself, the fact that typifications even arise in human consciousness, the fact that human beings themselves understand, live in, and act on the social world as the common matrix of their lives in terms of these typifications — all these point to a dimension of issues which undergird those of the social sciences and are systematically presupposed by them. These issues, I have argued, form the prime subject of phenomenological criticism. A truly radical discipline of criticism, then, is one that has that task of explication, and it relates to social science as the soil relates to the tree which is nourished by it, on and through which it can at all thrive.[71]

In short, for Zaner, phenomenological sociology is the critical or reflexive sociology for which he believes Gouldner is — or should be — seeking.

Two respondents to Zaner's paper, Kurt Wolff and Helmut Wagner, had reservations about the notion that the major issue should be one of transforming phenomenological sociology, forthwith, into a Gouldner-type reflexive or critical theory, with a thorough critique of both society and social science. Kurt Wolff's response was to suggest that one ought first to clarify the very nature of radical criticism, whether philosophical or political, and to insist that radicals face up to their moral and political responsibilities. "It calls for persuading political radicals, and for them persuading themselves, to recognize human beings and to understand and treat them as ends."[72] Wagner, tactfully and more by implication than by explicit formulation, shifted the essential issue faced by a phenomenological sociology to grounds other than those proposed by Zaner. Husserl's phenomenology came into being as a radically subjective individualistic (even solipsistic) enterprise. In his later work he sought to correct this. Schutz, who synthesized Husserl's phenomenology with Weber's theory of action, was not satisfied with Husserl's solution, but postulated intersubjectivity from the start and advanced analyses to prove that the other

---

[70]Psathas, *Phenomenological Sociology*, pp. 28–29.

[71]*Ibid.*, p. 42.
[72]*Ibid.*, p. 55.

actually rises directly and before the self, which can arise only reflexively. At the same time, he still maintained sociology is an enterprise primarily concerned with subjective analysis at a micro level. Using Berger and Luckmann to illustrate his point, Wagner made a case for expanding phenomenology's scope into a fully constituted sociological theory.

> It is our conviction that phenomenological sociology will make a relevant contribution to our knowledge of the whole range of social phenomena to exactly the degree to which it will manage to make inquiries not only into the certainly basic areas of social-psychological concerns but also into those of the broader, socially crucial aspects of modern society in perpetual change, upheaval, and crisis.[73]

A number of the other papers in the volume implicitly accept Wagner's suggestion that the major task facing phenomenological sociology is the application of its analytical principles to areas other than immediate experience (as in the essays by Spiegelberg, Psathas and Waksler, and Manning and Fabrega) or to new spheres (Blumensteil's *The Sociology of Good Times*), and secondary relationships (Jehenson's "A Phenomenological Approach to the Study of the Formal Organization").

A special issue for a phenomenological sociology was raised by John O'Neill in his essay, "On Simmel's 'Sociological Apriorities.'" As a neo-Kantian, Simmel had imaginatively raised the question whether one could not approach society in the same manner that Kant (in the *Critique of Pure Reason*) had approached nature by asking: How is nature a priori possible? The comparable question for society is: How is society a priori possible? Kant's answer for phenomena had been that there are certain formal requirements to be met before nature can be perceived (space and time, which are forms of apperception) and others to be met before it can be conceived (the categories). In asking the same question with respect to society, as a good Kantian, Simmel had assumed that all experience, including social experience, presupposes the existence of transcendental subjects. Society could only be some kind of arrangement between independent subjects, but an important question is why they should ever enter such an arrangement at all since, in the nature of the case, the individual is always more than any social arrangement. Simmel's answer was, if a type of arrangement could be found in which individuals, at least with respect to it, were transformed into something more than they were as isolated individuals, the condition of society could be realized. This, he had argued, was the peculiar significance of a *calling*. With the calling the individual is simultaneously realized and transcended. This argument, of course, brilliantly anticipated the rise from another starting point of the treatment of the social role as the great building block of social life.

John O'Neill undertook to translate Simmel's problem and questions into phenomenological terms.

> I want to show that by shifting Simmel's question away from the search for invariant categories or forms of social reality the real nature of the question may be proposed as an inquiry into the subjective constitution of social reality.[74]

The details of O'Neill's discussion need not concern us, for he simply translated Simmel's observations into phenomenological terminology, arriving at an identical conclusion: that is, certain formal conditions must hold if empirical social experience is to be possible in the first place. In O'Neill's words:

> Each of Simmel's antinomies, or, as we may call them, the *a prioris of typification, presentation, and symbiosis*, are constituent features of individual and social existence. They circumscribe the cognitive and expressive operations of social bonding but are prior to all empirical

---

[73]Wagner, in *Phenomenological Sociology*, p. 85.

[74]John O'Neill, "On Simmel's 'Sociological Apriorities,'" *Phenomenological Sociology*, p. 92.

patterns of motivation. However, these sociological a prioris taken as practical antinomies may also provide the sociological imagination with a critical or "experimental intentionality" in which the constituent practices of individual and social reality may be revealed.[75]

Presumably this means that if we ask a Kantian question we get a Kantian answer, but it is useful, still, to ask to what extent are individuals independent of and superior to society and in what ways may individuals be realized in an essentially new manner (transcending their old selves) when they undertake their callings — losing themselves only to find themselves once again in a new and more fulfilling experience.

A quite different issue was raised by Egon Bittner, the one self-styled ethnomethodologist among the contributors to the Psathas volume, whose major concern is the elimination of positivism from social science.

> Of the three positive reasons for the abandonment of the positivist idea of objectivity, the first consists of a version of the inherited views about the methodological contrast between the natural and the social sciences; the second advances the consideration that far from being practiced in the interest of building a science of society, positivist objectivity was partly a deliberate and partly an unwitting way of *not* facing the tasks of studying social reality; and the third — the most radical of the three — urges that efforts to impose positivistic objectivity on sociological inquiry involve a contradiction in terms inasmuch as the discipline is programmatically oriented to the study of matters that are inherently devoid of objective meaning.[76]

Bittner subscribes to the view extending back to Vico and transmitted to modern times by the neo-Idealists that there is a difference in principle between knowledge of nature and meaningful knowledge of humanity. Secondly, he agrees with those Marxists who have argued that compliance

with the ideas of positivist objectivity is a way of avoiding the serious analysis of society. Bittner quotes with approval Gouldner's suggestion that those who are enamoured of modern positivism and objectivism are seeking compensation for their crippled lack of the capacity to love and whose resentment is shackled by their timidity and privilege.[77]

> The third denial of the possibility of objectivism in sociology comes from an extraordinarily rigorous program of empirical research known as ethnomethodology. It is in the nature of this approach that it should seek to yield evidence in favor of the presumption against objectivity, rather than either proof or exhortation. The demonstration could be briefly stated as follows. All "accounts" (i.e., all manner of describing, analyzing, questioning, criticizing, believing, doubting, idealizing, schematizing, denigrating, and so on) are unavoidably and irremediably tied to the social settings that occasion them or within which they are situated.[78]

Bittner observes that recent members of the symbolic interaction school (like Goffman) have tried to develop a sociology free from positivism and objectivism, but he is skeptical about their success and feels that any serious hope lies rather with a phenomenological sociology.

The last essay of the collection, by Fred R. Dallmayr, professor of political science at the University of Georgia, on "Phenomenology and Marxism," surveys the historical relation between phenomenology and Marxism. The twentieth-century Marxists and neo-Hegelians, from Lukács to Habermas, and Gouldner have, by and large, been antagonistic to phenomenology. Lukács, for example, viewed phenomenological and existentialist thought as a manifestation of the disintegration of bourgeois culture during the phase of imperialism and Husserl's method of bracketing as a subjectivist maneuver to elude the question of objective social reality. Gouldner's denunciation of

---

[75]*Ibid.*, p. 102.
[76]Egon Bittner, *Phenomenological Sociology*, p. 113.

[77]*Ibid.*, p. 115. The references are to Gouldner's *The Coming Crisis*, pp. 103 and 440.
[78]*Ibid.*, p. 115.

Garfinkel's presumed sadism and cruelty and contribution to the social crisis is only the latest of the responses by a critical theorist to phenomenology as a decadent form of bourgeois culture. To be sure, some critical theorists, like Marcuse, who studied with Heidegger, dreamed of fusing Marxism and phenomenology, but this was never approved by Horkheimer and Adorno. On the other hand, some French phenomenologists for a time developed a school (Sartre, Merleau-Ponty and for a time the Vietnamese theorist Tran Duc Thao) which tried to fuse Marxism and phenomenology.[79] In Dallmayr's view, these early attempts at integration were never very convincing.

Dallmayr argues that this antagonism and divergence has been changed by the work of Enzo Paci, a professor of philosophy at the University of Milan and a leading member of a circle of left Husserlians or phenomenological Marxists. In *The Function of the Sciences and the Meaning of Man,*[80] Paci offers a running commentary on Husserl's *Crisis* and his elaborations of the *Lebenswelt* as a counterpoise to scientific objectivism. According to Paci, these elaborations unmistakably point to the direction of dialectical materialism — but without reaching this goal. Both the *Crisis* and Marx's analysis of the capitalist economy, he argues, are critical efforts designed to rescue human experience from reification and estrangement. Once the life-world is interpreted as incorporating the level of basic needs and of material production, phenomenology and Marxism are destined to converge.[81]

Dallmayr is convinced that Paul Piccone, one of the translators of *The Function of the Social Sciences* and editor of *Telos* (a social theory journal) and John O'Neill, translator and interpreter of Merleau-Ponty and author of *Sociology as a Skin Trade*, also illustrate the potential for a development of phenomenological Marxism.[82]

Both Piccone and O'Neill are committed to a critical Marxism and invoke the assistance of phenomenology in formulating this outlook; but both ultimately stop short of their goal, by retreating either into intuitive certainty or common-sense belief. In every instance, the incongruity seems to derive from the role assigned to phenomenology and from its somewhat indiscriminate fusion with Marxist thought.[83]

Dallmayr's personal solution, which he sees as approached by Paci, is that phenomenology and Marxism differ primarily in terms of scope: "phenomenology concentrates on special problems, the function of the sciences, to which Marxism offers a more general solution."[84] (In his earlier attempt at function, Marcuse had reversed this order, describing existential phenomenology as a general philosophy and Marxism as the application.) Dallmayr suggests that it might be wise to return to the counterpart of the proposal of Giambattista Vico in his *New Science* when he envisioned a relation between "philology" and "philosophy."

Although this moves outside the sphere of *Phenomenological Sociology* Dallmayr's discussion of the potential for a fusion of phenomenology and Marxism calls to mind Tiryakian's early suggestions for a fusion of sociologism and existentialism. After a review of sociologism (Durkheim's sociology) and existentialism (of Kierkegaard, Nietzsche, Heidegger, Jaspers, and Marcel), Tiryakian concludes: "A common compassion animates sociologism and existentialism: the predicament of the individual in modern society, who, cut off from his traditional ties, has become deracinated."[85] Furthermore, a little carpentry on their respective interpretations of the human predicament and their respective therapies, could work wonders.

Existentialism would not find its approach to man undermined by sociological considerations. On the contrary, without incorporating a genuine social dimension existentialism is threatened with failure in its

[79]*Ibid.,* p. 313.
[80]Enzo Paci, *The Function of the Sciences and the Meaning of Man*, trans. James E. Hansen and Paul Piccone (Evanston, Ill.: Northwestern University Press, 1972).
[81]Dallmayr, *Phenomenological Sociology*, p. 318.
[82]*Ibid.,* pp. 331–343.

[83]*Ibid.,* p. 343.
[84]*Ibid.,* p. 344.
[85]Edward A. Tiryakian, *Sociologism and Existentialism* (Englewood Cliffs, N.J.: Prentice-Hall, 1962), p. 162.

efforts to liberate integral man from the constraints of traditional philosophy. By abstracting man from society, by treating the individual and society as polar entities, existentialism may have built a magnificent edifice without some essential building blocks; instead of having arrived at a comprehensive understanding of the existential reality of man, modern existentialism leaves human being void of existential roots in the world . . . Finally, the benefit stemming from the interrelation of sociology and existential philosophy might not be confined to the theoretical level but may well be extended to the realm of the practical. If Durkheim and existential thought are correct in their diagnosis . . . it will require the joint efforts of sociology and philosophy to bring about a meaningful rehabilitation of the individual and society.[86]

SUMMARY

The first two systems of sociological theory, organismic positivism and conflict theory, took shape before sociology had become an institutionalized and professional discipline. Institutionalization standardizes a set of social relations and fixes social roles. Sociology as an intellectual discipline may be said to have become an institutionalized discipline when it achieved a standard form with an autonomy separate from that of any single person who might become a "sociologist." One of the surest signs of the social crystallization process called institutionalization is the speed with which sociology became a recognized department in the colleges and universities, taught by specially trained personnel.

For practical purposes, professionalization implies a peculiar kind of institutionalization characterized by the extensive self-determination of the activity by its own members. When the conditions of work, standards of performance, and standing of members are determined by some outside agency (as in the case of the wage worker, where these things are determined by industry, or the conditions of a civil service worker, where such af-

fairs are determined by the administrative bureau), we do not speak of a profession. The establishment of recognized scientific societies and journals was an aspect of the professionalization of sociology. To an extensive degree, sociologists themselves had usurped the right to say who was and who was not a sociologist and what is and what is not good sociology.

One of the conditions of institutionalization and professionalization was the necessity for sociology to abandon the imperialistic claims to areas and material of the founders. One could not maintain such claims and expect to live at peace with other disciplines. Institutionalization and professionalization thus coincided with the demand for a more restricted definition of sociological subject matter. Besides, as already noted, organismic positivism was beginning to disintegrate into its component parts, and the "progress" and "evolution" formulas were producing contradictory findings. Furthermore, while adding a powerful note of realism, conflict theory could hardly have universal appeal. The line between empirical theory and ideology was not clearly drawn. Some forms of social Darwinism could only appear to be crass justifications of current social abuses: racism was partly linked to political and economic imperialism, partly to class exploitation; eugenicism in part implemented a dangerous class snobbery. In terms of its normal anchorage, Marxism could only appear to the average sociologist of the times as an apocalyptic vision of social chaos. Conflict theory was thus too near to ideology to satisfy modified professional claims. Besides, the imperialistic compass of sociology was largely maintained among the conflict theorists.

The early formalists like Simmel and Vierkandt were quite self-consciously searching for a special and precise definition of their field. This search coincided with ground movements in nineteenth-century thought, in the neo-Kantian reaction to idealistic and romantic excesses. The ferment was not confined to sociology, but was a product of the late nineteenth century, appearing in philosophy, history, jurisprudence, and all the social sciences. In sociology, it meant, among other things, that

[86]*Ibid.*, pp. 168–169.

the search of the traditions of Western thought for new approaches was undertaken once again, and a whole new body of relatively unexploited sources was brought to bear upon sociological theory construction. The rationalistic traditions of Western philosophy came into prominence for sociological theory at this time. Of especial importance were the traditions of Kant, the neo-Kantians, and the phenomenologists. In sociology, all this took the shape of an attempted establishment of a "pure" or formal sociology.

The solution to the problem of obtaining a more restricted but more exact definition of the field by the neo-Kantians was to find the true nature of pure sociology in the study of forms. The great prestige the term "form" derived from Kantian philosophy was a component in the attractiveness of this term for various social sciences. Simmel himself saw that there were differences between his sociological forms and Kant's categories. He was unable to supply a convincingly exact explanation of just what the difference was. Moreover, he achieved his most imaginative brilliance precisely when he undertook the comparative study of the most varied social situations, disregarding the distinction between form and content. Simmel was by no means clear about the method to be followed in the discovery of forms. He wavered between the idea that they were only to be found by introspection and the notion that they were to be established by comparative study and induction.

The early American formalists perceived one tremendous advantage in the formalistic approach: it could serve as a vehicle for the systematization of all aspects of sociological knowledge without the need to appeal to older ideas (like progress and evolution) that had fallen into disrepute. But such students as Ross, Park, and Burgess, tended to lose sight of the theoretical problems posed by the formalists. In their zeal to carry out sociological systematization, such issues were cast aside. Judgment day was merely postponed.

Von Wiese shows one type of vigorous response to the methodological ambiguity of Simmel. The concept of form is re-expressed in the more anonymous language of relations. Moreover, the problem of method is posed in terms of pseudomathematical equations, and the elaborate dream of a thoroughgoing positivism of procedure is entertained. But the proposals for extreme empiricism were never carried out, and von Wiese presents a rather barren scheme of "relations" without any real justification for schematizing them in terms of "approach" and "avoidance." When systematization is carried out for its own sake, the results may be a kind of scientific curiosity. Such seems to have been the case with von Wiese, for he did not particularly promote the formation of those further hypotheses critical to the growth of science.

The close ties between the neo-Kantian and phenomenological branches of formalism are clear. Vierkandt, the phenomenologist, in part took Simmel's formalism as a starting point. Scheler, the phenomenologist, was the student of Simmel. Gurvitch, during his phenomenological phase was also influenced by Scheler, Bergson, and Husserl.

One could thus take Simmel as the common starting point for two types of later formulations: the extremely positivistic interpretation of von Wiese and the extremely subjectivistic interpretation of the phenomenologists. In a sense, the phenomenologists solved the problem of Simmel's methodological ambiguity in precisely the opposite way from von Wiese. Here the pretense that in the search of the immanent structure the a priori sociopsychic conditions that make society possible are performed inductively is dropped.

There is little doubt that Vierkandt's phenomenological sociology is a far more theoretically consistent solution to the problems of Simmel's neo-Kantianism than is von Wiese's *relational* formalism. The artificiality of von Wiese's procedure could not be more dramatically demonstrated than by the development of pseudomathematical formulas which are set down as ideas, lamely admitted to be quite empty, and ignored in practice. This means that, in fact, no method adequate to relational formalism has been provided, and the theoretical basis of the system is obscure. By contrast, Vierkandt is quite correct. If the real point of stability for sociology is to be found in a priori forms, we are likely to obscure them by reviewing varied historical circumstances. The theory that established the "forms" also consistently requires a method really appropriate to their discovery. Phenomenological method recommends itself as the true means of arriving at absolute knowledge of the forms in acts of immediate intuition.

The formalists developed a liberal conception of society as a legally ordered plurality of independent wills to counterbalance the conservative image of society of their predecessors. But as the inner course of the evolution of formalism from neo-Kantianism to phenomenology demonstrates, there was an implicit rebellion against the positivism of the previous theories as well as against their substantive social theory. The full implications of this for theory only gradually become clear.

The fusion of phenomenology and existentialism played a critical role in the transition of phenomenological sociology from its pioneering to its mature development. The existentialists directed interest to the predicament of contemporary human beings. Furthermore, in addition to bringing their alienation into focus, many of the existentialists assigned much of the responsibility for that alienation to science and technology. This varied, to be sure, from the qualified receptivity to science by Jaspers to the radical antipositivism of Heidegger. However, it is noteworthy that even Husserl was being dragged with the current. In his last work on *The Crisis of the European Sciences,* Husserl expressed antipositivist sentiments and proposed the refounding of phenomenology with its center of gravity in the life-world. Instead of bracketing existence, the suggestion was made to bracket philosophy and science.

During the time when the existentialists were threatening to steal the show from Husserl and Husserl was reorganizing his own approach, Alfred Schutz seized the idea of using Husserl's phenomenology to illuminate the formulations in Max Weber's interpretative sociology. Weber provided a systematic framework of ideas and methodological judgments intended for describing and explaining human interaction in objective value-neutral terms, for Weber's whole concept of science rested on separating scientific questions from political and ethical questions. The result was that Schutz managed by systematic application of Husserl's phenomenological procedures not only to enrich Weber's microsociology, but also potentially to establish a phenomenological sociology of everyday life that was not dominated by the sense of urgency, alienation, and ethical concern.

The relative neutrality of Schutz's phenomenology of the life-world was unquestionably a component in its later emergence at the heart of a refounded phenomenological sociology. During the war years and the relatively affluent milieu of the immediate postwar period, American sociology was not receptive to an urgent sense of alienation, whether on the part of critical (or reflexive) sociology or phenomenology. At the same time, when Schutz was part-time teaching at the New School for Social Research, he continued to extend and modify his phenomenological sociology, with extensive references to American social scientists (Dewey, James, Mead, W. I. Thomas), acquainting receptive students with possible alternatives to reigning structure-functionalism. Hence, when structure-functionalism began to lose its virtual monopoly over American sociology in the 1960s, the phenomenology of the life-world was waiting in the wings and better adapted to American needs than Schutz's original version. With the discovery of Schutz the way was open for students who had worked with him and had studied his work. Berger and Luckmann tried to extend Schutz's position to the solution of the problems of a sociology of knowledge. Garfinkel and other ethnomethodologists began to explore phenomenological alternatives to positivist methodologies. Robert Nisbet's *Sociology As an Art Form* appears to be an independent movement in the conceptual space opened by the new or refounded phenomenological sociology.

A major development in the 1970s has been the move to institutionalize phenomenological sociology with space on the agenda of ASA sessions, with a society of its own, with a newsletter, and even a publication of its proceedings. Accompanying this development has been the attempt to reconceptualize phenomenological sociology as a form of critical (or reflexive) theory which, of course, would either fuse or put it in conflict with the critical theory of the Frankfurt school. In fact, the proposals for an integration of phenomenology and Marxism, which have found sponsors, have this objective in view. However, the two traditions have tended, despite all efforts, to separate as oil and water, which is to be expected so long as phenomenological sociology remains elementaristic and the critical theory of the Frankfurt school and Marxism remain holistic.

PART VI

CONCLUSION

WHEN THE FIRST EDITION of *Nature and Types* appeared theory had somewhat ambiguous status in American sociology: it was thought to be an alien European philosophical preoccupation, on the one hand, and assumed to be unified by contemporary functionalism on the other. Talcott Parsons had emerged as the dominant figure in American sociology and in the immediate postwar period American sociology was ascendant in the world at large. Parsons and those who studied with him took his *Structure of Social Action* as a new departure in unified theory on the basis of its review and presumed synthesis of the sociologies of Pareto, Marshall, Durkheim, and Weber. Meanwhile theory courses in most colleges and universities were largely preoccupied with a review of historically outmoded social philosophies. Contemporary theory was dominated by functionalism, which held a sort of world cartel.

Toward the end of the 1950s, the major spokespersons for functionalism had become aware of the discrepancies between their monopolistic pretensions as sole legitimate heirs of theory and the content of most theory courses. Talcott Parsons, Edward Shils, Kaspar Naegele, and Jesse Pitts undertook a major assemblage of the materials on social theory with the intention of revealing its integration and fulfillment in functionalism. The *Theories of Society* (1961) was a parallel to Parson's *Structure of Social Action*, intended as a review of theories that had been integrated into a higher synthesis.

Nature and Types, which appeared the year before *Theories of Society*, had a different objective; not to bring theory to a climactic synthesis, but to explore the status of actual theories, cutting out deadwood and determining what alternatives were still being actively pursued. That the schools were true alternatives was established beyond doubt. They represented semi-independent systems of concepts that could not be arbitrarily mixed, a fact which appeared repeatedly whenever adherents of one theory sought to account for the evidence and ideas of another. For this reason, the task of applying the standards of modern logical and analytical philosophy to existing schools of theory was becoming a major trend.

Although that was not its intention, in the very act of establishing the existence of a variety of theoretical positions, the first edition of *Nature and Types* was a challenge to functionalism's monopolistic pretensions. At the same time, the wish expressed strongly by the functionalists for the unification of theory was recognized not only as legitimate, but in the best traditions of science. Hence, in the final chapter of the first edition we addressed the problem of the prospects for theoretical integration of social theory.

We called attention to the role of ideological elements in new departures in social theory. Sociology, for example, had arisen in the nineteenth century as a conservative alternative to socialism; and its original attempt to combine a positivism of method with an organismic conception of society provided the framework for institutionalization of scientific methodology in the study of social life. The first school of theory developed an array of ideas that have become the common property of all later schools of theory — though they have often been elaborated and altered in the process. Moreover, the first school of theory began to assemble facts, undertook to increase the precision of methods, and to separate values from facts, ideologies from empirical theories.

Each new theoretical development, often in response to some ideological preference, such as left-wing utopianism and liberalism, brought new areas of fact under review, presided over the formation of subfields, and became the focus of new research traditions. Conflict theory brought a more realistic conception of social life, attention to the sociology of law, class, politics, and economics and developed a tougher methodological program than that of the early positivistic organicists. The various forms of scientific elementarism established the field of social psychology, enriching sociology with the study of the sociology of personality, social behavior, and social relations and accelerating not only the collection of firsthand data, but also the development of statistical and case-history methods. Furthermore, alternative points of view, at a time when all parties subscribed to the norms of science, resulted in a competition of truth. Facts slighted by one point of view were often forced to attention by another; methods perfected by one group of theorists became available to others; alternative ideas often had a self-sharpening effect when cut against one another. In short, for all the alternatives, the field as a whole was accumulating a deepening body of shared knowledge as the growing edge of the discipline shifted to the unsolved problems.

The mistake of Parsons and the functionalists was not in desiring integration, but seeking to force it at the level of theory rather than working from the common body of ideas and shared body of factual knowledge. Furthermore, developments in modern mathematics and logic were among the tools available for the task of contemporary students of theory construction. And it was on this note that the first edition closed:

> From the perspective developed here, it is possible to offer neither easy solutions for the integration of theory nor utopian hopes for sociology as a boon to mankind. It is not even possible to offer that sop to the Western conscience—all things yield to hard work. In the cooperation of reason and energy, when the tinder is at hand and the sparks are struck from mother wit, sociology may yet find the ingredients for its synthesis. Sociology may yet produce a Newton or a Maxwell who will take the materials cast up by chance and worked up with patient labor, clarify them in the crystalline formations of his logic, and fuse them in the fire of his love.

Developments in the 1960s soon confirmed this estimate of the field of social theory. Homans, who had been a major architect of functionalism, defected to found behavioristic sociology. The easing of the Cold War along with domestic conflict over the civil rights issue encouraged a revival of conflict theory, including Marxism. Symbolic interactionism developed briskly into a full system of theory and not simply a special social psychology; phenomenology was developed as a sociology of everyday life. The hegemony of functionalism was destroyed. The analysis by historian Thomas Kuhn of science in terms of paradigms, rather than theories, was seized upon to account for a new pluralist vision of social theory, though opinion varied as to whether sociology was in a pre- or postparadigm stage, on the one hand, or a unique multiparadigm science on the other. And while the positivistic thrust toward theory construction in social science came to a climax in the 1960s, the entire positivistic tradition was going into a kind of remission and humanistic (even antiscientific) approaches to theory were becoming more popular.

In view of these developments the emphasis has been shifted in the final chapter of the second edition of *Nature and Types* from the integration to the problems of theory, for, in the long run, it is how these problems are solved that will determine the extent to which the field remains distributed in partially conflicting formulations or achieves the type of unity at which scientific explanation always aims. The humanistic preoccupation of sociology will have the effect of enlarging and enriching scientific methodology rather than replacing it as the institutional norm of thought in Western civilization.

XXV

The Conflicts of Sociological Theory

A peculiar irony accompanied the evolution of human beings. As happened to other higher creatures, their system of biological, preprogrammed (in older terminology, instinctive) responses weakened as their individual intelligence and adaptability increased. Human ancestors early reached the point of dependence on adults of their species until they could learn enough to survive on their own. But in the case of human beings, this went further than in any other species. The human species, moreover, developed cultural traditions of language and tool making, which marked the last stages of human evolution. The result was creatures whose prolonged dependence upon the society in which they were born was related to their lack of precommitment to society of any particular type or to any narrow or particular form of selfhood. There are few if any societies in which average human individuals of any other society could not fill all or most of the social roles available if they were born and raised in it.

Human society places unusual demands on socialization, for without the continuous manning of its positions as they become vacant through illness, retirement, and death, it would simply melt away. However, since most societies only require a fraction of what any given individual could offer, much human potential is unused. A major problem confronting every human society is to prevent unused human energy and imagination from being employed against it. All human societies also place demands on the means of social control. The more complex the society the more serious its control problem.

THE HOLISM-ELEMENTARISM DISPUTE

The representatives of every society inevitably seek to strike some kind of balance between the latitude or freedom permitted to the individual and the requirements of society. The theoretical limits represented by anarchism and authoritarian absolutism are rarely approached in practice. Furthermore, the line between individual and collective requirements is constantly shifting. In the formative period of a new collectivity[1] considerable scope is usually permitted the individual. Often when a collective is in danger of falling apart in a last attempt to retain control authorities may place a virtual straitjacket of restrictions on the membership. When this fails the result may be revolution or collapse into anarchism.

There are few decisions more basic made by students of human social life than the comparative importance they assign to the individual and to the collective. Do they take the social system or the individual to be the primary reality? All students of human social life inevitably recognize both. However, it makes significant difference whether one treats individuals as the primary reality, considering social life merely as what they do together (elementarism) or whether one sees the social system as a reality sui generis with laws of its own viewing the individuals who compose it as the raw materials from which a society is made. From the time of the origin of the conflict to the present, the tides of battle have surged back and forth between the holists and elementarists.

However, the conflicts do not end with these distinctions, for there are important subdifferences among the holists. Traditional Christian theologians assumed that there were two collectives: as St. Augustine put it, the city of God (the Church, the fellowship of believers) and the city of man (secular society). Human salvation rested with membership in the fellowship of believers. Augustinian theology was holistic. Hegel and other absolute idealists conceived the primary sociocultural reality to be human history, represented by the spirit or genius of peoples or national cultures. Nations were, in Hegel's words, concrete universals and the true individuals of history. Auguste Comte and other members of the first school of social theory subscribed to an organismic view of humanity. The early sociological conflict theorists

had envisioned society as a unit synthesizing the tensions of interest and ethnic groups. The structure-functionalists treated the equilibrating social system as the fundamental unit of study. The major property of all of these positions, whatever their other differences, was the vision of the whole as the primary reality. Whether sacred or secular in orientation, they saw in the whole the promise of order. It is not unfair to describe them as right-wing holists.

However, not all holists have envisioned the sociocultural whole in terms of a promise of order. For some, revolutionary holism has represented the primary hope for change and human betterment. As a young man, Hegel had been an admirer of Rousseau and had interpreted his theory in radical terms. After Hegel's death, the Left Hegelians, who counted Marx among their numbers, returned Hegelianism to something similar to Hegel's youthful position. Marx fused Left Hegelianism with the traditions of the French scientific socialists — who represented the radical tradition stemming from Saint-Simon in contrast to the conservative tradition of Comteian sociology. Classes, conceived as the revolutionary agents of progress, were the focus of interpretation. When, in response to the positivistic tendencies of orthodox Marxism and the revisionists, the conflict theorists of the Frankfurt school took up the tradition of revolutionary Marxism, moving it gradually toward Left Hegelianism once more, a revolutionary class again became the vehicle for hopes of human betterment.

In contrast to such nineteenth- and twentieth-century holism, the dominant trend in Western philosophy from Descartes to Kant was elementaristic, assuming that the individual was the primary reality in human social life. This tradition was also rationalistic, conceiving reason as the most important of human faculties and as distinguishing human beings among the creatures. When reaction in sociological circles eventually occurred against holism, rationalistic individualism was readily available. Four of the major elementaristic theories, behaviorism, sociological formalism, social-action theory, and symbolic interactionism

---

[1]Cult formations, to be sure, represent the opposite extreme — withdrawal from (though this may take place within) the wider collective into special groups that place extreme restrictions on their members.

are basically types of elementaristic rationalism. However, also among the major developments in recent thought has been the rejection of rationalistic conceptions of humanity. The emotions and drives of human beings were brought under scrutiny, their irrationality, their capacity for faith and for creativity became focal points for analysis. Phenomenological sociology and behavioristic sociology (which tends to approach human beings primarily as reactive mechanisms) are best conceived as forms of nonrationalistic elementarism.

The conflict between holism and elementarism in sociology has been crossed by another dispute, the ancient mind-body problem.

SOCIOLOGICAL FALLOUT FROM THE MIND-BODY PROBLEM

When people began to reflect upon their responses to the world they found themselves drawing a distinction between living and nonliving things. The general character of living things, Aristotle noted, was that they were able to move themselves. There was no question about the location of human beings, they were the most important of the self-movers. Even people in very primitive circumstances assumed the existence of some principle or inner entity or spirit which distinguished the self-movers and mysteriously departed when they died. Long before human beings invented complex civilizations they had elaborate notions about what happened to souls or spirits or ghosts when they left the body (and sometimes where they resided before they took up residence in a newborn individual) and began to engage in funeral and burial rites to prepare the soul for its journeys in the hereafter.

Self-reflection by human beings led to the notion that they had all sorts of properties not shared by nonliving things: perception, feelings, desires, concepts, and consciousness. Living things other than human beings had some of these, but apparently to a lesser degree. Human beings seem to

have long been convinced that anything they could name must be a thing of some sort, and since it did not make sense to view a given individual's perceptions, feelings, desires, and concepts as things that belong to his or her body, they were believed to belong to the spirit assumed to occupy the body.

In his thumbnail review of theories of the mind, Alan White treats Plato's theory in antiquity, Descartes's theory at the threshold of modern philosophy, and Freud's theory in the twentieth century as influential forms of the entity theory of mind.[2] In the fourth century B.C., in *The Republic* and *Phaedo,* Plato assumes that the mind (or psyche) is an invisible entity distinct from the body and capable of acquiring knowledge. His model for the mind was the political community which has a governing, executive, and productive element; similarly, the mind was thought to have cognitive, affective, and connative components. Plato's theories of the mind had a major influence on medieval Christian views of the soul.

In the seventeenth century Descartes restated this ancient and medieval entity conception of mind in a form that played an important role in modern thought. Anything in us, Descartes argued, that cannot be viewed as pertaining to the body has to be attributed to the soul. However, White notes, although Plato modeled the mind after the political constitution of the city-state, Descartes used physical processes as his analogy for the mind. Hence he describes Descartes's view as the physical theory since the language of physical phenomena was employed to describe things of the mind. Since Descartes, pictures of the mind have been successively modeled on physics, chemistry, physiology, and most recently cybernetics.

Minds can be deep or dirty, slow or tenacious, dull or flashing: they can be 'weighted down' by worry or 'lightened' by good news. We can 'bear' something in mind or 'cast it out.' We can be 'numbed' by desire or by an electric shock, 'torn' between patriotism and

[2]See Alan R. White, *The Philosophy of Mind* (New York: Random House, 1967), pp. 22–45.

ambition . . . We can 'display' courage . . . We can 'possess' plenty of ambition and little knowledge, or much property and little cash.[3]

The Freudian theory of mind, developed at the end of the nineteenth and in the early twentieth century, partly restored both the political and physical theories of mind. A word was thought of as an object, "mind" was taken as the name for the "psychical apparatus" and divided into provinces, agencies, regions, or systems which operated with and on energies or forces (instincts and ideas). Freud's Id, devoted to attaining pleasure, is like Plato's element of desire. The Ego and Superego are the counterpart to Plato's spirit and ruling elements of the mind. As the theories of Descartes which influenced the early psychologists, Freud's descriptions of mental phenomena are presented in physical metaphors. "What, in Freud's view, chiefly distinguished his picture of the mind from that of his predecessors was the concept of the *Unconscious*."[4] This was itself a product of Freud's physicalist approach to mental phenomena. Everything had a cause and the mind was conceived as an energy system. If an item appeared missing in the chain of causes, it had to be present in some region other than that of consciousness.

Entity theories of mind and matter proved to be a major stumbling block to the philosophic dream of a unified system of knowledge. Depending on where one started with mind or with matter, something tended to be left out and dualism was likely to be converted into idealistic or materialistic monism. Particularly troubling was the question of the interaction of mind and matter which were presumably manifest in the mind and body in a single individual. The common-sense notion that the mind can influence the body and vice versa implied that somehow or other these different eternal substances could turn into one another. Expedients with which to solve the mind-body problem such as the notion that mind and body

were independent but operated like preset clocks (an idea taken over in Leibnitz's monadology) had the properties of ad hoc inventions to salvage an untenable theory. In the empiricist tradition extending through Locke, Berkeley, and Hume, the successive breakdown of dualism — first into Berkeley's subjective idealism, then into Hume's skepticism and common-sense psychologism — was a major component in Kant's attempts to pull the rationalist and empiricist traditions together once more. But Kant ended separating, in principle, the problems of science, morality, and aesthetics. The distinction between mind and matter was transformed into a methodological opposition.

Unquestionably, one of the major attractions of nineteenth-century holism lay in its promise of a new attack on the task of systematic explanation of the world. In shifting the arena of explanation from the individual to the historical development of humankind, thinkers had presumably bypassed the mind-body problem. Comte declared an end of philosophy and metaphysical inquiry. The task of the proven best method of study, science, is to examine events as presented in experience, seeking laws of coexistence and succession between their manifestations without concern for some reality in itself. Early French and English sociological positivism draws no distinction between events based on their presumed anchorage in nature or the physical world rather than in the psychical or sociocultural world. By contrast, Hegel was first and last an idealistic metaphysician, visualizing ultimate reality as the development of the spirit in its historical attainment of autonomy and freedom. The effect of Comteian positivism was to treat ideas as if they were things; the effect of Hegelian absolute idealism was to treat things as if they were ideas. For neither position, at least for the moment, was the mind-body distinction a problem, although whenever absolute idealism and positivism were brought into confrontation conflict could be anticipated.

Little noticed in the nineteenth century was the long delayed discovery of Vico. Vico was a holist, hence he should have been of interest to collectivistic thought. Furthermore, he had envisioned

---

[3]White, *The Philosophy of Mind*, p. 32.
[4]*Ibid.*, p. 42.

the development of a science of society. However, Vico had also retained the traditional spirit-matter distinction and had proposed to found a science of society on traditional grounds. He had argued that all social and cultural events are human made, while nature is the creation of God. Human beings understand the social and cultural world from the inside, as its authors and as direct participants; their understanding of nature, on the other hand, can only be external. Although recognized as an interesting anticipation of nineteenth-century philosophy and sociology, Vico's proposal was set aside by the more philosophically minded absolute idealists and positivists who possibly sensed that Vico's point of view would reintroduce the mind-matter problem at the very heart of holism.

Positivistic organicism, the first school of sociology, soon began to develop as an independent social science in France, England, and America. Absolute idealism found its home in Germany in philosophy and history. While Comte proposed that his new science draw its primary materials from history, in accordance with his positivism he reduced history to overt happenings in human behavior and proposed that they be studied purely as phenomena without concern for what might lie behind them. John Stuart Mill agreed with Comte, the idea was to apply the methods of the natural sciences to social phenomena, establishing the natural laws of activities in human pluralities. Thomas Buckle began the application of positivistic methods to the writing of history. Reactions were not long in coming from German historicists.

Johann Droysen, who in 1852 developed a course in historical method at the University of Berlin, led the reaction. Droysen drew a sharp distinction between the methodology of the natural and historical science on the grounds that the sphere of history and science are quite distinct: history deals with moral judgment which eludes statistical and causal study. Statistical and causal methods, however, are appropriate to the study of things.[5] In the tradition initiated by Droysen, Dil-

they elaborated with considerable subtlety the difference between the method of the natural and of the human sciences. In the natural sciences we explain, in the human sciences we understand: explanation is external, understanding is internal; causal and statistical analyses are proper for explanation; the intuition of meanings generalized into types is basic for understanding. However, the problem grows complicated at those points where psychical and physical forces interact. At these points causal and statistical understanding tends to break down.[6] Moreover, direct intuitive understanding is clearly only fully possible in immediate experience. The primary task of the human sciences is to understand the objectification of life. The productions of the poet are unusually relevant for this purpose which is fulfilled in the development of a hermeneutic perspective.[7] In all this, it is clear, Dilthey was restoring the mind-body distinction and was being forced to deal with the issue of what to do when mind and body interact.

Dilthey's theories had considerable influence on both the critical theorists and phenomenologists. Repeatedly, members of both these schools have restored the distinction between mind and matter and have expressed the conviction that the social sciences require special methods of study adapted to their character as disciplines concerned with meaning. However, this is to get ahead of the story. Although the mind-body problem was beginning to take shape, for the holist it was the rise of elementaristic perspectives that made it inevitable that sociologists had to face up to the implications of the mind-body problem.

The neo-Kantians, as could be expected from the anchorage of their position in the tradition

---

[5]Johann Gustav Droysen, *Grundris der Historik*, trans. E. B. Andrews as *Outline of the Principles of History* (Bos-

ton: Ginn & Co., 1893) and "Zur Characteristik der europaischen Krisis," [The Nature of the European Crisis] in Felix Gilbert, ed., *Politische Schriften* (Munich, 1933), pp. 307–342.
[6]See Rudolf A. Makkreel, *Dilthey, Philosopher of the Human Studies* (Princeton, N.J.: Princeton University Press, 1975), p. 60.
[7]See *ibid.*, pp. 247ff.

extending from Descartes to Kant, tended to restore the dualism of mind-matter to the status of a major issue. The behavioristic sociologists made behavior the object of analysis, treating the problem of meaning more or less as an epiphenomenon which could be ignored (or treated as a kind of index to behavior). The social action theorists and symbolic interactionists (at least the early representatives of these schools such as Max Weber and George Herbert Mead) subscribed to what is at times called a functionalistic theory of mind which permitted them to take the position that it is important both to determine the meaning of social acts to their subjects and to explain behavior causally. This set aside the mind-body problem, treating mind as a function of the body.

In the classical world, Aristotle formulated a functional theory of mind or the soul. He had studied long with Plato, but on Plato's death his school was taken over by Plato's nephew. Aristotle did not get along well with the nephew and left Athens. On the Island of Lesbos, among other things, he spend considerable time observing and classifying forms of marine life. Aristotle accepted a position as tutor to Alexander the Great and after the death of Alexander's father Philip, when Alexander launched upon his military adventures, Aristotle returned to Athens, established the Lyceum, and continued for the next thirteen years to teach and organize research in a variety of areas. Aristotle was a scientist by temperament, in contrast to Plato who was a metaphysician. He approached the problem of mind from the standpoint of biological naturalism. Aristotle was dissatisfied with the notion of a realm of pure spirit.

> Now matter is potentiality, form, actuality . . . Of natural bodies some have life in them, others not; by life we mean self-nutrition and growth (with its correlative decay). It follows that every natural body which has life in it is a substance in the sense of a composite. But since it is also a *body* of such and such kind, viz. having life, the *body* cannot be soul; the body is the subject or matter, not what is attributed to it. Hence the soul must be a substance in the sense of the form of a natural body having life potentially within it. . . .

We can wholly dismiss as unnecessary the question whether the soul and body are one: it is as meaningless as to ask whether the wax and the shape given to it by the stamp are one.[8]

Aristotle envisioned all things as divisible into content and form. The form was provided by its purpose or function, which also constituted its essence or identity. The soul or mind was the function of a living body and had no existence apart from the formed material. The soul is to the body like cutting to an axe, seeing to an eye, or music to a violin.

The considerably lesser popularity of Aristotle's theory of the mind and soul than Plato's is understandable. From Aristotle's position there is no foundation for denying that all living things have souls; as he admitted from his point of view, even trees have souls. It is a poor doctrine from which to launch arguments for individual immortality. Developments in nineteenth-century philosophy and science posed serious obstacles in the path of the traditional conceptions of mind and matter. The materialists, such as L. Büchner in *Force and Matter* (1855), claimed that life and spirit were natural phenomena to be explained by mechanical laws. Karl Voght, in *Physiological Epistles* (1847), argued that the brain secretes thought in the same manner as the liver secretes bile. When it was discovered that even when its brain was removed a frog could carry out some apparently purposeful actions, it suggested the possibility that fundamentally, purposeful actions may actually be automatic reflex reactions to stimuli. Helmholtz (1847) applied the theory of the conservation of energy to organic as well as inorganic matter, indicating that the idea that human beings can influence events by free will may be illusory. L. A. Quetelet, *Sur l'Homme* (1835), demonstrated that many human activities such as crime, which have been taken as purposeful, occur with a statistical regularity that was hard for many persons to reconcile with traditional notions of free will. The Darwinian theory of evolution not

[8]Richard McKeon, ed., *The Basic Works of Aristotle* (New York: Random House, 1941), p. 555.

only indicated that all species developed over time by a long, slow process, but also struck a major blow against the notion that human beings were intrinsically different (and close to the angels) from other living species. And, worst of all, Darwin's principle of natural selection indicated that the rise and change of species could be explained by the operation of purely mechanical forces without any need for recourse to notions of plans or purposes or entelechies which guided the evolutionary processes.[9] One possible implication of such developments was that mind (and such associated phenomena as thought, feeling, value, and the like) had either to be explained functionally[10] or rejected altogether.

Among the forms of elementaristic social theory, both social action theory and symbolic interaction theory received from their founders (Weber for social action theory and G. H. Mead for symbolic interaction) a functional theory of mind. Max Weber had no doubt (in agreement with the neo-Idealists) that to ignore the meanings in human interaction was to miss its most distinctive feature; he believed (with the neo-Kantians) that the purpose of science was to explain phenomena causally, and that human behavior was a legitimate object of scientific study. Weber was temperamentally a nominalist and suspicious of the German philosophic tendencies toward reification and preoccupation with metaphysics. In his definition of the task of sociology he deliberately set aside the metaphysical problem of mind and matter and laid down the task of sociology as the meaningful understanding of social action with an aim of arriving at a causal interpretation of it. In his discussion of the implications of this, Weber displayed keen awareness of problems in this formulation but always pulled speculation up sharply at the point where there would have been a tendency to restore the mind-body problem as a major issue.

The pragmatic philosophers were moving in the same direction.[11] And George Herbert Mead, for example, had urged in *Mind, Self, and Society* that if we begin the analysis of human interaction with the assumption of psychophysical parallelism, no matter how far we carry the reasoning process we never manage to get them together. He proposed, rather, that ongoing interaction is given at the start (as it most certainly is for any individual at the time he or she is born) and then raises the question how the type of behavior we identify as mind could arise within it. Mead, then, suggested that language was the mechanism that made this possible. Mind, of course, becomes not a new entity, but the form in which behavior is reconstituted when it is remodeled from the inside by the mediation of language.

In Alfred Schutz's version of phenomenological sociology, he proposed to dismiss the mind-body problem in the same manner as Weber and the pragmatists and simply take the phenomena of both body and mind as manifestations of everyday interaction, without worrying about the question of whether they are manifestations of underlying entities. It is noteworthy that Schutz believed that Husserl's solution of the problem of solipsism was

[9]For a review of nineteenth-century materialism, naturalism, and agnosticism see John Passmore, *A Hundred Years of Philosophy* (Harmondsworth: Penguin Books, 1968).

[10]As biological functions, not as social functions.

[11]It is quite possible that the pragmatists through the English representative, F. S. C. Schiller, had some influence on Weber. Schiller was particularly concerned with the implications of the development of science for the traditional mythology, magic, and religion, and was never tired of pointing to new examples of the dismantling of such ancient beliefs as a result of the advance of scientific thinking. Weber was fond of quoting Schiller on the role of science in the disenchantment of the world. To be sure Weber was also impressed by Nietzsche's treatment of the same problem, which Nietzsche expressed with poetic force in his parable of the madman who appeared with a lantern in the marketplace at midday proclaiming that God is dead, and that we (members of a scientific world) have killed him. But, in any case, Weber could well have been directly influenced by the pragmatists' (particularly William James) inclination to set aside both mind and matter, taking the problem of interaction in its everyday form, and treating mind, thought, value, and the like simply as the way in which a creature with humanity's peculiar evolutionary history functions.

612 THE CONFLICTS OF SOCIOLOGICAL THEORY

unsatisfactory[12] — he had assumed that the ulti-mate reality was Descartes's self, and in the end never convincingly explained how one could be sure there was more than the one presumably known from the inside. Schutz, of course, was fol-lowing the practice of both Max Weber (whom he had undertaken to illuminate) and the prag-matists, and came to the conclusions that one knew the other directly and arrived at the self only by reflexion or secondarily. This was merely a spell-ing out of G. H. Mead's position.

The ordinary language philosophers have further elaborated functional theories of mind. Wittgenstein, for example, states:

> There is a temptation for me to say that only my own experience is real: "I know that I see, hear, feel pains, etc. but not that anyone else does. I can't know this, because I am I and they are they." On the other hand I feel ashamed to say to anyone that my experience is the only real one; and I know that he will reply that he could say exactly the same thing about his experience. . . . There are propositions of which we may say that they describe facts in the material world (external world). Roughly speaking, they treat of physical objects: bodies, fluids, etc. . . . . There are on the other hand propositions describing personal experiences. . . . At first sight it may appear . . . that here we have two kinds of worlds, worlds built of different materials; a mental world and a physical world. The mental world in fact is liable to be imagined as gaseous, or rather, aethereal. But let me remind you here of the queer role which the gaseous and aetherial play in philosophy — when we perceive that a substantive is not used as what in general we should call the name of an object, and when therefore we can't help saying to ourselves that it is the name of an aetherial object. I mean, we already know the idea of 'aetherial objects' as a subterfuge, when we are embarrassed about the grammar of certain words, and when all we know is that they are not used as names for material objects.

This is a hint as to how the problem of the two mate-rials, *mind* and *matter,* is going to dissolve.[13]

Gilbert Ryle, the best known Oxford ordinary lan-guage philosopher, develops the functional theory of mind at length in *The Concept of Mind* (1949). In everyday life, he urges, we get along well with mental concepts and know what we mean when we say someone is intelligent or stupid, joking and serious. The official Cartesian myth of mind-body must be destroyed. It is a mistake to assume that entities correspond to thoughts, feelings, values. When we speak of intellects it is to describe human behavior, not name an entity. When a person knows how to do something, for example to play chess, we are not describing an entity but a dispo-sition. We are misled when we follow Descartes and others who presume that human beings are com-posed of two disparate entities, a mind and a body, a ghost and a machine. As White summarizes Ryle's position:

> Functional theory regards mental concepts not as referring to mysterious inner entities and processes that affect our outward behavior, but as a way of referring to certain characteristics of that behavior. "The styles and procedures of people's activities," says Ryle, "*are* the way their minds work and are not merely imperfect reflections of the postulated secret processes which were supposed to be the workings of minds."[14]

However, even though founders of the social action, symbolic interaction, and phenomenologi-cal sociologies (Weber, Mead, and Schutz) all tried to avoid the mind-body problem, some of their followers have reinterpreted these traditions in a manner that would reintroduce it.

---

[12]Husserl, of course, has made the idealistic assumption of the existence of a transcendental ego in the first place. And he could be viewed as illustrating Mead's point: if you begin by assuming psychophysical parallelism you never overcome it.

[13]Ludwig Wittgenstein, *The Blue and Brown Books* (New York: Harper, 1965), pp. 46–47. See also *Philosophical Investigations* (Oxford: Blackwell, 1953).
[14]White, *The Philosophy of Mind,* p. 55. See also Gilbert Ryle, *The Concept of Mind* (London: Hutchinson, 1949).

THE METHODOLOGICAL DISPUTE

In addition to the holism-elementarism dispute and the mind-body or naturalism-spiritualism dispute, sociology has been haunted by a methodological conflict over the appropriateness of positivistic methodology to the study of its problems. Positivism is the doctrine that science, which proved its value in the natural sciences, is also the most appropriate method for studying social and cultural phenomena. Positivism has roots in British empiricism in the tradition extending from Bacon to Hume. Kant's *Critique of Pure Reason*, which undertook to demonstrate the scope and limits of scientific study, also had positivistic implications. Comte's positivism proposed: to confine analysis to things as presented in experience; to renounce metaphysics and the search for essences or hidden principles; to advance a program of the unity of science; and to envision the value of science as its contribution to human progress. Positivism was vigorously sponsored by Herbert Spencer and Thomas Huxley, and it was taken by John Stuart Mill as a starting point for the development of his logic of the moral science, completing the review of empirical methodology in his *System of Logic* (1843).

Mill's method, strongly influenced by David Hartley's associationism and Jeremy Bentham's utilitarianism, was analytical or, as he described it himself in his description of Bentham's procedure, a "method of detail," consisting of studying wholes by examining their parts, abstractions by examining things, and classes by the examination of the individuals which make them up. This procedure contrasted with that of such "intuitionists" as Carlyle and Coleridge, who approached issues as historically developing wholes. However, when he developed his logic of the moral sciences (or as we would say the methodology of the social sciences), Mill combined historical and analytical procedure into what he described as a method of "inverse deduction": first examining society directly, developing generalizations on the basis of historical observation, then connecting them with experimental laws of psychology.

A number of developments played a role in the transition from nineteenth-century to twentieth-century positivism. Some natural scientists had begun to turn their attention to problems of the logic of scientific procedure: Ernest Mach, Karl Pearson, Henri Poincaré, and Pierre Duhem were notable. The positivist spirit was manifest in their proposals for the establishment of science on a strict empirical foundation and the reduction of its formulations to rigorous deductions from clearly formulated axioms.[15] A second major development that played a role in the reconstituted positivism was a program that had roots in Leibniz's dream of a symbolism that would unite logic and science. This program was picked up by Bertrand Russell along lines suggested by Frege, and in *Principa Mathematica*, in collaboration with A. N. Whitehead (1910–1913), he developed a system of symbolic logic which was not only to unite logic and mathematics in a single system but supplied the language of positivism.[16] Meanwhile, Russell and G. E. Moore were attempting to reconstruct Mill's position, that is, that empirical knowledge ultimately is derived from particulars. Since, they reasoned, the philosopher is concerned with words about things, rather than things, this position was called logical atomism. One of Russell's students, Ludwig Wittgenstein, worked out the position of logical atomism in a form (*Tractatus logico-philosophicus*, 1921) that had influence not only on logical positivism (or logical empiricism), but on most other developments in twentieth-century philosophy.

In 1922 Moritz Schlick, a philosopher scientist and interpreter of Einstein, was appointed to Ernst Mach's old professorship at the University of Vienna. Around Schlick a circle of scientists, mathematicians, and Machians, took shape, constituting the nucleus of the Vienna Circle. Important members included Rudolf Carnap, Otto Neurath, and Herbert Feigl. Sometime later a Berlin group centered on Hans Reichenback formed. A British

---

[15]See Passmore, *A Hundred Years of Philosophy*, pp. 320ff.
[16]*Ibid.*, pp. 217f.

group also took shape around A. J. Ayer. In the 1930s, with the rise of fascism members of both the Vienna and German Circles were forced to emigrate. Carnap settled at the University of Chicago where, under the influence of C. W. Morris, American pragmatism was partly integrated with the positivist program.

Members of the original Vienna Circle in the 1920s were concerned with the problem of how the certainty of mathematics could be reconciled with the empiricist belief that meaningful propositions are based on experience. Using their interpretation of Wittgenstein's *Tractatus* as a guide, the positivists took the position that, except for identities, all intelligible propositions are based on experience. Mathematical and purely logical propositions are identities or tautologies; all other propositions derive their meaning from experience, meaning rests on verifiability. Carnap, who emerged as the leading member of the group, was a student of Frege, a system builder and formalist, making major attempts to present his ideas systematically in symbolic logical terms. Primitive ideas were cross sections of the stream of experience that can be arranged into quality classes and these, into sense classes. Under the influence of Otto Neurath, Carnap gradually abandoned phenomenalism, proposing — the thesis of physicalism — that everything meaningful can, in principle, be formulated in the language of things, in the language of physics. In the end, certain statements (protocol sentences) are accepted on the basis of experience. Truth is correspondence with fact as disclosed by experience.

A number of problems began to emerge for the logical positivists from the beginning. If the principle of verifiability was interpreted too narrowly, it clearly prematurely closed out as meaningless all sorts of ideas that later proved to be verifiable — for example, if one only accepted as meaningful what one had verified one had to abandon most of what one knew. If, however, verifiability was interpreted too loosely it opened the door once more to all sorts of magic, mysticism, myth, and metaphysics. Moreover, special problems emerged when the theories were admitted, for corre-

spondence rules had to be developed for reducing theories to protocol sentences and some of the most important theories of science have derived their value from the manner in which they have suggested new lines of factual exploration. Meanwhile, it became clear that theory had already entered the picture in the very description of fact. Finally, a member of the Vienna Circle, Kurt Gödel proved that any formalism rich enough to permit the formulation of arithmetic also allowed for the statements which, though true, cannot be proven to be true within that formalism.[17] Alfred Tarski proved that Gödel's principle holds in any formal logical system. In short, the principle of verification was shown to be anything but unambiguous, the lines between theory and fact were becoming blurred, and even the distinction between analytical and synthetic propositions was turning out to be less sharp than had been believed. Logical positivism has run its course. In Passmore's summary: "Logical positivism has marched in two different directions. At Carnap's hands, toward a realist account of perception and a physicalist account of minds; at Ayer's hands back to British empiricism out of which it developed. What has been discarded, in both cases, is the conception of a kind of empirical knowledge which is wholly trustworthy, free of any risk of error."[18] Karl Popper has done more to repair the positivist program than anyone else.

Karl Popper has denied that he is a positivist and has often pointed to his many criticisms of the logical empiricists, but he has been closely acquainted with developments of the Vienna school, he has advocated an analytical point of view, has appreciated the value of formalization — though, he insists — not as an end in itself, and has searched for a criterion, if not for eliminating metaphysics at least for drawing a clear line between science

[17]Kurt Gödel, "Uber formal unentscheidbare Sätze der Principia mathematica und verwandter System" [Concerning Formally Indeterminate Tenets of the Principia Mathematica and Related Systems] Part 1, *Monatshefte für Mathematik und Physick*, XXXIX, 173–198. Alfred Tarski, *Logic, Semantics, Metaphysics* (Oxford: Clarendon, 1956).
[18]Passmore, *A Hundred Years of Philosophy*, p. 393.

and pseudoscience. Finally, Popper has argued for the essential unity of science.

Even though not a positivist, Popper has tried to repair or find alternatives to those aspects of the positivist's program where they, in his opinion, have failed. The positivists have devoted, he believes, insufficient attention to the historical development of science, have tended to introduce the principle of testability prematurely and eventually were forced to substitute a degree of confirmation which is too vague to permit the rejection of anything, and have paid insufficient attention to the fact that the "facts" are already theoretically processed by the time we are ready to theorize about them. We do not work up from single observations to generalizations, we start thinking with all sorts of generalizations. Science really begins with the introduction of a critical attitude, which submits the generalizations with which we begin to the test of falsification. General hypotheses cannot be established by induction. If they are falsified, however, they can be rejected. If they prove in principle not to be falsifiable they can be rejected as nonsense.

The growth of science, Popper argues, occurs not through the gradual accumulation of truth, but in the replacement of theories by better theories. In this, the formulation of axiomatized deductive systems is helpful by aiding the comparison of competitive theories. Systematization is not an end in itself, but useful in the location of formulations, the falsification of which makes a difference. Neither essentialism, the attempt to offer ultimate explanations, nor instrumentalism, the treatment of theories as mere instruments, does justice to science. Essentialism sends it on a wild goose chase; instrumentalism generates complacency (an instrument can break down or go out of fashion, but cannot be refuted) about scientific theories which is fatal to progress. The social sciences operate with the same logic as the physical or natural sciences.[19]

What Herbert Feigl calls the "orthodox" view of scientific explanation[20] owes much to developments of the Vienna Circle, as may be seen in the accounts of Hempel and Oppenheim[21] and Ernest Nagel[22] (who, to be sure was also influenced by the pragmatic tradition). Scientific explanation, according to Hemple and Oppenheim, is "deductive-nomological." Explanation in science rests on a combination of general laws and information about specific circumstances in which the laws have application. The explanation is a deduction from the combination of these two types of statements. For the testing of a scientific explanation empirical confirmation of the statements describe boundary conditions and empirical confirmation of the laws, in terms of which the "explanandum" is deduced. The deduction must be logically consistent. Explanation and predication differ only in respect to the direction of interest. Explanations in the social sciences and history have the same form, as in the natural sciences, though, in the case of history, often only explanatory sketches are offered in which boundary conditions and relevant laws are suggested.

The principles of scientific explanation are the same also, according to Nagel, for all the sciences. Explanation is based on a combination of laws and specific conditions. The language of observation and of theory are mediated by correspondence rules. Explanation assumes a deductive form in which both the laws and observation statements are subject to logical criteria (so far as the deduction is concerned) and confirmation so far as both statements of fact and laws are concerned, whether we are dealing with mechanics, physics, biology, or the social sciences. The teleological or functional

[19]Karl Popper, *The Logic of Scientific Discovery* (New York: Basic Books, 1959); *The Poetry of Historicism* (New York: Harper & Row, 1964).

[20]See Herbert Feigl, "The 'Orthodox' View of Theories: Some Remarks in Defense as Well as Critique," in M. Radner and S. Winokur, *Minnesota Studies in the Philosophy of Science.* Vol. 4 (Minneapolis: University of Minnesota Press, 1970).
[21]Carl G. Hempel and P. Oppenheim, "Studies in the Logic of Explanation," *Philosophy of Science.* Vol. 14 (1948).
[22]Ernest Nagel, *The Structure of Science* (New York: Harcourt Brace, 1961).

explanations encountered in the social sciences also require observational evidence and laws. However, most of the generalizations in the social sciences are statistical, and functional generalizations are often diffuse. This may, in part, be due to the youth of the social sciences, in part, to the concern with problems close to everyday life, but there is no reason in principle to assume that explanations in the social sciences could not assume full deductive nomological form.

Such conventional accounts of scientific explanation show the strong influence of positivism.

The Influence of Positivism on Sociology. Conceptions of scientific method have largely been determined by positivistic notions. The ideas that if sociology is to be a science it must have a precise language, make more skillful use of logical and mathematical tools, develop hypotheses in a form that permits their empirical testability, and the like are all taken directly from positivistic approaches to scientific explanation. Also, the influence of positivism is manifest in the development of sociometrics and psychometrics, and the fascination with mathematical model building.

The logical positivists were the inspiration of some sociologists concerned with theory construction. Hans Zetterberg's *On Theory and Verification in Sociology*[23] appears to have been directly inspired by Carnap's version of logical empiricism. Zetterberg's approach to theory and research is more philosophical than investigative (as, in fact, is the approach of most students of theory construction). He is not so much interested in developing new ideas, as in arranging existing generalizations into axiomatic systems. He believes that there is no shortage of generalizations in sociology and envisions the major task of sociology as the completion of the program urged by older positivists such as Lundberg, that is, to develop a sociology matching the rigor of the natural sciences. This is conceptualized as entailing a deductively derived set of

laws to which any particular event within boundary conditions is referable. The primitive terms referring to behavior should be deductively subsumed under theoretical or second-order generalizations. The content of second-order generalizations, conversely, should be reducible to protocol sentences.

Although positivistic-minded students of theory construction have advanced the argument that their purposes are to reduce sociological generalizations to a more precise form susceptible to research and to discover new areas where research is needed, many of their writings demonstrate a nonempirical and nontheoretical tendency. The result of programs of theory construction has too often been the substitution of narrow methodological rationalism for the messy business of firsthand research for this manifestation to be accidental. Meanwhile, positivism, with its preference for an analytical methodology, has been a component in the problem of holism; and with its concern for objectivity has been a component in the problem of meaningfulness.

Positivism and Holism. In a monograph in 1976, *Holistic Thought in Social Science,* Denis Phillips reviewed the conflict between the holists and exponents of positivistic methods. It is common in holistic writing, he observes, to find attacks upon mechanistic and atomistic methods, that is, the explanation of complex entities in terms of the properties of their parts plus relevant covering laws.[24] Holism, however, exists in a number of versions which Phillips lists as holism 1, 2, and 3. Holism 1 consists in a set of ideas pertaining to organic wholes: (1) that analytical methods are inappropriate to the study of biological organisms, society, or even to reality as a whole; (2) that the whole is more than the sum of its parts; (3) that the whole determines the nature of its parts; (4) that the parts cannot be understood if considered in isolation from the whole; and (5) that the parts are

[23]Hans L. Zetterberg, *On Theory and Verification in Sociology* (Totawa, N.J.: Bedminster, 1966).

[24]Denis C. Phillips, *Holistic Thought in Social Science* (Stanford, Calif.: Stanford University Press, 1976), p. 2.

dynamically interrelated or independent.[25] Holism 2 accepts holism 1 and adds, that even after the whole is studied, it still cannot be explained in terms of its parts. Holism 3 is the thesis that science would be advanced by having special terms to refer to wholes and their properties.

The analytical method of studying any complex entity or system has been to examine its components separately or in combinations of two or more, gradually piecing the whole together as more precise knowledge is generated until one can examine their operation in the ensemble as a whole. The thesis of methodological individualism on which this procedure rests states that every complex social situation, institution, or event is the result of particular configurations of individuals, their dispositions, situations, beliefs, the physical resources at their disposal, and the limitations of the environment.[26]

Far from accepting the thesis of holism, the methodological individualists argue that only their methods permit the understanding of the whole. They agree that things in interrelation often display properties that could not have been anticipated from examining them separately. But when this is described as *emergence* the methodological holists are no better off than the methodological individualists. However, the individualists argue that the notion that the "whole is more than the sum of its parts" is obscure and arises from a misconception of analytical methods; and it is not true that even after one understands all parts in the arrangement of the whole, one still cannot explain the whole in terms of the parts. The whole cannot be more than all the parts and whatever properties they acquire in relation to one another. This concept of *reduction* is meaningless and holism 2 must be rejected. At the same time, it is of value to have a terminology for different kinds of wholes.

Phillips concluded that the analytical method in the form presented by such writers as Hempel and Nagel was so moderate and reasonable that no sci-entist, not even a holist, can avoid putting it into practice. "By contrast, holism — taken seriously — is an eminently unworkable doctrine."[27] It was Phillips's opinion that the positivist can accept some components of holism 1 and could accept holism 3, but must reject holism 2.[28] This, of course, can hardly be expected to end the dispute; in due time, no doubt, a rejoinder from the holists to Phillips will be forthcoming.

Positivism and the Meaningfulness of Sociocultural Phenomena. In *The Structure of Science* Nagel carefully reviewed the presumed irreducibility of explanation in terms of meaning to a hypothetic-deductive model. He urged that, although biologists interested in the activities of organisms or the operation of a part of an organism may find it convenient to talk in terms of purposes, goals, and functions rather than laws and limiting conditions, this does not prove that it is impossible to explain such phenomena in terms of laws and relevant conditions. He advocates that the same qualification holds for social scientists who are concerned with the means, aims, and purposes of their subjects. Many of the problems of interest to social scientists are close to everyday life. They are often primarily concerned with probability outcomes and with the interpretation assigned to their conduct by the individuals involved, rather than with universal laws. In a manner somewhat similar to Weber, who had urged that an explanation of human activity may be "adequate at the level of meaning" without necessarily being causally adequate, Nagel observed that social scientists are often content with discovery of the merely necessary rather than both the necessary and sufficient conditions of social phenomena.

When a person gives reasons for his or her conduct, say that he or she is taking a neighbor to court because the neighbor is trying to steal his or her property, it is essential to know something of

---

[25]*Ibid.*, p. 6.
[26]*Ibid.*, p. 38.

[27]*Ibid.*, p. 123.
[28]Incidentally, holisms 2 and 3 were attributed to the work of two Continental biologists, Paul Weiss and Ludwig von Bertalanffy.

both his or her circumstances, which were the occasion for such behavior and the laws of psychology if one is to explain the event. Litigiousness over minor social conflicts may be "explained," for example, by the individual's history of paranoia. In any case, explanation, according to Nagel, ultimately takes the form of deductions from laws and initial conditions.[29]

The Positivist Dispute in German Sociology. Not all holists are antinaturalistic or all antinaturalists holistic. The most dramatic confrontation that can be imagined, thus, is between a competent form of positivism and an able form of holistic antinaturalism. When Max Horkheimer and Theodor Adorno were invited to return to Frankfurt and head up the restoration of prewar German sociological tradition, critical theory emerged at the core of the German sociological establishment. With a fine sense of drama, the German Sociological Association in Tübingen in 1961 invited Karl Popper to present a paper on the logic of the social sciences and Adorno to reply. Ralf Dahrendorf was scheduled to summarize the discussion.

However, what had been planned as a major event turned out, as perhaps should have been expected, to be something of a disappointment. For one thing, Popper had always claimed to be critical of positivism and did not consider himself to be a positivist. Furthermore, Popper and Adorno were wary antagonists. By the time they finished paying respects to one another and denouncing positivism — though they meant quite different things by their respective concepts — the result had more the properties of a dance exhibition than a confrontation of titans. Dahrendorf, in his summary, was moved to speak of the third person in

the debate and Giddens to suggest that "the debate is like Hamlet without the prince."[30]

However, the controversy took a more serious turn when it was resumed by Habermas and Albert after 1963 and soon involved other thinkers on both sides. In 1969 *The Positivist Dispute in German Sociology* was published in German with considerable additional material by Adorno, which provoked an afterword by Hans Albert, who was distressed by the form the volume had taken. And when the English translation of the volume appeared, an additional essay, Popper's review of the German volume, was added.

In his paper on the "Logic of the Social Sciences," Popper had summarized his views on the nature of science and the place of social science within it. He had argued that the method of the social sciences, as that of the natural sciences, consists in (1) trying out tentative solutions to problems; (2) subjecting these solutions to attempts at refutation when they are open to pertinent criticism; (3) trying another when a proposed solution is refuted through criticism; (4) accepting it tentatively if it withstands criticism. Hence, (5) the method of science is a consciously critical development of trial and error and (6) the objectivity of science means that no theory is beyond critical revision and the main instrument of logical criticism — the contradiction — is objective.[31] Among the sciences, sociology can and must make itself independent of psychology. It has an objective method, the method of objective understanding, or a situational logic which consists in the analysis of the actions of people within their social situations.

In other words, the situation is analyzed far enough for the elements which initially appeared to be psy-

---

[29]For a review of attempts by Nagel and others to incorporate the social science problems of meaningful interpretation within the positivistic explanation of science, see Passmore, *A Hundred Years of Philosophy*, pp. 517ff. The antinaturalists have, as could be expected, revived all the arguments of their predecessors against such attempts.

[30]Theodor W. Adorno, Hans Albert, Ralf Dahrendorf, Jürgen Habermas, Harald Pilot, and Karl R. Popper, *The Positivist Dispute in German Sociology*, trans. Glyn Adey and David Frisby (London: Heinemann, 1976), p. ix. See also A. Gidden, ed., *Positivism and Sociology* (London: Heinemann, 1974), p. 18.

[31]Popper, *The Positivist Dispute*, pp. 90–91.

chological (such as wishes, motives, memories, and associations) to be transformed into elements of the situation. The man with certain wishes therefore becomes a man whose situation may be characterized by the fact that he pursues certain objective *aims;* and a man with certain memories or associations becomes a man whose situation can be characterized by the fact that he is equipped objectively with certain theories or with certain information.[32]

Popper's critical rationalism, thus, accepts a method of *verstehen,* but this is understood in an objective sense and subject to falsification in the same manner as scientific method in any other sphere. Popper's view is very similar to that of Max Weber.

Adorno's commentary on Popper's presentation danced around without ever quite coming to grips with the point that the critical theorist and Popper had different conceptions of positivism. From the perspective of the Frankfurt philosophers, Popper was a positivist because: of his view that social science, although admittedly autonomous, had the same method as the other sciences; his attempt to separate scientific meaning from nonsense involved the rejection of metaphysics; his method was analytical rather than dialectical; he was sponsoring a form of "bourgeois" individualism; and so forth. However, that was precisely what Jürgen Habermas began to do in his 1963 essay on the "Analytical Theory of Science and Dialectics."

> The analytical-empirical modes of procedure repeatedly attempt to test law-like hypotheses in the same manner, regardless of whether they are dealing with historical material or with natural phenomena. . . . A dialectical theory of society, on the other hand, asserts the dependence of individual phenomena upon the totality; it must reject the restrictive use of the concept of law. Its analysis aims beyond the particular dependent relations of historically neutral quantities, toward an objective context which also plays a part in determining the direction of historical development.[33]

And once he began to restate the old complaint of the Frankfurt philosophers when he contrasted a holistic philosophy operating with dialectical methods in the interest of revolutionary change with the "positivistic sciences," Habermas was not long in accusing Popper of retrogressive support of the status quo.

> The dualism of facts and decisions necessitates a reduction of permissible knowledge to strict empirical sciences and thereby a complete elimination of questions of life-practice from the horizon of the sciences. The positivistically purified boundary between cognition and evaluation naturally signifies less a result than a problem. For philosophical interpretations now take possession anew of the eliminated realm of values, norms and decisions precisely on the basis of labor divided between philosophy and a restricted science.[34]

And when Hans Albert defended the Popperian approach to science, Habermas repeated his charges against analytical rationalism.

> I do not dispute that the analytical theory of science has stimulated actual research and has helped to elucidate methodological judgments. At the same time, however, the positivistic self-understanding has restrictive effects; it silences any binding reflection beyond the boundaries of the empirical-analytical (and formal) sciences. I reject this masked normative function of a false consciousness.[35]

In his review of the German publication of *The Positivist Dispute,* reprinted in the English translation, Popper complained that his invitation to speak on the logic of the social sciences before the German Sociological Society had the properties of an ambush. He had presented his theses on the logic of the social sciences unambiguously, but his respondents had avoided direct confrontation of them. Then Jürgen Habermas, another member of the Frankfurt school, had produced a paper twice as long as his original address filled with criti-

[32]*Ibid.,* pp. 102–103.
[33]Habermas, *The Positivist Dispute,* pp. 137, 138.
[34]*Ibid.,* p. 145.
[35]*Ibid.,* pp. 198–199.

cism of him as a positivist, something he had always denied.

> But having been invited to speak about 'The Logic of the Social Sciences' I did not go out of my way to attack Adorno and the 'dialectical' school of Frankfurt (Adorno, Horkheimer, Habermas *et al.*) which I never regarded as important, unless perhaps from a political point of view; and in 1960 I was not even aware of the political influence of this school. Although today I should not hesitate to describe this influence by such terms as 'irrationalist' and 'intelligence-destroying', I could never take their methodology (whatever that may mean) seriously from either an intellectual or scholarly point of view.[36]

The debate continues.

THE SOCIOLOGY OF SOCIOLOGICAL THEORY

The continuous preoccupation of sociology from the time of its origin into the present with the same issues — holism versus elementarism and naturalism versus antinaturalism — and the same methodological disputes — analytic versus synthetic (dialectical) and value-neutrality versus value-commitment — suggests that they belong to the deepest problems of psychology and civilization (at least in the psychology and civilization of Western humanity) and cannot be settled once and for all. Temperament, for example, seems to play a role in a realistic versus a nominalistic interpretation of general ideas which, in turn, is manifest sociologically in the inclinations toward holism or elementarism. The nominalists seem by temperament to be doubting Thomases, inclined to accept only what they can see or touch; the realists eagerly embrace the universal as the really real. Furthermore, the range of temperament seems to be universal, for there are nominalists and realists in all known societies. At the same time, tradition and

local milieu also seem to play a role. In England, for example, since Renaissance times, analytical, nominalistic, and empirical preferences have predominated; in Germany, on the other hand, during the same period, numerous realistic and holistic systems of thought developed. Hence, while temperament may play a role in individual preferences in social theory, sociocultural traditions and activities seem to have a selective influence on which will dominate.

There is no question that sociological theory has been shaped by the humanistic-scientific methods of the contemporary West and by holistic-elementaristic interpretations of social reality. Humanism-scientism and holism-elementarism define the primary directions that one can take in interpreting sociocultural events so long as Western civilization preserves the character it has acquired in the development of the city and the nation-state. The various theories which have developed have represented the exploration of the explanatory power of different combinations of methodological and substantive assumptions about the nature of social life and how it is best studied. The first major sociological theory to win a following was positivistic organicism, a combination of holism and scientism; the most recent form of sociological theory to attract constituents, phenomenological sociology, combines elementarism and antirational humanism. In between, most other combinations have been tried at one time or other.

Once a social theory and its associated research tradition are established, that is, becomes the official explanation and procedure sponsored by a number of scholars, social factors may intervene to give the theory an autonomy and a history of its own. Charismatic teachers acquire a circle of student satellites. If a member of the circle obtains a strategic editorship in the periodicals or the staff of book publishers, he or she may give preference to works of other members of the circle. The theory then is institutionalized in a circle of power and vested interests. Ideas and research traditions transmitted from master to apprentice may be strengthened by material and other rewards. Oc-

[36]Popper, *The Positivist Dispute*, p. 289.

casionally the circle forms a special association and may establish a journal to serve as a house organ of the official point of view. Foundation or government support may be sought to endow research and publication approved by the leaders of the school. The members of the school may develop ideas both in response to internal problems arising from within the group and in response to problems and pressures from the outside. To break with the group may then entail the loss of publishing and research opportunities.

It was the scientific circle, in its role in both the promotion and obstruction of scientific growth, that Thomas Kuhn discovered in his notion of the revolutions of science. He had argued that paradigms were more fundamental than theories, or laws, or methods, or technologies in science. Paradigms dominated normal science (representing the sharing by individual scientists of a body of suppositions as to what constitutes exemplary scientific practice) reducing the activities of its members to puzzle solving (which Kuhn mistakenly described as the verification of hypotheses). This process, he thought, continues until so many anomalies, things that do not fit the paradigm, develop, that the paradigm itself is undermined and loses the adherence of the group. A period of chaos ensues, ended by the rise of a new charismatic leader who establishes a new paradigm. Progress in science is an illusion, for between one paradigm and another there is no legitimate comparison. Science, in fact, resembles the operation of political or interest groups, artists' cults, or even religious sects far more than anyone had ever dreamed.

However, upon close examination, paradigm, the central notion in Kuhn's interpretation, proved to be ambiguous. One philosopher traced out more than twenty different senses in which the term was used. Kuhn was forced to admit that he had used the term loosely, though he has been inclined to let his argument stand anyway. In the end, the scientific paradigm was — though Kuhn did not use these words — the reified spirit of the scientific circle: the alleged source of everything else.

Thomas Kuhn's concept of revolutions in sci-

ence is a distorted picture of the growth of scientific culture, but it can be interpreted as a fair account of the manner in which some social factors at times promote or retard the growth of science. Science does not always or only develop in circles but sometimes it does. However, the theories, laws, methodological or technological innovations, and discoveries of a scientific circle do not vanish with the dispersal of the circle, but may become permanent parts of the growing culture of science — to be employed, modified, or extended by other researchers. It is also true that scientific circles do at times succeed in taking areas of science under their management, dominating developments until they achieve their aims. However, they often do not know how to proceed or for a variety of reasons — for example, conflicts among the prima donnas — explode or run out of steam, causing interest to shift elsewhere. The particular arrangement of theories, laws, methodologies, and technologies characteristic of the circle may be dismantled, as its component parts become assimilated into common scientific culture.

Science, as a specialized development of culture, started with assumptions, instruments, ways of reasoning, and problems which were part of everyday life. As scientific culture accumulates, the opportunities presented by the problems of everyday life to initiate scientific study diminish, and scientific culture itself becomes the source of ideas for research at what is described as the "growing edge" of science. In this respect, too, science may be said to progress — a phenomenon also attacked by Kuhn as a sacred cow of science.

Since the social sciences remain close to everyday life, the problems to which they are addressed can be expected to be posed by the developments of general culture and contemporary society with far greater frequency than is true for the physical sciences. This may be a major clue to the apparently interminable disputes over holism versus elementarism, naturalism versus antinaturalism, and value-neutrality versus value-commitment — they are potentially contradictory currents in the Western mind, compromises between which define the Western way of life. Furthermore, there have been

Humanistic-Scientific and Individualistic-Collectivistic Components of the Sociological Theories

Basic Notion of Social Reality

METHODOLOGICAL ORIENTATION	Elementarism		Holism	
	RATIONALISM	NONRATIONALISM	LEFT-WING	RIGHT-WING
Humanism	4. Social-Action Theory 5. Symbolic Interactionism	12. Phenomenological Sociology	10. Critical Theory	Traditional Christian Social Theory Absolute Idealism, Hegelianism 8. Structure-Functionalism, Macrofunctionalism
Science	3. Neo-Kantian Sociology (Formalism)	6. Pluralistic Behaviorism 11. Behavioristic Sociology	7. Marxian Sociology	1. Positivistic Organicism 2. Conflict Theory 9. Structure-Functionalism: Microfuntionalism

major conflicts within individualism and holism over the character of each. In the seventeenth and eighteenth centuries, for example, the most crucial property of individuals was felt to be their reason; in the nineteenth and twentieth centuries, on the other hand, the essential properties of individuals have more frequently been located in their emotional lives, their capacity for faith, for creativity, and for intuition. In the holistic doctrines of the nineteenth and twentieth centuries theorists have split over the identification of the critical property of the whole: some took it to be its order, harmony, and equilibrium in contrast to others who have stressed its internal dynamism and potential for change. These contrasting positions have been described as right- and left-wing holism, respectively. The basic types of sociological theory are bound up with Western culture in a most intimate sense: they have arisen at the intersection points of possible combinations of the humanistic-scientific and holistic-individualistic traditions.

Tensions Within and Between Humanism and Science. In the medieval world between A.D. 400 and A.D. 1000 except for a few cities much reduced in size and importance around the Mediterranean, the dominant communities of Europe were peasant villages, manors, and monasteries. The seigniorial and monastic communities in general enjoyed hegemony over the peasant village and landlords, knights, and monks enjoyed political and ecclesiastical authority over the population as a whole.

By A.D. 1000 a wave of city formation was underway in Europe as cities revolted against the domination of their landed and ecclesiastical lords. City corporations were forming, demanding charters which granted a variety of political and economic rights. In the new cities a bustling society was forming with greater affinities with the urban communities of the ancient world than with the surrounding rural world. A wide spectrum of urban types appeared, requiring knowledge and skills quite different from those of either monk or knight. In these urban environments the artists-craftspeople-engineers found a new field for the development of their talents. It was from their circles that the scientific way of thinking developed. Meanwhile, particularly in upper middle-class spheres, a new view of the world, oriented to the problems of this world and urban life, was taking shape. This view was designated humanistic (it was human-centered in contrast to the God-centered thinking of the monk). The humanistic view was optimistic and visualized individuals in terms of their capacity to learn, to improve themselves and to realize their potential; the religious view was pessimistic, considering individuals as creatures born in original sin, fallible, subject to temptation, requiring the Church to mediate their salvation. New lines of cleavage appeared in the cities between humanist and priest replacing the older divisions between knight and monk.

Religion, too, was changing in the new urban communities. The secular clergy, serving the needs of the ordinary person in the city, became the focus of change. An era of church building was opened in the cities and the cathedrals quickly dominated the monasteries of the countryside. Cathedral schools expanded, in part to serve the needs of the average churchgoer, but more importantly to educate the secular clergy. As it became apparent that Christianity had to respond to the needs of urban humanity or be thrust aside, new monastic orders (the most important being the Franciscans and Dominicans) appeared, now not with the mission of establishing rural religious establishments outside the sphere of decaying cities, but of winning the urban common people for the Church and of revising traditional Church culture for the task. The recovery of ancient literary culture, which had been promoted by the humanists, was taken up by members of the new monastic orders. The great project that emerged was the synthesis of ancient philosophy (particu-

larly the philosophy of Aristotle) wth Christian theology. The most successful of the syntheses was completed by Thomas Aquinas; hence, the designation of the resulting system of thought as Thomism. Thomism can be recognized as a major revision of the outlook of Western intellectuals in response to the rise of the city. It marks an important stage in the development from medieval to contemporary thinking. Meanwhile, science was beginning to take shape as an intellectual adventure in its own right. The time was rapidly approaching when it would begin to develop pictures of the world contrary to those of both the traditional Church and Antiquity, which in various ways the humanists and priests were readapting to their respective needs.

By the fifteenth century, when the European city had reached the point of its greatest autonomy, and the urban mind was polarized between humanist and priest, a new development — the expansion and consolidation of the territorial powers as the monarchical state — was underway. Both the city and countryside were reorganized as the monarchies increased in power. The territorial princes played a major role in the division within Christianity between Protestantism and Catholicism. Partly out of conviction and partly as a strategy of consolidating their hold over their subjects and winning them for their own purposes, the princes of the various states took sides in the religious controversy and launched a series of religious wars which divided Christianity into national configurations, strengthened the hold of the princes over their populations, and generally weakened Christianity as an ideologically unifying force.

Meanwhile, many of the forces released by the emerging monarchical states expanded the scope of science. As the Western world moved toward a stage in which national revolutions would take the state out of the hands of the monarchs and, in theory, place it in the hands of the people, the redrawing of the divisions in Western thought was occurring. The old polarization between humanism and theology was collapsing: religion was becoming absorbed into the humanistic heritage. Meanwhile, the sphere of science was expanding. Seventeenth- and eighteenth-century Enlightenment rationalism, which emerged in the monarchical states, presented a major attempt at synthesis of Western thought: it combined a rationalistic individualism with trust in the powers of scientific methods. The rationalists were either atheists or Deists — convinced that God was remote from the day-to-day operations of society and nature, leaving the world to be explained in its own terms. Faith in secular progress had largely been substituted for traditional Christianity as a socially unifying ideology in three circles.

The rationalists supplied the ideology of the revolutionaries who ousted the monarchs and began the process of a reconsolidation of power in the nation-states. The middle classes obtained varying degrees of power in the new nations, but the revolutionary ferment had also extended to the lower classes. The national revolutions spawned the modern movements toward mass democracy and socialism.

Saint-Simon, the adventurous aristocrat and soldier of fortune who is generally recognized as a precursor of both sociology and scientific socialism in France, had a keen realization of the fact that Christianity had weakened to a point where it could no longer effectively supply the binding ideology of Western humanity. Saint-Simon envisioned a new Christianity under the guidance of a priesthood of scientists. In Germany, Hegel, the major architect of German (Absolute) Idealism and an enthusiastic student in his youth both of the Enlightenment and French Revolution, had a reaction similar to that of Saint-Simon — that traditional Christianity could no longer bring unity to Western society. Both Saint-Simon and Hegel, moreover, realized that in the postrevolutionary world, consolidation of the nation was essential if the promise of the self-fulfillment of humanity was to occur. Hegel, too, revised Christianity, reconceptualizing God as the Spirit of Reason, manifest in the Genius of Peoples achieving ever greater autonomy and freedom in the Dialectic of History.

Absolute idealism in Germany and sociology in France, England, and America with their combi-

nation of holism and humanism, on the one hand, and holism and positivism, on the other, represented adaptations of the Western cultural tradition to the needs of people in the nineteenth-century nation-states. One could anticipate tensions resulting from the contrast between both forms of holism and the traditions of individualism that had preceded them. Tension was also inevitable between the organicism and positivism of the first school of sociology. An internal evolution of positivistic-organicism got underway almost immediately in the attempt to resolve conflicts between them. At the same time, in German social philosophy the opposite problem emerged. Its dialectical methodology faced a powerful antagonist in the analytical character of the empiricist traditions which were closer to scientific practice. Above all, however, the social sciences were taking shape at a time when Christianity was losing its grip on the Western mind, and the founders of sociology were assigning an ideological mission to their new discipline. The so-called value problem was, thus, not only anchored in the general cultural traditions of the recent West, but saddled on the new discipline from the beginning by its creators. It is little wonder that these issues have pursued sociology as it has step-by-step explored almost every major combination of humanism-scientism and holism-elementarism. In the passion with which Habermas, the major critical theorist in the contemporary world, has defended radical holism of a Hegelian type against the analytical methodology of Popper and the intensity with which some phenomenological sociologists have justified antinaturalistic individualism and intuitive methodology against the positivism of the students of theory construction, one may perhaps discern twentieth-century versions of the search for God and the salvation of the soul.

As sociologists have explored social interpretations ranging from humanistic holism to positivistic behaviorism with numerous revivals of older formulations (that are basically new versions of the same old issues) there is a temptation to despair: no issue seems permanently settled. However, in the process of exploring possible alternatives, sociological culture has been continuously enriched. The positivistic organicists established the theory of social structure, the theory of institutions, and the theory of social change as basic areas of sociology. The conflict theorists added the sociology of social strata, the theory of power, and the sociology of law. The neo-Kantians made major contributions to the theory of social relations. The various branches of social behaviorism added the new field of social psychology and enriched many of the older areas with elementaristic interpretations of their areas of interest. The Marxian sociologists enriched the sociology of economic life and co-founded with the phenomenologists the sociology of knowledge. The functionalists have enriched the theory of social organization. The critical theories of the Frankfurt school have greatly enriched the sociologies of art, literature, and music. The phenomenological sociologists have illuminated many phases of microsociology. There are, of course, many other areas that have been added, but the purpose of this listing is intended to be illustrative rather than exhaustive. The point is: despite the superficial impression that sociology spins its wheels and, instead of moving ahead, mires itself ever deeper in the same mud, it has generated a wealth of understanding that has become part of the common culture not only of sociologists, but of all people.

Sociology in a Postnational, Postindustrial, and Postpositivistic Age.

The diversity of sociological theory is, in part, a product of the fact that it arose in response to the needs of the nation-state; it was developed by individuals and circles in different countries at different times. Comte's fusion of organicism and positivism was adapted to the needs of the French milieu as Hegel's combination of holism and humanism to the German. Gumplowicz's conflict theory was addressed to ethnic conflicts in the Austro-Hungarian empire and the peculiar role of law among its social sciences. Marxian theory was directed to problems in German society in the revolutionary stirrings of 1830 and 1848 and to problems of scientific socialism in France, where Marx spent time in exile from Germany. Neo-Kantian sociology and some forms of social behaviorism arose in response to individualist reaction to nineteenth-century collectivism in the last quarter of the nineteenth century. Symbolic interactionism was adapted to the American milieu and to American pragmatism. Structure-functionalism, America's first native form of sociological holism, was as clearly a response to the national euphoria of the United States after a victorious war and the emergence of the United States as the foremost world power as the interest in American forms of critical theory (so-called reflexive sociology) and ethnomethodology are responses to the social upset and disillusionment of the 1960s and 1970s.

Without pursuing further examples, it is evident that some of the diversity in the various sociological theories arises from the fact that they have been addressed to conditions in different nation-states and over a time when the nation-state itself has been changing. Furthermore, although more new nations have formed since World War II, the nation-state may be declining as a workable community. Major wars are no longer fought by single nations, but by power blocs. Multinational corporations at times acquire more power than the smaller nations, and are often able to play nations off against one another. The elaborate bureaucracies and growth of welfare statism in the democracies has made them more similar to the communist nations than was true in the past; meanwhile, in the communist nations some features of a free market economy have been permitted to reappear. Such politicoeconomic developments, when added to the growth of the world population, the approaching exhaustion of fossil fuels, and the development of atomic weapons and an atomic energy industry (with its lethal by-product of atomic waste), have led some students to propose that we are entering upon a postnational, postindustrial society. Much of the theorizing, based on the assumption that its object was the national and industrial society, is proving to be inadequate.

Twentieth-century philosophy may also influence theorizing in new directions during the next decade. It has generally taken from ten to fifteen years for developments in philosophy to become manifest in sociology. Logical positivism, which eventually was demonstrated in sociological theory construction, was most rapidly expanded during the 1920s and 1930s. By the 1940s the movement was beginning to bog down in difficulties and to break up. Theory construction only began to come into its own in sociology in the 1960s, at a time when philosophy had already moved on to other things.

One trend in twentieth-century philosophizing is the view that if there is a place left for philosophy it is as a metadiscipline, a study not of things (that is the province of sciences) but the study of the study of things. Specifically, this meant that its object is the study of the language and logic of the disciplines.

The fundamental argument common to both nineteenth- and twentieth-century positivism is that scientific thinking is the best human beings are capable of and science provides the standard for measuring all forms of thought. Positivistic philosophy saw its task as similar, but once removed: to study the language of science and employ it as the norm for all other languages. Ludwig Wittgenstein's *Tractatus,* in which he formulated the presumed limits of scientific thought on the basis of the logical atomism of Bertrand Russell and G. E. Moore, became the bible of the logical positivist movement, However, at the conclusion of the *Tractatus* Wittgenstein observed that having said what one can say legitimately within the language of fact, everything important remains outside. While the logical positivists took this to mean that anything that cannot be formulated in the language of science was metaphysical and had, at best, purely expressive significance and could be dismissed, Wittgenstein interpreted this, rather, as indicating that the language of science cannot be taken as the norm of all other language without immeasurable loss.

In his lucid review of Wittgenstein's thought, David Pears interprets Wittgenstein's aim in both the early period (that of the *Tractatus*) and later

period (that of *Logical Investigations*) as the understanding of "the structure and limits of thought," and his method as the study of "the structure and limits of language."[37] Pears interprets the *Tractatus* as similar in purpose and scope to Kant's critique of thought, but carried out in the form of a critique of language. The object was to discover the exact line dividing sense from nonsense and to understand the structure of what can be said. All his doctrines are based on the notion that language has limits imposed by its internal structure.

> There are two main changes in Wittgenstein's doctrines between his early and his later periods. First, he abandoned the idea that the structure of reality determines the structure of language, and suggested that it is really the other way round: our language determines our view of reality, because we see things through it . . . The second main doctrinal change is in Wittgenstein's theory of language. In the *Tractatus* he had argued that all languages have a uniform, logical structure. . . Early in his second period . . . he came around to the diametrically opposite view. The diversification of linguistic forms, he now thought, actually reveals the deep structure of language, which is not at all what he had taken it to be. Language has no common essence, or at least, if it has one, it is a minimal one which does not explain the connections between its various forms. They are connected with one another . . . like games, or like the faces of people belonging to the same family.[38]

Wittgenstein was one of the major influences in the shift from logical positivism to ordinary language philosophy, which tends to draw its examples from the language of law, morality, religion, and aesthetics more often than from science. Along with the existentialists the ordinary language philosophers bear some of the responsibility, in turn, for the increased popularity among sociologists of the study of everyday life, with new respect for common sense.

In view of the trends in contemporary social

[37]David Pears, *Ludwig Wittgenstein* (New York: Viking, 1969), p. 2.
[38]*Ibid.,* pp. 3, 4.

theory which include: antiscientism; antipositivism; disillusionment with holism and rationalistic forms of elementarism; an inclination to erase the distinction between fact and value and with it the distinction between scientific theory and ideology; interest in irrational components of individual personality; and, finally, an inclination to place the sociology of everyday life in the center of analysis, the entire Western intellectual tradition would appear about to come apart at the seams. On the other hand, there was never a time when there has been so much activity in virtually every area of sociological theory as has been true in the 1970s and early 1980s. Since the 1960s there has been an increasing inclination for consensual and conflict theorist, holist and elementarist, formalist and substantialist, positivist and antipositivist, humanist and scientist to reconcile themselves to the fact that others are vigorously promoting alternatives to their interpretations and explanations. Moreover, the lesson has repeatedly been driven home that too vigorous attempts to secure an institutional monopoly (as illustrated by the efforts of the American Sociological Association to control the profession and of a single clique to retain control of the Association by co-optation no longer work. Repeated revolts from the rank and file membership have lifted individuals who did not have the approval of the dominant clique to presidency of the ASA. Furthermore, the hegemony of the ASA over professional sociology has been challenged by the formation of alternative and subassociations (The Society for the Study of Social Problems, The Society for the Study of Symbolic Interaction, The Phenomenological Society, and newly invigorated regional and state sociological associations).

Those persons inclined to throw up their hands in dismay at the theoretical fragmentation and institutional counterformations of contemporary professional sociology are employing social and political criteria to a sphere where they are inappropriate. Professional sociology is not — or at least should not be — a political party in dire need of ideological unity if it is to have realistic hope of winning an election. In the world of the mind variety is the essence and not simply the spice of life. Theorists who must defend their ideas before intelligent alternatives cannot hope to win acceptance if those ideas are logically loose or inconsistent and empirically unverifiable. New concepts have always been generated at points where older concepts conflict. The frequency with which attempts have been made to find new ways of integrating former approaches is itself one of the most promising features of social theory in the 1980s. Even the return to the sociology of everyday life and renewed respect for common sense is hopeful: sociology has been seeking renewal by contact with the matrix of its origin.

Although antiscientism and irrationalism (calls for setting aside the program of objective understanding of the social world and replacing it with passionate advocacy) have tended to set the tone for much recent sociological work, it would be a serious mistake to view them as harbingers of the future. Scientific thinking remains the norm of Western civilization, although the uses to which science has been put have unquestionably been an important component in the dilemmas that face the contemporary world. And we have, indeed, made a Faustian bargain with our technologists in which an atomic war or even the peaceable uses of atomic energy (which creates waste deadly for up to a quarter of a million years, waste we have found no safe way to dispose of) could destroy all higher forms of life on earth. The scientific mentality, which has made possible such awesome control of nature, has tended to dissipate all mythologies, religious or other, which in the past were ultimately relied on to hold human beings together in war and peace groups. But there is no going back to a prescience world. Those who attempt this simply place themselves under the power of whichever persons or organizations decline to abandon science. The only reasonable alternative is to equip one's self with sufficient scientific competence to understand what is going on.

However, the ironies do not end when the individual decides to acquire scientific training to understand the world that science has brought into being. Not only is science organized in specialties which are so complicated that even competence in the full range of a single specialty is growing rare, but the world has developed to a stage where scientific research is so extensive in scope and so costly that only powerful corporations and the bureaucracies of national states can support it. Even the most able scientist can understand with any completeness only a limited amount of what goes on and is virtually helpless in controlling the direction the scientific enterprise as a whole will take. By the time the consequences of such big science, as it is sometimes called, reach ordinary citizens in a form they can understand, it is too late to do much to alter the course of sociocultural events.

However, the problem may not be as bad as it looks. The suggestion has been advanced by some students, a notable example is the molecular biologist Gunther Stent,[39] that we have no reason to suppose that scientific innovation and discovery can continue to accelerate at the same rate forever. As a matter of fact, Stent argues, we are rapidly approaching the point where all of the most fundamental discoveries of science will have been made. About half the people who ever lived are alive today; around 95 percent of the scientists and technicians who have ever lived are alive today. Big science, sponsored by powerful bureaucracies of business and government, has taken over the thrust of research. There may be significance in the fact that a mountain of federal funds is required to produce a molehill of pure scientific findings. At the level of individual understanding we may possibly be approaching the limits of what the human mind has been biologically preprogrammed to comprehend. This type of appraisal of our situation has led Stent to subscribe to a form of up-dated neo-Kantianism or structuralism.

If this should turn out to be the best appraisal of where we stand today, there is a possible message in it for the social sciences. The major task of the social scientist will consist of the codification of scientific findings and then translation into terms that

the ordinary person can understand, equipping the average person with sufficient competence at least to ask the right questions.

Sociology arose in the first place in response to the realization that in a culture based on science no mythology could in the end be safeguarded from the disenchanting clarification of the scientific attitude. Hence, the days of the old collective myths, particularly religious myths, that had once held the social world together were numbered. The charge that the early sociologists assigned to themselves was, in an age of science, to find a way to maintain sufficient social unity to get the collective work of the world accomplished. It would seem to be time for sociologists to rededicate themselves to this task, but enriched by all they have learned in the meantime. Possibly the renewed interest in the sociology of everyday life is a move in the right direction: dedication to a task of communication, raising the level of understanding of the ordinary people to a point where they comprehend the fundamentals of science and society and are able — without need for recourse to collective mythologies — to participate directly in the management of their futures.

POSTSCRIPT: A MYTH

If the age of mythology were not at an end it is conceivable that some priest, shaman, sage, or natural philosopher might observe:

In the beginning was Plasma. Our Universe is merely a state of Plasma, born in an explosion twenty billion years ago. It is still exploding: its fragments rush away from one another at great speed and the noise of the explosion that gave birth to the Universe echoes as a soft background noise from outer space. In some prior state the Plasma was locked into an egglike mass by powerful forces for unity with enormous internal pressures toward separation, dispersion, and the autonomy of some smallest unit which blew the egg apart, setting in motion the differentiation of a Universe.

---

[39]Gunther S. Stent, *Paradoxes of Progress* (San Francisco: W. H. Freeman and Company, 1978).

In the course of the explosion the forces for differentiation and synthesis continue to operate. Hence, even as it exploded the Plasma condensed into galaxies, stars, and planets; gases cooled to liquids, liquids froze into solids. The elements appeared, with every crystal reflecting the joint operation of forces for repulsion and for synthesis. How else can one explain the enormous energies released by the fission and fusion of matter. How else explain black holes, nuclei of the original force for synthesis so powerful that they suck up stars and pull the very light into their vortexes? And is it not possible that the plasma in such black holes is once more formed into egglike masses that explode to form new galaxies, repeating on smaller scale the birth of the Universe?

And in those planets which like our World spin around and are heated by their star-suns, and have cooled to the range where water remains in liquid form, and have sufficient gravitational force to hold an atmosphere, molecules sooner or later appear — themselves structures or combinations of the forces for differentiation and for synthesis — which separate and duplicate themselves whenever they have accumulated sufficient material to do so. So subtly do these molecules balance the forces for differentiation and synthesis that they grow ever more complex, differentiating into the endlessly varied fragile structures of life. For what is life, if not a gauzy structure, in which the conjoint operation of conflicting forces are manifest? And what is an individual if not a form of life in which the force for differentiation and autonomy dominates the force for synthesis with other like forms? And what is a community, if not a product of the force for synthesis of like living forms with others, limited by the immunology mechanism set in motion whenever the force for community threatens the residual identity of the individual? And what are mind, consciousness, ambition, jealousy, envy, spite, and the desire for recognition and love, other than rays cast by the conjoint operation of forces for individuality and for community? And, in the end, is there anything but Plasma?

BIBLIOGRAPHY

Detailed bibliographic information was supplied throughout the text in connection with discussions of specific theorists. The present bibliography is concerned only with general matters that might otherwise have been missed: other treatments of theory, the historical sources of theory, considerations in the shaping of theory, and the perennial problems of theory.

GENERAL

Abel, Theodore. *The Foundation of Sociological Theory.* New York: Random House, 1970.

Abraham, J. H. *The Origins and Growth of Sociology.* Harmondsworth: Penguin Books, 1973.

Abrams, Philip, ed. *The Origins of British Sociology.* Chicago: University of Chicago Press, 1968.

Andreski, Stanislav. *Social Sciences as Sorcery.* New York: St. Martin's Press, 1972.

Aron, Raymond. *Les Etapes de la pensée sociologique.* Paris: Gallimard, 1967.

————. *Main Currents in Sociological Thought.* Harmondsworth: Penguin Books, 1970.

————. *La Sociologie allemande contemporaine.* Paris: P.U.F., 1950.

Barbano, F. *Lineamenti di storia del pensiero sociologico.* Torino: Giappichelli, 1970.

Barnes, Harry Elmer, ed. *An Introduction to the History of Sociology.* Chicago: University of Chicago Press, 1948.

Beach, Walter Greenwood. *The Growth of Social Thought.* New York: Scribner's, 1939.

Becker, Ernest. *The Lost Science of Man.* New York: Braziller, 1971.

Becker, Howard, and H. E. Barnes. *Social Thought from Lore to Science.* 3 vols., 3d ed. New York: Dover, 1961.

Benton, Ted. *Philosophical Foundations of the Three Sociologies.* London: RKP, 1977.

Bernal, J. D. *Science in History.* London: Watts, 1956.

Bernsdorf, Wilhelm, ed. *Internationales Soziologen Lexikon.* Stuttgart: F. Enke, 1959.

Bogardus, Emory S. *The Development of Social Thought.* New York: Longman, 1940.

Bouthoul, Gaston. *Histoire de la sociologie.* Paris: P.U.F., 1956.

Braunleuther, Kurt. *Probleme der Geschichte der burgerlichen Soziologie.* Berlin: Akademie Verlag, 1975.

Brett, George Sidney. *History of Psychology.* Edited and abridged by R. S. Peters. London: Allen and Unwin, 1952.

Brunschvicg, Léon. *Le Progrès de la conscience dans la philosophie occidentale.* 2 vols. 2d ed. Paris: P.U.F., 1953.

Bryant, Christopher G. A. *Sociology in Action: A Critique of Selected Conceptions of the Social Role of the Sociologists.* London: Allen and Unwin, 1976.

Catton, William R., Jr. "The Development of Sociological Thought." In Robert E. L. Faris, ed., *Handbook of Modern Sociology.* Chicago: Rand McNally, 1964.

Cazeneuve, Jean, and David Victoroff. *La Sociologie: Les idées, les oeuvres, les hommes.* Paris: P.U.F., 1970.

Chambliss, Rollin, ed. *Social Thought from Hammurabi to Comte.* New York: Dryden Press, 1954.

Châtelet, François, ed. *L'Histoire des idéologies.* 3 vols. Paris: Hachette, 1977.

Collins, Randall, and Michael Makowsky. *The Discovery of Society.* New York: Random House, 1972.

Coser, Lewis A. *Masters of Sociological Thought: Ideas in Historical and Social Context.* New York: Harcourt Brace Jovanovich, 1971.

Cuvillier, Armand. *Manuel de sociologie.* 2 vols. Paris: P.U.F., 1954.

Cuzzort, Raymond Paul. *Humanity and Modern Sociological Thought.* New York: Holt, Rinehart and Winston, 1969.

Easthope, Gary. *History of Social Research Methods.* London: Longman, 1974.

Eisenstadt, S. N., with M. Curelaru. *The Form of Sociology: Paradigms and Crises.* New York: Wiley, 1976.

Ellwood, Charles Abram. *The Story of Social Philosophy.* Englewood Cliffs, N.J.: Prentice-Hall, 1938.

Fay, Brian. *Social Theory and Political Practice.* London: Allen and Unwin, 1975.

Ferrarotti, F. *Il pensiero sociologico da Auguste Compte a Max Horkheimer*. Milano: Mondadori, 1974.

Fletcher, Ronald. *The Making of Sociology: A Study of Sociological Theory*. Vol. 1, *Beginnings and Foundations*; vol. 2, *Developments*. London: Nelson, 1972.

Freund, Julien, *Les Théories des sciences humaines*. Paris: P.U.F., 1973.

Furfey, Paul H. *A History of Social Thought*. New York: Macmillan, 1942.

Gella, Aleksander, Sue Curry Jansen, and Donald F. Sabo, Jr. *Humanism in Sociology: Its Historical Roots and Contemporary Problems*. Washington, D.C.: University Press of America, 1978.

Gide, Charles, and Charles Rist. *Histoire des doctrines économiques depuis les physiocrates jusqu'à nos jours*. Paris: Librairie du Recueil Sivey, 1929.

Goldmann, Lucien. *Sciences humaines et philosophie*. Paris: P.U.F., 1952.

Goudsblom, Johan. *Sociology in the Balance: A Critical Essay*. Oxford: Blackwell, 1977.

Gough, J. W. *The Social Contract: The Critical Study of Its Development*. 2d ed. Oxford: Clarendon Press, 1957.

Gouldner, Alvin W. *The Coming Crisis of Western Sociology*. New York: Equinox Books, 1971.

Gurvitch, Georges. *La Vocation actuelle de la sociologie*. 2 vols. Paris: P.U.F., 1963.

————, ed. *Traité de sociologie*. Vol. 1, sec. 1. Paris: P.U.F., 1958.

Gurvitch, Georges, and Wilbert E. Moore, eds. *Twentieth Century Sociology*. New York: Philosophical Library, 1946.

Habermas, Jürgen. *Knowledge and Human Interests*. Boston: Beacon Press, 1972.

Harris, Marvin, *The Rise of Anthropological Theory: A History of Theories of Culture*. New York: Crowell, 1968.

Hawthorn, Geoffrey. *Enlightenment and Despair: A History of Sociology*. Cambridge: Cambridge University Press, 1976.

Herpin, Nicolas. *Les Sociologues américains et le siècle*. Paris: P.U.F., 1973.

Hinkle, Roscoe C., Jr., and Gisela J. Hinkle. *The Development of Modern Sociology: Its Nature and Growth in the United States*. Garden City, N.Y.: Doubleday, 1954.

Horowitz, Irving K. *Professing Sociology: Studies in the Life Cycle of Social Sciences*. Chicago: Aldine, 1968.

House, Floyd Nelson. *The Development of Sociology*. Westport, Conn.: Greenwood Press, 1970.

Israel, Joachim. *Alienation: From Marx to Modern Sociology: A Macrosociological Analysis*. Boston: Allyn and Bacon, 1971.

Janet, Paul. *Histoire de la science politique dans ses rapports avec la morale*. 2 vols. Paris: Librairie philosophique de Ladrange, 1872.

Jarvie, J. C. *The Story of Social Anthropology*. New York: McGraw-Hill, 1971.

Jonas, Friedrich. *Geschichte der Soziologie*. 4 vols. Munich: Rewohlt, 1969.

Keat, Russell, and John Urry. *Social Theory as Science*. London: RKP, 1975.

Kinloch, Graham C. *Sociological Theory: Its Development and Major Paradigms*. New York: McGraw-Hill, 1977.

Kiss, Gabor. *Einfuhrung in die Soziologischen Theorien*. 2 vols. 3d ed. Opladen: Westdeutscher Verlag, 1977.

Kuhn, Thomas S. *The Structure of Scientific Revolutions*. 2d ed. Chicago: University of Chicago Press, 1970.

Lengermann, Patricia H. *Definitions of Sociology: A Historical Approach*. Columbus, Ohio: Merrill, 1974.

Lerner, Daniel, ed. *The Human Meaning of the Social Sciences*. New York: Meridian Books, 1959.

Lichtenberger, J. P. *Development of Social Theory*. New York: Century, 1923.

Lowie, Robert H. *The History of Ethnological Theory*. New York: Holt, Rinehart and Winston, 1937.

Madge, John. *The Origins of Scientific Sociology*. London: Tavistock, 1963.

Manuel, Frank E., and Fritzie P. Manuel. *Utopian Thought in the Western World*. Cambridge, Mass.: Belknap Press, 1979.

Martindale, Don. *Prominent Sociologists Since World War II*. Columbus, Ohio: Merrill, 1975.

————. *Sociological Theory and the Problem of Values*. Columbus, Ohio: Merrill, 1974.

Maus, Heinz. *A Short History of Sociology*. New York: Citadel Press, 1966.

Mercier, Paul. *Histoire de l'anthropologie*. Paris: P.U.F., 1971.

Merton, Robert K. "On the History and Systematics of Sociological Theory." In Merton, *On Theoretical Sociology: Five Essays, Old and New*. New York: Free Press, 1967.

Mihanovich, C. S., ed. *Social Theorists*. Milwaukee: Bruce Publishing, 1953.

Mills, C. Wright. *The Sociological Imagination*. New York: Oxford University Press, 1959.

————, ed. *Images of Man: The Classic Tradition in Sociological Thinking*. New York: Braziller, 1960.

Mitchell, G. Duncan. *A Hundred Years of Sociology*. Chicago: Aldine, 1968.

Mongardini, Carlo. *L'epoca, della societá: Saggi di storia della sociologia*. Rome: M. Bulzoni, 1970.

Murphy, Gardner. *An Historical Introduction to Modern*

Psychology. 2d ed. London: Kegan Paul, Trench, Trubner, 1930.

Naroll, Raoul, and Frada Naroll, eds. *Main Currents in Cultural Anthropology.* Englewood Cliffs, N.J.: Prentice-Hall, 1973.

Nisbet, Robert A. *Social Change and History: Aspects of the Western Theory of Development.* New York: Oxford University Press, 1969.

———. *The Social Philosophers: Community and Conflict in Western Thought.* New York: Crowell, 1973.

———. *The Sociological Tradition.* London: Heinemann, 1967.

———. *Sociology as an Art Form.* London: Heinemann, 1976.

Oberschall, Anthony, ed. *Establishment of Empirical Sociology: Studies in Continuity, Discontinuity, and Institutionalization.* New York: Harper and Row, 1972.

Odum, H. W. *American Sociology: The Story of Sociology in the United States Through 1950.* New York: Longmans, Green, 1951.

Ossowski, Stanislaw. *O osobliwościach nauk spolecznvch. Dzieta,* vol. 4. Warsaw: PWN, 1967.

Parsons, Talcott. *The Structure of Social Action: A Study in Social Theory with Special Reference to a Group of Recent European Writers.* 2 vols. New York: Free Press, 1968.

Penniman, T. K. *A Hundred Years of Anthropology.* 3d ed. London: Duckworth, 1965.

Phillips, D. C. *Holistic Thought in Social Science.* London: Macmillan, 1976.

Plamenatz, John. *Man and Society: A Critical Examination of Some Important Social and Political Theories from Machiavelli to Marx.* London: Longman, 1969.

Poirrier, Jean. *Histoire de l'ethnologie.* Paris: P.U.F., 1969.

Raison, Timothy, ed. *The Founding Fathers of Social Science.* Harmondsworth: Penguin Books, 1969.

Reynolds, Larry T., and Janice M. Reynolds, eds. *The Sociology of Sociology.* New York: McKay, 1970.

Ritzer, George. *Sociology: A Multiple Paradigm Science.* Boston: Allyn and Bacon, 1975.

Rossides, Daniel. *The History and Nature of Sociological Theory.* Boston: Houghton Mifflin, 1978.

Runciman, W. G. *Sociology in Its Place and Other Essays.* Cambridge: Cambridge University Press, 1970.

Russell, Bertrand. *History of Western Philosophy and Its Connections with Political and Social Circumstances from the Earliest Times to the Present Day.* London: Allen and Unwin, 1946.

Sabine, George H. *A History of Political Theory.* 3d ed. London: George G. Harrap, 1951.

Sahay, Arun. *Sociological Analysis.* London: RKP, 1972.

Salomon, Albert. *The Tyranny of Progress: Reflections on the Origins of Sociology.* New York: Noonday Press, 1955.

Schilling, Kurt. *Histoire des idées sociales: Individu — Communauté — Société.* Paris: Payot, 1962.

Schoeck, Helmut. *Soziologie: Geschichte ihrer Probleme.* Munich: K. Alber, 1952.

Schumpeter, Joseph A. *History of Economic Analysis.* London: Allen and Unwin, 1972.

Shils, Edward. "Tradition, Ecology, and Institutionalization in the History of Sociology." *Daedalus* 99 (Fall 1970): 760–825.

Sills, David L., ed. *International Encyclopedia of the Social Sciences.* 17 vols. New York: Macmillan, 1968.

Sklair, Leslie. *The Sociology of Progress.* London: RKP, 1970.

Small, Albion W. *Origins of Sociology.* Chicago: University of Chicago Press, 1924.

Sorokin, Pitirim A. *Contemporary Sociological Theories.* New York: Harper and Row, 1928.

———. *Sociological Theories of Today.* New York: Harper and Row, 1966.

Stark, Werner, *The Fundamental Forms of Social Thought.* London: RKP, 1962.

———. *Social Theory and Christian Thought: A Study of Some Points of Contact.* London: RKP, 1959.

Stern, Fritz, ed. *The Varieties of History from Voltaire to the Present.* New York: Meridian Books, 1956.

Strasser, Hermann. *The Normative Structure of Sociology: Conservative and Emancipatory Themes in Social Thought.* London: RKP, 1976.

Suchodolski, Bogdan. *Narodziny nowozytnej filozofii czlowieka.* Warsaw: PWN, 1963.

———. *Rozwój nowozytnej filozofii czlowieka.* Warsaw: PWN, 1967.

Szacki, Jerzy. *History of Sociological Thought.* Westport, Conn.: Greenwood Press, 1979.

Szczepański, Jan. *Socjologia: Rozwój problematyki i metod.* 3d. ed. Warsaw: PWN, 1969.

Thompson, J. W. *A History of Historical Writing.* 2 vols. New York: Macmillan, 1958.

Timasheff, Nicholas S. *Sociological Theory: Its Nature and Growth.* 3d ed. New York: Random House, 1967.

Tiryakian, Edward A., ed. *The Phenomenon of Sociology.* New York: Appleton-Century-Crofts, 1971.

Truzzi, Marcello, ed. *Sociology: The Classic Statements.* New York: Random House, 1971.

Vaughan, C. E. *Studies in the History of Political Philosophy Before and After Rousseau.* 2 vols. Manchester: Manchester University Press, 1939.

Voget, Fred W. "A History of Cultural Anthropology."

In John J. Honigmann, ed. *Handbook of Social and Cultural Anthropology*. Chicago: Rand McNally, 1973.

Wagner, Donald O. *Social Reformers: Adam Smith to John Dewey*. New York: Macmillan, 1934.

Walicki, Andrzej. *Rosyjska filozofia i myśl społeczna od Oświecenia do marksizmu*. Warsaw: Wiedza Powszechna, 1973.

Widgery, Alban G. *Interpretations of History*. London: Allen and Unwin, 1961.

Wiener, Philip P., ed. *Dictionary of the History of Ideas: Studies of Selected Pivotal Ideas*. 5 vols. New York: Scribner's, 1973.

Wiese, Leopold von. *Soziologie: Geschichte und Hauptprobleme*. 6th ed. Berlin: Walter de Gruyter, 1960.

Wolin, Sheldon S. *Politics and Vision: Continuity and Innovation in Western Political Thought*. London: Allen and Unwin, 1961.

Zeitlin, Irving M. *Ideology and the Development of Sociological Theory*. Englewood Cliffs, N.J.: Prentice-Hall, 1968.

Znaniecki, Florian. *Cultural Sciences: Their Origin and Development*. Urbana: University of Illinois Press, 1952.

PART 1/THE CONTEXT

Althusser, Louis. *Politics and History: Montesquieu, Rousseau, Hegel and Marx*. London: NLB, 1972.

Aristotle. *The Works*. Tr. into English under the editorship of W. D. Ross. 12 vols. Oxford: Clarendon Press, 1910–1937.

Augustine, Saint. *The City of God*. Trans. M. Dods. Edinburgh: T. & T. Clark, 1872.

Barker, Ernest. *Greek Political Theory: Plato and His Predecessors*. London: Methuen, 1957.

———. *The Political Thought of Plato and Aristotle*. New York: Russell, 1959.

Becker, Carl. *The Heavenly City of the 18th Century Philosophers*. New Haven: Yale University Press, 1932.

Blumfitt, John H. *Voltaire: Historian*. London: Oxford University Press, 1958.

Bongie, Lawrence L. *David Hume: Prophet of the Counter-Revolution*. Oxford: Clarendon Press, 1965.

Bredvold, Louis J. *The Brave New World of the Enlightenment*. Ann Arbor: University of Michigan Press, 1961.

Bryson, Gladys. *Man and Society: The Scottish Inquiry of Eighteenth Century*. New York: Kelley, 1968.

Burckhardt, Jacob. *The Civilisation of the Renaissance in Italy*. 2d ed. London: Allen and Unwin, 1944.

Carlyle, A. J., Sir Robert Warrand, and Alexander James. *History of Mediaeval Political Theory in the West*. 6 vols. Edinburgh: Blackwood, 1903–36.

Cassirer, Ernst. *The Philosophy of the Enlightenment*. Princeton: Princeton University Press, 1951.

Chitnis, Anand. *The Scottish Enlightenment*. London: Croom Helm, 1977.

Clark, Robert T., Jr. *Herder: His Life and Thought*. Berkeley and Los Angeles: University of California Press, 1955.

Cobban, Alfred. *In Search of Humanity: The Role of the Enlightenment in Modern History*. London: Cape, 1960.

———. *Rousseau and the Modern State*. London: Allen and Unwin, 1934.

Cochraine, Charles Norris. *Christianity and Classical Culture: A Study of Thought and Action from Augustus to Augustine*. New York: Oxford University Press, 1957.

Crombie, A. C. *Augustine to Galileo: Medieval and Early Modern Science*. 2 vols. London: Mercury Books, 1961.

Dunn, John. *The Political Thought of J. Locke*. Cambridge: Cambridge University Press, 1969.

Dunning, William A. *A History of Political Theories Ancient and Medieval*. New York: Macmillan, 1902.

Edelstein, Ludwig. *The Idea of Progress in Classical Antiquity*. Baltimore: The Johns Hopkins Press, 1967.

Effrat, Andrew. "Power to the Paradigms: An Editorial Introduction." *Sociological Inquiry* 42 (1972): 3–33.

Fairchild, H. N. *The Noble Savage: A Study in Romantic Naturalism*. New York: Columbia University Press, 1928.

Farrington, Benjamin. *Greek Science: Its Meaning for Us: Thales to Aristotle*. Harmondsworth: Penguin Books, 1944.

Ferguson, Adam. *An Essay on the History of Civil Society*. Edinburgh: Edinburgh University Press, 1966.

Finley, Moses J. *The Ancient Greeks*. London: Chatto and Windus, 1963.

———, ed. *The Greek Historians: The Essence of Herodotus, Thucydides, Xenophon and Polybius*. London: Chatto and Windus, 1959.

Foley, Vernard. *The Social Physics of Adam Smith*. West Lafayette, Ind.: Purdue University Press, 1976.

Forbes, Duncan. *Hume's Philosophical Politics*. Cambridge: Cambridge University Press, 1975.

Frankel, Charles. *The Faith of Reason: The Idea of Progress in the French Enlightenment*. New York: King's Crown Press, 1948.

Friedrichs, Robert W. *A Sociology of Sociology*. New York: Free Press, 1970.

Fromm, Erich. *Escape from Freedom.* London: RKP, 1941.

Gierke, Otto, *Natural Law and the Theory of Society, 1500 to 1800.* Boston: Beacon Press, 1957.

———. *Political Theories of the Middle Ages.* Boston: Beacon Press, 1958.

Gilson, Etienne. *The Christian Philosophy of St. Thomas Aquinas.* New York: Random House, 1956.

———. *History of Christian Philosophy in the Middle Ages.* London: Sheed and Ward, 1955.

———. *Introduction à l'étude de Saint-Augustin.* Paris: J. Urin, 1929.

———. *The Spirit of Medieval Philosophy.* New York: Scribner's, 1936.

Gitler, Joseph B. *Social Thought Among the Early Greeks.* Athens: University of Georgia Press, 1941.

Goldsmith, Maurice M. *Hobbes' Science of Politics.* New York: Columbia University Press, 1966.

Gouldner, Alvin W. "Anti-Minotaur: The Myth of a Value-Free Sociology." In Alvin W. Gouldner, *For Sociology: Renewal and Critique in Sociology Today.* New York: Basic Books, 1973.

———. *Enter Plato: Classical Greece and the Origins of Social Theory.* New York: Harper and Row, 1971.

Halévy, Elie. *The Growth of Philosophic Radicalism.* London: Faber and Faber, 1972.

Hazard, Paul. *The European Mind, 1680–1715.* London: Hollis and Carter, 1953.

———. *European Thought in the 18th Century from Montesquieu to Lessing.* London: Hollis and Carter, 1954.

Hearnshaw, F. J. C., ed. *The Social and Political Ideas of Some English Thinkers of the Augustian Age, A.D. 1650–1750.* London: Dawsons of Pall Mall, 1967.

———, ed. *The Social and Political Ideas of Some Great Mediaeval Thinkers.* London: Dawsons of Pall Mall, 1967.

———, ed. *The Social and Political Ideas of Some Great Thinkers of the Sixteenth and Seventeenth Centuries.* London: Dawsons of Pall Mall, 1967.

Hearnshaw, F. J. C., and Ernest Barker, eds. *The Social and Political Ideas of Some Great Thinkers of the Renaissance and the Reformation.* London: Dawsons of Pall Mall, 1967.

Hemple, Carl G., and Paul Oppenheim. "The Logic of Explanation." In Herbert Feigl and May Brodbeck, eds., *Readings in the Philosophy of Science.* New York: Appleton-Century-Crofts, 1953.

Hertzler, J. O. *The Social Thought of the Ancient Civilizations.* New York: McGraw-Hill, 1936.

Hobbes, Thomas. *Leviathan.* In *Great Books of the Western World,* vol. 23. Chicago: Encyclopaedia Britannica. 1952.

Hodgen, Margaret T. *Early Anthropology in the Sixteenth and Seventeenth Centuries.* Philadelphia: University of Pennsylvania Press, 1964.

Huizinga, Johan. *The Waning of the Middle Ages.* Garden City, N.Y.: Doubleday, 1956.

Hume, David. *Essays Moral, Political and Literary.* London: Oxford University Press, 1963.

———. *A Treatise of Human Nature.* 2 vols. London: Longmans, Green, 1898.

Jaeger, Werner. *Paideia: The Ideals of Greek Culture.* 3 vols. Oxford: Blackwell, 1939–45.

Jarrett, Bede. *Social Theories of the Middle Ages, 1200–1500.* London: E. Benn, 1969.

Kettler, David. *The Social and Political Thought of Adam Ferguson.* Columbus, Ohio: Ohio State University Press, 1965.

Kitch, M. J., ed. *Capitalism and the Reformation.* London: Longman, 1967.

Krieger, Leonard. *The Politics of Discretion: Puffendorf and the Acceptance of Natural Law.* Chicago: University of Chicago Press, 1966.

Kuhn, Thomas. "Reflections on My Critics." In Imre Lakatos and Alan Musgrave, eds., *Criticism and the Growth of Knowledge.* London: Cambridge University Press, 1970.

———. *The Structure of Scientific Revolutions.* Chicago: University of Chicago Press, 1962. 2d rev. ed., 1970.

Lehmann, William C. *Adam Ferguson and the Beginnings of Modern Sociology.* Columbia University Studies in History, Economics and Public Law, no. 328. New York: Columbia University, 1930.

———. *John Millar of Glasgow (1735–1801): His Life and Thought and His Contributions to Sociological Analysis.* Glasgow University, Sociological and Economical Studies, no. 4. Cambridge: Cambridge University Press, 1960.

Locke, John. *On Politics, Religion and Education.* Edited by Maurice Cranston. New York: Collier Books, 1965.

———. *An Essay Concerning Human Understanding.* 2 vols. Oxford: Clarendon Press, 1894.

———. *Two Tracts on Government.* Cambridge: Cambridge University Press, 1967.

Lovejoy, Arthur O., et al. *Documentary History of Primitivism.* Baltimore: The Johns Hopkins Press, 1935.

McKinney, John C. *Constructive Typology and Social Theory.* New York: Appleton-Century-Crofts, 1966.

Macpherson, Crawford Brough. *The Political Theory of Possessive Individualism: Hobbes to Locke.* London: Oxford University Press, 1962.

Manuel, Frank E. *The Eighteenth Century Confronts the*

Gods. Cambridge, Mass.: Harvard University Press, 1959.

——. *The Prophets of Paris.* Cambridge, Mass.: Harvard University Press, 1962.

Martin, Basil Kingsley. *French Liberal Thought in the 18th Century: A Study of Political Ideas from Bayle to Condorcet.* London: Turnstile Press, 1954.

Martin, John. *Sociology of the Renaissance.* New York: Oxford University Press, 1944.

Martindale, Don. *Sociological Theory and the Problem of Values.* Columbus, Ohio: Merrill, 1974.

Masterman, Margaret. "The Nature of a Paradigm." In Imre Lakatos and Alan Musgrave, eds., *Criticism and the Growth of Knowledge.* London: Cambridge University Press, 1970, pp. 59–89.

Meek, Ronald L. *Social Science and the Ignoble Savage.* Cambridge: Cambridge University Press, 1976.

——, ed. *Turgot on Progress, Sociology and Economics.* Cambridge: Cambridge University Press: 1973.

Meinecke, Friedrich. *Historism: The Rise of a New Historical Outlook.* London: RKP, 1972.

Montesquieu. *The Spirit of Laws.* In *Great Books of the Western World,* vol. 38. Chicago: Encyclopaedia Britannica, 1952.

Plato. *The Dialogues.* In *Great Books of the Western World,* vol. 7. Chicago: Encyclopaedia Britannica, 1952.

——. *The Republic.* Trans. A. D. Lindsay. London: J. M. Dent/New York: E. P. Dutton, 1937.

Popper, Karl R. *The Open Society and Its Enemies.* Vol. 1, *The Spell of Plato.* Princeton: Princeton University Press, 1971.

Reynolds, Paul D. *A Primer in Theory Construction.* Indianapolis: Bobbs-Merrill, 1971.

Ritzer, George. *Sociology: A Multiple Paradigm Science.* Boston: Allyn and Bacon, 1975.

Sampson, R. V. *Progress in the Age of Reason.* London: Heinemann, 1965.

Schneider, Louis, ed. *The Scottish Moralists on Human Nature and Society.* Chicago: University of Chicago Press, 1967.

Skinner, Andrew S., and Thomas Wilson, eds. *Essays on Adam Smith.* London: Oxford University Press, 1976.

Slotkin, James Sydney, ed. *Readings in Early Anthropology.* Viking Fund Publications in Anthropology, no. 40. New York: Wennergreen Foundation for Anthropological Research, 1965.

Small, Albion. *Adam Smith and Modern Sociology.* Chicago: University of Chicago Press, 1907.

Smith, Adam. *Theory of Moral Sentiments.* London: Oxford University Press, 1976.

Stark, Werner, *Social Theory and Christian Thought: A Study of Some Points of Contact.* London: RKP, 1959.

Stephen, Leslie. *History of English Thought in the Eighteenth Century.* 2 vols. London: Murray, 1927.

Stewart, John B. *The Moral and Political Philosophy of David Hume.* New York: Columbia University Press, 1963.

Strauss, Leo. *Thoughts on Machiavelli.* Glencoe, Ill.: Free Press, 1958.

Troeltsch, Ernst. *The Social Teaching of the Christian Churches.* New York: Harper Torchbooks, 1960.

Vyverberg, Henry. *Historical Pessimism in the French Enlightenment.* Cambridge, Mass.: Harvard University Press, 1958.

Waddicor, Mark H. *Montesquieu and the Philosophy of Natural Law.* The Hague: M. Nijhoff, 1970.

Wade, Ira O. *The Intellectual Development of Voltaire.* Princeton: Princeton University Press, 1969.

——. *The Intellectual Origins of the French Enlightenment.* Princeton: Princeton University Press, 1971.

Wasserman, Earl R. *Aspects of the Eighteenth Century.* Baltimore: The Johns Hopkins Press, 1965.

Watkins, J. W. N. *Hobbes' System of Ideas: A Study in the Political Significance of Philosophical Theories.* New York: Hutchinson, 1968.

Weber, Max. *On the Methodology of the Social Sciences.* Trans. Edward A. Shils and Henry A. Finch. Glencoe, Ill.: Free Press, 1949.

——. "Politics as a Vocation." In *From Max Weber.* Trans. H. H. Gerth and C. Wright Mills. New York: Oxford University Press, 1946, pp. 77–128.

——. *The Protestant Ethic and the Spirit of Capitalism.* London: Unwin University Books, 1930.

——. "Science as a Vocation." In *From Max Weber.* Trans. H. H. Gerth and C. Wright Mills. New York: Oxford University Press, 1946, pp. 129–156.

Zetterberg, Hans. *On Theory and Verification in Sociology.* Stockholm: Almquist and Wiksell, 1954.

PART 2/THE PROBLEMS OF SOCIOLOGICAL THEORY

Abel, Theodore F. "The Operation Called *Verstehen.*" *American Journal of Sociology* 54 (1948): 211–218.

Achinstein, Peter, and Stephen F. Barker, eds. *The Legacy of Logical Positivism.* Baltimore: The Johns Hopkins Press, 1969.

Adorno, Theodor W., Hans Albert, Ralf Dahrendorf,

Jürgen Habermas, Harald Pilot and Karl R. Popper. *The Positivist Dispute in German Sociology.* Trans. Glyn Adey and David Frisby. New York: Harper & Row, 1976.

Antoni, Carlo. *From History to Sociology: The Transition in German Historical Thinking.* London: Merlin Press, 1962.

Bottomore, Tom. *Marxist Sociology.* London: Macmillan, 1975.

Bottomore, Tom, and Robert Nisbet, eds. *A History of Sociological Analysis.* New York: Basic Books, 1978.

Bruun, H. H. *Science, Values and Politics in Max Weber's Methodology.* Copenhagen: Munksgaard, 1972.

Charlton, Donald G. *Positivist Thought in France during the Second Empire, 1852–1870.* Oxford: Clarendon Press, 1957.

Coker, F. W. *Organismic Theories of the State: 19th Century Interpretations of the State as Organism or as a Person.* New York: Columbia University Press: 1910.

Feyerabend, Paul K. *Against Method.* London: New Left Books, 1975.

Giddens, Antony. "Positivism and Its Critics." In Tom Bottomore and Robert Nisbet, eds., *A History of Sociological Analysis.* New York: Basic Books, 1978, pp. 237–286.

Giddens, Anthony, ed. *Positivism and Sociology.* London: Heinemann, 1975.

Gouldner, Alvin W. *The Coming Crisis of Western Sociology.* New York: Basic Books, 1970.

Henn, T. R. "The Arts v. the Sciences." In Alan S. C. Ross, ed., *Arts v. Science.* London: Methuen, 1967, pp. 1–19.

Kolakowski, Leszek. *Positivist Philosophy: From Hume to the Vienna Circle.* Harmondsworth: Penguin Books, 1972.

Kuhn, Thomas. *The Essential Tension: Selected Studies in Scientific Tradition and Change.* Chicago: University of Chicago Press, 1977.

———. *The Structure of Scientific Revolutions.* 2d ed. Chicago: University of Chicago Press, 1970.

Lewis, John. *Max Weber and Value-Free Sociology: A Marxist Critique.* London: Beekman Publishers, 1975.

Lynd, Robert S. *Knowledge for What? The Place of Social Science in American Culture.* Princeton: Princeton University Press, 1939.

MacIver, R. M. "Is Sociology a Natural Science?" *American Sociological Society* 25 (1932): 25–35.

Mandelbaum, Maurice. *The Problem of Historical Knowledge: An Answer to Relativism.* New York: Liveright, 1938.

Maslow, Abraham H. *The Psychology of Science.* New York: Harper & Row, 1966.

Meinecke, Friedrich. *Historism: The Rise of a New Historical Outlook.* London: RKP, 1972.

Mills, C. Wright. *The Sociological Imagination.* New York: Oxford University Press, 1959.

Nisbet, Robert. *Sociology as an Art Form.* New York: Oxford University Press, 1976.

Palmer, Richard E. *Hermeneutics: Interpretation Theory in Schleiermacher, Dilthey, Heidegger and Gadamer.* Evanston, Ill.: Northwestern University Press, 1965.

Passmore, John. *A Hundred Years of Philosophy.* New York: Penguin Books, 1978.

Pears, David. *Ludwig Wittgenstein.* New York: Viking, 1969.

Rex, John. *Key Problems of Sociological Theory.* London: RKP, 1961.

Rickert, Heinrich. *Science and History: A Critique of Positivist Epistemology.* Princeton: Van Nostrand, 1962.

Ryle, Gilbert. *The Concept of Mind.* London: Hutchinson, 1949.

Shaw, Martin. "The Coming Crisis of Radical Sociology." In Robin Blackburn, ed., *Ideology in Social Science.* New York: Vintage Books, 1973, pp. 32–44.

Snow, C. P. *The Two Cultures and A Second Look.* Cambridge: Cambridge University Press, 1959.

———. *Science and Government.* Cambridge, Mass.: Harvard University Press, 1960.

Stent, Gunter S. *Parodoxes of Progress.* San Francisco: W. H. Freeman and Company, 1978.

Thackray, Arnold, and Everett Mendelsohn, eds. *Science and Values.* New York: Humanities Press, 1974.

Tiryakian, Edward A. *Sociologism and Existentialism: Two Perspectives on the Individual and Society.* Englewood Cliffs, N.J.: Prentice-Hall, 1962.

Truzzi, Marcello, ed. *Verstehen: Subjective Understanding in the Social Sciences.* Reading, Mass.: Addison-Wesley, 1974.

Wann, T. W. *Behaviorism and Phenomenology: Contrasting Bases for Modern Psychology.* Chicago: University of Chicago Press, 1964.

Warshay, Leon H. *The Current State of Sociological Theory. A Critical Interpretation.* New York: McKay, 1975.

White, Alan R. *The Philosophy of Mind.* New York: Random House, 1967.

Wittgenstein, Ludwig. *The Blue and Brown Books.* New York: Harper & Row, 1965.

Zeitlin, Irving M. *Rethinking Sociology: A Critique of Contemporary Theory.* Englewood Cliffs, N.J.: Prentice-Hall, 1973.

INDEX

Page numbers set in boldface indicate passages in which the entry is the principal topic of discussion.